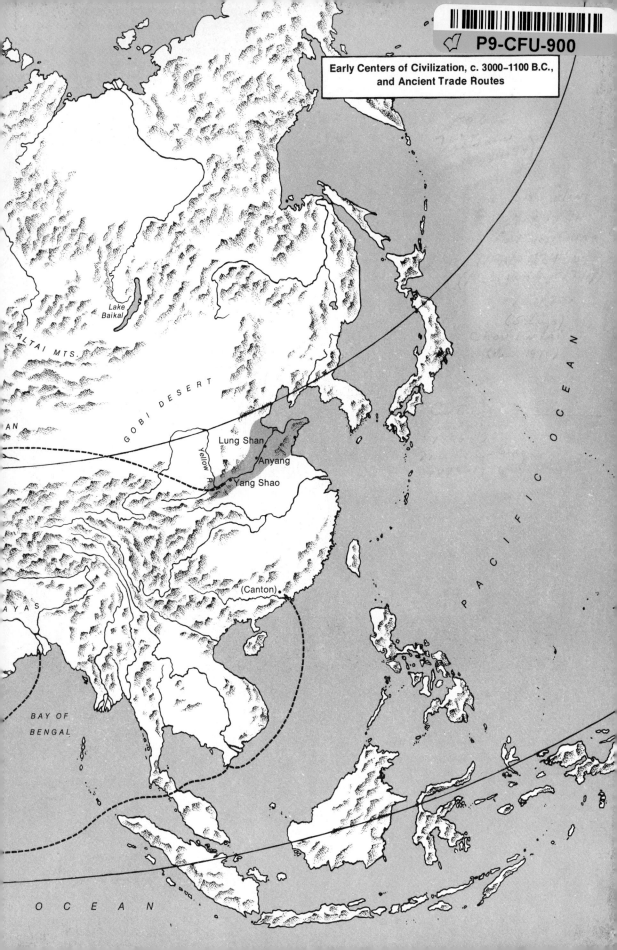

Early Centers of Civilization, c. 3000–1100 B.C., and Ancient Trade Routes

Lake Baikal

ALTAI MTS.

GOBI DESERT

Yellow R.

Lung Shan

Anyang

Yang Shao

(Canton)

PACIFIC OCEAN

BAY OF BENGAL

OCEAN

A History of EASTERN CIVILIZATIONS

A History of
EASTERN CIVILIZATIONS

GUILFORD A. DUDLEY- *deceased 1972*

Arizona State University

Tempe, Az.

JOHN WILEY & SONS, INC., New York · London · Sydney · Toronto

Library of Congress Cataloging in Publication Data:

Dudley, Guilford A. 1921- 1972
Eastern civilization [by] Guilford A. Dudley.

1. Asia—Civilization. 2. Asia—History. 3. Near East—Civilization. 4. Near East—History. I. Title.
DS12.D76 915'.03 72-6744
ISBN 0-471-22365-4

Printed in the United States of America

10 9 8 7 6 5 4 3 2 1

PREFACE

This book is designed to provide a basic understanding and appreciation of the major Eastern civilizations for students who are able to take only one course on this area. It is also an introduction and background for advanced courses on Asia which concentrate on a specific country or topic.

Criteria of selection and emphasis are necessary to make a survey of this vast scope coherent and meaningful to students. The central theme of this work is the identification of the enduring ideals, values, and attitudes that distinguish each of these civilizations and that continue to influence the way their people and their leaders think, act, and react to contemporary issues. Underlying this theme is a belief in the essential persistence of the fundamental ideals and values that give cohesion to each civilization, no matter how much they are being modified and altered to meet the challenges of the modern world. Moreover, it is shown that an attempt must be made to understand the distinctive outlooks of each of these civilizations if we wish to appreciate their attitudes and actions today and tomorrow. The result is an emphasis on the creative elites and only a limited attention to popular culture and institutions. In addition, the more mature phases of each civilization may seem to be given less attention than they deserve because the principal concern is with the introduction of new elements or significant modifications of traditional values and institutions.

The book is organized in six parts. To encourage a comparative approach, the chapters in each part carry the respective civilizations or areas through a roughly equivalent stage of development. The first three parts concern the emergence and development of these civilizations and areas and their reactions and modifications to the challenges that confronted them to about the mid-nineteenth century. The last three parts concentrate on the interaction with the West and the varying responses and adaptations to this unprecedented challenge. Since the painful process of adaptation is still in progress, the story is an unfinished one, and the final chapters must be largely descriptive and inconclusive; only future events will reveal the ultimate course of development.

In the transliteration of foreign names and words the spelling closest to the phonetic pronunciation has been followed while avoiding confusion with the standard usage in other works. For Indian words, diacritical marks have been left out except for *a* (pronounced *ah* as in *car*). The short *a* is pronounced *uh* as in *but*. In cases of familiar usage, such as *Punjab*, however, the familiar form has been used rather than the formal *Panjab*. In addition, the Indian *s* with a diacritical mark below it has been transliterated *sh*, which closely approximates the actual pronunciation. Chinese represents a necessary exception because of the almost universal use of the Wade-Giles method of romanization in English language works; otherwise, the phonetically much closer *pin-yin* method used in the People's Republic of China would have been employed. The aspirated consonants indicated by following apostrophes (*ch'*, *k'*, *p'*, *t'*, *ts'*, *tz'*) are pronounced like their English equivalents; without following apostrophes they are unaspirated: *ch* sounding something like the English *j*, *k* like *g*, *p* like *b*, *t* like *d*, *ts* and *tz* like *dz*. In addition, *j* sounds like *r* (*jen* like *run*) and *hs* like *sh*. A few examples of English equivalents may be helpful: *Cha'ao* = Chow, *Chou* = Joe, *K'in* = Keen, *Ku* = Goo, *P'en* = Pun, *Pei* = Bay, *T'ang* = Tong, *Tao* = Dow. Since many Chinese place-names refer to cardinal directions or physical features, some of the more common ones help in identification: *pei* = north (as in *Peik'ing* = Northern Capital), *tung* = east, *nan* = south, *hsi* = west, *shan* = mountain, *ho* = river, *hu* = lake.

In a work of this scope, of course, I have had to rely on the research of specialists, many of whom are recognized in the bibliography, but I am entirely responsible for any errors in fact and weaknesses in interpretation. I am also indebted to my colleagues in the history department and in Asian Studies for their support and encouragement, particularly to Professors B. Winston Kahn and Stephen R. MacKinnon for ably offering additional sections of the growing Eastern Civilizations course. I also express my appreciation to my wife and to the departmental secretaries past and present, Grace Skinaway, Dorothy Score, Nancy Henderson, and Jane Einhorn for their contributions in typing the manuscript, not once, but several times. Most of all, I am grateful to my wife, Anne, and to my son, Ford, for their patience in putting up with my neglect and my moods during the years that this book has been in preparation.

Guilford A. Dudley

(Assistance rendered by)
(Audrey Massie)
(during completion).

Before my husband's death, he was able to complete this text and to do most of the proof reading. The book deals with a field that he felt was necessary, important, and of great interest. He spent many years researching, writing, and rewriting this book and maybe the hardest part was keeping it up to date in these changing times. Our son, Ford, spent his summer helping his Dad for which we were both grateful and proud. Also I especially thank the History Department at Arizona State University for their final help in finishing this book and for their time and moral support. The people at Wiley who have been working on this book have been extremely helpful to me and have made my small part so very much easier.

Anne S. Dudley

CONTENTS

MAPS
BY JOHN V. MORRIS

A History of EASTERN CIVILIZATIONS

PART ONE
EMERGENCE OF MAJOR EASTERN CIVILIZATIONS

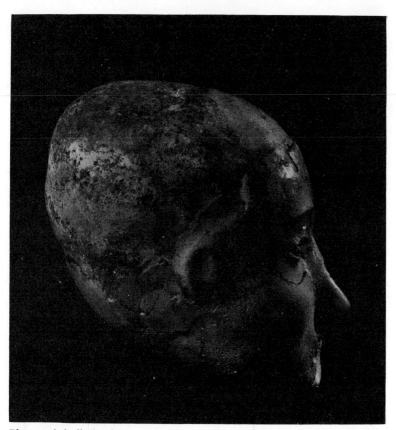

Plastered skull, Jericho, c. 6000 B.C. (*British School of Archaeology, Jerusalem*)

Neolithic "Mother Goddess" or fertility figurines (*Deutsches Archäologisches Institut, Athens*)

Earliest example of writing on limestone tablet, Kish, c. 3500 B.C. (*Department of Antiquities, Ashmolean Museum*)

The great Ziggurat at Ur, C. 2100 B.C. (*Douglas R.G. Sellick, London/British Museum*)

Gudea of Lagash, c. 2200 B.C. (*Douglas R.G. Sellick, London/ British Museum*)

Upper portion of stele showing Hammurabi before the sun-god, Shamash, 18th century B.C. The "code" is engraved in cuneiform script on the shaft of the stele. (*Cliché des Musees Nationaux*)

Obverse and reverse of the palette of King Narmer,
c. 3100 B.C. *(Egyptian Museum, Cairo)*

Step pyramid of Djoser at Saqqara, c. 2770 B.C. (*Bernice Q. Johnson/FPG*)

Daily life in Egypt as illustrated in tomb decoration. (*The Oriental Institute, University of Chicago*)

Egyptian prince and princess, c. 2660 B.C. (*Hirmer Fotoarchiv*)

Bronze dancing girl, Mohenjo-daro. *(National Museum of Pakistan)*

Seal impression of humped bull with undeciphered symbols, Mohenjo-daro. *(National Museum of Pakistan)*

Bearded figure, possibly high priest, Mohenjo-daro. *(National Museum, New Delhi)*

Lung-shan burnished black tripod pot, c. 2000 B.C. (*Academia Sinica, Formosa*)

Yang-shao burial urn, c. 2000 B.C. (*Seattle Art Museum, Eugene Fuller Memorial Collection*)

Shang bronze ritual pouring jug; note intricate design. (*Collection of the National Palace Museum, Taipei, Taiwan*)

Shang oracle bone with early Chinese writing. (*Douglas R.G. Sellick, London/British Museum*)

Late Chou bronze bell. *(Freer Gallery of Art)*

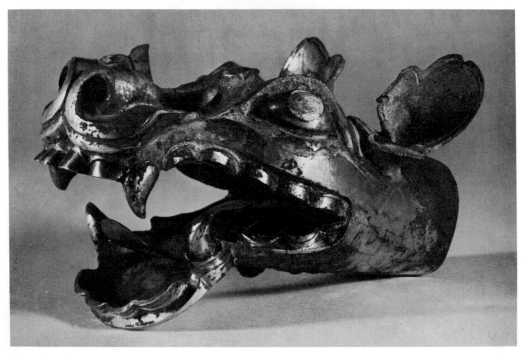

Late Chou dragonhead. *(Freer Gallery of Art)*

CHAPTER ONE

BACKGROUND TO CIVILIZATION

Before World War II, despite the growing pressures of nationalism, the West viewed the East as a subordinate, backward, and peripheral adjunct of Western civilization. Few Western scholars knew or cared much about this area which had produced great civilizations while the West was still in swaddling clothes. Since World War II events have precipitated an awakened interest and revised attitude regarding this part of the world. Thanks in large measure to the cold war, our government has become deeply involved in its present and future. Yet the disappointment, bewilderment, and frustration frequently expressed concerning Eastern actions and reactions document our lack of depth in understanding the various ancient heritages of ideals and values that influence and explain their current actions and attitudes. The "mysterious East" remains for most of us a mystery that needs to be dispelled.

The so-called "revolution of rising expectations" is one indication of the revived vitality that is coursing throughout the East. Each day more people in Asia and Africa are becoming self-consciously aware of the inadequacy of their material conditions in comparison with those of the West. Political independence has not, as they had hoped, automatically produced economic equality and independence. With growing insistence they are demanding from their leaders a rapid improvement of their economic deficiencies. These demands lead to social and political changes, sometimes peaceful, but often violent.

For many reasons this awareness of economic inequality is not evenly distributed. Naturally it is strongest in rapidly modernizing urban centers and among the educated elite. In rural areas it varies according to the quality and quantity of the facilities for communication and education. Often the older generation with its traditionally narrow horizon is thoroughly puzzled by the broader horizons and interests of its educated offspring. Another variable factor is the amount of interest and involvement in each country of the contestants in the cold war. In addition, the degree of population pressure on the traditional means of subsistence tends to contribute to a greater or lesser sense of the immediacy of the need for change. But of most importance is the cultural stage of development of any particular area. Primitive societies, while internally complex, are strongly wedded to custom and extremely resistant to external pressures for change. More complex and unified societies have a greater built-in potentiality to adapt to change both because of their larger unity and because of their greater internal diversity of skills and ways of living. These latter societies with their proud and distinguished heritages of civilization will be our primary concern.

The picture of contemporary Asia and Africa thus far drawn is one of dynamic change, instability, discontent, and alas —frustration. While no one can predict events, some broad assertions of probable developments can be set forth with reasonable confidence.

When one realizes that this area contains well over one half of the world's people, the concern and attention of the parties to the cold war can be expected to grow greater in the future fertilizing and expanding their awakening. Even if the cold war contestants should succeed in negotiating an end to the military aspects of their struggle, no reduction in their attention to the area can be forecast. On the contrary, the most likely result would be the release of additional resources for an acceleration of this contest for the alle-

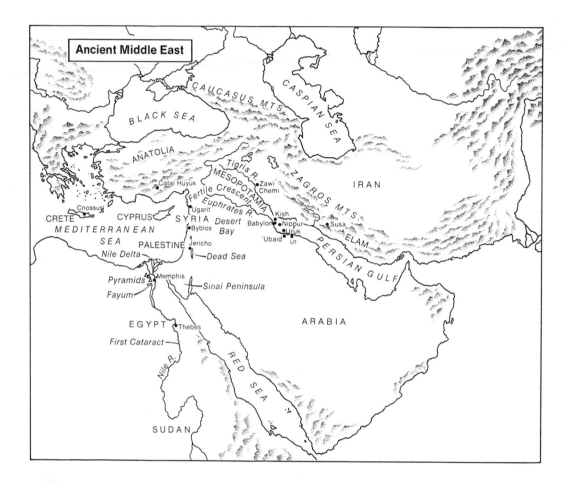

giance of mankind. Thus a larger, and not a smaller, involvement by the superpowers can be predicted. This means that under our system of popular control of the government every American needs a better knowledge and understanding of these different and differing civilizations.

Also predictable in general terms is the fact that their goal of matching the West in material accomplishments will result in continuing disappointment that will stimulate tension and turmoil, both internal and external. Few of these people have any appreciation of the centuries of hardship, exploitation, and sacrifice that the people of the West invested first in building their nations and second in constructing the industrial foundation of their way of life. Too many believe that, like political independence, the mere acquisition of machinery will produce a miracle overnight and fail to appreciate the social and educational transformation essential for the efficient use of this equipment. Too few realize the handicap involved in producing a modern industrial society in competition with the established industry of the West. They have one successful Asian example in Japan, but the Japanese would find their transformation into an industrialized state much more difficult today. The problems of modernization are not insurmountable, but their solution will take time—more time than the peoples of Asia and Africa are yet ready to accept. Moreover, more than machines will be needed: each society will have to make its own adaptations and alterations of its traditional culture and social structure to meet the demands of a mechanized society.

This point cannot be too strongly emphasized: no Westerner should expect any of the Eastern civilizations to abandon its past and refashion itself wholly in any Western image. Such expectations will only lead to misunderstanding, disappointment, and disillusionment. Borrowings and similarities there will be, but on closer examination these changes will prove to be superficial additions or adaptations that involve at most a modification in the essence of the cultural heritage.

On the other hand, similar problems in modernization can be expected to produce familiar solutions. For example, the problem of unification involved in nation-building in the West resulted in the enhancement of the arbitrary authority of the government. Already answers of a similar nature have been found necessary for the solution of the same problem in the East. Again, protectionist policies for industrial development in competition with established industry were deemed essential by our own country as well as other Western states. Should we be surprised or alarmed if developing Eastern states have recourse to the same policies? Until very recently America was so completely absorbed with its internal development that its cardinal policy was one of no entangling alliances. Are we justified in criticizing Eastern states that pursue a similar policy?

Finally, before becoming too self-righteous or confident, let's examine briefly for perspective the accomplishment of Western civilization, the latest to develop. Without question Western civilization has surpassed all its predecessors in material achievement and has created greater material comfort for the many as well as the few. This task has been accomplished primarily by harnessing the forces of nature to serve man. Success in this endeavor has involved costs both to man and his environment. But so monumental has this success been that many Western authors wax eloquent over the conquest of nature which is singled out as man's ultimate objective and, indeed, the very reason for his existence. If *human* nature was included in this definition, I might agree.

Actually the conception of the conquest of nature is a product of the modern West along with the idea of progress. Modern man's predecessors, both civilized and savage, sought to live in harmony with nature. They did alter their environment unconsciously but not intentionally. While Western mastery of the forces of nature is a magnificent achievement of vital importance to the future welfare of mankind, perhaps Western dedication to this essentially material objective represents a case of overspecialization.

A larger challenge that has confronted man from the beginning is the mastery of man himself. From the time when a few families banded together man has faced the need to tame his wild and independent spirit, to develop institutions and ideals for cooperative effort on a larger and larger scale. Although the modern West has made significant contributions in this area, especially in communications technology, its overall record is one of neglect and secondary or unconscious interest. Indeed, its most dynamic contribution, the conception of nationalism that has so enhanced unity within the boundaries of the state, works against the development of any larger unity except in terms of power. The major Eastern civilizations all gave greater attention to the problem of human relations. In this field the West may very well have something to learn from the East. Eastern experience in human relations combined with Western technology may someday provide the solution to the dilemma of potential destruction with which the West's progress in the conquest of nature confronts us today.

This then is our task: first, to examine and explain the rise and development of the first civilizations in the valleys of the Nile,

Tigris-Euphrates, Indus, and Yellow rivers, identifying those institutions and values that are still influential; second, to analyze the expansion into neighboring areas and the alterations brought about by interaction with other peoples and other sets of values; third, to pay special attention to the interaction between East and West that began in 1500 and has progressed at a greatly accelerated tempo during the past century; and last, to survey the recent developments throughout the East. Primary attention will be given to the appearance, development, and modification of those institutions and values with enduring significance. Specific historical events will not be ignored, but they will be drawn on selectively to provide a frame of reference in support of the overall objective of gaining a knowledge and understanding of how and why the current possessors of these various and complex heritages view the world today, both internally and externally, as they do.

This book is organized into six parts in each of which separate chapters bring the story of the major civilizations to an equivalent stage of development. Later, the accounts of secondary civilizations in Japan and Southeast Asia will be introduced. This method of organization, in contrast to separate treatment of each civilization from beginning to end, is intended to encourage comparative analysis that will give a deeper understanding and appreciation of the distinctive characteristics of each civilization and the difficulties involved in reaching a meeting of minds in our rapidly shrinking, modern world.

After an abbreviated look in this chapter at the probable factors behind the movement toward civilization, Part One will successively examine the emergence of the civilizations of the Middle East, India, and China and the articulation of their distinguishing ideals, values, and practices with particular attention to those that have proved most enduring. Since these civilizations arose at differing dates and each evolved at its own rate,

the concluding dates will not coincide but will vary according to when each arrived at a somewhat similar stage of development, having worked out its basic precepts and practices. The subsequent parts will approach a greater chronological similitude.

GEOGRAPHICAL LIMITS AND FACTORS

Before attempting to explain how men became civilized, some remarks on the geographical scope and conditions of this study are needed. In maximum extent, including peripheral regions, the area concerned is a broad arc stretching from Sakhalin Island in the northeast to the Atlantic coast of Africa in the west. The northern edge from east to west sweeps through Russian territory along the northern watershed of the Amur River, Lake Baikal, the northern tip of Outer Mongolia and then of the Caspian Sea, through the Black and Mediterranean seas, and including the Iberian Peninsula during the period of Muslim domination. The southern edge initially bulges far to the south to include the island states of the Philippines and Indonesia, passes south of Ceylon and the Arabian Peninsula, and thence across Africa to the Atlantic coast.

This is a vast area that includes the full range of physical and environmental possibilities, from burning desert wastelands to rain-soaked tropical forests and from the world's highest snowcapped mountains to areas well below sea level. In it also live representatives of every form of the human race. Many waves of migration have washed back and forth promoting mixtures of peoples and cultures and in other instances leaving pockets of primitive societies in many places.

This area contains more than 60 percent of the world's population with 90 percent of this figure concentrated in the great bulge east of Iran, thanks mainly to the multitudes living in India and China. The majority of the whole area, however, is thinly populated for geographical reasons. Extensive desert, steppeland, jungles, and mountains simply cannot support many people. Too much rain leaches the fertility out of the soil. Too little water will not maintain men or beasts in any great numbers. Even with modern technology it is doubtful if more than 20 percent of the area can be claimed for agriculture. From an overall point of view most of it is exceedingly unattractive for human occupation. Yet through human ingenuity certain parts have supported large populations from ancient times, and in these regions agriculturally based civilizations first arose and prospered. Through trade these civilizations radiated their influence to their neighbors near and far, and also acted as magnets attracting less advanced peoples into their orbit, often peacefully, but frequently forcefully.

The eastern, most heavily populated part of the area is dominated geographically by the forbidding Tibetan plateau girdled by the greatest mountain ranges in the world, which separate rather than unite its major regions. The snowcapped Hindu Kush, Pamirs, Himalaya, Karakoram, Altyn Tagh, and T'ien Shan ranges are the sources of the great rivers that spiral outward from the Tibetan hub to water and fertilize the plains of Pakistan, India, Southeast Asia, and China. Today the Chinese colossus stands astride this geographical center and looks down on its Asian neighbors below. The barrier nature of Tibet now seems to be belied by the successful movement of substantial numbers of Chinese troops across this "roof of the world."

An entirely opposite quality characterizes the western part of the area, known as the Middle East (the inappropriate but current title of Southwest Asia and North Africa). Its outstanding feature is the function of its core as a crossroads between the continents of Europe, Asia, and Africa. Thus its geographical heart serves to join rather than to separate. As peoples and trade have converged on this region, a selection from only a few routes was possible. During the 5000

years of recorded history, efforts to control these routes have been a key factor in the relationships of Middle Eastern states. Perhaps the initial development of civilization in such a strategic center is to be expected in those river valleys suitable for the support of substantial populations by intensive agricultural production.

For the moment these broad geographical generalizations will suffice. Later, when dealing with specific parts, a more detailed examination of the peculiarities of each one will be made. Two contrasting regions within our area have been defined: the one, divided by a frigid mountain mass, while it has provided the rivers that support civilized life in their lower reaches, has served to separate and largely isolate the chief centers of civilization; the other, united by a crossroads between continents and seas, has drawn people into contact to mix and interchange themselves, their ideas, and their products. Modern technology has brought into question the effectiveness of each of these qualities, just as it has also brought into question the continued separate development of peoples the world around. Geographical conditions can limit and check man's development in a particular direction but, as has been well-stated, "ideas have wings" which geographical barriers can only impede. Contact with other people with other ideas has led man to alter his way of life in the past and can be confidently expected to exercise such an effect in the future.

CULTURE AND CIVILIZATION

Before looking at the development of early man two troublesome terms, culture and civilization, need to be defined. The multitude of ways in which these two vital words have been used by social scientists have made them almost meaningless. As used here, *culture* refers to everything *learned* after birth from someone else, including habits, customs, skills, and values. By this definition all human—and even some animal—societies, no matter how primitive or advanced, have cultures varying in degree but not in kind from one another. The central purpose of any culture is to enhance the survival of the group. Therefore, differing environments will call for different cultures. The culture of a worker in an electronics factory will scarcely be suitable for an Eskimo; their respective conditions for survival are altogether different, and this difference in environment makes each culture wholly valid and appropriate for its members. Of course, each may find some facets of value to survival to borrow from the other's culture. In this way cultures in contact with each other may become modified.

The fundamental feature of culture, then, is learning, a characteristic not wholly the monopoly of human societies. Birds and men share the need to teach their young, respectively, to fly and to walk, but beyond this point all similarity ceases. Biologically the child of man is dependent on his elders for many years. These long years of dependence are required not only for his physical development but also to learn the complex culture of his group essential to the survival both of himself and his society. The more complex the culture, the longer becomes the period of dependency. In our culture some graduate students, 30 years of age, have yet to become productive members of society. Moreover, in human society the need for cooperative effort precluded the possibility of complete independence. Every man—even the member of a primitive hunting band—must learn and obey the discipline of the group.

Civilization is an arbitrary term used to distinguish those comparatively large, settled societies that have surpassed the tribal stage in size and have developed complex governments usually associated with the skill of writing to supplement memory as a means of maintaining and transmitting the essential records and knowledge of the group. The potentialities of human memory, however, have often been underestimated. Indian priests performed prodigious feats of memorization. The use of written records reflects a more impersonal, institutionalized stage in human relations. In addition, such a society normally requires an administrative center—a city—that must have an extensive domain or an extensive trade for its support. Moreover, the growth of civilization is accompanied by greater specialization and division of labor, not only in governmental but also in economic activities. Such a development, as will be seen, came about by need, not by chance. When the requisite raw materials are close at hand, an agricultural village can exist by itself or a group of villages may fulfill its needs with one, centrally located town which serves as a market without taking on the attributes of civilization. Other factors are required to explain the rise of a city and a civilization.

EARLY MAN

The story of early man is beset with many problems. The remains thus far discovered are too few and too scattered. Moreover, these finds are for the most part fragmentary—a part of a skull or sometimes only some teeth. The dating of these fragments is frequently the subject of wide-ranging disputes between the experts. Any story of early man's appearance and development reconstructed from such evidence should for the present be viewed with extreme caution and recognized as no more than a tentative working hypothesis. However, the increasing number of recent discoveries, especially those of Lewis Leakey in Olduvai Gorge in Tanganyika, Africa, holds the promise of more plentiful finds to work with in the future. Moreover, a new method of dating, the potassium-argon technique, suggests the possibility of greater certainty through multiple sampling. The better known carbon 14 method, so useful for dating more accurately recent prehistoric discoveries, is limited to items less than 40,000 years old. Therefore, while the story of early man may become much clearer in a few decades, the one told here is only a tentative account that is indicated by present knowledge.

Recognizable ancestors of both men and apes lived as long as 25 to 30 million years ago. One example was Proconsul who existed in several sizes in East Africa about 25 million years ago. Another example, Kisumu, with some manlike features, lived in the same region about 14 million years ago. A number of other samples of ancient primates have been found in other areas.

One of the chief features that distinguishes man-types from other primates is the production of tools rather than the mere use of natural items. Apes will make intelligent use of things at hand to get what they need, but only manlike creatures have demonstrated the forethought to fashion what nature provides to serve a specific future purpose in more than a temporary ad hoc manner. Finding such consciously fashioned stones in conjunction with manlike remains does not mean that that species necessarily did the work: he may merely have been the victim. But, if the site can be dated, tool-making creatures may be claimed to have lived at that time.

Such a site is Olduvai Gorge in Tanganyika where Lewis Leakey uncovered remains belonging to a general group found in other parts of the world and called Australopithecines. The form of the foot suggests that he walked erect, and his teeth were essentially human in type, though large in proportion to his pygmy size. His brain relative to his body size was larger than any ape's. The first date obtained by the potassium-argon method gave an age of one and three-quarter million years with a possible error of one-half million years either way.

On the basis of present evidence then there is a good possibility that manlike primates, walking erect, fashioning crude tools, and hunting small game, lived in suitable environments at the beginning of the Pleistocene epoch more than one million years ago. During this epoch, which lasted until approximately 10,000 years ago, drastic cli-

matic changes occurred as a result of at least three major glaciations along with many lesser retreats and advances of the ice sheets. During this time many types of manlike creatures must have developed, while others became extinct. Some may have been wiped out by weather changes, others may have been extinguished by more competent types, and still others may have been absorbed in mixtures leading to more advanced types. Remains of exceptionally large sizes as well as other aberrations have been found. This epoch was nature's great experimental period with man, as well as his fellow animals, until identifiably modern types appeared 250,000 years ago.

There is no need to catalogue the many types and their peculiarities. What is important are the overall trends of development that were to culminate in civilized societies.

Biologically, man evolved as a hunter in contrast with the apes who remained primarily vegetarians living off the fruits of their forest homes. No significant physical changes have become manifest since man began to settle down to a more sedentary life during the past 10,000 years. The basic role of the hunter is attested by the association of small game fossils with the early Australopithecines. The improvement of the skills of the hunter is illustrated by the location of bones from the largest game with later manlike types. Incidentally evidence of the use and control of fire have been found in these later sites.

Physically men may not appear especially well adapted to be effective hunters. The erect posture provided a wider horizon, but did not contribute to speed. On the other hand, the freeing of the arms from the task of locomotion made possible the manipulative development of the hands for the production and use of tools and weapons. The progressive utilization of this ability to provide extra-bodily adaptations to the environment could not have proceeded very far without an even more important development: the gradual increase of the size of the brain in proportion to the size and weight of the body. To illustrate this point the brain space of the Australopithecines averaged about 650 cubic centimeters, the range of succeeding types extended from 775 to 1225 cubic centimeters, and that of modern man varies from less than 1100 to more than 1800 cubic centimeters. The growth of the brain called for a change in the skullcap from a low to a high vault and from a sloping to a vertical forehead. With the development of a more vertical forehead the heavy eyebrow ridges that had protected the eyes were no longer necessary. Other related physical changes also took place that we need not describe here. The most important point is that the reliance on extra-bodily adaptations freed man from the trammels of a specific environment, an advantage not shared by any other animal.

One vital feature, which must have developed at an early date, but for which there is no direct evidence, is speech, a necessary attribute for the transmission of culture and the planning and organization of the hunt. Thought, and especially forethought, is inconceivable without the identification and abstract classification represented by words. When we think, we carry on a silent conversation concerning objects that may or may not be in sight. With speech and thought, not only can a group's culture be transmitted but also experiences can be pooled and accumulated to produce cultural change and improvement.

For success as a hunter, then, man depended less on strictly physical attributes, such as fangs and claws, and more on the development of skill and cunning in dealing with the animal environment. As the environment changed, he moved after his prey or adapted his techniques to the new conditions. In addition, he early learned to cooperate in hunting bands to overcome the advantages of his fleet-footed or larger quarry. Throughout the hundreds of thousands of years that man was evolving he was gradually improving his tools and his weapons.

Unfortunately only the more durable ones made of stone have survived, but many others of perishable materials can be imagined, especially in the later stages.

Finally, some later examples of early men provide the first clear evidence of a concern with life and death (a basic factor in spiritual development) in burials and pictorial representations. Undoubtedly, man's emotions and thoughts had previously been stirred by considerations of this kind, but the only tangible evidence, of questionable interpretation, are tools fashioned with excessive care or whose usefulness cannot easily be explained except as cult objects. Although for a million years modern man's predecessors were fully occupied with the problem of survival, it is difficult, if not inconceivable, to imagine any group with tools, speech, and thought that did not devise some kind of explanation for the anxieties and tensions generated by the life they lived. In other words, every society, no matter how primitive, requires the cultural cement of a satisfying ideology of assorted, but comprehensible, superstitions, beliefs, ideals, and values. Without an integrating ideology suited to its way of life, social discipline breaks down, the group disintegrates, and the members perish. This is just another way of saying that man with speech and thought is a social animal dependent on cooperation in a group for survival.

The story of man involves the progressive formation of larger and larger groups. During the first million years little evidence of progress of this kind is apparent. Dependence on a hunting and food-gathering economy is not conducive to the growth of population in a prescribed area or to the grouping of numbers larger than those required by the way of life. This step has to await a revolutionary change in the way of living: the shift from food collecting to food producing made possible by the domestication of plants and animals.

Just who took the first step in this revolution and when, where, and why it took

place will never be precisely known. Possibly the young of animals killed in the hunt had been kept and cared for from the beginning, but there is no evidence that this led to domestication. Those men who enjoyed lush hunting conditions during the fluctuations of the latter part of the last glaciation appear to have taken the first step by domesticating the dog as a hunting partner. Wild dogs following hunters as scavengers had probably become so used to being near men that the transition was not difficult.

The first crops and food animals domesticated existed in their wild state only in the upland areas of Southwest Asia. Here wheat, barley, goats, and sheep were first mastered by men. Exactly when, where, and why is a subject of wide dispute. For thousands of years men had been showing signs of settling down rather than following game as the climate changed. In addition, more complex cultures had been developing as represented in tools, burials, and religiously inspired art forms. Greater skills in hunting and food-gathering were required to feed a larger and more settled population. Evidence of the shaman and his imitative magic that was supposed to induce greater animal reproduction and success in the hunt became more widespread. Perhaps we can gain small comfort from the realization that population problems are not something new in the world.

At the same time the climate was changing in ways that are not yet fully understood. About 12,000 B.C. the ice sheet began to retreat for the last time. The newly exposed, well-watered land provided plentiful forage for the herds of animals pursued by the hunters, while the sea, gradually rising approximately 3 feet a century, took other land away. The pattern of rainfall shifted northward, leading to a drier environment in the Middle East, similar to the present, between 8000 and 6000 B.C. The landscape, however, was not so desolate then because man had only begun to alter nature by felling trees with the consequent damage to the soil.

At the same time in Northern Europe, between the advance of the forests and human attrition, the herds of large animals dwindled or disappeared, and the hunters had to adapt to a different and more difficult environment. The warming trend did not end in 6000 B.C. but continued to a maximum around 4000 B.C., creating denser forests in Northern Europe and, because of a shift in the weather pattern, wetter, less arid conditions in the Middle East. Against this background of climatic and cultural change, which was accompanied by an apparent growth in population, the shift from food collecting to food producing and the ultimate rise of the first civilizations must be viewed.

In the hill country of Palestine, Syria, and Iraq the earliest evidence has been found that suggests the development of food production as part of a mixed agricultural and hunting economy. The dating of these finds with greater precision has been made possible by the carbon 14 technique, devised by Willard F. Libby in 1948. This procedure i based on the knowledge that plants live o carbon dioxide, which is subject to cosm radiation. When the plant dies, it ceases absorb radioactivity. The disintegration the radioactive carbon 14 atoms then p ceeds at a fixed rate, and with a Geiger co ter the date when a piece of charcoal or o suitable sample died can be determ within a reasonable margin of error as as 40,000 years ago. In a numbe sites—and there are many more pot ones to be excavated—flint sickle tee the bones of possibly domesticated a have been excavated. The flints are kn have been used to cut wheat or other because they have been shined by th contained in the stems of all Whether these sickles harvested ticated or wild grain is disputed, bu for the former notes that wild wh burst and throw out their seed, wh mesticated wheat pod is a mutatio mains closed and thus can be harv a sickle. The only efficient way

wild wheat is with a stick and a basket. This argument seems convincing and, if accepted, means that wherever and whenever sickles are found wheat had been domesticated. The earliest carbon 14 date for such an association is 8900±300 B.C. at Zawi Chemi in northern Iraq. At a number of sites in Palestine a sickle culture, named Natufian, may be somewhat later in date. In the bottom layer of the Jericho mound a burned building, which appears to have been a Natufian shrine, has yielded a date of 7800±210 B.C.

JERICHO: THE EARLIEST SETTLEMENT

These early farmers, if indeed they were, apparently did not appreciate the significance of their discovery. Hunting was still their main source of livelihood, and the many bones of the gazelle, which lives in a more open, drier climate than the deer, as well as those of other game, are also informative about the environment. Most of the sites represent temporary encampments indicating the need to follow the game according to the seasons. The supposed Natufian shrine is doubly significant because it is the earliest solidly built structure. It was an 11 by 21 feet rectangular building with substantial stone walls in which wooden posts were set at intervals. Unlike other sites Jericho is 900 feet below sea level. What attracted the Natufian hunters—and their quarry—was the reliable spring. A shrine at such a spot in an area extremely hot and arid in the summer and wholly dependent on the reliable spring is understandable. The time of a settled agricultural life in permanent villages had not yet arrived. On the other hand, the presence of seashell ornaments in burials on the eastern slopes of the Judaean hills suggests that trade was already carried on over substantial distances.

Although other sites provide supplementary evidence, Jericho is invaluable for presenting a picture of continuous development from hunting site to village to walled town with an economy that supported several thousand inhabitants. For several centuries or more, hunters living in flimsy huts continued to occupy the site until solid round houses, made of hand-molded bricks and having domed roofs, indicate a permanent village settlement. Moreover, with the advent of solid structures the area occupied was expanded to 8 to 10 acres. To support this enlarged population, irrigated agriculture or extensive trade, or a combination of both, must be presumed. Since the surrounding area has been continuously farmed or occupied, the chances of discovering positive evidence of such an ancient irrigation system are extremely unlikely.

Not long after the site was fully occupied, massive walls were constructed around it, which introduces a new element. Fortifications of this kind imply the presence on occasion of hostile forces of substantial size, as well as a prosperous population that is large enough to supply the surplus labor for such a major public work. The wall was built of solid stone, 6½ feet wide and preserved at one point to a height of 12 feet. Here it included a stone tower, still standing 30 feet high. Two successive building phases added a ditch 27 feet wide and 9 feet deep cut into the rock and a raising of the wall, which survives to a height of 25 feet. A carbon 14 date from the third phase of 6850±210 B.C. suggests that the original wall may have been built before 7000 B.C. In the thousand years since the Natufian shrine the people of Jericho had made the full transition from a hunting economy to a settled community with a mixed economy and an efficient organization of substantial complexity. The maintenance of the same general style suggests that this development was carried out by successive generations of the same people cumulatively adding to their cultural heritage. Then comes a break. The evidence of burning may mean that the great defensive ramparts not only were needed, but also proved inadequate. On the other hand, the subsequent erosions, indicating a period of

unknown duration when the site was unoccupied, may mean that this prepottery neolithic culture was terminated by a natural disaster.

When the town was rebuilt, the work was done by a different people. Every aspect of style was entirely different. Many-roomed, flat-roofed houses of rectangular shape built around courtyards replaced the round, domed houses of their predecessors. The handmade bricks and almost every utensil were radically different in style. Tools made of obsidian, probably from the Anatolian plateau in modern Turkey, and other items not locally available suggest a substantial trade in luxury goods over considerable distances. A figurine of a woman with a flowing gown gathered at the waist, arms akimbo, and hands beneath her breasts is similar to the much later representations of the Mother Goddess and indicates the existence already of the idea of a personified deity. A small shrine contained a pedestal on which was mounted a conical pillar similar to those found in many later Semitic sanctuaries. Most unique and interesting from both a religious and artistic point of view was the treatment of skulls of the dead. The features of the face were reconstructed with plaster, using shells for the eyes, for a truly portraitlike appearance. Previous to the production of these unusual "sculptures," defenses apparently were deemed unnecessary. Immediately thereafter, about 5850±160 B.C., massive walls using even bigger stones and encompassing as large an area as the prior ones were built.

Our attention has been concentrated on Jericho for a picture of the transition from a hunting to a settled agricultural community supporting a substantial population because to date this picture is unparalleled anywhere else. Certainly future excavations will uncover similar settled societies of early date, although not all groups shared such a remarkable development. Most people were probably still following an unsophisticated way of life relying primarily on hunting sup-

plemented by occasional farming. Yet during the thousand years of this last-studied phase at Jericho (c 6500–5500 B.C.) most known sites had become permanent ones of village size with some, such a Catal Hüyük on the southern Anatolian plateau, reaching the size of towns.

The stimulus to the development on the Anatolian plateau in modern Turkey appears to have been the demand for obsidian obtained from the volcanoes in central Anatolia and a general growth in trade throughout the Fertile Crescent. In short, the tempo of life was picking up. A further notable Anatolian contribution was handmade pottery which was of a high quality from its first known appearance in the latter part of the seventh millennium. By 5500 B.C. its use was universal throughout the area as well as the obsidian goods produced in its workshops. Another example of cultural diffusion was the appearance of female figurines representing a Mother Goddess in almost all sites of this date, illustrating the general concern for human, animal, and plant fertility on which the survival of every community depended.

Another stimulus to exchange was the discovery of the first metal, copper, which was used and traded in small amounts between 5500 and 5000 B.C. in Anatolia and Iran. During this period the arid lowlands of Elam (southwest Iran) and Iraq were first settled. In southern Iraq irrigation was essential to raise a crop because the winter rainfall was insufficient. In addition, stone or copper for tools had to be imported. Surplus crops had to be raised or other goods produced to pay for these imports. The first steps toward civilization had been taken.

Although the first steps toward civilization had been taken, however, its arrival was maddeningly slow. For the next 1500 years the gains made were slowly consolidated and expanded, the population grew, and new peoples from the hills entered the area. The brew was simmering at a low heat.

Perhaps the most significant development was in the field of religion as represented by the temple architecture on a monumental scale that was produced by the 'Ubaid culture of Mesopotamia in the last centuries of the fifth millenium. The social and political organization implied by these temples, or possibly some other factor, made it possible for these vigorous newcomers within a few centuries to impose their culture over the whole of the Land of the Two Rivers (Tigris and Euphrates) and to extend their influence into Syria. As in later civilizations, the wheel-turned pottery became utilitarian and dull compared to the often brilliantly painted wares of less civilized folk. Even so, its wide dispersion further testifies to this people's widespread influence. This culture, which precedes the birth of civilization, strictly defined, reflects the development of an urban, materialistic outlook that was demonstrated by expanding trade and a religiously sanctioned political authority, illustrated by increasingly monumental temple architecture.

The story of the development of early man, who evolved as a hunter during the million or more years of the Pleistocene epoch, has concluded with his transition from a food collector to a food producer, relying more on his newly acquired skills as a farmer and

shepherd. The information on which this sketch is based is provided by the anthropologists and archeologists who excavate and analyze the material remains of man and his cultures. What men said and thought and believed can be only vaguely inferred from these fossils and material goods. Beyond orally transmitted myths no historical account of persons and events, thoughts and beliefs, is possible without the invention of writing to record these ephemera. The earliest known example of writing is a small limestone tablet, dated about 3500 B.C. found at Kish near Babylon on the Euphrates River. This record marks the threshold of history and civilization, but for another thousand years major reliance must still be placed on the archeologists, not only for the written records but also for the development of cities and civilizations. The written records, which become prolific and decipherable by 3000 B.C. both in Mesopotamia and later in Egypt, are but brief economic or political accounts that are intended to supplement the memory of the businessmen and officials of the growing states. Not until after 2500 B.C. are there literary accounts of sufficient length to expand and explain the archeological record in human terms.

SIGNIFICANT DATES

c.	1000000 B.C.	First tool-producing primates (*Australopithecines*)
c.	250000 B.C.	First "Modern Types"
c.	12000 B.C.	Retreat of last ice-sheet
c.	8900 B.C.	Earliest evidence of domesticated (?) wheat
c.	8000 B.C.	Maximum aridity in Middle East
c.	7800 B.C.	First Stone Building at Jericho
c.	7000 B.C.	Jericho is first known walled town
c. 6500–5500 B.C.		Many towns and evidence of trade
c. 5500–5000 B.C.		Trade in copper and indication of irrigation
c.	4000 B.C.	Climatic optimum—maximum rainfall in Middle East
c. 4100–3100 B.C.		'Ubaid period—monumental temples
c.	3500 B.C.	First writing found at Kish

SELECTED READINGS

No individual can be fully versed in the history and culture of the vast area that this study covers and, therefore, he must draw heavily on the works of specialists. These selections represent the studies that have been found most stimulating and readable. Particular attention should be given to the source readings listed in subsequent chapters. There is no better way of gaining the "feel" of an alien civilization than to immerse oneself to the greatest possible extent in its own writings, even in translation. To encourage the building of a personal library, useful paperback books are stressed in these selections and are indicated by an asterisk (*).

*Childe, V. Gordon, *What Happened in History*. Baltimore: Penguin Books, 1964.

*Clark, Grahame, and Piggott, Stuart, *Prehistoric Societies*. Baltimore: Penguin Books, 1970.

*Clark, Grahame, *World Prehistory*. Cambridge: Cambridge University Press, 1961.

Coon, Carleton S., *Caravan*. Rev. ed.; New York: Holt, Rinehart and Winston, 1966.

————, *The Origin of Races*. New York: Knopf, 1962.

————, *The Story of Man*. New York: Knopf, 1962.

Cressey, George B., *Asia's Lands and Peoples*. New York: McGraw-Hill, 1963.

————, *Crossroads*. Chicago: Lippincott, 1960.

Ginsburg, Norton, ed., *The Pattern of Asia*. Englewood Cliffs, N.J.: Prentice-Hall, 1958.

Howell, F. Clark, *Early Man*. New York: Time-Life Books, 1970.

*Kenyon, Kathleen M., *Archeology in the Holy Land*. London: Ernest Benn, 1960.

*Leakey, Lewis S., and Goodall, Vanne M., *Unveiling Man's Origins*. Cambridge, Mass.: Schenkman, 1966.

Piggott, Stuart, ed., *The Dawn of Civilization*. New York: McGraw-Hill, 1961.

CHAPTER TWO

THE FIRST CIVILIZATION: MESOPOTAMIA AND EGYPT

Iraq

In fairly close succession the two earliest known civilizations emerged in the later fourth millennium and the early third millennium in the valleys of the two principal flood river basins of the Middle East: the Tigris-Euphrates and the Nile. In both regions men in small numbers had been living a comparatively primitive existence for several thousand years. Just what caused them to break out of this pattern—increasing aridity, a growing population, the arrival of new peoples, or other factors—cannot be clearly determined. While the fertility of the soil was annually renewed by flood deposits of rich silt, dikes and irrigation, utilized to realize its agricultural potential, required a heavy human investment in disciplined labor. For the mobilization and direction of manpower more advanced institutions than those of the tribe had to be developed.

Because of varying conditions, however, this development followed a different and distinctive course in each region. In Egypt, civilization and unity arose at the same time and cities were very slow in evolving, thanks in large part to the ease of two-way communications on the Nile which facilitated unification. Moreover, the comparative rarity of external threats reduced the need for a fortified urban concentration as a ruling center. In Mesopotamia, on the other hand, a number of city-states developed their respective territories and only after long centuries of conflict was unification achieved. Even then, the city-state heritage limited the authority of the ruler as compared to the theoretical monopoly of power concentrated in the person of the Egyptian pharaoh.

Despite contacts and exchanges, both civilizations also followed their own distinctive paths in cultural and religious development to meet their differing conditions and needs. While here we emphasize these differences, the many features and attitudes that they shared are, perhaps, more important because the subsequent development in the Middle East drew eclectically on both heritages. Nevertheless, the Middle East is unique in the East in its possession of two centers of civilization, and the later history of the region, even to the present day, can frequently be explained in terms of the contest between them for influence and dominance over the entire area, particularly the strategic Syria-Palestine buffer zone that separates them.

EARLY SUMERIAN ERA (C. 3500 – 2900 B.C.)

After 1500 years of preparation the appearance of writing about 3500 B.C. signaled the emergence of the first civilization in that most inhospitable region, the hot and swampy lower reaches of the Tigris and Euphrates rivers as they made their way to the sea. Of course, both the large-scale communal efforts required to control the erratic and devastating floods of these rivers and the broader outlook demanded by the local lack of essential materials, such as wood, stone, and copper provided the preconditions that were conducive to the development of civilization. Moreover, it was probably no mere accident that the first signs of civilization coincided with the arrival on the scene of a new people, the Sumerians, who contributed new vigor and stimulated a renewed cultural advance. The clearest symptom of cultural change and expansion was a new pottery style of red and grey burnished ware that was turned on a fast potter's wheel and spread rapidly over Mesopotamia, supplanting the last painted pottery cultures throughout the area. An unfortunate casualty of civilization, here and elsewhere, has been the artistic painted pots in favor of monotonous, but more advanced ware that is mass-produced on the fast potter's wheel.

Precisely who the Sumerians (called the black-headed people) were, or where they came from, cannot be ascertained as yet. Their agglutinative language, preserved in their writings, cannot be related to any other language in the Middle East. What seems certain is that they did not liquidate their predecessors, the 'Ubaid people, but mixed with them and built the Sumerian civilization on the foundations that had already been laid.

Sumerian civilization was truly the gift of its two rivers which poured into the Persian Gulf some 150 miles north of the present shoreline. Irrigation water drawn mainly from the slower moving Euphrates was essential to farming, the key to the support of larger populations. The Tigris, anciently called Idiglat meaning "swift as an arrow," was less predictable and controllable and, therefore, less inviting to settlement.

As irrigated farming made possible the support of more people in relative prosperity, the area served as a magnet and stimulant to the people of surrounding areas. The lack of stone, minerals, and wood needed by the growing cities encouraged trade and consequent interaction with the upland regions to the north and the east. Mountain-girt Iran to the east looks down on Mesopotamia from the rugged Zagros range. In isolated valleys melting snow and springs supplied, then and now, adequate water for limited, self-sufficient communities. The interior plateau, into the salt flats of which drained the surplus runoff, was inhospitable to more than scattered settlements. No rivers united any large areas. All the forces of nature worked for disunity. But Iran had an abundance of assets needed in Sumer: stone, minerals, timber, and a sturdy people. The early records illus-

trate trade relations with Iran, and via Iran with the source of lapis lazuli, a much-valued semiprecious stone, in Afghanistan. The surplus products of the plain were exchanged for those of the mountains, and international relations of the Mesopotamian city-states often involved gaining control of a good source of supply. In addition, surplus population in the mountains was peacefully absorbed into the growing economy of the plain, though on more than one occasion, the mountaineers found opportunities to intervene militantly in the affairs of the plain.

The northern part of the plain, centered on the point where the two rivers come within 30 miles of each other, was settled by Semitic people and known as Akkad. Emulating their southern neighbors, they, too, developed powerful city-states. The names of the rulers of these northern states preserved in the king-lists are mostly Semitic, and eventually these defenders of Sumerian civilization against pressures from the north were to bring an enforced unity to the whole Mesopotamian region. In addition to being middlemen in trade with northern Iran, they served as intermediaries for trade with the north and the west.

Indeed, northern Mesopotamia rather than Arabia may have been the original home of the Semitic people who moved into the grazing lands of the Desert Bay embraced by the Fertile Crescent and the Arabian peninsula only after the domestication of sheep and goats had made such a nomadic existence feasible. Whether this was the case or not, a constant theme in the history of the Middle East has been the contest between the desert and the sown, between the nomadic herdsmen and the sedentary farmers. Most of the time a balance has prevailed, the economy of each complementing the other. On other occasions this balance has been disturbed in favor of one or the other. Much later the introduction of the "ship of the desert," the camel, about the twelfth century B.C., added a new dimension to the Bedouin economy; new trade routes across the desert provided them with a new source of livelihood.

The ancient trade with southern Anatolia was further developed by the defenders of Sumerian civilization. Their merchants penetrated the central plateau of modern Turkey, which is another mountain-girt internal drainage area only slightly more hospitable than the lower one of Iran. The annual rainfall of 10 to 17 inches made marginal agriculture possible and encouraged militant activity from this assembly area in times of drought.

Mesopotamian merchants early made contact with the favored entrepots, Ugarit and Byblos, on the Syria-Lebanon coast. Here they met Egyptian traders seeking the famed cedars of Lebanon as well as other needs. The central crossroads nature of the area indicated by its physical position has been reflected in the varying cultural and political influences of Egypt, Anatolia, and Mesopotamia throughout the history of its many states. As in Mesopotamia, its history also illustrates the contest between the desert and the sown.

The early history of Sumer and Akkad from roughly 3500 to 2900 B.C. is only vaguely sketched in later written records. A Sumerian king list starts, "when kingship was lowered from heaven, the kingship was in Eridu," and then names five cities and their rulers. Since the reigns ascribed to these sovereigns are of fantastic length, this account appears to be a projection into the past of the type of political organization that had evolved when the list was compiled.

Whatever the case may be, this period seems to have been prosperous and expansive with plentiful virgin lands to be brought under the plow by new irrigation canals and drainage ditches. Each city had its patron deity, and the citizens were the servants of their particular god or goddess in the Sumerian pantheon. Temples of sunbaked brick sometimes on stone foundations were the headquarters of the priests and priestesses who interpreted the will of the deity

and organized and directed the labors of the people in public works, such as the reclamation of land by irrigation works. Naturally those who farmed these lands and depended on the temple's control and regulation of the irrigation works owed a debt to the deity, whether or not ownership was vested in it. In this fashion the priests, especially if they became hereditary, were in a position to abuse their authority and assume what amounted to a combination of kingship and chief priesthood supported by religious sanction and economic control. Initially, with plenty of land to be developed, boundary quarrels between these city-states were probably rare. As the limits of cultivation were reached and older lands became less fertile, interstate friction encouraged the centralization of authority in the hands of a single individual. The demands of war called for new or enlarged sources of revenue. Thus tyranny evolved, and the conditions for the succeeding dynastic era were prepared.

Since the temple represents the heart and soul of the civic and cultural achievement in the predynastic era, it deserves detailed consideration. The city of Uruk (biblical Erech), which has given its name to this period because the discoveries made there best illustrate its development, reached a golden age of temple architecture about 3200 B.C. A whole array of temples, of which the White Temple and the Pillar Temple are most impressive, towered over the plain on raised platforms that were composed of the remains of innumerable predecessors. The erection of temple after temple on the same site with little alteration of the general plan suggests the religious conservatism of the Sumerians. Each site was the sacred preserve for eternity of its particular deity, and liturgy prescribed the pouring of libations over the remains of the old temple before beginning the construction of its successor. Security in this uncertain life was sought through religious continuity.

The White Temple, so-called because its mud-brick walls were whitewashed, was erected on a 40 foot high terrace scaled by a steep flight of stairs and then a ramp that provided a panoramic and awe-inspiring approach for the worshiper. Both the exterior and interior walls of the temple were designed with the buttresses and recesses typical of Sumerian temple construction, which probably reflected an ancient tradition of wood construction in a forested country. Indeed, the imprint of a wooden stockade on the north suggests the use of this expensive import for decoration. The interior of the temple was composed of one long central room with a table for burnt offerings and was flanked by storerooms. Stairs gave access to the roof where the priests intoned prayers at sunrise and other times.

The Pillar Temple is notable for a raised platform with a double row of eight mosaic-covered columns through which the worshiper passed to the inner building. These earliest known columns measure as much as a monumental $8^1/_2$ feet in diameter and with the accompanying polychrome mosaic decoration must have presented a brilliant effect. The mosaic patterns used on this and other temples were composed of hundreds of thousands of black, red, and occasionally white clay cones imbedded in the wall plaster like nail heads. Again, this decoration probably was derived from an older tradition of wooden construction.

As might be expected, other arts such as sculpture achieved at this time an artistic peak not to be matched for many centuries. Also interesting and significant is the evidence of contact with predynastic Egypt provided by the finds in Egypt of Sumerian cylinder seals of this period as well as other items indicating Sumerian influence. But most significant is the increased use of writing found on clay tablets and the advance from pictographs to simplified signs representing phonetic sounds as well as meanings. However, the Sumerians never made much progress in developing a syllabic script because their essentially monosyllabic language did not require such a development.

Conversely, the number of signs that a scribe had to learn was reduced by having one sign serve for several related meanings. For example, the sign, DU, meaning leg, was also used for GUB, to stand; GIN, to go; and TUM, to carry off. On the other hand, a single syllable might have several entirely different meanings for which the same sign would be used with usually prefixed or suffixed signs to indicate the meaning intended. In the course of development the original pictographs were simplified into stylized forms that could be rapidly inscribed in a clay tablet with a standardized stylus. In this way a cursive system of writing evolved, composed of symbols only remotely related to the former pictographs. The Sumerian writing system, known as cuneiform, survived the death of the language and was adapted for the writing of the languages of succeeding Semitic and Indo-European peoples until replaced by alphabetic scripts.

Most of the clay tablets of the early Sumerian period, insofar as they can be deciphered, are economic memoranda that with other evidence help to provide a picture of the life of the times, especially as it concerns the activities of that central institution, the temple. One important feature of the Sumerian economy was the equal, if not greater, part played by the raising of livestock compared with the tilling of fields. Vast herds of sheep were a major source of income, supplemented by cattle and dairy products. An important deity in the Sumerian pantheon was Dumuzi, the shepherd-god, who according to one myth defeats the farmer-god in the contest for the hand of Inanna, the goddess of love and queen of heaven. Ultimately he dies and becomes a god of the nether world in order that his wife may be released to return to her role in the world above. Thus the shepherd-god plays an important role in an early form of the story of death and resurrection. In this religious myth the importance of the pastoral aspect of the Sumerian economy is confirmed.

Both wheat and barley were major

crops. Barley was later to become the dominant crop as excessive irrigation and inadequate drainage raised the salt content of the soil in the older fields. Beer appears to have been part of the daily ration, at least of the priests.

Copper is frequently mentioned, and seed-ploughs, nails, and a wide variety of household utensils were in daily use. The armory included the recurved bow and arrow, the socketed axe, the spear, and the dagger. Boats and both two- and four-wheel wagons were in common use. Wagons drawn by asses—the horse was not introduced until the second millennium—may have provided some mobility in military campaigns, but the major contribution of the Sumerians to military tactics was the development of a disciplined infantry phalanx in place of the former mad melee of individual duels. The impact of a massed body of drilled troops must have given them a decided advantage in battles with more primitive tribal forces.

In addition to the priest, major professions included those of carpenter, smith, and shepherd. At this time scribe and priest were probably one and the same, although at other sites tablets have been found in private homes which suggest that priests did not have a complete monopoly of literacy. Mathematical calculations used both the sexagesimal system, based on the unit of 60, and the decimal system. The former is especially flexible, since it is divisible by 30, 20, 15, 12, 10, 6, 5, 4, 3, and 2. On it is based our 360° circle and a number of our divisions of time. These early mathematicians also understood and used fractions. Recent excavations have uncovered proof that the Semitic heirs of the Sumerians mastered the fundamental laws of mathematics not long after 2000 B.C., if not earlier. Most striking is the recovery of a clay tablet at Baghdad in 1962 B.C. that gives a full and clear demonstration of what has been known as the "Pythagorean" theorem after the Greek philosopher and mathematician of the fifth century B.C. Future discoveries will undoubtedly expand our knowledge and appreciation of ancient Mesopotamian mathematical prowess.

Texts classifying and compartmentalizing various branches of knowledge represent the beginnings of science.

The need of temples and rulers for trained clerks and officials generated formal education, and reading, writing, and arithmetic established that inevitable association of teacher and pupil with the endless exercises essential to the mastery of these civilized disciplines. Many tablets obviously represent student exercises by the range of writing competence they demonstrate. Although education was for the wealthy few, several homely stories show that the relationships of parents, pupils, and teachers have changed little through the ages. Discipline was rigorous and Sumerian pedagogy did not believe in sparing the rod. One story relates a typical student's day in which he made his recitation, ate a lunch of two rolls his mother had given him, and did more written and oral work in the afternoon. In the evening his father praised his written work and his recitation. But the next day the monitor said he was tardy and with a quaking heart he entered the classroom and bowed to the teacher. Despite this demonstration of respect, however, he had a bad day, and that evening he persuaded his father that his schoolwork might improve if the teacher were invited to dinner and given gifts. The teacher accepted and, after dinner and gifts, rhapsodized on the promise and diligence of his student. Apparently, teachers were inadequately paid and welcomed gratuities.

Another story about the problem of an indulgent parent and a delinquent child is as old as civilization. After upbraiding his son for truancy, the father told him how to behave in school and then required him to repeat these instructions. The father proceeded to berate his son for his ingratitude pointing out that he never made him work as the sons of other fathers did. And how did his son repay his kindness? He neglected school and wasted his time wandering in the streets and searching out pleasures. Instead, he should emulate his brothers or even his closest friend and win the respect of his kinsmen. Finally, like fathers throughout the ages, he asserted that dutiful sons should follow in their fathers' footsteps, adding that the scribal art was the most honored of professions.

THE EARLY DYNASTIC ERA
(C. 2900 – 2340 B.C.)

The period after about 2900 B.C., is labeled the dynastic period because of the intensified struggle for hegemony over all the city-states by clearly identified hereditary rulers. This struggle culminated in the short-lived empire established by the Semitic ruler of Akkad, Sargon, about 2340 B.C. The period is also known as the heroic age because later poets found the setting for their epic tales in this era, which raises doubts about their reliability, but clearly a new age had begun.

Militant competition for supremacy began in earnest, the two initial rivals being the city of Kish in the north and the city of Uruk in the south. The seriousness of their rivalry is attested in a poem concerning an ultimatum delivered by Agga, the last ruler of the first dynasty of Kish, to the epic hero Gilgamesh, fifth ruler of the first dynasty of Uruk. (Enough evidence suggests the reality of this ruler.) The reaction of Gilgamesh to the demand for capitulation indicates that the authority of rulers was something less than absolute at this date. First, he sought the advice of the elders who recommended submission to Kish rather than to face the possibility of destruction. Dissatisfied with this advice, he then turned to an assembly of the men of the city who declared themselves ready to fight to the finish for their independence. Thus from as early as 2800 B.C. comes an example of a people confronted with the classic decision of accepting peace at any price or of facing possible destruction in defense of freedom.

Although this poem suggests somewhat democratic institutions, the trend of the times was in the direction of authoritarianism. Indeed, in another poem Gilgamesh himself is pictured as an oppressive tyrant. A general condition of fully developed lands of declining fertility appears to have provided the chief stimulus to intercity competition. Further reclamation efforts demanded larger resources than any single city could command. Moreover, a slight decline in rainfall combined with the long-term consequences of overgrazing may have led to a shrinkage of the available pastureland. In these circumstances the larger cities with the strongest rulers, the most skilled and abundant craftsmen, and the best developed trade would tend to extend their authority over the less favored cities. The *lu-gal* (great man or king) living in the *e-gal* (great house or palace) gradually assumed a position of wealth and authority far above that of his subjects, and some of these rulers even called themselves gods. As their authority was extended and elevated above their subjects, a bureaucracy, demonstrating the customary corruption and venality, was needed to manage the day-to-day relations with the people. The wealth and power of rulers is well illustrated by the construction and contents of the Royal Cemetery of the first dynasty of Ur where chariots, large numbers of retainers, and abundant works of art were buried with the rulers in tombs of stone and brick. Architecturally these tombs are interesting because of the use of the barrel vault and the dome, illustrating the Mesopotamian invention of these basic structural forms.

Cultural and religious cohesion and continuity were maintained by the practice of each ruler obtaining religious confirmation of his authority in return for gifts to the centrally located city of Nippur, sacred to Enlil, the chief Sumerian god. Since religion played a very important role in the organization and control of Sumerian life, an effort must be made to explain the Sumerian's unsystematic and often ambiguous interpretation of the universe and man's position in it.

Originally all that had existed was a boundless primeval sea that was envisioned as still encompassing the universe. Varying accounts explain how heaven, earth, and the constantly moving and changing atmosphere in between were created out of the sea. The earth was conceived as a flat disk separated from a dome-shaped heaven by the atmosphere. Subsequently, the moon, sun, and myriad stars were created, followed by plant, animal, and human life.

For religious purposes and to explain the operation of the universe, each of its components was associated with an immortal being conceived in human form and instilled with human interests and appetites. According to the cosmic plan, each deity was responsible for the proper functioning of its part. Thus there was a whole hierarchy of gods and goddesses of varying ranks of whom the most important were the three who controlled heaven, air, and earth and freshwater. These were the creating deities, and the creative technique attributed to them was the power of the divine word; they uttered the command and it was. Thereafter, this conception of creation was generally followed in religious thought throughout the Middle East. Of course, earthbound poets often provided a more human explanation of creation.

The three chief deities were the heaven-god An, the air-god Enlil, and the earth and freshwater god Enki. At one time the patriarchal An may have been the most important, but in the dynastic period Enlil, whose Sumerian home was the sacred city of Nippur, had become supreme, perhaps, because he was the beneficent deity credited with the creation and control of the productive features of life on earth through a host of lesser deities. He gave kings their crowns and determined whether or not their works would prosper. A prayer to Enlil by Lugalzaggisi, who conquered an ephemeral empire about 2400 B.C., demonstrates the veneration in which Enlil was held.

When Enlil king of the countries had granted to Lugalzaggisi the kingship of the land; had turned the eyes of the land toward him; had prostrated the countries at his feet: then did he make straight his path for him, from the Lower Sea, by Tigris and Euphrates, to the Upper Sea. From East to West Enlil nowhere allowed him a rival . . . May Enlil king of the countries prefer my prayer before his dear father An. May he add life to my life, cause the country to rest at peace with me.
[Carleton, Patrick, *Buried Empires* (New York: E. P. Dutton and Co., Inc. 1939), p. 118.]

A portion of a paean in praise of Enlil gives him the chief credit for providing the essentials of Sumerian civilization.

Without Enlil, the great mountain,
No cities would be built, no settlements founded,
No stalls would be built, no sheepfolds established,
No king would be raised, no high priest born,

. . . . .

In heaven the drifting clouds would not yield their moisture,
Plants and herbs, the glory of the plain, would fail to grow,
In field and meadow the rich grain would fail to flower,
(Kramer, *History Begins at Sumer*, pp. 93–94.)

The earth and freshwater god Enki, besides being the special protector of seafarers, was the chief agent in carrying out the general plans of Enlil and assigning specific responsibilities to a whole host of lesser deities. This idea of a divine prime minister must be a late one because such delegation of responsibility presumes advanced political development.

At one time the mother goddess Ninhursag, also known as Nintu (the lady who gave birth), was more important than Enki.

In one poem she plays an important part in the creation of man from clay fashioning him in the image of the gods. In another poem with "Garden of Eden" and "forbidden fruit" motifs she condemns Enki to death and only relents at the last moment. In this work she is playing her primary role of control over life and death as the presiding deity of the nether world, the world of death.

Sumerian writers never cease reiterating their conviction that immortality is only for the gods and goddesses, not for mortal man. Man was created to serve the gods, not the reverse, and is at the mercy of the whim of the gods. Even the mighty hero Gilgamesh was defeated in his quest for immortality. Only one man, the Sumerian "Noah," was rewarded for his exceptional services by the grant of "life like a god" and eternal residence in the Sumerian paradise, Dilmun, "the place where the sun rises." Although Semitic successors expanded, embellished, and incorporated the story in their version of the Gilgamesh Epic, the original Sumerian composition is partially preserved in a single badly damaged tablet from Nippur.

Although at the beginning and subsequently large portions of the text are missing, it is clear that man was created and given cities as religious centers in which to worship according to divine rites and laws. Another long break probably dealt with the debate and decision to destroy man by flood, presumably for failing to maintain the rites and laws. Obviously the decision was not unanimous, and some of the deities lamented the loss of their human servants. In a dream King Ziusudra, the Sumerian Noah, is advised to stand by a wall for instructions. He does so and is told of the decision of the assembly of the gods to destroy the seed of mankind. Another break must have informed the king how to avoid destruction by building a giant boat. Then follows the description of the flood. The flood and storms tossed the boat for seven days and seven nights before it subsided.

When the seventh day arrived,

The flood (-carrying) south-storm subsided in the battle,
Which it had fought like an army.
The sea grew quiet, the tempest was still, the flood ceased.
I looked at the weather: stillness had set in,
And all of mankind had returned to clay.
The landscape was as level as a flat roof.
I opened a hatch, and light fell upon my face . . . .
The raven went forth and, seeing that the waters had diminished,
He eats, circles, caws, and turns not round.
Then I let out (all) to the four winds
And offered a sacrifice.
I poured out a libation on the top of the mountain.
(Selections from "Akkadian Myths and Epics," translated by E. A. Speiser in James B. Pritchard, *Ancient Near Eastern Texts Relating to the Old Testament*, 3rd ed., with Supplement, copyright © 1969 by Princeton University Press, pp. 94–95. Reprinted by permission of Princeton University Press.)

The moral seems clear. The very existence of man depends on the favor of the gods. The best way to retain their favor is to serve them faithfully and to observe rigorously the divinely established rites and laws, but the most faithful service provides no guarantees. Moreover, the suggestion seems to be made that kings would be well advised to pay special attention to dreams and omens.

Religion generally reflects the moral ideals and values of a society. In the case of the Sumerians this is especially true because the life of the gods was fashioned after life in Sumer, the main difference being the immortality of the gods. This view left the Sumerians less than confident of their destiny. The flood story encouraged belief in the fickleness of the gods. Thus life, dependent on the favor of the gods, was uncertain and insecure. The only hope was prayer. While a major deity might heed the supplications of a ruler, he would obviously be too busy to listen to the ordinary man. Therefore, each common man took a minor deity to act as his intercessor with the major gods. But man was warned not to put too much faith in this procedure, as illustrated in a Job-type story. The wealthy, wise, and righteous principal in the tale is overwhelmed by misfortune. Instead of questioning or cursing his personal god for neglect and desertion, he puts his heart and soul into prayer and supplication with ultimately favorable results. The message of the poet is that man's sole recourse in dealing with the unpredictable gods is prayer.

Since the gods had created all things, the Sumerians with eminent logic concluded that they had created evil as well as good, immorality as well as morality. Generally, however, the gods were represented as favoring those values most esteemed by Sumerian civilization—goodness and truth, law and order, justice and freedom, righteousness and sincerity, mercy and compassion—while they abhorred their opposites. Rulers always claimed to uphold these virtues. Urukagina, a ruler of Lagash in the twenty-fifth century B.C., was pictured by his historian as a social reformer who had restored these virtues. Specifically, he eliminated a host of bureaucrats with their innumerable exactions. No longer was there a boat inspector, a cattle inspector, a fisheries inspector, a wool inspector. Fees paid for various permits, such as for divorce, were ended and other charges were drastically reduced. Oppression and exploitation of the poor by the rich and the plague of usurers, thieves, and murderers were eradicated. Officials were to cease stealing fruit from the garden of a "poor man's mother." In collaboration with the city god, Urukagina protected widows and orphans against "men of power." But his reforms were in vain. In an age of dynastic strife victory went to the most resourceful and ruthless ruler. In less than 10 years he was overthrown by Lugalzaggisi,

and his city became part of that ruler's short-lived empire. Nevertheless, his efforts and the boasts of other rulers served to establish the ideal that despotism should be tempered with benevolence, that the care and protection of the poor, the weak, the widow, and the orphan were the moral responsibility of every ruler. Hereafter, this ideal was stamped on the public image of what has been called "oriental despotism." The "freedom" of the individual from oppression, which Urukagina had failed to maintain, was proclaimed and enshrined in a set of values that subsequent rulers ignored at their peril. Finally, in Sumerian civilization the emphasis on obedience to divine law contributed to the development of codes of human laws. Fragments of several Sumerian law codes were obviously precedents for the famous compilation of Hammurabi.

Political and economic problems had for several centuries become more than the individual city-state could cope with. Leading cities had been taking turns in asserting supremacy. Such assertions were possible because of the emergence of authoritarian kingship which exerted greater and greater economic control. Architectural evidence is provided by the appearance of royal palaces separated from the temple enclosures. However, no written record of the separation of the functions of king and priest exists before 2400 B.C.

MESOPOTAMIAN IMPERIALISM (C. 2340 – 1500 B.C.)

After the assertion of dynastic authority over Sumer and Akkad the next step would be imperialism, the assertion of authority beyond the plain. The possibilities of expanding the economic base through control of commerce was not a new idea. Lugalzaggisi claimed such conquests, but the Semitic Sargon of Akkad and his successors appear to have been the first to establish more than a temporary supremacy. That this new departure was pioneered by a non-Sumerian ruler of a city on the fringe of Sumerian civilization is not surprising. Unification and expansion at the hands of a vigorous frontier state is a recurrent theme in the history of civilizations.

As an inscription dealing with his defeat of Lugalzaggisi testifies, Sargon was a supporter of Sumerian civilization. He brought his captured predecessor "in a dog collar to the gate of Enlil [Nippur]" and thus followed the established format for obtaining confirmation of his succession to authority. His empire extended from Elam in the east to Syria in the west. Tablets telling of trade throughout the area are witnesses to the achievement of his economic objective. His able grandson who called himself "The divine Naram-Sin, the mighty, god of Akkad, king of the Four Quarters," expanded the empire in the east and the west, especially into the highlands of Iran. Wealth from tribute and trade financed large-scale public works and a new peak in art. Apparently, however, the empire had become overextended. Perhaps the campaigns stimulated the growth of unity among the scattered tribes in the Zagros Mountains to the east who cast envious eyes down on the prosperity of the plains below. In any case, a little-known people, the Guti, descended from the hills, ravaged the heart of the empire, and caused its disintegration about 2180 B.C.

After a century of disorder the Gutians were driven out and various cities managed to restore temporarily a measure of their former prosperity. A new dynasty at Ur generated a Sumerian renaissance and erected the best-preserved, step-temple (ziggurat) on a vast scale. A fascinating feature of this building is the calculated curving of the lines of the walls to give the appearance of lightness and strength, a technique to be followed much later in the renowned Parthenon of Athens. Incidentally, one of the rulers of this dynasty followed Naram-Sin's example, having himself worshiped as a living god. Rulers were no longer so scrupulous in adhering to the religious distinction between the immortality of the gods and the mortality of men.

This revival in the plains was terminated by new invaders who established alien regimes lasting several centuries, Elamites from the east and a Semitic people known as Amorites from the north. These foreign rulers maintained with little alteration the religious and economic aspects of Sumerian civilization. In their intercity strife they even continued to recognize the special position of Nippur as the home of the chief deity, Enlil. Finally, the Amorite dynasty of a previously insignificant city near Kish called Bab-ilu (Babylon) produced the military and administrative genius who was to restore unity to the plain and revive the long-defunct empire. This was Hammurabi (c 1792–1750 or 1728–1686 B.C.).

The orderly quality of his mind is shown by the planned layout of his capital city. Until that time Sumerian cities had been unplanned warrens of concentrated human habitation, which had grown in a haphazard fashion without municipal regulation. The irrigation of the plains was reorganized according to a unified plan, new canals being dug and old ones reopened. "Lasting water I provided for the land of Sumer and Akkad. Its separated people I united. With blessings and abundance I endowed them." His deeds were as good as his words. The agriculture and trade of the plain prospered as never before.

Religion, too, received the touch of his organizing hand. By a typical act of reorganization a new myth elevated his patron deity, Marduk, to the position of supremacy in the ancient pantheon. In this myth the creation of all the gods is assigned to two personalized qualities; the male Apsu representing the primeval sweetwater ocean and the female Tiamat representing the primeval saltwater ocean. Irritated with their offspring, Apsu decides to destroy them, but the Sumerian Earth god slays Apsu. Tiamat organizes her forces to avenge Apsu. The gods are terrified. Enter Marduk, city god of Babylon, who

volunteers to be their champion if he is accepted as supreme. The gods agree and he
prepares his weapons for the titanic encounter.

> Then joined issue Tiamat and Marduk,
> wisest of gods.
> They strove in single combat, locked in
> battle.
> The lord spread out his net to enfold
> her,
> The Evil Wind, which followed behind,
> he let loose in her face.
> When Tiamat opened her mouth to con-
> sume him,
> He drove in the Evil Wind that she close
> not her lips.
> As the fierce wind charged her belly,
> Her body was distended and her mouth
> was wide open.
> He released the arrow, it tore her belly,
> It cut through her insides, splitting the
> heart.
>   . . . . .
>
> Then the lord paused to view her dead
> body,
> That he might divide the monster and do
> artful works.
> He split her up like a shellfish into two
> parts:
> Half of her he set up and ceiled it as
> sky, . . .
> (Pritchard, ed., *Ancient Near Eastern
> Texts*, trans. by E. A. Speiser, p. 67.)

After slaying Tiamat, Marduk then created
the earth and continued by assigning the
gods to their respective spheres. From the
blood of Tiamat's chief supporter man was
created. To demonstrate their loyalty, the
gods of heaven and earth built Marduk a
great stepped-tower temple as a home and
then prescribed the following pledge for gods
and men.

> Most exalted be the Son, our avenger
> (Marduk);

> Let his sovereignty be surpassing, hav-
> ing no rival.
> May he shepherd the black-headed
> ones, his creatures.
>   . . . . .
> May he order the black-headed to
> re(vere him),
> May the subjects ever bear in mind their
> god,
> And may they at his word pay heed to
> the goddess.
> May food-offerings be borne for their
> gods and goddesses.
> Without fail let them support their
> gods!
> Their lands let them improve, build their
> shrines,
> Let the black-headed wait on their
> gods.
> As for us, by however many names we
> pronounce, he is our god!
> Let us then proclaim his fifty
> names . . . .
> (Pritchard, ed., *Ancient Near Eastern
> Texts*, trans. by E. A. Speiser, p. 69.)

Thus, while elevating his own city god
to supremacy, he also acknowledged the respective deities of his conquered subjects, a
true act of statesmanship. So methodical is
this religious reformulation that it seems as
though it must have been composed by
Hammurabi himself.

Although these organizational works
were great in themselves, his most renowned
achievement was his law code found almost
intact inscribed on a diorite stele at Susa. The
religious sanction is illustrated in a low relief
at the top which pictures Hammurabi receiving his law-giving power from the god of justice enthroned on a mountain. In the pro-
logue Hammurabi typically asserts that the
gods An and Enlil "named me to promote the
welfare of the people, me Hammurabi, the
devout, god-fearing prince, to cause justice
to prevail in the land, to destroy the wicked
and evil, that the strong might not oppress
the weak . . . ." In the epilogue the purpose

of all law codes is clearly and forcefully defined: to maintain good government and protect the weak from oppression by the strong. (Pritchard, *Ancient Near Eastern Texts*, pp. 164 and 178.)

The code containing 282 laws is especially enlightening about the social, economic, domestic, and moral conditions of the time. By modern standards the penalties appear harsh. The death penalty in various forms was obviously prescribed as a deterrent. The ancient doctrine of "an eye for an eye and a tooth for a tooth" was moderated in some instances by the substitution of set fines that compensated for the material loss. The differences in penalties according to class illustrate the stratified nature of society. The operation of the legal system and the relative seriousness with which the crimes were viewed are indicated by the ordering of the laws; the most important came first and the rest followed in a descending order of significance and frequency.

In most cases the city council sat in judgment on cases brought before it. The first four laws prescribed the assessment of the penalty of the crime against those who made false accusations or offered false testimony. These provisions obviously operated to keep the court's docket from being cluttered with frivolous accusations and they also suggest that there was no public prosecutor for cases between individuals. The fifth law placed a heavy penalty on a judge who later altered a verdict. Apparently decisions that were sanctioned by the city deity were final without the possibility of appeal. As one would expect, the first positive law concerned those civic entities, the church and the state, and laid down an unequivocal sentence of death for theft of the property of either one. Apparently, however, the theft of animals was less serious because the eighth law required only a payment of thirty times the value. In the case of the same theft from a private citizen the penalty was only ten times the value. In both cases, however, inability to pay the fine meant death.

The seventh law is surprising. It prescribed the death penalty as a punishment for anyone purchasing goods from a freeman's son or slave without a contract and witnesses. This law illustrates the father's sole ownership of the family's property, and its prime position in the code indicates the importance attached to maintaining paternal authority.

The emphasis at the beginning and throughout the code on the protection of property and the definition of property rights demonstrates the materialistic orientation of this society. A large proportion of the fields and orchards was inalienably owned by the church or state and was granted to individuals in return for service or rent. Yet a substantial amount of land was privately owned and salable.

A series of laws concerned the duties and rights of soldiers. Apparently all those who held fields and orchards from the state or church owed military service. All others were free from conscription. A common subterfuge carrying the death penalty was to hire a substitute. Officers who abused their power by despoiling a soldier under their command were to be put to death. A captured soldier's ransom was ultimately an obligation upon the state. If a soldier abandoned the obligations of his estate and someone else took over and fulfilled them for 3 years, the former could not regain it. Thus a 3-year statute of limitations was provided.

Although the positions of husband and sons received preferential treatment, wife and daughters enjoyed protection and support under the law. Marriage was arranged by the parents, the groom's father providing a marriage price and the bride's father providing a dowry. No marriage was valid without a written contract. Those caught in an act of adultery were both drowned unless the husband relented; then the king might pardon the wayward wife. A wife accused by her husband but not caught in the act could affirm her innocence before god, and the husband must take her back into his house. If someone else accused her, she must throw herself into the river. If she survived, the divine judge had proved her innocence. Either party could obtain a divorce for various reasons, the woman being additionally required to be a good wife and not a gadabout, neglecting her house and humiliating her husband. In the latter instance, she was to be drowned. If a wife brought about her husband's death because of another man, she was impaled on stakes. The wife, as a mother, gained the management and use of her deceased husband's estate which she held in trust for his sons. Normally the sons shared equally in the inheritance, and a son could only be disinherited if the father on two occasions could prove grave wrongs before the judges. A daughter was only entitled to support and a dowry.

Family morality is illustrated by several laws. Incest was punished only by exile for the father. If the son had had intercourse with his chosen bride and then his father cohabited with her, the father was drowned. If the son had not had intercourse with her, the father only paid a fine and returned her with her dowry to her father's house. If a son cohabited with his mother after his father's death, both were burned to death. But if she was only a stepmother who had borne children, the son merely lost his inheritance. If a son should strike his father, his hand was cut off.

Both physicians and veterinarians practiced surgery under a scale of fixed fees for successful operations, but the scale of penalties for failure made the former profession hazardous. If an upper class patient died or lost his sight as a result of a common eye operation, the surgeon's hand was cut off. On such terms there would probably be few surgeons today.

The establishments of women wine sellers—the saloons of the day—were places of such ill-repute that special laws were required for their regulation. The woman wine seller was apparently a common cheat and her shop was the customary hangout of criminals and other undesirable elements. Any woman connected with a temple who even opened the door of a wineshop was to be burned to death.

The normal legal procedure was for the judges to hear the accusation in a courtroom in the temple, to examine the evidence and witnesses and, if necessary, require solemn affirmations before the god. Then they would deliberate in the temple of the god before handing down a religiously sanctioned verdict.

On the accumulated experience of the past Hammurabi constructed a well-ordered empire in which the state and its adjunct, the church, played a large role. Yet despite state regulation most men were free to pursue their destiny within reasonable limits. A few men were wealthy and could pass their wealth on to their sons in equal shares. A substantial middle class provided the backbone of the urban economy. The abundance of still extant correspondence suggests that literacy was relatively widespread. The labors of a large number of poorer freemen and a perhaps even larger number of slaves supported this literate civilization.

The gradual evolution of the first civilization with the challenges it confronted and the solutions it found has been briefly described. By 5000 B.C. small communities primarily dependent on hunting and fishing had moved into the almost rainless plain and marshland bordering the lower Tigris and Euphrates. In time, they learned how to convert this waste into exceptionally productive farmland by digging drainage and irrigation canals to service diked fields. Since the land lacked stone, minerals, and timber, the development of trade with upland sources of supply was essential. Thus in this productive land evolved an agrarian-pastoral economy supplemented by a growing commerce that demanded large-scale cooperative effort to realize its potential. These conditions encouraged the development of a number of city-states that were fully engaged for a long time in land reclamation. The need for co-operation required a unifying institution to direct and control human activities. The solution was found at first in the development of a religion that commanded the loyalty and labor of all the citizens. At the same time the temple administrators came to need written records to supplement human memory.

As the limits of development at the city-state level were reached, further growth became dependent on achieving a larger scale of cooperation and unity. Interstate conflict brought to power hereditary kings supported by religious sanctions who for military purposes concentrated more and more economic and political authority in their hands. The more successful dynasties as-serted successive hegemonies over other cities, gaining religious confirmation from Nippur, the city of the chief god Enlil. In ad-dition to utilizing the combined resources of the cities they controlled to enlarge the irri-gated area, these rulers also exploited their enhanced power for the expansion of domes-tic and foreign commerce. This last step log-ically led to adventures in empire building that culminated in the Babylonian Empire of Hammurabi.

When efficiently administered, the sys-tem that was finally worked out provided a reasonable compromise between freedom and authority, fulfilling the needs of both the state and its citizens. Meanwhile, commer-cial and imperial expansion diffused widely the features of Mesopotamian civilization, both material and spiritual, and stimulated by example the advancement of both old and new peoples throughout the Middle East.

In the thousand years after the over-throw of Hammurabi's dynasty (c 1530 B.C.) a confusing array of states arose and sought control of the trade routes. Methods of gov-ernment varied from ruthlessness to toler-ation, but the most significant feature was the overall trend toward the creation of a larger, all-encompassing entity. The Sume-

rians blazed the trail of civilization which others have followed with variations of their own.

EGYPTIAN CIVILIZATION: THE SETTING

A second distinctive civilization bene-fiting from Sumerian example and influence emerged not long afterward in the valley and delta of another flood-river, the Nile. For various reasons, including geographical fac-tors, Egyptian civilization developed and reached maturity much more rapidly than Sumerian civilization.

Like Sumer, Egypt has been styled as the "gift" of its river. This "greatest single stream on earth" begins at the equator, where daily tropical rains maintain a con-stant volume of water, and meanders 4000 miles before flowing into the Mediterranean Sea. At Khartoum, the White Nile, as the main stream is called, is joined by the Blue Nile which rises in the mountains of Ethiopia. The Ethiopian rainy season supplies the flood waters that cause the annual in-undation on which Egyptian civilization relies. At the first cataract, where the waters tumble turbulently over a granite ridge, Egypt proper begins. For some 500 miles a narrow ribbon of cultivated land, seldom more than a dozen miles wide, is irrigated and fertilized by the silt-laden waters of the Nile. On either side of this continuous oasis desert conditions prevail. Then for the last 100 miles the river divides to produce the rich alluvial fan of the delta.

While the dependable annual flood made possible the intensive cultivation es-sential to the support of an agricultural civili-zation, the river served as a year-round high-way. Two-way traffic is uniquely facilitated by a reliable wind that blows upstream from the Mediterranean for the greater part of the year. At an early date Egyptians learned to use the sail to take advantage of this natural blessing. This favor of nature which facilitated communications was mainly responsible for Egypt's early unification.

Much has been written about how the regularity of the Nile and the relative isolation from other peoples contributed to the cultural stability and optimistic outlook of the Egyptians. These arguments seem exaggerated. Although the annual flood always arrives in July, its volume fluctuates widely in an unpredictable fashion. A low flood could cause drought, and a high flood could ravage the fields destroying dikes, canals, and reservoirs. In either case famine would be the result. Other natural catastrophes, such as a plague of locusts, could also contribute to the uncertainty and insecurity of life from year to year. Although nature has been kinder to Egypt than other early centers of civilization, it was by no means wholly benign. Egyptian attitudes cannot be attributed entirely to nature's bounty.

In addition, Egypt has never enjoyed complete isolation, even if such a condition were desirable. In predynastic times physical anthropologists can show evidence of the frequent arrival of new people. In dynastic times not only alien peoples, but even dynasties, entered Egypt from the east, the west, and the south. Desert or near-desert approaches might deter, but not prevent, invasion. Conversely defense and trade encouraged the rulers to engage in imperialistic adventures abroad. Even during the Old and Middle Kingdoms evidence remains of foreign relations and military campaigns in all directions. The term Empire only designates a period of relatively greater, more fully documented imperial activity. Any evaluations of Egyptian civilization based on its relative isolation must be tempered with generous qualifications.

After all this has been said, however, it must be admitted that geography did give Egypt a comparative advantage over Mesopotamia. Stone for building and for tools was immediately available, and copper could be mined in the Sinai Peninsula. Although the northern part of the Red Sea is not hospitable to navigation by sail, seafaring expeditions to the south and the east could be launched from a coastal point opposite the important center of Thebes in Upper Egypt. From points in the delta sea trade in the early dynastic period, if not earlier, filled the need for timber with the renowned cedars of Lebanon. Therefore, from its beginning and throughout its history, Egypt was subject to influences and ideas from the outside world, but they were refashioned and adapted to satisfy the distinctive and unique Egyptian personality and culture.

Agriculture was most probably introduced into the Nile valley from Palestine. A Natufian culture site at Helouan, 20 miles south of Cairo, supports this hypothesis. For a long time, however, the potentialities of this fertile river valley were not recognized by a succession of primarily hunting and fishing cultures which only briefly settled in a single spot just long enough to raise a crop. The earliest sites according to carbon 14 dates are from the later fifth millennium in the Fayum basin, whose lake level during this wetter period was 180 feet higher than today. Forest and swamp must have covered much of what is now an arid area. By 4000 B.C. a similar way of life existed throughout the valley as far south as Khartoum. These people kept sheep and goats—and pigs in the north—and cultivated wheat, barley, and flax from which linen was woven. No signs of substantial structures have been found. Handmade pottery was used. The presence of seashell and copper ornaments indicates the existence of some trade.

EGYPT: THE PRE-DYNASTIC ERA (C. 3600 – 2900 B.C.)

By about 3600 B.C. larger, more permanent settlements indicate that the advances in social and political organization necessary for exploiting the possibilities of irrigated farming had been begun. Improvement in technology is illustrated by well-made stone vessels. While this culture, known as Amratian, centered in Upper Egypt, its successor, the Gerzean culture, is best represented in Lower Egypt.

Actually, the Gerzean culture seems to have been a further development and refinement of the Amratian under the impact and stimulus of alien influences. A major innovation was metallurgy. Previously the Egyptians had shaped raw copper into pins and beads; now they could cast copper in any form they wished including axes and daggers. Copper goods became plentiful indicating an expansion of trade. Another innovation, probably from abroad, was the use of mud-bricks to build solid structures. In late Gerzean times the appearance of monumental buildings designed with Mesopotamian-type buttresses and recesses is suggestive of foreign influence. More striking is the use of Mesopotamian themes in murals and other art objects. Positive proof of contact is the presence of Mesopotamian cylinder seals at Nakada in Upper Egypt. Gerzean culture had soon spread to the south, but was surprisingly absent in the delta. Hieroglyphic writing already utilizing ideograms and phonograms also suggests Sumerian inspiration. Perhaps it is no accident that the appearance of writing in Egypt coincided with an increase of the Semitic element in the racial and cultural composition of the Egyptians. Nevertheless, it should be emphasized that these alien ideas and practices received a distinctively Egyptian expression.

During the Gerzean period, which may be roughly dated 3400 to 2900 B.C., a regional division (later called nomes by the Greeks) began to form, indicating a further development in social and political organization. Also a larger division began to be recognized between Upper Egypt, composed of the long, narrow valley stretching northward from the first cataract, and Lower Egypt, where the river divided and fanned out to form the broad, alluvial plain and marshland of the delta. Although no essential differences in culture developed, this distinction between Upper and Lower Egypt persisted throughout its history.

The ease of contact by sea leads to the inference that the delta region was initially more advanced in cultural and political development, but the available archeological evidence does not support this hypothesis. The difficulty of mastering the swampland and the many riverine divisions may have delayed the delta's development and unification. A stele commemorating unification by a ruler of Upper Egypt suggests that Lower Egypt was divided at that time into two or more states. On the other hand, a later historical chronicle hints at an earlier temporary unification of the Nile valley by a ruler of Lower Egypt.

Although future archeological work in the delta may alter the picture, the weight of present evidence favors the initiation of the first important advances in the vicinity of Gerzeh, just south of the delta. These advances moved upstream reaching a peak of development at sites not far from the historically important Thebes. Certainly, there is no doubt that enduring unification was accomplished by a ruler of Upper Egypt who operated from a capital 300 miles south of the delta. With the removal of the capital to the strategic location of Memphis, the approximate point of demarcation between Upper and Lower Egypt, the north with its more cosmopolitan population and control of most foreign trade established and maintained a cultural advantage over the south. It became a center of the arts and crafts drawing on foreign artisans to produce the quality products demanded by the ruler and his courtiers.

The steps and struggles that led to the unification of Egypt are obscure, but war and the subsequent consolidation of conquests must have required the growth and centralization of political power in the hands of the rulers and their staffs. A growth in population requiring the utilization of higher land would also have stimulated the extension of social and political organization to construct the works necessary to bring water to these additional fields. As in Mesopotamia, religious sanction became the most important support of monarchical authority.

EGYPTIAN THEOLOGY

Although a number of similarities may be found in the Mesopotamian and Egyptian interpretations of the universe and its creation, a basic difference in outlook and emphasis can be identified. Both imagined an original formless chaos, described as the primordial waters, out of which form and substance issued. The components of the universe were visualized similarly with the dome of the sky separated by the atmosphere from the flat disk of the earth, and below the earth, the waters. But here came an important difference; the Egyptian insistence on harmony and symmetry demanded a countersky below to balance the sky above.

Both agreed that there was a divine order in the universe with each god responsible for the proper functioning of his component. But to the Sumerians this divine order was generally interpreted as beyond the understanding and control of mere mortals. What impressed them most was the fact of unpredictable change as illustrated by their elevation to the position of primacy among the gods of Enlil, the god of the atmosphere, of the storm, of constant change. On the contrary, what impressed the Egyptians most was the regularity, the harmony, the symmetry that they could observe in the operations of the universe.

How can this contrast in the interpretations of observed natural phenomena as translated into religious terms be explained? Obviously, no positive and assured explanation can be offered. Neither the Sumerians nor the Egyptians have provided reasoned analyses in support of their respective points of view. Most modern interpreters have sought to explain the difference in terms of the respective physical environments of Mesopotamia and Egypt, and certainly these arguments are validly based

on the relatively more regular and dependable nature of the Egyptian environment. But, as has been noted, the dependability of natural phenomena in Egypt has been exaggerated. Constant toil and struggle are the perpetual burden of the people. Prosperity is by no means certain and secure. Some other reason to explain the emphasis on regularity, balance, and symmetry seems to be required.

This other reason may be the existence of an altogether different social and political situation. In Egypt, civilization and unity were coeval developments, both born at the same time. In the predynastic era, there was no long history of city-states as in Sumer with their divisive effect as foci of local loyalties. Indeed, in Egypt, urbanization never developed in the Sumerian sense. Instead, the countryside was composed of strings of compact villages interspersed with administrative and market towns that occupied as little arable land as possible. In likely locations here and there were temple towns. Until they settled in Thebes, the pharaohs* tended to move their residence from place to place. Memphis was a ritual center symbolizing unity rather than a true urban capital. The picture is one of rural dispersion in contrast to the urban concentrations of Mesopotamia.

The absolute rulers of a unified domain desired that emphasis be placed on cohesion and stability. The advocacy of change was not in their interest. Therefore, they encouraged a unification and stabilization of predynastic religious views which may have differed considerably from one end of the Nile valley to the other. There are hints of a number of previous clanlike organizations with

---

*This title for the rulers of united Egypt was derived, via Hebrew, from the name of the rulers' palace, "Great House," and reflects the belief that the living god could not be referred to directly by name. But similar indirect usages without such august connotations are common today, such as "the White House," "10 Downing Street," or "the Kremlin."

distinctive totemic symbols. Whatever the prior religious views may have been, certain views demonstrating regularity were singled out and integrated by absorbing differing myths as manifestations of the same underlying concept, and these were concentrated in the living god, the ruler, who comprehended all deities at one and the same time.

Two natural phenomena were obvious examples of the regularity important to the Egyptian way of life—the Nile with its annual flood and the sun with its daily passage from east to west. Surprisingly the Nile never received the attention that the sun did, perhaps, because it was not so dependable. In any case, the sun-god Ra-Atum soon became the chief deity and the pharaoh was his son, Horus. Each day the sun died in the west (to the Egyptians darkness was like death), passed through the primordial waters under the earth, and was reborn daily from this source of all creation. The sun was also the son of the sky-goddess represented as a great cow and as such was pictured as a mighty bull born each day. A number of other manifestations for the sun-god were also devised that seem confusing and wholly illogical to us but are entirely complementary in the Egyptian view of nature. All things, including gods, were created and, therefore, all partook of the same nature that was freely transferable. Thus there was nothing contradictory to the Egyptians in the conception of being ruled by a living god, and this ruler could be conceived in a number of manifestations at one and the same time. In one instance the pharaoh was entitled the sun, a star, a bull, a crocodile, a lion, a falcon, a jackal, and the two tutelary gods of Egypt, each being merely different aspects of his godhead. Being divine, the king was in fellowship with the gods and could exercise the function of any one of them—indeed actually *be* any one of them—in promoting the welfare of Egypt.

This conception of a god-king contributes to another range of development in Egyptian religious thought. As a living god, the ruler at death would join his fellow gods in immortality. At first he was believed to take with him to heaven those who had served him well. If the king and a select few could achieve immortality, however, why could not all good Egyptians join them? Later this idea was fully expressed in the Osirian cult. This belief in the essential unity of all nature, including men, stands in sharp contrast to Mesopotamian doctrine, which never tired of proclaiming the mortality of men as servants of the gods; only gods were immortal. It is true that some Mesopotamian rulers declared themselves to be gods, but these assertions were fundamentally contrary to Mesopotamian theology.

In addition to regularity, Egyptian religion also sought balance and harmony. For each god there was created a goddess who according to the Egyptian conception was both sister and wife. The first couple, air and moisture, produced earth and sky which in turn bore two couples, Osiris and Isis and Set and Nephthys, who were concerned with the creatures of the earth, animate and inanimate, human and divine. This pairing of deities was applied also to the things of this world to achieve balance and harmony. Even the idea of the two lands of Egypt with its two crowns and two tutelary gods, although it probably had a more mundane origin, was maintained throughout Egyptian history as an expression of the doctrine of balance and harmony.

Another aspect of the emphasis on divine harmony was the god-king's responsibility to maintain *ma'at*, usually translated as "justice," in his earthly realm. *Ma'at*, however, meant something more than justice. It was the application of the principles of divine harmony to Egyptian affairs and, thus, included the ideas of truth and righteousness in its administration. Cold-blooded law was not enough. The ruler, and through him his deputies, was required to keep in mind the need for harmony in his decisions and to go beyond simple justice in evaluating in each case what truth, righteousness, and the welfare of Egypt demanded. Therefore, the living gods of the early dynasties at least were encouraged and had the power to exercise initiative in dealing with the problems and needs of the people and the country, utilizing their divine insight to implement harmony on earth. Under these circumstances the absence of written law codes is not surprising. Divine justice emanated from the pharaoh and was applied by his deputies. Indeed *ma'at* required action to forestall injustice or disharmony.

According to the Osirian myth, Osiris was the original god-king who had taught the people agriculture and the arts of civilization. His wicked brother Set, representing the forces of destruction, slew him, cut him in pieces, and scattered them. Osiris' sister and wife, Isis, found the pieces, put them together, and miraculously restored him to life. The resurrected god ruled again for a time and then became judge of the dead, his posthumous son Horus taking his place as god-king. This story is another familiar account of death and resurrection, explaining the annual regeneration of plant and animal life. As utilized by the pharaohs to support their authority, each new king was a reincarnation of the god Horus and upon death was joined with his father Osiris as judge of the dead. In the later development of the Osirian myth as a salvation cult, each Egyptian after death was judged on his conduct in this life. As in most religions, this procedure became ritualized under the control and for the benefit of the priesthood.

On the stone palette that is believed to commemorate the initial enduring unification of Egypt, King Narmer is represented as the falcon-god Horus, son of Osiris, and the mighty bull, son of the sky-goddess cow. Thus the divinity of the ruler is proclaimed from the beginning. As a god-king the pharaoh's rule by benevolence through justice was traditionally described as balanced by the inculcation of absolute obedience through fear of him who by divine power controlled the destiny of Egypt and every Egyptian. These dual aspects of the pharaoh

were stressed in an official's admonitions to his children to revere the living god who gives life to everything in Egypt and who, if displeased, can likewise take it away.

> The king is the *ka*, and his mouth is abundance. That means that he brings into being him who is to be . . . He whom the king has loved will be a revered spirit, but there is no tomb for him who rebels against his majesty.
> (Frankfort, ed., *Before Philosophy*, trans. John A. Wilson, pp. 95–96.)

The reference to *ka* introduces another Egyptian conception that needs an explanation. The *ka* was conceived as an identical twin, born with each person, who provided energy, guidance, and protection throughout life and led the way into the next world. It may be imagined as the individual's contact with the divine way, steering him in the path of a prosperous, constructive, and righteous life and protecting him against evil influences. In short, the *ka* was the force in the individual that made possible the good life, here and hereafter. As used in the above context, the king's *ka* was the source of the good life for all Egypt.

Before we reconstruct a picture of Egyptian civilization during the Old Kingdom, an interesting theological work that was composed to justify the establishment of the ritual capital at Memphis should be considered. The Memphite Theology, as it is called, is valuable as an illustration of intellectual precocity and as an example of conscious theological manipulation. Why the first pharaoh felt it necessary to establish a new center when Heliopolis, sacred to the sun-god, was nearby is hard to say. Perhaps the sun-god was too closely associated with conquered Lower Egypt. This hypothesis is supported by the title of "city of the white wall," the color of Upper Egypt, given to Memphis and by the subordination of the sun-god to Ptah in the Memphite Theology. In this work Ptah, rather than the sun-god is credited as the giver of life, as well as their *ka*, to all the gods through the mind and tongue of Atum, the original creator of undifferentiated life, out of the primordial sea. Thus, Ptah is put between Atum and the rest of the gods as the intermediate creator. Also notice the mode of creation, by the mind and the tongue, that is, by the divine word. From this premise it is argued that the mind and tongue control every member of the body and thus as mind and tongue Ptah controls and commands every being, the tongue announcing what the mind commands. From this assertion it follows that Ptah is in every god and every man and in everything they created, that is, Ptah is omnipresent and omnipotent throughout the universe.

At Memphis each new ruler celebrated his accession by a ritual feast of the "union of the Two Lands" which was symbolized by tying together the Lotus of Upper Egypt and the Papyrus of Lower Egypt. Tombs from the first dynasty have been excavated at nearby Saqqara and near their home town far to the south in Upper Egypt. The arrangement of the burial chamber surrounded by storage rooms with the lesser tombs of retainers placed around the main tomb shows that the pattern to be followed in the great pyramids was already set on a much smaller scale.

EGYPT: THE OLD KINGDOM
(C. 2900 – 2200 B.C.)

The relatively unimpressive mud-brick and timber tombs of the first two dynasties have suffered so much from deterioration and plundering that there is little evidence left on which to reconstruct a picture of the times. Other than the Memphite Theology the only literary work thought to have been composed in this period is a surgical treatise with a surprisingly experimental approach that epitomizes the questing spirit of a daring young society on the move.

A type of writing paper made from the pith of papyrus reeds was invented at least as early as the first dynasty which greatly facilitated the keeping of accounts. A simplified cursive script was also devised to ease the task of record keeping. Nevertheless, throughout Egyptian history, tradition and religion demanded the continued use of hieroglyphic writing for tomb inscriptions because of its sacred character.

For pragmatic purposes the study of mathematics and astronomy was fostered. Mathematical development was needed for accurate measurement in a land where the annual flood often eradicated boundaries, for the assessment of a complex system of taxation, and for the calculations needed in engineering irrigation works and tombs. Astronomical development was needed for the accurate directional orientation of tombs and temples and for the construction of reliable calendars to forecast the seasons and to determine the correct time for religious observances. During the first two dynasties a solar calendar of twelve 30-day months plus five feast days was invented to supplement the old lunar calendar. Not much later, however, a third, more accurate calendar was devised.

The scanty remains of arts and crafts demonstrate not only sharply improved skill but also bold experiments and daring innovations that substantiate the vitality of this new civilization. As has been observed in Sumer and will be observed again, however, the typical decline in pottery as an art form characterized this period in Egypt. As elsewhere, the utilitarian attitude toward pottery was in part a result of the introduction of the fast potter's wheel and the consequent emphasis on mass production. Mass production and artistry rarely go hand in hand.

The picture of society in the early period of the Old Kingdom is one of a busy and industrious people taking the fullest possible advantage of the opportunities for expansion and development offered by unification. A new, go-getting energy had been released that would carry over into the next period. The god-kings were proving their ability to advance the earthly welfare of the people and, for the moment, the people were chiefly concerned with the opportunities for the good life here and not much concerned about the hereafter. Even the kings, who relied on relatives to fill the chief administrative posts, shared and, indeed, inspired this enthusiasm by plowing back their wealth, derived from a taxation system that took an average of one fifth of production, into productive public works that would further increase their income.

The momentum and exuberance generated in the first two dynasties carried over into the third, but constructive outlets for the vastly increased revenue pouring into the royal coffers were becoming harder to find. The expansion of the material base of Egyptian civilization continued, but the pace slowed down. Sufficient surpluses existed for the construction of Djoser's Step Pyramid (c 2650 B.C.), the first "house of eternity" constructed entirely of stone. In six steps it stood 190 feet high overlooking a complex of dummy buildings in imitation of those in which the living ruler performed various ceremonies. False doors concealing solid rubble interiors emphasize the unreal quality and magical purpose of this "city of the dead." What in real life was made of wood or some other perishable material was faithfully reproduced in eternal stone. The whole area was surrounded by a massive wall more than one mile in circumference, with fourteen gateways only one of which was real. The effect of the whole seems to have been to guarantee by imitative magic the permanence, stability, and harmony of the united realm of the two lands of Egypt. The pyramid form, which was to be repeated on a more massive scale in the great pyramids of the fourth dynasty, appears to recognize the achievement of primacy by the sun-god in the Egyptian pantheon.

The architect of this vast work, Imhotep, is the first example of a universal genius whose reality is not lost in legend. In addition to his genius as an architect, preserved for all time in the Step Pyramid, this chief minister of Djoser was renowned as an astronomer, a priest, a writer and sage, and a physician. His reputed skill as a physician was so great that it led to his later deification as the god of medicine.

With such a servant Djoser's reign must have prospered greatly. His successors in the third dynasty were apparently not so well endowed. Several tried to emulate his tomb-building effort but were unable to complete their undertakings. Not until the fourth dynasty was a succession of rulers able to marshal the resources and skills needed to repeat this feat on an even more grandiose scale in the famous pyramids at Giza, the tombs of the Pharaohs Khufu, Khafre, and Menkaure.

Whether, as some authorities have suggested, these pyramids were vast public works designed to ameliorate an unemployment problem, their scale clearly indicates that the pharaohs had reached a pinnacle of power and wealth. The possibility that the diversion of resources to such nonproductive works may have contributed to subsequent decline does not alter this conclusion. In any case, the decline was gradual and not precipitous, reflecting a slow shift in power from the pharaoh to a self-assertive nobility, rather than a breakdown of the economy.

The pyramid of Khufu was erected on a square base of 13 acres to a point 481 feet high. More than 2 million huge blocks of limestone averaging $2^{1}/_{2}$ tons each were carefully fitted to form the core which was then faced with finer limestone blocks. The seams were cut to a precision of one ten-thousandth of an inch. The engineering achievement was magnificent and modern scholars have tried to reconstruct the technique used in view of Old Kingdom technology. Perhaps their most significant conclusion is that the numbers employed would have been large only when the stones were floated to the site during the annual flood. At that time of year farmers were in any case idle.

The pyramid of Khafre was built on a

somewhat smaller base, but the sides arose at a slightly steeper angle achieving almost the same height. The third pyramid is substantially smaller, and those of succeeding pharaohs of the fourth and fifth dynasties were on a much smaller scale. A shift in outlook may be reflected in the greater effort put into the construction of temples to the sun-god, especially in the fifth dynasty. Inscriptions in these later pyramids emphasized the sun-god whom the deceased ruler would join in a glorious hereafter. Nevertheless, the great pyramids of Giza remain a permanent memorial to the power and achievement of the Old Kingdom.

In the arts and crafts, as in architecture, the greatest effort and skill were devoted to productions in enduring materials, especially stone, whether the products were stone vessels and ornaments or sculptures and reliefs. Despite the adoption of pictorial conventions similar to the Sumerians', the Egyptians' sense of oneness with nature inspired a restrained naturalism in contrast with the more abstract and symbolic treatment of the Sumerians.

The people, both lords and commoners, of the Old Kingdom enjoyed a gay, materialistic, this-worldly set of values. When they thought of the next life, they expected it to be just as happy, well-equipped, and vigorous as this life. This point of view is confirmed by inscriptions and reliefs in tombs which provide a picture of life at the time. One lord who lived about 2400 B.C. is pictured engaging fully in an active, constructive life of hunting, fishing, farming, herding, and building with both humor and humanity as common themes. This outlook contrasts sharply with the almost morbid concern with death and the next life that characterizes the tomb inscriptions in the last stages of ancient Egyptian civilization.

Throughout the era of the Old Kingdom materialism vied with morality in shaping the ethics of a self-confident, optimistic people more concerned with this life than the next. This contest is well-illustrated by the advice the vizier Ptah-hotep (c 2450 B.C.) delivered to his son, in which cynical success formulas are mixed with moral injunctions.

Despite his superior knowledge the young man is advised to be modest and listen to others, the ignorant as well as the wise, because no man is all-knowing and much can be learned. As an official, do justice to those under your command because, while fraud may gain riches, a reputation for justice will secure more enduring benefits. In the company of a superior, be modest, avoid staring at him, keep your face cast down when he speaks to you, and laugh when he laughs. When you are sent with a message, deliver it exactly as it was spoken to you and avoid adding your own words which could make matters worse. Respect a man for what he is today and forget about his former lowly status. Listen patiently to petitioners because a petitioner appreciates a good hearing even more than the redress of his complaint. Avoid the appearance of covetousness for more than your share at any division, such as an inheritance. Above all, if you wish to keep a friend, stay entirely away from his women. On the other hand, be unstinting in lavishing attention on your wife because she is the foundation of your family (Pritchard, *The Ancient Near East*, pp. 234–237).

With some modifications and modernization of language the same ideas and advice might be expressed by today's "organization man."

The general trend, at least among the lords, was a progressive development of self-confidence and individualism. The early desire to be buried around the pharaoh's tomb in order to share in his immortality was abandoned as lords became hereditary officials in the later fourth dynasty. The self-assured governor who ruled his province like a petty pharaoh confidently built his tomb near his residence. As the grip of the pharaoh over the affairs of the realm relaxed, the corruption and self-seeking of local lords created conditions of oppression that belied the continued claims of beneficent justice. The resources and power of the pharaoh were sapped by the alienation of property and income to support temples and the "cities of the dead." Ruthless competition before long produced the decentralization and ultimate anarchy that for the moment undermined and overthrew the ideals of regularity, balance, harmony, and unity that had characterized the government, religion, and way of life of the old Kingdom.

The collapse of central authority ushered in an extended era (c 2200–1991 B.C.), of social upheaval and internal turmoil, complicated by alien intrusions, which many contemporaries bewailed in personal accounts that have survived.

One such account noted that servants had abandoned their posts to go forth and seize the property of the rich, while nobles and their ladies were forced to labor in the fields or in workhouses. Farmers neglected their fields because they had no idea what the morrow might bring. The ruler himself had been carried off by poor men. Sons even turned their hands against their fathers, and virtuous men threw themselves to the crocodiles in despair. To cap this tale of disintegration whose worst effects were apparently limited to lower Egypt, barbarians had joined in the pillaging, turning fertile fields into desert. Overwhelmed by this disaster, the author exclaimed: Ah, would that it were the end of men, no conception, no birth! (Pritchard, ed., *Ancient Near Eastern Texts*, trans. by John A. Wilson, pp. 441–443.)

In despair many resorted to suicide in the belief that this life was so bad that the next must be better. The crocodiles were said to be sated on the flesh of men. Some became so skeptical that they endorsed outright hedonism.

> Make holiday and weary not therein! Behold it is not given to a man to take his property with him. Behold, no one who goes (over there) can come back again!

(Frankfort, ed., *Before Philosophy*, trans. by John A. Wilson, p. 115.)

EGYPT: THE MIDDLE KINGDOM (C. 1991–1786 B.C.)

Eventually unity was restored and the frontiers regained by the rulers of Thebes, 440 miles south of Memphis. Again, as so frequently recurs in history, unity was achieved by vigorous leaders from the fringe area of Egyptian civilization.

The form of social and political organization had been set by the Old Kingdom. The Middle Kingdom followed this form, but the disorders and difficulties of the last days of the Old Kingdom and the Interregnum contributed to a change in the substance of royal authority and in the essence of social values and practices. The extent of this alteration may be debated, but the existence of, at least, a shift in emphasis is generally agreed on.

The aristocracy who had survived the upheavals of the interregnum were too well established in their own areas to be completely liquidated. They were disciplined into acceptance of subordination to the crown, but retained sufficient local influence to check the full assertion of power by the pharaohs. On the other hand, the pharaohs, to obtain greater independence of action, opened the ranks of the administrative hierarchy to all qualified comers and subsidized education in order that able and ambitious commoners might qualify for positions. In this way the rulers sought to minimize the effects of social stratification, opening avenues of advancement to all their subjects.

During the Middle Kingdom the doctrine *of ma'at* received special emphasis in terms of securing social justice. Officials were regularly admonished to give particular attention to the welfare of society's unfortunates: the poor, the widow, and the orphan. Proof that this stress on ethical behavior was not a mere facade comes from tomb and coffin texts and other writings of the time. In one story a peasant appealed for social justice as a moral right. Yet the repeated appeals he had to make before obtaining justice suggest the continued abuse of power by officials. Indeed, the general view was that all subjects had rights as well as duties under the overall protection of the pharaoh. As the shepherd of his people the king had the duty to see to it that his deputies protected these rights in addition to obtaining compliance with the duties. Many writings emphasized that the gods were more impressed with righteous conduct than with the material works dedicated to them.

A change in religious outlook reciprocally supported the emphasis on ethical conduct. Implicit in the idea of the *ka,* that other self and guiding spirit of every individual, is the idea that every person is invested at birth with a divine spark which he may obey or not at will. During the Old Kingdom immortality had been assured only to the pharaoh. During the Middle Kingdom the belief developed that every person by proper conduct could prepare for individual salvation. The deceased person would appear before a tribunal of gods where his good deeds would be weighed against his bad deeds to determine his fate. And this fate was dependent on the individual's behavior in this life, not on the benevolence of the pharaoh. Texts were written inside coffins for the guidance and protection of the deceased. Thus the gods came to be viewed as concerned with all mankind, not just their earthly agent. The cult of Osiris as the specific judge of the dead was only beginning to evolve at the end of this period. The full development of the Osirian cult did not take place until the period of the New Kingdom or Empire.

These changes only represent a shift of emphasis in values. They merely modified the approach to life and death which was still characterized by a materialistic, individualistic, this-worldly attitude. The worldly outlook was simply tempered by a greater recognition of ethical restraints on human relations. The continued emphasis on the active life, and the expectation that the next life would mirror it, is depicted in the tombs of this period by the abundance of lively scenes of all aspects of human activity. The addition of funeral and religious scenes is just a modest modification of the former outlook.

In a sense the value system had not been changed at all. The values implicit at the outset of Egyptian civilization were only given a more refined, a more civilized expression during the Middle Kingdom. The original Egyptian conception of balance, harmony, and justice were merely extended and more fully implemented. The large literary output of the Middle Kingdom included secular as well as religious and ethical works. Particularly notable is the touching story of Sinuhe, a voluntary exile in Palestine, because it illustrates the strong Egyptian attachment to the land they knew and revered. Even though he had prospered greatly in Palestine and won the highest honors, he yearned in his old age to return and be buried in the land of his birth. To his great joy the pharaoh granted his wish.

The refinement of Egyptian civilization in this period was also reflected in a greater interest in foreign trade, largely under the auspices of the pharaohs. Overseas expeditions on a larger scale were organized. The Sinai copper mines were developed on a continuing basis. A canal connected the Mediterranean and Red Seas via the Nile. Egyptian trading connections spread far and wide, especially with Crete. The remarkable skill of Egyptian craftsmen created a foreign demand for their products, and knowledge of Egyptian wealth naturally aroused the covetous instincts of less prosperous peoples.

Near the end of the Middle Kingdom broken pottery inscribed with curses of foes, both foreign and domestic, were an attempt to exorcise by magic the growing threats at home and abroad. The inclusion of hostile Egyptians indicates the deterioration of the pharaohs' authority within the land, which would also result in an inability to maintain the defense of the frontiers. In any case, increasing weakness invited the invasion of

Egypt by a mixed horde whose leaders were the Hyksos (rulers of foreign lands). Whether the Hyksos were Semites or people of more distant origin cannot be determined. Apparently, they enjoyed a military advantage by using horses to give greater speed and mobility to their war chariots.

For many centuries peoples outside the centers of civilization had been moving about and interacting peacefully or forcefully with their civilized neighbors. Many settled peacefully within civilized frontiers, while others found temporary occupation as mercenaries. By 2000 B.C. Indo-Europeans from beyond the Caucasus Mountains and the Caspian Sea began to press into Anatolia, Iran, and the mountainous terrain in-between conquering or pushing before them the residents of these areas. The Indo-Europeans appear to have been the first to utilize the horse to draw light, spoked-wheel war chariots, but this practice could and was rapidly transmitted to those with whom they came into contact.

EGYPT: THE NEW KINGDOM AND EMPIRE (C. 1570 – 1100 B.C.)

The Hyksos, who are described as "a blast of God" who ruled "in ignorance of Ra," plundered and exploited Egypt for more than a century (c 1700–1570 B.C.) before being expelled by a resurgence of Egyptian spirit again under the leadership of Theban princes. The long domination by barbarians who failed to appreciate Egyptian civilization was a traumatic experience to the hitherto self-confident soul of Egypt, and it left its scars. Either the gods had failed Egypt, or the Egyptians had failed their gods and suffered punishment.

One result was a fanatical pursuit of the Hyksos using horse-drawn chariots into Palestine, Syria, and even beyond the Euphrates to forestall any revival of their threat to Egypt. This campaign involved the New Kingdom in imperialistic adventures that have given the next several centuries the ad-

ditional label of the Empire. The military forces concentrated in the hands of the pharaohs for campaign after campaign gave them greater absolute power than ever before. Plunder filled the royal coffers. One form of plunder, large numbers of captives, introduced a new element into Egyptian society, slavery on a significant scale.

A more important result was the development of extreme religiosity. Rulers gave thanks to the gods for their victories by the construction of temples supported by lavish endowments of land and people. Eventually, the temples are estimated to have owned one third of the land, while the serfs and slaves who labored in temple factories produced possibly one half or more of the manufactured goods. Naturally, in return for favors rendered, the priesthood supported the absolute power of the pharaohs until they came to rely more on the priests than the priests did on them.

The growing concern of the people about the next life was also served by the priesthood, especially the priests of the cult of Osiris who fully defined their doctrine during this period. With magic formulas that, indeed, stressed high moral standards, they stood ready to grant forgiveness and ease the passage for the worst sinner—for a fee. The fullest expression of the belief in universal immortality is preserved in a poem found in a New Kingdom tomb. Its author has overcome all the doubts that caused most Egyptians to patronize the priests. He acknowledges having heard the songs celebrating this life and wonders how Egyptians can so belittle the land of eternity where truth and universal love prevail, where there are no enemies, and where all our kin from the beginning of time have gone and all future generations are destined to go:

> There exists none who may tarry in the land of Egypt; there is not one who fails to reach yon place.
> (Pritchard, ed., *Ancient Near Eastern Texts*, trans. by John A. Wilson, p. 34.)

The ethnocentric reference to Egyptians brings out an important feature of their ideological outlook: their excessive attachment to the homeland. Many stories, such as the already-mentioned story of Sinuhe, illustrate how those who served abroad under the Empire yearned to return to Egypt and how vital they believed death and burial in the homeland to be. No Egyptian, it seems, ever felt comfortable abroad amid unfamiliar surroundings. Only the valley of the Nile provided the regularity and rhythm on which his entire set of ideals and values were built. This attitude, first apparent in ancient times, still prevails today, as witnessed by the reluctance of Egyptians to stay in new settlements irrigated by well-water outside the Nile valley despite the greater, government-supplied amenities. It is an example of the persistence of traditional conceptions which hinder progress in modernization.

During the first two centuries of the Empire the command to obedience insisted on by both the state and the priesthood brought about a gradual revolution. The old lust for life and spirit of individualism, although still depicted in tombs, were subordinated to the demand for conformity to the needs of the group and the nation. Intellectually and emotionally individuals yearned for the freedom and independence that was past and gone forever. Their fate in the next life, the priests told them, depended not on their own actions but on the intervention of the priests. The long list of sins that had developed made every man a sinner dependent on divine mercy. The ethical standards established were beyond human accomplishment. The former balancing of good against bad deeds at the final judgment was replaced by weighing the heart against a feather. Conformity and submission in this life were advocated in the hope for a better life after death. The "Book of the Dead" was a scroll to be included in the coffin for the deceased's presentation before the judgment tribunal and illustrates the ethical code that men were supposed to match up to in life. It asserts in detail that the defendant had never throughout his lifetime committed a wrong of any description against any of his fellowmen or the gods and that he presents himself for judgment wholly pure in mind and body.

Obviously no man could be so pure. Reliance on such magical methods for salvation must have debased the more realistic religion of the Middle Kingdom into a ritualistic superstition inspired by fear and despair. A generalized and unorganized dissatisfaction and frustration with this state of affairs may have encouraged Akhnaton to attempt a religious revolution, but other factors provided additional incentives.

The requirements of imperialism had concentrated social, economic, and political control in the hands of the ruler, but religious development, despite royal assertions to the contrary, had weakened the religious sanction of the god-king. He was no longer viewed as the single, or even the most important, source of individual salvation. Even though the rulers of the New Kingdom made every effort to raise Amon-Ra, a combination of the Theban deity and the sun-god, and the pharaoh as his chief priest to the headship of the Egyptian pantheon and lavished funds on the magnificent temples at Karnak and Luxor, the popularity of the other cults had to be recognized by generous royal gifts. Egyptian religious establishments had not only become largely independent of the crown, they had also gained control of such a large proportion of Egypt's economic resources that they could deal on equal terms with the living god. Therefore, there was ample political justification for religious reform.

Modern interpreters are perhaps too ready to attribute religious action to secular needs and to discount the possible genuineness of spiritual inspiration. Akhnaton's thoroughgoing dedication to his religious work in spite of resistance at home and serious setbacks abroad seems to vouch for his religious conviction and sincerity. If he had succeeded, however, the power of the priesthood would have been broken, and all sources of authority, both spiritual and secular, would have been concentrated in the pharaoh. There would have been no check on the absolutism of the ruler.

Akhnaton (c 1370–1353 B.C.) replaced the whole pantheon with the worship of the sun, Aton, conceived abstractly and not anthropomorphically. In a wholly new city dedicated to Aton, the deity was represented by a sun disk whose rays ended in hands holding the hieroglyph meaning "life." Before this symbol stood the surprisingly realistic figure of Akhnaton as the sole intermediary between this universal deity and all mankind. Indeed, one of the significant byproducts of this reform was the Egyptian artists' temporary release from traditional conventions with the result that they expressed their innate talent for naturalism in artistic works. Such an abstract universal monotheism was an entirely unprecedented conception which died with its creator. This religion was too radical for the times. It was too abstract for popular comprehension and, for obvious reasons, was solidly opposed by the priesthood. The mere fact of its implementation during the reign of Akhnaton, however, demonstrates how much power the pharaoh still wielded. An idea of this lofty conception is conveyed by one hymn in praise of Aton, which contains significant parallels to the later 104th Psalm. A few excerpts may suggest the feeling and power of its message, but it should be consulted in its entirety.

Thou appearest beautifully on the horizon of heaven,
Thou living Aton, the beginning of life!
When thou art risen on the eastern horizon,
Thou hast filled every land with thy beauty.
Thou art gracious, great, glistening, and high over every land;
Thy rays encompass the lands to the limit of all that thou hast made:

. . . . .

O sole god, like whom there is no other!
Thou didst create the world according to thy desire,
Whilst thou wert alone:

. . . . .

The world came into being by thy hand,
According as thou hast made them,
When thou hast risen they live,
When thou settest they die.
Thou art lifetime thy own self,
For one lives (only) through thee.
(Pritchard, ed., *Ancient Near Eastern Texts*, trans. by John A. Wilson, pp. 370–371.)

Subsequent Egyptian development is a part of the imperial conflicts and experiments that will be considered later. The creative period of Egyptian civilization had seen its most significant days. Emerging suddenly as a unified state with a unique interpretation of man's relationship to nature and the universe, it proceeded to work out a fuller expression of the conceptions implicit from the beginning. On two occasions unity was lost, but both times Egypt regained unity, employing with modifications the form that best fulfilled the ideals and values of its civilization. In the Egyptian view man was a part of nature, not a separate creation, and should live in harmony with nature which had provided physical manifestations of divine order, regularity, and balance. Man's proper course was to evolve institutions that would provide for human affairs this divinely demonstrated regularity, harmony, balance, and stability. Justice was understood as part of the provision of harmony, not limited to temporal affairs, but an eternal verity coeval with creation.

At first the ruler as a living god had the sole responsibility for implementing these ideals on earth. Gradually, responsibility was extended until it reached each individual. Each man because of the divine spark within him thus shared the responsibility for providing justice and harmony on earth, and his salvation depended on his performance of this duty to man and nature. As a result, such extremely high ethical standards of human conduct were enjoined that few, if any, human beings could expect to meet them. Before scoffing at such a demanding code of morality, it should be remembered that every society has ideals and values that are more often preached than practiced. The mere existence of such a code may stimulate a higher level of moral behavior than would otherwise be the case. Perhaps the Egyptians of the New Kingdom sought to deceive the gods of judgment, but plentiful evidence indicates that in relations with their fellow Egyptians, at least, a greater generosity and humaneness were commonplace.

In the two Middle Eastern civilizations we have examined, the intimate relationship of religion and political authority, though distinctively different, is evident. This feature, conceived as early as 4000 B.C., has been followed by almost every succeeding regime in the area to the present day. Indeed, any wholly secular solution to the political problems of the contemporary Middle East, after some Western model, seems unlikely; the role of religion in political theory and practice, however modernized, must be recognized. Thus it has proved to be an enduring heritage that exercises an important influence. In addition, the techniques of water control, devised to support an intensive agricultural economy, have continued with little alteration or technological improvement to provide the basis for civilization in the Middle East until today. Whenever water control has been neglected or has deteriorated, civilization, too, has suffered. Finally, the fostering of trade, pioneered by the earliest civilizations of this crossroads region, has provided a vital supplement for the support of its cities as trading centers. Many of the difficulties in modern times, until oil became a precious product, can be attributed to the development of sea routes that bypassed the Middle East. In these terms the Egyptian concern for control of the Suez Canal and the leading role of Egypt in Middle Eastern affairs can largely be explained and understood. To a large degree the religio-political, the economic, and even the social creations of the earliest civilizations are still reflected in the life and livelihood of the peoples of the Middle East. Only the more isolated civilizations of India and China possess heritages with greater continuity.

SIGNIFICANT DATES—MESOPOTAMIA

c.	5000 B.C.	First settlement of Lower Mesopotamia
c.	4100–3500 B.C.	Precivilization development of 'Ubaid Period
c.	3500 B.C.	First writing and arrival of Sumerians
c.	3500–2900 B.C.	Early Sumerian era
c.	2900–2340 B.C.	Early Dynastic era
c.	2340–2180 B.C.	Empire of Sargon of Akkad
c.	2180–1792 B.C.	Foreign invasions, domination, and political disorder
c.	1792–1750 or 1728–1686 B.C.	Reunification by Hammurabi of Babylon
c.	1530 B.C.	Overthrow of Babylonian Empire

SIGNIFICANT DATES—EGYPT

c.	4200 B.C.	Earliest evidence of agriculture in Nile valley
c.	3400–2900 B.C.	Predynastic Gerzean culture
c.	2900–2200 B.C.	Old Kingdom
c.	2650 B.C.	Djoser's Step Pyramid
c.	2550–2450 B.C.	Great Pyramids at Giza

c. 2200–1991 B.C.   First collapse of central authority
c. 1991–1786 B.C.   Middle Kingdom
c. 1700–1570 B.C.   Hyksos domination
c. 1570–1100 B.C.   New Kingdom and Empire
c. 1370–1353 B.C.   Religious revolution of Akhnaton

SELECTED READINGS

*Covensky, Milton, *Ancient Near Eastern Tradition*. New York: Harper & Row, 1966.

*Edwards, I. E. S., *The Pyramids of Egypt*. Baltimore: Penguin Books, 1952.

*Emery, Walter B., *Archaic Egypt*. Baltimore: Penguin Books, 1961.

*Finegan, Jack, *Light from the Ancient Past*. Princeton: Princeton University Press, 1959.

*Frankfort, Henri, *The Art and Architecture of the Ancient Orient*. Baltimore: Penguin Books, 1958.

*———, *The Birth of Civilization in the Near East*. Bloomington: Indiana University Press, 1951.

*Frankfort, Henri, et al., *Before Philosophy*. Baltimore: Penguin Books, 1951.

*Gardiner, Alan Henderson, *Egypt of the Pharaohs*. London: Oxford University Press, 1962.

*Kramer, Samuel Noah, *History Begins at Sumer*. Garden City, N.Y.: Doubleday, 1959.

*———, *The Sumerians*. Chicago: University of Chicago Press, 1963.

*Mallowan, M. E. L., *Early Mesopotamia and Iran*. New York: McGraw-Hill, 1966.

*Moscati, Sabatino, *The Face of the Ancient Orient*. Chicago: Quadrangle Books, 1961.

*Oppenheim, A. Leo, *Ancient Mesopotamia*. Chicago: University of Chicago Press, 1964.

Piggott, Stuart, ed., *The Dawn of Civilization*. New York: McGraw-Hill, 1962.

Pritchard, James B., ed., *Ancient Near Eastern Texts*. Princeton: Princeton University Press, 1955.

*Pritchard, James B., ed., *The Ancient Near East*. Princeton: Princeton University Press, 1958.

*Roux, Georges, *Ancient Iraq*. Baltimore: Penguin Books, 1964.

Van Seters, John, *The Hyksos*. New Haven: Yale University Press, 1966.

*Wilson, John A., *The Culture of Ancient Egypt*. Chicago: University of Chicago Press, 1956.

*Wittfogel, Karl A., *Oriental Despotism*. New Haven: Yale University Press, 1957.

CHAPTER THREE

THE INDUS CIVILIZATION AND THE ARYAN INVASION

The Indus civilization is at once fascinating and frustrating because knowledge of it depends entirely on incomplete archeological examination. Of the early civilizations, it was the most extensive, covering with a uniform culture an area, on present evidence, of almost 500,000 square miles. In addition, it possessed the two largest urban centers yet known for this period, the city of Mohenjo-daro 250 miles north of the present mouth of the Indus River and the city of Harappā nearly 400 miles farther north and east on the Ravi tributary of the Indus. A further feature is the amazing continuity and conservatism of style and technology that characterized this civilization from beginning to end, an attitude shared by later Indian civilization. Finally tantalizing hints suggest that its religion, ideals, and values were somehow transmitted to become vital ingredients of later Indian civilization. Unfortunately, without decipherable written records to explain and elucidate the archeological picture, the formulation of these connections must remain extremely speculative and hypothetical. Probably, the work of archeologists will greatly clarify our understanding of the Indus civilization in the next decade or two. This account must be considered as only tentative.

Like its predecessors, this civilization arose on the alluvial plain of a flood river, the Indus and its tributaries in the Punjab (the land of five rivers). As elsewhere, geography and especially the weather provided the conditions that encouraged large-scale cooperation under able and determined leadership. Rainfall of this region was greater then than it is today and greater than that in Egypt or Mesopotamia. The result was vast marshes and jungles in which fever and wild beasts flourished. Even today, the Punjab averages more than 20 inches of rainfall annually, although Sind to the south is now almost rainless. The wetter condition in ancient times caused the rivers to flood and change their courses unpredictably bringing destruction to the works of men who dared to challenge nature in this environment.

But the physical conditions attracted, as well as deterred, settlement. Here was fertile land annually renewed by the rivers that were natural highways and sources of fish and fowl. Settlement was also encouraged by the generally drying conditions which made it difficult for the nearby hill and lowland agricultural communities to support growing populations and by the example of the two other successful riverine societies. In any case, the Indus civilization suddenly emerged about 2500 B.C. with signs of only a brief pioneering period by settlers from these communities to the west. The distinctiveness of this culture preludes the possibility of direct colonization from Mesopotamia, although a knowledge of that civilization probably inspired the effort in the Indus valley. The most reasonable hypothesis is that, following hunting expeditions and a few small-scale attempts at settlement by those communities to the west, a major effort was undertaken by these people who had a knowledge of metallurgy, ceramics, and agriculture. Because of the need for manpower they mixed freely with the proto-Australoid people previously living a primitive, hand-to-mouth existence in the valley and thus established an open society from the beginning. After initial success they spread rapidly up and down the river highways as they sought sources of raw material. Before long, trade led them to take to the sea

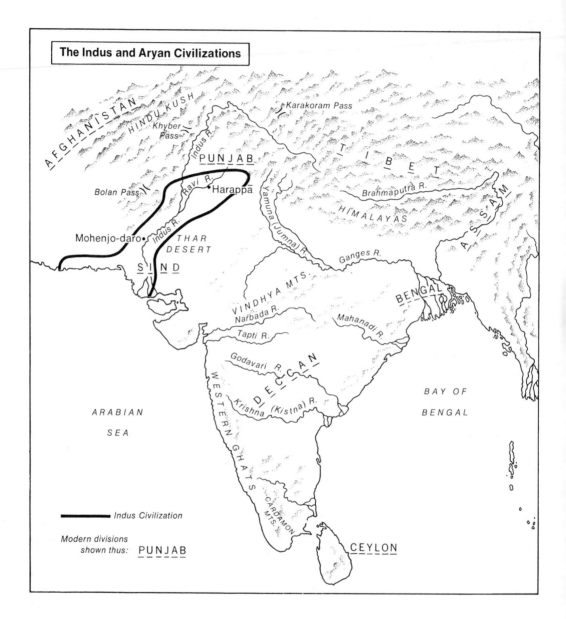

The Indus and Aryan Civilizations

Indus Civilization

Modern divisions
shown thus: PUNJAB

and establish coastal outposts some 300–400 miles east and west of the mouth of the Indus. By about 2350 B.C. trade with Mesopotamia is attested by Indus products found there. In short, success followed success in a chain reaction that developed and spread this civilization in only a few generations. Perhaps the penalty of such early and outstanding success was the determination to preserve it by rejecting all innovation.

THE GEOGRAPHICAL SETTING

Before proceeding to an examination of the features and characteristics of the Indus civilization, something must be said about the geographical factors that have been influential in Indian history and civilization as a whole. The Indo–Pakistan area has been described as a subcontinent largely because of the mighty Himalaya mountain range that bars easy access for 1600 miles along the northern frontier. The moisture-laden clouds of the summer monsoons from the south are broken on this barrier that also effectively protects India against the winter cold wave from the north.

Other than by sea the subcontinent is open to trade and invasion in force only from the northwest. Several passes, such as the Karakoram in the extreme north, the renowned Khyber, and the Bolan, grant access to the Indus plain. Once past the Indus, invaders were forced far to the north by the Thar Desert. Here a relatively narrow passage leads to the Gangetic plain and here many a decisive battle has been fought. An invader had the advantage of conquering northern India piecemeal: first, the Punjab and the Indus plain, and then, the Gangetic plain. Seldom was a unified defense mounted in the Indus basin or the mountains to the west.

In ancient times, because of heavier monsoon rains, the Gangetic plain was more difficult to settle and develop than the Indus, the first cities rising sometime after 1000 B.C. The delta region of Bengal presented an even greater challenge and was not incorporated till the third century B.C. Assam, through which the Brahmaputra (son of Brahma) flows, only really began to be developed under the British Raj.

Below the Gangetic plain the Vindhya Range, rising to only 3000 feet, separates northern India from the peninsula. In ancient times its dense forests peopled by primitive, but savage, tribes deterred the southward penetration of civilization. Many military and romantic legends take as a theme struggles with the forest peoples of this region. In a number of pockets in these mountains and hills tribal groups still maintain their primitive way of life.

The heart of the peninsula is the Deccan, a plateau that slopes gently eastward from a weathered mountain ridge called the Western Ghats, paralleling the west coast for 600 miles, and is bounded on the east by a lower and irregular ridge called the Eastern Ghats. Geologically the oldest part of India, the Deccan is severely weathered and eroded and farming depends on conserving the water of the erratic summer monsoon with an average duration of only 6 weeks. This rainfall is returned to the Indian ocean by eastward-flowing rivers, such as the Mahānadi, the Godāvari, and the Krishna (Kistna), that have built up broad alluvial plains on the east coast supporting large populations. Thanks to the interception of the southwest monsoon by the steep escarpment of the Western Ghats, a narrow, but fertile and well-watered plain faces the Arabian Sea.

South of the Deccan the tropical land of the Tamil people is centered around the Nilgiri and the Cardamon Mountains, reaching heights of 8000 feet. The weather pattern is complex, but a secondary monsoon, as in Bengal and Assam, provides an abundance of moisture in much of the region, including Ceylon, that encourages the production of tropical products. During the Roman principate Western merchants pursued an extensive seaborne trade with this region which, in turn, developed overseas trade with Southeast Asia.

Thus, geographical conditions dictated the initial arrival of the idea of civilization in the Indus basin from the northwest. Until the approach of Europeans by sea, the most important waves of people and ideas entered India from the same direction. People and civilization next pressed through the narrow gap between the desert and the Himalayas to conquer the Gangetic plain. Thereafter, Bengal to the east and the peninsula to the south were gradually brought into the orbit of the Indian civilization of the northern plains. In the extreme south the Tamil peoples adapted the influences from the north to evolve a culture that remains in many ways distinctive today.

THE INDUS CIVILIZATION
(C. 2500–1500 B.C.)

The Indus civilization is best known from the excavations at its two chief cities, Mohenjo-daro on the Indus and Harappā to the northeast on the Ravi River. The regular layout of city blocks, each 200 by 400 yards, and the wide, straight streets is unique at this date and implies a strong municipal organization to regulate the activities and to look after the welfare of the citizens. Each city was more than three miles in circumference and was flanked on the west by a fortified citadel built on an artificial mound 40 to 50 feet above the plain. Construction in both cities utilized for the most part kiln-fired bricks of identical pattern, suggesting a plentiful supply of firewood. Homes of two and perhaps three stories were designed with rooms opening on a central courtyard and presenting a solid face to the street. Each was equipped with a bath that connected with municipal brick-lined drains under the streets that were provided with regularly spaced inspection holes for the removal of debris. The homes, all substantial, varied in size suggesting a prosperous middle-class society with a measure of individual opportunity for improvement. At both cities very large public granaries of similar design with ventilation ducts under the floors provide further evidence of municipal organization and supervision. Barrack-type buildings next to the granaries may have housed workers, possibly slaves, or soldiers. Identifying seals found in the ruins of a granary at another site could mean that the municipality furnished storage facilities as a public service, but the more probable hypothesis is that the size of these granaries reflects the extent of governmental control and taxation.

The most interesting structure on the citadel of Mohenjo-daro is a large pool, 39 by 23 feet, made watertight with asphalt and entered by steps at either end. Facilities for filling and emptying the pool were part of the design. Around the pool were rooms and baths for the bathers. Nearby, a long building, 230 by 78 feet, could have been a royal palace or priestly residence.

Whatever may have been the form of government, the citadel was certainly its headquarters. The great pool, so similar to the ritual tanks of medieval and modern India, may have served a religious purpose for purification. If this interpretation is correct, political and religious authority may have been joined together in the Indus civilization as they were during the third millennium in Egypt and Mesopotamia. To date, however, no monumental temples have been identified to support such a view.

While methodically planned, the absence of monuments or parks and the solid, undecorated exteriors of the houses must have made a stroll through the streets a dull and uninspiring experience, possibly enlivened only by people wearing colorful cotton clothing. For the most part, the artistic expression of this utilitarian society appears to have been personal and religious, involving small, but often finely modelled, objects.

Most abundant are the flat seals or amulets carved from soft stone that could then be hardened by baking. Holes on their backs suggest that they were worn around the neck. Many kinds of animals which must have been familiar to the inhabitants are pictured realistically on these seals: elephants, rhinoceros, tigers, antelopes, crocodiles, and most common of all, the humped bull native to India. The fact that the bull accounts as well for more than three quarters of the terracotta animal figurines strongly suggests his probable association with religion. The total absence of representation of the cow further emphasizes the special significance attached to the bull. The seals commonly include writing in as yet undeciphered symbols. Of course, these brief accounts can be no more than names, titles, or religious invocations. Other examples of writing thus far found are also brief, running at most to 20 signs. Although the Indus people were literate, they apparently used perishable material for lengthier accounts. The uniqueness of their writing is further evidence of the distinctiveness of their civilization.

Composite renderings combining human and animal parts are suggestive of later Indian religious art. Especially interesting are examples of what appears to be a prototype of the Hindu god Shiva that is provided with horns and seated in the typical Indian position of meditation. This hypothesis is supported by the many bulls who are Shiva's traditional means of transport as well as by the association of the phallic symbol with the god. Numerous representations of the Mother Goddess, whose cult was common throughout the ancient world, have also been found. The religion of the Indus civilization, insofar as it can be surmised from these remains, concerned nature and especially the problem of fertility and reproduction.

A charming human touch is given by terra-cotta and occasionally metal toys including comic figures and solid-wheeled carts identical with those still used to haul goods today. Several types of dice indicate that gambling was as common an amusement then as later.

Artistically, one of the finest finds is the lively figure of a dancing girl cast in bronze. The slim figure is entirely nude except for a necklace and a string of bracelets. The gracefully tilted head has proto-Australoid features.

Metal tools and weapons illustrate the conservatism of this society. Even though their technology was in no way inferior and samples of improved products were occasionally imported, the Indus craftsmen clung doggedly to the old forms. As an example, the shaft-hole axe had been adopted throughout western Asia, yet the Indus smiths continued to produce the flat axe to which the shaft had to be bound. Likewise, although the strengthening of knives and spearheads with midribs was common practice elsewhere, weaker flat blades persisted

to the end of the Indus civilization. Such military conservatism will also be found to characterize later Indian civilization.

On the other hand, a distinctive invention was the saw with offset teeth. Such an improved tool suggests a special attention to woodworking, a skill for which India was later to be renowned. Probably a great deal of artistic effort was put into woodcarving, all examples of which time has destroyed.

The economy of the Indus civilization, as of all Eastern civilizations, was based on intensive farming in an environment that requires large-scale cooperation in water control projects. Possibly rainfall was relied upon but, even so, the marshes would have required drainage ditches, and the fields would have needed the protection of dikes. Considering the size of the population and the great granaries, a full-scale irrigation system was probably built and maintained. Besides wheat, barley, and vegetables, one new crop, cotton was grown. Cotton and cotton cloth probably bulked large as exports.

The rearing of domesticated cattle, buffaloes, and possibly pigs and asses supplemented farming. Fowl were first domesticated in the Indus valley, and the egg-laying hen became a valuable addition to the barnyard community. The frequency with which the peacock is depicted on pottery indicates the esteem felt for his beauty. Hunting further supplemented the diet and, in the case of the elephant, provided ivory for skilled carvers.

Like the other civilizations, the Indus civilization was not wholly self-sufficient and self-contained. Farming and livestock raising were supplemented by an extensive trade that reached distant Mesopotamia by sea. The natural river highways encouraged exchange as well as unity. Gold, silver, semiprecious stones, and especially copper and tin had to be sought outside the valley proper. These supplies were purchased with the surplus products of Indus agriculture and artisans. In the time of Sargon of Akkad (c. 2350 B.C.) Indus merchants sailed their vessels along the coast and up the Euphrates to deal directly at his capital. By about 1950 B.C., if Mesopotamian tablets of that date have been properly interpreted, merchant-pirates on the island of Bahrain in the Persian Gulf had gained control of the trade with the Indus valley, acting as transshippers. Among the goods listed as coming from the Indus area were copper, stone, wood, and ivory objects as well as various animals.

How did this flourishing civilization come to an end—with a bang or a whimper? Were internal or external factors more important in its downfall? What happened to these skilled and talented people? Were they wiped out or enslaved, or did they migrate elsewhere? Various hypotheses have been advanced emphasizing one factor or another, but the most reasonable one incorporates all these possibilities in a picture of gradual decline punctuated by sharp blows.

By about 2000 B.C., it will be recalled, primarily pastoral peoples speaking Indo-European dialects were conquering the outlying areas on the northern and eastern frontiers of the Middle East and settling down as petty rulers, at least temporarily, until they could digest their conquests. Among them were a group of related tribes who came to call themselves Arya (anglicized as Aryan), a generic term meaning "kinsmen," preserved in the names of Iran for modern Persia and Eire for Ireland. Like their brethren, they paused for a period, probably in eastern Iran, before pressing into the inviting pastures in the high valleys of Afghanistan. Naturally the pressure of the invaders helped to set other peoples in motion, ultimately bringing turmoil to the villages on the western frontier of the Indus civilization. Sometime after 2000 B.C. one of these villages was burned, and then the site was occupied by a less advanced people—probably the invaders—as indicated by the cruder pottery they produced. Similar evidence of newcomers has been found at many other sites.

Meanwhile, signs of difficulties and fear appear in the latest levels of the Indus cities. They had suffered damage and destruction

a number of times from exceptionally severe floods, but each time a city was rebuilt the building code and city plan had been maintained. Apparently this essentially open society now admitted refugees who were accommodated by the subdividing of rooms and the putting up of shoddier buildings. Construction pressed into the streets indicating the pressure of population and the problem of integrating less disciplined settlers. Alien pottery of the type used in the villages to the west supports the probability that much of the population increase represents refugees from this area outside the Indus civilization proper. Within the Indus area fear of raids may have encouraged farmers to abandon their undefended villages and fields and to seek safety in the cities. Without daily care agricultural production would suffer, adding a new dimension to the problem of overpopulation in the cities. Lack of maintenance of dikes and canals by absentee farmers could bring devastation during the annual flood with consequent famine and epidemic in the cities. In other words, the delicate balance of the Indus economy was seriously disturbed by one or more of many possibilities.

At this time, the defenses of the citadel were substantially strengthened. The massiveness of these fortifications seems to have exceeded the needs of protection against raiders. It is notable that no effort was made to fortify the cities themselves. Perhaps, the rulers were inspired more by fear of discontent in the city below.

The only evidence of a violent end comes from Mohenjo-daro. There, on the last level, skeletons of persons cut down in attempted flight are strewn in contorted positions with plentiful signs of mortal wounds. The failure to clean up after the slaughter is proof that this disaster was inflicted by aliens. The Aryans may very well have delivered this final blow. In the Rigveda the Aryan war-god is described as the "fort destroyer," and where else, except in the Indus cities, were there forts to destroy?

Meanwhile, what happened to the people of the Indus civilization? The civilization was not destroyed overnight. Even in the Rigveda the struggle is long and drawn out, possibly lasting several centuries. Many were captured and enslaved, but others may have moved before the storm. The identification of an Indus-type settlement near Delhi opens up the possibility of migration into the Ganges valley. In the southeast, around the Gulf of Cambay and the mouths of the Narbadā and Tāpti rivers, Indus-style towns and villages continued to flourish beyond the reach of the invaders. Gradually they were transformed by about 1000 B.C. into successor cultures without any sharp break. Here then the Indus civilization did not die as it did in the north; it just slowly faded away. Nevertheless, as interesting as these outlying attenuations may be, the collapse of the two chief cities cut the heart out of the Indus civilization.

THE VEDIC AGE (C. 1600 – 900 B.C.)

Historically, the subsequent centuries until well after 1000 B.C. are India's Dark Ages. Thus far archeology has found little to fill the gap. The chief source of information is the Rigveda, a collection of poetic accounts describing the activities and religious view from about 1600 to 900 B.C. of those Aryan tribes that revived civilized life in the Gangetic plain between 900 and 500 B.C. Since the 1028 hymns of the Rigveda were only finally selected and declared about 900 B.C. a sacred literature to be transmitted orally without alteration by the priestly caste of *brāhmans*, the extent to which they accurately portray conditions and events in the previous centuries remains uncertain. Yet, as the only records, they must be interpreted generously to fill the gap of this long Dark Age.

Geographical references indicate that the earliest poems were composed when the tribes were settled in eastern Afghanistan and were raiding the upper Indus valley. The bulk of the poems, however, concern the period when they had reached the eastern Punjab and were pressing into the upper part of the Ganges' basin.

The society pictured was composed of pastoral tribes whose main interest was warfare. Although their first concern was to defeat the non-Aryan Dasyu, they were as frequently engaged in power struggles among themselves. Therefore, the tribal "system" was confusingly fluid, some tribes disappearing and others appearing, while several cases of amalgamation occurred. Chieftains called rājās were selected for their military prowess by assemblies of the warriors, although a trend toward hereditary succession is clearly apparent. A noble class went to war in horse-drawn chariots. Free commoners served as foot soldiers with whatever weapons they could obtain. At the bottom of society were the slaves, mostly non-Aryan captives. Women still enjoyed considerable prestige and respect, although they were very definitely subordinated to men in this patriarchal society. In the later hymns a priestly class who were responsible for performing properly the increasingly complex rituals had evolved as advisors to the chiefs. At this time, class distinctions were still loose, and movement from one to another was relatively easy. Castes as rigid classifications had not yet developed, but the taboos on relationships with the conquered natives, which emphasized purity of blood, plus the example of the priests who sought to set themselves apart as a privileged class led to the earliest delineation of the four major classes: priest (brahman), warrior (kshatriya), peasant (vaishya), and serf (shūdra). Religious sanction for this division is given by a hymn describing the sacrificial dismemberment of primeval man by the gods.

When they divided the Man
into how many parts did they divide him?
What was his mouth, what were his arms,
what were his thighs and his feet called?
The brāhman was his mouth,

of his arms was made the warrior,
His thighs became the vaishya,
of his feet the shūdra was born.
(Basham, *The Wonder that was India*, p.
241)

The descriptions of their chief foes, the dasyus or dāsas (slaves), allowing for the normal exaggeration when depicting enemies, give a fairly accurate portrait of the Indus people and their way of life. They are short and swarthy demons with such unbecoming features as thick lips and flat noses. They were wealthy, living luxuriously in fortified places. Despite their skill in black magic, the war-god Indra had successfully led his people in storming and destroying their forts. Most loathsome and revolting was their worship of the phallus.

In spite of these expressions of contempt, interaction and exchange could not be prevented. Many Aryans mixed with their female slaves. Reference is made to a dāsa chief who adopted the Aryan religion, while frequent references are made to Aryans who had left the fold. Of course, the Aryans were a mixed people when they arrived in India. The fruit of this mixture and that with the dāsas is apparent in the non-Indo-European words included even in the Rigveda. Religious and cultural influences must also have had their effect, but they are very difficult to identify in the early stages. Much later, non-Indo-European characteristics gradually predominate and almost submerge the Aryan culture, but here again basic Indian conservatism has preserved the first of the Vedas as the primary sacred text.

Aryan social organization was built on the fundamental unit of the family in which the father exercised absolute authority limited only by custom. The family cult centered on the hearthfire at which both father and mother made daily offerings and prayers. A group of related families formed a clan which later, after settling down, became synonomous with "village." A group of clans formed a tribe.

Although simple agriculture was practiced, it is rarely mentioned in the Rigveda and was obviously viewed as subordinate to the major respectable occupation, the raising of cattle. Indeed, cattle played the leading role in Aryan tribal life, providing a kind of currency as a unit of value. Incidentally, they were not yet sacred and served as the main course on festive occasions. Feasts were frequent, whether connected with a religious ceremony or not, and were the occasion of free and unrestrained consumption of inebriating beverages. Music played on flute, lute, and harp, accompanied by cymbals and drums, the singing of heroic songs about great deeds, and dancing with dancing girls, enlivened these occasions. In addition, like all Indians before and since, the Aryans were addicted to gambling and, as the "Gamester's Lament" points out, the sky was the limit.

In this moving poem the victim bewails his passionate and unbreakable addiction to the dice. His devotion to them has forced him to forsake a loving wife who has found comfort in the arms of another man. His mother, father, and brothers have given him up and no longer recognize him as a member of the family. Even lady luck has rejected him, and he wanders afar in debt and in fear, seeking sanctuary. At the close the moral is clearly set forth.

Don't play with dice, but plough your furrow!
Delight in your property, prize it highly!
Look to your cattle and look to your wife . . . .
(Basham, *The Wonder that was India*, pp. 403–405)

In essential skills a beginning of specialization can be recognized from references in the Rigveda. Naturally those artisans who produced the tools of war were most highly regarded. Although not highly developed culturally, Aryan society enjoyed a clear superiority in military technology. Their bronze-smiths produced shaft-hole axes, swords and spearheads with strengthening midribs, and other weapons far superior to those of the Indus artisans. Aryan warriors were particularly deadly with their sophisticated bows. Their carpenters and chariot-makers manufactured lightweight chariots with spoked wheels that were far more mobile and speedy than the heavy, solid-wheeled vehicles produced by Indus craftsmen. Although iron, the cheaper "metal of the masses," came into common use during this period in western Asia, the rarity of iron objects emphasizes the isolation of India at this time. Not until the expansion to India of the Persian Empire in the late sixth century did the use of iron become common.

The Rigveda, being a sacred work collected by the brāhmans, relates much more about Aryan religion than Aryan social and political life. The later Sāma and Yajur Vedas are chiefly significant as illustrations of the growing domination of religion by the brāhmans through an emphasis on the precise performance of complex rituals demanding a lifetime of study. The Atharva Veda is interesting because, relying chiefly on magic invocations, it reflects the religious beliefs and practices of the masses, which include many non-Aryan elements. The Brāhmanas, composed between about 900 and 600 B.C. with interpolations of later date, are lengthy prose commentaries on the Vedas seeking to explain and justify the ritualized religion that had evolved. The mere composition of such works documents the development of some doubt and questioning of the ritual basis of brāhman supremacy and the altered needs of a society that was settling into a more civilized way of life. Much more illustrative of the searching for a fuller and more satisfying explanation of the role of the individual in a society becoming detribalized are the Aranyakas and Upanishads, composed after 700 B.C. and extending in time in some parts into the Christian Era.

The central feature of the Vedic religion was sacrifice, for the most part to obtain some worldly favor from the specified god. The most common, but by no means the only, procedure was placing the offering in a fire sacred to the god of fire, Agni (cognate of "ignite"), who would then deliver it to the appropriate god in heaven. At first the sacrifice was a comparatively simple procedure that any good Aryan could perform, and most of the gods were looked on as generous, benevolent, and cooperative in helping their people to achieve their worldly desires. In time, however, the development of brāhmanism surrounded the sacrifice with an aura of magic requiring the services of the trained brāhman who by a simple error in the ritual could destroy his patron. In other words, the efficacy of the sacrifice came to depend on the magical utterance of the proper formulas by the inspired brāhman in spiritual communion with the god.

The Aryan pantheon contained obvious parallels to those of other Indo-European peoples. Dyaus-piter, the father of the gods, is clearly cognate to the Greek Zeus and the Roman Jupiter, but by Vedic times his importance had become subordinate to other deities. The single, most important Vedic deity was Indra, god of storms and war, whose chief weapon was appropriately the thunderbolt. In their own image the Aryan warriors pictured Indra as a spirited, lusty deity, especially addicted to feasting and drinking. The inebriating beverage, *soma*, prepared from some unidentified plant growing on the mountainsides, was sacrificially imbibed by the god and his communicants, inducing hallucinations and visions. The sacred *soma* was also used in the sacrifices to other gods and helped to create a sense of fellowship and communion with these representatives of the forces of nature. Otherwise fearful phenomena thus became congenial companions who were believed to share in the festivities.

Several gods were related to the sun. A verse to one of them was and still is the most esteemed verse in the Rigveda, recited at every religious ceremony. It is particularly associated with the initiation of an Aryan between 8 and 12 years of age by which he gains the distinction of being "twice-born."

Let us meditate on the lovely splendor of the sun-god:
may he enlighten our understanding.

Another god connected with the sun was Vishnu, pictured as crossing the earth in three giant strides, who was to play a major role in later Hinduism. Of a different nature were the gods Varuna and Rudra.

Varuna, second only to Indra, was the master and guardian of the cosmic order and, as such, punished men for sinful acts. Unlike the rowdy Indra, he sat in serene majesty in heaven receiving reports of human misconduct from his spies. Thus, he was an all-knowing, omnipresent god whom mere mortals approached with fear and trembling. Sacrifice alone would not be sure to appease him; the sinner must do penance. In addition to ritual sin, he abhorred lying, inhospitality, violation of friendship, and immoral acts, especially those induced by anger, alcohol, or gambling. He inflicted diseases on men for their sins, and even for their fathers' sins. After death the hapless sinner was consigned to the sombre "House of Clay," the counterpart of the carefree "World of the Fathers." The divine archer Rudra, though no upholder of virtue, unpredictably fired arrows carrying plague and disaster wherever they struck. Therefore, he, too, was viewed with fear and urged in prayers to fire his shafts elsewhere. He had, however, a good side. As the guardian of healing herbs he could, if he so wished, grant the gift of health.

By the end of the Vedic era the brāhmans had convinced most, if not all, believers that the very existence of the universe depended on their regular performance of the prescribed sacrifices. Without them chaos would ensue. At the same time, however, a fresh spirit of inquiry for answers beyond the gods, who themselves had to conform to the cosmic order, is manifested in one of the last hymns of the Rigveda, a creation hymn whose conception and uncertain conclusion strike a new note seemingly at odds with the rest of this work. Perhaps it was a late addition.

Nor Aught nor Nought existed; yon bright sky
Was not, nor heaven's broad woof outstretched above.
What covered all? What sheltered? What concealed?
Was it the water's fathomless abyss?
There was not death—yet was there nought immortal;
There was no confine betwixt day and night;
The only One breathed breathless by itself,
Other than it there nothing since has been.
Darkness there was, and all at first was veiled
in gloom profound—an ocean without light—
The germ that still lay covered in the husk
Burst forth, one nature, from the fervent heat.

Who knows the secret? Who proclaimed it here?
Whence, whence, this manifold creation sprang?
The Gods themselves came later into being—
Who knows from whence this great creation sprang?
He from whom this great creation came,
Whether His will created or was mute,
The Most High Seer that is in Highest heaven,
He knows it—or perchance even He knows not.
(Max Muller, *Chips from a German*

Workshop [N.Y.: Charles Scribner's Sons, 1881], I, pp. 76–77.)

Certainly this hymn threw wide open the gates for speculation and inspired the search for ultimate answers that characterizes the Aranyakas and Upanishads and, in fact, the bulk of subsequent Indian intellectual activity. Setting the stage for this quest, however, were the political, social, and economic developments after 900 B.C.

THE RISE OF INDO-ARYAN CIVILIZATION (C. 900 – 500 B.C.)

Perhaps pushed from behind by new invaders, the Aryans took up the challenge of the Ganges basin and under the leadership of increasingly powerful hereditary rulers gradually pressed forward along the north bank to the edge of the delta in Bengal. The challenge of the jungle demanded larger scale cooperation and more authoritarian leadership than the customary tribal organization provided. Tribes merged, accepting more absolute rulers, and the brāhmans, in return for royal patronage, cooperated in elevating the prestige and authority of the rulers. The struggle for supremacy involved bitter wars the vague memories of which are preserved in the heroic epics composed in their final form at a much later date. The *ashvamedha*, a horse sacrifice, was developed to justify the aggressive extension of the royal domain. A consecrated horse was released to roam for a year followed by the king's warriors. Whenever he set foot on another ruler's territory, that ruler had the choice of submission or war. Other royal sacrifices to enhance the power of the ruler were also devised by the brāhmans. In this way the status of rulers and brāhmans came reciprocally to depend on the mutual support of each other. Naturally, tribal assemblies tended to disappear as this alliance became predominant and geography replaced tribal kinship as the basis of political division. In peripheral regions, however, a few tribally organized states that

may not have been Aryan managed to persist for several centuries, particularly in the Himalayan foothills.

Meanwhile, the clearing of the jungle for cultivation brought about significant social and economic changes. A story in one of the Brāhmanas alludes to the use of fire, on the instruction of the fire god Agni, to clear the jungle. This tale illustrates both the Aryan advance to the east and one method used to overcome the jungle. To exploit such terrain more or less permanent settlements that devoted more attention to agriculture were necessary. Administrative demands required the establishment of towns and cities for the localities under settled development. The transition from a tribal to a territorial society undermined tribal organization. The breakdown of the tribal sense of community and kinship threw the individual more on his own, and on the central government. The consequent feeling of insecurity may have encouraged the growing asceticism and pessimism that accompanied this advance toward civilization. As prosperity stimulated the formation of larger political units under autocratic rule, the increased gap between ruler and ruled created a spiritual malaise that was reflected in the speculations of sensitive souls.

The dominant characteristic of the new thought was religious individualism. The ritual ministrations of the brāhmans no longer provided satisfaction. The quest for mystic knowledge and enlightenment above and beyond the sacrifices to the gods reflected a more sophisticated attitude toward the here and the hereafter. Undoubtedly, non-Aryan doctrines were exercising a greater influence. Among them were the doctrine of *samsāra*, the transmigration of souls in rebirth after rebirth, and the associated concept of *karma*, whereby the good and bad acts of this life determine the condition of the next life. Although the source and evolution of these two doctrines are not clear, they were fully developed and generally accepted by the end of this period. All forms of animal life, and in some sects even plants, were incorporated in this perpetually revolving "wheel of life." Even the gods were included in this process.

For the average man such a conception was not unattractive. It placed the burden for a humble station in this life on the misdeeds of a former life and offered the promise of a better future life to those who behaved well in this one. But some found the prospect of perpetual rebirth appalling. The ascetic was dedicated to the search for the secret that would release him from this endless cycle of birth and death, a goal that the sacrifices of the brahmans could not secure.

The Aranyakas (forest texts) are transitional teachings of ascetics who went to meditate in the forests, a dangerous and uncongenial environment from the Aryan point of view. While recognizing the need for the brāhman sacrifices, they sought to explain the symbolic meaning of the ritual, and to them this meaning was more important than the act of sacrifice itself.

The Upanishads also recognized the gods, but sought the larger, more encompassing truth that, they taught, each man possessed within himself—if he could but discover it. This conception was the microcosmic Self, Ātman, the counterpart in each individual of the macrocosmic Reality, Brahman. As conceived by these mystics, the two are identical and eternal. Those who concentrate on sacrifices and the accumulation of worldly merit fail to understand the higher, universal truth that is unchanging reality. As a consequence, they are reborn and do not escape this illusory life with all its pains and passions. In contrast, those who go into the forest with a heart full of penitence and faith in Brahman find tranquility and discover their imperishable souls (Ātman) and oneness with Brahman. A student in search of this knowledge should seek out a teacher (guru) well-versed in the Vedas, who recognizes the inadequacy of sacrifices and knows Brahman. If the student has achieved peace of mind and approaches him in all humility, the knowing teacher can reveal the

knowledge of Brahman through which the student can gain awareness of the only reality, the "imperishable Soul" (Ātman).

An account in the form of a conversation between father and son illustrates and explains by a readily recognizable example the identity in essence of both the Self and universal Reality. The father begins by explaining to his son that in the beginning there was only undifferentiated being, one without a second. Some claim that at first there was just undifferentiated nonbeing out of which being was created, but how, the father asks, could being be produced from nonbeing. Such an argument is simply not logical. The father then asks the son to put salt in a container of water. The next morning he asks for the salt, but it has been completely dissolved in the water. Then he instructs his son to sip the water in different parts of the container and report the taste, which in each instance is salty. Following this experiment, the father points out that the salt, although unperceived, exists throughout the water, and likewise, Being, although unperceived, permeates the world. Indeed, "this whole world has the essence for its Self. That is the Real." (Wm. T. deBary, *Sources of Indian Tradition*, pp. 35–36).

The objective of these mystics was release (*moksha*) from the chain of matter, the wheel of life. Release could only be obtained by penance, study, and meditation leading to the individual realization that the inner Self and the ultimate Reality were one and the same, now and forever. This realization would end the endless cycle of birth and death by means of a mystical merger of one's Self and the eternal Truth. The tie to ever-changing and, therefore, illusory matter would be terminated. The path to this goal prescribed the minimizing of one's dependence on the material things of this life by living the minimal life of the ascetic in which even life or death was inconsequential. The necessity of reducing the connections with this world to a minimum led in time to the formulation of systematic exercises, called Yoga.

Although the Upanishads reflect the intrusion of non-Aryan elements and substantially altered the intellectual outlook and emphasis of the Vedic religion, most of the mystics were brāhmans who considered their teachings as a continuation and culmination of the doctrines implicit in the Vedas. Each Upanishad was directly linked to the Vedas, and the total accomplishment was interpreted as the completion or end of the Vedas, the Vedānta.

Recognizing the importance and popularity of this mystic development, the brāhmans later demonstrated the traditional flexibility, tolerance, and absorptive character of Indian religion by providing a place for asceticism in the last two of the four stages (āshrama) of life. Following initiation, the young brāhman as required by the first stage, attached himself as a disciple and student to a teacher (guru) and studied the Vedas for 10 to 12 years. The second stage involved marriage, worldly endeavour, and the raising of a family. In the third stage he retired and abstained from worldly activities in preparation for the fourth stage of ascetic search for the ultimate Reality. This practical and realistic organization of life is still influential today.

The growth of mysticism resulted necessarily in a reorientation of religious values. The sacrifice, which had been spiritually elevated by the brāhmans to the point where its proper and regular performance was equated with the maintenance of the cosmic order, was now reduced to its original import as a means of obtaining worldly favors from the gods. Spiritual power and respect were transferred from the sacrifice to the seer, who by asceticism had gained transcendental knowledge and wisdom. The popular reverence for these persons was a powerful reinforcement and inducement to the further development of asceticism. The spiritual ground was thus fertilized for the nourishment of the more radical teachings of Buddhism and Jainism.

This shift in religious outlook was naturally accompanied by an alteration in ethical standards. The old virtues of a tribal society of warriors were transformed by the doctrines of transmigration and *karma* to suit a settled agricultural society living cheek to jowl. The requirement of virtuous conduct deprecated violence in favor of gentleness, kindliness, and cooperativeness—qualities of greater value to civilization. If the status of the next life depended on the deeds of this life, then there was a strong incentive for the practice of high standards of human behavior. These two doctrines also supported the dedicated performance of the duties of one's station in this life, which helped greatly to maintain social and political stability. Such an ethical attitude reduced to a minimum the frictions associated with individual jealousy, ambition, and discontent and eased the task of government. The channeling of the highest intellectual endeavor into the ascetic's search for transcendental knowledge above and beyond the pains and pleasures of this life also contributed to social and political stability and quietude. The best minds were thus diverted from active agitation. In the later Upanishads the extinction of all desires became the ultimate goal.

This picture, however, should not be overdrawn. Autocratic rulers advised and supported by brāhmans carried on a continuous struggle for worldly supremacy. But autocracy and warfare were tempered by the prevailing religious values. Rulers were expected to be benevolent and just, and warfare was to abide by a chivalric code that proscribed unnecessary cruelty. Probably, as elsewhere, these ideals of government were honored more in the breach than in practice.

By the end of the sixth century B.C. the Aryan conquerors had collaborated with their non-Aryan subjects in producing a civilization in the Ganges valley with substantial states, cities, and towns that were supported by intensive, irrigated agriculture. A new crop, rice, had been domesticated which was destined to have an important future throughout Asia. In government, the elected Aryan chief had evolved into the hereditary ruler whose authority was checked mainly by the brāhman religious monopoly. However, the relationship between ruler and brāhmans was one of cooperation and reciprocal support for their mutual benefit rather than a contest for power. In religion, control of the simple Aryan sacrifices to their gods had fallen into the hands of the hereditary class of brāhmans through the development of a complex ritual requiring professional priests. But, aided by non-Aryan influences and the uncertainty instilled by the transition from a tribal to a territorial society, a whole new religious dimension had been opened by theosophical speculations that sought ultimate answers beyond the gods and outside of ritual. The answers offered by the end of this period were diverse and often inconsistent concerning basic problems, such as the origin of the universe and the nature of the Self, but they agreed that an eternal Reality, often called Brahman, pervades all space and time and that the Self, called Ātman, within each individual is identical with it. The problem was how to attain consciousness of the

Self, and the variety of ways proposed contained the seeds of all subsequent Indian religious development. The ultimate goal of release (*moksha*) from the chains of matter became the common objective of orthodox as well as unorthodox sects, such as Buddhism and Jainism.

Too often an emphasis on the conception of release has implied that the basic Indian outlook on life is one of negation and renunciation. This is far from the truth. Even the brāhman is obligated to marry, raise a family, and provide for it to the best of his ability before turning to asceticism. As we shall learn, all Indians from the highest to the lowest are very much interested in the maximum enjoyment of this life. For the mass of the people this life is very real—often too real.

The fundamental ideals and values of Indian civilization, which still direct it today, have been described. Subsequently, we shall examine the fuller development and expression of these ideals and values.

SIGNIFICANT DATES

c.	2500 B.C.	Emergence of the Indus civilization
c.	2350 B.C.	Evidence of trade with Mesopotamia
c.	1500 B.C.	Destruction of major Indus cities
c. 1600–	900 B.C.	Aryan Invasions and era of Vedas
c. 900–	600 B.C.	Era of Brāhamanas and settlement of Gangetic Valley
c. 600–	500 B.C.	Emergence of Indo-Aryan civilization

SELECTED READINGS

*Allchin, Bridget and Raymond, *The Birth of Indian Civilization*. Baltimore: Penguin Books, 1968.

Auboyer, Jeannine, and Goepper, Roger, *The Oriental World*. New York: McGraw-Hill, 1967.

*Basham, A. L., *The Wonder That Was India*. New York: Grove Press, 1954.

*DeBary, Wm. Theodore, et al., *Sources of Indian Tradition*. New York: Columbia University Press, 1958.

Goetz, Hermann, *The Art of India*. 2nd ed.; New York: Crown Pubs., 1964.

*Kosambi, D. D., *Ancient India*. New York: Pantheon Books, 1966.

*Nehru, Jawaharlal, *The Discovery of India*. New York: Doubleday, 1959.

Piggott, Stuart, ed., *Dawn of Civilization*. New York: McGraw-Hill, 1961.

*————, *Prehistoric India*. Baltimore: Penguin Books, 1950.

*Rawlinson, H. G., *India*. New York: Praeger, 1952.

Riencourt, Amaury de, *The Soul of India*. New York: Harper, 1960.

*Smith, Vincent A., *The Oxford History of India*. 3rd ed.; London: Oxford University Press, 1966.

*Thapar Romila, *A History of India*. Vol. I. Baltimore: Penguin Books, 1966.

Wheeler, Sir Mortimer, *Civilizations of the Indus Valley and Beyond*. London: Thames and Hudson, 1966.

————, *Early India and Pakistan to Ashoka*. New York: Praeger, 1959.

*————, *The Indus Civilization*. 3rd rev. ed.; Cambridge: Cambridge University Press, 1968.

Lin, Yutang, ed., *The Wisdom of China and India*. New York: Random House, 1942.

*Zimmer, Heinrich, *Philosophies of India*, ed. by Joseph Campbell. New York: Meridian Books, 1956.

CHAPTER FOUR

THE RISE OF CHINESE CIVILIZATION

Chinese civilization, isolated from its predecessors, arose at a much later date in the flood basin of the lower reaches of the Yellow River (Huang Ho). Except for a much cooler climate, the physical conditions were analogous to those that had cradled the previous civilizations.

The Yellow River rises in Tibet, loops far to the north around the desolate Ordos, and then drops due south, passing through a region of heavy loess deposits that feed it with the fertile silt that gives this river its name. Finally, the river turns eastward through a corridor in the loess plateau and issues into the broad North China Plain, which its silt-laden waters have built. Loess is a fine-grained, extremely rich loam that through hundreds of thousands of years has been deposited by the northwest winds, reaching depths in some places of several hundred feet. Its friable nature subjects it to easy erosion by the tributaries of the Yellow River. Such soil is so easy to work that it encourages the development of farming. The absence of a forest cover even in ancient times was an added inducement to agriculture. On the other hand, the silt continually raises the riverbed, which has been as much as 50 feet above the surrounding plain. As a result, men's efforts to contain the river have only caused it repeatedly to burst its dikes with catastrophic results. For this reason, the Yellow River is popularly labeled "China's Sorrow."

On the seaward side, the North China Plain is divided by the hilly Shantung (Eastern Mountains) Peninsula where sacrifices to heaven invested the area at an early date with religious signifcance. Throughout history the Yellow River has shifted its course numerous times, emptying into the sea sometimes north and sometimes south of this peninsula and spreading its alluvium throughout the plain.

To the north and west, the plain and loess plateau are hemmed in by mountains, deserts, and steppes that support nomadic herdsmen of Turkish and Mongol-speaking groups. This vast area of difficult terrain has shielded China from substantial alien influences and has encouraged Chinese ethnocentrism. Until modern times the warlike nomads of this frontier have presented China with its major defense problem. During periods of greater rainfall Chinese farmers have pushed into this region, depriving the nomads of grazing land, but on these occasions the impact on the nomads has been reduced by an equivalent expansion and enrichment of the grazing area. During periods of lesser rainfall these pioneers have been forced to retreat, while the shrinkage of pasture has encouraged the nomads to mobilize organized invasions of northern China. Here again, much of history is characterized by the classic contest between "the desert and the sown." Today's technology has decisively tipped the scales against the hardy, but less numerous nomads.

To the south, the Yellow River basin is separated from the Yangtze River basin physically and climatically by a line through the Ch'in Ling Mountains and then along the Huai River to the sea. Not until the northern plain was fully occupied did the Chinese press into the heavily forested Yangtze region, conquering or pushing southward the more primitive inhabitants.

The Yangtze too rises in Tibet, jogging to the south before turning north and emerging in the well-watered, mountain-girt plateau of Szechuan. The surrounding mountains protect Szechuan from weather extremes maintaining an equable year-round climate. To-

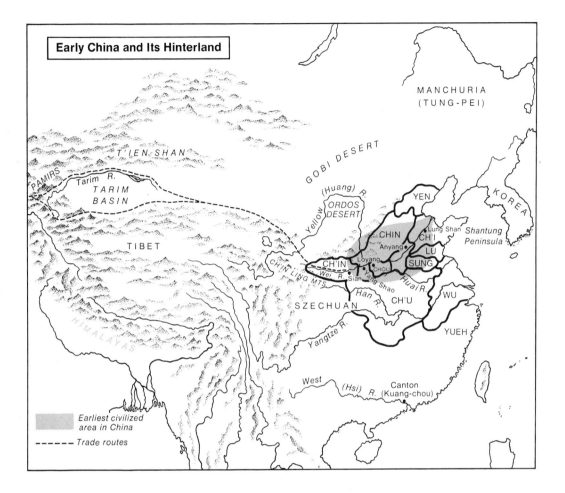

Early China and Its Hinterland

Earliest civilized area in China

— — — Trade routes

day this province with more than 72 million people is China's most populous province. After gathering the drainage of this basin the supplemented waters of the Yangtze, constrained within the one- to two-thousand-feet walls of rocky gorges, tumble, and race to the basin below where this deep river resumes a sedate course for approximately 1000 miles to the sea. Although several lakes serve as flood reservoirs, the combination of melting snow and heavy rains has frequently caused devastating floods. But the main function of the Yangtze, in contrast to the Yellow River, is as a great drainage system and transportation artery, not as a flood river. The surrounding terrain receives adequate rainfall for irrigation which the Yangtze then carries

to the sea. The tremendous load of silt that it picks up from its tributaries is currently extending the delta at a rate of one mile every 70 years. Also it is deep enough to accommodate ocean-going vessels as far inland as Hankow, some 650 miles upstream. For smaller craft it is navigable for an additional 1000 miles into Szechuan.

Below the Yangtze stretches a broad belt of hilly terrain extending from the mountains to the sea. A multitude of relatively isolated valleys encourages the persistence of parochial peculiarities in language and customs. Poor and difficult communications have deterred the full development of this region.

The southern boundary of this region is vaguely indicated by the third major river system composed of the West River (Hsi Kiang) and its tributaries that tap the hill country and have built a fertile delta around the port of Canton. The winterless climate makes possible three crops a year which are still not enough to support China's densest agricultural population, more than 3100 people per square mile of cultivated land.

In this southern region many are minority peoples who have been more or less culturally absorbed. On the infertile and thinly populated plateaus of the Southwest, the Chinese are a minority among Thai, Lolo, and other peoples, many of whom still cling to their own tribal way of life. The present regime by means of "autonomous districts" is seriously attempting to complete the cultural conquest of the south that began 2800 years ago with the expansion into the Yangtze basin.

In the Northeast, the whole of Manchuria was effectively occupied by the Chinese only after 1900. In recognition of the total submersion of the remaining Manchus by 50 million Chinese, the region is now known simply as Tung-pei, "The Northeast." Although the growing season is short, the soil is relatively fertile and, if fully developed, could support twice the present population. In addition, thanks to Japanese development, the Northeast is still the major center of Chinese heavy industry.

In the east, the high Tibetan heartland of Asia was for the first time fully incorporated as a part of China by the Communist regime. Roads and Chinese settlers have been pushed into Tibet under a forced draft program that seeks to sinicize the area in the shortest possible time. Before long there may be more Chinese than Tibetans in Tibet.

Historically, however, Chinese civilization, tied intimately to intensive agriculture, was in fact limited by natural conditions in its expansion. The areas to the west and the north were for the most part unsuited for Chinese agriculture, and while for defensive reasons the government sought in various ways to control these regions and even to sinicize their peoples, it held no other permanent, vested interest in these areas, which were considered fundamentally outside the pale of Chinese culture until recent times. Weather and terrain, then, have been major factors in determining the extent of China proper. Outside China proper, most of its governments, with the notable exception of non-Chinese regimes, were content with acknowledgement of Chinese suzerainty by its "barbarian" neighbors. Parenthetically, it should be observed that anyone who did not fully accept Chinese culture was by definition a "barbarian."

The weather in most of China is dominated by the moisture-bearing monsoon pressing northward in the summer and the cold, dry Siberian air pressing southward in the winter. Normally, when the sun moves north of the equator, the warm front pushes northward passing over southern China in April and May and giving the Yangtze basin its heaviest rainfall during June and July. Finally, with much moisture removed, it arrives in the Yellow River basin in late July and August and in the Northwest often reaches the Gobi Desert before it retreats in September in front of the advancing Siberian cold front. During the retreat, central and southern China receives more rain. Unpredictable typhoons frequently reach China and provide additional rain and high tides with often devastating effects along the coast.

The big problem is that actual performance rarely adheres to this ideal weather pattern. Sometimes the warm front hovers over the Yangtze and reaches the Yellow River basin with almost no moisture left. This situation can result in drought and famine in northern China and in destructive floods in much of central China. On other occasions, the monsoon will advance too rapidly bringing floods to the north and relative drought to the central region. Flood, drought, and consequent famine occur annually in one or another part of China. Only when such an affliction is widespread and repeated does peasant discontent become menacing.

YANG SHAO AND LUNG SHAN CULTURES

Chinese civilization, based on the cultivation of hardy millet, later supplemented by wheat, developed in the loess plateau and fertile plain of northern China where the severity of the winters and erratic water supply presently preclude the growing of rice. The southern boundary of the Ch'in Ling-Huai River line marks the northern limit of rice farming today.

Two indigenous neolithic cultures of uncertain dates have been identified in the Yellow River valley: the Yang Shao in the west with painted pottery and the Lung Shan in the east with finer, burnished black pottery, frequently turned on a fast potter's wheel. Most distinctive, however, are the angular shapes of the finest Lung Shan ware that offers a preview of later bronze vessels. Where the products of the two cultures are found together, the Lung Shan lasts longer and, therefore, presumably represents a later, more advanced culture that moved westward from the vicinity of the Shantung Peninsula and continued into the bronze age. If this hypothesis is correct, it rules out the possibility of early Chinese development being significantly stimulated by influences from the older civilizations to the west.

Several sites of both cultures are large, covering areas up to 250 acres. Therefore, although the closely concentrated buildings are relatively primitive in construction, the size of the settlements indicates a comparatively advanced degree of social and political organization. Besides farming, both cultures bred dogs, pigs, goats, sheep, and cattle. Notably absent was the horse, introduced later through contact with the nomads. Both cultures supplemented their larders by hunting. Perhaps the clearest evidence of continuity between the Lung Shan culture and the succeeding Shang dynasty is the discovery of oracle bones. Although, they bear no inscriptions, suggesting that writing had not yet been devised, the technique of heating the bones until cracks appeared, which could then be interpreted, is identical with the Shang procedure.

The unique and distinctive characteristics of these two cultures, which broke the ground for Chinese civilization, and the evidence of cultural continuity make it possible to assert that civilization in China was developed independently by indigenous peoples and was not a result of any migration from the west. Of course, ideas and products may have been, and probably were, received from the outside but, where fashioned by human hands, they were given an entirely Chinese character. Imports possibly included the idea of pottery, bronze, the wheel, grain seeds, and domesticated animals, but no one can be certain that they were not independently discovered and developed.

Chinese tradition, compiled at a comparatively late date, ascribes the foundation of a unified Chinese state to the year 2852 B.C. Although these accounts vary substantially in detail, they generally agree that the creator, P'an-ku, was followed by three sequences of brothers who are designated, respectively, as the twelve Heavenly Rulers, the eleven Earthly Rulers, and the nine Human Rulers. These three groups represent symbolically the basic elements of Chinese cosmology—heaven, earth, and man—and should not be taken literally. Notice also the Chinese penchant for numerology. Following them came five rulers who are personified culture-heroes credited with the invention of various aspects of Chinese civilization, such as fire, agriculture, the calendar, and the Chinese characters in place of an older means of keeping records by knotted ropes. The last two rulers broke the practice of succession in the family by choosing the most able and experienced ministers to succeed them.

Little credence can be given to this imaginative explanation of the origin of

Chinese civilization which was created by later scholars. Indeed, the succession story smacks strongly of special pleading on the part of scholar-ministers who sought certification for the importance of their roles. On the other hand, the literal acceptance of this account and the norms of conduct it prescribed exercised a significant influence on later governmental behavior. Scholars and officials drew on these tales to buttress their criticisms of the conduct of government.

The next ruler returned to succession within his family and thus established the Hsia dynasty, traditionally dated 2205 to 1766 B.C., but one account dates it 1994 to 1523 B.C., which agrees closely with currently accepted chronology. Although there is no archeological evidence in support of this dynasty's existence, the durations attributed to individual reigns are reasonable compared to the incredible number of years ascribed to the preceding rulers. Someday archeology may connect this dynasty with one of the neolithic cultures, possibly the Yang Shao. The last ruler of this dynasty is described as a thoroughly vicious and profligate despot— a standardized historical convention applied by Chinese historians to the last ruler of every dynasty. Naturally, scholar-officials would not blame their own class for maladministration.

THE SHANG DYNASTY (C. 1766 – 1122 or 1523 – 1072 B.C.)

The new ruler established the Shang dynasty which, like its predecessor, practices succession from brother to brother as well as father to son. This mode of succession suggests a society in which maturity and military ability were at a premium, a state in which the ruler's authority depended on the respect he could command.

For the latter half of the Shang dynasty archeology has furnished confirmation of traditional Chinese history by excavations of the capital at Anyang in northern Honan Province. Suddenly, chronologically speaking, we are confronted with a literate civilization with an exceptionally advanced bronze metallurgy. No other site that illustrates a transitional state of development has yet been clearly established.

Perhaps the most valuable discovery was more than 10,000 oracle bones inscribed with Chinese characters that confirmed the names of most of the rulers in the traditional Shang king-list. In this first example of the ancestral cult the rulers called on the spirits of their predecessors for advice and guidance. Most of the bones are shoulder blades of oxen and tortoise undershells. Insofar as the questions and answers on them can be deciphered, they present a picture of the beliefs, practices, and problems of the times.

A large proportion of the questions concerned agriculture. Would it rain soon or would a sacrifice induce rain? Would the crops prosper this year? Another large group of questions concerned whether or not to undertake a particular military campaign. Apparently, in addition to assuring good crops, the ruler was regularly occupied by warfare in which the loyal support of subordinate lords was by no means certain. Frequent queries concerned the timing of hunts and other royal activities. Most often the appeals were made to the king's ancestors, indicating the belief that, at least, royal ancestors were believed to be able to bring about desirable or undesirable results in the world of their descendants. Whether ancestor worship at this time extended beyond the royal family cannot be ascertained. In addition to ancestral spirits, other forces or gods received sacrifices. Most important was Shang Ti (supreme ancestor or spirit) who may have been conceived abstractly as the force of nature or more concretely as the supreme god.

The Chinese writing system, first illustrated on the oracle bones, is of great significance. More than any other single element it has influenced and shaped Chinese civilization as well as those neighboring civilizations that developed under Chinese influence. No other civilization outside eastern Asia has been so deeply affected by its method of writing.

The method of writing that appears on the oracle bones is clearly the forerunner of the one which still prevails in China, Korea, and Japan. In addition, all the fundamental principles of Chinese writing had already evolved. This suggests, but by no means proves, that Chinese writing had gone through a long period of evolution before these first known examples. It could just as logically have developed rapidly after the initial breakthrough, and the absence of prior evidence of writing supports the likelihood of this hypothesis. Approximately 5000 different characters have been identified of which more than 1500 are clearly related to their counterparts today. This vocabulary compares with the 50,000 characters of a recent dictionary. The direct relationship of today's written language with that of the Shang period has fostered the Chinese sense of cultural identity with their ancestors and has reinforced a feeling of historical continuity and reverence for the past.

For the most part, the Chinese characters are ideographs compounded from what were originally pictographs. For example, the character meaning "bright" is a compound of the two pictographs for "sun" and "moon." In other instances, the first part of a character signifies the general category of meaning and the second part indicates the syllabic sound. Generally, the ideographs represent uninflected monosyllables indicating a specific meaning.

The Chinese language has often been described as wholly monosyllabic. This is not strictly correct. Each character is a single syllable, but to create new words two or more characters are frequently used. Since the number of syllables available is limited, the formation of such multisyllabic words has been even more necessary for clarity in the spoken language. A single syllable may have hundreds of different meanings. In the writ-

ten form the particular character clearly indicates the meaning intended, but in the spoken form an added syllable helps to single out the meaning desired. The problem of an essentially uninflected, monosyllabic language has led to a substantial differentiation between its written and spoken forms. Because the basic meaning of each character is clear, the classic written account is almost unintelligible to the listener. This difference has helped to invest the written language and its mastery with a certain mystique and prestige that has been attached to no other written language. A premium was placed on literacy because of the status it conferred.

Furthermore, the writing of the characters with a brush, which was already used in the Shang period, has made it a highly regarded form of artistic expression. Illiterate peasants decorate their homes with reproductions of prized examples of calligraphy. These works have the double appeal of the mystique of writing and high art.

The handicaps of the Chinese system of writing are manifest. The achievement of literacy, which is so essential to a modern industrialized society, is a monumental chore. Thousands of characters must be memorized, and writing requires the mastery of considerable skill with the brush. Moreover, though well-adapted to artistic and literary expression, the Chinese language does not easily lend itself to the precision and clarity demanded by modern science and technology. Finally, despite the fact that the Chinese invented printing, it involves an immensely more complex process than in the West. No simple typewriter can be devised to reproduce Chinese characters. In an effort to overcome these handicaps, China has tried to adapt the Roman alphabet to speed up the spread of literacy, but the cultural revolution represented by such an experiment militates against its acceptance even more than similar linguistic experiments; Chinese characters are the bearers of too much cultural baggage for ready rejection. Much more acceptable is the simplification of the most commonly used characters, a reform that has many precedents in China's past.

The Chinese writing system, however, possesses distinct advantages, more important in the past, but still important today. The very difficulty of mastering the written language gave a special status to the educated elite which came to be synonymous with the ruling class. Thus, in the popular mind, literacy enveloped Chinese rulers in an aura of legitimacy in place of the religious sanction that supported political authority in other civilizations. In addition, the strong value attached to literacy promoted both education and scholarship, even if the emphasis on the past tended in the long run to stifle creativity. As a result, the higher literacy rates in eastern Asia than in the rest of the East are perhaps no mere coincidence. Moreover, every literate Chinese is, in a sense, an artist. The writing system has stimulated the artistic and esthetic qualities latent in the Chinese, and in all those who utilized their writing system, to produce works of art in all media. Indeed, it may be asserted that the outlook and attitude toward art of both literate and illiterate East Asians has been deeply influenced by this writing system.

Undoubtedly, however, the most important contribution of the Chinese method of writing has been its promotion of cultural cohesion through its unique ability to overcome differences in dialect and even language. Even though two persons may speak mutually unintelligible dialects, they can communicate freely and easily in the written language. The Chinese character indicates meaning; any syllable or syllables may be associated with it. If the West had such a system of writing, the written form of "no," for example, would be identical whether it was pronounced "non," "nein," "nyet," and so forth. In other words, in writing there would be no language barriers nor the cultural barriers that they promote. Not only has the Chinese writing system facilitated cultural diffusion and unity, helping to create the largest aggregation of people on earth, but also it has promoted a sense of community with those states that borrowed and adapted it to their languages: Korea, Vietnam, and Japan. The Chinese language carried with it a large cultural cargo that affected the cultural development of these countries to a greater or lesser degree. Indeed, until a century ago a large proportion of the literary works produced in these countries was composed in the Chinese language. And even today, well-educated Koreans or Japanese can read the title of a Chinese work without difficulty and with somewhat less facility glean the essence of the text. In this sense, eastern Asia is identifiable as a distinct cultural unit in the world, with parochial variations. The common denominator has been, and still is to a large degree, the Chinese writing system, not a common religion as is the case in other areas.

To return to the Shang oracle bones, the picture of royal life given by these records is one of vast activity in which every action required ritual endorsement. Under these circumstances the royal diviners must have wielded great influence. The concern with appeasing the unseen forces of the spirit world is further illustrated by the practice of human as well as animal sacrifices in connection with the construction of major buildings and what are presumed to be royal burials.

At Anyang large buildings up to 90 feet in length were constructed around a rectangular court. At the gates and at intervals around the buildings human victims, presumably war captives, were buried, some holding halberds and others sacrificial bronze vessels. Elsewhere, dogs were buried in the foundations. In the courtyard five chariots and their drivers have been excavated. The latter as well as the burial of horses in the royal tombs show that the Shang had learned to use light chariots with spoked wheels drawn by horses. The huge tombs outside the city were dug out in the shape of a cross. The deep central pit containing the "royal" wooden coffin placed over a sacrificed dog was approached by downward sloping ramps 45 to 60 feet in length. Bordering the ramps and the central pit were slaughtered horses and humans who were to serve their deceased master in the spirit world. Some of the human victims had been decapitated which helps to explain the representations on bronze vessels of headless humans under a large axe.

While practices of this kind may suggest a barbarous, scarcely civilized society impregnated with the basest superstitions, the unparalleled skill and artistry of its bronzesmiths counteracts this impression. The advanced stage of metallurgy, for which no preceding period of development has been found, is illustrated in the varying proportions of copper, tin, and lead used in the alloy. The large amount of lead was essential for the free flow of the molten metal needed to produce successfully the complex and intricate designs and decorations. The unique ornamentation of the Shang bronzes reflects a highly developed tradition of carving in wood and other soft materials for which Chinese artisans are still renowned. The translation of this style to the completely unrelated technique of metal casting is a magnificent achievement unequalled elsewhere at any time. Obviously these masterpieces could have been produced only by full-time specialists who felt free to experiment with their materials. Furthermore, while the religious purpose of these vessels prescribed standardized shapes and ornamentations, the genius and artistry of the individual bronzesmith is readily apparent in the adaptation of the conventional motifs to gain the maximum esthetic effect within the limitations of his material. From this point of view, the best examples of Shang bronzes are works of art of the highest order.

Drawing on the combined resources supplied by archeology and tradition, Shang civilization may be portrayed as a settled agricultural society which retained a strong patriarchal organization based on the family and the clan. As today, the family name came first, followed by the personal name. The society was further divided by a great gulf between commoners and aristocrats. The contrast between the two is brought out by the continued use of pit dwellings for commoners as compared with the large buildings that housed their lords. The aristocrats maintained their authority and prestige not only by their military function and a monopoly of expensive weapons but also by the magical cult of their ancestors. The strength of the belief in the spiritual powers of the lords was also reinforced by the human sacrifices that continued to be practiced occasionally in the succeeding dynasty.

The direct authority of the ruler probably did not extend any great distance from his capital. Many other kings are mentioned against whom the Shang ruler had to conduct frequent military campaigns to maintain his supremacy. At best, he was the "first among equals," exacting homage and some tribute from the other lords throughout the North China Plain. He also organized joint expeditions against sheepherding nomads who were constantly intruding into Chinese territory.

The climate was considerably warmer and wetter in Shang times as indicated by the references to elephants and bamboo. Although flood control and drainage probably required the organization and planning of substantial public works, rainfall was normally sufficient to bring the crops to maturity. There is no positive evidence of irrigation until much later. Needless to say, labor had to be conscripted in large numbers for works such as pounded-earth walls, royal buildings, and royal tombs. But Anyang was a populous city, measuring roughly one-half by one-quarter miles, easily capable of providing the troops and labor battalions needed.

THE CHOU DYNASTY (C. 1122 or 1027 – 256 B.C.)

Typically, tradition describes the last Shang ruler as a wholly evil and immoral tyrant reluctantly overthrown by the King of Chou, a frontier agricultural state in the loess basin of the Wei River which joins the Yellow River at its eastward bend. This highly strategic region has more than once been the base of operations for the unification of China under a new leader, the latest example being the Communist conquest from its Shensi headquarters. Protected by mountains from easy incorporation into the Chinese domain, the region could cultivate a parochial sense of independence which was subject to the limited influence of Chinese culture. Yet the Yellow River encouraged contact and exchange with the North China Plain, besides providing a natural thoroughfare for attack. The fertile loess soil of the Wei River basin and the small neighboring valleys invited intensive agricultural development which supported a large enough population to supply the manpower requirements of military operations. Furthermore, direct contact with nomadic peoples to the north and west stimulated a martial spirit and provided a source of military experience and alien ideas that were often invigorating. Finally, this region was the eastern terminus of the natural trade routes with the west. This trade not only supplemented the economy but also nourished a more receptive and flexible outlook. With all of these advantages, the prominent part in Chinese history played repeatedly by this region, defending the most dangerous frontier, is understandable.

The Chou state was peripherally subject to Shang culture, and the Chou ruler nominally accepted Shang supremacy. Therefore, the Chou conquest (1122 or 1027 B.C.) did not cause any sharp break in the evolution of Chinese civilization. The capital was maintained at the center of the source of Chou strength in the Wei River valley near modern Sian. The decentralized system of political organization was continued with some modifications. Several states in the plain were given to relatives or loyal retainers, but in many other cases the former rulers, after pledging allegiance, were confirmed as rulers of their territories. Even the ruling families that were displaced from their former possessions were usually granted

lesser estates to support the continuance of their ancestral cults. The customary political and economic unit, as in the past, was the walled city with the neighboring villages and towns dependent on it. The primitive state of communications militated against a greater centralization of power. Therefore, as in the Shang dynasty, the authority of the Chou rulers ultimately rested on military strength, supplemented by the belief in their religious functions as essential to the general welfare.

According to Chinese tradition the Chou rulers took the title of "Son of Heaven" and justified their assumption of power on the doctrine that the mantle of the "Mandate of Heaven" had been transferred to them. Simply stated, this mandate was conferred on the ruler by Heaven operating through the people—"Heaven sees as the people see; Heaven hears as the people hear"—and was withdrawn by Heaven similarly operating through the people after a series of bad omens and natural catastrophes demonstrated the ruler's loss of favor with Heaven. This doctrine, which later became the standard political theory for justifying successful rebellion and the establishment of a new dynasty, may have been attributed by scholars to the Chou conquest to gain the respectability conferred by antiquity; but it nevertheless reflects the belief in divine intervention and authorization for the exercise of political power. The title, "Son of Heaven," illustrates the essential function of the divinely appointed ruler as the intermediary between men and the controlling forces of nature. The chief deity to which the ruler had to make regularly prescribed sacrifices was Heaven (*T'ien*) which, however, was probably still conceived in human form as its Chinese character indicates. Sacrifices to other deities, such as Earth and the royal ancestors, continued to be the specific responsibilities of the ruler in his capacity as chief priest. Today two of the most impressive structures in Peking are the square altar to Earth and the round altar to Heaven built during the Ming dynasty.

Further evidence of continuity was the continued use and development of the Chinese system of writing and the continued practice of divination with oracle bones. In addition, magnificent bronze vessels continued to be cast of the same style and technology. Gradually, however, the technique deteriorated and the style became plainer. No good reason can be assigned for the regression in technique, although a lesser sacrificial emphasis on the ornamental representations has been suggested as a factor. Certainly there is no sign of economic decay. On the contrary, the expansion of the frontier suggests an increase in population and prosperity.

Little can be said with certainty about events during the Western Chou dynasty, the period that lasted until the removal of the capital eastward to Loyang in 769 B.C. The first reliable date is 841 B.C., and after this date the accuracy of traditional chronology is attested by the correlation of eclipses with the dates given for them.

Generally speaking, political development was characterized by the gradual decline of the ruler's authority, while expansion and consolidation absorbed the activities of the more successful lords. Some lords expanded by subordinating neighboring lords, but the most successful ones were those in a position to conquer and incorporate the territories of people not yet deemed to be within the pale of Chinese civilization. The gentlemanly rules of warfare that evolved under the influence of reverence for the ancestral cults frowned on the liquidation or disinheritance of Chinese lords. Such unchivalric conduct, it was believed, would bring untold woe to the offending lord and his people. No such limitations were placed on actions against those considered to be "barbarians." Under these conditions frontier states enjoyed a growth potential not shared by interior states. As an example, the state of Ch'i grew at the expense of hitherto unconquered tribes in the Shantung Peninsula.

Within the area of Chinese civilization the relative power of the various lords was distinguished by the development of a hierarchy of ranks usually translated in accord with Western feudal titles as duke, marquis, count, and baron; but in the course of shifts in power these titles came no longer to accord with the real power of their possessors.

Originally all lords apparently had to travel to the Chou court to be invested with their authority by the ruler. This practice implied royal ownership of all land with the right to dispose of it as the ruler saw fit. The ceremony also involved a pledge of loyalty that strengthened the real authority of the ruler. By the eighth century the general neglect of the investiture ceremony and the lack of court attendance for any reason underlined the decline in royal authority and prestige.

Meanwhile expansion was encouraged by the natural increase of the lord's family as well as by that of his subjects'. Both required the development or acquisition of additional resources to provide for their livelihood. Moreover, expansion and closer control to wring the maximum income out of the land required the development of a more complex system of administration and taxation. This demanded the services of a bureaucracy that was composed of literate officials. Perhaps this picture is being prematurely a bit overdrawn. Certainly its extent and degree of refinement varied widely according to the size and nature of the lord's domain. This development would be more advanced in states such as Ch'i which had grown at the expense of "barbarians." But these very circumstances of frontier states help to explain the prominent role that they were later to play. In contrast with the lords of interior states, these lords were freer to experiment and less bound by traditional and hereditary claims. In other words, by the eighth century, distinctive differences in governmental practices and the power of the lord had begun to differentiate the administrations of interior and frontier states.

Keeping in mind the substantial degree of differentiation that had evolved, a general picture of conditions and relationships within a state can be sketched. Under a hereditary lord with absolute power, who performed the sacrifices necessary for the welfare of his state, was a hereditary class of aristocratic warriors who doubled as administrators and tax collectors. These specialists were socially separated by a wide gulf from the peasants who supported them by their manual labor. Although the social separation may not have been so extreme during this early period, its essence is well illustrated by the later adage: "The ritual does not extend down to the common people; punishments do not extend up to the great officers" (from *Book of Rites*). Without rights, the peasants were conscripted for public works or war at the lord's will. Without ancestral cults of their own, both the spiritual and worldly welfare of the peasants depended on the lord's beneficence. Again, however, the picture should not be overdrawn. The welfare of the lord reciprocally depended on the loyal and devoted service of his subjects. Unreasonable tyranny, contrary to custom, was not in his interest. The injunctions to virtuous conduct applied equally to the ruler and the lord. He, too, could lose the "Mandate of Heaven." As the lords usurped in practice the prerogatives of the ruler and engaged in contests for power with other lords, this became even more the case.

One of the last rulers of the Western Chou period, Hsüan (827–782 B.C.), attempted vigorously to reassert royal authority. His reign is a record of continual campaigning in all directions, but the challenge was too great and the effort too strenuous for the resources at his command. In 822 B.C. nomads from the north seized and sacked the royal capital. Although the king assembled his forces and routed the nomads in the same year, their appetite for plunder had been whetted. In other campaigns he expanded Chou authority temporarily to the south into the Yangtze and Huai River valleys. The next ruler could not maintain these achievements and was killed in 771 B.C. in defense of his capital against another nomadic invasion in

alliance with Chinese rebels. In 769 B.C. his successor took the fatal step of divorcing the dynasty from its ancestral land and people by moving the capital eastward to the less exposed site of Loyang in the North China Plain.

The Eastern Chou period (769–256 B.C.) was a time when the ruler was reduced to the status of a ceremonial figurehead while the major frontier states gradually usurped all the attributes of sovereignty, including even the title of king. As time passed, the political picture took on all the characteristics of international relations among a number of independent states, both large and small. The only semblance of unity was provided by the heritage of a common culture, but in the expanding frontier states, especially in the south, Chinese culture at best was no more than a thin veneer over a more barbarous base.

The political history of the Eastern Chou period presents a thoroughly confusing picture of the rise, fall, and dismemberment or extinction of one leading state after another in the contest for power. A kaleidoscope of shifting alliances and treaties punctuated the alterations and upheavals of this era of disorder and disunity. Some sense of the overall development that led to the establishment of the first empire can be conveyed, first, by dividing the period into the two parts devised by Chinese historians, the "Spring and Autumn" period from the eighth to the fifth centuries and the "Warring States" period from the fifth century to the establishment of the empire (221 B.C.) and, second, by arbitrarily singling out for notice the most significant developments as illustrations of the overall trends.

The Spring and Autumn era, named after a classic historical work covering the years 722 to 481 B.C., is characterized by the setting up of leagues of Chinese states under successive hegemons to fill the vacuum left by the demise of the Chou ruler's power. In addition, the conduct of war tended to be restrained by a code of aristocratic honor that was inspired by reverence for the maintenance of ancestral cults. Peasants might be slaughtered, but aristocratic warriors were concerned about their mutual survival. Gradually the observance of the code broke down merging into the ruthless fights to the finish that characterized the intensified struggle for survival of the Warring States era.

The first league was formed in 681 B.C. under the command of the Prince of Ch'i. This state, under a series of able lords, had taken advantage of the collapse of Chou power to expand vastly its already large domain. Within a few years most of the plain's states had accepted Ch'i's leadership to check the militant expansionism of the southwestern state of Ch'u. The success of this first league depended on the exceptional talents of its hegemon. On his death in 643 B.C. internal quarrels prevented a united front, and Ch'u happily engaged in reducing one member state after another.

The desperate members of the league in 634 B.C. found a new hegemon in the prince of Chin, a large upland state on the northwest border of the plain. Although Ch'u was temporarily repulsed, it gradually built up its own league. In addition, by the mid-sixth century B.C., a new major state had entered the lists, the state of Ch'in, which had taken over the old Chou base in the Wei River valley. Beset by both Ch'in and Ch'u, Chin accepted the proposal that the contending leagues of Chin and Ch'u join in a treaty whose basic provision would be a mutual renunciation of war as an instrument of policy. This valiant experiment with such a modern ring to it was consummated in 546 B.C., but it did not last long. As soon as the further decay of Chin power became apparent, Ch'u repudiated the agreement. Later, two of the least civilized states in the southeast asserted successive, short-lived hegemonies. That such "barbarous" powers should be accepted as the "guardians" of Chinese civilization against barbarian domination carried the league concept to the ultimate point of absurdity. Actually the position of hegemon had for some time become merely a pious fraud to legalize and mask the exercise of military domination based on military strength. But even a deception establishes moral restraints on the exerciser of power. Now, in the mid-fifth century, the deception was dropped, and an open struggle for supremacy ensued, marked by increasingly callous ruthlessness and cruelty. Almost all moral restraints were lost in the growing tempo of bitter struggle of the Warring States era.

Legitimacy no longer commanded the respect that had formerly protected the weaker lords. Not only were states gobbled up but their ruling families were extinguished. Following the example of Ch'u, the leading contestants had by the mid-fourth century taken the title of king, thereby announcing their rejection of the last vestiges of respect for the legitimacy of the Chou rulers.

There is no need to follow the complex details of the ups and downs of the various states. By the end of the fourth century the two principal rivals were obviously the great states of Ch'in and Ch'u. Two significant innovations had altered the nature of warfare, and in both cases Ch'in, because of its location, had been the initial beneficiary. One innovation was the introduction of iron that not only revolutionized warfare but also farming with the iron-tipped plow. In the fifth century the sword supplemented the spear and halberd as a weapon for close combat. The second innovation was cavalry, learned undoubtedly from the nomads who with this technique put renewed pressure on the chariot-equipped forces of the northwestern frontier states, such as Ch'in. Evidence of nomadic pressure as well as enlarged resources was the construction of substantial walls along the borders to check raids by small mounted bands and to delay and give warning of major nomadic incursions.

In spite of the political disunity and disorder of the Eastern Chou period and the increasing amount of resources channeled into wasteful and destructive warfare, Chinese civilization was growing and maturing at a continuously accelerating pace. Social, economic, and even political development took place not only within the heartland, but also in the new additions which more than doubled the area of Chinese civilization. In addition to territorial expansion, China also grew greatly in population thanks to advances in both technology and communications. A frequent paradox of history is the appearance of rapid growth and development amid increasingly bitter political strife.

Success in war demands superior political organization, maximum economic development and utilization of resources, and whatever social changes and cultural development will best implement these objectives. Territorial expansion by the successful contestants caused the streamlining of administration and the improvement of communications. On the other hand, the marshaling of talent and the premium placed on productiveness stimulated social and cultural change and development. Heredity carries no assurance of talent and, therefore for efficiency hereditary officials had either to be replaced or assisted by educated officials of proven ability. Thus there developed the prospect of a career open to talent, and the barrier of class became less absolute. Also the need for education promoted the profession of teaching of which the outstanding example is the career of Confucius.

In the area of social change the state of Ch'in is credited with the most radical innovations under the inspiration of authoritarian Legalist political doctrines. Actually most of the reforms appear to have been initiated pragmatically before Legalism had evolved into a recognized school of political thought. To centralize all authority in the person of the ruler, hereditary nobles and officials were replaced by an appointed bureaucracy. The former practice of communal farming was supplanted by the assignment of fields to individual families who could be held separately responsible and could be rewarded or punished according to their pro-

ductive contribution to the resources of the state.

Moreover, Ch'in took the lead in the fuller development of irrigation and water control works to produce the food needed for a growing population. In addition, canals were built to facilitate the delivery of the grain tax. At all times the size of armies and the duration of campaigns have depended on the surplus food resources at the command of the state. Certainly the increased yields achieved by these public works gave the state of Ch'in a military advantage and promoted the scale and intensity of warfare by making possible larger armies and longer campaigns.

Canals and other communications' improvements, as well as the overall growth in population and production, stimulated as a by-product the growth of trade and the accumulation of wealth through commerce. Increasing aristocratic complaints testify to the development of a wealthy merchant class in the latter centuries of the Chou era that added a new dimension and function to the social classification. Highest prestige was accorded to the literate elite who excelled as military commanders, scholars, and administrators; second in social status came the peasant farmers as the backbone of the state; third in rank were the artisans who also made a productive contribution to society; the bottom rung of the social ladder was occupied by the merchants who were viewed as living parasitically off the fruits of other men's labor.

In spite of the contempt in which the merchant class was held, its importance as a source of wealth was recognized early by the state. As early as the seventh century B.C. the government of Ch'i established standard weights and measures and sought to control prices and trade. It is even credited with the initiation of governmental monopolies of vital products, such as salt and iron. Chinese state monopolies limited trade in a specified product to licensed and regulated operators. Since knowledge of iron at such an early date is unlikely, doubt is cast as well on the attribution to Ch'i of all these reforms. Whether Ch'i initiated them or not, similar policies of state control and regulation of economic activities were introduced later to a greater or lesser degree in all the contending states. In fact, Ch'in instituted full state control and direction of commerce.

By the time of Confucius, and much more by the time of unification by the ruler of Ch'in, Chinese civilization had come a long way in the course of the Chou era. Territorially, it had reached northeast into southern Manchuria, filled in all the arable areas bordering its Yellow River cradle, incorporated the whole Yangtze River region from Szechuan to the sea, and had even pushed into the hill-girt valleys of the southeast coast. Economically, the contest for power had stimulated the Warring States to carry out vast public works which made possible the support of a much larger population and the production of much greater wealth. By the later third century B.C. the area encompassed by Chinese civilization probably already contained the largest concentration of population in the world—as it still does today. Politically, the same contest for power had promoted the development of a much more sophisticated type of government in which the ruler depended on the services of

an educated officialdom dedicated to the solution of day-to-day problems. The need for able military officers and civil officials brought into existence a degree of social mobility. Although the gap between the ruling and common classes remained wide, it could be bridged by the exceptional individual. Naturally the successful aspirant, as in all societies, adopted the role and outlook of the ruling elite he had joined. Although sacrificial rites, divination, and ancestral worship were maintained, the pressing problems of interstate strife tended to concentrate the attention of the best minds on solving pragmatically the problems of the governments they served. A most important value, which has persisted throughout Chinese history, established government service as the most highly regarded career. No other career commanded anywhere near the same respect and prestige. As a result, social and political organization monopolized the blossoming of intellectual activity during the latter centuries of the Chou period. This was the era when the hundred flowers bloomed; when the hundred schools of thought contended. To this most creative period of the Chinese mind we shall return after examining the comparable developments in the Middle East and India.

SIGNIFICANT DATES

2852 B.C.	Traditional founding of Chinese state
c. 1994–1523 B.C.	Hsia dynasty (?)
c. 1523–1027 B.C.	Shang dynasty
c. 1027– 256 B.C.	Chou dynasty
c. 1027– 769 B.C.	Western Chou dynasty
841 B.C.	First reliable date
769– 256 B.C.	Eastern Chou era
722– 481 B.C.	"Spring and Autumn Annals" era
403– 221 B.C.	"Warring States" period
256– 221 B.C.	Consolidation of Ch'in authority
221– 207 B.C.	First Chinese empire—Ch'in dynasty

SELECTED READINGS

Auboyer, Jeannine, and Goepper, Roger, *The Oriental World.* New York: McGraw-Hill, 1967.

*Birch, Cyril, ed., *Anthology of Chinese Literature.* New York: Grove Press, 1967.

*Creel, H. G., *The Birth of China.* New York: Frederick Ungar, 1954.

———, *The Origins of Statecraft in China.* Chicago: University of Chicago Press, 1970.

Cressey, George B., *Land of the 500 Million.* New York: McGraw-Hill, 1955.

*DeBary, Theodore, et al., *Sources of Chinese Tradition.* New York: Columbia University Press, 1960.

*Fitzgerald, C. P., *China: A Short Cultural History.* 3rd ed.; New York: Praeger, 1954.

Gernet, Jacques, *Ancient China.* Berkeley: University of California Press, 1968.

*Goodrich, L. Carrington, *A Short History of the Chinese People.* 3rd ed.; New York: Harper and Row, 1963.

*Hsu, Cho-yun, *Ancient China in Transition: An Analysis of Social Mobility, 722–222 B.C.* Stanford: Stanford University Press, 1965.

Karlgren, Bernhard, *The Chinese Language.* New York: Ronald Press, 1949.

Latourette, Kenneth Scott, *The Chinese: Their History and Culture.* 4th rev. ed.; New York: Macmillan, 1962.

*Levenson, Joseph R., and Schurmann, Franz, *China: An Interpretive History from the Beginnings to the Fall of Han.* Berkeley: University of California Press, 1969.

*Li, Chi, *The Beginnings of Chinese Civilization.* Seattle: University of Washington Press, 1968.

Lin, Yutang, ed., *The Wisdom of China and India.* New York: Random House, 1952.

*McNeill, William, and Sellar, Jean W., eds., *Classical China.* London: Oxford University Press, 1970.

Needham, Joseph, *Science and Civilization in China.* 7 vols.; Cambridge: Cambridge University Press, 1954 —.

Reischauer, Edwin O., and Fairbank, John K., *East Asia: The Great Tradition.* Boston: Houghton Mifflin, 1960.

*Swann, Peter C., *The Art of China, Korea, and Japan.* New York: Praeger, 1963.

*Waley, Arthur, trans., *The Book of Songs.* New York: Grove Press, 1960.

Watson, Burton, *Early Chinese Literature.* New York: Columbia University Press, 1963.

Watson, William, *China: Before the Han Dynasty.* New York: Praeger, 1961.

*———, *Early Civilization in China.* New York: McGraw-Hill, 1966.

PART TWO

ELABORATION, EXPANSION AND DIFFUSION

Ishtar Gate, Neo-Babylonian. *(Staatliche Museen zu Berlin)*

Ruins of Persepolis, a major capitol of the Persian Empire. (*Paolo Koch/Rapho Guillumette*)

Bodhisattva, fresco from the Ajanta Caves, 6th to
7th century. (*Archaeological Survey of India*)

Descent of the Ganges, monumental Indian relief, 7th century.(*New York
Public Library*)

The god Shiva in dance of destruction, a 14th century bronze. (*Collection of William Rockhill Nelson Gallery of Art, Kansas City, Missouri*)

Lion capital from the Ashoka column; symbol of the Republic of India. (*Raghuber Singh/Nancy Palmer Agency*)

Great Buddhist Stupa at Sanchi, India. (*Archaeological Survey of India*)

Borobudour, Java, a monumental Buddhist temple carved from rock, late 8th century. (*Van Bucher/Photo Researchers*)

Angkor Wat, Cambodia, early 12th century. (*Georg Gerster/Rapho Guillumette*)

Part of Great Wall of China. *(René Burri/Magnum)*

Colossal Buddha, Yunkang, China, late 5th century.

T'ang dynasty horse. (*Cleveland Museum of Art, anonymous gift*)

Translucent Sung celadon with delicate lavender glaze and bell like tone—a masterpiece of porcelain. (*The Metropolitan Museum of Art, gift of Mrs. Samuel T. Peters, 1926*)

Six Persimmons by Mu-ch'i, 13th century, Southern Sung. (*Daitoku-ji, Kyoto*)

Buddhist guardian deity in Todaiji, Nara, 8th century. (*M. Sakamoto*)

Great bronze Buddha of Kamakura, 1253.
(*M. Sakamoto*)

Haboku Landscape by Sesshu (1420–1506). (*The Cleveland Museum of Art, Norweb Collection*)

Garden of Daisen-in, Daitoku-ji, Kyōto.
(*M. Sakamoto*)

In Part One of this book the emergence of the respective civilizations of the Middle East, India, and China has been examined and carried to roughly equivalent stages, insofar as a general comparison is possible for such distinctively different courses of development. Although all four of these earliest civilizations arose in similar environments and faced similar problems, each one found unique, though comparable, answers and in the process evolved its own set of ideals and values, illustrating the fallacy of any single solution for human organization and cooperation in a civilized society. Moreover, it has been shown that these ideals and values, once imbedded in a civilization, have proved extremely resistant to change. As the vital cement of a society, they may only be adapted and modified to meet new circumstances; they can be rejected only at the risk of total societal collapse.

The crossroads area known as the Middle East was unique in spawning two almost contemporaneous civilizations. Both of them, though distinctively different, relied heavily on divine sanction in the form of unpredictable gods in the case of Mesopotamia or of a living god in the case of Egypt. The dominant role of religion and religious sanction continues to characterize this region. India was exceptional in witnessing the rise and extinction of an advanced civilization in the Indus River valley. The demise of this civilization was separated by a dark age of more than half a millennium before the emergence of Indo-Aryan civilization in the Ganges River valley, which incorporated important elements from the long-defunct Indus civilization. This experience suggests that a civilization, no matter how advanced, can be destroyed, and yet its ideals and values can survive long centuries of barbarism and can reassert themselves. As in the Middle East, religion was at the core of civilization in India but was not as pervasive in its authority. Political authority, while buttressed by religious authority, maintained its identity separate from the religious establishment. Chinese civilization offers the one example of unbroken continuity since its inception. It is also the only example among the earliest civilizations in which secular rather than religious ideals and values become predominant. Of course, no correlation between its secular outlook and its continuity can be claimed; its comparative isolation may be just as important a factor in its persistence. Nevertheless, the durability of Chinese civilization does invite careful consideration.

Now that the features of the major eastern civilizations have been delineated, Part Two of this study will concentrate on their maturation as reflected in ideological elaboration, imperial expansion, and cultural diffusion.

The next chapter on the Middle East provides essentially a bridge between its ancient civilizations and the rise of Islam with particular attention to its principal contributions: the perfection of imperialism, the accompanying development of commercial and cultural exchange so characteristic of a crossroads region, and most important, further advances in religion. The chapter on India concentrates on its adventures in transcendental thought: Jainism, Buddhism, and Hinduism. Similarly, the chapter on China gives major attention to the intellectual development of China from Confucius to Chu Hsi as well as the development of imperial administration. A chapter on that buffer region, Southeast Asia, examines the emergence of successive centers of lesser civilization as examples of cultural diffusion via trade, emanating principally from India. Another chapter takes up a major example of cultural diffusion: the adoption and adaptation of Chinese conceptions in the creation of a distinctive civilization by the Japanese.

In the study of this part attention should be focussed on the further elaboration of the distinctive ideals and values of each civilization, the expansion of the area which each one encompassed, the way in which its uniqueness in outlook influenced its approach to comparable situations, and the diffusion of its influence to areas beyond its direct rule.

CHAPTER FIVE

EXPANSION AND DIFFUSION IN THE MIDDLE EAST: 1570 B.C – 632 A.D.

The period covered by this chapter contains a bewildering array of events. Many peoples move to the center of the stage and new empires rise and fall, as the old centers of civilization lose control of affairs. To simplify this picture we shall emphasize those events and developments that contribute something new or add significantly to the heritage of the Middle East. Underlying the confusing kaleidoscope of political events is the reality of economic and cultural growth and diffusion.

During this time, the area of civilization was vastly expanded, generating new wealth and markets for a growing trade. The tentacles of trade following new and old routes stretched out to the Atlantic Ocean in the west and to the Pacific in the east. Improved communications and trade stimulated imperial expansion, and imperial expansion in turn provided the conditions for better communications and an enlarged trade. Agriculture remained the heart of the economy, but trade supplied the tempting sugarcoating.

Although the empire builders may have been most deeply inspired by economic and political considerations, they could not ignore the religious heritage that provided the major support and justification for the acceptance of their authority. Most of them accepted with minor modifications the traditional religions of the regions they ruled. Indeed, the eclectic cross-identification of the gods of one area with those of another became more general, and the erection of temples to alien gods was further evidence of the interaction and exchange that was reducing the differences between peoples and was preparing the ground for a larger, more comprehensive community and state. In the advancement of religious speculation, however, the prophets of two little-known peoples

shared the honor of elevating religion to the highest plane yet achieved in the Middle East: the legendary Zoroaster (Zarathustra) of Persia and the series of inspired men responsible for the development of the ethical monotheism of the Hebrews. Both of the religions these prophets represented prepared the ground for their successor, Islam, the religion that prevails throughout the Middle East today.

ANCIENT IMPERIALISM

In the broadest sense imperialism may be defined as the extension of the authority of one independent group over another independent group. By this definition it would be as old as man and society, and the assertion of hegemony by one Sumerian city-state over others or the unification of Egypt would be examples. In fact, imperialism refers to the enforced submission of one culture to another culture, and the first clear case of imperialism is the alleged conquests of Sargon of Akkad of lands outside Sumer and Akkad. Succeeding examples in Mesopotamia culminated in the more enduring empire of Hammurabi and his successors (c 1792–1530 B.C.). Meanwhile, Egypt, which had some limited external conquests during the Middle Kingdom, became fully engaged in imperialism following the expulsion of the Hyksos (c 1570 B.C.).

The reasons for imperialism are manifold, varying from case to case, and any effort to single out a single one as most important can only lead to invidious distinctions and historical distortions. Economic factors in one form or another have always been important considerations. The desire to control vital trade routes and sources of essential materials appears to have inspired Sumerian mil-

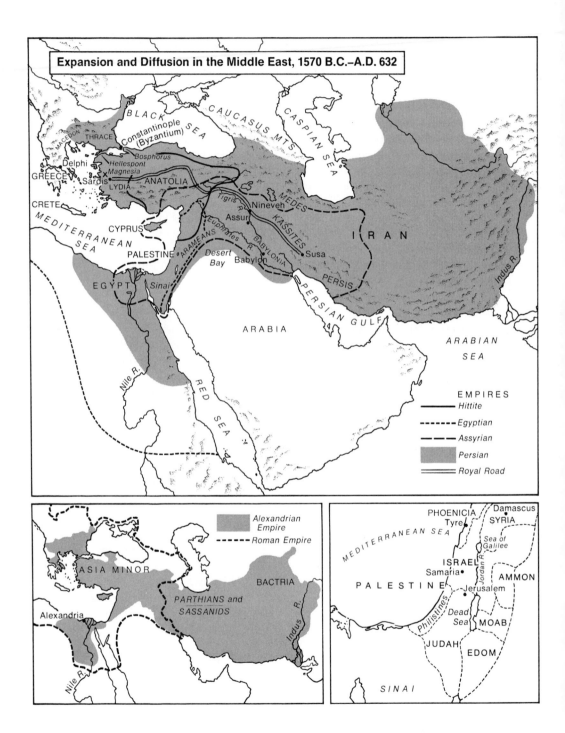

Expansion and Diffusion in the Middle East, 1570 B.C.–A.D. 632

EMPIRES

—— Hittite

----- Egyptian

– – – Assyrian

▓ Persian

══ Royal Road

▓ Alexandrian Empire

----- Roman Empire

itary campaigns at an even earlier date. From a negative point of view, external conquests to forestall raids may be described as in part economically motivated. Again, expansion may be prompted by the need to gain new lands to accommodate a growing population or to offset the economic strains caused by a decreasing fertility of the soil of the homeland. Of course, less favored peoples on the periphery of a prosperous civilization are constantly tempted to plunder and conquest at the first sign of weakness—the age-old story of the "have-nots versus the haves." All these and other economic factors played a part in the imperial activities already surveyed.

On the other hand, other reasons, sometimes nonrational, were as influential, if not more influential, than the economic ones. Power begets power, and the military force that had achieved unification had to be maintained. What better way was there to employ such a force than in foreign conquests which reinforced the power and prestige of the ruler? The records reflect the quest for power and glory in the grandiose titles that were devised to enhance the majesty of the ruler. Pride is another related factor, well-illustrated by the Egyptians' relentless pursuit of the Hyksos. The well-ordered world of the Egyptians had been turned upside down by these untutored barbarians. Nothing would satisfy Egypt but their total annihilation. This emotionally inspired motive was supplemented by the equally emotional demands of fear and revenge. Economic factors played hardly any part in the conquest of Palestine and Syria and little part in the decision to retain this area as an imperial possession. Much more decisive was the determination to maintain a buffer against any recurrence of alien assault. Military strategy on alien soil can be much more flexible than when it is used in a desperate defense of one's native land. Most of the plunder from these campaigns was put into temples erected to the gods who had smiled on Egyptian arms, which introduces another factor.

In each civilization the dominant char-acteristic of its world view deeply influences, if it does not absolutely control, all decisions and actions, including military actions. Rulers' references to such a factor should not be passed off as mere rationalization for acts otherwise motivated. It carries a deeper imperative. For every important action that involves the employment of public resources and manpower, the leader needs a measure of public acceptance and support. In other words, he must appeal, or submit, to public opinion.

In the civilizations of the Middle East religion played the dominant role, and every action, including imperialism, had to be religiously sanctioned. Whether the ruler was the agent of the gods, as in Mesopotamia, or the living god himself, as in Egypt, his actions were expressions of the will of the gods. In conquests, the gods commanded him to act, and victories were credited to their active support and participation. Thus the command of the gods to expand their domain was an important motivating factor in imperialism. Sometimes their will, interpreted by the priests, may have compelled the ruler to take action against his own will. Perhaps the attempted religious revolution of Akhnaton was partly inspired by a pacifistic desire to escape from the commands of a militant priesthood.

The next consideration is how were campaigns carried out and how were conquests consolidated. First it should be recognized that the mobilization of large citizen armies for extended compaigns was generally beyond the resources of the early civilizations. The one notable exception was the initial pursuit of the Hyksos whose rule in Egypt had stimulated deep and bitter national emotions. The prominence given in Hammurabi's law code to the "crime" of hiring a substitute suggests that obligatory military service was deemed as much of a nuisance and burden then, as now.

If possible, persuasion and threats were used to induce submission and the acceptance of a tributary status by the foe. If this failed, internal dissidents and external allies were sought to assist in overthrowing the enemy. Finally, mercenary allies were recruited from the nearby tribal nomads who were constantly seeking opportunities to supplement their meager and uncertain income.

These Semitic peoples living on the desert fringes of settled areas and gaining a livelihood by exchanging their livestock for needed goods and grazing rights during the blistering heat of summer were already collectively known as Habiru or "wanderers," a term from which, some assert, the name of Hebrew for a specific group of tribes originated. They provided a labor as well as a warrior reservoir and can be described as the original migrant workers, although their services were more extensive than those of their counterparts today.

Therefore, the ancient eastern armies must have been motley hosts stiffened by a small disciplined phalanx and, after the introduction of the horse, a corps of war-chariots to break the enemy line. Their successes must have been due to the even less-organized character of their foes.

In most instances, conquered areas were turned over to a local prince who paid tribute. Frequently he was supported in power by a small garrison force which discouraged revolt by the threat of massive retaliation it represented. Occasionally fortified positions were established to overawe the area and to serve as a base of operations. Only rarely was a conquered region colonized and incorporated politically into the state. Therefore, for the most part ancient imperialism was limited to the establishment of an uncertain suzerainty which might be overthrown at the first sign of weakness. Nevertheless, this relativeley weak control stimulated the expansion of trade and cultural diffusion which, in turn, dampened the desire for independence because of the mutual benefits and bonds that grew between suzerain and vassal.

On the other hand, imperialism of this nature was restricted to settled areas and

committed the imperialist power to the defense of greatly expanded frontiers against semi-nomadic marauders. Reliance on local forces for defense often proved inadequate, and comparatively small parties, reinforced by malcontents, could bring about the rapid overthrow of this type of empire.

THE HITTITES

About 2000 B.C. or earlier, an Indo-European speaking people known as the Hittites migrated across the Caucasus and settled on the Anatolian Plateau mixing with peoples there and en route. After 1900 B.C. they extended their political authority over the entire region. The ancient trade between Anatolia and Mesopotamia was continued and attracted the attention of the Hittite rulers to the fabulous wealth of Hammurabi's empire. About 1530, a Hittite king launched a raid that to his surprise met almost no opposition, and almost before he realized what he was accomplishing, he had entered the imperial capital, Babylon, and had slain the last of Hammurabi's successors. Wholly unprepared to consolidate his success, his destruction of the Babylonian dynasty only opened the way for the domination of lower Mesopotamia by the neighboring Kassites, probably a mixed people with Indo-European rulers. The Kassites merely absorbed and preserved Babylonian civilization without making any important contributions to Middle Eastern development.

By the fourteenth century B.C., the Hittites had secured their flanks and were prepared to challenge Egyptian ascendancy in Syria and Palestine. The clash of imperialisms that ensued was the largest and longest struggle the world had yet seen. Vast hosts marched back and forth and clashed in mighty battles. Siege and counter-siege promoted the arts of war and fortification. The end result was stalemate, proclaimed by a series of treaties in the thirteenth century B.C. which divided Syria, provided mutual extradition, stipulated a defensive alliance between the two powers, and declared in good diplomatic parlance "peace and good brotherhood between the contending parties forever." Egyptian monopoly of the major trade routes had been broken, but both parties were exhausted by the struggle.

Before 1200 B.C., the Hittite homeland was overwhelmed by fresh invaders who were part of another wave of Indo-Europeans that created confusion throughout the Middle East at this time. Among them were the "Sea Peoples" of uncertain antecedents who failed in an invasion of Egypt but left an impression in the Philistine settlement on the coast of Palestine. Knowledge of iron technology now became general, ushering in what is called the "Iron Age." Meanwhile, lesser Hittite city-states persisted for centuries in northern Syria reflecting a thoroughly mixed culture.

Culturally the Hittites contributed little that was new other than a certain primitive freshness and vitality in their otherwise crude reliefs and sculptures. To fill the needs of an imperial power they leaned heavily on borrowings from Mesopotamian civilization. Their religion was infused with the familiar Indo-European reverence for nature and natural forces and phenomena. Of their pantheon of a thousand or more deities the two chief figures were the sun-god and the typical Indo-European storm-god. Other deities and cults were freely borrowed and adapted from their more civilized contacts. For writing, Sumerian cuneiform was supplemented by their own hieroglyphs.

The collapse of the Hittite Empire and the exhaustion of Egypt was followed by an interlude of four centuries during which a number of lesser states (such as the Phoenician, Aramean, and Hebrew states) were able to form and prosper in the Syria-Palestine buffer region. During this period east-west trade continued to grow despite political disunity. The Phoenicians were the successors of Crete in the domination of the maritime trade of the Mediterranean, while

the Arameans specialized in the overland trade between the Persian Gulf and the Phoenician ports. The camel facilitated the development of new routes across the hitherto forbidding desert. Damascus under the Arameans became an important distribution center. For a time the unified Hebrew state benefited from the control of caravan routes from Arabia, which bypassed Egypt. As might be expected in such a crossroads area, the cultures of the Semitic peoples of Syria-Palestine were an eclectic adaptation of influences from abroad and demonstrated little originality, with one notable exception. The Hebrews' outstanding contribution was in the field of religion which will be dealt with below. Finally, a new imperial power arose which created by dubious methods a larger empire than any of its predecessors and set in motion a movement towards the development of a larger unity.

THE ASSYRIANS

As early as 3000 B.C., a Semitic people known as Assyrians after their chief city, Assur, had settled down to a predominantly pastoral life in the foothills along the upper Tigris River. During the subsequent millennia they adopted Mesopotamian culture and can be designated a fringe area of Mesopotamian civilization. Constantly they were assailed by other peoples whose movement toward Mesopotamia they blunted and with whom they mixed creating a racial amalgam. Thus, Assyria unwittingly defended Mesopotamian civilization against barbarians whom they also partially civilized. The transformation of a relatively peaceful pastoral people into militant defenders of civilization was economically rewarded by their role as intermediaries in trade. At the same time, their military function promoted the centralization of political authority, although throughout their history the support of a military aristocracy had to be recognized and rewarded by the rulers.

At the end of the twelfth century B.C.,

Assyria made its first essay at imperialism, hoping to take advantage of the political fragmentation in northern Syria, but the effort proved to be premature. Not until the ninth century did a series of able rulers begin to build a new type of empire that was based on military power and took advantage of improved means of transportation and communications to exercise a more direct control over conquered territories. The Assyrian Empire reached its greatest extent near its sudden and fatal end in the seventh century B.C., incorporating all the civilized and economically valuable areas of the Middle East, including Mesopotamia and Egypt.

Thanks in large part to the biblical record and their own boasts the Assyrians have come down in history as the epitome of ruthlessness, cruelty, and barbarity, and moralists have never tired of pointing out the object lesson of their sudden and complete overthrow by their enraged and embittered subjects. Such an interpretation is not supported by the facts.

First, ruthlessness was nothing new in Middle Eastern warfare. Before institutional and communication advances made possible the maintenance of direct control over conquered areas, slaughter and mass enslavement, in which human beings were classified along with other plunder, were commonplace. As examples, both Egyptian and Hittite records boast of slaughter and human loot. In fact, for the first century and a half the practice of Assyrian imperialism appears to have been more humane in this respect. Like their predecessors, they sought to establish their suzerainty over the trading centers and to extract tribute from vassal princes; they did not yet attempt to establish the fuller institutional control that characterized the last century and a half of their empire. A dead people cannot pay tribute. Therefore, the Assyrians did their best to promote trade, although they left the trading activities to the more experienced Arameans and Phoenicians.

The Egyptians, however, had never become reconciled to their loss of the control of the major trade routes and fomented rebellions among Assyria's tributary states in the Syria-Palestine region. In reaction, the Assyrian ruler Tiglath-Pileser III (745–727 B.C.) initiated the policies of terror, mass deportation of rebels, and the establishment of directly administered provinces. The last-mentioned step ushered in a wholly new stage in imperial development. Some loyal local lords were allowed to stay in power, subject to the authority of the local governor, but other vital areas and cities, such as Damascus, were placed under Assyrian administrators. Assyria's approach to governing its empire, however, was still flexible and experimental.

In Mesopotamia the Assyrian ruler accepted the supreme Babylonian god, Marduk, and took the position of its king. In 721 B.C., Samaria, the capital of Israel, was taken after a 3-year siege and a mass deportation ended its independence. Sennacherib (705–681 B.C.), the most ruthless of Assyrian rulers, thoroughly reduced the Phoenician cities which Egypt had encouraged to revolt, ravaged Judea, and razed Babylon to punish rebellion. His son and successor tried a different approach by rebuilding Babylon and placing it under a local ruler. This effort to mollify the Mesopotamians ultimately failed when, under their local ruler, they joined the Medes of Iran in destroying the Assyrian Empire and state. Meanwhile, the principal thorn in Assyria's side, Egypt, was conquered in successive campaigns.

The success of the later campaigns was made possible by the development of a new military arm, a cavalry of mounted warriors, which greatly increased mobility and impact. Mounted messengers had been used for some time to speed communications and thus to facilitate imperial administration. Royal post roads tied together the chief administrative cities of the empire. Indeed, without this improvement in communications the effective organization of provincial administration is difficult to conceive.

Ashurbanipal (668–626 B.C.), the ruler who completed the conquest of Egypt, is also renowned for building up and beautifying the imperial capital, Nineveh. His most valuable contribution to later times was the collection and storing in a great library of the literary works of all his subjects. The site, accursed and undisturbed since its overthrow, has provided scholars with a treasure trove for the recovery of the past.

At its zenith, when Assyria had apparently reduced all its foes and had instituted an efficient imperial administration, its military strength rapidly evaporated. The Assyrian people, it appears, had been bled white in the centuries of incessant campaigns and could no longer supply the forces needed to maintain the empire. The government could not find loyal non-Assyrian troops to reinforce the depleted ranks of its army which, in any case, was dispersed in far-flung garrisons. The successful revolt of Egypt demonstrated the inherent weakness of the empire and encouraged rebellious intrigue in every province. The deathblows were delivered by the joint forces of the tributary Medes of western Iran and the Mesopotamians under their local ruler. Notably both of these areas were ruled by native princes and were not subjected to Assyrian governors. In 612 Nineveh was razed, and 6 years later the allies destroyed the last Assyrian army. As a people, the Assyrians disappear from the pages of history, but the trail they had blazed in military and imperial development was not forgotten and was immediately followed by their successors. They had brought the fragmented territories of the Middle East together into a genuine and prosperous unity. Through their efforts imperialism had come of age.

With tribute pouring into the royal coffers from the far-flung empire the later Assyrian rulers were able to dedicate large sums to the arts. Nineveh and other cities as well were benefited by the royal bounty. The temples built in Mesopotamia were larger and more luxuriously decorated than any of their predecessors. In relief and sculpture the artists achieved greater and more effective natural effects than ever before. The geometrical and floral forms for decoration developed under Assyrian auspices were to be copied and elaborated much later in Islamic art. In art, literature, religion and, indeed, in all aspects of culture the Assyrians were the true heirs, preservers, and developers of Mesopotamian civilization, which was to be continued on an even grander scale by the short-lived Neo-Babylonian Empire.

NEO-BABYLONIAN AND PERSIAN EMPIRES

The Babylonian ruler took as his share of the spoils the more civilized heartland of the Assyrian empire with the major trade routes, while the Medean king inherited the less tamed areas to the north and east of the Tigris. The new Babylonian ruler, Nebuchadrezzar II (605–562 B.C.), however, was not unopposed in his claims. A revived Egypt, fearful of allied success, had announced its intention of contesting the Babylonian claim by fighting on the side of the Assyrians at the last decisive battle. National interest, not principle, dictated Egyptian support of their recent oppressors. Obviously, a consideration of the balance of power in determining international alignments is not an original contribution of the modern West.

Like the Assyrian rulers, Nebuchadrezzar of biblical renown had to deal with Egypt's effort to reassert its influence in Syria-Palestine. Although his forces regularly defeated the Egyptians and their allies in the field, the struggle was long and hard, not being concluded until the fall of the Phoenician city of Tyre in 572 B.C., after a siege of 13 years. One result of this contest, which looms large in the Old Testament, was the capture of Jerusalem after repeated rebellions and the carrying off (in 586 B.C.) of the Hebrew elite to what is known in biblical annals as the "Babylonian Captivity."

Judging by his inscriptions, Nebucha-drezzar was much less proud of his military exploits than of his public works which included irrigation, canals, caravan roads, temples, and palaces. After almost a millennium Babylon was once more an imperial capital and the chief seat of civilization in the Middle East. National pride in this rebirth stimulated an artistic and cultural renaissance, drawing heavily on tradition, which made Babylon surpass all its predecessors in size and in the grandeur and beauty of its monumental temples and palaces. This was the city of the famous "hanging gardens" (one of the seven wonders of the world selected by the Greeks)—apparently a series of watered terraces on which were cultivated the most exotic plants and flowers of the East. This was the city harboring every vice and depravity that tortured the puritanical consciences of the religious leaders of the Hebrew exiles. They dreaded the temptations to sin which the city offered to their followers and reacted by developing a more rigorous outlook than they had had before.

The ancient Mesopotamian religious doctrine which reduced men to mere slaves of the gods received renewed emphasis and stimulated the study of the stars as a means of discovering one's destiny in place of the old dependence on sacrifices and the interpretation of dreams and omens. As a result of the accent on astrology, the heavenly bodies were charted and catalogued with a greater accuracy than ever before, providing a foundation of precise data for the later development of astronomy. Religiously, the development of astrology made the individual more dependent for guidance on experts whose calculations were well beyond ordinary comprehension; no longer could the individual rely on supplications and sacrifices to his personal patron deity. Moreover, the astrologists, then as now, seldom gave direct advice; usually they simply indicated those days that were favorable or unfavorable to specific actions. There were no guarantees. A man's fate still rested on the whim

of the gods.

While the Neo-Babylonian empire was luxuriating in its revived power and achieving a new peak of prosperity, its end and absorption into a far larger empire were being prepared by poorly understood events transpiring among the Indo-European speaking peoples who had settled in western Iran. A vassal-king, Cyrus of Persis, supplanted his Medean overlord in 550 B.C. and led the united peoples in a series of amazingly rapid conquests. The rulers of the major states (Nabonidus of Babylonia, Amasis of Egypt, and Croesus of Lydia) were not unaware of the coming storm and attempted in vain to coordinate a common defense. Cyrus, the Persian, and his successor were enabled to conquer them one by one starting with the weakest, the fabled Croesus of Lydia in Asia Minor. Croesus consulted the Greek oracle of Delphi which advised him that if he went to war with Cyrus a great empire would be destroyed. He never dreamed it would be his own. In any case, his only choice was to fight or submit. In 546 B.C., the conquest of Lydia gave Cyrus control of the whole of Asia Minor. For a few years he campaigned in the east to forestall nomadic raids and then took advantage of the Babylonian priesthood's discontent with Nabonidus. After routing the Babylonian army, the capital city was taken without a struggle in 538 B.C. The balance of his reign was occupied with the consolidation of these conquests. Then his son, Cambyses (529–521 B.C.), added Egypt to the Persian Empire.

Wisely Cyrus had adopted a moderate and tolerant policy toward the conquered territories allowing them to retain their religions while he, as their new king, performed their religious ceremonies and subsidized their temples and priests. At the same time, all exiles, such as the Jews, were permitted to return to their homelands and even assisted in rebuilding their temples. But the Persian conquerors carried in their cultural baggage a vigorous religion infused with a high ethical content and a sense of mission.

ZOROASTRIANISM

Just when Zoroaster (Zarathustra) preached his new revelation and just what the nature of his original teachings were are not known. Since there is no clear evidence of his religion before the establishment of the empire, he probably lived not long before, about 600 B.C. The Zend-Avesta, which purports to represent his teachings, was not compiled in its present form until the opening of the Christian Era. To what extent the priests, called magi, altered his original message cannot be determined. The major point in dispute is whether he taught a monotheistic faith in Ahura-Mazda, the god of light, or a dualistic doctrine in which Ahriman, the god of darkness, is locked in continuing conflict with Ahura-Mazda. In fact, the earliest evidence indicates that Ahura-Mazda was viewed as the supreme, if not the sole, god who would ultimately prevail. Darius I (521–485 B.C.), who gained the throne in the strife following the premature death of Cambyses, clearly declared his debt to Ahura-Mazda and established his worship as the state religion. Perhaps the death of Cambyses and the succeeding turmoil were instigated by Zoroastrian priests discontented with the imperial policy of religious toleration established by Cyrus. Whether a result of imperial patronage or the tired and uninspired condition of the other religions, Zoroastrianism spread rapidly and became popular throughout the empire. Certainly, on its merits alone, it had a strong appeal.

Zoroastrianism was the Iranian version of the reform of the ritual-ridden Indo-Aryan religion which was mixed with local cults and priestly domination. A central feature was the sacred fire that has already been noted as the central element of the Aryan religion. While preserving the idea of a sacred fire, however, Ahura-Mazda's revelation to Zoroaster created a wholly new and dynamic religion in which the forces of the universe were in conflict, preparing the world and

man for the ultimate day of judgment.

As taught, this was a universal religion. All men were invited to support the forces of good, commanded by Ahura-Mazda, against the forces of evil, led by Ahriman. The active participation demanded of each individual preserved freedom of choice, and the prescribed course of action required virtuous conduct, involving positive acts of will and self-denial on the part of the believer. Practical virtues included hard work, the keeping of contracts, obedience to superiors, tilling of the soil, and the begetting of many children to enlarge the ranks of the army of good. More abstract injunctions enjoined honesty, brotherly love, hospitality, and alms for the poor. A negative statement of the Golden Rule charged one not to do to others what would not be for one's own good in the ethical sense of the term, "good." A long catalogue of sins to be abjured left no doubt about the kind of behavior required of the believer. The broad categories of sin included selfish pride, gluttony, laziness, covetousness, lust, anger, slander, and waste. Specific sins included adultery, abortion, and usury. With its emphasis on the active life, Zoroastrianism forbade ascetic practices, such as self-punishment, fasting, and excessive grief, as essentially selfish and contrary to the communal virtues as well as the obligations to produce food and children.

Zoroastrianism was the first religion to set a definite goal when Ahura-Mazda would finally prevail and establish an eternal paradise. As fully developed, a regular timetable was laid down. In 9000 years Zoroaster would come again as a promise of ultimate redemption. He would be followed by the miraculous birth of a messiah whose task was to make the final preparations for the conclusion of the struggle at the end of 12,000 years. On that date would occur the resurrection of the dead and the day of judgment. The righteous would cross the bridge to paradise, while the sinners would join Ahriman in the fiery abyss. However, according to the weight of their sins, the wicked would be sentenced to a longer or shorter period of suffering. Ultimately all, both saints and sinners, would enjoy eternal life in paradise. The appeal of this religion and its influence on its successors are self-evident and do not need elaboration.

Like other universal religions, Zoroastrianism in the course of time lost its pristine purity. The organized priesthood reintroduced ritualistic magic based on old superstitions. Moreover, as the religion spread, it picked up alien elements from the older religions it sought to replace. Out of these alterations evolved subsidiary cults.

One of the earliest and most popular of these cults was the worship of Mithras who was conceived both as the commander of Ahura-Mazda's human host and as a sort of culture hero who miraculously created the conditions for the transition from a pastoral to an agricultural way of life. When Ahriman first sought to thwart his work by causing a drought, Mithras caused waters to gush forth by driving his spear into a rock. Then Ahriman tried a flood, but Mithras had an ark built. Both of these feats attributed to Mithras are clearly based on older myths. After completing his tasks on earth, he achieved mystic union with the sun by consuming a joint sacramental meal. Eventually Mithras would return to earth to confer eternal life on all his followers.

The objective of Mithraism was the achievement of individual mystic union with the god by going through extreme asceticism, connoting renunciation of things of the flesh, and elaborate rituals, including baptism and sacramental meals of bread and water. Sacred chants and incense were part of the ceremonies. The days of the week, following Neo-Babylonian practice, were named after the major heavenly bodies, and the day of the sun, Sunday, was the chief holy day. December 25th, as the approximate date when the sun began to move to the north, was the most sacred day of all. This cult conveying, as it did, a sense of personal

union with the divine to its initiates became very popular and spread throughout the later Roman Empire. Again, its influence on other religions needs no elaboration.

In the third century A.D. a Persian priest, Mani, attempted to reform the corrupted practice of Zoroastrianism and was crucified for his effort by his countrymen. Nevertheless, his teachings, known as Manicheism, gained large followings in the rest of the Middle East and the West. Starting with Zoroastrian dualism, he divided the universe into the realm of the spirit presided over by the god of good and the realm of matter ruled by the god of evil. Since mankind was essentially material, endowed with physical desires and material needs, it was the creation and subject of the god of evil. Only the souls of men had been created by the god of good.

As this doctrine implies, all those who seek "perfection" must abstain from all material entanglements by following a program of extreme asceticism. In contrast with Zoroastrian teaching even marriage was forbidden because its fruits would increase the forces of the god of evil. An interesting concept, which recurs later in Islam, is the recognition of a number of prophets of whom Mani was asserted to be the last and the greatest. Such a point of view sets up a sort of religious genealogy that reinforces the validity of the last prophet's revelation.

Although Darius I declared Ahura-Mazda to be his patron, and undoubtedly subsidized Zoroastrian development out of imperial revenues, there is no indication that he added religious to territorial imperialism. Toleration, if no longer active support of the local religions, laws, and customs, remained the imperial policy. On the other hand, the problem of a number of insurrections which he had to suppress to secure his succession made Darius well aware of the need for a more efficient system of imperial administration, a chore to which the conquerors, Cyrus and Cambyses, had been too busy to give their serious attention. Not that Darius neglected imperialism, he extended the frontiers in the west across the Hellespont into Thrace and in the east into the Indus valley. But his most important contribution was in the sphere of imperial government.

PERSIAN IMPERIAL ADMINISTRATION

First, the status of the "Great King" was elevated from that of a simple warrior to that of an omnipotent despot whose word was law and whose person could be approached only through a maze of intermediaries amid much pomp and circumstance. This creation of an "oriental" court not only protected the ruler against assassination but also instilled a deeper respect for his person and power among the many different subject peoples encompassed within the Persian state.

Second, he divided the empire into more than 20 provinces (satrapies). While he retained the position of direct ruler over the two centers of civilization, Babylonia and Egypt, the other provinces were placed under civil governors (satraps) who were either royal relatives or trustworthy associates of the king. Associated with the satrap was a separate commander of the garrison troops. Each had to cooperate with the other and was required to report directly to the king on the other's activities. As an additional check, a provincial secretary was directly appointed by the king to inspect the mails. A final precaution was the setting up of a system of traveling inspectors known as "the eyes and ears of the king." By this division of authority and additional safeguards, Darius sought to minimize the possibilities of a menacing concentration of power.

The satrap was responsible for collecting the taxes to be forwarded to the royal treasuries, and the fixed assessment was usually lower than it had been in the past. But the extra exactions of the Persian officials, their monopoly of the higher offices, the military conscription, and the frequent disdain for the subject peoples combined to generate discontent that often resulted in futile rebellions.

Communications have always governed the size and the method of administration of empires. Darius sought to solve this problem for his vast realm by the construction of post roads between the administrative capitals. Best known is the 1500-mile road between the chief imperial capital, Susa, and the capital of Lydia, Sardis, over which royal messages carried night and day by mounted relays could be delivered in 10 days. These roads also promoted an accelerated growth of trade within the largest political entity yet devised. The Aramean merchants expanded the range of their commerce carrying with them their language and their alphabet. Cuneiform was replaced and an alphabet of 39 letters, based on the Aramean, was used to write Persian.

The army illustrates well the problem of a loosely organized, tolerant empire unable to institute a centralized administration and enforce a measure of cultural uniformity. It relied, as the Assyrian army had, primarily on native Persians and the elite corps of "10,000 Immortals" to provide the reliable core. This relatively small body was supplemented by contingents from the subject peoples armed and equipped after the local manner. A vast and colorful host of this nature might overawe a foe, but in combat it was not only unwieldy but also was uninspired by any deep loyalty. The first reverse could precipitate a general rout.

Nevertheless, this decentralized empire, tolerant of its diverse components and dependent on an unwieldy army, managed to suppress the all-too-frequent rebellions and to maintain its frontiers for two centuries. The system of imperial organization and administration, which drew on Assyrian precedents, served as the model, with modifications, for succeeding empires in the Middle East.

Perhaps its greatest weakness has not yet been mentioned. This was the Great King himself. The effective functioning of the government depended on the ability and conscientiousness of this single figure with unlimited power. No device could be devised to assure the efficiency of his administration or to provide for the removal of an inefficient ruler. Also the wealth accumulating in the royal treasuries furnished a powerful temptation for the diversion of his efforts from the responsibilities of government to the pleasures of luxurious living. Thus the key to this system of checks and balances was himself unchecked.

As might be expected, the Persians utilized the skills and talents of their more advanced subjects. Artists and architects were assembled from the whole empire and the regions beyond, to build and beautify the imperial capitals. While these aliens naturally introduced their own motifs in their works, the columnar style of architecture was derived from the Persian tradition in wood of columned porticoes, not from Greek or Egyptian precedents as has sometimes been supposed. In the other amenities of civilization the Persians were fully occupied by the adoption and spread of the achievements of their more cultured subjects and added nothing of their own except an inborn sense of esthetic appreciation which has always characterized the people of Iran and their products. The pedestrian products of mass production that satisfied the needs of Babylonians and Egyptians held no appeal for them. Even in products of common use the artistic expression of the artisan was highly prized. Mass-produced coinage, however, was of such obvious utility that it was borrowed from Lydia and carried throughout the realm and abroad by trade.

THE HEBREWS

A minor people known as the Hebrews were responsible for a major contribution to what has been singled out as the most in-fluential element in Middle Eastern civilization—religion. In addition, they produced the first substantial historical work in the Old Testament. This was no mere chronicle of events, but a conscious selection compiled to illustrate and explain in a meaningful fashion what the Hebrews considered the most important aspect of their history—the course of their religious development. Subsequent historians have concentrated their attention on other aspects of historical development, such as politics, economics, or civilizations, in their search for meaning in history, but their efforts in no way undermine the validity of the theme selected by the Hebrew historians. Indeed, in the light of their principal contribution, they selected the most important theme around which to organize the study of their history. The selection and suppression of facts may disappoint the modern historian interested in other secular aspects of Hebrew development, but they were entirely justified from the Hebrew point of view. Since our chief concern here is the Hebrews' contribution to Middle Eastern religious development, scant attention will be paid to the other aspects of their history.

The group of pastoral nomads, eventually known as Hebrews, may have moved into Palestine, already occupied by a related Semitic people called Canaanites, about 1800 B.C. or later. The Old Testament contains evidence indicating that their religion was at this time a typical amalgam of animistic worship and magical practices. Contact with the culturally more advanced Canaanites introduced them to polytheistic doctrines, especially the prevalent fertility cults. Several centuries later, famine may have driven some groups to seek refuge in Egypt where they were enslaved. The Exodus from Egypt under Moses' leadership probably occurred in the years around 1250 B.C. While passing through the Sinai Peninsula, Moses persuaded his followers to accept Yahweh, who may have been the deity of Hebrew nomads in the area, as their supreme god and protector. Through the common acceptance and worship of Yahweh the various tribes were brought together in a loose confederation to accomplish the gradual conquest and unification of Palestine over the next several centuries.

During this period, Yahweh was conceived in human form as the folk god and champion of his chosen people who acted in an arbitrary and unpredictable fashion and had to be appeased by ritual sacrifices. He was not an exclusive god—only the god of the Hebrews—and not much of a promoter of spiritual or ethical conduct—only a dispenser of rewards and punishments in response to loyalty or disloyalty. His chief function, then, was to unify and lead his people to victory in their struggles with other peoples and other gods. He was the supreme lawgiver, but the purpose of his laws was to induce political cooperation and social order. Any promotion of ethical behavior was an incidental result. Old Testament scholars generally doubt that the Ten Commandments, in their present form, are older than the eighth century B.C.

Shortly before 1000 B.C., Saul was the first king of the united Hebrew tribes who had been elected on the recommendation of the Judge, Samuel, but his reign ended in suicide after a defeat in which he lost his son. The founder of the short-lived Kingdom of Israel was the hero David (c 1000–961 B.C.) who drove the Philistines back, reduced the Canaanite cities, and extended his realm across the Jordan to the east and to Damascus in the north, gaining control of the overland trade routes. In these conquests he was aided by an alliance with the Phoenicians who dominated the overseas trade routes. Jerusalem, an old city with natural defenses, was chosen as the political and religious capital because it represented neutral ground between the two halves of the Hebrew kingdom, Judah and Israel. David, the warrior, was succeeded by his son Solomon, the builder (961–922 B.C.), who brought great wealth to the realm by fostering trade, though he lost some outlying areas such as Damascus to the Arameans. He is famed for

his luxurious "oriental" palace harboring 700 wives and 300 concubines, who reflected his diplomatic vigor, and for constructing a great temple to house the Hebrew Covenant with Yahweh. This era also saw a blossoming of literature. But the people were unhappy with the rapid transition from tribal life to a bureaucratic state with heavy taxation to support it, and on Solomon's death the tribes of Israel rebelled, bringing to an end the glory of a united realm. The rest of Hebrew *political* history is an epilogue until the recreation of Israel after World War II. The greatest religious achievement, however, was yet to come.

In the course of their conquests many Hebrews borrowed a number of exotic cults that diverted religious energies from the worship of Yahweh. This wayward condition inspired religious reformers, first, to drive out the alien cults, and second, to initiate the era of the prophets (eighth and seventh centuries B.C.) who revolutionized the conception of Yahweh and his worship. The teachings of these inspired men, which carried Hebrew thought to its zenith, cannot be done justice in a brief summary. They should be directly consulted in the Old Testament.

First, Yahweh came to be viewed by the prophets as transcendent. He was the sole god of the universe, not just the god of the Hebrews. There was no other god beside him. This was the first assertion of pure and unalloyed monotheism. Furthermore, Yahweh was a god of goodness, justice, and mercy, who used his power to guide men back to the path of righteousness. Probably these ideas stemmed from the need to explain the reverses and threats the Hebrews suffered during these centuries. A god of all mankind directed the actions of Assyrians as well as Hebrews. Thus he used the Assyrians to punish the Hebrews for their sins or visited the invincible host of Sennacherib with a plague as an act of mercy toward his Hebrew people.

Finally, sin was not merely the violation of a law of the Book, but included any unjust act, or even thought. In this way the conception of sin was expanded from a legalistic to a humanistic doctrine. Obedience to the letter of the law was not enough; observance of the spirit of the law was just as necessary. The prophets deprecated and even rejected mere fulfillment of ritual requirements. By caring for the oppressed and unfortunate, men could demonstrate far better their love of Yahweh. Men were urged to look inside themselves and honestly assess and reform their actions and attitudes toward their fellow men. On this basis, the all-knowing Yahweh would judge them; and punish, reward, or show mercy toward them. The poetic instruction of the Prophet Micah sums up well this attitude.

> Wherewith shall I come before the Lord,
> And bow myself before the high God?
> Shall I come before him with burnt offerings,
> With calves of a year old?
> Will the Lord be pleased with thousands of rams,
> Or with ten thousands of rivers of oil?
> Shall I give my firstborn for my transgression,
> The fruit of my body for the sin of my soul?
> He hath showed thee, O man, what is good;
> And what doth the Lord require of thee,
> But to do justly, and to love mercy,
> And to walk humbly with thy god.
> (Micah 6: 6–8)

The command to social justice reflected the growth of inequities in Hebrew society and also the need that was felt to eliminate these inequities to unify the nation in the face of the Assyrian threat. In the circumstances, which had already seen the extinction of Israel, utopian visions of a future time when a "Prince of Peace" would cause wolves to lie down with lambs and when complete justice would prevail are not surprising. This dream, poetically expressed by the Hebrew proph-

ets, is still the dream of mankind today. The deliverance the prophets envisioned was an earthly salvation. No Hebrew thinkers as yet entertained any idea of an afterlife.

During the "Babylonian Captivity" the intellectual elite were exposed to the full force of Babylonian pessimism and fatalism as well as the more fleshly temptations of that cosmopolitan center. In reaction, the priests to maintain discipline placed a heavier emphasis on the law and ritual practices than had ever existed before. At the same time, unable to justify their misfortunes in any other way, the transcendental character of Yahweh was elevated beyond human understanding. Man had no choice but to submit without question to whatever was his will. Yahweh alone understood his divine purpose. Although the Book of Ezekiel and other compositions of the period of exile illustrate the development of this conception of the remoteness of Yahweh, it is most forcefully expressed in what was probably the supreme literary achievement of the Old Testament, the story of Job. Utilizing an ancient Babylonian theme, Yahweh accepts Satan's challenge by permitting him to test the steadfastness of the righteous Job by inflicting every type of calamity on him. While remaining firm in his faith despite the mounting afflictions, Job explores every avenue in search of an explanation for his sufferings. Finally, in despair, he appeals to Yahweh who speaks to him from a whirlwind chastening his loyal servant for his presumptuous wish to understand the ways of God. Job is shown how limited is man's knowledge of the universe and is convinced to keep faith and accept humbly the dictates of the Almighty.

On their return from exile, the priests, reinforced by the law, which was given the sanctity of revelation, and supported by the Persians, gradually asserted their religious supremacy. The rigidity of their outlook, however, as well as the influence of Zoroastrian ideas, stimulated the development of splinter movements. Some transferred the source of evil from man to Satan. Some looked for salvation from the woes of the world in an afterlife. Along with these conceptions developed the ideas of a spiritual messiah, resurrection of the dead, and a last judgment. Although these doctrines were rejected by the orthodox faith, they were a fertile source of further expressions of spiritual vitality.

Shortly before the Christian Era there were three major sects: the Sadducees, the Pharisees, and the Essenes. The Sadducees, composed of the priests and the upper class, insisted on rigid adherence to the ancient laws and customs and condemned the new ideas of resurrection and rewards and punishments in an afterlife. The middle class Pharisees, while upholding full observance of the law and ritual to maintain national unity, also entertained beliefs in an afterlife and a political messiah who would lead his people to their destined role of leadership in this world. The essence of the Essene doctrine was the subordination of all earthly activities to the single goal of spiritual preparation for the next life. They lived the simplest possible life in communal groups in which they shared their goods and the labor necessary for survival. Because they looked forward to the coming of a spiritual messiah and the imminent end of the world they renounced all political ties and obligations, even refusing to take oaths. Any diversion from concentration on devotional activities was frowned on, even marriage, which was considered no better than a necessary evil. How much influence the ideas of this sect may have exercised on Jesus of Nazareth cannot be determined. John the Baptist, who first recognized the mission of Jesus, may have been a member, although he later denounced them for their selfish concern with their own salvation and their failure to work for the salvation of the whole nation.

The teachings of Jesus are important not only for their contribution to Christianity, which gained large followings in the East, but also because Muhammed recognized the prophetic role of Jesus and was influenced by them, and by those of Christianity. Furthermore, Jesus' teachings, insofar as they can be determined, sought to restore the most ethical aspects of the Hebrew religious tradition, especially the prophets' emphasis on the spirit of the law and the universality of God.

In the absence of contemporary accounts the only reliable sources for the views of Jesus are the four Gospels of Matthew, Mark, Luke, and John, none of which appears to have been composed less than a generation after his death. Generally scholars believe that those views commonly expressed in all four Gospels to be the most valid. Whether Jesus considered himself divine is a subject of wide disagreement, but he does appear to have felt that he had a divinely inspired mission to save man from the error of his ways. His central doctrine, from which all his other teachings naturally followed, described God as a God of love whose chief commandments to his believers were to love God and to love their fellowmen who were the subjects of God's universal love for mankind. Such a religion, it was emphasized, came from the soul of each man and could not be attested by mere ritual observance. Jesus did not reject the Hebrew law, but as he said, he had come to fulfill it, to proclaim in the fullest sense the spirit of the law. From the doctrine of love and the personalized conception of worship stemmed other major teachings, such as the Golden Rule, turning the other cheek, and repaying evil with good, scathing criticisms of selfishness and greed, and contempt for religious hypocrisy. In addition, he taught the imminent end of the world, the resurrection of the dead, and the establishment of the Kingdom of God.

ALEXANDER THE GREAT AND THE HELLENISTIC ERA

In 334 B.C. the Hellenized Macedonian ruler, Alexander, at the head of only 30,000 infantry and 5000 cavalry had the audacity to challenge the vast distances, immense wealth, and apparent military strength of the Persian empire. In less than 10 years, with scarcely any assistance from his Greek allies, he carried out this dream and more, extending his march beyond the Indus River into the Punjab before he was forced to retire by a mutiny of his tired troops.

What was the significance of this achievement? First, it created the largest political entity the world had yet seen. But this political unity died in 323 B.C. with the death of its creator to be carved up by his successors into several states that constantly contended for control of the trade routes. Second, it ushered in the so-called Hellenistic Era, which implies that Greek culture was the dominant element in the cultural mixture that ensued.

From the beginning the younger civilization of the Greeks, especially in Asia Minor, had been subject to the influence of the older Eastern civilizations. In the eighth century B.C. when Greek merchants began successfully to challenge the maritime monopoly of the Phoenicians, they brought back ideas as well as goods in their cargoes. Before the creation of the Persian Empire, Greek mercenaries were gaining an even more intimate knowledge of the East. Although the Greeks repulsed the military assaults of the Great King, his gold was able to keep their quarrelsome states in continuous turmoil until the time of Alexander. Alexander's conquest of the Persian Empire released the hoards of gold in the royal treasuries to stimulate a commercial boom and threw open this eastern wonderland to the exploitation of Greek adventurers. In the process, however, the Greeks, and subsequently their Roman successors, were far more "easternized" than their Eastern subjects were "westernized."

This does not mean that Greek (Hellenic) influences were without effect. Greek culture was essentially urban in nature and left deep and enduring impressions, especially in the art and architecture of the new cities. Not until the Byzantine period did the Eastern artistic heritage reassert itself strongly enough to play a prominent role. Temples dedicated to Eastern deities were Hellenic in design, but both art and architecture, while retaining Hellenic form, became ornate and monumental under Eastern influences. The Greek language also prevailed in the Greek cities and in much of the trade, but it could not supplant Aramaic which actually spread with the expanded opportunities provided under the Roman Empire to Aramean merchants. Aramaic even displaced Hebrew as the language in which Jesus delivered his message. Hellenic rationalism also exercised a perceptible influence on Eastern and Christian thought. Even in the cities, however, the extent, depth, and duration of Hellenic influence varied from region to region, being strongest in Western Asia Minor and Syria and much weaker in Egypt and the rest of the Seleucid realm.

In whatever area one examines—political, social, economic, philosophical, religious—the West was eventually taken culturally captive by the East. Oriental despotism with all its attributes, including royal divinity, was adopted by the new rulers. With modifications the Persian provincial system of imperial administration was applied not only in the East but also in the Western territories of the Roman Empire. Although Alexander and his successors founded many new cities after the Greek model, they never gained the degree of independence and political vitality of Greek cities and their settlers soon succumbed to Eastern religions and luxury. Greek austerity and the idea of moderation could not resist the temptations of the Eastern way of life. The Greek forms of city-state government might be maintained, but their substance was in practice thoroughly subverted. Eastern religions not only captivated Greek settlers but also they spread and became dominant eventually throughout the West. Even in the Greek area of greatest originality and renown, philosophy; Stoicism, founded by a

Cypriot Syrian, incorporated facets of Eastern provenance. Eastern influence was even more apparent in the later transcendental philosophies of neo-Pythagoreanism and neo-Platonism. In sum, then, the term, Hellenistic, as a description of the new cultural mixture, seems singularly inappropriate and misleading.

To illustrate the ebb and flow of power, the major political developments in the Middle East from the death of Alexander to the rise of Islam must be briefly surveyed. Following Alexander's premature death in 323 B.C. his unconsolidated conquests broke up into three major successor states: Macedonia with its domination of Greece and territories in Asia Minor, the Seleucid state with the bulk of Alexander's conquests stretching from the Mediterranean Sea to the Indus valley, and Ptolemaic Egypt with territorial interests in Syria-Palestine and an ambition for maritime supremacy and the control of trade. With their control of the major trade routes the last two states with capitals in the Middle East were by far the most prosperous. While the Ptolemies maintained the Egyptian frontiers, with fluctuations in their imperial possessions and power, the Seleucids gradually lost control of their eastern territories as Parthian power waxed and waned after its establishment in 248 B.C. Parthian authority, although little more than a military hegemony over virtually independent lords, effectively cut off the Greek state in Bactria, whose subsequent history followed an independent course, ultimately moving influentially into India. Since most trade with India came by sea through the Persian Gulf and Red Sea, perhaps, the Seleucids felt that their military efforts might be more profitably employed elsewhere than in the eastern extremities of their empire.

Roman imperialism began in the Middle East at the Battle of Magnesia (190 B.C.) and was pursued until the annexation of Egypt in 30 B.C. For the first time in history the political center moved out of the Middle East. But with some temporary fluctuations Rome accepted a frontier marked by the northern Euphrates and buffer client states in the Desert Bay, leaving Parthia in control of Mesopotamia and the lands to the east. This decision was probably dictated by Roman development and the expansion of direct trade with southern India via Egypt and the Red and Arabian seas. With this connection Rome felt no great need for control of Mesopotamia and the Persian Gulf.

Recognition of the "easternization" of Roman culture and the greater economic value of the Eastern provinces was reflected in the removal of the imperial capital in 330 A.D. to the "new Rome," Constantinople, strategically located on the European side of the straits of the Bosphorus. While the western half of the empire deteriorated into the political and economic disorders of the Middle Ages, this almost impregnable city repulsed all Eastern assaults until 1453. Meanwhile, the East had gained a far more formidable champion when the last Parthian ruler was slain and the Sassanid dynasty (226–651 A.D.) was established. Reviving Zoroastrianism as the state religion and the Persian system of government, the Sassanids created a far stronger state with greater resources than their Parthian predecessors. Taking the Persian title "king of kings" (*shahanshah*), they asserted their claim as heirs to all the territories of the old Persian Empire. Such a claim precipitated full-scale wars with the Roman empire in which the Sassanids almost gained total victory. The long-range result, however, was the military and economic exhaustion, accompanied by widespread discontent, of both sides, which prepared the way for the conquests of Islam.

The Zoroastrianism of the Sassanids and the Christianity of the Byzantines infused their conflicts with the character of holy wars. Like the Byzantines, the Sassanids occasionally sought to enforce conformity by religious persecution until they realized that toleration would gain them support among heretical Nestorian and Monophysite Christians at home as well as in Syria and

Egypt. In 555 A.D. the Sassanid ruler founded an academy of medicine and philosophy which employed Christian professors who taught in Syriac (derived from Aramaic). These professors and their descendants performed an important service by translating Greek works into Syriac whence later they could be translated into Arabic. In this way Persia and Islam were able to utilize the elements of the intellectual heritage of Greece that were found useful.

The Parthian language, *Pahlawi* (middle Persian), which is the descendant of old Persian and the parent of modern Persian, was continued in use in the cultural renaissance promoted by the Sassanids. The cultural vigor of the period was stimulated by imports from India as well as the Byzantine realm. Two Indian imports of this era which eventually reached the West via Islam were the famous Bidpai animal fables and the game of chess.

In art and architecture the Sassanid era saw the elimination of the last remnants of Hellenic influence. Although few buildings remain from this period, Sassanid architects are believed to have solved the problem of placing a dome on a square base by the use of squinches. However, the most characteristic architectural form was the barrel vault which may still be seen roofing over the old bazaars of Iranian cities and towns. Examples of metalwork, carpets, and textiles preserved in museums illustrate the high level of excellence already achieved by Iranian artisans and for which they are still renowned today. This cultural revival was not extinguished but, instead was stimulated to greater achievement, by the greatly enlarged market provided by the Islamic conquest.

Many may be shocked at this abbreviated condensation of some 2000 years that are laden with well-documented events and personalities, most of which have been ignored. For the purposes of this study of Eastern civilizations, however, only three significant developments of this era of Western intrusion warrant attention, and all three are only fuller realizations of characteristics already evident in the civilizations of the Middle East. For this reason, this period has been labeled an era of expansion and diffusion.

First, the necessary administrative techniques and communications were worked out for the satisfactory control of extensive empires in terms of the technology available. Thus the desire to control trade routes could be effectively implemented. From this point of view, this era could be called the age of imperialism. One result of empire building was the diffusion of civilization both within and beyond imperial frontiers.

The second major development, directly related to the first, was the expansion of commerce and the widespread diffusion of a more active economic life. With the exception of the last few centuries when the Roman Empire in the west underwent a rapid decline, the volume and area of commercial activity continuously grew, enriching the trading cities and their rulers. Along with trade went the diffusion and exchange of ideas, creating a more integrated outlook—at least in the cities—over a wider area than the world had previously known.

Finally, that area of special concern in the Middle East, religion, gained new universal dimensions of long-range significance at the hands of Persian and Hebrew prophets. The spread of Zoroastrian and Christian doctrines, as well as those of numerous cults, was facilitated by the development of a larger political and economic community and provided an influential background to the rise and spread of Islam.

The Hellenic role in that amalgam labeled Hellenistic civilization by Western scholars has been downgraded. This interpretation is contrary to the generally accepted view but it is possible to state that in the total picture of civilization in the Middle East Greek influences were temporary and minor phenomena while, conversely, Eastern influences have exerted a relatively greater effect on Western development. Hopefully this account will stimulate the reader's critical examination of the Hellenic role.

SIGNIFICANT DATES

c.	2000–1600 B.C.	First Wave of Indo-European penetration: Introduction of horse-drawn war chariot
c.	1570–1100 B.C.	Egyptian Empire
c.	1400–1220 B.C.	Rise and fall of Hittite Empire
c.	1300–1200 B.C.	Second Wave of Indo-Europeans
c.	1200– 800 B.C.	Age of fragmentation and rise of lesser states
c.	933– 605 B.C.	Rise and destruction of Assyrian Empire
	625– 538 B.C.	Neo-Babylonian Empire
	586 B.C.	Capture of Jerusalem and Babylonian Captivity
c.	600 B.C.	Zoroaster (Zarathustra)
	550– 330 B.C.	Persian Empire
	334– 323 B.C.	Conquests of Alexander the Great
	190 B.C.	Battle of Magnesia (Rome enters the Middle East)
	248 B.C.–226 A.D.	Parthian Empire
	226– 651 A.D.	Sassanid Empire
	330 A.D.	Constantine dedicates "Eastern" capital of Constantinople: Byzantine era begins

SELECTED READINGS

See Chapter Two for additional selections.

*Conteneau, Georges, *Everyday Life in Babylon and Assyria*. New York: Norton, 1966.

*Finegan, Jack, *Light from the Ancient Past*. Princeton: Princeton University Press, 1959.

Fisher, Sydney Nettleton, *The Middle East*. 2nd ed.; New York: Knopf, 1969.

*Ghirshman, R., *Iran*. Baltimore: Penguin Books, 1954.

*Gurney, Oliver R., *The Hittites*. Baltimore: Penguin Books, 1952.

Hitti, Philip K., *History of Syria Including Lebanon and Palestine*. New York: Macmillan, 1957.

*———, *The Near East in History*. New York: Van Nostrand, 1961.

Huart, Clement, *Ancient Persian and Iranian Civilization*. New York: Knopf, 1927.

*Moscati, Sabatino, *Ancient Semitic Civilizations*. New York: G. P. Putnam's Sons, 1957.

Olmstead, A. T., *History of Assyria*. New York: Charles Scribner's Sons, 1923.

*———, *History of the Persian Empire: Achaemenid Period*. Chicago: University of Chicago Press, 1948.

Pritchard, James B., ed., *Ancient Near Eastern Texts*. Princeton: Princeton University Press, 1955.

*Pritchard, James B., ed., *The Ancient Near East*. Princeton: Princeton University Press, 1958.

Rostovstzeff, M. I., *Social and Economic History of the Hellenistic World*. 3 vols.; Oxford: Clarendon Press, 1941.

*Sachar, Abram Leon, *A History of the Jews*. 5th ed.; New York: Knopf, 1967.

*Stark, Freya, *Alexander's Path*. New York: Harcourt, Brace & World, 1968.

*Tarn, W. W., *Alexander the Great*. Cambridge: Cambridge University Press, 1951.

*———, *Hellenistic Civilization*. 3rd ed.; London: Longmans Green, 1952.

*Wilson, John A., *The Culture of Ancient Egypt*. Chicago: University of Chicago Press, 1956.

Zaehner, Robert C., *The Dawn and Twilight of Zoroastrianism*. New York: G. P. Putnam's Sons, 1961.

CHAPTER SIX

INDO-ARYAN CIVILIZATION

We left the story of India in the sixth century B.C., during a period of great intellectual, spiritual, and political ferment and turmoil. This condition had built up in intensity over the preceding centuries as a result of the culmination of the Aryan migration into the Gangetic plain and the consequent settling down into a civilized way of life characterized by the development of cities, territorial states, and irrigated agriculture. This growth of a settled, civilized way of life undermined tribal organization and social ties and contributed to a growing feeling of individual insecurity in response to which new answers were sought, especially in the spiritual realm. Moreover, the Aryans in the course of their prolonged migration from west to east across northern India had inevitably been subjected to non-Aryan influences that had altered their culture as well as their racial purity. They had to come to terms with the more numerous indigenous peoples whom they ruled and, in the eastern Ganges, to accept the existence of some non-Aryan states that did not fully adopt Aryan culture. Thus, by the sixth century B.C., Aryan culture was being seriously subverted from within and threatened from without.

How much of the change was a result of the transition to civilization and how much was due to the assertion of non-Aryan views cannot be determined. No written records have been preserved of a date earlier than the third century B.C., and the accounts on which the historian must rely are often compilations of a much later date, drawing on many centuries of oral transmission. Indeed, the whole period to the Muslim conquest abounds in chronological uncertainties. Most governmental records were written on perishable materials with the exception of significant grants of land that were inscribed on copper plates. The only certain dates are connected with alien contacts and visits. Therefore, any reconstruction of pre-Muslim Indian history must be built on very flimsy documentary foundations. Even the course and chronology of cultural developments, though abundantly documented, cannot be set forth with precision and certainty as to time and place.

This qualification should not be taken to mean that Indians were unconcerned with the problems of this life and their solution. Then, as now, the energies of both rulers and people were almost wholly absorbed in dealing with the problems of this life. But an awareness of its impermanence and constant change worked against the development of a feeling for history.

Politically, India under more autocratic rulers was engaged in increasing interstate warfare that was reducing the number of independent states. At the end of the sixth century B.C. the potential scale of warfare was increased by the knowledge of iron metallurgy gained from the Persians, probably as a result of the subjugation of northwest India by Darius I. This was the beginning of fruitful exchanges between India and Iran. Knowledge of the Persian Empire and administrative techniques subsequently stimulated the growing imperial ambitions of the leading Indian states. However, two centuries of struggle were to pass before the rise of the Maurya Empire, which eventually incorporated all but the southern tip of India.

Possibly instrumental in precipitating the Maurya rise to power was another alien incursion, that of Alexander the Great in 325 B.C. One story represents the founder of the Maurya empire, Chandragupta, as urging Alexander to march into the Gangetic plain where he might easily overthrow the corrupt and unpopular ruler of the paramount state.

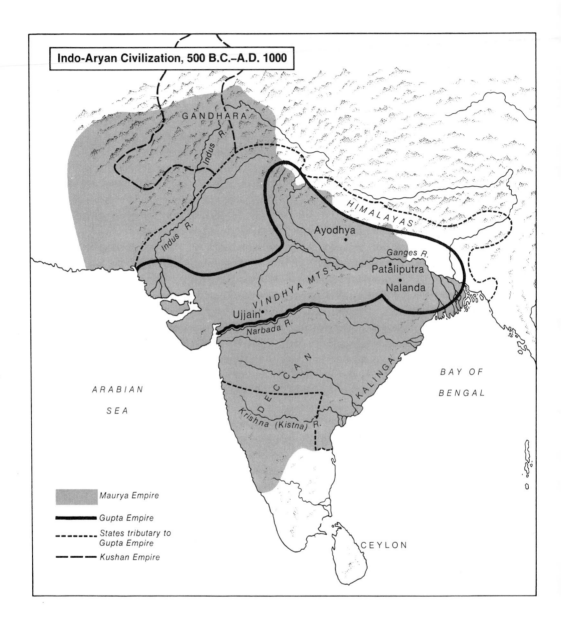

Indo-Aryan Civilization, 500 B.C.–A.D. 1000

GANDHARA

Indus R.

Indus R.

HIMALAYAS

Ayodhya

Ganges R.

Pataliputra

Nalanda

VINDHYA MTS.

Ujjain

Narbada R.

D E C C A N

KALINGA

ARABIAN

SEA

Krishna (Kistna) R.

BAY OF

BENGAL

Maurya Empire

Gupta Empire

States tributary to
Gupta Empire

Kushan Empire

CEYLON

Although this intrigue was frustrated by the mutiny of Alexander's army, Chandragupta did manage to conquer both the Gangetic plain and northwest India, uniting all of northern India for the first time. Finally, he repulsed an effort of Seleucus to regain Alexander's Indian provinces and made an alliance, confirmed by a marriage, with him. In return, Seleucus received a gift of India's chief contribution to warfare, a contingent of 500 war elephants.

Chandragupta's little-known successor moved south of the Vindhya Mountains, conquering the Deccan, and his renowned son, Ashoka, conquered the southeast before being converted to Buddhism and pacifism as an imperial policy. Maurya imperial organization and administration were clearly modeled on Persian precedents, and Iranian influence is also evident in the numerous pillars erected by Ashoka to carry his Bud-dhist-inspired injunctions. Buddhism under Ashoka will be examined later.

RELIGIOUS PHILOSOPHY

The Upanishads, it will be recalled, re-vealed a growing dissatisfaction with the sacrificial worship of the Vedic deities and the ritual domination of the brāhman priest-hood. Individual ascetics, probably inspired by non-Aryan religious practices, sought the ultimate reality behind the gods. The univer-sal soul, Brahman, which transcends the constant change of this world and its gods, was found to reside within each individual as his imperishable self, ātman. By ascetic in-troversion, full self-consciousness of the self as identical with the universal soul and be-yond the phenomenal changes of life and death could be achieved. From this point of view the ultimate reality is eternal, unchang-ing, and unperceived consciousness. What the senses perceive is constantly changing, ephemeral, and essentially unreal. Such transcendental knowledge cannot be gained by Western-type reason, which is limited to the study of subject and object.

While this transcendental religious phi-losophy was evolving, other fundamental conceptions, probably of non-Aryan origin, were gaining prominence as dominant doc-trines of all subsequent Indian religious and philosophical development. The doctrine of samsāra, of perpetual rebirth of the soul, was firmly established by 500 B.C. For the aver-age man, belief in this doctrine, at least re-moved the fear of death and guaranteed a form of individual immortality. Associated with it, however, was the doctrine of karma (action) according to which one's deeds, good or bad, determined the status in which one would be born again. The karmic theory had the advantage of enjoining the ideals of virtuous conduct. It also explained one's status in this life and eliminated social dis-content while it held out hope for a better status in the next life to come. Naturally, this doctrine led to the development of dharma (moral law) generally prescribing the rules of virtuous conduct and particularly setting up regulations for each class and caste.

Although obedience to the moral law in preparation for a better status in a future life probably satisfied most Indians, many found the prospect of a perpetual round of rebirths appalling and sought some avenue of imme-diate release (moksha). The authors of the Upanishads, deeply disillusioned with life, were probably influenced by the contem-porary elaboration of the doctrines of rebirth and karma. Certainly, Jainism, Buddhism, and Hinduism were all affected by them.

JAINISM

Jainism and Buddhism were only the more enduring of many unorthodox teach-ings of the sixth and fifth centuries B.C. For the most part knowledge of the other phi-losophies is preserved only in the Jainist and Buddhist denunciations of them and, there-fore, is not reliable. However, these biased descriptions can furnish a general idea of the range of intellectual speculation and ferment in this era.

Generally these thinkers were dis-turbed by the doctrines of rebirth and karma and the possibilities of release from the chains of everchanging matter. One rejected the effect of good or bad deeds and argued that release could be achieved simply by faith. Another repudiated the possibility of attaining transcendental knowledge and adopted an agnostic position. In response to the question of whether there was another world, he replied that he could not say whether it existed or not. A third was an atomist who believed that everything was composed of seven uncreated, unfeeling, in-destructible elements. Consequently, no hu-man action added to, took away from, or al-tered in any way the basic constituents of reality. A fourth was a less subtle materialist who simply excluded any reality for man be-yond this life.

Gosala, an early associate of the establisher of Jainism, founded the Ajivika sect, teaching determinism which gained wide popularity during the pre-Christian era and lasted as an organized faith until the fourteenth century. Each man, he taught, is destined to pass through a predetermined schedule of rebirths whose course cannot be speeded up or slowed down by any acts, good or bad. However, the desire to avoid damaging acts and to practice extreme asceticism is by itself evidence that one is nearing the end of one's scheduled round of rebirths. Hence this doctrine indirectly encouraged ethical behavior.

Mahāvīra (c 540–468 B.C.) is believed by Jains to have been the twenty-fourth and last inspired teacher during this long period of decline in the cosmic cycle. Therefore, his doctrine is not considered original, but, rather a restatement of ancient teachings that had been largely forgotten. Like his contemporary, the Buddha, Mahāvīra, was the son of a chieftain of one of the tribal states north of the lower Ganges which probably were largely non-Aryan in blood and culture. The prevalence of animism is reflected in Mahāvīra's view that not only animals and plants but even inanimate objects possess souls.

His philosophy was essentially materialistic and dualistic. The universe is composed of an infinite number of separate and finite souls, called jīva (life), which to a greater or lesser extent mixed with matter, and it is conceived as ovate in shape in which these souls float upward or downward according to their material weight. Eternal bliss is to be obtained by eliminating this material burden until the soul floats to the top of the universe and adheres there like a drop of pure water. Pursuing this analogy, the soul is burdened by actions (karma) which are lighter or darker in color according to the seriousness of the action. Life is pictured as a fire in which karma are constantly being consumed, but fresh karma resulting from selfish and cruel thoughts and actions are constantly providing fresh fuel, generally in excess of that burned up. The path to bliss, then, requires a regimen of extreme asceticism with fasting and penance to burn up the darker karma and to minimize the influx of fresh karma. The ultimate form of asceticism would result in death by starvation.

Of all Indian philosophies, Jainism has placed the heaviest emphasis on nonviolence (ahimsā) because the soul incurs the darkest stains by the destruction of life. But the darkness of the hue is graded downward from human life through animal and plant life to inanimate "life." This gradation has encouraged vegetarianism as the least damaging means of sustaining life. Moreover, this doctrine has led Jainists to avoid farming and to specialize in commerce as the source of livelihood that involves the least destruction of life. Jainist commercial success has been enhanced by the emphasis placed on honesty and austerity. The 2 million Jainists of India today are especially prominent in the business community. Nonviolence and the other ethical teachings of Jainism lack the attractiveness of those of other religious philosophies because virtuous behavior is dictated for the selfish benefit of the individual Jainist's soul, not because of any consideration or compassion for his fellowman. Indeed, involvement of one's own feelings with others is believed positively to endanger one's own spiritual welfare. Good deeds, charity, nonviolence, all are motivated by the selfish end of individual salvation.

In contrast with other doctrines, Jainism has undergone no fundamental alterations. It divided into two sects over the issue of whether monkish renunciation prescribed nudity or permitted the wearing of a white robe, but there was no basic difference in doctrine. Today the "space-clad" sect avoids offense by wearing garments in public. It is essentially nontheistic, recognizing no deity, but in practice icons of Mahāvīra and his predecessors are revered, and often Hindu gods are given, with typical Indian tolerance, supplementary worship for the temporal blessings that they may bestow. None of these deviant practices, however, have changed the doctrine and discipline of Jainism whose dedicated monks, according to Mahātmā Gāndhi's own admission, deeply influenced his youthful mind.

BUDDHISM

Siddhārtha Gautama (c 536–483 B.C.) was the son of the chief of the Shākya tribe, which was also located north of the lower Ganges and only weakly influenced by Aryan culture. Unlike the teachings of Mahāvīra, those of Gautama underwent so much change that their original form and content cannot be delineated with certainty except in the broadest terms. Clearly, both he and Mahāvīra were disturbed by the doctrines of rebirth and *karma* and were inspired to analyze the reality presented by the senses to discover the avenue to release from the bondage and suffering of existence. But, although the problem they confronted was the same, their answers were poles apart.

According to tradition, Gautama, appalled at the extent of human suffering, abandoned his life of princely comfort at the age of twenty-nine and for six years pursued a program of extreme asceticism in the hope of discovering the ultimate truth. Finally, realizing that all of his suffering and penance had been in vain, he gave up extremism, regained his health, and then sat down under a pipal (fig) tree, determined to remain there in meditation until he learned the secret of existence. After resisting every type of temptation, he achieved enlightenment and became the Buddha (the Enlightened One). At first, convinced that it would be impossible to convey this knowledge so indescribable in words with their sensate connections, he decided to remain silent. But, at last, he became persuaded that he must at least attempt to show others the path he had

discovered to enlightenment. Therefore, the bulk of his teachings concerned the means of gaining enlightenment and only suggested by imperfect parables the indescribable and ineffable end.

His fundamental doctrine is summed up succinctly in what are called the "Four Noble Truths." First is the noble truth of sorrow or suffering, and its inextricable connection with existence. The second noble truth concerns the cause of sorrow which is identified with the blind desire of the ego for satisfaction and permanence, "the craving for sensual pleasure, the craving for continued life, the craving for power." From these two truths logically follows the answer for eliminating sorrow. "It is the complete stopping of that craving, so that no passion remains, leaving it, being emancipated from it, being released from it, giving no place to it" (de Bary, *Sources of Indian Tradition*, p. 102). However, this cure is more easily prescribed than achieved; and the fourth noble truth lays down a program, called the "Noble Eightfold Path," which will be most conducive toward the end of extinguishing the desire of the ego and eliminating the ignorance that prevents men from gaining the ultimate knowledge.

Up to this point the doctrine appears to present a negative renunciation of this life. Now a positive program of thought and action is prescribed. "Right View," or outlook, merely requires recognition of the desires of the ego as the source of sorrow. "Right Resolve" is the determination to extinguish this source of sorrow. "Right Speech" and "Right Conduct" involve the exercise of positive virtues—the four cardinal virtues of Buddhism: love, compassion, joy, and serenity. The true disciple loves all his fellow creatures, not just humans and would do nothing to cause any one of them a moment of suffering. Also he feels deep compassion for their sorrow and does all he can to alleviate it. Such actions have the cathartic effect of diminishing the novice's concern for himself by diverting it to others, in contrast to the self-centered altruism of the Jainist. Thus "Right Speech" and "Right Conduct" are important steps on the path from ignorance to knowledge.

The fifth step, "Right Livelihood," concerns the obtaining of food by begging and the semi-ascetic dietary regulations, especially the prohibition of food after midday. Naturally the Buddhist monk renounces all worldly goods, which are only the fruit of human craving. "Right Endeavor" prescribes acting and thinking in terms of the goal of extinguishing desire by becoming fully aware of the transient nature of all living things. This awareness is to be aided by "Right Consciousness" of every personal thought and action. In other words, every individual thought and action should be carried out deliberately with full awareness of its effect and its transient quality. After these preparatory steps have been faithfully fulfilled, the novice should be ready for the final step of "Right Contemplation" of the transitory nature of all existence which may lead him to that enlightenment which is the final goal of the Noble Eightfold Path and which is essentially indescribable.

Unlike other forms of Indian asceticism, Buddhism emphasized moderation and decried extremism either in asceticism or the pursuit of worldly pleasures, because both enhanced rather than diminished egoism. The middle path and the practice of altruism were deemed most conducive to attaining the end of enlightenment.

What enlightenment was, or is, could only be hinted at. To give it a name, such as Nirvāna, is an error because it implies that a finite term can define that which is not only infinite but beyond description and definition with reference to human experience. The Buddhist philosophy of nature provides one suggestion. Everything in nature is composite and involved in constant change never being the same from one moment to the next. The composite nature of any thing is not limited to material substance but includes mind

and soul, or individual consciousness. All change is a result of the "Chain of Causation," and each thing is changed by causes outside itself. Therefore, there is no permanent individuality and certainly no eternal soul within the individual (ātman), as Hinduism taught. As it is explained in one passage, the individual existence of all beings, past, present, and future, is a consequence of craving for the essential supports of life: food, sensate contact, thought, and individual consciousness. And such craving arises ultimately from ignorance of the oneness of the unchanged and unchanging universe, from ignorance of the external causation of the awareness of finite individuality, out of which come attachment, birth, death, and all the accompanying ills of suffering, grief, and despair. Once such ignorance is dispelled, all ills will cease.

If everything is composite and constantly changing, Buddhist acceptance of the doctrine of rebirth appears inconsistent. Yet while Buddhism denied the transmigration of souls, it insisted that the basic doctrine of rebirth was explained by the "Chain of Causation." The famous lamp analogy was frequently cited in support of this argument. When a man lights one lamp from another, there is no transmigration but there is rebirth with the man acting as the external cause.

Enlightenment, then, involves, as one aspect, the realization of the transient nature of all existence. With this knowledge the Buddhist disciple is released from the ignorance that results in clinging to life and individuality. However, there is no renunciation of life or of the reality of sorrow and suffering, at least, not in early Buddhism.

Another common analogy used to convey some idea of the quality of enlightenment and its remoteness from human understanding is the description of the doctrine as a vehicle (yāna), specifically a ferryboat. In the Buddhist metaphor, the river is pictured as so wide that the far bank can scarcely be perceived. The near shore, on which one is standing, represents life filled with desire, suffering, and death—all due to ignorance. By analogy, when one boards the ferryboat, one is entering on the Noble Eightfold Path of the Buddhist discipline without any idea of what will be found at the end of the journey. As the ferryboat reaches midstream both banks, the bank of life, and the bank of enlightenment, have become indistinct in detail. All that has genuine substance is the ferryboat, the fellow passengers, and the swirling waters that must be overcome. Finally, the far shore is reached, the shore of life is lost in the haze, and the passengers disembark. The ferryboat is left and forgotten because it, like the Buddhist discipline, is a mere vehicle no longer of use to those who have gained enlightenment. The discipline is for pupils; it is of no use except as a tool to teach others how to find the way. Each individual must use it and, having achieved the goal, discard it. Thus the parable concludes paradoxically that for those who have reached the far shore there is no shore, neither near nor far; there is no river, no crossing, no ferryboat because there can be no duality in perfection. There is no rebirth and no enlightenment. All such perceptions are illusions of life. This is the great awakening, the achievement of perfect knowledge. Essentially, then, the teachings of Buddhism are psychological, and are not theological or even metaphysical.

After the Buddha's death at the age of eighty after a meal of spoiled pork, his followers in the course of time developed varying interpretations of his teachings and eventually divided into a number of sects. Several councils were reportedly convened to preserve the pure doctrine, to reconcile differences, and to define the orthodox creed. Two clearly divergent schools of Buddhism gradually emerged: one labeled derogatively by its opponents Hīnayāna (the Lesser Vehicle) and the other calling itself Mahāyāna (the Greater Vehicle).

The Hīnayāna, known as Theravāda Buddhism, prevails today, with local variations, in Ceylon, Burma, Thailand, Laos, and Cambodia. It purports to adhere more closely to the teachings of the Buddha by asserting that enlightenment can be achieved only by arduous individual effort via the Noble Eightfold Path. Those believed to have reached this goal are venerated as arhants (perfect beings) who have set the example for others to follow.

The Mahāyāna school is represented by a number of sects that gained the greatest followings in China, Korea, Japan, and Vietnam. The Mahāyānists, perhaps, influenced by Middle Eastern religious ideas brought into India by invaders after the third century B.C., decried the limited opportunity of enlightenment offered by the Hīnayānists only to their intellectual athletes and taught that no small ferryboat but, instead, a superliner was ready and waiting to transport all the faithful. This ship was manned by Bodhisattvas, those who had reached the edge of nirvāna but who out of overwhelming compassion for suffering mankind would forego the final step until all had been saved. Stopovers in heaven were provided for the faithful, where final preparation for enlightenment would take place. In one sect a mere declaration of faith in one's dying breath guaranteed a passport to this heaven. Thus the transition from a philosophy to a theistic religion of faith and salvation was achieved. In some sects, the nature of heaven as merely a convenient way station en route to full enlightenment was lost sight of in the popular mind and became the ultimate goal to be reached by worship and simple declarations of faith.

The foregoing statement by no means does justice to the philosophical development that led to this religious conclusion, and only a few sects went this far. Mahāyāna Buddhism represents rather a natural development of the emphasis on altruism that permeated the teachings of the Buddha, especially the four cardinal virtues of love, compassion, joy, and serenity. How could one unselfishly and genuinely observe with love and compassion the sufferings of mankind and yet remain se-

renely detached in pursuit of one's own enlightenment? Small wonder, then, that the
individual austerities prescribed by the
Noble Eightfold Path were in time subordinated in importance to the consideration of the
ultimate goal of release for all from the sorrow
and suffering of the "wheel of life" with
its perpetual round of rebirths.

Buddhism had never rejected the gods;
it had only reduced them to the realm of this
ever-changing universe, subject like everything else to dissolution and rebirth. Since
the Buddha, the Enlightened One, had
passed into that transcendent, ineffable condition that could not be described as existence or nonexistence, he surpassed the
gods, but could not be adored in an icon because he was beyond form. His memory and
teachings, however, were venerated from an
early date in symbols, such as the Wheel of
the Law, footprints, a vacant throne, or the
trident-shaped symbol representing the
early Buddhist declaration of faith, called the
Three Jewels: "I take refuge in the Buddha,
I take refuge in the Doctrine, I take refuge
in the Order." To take refuge, as the first
Jewel prescribes, in something that is no
longer something appears meaningless; yet,
linked with the alleged declaration of the
Buddha that all who acknowledged him with
genuine faith and devotion would be reborn
in heaven, it encouraged worship of the Buddha who was represented by icons in human
form by the first century A.D. Of course, representations of Bodhisattvas presented no
such philosophical dilemma.

By the end of the first century A.D.
Mahāyāna Buddhism had reached full vigor.
Mahāyānists, Hīnayānists, and even brāhman ascetics were still able to coexist, even
in the same monastery, but their views had
completely diverged in emphasis.

BUDDHISM AND ASHOKA

Buddhism did not come into its own until
it gained as a convert the great emperor of
the Maurya dynasty, Ashoka (c 269–232

B.C.), who left permanent memorials testi-
fying to both his conversion and the vast extent of his empire. Edicts were inscribed on
rocks and pillars as far apart as Gandhara in
the northwest and below the Krishna River
in the south, a distance of about 1500 miles.
One of these inscriptions describes his remorse at the blood spilled in rounding out his
domain on the southeastern coast and his
unique political views. After conquering Kalinga at a cost of more than 100,000 lives, "the
Beloved of the Gods" was converted to the
path of righteousness and became the champion of peace. Now, if even a thousandth part
of such slaughter and suffering should occur,
he declared that he would be grief-stricken.
Henceforth forgiveness, so far as possible,
would be the guideline of his government.
He even sought to reform the wild forest
tribesmen by reasoning with them. Nevertheless he warned them and all would-be rebels to beware of testing his compassion too
far for fear of being slain. Thus Ashoka's
pacifism and idealism were pragmatically
limited in terms of the welfare of the state
and his subjects. His interest in security, self-
control, justice, and happiness led him to
recognize the need for enforcing law and order. Finally, this inscription expressed his
belief that "the greatest of all victories is the
victory of Righteousness," but note that he
never thought of relinquishing conquered
Kalinga to its former rulers. Moreover, there
is no record of any reduction in the size of the
army.

Nevertheless, as much of a political
realist as he was, Ashoka did represent the
Indian ideal of the *Chakravartin*, the benevolent universal emperor, extolled in all the
religions and philosophies of India. He set an
example of enlightened, humanitarian government, relaxing the sterner justice of the
past. Capital punishment was retained, but
the condemned were granted a three-day
stay of execution to prepare themselves for
the next world. The former secret police were
converted into "officers of righteousness"
who censured provincial administration and

fostered more humane relations between man and man. Ashoka considered himself the gentle father of his people and frequently reproved local officials for failing to maintain this principle in their governmental actions. He encouraged the doctrine of nonviolence (*ahimsā*) which was becoming general in all Indian religions and philosophies by prohibiting animal sacrifices, regulating animal slaughter for food, substituting royal pilgrimages to Buddhist shrines for the grand hunts that had been the traditional sport of kings, and almost eliminating the eating of meat in the royal household. Although royal approval, perhaps, accelerated the development of vegetarianism, Ashoka mainly capitalized on a trend that was already well underway.

In the area of public works Ashoka displayed tolerance and political wisdom by granting royal patronage to the construction of non-Buddhist as well as Buddhist shrines. Roads were extended and improved by planting fruit trees for shade and food, digging wells, and building hostelries. The cultivation of medicinal plants to be supplied free of charge to both men and animals received royal support, and medical clinics were set up. Finally, he supported Buddhist missionary activity by which he sought to extend his moral authority to foreign lands. Despite the claims in his inscriptions, the only important spiritual conquest was the island kingdom of Ceylon whose conversion was reputedly accomplished by his son. According to the Ceylonese Chronicle, which would scarcely err on such a subject, the king even acknowledged the suzerainty of Ashoka, providing him with his only known "victory of righteousness."

The net effect of Ashoka's reforms, then, tended to enhance paternalism and the centralization of imperial authority, regardless of Buddhist influences. Indeed, it could be argued that Ashoka used Buddhism to advance his own ends as a ruler.

While he was clearly a Buddhist, Ashoka's understanding of Buddhism was shallow and superficial and probably reflects the popular knowledge and appreciation of this philosophy. Certainly, the emperor was in a better position to learn its precepts than the ordinary layman. Yet his inscriptions indicate that it meant to him mainly a system of morality and altruistic behavior that was conducive to promoting peace and goodwill on earth and entrance into heaven after death. Moreover, he believed that the moral uplift inspired by his reforms had attracted the gods into manifesting themselves on earth in support of the public welfare. The frequency of his references to heaven suggest that Mahāyānist conceptions were already emerging.

Whatever benefits may have accrued to the Indian people and Ashoka through his support of Buddhism were rapidly dissipated after his death when the provincial governors who were drawn primarily from the royal family asserted their independence. Buddhist altruism disappeared from government, which reverted to the Indian "law of the fishes" according to which the little fish is the natural prey of the big fish. But, while Ashoka lived, India enjoyed greater peace and prosperity over a larger area than under any successor until modern times. The use of the capital of an Ashokan pillar as the central feature on the seal of the Republic of India is only an appropriate recognition of India's greatest ruler.

The dissolution of the Maurya Empire was complicated by a succession of alien incursions from the northwest; first came Bactrian Greeks in the second century B.C., then Scythians known as Shakas in India, and then the Turkish-speaking Yueh-Chih who had been pushed westward from the Chinese frontier. Some patronized one religion, some another. Some created fairly large, but ephemeral, empires. Politically these empires were no more than loose suzerainties which generally began to dissolve on the death of the able leader who had founded them. The bureaucratic empire of the Maurya type was not easily recreated.

Sometime in the last half of the first or the first half of the second century A.D. the Yueh-Chih under Kanishka created an empire known as the Kushān, which included northwestern India and much of central Asia. This empire and its ruler are important for the patronage and transmission of Mahāyāna Buddhism to China over the major trade routes under Kushān control. The Kushān period is also notable for the promotion of the Gandhara school of Buddhist art which transmitted Greek artistic motifs to China. Paradoxically, a Turkish and not a Greek Indian dynasty carried out this achievement, utilizing some Western-style sculptors attracted to India by the growth of East-West trade.

THE GUPTA EMPIRE

In 320 A.D. another Chandragupta, unrelated to the founder of the Maurya empire, rose to prominence in the former Gangetic center of power and founded the Gupta dynasty, which restored the glory of empire on a lesser scale and the prosperity necessary to carry Indian culture to a new peak of achievement. The Guptas (c 320–480 A.D.) aspired to eliminate other rulers and to establish a centralized government on the Maurya model, but most of the other rulers and their states were too well developed to make this goal an easy task. Except in the Gangetic plain they had to settle for the acceptance of a temporary tributary status on the part of most other rulers. Although the Guptas extended no special patronage to Buddhism and, in fact, favored the brāhmans, Buddhism was flourishing as witnessed in the record of a six-year sojourn in India that was written by the Chinese Buddhist monk, Fa-hsien. The few non-Buddhist references in this work present the picture of a humane society, thanks to the moderating influence of Jainist and Buddhist ethics. All but the members of the lowest strata of society were vegetarians. Adminis-

tration was mild and crime was rare. Fa-hsien was able to travel safely throughout the country without a passport. Hinduism had evolved out of sacrificial Brahmanism, incorporating or adapting much of the ethical and other teachings of the unorthodox philosophies.

After the disintegration of the Gupta Empire, northern India once more gained a brief measure of unity under the brilliant ruler, Harsha (c 606–647), but his regime was even less centralized and more feudal than the Guptas' had been. Again, we are indebted to a Chinese pilgrim, Hsuan Tsang, for a picture of this era. He was more observant of worldly affairs, and his chronicle tells about the ruler as well as the social conditions. He describes in glowing terms Harsha who admitted the alien monk to a place of honor in his court. In fact, in his later years the ruler appears to have come under strong Buddhist influence. But Hsuan Tsang's account indicates that Buddhism was declining in the land of its birth and tantric influences from southern India were infecting both Hinduism and Buddhism with a more emotional and devotional outlook. Travel was no longer safe. The monk was twice robbed and once almost sacrificed to the goddess Durga by river pirates in the heart of the empire.

Although Indian political development had passed its peak, this era from the fourth to the eighth centuries produced the greatest achievements in literature and art, which continued in a less vigorous, more stilted form through the Muslim conquest. Since the authors depended on patronage, their works tended to reflect the high culture of the courts and the wealthy. While their names and works are legion, one figure stands out, the poet and dramatist Kālidāsa, whose role has been appropriately compared to that of Shakespeare in English literature. Like Shakespeare, he appeared early in the era of secular Sanskrit literature, flourishing from 380 to 450 A.D. during the heyday of the Gupta Empire. Although he is acknowledged by Indian and Western critics alike to have been India's greatest poet and greatest dramatist, he, like Shakespeare, is most renowned as a dramatist and *The Recognition of Shakuntalā* is considered his masterpiece. Indian dramatic convention prescribed a happy ending, though the principals went through all sorts of emotion-packed travails before reaching this goal. The stock characters, as in English drama, were hero, heroine, and villain plus a buffoon for comic relief and other character roles to set off the principals. Although the stories frequently dealt with gods and demigods, these figures were treated in a wholly secular fashion with the full range of human desires and weaknesses. Thus, like the murals in the contemporary cave-temples at Ajantā, these plays were packed with realistic delineations of everyday life, further examples of the happy marriage in India of religion and real life. None of the Indian dramatists surpassed Kālidāsa in characterization particularly of the supporting figures, another feature that encourages comparison with Shakespeare. In his famous play, a king, while hunting in a forest, meets, falls in love with, and marries by simple mutual consent Shakuntalā, the illegitimate daughter of a woodland nymph, in the absence of her hermit foster-father. The villain, an evil-tempered hermit, places a curse on her by which her husband will not recognize her until he sees the wedding ring. When her foster-father returns, he sends the now pregnant Shakuntalā to the king, but she has lost the ring and in a moving confrontation the king denies any memory of her. Subsequently the ring is delivered to the king, and he immediately recalls his marriage, but she has been taken away by her mother. In the final act, which takes place several years later, the king, returning from battle, runs into a small boy, and is told that he is Shakuntalā's son. Thus the lovers find each other again. The moving emotions of love and the touching pathos of this drama can only be suggested in this sketch. The play itself should be read. Even in translation the quality of the prose and poetry comes through. It is truly one of the world's literary masterpieces.

INTRODUCTION TO HINDUISM

What is called Hinduism evolved after 500 B.C. out of Brahmanism under the influence of internal criticism and the stimulus provided by the non-Vedic teachings, such as Jainism and Buddhism. As it evolved, the complex and imperfectly understood interplay, adaptation, and exchange of conceptions produced a number of philosophies, religions, and deities united only by the common acceptance of the Vedas as sacred revelation and of the class and caste system as the device supposedly prescribed in the Vedas for the organization and integration of the social hierarchy from the brāhman class downward. The general moral law (*dharma*), which the top brāhman castes were supposed to observe in full, was modified in part according to the conditions of each class and caste so that each one had its own set of rules and regulations. In particular, the ruler was integrated into this system by the obligation to enforce *dharma*, a power and function symbolized by the white umbrella carried over his head. Thus Hinduism encompassed more than religion and philosophy, providing a whole way of life that has demonstrated remarkable flexibility and adaptability during the past 2000 years.

New doctrines and cults have been incorporated and given a place alongside older practices and beliefs by means of the tolerant and, perhaps, condescending doctrine that there are innumerable valid and appropriate levels of truth from primitive animism to the most esoteric philosophies. A multitude of deities are comprehended as specific manifestations of the manifold aspects of the ultimate truth, and each one with its rites is believed to be helpful in guiding men along the path to truth. This comprehensive attitude has supplied a measure of social and cultural unity amid the political, linguistic, racial, and even doctrinal diversity of India. Only Islam and Christianity have resisted integration. While the development of system, order, and classification will be stressed here, it should be recognized that the existence of diversity has been, and still is, very real and has prevented the development of the degree of unity which, for example, China has enjoyed.

In addition to class and caste, the secular and religious life of man was regulated by two fourfold systems of classification which were developed to comprehend all aspects of life. The first, already mentioned, prescribed the four stages (*āshrama*) of life from youth to death and was inspired by the need to regularize and legitimize the ascetic quest for realization of the identity of the inner Self, Ātman, and the universal Soul, Brahman, as reflected in the Upanishads.

The first stage was devoted to the study and memorization of substantial portions of the Vedas under the strict discipline of a *guru* (teacher). This apprenticeship was entered between the ages of eight and twelve, when a boy of the upper three classes was initiated as "twice-born," and it lasted normally until the age of twenty. The student fully subordinated himself to his teacher and faithfully carried out all assignments and accepted without question all knowledge that was communicated to him. To what extent this stage was observed outside the brāhman class is difficult to say. For most Indian youths it probably involved mastering his trade and the rules and regulations of his caste.

In the second stage of life he married, raised a family, and dedicated himself to the promotion of its welfare within the rules of his caste. When this stage was completed, he was then free to turn over family affairs to his sons and retire, with or without his wife, to pursue a life of meditation and asceticism as a hermit in quest of the ultimate truth. How many Indians entered this third stage is impossible to determine, but the desire of sons

to take over their inheritances and the management of family affairs probably propelled more fathers into it than spiritual considerations alone might have induced. The fourth stage involved complete separation from dependence on the family by taking up the life of a wandering beggar as a final renunciation in preparation for death.

This system of the four stages of life regularized religiosity so that it would not interfere with the normal and necessary functions of society. By prescribing a time and place for both secular and religious duties it provided a proper balance and moderation that gave appropriate weight and importance to secular obligations.

Also supporting moderation and complementing the four stages of life was the fourfold classification of the ends of man. First, was the sacred law (*dharma*), covering man's religious, social, and moral obligations. This category included the four stages of life that were thus integrated with the ends of man. Therefore, the sacred law differs according to age as well as class and caste. Indeed, in the broadest sense this law regulates all aspects of human relationships, but in practice three other ends of man became differentiated: *artha* (material gain), *kāma* (pleasure and love), and *moksha* (release from rebirth that was the goal of the last two stages of life). *Artha* and *kāma* will be given special consideration to offset the too common Western misconception that Hindus are wholly otherworldly and unconcerned with this life.

ARTHA: MATERIAL GAIN

In fact, the study of *artha* was principally limited to political science because the material welfare of the people depended on the activity and effectiveness of the government. This point is clearly expounded in the *Arthashāstra (Treatise on Material Gain)*, which was presumably written by Kautilīya, based on his experience as chief minister of the founder of the Maurya Empire.

According to the author, the entire structure and stability of society depend on the rational exercise of political power, that is, "the science of polity." The acquisition, maintenance, and advancement of material gain, the sacred law, and pleasure and love are the responsibility of the ruler. Of these three ends of human life the last two, *dharma* and *kāma*, can only be realized through material gain. Thus the author justifies his concentration on material gain as the fundamental task of the ruler in this treatise on political science.

Like Machiavelli, in *The Prince*, Kautilīya is exclusively concerned with the modes of political behavior that will succeed, given the existing condition of interstate rivalry and conflict. Ethics or morality as such do not enter into the picture.

First, the ruler must be active and full of energy, devoting almost every waking hour to affairs of state. Unless he sets an active example, his officials will be equally indifferent to their responsibilities, and the welfare of his subjects, and thus his own, will consequently suffer. Kautilīya reminds the ruler that his welfare and happiness are rooted in the welfare and happiness of his subjects.

Therefore, the wise ruler will make himself always available to hear the complaints of his subjects and will not permit his bureaucracy to separate him from them. Moreover, the wise ruler will give attention to the customs and religious beliefs of his people and will consult the brāhmans—"Lest these become enraged." In addition, to gain the affection of his people he will personally care for all unfortunates, such as minors, the aged, the sick, the helpless, and women—already a familiar precept of Eastern government. In other words, whatever his personal views, his intelligent self-interest directs him to uphold and patronize the cultural and religious views of his people. Certainly he would do nothing to alienate them because his strength is their strength.

After saying these things, Kautilīya ad-

monishes the king to rule with a firm hand administering impartial, consistent, and severe justice. But this is not enough. A thorough secret service of spies and agents provocateur employing prostitutes and professional assassins must be maintained to uncover and eliminate every dissident element. Moreover, the spies are not to be trusted. They have a vested interest in supporting a measure of subversion to justify their continued employment. Therefore, the ruler needs spies to spy upon the spies. What is being advocated as early as the fourth century B.C. is a thorough police state in which all potential opposition will be ferreted out and liquidated.

Such an internal policy is justified by Kautilīya's assumption that every ruler was intent on conquering his neighbor and, therefore, the wise king will develop his human and economic resources to the maximum degree. The seven basic constituents of the state are listed as the king, the ministers, the country, the forts, the treasury, the army, and the allies. Without a dispassionate, intelligent, and ruthless king the state would be in danger of being overthrown. Without able and loyal ministers, the state would be weak and vulnerable. Without a prosperous country supported by public works the resources of the ruler would be inadequate. Without well-maintained frontier fortifications the most prosperous state would invite invasion. Without a well-stocked treasury neither defensive nor offensive operations could be adequately supported. And, of course, without a strong and well-equipped army an effective foreign policy could not be implemented nor allies retained.

Notice that four of the seven constituents of the state concerned the military support of foreign policy. Survival and expansion in a world of contending states were clearly the chief concerns of Kautilīya's science of politics as shown in his analysis of foreign relations.

An apparently simple and formalistic

theory of circles of states becomes on examination complex and realistic, especially when combined with the six types of foreign policy that he defines. Taking the king's state as the center, the circle of immediately surrounding states are always to be recognized as his natural enemies, regardless of the policies that may be pursued toward any one of them at any particular moment. These adjoining states are the obvious source of any territorial "acquisition." The next circle of states provides the king's natural friends, since each shares at least one mutual enemy, and so forth. This picture of normal interstate relations becomes much more complex when it is realized that each natural enemy or friend is the center of another system of circles. Obviously one natural enemy who also has a frontier with one of your natural enemies may be utilized as a temporary ally. Moreover, successful conquests will alter one's system of circles, converting natural friends into natural enemies and vice versa. Finally, the relative strength or weakness of enemies and friends must be taken into consideration in the manipulation of foreign policy. When the neighboring ruler, the natural enemy, is strong, he should only be "harassed or weakened." When he is in trouble, he should be attacked. When he is weak and without strong allies, he should be liquidated and his territories annexed.

The six modes of policy in dealing with an enemy are peace, war, marking time, attack, seeking refuge, and duplicity. When you are weaker, make peace, if possible, and if not, seek refuge. When you are stronger, make war. When you are evenly matched, mark time. When you possess overwhelming strength, make an all-out attack. When success depends on the aid of an ally, utilize duplicity.

Such a thoroughgoing materialistic and realistic organization and operation of a state probably never was implemented in practice. The Seleucid envoy, Megasthenes', description of the regime of Chandragupta Maurya, whom Kautilīya reputedly served, approaches most closely this system of govern-

ment. The power of Indian rulers, however, was too circumscribed by custom, taboos, and ethical imperatives. Ministers tended to become hereditary, supported by grants of estates. The liquidation of ruling and noble families and states was frowned on by Indian ethics. The power of rulers was checked by brāhman prestige. Although minor divinity was attached to rulers, divinity in India was cheap. Every brāhman was semidivine. Rulers were recognized and justified mainly as protectors and maintainers of the status quo against anarchy in this age that all philosophies agreed in describing as one of decay and decline.

KĀMA: PLEASURE AND LOVE

Although the word *kāma* embraces every aspect of human pleasure, in India, as elsewhere, its sexual connotation received the greatest attention. In its connection with the second stage of life, which many literary references deemed the most important of the four stages, *kāma* as love was invested with more than secular significance; it was a sacred duty essential to the perpetuation of the wheel of life. Hindu literature and art are filled with sexual motifs and often with outright eroticism. The Tantrism of the Middle Ages which made of sexual union a sort of sacrament, illustrating the unity that transcends duality, promoted an exaggeration of the religious obligation attached to producing a family.

The *Kāmasutra* (Aphorisms on Love) compiled in the early centuries of the Christian Era, is the best known of a number of works that provide detailed guidance for cultured members of the upper classes, not only on human love but also on the social graces and the esthetic appreciation of art forms. In dealing with love, it reveals exceptional sensitivity for the feelings of the female partner, in part, inspired by the fact that marriages were arranged by the families and husband and wife were frequently complete strangers and, in part, reflecting the refined level of taste and culture achieved by Indian civilization. In other words, lovemaking had been developed into a high art whose end was the achievement of maximum pleasure for both parties. The means to this end called for the mastery of complex skills. For example, sixteen types of kisses were delineated. Instructions to the groom on how to approach his bride illustrate both the concern for the bride and also the lack of premarital familiarity in the customary Indian marriage.

During the first three days the newlyweds should abstain from intercourse and undue familiarity. The next seven days should be devoted to getting to know each other by bathing, dressing, and dining together under the pleasantest conditions and spending the rest of their time visiting relatives and friends. By the evening of the tenth day the couple should know each other well enough for the husband to approach his wife with gentle words to give her confidence. In any case he should restrain himself until he has gained her confidence. If he should force himself on his wife, she might end up abhorring intercourse and men in general or turning in hatred from him to another man.

Indian custom classified all women as minors under the protection of some man. Wives were instructed to devote themselves entirely to their homes and husbands whom, regardless of any shortcomings, they should worship as gods. On the other hand, the husband is admonished to honor and treasure his wife as his better half from whom all the benefits of companionship, comfort, encouragement, love, and happiness flow.

Moreover, as in other cultures, women were also viewed as creatures of pleasure with insatiable sexual appetites who needed not only constant attention but also constant surveillance.

> The fire has never too many logs,
> the ocean never too many rivers,
> death never too many living souls,
> and fair-eyed woman never too many men.
> (Basham, *The Wonder That Was India*, p. 182)

Although the treatises on *kāma* devoted the most space to the relationship of man and woman, the esthetic appreciation of art, drama, and music also received substantial attention. While the themes of the various art forms were almost wholly drawn from religion, it has been noted that religion and life were very closely integrated in Indian thought. Sensual pleasure was not sharply separated from religious feeling, as has frequently been the case in the West with consequent inhibitions. To the Indian mind there was nothing incongruous in the voluptuous proportions of the female deities enshrined in the temples. In short, nature in all its manifestations was deemed a divine work of art, and an artist sought to distill in his work the divine essence in the natural event or story by which he delivered his religious message. In esthetic appreciation of a work of art, then, the object, character, or story were considered only incidental. What was most important was through sensitivity and emotion to appreciate the aspect of ultimate truth the artist meant to convey. Thus esthetic appreciation involved spiritual appreciation, at least for the cultured individual with an "attuned heart" and sense of taste. Thus Indian art forms were able to accomplish a happy marriage of religiosity and naturalism because the Indian outlook saw in them no contradiction, but rather an essential unity.

MOKSHA: RELEASE

With the acceptance of the doctrine of rebirth the fourth end of man, the quest for release (*moksha*) from the wheel of life, became and has remained a fundamental facet of Indian religious and philosophical thought, both heterodox and orthodox. This quest for permanence amid the impermanence of existence, for ultimate truth amid the delusions of this world, has already been observed in the Upanishads, Jainism, and Buddhism. In the development of Hinduism it has produced answers in the form of religion, theistic philosophy, and nontheistic philosophy—the path of religion emphasizing devotion and the path of philosophy emphasizing knowledge.

The oldest Hindu philosophy, Sānkhya, was nontheistic and, perhaps, shared the same non-Aryan background that produced Jainism. In any case, their basic doctrines were similar. Like Jainism, Sānkhya envisioned the universe as a duality composed of "matter" (*prakriti*), including intelligence and self-consciousness as well as more material elements, and as an infinite number of inactive "souls" (*purusha*). All change, all experience, stems from "matter" with which the "souls" become erroneously involved. Yet neither one is dependent on the other. Without "souls," "matter" can and does produce everything. Release is obtained by the realization that the inactive "soul" has nothing to do with matter.

Yoga in its broad meaning of "spiritual discipline" is well-known and played a part as preparatory exercises in all Indian religions and philosophies. But originally it was the name of a school closely related to Sānkhya, the main difference being the recognition of a god who served as an example by never having become enmeshed with "matter." In other words, like the Buddhist Noble Eightfold Path, Yoga provided a means of achieving the Sankhya goal of realization of the eternal and inactive "soul." The prescribed stages included selfless moral conduct as well as the familiar posture, breath control, and intense concentration and meditation which led to temporary dissolution of the personality of the yogi. Subsequently, variant Yogic techniques were devised, some of which yield results yet to be explained by modern science.

BHAGAVAD GĪTĀ

The basic renunciation of the value and reality of this life involved in these early doctrines, both orthodox and unorthodox, was in time overcome by the most revered work, after the Vedas, of Hinduism, the Bhagavad Gītā (Song of the Lord), which was in-

corporated in the world's longest epic poem, the *Mahābhārata*. The setting for the doctrine, which reconciled action with knowledge and devotion and *dharma* with *moksha*, was the period before a great battle when the warrior Arjuna was overcome with remorse at the prospect of slaying his relatives in the ranks of the foe. His charioteer, Krishna, the god incarnate, then explained at great length why Arjuna must do his duty as a warrior.

The warrior who believes he is a killer and that his victim has been killed is still in ignorance of the real truth. He is confusing the material body, which is born, grows, changes, and dies, with the eternal soul, which is unborn, unchangeable, and indestructible. For everything that is born death is certain and for everything that dies rebirth is certain. Therefore, the warrior should not grieve about his part in what is inevitable. Indeed, the *dharma* of the warrior commands him to fight and to kill, and if he should fail to do his duty, he would incur sin.

Having explained the noncontradictory nature of the demands of *dharma*, Krishna then went on to explain that in this life action of some sort cannot be avoided. What is important is not the action but one's attitude toward it. The proper attitude is one of selfless detachment from the fruit of the action.

To live means to act, even if this action should be limited to the normal needs of the body. But beyond such simple actions, essential to individual survival, a man whose mind controls his body is obligated to fulfill his prescribed role in society, particularly if he desires to achieve his spiritual goal. To give himself up to mere sensate pleasures and to ignore his tasks in rotating the wheel of life would be to lead a sinful life and, indeed, to live in vain. Therefore, by doing his prescribed tasks without attachment to the fruits of his actions, a man will attain his highest goal. Moreover, as a leader, he is under the additional obligation to set an example of superior conduct because, as he leads, people will follow. Krishna pointed out that even he as a god must continue to act without weariness or else "these worlds would fall into ruin," and then he would be a creator of chaos, a destroyer and not a creator.

The Gītā was a synthesis and reinterpretation of current doctrines that were carried out by brāhmans over a long period of time. Therefore, it is not surprising to find incorporated and integrated into its teachings the cosmological doctrine of Sānkhya, the class system promoted by the brāhman class, and both the nontheistic philosophy of knowledge and the devotional theism that was gaining strength in the upper classes. More over, Indian pantheism, whereby every god is but a manifestation of the Supreme One and worship of the least of them is worship of Him, is set forth. In fact it is asserted that all things in this world are pervaded by Him in His nonmanifest form. "All beings abide in Me, but I do not abide in them." Furthermore, even the lowliest, women and *shūdras*, who are not twice-born, are eligible for salvation through worship of Him, no matter how indirectly or improperly performed. This doctrine countered Jainist and Buddhist criticism of the exclusiveness of Vedic religion. Indeed, one of the reasons for the high regard in which this work is held is that every school can find in it support for its position.

LATER HINDU PHILOSOPHIES

Although Indians, with their penchant for classification, distinguished at an early date six orthodox schools of thought, interpreters were constantly modifying their doctrines under the pressure of other philosophies and the growing popularity of devotional theism. Therefore, any description of the doctrine of a particular school can be wholly valid only for a particular time and a particular expounder of that doctrine. Only one school because of its continued prominence requires description.

The Vedānta (End of the Vedas) school, in the hands of the brilliant theoretician, Shankara (c 788–820 A.D.), became the premier school of philosophy—a position it still

retains today. This school drew its major inspiration from the Upanishads. As interpreted by the South Indian brāhman Shankara, the only reality, the ultimate truth was Brahman, the impersonal Universal Soul of the Upanishads with which the individual soul, ātman, was identical. Everything else—the world, the universe, the gods—was illusion (*māyā*) and unreal. This is strict monism and Shankara's followers distinguished themselves from other Vedantists by the label *advaita* (allowing no second).

In developing this monistic philosophy, however, Shankara had to reconcile inconsistencies with it in the Upanishads as well as in the Vedas. To do this he utilized the old Indian device of differing levels of truth. On a lower level of relative truth the Lord Brahmā created the phenomenal universe which evolved in a manner similar to that taught by the Sānkhya school. Indeed, Shankara himself worshipped Shiva, the supreme god from whom Brahmā arose. But the ultimate and absolute truth transcended deity and form. As his opponents were quick to point out, his conception of Brāhman did not differ in essence from the ultimate truth of Buddhism, and he was accused of being a crypto-Buddhist.

Regardless of criticism, however, his philosophy has proved most convincing to Hindu intellectuals. Today most educated Hindus are adherents of Advaita Vedānta. In Vedānta, release can be obtained only by introspective meditation that leads to the intuitive realization of the oneness of the self and the universal soul, but religious devotion can help in preparing and purifying the mind for the attainment of liberation; and in a condescending fashion Vedāntists concede that any worshipper has, at least, put his foot on the bottom rung of the ladder to ultimate truth.

THEISM

The frequency of references to the worship of deities has probably already suggested the growing influence on the educated classes of the way of devotion (*bhakti*) to salvation as distinguished from the way of knowledge which was emphasized by the various schools of philosophy. As has been observed, even the philosophers were not immune to theism and had to find a place for it in their teachings. Although there is little literary evidence, it is reasonable to assume that the worship of deities and impressive aspects of nature prevailed among the lower classes from the beginning and gradually penetrated the upper classes, who refined it and gave it a philosophical foundation. By the time that literary works—first, the two epic poems, the *Mahābhārata* and the *Rāmāyana*, and then the many Puranas that describe the missions performed in the manifold incarnations of the gods—furnish substantial evidence, worship had replaced sacrifice, and various levels of worship had already evolved.

Perhaps most common was simple adoration and service of the icon in which the deity was believed to dwell. The icon was fed, bathed, given flowers, and even put to bed with his wife. This type of devotion may be said to be characterized by respect and awe. Already, however, for the more advanced worshiper the icon was merely a symbol to remind him of the godhead who loved men and could be loved in return. Of course, it followed that the devotee demonstrated his love of god by love of his fellowmen who were also subjects of god's love. This personalized love between man and immanent deity received its earliest and most fervent expression in the Dravidian south, whence it spread to the north.

Southern India had only been brought within the orbit of Aryan civilization by the Maurya conquests and, undoubtedly, contributed its own religious attitudes and practices as well as new deities to the development of the Vedic religion. Indeed, as elsewhere, these darker-hued southerners who were the last to be brought into the orbit of Indo-Aryan civilization contributed the bulk of new creative vigor after the opening of the Christian Era, drawing inspiration from their own distinctive heritage. In addition, under the stimulus of trade with the Roman West their merchant adventurers carried the South Indian version of Indo-Aryan civilization overseas to Southeast Asia where, in time, several impressive maritime empires based on trade were developed, as witnessed by the substantial monumental remains.

By the Christian Era, if not earlier, two supreme gods, Vishnu and Shiva, whose incarnations accounted for a number of other gods, had become generally recognized by the educated class. Vishnu is visualized as wholly benevolent. He has incarnated himself in one form or another on many occasions because of his concern for the welfare of the world. The character of Shiva is less clearcut. He is fierce as well as paternal and will in time destroy all things. In this latter aspect he is frequently depicted engaged in the "dance of death" which will end a cosmic cycle. He also incorporates the pre-Aryan fertility cult and is most frequently worshiped in the form of phallic symbols.

Hinduism is fundamentally tolerant. The followers of Vishnu or Shiva accept the reality of the other, only relegating each one to a secondary position as an emanation of their god. This comprehensive tolerance has contributed to a large amount of assimilation in the course of Indian religious history. Indeed, there has been no serious antagonism to those of alien religions which have resisted assimilation, such as Christians, Zoroastrians called Pārsees, Jews, and even Muslims.

TANTRISM

A final, ecstatic state in the development of Hinduism in the post-Gupta era also originated in the south and is known as Tantrism after their scriptures, called Tantras. It was characterized by the worship of the female counterparts of the gods, called *shakti*, who were believed to represent the active energy of their passive partners. Although mixed in practice with the quest for magical power by means of symbols and formulas, the underlying doctrine was that release was attainable in this life for the initiate through the transcendental realization of the essential identity of bondage and release. For the tantrist the two terms were meaningless; a distinction without any difference. While accepting the monism of Advaita Vedānta, Tantrism shifted its emphasis to the world as the dynamic manifestation of the divine truth that was to be approached through love of the goddess (*shakti*) as the dynamic aspect of divinity.

Not only were bondage and release subsumed in the monism of the Tantrist, but when engaged in worship, all ritual restrictions and taboos were eliminated as also meaningless. Without restraint, therefore, the participant in tantrist rituals experienced all aspects of this world normally prohibited, such as alcohol, meat, fish, and sexual intercourse. Also, all distinctions of class and caste were set aside for the initiates. Such overstepping of the bounds of the moral and social order prescribed by *dharma* was permitted only during Tantric worship and only after a long period of spiritual training and under the guidance of a spiritual teacher (*guru*). *Dharma* still applied when the celebrants returned to the world of ego-consciousness and left the world of purity and perfection.

Naturally, these rites have been decried as decadent by critics, especially Westerners. But they represent a world-affirming outlook in contrast with the world-negating outlook of ascetic renunciation. Ascetic renunciation had been brought into balance with the demands of society by the four stages of life. Now a more positive world-affirming viewpoint was developed in the Tantric doctrine that enlightenment was to be gained by the full appreciation, and not by the rejection or setting aside, of nature. In this way, every natural act is only a part of

the dynamic aspect of divinity and becomes not a mere animal act but a religious rite.

The emphasis on the worship of the consort of the god as his dynamic aspect revived the ancient conception of the Mother Goddess. Each female deity was considered a manifestation of the Mother Goddess and responsible for the functioning of this world regardless of the different names, such as Devī, Durgā, Kali, and the like. Even a worshipful approach to one's wife as a symbol of *shakti* was encouraged. The emphasis on sexual intercourse symbolized the identity, the oneness in duality, of god and goddess.

CLASS, CASTE AND FAMILY

Enough has been said about the four classes—brāhman, kshātriya, vaishya, and shūdra—to demonstrate their integral relationship with religion, regardless of how they may have originated. Caste may have developed later and should not be confused with class. The four classes have remained essentially unchanged, while castes are constantly being formed and dissolved on many bases including occupation, religion, race, and locality. In the post-Gupta era castes multiplied and became more prominent, a tendency that accelerated under alien rule.

Every class, including the brāhman, is subdivided into castes that total in the thousands, but caste is far more influential and important among the lower than the higher classes. This difference in emphasis suggests the probable origin of castes as protective groupings of less secure elements in a complex society. Castes are ruled by committees of elders, normally hereditary, who can enforce caste rules by ostracism. In other words, castes are small-scale units of self-government that protect the interests of the group against outside forces and absorb the loyalty directed in Western countries toward the state. Under alien rulers they were vital factors in preserving Hindu culture and its diversity.

As in other early agricultural civilizations, the basic unit of Indian society was, and still is, the extended family which jointly owns the immovable property under the administration and control of the father. The father's authority, though limited by law and custom, was reinforced by the ancestral rites over which he presided. From youth the individual was trained to subordinate himself and to find his security and rewards in the family.

Hemmed in by class, caste, and family restrictions upheld by religious sanctions and taboos, the ordinary Indian led a closely circumscribed life, but he also enjoyed the security that membership in these groupings provided. In turn, his industriousness supported the exceptionally luxurious and sophisticated life of his rulers.

In this chapter the major factors in the complex evolution of Indo-Aryan civilization have been briefly surveyed to convey some understanding of its uniqueness without losing the Western student in too detailed an elaboration of unfamiliar Indian conceptions and attitudes. It should be recognized that this oversimplification cannot do justice to the depth and diversity of Indian thought and creative development. Moreover some subjects, such as mathematics and science, have been omitted because their contribution, transmitted to and developed by other civilizations, does not play a significant role in modern India.

The overriding feature of Indo-Aryan civilization is the failure to gain the respect for political authority achieved in other civilizations by religious or cultural sanctions. This failure cannot be attributed to political ineptitude (witness the *Arthashāstra*), or racial and cultural diversity (although these factors are more pronounced in Indo-Aryan than in other civilizations), or obviously to any lack of religious development. Indeed, it was the subordination of political authority to religious authority, as represented by the Aryan brāhman class and its heirs, and the subordination of temporal affairs to spiritual and transcendental considerations that proved to be the major stumbling block to the establishment of enduring political unity on a large scale. The caste system also isolated the rulers from their subjects. Although the brāhmans with their near monopoly of literacy and scholarship played a large role in government from the beginning, they maintained their separateness as a class that was dedicated primarily to religious affairs. Rulers were rarely brāhmans. They met successfully the challenges of Jainists, Buddhists, and other rebels and by comprehensive adaptability absorbed the major elements of these heresies in that tolerant and diverse religious amalgam known as Hinduism. To meet the challenges of alien conquests and internal anarchy, a multitude of ever-changing castes evolved, compartmentalizing the Indian people into essentially self-governing units that provided group protection and regularized external relations with other castes and with the political powers existing at any particular time. This fundamentally defensive technique of organizing human relations has proved so successful and durable that it presents a major problem to the assertion and maintenance of the political unity of India today. In a subsequent chapter we shall examine the impact of the Muslim and British conquests on Indo-Aryan civilization.

SIGNIFICANT DATES

c.	563– 483 B.C.	Siddhārtha Gautama, the Buddha
c.	540– 468 B.C.	Mahāvīra, founder of Jainism
	327– 325 B.C.	Invasion of Alexander the Great
c.	322– 183 B.C.	Maurya Empire
c.	269– 232 B.C.	Ashoka, patron of Buddhism
c.	320– 480 A.D.	Gupta Empire

606– 647 A.D.	Harsha
788– 820 A.D.	Shankara, founder of Advaita Vedānta sect
712 A.D.	Muslim conquest of Sind
999–1026 A.D.	Raids of Mahmūd of Ghaznī
1192 A.D.	Muslim conquest of northern India

SELECTED READINGS

See Chapter Three for general accounts.

Auboyer, Jeannine, *Daily Life in Ancient India*. New York: Macmillan, 1965.

*Brown, D. Mackenzie, *White Umbrella: Indian Political Thought from Manu to Gandhi*. Berkeley: University of California Press, 1969.

Brown, W. Norman, *Man in the Universe*. Berkeley, University of California Press, 1970.

*Conze, Edward, *Buddhism: Its Essence and Development*. New York: Harper, 1959.

*————, *Buddhist Texts through the Ages*. New York: Harper, 1964.

*————, *Buddhist Thought in India*. Ann Arbor: University of Michigan Press, 1967.

Derrett, John D. M., *Religion, Law and the State in India*. New York: Free Press, 1968.

Drekmeier, Charles, *Kingship and Community in Early India*. Stanford: Stanford University Press, 1962.

*Egerton, Frank, *Bhagavad Gita*. New York: Harper and Row, 1968.

Gokhale, B. G., *Ashoka Maurya*. New York: Twayne, 1966.

*Humphreys, Christmas, *Buddhism*. Baltimore: Penguin Books, 1962.

*Hutton, J. H., *Caste in India*. 3rd ed.; London: Oxford University Press, 1961.

Kautilya, *Arthasastra*. 5th ed.; Mysore: Sri Raghuveer, 1956.

*McNeill, William H., and Sedlar, Jean W., eds., *Classical India*. London: Oxford University Press, 1969.

*Nikhilananda, Swami, *The Upanishads*. New York: Harper and Row, 1968.

*Prabhavananda, Swami, *The Spiritual Heritage of India*. New York: Doubleday, 1964.

*Radhakrishnan, Sarvepalli, *The Hindu View of Life*. New York: Macmillan, 1939.

*————, *Principal Upanishads*. New York: Humanities Press, 1953.

*Rahula, Walpola, *What the Buddha Taught*. New York: Grove Press, 1962.

*Renou, Louis, *Hinduism*. New York: Washington Square Press, 1961.

*————, *Religions of Ancient India*. New York: Schocken Books, 1968.

*Rowland, Benjamin, *The Art and Architecture of India*. Baltimore: Penguin Books, 1970.

*Sen, K. M., *Hinduism*. Baltimore: Penguin Books, 1962.

Spellman, John W., *Political Theory of Ancient India*. Oxford: Clarendon Press, 1964.

*Suzuki, Daisetz T., *On Indian Mahayana Buddhism.* New York: Harper & Row, 1969.
*Vatsayana, *Kama Sutra.* New York: Dutton, 1962.
*Weber, Max, *Religion of India.* New York: Free Press, 1958.
Zaehner, Robert C., *The Bhagavad-Gita with a Commentary based on Original Sources.* London: Oxford University Press, 1969.
*———, *Hinduism.* London: Oxford university Press, 1966.

CHAPTER SEVEN

DIFFUSION IN SOUTHEAST ASIA

Southeast Asia is a conveniently comprehensive label for the geographically, ethnically, culturally, and politically complex and diverse buffer region that, as a southeastward extension of the Tibetan massif, separates the Indian and Chinese centers of civilization. Indeed, since the early centuries of the Christian Era, difficult and hazardous land and sea routes have permitted trade between the major, mature civilizations and have fostered the emergence of civilizations and empires in this region, dependent as much on the control of trade routes as on intensive rice agriculture to support substantial concentrations of population in favored areas. In addition, various parts of Southeast Asia have been the chief sources of spices and other tropical products desired by the entire world, not just by the neighboring civilizations. Thus trade with and via this region has been significant for nearly 2000 years.

Our consideration of this area has been reserved until this time for several reasons. Although in prehistoric times it may have made important contributions to the development of its great neighbors, such as rice cultivation and the East Asian variety of pig, most of its historically important peoples have migrated southward into the region from eastern Tibet and southern China and most of its development has been stimulated by external influences. Moreover, although distinctive civilizations in this area have demonstrated creative talent, they have been secondary in nature, representing varying blends of alien, especially Indian, cultures and indigenous beliefs and customs and have exercised no radiating influence outside the area. In short, the region has been an absorber and not a dispenser of cultural influences. Finally, none of these "twilight" civilizations has been able to unite the diverse peoples

and cultures of the area into a single whole. Diversity, and not unity, has characterized the peoples and cultures subsumed under the deceptively singular title of Southeast Asia.

Even under the pressure of today's worldwide power politics Southeast Asia, defined as the non-Western region separating China from India, is divided into nine independent states plus two diminutive Western controlled enclaves, the oil-rich sultanate of Brunei and Portuguese Timor. The independent peninsular states consist of Burma, Thailand, Laos, North Vietnam, South Vietnam, Cambodia, and the hybrid state of Malaysia, including the southern Malay Peninsula and former British territories in northern Borneo; the wholly insular states are the Philippines and Indonesia. Of the total population of 285 million, 125 million live in the scattered islands of Indonesia with its majority concentrated in the central island of Java.

Geographically, the mainland features are for the most part mountain ranges that extend southward from eastern Tibet and are a severe handicap to east-west communication by land. Between the mountain ranges tropical valleys, generally subject to excessive rainfall during the monsoon season, cradle mighty rivers that in their lower reaches and deltas possess silt-laden areas which support concentrated populations by rice farming. Down these valleys wave after wave of peoples from Tibet and China have pushed many of the previous inhabitants further southward, mixed with others, and have isolated a wondrous variety of primitive peoples in mountainous or other undesirable pockets. The major islands of Indonesia are connected to the mainland by a continental shelf that provides a comparatively shallow and sheltered sea suitable for easy communication by sea. A volcanic mountain arc from

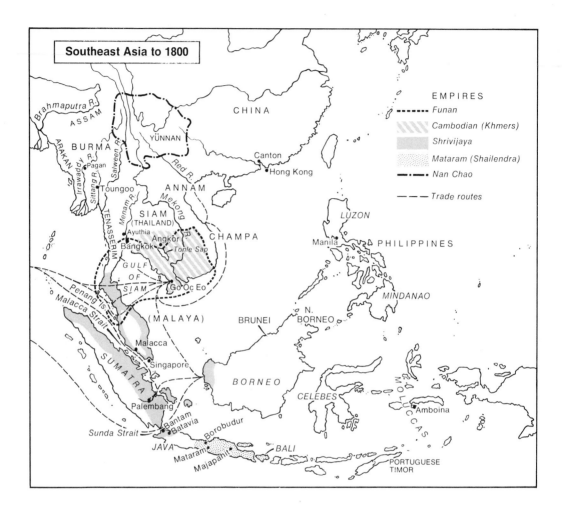

Southeast Asia to 1800

EMPIRES
- - - - - - - *Funan*
///// *Cambodian (Khmers)*
░░░░ *Shrivijaya*
∴∴∴∴ *Mataram (Shailendra)*
—·—· *Nan Chao*
— — — *Trade routes*

Burma to the Philippines and northward supplies the backbone of the main islands of Indonesia and the geological, though not the territorial, southern limit of Southeast Asia.

Most of Southeast Asia receives excessive rainfall during one period of the year or another according to the monsoon pattern, and some places such as Singapore have almost daily rains the year around. As previously mentioned, however, although an adequate and reliable water supply is essential to the development of civilizations based on intensive agriculture, there can be too much of a good thing, if it cannot be controlled. This is the case in most of Southeast Asia. In upland areas torrential rains wash away potentially rich volcanic ash and top-

soil, causing extensive erosion and clogging the valleys into great sponges. In the tropical lowlands where soil temperatures regularly exceed 75°, the stone and mineral content of the soil is broken down and along with organic materials is filtered to lower levels by the rains, leaving a porous surface of heavy clay and iron called laterite. Although this soil makes excellent sun-dried building bricks, it is notoriously deficient in plant nutrients. On the other hand, where the soil temperatures are normally below 75°, heavy rains dissolve even the clay and iron, leaching the soil surface of needed iron oxides. As a result, most of the rain-drenched soils of Southeast Asia are unsuited for intensive food production and are suited only for deep-rooted trees and plantation crops which can tap the water tables far below the surface. The notable exceptions are semiarid regions such as central and eastern Java where cooperative endeavor in the construction of terraces and canals has preserved the topsoil and the floodplains and deltas of major rivers where the annual inundation deposits heavy layers of rich silt. Even in the latter regions large-scale cooperative labor in the construction of dikes and canals to control the flood waters and provide drainage is essential. With the exception of purely commercial powers, which could pay for food imports and mercenaries out of trading revenues and levies, all empires and civilizations grew up in these areas where large populations could be supported and the necessity of social control encouraged political development and discipline. Most important were the island of Java, the basin and delta of the Irrawaddy River in Burma, the Menam drainage area of lower Siam, the Red River delta of northern Vietnam (Annam), and the Mekong River delta with its unusual Tonle Sap basin which, by reverse flow during the Mekong flood, is raised 40 feet providing the agricultural basis, with the aid of complex irrigation facilities, of present-day Cambodia.

While intensive cultivation of rice in the fields of these areas of water management furnished the foundation of concentrated population and political development characteristic of civilization, trade with its cultural contacts provided the incentive for expansion and the fuller delineation of the various aspects of civilization. Under the stimulus of the demands of the Roman Empire, Indian merchants early in the Christian Era developed trading contacts with Southeast Asia, but the problem of discovering relatively swift and safe routes was not easily solved. The natural all-water route via the Malacca Strait between lower Malaya and Sumatra presented many difficulties for sailing ships. The passage from Ceylon to the Malay Peninsula with the summer monsoon was easy enough, but the negotiation of the strait with its erratic and unreliable winds was a major challenge. There were no safe ports and the narrow waters were full of island hideouts that were infested with pirates who were ready to pounce on the becalmed merchantman. As a result, several portage routes across the Malay Peninsula south of the narrow isthmus of Kra prospered. Contests for the control of these portages have been a recurrent feature of Southeast Asian history. An alternative route for the daring navigator passed south of Sumatra to the Sunda Strait where several ports of call in western Java and western Borneo developed to accommodate ships waiting for favorable winds. This was a long voyage of about 90 days at sea and required precise timing to catch favorable winds because there were no safe ports on the long southern coast of Sumatra. Few captains and fewer passengers looked forward to such a long ordeal at sea.

From the later first to the early fourth century, Chinese merchants developed an extremely difficult land route from Yünnan in the southwest across the mountains and gorges of the upper Mekong and Salween rivers and thence down the Irrawaddy into Burma, but most Chinese traders preferred the longer but less difficult overland route through Central Asia. Not until Sung times (the late tenth century) did the Chinese become prominent in the seaborne commerce of Southeast Asia, preferring to let Southeast Asian ships carry goods to and from the ports of Annam (North Vietnam) in the Red River delta, which was an integral part of China from its conquest by Han Wu Ti in 111 B.C. to the collapse of the T'ang dynasty in the tenth century. Alien trading communities here, and later at Canton, were closely controlled by Chinese officials and held jointly responsible for their actions, just as European merchants were to be when they were admitted to trade with China. As a result of Chinese reluctance to trade directly with Southeast Asian markets, except as passengers in foreign ships, the field for the first half of the Christian Era was left open to the daring Indian merchants for the propagation of Indian culture and influence throughout the rest of Southeast Asia.

Several reasons have been advanced to explain Chinese backwardness in overseas endeavor, including the less seaworthy character of Chinese junks and poorer navigational skills until the widespread use of the Chinese-invented compass in the tenth century. Other reasons given point out the governmental neglect of the pirate-infested sea frontier in favor of the more menacing land frontier and the belief that Southeast Asia was, in any case, beyond the pale of Chinese civilization and need only dispatch tribute missions in acknowledgement of Chinese superiority and suzerainty. In addition, the lack of official control by Indian mercantile kingdoms over merchants has been contrasted with the close control of Chinese officials over the despised merchant class. Actually, Chinese officials could profit as much, if not more, from their absolute authority over alien traders than from the measure of justice they would have been compelled to extend to Chinese merchants, while the Court benefited directly from the tributary missions that were thinly disguised trading operations. Under the internationally minded T'ang dynasty (618–907 A.D.) more Chinese ships engaged in Southeast Asian trade, but not until the accession of the commercially minded Sung dynasty (960–1279 A.D.) did they become a predominant factor. Finally, the minimal radiation of Chinese culture can also be partially explained by Confucianism's absence of missionary zeal in comparison with Buddhism and even Hinduism. Non-Chinese were left free to adopt Chinese civilization or not, as they saw fit. Generally, China, self-confident in its superiority, did not engage in the aggressive imperialism with which we are familiar.

Only the major civilizations and commercial empires can be briefly surveyed in this account. The lesser civilizations and states that rose and fell must be ignored. An-nam can be passed off with the observation that it was heavily sinicized during the millennium of Chinese rule (111 B.C.–939 A.D.). Its southern neighbor and foe, the Indianized state of Champa, occupying the coastal region between Annam and the Mekong delta, profited from organized attacks on the merchant ships passing off its coast, but was eventually extinguished by the expansion of its more civilized neighbors.

FUNAN

The first major civilization and commercial empire, known as Funan by the Chinese, was the creation, beginning in the later second century, of a predominantly Malayan people who, like their Khmer successors, developed the Tonle Sap and Mekong delta region as an agricultural base to feed a large, disciplined population. The rise of Funan to commercial predominance was based on the development of the strategic port of Go Oc Eo in the southern part of the delta, about 120 miles downstream from the capital, where merchant ships could assemble and refit before making the dangerous northward passage to China or the westward passage across the Gulf of Siam. During the third century, military expeditions reduced to vassalage the states around the Gulf of Siam which included all those that controlled the portage routes across the Malay Peninsula. Thus Funan at its height controlled all seaborne trade between India and China, and its ships dominated the Gulf of Siam. Even Indian ships using the Malacca and Sunda straits, if they wanted Chinese goods, had to stop at Funan's port, which became the commercial entrepot of Southeast Asia.

The report of a Chinese mission in the mid-third century confirms the heavily Indianized character of Funanese civilization. Funan means "king of the mountain," a reference to the Indian conception of Mount Meru as the cosmological center of the universe. Frequently, subsequent Southeast Asian rulers employed brāhman cosmologists to locate the center of the universe, identified as a symbolic mountain, to give magical and divine support to their political authority. The Khmer word for mountain, *Phnom*, is still part of the name of the Cambodian capital city. The Funanese foundation legend, which describes the marriage of a brāhman conqueror to a local queen, daughter of the nine-headed Naga cobra, god of the soil and the waters, is obviously derived from a similar south Indian legend and reflects the predominance of south Indian merchants in the portage trade. The cult of the Naga snake along with the conception of descent from his daughters was prominent in the Khmer and Thai successors of Funan, as well as in other Southeast Asian states, because it supplied divine sanction for royal ownership of the land, blended well with indigenous fertility cults, and fitted the general genealogical preference for matrilineal descent. On the other hand, the use of Sanskrit writing and the patronage of Buddhism probably reflect the influence of the conquered Mons of lower Siam, the pioneers of cultural development in peninsular southeast Asia outside Annam. The Chinese report indicates a sharp social stratification, that was partially based on racial differences. The educated elite were Malayans, while the people were described as ugly and black with frizzy hair, suggesting Negrito and Melanesian types. Bricks covered with lime plaster were used in the construction of governmental buildings and the wall around the capital. The major crops were rice, cotton, and sugar cane, and the major sports were cock and pig fighting.

In the later fourth and fifth centuries, Funan reached its peak of power and Indianization. One ruler, presumably from one of the portage states, introduced the fertility cult of the Shiva linga to reinforce the divine sanction for his rule and associated it eclectically with Mahāyāna Buddhist worship. This south Indian Hindu cult also proved popular in later Southeast Asian states because it blended well with the native fertility cults. Gupta influence is also apparent in re-

ligious images and a minor interest in the Vishnu cult. Other Hindu practices in evidence were the prohibition of remarriage, throwing the ashes of the dead in expensive containers into the waters, and royal processions in which the ruler rode on an elephant under a white umbrella symbolizing his authority as guardian and implementer of the cosmic law.

After 550 A.D., under heavy Khmer attacks accompanied by internal dissidence, the empire rapidly disintegrated, leaving a host of successor states. But Funan had developed the social, economic, and political techniques and had set the cultural pattern that the succeeding Khmer civilization would emulate and spread after several centuries of weakness and near chaos.

SHRIVIJAYA AND SHAILENDRA

Coincident with the collapse of the Funanese Empire and the decline of its maritime enterprise were the rise of the commercial empire of Shrivijaya from its port capital on the Palembang River in southeastern Sumatra and the rise of the wealthy and culturally creative Shailendra dynasty of the agricultural state of Mataram in the interior of central Java, both of which became for a long time important Buddhist centers. One factor that stimulated the development of these two states was an increased interest in fostering direct trade, exhibited by the emergence of strong states at both ends of the trading arc. In the Middle East, first, the Sassanid Empire of Persia in its last century thrust its authority southward, gaining control over south Arabia, and its merchants with a stranglehold on trade with eastern Asia were no longer content to limit themselves to trading through Indian middlemen; and then the Muslim conquests opened up even larger markets for Persian and Arab merchants. At the other end of the arc, the internationally minded T'ang emperors of a reunited China also encouraged more direct trade both by land and by sea. Chinese junks appeared in numbers in all significant Southeast Asian ports, although few seem to have ventured beyond Sumatra. Persian and Arab merchants with improved ships and navigational knowledge proved more enterprising, trading directly with Chinese ports in growing numbers, once Shrivijaya could assure a reasonable degree of security for passage through the Malacca Strait. Another factor was the desire of north Indian merchants to bypass the portage markets and establish direct trade via the Malacca Strait with the port cities of central and east Java, carrying with them a vigorous Mahāyāna Buddhism.

With this encouragement a vigorous line of rulers of the old port of call in southeastern Sumatra, Shrivijaya, schemed and fought after the mid-sixth century to extend its authority over the Malacca Strait and the portage states, until by the last decades of the seventh and the eighth centuries it had replaced the broken maritime power of Funan with its own. Shrivijaya's special asset was its ideal location where eastbound ships could lay over awaiting the summer monsoon to continue their voyage to China. This imperial city-state, which produced only pepper for export and depended on imports of food and manpower, prospered with ups and downs according to the volume of trade for six centuries, demonstrating the importance of commerce via and with Southeast Asia.

Shrivijaya was also an important center of Buddhist studies which contained, according to the account of the Chinese Buddhist pilgrim, I-Ching, a thousand scholarly Buddhist monks of both Hīnayāna and Mahāyāna sects in the latter seventh century, though the Mahāyāna school apparently was predominant. I-Ching's high regard for this Buddhist center is reflected in his sojourns there totaling nearly 9 years, during which he translated a monumental number of Buddhist works. In spite of the early dedication of the rulers to Buddhism, it appears to have been wholly borrowed and to have stimulated no creative development at Shrivijaya that was comparable to that in

central Java. No impressive monuments have been found, and the images were imports or imitations of works produced in northern India, especially the center at Nālandā. Apparently the political tour de force represented by this commercial empire lacked the indigenous cultural development that might have generated a creative response, and the rulers became preoccupied with maintaining their control of the trade routes.

In contrast, central Java had for several centuries, before receiving direct Indian influence, developed an advanced economy and indigenous culture based on cooperative development of intensive irrigated agriculture. Characteristics found elsewhere in Southeast Asia were an emphasis on ancestor worship and a fertility cult connected with the soil and crops, as well as a variety of animistic cults. A hierarchy of local chieftains recognized the overlordship of the ruler. The ruler reinforced his authority by the Hindu cults of Shiva and the Naga snake-god of soil and waters, perhaps borrowed from Funan. The first prominent ruler of Mataram, Sanjaya (732–750), the ninth in his line, was a worshiper of Shiva and bore the dynastic title of Shailendra meaning, like Funan, "king of the mountain." These factors suggest the possibility that this line may have been founded or, at least, influenced by refugees from the ruling family of Funan.

The interior Javan state of Mataram was then exposed to the full impact of the Mahāyāna Buddhism and culture of the north Indian Pala script and Pala art, but was not submerged by it. The outstanding monument to this influence is the cosmic mountain of Borobudur carved out of rock beginning in the 770s. Five squared terraces were surmounted by three circular ones and topped by a domed stupa 100 feet high. Almost 3 miles of terraced walks were decorated with edifying relief scenes that illustrated the peaceful and compassionate ethics of Mahāyāna Buddhism, as represented by episodes in the life and teachings of the Buddha and the bodhisattvas. Only the unfinished bottom tier depicted the violence of life and the torments of hell. Most notable in this work is the creative blending of Indian technique and motifs with native scenery and human types, such as brāhmans performing their role in support of kingship. These native scenes, interspersed with the Buddhist tales, illustrate the indigenous culture that continued in all its vigor after the decline of Buddhism. After the expulsion of the Shailendras in the mid-ninth century, Buddhism in a corrupted form became subordinated to the revived Hindu cult of Shiva, which gave greater support to the exercise of royal authority than the compassionate ideals of Mahāyāna Buddhism. A modified Hindu-Buddhist blend, in which Buddhism is almost submerged, persists today on the neighboring island of Bali.

During their century of power in Java the Shailendras supplemented their agricultural wealth by trading with T'ang China and by a vigorous foreign policy in order to dominate the states en route to China. For example, in 802 a Khmer prince was aided in seizing power and unifying Cambodia. In addition, the Shailendras apparently exchanged surplus food and other products for the spices of the Moluccas and other spice islands, and with the addition of Indian products loaded their ships for direct trade with China during a period when Shrivijayan relations with China were broken. In a dynastic upheaval the Shailendras were displaced, but the Shailendra prince took refuge in Shrivijaya and became its ruler in 860.

The change of dynasty and the shift of emphasis to Hinduism did not diminish Javan cultural vitality. Under new rulers the synthesizing of Javan and Indian culture continued with, perhaps, a greater respect for the native tradition. Hindu temples and mausoleums continued to display the same Javanese architectural and artistic skill and creativity, although on a smaller scale and based on the Hindu Rāmāyana rather than Buddhist stories. The Rāmāyana and later the entire Mahābhārata were translated into the local language. The shadow play cele-brating ancestor worship, which still is a distinctive feature of Javanese culture, had been represented in some of Borobudur's panels by utilizing distortion to cast shadows, and its continued development included modified tales from the Hindu classics. Economic expansion in the tenth century is indicated by the draining of swamps for cultivation in east Java and an expansion in the volume of trade. Gradually the full development of Javanese civilization led to a decline in creativity and a routine perpetuation and maintenance of the accomplishments of the past.

On the other hand, Shrivijaya, almost totally dependent on trade, suffered hard times for more than a century as a result of the nearly simultaneous decay of the two major empires of the East, the Abbasid and the T'ang dynasties, the lowest point being reached in the second and third quarters of the tenth century. Then arose the even more prosperous Sung dynasty, which actively encouraged the expansion of Chinese seaborne trade and developed a seemingly insatiable appetite for imports during the eleventh and twelfth centuries. Although never as dominant as before, Shrivijaya by desperate diplomacy and militancy did manage to retain its grip on a major portion of the trade for more than two centuries.

THE KHMERS

The Khmers, ethnic cousins of the Mons of lower Burma and lower Siam, had originally settled in modern Laos and upper Siam and then filtered into Funan as warriors, military aristocrats, and peasants. Therefore, they were thoroughly familiar with the Funanese culture and political system of divine rulers which they gradually overthrew between 550 and 650 as much by subversion as by conquest. As well integrated as they were into the social, economic, and political structure of Funan, the Khmers proved unable to maintain its political unity and broke up into a number of feuding principalities. This resulted in economic decline because of the neglect of the irrigation works and the loss of control of trade.

Not until the beginning of the ninth century was the process of reunification successfully initiated by a refugee prince who was supported by the Shailendras. By 819 he had secured control of Angkor, just north of Tonle Sap, and had revived the royal Shiva cult by which the ruler in his person was regarded as a divine manifestation of the universal ruler symbolized by the erection of a temple in the center of the capital to house the royal linga. The Shiva cult was supplemented by the revival of the Naga snake cult in which the royal queens were conceived as daughters of the god of the soil and each night had intercourse with the divine ruler on top of a pyramidal tower representing the cosmic mountain at the center of the universe. As a result, all royal offspring by the king's five wives, symbolizing the five cardinal directions, were doubly divine. This situation as fully developed by succeeding rulers presented a succession problem, additionally complicated by the practice of tracing descent in the female line. Not only were all of the deceased ruler's offspring eligible but also the descendants of previous queens for five generations. To resolve the issue, a Great Council that was composed of hereditary officials met to designate the successor, but even then most new rulers felt compelled to liquidate potential pretenders. The concept of a divine ruler proved compatible with Mahāyāna Buddhism by considering the ruler to be a bodhisattva. However, it must be emphasized that the Cambodian conception of royal incarnation as a living deity, reinforced by indigenous ancestor worship, was far more personalized and forceful than the generalized Indian conception. The king, aided by hereditary high priests, headed what amounted in large part to a theocracy in which his major function was the maintenance of religious rituals and law. As a descendant of the Naga snake, he was the absolute owner of the soil and, consequently, of the products of his people. Therefore, he was

responsible for constructing and maintaining the water-control projects that stored the waters of the 4-month summer monsoon to support rice growth during the 7-month dry season. The intricacy of the waterworks of the Khmer state in its prime demonstrated an exceptionally high level of technological achievement.

The first reunifier of the Khmer state tended to vitiate his absolute authority by granting estates to his loyal supporters in conquered areas. His successors in the later ninth century worked to eliminate this decentralization, so that by the end of the century unification was completed and the authority of the ruler was absolute and exercised largely through appointed officials. In addition, imperial expansion eastward against Champa and westward against the Mon states of lower Siam and the portage states of the Malay Peninsula was initiated. Overall, Cambodia was characterized by growing internal strength and substantial success in reasserting the Funanese imperial limits.

But more significant was the expression of cultural vitality represented by the temple of Angkor Wat which was built during the vigorous rule of Suryavarman II (1113–1150) who, in addition to other campaigns, met and checked the first southward movement of the Thai peoples employing mercenary Thai warriors to aid in the task. As the civilized Funanese, more interested in the peaceful pursuits of agriculture and commerce, had employed the warlike Khmers to fight their battles so, too, the now civilized Khmers came to rely more and more on Thai soldiers to defend their empire.

The Vishnu temple of Angkor Wat, designed as the tomb of its builder, does not represent a sudden flourishing of Khmer art and architecture but rather is the most impressive, monumental culmination of Khmer artistic creativity in stone. Some of the most exquisite work had been executed in the Banteay Srei temple, completed in 968. Already the solid pyramidal mass had been supplanted by the vaulted stone gallery, which was open on one side and supported by pillars to admit light for the illumination of deep relief sculptures on the opposite wall. Already the architects had mastered the technique of precisely cutting stone according to plan to fit the stone blocks together without mortar. Already Indian motifs, as in Java, had been blended with native scenery, figures, and tales in an original and creative manner. This temple was succeeded by a great number of temples and lesser shrines that increasingly reflected Khmer culture until it received a major expression in Angkor Wat.

This temple area, enclosed by a colonnaded wall, measured 920 by 1100 yards and was surrounded by a moat more than 200 yards wide. Causeways across the moat gave access to the temple area through colonnaded gateways that were elaborately decorated and guarded by towers. Within the temple area a raised approach, nearly 500 yards long and bordered by stone balustrades carved in the form of elongated Naga snakes, led eyes and feet to the temple proper. The temple was composed of three rectangular galleries surmounted by a central tower 210 feet high surrounded by lesser towers. Originally all these towers glistened with gold gilt. The inner walls of the galleries were covered with carved reliefs in multiple levels that depicted the stories of Vishnu and his major incarnations, Rāma and Krishna, as well as elements of the Shiva story and many representations of everyday Cambodian life, including military arrays, royal processions, and the life and work of the people. The vigor and realism of these scenes reflect the high esthetic development of the artists and the vitality of the Khmer civilization at its height. Finally, the ability to marshal the talent and wealth that went into the construction of Angkor Wat is proof of the strength of the government, the availability of skilled artisans, the high level of artistic values, and the great prosperity essential to such an endeavor.

Another ruler, Jayavarman VII (1181–1219), who fancied himself a bodhisattva, built the Mahāyāna Buddhist temple of Bayon as an integral part of his capital city, Angkor Thom. Although in size it is only surpassed by its predecessor and its design was more intricate, its dependence on timber for its superstructure suggests the weakening of the Khmer regime as a result of increasing attacks and a reduction in Sung trade.

The social structure was strictly stratified, although not as rigidly as the Indian caste system, with the brahman high priests of the Shiva cult at the top of the hierarchy, limiting and supporting the absolute authority of the ruler. Perhaps the championship of Vishnu by Suryavarman II and of Mahāyāna Buddhism by Jayavarman VII represent efforts to minimize brahman influence. In particular, the advocacy of Mahāyāna Buddhism with its belief in salvation for all and its ideal of a benevolent rule in the service of all the people may have been intended as a calculated appeal for broad popular support against the entrenched classes. If so intended, it failed as did other efforts. Always the Shiva cult and its adherents returned to power after these episodes. Herein lay the weakness of this religiously oriented civilization which supported approximately 300 thousand holy men and a multitude of shrines, temples, and monasteries. Any decline in agricultural and commercial revenue or extended additional military expenses could easily upset this luxurious economy.

Before going on, another unique feature should be mentioned: the comparatively high standing and prominent part of women in Cambodian life. They practically monopolized the trade in local products. They staffed the palace as servants, as entertainers, and even as an Amazon military guard. Those of higher status were prominent in scholarship and sometimes were appointed judges and royal secretaries.

During the thirteenth and succeeding centuries the Cambodian empire shrank gradually under the increasing pressure of the Thai (Free) peoples who lost their independent state of Nan Chao in Yünnan to the Mongol forces of Khubilai Khan that were carrying out a flanking attack on the Southern Sung domain. Not until the fifteenth century, however, did the Angkor region fall to Thai forces. During this era of decline Hīnayāna Buddhism gradually gained ground until it predominated in the fourteenth century. In due course it captured the militant Thai as well.

PAGAN BURMA

The Burmese state with its capital at Pagan on the middle reaches of the Irrawaddy River warrants brief attention because in its career it not only gave a measure of unity to Burma but also established the social and religious structure that prevails today, constructing temples under the inspiration of Hīnayāna Buddhism which are architecturally comparable to the great works of the Khmers.

The Mons, ethnically related to the Khmers, had from earliest times been a cultured, but not a particularly creative, people transmitting their adopted Indian culture to more primitive peoples. In Burma, as well as lower Siam, they had occupied and developed most of the areas suitable for irrigated agriculture. During the ninth century primitive Tibeto-Burman tribesmen poured into the central Irrawaddy valley, overrunning Mon settlements and gradually learning the rudiments of civilization from their Mon tutors. Even when a strong state was established in the 1050s through the military talents of Anawratta (d 1077), however, it depended on Mon scholarship and talent in all areas except military and political power. Indeed, Anawratta and his unlettered people had come to the fore as allies of one of the Mon states to meet the challenge of Cambodian imperialism. Once victorious, he used his military power to reduce the rest of Burma but had to rely on his Mon junior

partners to organize his government and provide the religious sanctification of his rule. Although in contrast to the predominance of the Shiva cult at the Javan and Cambodian courts the Burman ruler was invested with divine authority by brāhman proponents of the Vishnu cult, popular support was based on the lavish patronage of Hīnayāna Buddhism which reflects Mon influence and the development of close ties with Ceylon, the seat of Hīnayāna Buddhism.

Ceylon's gift of a replica of a tooth of the Buddha in appreciation of Burmese assistance inspired Anawratta to begin the construction of the first of a sequence of mighty pagodas that has caused them to be named "the dynasty of temple builders." The Shwezigon pagoda, completed by his successor, was a pyramidal-type structure, similar in basic design to Borobudur, with square-shaped lower stages surmounted by circular ones from which arose an enormous bell-shaped stupa and spire gilded and topped by a jewel-encrusted umbrella. Passages in the various levels of the base accommodated hundreds of niches for idols and terracotta plaques. The massiveness of the whole structure is still impressive as a monument to the power and piety of the founders of the Pagan dynasty, but equally significant are the 37 shrines dedicated to Burmese spirits which represent a blending of native beliefs with Hīnayāna Buddhism. Three successive temples illustrate the progressive development of Burmese architectural skill and esthetic talent. Dimly-lit, vaulted corridors that were decorated with paintings, instead of open staircases, led the worshiper to elevated gilded Buddhas effectively lighted from above to enhance the spiritual effect. Although terracotta plaques were still used, the increased amount of relief sculpture indicates the greater number and skill of Burmese artisans. Other architectural and decorative innovations suggest a decreasing dependence of the Burmans on their Mon mentors. A final, major temple, built in the thirteenth century, reverted to the design of the first one and reflects the exhaustion of the resources and creative talents of the Pagan dynasty.

The five great pagodas and the thousands of lesser shrines dotting the landscape are significant not only as memorials to the wealth and piety of the Pagan rulers but also as an indication of the extent to which the peoples of Burma were captured by Hīnayāna Buddhism. Almost every village could boast a contingent of monks provided with quarters by well-to-do donors and supported by the contributions of the peasants. A number of major centers were equipped with libraries and endowed by princes with grants of enslaved villages. In addition to setting examples of scholarship and piety according to Hīnayāna doctrines, the monks furnished education and indoctrination for the youth and utilized religious beliefs to assist in the maintenance of law and order in the villages. The growth in the number of monks, the allocation of resources for their support, and the construction of religious edifices appear to have contributed to the weakening of the Pagan dynasty by diverting much potential revenue from the government. On the other hand, Buddhism's emphasis on brotherly compassion and cooperation may have encouraged sufficient economic expansion to pay its way, and its real contribution to military weakness may have been more psychological than economic by undermining the martial spirit of the Burmese people. The Burmese who occupied irrigated royal lands owed specified services, largely military, to the crown instead of taxes. In the rest of Burma various taxes, as well as military service, were assessed on the families or village communities that owned the land. As in other areas of Asia, the group, governed by hereditary officials or elders, was entrusted with the care and maintenance of its property, and the individual was dependent on the group for his livelihood. Over these locally self-sufficient units stood appointed provincial governors whose main function was to collect royal revenues and uphold royal authority. This system of social, economic, and religious organization has persisted, with some modifications, into the twentieth century.

In campaigns from 1283 to 1287 the Mongols broke the power of the Pagan dynasty and occupied the capital where a puppet ruler was established in 1289, after a period of fratricidal slaughter. Mongol authority did not last long, however, and Burma was divided into a confusing array of successive feuding states until a measure of unity was restored in the mid-sixteenth century by a Burmese dynasty that ruled from Toungoo in the valley of the Sittang River.

THAI-SHAN MIGRATION

The Thai (Free) peoples, known as Shan in Burma, were the last major group to move southward from southwest China into Southeast Asia. This movement in small tribal groups began centuries before their state of Nan-Chao was overrun in 1253 by Mongol forces under Khubilai Khan, and today their descendants still represent a significant minority in this region of southernmost China. Frequently, as in the case of the Khmer Empire, they found service as mercenaries and secured peaceful acceptance as settlers. In the early thirteenth century, before the Mongols appeared on the scene, the tempo of migration picked up, extending into Assam in the west, the Shan plateau in Burma, and especially into the upper Menam and middle Mekong valleys as the Khmer grip weakened. The most vigorous expansion and the creation of the first Thai empire came in the last quarter of the thirteenth century when, utilizing military methods learned from the Mongols, the Thai under an able leader overran all of modern Thailand and Laos, secured recognition by the ruler of Mon Burma, marched down the Malay Peninsula as far as Penang Island, and laid claim to all of Malaya. The ruler adopted the religious rituals of the conquered, borrowed from the Mons and Khmers in reducing the Thai language to writing, and most importantly took over from the Mons the patronage of Hīnayāna Buddhism which, under Thai auspices, spread to the Khmer.

Nevertheless, the ease of these conquests was only made possible by the Mongol destruction of Pagan Burma, the deterioration of the Khmer Empire, and the inability of any of the lesser states to combine their resources in resistance. The Thai rulers' military strength rested on the loose and uncertain loyalty of tribal chieftains. This power did not begin to be consolidated until the establishment of a new capital at Ayuthia in the midst of the agricultural resources of the lower Menam. Even then the empire was continuously racked by rebellious Thai chieftains in the north and persisted only because of the impotence of its neighbors. The strongest neighbor remained Cambodia and, when a surcease of internecine strife permitted, attacks were made on the Khmer state until the Angkor capital and its irrigated hinterland were seized in 1431 to 1432. When Burma regained its strength under the Toungoo dynasty and with the aid of Portuguese mercenaries attacked Ayuthia repeatedly after the late 1540s, the Khmers were temporarily able to regain the Angkor region and to renovate its waterworks as well as its temples, but by the end of the century the Thai state had regained its vigor and its territories. Beyond the restoration of a measure of political order and unity, the warlike Thai did nothing conspicuously creative, being content to perpetuate and propagate the religious and cultural achievements of the con-

quered peoples with whom they mixed.

From the early Christian Era to the fifteenth century, Southeast Asia as a source of spices and a transit route for a fluctuating volume of seaborne trade produced several centers of "twilight" civilization, the Chinese-dominated region roughly equivalent to modern North Vietnam and the Indian-dominated areas of Burma, the lower Menam, Cambodia, Java, and the Sumatran empire that controlled the Malacca and Sunda straits. All except the last possessed sound agricultural bases and indigenous cultures that were never totally submerged by Hindu and Buddhist doctrines. Instead, these Indian institutions were superimposed on the native cultures to reinforce the authority of the rulers. Local customary law and religious beliefs were in varying degrees retained in each area: most vigorously in Java and least so in Burma, reflecting the strength of indigenous cultural development prior to full exposure to Indian influences. A more important observation, however, was the inability of any of these "twilight" civilizations to radiate an influence of their own outside the confines of Southeast Asia; they were essentially receivers rather than disseminators of civilization, regardless of the vigor and persistence of their indigenous cultures. Finally, none of these synthesized civilizations was able to integrate the whole region, even for a brief period. Therefore, Southeast Asia, destined to confront the challenges of Islam and the West, was a divided area characterized by cultural and political plurality.

SIGNIFICANT DATES

	111 B.C.	Chinese conquest of Annam (North Vietnam)
c.	180– 650 A.D.	Funan Empire
c.	650–1250 A.D.	Shrivijaya controls Malacca Strait and trade
c.	650– 832 A.D.	Shailendra in Java followed by successor states
c.	775– 832 A.D.	Construction of Borobudur

c.	819–1431 A.D.	Khmer Empire
c.	1113–1150 A.D.	Construction of Angkor Wat
c.	1050–1287 A.D.	Pagan Burma
c.	1275 A.D.	Founding of Siam (Thailand)

Briggs, Lawrence Palmer, *The Ancient Khmer Empire*. Philadelphia: American Philosophical Society, 1951.

*Buttinger, Joseph, *Vietnam: A Political History*. New York: Praeger, 1958.

Cady, John F., *Southeast Asia: Its Historical Development*. New York: McGraw-Hill, 1964.

*———, *Thailand, Burma, Laos, and Cambodia*. Englewood Cliffs, N.J.: Prentice-Hall, 1966.

Coedè, George, *The Indianized States of Southeast Asia*. Honolulu: East-West Center Press, 1968.

*———, *The Making of South East Asia*. Berkeley: University of California Press, 1966.

*Corpuz, Onofre D., *The Philippines*. Englewood Cliffs, N.J.: Prentice-Hall, 1965.

Donnison, Frank S. V., *Burma*. New York: Praeger, 1970.

Giles, Herbert Allen, *The Travels of Fa-hsien, 399–414 A.D.* London: Routledge and Kegan Paul, 1956.

Groslier, Bernard, *Indochina*. New York: World Pub. Co., 1966.

Groslier, Bernard, and Arthaud, Jacques, *Angkor*. Rev. ed.; New York: Praeger, 1966.

*Hall, D. G. E., *A History of South-East Asia*. 3rd. ed.; New York: St. Martin's Press, 1968.

Harrison, Brian, *South-East Asia: A Short History*. New York: St. Martin's Press, 1954.

Hourani, Georges F., *Arab Seafaring in the Indian Ocean in Ancient and Medieval Times*. Princeton: Princeton University Press, 1951.

Htin Aung, Maung, *A History of Burma*. New York: Columbia University Press, 1967.

*Legge, J. D., *Indonesia*. Englewood Cliffs, N.J.: Prentice-Hall, 1964.

*Myrdal, Jan, and Kessle, Gun, *Angkor: An Essay on Art and Imperialism*. New York: Random House, 1970.

*Purcell, Victor, *Malaysia*. Rev. ed.; New York: Walker and Co., 1967.

*Rawson, Philip, *The Art of Southeast Asia*. New York: Praeger, 1967.

Toussaint, Auguste, *History of the Indian Ocean*. Chicago: University of Chicago Press, 1966.

*Winstedt, Richard, *Malaya and its History*. Rev. ed.; New York: Hillary House, 1966.

Zainuddin, Ailsa, *A Short History of Indonesia*. New York: Praeger, 1970.

CHAPTER EIGHT

IMPERIAL CHINA

In Chapter Four, the greatly enlarged area of Chinese civilization was left on the verge of unification by force at the hands of the strongest single state. From the eighth to the third centuries B.C. the authority of the Chou rulers had been undermined by revolutionary social, economic, and political changes. Internally this period was characterized by a vast population growth that put increasing pressure on the means of subsistence. This pressure forced changes that took different forms in the different states.

The interior states, where the traditional heritage of a hereditary aristocracy was strongest, resisted change and, as a result, lagged in social, economic, and political development, becoming pawns in the growing struggle for power. Yet, their very hardships inspired their best minds to examine critically and creatively the Chinese heritage that they sought to preserve in order to find solutions to their dilemma. Many aristocratic families in these states suffered a loss of wealth, if not status, and had to turn to education and training as preparation for employment on the basis of merit as civil servants or warriors. Since opportunity was limited at home, they had to look to the peripheral states for careers. An incidental by-product of this aristocratic emigration was the inculcation of Chinese culture in newly incorporated regions. Although direct evidence is lacking, it may be assumed that the younger sons of commoners greatly supplemented this exodus, carrying with them their agricultural and technical skills, as well as their sense of social discipline.

The peripheral states were first of all less burdened by the incubus of Chinese tradition, and able rulers felt freer to employ able ministers to carry out programs of economic and political reform. Generally the trend was in the direction of centralized government staffed by a bureaucracy selected on the basis of merit. To build up their resources, these states invested in public works, such as irrigation and canal projects. Second, they were in a position to ease the population pressure by expansion into hitherto non-Chinese areas. The end result of both developments was the creation of larger, more prosperous, and more populous states with more efficient governments able to mobilize and maintain larger armies in the field.

By the later sixth century the social, economic, and political conditions had altered enough to gain frequent recognition in historical records. Under these circumstances, the rise of schools of thought in the fifth century that attempted to supply solutions to the growing turmoil and tension is not surprising. Furthermore, the almost total concern with social, economic, and political problems is what one would expect, especially in view of the comparatively undeveloped state of Chinese religion. In contrast with the civilizations of the Middle East and India, Chinese thought was overwhelmingly secular in orientation.

Three broad schools with their individual variations dominated the amazingly creative thought of the later Chou era: Confucianism, Taoism (pronounced dowism), and Legalism (perhaps more accurately defined as Statism). All three were predominantly concerned with human relationships, the relationship of man to man and man to the state and, from this point of view, may be described as humanistic. Of course, each also sought to find in nature the universal rules that should govern human relations and thus was influenced to a greater or lesser extent by the Chinese cosmological triad of

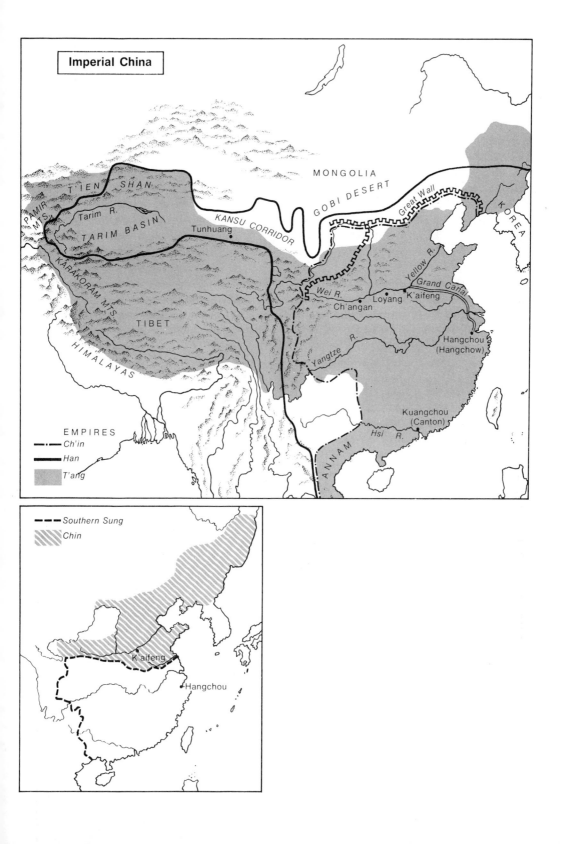

Imperial China

MONGOLIA

GOBI DESERT

T'IEN SHAN

PAMIR MTS.

Tarim R.

TARIM BASIN

Tunhuang

KANSU CORRIDOR

Great Wall

KOREA

KARAKORAM MTS.

Yellow R.

Grand Canal

Wei R.

K'aifeng

Ch'angan

Loyang

TIBET

HIMALAYAS

Yangtze R.

Hangchou
(Hangchow)

Kuangchou
(Canton)

Hsi R.

ANNAM

EMPIRES
—·—·— Ch'in
———— Han
░░░ T'ang

——— Southern Sung
▨▨ Chin

K'aifeng

Hangchou

heaven, earth, and man. Of these three, however, man was clearly their central concern.

The three schools may be considered as representing three views of Chinese society. Confucianism looked to the family as the fundamental unit of society whose regulation would produce harmony in both society and the state. Taoism looked to the individual whose proper regulation would produce harmony with nature and thus bring peace to society. Legalism, decrying the basically evil nature of man, looked to the state to regulate human relations by a rigorous code of punishments and rewards that would mobilize human resources for the benefit of the state and its subjects. Confucianism and Taoism looked to a golden age in the past as the model for reform. Legalism realistically insisted that the conditions of the present must be met by contemporary solutions. Past precedents were without pertinence for present problems. All three schools represent reactions to the rapid change and growing disorder.

CONFUCIUS (C. 551–479 B.C.)

Confucius, the founder of Confucianism, was the first and, in the long run, the most influential of the Chinese philosophers and teachers. Because he left no writings of his own, the most reliable information on his life and teachings must be derived from the *Analects*, a purported compilation of his sayings as recalled by his immediate disciples. How much this work may have suffered from interpolations and editorial alterations can never be determined.

Confucius was born in the old state of Lu into a family of the minor aristocracy which, like so many others in this era of upheaval, had lost its hereditary status and fallen on evil days. His father, who apparently had been employed as a military officer, died when Confucius was only four years of age, leaving his family in a condition of genteel poverty. Nevertheless, in accordance with

family tradition, Confucius was educated and obtained minor posts in the civil service. Later, after having gained renown as a teacher whose pupils secured important positions, he was provided with an honorable sinecure. In the conviction that he was wasting his talents as a statesman, he left Lu and moved with his disciples from state to state for more than a decade in a fruitless quest for a ruler who would give him the authority to put his principles into action. But, while treated everywhere with respect, he was too independently minded to make a suitably servile civil servant. Finally, he returned to Lu and died shortly thereafter in the belief that his life had been a failure.

The primary assumption, from which his other teachings stemmed, was the belief that the troubles of his time were the result of a falling away from the virtuous behavior and observance of the rules of social order that had prevailed in the early Chou period. The cure was to restore this ancient order. Therefore, he devoted his study to the records of the past and insisted that he was a transmitter and not an originator, a conservator and not a revolutionary. Moreover, he did not concern himself with metaphysics and would have rejected the title of philosopher in favor of that of a teacher of proper social and political practice. In reaction against the superstitions of his times he struck a note that can be described as agnostic. He did not by any means repudiate religion and, indeed, emphasized the vital importance of the proper performance of the traditional religious rituals, but beyond this he asserted that the ways of heaven were beyond human knowledge and control. A true scholar would concentrate his attention on the management of worldly affairs. Generally he opposed extremism and favored moderation.

If the teachings of Confucius had been as conservative and reactionary as at face value they appear, his influence on subsequent Chinese development would have been much less than it became. In spite of his citation of ancient precedents in support of his views, he was in fact proposing revolutionary solutions. Although he upheld the restoration of the ancient hierarchy as a prophylaxis for the disorders of his time, he placed an equal emphasis on virtuous conduct as the source of stability for society and the state. This advocacy of ethics as basic to good government and the good life was an original contribution, despite his idealization of the ancient past. His program called for the employment by the hereditary rulers of civil servants so educated as to appreciate fully the paramount virtue of public service, emphasizing both loyalty to the ruler and dedication to the welfare of the people. This "cultivated gentleman" (chün-tzu) would have developed through education both the inner virtues of integrity, righteousness, and conscientiousness and the external virtues stemming from them of loyalty, altruism, and human-heartedness. As a realist, he fully realized that practice must reflect doctrines and, therefore, prescribed for his "gentleman" a thorough understanding and performance of the rituals, etiquette, and proper relationships institutionalized in Chinese society—if not often practiced—as essential to the promotion of social and political harmony. As he reportedly said "Uprightness uncontrolled by etiquette becomes rudeness."* Western philosophers have generally neglected the importance of "teaching by doing" emphasized by Confucius.

This emphasis on the employment of "gentlemen" cultivated by education accepted implicitly the idea of the bureaucratic state in which hereditary status was limited to the ruler. Whether Confucius realized it or not, this doctrine stood in fundamental contradiction with his praise of the early Chou period with its hereditary hierarchy. Moreover, he explicitly asserted that lowly birth

* *Analects* of Confucius, Book VIII, Chapter 2. The quotations in these sections generally follow the translation in Wm. Theodore de Bary, et al. (comps.), *Sources of Chinese Tradition* (N. Y.: Columbia University Press, 1960).

was no bar to becoming a gentleman and, on the contrary, insisted that aristocratic birth by itself did not qualify a man to be accepted as a student. As he said, "In education there are no class distinctions" (XV, 38). His rigorous admission and retention standards would close the door to higher education for many students today. Confucius said: "I won't teach a man who is not anxious to learn, and will not explain to one who is not trying to make things clear to himself. If I hold up one corner of a square and a man cannot come back to me with the other three, I won't bother to go over the point again" (VII, 8).

In these two ways—by advocating a civil service of "cultivated gentlemen" and by ignoring class distinctions in the selection of candidates—Confucius actually broke with the ancient past. Nevertheless, he was no egalitarian. He recognized the mutual distinction and relationship between rulers and ruled on the basis of innate qualifications. Some were fitted by nature to be trained as rulers; the rest were equipped by nature to labor in the fields for the support of themselves and their rulers. Each worked reciprocally for the benefit of the other. The rulers earned their support by guiding and directing benevolently the work of the ruled for their mutual benefit, and the ruled accepted willingly the guidance of enlightened and virtuous rulers. Obviously, Confucius argued, the troubles of the times arose from the failure to observe and practice the proper rules regulating human relationships. Therefore, he pictured an ideal society of graded relationships in which observance of the rules of human relationships would create stability and harmony.

Human relationships as taught by Confucius prescribed five basic relationships only one of which was equal, that of friend and friend. The other four were absolute relations of superior and inferior: husband and wife, father and son, elder brother and younger brother, ruler and subject. Although absolute obedience was required of the inferiors, the superiors in each case were obligated to protect and benevolently look after the welfare of their inferiors. In the natural course of events superiors might sometimes abuse their authority, and in the case of a father who so oppressed his son Confucius was asked what recourse remained to the son. Confucius somewhat equivocably replied: "In serving his parents, a son may gently remonstrate with them. If he sees that they are not inclined to follow his suggestion, he should resume his reverential attitude but not abandon his purpose. If he is belabored, he will not complain" (IV, 18). Clearly he believed there was no possibility of a harmonious society unless the rule of filial piety was maintained, and thus any abuses must be endured for the sake of the general welfare.

Furthermore, he believed that reform must take place from the top downward. The ruler must not only set an example, but by his actions serve as a positive force for the moral regeneration of society. First, he must practice virtue and filial piety within his own family. Second, he must select virtuous ministers. And third, he must give constant attention to the welfare of his subjects. "To govern is to set things right. If you begin by setting yourself right, who will dare to deviate from the right" (XII, 17). He further suggested that a state so governed need not fear its neighbors because their subjects would gladly surrender to such a virtuous prince, the implication being that the territory of a truly virtuous ruler would expand without aggression on his part.

A cardinal conviction of Confucius was his belief in a government of men, not of laws. This doctrine followed logically from his argument that power should be put in the hands of gentlemen educated in virtue who would naturally seek to do justice in every case. "Lead the people by laws and regulate them by penalties, and the people will try to keep out of jail, but will have no sense of shame. Lead the people by virtue and restrain them by the rules of decorum, and the people will have a sense of shame, and more-

over will become good" (II, 3). Harmony and happiness would radiate from the virtuous prince's reaching and reforming every subject through his virtuous officials.

In addition to ethical, altruistic behavior and filial piety in dealing with others, Confucius also emphasized for the same reason the importance of the correct observance of the institutionalized rites of Chinese society as a stabilizing influence and an expression of respect for the feelings of others. This emphasis on rites, like that on conduct, was inspired by the growing neglect of these forms and the selfish individualism of his times. In other words, it was another means by which Confucius sought to revitalize the decaying morality in human relations. However, he insisted that the mere perfunctory performance of rites without the proper spirit of reverence would be of no more value than a cold obedience to the other rules of conduct. He upheld the ancient rule of three years' mourning for the death of a parent—a position that was particularly singled out for attack by his later critics—on the ground that each child was dependent for his very life on his parents for, at least, this length of time.

Much use has been made of the term virtue. Even by Confucian usage this is a very comprehensive word. The first objective is to achieve inner integrity and sincerity by careful study and practice. Learning by the reverent study of the past and its comparison with the present is the only path to virtue. His insistence on the study of the past as a guide to present action reinforced the already strong Chinese sense of history and its value. Confucius clearly denied the value of meditation without study. "Sometimes I have gone a whole day without food and a whole night without sleep, giving myself to thought. It was no use. It is better to learn" (XV, 30). A critic might justly observe that a day and a night are not much of a test. But learning was for him no mere feat of memorization. A piece of advice that he passed on might well receive serious consideration by today's students: "Learning without thinking is labor lost; thinking without learning is perilous" (II, 15). As a teacher, he sought to develop in his students open minds. Four obstacles to the achievement of virtue which he singled out were "a biased mind, arbitrary judgments, obstinacy, and egotism" (IX, 4). Objectivity and sincerity with oneself were essential. Moreover, each individual had to find virtue for himself. The teacher could be no more than a guide.

After attaining the goal of complete honesty with himself, the student was then prepared to consider his relationship with mankind. Actually, the quest for inner virtue and outer virtue was not arbitrarily separable in this manner; the one was integrally related to the other. If one had respect for himself, he must have an identical respect for all others. It was a simple fact that men lived in society and constantly interacted with each other. When asked for a single principle as a guide to conduct, Confucius replied: "Do not do to others what you would not want others to do to you" (XV, 23). This negative statement of the Golden Rule, however, was positively supplemented by his entreaty to his disciples to practice the five humane virtues: "courtesy, magnanimity, good faith, diligence, and kindness. He who is courteous is not humiliated, he who is magnanimous wins the multitude, he who is of good faith is trusted by the people, he who is diligent attains his objective, and he who is kind can get service from the people" (XVII, 6).

Virtue, then, consists first of being honest with yourself so that you may objectively examine with humanity your relationship with your fellowmen in the expectation that they will recognize and reciprocate your benevolence. Certainly, inhumane actions can only result sooner or later in inhumane reactions. Therefore, in spite of any immediate disappointments, "the gentleman cherishes virtue; the inferior man cherishes possessions" (IV, 11). The gentleman, subordinating his personal desires, exercises altruism always upholding the right, regardless of personal success or failure, in recognition of the fact that his welfare and that of his descendants are integrally tied up with the welfare of the people.

Such a philosophy with its moderation and emphasis on duty was ideally suited to the production of able civil servants. For this reason, and not because it sought stability by looking to an idealization of the ancient past for precedents, it was well adapted to the wave of the future in China and ultimately prevailed, albeit with significant modifications and alterations. Admittedly, the ideal of the cultivated gentleman for public service was frequently violated in practice, but it at least served as a restraint against gross abuses. Once established, it provided a measuring stick against which the performance of government could be evaluated. In Chinese development this function alone justified the Confucian ideal, providing greater institutional stability and continuity than can be found in any other civilization. Even in eras of political fragmentation and distress no successor regime could for long afford to lose sight of or reject this ideal of a civil service staffed by gentlemen educated in the Confucian virtues.

MO-TZU (C. 479 – 381 B.C.)

The teachings of Confucius were by no means immediately accepted as final. In fact, they stimulated other thoughtful men to give theoretical consideration to the overriding problem of human relationships he had singled out. Some struck out on radically new trails, while others, including his disciples, made further elaborations that put new content into the Confucian tradition. One of the earliest whose doctrines have been substantially preserved is Mo-tzu. He was educated in the traditional rites and, perhaps, in Confucianism. In any case, he concentrated his critical attacks against the formalism and coldness of Confucian doctrines and, therefore, his teachings may be deemed a Confucian heresy. Because of the need to refute Confucius he developed a dialectical method of argument that served as an example and inspiration for the later school that specialized in dialectics.

In contrast with the moderation of Confucius, his thought is characterized by extremism, a position he may have been forced into by the use of dialectic. In his attacks on Confucius he distorted the Master's teachings, ascribing to them a more positive position than they actually maintained. For example, he condemned Confucius as a defender of an aristocratic, hierarchical order in contrast with his own more egalitarian outlook. Yet he, too, wanted virtuous men appointed to positions of authority. Furthermore, he attacked the Confucianists for religious skepticism and rigid ritualism, where Confucius had advocated moderation in both respects.

Much more important differentiations from Confucius were Mo-tzu's doctrines of universal love and utilitarianism. Criticizing Confucius' graded love according to the rules of filial piety for its coldness and lack of genuine humanity, Mo-tzu advocated equal love for all men on the ground that by its support Heaven demonstrated its equal love for all men. He argued that the limited and partial love taught by Confucius left room for the hatred that was the cause of disorder in the world. If everyone regarded all others as he regarded himself, then hatred would cease and universal peace would prevail. Therefore, he denounced aggression and devoted a great deal of attention to defense as necessary until his doctrine of love was universally accepted. He realized that an active program of conversion would be necessary and argued that as Heaven guides men by rewards and punishments the state, too, must devise a system of rewards and punishments to guide its subjects. This initial break with the Confucian ideal of a government of men rather than laws prepared the ground for the later authoritarian doctrines of the Legalist school. In contrast with the open-mindedness taught by Confucius, an evangelical sense of mission led Mo-tzu to demand from his disciples

absolute conformity and discipline. Both his doctrine of universal love and his insistence on authority are examples of his extremism.

Although Mo-tzu appealed both to Heaven and to the legendary Hsia dynasty and its predecessors for sanctions, he also found support for his arguments on the grounds of utility. On this basis, he denounced all activities that did not contribute to the material welfare of the people, such as militarism, luxury, and expenditures on rituals. All resources should be husbanded to meet the three essential needs of food, clothing, and housing, and all waste should be eliminated. In this connection he particularly denounced the waste of money in expensive funerals and the waste of productivity in the three year's mourning for parents prescribed by Confucius.

Although he proclaimed egalitarian ideals, his support of the authority of the ruler and his officials, backed up by rewards and punishments, left the people with less freedom than Confucius advocated, and provided a precedent for the Legalists. Moreover, his assertion that a ruler's power came from Heaven contributed to the later elaboration by Mencius of the doctrine of the Mandate of Heaven. In sum, then, Mo-Tzu's teaching may be considered an extremist and heretical offshoot of Confucianism which developed new techniques and doctrines, such as dialectical argument, utilitarianism, and authoritarianism, which were to influence various later schools of thought. In addition, the cohesion of his disciplined disciples persisted for several generations after his death, serving to preserve and spread his views.

TAOISM

The origin of this second most important school of thought is shrouded in the obscurity of the past. The traditional founder, Lao-tzu, cannot be clearly identified, and the *Tao Te Ching (The Way and the Power Classic)* attributed to him is obviously the product of several minds and of uncertain date. In its present form it is probably no older than the late fourth century B.C., although portions of it may have been composed a century or more earlier. Essentially it is an anti-intellectual protest against an increasingly complex society and government and an appeal for a return to the primitive simplicity of a mythical past when men followed and accepted the Way (*Tao*) of nature without making the futile attempt to control and manipulate man and nature for selfish ends. The second classic work of Taoism written by Chuang-tzu (c 369–286 B.C.) carries a substantially different message. It is even more mystical and, instead of trying to reform society, takes as its central purpose the salvation of the individual.

Although both of these aspects of Taoism made important contributions to the development of Chinese civilization, Chuang-tzu's conception of the mystical recluse communing with nature in quest of the eternal truth probably exercised a greater influence. It provided the scholar with the perfect counterpart or complement to the Confucian call to duty. As a Confucianist, the scholar was a sober and responsible family man and a conscientious bureaucrat; as a Taoist, the same man felt free to relieve himself of the burdens of family and office and retire to some place of natural beauty for meditation—perhaps with the aid of a little wine. In other words, Taoism provided the scholar with an ideal safety valve. When he lost office or suffered any other worldly setback, he could turn to the solace of Taoism. In addition, the Taoist emphasis on the beauty of all creation countered the man-centered humanism of Confucianism and furnished a vital esthetic inspiration for Chinese literature and art.

Like Indian transcendental conceptions of the same type, the Way (*Tao*) is essentially indescribable in human terms. It is timeless, eternal, and formless. "The Tao that can be told of is not the eternal Tao; the name that can be named is not the eternal name" (*Tao Te Ching,* I). The means of fol-lowing the Way, generally translated as "doing nothing," have frequently created the misunderstanding that the concept is wholly negative. While this interpretation may be valid for the teachings of Chuang-tzu, it is less than accurate for the doctrine of the *Tao Te Ching*. A better translation would be "doing nothing contrary to nature." In this sense it is a condemnation of bureaucratic meddling with the life of the people and an advocacy of a positive program of laissez-faire in government on the ground that the source of disorder within and between states is selfish striving and ambition.

> Refrain from exalting the worthy,
> So that the people will not scheme and contend;
> Refrain from prizing rare possessions,
> So that the people will not steal;
> Refrain from displaying objects of desire,
> So that the people's hearts will not be disturbed.
>
> Therefore a sage rules his people thus:
> He empties their minds,
> And fills their bellies;
> He weakens their ambitions,
> And strengthens their bones.
>
> (*Tao Te Ching,* 3)

Similarly, foreign policy should be characterized by softness and nonassertion. Avoid antagonizing one's neighbors and give them no cause to covet your territory. The path of violence will inevitably lead to a violent end. A frequent Taoist analogy observed that, while water was soft, it could wear away the hardest substance.

While the *Tao Te Ching* sought to reform society by advocating the virtue of selfless nonassertion, Chuang-tzu was almost exclusively concerned with freeing the individual from the bondage of life. Perhaps he believed that the society of his day was so sunk in degradation and depravity that it was beyond the possibility of reform. In his view of the transient and relative nature of all material things, including man, he approached very closely Buddhist and Vedantist philosophy.

All life, he wrote, is involved in continous change and "passes by like a galloping horse" (*Chuang-tzu*, 17), taking its own course despite any efforts to alter it. The ever-changing phenomena of the external world are essentially unreal; what is real and natural comes from within where true virtue abides. Since virtue resides within each individual, while everything external is artificial, the true sage will dedicate himself entirely to seeking to comprehend this inner virtue, which is the only path to knowledge of the Way. When he realizes the essential oneness of all nature, he will rise above the bondage of the temporary and changing phenomena of life and death. The study of things, which are constantly changing and can only provide relative knowledge, is obviously futile. For the same reason, government service serves no useful purpose for the individual. Meditation and intuition are the only way to realization of the ultimate truth, the knowledge of the *Tao*. It may readily be appreciated how this aspect of Taoism prepared Chinese intellectuals for the reception of Buddhism.

MENCIUS (C. 372 – 289 B.C.)

The single, most important interpreter of Confucianism was Mencius who, like its founder, failed to find significant employment and is best known as a teacher. Unlike Confucius, he had to contest the field with other well-established schools, especially the disciplined followers of Mo-tzu's teaching. Furthermore, political strife had become much more ruthless in his day. Both of these factors probably influenced his development of new ideas and emphases, although he believed himself to be merely an expounder of Confucian doctrine.

Although he, too, looked to the ancient past for precedents, he was far more concerned than Confucius with the present, material foundations of society. Indeed, he as-

serted that virtuous conduct and government would be of small avail if the material prosperity of the people had not been adequately provided for. His concern for the material welfare of the people led him to urge a land reform program based on the ancient well-field system. According to this system, which may never have functioned as described, a section of 150 acres of arable land was divided into nine equal portions. Eight families each had a plot and commonly farmed the ninth for the support of the government.

With his special concern for the people Mencius is noted for his elaboration of the doctrine of the Mandate of Heaven, which became an integral part of Confucianism. When Heaven-sent calamities and maladministration caused a rebellion that overthrew the ruler, he had lost the Mandate of Heaven. In support of this doctrine Mencius could quote from the *Book of History*: "Heaven sees as the people see; Heaven hears as the people hear" (V, I, 5). Thus successful rebellion was given divine sanction. Again, in support of the importance of the people, Mencius said: "[In the constitution of the state] the people rank the highest, the spirits of land and grain come next, and the ruler counts the least" (VII, II, 14). Where Confucius had upheld the hereditary right of rulers, Mencius, perhaps influenced by Mo-tzu's teaching, reduced them to replaceable servants of the people whose tenure depended on just and effective administration.

Mencius is best known, however, for his thesis that man is by nature good but subject to infinite corruptibility in the same way that the ancient perfection of the social and political order had become corrupted. Therefore the innate goodness in man must be cultivated by education and virtuous government. Mencius asserted that those who are more virtuous than others have become so because they have developed more fully their original capability. Those who have become evil have neglected the development of their innate virtue.

The issue of whether man is by nature good or bad apparently never crossed the pragmatic mind of Confucius and, if it had, he probably would have treated it as meaningless. Mencius' position would perhaps have been forgotten if it had not been challenged by the more radical and somewhat heretical Confucianist, Hsün-tzu.

HSÜN-TZU (FL. 298–238 B.C.)

By the time of Hsün-tzu the old order was so decayed that any hope for its reestablishment appeared futile. To his way of thinking the time had arrived for a realistic and rational reappraisal of the fundamental tenets of Confucianism in the light of contemporary conditions. Moreover, in contrast with Confucius and Mencius, he was a practicing politician holding high office in the states of Ch'i and Ch'u and, therefore, could not afford to ignore the desperate realities of the times. At least, these two factors appear to explain the cold-blooded realism of his writing, which led to his denunciation as a heretic by later Confucianists. A further basis for denouncing him was the fact that two of his students became the outstanding exponents of Legalism.

In his time, the desperate nature of the political struggle had encouraged the growth in importance of diviners who purported to predict the course of events. The rulers, engaged in ruthless conflict, patronized every source of guidance, including these men who posed as interpreters of the will of Heaven and the spirits. Hsün-tzu utilized rational argument in an effort to undermine the faith placed in these charlatans. He did not deny the operation of Heaven in human affairs, but he insisted that it was beyond human prediction and control, at least by such superstitious practices. The true sage, he asserted, is an activist who will concentrate his attention on those human affairs that he can manipulate and control. Furthermore, he was a positive advocate of progress through human effort, arguing that man can improve his environment and livelihood through positive, rational efforts.

From this overriding humanistic emphasis in his thought Hsün-tzu was led to a consideration of the fundamental factors governing human nature. His analysis resulted in a conclusion diametrically opposed to that of Mencius. According to Hsün-tzu, man is by nature evil and, under the influence of his passions, is filled with selfishness, covetousness, envy, and hatred. His goodness is acquired as a result of the rules and regulations of society, the laws of the state, and the discipline of education, both informal and formal. Although initially evil, man and society are infinitely perfectible. Later Confucianists were repelled by his analysis of human nature as evil and failed to appreciate the progressive vista for mankind opened up by his doctrine of infinite perfectibility.

His emphasis on the need to regulate, guide, and control man in order to overcome his evil propensities provided a philosophical foundation for the importance attached to laws by the Legalists. Thus Hsün-tzu shifted subtly away from the Confucian emphasis on a government of morally trained men to a government of laws administered by men. In essence, however, this ideological conflict between Mencius and Hsün-tzu on the original nature of man was superficial. Both agreed that the development of goodness depended on education that inculcated moral discipline and ethical conduct.

THE GREAT LEARNING AND THE MEAN

Two brief works of uncertain authorship were later classified with the *Analects* and the *Mencius* as the four basic works to be studied and memorized by every aspiring Confucian scholar. *The Great Learning* emphasized the necessity of self-cultivation and self-discipline as preparation for governing others and for maintaining social order. A frequently quoted passage illustrates the

Confucian conception of government by virtuous men as well as the Chinese penchant for orderly classification and organization.

> The ancients who wished clearly to exemplify illustrious virtue throughout the world would first set up good government in their states. Wishing to govern well their states, they would regulate their families. Wishing to regulate their families, they would first cultivate their persons. Wishing to cultivate their persons, they would first rectify their minds. Wishing to rectify their minds, they would first seek sincerity in their thoughts. Wishing for sincerity in their thoughts, they would first extend their knowledge. The extension of knowledge lay in the investigation of things. For only when things are investigated is knowledge extended; only when knowledge is extended are thoughts sincere; only when thoughts are sincere are minds rectified; only when minds are rectified are our persons cultivated; only when our persons are cultivated are our families regulated; only when families are regulated are states well governed; and only when states are well governed is there peace in the world.
> (de Bary, ed., *Sources of Chinese Traditions*, p. 129.)

Although the title of *The Mean* concerns the Confucian doctrine of moderation and self-discipline, this work goes much farther, developing a cosmology to demonstrate that by ethical conduct man can achieve a transcendental unity and harmony with heaven and earth. Apparently this was the Confucian answer to the Taoist dismissal of social ethics as irrelevant. Later, however, this exercise in metaphysics was utilized to bridge the gulf between Confucianism and both Taoism and Buddhism.

What should be apparent by now is that, as in other civilizations, the "Hundred Schools of Thought" in China were interacting on and borrowing from each other in

preparation for later synthesis. Almost every strain of thought was represented and exercised its influence to a greater or lesser degree. The works of these other schools are lost, and they are known by the references to them in the works of the major schools. These references alone indicate their influence.

THE YIN-YANG SCHOOL

One of the most important of these other schools was one that sought to explain the workings of nature on the two opposed, but complementary, principles of Yin and Yang. The attributes of Yin are female, dark, cold, and negative; the attributes of Yang are male, light, hot, and positive. Unlike Western dualism, these two principles are not separate and distinct, but essentially united in a shifting relationship in which one prevails for a while and then the other. This conception contributes to the fundamental optimism of the Chinese people because it supports the belief that the worse things become the nearer they are to shifting for the better. The Yin-Yang doctrine combined with the complex combinations of the "five elements" of wood, metal, fire, water, and earth and their cosmic correlatives has been an important factor in philosophical as well as popular thought throughout Chinese history.

LEGALISM

The last major school of thought was Legalism. Although it drew on the accumulated ideas of its predecessors, it broke radically with the common emphasis of the older philosophies on the welfare of the people. In their emphasis on the state, the Legalists were only giving philosophical rationalization for the actual state of affairs in the third century B.C. The larger states, locked in a fight to the finish, had naturally stressed centralization of power in the hands of the ruler and the development of government by laws rather than men. The looser, personalized relationship possible in the many small states of former times was no longer feasible. More than any other, the state of Ch'in epitomized this development and, therefore, it is not surprising that the two chief exponents of Legalism should find employment there.

Both Han Fei-tzu (d 233 B.C.) and Li Ssu (d 208 B.C.) had been students of Hsün-tzu and were deeply influenced by his rationalism as well as by his low estimation of human nature and his belief in the need for specified rewards and punishments. But they were also influenced partially by Mo-Tzu's authoritarianism and utilitarianism and even more by the Taoist disdain for conventional morality and scholarship. Their ideal state, in which well-cared for, but ignorant, subjects blindly obeyed the dictates of an absolute ruler, was not unrelated to the policy prescribed in the *Tao Te Ching*. Indeed, in their well-ordered state, once the law code had been fully elaborated, the ruler, like the Taoist ideal, would do everything by doing nothing. The machinery of government would function automatically without any need for his intervention.

As a hardheaded realist, Han Fei-tzu repudiated the other philosophies' appeals to the ancient past for guides to present action on the relativistic grounds that different times and different circumstances require different answers and actions. He ridiculed the other philosophers for their failure to examine and deal with things as they are. Moreover, he criticized the patronage extended to these men of learning, who not only were unable to solve current problems but also were constantly at odds with each other, and more concerned with the supposed welfare of the people than with that of their patron. They would destroy incentive and weaken the state by taxing the rich and giving to the poor. "Therefore, the intelligent ruler upholds solid facts and discards useless frills. He does not speak about deeds of humanity and righteousness, and he does not listen to the words of learned men" (*Han Fei-tzu*, Chapter 50).

He pointed out that the people in their ignorant shortsightedness are bound to object to those measures that are best for them in the long run. Regardless of the people's complaints, the ruler should conscript labor to expand the arable area, fill his granaries and treasuries by taxation in preparation for famine and war, exact harsh penalties to eliminate the unruly, and require universal military training and service without favoritism.

Legalist doctrines were most thoroughly implemented in the state of Ch'in which, in part because of them, seized the Chou territory and symbols of authority in 256 B.C. and completed the conquest of all the Chinese states in 221 B.C. Although many of the measures had been adopted in practice before the Legalist theories were set forth, the work was completed and applied to the Ch'in empire by Li Ssu as prime minister.

The hereditary aristocracy supported by landholdings was eliminated, and all land was reclaimed and granted directly to its tillers by the ruler. All officers, both civil and military, were appointed and paid by the ruler. An extensive law code and standard weights and measures were prescribed. Large water control and irrigation projects expanded agricultural production and facilitated communication. As the economic foundation of the state, agriculture was favored, while industry and especially commerce were held in low regard. All aspects of the economy, however, were put under state control and regulation. In particular, foreign trade, as a part of foreign policy, was closely controlled. In sum, then, the interests of individuals and families were wholly subordinated to those of the state, and all power was concentrated in the ruler and his select group of Legalist advisers.

THE CH'IN EMPIRE (221 – 207 B.C.)

On the establishment of the Ch'in Empire these reforms with some additional refinements were applied to all of China, completing the first of two major "revolutions" in

Chinese history. The second Chinese revolution began with the overthrow of the Manchu dynasty in 1912 and is still developing under Communist auspices. It is interesting to observe the similarity between Legalist and Communist procedures, although they are separated in time by almost 2200 years. In making such a comparison, however, we must keep in mind the very great differences in conditions.

Aristocratic families, reportedly numbering 120,000 persons, were separated from their lands and placed in what amounted to a concentration camp near the imperial capital. The lands taken over by the state were redistributed to the peasants who were urged and aided to increase production in order to pay larger taxes for the support of the government. Peasant families were made collectively responsible for the activities of their members. Moreover, a traditional puritanical tendency in Chinese society was reinforced by prohibiting the remarriage of widows and decreeing the death penalty for adultery. Confiscation of the property of rich merchants and manufacturers underlined the Legalist emphasis on agriculture as the backbone of Chinese civilization and the state. The country was divided and subdivided into administrative units ruled by appointed and salaried officials. Ch'in Shih-Huang-Ti (the First Emperor of Ch'in) kept as close a check as possible on local administration by constant tours of inspection, while a vast roadbuilding program which utilized conscripted labor was undertaken to improve communications and make it possible for the army to move rapidly to any threatened area. However, highways radiating from the capital could also facilitate a swift advance on the imperial center by rebels or invaders.

The armies of the old states were disarmed and demobilized, releasing large numbers of soldiers who found it difficult to adapt to civilian life. Many former soldiers and other dissidents could not keep out of trouble and were condemned to hard labor, especially in the construction of the Great Wall of China where many died as a result of inadequate food rations. To overcome local patriotism and resistance and for purposes of defense, large numbers were moved in mass from their homes and were resettled in newly acquired frontier areas. As this implies, the vigorous emperor engaged in almost continuous military campaigns to expand the territory of the empire and to eliminate all threats to his regime.

Legalist doctrine prescribed uniformity of all instruments of nationwide use and ideological conformity. Instruments such as weights and measures, axle widths, and the written language were standardized throughout the realm, providing permanent ties. On ideological conformity a great debate ensued at court. The eldest son of the emperor favored a more liberal policy, probably because of the shortage of trained Legalists to fill governmental positions, but the hard line advocated by Li Ssu prevailed. Naturally, many scholars of the other schools of thought found it very difficult to accept Legalist doctrines. They were embittered by the loss of their civil service posts as well as their landholdings. The most outspoken were either executed as examples to the rest or were condemned to labor gangs. Many more conformed outwardly, and some obtained governmental posts, while they seethed inwardly with resentment which they stored up for the future. The most notorious Legalist device intended to ensure the eradication of opposing doctrines was the so-called "Burning of the Books" advocated by Li Ssu. All works of other schools, all histories of other states than Ch'in and, indeed, all works of a non-practical nature, except those in the hands of an approved list of safe Legalist scholars and one copy of each in the imperial library were ordered to be burned. Furthermore, anyone who referred to the past to criticize the present was to be executed along with all members of his family, and any who failed to carry out the book-burning decree within 30 days was to be branded and condemned to labor on the Great Wall.

Even under modern conditions with

much larger bureaucracies supported by the vast resources of industrial economies, a thorough enforcement of such a decree would prove extremely difficult. In the less developed circumstances of the Ch'in Empire, the effectiveness of this decree must have been limited. Moreover, the short life of the Ch'in dynasty was survived by many scholars who had studied and memorized many of the more important works. Perhaps most damaging to the Chinese literary heritage was the destruction of the imperial library by the rebels who captured the capital.

At the death of the first emperor in 210 B.C. his liberally inclined eldest son was deceived into committing suicide, and the government fell into the control of Li Ssu and the eunuch Chao Kao. Before long, Chao Kao with true Legalist ruthlessness liquidated Li Ssu and, confronted with mounting discontent and rebellions, sought to shore up the government by relaxing some of the more stringent Legalist measures. But the time had passed when steps of this kind might have succeeded. Oppression and the burdens of public works and wars had alienated all elements of society, even the peasantry who had initially benefited from land redistribution. Oppressive taxes and conscription had persuaded many of them to abandon their lands and take to banditry under leaders drawn from their own ranks or surviving aristocrats. In 207 B.C., less than 15 years after its triumphant establishment, the mighty Ch'in Empire was violently overthrown. In 202 B.C. an untutored peasant leader, Liu Pang, established the more moderate and enduring Han dynasty.

THE HAN DYNASTY
(202 B.C. – 220 A.D.)

Although the new regime backed away from the more severe features of Legalism, the "revolution" under Ch'in auspices had been too thorough to permit a return to the pre-Ch'in way of life. In spite of the partial revival of political decentralization, this type

of political organization had been discredited by the development of bureaucracy even before the "revolution." The wars of unification, liberation, and reunification, plus Ch'in policies, had all but destroyed the hereditary aristocracy, opening a wide avenue to advancement for commoners. Although the reaction to Ch'in oppression discredited Legalism as a recognized school, its doctrines in a modified form were incorporated into the philosophical synthesis that evolved under the label of Confucianism. The Legalist conception of a single, absolute ruler served by appointed and salaried officials and empowered to make law by imperial decree was retained. The idea of a unified state with a standardized written language provided the basis for the persistence of a sense of cultural identity, even during later periods of political fragmentation. The principle of the farmer as the backbone of the state requiring equitable land distribution and supported by public works, though regularly abused, was reasserted at the establishment of each new dynasty after the Han. In short, the Legalist heritage, which has never been lost for long, was the doctrine of an authoritarian, bureaucratic empire based on a prosperous peasantry controlled, aided, and protected by the state.

The founder of the Han dynasty had little respect for scholarship. His roots were in the peasantry who had been so grievously exploited under his predecessors. A story, possibly apochryphal, is told that illustrates his earthy outlook. When approached by a contingent of Confucian scholars whose leader informed him that an empire could not be successfully ruled by force alone, he ordered the leader to remove his hat, urinated in it, and then ordered him to put it back on his head. Obviously he intended to rule and not be ruled by his bureaucracy.

Perhaps because of his peasant distrust of scholar-officials, as well as the need to reward his chief supporters and to relax the strict centralization of the Ch'in, he granted out much of China in new estates or "kingdoms." In view of the vast extent of the empire, the primitive nature of communications, and the limited income that could reasonably be extracted from an agricultural economy, the only alternative appeared to be a large bureaucracy that was supported by heavy taxes on the peasantry. The ruler soon regretted this decision, however, and spent the rest of his life eliminating the seven "kings" who were not members of the imperial family. Also he initiated the policy of transferring actual power in these domains to imperial governors. His successors spent the next 50 years reducing the remaining lords to impotence by various devices. In spite of this limited revival of decentralization, which, at least, reduced the cost of the central government and transferred the odium for exploitation to the lords, Liu Pang and his successors retained in a modified form the machinery of imperial government developed by the Ch'in dynasty.

The limited bureaucracy developed even in his reign thereafter increasingly drew on the supply of Confucian scholars. However, the Confucianism of the Han era had to be modified to fit the requirements of an empire and absorbed elements from other schools that gave it a distinctive quality. Before considering imperial Confucianism, two other typical problems should be mentioned briefly.

While Liu Pang's court was exceptionally frugal and his decentralization provided an economic breathing spell after the heavy costs of the Ch'in dynasty, he and his successors were confronted by the external threat of the nomadic Hsiung-nu (known later in Europe as the Huns), the strong tribal confederation that had caused the Ch'in ruler to undertake the construction of the Great Wall. The Hsiung-nu leader had gained control of almost all the tribes between the Chinese frontier and the Pamirs and was reputed to be able to mobilize a skilled cavalry force of 300,000. Desperately needing peace to deal with internal problems, Liu Pang bought him off by the flattering gift of an imperial princess and a supply of silk and other products of Chinese civilization in return for horses to mount his cavalry. This became a characteristic stratagem to protect the frontier against nomadic incursions. But it did not eliminate the menace whose seriousness varied with the changes in weather that provided adequate or inadequate pasturage for their flocks. Another technique was to support one or another tribal leader to encourage internal division and tribal strife. Only as a last resort was military conquest attempted and, even when it was successful, the gains seldom lasted for long. The steppes were not suited for the intensive agriculture that was the basis of Chinese civilization. Trade and the tendency of Chinese political dissidents to offer their services to nomadic chieftains did have the useful effect of acculturating to some degree these neighbors of the Chinese. In periods of political weakness or disunity, northern China was frequently overrun and "barbarian" dynasties were established without serious change in the imperial system of government. Therefore, until the arrival in strength of Europeans by sea in the nineteenth century, the nomads to the north and west provided the only serious external menace to the Chinese Empire.

A frequently recurring internal problem concerned the succession. The founder of a dynasty was naturally a vigorous individual who was busily engaged in the establishment of his regime and, therefore, fully conversant at first hand with its problems. His successors, however, tended to be raised in the harem with little or no contact with the outside world. If at their accession they were minors, their mothers as Empress Dowagers wielded great, and often decisive, power and, under the pressure of family loyalty, frequently utilized their influence to put their relatives in control of the government. The first notable example of this problem was Liu Pang's widow, the Empress Dowager Lü Hou, who did such a thorough job that she almost succeeded in displacing her husband's family altogether. She had shared all her husband's hardships in his rise to power, and her dynamic and ruthless character may have made an important contribution to his success. She disfigured, tortured, and dispatched her husband's favorite concubine with the extreme cruelty of vengeance and then ruled the realm with an iron hand for 15 years. Her major contribution was increased recognition of Confucian scholars by their appointment to offices. At her death those loyal to Liu Pang rose and wiped out her family, restoring another of his sons to the throne. But the problem of court intrigue and the cloistered life of the rulers was never solved throughout the history of the empire.

HAN CONFUCIANISM

Brief as it was, the rigors and oppression of the Ch'in dynasty threw the schools of thought into disarray from which recovery was a slow and prolonged process. Only gradually was Confucianism able to rise and gain recognition as the orthodox doctrine of state and society. Its complete success, which was not achieved until the Later Han dynasty (25–220 A.D.), was facilitated by the eclectic way in which it adapted and adopted many features of the other schools, including the Legalist, Taoist, and Yin-Yang. In this synthesis, however, Confucian doctrines furnished the predominant elements and, therefore, the title of Confucianism is appropriate.

Even Liu Pang, in spite of his distrust of scholars, recognized his need for their services and issued a call for the recommendations of educated and able men to staff the civil service. During his widow's "reign," the Ch'in prohibition of philosophical and historical works was raised, and the reconstitution and study of classic texts was begun. Eventually five of these classics were singled out as essential to the education of a Confucian scholar: the *Classic of Songs* containing 305 selected poems of the tenth to seventh centuries B.C. which were given philosophical interpretations; the *Classic of Documents*

consisting of a selection of semihistorical documents that were supposedly composed in the early Chou period, but containing many later forgeries or what some Chinese scholars prefer to call "imaginative reconstructions"; the *Classic of Changes*, a work on divination for the interpretation of the eight trigrams and 64 hexagrams; the *Spring and Autumn Annals*, a terse chronological account of events at the court of Lu, 722–481 B.C., into which Confucius and his successors had read great significance; and the *Book of Rites*, a later compilation for the proper performance of appropriate rites and rituals. Although these works received the sanctity of scripture, their terseness, which made their meaning obscure, and the need to adapt their message to the very different circumstances of a unified state required the composition of extensive explanatory, and often fanciful, commentaries.

The world of man organized into a single central state under an absolute ruler called forth a cosmological intrepretation in terms of the traditional triad of heaven, earth, and man. In the process of fashioning this ideology much Taoist and Yin-Yang theory was drawn on, in contrast with Confucius' more limited concern with the regulation of human affairs on an ethical basis. Although subsequently modified, especially by Buddhist influence, the general formulation during the Han era of what was labeled Confucianism provided the intellectual and cultural foundation until recent times not only for China but also, to a substantial degree, for Korea, Vietnam, and Japan.

The empire under an absolute ruler responsible for the orderly relationship of man with earth and heaven was interpreted as having always existed and as having undergone cyclical ups and downs according to the Yin-Yang theory and the proper exercise of the rulers' responsibilities. One function of the ruler was to perform correctly the rites essential to maintaining harmony with earth and heaven and to keep a weather eye out for omens and portents that might indicate malfunctioning. This conception encouraged serious study and analysis to discover the laws governing natural relationships that were intended to be "scientific" but that, in fact, led to the growth of pseudoscientific superstition. A second function of the ruler was the protection of the people against threats, both internal and external, by the maintenance of an adequate military force. Finally and most importantly, the ruler was responsible for the material and moral welfare of the people, but with a minimum of meddling in their affairs. This responsibility involved the construction and maintenance of essential public works and the delegation of his authority to appointed scholar-officials who, from Wu Ti's reign (141–87 B.C.), were increasingly selected on the basis of examinations that emphasized proficiency in Confucian doctrines.

The inability of an agricultural economy to support a large bureaucracy, reinforced by the Taoist emphasis on laissez-faire, inspired the doctrine that the people were expected to manage their own affairs with a minimum of recourse to the state. In fact, however, vigorous emperors like Wu Ti did intervene extensively in the economic life of the people to gain the revenues to support their activities. Such activist policies, including military expansion, were constantly decried by the Confucianists as sapping the economic strength of the state and, in fact, they generally did contribute to eventual decline. Naturally, the scholar-officials preferred the type of emperor who submitted to their direction and permitted them to pursue a program of peace and prosperity.

In short, the emperor as head of the human hierarchy was held responsible for maintaining order and well-being among men and harmony between man, earth, and heaven; yet he was supposed to accomplish this task with a minimum of active intervention, laws, and expense. If things went well, he enjoyed the Mandate of Heaven. If they went badly, he—and not the scholar-officials who only exercised delegated authority—was solely to blame and in danger of losing his mandate. In practice, under Han Confucianism weak emperors became the puppets, captives, and scapegoats of the Confucian scholar-official class. This reciprocal relationship could be destroyed only by external force or internal rebellion caused by excessive economic oppression and calamities.

Economic theory inherited from the Ch'in dynasty emphasized the primacy of agriculture and discriminated against trade. Merchants and their descendants were legally barred from public office, and rulers were admonished to reckon their wealth in reserves of grain, not gold. Merchants were forbidden the ownership of land. This regulation also reserved moneylending to the scholar-gentry class. Under the governmental policy of nonintervention, land tended to fall into the hands of landlords through foreclosure and this constantly raised the problem of land reform. Since scholars and great landed families enjoyed privileged status and the support of those among them who held office, land-reform proposals encountered stiff resistance and were seldom put into effect. This was, perhaps, the most serious weakness of the Confucian system of government and frequently the key factor in the overthrow of a dynasty. Wu Ti's chief advisor sought without much success to carry out a measure of land reform.

WU TI (141 – 87 B.C.)

By the time of the accession of this energetic ruler, China had enjoyed 60 years of comparatively mild government in which to recover from Ch'in oppression and the ravages of rebellion. The growth in both population and wealth was reflected in the need for land reform. Before Wu Ti's accession the last kingdoms had been broken up, and it seemed to him to be time for greater centralization of authority. Costly campaigns in almost every year culminated in the conquest of North Vietnam in the south, North Korea in the northeast, and the Kansu corridor and Tarim Basin vital to the control of trade with the west. In 104 B.C. one daring general successfully led armies across the Pamirs and subdued Ferghana. These military expeditions extending more than 2000 miles from the capital across desert wastes represent a spectacular, but expensive, achievement.

To pay for them and to check local corruption, Wu Ti instituted extensive state intervention into economic affairs at home. Vast irrigation, canal, and road-building programs were carried out with conscripted labor in addition to heavier taxes. To maintain his conquests, great numbers were forced to colonize the new areas. For example, some 700,000 were transported to occupy the arid Kansu corridor. Colonization, however, may have eased the pressure on the available arable land. Further measures were the establishment of state monopolies for vital products, such as iron, salt, liquor, and coinage. In addition, the government entered commerce through the bureau of "Equalization and Standardization," which set up marketing offices to purchase goods in oversupply at low prices for storage and resale elsewhere where they were in short supply. Of course, this practice and the monopolies were justified as protection against private exploitation and a means of stabilizing both prices and supplies. Although this may have been the sincere intention, the price record suggests that profit for the government was an added motive.

Wu Ti also expanded imperial support of Confucianist scholarship and relied more and more on competitive civil service examinations to staff a growing bureaucracy; he was interested in promoting an efficient corps of officials indoctrinated in loyalty to the throne. On the other hand, his concern for finding the elixir of eternal life and interpreting omens reinforced the already strong Taoist and pseudoscientific ingredients in Han Confucianism.

For the rest of the Early Han dynasty (202 B.C.–9 A.D.) the character of the government fluctuated between strong rulers and weak rulers under dominant bureaucracies, but none of these regimes had the ability or the will to cope effectively with the mounting pressure of internal problems. Finally, an exceptionally energetic scholar-official succeeded via the "petticoat" route in obtaining control of the government and displacing the Han family on the throne.

WANG MANG AND THE NEW DYNASTY (9 – 23 A.D.)

After the founder of the Ch'in Empire two other radical reformers in the course of Chinese history have received special attention from modern historians as precedent-setters for contemporary socialist and statist doctrines. In their own times both ultimately failed because of their inability to win sufficient support from the scholar-official class. Both were dedicated exponents of Confucianism, but their similar programs bear a closer relationship to Legalist statism. The first reformer, Wang Mang, has been condemned by Confucian historians as a usurper. The second, Wang An-shih (1021–1086), although he sought to carry out his program under Sung imperial auspices, has been seriously criticized as a heretic whose reforms would have subverted the Confucian philosophy and practice of government. In both cases, their reforms illustrate basic weaknesses in the Confucian system of government that might have been overcome by greater centralization.

Wang Mang's rise to power was another instance of female influence at court. In 48 B.C. a female member of the Wang family became the favorite concubine of the heir apparent. At his accession she was named empress and her son, heir apparent. In 33 B.C. her son, still a minor, succeeded to the throne and, as Empress Dowager, she filled the important ministries with her relatives, including her nephew, Wang Mang, who was already noted for his scholarship, temperate living, filial piety, and patronage of learning. In short, by Confucian standards he was a true gentleman, cultivating virtue and practicing altruism. For more than 20 years he was a powerful, able, and diligent minister until the emperor died childless and the new ruler's mother replaced Wang's relatives with her own. But Wang Mang had gained too high a reputation to be ignored for long. At the accession of a new, eight-year-old emperor in 1 A.D., he was appointed regent and began to assert himself by giving generous support to the poor and by setting up a new university staffed with scholars who were instructed to develop accurate texts of the Classics. In 5 A.D. this boy emperor died, possibly poisoned, and was succeeded by an infant, while Wang Mang took the title of acting emperor. Finally, in 9 A.D., he deposed this puppet and declared his New (Hsin) dynasty.

This drastic step was inspired by his conviction that only a program of radical reform could save the empire. One of his first decrees confiscated huge estates and redistributed them to peasant farmers. At the same time he decreed the abolition of slavery. The enforcement of these two decrees and those that followed depended on the cooperation of the scholar-official class drawn largely from the great landed families. Within 3 years he had to concede defeat by withdrawing them, although he placed a prohibitive tax on slaveholding.

As a further assistance to the peasants he tried to fix and maintain fair prices by restoring governmental purchase and storing of surpluses. This action alienated the merchants. In addition, he provided state loans without interest for funerals and other Confucian rites and loans at lower than customary interest rates for productive activities. This reform, if effective, would have undermined the lucrative moneylending activities of the landlords. To transfer the burden of taxation from the back of the peasants, he tried to introduce an income tax. To solve the financial problems of the government, he debased the currency, causing severe in-flation, and added new state monopolies.

Recognizing that his chief need was a civil service sympathetic to his reforms, he built dormitories and provided scholarships for thousands of students, vastly expanding state support of education. This educational program, if maintained long enough, might have broken the grip of the landlord class on education and government service.

Much to Wang Mang's dismay his reforms were followed by peasant rebellions which were generated by the failure and official abuse, such as enforced borrowing, of his drastic reforms. Internal disorder was compounded by nomadic incursions. A feature common to Chinese peasant rebellions was their organization under the leadership of a secret society, in this case the Red Eyebrows inspired by popular Taoist beliefs. Excluded from participation in government and largely left to their own devices by laissez-faire policies, Chinese peasants and merchants have always felt a need for mutual aid societies which, unrecognized and seen as a menace by the government, have necessarily had to be secret and conspiratorial. Although devoted to peaceful purposes in normal times, those societies with widespread memberships could be converted to anti-dynastic purposes in times of severe distress by rebel leaders who played on the people's superstitions and belief in magic. Although these societies have frequently succeeded in overthrowing a dynasty, their efforts to establish a new dynasty have always significantly failed. Successful administration in China has always required the services of an adequate number of the educated elite. In Wang Mang's case, his reforms had not only failed to be implemented in an honest and effective fashion by the bureaucracy but had also positively contributed to the increase of economic distress. With rebellions ravaging the country and the capital besieged, this dedicated reformer was dispatched by his own troops. After two more years of chaos a scion of the Han dynasty was restored to the throne.

The civil strife had eliminated enough of

the wealthy families to allow the revival of prosperity and the regaining of lost conquests under able rulers of the Later Han dynasty (25–220 A.D.), but the basic problems which Wang Mang had sought to reform were never squarely faced and corrected. The chief device developed by the Later Han emperors to offset the monopoly of power held by the Confucian bureaucracy was a reliance on eunuchs as advisors and ministers. This cure, however, proved worse than the disease. The playing off of eunuchs against bureaucrats and clique against clique only resulted in bloodbaths at court, which undermined what little Confucian virtue remained in the central government. The ultimate beneficiaries of this breakdown of governmental morale were the generals of large landed families who maintained private professional armies following the collapse of the system of conscription.

THE DYNASTIC CYCLE

As a result of the Confucian emphasis on looking to the glorious past as a guide to present action, the study of history in China received a greater stimulus to development than in any other civilization. This same emphasis also encouraged Chinese historians to look for repetitive patterns and motifs rather than the unique in history. A direct consequence was their elaboration of a cyclical, rather than a progressive, interpretation that sought to explain the ups and downs of history in terms of the Confucian conception of the virtue or lack of virtue of individuals, especially emperors. Therefore, following the example of the great Han historian, Pan Ku (d 92 A.D.), Chinese historians have organized their histories according to dynasties and have laid great stress on biographies that illustrate the virtuous or unvirtuous conduct of individuals. Economic and cultural developments have not been ignored but have been subordinated and evaluated according to Confucian values. Western students of Chinese history, dependent on Chinese sources, naturally have tended to accept this

cyclical interpretation, although they have searched for impersonal social, economic, and cultural factors to fill out the personalized Chinese interpretation. Some Western scholars have directed their quest toward evidence of change and progress but, while many instances of new and progressive developments have been uncovered, the domination of Confucian orthodoxy with its insistence on returning to past practice gives validity to the cyclical view of Chinese history—even if the emphasis on individual responsibility is rejected.

Thanks to the circular nature of the cyclical theory, a generalized analysis of its common features may be begun at any point, with the establishment of a new dynasty being perhaps the logical starting point. An energetic conqueror can only succeed in establishing a dynasty if he can obtain the administrative assistance of an adequate number of the educated elite. The empire was too large and the civilization too complex to be administered effectively by illiterate warriors. Even nomadic conquerors who wished to perpetuate their control and not merely gain plunder recognized this necessity. Since all educated persons were Confucianists who looked to past example, the government of each new dynasty was modeled on its predecessors with only those modifications that the new ruler could introduce.

The founder's military strength and the vigor of his immediate successor, who often had played a vital role in his father's success, kept the Confucian bureaucracy temporarily under control. Later emperors, isolated in the court, frequently were reduced to tools of the bureaucracy. Vigorous rulers might assert their authority through favored ministers or eunuchs, or by playing off one clique of officials against another because there were never enough posts to please all. But hereditary succession assured the accession of weaklings. Indeed, the incidence of able and conscientious rulers was higher than might be expected, considering the temptations to debauchery and dillettantism. According to the traditional Chinese interpretation, extreme inattention to duty and virtue would finally result in a spate of natural portents and calamities that indicated the withdrawal of the Mandate of Heaven.

According to the extent of disasters, hardship, and civil strife during the decline and after the fall of a dynasty, the total population and the number and wealth of the educated class had been reduced, easing the problems of the new dynasty. Frequently, however, a land reform measure was carried out to put more peasants on the tax rolls. Greater revenues made possible the restoration of essential public works that, in turn, produced more income. In addition to public works, more food to feed a growing population might be produced by territorial acquisitions and favorable weather. Favorable weather also tended to reduce the nomadic menace by providing better pasturage. But there was a definite limit to the extent of arable land and the duration of good weather.

Eventually peace and prosperity encouraged the increase in numbers that resulted in intense pressure on the means of subsistence. Unable to support their families on smaller plots of land the peasants had to resort to the moneylender, and once in his grip the ultimate result was reduction to tenancy. But as a tenant the peasant's condition was worse. He had to pay up to 50 percent of his crop in rent, while the official tax had only amounted to one thirtieth to one fifteenth of the normal crop. As a result, many peasants had no recourse but to abandon their lands and take up the precarious career of banditry. An unfavorable turn of the weather forced those farming marginal lands to follow the same career.

Meanwhile, scholar-officials, sensing the impending end of a dynasty, falsified records or by other means withheld imperial revenues for their own benefit. At the same time they diverted into their own pockets revenues that normally were allocated to the maintenance of public works. In time this neglect provided the conditions for "natural"

disasters, such as floods and famines due to the breakdown of water control and irrigation works. A further device by which the official enriched himself was the charging of exorbitant prices for grain stored in the public granaries he controlled. Finally, the official was responsible for maintaining peace in his territory. When the cost of suppressing bandits became excessive, collaboration, advice, and protection in their activities directed toward another official's territory in return for a share of the plunder were not unknown. By this means the official provided himself with the nucleus of a personal army to advance his interests in the ensuing chaos. In short, the official was making the transition to warlord.

Thus in a period of declining revenues the government was confronted with growing military expenses to suppress rebellions and defend the frontiers. The bad weather which precipitated the growth of banditry also stimulated organized nomadic assaults on the settled lands of China and further aggravated the economic decline. To meet this challenge, the government tried to increase the levies on those peasants who remained on the tax rolls and also devised new taxes, such as tolls on trade and new monopolies. While such measures might temporarily provide the necessary revenue, they ultimately caused a further shrinkage in the economy. The dynasty was in its deaththroes; the Mandate of Heaven was about to be lost.

The deliverer of the deathblow might be strong enough to establish a new dynasty, or an interregnum might ensue in which warlords struggled for the power to reunite the realm. No matter how long this period of disunity might last, the ideal of unity inculcated by Confucianism was never lost. Sooner or later, under alien or indigenous auspices, the empire was reconstituted under a new dynasty that employed essentially the same machinery of government. Therefore, both the unity of China and the so-called dynastic cycle drew their vitality and reality from the cultural cement of Confucianism so thoroughly formulated during the Han era. When the Chinese call themselves men of Han, this label carries a deep and enduring meaning.

BUDDHISM

The conquest under the Han dynasty of the south coast and the Kansu corridor and Tarim Basin in the northwest, although interrupted during periods of weakness, greatly facilitated the growth of foreign trade. In company with the exchange of goods, ideas and techniques were also traded by land and sea. Under the successors of Han Wu Ti, military control was temporarily extended beyond the Pamirs into Central Asia. During the Later Han dynasty Chinese control was established over the whole region between the Pamirs and the Caspian Sea, thanks to the genius and determination of one general Pan Ch'ao (32–102 A.D.), the military representative of an outstanding family. His father, Pan Piao, began a dynastic history of the Early Han dynasty which was mostly written by his brother, Pan Ku, and completed by his sister, Pan Chao, China's first and still foremost female scholar.

Over the trade routes thus established, China received the one substantial alien influence prior to modern times—Buddhism. The Mahāyāna form transmitted initially over the land route from the Kushān dynasty of northwest India received the widest acceptance and popular support in China. Just when Buddhism first arrived in China is a subject of scholarly controversy, but by the last years of the Later Han era, when the disorders of the times were contributing to the growth of Taoism, Buddhism became a significant influence among scholars who were searching for new answers.

At first, this alien faith was accepted as a variant form of Taoism and, in fact, for the purposes of translation borrowed Taoist terminology. In the period of its greatest influence in China, from the fourth to the ninth centuries, Buddhism was approached selectively and adapted to fit the conditions of Chinese civilization. Although after the fall of the Han dynasty the dominance of Confucianism in government was lost with the revival of aristocracy in the form of great landed families, Confucian ideals and ethics continued to influence the development of Taoism and the adaptation of Buddhism to the Chinese way of life. The anti-social and otherworldly aspects were resisted, if not wholly rejected, and emphasis was placed on those features and values that could ease the sufferings of this life and could make a positive contribution to society. Even if Buddhism had not arrived, the political failure of Confucianism would have diminished its influence, and those Buddhist features that gained widest support would, in any case, have been sponsored by Taoism. Therefore, the alien character and impact of Buddhism should not be overemphasized. To say that China altered Buddhism more than Buddhism altered China is not an unjust statement.

But Buddhism did make some important contributions. Monasticism, though the Indian emphasis on clerical celibacy was modified in the course of time, was a permanent addition to Chinese culture. The growth of monasticism and its acquisition of vast tracts of tax-free land compelled the government later to limit and regulate it. New Yogic exercises and meditative disciplines as a means of preparing for enlightenment were welcome supplements to techniques that had already been evolved by Taoism. New magical practices were also seized on as additions to the Taoist stock of such lore. Many new deities supplied with Chinese attributes furnished variety and stimulation to popular religion. The Indian ideas of transmigration, *karma*, and *nirvana* proved somewhat abstruse for popular appreciation, but the idea of an afterlife in paradise gained great popularity. Chinese ethics, emphasizing kindness and regard for human life, were reinforced by Buddhism and extended to all animate life, a quality already latent in the Taoist regard for nature. In particular, the doctrine of charity and good works left a permanent imprint on Chinese morality. Chinese art had already been stimulated by nomadic art in the direction of less stylized and more realistic representations. The Greek-influenced Gandhara style of northwest India was transmitted to China, while Buddhist iconography stimulated the development of sculpture. Indeed, Buddhism provided a whole host of new subjects and themes to fire the imagination of Chinese artists. The Chinese with their ingrained respect for scholarship were impressed by the sheer volume of Buddhist literature, although they were puzzled by the diverse and contradictory nature of different works. With characteristic industriousness Chinese Buddhist scholars selected, classified, and sought to reconcile divergent doctrines. For this purpose they welcomed the Indian conception of relative levels of truth. Concerned with obtaining accurate editions of Buddhist writings, a large number of Chinese Buddhist scholars traveled to India beginning with Fa-hsien who left in 339 and returned in 414. He and a number of successors kept diaries that are invaluable both for Indian chronology and for their pictures of Indian life.

Buddhism made its first appeal to the educated, but frustrated, Chinese scholar class and only later gained popularity with the masses. It initially appealed also to the "barbarians" who began to overrun northern China at the beginning of the fourth century and who were not deeply imbued with a belief in the superiority of Chinese civilization. Following these conquests, many Chinese, both aristocrats and peasants, fled to the south carrying Buddhist views with them to reinforce the foothold already achieved. Incidentally, this continuing movement to the south greatly increased the population and wealth of the region and made it much more "Chinese" both in race and culture. Later, under the Southern Sung dynasty, the south clearly became the most populous,

wealthiest, and most "Chinese" part of China.

Space does not permit an analysis of the development and demise of the numerous sects of Chinese Buddhism which, in any case, tended to be tolerant and not exclusive of each other. Here we shall consider only those that were more enduring and popular because they were well adapted to Chinese views.

The T'ien-t'ai (Japanese, Tendai) sect, founded in the sixth century by a Chinese monk drew together those elements of Buddhist thought that were least inimical and most appealing to Chinese intellectuals. By stressing the Indian conception of different levels of relative truths, it was enabled to classify and organize many conflicting Buddhist doctrines in the kind of eclectic structure preferred by the Chinese mentality. In this manner, the Confucian scholar's love of ritual, study, and moral discipline was wedded to the Buddhist stress on meditation, concentration, and intuition. The first steps were deemed essential preparation for the last. Although such a regimen would limit the number of elite members, the doctrine of relative truths extended membership to the less educated, and emphasis on the Lotus Sūtra aided in its establishment as the most popular scripture of east Asian Buddhism.

Numerically largest was the Pure Land sect which traced its origins back to a Chinese monk of the late fourth and early fifth centuries. It stressed the devotional aspect of Mahāyāna Buddhism which required only a sincere declaration of faith in the Buddha Amītabha (Chinese: O-mi-t'o Fo; Japanese: Amida Butsu) to gain admission to his Western Paradise. Once freed from earthly bondage, this doctrine believed that final enlightenment would not be difficult to attain, but most ordinary believers did not look beyond paradise. As a balance to paradise, artists were free to depict in the most terrifying forms the characteristics of hell. Subsequently, popular rebellions, which had previously gained religious inspiration from Taoism, found their inspiration in this or other popular forms of Buddhism.

The later True Word sect gained popularity through its use of magic, incantations, and ceremonies—especially its masses for the dead. Its basic doctrine taught that all phenomenal existence, including man, was an emanation of the Eternal Buddha. This sect appealed to both the Taoist love of magic and the Confucian reverence for ritual.

Finally, the last to develop was the almost exclusively Chinese Ch'an (Japanese, Zen) sect which drew its major inspiration from the Taoist love of nature and simplicity. In addition, it represented a reaction against the complex ritual and philosophy of the other Buddhist sects. By sheer accident, its stress, drawn from Taoism, on meditation and intuitive realization of the Buddha nature within oneself approached closely the original teaching of Gautama. In other words, each individual must find enlightenment within and for himself. The anti-intellectual, anti-scholastic emphasis of Ch'an Buddhism relegated good works, asceticism, ritual, and study to the realm of the objective and transient world. Therefore, endeavors of this kind were considered to be largely futile exercises. Enlightenment could only come by a rigorous course that would relieve the mind of the dependence on ordinary logic and sensate perceptions. In place of the study of texts, the Ch'an technique relied on oral instruction by a master. Because of this procedure several techniques were developed by different masters, but the most common was the posing of meaningless problems which was intended to break the pupil's reliance on logic. Such a program emphasized the self-discipline and self-reliance that was to have a special appeal to the military class in Japan. On the other hand, the aim of finding the macrocosm in the microcosm inspired the approach to nature that so deeply influenced artistic and poetic expression, the artist seeking to present in each work the universal and eternal truth. This attitude encouraged

an impressionistic rather than realistic representation, characterized by brevity and simplicity.

SUI DYNASTY (589 – 618 A.D.)

The dynastic breakdown that left China disunited politically for more than 350 years was not as chaotic as it appears on the surface. Even before the official end of the Later Han dynasty in 220 A.D. the practical control of affairs at the local level had been usurped by great landed families, and the peasants had been reduced to virtual serfdom. Subsequently, these families extended their authority and many new families arose to replace those that declined, but no substantial change in the location and exercise of power took place during these centuries. At the dynastic level there was less turmoil in the south than in the north where nomadic inroads ravaged the land. In the south, every dynasty at least paid lip service to restoring the imperial machinery of government in their territory, and some energetic rulers did even more. None, however, could overthrow the great landed families. In the north, many nomadic conquerors had already begun to settle down and, in any case, realized that the Chinese administrative machinery was essential to collecting revenue from a settled peasantry. Before their conquests most had been served by Confucian officials and had intermarried with ruling or great families, becoming largely sinicized in the process. Every ruler, both north and south, kept alive the dream of restoring the unity of the empire. While the economy of the north may have suffered some deterioration, the economy of the south actually underwent substantial growth.

After the "barbarian" invaders had been thoroughly sinicized in language, customs, and dress, it was only a question of when, not if, China would be reunited. The strongman who accomplished this task was Yang Chien, a general of mixed ancestry who established the Sui dynasty (589–618). In many ways, the role and actions of this short-lived dynasty are analogous to the Ch'in dynasty. Like the Ch'in, it established a strong and severe centralized government, rebuilt the Great Wall, tied China together by canals and roads constructed by forced labor in vast numbers, and restored imperial prestige and authority by extensive and costly military campaigns. As in the case of the Ch'in, this full mobilization and exploitation of human resources, which laid the foundation of the succeeding dynasty's prosperity, alienated all elements of Chinese society and, at the first sign of weakness, inspired rebellions.

T'ANG DYNASTY (618 – 907)

Li Shih-min, the able, ambitious, and ruthless second son of a frontier official, goaded his father into rebellion and set him on the throne as the founder of the T'ang dynasty, the most vigorous, and cosmopolitan of Chinese dynasties. Unlike the early years of the Han dynasty, the first T'ang rulers gave the Chinese people little rest.

After liquidating his brothers, Li Shihmin (626–649) persuaded his father to abdicate in his favor. The first decade of the dynasty was occupied with the subjugation of dissidents. Then this restless ruler turned to an intensive program of internal improvements and external conquests. Both the public works of the Sui and his additions provided the surplus resources for such an active program. In spite of occasional setbacks, this ruler and his abler successors established Chinese control over a larger area than ever before.

Direct control over the Tarim Basin was regained, and military campaigns secured recognition of Chinese suzerainty in Tibet, the Trans-Pamir region, and even the upper reaches of the Indus River in modern Afghanistan. A Chinese ambassador to north India who was mistreated recruited Tibetan and Nepalese troops, captured the offending king, and delivered him as a prisoner to the imperial capital. To the south, North Vietnam was reconquered, and to the northeast, the king of the Korean kingdom of Silla, aided by Chinese troops, defeated the other Korean states, including their Japanese allies. Thereafter, a unified Korea remained a faithful subordinate of the T'ang dynasty. To maintain control of these areas, special military administrations were set up. They were: An-hsi (Pacify the West), An-pei (Pacify the North) in Mongolia, An-tung (Pacify the East) in southern Manchuria, and An-nam (Pacify the South) encompassing contemporary North Vietnam. In 751, after earlier successes, the decisive defeat of a Chinese army in the Trans-Pamir region by the rising power of the Arabs signaled the decline, though by no means the overthrow, of T'ang military strength.

Internally, neither the Sui nor early T'ang rulers were able to eliminate the aristocracy of great landed families, but the turmoil preceding and following the Sui dynasty did substantially reduce the number and influence of these almost autonomous units. Furthermore, both regimes vigorously reinstituted the civil-service examination system and developed additional measures to check the reassertion of aristocratic power. Every effort was made to develop and maintain a free, tax-paying peasantry. For the most part, this was achieved by opening new lands to agriculture and by reclaiming abandoned lands. A free peasantry not only provided taxes and conscript labor but also conscript soldiers and a militia. The growth of population and wealth in the south explains in large part the expensive canal-building program that was essential to the transportation of tax-grain to the north and the endangered frontiers.

By the eighth century the T'ang regime was faced with the traditional dilemma of the dynastic cycle: the growing costs of government at a time when revenues were declining as a result of the reduction of free peasants to tenant status. By the mid-eighth century this development had virtually eliminated the valuable conscript labor and peasant soldiery, and the government had to find the funds to hire labor and mercenary troops. Since the cheapest troops were "barbarians," Chinese military ability deteriorated and the survival of the regime became increasingly dependent on non-Chinese of questionable loyalty. Meanwhile, the Confucian civil service developed increased disdain for the military, furnishing cultural confirmation for the anti-militaristic outlook that from that time on became one of its predominant features.

To meet the fiscal problem, a tax reform was introduced of very large, but perhaps exaggerated, significance. Until this time, the direct levy of taxes in grain, labor, and military service on free peasant producers had been the major source of governmental income, supplemented by a small land tax, state monopolies, and sundry levies on wealth and commerce. The low taxes on trade combined with the vast empire, the extrovert and tolerant attitude toward foreigners, and the improvements in internal communications had stimulated a rapid expansion of trade and a money economy. In consideration of this background, the government gradually abandoned the direct levy on free peasants, greatly increased the land tax, and devised a number of new taxes on trade and wealth. The major source of revenue became the land tax assessed on all land according to productivity and regardless of ownership. In theory, the great landholding families lost their almost tax-free status and paid their fair share out of the rents collected from tenant farmers. In fact, however, prestige and privilege permitted them to discover ways of evading, in part, their obligation. Because the government had to hire labor to transport grain, every effort was made to get payment of taxes in cash rather than in kind. This new tax system propped up the finances of the government and helped to accelerate the decline of the great families, but a more important factor in this decline was the revival of an effective bureaucracy, staffed mostly by successful contestants in the Confucian-oriented examinations. In what has been described as a socioeconomic "revolution," the large, semiautonomous landholding families were gradually replaced in a process not completed until Ming times by a ruling elite of small landholders, called the "scholar-gentry," who looked to government service as the most prestigious career. The revival of Confucianism was further evidenced by successive attacks on Buddhist monasticism and the general decline of Buddhist and Taoist influence in the latter half of the T'ang dynasty.

Confucianism had come to prevail in theory, if not in practice, during the Han dynasty. During the long centuries of disunity it had been eclipsed by the political domination of the great families and the cultural predominance of Taoism and Buddhism. By the last half of the T'ang era it had regained its stature and was destined to achieve unquestioned supremacy under the Sung dynasty. In the process, the proponents of Confucianism rethought and elaborated its doctrines to incorporate the cultural and intellectual contributions of Taoism and Buddhism. In short, the "perfection" of Confucianism by Sung scholars involved the fuller realization in a general synthesis of qualities inherent for a long time in Chinese culture. Such "perfection" tended to stifle any further quest and to resist the introduction of alien conceptions. Any drastic change might subvert the firm control that the Confucianists had gained over the functioning of society and the state.

SUNG DYNASTY (960–1279)

The fiscal reform did no more than check the declining phase of the dynastic cycle into which the T'ang regime had entered. Indeed, the dependence on foreign mercenaries for military strength did nothing to popularize the regime, especially when these troops had to be used to suppress popular rebellions brought on by impoverishment. In 907 the

T'ang dynasty was overthrown and during a 50-year interregnum China was fragmented into contesting states. Finally, in the north, a Chinese general seized power and by exceptionally diplomatic and generous treatment of friend and foe gained control of most of China for the Sung dynasty which he founded. In every way he stood out as an ideal example of the virtuous Confucian ruler and thus won widespread support. The acceptance by him and his successors of Confucianist guidance made the Sung the least aggressive of Chinese dynasties. In any case, the great growth of trade by sea since the eighth century made control of the northwest no longer so desirable and essential, and the abandonment of reliance on a peasant militia and alien mercenaries discouraged militancy. The payment of tribute to "barbarian" states seemed a cheaper expedient than war with all its uncertainties. Yet the maintenance of a larger and larger army, untried in war and apparently dependent on the sheer weight of numbers, increasingly absorbed a larger and larger portion of imperial income. On the other hand, careful fiscal administration under greater centralized authority produced an income three times that of the T'ang at its height. The bulk of additional income came from the rapidly developing south.

Again, however, the inevitable problems of the dynastic cycle—growing costs and population combined with a declining tax yield—caught up with the Sung regime. The result was budgetary deficits. The great increase in the size of the army, which because of the hostile attitude toward aliens was primarily recruited from Chinese paupers, came to absorb 80 percent of the government's income in what amounted to a massive welfare program. In an effort to overcome these problems Wang An-shih (1021–1086) was given an opportunity to introduce a series of drastic reforms. For the most part, the proposals of this second great reformer in Chinese history were similar to those of Wang Mang, and as a good Confu-

cianist he also defended them on the basis of the Classics.

Among the proposals instituted by imperial decree were measures to assist the peasants in regaining economic independence and prosperity and "soak the rich" measures to recapture for the government the wealth that was increasingly being diverted into the pockets of the Confucian scholar-gentry class. Prices were fixed and stabilized by the revival of a vigorous government marketing program for surpluses. Government loans to peasants at lower than prevailing interest rates and government pawnshops were instituted. A revaluation of all land in terms of productivity was the basis of revised land-tax assessments. The remaining conscript labor obligations were abolished and replaced by a graduated tax that fell more heavily on the wealthy. Movable as well as immovable wealth was included in the assessment of a graduated tax. Wang An-shih tried to meet the military problem by reviving the peasants' military obligation. Every peasant family with more than one son was required to provide one for military training and service. In addition, to overcome the traditional Chinese weakness in cavalry, peasants in suitable areas were required to care for a horse which was provided along with winter fodder by the government.

To support his program with properly trained civil servants, Wang An-shih multiplied the number of government schools and revised the civil service examinations to place a greater emphasis on the selection of men versed in the contemporary problems of policy and administration. This shift reflected his philosophical position that so-called natural disasters were not heaven-sent but, instead, were the result of human errors and natural causes which should and could be avoided by able administrators.

His reforms, which were not notably original, were vigorously opposed by most of the outstanding scholar-officials for numerous reasons—political, personal, and ideological—but underlying their concern was the reinforcement of the Sung inclination toward greater autocracy. This threatened to limit and regulate the independence and vested privileges of the scholar-official class. As a consequence, contemporary Chinese historians gave Wang An-shih a "bad press." Nevertheless, the problems of the time led to the reintroduction of his reforms in whole or in part on a number of occasions, even after his death. Perhaps it is significant that even the hostile historians record no revolts when his reforms were operative. Yet they were never in force long enough or implemented sincerely enough by the bureaucracy to have a permanent effect. Confucian scholar-officials resisted, perhaps for good reasons, any radical reordering of the system that had put them in power.

Chinese diplomacy made the mistake of supporting barbarian attacks on one of the semi-sinicized states to whom tribute was being paid. Dissatisfied with their share of the spoils, the victors, who had taken the dynastic name of Chin (Golden), rewarded themselves by overrunning northern China. As a result, the Southern Sung dynasty (1127–1279) was forced to accept a boundary just north of the Yangtze, which it agreed not to defend, and the status of a tributary.

In spite of the loss of northern China, the greater attention given to the south resulted in such tremendous economic growth that this smaller state became actually wealthier than its larger predecessor had been. In addition to rural development, the Southern Sung era was characterized by rapid urban expansion that was supported by the growth of trade, despite the continued Confucian disdain for the merchant class.

T'ANG AND SUNG ECONOMIC AND CULTURAL DEVELOPMENT

The development of the south had been accelerating for several centuries. Between the eighth and twelfth centuries its population probably tripled, reflecting the investment in water-control projects, the introduction of improved seeds, crop diversification, and the more intensive cultivation of all arable land. Although the prosperity of the south was founded on agricultural development, a more important source of wealth was the huge growth of trade, particularly overseas trade, that was based on the demand for improved Chinese products. Technical advances increased the quality and quantity of silk, lacquer, and porcelain production. Muslim ships had initiated the trade, but by the twelfth century large Chinese vessels carrying up to 200 passengers became major participants, thanks in part to the development of the compass. The use of gunpowder in explosive weapons, though not a factor in trade, illustrates the technological vigor of this era. The expansion of cities and the growth of commercial quarters, the development of transport operations and the multiplication of trade guilds are yardsticks of the greater volume and specialization of commerce. Another index of economic growth are tax returns measured in strings of 1000 copper coins, although they also reflect greater governmental efficiency in cash collections. At the height of the T'ang dynasty in 749 only 2 million strings were collected compared with 37 million strings in 1065 under the Sung. Indeed, the use of money multiplied rapidly as illustrated by the minting of 200,000 to 300,000 strings a year by the T'ang compared to more than 1 million strings a year by the Sung. Even then the demand for cash exceeded the supply, and both the government and private bankers issued paper money drafts and certificates of deposit to get around the transportation of bulky coinage from one place to another. In 1024 when the government took over the issue of certificates of 200 to 1000 cash each, they became the first real paper money. Government acquisition and monopolization of important advances like this maintained state control of the economy and checked the potential assertion of entrepreneurial influence as a factor to be reckoned with. Thus the Confucian scholar-official class defended its supremacy in the state and society.

In the face of such economic change the great landed families gradually faded away and were replaced in influence by Confucian scholar-landlords with smaller and often fragmented landholdings, who vied for public office. Many of these families had probably made their money in trade, which they conveniently forgot. Attracted by the sophisticated pleasures of the cities, they tended to live there much of the time in a community of scholars, and the higher culture reflected urban tastes. During the Sung the introduction of foot-binding for upper class women perhaps reflects a decline in their usefulness in an urban as opposed to a rural environment.

A wealthy urban society demanded and financed a greater cultural sophistication than China had yet enjoyed. Art and literature which had flourished under the T'ang and Northern Sung achieved a peak of refinement esthetically unsurpassed since this time. Both T'ang and Sung art have their respective champions among the critics, but all agree that in vigor, variety, sensitivity, and creativity this era overall is without comparison in architecture, sculpture, painting, and porcelain.

China's greatest lyric poets were products of the T'ang period. Li Po (701–762), a Taoist individualist, was inspired by the desire to live life to the fullest extent, employing the pleasures of wine, women, and song. His contemporary and friend, Tu Fu (712–770), was a conscientious Confucian moralist only too well aware of human suffering and injustice. Po Chu-i (772–846) is noted for breaking down the literary conventions and composing his poems in a simpler, more popular style.

In prose, this era produced a tremendous volume of writing. A much larger interest in literacy was reflected in the expansion of educational institutions, both private and government sponsored. Under imperial patronage vast encyclopaedic works

were composed that collected and classified for ready reference the accumulated wisdom of Chinese civilization. Such monumental efforts were encouraged by the development of printing which made them available to a larger audience. The invention of paper and printing, two vital foundations of modern civilization, by the most literary civilization of all should be underlined. The Sung era is renowned for a number of outstanding historians of whom the most famous was Ssu-ma Kuang (1018–1087). He wrote the first comprehensive history since the Early Han historian, Ssu-ma Ch'ien, covering the period 403 B.C. to 959 A.D. under the appropriate Confucian title, *The Comprehensive Mirror for Aid in Government*. In his work and in that of his contemporaries the greater attention to institutional development reflects the greater concern for the functions of a fully bureaucratized government. Even though Ssu-ma Kuang was a leading opponent of Wang An-shih, he would have agreed that a well-trained official should and could prevent natural disasters through full knowledge of his responsibilities and a conscientious performance of his duties.

NEO-CONFUCIANISM

The pinnacle of Sung intellectual achievement, however, was the reworking of Confucianism that has been labeled Neo-Confucianism, and the outstanding scholar who completed this work of synthesis was Chu Hsi (1120–1200), also noted for his abridgement of Ssu-ma Kuang's history to emphasize the moral lessons of Chinese history. Although Chu Hsi's synthesis gained the final stamp of approval as the orthodox doctrine of Confucianism, the stimulating realization of the altered milieu since Han times inspired other interpretations as well in this vibrant age of intellectual reassessment and reformulation. As good Confucianists, all schools accepted the validity of the Classics as the basis of Confucianism. In fact, the standard canonization of the Classics and the

Four Books was drawn up in this era. But vital new elements that could not be ignored had been added since Han times to the stock of Chinese intellectual material—Buddhism and the Buddhist-influenced development of Taoism. In addition, the cosmological doctrines of Han Confucianism were deemed no longer satisfactory or satisfying. Merely to reject Buddhist and Taoist doctrines was not enough; a convincing Confucian answer to their intellectual as well as their spiritual challenge needed to be worked out that would confirm the this-worldly, secular characteristics of Confucianism.

The Neo-Confucian metaphysics of Chu Hsi accepted the eternal and infinite "Supreme Ultimate" of the *Classic of Changes* as the underlying principle of all existence and change and went on to assert that everything has its fundamental principle of form (*li*), regardless of whether it materially exists or not at any particular moment. This conception may be fruitfully compared with Plato's doctrine of ideas or Thomas Acquinas' principle of "substantial form." Incidentally, this principle of eternal "forms" or "laws" supported a reinterpretation in support of Mencius' doctrine of man's innate goodness which might become perverted or perfected in a man's actual existence. Complementing the principle of "forms," Chu Hsi postulated *ch'i*, which may be freely translated as "matter," by a combination of which the "form" takes material shape in the phenomenal world. Thus Chu Hsi's metaphysics was an inseparable dualism of *li* and *ch'i* (form and matter), which though appearing to change constantly, represented the eternal unity of the "Supreme Ultimate." With *li* were associated Confucian ethics, always latent, but which required cultivation by education, study, and "enlightenment," reminiscent of Ch'an Buddhism, to gain the full realization of the potentiality for perfection. In other words, man's physical existence is a rough replica of his ideal form requiring extensive polishing to achieve his innate potentiality for perfection. On the basis of his dualism of

li and *ch'i*, Chu Hsi then elaborated his metaphysical exposition to incorporate the traditional Chinese conceptions of *yin* and *yang* and the five elements.

In the long run, Neo-Confucian metaphysics occupied little of the attention of the Confucianists who generally accepted without question or much study Chu Hsi's formulation and concentrated on the Confucian Classics, ethics, and their application to government. Neo-Confucian ethics reaffirmed the family-oriented doctrine of filial piety as the guide to proper human relations. The family conception was applied to the government of the empire over which the ruler exercised the autocratic authority of a father according to the family ideal of benevolent paternalism. But, as the father was to be aided and courteously criticized for any shortcomings, by the same token the ruler was to be aided and guided in government by a bureaucracy of officials whose moral excellence and knowledge of the principles of good government had been proved by successful passage through the civil service examination system. The bureaucratic ideal, egalitarian in principle, in fact, favored those scholar-gentry families who could afford the needed education. Furthermore, a substantial proportion of the bureaucracy were appointees who had not passed through the examination system. Thus, as in every civilization and every institution, Chinese political practice fell short of full compliance with its expressed ideal.

Neo-Confucianism, as synthesized by Chu Hsi, in time became firmly established as the orthodox doctrine enshrined in the examination questions. Even his stress on the "investigation of things" was interpreted to mean the study of the Classics and history according to his commentaries on them, and this effectively forestalled any creative thought, let alone investigation in other field. An appreciation of the character and sacrosanct nature of Neo-Confucianism is necessary to an understanding of the obdurate official resistance at a later date to new ideas from the West. The expansive creativity and extroverted curiosity of the T'ang was submerged by the introverted scholasticism of the Sung. To the Confucianist mind the Middle Kingdom was the source and center of civilization that was surrounded and menaced by a sea of "barbarians." The "barbarians" might overrun the realm, but only by adopting Chinese civilization could they gain recognition and acceptance from the Confucian scholar-elite.

In this chapter, the major features that contributed to the full realization of Chinese civilization have been traced from the creative intellectual ferment of the pre-imperial period of strife to the peak of Chinese cultural achievement under the T'ang and Sung dynasties. Subsequently, the alien Mongol and Manchu dynasties, as well as the native Ming regime, were to add some new elements, but for the most part they operated within the established framework.

The single, most important development of imperial China was the synthesis of political and cultural ideas and practices labeled Confucianism which, as finally worked out, incorporated significant elements from all schools, including Taoism and Buddhism. Basic theory pictured the Middle Kingdom as the center and source of civilization surrounded by barbarians who were expected to recognize the superiority of China by accepting tributary status. At the head of the state, and in theory of all mankind, stood the Son of Heaven with absolute authority and ultimate responsibility for maintaining harmony between heaven, earth, and man. Any sharp increase in natural disasters and other abnormalities was a sure sign that the emperor was losing the Mandate of Heaven. In practice, however, his powers were to be exercised, supposedly under his scrutiny, by appointed bureaucrats who were selected through examinations that demonstrated their proficiency in Confucian ethics. As the Son of Heaven was to rule according to the

doctrines and practices of Confucianism inherited from the past, so, too, the scholar-officials were to keep uppermost in their minds what the maintenance of social harmony required according to Confucian ethics and to judge each case on its merits. In other words, each official, like the emperor, was absolute in power and responsible for the maintenance of harmony in his territory in accordance with the ideal of a government of men, not of laws. Indeed, each official's administration was judged on his ability to keep the peace and forward the assessed taxes without having recourse to his superior. Disorders or inability to meet the tax requirements was proof positive that he had lost his "mandate" and must be replaced. This decentralization of authority extended downward through each grade of the official hierarchy, and even to the people who were expected, if possible, to settle their disputes, solve their problems, and collect the prescribed taxes without resort to the authority of the district magistrate. Only by this step-by-step delegation of responsibility, which at the bottom of the ladder left the villages and the city sections and guilds essentially self-governing, could China be governed by such a small civil service. Only by the common acceptance of the social and political precepts of Confucianism, which were founded on the family, could such a system be made to work effectively. Thanks to this system, even when the political fabric was rent by disorders, life and government at the local level continued to function, providing a sound basis for the reestablishment of order and unity. Fundamental to the stability over such a wide area and for such a long period of time was the cultural conformity that resulted from the inculcation of Confucianism with its emphasis on looking to the past.

Both the emphasis on the rules of filial piety and the evaluation of occupations, which placed the scholar-official at the top and the merchant near the bottom, stressed social order and gave priority to ethics in human relationships. This value system attracted the best minds to government service, which carried the highest prestige and privileges. Of course, the Confucian ideal could not eradicate the human desire for material rewards and, in fact, the scholar class exploited their privileged status for the acquisition of landed estates. Indeed, the dynastic cycle can be largely explained in terms of the central government's effectiveness in checking the extent of this acquisitiveness. The very decentralization in the Confucian theory of government invited abuses whenever the scrutiny of the central government was relaxed. Nevertheless, with all its weaknesses, the Confucian conception of society and government made possible the most durable and stable preindustrial society and government of the largest aggregation of human beings in the world, then and now.

Although Industrialism has greatly increased the resources of the state and has altered the relationship of the government and the people, the merits of this social and political theory with its stress on human relationships warrants careful consideration.

A major weakness of fully developed Confucianism, which was never satisfactorily resolved, was its inability to deal effectively with the problem of military defense. The high value placed on scholarship proved incompatible with a militant outlook and, indeed, encouraged pacifism. As we shall see, long before the arrival of Europeans in China, the Chinese, though vastly superior numerically, were incapable of defending themselves against conquest by militant aliens, as shown first by the Mongols and then by the Manchus.

SIGNIFICANT DATES

c.	551– 479 B.C.	Confucius
c.	479– 381 B.C.	Mo-tzu
	403– 221 B.C.	"Warring States" period
c.	372– 289 B.C.	Mencius
c.	369– 286 B.C.	Chuang-tzu
fl.	298– 238 B.C.	Hsün-tzu
	221– 207 B.C.	1st Empire (Ch'in dynasty – peak of Legalism)
	202 B.C.–9 A.D.	Early Han dynasty
	141– 87 B.C.	Reign of Wu Ti
	9– 23 A.D.	Wang Mang – Hsin (new) dynasty
	25– 220 A.D.	Later Han dynasty
	589– 618 A.D.	Sui dynasty
	618– 907 A.D.	T'ang dynasty
	960–1279 A.D.	Sung dynasty
	1021–1086 A.D.	Wang An-shih
	1127–1279 A.D.	"Southern" Sung era
	1120–1200 A.D.	Chu Hsi Neo-Confucianism

SELECTED READINGS

See Chapter Four for general accounts.

*Balazs, Etienne, *Chinese Civilization and Bureaucracy*. New Haven: Yale University Press, 1964.

Bodde, Derk, *China's First Unifier*. Hong Kong: Hong Kong University Press, 1967.

Ch'en, Kenneth K. S., *Buddhism in China*. Princeton: Princeton University Press, 1964.

*Creel, H. G., *Chinese Thought from Confucius to Mao Tse-tung*. New York: Mentor Book, 1961.

*——, *Confucius and the Chinese Way*. New York: Harper, 1960.

*Eichhorn, Werner, *Chinese Civilization*. New York: Praeger, 1969.

Fung, Yu-lan, *A History of Chinese Philosophy*. 2 vols.; Princeton: Princeton University Press, 1952–53.

*——, *The Spirit of Chinese Philosophy*. Boston: Beacon Press, 1962.

*Gernet, Jacques, *Daily Life in China on the Eve of the Mongol Invasion, 1250–1276*. Stanford: Stanford University Press, 1970.

*Grousset, René, *The Rise and Splendour of the Chinese Empire*. Berkeley: University of California Press, 1953.

*Kaltenmark, Max, *Lao-tzu and Taoism*. Stanford: Stanford University Press, 1969.

*Lattimore, Owen, *Inner Asian Frontiers of China*. Boston: Beacon Press, 1962.

*Liu, James, J. Y., *The Art of Chinese Poetry*. Chicago: University of Chicago Press, 1962.

Liu, James T. C., *Reform in Sung China: Wang An-shih (1021–1086) and his New Policies*. Cambridge, Mass.: Harvard University Press, 1959.

*Liu, James T. C., and Tu, Wei-ming, eds., *Traditional China*. Englewood Cliffs, N.J.: Prentice-Hall, 1970.

*Loewe, Michael, *Everday Life in Early Imperial China during the Han Period 202 B.C.–A.D. 220*. New York: Harper and Row, 1970.

*——, *Imperial China*. New York: Praeger, 1966.

*Nivison, David S., and Wright, Arthur F., eds., *Confucianism in Action*. Stanford: Stanford University Press, 1959.

Pulleyblank, Edwin G., *The Background of the Rebellion of An Lu-shan*. London: Oxford University Press, 1955.

Reischauer, Edwin O., *Ennin's Diary*. New York: Ronald Press, 1955.

——, *Ennin's Travels in T'ang China*. New York: Ronald Press, 1955.

Twitchett, Denis C., *Financial Administration under the T'ang Dynasty*. Cambridge: Cambridge University Press, 1963.

——, *Land Tenure and the Social Order in T'ang and Sung China*. London: School of Oriental and African Studies, 1962.

*Waley, Arthur, *Three Ways of Thought in Ancient China*. New York: Doubleday and Co., 1956.

——, trans., *Analects of Confucius*. New York: Random House, 1966.

*——, *The Way and its Power*. New York: Grove Press, 1958.

*Wang, Gung-wu, *The Structure of Power in North China during the Five Dynasties*. Stanford: Stanford University Press, 1967.

Watson, Burton, *Ssu-ma Ch'ien: Grand Historian of China*. New York: Columbia University Press, 1958.

*Watson, Burton, trans., *Chuang Tzu: Basic Writings*. New York: Columbia University Press, 1963.

*——, *Han Fei Tzu: Basic Writings*. New York: Columbia University Press, 1964.

*——, *Mo Tzu: Basic Writings*. New York: Columbia University Press, 1963.

*Weber, Max, *The Religion of China: Confucianism and Taoism.* New York: Macmillan, 1964.

*Wright, Arthur F., *Buddhism in Chinese History.* Stanford: Stanford University Press, 1970.

*Wright, Arthur F., ed., *The Confucian Persuasion.* Stanford: Stanford University Press, 1960.

*————, ed., *Studies in Chinese Thought.* Chicago: University of Chicago Press, 1953.

*Wright, Arthur F., and Twitchett, Denis C., eds., *Confucian Personalities.* Stanford: Stanford University Press, 1962.

CHAPTER NINE

DIFFUSION IN EAST ASIA: JAPANESE CIVILIZATION

In contiguous areas, suited to settled agriculture, the Chinese cultural impact was so overwhelming that it all but obliterated indigenous cultures. To the south, where most of this expansion took place, it penetrated North Vietnam and then was checked by a combination of distance, climate, geography, and the counterspread of Indian civilization in Southeast Asia. After the more easily developed lowlands of the south were occupied, the neighboring uplands, including the valleys of eastern Tibet, were absorbed. The only alternatives for indigenous peoples were to become sinicized, to hold out in isolated pockets in the uplands, or to migrate to the south or overseas. In this way, the expansion of Chinese civilization put peoples in motion, a notable example being the Thais, who significantly affected the regions to which they moved.

To the north and west, climatic factors limited the possibilities of expanding the area of settled agriculture, and thus the extension of Chinese civilization, except in oases. During favorable weather cycles Chinese farmers would encroach on nomad territory, but with unfavorable weather they could be forced to retreat. Although political control over the pastoral nomads might be achieved by intrigue and force for a longer or shorter period of time, the thorough siniciza- tion of these "barbarians" was only possible where they were converted to settled agri- culture. In short, Chinese civilization and settled agriculture were synonymous terms.

To the northeast, Chinese expansion in- troduced settled agriculture to southern Manchuria on an unstable basis, contin- uously menaced by the threat of barbarian destruction. Nevertheless, this shallow and

tenuous foothold provided a route for the penetration of Chinese influence into Korea and for its ultimate transmission to the is- lands of Japan. As a result, two variant forms of Chinese civilization evolved that were re- mote enough from direct Chinese control to preserve distinctive features.

KOREA

Korea, as a Chinese tributary state for most of the time from the T'ang dynasty to the present, came increasingly under Chi- nese influence and, therefore, is less unique and interesting than Japan which maintained its total independence. Chinese influence was probably first introduced into northwest Korea in the fourth and third centuries B.C. from the most northern of the Chou states, which had pushed its frontier into southern Manchuria. The dislocations that accom- panied the unification of China under the Ch'in and then the overthrow of this dynasty produced political refugees, some of whom fled to northwest Korea, overthrew the na- tive prince (c 190 B.C.), set up a strong gov- ernment at P'yongyang (the present capital of North Korea), and extended their control over a large part of the peninsula.

As part of his strategy for outflanking the Hsiung-nu, Han Wu Ti in 108 B.C. con- quered this sinicized state and established direct government over most of northern and central Korea. Although imperial control of this area soon proved to be too much of a mil- itary strain, P'yongyang remained the center of a prosperous Chinese colony until 313 A.D. The Korean successor states were to a greater or lesser extent sinicized and utilized Chinese-type systems of government. Chi- nese Buddhism was introduced in the late

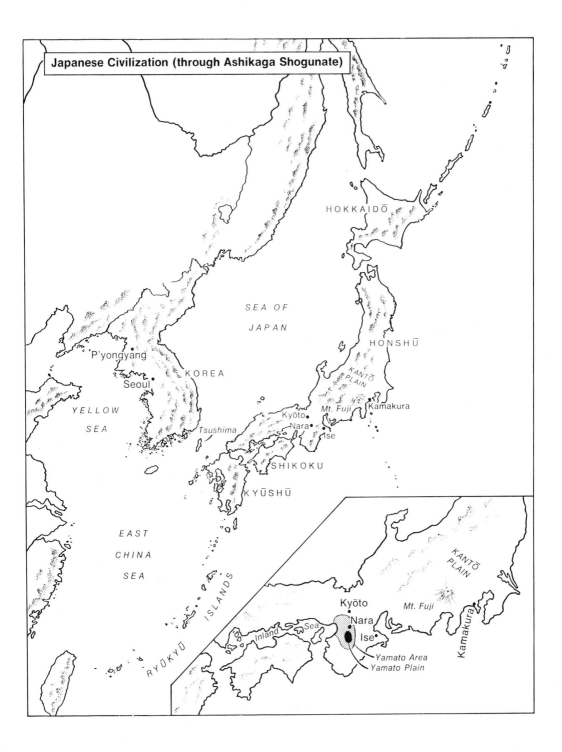

Japanese Civilization (through Ashikaga Shogunate)

fourth century, and commercial and cultural exchange enhanced Chinese influence. Finally, T'ang forces collaborated with the state of Silla to unify Korea in 668.

Although accepting tributary status, the Korean state has remained autonomous and unified, except for brief periods of division, until modern times. The close political and commercial relationship with China accounted for a growing emulation with variations and adaptations to fit the Korean social and economic structure. These differences, however, are not great enough to warrant detailed attention here.

JAPANESE: GEOGRAPHICAL FACTORS

Of much greater interest is the unique civilization developed by the Japanese under the stimulus of Chinese civilization. The chief factor that made it possible for the Japanese selectively to adopt and adapt those facets of Chinese civilization best suited to Japanese culture was geography. Like the British Isles, the islands of Japan are protected, but not isolated, from continental influence by a saltwater moat. But, while the Straits of Dover are narrow enough to provide a view of the opposite shore on a clear day, the southern island of Kyūshū is separated from Korea by more than 100 miles of open water. Moreover, Britain presents her most attractive face to the European continent, while the heart of Japan is on another island well removed from the Straits of Tsushima. Finally, while the part of the continent opposite Britain became a major political and economic center, Korea was a comparative backwater and the core of East Asian civilization was far away over a much broader stretch of hazardous seas. Thus Japan was separated to a much greater extent than Britain from continental intervention and influence and was comparatively freer to evolve its own civilization in its own way.

Unlike Korea, Japan was never subjected to Chinese political control. Until World War II, two Mongol invasion attempts were the only external challenges. Therefore, change came to Japan only as a result of internal and indigenous pressures, and foreign borrowings were generally deliberate and easily identified. This condition provided the Japanese people with a much greater sense of continuity than that enjoyed by other peoples and helps to explain the unique retention of anachronistic and outmoded institutions and practices along with often contradictory innovations. Indeed, their freedom from external pressure and the opportunity to be masters of their own destiny have encouraged them to be culturally progressive and conservative at the same time, a quality that they still retain and that other peoples find very difficult to understand and appreciate. Primitive Shintō beliefs are still maintained and observed. Ancient musical, architectural, and dramatic forms are preserved and revered alongside the most modern importations from the West. The imperial institution is retained and enshrined, although it has not exercised any significant political power for nearly a millennium. This trait may partially be explained by their sensitive awareness of their separateness and distinctiveness as a people. They are also conscious of the fact that many of the building blocks of their culture have been imported. To counter this sense of dependence on imports, they have preserved, cultivated, and often exaggerated the importance and stature of the "native" elements in their culture.

In addition to isolation, other geographical factors help to explain the historical development and peculiarities of Japanese civilization. Composed of a string of volcanic islands, the rugged terrain possesses great natural beauty, which stimulates esthetic development but restricts the possibilities of settled agriculture to less than one fifth of the land. Moreover, with a few exceptions the agricultural land is divided into a multitude of relatively isolated valleys traversed by short, swift streams that tumble from the mountains to the sea. This division into islands and valleys has made communication and unification difficult and has encouraged the Japanese people to utilize the sea as a highway.

The sea also dominates the climate. A warm current bathes the southeast coast providing the warm and wet weather essential to intensive rice farming. Double cropping of rice is practiced as far north as the Kantō Plain at the base of which is located today's largest metropolitan center, Tōkyō. The combination of weather, modern methods, and Japanese skill has made their fields the most productive farmland per acre in the world.

Nature, however, is not always kind and the same warm current brings destructive typhoons to batter the southeast coast during the late summer and fall of almost every year. In addition, the frequency of earthquakes, sometimes devastating, contributes to a sense of insecurity. Thus Japanese peasants have always been made well aware of both the bounty and the awesome power of nature. The heavy rainfall in the mountains supports not only complex irrigation systems but also large stands of timber. Japanese skill in woodworking is no accidental phenomenon.

The northeastern half of Japan comes under the influence of cold ocean currents flowing from the north, but the island nature of Japan helps to moderate the severity of the weather. Only Hokkaidō, the most northern major island of the Japanese chain and the last refuge of the disappearing Ainu, has resisted the development of settled agriculture.

The mixing of warm and cold currents has made the seas off the coasts of Japan extremely rich in sea life. Since prehistoric times the Japanese have exploited this natural resource for their chief supply of protein. Buddhism's prohibition of the eating of meat was never extended to seafood and, in fact, has intensified attention to fishing. This accumulated seafaring experience has contributed to making Japan the world's first fishing nation today as well as a leading shipbuilder and maritime operator.

Considering the difficulty of overland communications, it was natural for the early development of Japan to take place around the Inland Sea, sheltered from the Pacific by the island of Shikoku. Furthermore, it was natural for the first steps toward political unification to be taken by those who wrested the fairly large plain at the northeastern end of the Inland Sea from the Ainu and pressed the Japanese advance from this base. Again, as on so many other occasions, an aggressive frontier state proved best suited to the task of unification.

THE JAPANESE PEOPLE

Although the precivilized development of Japan is of little concern to us, the exceptional effort made by modern Japanese scholars in trying to unravel their racial origins is indicative of their national sensitivity about the native elements in their culture. The most significant result of this interdisciplinary assault on the prehistoric past is the fact that the more that is learned the more confusing and uncertain the picture becomes. All that can be asserted with confidence is that the Japanese people derive from a highly complex blend of diverse peoples and cultural influences. Probably a similar effort devoted to determining the origins of any other people would yield the same sort of uncertain and complicated picture.

The indigenous "hairy" Ainu of proto-Caucasian type obviously contributed an important element to the Japanese racial composition, but a comparative skeletal study of ancient and modern Ainus indicates that they too have undergone substantial physical change. Cultural, linguistic, and historical studies furnish plentiful evidence of substantial northeast Asian influences via the Korean Peninsula, but anthropological considerations also indicate generous infusions of a southern strain.

One theory—and it is no more than that—proposes that Chinese expansion forced native peoples to take to the sea from the southern coasts of China. Some settled in the islands of Southeast Asia, some reached the islands of the central Pacific, and the forebears of the Japanese found refuge in Kyūshū and southern Korea, where they mixed with the existing population.

Whatever the origins of the Japanese people may have been, the first recognizable reference in a Chinese history of the first Christian century describes an agricultural people who were divided into 100 political units and resided in southern Korea and Kyūshū. They ate with their fingers, went about barefooted, and bedaubed their bodies with paint. In addition to borrowed Chinese practices, such as divination by baking bones, they already practiced ritual purification by bathing in water. They had hereditary rulers, frequently women who were believed to be possessed of magical powers. Class distinctions were already important. These characteristics, and those given in this and subsequent Chinese histories which comment on the people's honesty and their reverence for the sun, the sea, and the mountains, are clearly recognizable as traditional Japanese traits. Although later Japanese historians dated the beginning of the empire at 660 B.C., this assertion was an imaginary and arbitrary construction made under Chinese influence. The Japanese state does not begin to emerge as a historical reality until the fifth century A.D., and the picture of development is not filled in with adequate or reliable detail until the later sixth century.

EARLY JAPANESE CIVILIZATION

The early references in the Chinese histories indicate a stratified, agricultural society headed by a hereditary aristocracy. By the later third century the construction of large earthen tombs reflects the growth in wealth and power of the political units, which had been reduced in number from 100 to about 30. This tomb culture is closely related to one in Korea and is an example of Korea's importance as a bridge for the transmission of cultural innovations to Japan. Until 562, the Japanese maintained a foothold in southern Korea which facilitated this movement and participated militarily in the internal affairs of Korea. At the same time, Koreans, many of whom were deeply imbued with Chinese culture, were permitted to settle in Japan, often achieving aristocratic status. Tomb figurines make it clear that the aristocracy were already mounted and armored warriors equipped with iron weapons. Indeed, as elsewhere, the high cost of a warrior's arms and equipment was the foundation of the aristocracy.

At an uncertain date, one militant group had sailed from Kyūshū to central Honshū and carved out the Yamato state. The ruling clan claimed priority over other clan chieftains on the ground of descent from the grandson of the sun-goddess and by the mid-fifth century had apparently gained a hegemony over a majority of the Japanese states. A late fifth century Chinese history relates a Yamato envoy's claim of the conquest of "fifty-five countries of hairy men," sixty-six "countries" in western Japan, and ninety-five "countries" in Korea. The administrative problems presented by these larger responsibilities required written records, and Korean scribes versed in Chinese, the only known system of writing, were employed. Their records give a greater measure of reliability to that portion of later histories dealing with events after 400 A.D.

Even though Yamato suzerainty was recognized, local political authority resided in ruling "clans" (uji) claiming descent from a common ancestor and worshiping a common deity. In the larger, more complex political units, hereditary subunits under their own chiefs were subordinated to the uji. Yamato power seems to have been based on its ability to subordinate a number of uji, giving them specialized hereditary functions of a military or religious nature, and to supplement this strength by the creation of a large number of subunits. Each of these units was supported by a generous grant of the plentiful agricultural land available in the Yamato territory. At this stage of Japanese development, and for many centuries to come, there was still plenty of good, undeveloped land, and political power was measured in terms of manpower rather than in territory.

Another means of extending the power of the Yamato rulers was by gaining control of local cults and organizing them into a hierarchy headed by the sun-goddess whose chief shrine was located at Ise on a point of land facing the rising sun. Later, this agglomeration of native cults dedicated to striking aspects of nature and mythological ancestors was given the Chinese-derived general title of Shintō, the "Way of the Gods." In striking contrast with other examples of primitive nature worship, including the Korean, Shintō worship stresses the beautiful and beneficial, and not the menacing and terrifying, aspects of nature. In spite of the incorporation of involved genealogies that were worked out to support the prestige of aristocratic families, it remained a simple, amoral, and cheerful form of worship with its chief emphasis placed on ritual cleanliness. After ritual purification the worshiper claps his hands to announce his presence, bows, and makes an offering at the shrine. The annual shrine festivals are gay, bibulous affairs at which everyone, including the deity, has a good time. This simple and straightforward religion with shrines in impressive natural settings still possesses an almost universal appeal for the Japanese people.

THE CHINESE IMPACT

From earliest times some Chinese influences had filtered into Japan via the semi-sinicized Korean states. As the Yamato state grew in strength and authority during the fifth century, Korean immigrants in large numbers were attracted not only by the need for scribes but by the need for the other skills they possessed as well. Many of them came as members of fairly large and influential groups. In a ninth century register of the Yamato aristocracy, more than one third were of foreign origin. The influx of these sinicized aliens, whose talents gained them status, was bound to stimulate the rate and extent of cultural borrowing. Also, economic and political development was preparing the Japanese for the reception of the more sophisticated aspects of Chinese civilization that had already been established in Korea. The social dilemma that these changes were creating reached crisis proportions with the loss of the Japanese foothold in Korea in 562—a loss that the Yamato government was not ready to accept and attempted to recoup. Some means had to be found to increase the power and authority of the central government. As a result, borrowing shifted from unconscious acquisitions to a conscious quest for suitable innovations.

The first such conscious borrowing was Buddhism. If a religion of this kind were successfully introduced, subsidized, and controlled by the central government, it could greatly enhance the spiritual authority of the Yamato ruler and would undermine that of the local cults still under the control of *uji* chieftains. The first effort, before the Korean debacle, failed largely because of the natural opposition of Shintō and other conservative chieftains. Although one major clan was permitted to adopt Buddhism, a subsequent epidemic was blamed on this alien worship and the image was cast into a canal. The same clan was allowed to carry out the same experiment on a larger scale in 585 with suspiciously identical results, even to the casting of the image into a canal. However, in a confusing series of palace revolutions and intrigues Buddhism along with other reforms, prevailed under the brilliant leadership of the Yamato prince, Shōtoku (regent, 592–622), who was closely related by blood to this clan.

Even if he may not have been the universal genius that later eulogies have made him out to be, Shōtoku as regent did take the steps necessary to bring about overdue measures of reform. He is reported to have been uniquely well versed in Buddhist philosophy and to have expounded at length on its meaning. During his regime Buddhism became firmly entrenched at court, and all serious opposition to it was overcome. More importantly, he appreciated the advantages of the Confucian conception of government and in 604 issued a "17 Article Constitution" stressing those features that he believed to be most essential to a reform program.

Only the second article of the constitution concerned the value of Buddhism. In true Confucian style all but two of the rest were general ethical admonitions which stressed the type of behavior that would be most conducive to enhancing the authority of the central government. Harmony as opposed to wanton opposition, absolute obedience to imperial orders, decorum in the relations of superior and inferior, selfless devotion to duty, impartial administration of rewards and punishments, appointments to office on the basis of merit and wisdom, suppression of emotions like envy and anger which encourage dissension were some of the Confucian virtues enjoined in this document. Notice that all of them were aimed against the characteristic self-seeking of hereditary clansmen and were intended to enhance the efficiency and power of the central government in the interests of a unified Japan. One of the specific injunctions forbade the levying of taxes by the nobility—a function reserved to the appointed officials. The other specific article borrowed the Chinese system of conscript labor as part of the peasants' obligation to the state. With it, Shōtoku had roads constructed to improve overland communications. The final article appears to represent an early statement of the traditional Japanese preference for joint responsibility and rule by committees rather than individuals. It prescribed joint consultations on weighty affairs, leaving only lesser matters

to individual decision. In this clause a Japanese modification of a borrowed doctrine may be detected.

To implement the Confucian idea of an institutionalized bureaucracy, Shōtoku had the year before set up a court hierarchy of 12 graded ranks. Although further elaborated later, this revolutionary attempt to substitute merit as the basis of status was in time overcome by the Japanese preference for hereditary status. A further innovation in 604 was the adoption of the Chinese calendar, deemed so important for the accurate ordering of terrestrial affairs in accordance with the Heavenly order.

A more important step for the future was the sending of an embassy to the Sui court in 607, only the first of many such embassies. Shōtoku realized the need for informed personnel to carry out his program and sent students of both Buddhism and government with these missions. Although the numbers in his embassies were modest, a century later they numbered in the thousands. His ambitions and pretensions are indicated by the address of his first message from "the Son of Heaven in the land where the sun rises" to "the Son of Heaven in the land where the sun sets." Naturally the Chinese emperor took umbrage at this presumptuous claim of equality. The long-run impact of these Chinese studies is underlined by the important role that returned students played in the more radical Taika Reforms (646).

The clan that Shōtoku brought to power had become overbearing and threatened to usurp the throne. With the support of an imperial prince Nakatomi no Kamatari, ironically a member of the Shintō priest clan which had most adamantly opposed the introduction of Buddhism and the other reforms, engineered a coup d'etat. For his services he was awarded the surname of Fujiwara. His descendants grew in numbers and prestige, maintaining their position as the leading noble family until World War II.

Sometimes all-powerful, sometimes powerless, the Fujiwara family never lost its precedence in rank.

Thanks to the pioneer work of Shōtoku—especially the corps of students returned from Chinese studies—the new leaders were in a position to propose a more radical and specific program of reform. First, they sent out government appointees to take a census of the people and the cultivated land. On the basis of this census, an imperial edict of 646 in effect ordered the nationalization and redistribution of the land in equitable portions to the peasants who farmed them. Only government-appointed officials were to be granted the income of specified lands for their support. The rest of the taxes were supposed to accrue directly to the central government, although these funds might be largely expended on authorized local projects. Taxes were assessed not only in kind but also in goods and services. A subsequent edict followed the logic of its predecessor by ordering the aboliton of all hereditary units whose members should henceforth become loyal subjects of the state, gaining rank only by government appointment.

If these reforms had been fully implemented, a centralized regime on the Chinese model would have been established. But the wording of the edicts illustrates that this was a long range program whose full implementation applied immediately only to the six home provinces in the neighborhood of Yamato. To what extent these reforms were ever put into operation outside the home provinces is difficult to determine. Initially, local chieftains were appointed as local officials and were thus enabled to retain both their income and their prestige, although nominally accepting subordination to the central government. On the other hand, during the eighth century when these reforms achieved their widest application, detailed land and population registers were maintained, and the opulence of the court at the first capital

city of Nara testified to the collection of a large income. During this era, the almost verbatim reproduction of the T'ang law code also suggests the exercise of greater authority by the central government. Nevertheless, court officials sought appointment as provincial governors primarily for profit and frequently stayed in Nara, governing through a local deputy. This practice subverted the theoretical centralization and contributed to the maintenance and growth of locally based power.

THE NARA ERA (710 – 784)

In spite of the imposing facade of imperial government, Japan was still economically far behind China and even Korea in development. Until the ambitious layout of Japan's first capital at Nara in 710 the center of government was moved at the accession of almost every new ruler. Nara was not only the first fixed capital but, even in its stunted development, the first center large enough to warrant the title of city. Planned as a smaller scale replica of the T'ang capital, Nara was supposed to occupy an area of $2^2/3$ by 3 miles. Although never built up as proposed, it did accommodate a population in the tens of thousands. In this urban atmosphere students returning from periods of study in China stimulated the rapid adoption of the more refined elements of Chinese civilization, including Buddhism and the arts. Great Buddhist monasteries were constructed on the hills around the city and Buddhist influence in government grew. Chinese art and literature were faithfully imitated. The government authorized the establishment of branch monasteries and convents which were supported by grants of land in every province. In 749 an immense bronze Buddha, 53 feet high, was completed that is estimated to have required a million pounds of copper, tin, and lead and 500 pounds of gold for gilding. The great wooden hall, originally 152 feet high, in which it was housed remains the largest wooden structure in the world. In the course of time, the Japanese "domesticated" Buddhism by incorporating Shintō deities into the Buddhist pantheon. In 749 the first significant step in this direction was taken when Hachiman, the Shintō god of war, was ceremoniously installed as a bodhisattva.

The Chinese system of writing with ideographic characters was extremely ill-suited for adaptation to the writing of in-flected, polysyllabic languages, such as Japanese and Korean. Various makeshift techniques were evolved for writing Japanese, but the difficulties involved encouraged writing in the Chinese language as the simpler course. Naturally, the study and use of Chinese greatly aided the dissemination of Chinese ways of thought both Buddhist and Confucian. Two histories, the *Kojiki* (712) and the *Nihon Shoki* (720), clearly reflect Chinese influence in the legendary and mythological reconstruction of Japanese antiquity. More originality is demonstrated in the poetry of this era which utilized Chinese characters phonetically in the composition of 31 syllable poems. The brevity of their poetic form promoted a kind of suggestive impressionism.

In the imitation of Chinese government several vital modifications had to be made to adapt it to the conditions and predispositions of Japanese society and culture. To extend the government's control over Shintō cults a top-level Office of Deities was added to the borrowed Chinese structure of government. More significant was the failure to institute civil service examinations for the selection of officials. The tradition of hereditary authority was too deeply rooted in Japanese society to tolerate such a radical reform in which status would be determined by demonstrated ability rather than by birth. Although an imperial university was founded, enrollment was limited to the aristocracy. After the initial era of reform governmental positions again came to be filled according to hereditary rank with scarcely any opportunity for advancement. Thus, the very foundation of

the Chinese system of government was never established in Japan. As a result, the apparent similarity was from the beginning little more than a hollow facade. To expect a complete revolution in Japanese society without the application of external force, however, would be naive.

An interesting by-product of the retention of hereditary status in government was the diversion of men of natural talent into the Buddhist monasteries. Although hereditary factors influenced the monastic hierarchy, this was the one area of intellectual activity where careers were open to talent. The accumulation of brainpower and wealth by the great monasteries near the capital allowed them to exercise political influence. In fact, the decision to relocate the capital seems to have been largely a result of this influence, which almost led to a Buddhist usurpation of the throne.

THE HEIAN ERA (794 – 1185)

After the abandonment of Nara, a new capital was laid out on an even grander scale at Heian (Kyōto) where the imperial residence was to be maintained until the Restoration in 1867. For the first 50 years of the Heian period, the tide of Chinese cultural influence still flowed strongly, marked by the introduction of two important sects of Chinese Buddhism. Subsequently, official relations with China were ended, and the court reexamined and reinterpreted its acquisitions from a Japanese point of view. One result was the development of a more and more sophisticated and effete way of life in the capital which came to be increasingly out of touch with the vigorous development taking place in the countryside. Eventually this divergence between court and country had to be reconciled by force.

One of the new sects, Tendai (T'ien-T'ai), was brought back from China by a Japanese monk who had already gained imperial favor. In basing its teachings on the Lotus Sūtra, it had the advantage over its predecessors of asserting that its authority was drawn from the Buddha's own words, while the former sects all relied on secondary authorities. Its emphasis on relative levels of truth appealed to a large Japanese audience, as it already had done in China, because it opened the gates of salvation to all. In addition, the regulations issued by the founder of the Tendai sect commanded a combination of religious dedication with the Confucian ideal of service to society and the state. This emphasis encouraged the monks to promote secular as well as religious scholarship.

The founder of the Tendai sect, however, was soon overshadowed by his more brilliant contemporary, Kōbō Daishi, who brought back from China the esoteric doctrines of the Shingon or True Word sect. In China, the emphasis on the personal transmission from master to disciple of its secret knowledge had precluded the formation of a formally organized sect, but the Japanese master in extensive writings systematized the doctrine and thus established the sect as a formal body. The mysteries, rituals, and masses for the dead appealed as much to the Japanese as they had to the Chinese people. In a brilliant essay entitled the *Ten Stages* he classified and evaluated all forms of religious observance known to him, including Confucianism, Taoism, Hīnayāna, and Mahāyāna Buddhism. Naturally, as the only completely esoteric form, his teachings were placed at the top of the list, and insult was added to injury by relegating his rival's Tendai teachings to third place. Finally, in the mid-ninth century the Tendai sect prevailed when another noted monk and diarist, Ennin, incorporated the rituals and esoteric teachings of Shingon into Tendai doctrines. One of the most important contributions of esoteric views was the stimulus and support they gave to Japanese artistic and esthetic development. What could not be easily expressed in words, its exponents believed, could be illustrated in art forms.

Both sects with their more popular doctrines stimulated the spread of Buddhism among the people. The popularization of Buddhism was characterized by a decline of interest in its intellectual and philosophical content and a typically Japanese emphasis on rituals and evangelical preachings of salvation by faith among the people. This latter development, destined later to grow in importance, was inspired by Chinese Pure Land doctrine with its attractive Western Paradise which all filled with sincere faith might enter.

As Buddhism during these centuries was "domesticated" to reflect Japanese outlooks and attitudes, art and literature too turned away from Chinese models to find native inspiration for creative expression. Of course, with typical Japanese cultural conservatism Chinese forms continued to be produced and to influence the new styles. The Japanese rarely, if ever, have totally rejected past traditions and practices, preferring to preserve, modify, and blend the old and the new, no matter how logically inconsistent they might appear to be.

During this period the T'ang architectural style was modified to produce the distinctively light and airy structures, blending with natural settings, that have come to characterize Japanese architecture, both public and private. While religious art showed some changes that reflected the development of more popular forms of Buddhism, the most striking departure from Chinese models took place in secular painting. A simpler style of line drawing with flat, colored surfaces evolved, known as Yamato-e (Yamato pictures). This style was ideally suited to the popular device of pictorial storytelling on an scroll. An interesting and characteristic development of this era was the extension of the hereditary principle to schools of art. If an artist's natural son lacked talent, adoption was utilized to perpetuate the style of art in the artist's family. Indeed, the hereditary principle came to be applied to a wide variety of new professions and occupations.

In literature, the desire to compose poetry and prose in Japanese led to the development in the ninth century of two phonetic syllabaries that utilized simplified forms of Chinese characters, *hiragana* and *katakana*. The availability of these means of writing in Japanese made possible in the early eleventh century an unprecedented and remarkable blossoming of prose compositions by the highly cultivated and sensitive ladies of the court. Most famous is the lengthy novel by Lady Murasaki, *The Tale of Genji*, which remains Japan's greatest literary work. The sensitivity and psychological discernment with which she fathomed and delineated the character of her hero in the course of his amorous exploits have set an incomparable standard against which all subsequent Japanese novelists have had to measure their work. By her own definition, the novel should deal with life as it is, its virtues and its vices, its wisdom and its follies, and not create a fairyland beyond reality. Incidentally, her picture of the highly sophisticated, esthetically effete, and wholly amoral life of the court contrasts with the stern, military virtues of later Japan which were currently evolving outside the court. The one common characteristic of this and subsequent Japanese culture is the all-pervading sensitivity to beauty in all its natural forms.

While the culture of the court was achieving an extremely high level of refinement and sophistication, more mundane, but enduring, developments were taking place in the countryside. At best, the centralization of national power and resources envisioned by the Taika Reforms had only been partially realized. The authority of the government had been asserted over the whole of Kyūshū only in the eighth century and over northern Honshū in the ninth century. Nationalization of the land, even where implemented, was limited only to cultivated fields. Moreover, tax-free estates had been granted to aristocrats and monasteries, and their influence at court usually made it possible for them to obtain tax-free status for any new acquisitions or donations. Meanwhile, the growth in population required the development of new

lands. Intensive irrigated agriculture could be promoted only by those local lords who had at their command the necessary capital and manpower. A series of edicts culminated in 772 in the complete removal of all restrictions on the incorporation of wasteland into tax-free private holdings. The fertility, better irrigation, and relatively lower burden of rent persuaded peasants to move to the newly developed estates, abandoning their taxable lands. In due course, court aristocrats or monasteries were able to have these abandoned lands declared waste and thus opened to redevelopment as tax-free estates. In other instances, corrupt local officials could achieve the same result by manipulation of the land registers. Local lords who owned taxable lands also found it to their advantage to commend themselves and their estates to influential monasteries or court aristocrats in return for tax-exemption and legal protection.

The cumulative result of these various means of evading taxation was a progressive drying up of imperial revenues and the building of substantial estates by the ablest local lords who acknowledged either great monasteries or court aristocrats as patrons and protectors. By the ninth century the income of court aristocrats was derived primarily from estates rather than official salaries, and by the tenth century the bulk of the peasantry and the agricultural land had been redistributed among the tax-free estates. Also proliferation and financial pressure had forced the emperors to disinherit their younger sons and send them out to make their fortunes under the new family names of Minamoto or Taira. Thanks to paternal support and the prestige attached to scions of the imperial line, most of them succeeded in carving out estates and gaining local influence, especially in the Kantō region.

Meanwhile, at court, where the decline of imperial authority reduced official functions to largely meaningless ceremonies, the Fujiwara family by the latter half of the ninth century had reduced the emperors to puppets. Minors born of Fujiwara mothers were enthroned under Fujiwara regents. When the emperor came of age, he frequently was persuaded to abdicate and retire to a monastery. Beginning in the late eleventh century certain vigorous retired emperors challenged the Fujiwara monopoly of power, drawing on monastic intellectual and military resources. But by this time all real power resided outside the court as reflected in the military forces the monasteries could muster to attack each other or to dictate to the government. In the countryside the leading lords were engaged in militant struggles for power in their areas. It was only a matter of time before they would be invited to participate in the struggles at court. Although the central government had become powerless, the imperial tradition was too thoroughly entrenched for any power-seeker to raise the question of usurping the throne. In any case, the Fujiwara had established the tradition of exercising power by delegation—a tradition that was to be greatly elaborated in the next period.

As the authority of the central government deteriorated, a rural military aristocracy arose as the only source of law and order. The mounted and armored warrior-aristocrat supported by the income from an estate is a figure similar to the medieval knight in Western Europe. Successful military lords attracted knights, called *samurai* (servants), and rewarded them with lands. Although the relationship of lord and samurai was based on reciprocal protection and assistance, the material bond was subordinated to an ethical code of honor and loyalty. As in Europe, however, the ties of honor and loyalty were frequently violated in practice and the outcome of battles was often determined in advance by prearranged desertions.

THE KAMAKURA SHOGUNATE

In 1156 the inevitable occurred; each side in a struggle for power at court mustered all the military support that they could get from the countryside. The victor, leader of the branch of the Taira family whose base of power was the Inland Sea area close to Kyōto, retained control of the court instead of dutifully retiring to the country. He did not disturb the relationship of emperor, Fujiwara regent, and retired emperor, but simply exercised actual power founded on his military strength. His opponents, whom he could reach, were ruthlessly exterminated, but he was not strong enough to assert his control over much more than the central area of Honshū. His followers were rewarded with confiscated estates and provincial governorships, which were still useful in building up local power.

Minamoto Yoritomo, a son of one of the eliminated opponents, had been spared because of his youth and was entrusted as a ward to a supposedly loyal retainer of the Taira family, Hōjō Tokimasa. But this ambitious lord married his daughter to Yoritomo and ably advised and assisted him in gaining final control of a rebellion that began in 1180. Yoritomo's chief strength was centered in the Kantō Plain, the largest in Japan. From this date, control of this agricultural unit, which supported the largest number of samurai, became the main key to political power. Unlike his predecessor, he was not seduced by the effete life of the court but maintained direct control of the Kantō from his headquarters at Kamakura. As his arms swept to victory, lords and samurai throughout the country rushed to swear allegiance to him. Not only did he liquidate the Taira and award their estates to his followers, but by the time of his death in 1199 he had eliminated all close adult relatives. All Japan had been forced to acknowledge his authority and, through the government he developed, his victory was consolidated.

This government, called the *Bakufu* (Tent Government) in contrast to the court at Kyōto, was a relatively simple system for governing the retainers through whom military control of Japan was maintained. In fact, it was merely the application on a larger scale of the house law evolved for the control of his own estate. An Administrative Board was the central policy-making body. The Board of Retainers assigned, rewarded, and punished lords and samurai. The Board of Inquiry, as a court of appeal, applied the Minamoto house law in all disputes involving persons who had sworn loyalty to Yoritomo and his successors. In fact, as the only law that was enforced, all notables, including the court aristocrats, brought their cases before this board.

At the local level, a not altogether uniform system in two levels was applied to most of Japan to assure a measure of direct authority. Over most estates a retainer was appointed as Steward who received a share of the produce for managing the interests of the owner and of others with a share in the income, for maintaining law and order, and for collecting the small levy of one fiftieth of the yield as a symbol of Kamakura's authority. Above the stewards at the provincial level, Protectors were appointed to supervise affairs in peacetime and to command the provincial contingent of samurai warriors in war. Since both stewards and protectors tended to become hereditary, they were essentially local lords whose interests and loyalty in time shifted from Kamakura to the local enhancement of their own power.

In 1192 Yoritomo's military control of Japan was recognized and confirmed by the imperial grant of the title of *Shōgun* (Generalissimo). This delegation of the emperor's military authority on a permanent basis in effect established a military government with imperial approval. The full picture of the delegation of power, however, was not completed until 1219 when the last of Yoritomo's sons and relatives was eliminated and the Hōjō family became firmly established as regents for puppet shōguns. Finally, the Hōjō regent usually accepted control by a policy-making committee that was composed of the leading members of his family. This typically Japanese technique of delegating power without eliminating any traditional positions presents the following picture of progression from the source to the actual location of au-

thority: Emperor, Fujiwara Regent, Retired Emperor, Shōgun, Hōjō Regent, Hōjō family committee. During the times when a family committee controlled the Hōjō regent, actual power was thus removed six steps from its source. Only the Japanese with their exceptional reverence for tradition and hereditary status could have devised such a system of government and, what is more, made it function effectively.

THE KAMAKURA CULTURE

Although official contact with China had been severed during the last three centuries of the Heian era and the court had been engaged in remolding Chinese cultural contributions into a distinctively Japanese creation, private trade conducted by both Chinese and Japanese principals continued to contribute to Japanese development, especially in the provinces; and in the twelfth century this trade grew substantially in volume. Under Kamakura auspices this trade further expanded and brought new influences, but the feudal-type ethic which stressed martial virtues would permit no more than a highly selective adaptation of new Chinese religious and cultural importations. The military code of conduct, labeled much later *Bushidō* (The Way of the Warrior), placed the highest value on loyalty to the lord even to the sacrifice of oneself and one's family. The warrior preferred death to dishonor, and in the late twelfth century death by disembowelment (*seppuku*), vulgarly known as *harakiri* (bellyslitting), became a ritual. Such an ideal, even though often ignored, was wholly at odds with the Confucianist's prime obligation to his family.

In literature and the arts, the samurai impact was apparent in the vigorous stories and paintings that deal with military deeds of valor. The scholars and artists who were lured from the court to Kamakura maintained cultural continuity, but they also had to produce the type of works demanded by their new patrons. Indeed, the new dimension added to their outlook provided a source of creative inspiration that restored vitality to their work, regardless of subject. Moreover, Japanese culture not only gained new vitality and direction from its extension to Kamakura but also it was diffused more widely in Japanese society by the rural lords and samurai. A national culture began to replace the "hothouse" variety of the imperial court at Kyōto.

BUDDHIST EVANGELICISM

In spite of the sharp social cleavage between nobles and commoners, the peasants appear to have become socially more significant than they had been before, when society had been monopolized by the absentee court aristocracy. Now their rulers lived on the estates and had a close paternal interest in the peasants' welfare. In this sense, Kamakura society narrowed the gap between peasant and lord.

Another factor that contributed to bringing the peasants more actively into the cultural life of the country was the growth of egalitarian Buddhist sects whose inspired preachers evangelized the land. The Pure Land sect preached that salvation was open to all through simple faith in the Western Paradise of the Buddha Amida. All the sincere devotee need do was call on his name. Salvation was an individual achievement without any need for priests, rituals, or temples. The nobility was sufficiently disturbed by the radical implications of these teachings to exile the leader and behead some of his followers. This was the first instance of violent persecution in East Asian Buddhism, but it was not to be the last.

One of his disciples took the next logical step, asserting that repetitions of Amida's name were superfluous; all that was necessary for salvation was a single sincere calling on the Buddha's name, even on one's deathbed. In fact, he was fired by a

fervent desire to save the wicked. His enthusiasm led him to repudiate both scriptures and monasticism and to allow his priests to marry and form congregations of believers. Today his True Pure Land or simply True (*Shin*) sect has the largest following in Japan with the Pure Land sect in second place.

The most ardent evangelist was Nichiren (1222–1282) whose followers invoked the Lotus Sūtra in the chant, "Hail to the Sūtra of the Lotus of the Wonderful Law." Like his Pure Land predecessors, he appealed to the emotions of the Japanese people. The most significant and un-Buddhistic feature of his preaching was his intolerant condemnation of all rival sects for leading their believers straight to perdition, as well as bringing every kind of calamity on Japan. He damned the teachings of the other sects as false doctrines because they concentrated only on one or another of the threefold aspects of the Buddha enshrined as a single unity in the Lotus Sūtra, and he brought the wrath of the Shogunate on his head by attacking its dereliction of duty to both Buddhism and Japan by failing to suppress these "heretical" doctrines. His miraculous escape from execution and his prediction of the Mongol invasion attempts, as well as his impassioned and fearless preaching, gained renown for his teachings and a large popular following. The Japanese have always admired selfless courage. Furthermore, he appealed to innate national feeling by asserting that in this age of world degeneration Japan had the opportunity to become the home and champion of the true Buddhist faith.

The missionary and militant fervor of Nichiren and the various Pure Land sects led to the formation of fanatical, church-led communities of believers who defended themselves against aristocratic suppression. The vigor, single-mindedness, intolerance, militancy, and even the doctrines of the Buddhist evangelicals can bear fruitful comparison with the later Protestant movement in the West.

ZEN BUDDHISM

Zen (Ch'an) Buddhism shared with the other new sects the appealing tendencies toward simplicity, anti-scholasticism, and emphasis on the individual, but its stress on this-worldly self-realization through a rigorous self-discipline was in sharp contrast to the other sects' simple call for otherworldly faith. Obviously such a demanding curriculum limited its potential popularity. Although it gained some adherents among the lower classes, Zen found an especially sympathetic audience among the aristocracy whose martial ideals were complementary to those of Zen Buddhism. Both stressed self-reliance and self-discipline and the superiority of moral to intellectual attainments.

Under the command and guidance of a master, who was accepted as a living embodiment of truth, the novice sat erect, cross-legged, and motionless in concentration whose objective was to achieve for himself the realization of the Buddha-nature within himself. Once having gained this suprarational "enlightenment" of his oneness with the universe, there was no need to look outside himself for knowledge or for strength. This did not, however, mean a rejection of this-worldly duty or even study. The enlightened one actively carried out his assigned role with the realization that he was his own master maintaining the highest ideals. When engaged in study, he mastered the work and did not let the work master him.

Two Zen sects developed in Japan in emulation of the two main ones in China. The first emphasized sudden enlightenment through focusing attention on a problem that was insoluble by ordinary logic. The second deprecated this method as too self-assertively directed at a specific objective and too specialized on mental perception alone, instead of utilizing all human faculties. This sect favored meditation without concentration on a specific problem or objective through which a gradual, but fuller, realiza-

tion would be gained by the total utilization of all physical, mental, and moral faculties. Indeed, according to this doctrine, regular and routine meditation became an integral part of a disciplined attitude toward the whole of life, not just a single, sudden, illuminating experience.

As it evolved in Japan, Zen was not just another religious doctrine but a whole way of life. Its influence extended far beyond its immediate adherents and significantly shaped the ideals and values that characterize and distinguish Japanese civilization. Although numerically smaller than the more popular "faith" sects, Zen attracted strong support not only from the military aristocracy but also from artists and intellectuals. Probably the single, most influential feature of Zen on other areas of Japanese culture was the stress on finding the ultimate truth within oneself, on discovering the macrocosm within the microcosm. If the self can contain the whole truth of the universe, any part of nature can contain the whole. This point of view inspired an entirely new approach to the world of nature, which had always held a special appeal for the Japanese, and supplemented the native esthetic sensitivity and love of form and ritual. This attitude may be described as the cultivation of the small, the simple, and the natural in preference to the large, the complex, and the artificial. The full elaboration of this outlook took place in the Ashikaga period which, for this reason, has been dubbed the age of Zen culture.

One ritualized expression of Zen culture was the tea ceremony in which the small group, the austere setting close to nature, the slow, graceful, and prescribed motions of serving, and the simple and even coarse pottery were intended to induce a mental state of tranquility in contrast to the hurly-burly activities of daily life. Another example was landscape painting in which the artist sought to convey the essence of his subject by bold brushstrokes, ignoring details. Often the artist selected some small part, such as a branch in bloom, as the epitome of the whole.

Another development in the same vein was the replacement of the icon in the niche in the main room of a home with simple art objects or flower arrangements which were frequently changed to provide fresh subjects for concentrated esthetic appreciation. Needless to say, the rest of the room was left bare of ornament in order to concentrate attention on the single object of beauty and perfection. Similarly, Zen influence cultivated a preference for natural rather than painted finishes and for natural and gnarled timbers rather than milled lumber. Another art that was developed under Zen influence was landscape gardening in which the garden setting was considered as important as the building. Each garden was designed to represent the essence of nature on a small scale. Zen esthetics also inspired the arts of growing dwarfed trees and of creating miniature landscapes planted in bowls. Finally, although the Nō drama drew its subjects mainly from popular Buddhism rather than Zen, the form of the drama and the sensitive treatment of the subjects reflect the influence of Zen esthetics.

THE DECLINE OF KAMAKURA

Although the Mongol invasions of 1274 and 1281 put a severe strain on Japanese resources, particularly in the southwest, without any compensating material rewards, internal problems were primarily responsible for the deterioration of the Kamakura shogunate. The loose-knit, decentralized regime was held together chiefly by the bonds of personal loyalty to Kamakura, and rewards and punishments could be enforced only so long as vigorous shogunal leadership commanded a superior military force. The hereditary position of protectors and stewards allowed them to consolidate local power and to become virtually independent of Kamakura. Also peace permitted samurai families to increase their numbers without an equivalent increase in income. As yet no system of primogeniture to conserve estates had been

devised, and both sons and daughters shared an inheritance with the result that many samurai descendants possessed inadequate incomes to support their status. This increasing number of impoverished and indebted samurai was ready for any military adventure that might offer the opportunity to improve their fortunes.

On the other hand, the Kamakura period was a time of substantial economic development and cultural diffusion not only at Kamakura but throughout the country. Indeed, decentralized diversity and competition acted in this era, and later, as a positive stimulus to social and economic development. Ambitious lords realized that the more production they could get from their estates the stronger they would be. Less foresighted lords became relatively weaker and were ultimately eliminated.

The emperor, Go-Daigo, who dreamed of reasserting imperial authority, provided the rallying point for the rebellion that destroyed the Kamakura shogunate. The great monasteries and a number of lords, seizing the chance to fish in troubled waters, gave him military support; but the decisive factor was the defection with his army of the Kamakura general, Ashikaga Takauji, who had been sent to put down the rebels. Unfortunately for Go-Daigo's anachronistic dream, the realistic Takauji was prepared to settle for nothing less than the establishment of a new shogunate in his family. In 1336 he captured Kyōto, and the emperor escaped to the mountains where he and his successors maintained a rival court at Yoshino until 1392.

THE ASHIKAGA SHOGUNATE

Although the Ashikagas held the shogunal title from 1338 to 1573 and operated a government with headquarters at Kyōto that was almost identical in form to that of Kamakura, they never exercised authority over the whole land and frequently even failed to keep the peace within the immediate vicinity of their capital. The basic problem that they were unable to overcome was the loss of direct control over the samurai. Japanese political development had reached a stage where local lords, later to be called *daimyō* (great names), commanded the loyalty of the samurai under their protection, and the more samurai they commanded the greater the power and influence they wielded. In fact, the extent to which this new lord-vassal relationship had already developed largely explains the overthrow of the Kamakura shogunate. What power the Ashikaga shōguns possessed depended not on the direct loyalty of the warrior class but on the uncertain support of ambitious local lords who can be described as little more than allies of doubtful allegiance. In addition, the shoguns tried to maintain their position as the strongest lord through control of their own extensive estates and through kinship by obtaining large estates for their relatives. More than their predecessors they were almost entirely dependent on their own estates for income. Every other lord kept for his own use every ounce of income he could extract from his own lands.

Like the "Warring States" period in China, Japan was carved up into a number of territorial domains under autonomous lords intent on expansion. Warfare was endemic and in the last century of the Ashikaga period became increasingly bloody and ruthless. For the first 50-odd years the existence of two rival imperial courts furnished a cloak of legitimacy for opportunistic lords who did not hesitate to switch sides when such disloyalty appeared to be in their interest. After all, Takauji had demonstrated how profitable such an act of treason could be. In this era of ruthless competition, talent, skill, and luck were what counted. Many noble families disappeared, and new lords of humble origins rose to power. Many may have been humbler in origin than their genealogies admit.

As civil strife intensified, the pace of social and economic growth and change was accelerated, not checked. Under lords who were motivated by enlightened self-interest the agricultural production per acre was doubled and in some cases tripled. An improved standard of living promoted a great increase in industry and trade. And the growth in trade stimulated the development of a money economy. For the most part, Japanese commerce relied on copper cash that was imported in large quantities from China. The highly prized Japanese swords loomed large on the list of exports to China. Zen monasteries which maintained contact with China for religious reasons frequently sponsored commercial expeditions and utilized the profits for building programs. Commerce needed credit that was, at first, provided by prosperous monasteries and, then, by professional moneylenders and moneychangers.

In such unstable times manufacturers and merchants needed protection. Markets and towns developed under the patronage of lords, temples and monasteries; and merchant and professional guilds were formed to bargain for privileges and protection. In such an age of uncertainty, perhaps it was no accident that many family fortunes were founded on an initial adventure in brewing sake. Whatever the reason, there appears to have been a growing demand for alcoholic beverages.

As the scale and scope of warfare expanded in the last century of the Ashikaga period, enterprising lords for military purposes took a step with significant social and political potentialities. Each mounted samurai had always been served and aided in battle by several peasant attendants. Confronted with a conquer-or-die situation, the great lords had to mobilize every ounce of military potential in their territories. The logical step was the formation of large bodies of peasant infantry who were armed with pikes and commanded by mounted samurai. The highly trained professional warrior was supplanted by masses of conscripted peasants, and warfare came to require the full utilization of all the physical and human resources of the daimyō's domain. Consequently, peasants with military talent rose rapidly in the ranks, becoming generals and gaining grants of land. The hereditary monopoly of the samurai appeared broken and its check on social mobility removed. In the towns and villages popular risings aimed at moneylenders led to the cancellation of debts. The military role of the common man gave him a new importance that the daimyō could not afford to ignore. Both military and social considerations were forcing the daimyō to develop more absolute and efficient governments for their realms.

This was the Japan that the Portuguese discovered in 1543: a land divided into more than a dozen major principalities that were ruled by lords dedicated to the military ideal. This was a land whose political and social structure was far more understandable than China's to sixteenth-century Europeans. The

Chinese appeared cold and strange; the Japanese friendly and familiar. Although the rise of Japanese civilization had relied heavily on borrowings from China, even Europeans could easily recognize its distinctive differences. Moreover, it was a civilization which, like that of Europe, was still in the stage of dynamic growth and development in contrast to the long-established sense of self-satisfied fulfillment that characterized Chinese civilization. In contrast with the Chinese, the Japanese welcomed new ideas and implements and were eager to explore and exploit their potentialities. Naturally, Europeans found this open-minded attitude much more congenial and profitable. But the Japanese tendency to permit their emotions to lead them from one extreme to another was before long to slam shut the door that had been thrown so widely open to the West.

SIGNIFICANT DATES

	660 B.C.	Mythological foundation of Japanese state
c.	190 B.C.	Founding of Chinese colony at P'yongyang
	313 A.D.	Overthrow of Chinese Colonial State in Korea
	562 A.D.	Expulsion of Japanese from Korea
578–	621 A.D.	Regency of Prince Shōtoku: establishment of Buddhism and Chinese influence
	604 A.D.	Seventeen Article Constitution
	646 A.D.	Taika Reforms
	668 A.D.	Unification of Korea with T'ang aid
710–	784 A.D.	Nara era
794–	1185 A.D.	Heian (Kyōto) era
1192–	1333 A.D.	Kamakura shogunate
1338–	1573 A.D.	Ashikaga shogunate
	1543 A.D.	Arrival of Portuguese in Japan

SELECTED READINGS

*Aston, William G., trans., *Nihongi*. London: Allen and Unwin, 1956.

*Dumoulin, Heinrich, *A History of Zen Buddhism.* New York: McGraw-Hill, 1965.

*Hall, John Whitney, *Japan from Prehistory to Modern Times.* New York: Dell Pub. Co., 1970.

———, et al., *Twelve Doors to Japan.* New York: McGraw-Hill, 1965.

*Hatada, Takashi, *A History of Korea.* Santa Barbara, Calif.: ABC-Clio, 1969.

Henthorn, William E., *A History of Korea.* New York: Free Press, 1972.

*Humphreys, Christmas, *Zen Buddhism*. New York: Macmillan, 1967.

*Keene, Donald, ed., *Manyoshu*. New York: Columbia University Press, 1969.

*———, trans. and ed., *Anthology of Japanese Literature from the Earliest Era to the Mid-nineteenth Century*. New York: Grove Press, 1960.

Kitagawa, Joseph Mitsuo, *Religion in Japanese History*. New York: Columbia University Press, 1966.

McCullough, Helen Craig, trans., *The Taiheiki: A Chronicle of Medieval Japan*. New York: Columbia University Press, 1959.

*Morris, Ivan, *The World of the Shining Prince*. New York: Knopf, 1961.

*———, trans., *The Pillow Book of Sei Shonagon*. 2 vols.; New York: Columbia University Press, 1967.

Philippi, Donald L., trans., *Kojiki*. Princeton: Princeton University Press, 1969.

*Reischauer, Edwin O., *Japan: The Story of a Nation*. New York: Knopf, 1970.

*Sansom, Sir George Bailey, *A History of Japan*. 3 vols.; Stanford: Stanford University Press, 1969.

———, *Japan: A Short Cultural History*. Rev. ed.; New York: Appleton Century, 1962.

Shinoda, Minoru, *The Founding of the Kamakura Shogunate*. New York: Columbia University Press, 1967.

*Storry, Richard, *A History of Modern Japan*. Rev. ed.; Baltimore: Penguin Books, 1963.

*Suzuki, D. T., *Zen Buddhism*. New York: Doubleday, 1956.

*Tsunoda, Ryusaku, ed., *Sources of the Japanese Tradition*. New York: Columbia University Press, 1958.

Varley, H. Paul, *The Onin War*. New York: Columbia University Press, 1961.

*Waley, Arthur, trans., *The Tale of Genji*. 2 vols.; New York: Doubleday, 1955–1959.

*Warner, Langdon, *The Enduring Art of Japan*. New York: Grove Press, 1958.

*Watts, Alan W., *The Way of Zen*. New York: Random House, 1965.

PART THREE
THE ERA OF ALIEN ASSAULTS

Great Mosque and Kaaba, Mecca. *(Popperfoto, London)*

The Dome of the Rock, Jerusalem, 691. *(Louis Goldman/Rapho Guillumette)*

Great Mosque, Damascus, 715. Detail of mosaics and interior. (*Above: L. Powell/ M. Grimoldi; below: Paul Keel/Photo Researchers*)

Persian miniature. Camp scene from Nizamis *Khamsa* manuscript. (*Fogg Art Museum, gift of John Goelet*)

Court of Majjid-i Jami, Isfahan, 1088. (*I. Powell/M. Grimoldi*)

Fathpur Sikri, "City of Victory," built by Akbar in the 16th century. *(Indian Government Tourist Office)*

Miniature from Saadi's *Gulistan*, c. 1610.
(Private collection, Cambridge, Massachusetts)

Tāj Mahal, Agra, India, 17th century. (*Indian Government Tourist Office*)

Temple of Heaven, Peking, Ming Dynasty. *(Audrey Topping/Rapho Guillumette)*

Emperor Kuang Wu Fording a River by Ch'iu Ying, Ming Dynasty. *(The National Gallery of Canada, Ottawa)*

The Hall of Supreme Harmony, Peking, Ming Dynasty. (*Audrey Topping/Rapho Guillumette*)

Ni-jo Castle and gardens, Kyoto, 17th century. (*M. Sakamoto*)

The Great Wave, a woodblock print by
Katsushika Hokusai (1760–1849), Ukiyo-e
school. *(Museum of Fine Arts, Boston, Series
Fujaku Sanjurok'kei Fund)*

Woodblock print of Kabuki actor by Tosh-
usai Sharaku, 1794. *(Staatsbibliothek, Berlin)*

Detail from hand-woven Persian carpet, Herat. *(Collection of Mr. and Mrs. Louis E. Seley, Hervey Seley and Eliot Jay Seley)*

Sulaymaniya Mosque, Istanbul, 16th century. *(J. Powell/M. Grimoldi)*

In Part Two the growth and development of the major civilizations to full maturity have been described with particular attention to their enduring contributions and qualities. The cultural ideals and values that distinguished each one, already apparent in the first part of this study, have been more completely worked out and expressed in their respective religions and philosophies, making clearer the uniqueness that characterized the whole range of thought and action peculiar to each civilization. The expansion of the area directly controlled by each one and the diffusion of its influence among less advanced neighbors, who were attracted by its wealth, if not its sophistication, have also been observed. Indeed, the growth of trade in the prized products of each civilization was bound to arouse the covetous instincts of less favored, but warlike, peoples. The progress of the great civilizations as compared to the relative stagnancy of the tribal way of life accentuated the contrast between them. Also each of these civilizations had passed its zenith of political vigor and, to a greater or lesser degree, invited assault.

The first great eruption in the confrontation between "the desert and the sown" came out of the deserts of Arabia under the inspiration of the message of the Prophet, Muhammed. Arab warriors quickly overran the ancient centers of civilization in the Middle East, Mesopotamia, and Egypt, and ultimately carried their conquests from Spain in the West to India in the East, creating the largest ideological entity the world had yet known. Needless to say, the ideology of this civilization, as befitted the heir of the earlier centers of civilization in the Middle East, was founded on a religion, Islam. In turn, however, the empire of the Arabs fell prey to subversion and conquest by Mongols and Turks from the steppes of Central Asia under the borrowed banner of Islam. Moreover, the Ottoman Turks revived the imperial vigor of Islam, conquering much of Eastern Europe and carrying Muslim arms to the gates of Vienna, the capital of the Holy Roman Empire, while other Turkish-Mongol conquerors from Central Asia completed the conquest of the subcontinent of India for Islam.

India, as noted above, was also a victim of Islam politically, although Hinduism proved too resilient to be engulfed, and it carried the burden of Indian culture. The more exposed Indus valley, relatively isolated from India proper, fell first in the eighth century, as it had fallen many times before to foreign conquerors since the time of the Aryan invasions. The

Ganges valley was finally overrun in the late twelfth century and subsequently was most of southern India.

China also fell politically but not culturally to the Mongol host under Khubilai Khan in the later thirteenth century, but it mustered enough indigenous strength to expel the conquerors less than a century later. This resurgence had lasted three centuries when internal rebellion opened the gates to a more durable conquest by the Manchus in alliance with the Mongols.

The next alien assaults, which came from Western Christendom, were also initially inspired by the desire for trade in the exotic products of the East, but in the long run these assaults by the dynamic civilization of the West were to prove far more disruptive to the traditional ways of life of the older agricultural civilizations of the East than those of the comparatively unsophisticated Arabs, Turks, Mongols, and Manchus who had been content to inherit and exploit without the social, economic, and political structures of their civilized victims. By the mid-nineteenth century, the point at which Part Three concludes, only India and some lesser outposts had fallen prey to Western imperialism, but unequal treaties, enforced on all, had exposed the regions of Eastern civilization to the impact of economic penetration and subversion powered by the Industrial Revolution. Eventually, this exposure would be intensified and expanded by the combination of steamships and the opening of the Suez Canal, which greatly reduced the distance in time and cost between East and West. The reactions that this much broader assault engendered in the East are described in the second half of this book.

CHAPTER TEN

THE RISE AND SPREAD OF ISLAM: 610–750

Since the death of Alexander the Great (323 B.C.) the political unification of the Middle East that had been accomplished by the Persians had been broken for nearly a millennium. At first the land had been divided between the Greek-ruled successor states of Alexander's empire, and then, a shifting, but fairly stable, frontier had separated the Roman and Byzantine empires from the Parthian and Sassanid empires. Now, a thousand years later, the hitherto disunited and warlike Arab tribes that thinly populated the vast and harsh lands of the Arabian peninsula and the Desert Bay were to be welded together for the first time into an effective political force by the inspired message of Muhammed, the Prophet of Allah. A century after his death, the momentum imparted by his teachings was to carry the arms of the Arabs and their allies across North Africa to the Atlantic and to southern France in the West and through Iran to the Indus River and to the steppeland of central Asia in the East, creating a theocratic state of greater extent than the world had yet known.

Although the Arabian peninsula and the Desert Bay bounded by the Fertile Crescent can generally be described as desert, only a few areas are unable to sustain life, notably the vast and mountainous sand dunes of the "Empty Quarter" in the southwest. The interior plateau, which tilts from west to east, receives an average winter rainfall of 5 inches or less which brings forth vegetation sufficient to support a wide-ranging pastoral economy. In favored places the underlying limestone has been formed into storage pits, catching the run-off that is tapped by wells to water the stock and, where adequate, to make possible settled agriculture by irriga-

tion. In recent years, irrigated farming has been substantially increased by the use of oil-powered pumps. Nevertheless, the shortage of water has been the chief factor limiting and molding the way of life of the nomadic Bedouins.

Throughout history the difficulties of desert life had created continuous interaction between the "desert and the sown." The desert had always provided a reservoir of manpower for the settled areas, and before the Arab explosion tribal powers of substantial size and duration had maintained themselves in the Desert Bay.

The most important factor in their power and in the habitation of the desert was the camel, the "ship of the desert," probably introduced in the thirteenth century B.C. Most Westerners immediately associate the horse with the Arabs, but the horse was an expensive luxury, ill-adapted to life in the desert. On the other hand, the camel with its ability to go for a week without water and to subsist on almost any kind of plant life supplied man with the mobility needed to overcome the waterless stretches of the desert. In addition to grazing herds of sheep and goats, the nomads gained a new source of income by operating, raiding, or protecting the camel caravans that opened new and shorter trade routes across the desert from oasis to oasis. A Bedouin's wealth and prestige was measured by the number of camels he possessed, and the traditional status conferred by camel ownership is reflected in their recent sharp increase in numbers, even though motorized transport has largely undermined their economic utility. When the followers of Islam swept out of the desert to assault the Byzantine and Sassanid empires, the camel, and not their few horses, furnished the mobility

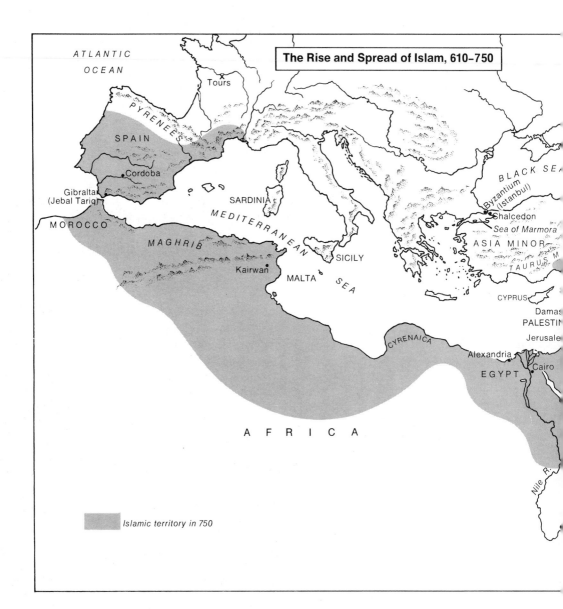

The Rise and Spread of Islam, 610–750

Islamic territory in 750

for surprise attacks that compensated for their smaller numbers. Like all valuable assets, however, the camel has, at least, one drawback. His close and indiscriminate grazing kills off the vegetation contributing to progressive dessication.

Facing the Red Sea in the west, mountain ranges that are a continuation of those in Palestine rise from 3,000 feet near Mecca to more than 14,000 feet in the Yemen. These mountains capture most of the moisture from the clouds blowing in from the Mediterranean and Red Seas during the winter months. The high mountains of the Yemen are also buffeted by a summer monsoon and receive a total annual rainfall of as much as 40 inches. As a result, this corner of the Arabian peninsula supports a present population of about 5 million, almost as much as the rest of Arabia combined. In ancient times large

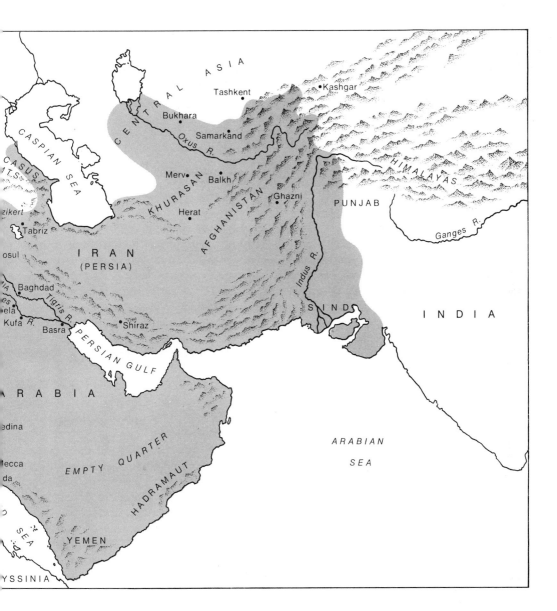

dams and irrigation works may have supported an even larger number. Spices, incense, and other exotic commodities made possible a prosperous caravan trade from this region via Mecca, Medina, and other transit towns to markets in the north. East of the Yemen, a similar mountain range of declining altitude separates the Hadramaut from the dunes of the "Empty Quarter" and the interior plateau.

The Arabs along the coasts have been notable seafarers. Their light, swift-sailing vessels served pearl divers, fishermen, traders, and pirates—the distinction between these occupations still being scarcely perceptible. Islamic conquests on land inspired them to adventure farther overseas, establishing a substantial colony in the chief port of China and developing navigational instruments, such as the astrolabe.

ARAB SOCIETY

Whether or not Muhammed's message is believed to have been the divinely revealed word of God, an appreciation of the society into which he was born is necessary because he had to express himself in the language and terms familiar to him and his audience. Arabic was no exception to the rule that the form and vocabulary of every language are molded by the way of life of the people it serves.

The nomadic Bedouins, who comprised the bulk of the Arabs, were divided into a multitude of politically independent tribes, each composed of several extended families and ruled by a shaykh (sheik), normally elected on the basis of leadership from the leading family. The shaykh's absolute authority was limited by tribal customs and traditions, called *sunna*, whose applicability was declared on any issue by the elders. Wholly illiterate, the perpetuation of the tribe's rules and regulations depended on the joint memory of the group. To aid memory, poems were composed and memorized utilizing repetition for emphasis. Even in the important trading and religious center of Mecca only 17 men were said to have been literate in the time of the Prophet. Muhammed himself is believed to have been illiterate and yet to have managed caravans in his early years. The themes and rich vocabulary of Arabic demonstrated the flexibility of the spoken language of a warlike people who valued individual courage, honor, and hospitality and yet permitted any deception or tactic in dealing with a foe. The vocabulary of invective was highly developed because of the prevalence of blood feuds and intertribal raids.

Boys because they grew up to become warriors were more highly regarded than girls. Able and faithful wives, however, were treated with honor and granted considerable dignity of status, especially those who had produced sons. Polygamy was the customary practice, and a warrior's first obligation was the protection of his family.

Each tribe had its own roughly demarcated grazing range, but the pressures of population, drought, and the very pattern of life called for constant incursions and raids beyond the ill-defined boundaries. Each tribe had its own watering holes and obtained its other necessities by raiding or trading with passing caravans or oasis towns. Not infrequently, traditional foes made a temporary truce bound by oaths in order to trade and enjoy festivities in a common market town and, in some cases, these arrangements had become sanctified by tradition as annual affairs. Each tribe had its own cult, often centered on a sacred stone or place where animal sacrifices were made.

This "system" of ordered anarchy was not limited to the Bedouin tribes. Although somewhat moderated by the requirements of settled life and trade, tribal organization and practices applied to the towns as well. In the absence of any larger political entity the individual Arabs depended on the clan and tribal unit for protection and justice.

Mecca, the birthplace of Muhammed, belonged to the Quraysh tribe. Located in a desolate valley, its only natural blessings were a reliable, if saline, spring and a commercially strategic situation. Forty-eight miles inland from the port of Jidda, the last easily accessible harbor for sailing vessels before facing the frustrating headwinds from the north, Mecca also enjoyed the advantage of being at a low point in the coastal mountain range. Thus it was a natural crossroads for goods that were being sent north or south by land or sea and east or west across the desert to southern Mesopotamia. The shrewd Quraysh merchants had supplemented this natural advantage by making Mecca a place of pilgrimage. A simple structure called the Kaaba (cube) housed a sacred black meteorite and 360 different deities catering to every possible cult. Pilgrims were protected by a holy truce in Mecca. Thus the Quraysh had capitalized on its natural setting to make Mecca the nearest thing the Arabs had to a cultural center. Indeed, fear of the loss of the pilgrim trade partially explains the hostility of the Quraysh to their fellow tribesman's monotheism. How could they foresee that Islam would bring far greater numbers of pilgrims to their town?

Trade and persecution had brought Jewish and Christian colonists and their religions to Arabia. Although they appear to have gained no foothold in Mecca, a Jewish colony (mostly Arab converts) accounted for a large part of the population of Medina to the north, and a number of Jewish and Christian communities were well established to the south. Arab traders and town dwellers were well aware of these more advanced religions, and discontent with their primitive cults had already stirred some to attempt religious reform. To this extent the ground had been prepared for the unique genius of Muhammed. But the Bedouins had been little affected and were to be lured into the fold less by the religious appeal than by the opportunity for plunder offered by confederation. Muhammed's special discovery was the winning combination of religion and militancy.

MUHAMMED, THE PROPHET OF ALLAH (C. 571 – 632)

No special or unique events or circumstances are related about the birth of the future Prophet. His father, a camel driver, died before he was born and his mother died when he was 6 years of age, leaving him in the care of an uncle. When he came of age, he entered the service of a shrewd, prosperous, and twice-widowed lady, Khadija, who operated a caravan business. Muhammed was described as a shy, but handsome, young man and, whether because of his good looks or some other reason, Khadija, who was fifteen years his senior, married him when he was 25 years old. In any case, they were bound by a genuine and deep mutual affection. She bore him four daughters and two sons, both of whom died at an early age. While she lived, he took no other wife, and she became

his first convert. By this marriage he had gained both a good wife and economic security. Yet he continued to live simply and was accustomed, when troubled, to retire for meditation to a cave in a hill outside Mecca.

Many years of troubled searching passed before he received his first revelation, and at first he believed he was possessed by a spirit and considered suicide. Finally, he became convinced that he was the Prophet of Allah—a creator deity in the Kaaba assemblage of gods—divinely appointed to receive His words transmitted by the angel Gabriel. In the first revelation Gabriel in a voice reverberating like a bell commanded him thusly:

Proclaim: *In the name of thy Lord who created— Created man from a clot of blood.*

Proclaim: *And thy Lord is the most bountiful, Who taught by means of the pen— Taught man what he knew not.*

This revelation was received in the year 610. The reference to teaching by the pen indicates his belief in the essential truth revealed to prior prophets, such as Abraham, Moses, and Jesus, and recorded in the Old and New Testaments and his conviction in his mission to deliver to mankind, as "the Seal of the Prophets," the final uncorrupted word of God. The Qur'an (Koran) is the collected revelations received by Muhammed and is believed to represent directly the words of God, not those of his messenger, Muhammed. They were collected, collated, and transcribed in a single, authenticated version not many years after his death.

No translation, it is said, can do justice to the poetic vigor and color of the Arabic, but it is interesting and, perhaps, significant to follow the unfolding and elaboration of the theme. The more detailed and confident nature of the later revelations does not necessarily raise any question about their divine origin. It can be explained by the Prophet's change of circumstances from a persecuted missionary to a successful leader and also by the clearer and fuller understanding of the messages transmitted to him. Furthermore, the Qur'an is a very different work and cannot be compared with either the Old or New Testaments. Although it contains copious accounts of the problems that were confronted by prior prophets, it is not a history like the Old Testament. Nor is it a story of the life and teachings of a religious leader, like the Gospels of Matthew, Mark, Luke, and John in the New Testament. Instead, it purports to be the final and complete revelation for the guidance of mankind of the eternal word of God which had been only imperfectly understood and appreciated by the followers of prior prophets. Finally, the 114 revelations, spread over 22 years, were delivered orally by the Prophet to his followers and were intended to re-emphasize and elaborate the basic message, although the length and complexity of the later ones would seem to have required written preparation. As a result, they seem inordinately repetitious to the Western reader. But remember, they were meant to be recited, not read.

For the first 12 years of his mission (610–622), Muhammed stayed in Mecca as the religious leader of a small group of believers who was despised and later persecuted by the leaders and the majority of his fellow Quraysh tribesmen. Most of the revelations of this Meccan period are comparatively brief, dynamic, and poetic, concentrating on countering the denunciations leveled at him. Repeatedly they pound home the major theme that there is only one God who has created everything in Heaven and Earth and that he, Muhammed, has been designated to warn the Arabs of the error of their ways in worshiping other gods and in selfishly pursuing the acquisition of worldly goods. Not only can you not take it with you, everything you possess, including your body, is God's creation and belongs to him alone. At a single blast of the trumpet, accompanied by other cataclysmic signs, God will bring about the bodily resurrection of all mankind and the final day of judgment. For Him who has created all things, resurrection presents no problems. No intermediary can save the evildoers because God is omniscient and every act, good or bad, of every man has been recorded from the beginning of time. Nothing can be concealed from Him.

Yet God is compassionate and merciful and will forgive the sins and shortcomings of true believers, especially those unconsciously committed. Indeed, each revelation opens with the invocation: "In the Name of Allah, the Compassionate, the Merciful." Moreover, God does not place unreasonable demands on the faithful. Necessary deviations from the prescribed practices are permitted, and serious shortcomings may be compensated for by penances. Even dissimulation of one's faith to protect one's life is allowed because God knows whether you believe in your heart or not.

Colorful descriptions of the pleasures of paradise and the horrors of hell are part of most of the revelations. Paradise contains a plenitude of all those things dear to Arabs: water, gardens, fruit, wine, an eternal supply of virgin maidens with swelling breasts and large dark eyes, and a complete absence of quarrels and vain discourse. In hell, the bodies of the nonbelievers will be eternally scorched by flames and forced by thirst to consume boiling water that will burst their bowels.

The Meccan revelations are filled with references to the aristocratic objection that God would not have chosen such a humble and ignoble messenger as Muhammed and, therefore, he must be an imposter, sorcerer, and a crazed poet who would lead them to abandon their gods. In reply, the doubting aristocrats were told that the mere fact of wealth, which they had not given away to the poor and needy, was a sure sign that they were destined for damnation. Moreover, they were told that the rejection of previous prophets, such as Noah, Moses, Jesus, and several Arab prophets by the prosperous, had brought destruction on their cities. Distribution of wealth as alms to the poor was prescribed as a recognition that all wealth came from God.

Naturally, this social gospel did not rest well with the wealthy Meccans and, as the number of believers grew, stimulated an increase of persecution. Some of the faithful left for Abyssinia and others took refuge in Yathrib (later renamed Medina, "the city" of the Prophet) where he had gained some converts and where a substantial Jewish settlement was an assurance of toleration. The city was torn by civil strife, and the Prophet's followers persuaded the disputants to accept Muhammed as a mediator. In June, 622, Muhammed and his closest associate, the well-to-do Abu Bekr, escaped from Mecca and made their way to Medina. This turning point in the Prophet's career was the famous Hijrah (migration or flight) from which the Islamic Era is dated.

The authority gained as a mediator was not surrendered, and the Medinan revelations reflect his new role as the political organizer of a theocracy. The abstract and poetic qualities of the persuader, which had already begun to diminish in his last years at Mecca, were replaced by the precise and positive statements of the legislator and commander and the increasingly confident assertions of God's word against the enemies of the faith. Although poetic qualities occasionally recur, the busy Prophet relied much more on prose.

His militancy emerged when he overrode Medinese objections to attacks on Meccan caravans for the benefit of the faith. Temporary alliances with warlike Bedouins, always eager for plunder, supplemented his forces. Naturally the Meccans reacted by counterattack. When the Medinese Jews, whom he had sought to convert, failed to support him, and even collaborated with the foe, he turned his wrath on them, driving them out of Medina and confiscating their goods. The tone of his revelations shifted in accordance with military success or defeat. Those able-bodied converts who failed to take the

field with him were berated after victory as hypocrites who did not believe that God determined the time of everyone's birth and death. His puritanism was set forth in a single verse that condemned the favorite Arab diversions of wine and gambling as works of Satan (Qur'an 5 : 92). Perhaps most enlightening about his heady sense of authority was his linking of himself to God as in his command of obedience to God *and* His Prophet. Attributes hitherto associated only with Allah were now attached to the Prophet as "the Compassionate, the Merciful" (Qur'an 9 : 129).

In 628 he gained safe conduct for his followers to make a pilgrimage to the Kaaba. Finally, in 630 he was strong enough to force the submission of Mecca. He entered his birthplace in triumph and, as his first act, destroyed the 360 idols in the Kaaba. News of his success, plus the threat of attack, brought a swarm of submissions and apparent conversions from one tribe after another: Arab, Christian, and Jew. The year 631 went down in Islamic annals as "the year of embassies and deputations," but the year of his death, 632, saw the important submissions of the Yemen and Hadramaut.

In the full flush of victory, the Prophet died, but what had he achieved? He had developed a religion that could transcend the tribal anarchy of Arabia by transferring the ultimate loyalty of the individual from the family and the tribe to the one God, Allah, but success in this transferral had been gained only through victorious military leadership. Tribal society had not been transformed and the individual's prime source of security remained the tribe. The only physical bond beyond military strength was the alms tax, and its collection was dependent on genuine conversion. At best, Muhammed, who was planning to divert Arab militancy to attacks on the Byzantine and Sassanid empires, had created a confederation of tribes that grudgingly accepted his religion because of his demonstrated military ability. In short, Muhammed had established a personal hegemony that on his death suffered defections much more rapidly than the submissions he had previously received. Furthermore, he had made no provision for succession to his religious and temporal authority. Nevertheless, a sufficient number remained firm in their faith to re-establish military authority under an able successor (*caliph*). Before we consider the problem of succession, however, the religion as finally delineated by the Prophet requires analysis.

ISLAM

The religion preached by Muhammed is called Islam, meaning "submission to the will of God," and the faithful are called Muslims, "those who submit to God's will." The idea of submission stems from the belief that God is the sole creator of all things. As the creator, it follows that He is the sole destroyer. His will alone determines what will *be* and what will cease to *be*. In the Qur'an the faithful are constantly admonished to fear God and provided with examples of His wrath in the past.

The body of the faithful constitutes a brotherhood (*umma*) in which all are spiritually equal in their common belief in God and His Prophet, regardless of race or class. A demonstration of this tolerance was Muhammed's marriage to a negress. Any difference in race or status, whether slave or ruler, is merely God's will to which the believer would submit without complaint. Since all Muslims are spiritually equal and each is individually responsible to God, there is no need for a spiritual hierarchy or organization. Each Muslim needs only to know and follow the prescription delivered by God to the Prophet and enshrined in the Qur'an. The basic religious obligations of the Muslim are generally known as the "Five Pillars."

The first pillar is the profession of belief in a formula that may be freely translated: "There is no God but Allah, and Muhammed is His Prophet." This is the most commonly

heard sentence throughout the life of a Muslim. It is uttered as a blessing and direction to the newborn child and is part of the muezzin's call to prayer five times a day. By it the Muslim acknowledges the singleness of God and the role of Muhammed as "the Seal of the Prophets," the deliverer of the final and undistorted version of the eternal word of God.

The second pillar is prayer to be performed five times a day according to a ritual involving standing, kneeling, and prostrate positions and orientation in the direction of the sacred center of Mecca. Since this is an individual act of devotion, the believer prays at the prescribed times wherever he may be, but he must be pure in mind and body. Bodily purity requires bathing of the extremities. In the absence of water, which might often be the case on the desert, the substitution of sand is permitted. On each occasion, the Muslim equivalent of the Lord's Prayer, which is the first revelation in the Qur'an, is repeated four times.

> In the name of God, the merciful, the compassionate.
> Praise be to God, lord of the universe,
> the merciful, the compassionate,
> ruler on the day of judgment.
> Thee alone we worship; thee alone we ask for aid.
>
> Guide us in the straight path,
> the path of those whom thou hast favored,
> not of those who have incurred Thy wrath,
> nor of those who go astray.
> (Quoted by Philip K. Hitti,
> *The Near East In History*,
> p. 199)

On Friday a complete bath and attendance at a mosque for noon prayer, if possible, are prescribed. There, a prayer leader (*imam*) normally delivers an address following the prayers. At the mosque, noble and slave, rich and poor, light and dark pray side by side as a reminder that each Muslim is an equal member of a spiritual brotherhood. Needless to say, the prayers must be said in Arabic, the language in which God's word was delivered to the Prophet. The prohibition of worship in translation was the basis for the spread of Arabic usage.

The architecture of the mosque evolved into a structure of exceptional beauty, but the essential features have remained the same. Of course, the mosque is precisely oriented in the direction of Mecca. No pictures or icons that might suggest the existence of other deities are allowed. Decoration is limited to the artistic use of Arabic script which gives passages from the Qur'an and, in the hands of artists from the conquered and converted civilizations, this medium was developed into an exceptionally esthetic art form. There are no pews or altars, the only unique feature being the pulpit from which the *imam* addresses the congregation. Normally a section is screened off for women. At the entrance a facility for ritual washing is provided. The site of each mosque is sacred and is supported by a perpetual endowment. From the outside, characteristic features are the bulbous dome sheathed with brilliantly hued tiles, which evolved later and have no religious significance, and the minarets from which the muezzins issue their calls to prayers.

The third pillar of the faith is alms for the support of the unfortunates. It is based on the doctrine that all property belongs to God and man is granted the use of it only to fulfill his earthly needs. By giving alms, the believer acknowledges this doctrine and purifies the use of the rest of his property.

The fourth pillar is fasting on special days and throughout the month of Ramadan as a reminder of mankind's total dependence on God's bounty. Today, fasting is required from dawn to dusk—when a black thread can be distinguished from a white thread—during the lunar month of Ramadan when the Prophet's mission was first revealed to Mu-

hammed. The prescribed abstinence is so total that in 1949 in Egypt a ruling had to be made that necessary medicine does not constitute a breaking of the fast. During the nights, dedicated Muslims eat sparingly, but today some urbanites utilize the nights for gluttonous indulgence and bacchanalian festivities.

The fifth pillar is the obligation for all who can afford it to make a pilgrimage to Mecca, at least once in a lifetime at the prescribed time of the year. Although Muhammed could not have imagined the vast distances the faithful would have to travel, hundreds of thousands converge on Mecca by every mode of transportation each year. For 1958 the government of Sa'udi Arabia claimed a total of 600,000 pilgrims, a figure that would have made the Prophet's Quraysh opponents much more eager to embrace Islam. On a worldwide scale this annual pilgrimage emphasizes the conception of brotherhood. In addition, the pilgrim gains local prestige and status by adding to his name the authorized title of *Hajji*. A complex, traditional set of ritual procedures culminates in a feast of sacrifice that is celebrated simultaneously throughout the Islamic world as a three-day festival in recognition of the worldwide spiritual brotherhood of Muslims.

Finally, the Qur'an commands obedience of all able-bodied male Muslims to the call to a holy war (*jihad*). Only the Khariji sect considers this the fifth pillar, dropping the first as self-evident. As defined in the Qur'an, the declaration of a holy war is limited to the defense of the faith. Yet the Prophet justified his struggle with Mecca on this ground. As any serious student of history knows, the assessment of guilt for aggression is well-nigh impossible to determine. Every aggressor can find some ground to explain his actions as defensive. Islam, like modern Communism, has pictured the world as divided into the land of peace or Islam (*dar al-Islam*) and the land of war or nonbelievers (*dar al-harb*). The tension between the two could always be drawn on to justify the declaration of a holy war. Death for a warrior in a holy war was martyrdom assuring entrance into paradise.

The wars of Islam were by no means the ruthless wars of extermination or conversion so often depicted in Western accounts, although in the heat of battle Muslims, like any others, sometimes were carried away. Muhammed's lack of success in converting the Jews of Medina led him to devise a policy whereby "people of the book" (Jews and Christians) could become wards of Islam in return for the payment of tribute. This device proved so lucrative that it was extended to others. In time, however, this economic disability encouraged conversions, though the process took about three centuries to complete, and the state was eventually forced to assess new taxes on the faithful.

Islam, as proclaimed in the Qur'an, was more than just a spiritual prescription; it was a way of life laying down rules and regulations for the relationships not only of man and God but also of man and man and of man and community. It may be said that, like Moses, Muhammed received a code of law from God, and in some facets the two are quite similar.

The Qur'an did not destroy, but supplemented and reformed, tribal custom. For example, tribal law prescribed equal retaliation for bloodshed, a free man for a free man, a slave for a slave, a woman for a woman. The truth of this law as the basic security for life was upheld, yet was supplemented by the command to accept a fine in payment for the loss of a life. The liquidation of female infants was condemned and, indeed, the number of prescriptions concerning women shows the concern for improving their status. Daughters and wives gained a prescribed share in an inheritance. Marriage was a civil contract—not a sacrament—and no free woman could be forced into marriage against her will. Detailed provisions were laid down concerning marriage and divorce that were based on the precepts that the husband must

support his wife and children and the wife must be faithful and obedient. Because of a scandal involving one of the Prophet's wives, a charge of adultery was proclaimed to require four witnesses, an unlikely prospect. On conviction, the penalty was stoning, which may seem barbarously cruel, but was actually milder than the customary punishment. Polygamy was moderated by setting a maximum limit of four wives at one time, except for the Prophet, and by prescribing equal treatment both physically and spiritually for each one, a requirement that has encouraged the practice of monogamy in recent times. Of course, a man could keep as many female slaves as he could afford. In case of divorce each partner kept property acquired before marriage or acquired since marriage as an individual, including the dowry paid by the husband to the wife.

The eating of animals killed in certain proscribed ways and swine's flesh was forbidden, which would seem to reflect Jewish influence. Usury was prohibited, which is today a major stumbling block to modernization. Thieves, whether men or women, were to have their hands cut off as a warning from God. In recent times this law has been literally enforced only in Arabia. Contracts were taken very seriously. Witnesses were required, and any intentional violation carried heavy penalties.

The political philosophy or doctrine of Islam is less easy to discern in the Qur'an, yet the subordination of man and the community to the transmitted word of God, the creator and destroyer of all things, is clearly proclaimed. As a practicing politician in Medina, Muhammed commanded the obedience of the faithful to both God and his Prophet. Thus he followed the precedent of previous Middle Eastern states by basing political authority on religious sanction. However, as the final Prophet, he left unresolved the question of who or what would exercise power at his death.

While God would be the final arbiter at

judgment day and determined the destiny of man in day-to-day life, he had delivered through Muhammed a divine code of laws that required enforcement by some earthly authority. Therefore, some sort of government for the faithful was required, but its form was not specified. Moreover, even a society of Muslims could not exist without authority because God admitted the existence of human frailties and shortcomings in the provisions and penalties of the law. The Qur'an had proclaimed the spiritual equality of Muslims, which might suggest democracy, but material inequality had also been attributed to God's will. Even if democracy in the modern sense were conceivable in the Arab society of the seventh century, legislative authority would have been limited by God's law. Since the Qur'an was the eternal word of God and, therefore, prior to the state, no government could be more than a subordinate instrument devised to enforce the religious law sent down to guide the individual on the path to salvation. In other words, the state can exist merely to aid the believer in conforming to divine law and, therefore, there can be no separation of state and church. At least, this has been the theoretical conclusion of most Muslim jurists.

In fact, Muhammed was necessarily a product of the tribal society into which he was born. The Muslim brotherhood (umma) was conceived as a vastly enlarged tribe in which each would loyally support and aid the other, settling any differences that might arise peaceably. Muhammed had not overthrown tribal custom (sunna); he had only supplemented and reformed it. As the influential members of a tribe selected by consensus a new shaykh who was confirmed by the tacit acceptance of the tribesmen, so logically the close associates of Muhammed agreed on a successor (caliph) who was tacitly accepted by the faithful. Any who disagreed with the selection could and did seek God's decision on the field of battle.

As the authority of the shaykh was re-stricted by the tribal sunna, so the caliph's authority was limited by the Qur'anic sunna later supplemented by the juridically accepted hadith, sayings attributed to the Prophet and his influential associates. Thus, by implication, the caliph had no legislative power, and no Muslim could be compelled to obey an order contrary to the law. Only the jurists, corporately called the ulema, could interpret the sunna, which included the Qur'an and the hadith, to deal with a new situation.

Later, the jurists formulated the theory of the Caliphate on the basis of actual practice. As the head of the temporal state the caliph was responsible for administration and appointed the chief officials. As the head of Islam, he was the supreme judge responsible for the enforcement of the law. As the protector of the faith he was commander-in-chief with the sole authority to declare a holy war. But in all three roles he was theoretically limited by the law, as interpreted by the jurists.

The classical period when the tribal pattern of selection prevailed had four caliphs: Abu Bekr, 632–634; Umar, 634–644; Uthman, 644–656; and Ali, 656–661. If Muhammed had left a son, the succession would probably have caused no problem, but without a clear claimant several parties arose. The original Quraysh converts who had fled with the Prophet to Medina believed blood kinship and earlier faith gave them a preferential claim. The Medinese asserted that without the refuge and support that they had supplied Islam would have failed. Another group supported a collateral hereditary claim for Muhammed's paternal cousin, Ali, and his sons by the Prophet's daughter, Fatima. Finally, the claim of the influential, aristocratic Umayyad clan of the Quraysh, which controlled Mecca, could not be ignored, even though their conversion had been compelled by superior military strength. The disagreement was settled when Umar, another Quraysh emigrant, placed his hand in that of

Abu Bekr, one of the Prophet's first three converts and his closest associate, and said, "I offer you as caliph." The rest accepted this nomination, and he was confirmed by the immediate community of the faithful.

THE FIRST CONQUESTS

Abu Bekr's first task, in which the young general Khalid ibn-al-Walid distinguished himself, was to suppress the tribal defections and dragoon all the Arabs of the peninsula into the ranks of Islam. Only when this chore was accomplished in record time, was the caliph ready to send forth his forces for campaigns of conquest to the north. Five thousand warriors of the faith under the command of Khalid gained Islam's first victory when they seized the capital of a Christianized Arab state on the Sassanid frontier. Khalid was about to follow up this success by invading Mesopotamia when he received orders to succor another army that was hard pressed by the Byzantine defenders of Syria-Palestine. In a daring march he led 700 picked troops across 500 miles of desert in 18 days and took the Byzantine forces by surprise in July 634. The death of the first caliph caused no pause in the campaign for Palestine and Syria because Abu Bekr returned the favor by nominating Umar as his successor. After a six-month siege Damascus fell in September 635 through internal treachery. But the decisive battle for Syria occurred almost a year later on a hot and windy day of August 636. Khalid in command of 25,000 troops faced a Byzantine army twice that size. Skillfully maneuvering his forces until the wind blew dust in the enemy's faces, he launched his attack from which few of the foe escaped with their lives. For this victory at Yarmuk Khalid was rewarded with the title "the sword of Allah."

Meanwhile, after Khalid's departure the Persian campaign had to await reinforcements. Finally, they arrived, the Persian army was routed, the Sassanid ruler abandoned his capital on the Tigris, and the Arab forces made a triumphant entry into the city in June 637. The naive Arabs were overwhelmed at the wealth of booty they found. One Arab, when criticized for selling an aristocratic woman who was his booty for only 1000 silver pieces, answered that he never knew that there was a larger number. The total treasure was estimated at 9 billion silver pieces. In a few years the rest of Persia was overrun in the face of minimal resistance. Apparently the tribute levied on nonbelievers was less than the oppressive taxes formerly assessed, and the Arabs were welcomed as deliverers. In 651 the Sassanid ruler was murdered by one of his own people for what treasure he still had, bringing an end to the Sassanid dynasty.

Another commander had been advocating for some time the advantages of a campaign in Egypt to cut off the major Byzantine granary. Finally, in the fall of 639, after Syria had been secured, he gained permission to proceed with a small force. As a former leader of caravans to Egypt he knew the terrain. After initial successes in several campaigns he received sufficient reinforcements to justify an assault on the mighty capital city and naval base of Alexandria. In the summer of 642 his force of 20,000 warriors without adequate siege equipment or ships arrived below the great walls of the second city of the empire which was defended by a 50,000-man garrison. In September the garrison withdrew and the city surrendered. With still fresh forces eager for battle he overran Cyrenaica in the following year, setting the direction for the subsequent conquest of all of North Africa and ultimately Spain and Sicily.

In less than a decade the first wave of Muslim conquest with comparatively small armies had destroyed one civilized state and had seriously crippled a second, creating an empire that extended from Iran in the east to Cyrenaica in the west and from the Taurus Mountains in the north to the Arabian Sea in the south. How can this phenomenal achievement be explained. In essence, a combination of factors in both areas had tipped the balance in the age-old confrontation between "the desert and the sown." When expansion was resumed, after a period of civil strife, it was to be directed in a more organized manner by a partially acclimatized Caliphate which was domiciled in Damascus, outside the Arabian homeland, and was to draw heavily on the manpower and resources of the conquered areas.

The outstanding internal factor in the initial conquests was Islam, not so much as a religion but, rather, as a political device to transcend tribal anarchy for a unified Arab effort. It was Muhammed the military leader, and not Muhammed the Prophet, who impressed and won the allegiance of the tribal shaykhs. Nevertheless, the Arabs could not help feeling that a God who made possible such success was potent and worthy of veneration, although they did not understand or appreciate as yet the full meaning of His message. Since Islam opposed the favorite Arab pastime of intertribal warfare and urged on Muslim brothers the peaceful settlement of their differences, some other outlet had to be found for their warlike propensities. What better release for this energy than the bringing into the fold of the Desert Bay Arabs and the conquest of Jerusalem whence the Prophet was believed to have made a journey to the seventh heaven. Needless to say, such expeditions could also provide opportunities for plunder rich enough to satisfy the greediest Arab.

Whether by accident or design, a more astute strategy would be hard to conceive. The weakest sector of the frontier between the Byzantine and Persian states was the Desert Bay, where each maintained loose suzerainties over Christianized Arab states. In addition, these Arabs of the Desert Bay had been an important source of mercenaries for both empires. During the first decade the total number of warriors in the field at any one time does not appear to have exceeded 100,000. At the highest estimate this figure would amount to no more than 10 percent of the able-bodied Arabs of military age, leaving 90 percent to attend to affairs at home. By any yardstick this does not amount to exceptional mobilization or an Arab military inundation. On the other hand, it does represent the largest Arab force ever assembled under one command, and credit for this achievement must be given to Islam. Whether for religious or strategic reasons, the selection of Syria-Palestine with its narrow width and long desert frontier on the east and the south as the first external objective was the ideal choice for Arab tactics and the small forces initially employed. For the same reasons Mesopotamia and Egypt, with Alexandria and the Sassanid capital not too far from the desert frontiers, were the logical secondary targets, once Syria had been won and the victories there had brought more Arab recruits to the banners of Islam. Some credit, but not too much, must be given to the spiritual inspiration to valor of the Islamic promise of salvation for warriors who gave their lives on "the path of God."

Just as important among external factors was the exhaustion of the Byzantine and Sassanid states, which had been locked in sporadic, but bitter, warfare for centuries, and the comparatively poor morale of the mercenaries on which they mainly relied. Even though they could field larger armies, these forces were not as large as in the past and with the defection of Arab mercenaries were unable to cope with desert-based tactics. Essentially on the defensive, they had to distribute their forces in garrisons, while the Arabs from their secure desert refuge were free to concentrate their attacks wherever and whenever they willed.

Furthermore, the regions under initial assault were populated by peoples bitter with discontent who welcomed the Arabs as liberators. This discontent was both economic and religious. They were tired of the heavy taxes and exploitation imposed to support the imperial wars of alien rulers. Monophysite Christians in Syria and Egypt felt oppressed by the hostile domination of the official Byzantine church, and the Nestorian Christians, though better treated, recognized a closer affinity in Islam than in Persian Zoroastrianism. Finally, the predominantly Semitic population of the Fertile Crescent and the related Hamitic population of Egypt perhaps saw in Arab liberation an opportunity for the restoration of glory to the ancient Middle Eastern centers of civilization. The Arabs offered a triple option: Islam, protected tributary status without military obligation, or death. The second option was welcomed as a relief. Damascus, it will be recalled, fell through internal treason, Alexandria was evacuated by a superior force in the absence of native Egyptian support, and the Sassanid capital was abandoned in the hope of finding native support in the Iranian highlands.

Remembering the Qur'anic injunction against mingling or becoming friendly with Christians or Jews, the second caliph instructed the armies to live apart from the subject peoples and especially to stay away from the corruption and vice of the great cities. In any case, the nomads felt ill at ease and lost in the alien culture of a city. In Egypt, al-Fustat (the tent city) was destined to become part of Cairo. In Mesopotamia, the tent cities of Kufa and Basra became centers of Arab life and rule. Later, in Tunisia, a similar Arab base was established called Kairwan.

Meanwhile, the conquest of vast areas of settled civilization presented the Arabs with the problem of administration for which they were wholly unprepared and unequipped. At first, there was a measure of confusion, but soon intelligent governors of these territories, alien both in culture and religion, realized that the only logical solution was to maintain their predecessors' administrative apparatus and staff with whatever modifications Islam required. Actually, the governor was the head of two regimes. The first was the Arab occupation forces and converts governed by the *sunna* with the aid of Muslim jurists. The second was the vastly

larger community of non-Muslims who were ruled according to their own law by their own judges and officials. The governor's primary concern was the maintenance of order and the regular collection of the taxes on non-believers—not the promotion of conversions to Islam.

The problems of conquest were not limited to the conquered territories and peoples. The fruits of plunder and the remainder of tribute after meeting local expenses inundated the relatively simple headquarters of the Caliphate at Medina. The caliph not only had the responsibility of distributing this largesse but also the task of appointing officials and of developing a governmental hierarchy far more complex than anything the Arabs had previously known. His temporal function tended to outdistance his spiritual leadership and occupied much more of his attention. The vastly enhanced wealth and power wielded by the caliph made the post an even stronger center of jealousy, intrigue, and competition. As the simplicity and virtues of the Caliphate were corrupted by the influx of wealth from abroad, so, too, was the tribal way of life undermined by the shares of booty brought back by the warriors of the faith and by the pensions paid out to the families of those who had died for the cause.

Naturally, some were unhappy with their share and charges of favoritism arose. As the economic incentive to cooperation was eased, the tribes and their shaykhs chafed at the growing centralization of authority in the Caliphate that was necessarily consequent on the establishment of an empire. In other words, imperial success demanded institutional development contradictory to the loose tribal confederation with which the expansion of Islam had begun. Old tribal hostilities and techniques, which had been temporarily transcended, were rearoused. Umar was the first, but by no means the last, caliph to be eliminated by assassination. His two immediate successors, Uthman and Ali, and many more to follow met the same fate. To a substantial degree it is true to say that Islam's greatest failure was its inability to overcome the Arab penchant for tribal jealousy and personal politics—a problem that still plagues the Arab world today. Arab annals are filled with coup d'états. By Muslim law a caliph could not legally be removed, unless proven unsound in mind and body.

The result, then, of the internal adjustments required by imperial success was the cessation of imperial expansion, while Arab energy was diverted to civil strife within the brotherhood of Islam. Caliph Umar had appointed a six-man committee to select a successor from themselves. They could not agree on one nominee and presented both Uthman and Ali to the congregation in the Medina mosque. Uthman had the advantage of age as well as being the candidate of the Umayyad clan. In addition, the influential favorite wife of the Prophet, Ayesha, daughter of Abu Bekr, was bitterly hostile to Ali.

As caliph, Uthman took full advantage of his wealth and authority, living a life of luxury and appointing his relatives to important posts throughout the empire. The major achievements of his rule were the completion of the official version of the Qur'an, the conquest of Cyprus (649), and the destruction of the Byzantine fleet (655). The last two accomplishments were the work of his able kinsman, Mu'awiyah, as governor of Syria. Appreciating the importance of seapower, he built Islam's fleet in the captured Byzantine naval arsenals of Alexandria and Acre and gained his naval victories by lashing his ships alongside the Byzantine ones so that Muslim warriors could convert the conflict into the type of land battle at which they excelled. Thus he was Islam's first great admiral, a word of Arabic origin.

Uthman's rule was filled with intrigues, plots, and counterplots with the tribes picking and shifting sides. Rebellions among the garrisons in Egypt and Mesopotamia led finally to his assassination by a band led by a son of Abu Bekr. Yet Mu'awiyah challenged the new caliph, Ali, to produce the assassins or share the guilt as an accomplice. The fact that a son of Abu Bekr had led the assassins of Uthman while a daughter of Abu Bekr hated Ali with an undying passion illustrates how involved Arab intrigue can become. Small wonder that Western observers are unable to unravel contemporary Arab intrigue!

After several years of confrontation and arbitration Mu'awiyah's path to the Caliphate was cleared when one of Ali's own men assassinated the caliph in 661. Without seeking nomination or confirmation at Medina, Mu'awiyah broke with precedent by simply declaring himself as caliph. Again, by simple fiat he transferred the capital of Islam to his headquarters and center of strength at Damascus. Later, he established the hereditary principle and the Umayyad dynasty by declaring his son as his successor and by commanding Arab acceptance of his decree. The classical Caliphate of Medina, which had won an empire for Islam and then had been torn by internal strife over how to organize the victories, was replaced by a centralized monarchy drawing on non-Arab as well as Arab sources of strength.

THE UMAYYAD CALIPHATE (661-750)

The Umayyad era may best be described as a period of transition during which Islam gradually became "civilized," adapting to, mingling with, and absorbing the advanced cultures of its subjects. The focus of power shifted from the tribal society of Arabia to the ancient centers of civilization. The creative flowering of this cultural blend had to await the succeeding Abbasid era. Under the Umayyads, Islam was going to school. This era also saw a new wave of expansion in which disciplined armies, no longer dependent on tribal organization and composed largely of non-Arab converts, carried Islam to its greatest extent as a unified state. Mu'awiyah as caliph (661–680) was the organizer of this new state.

As a martyr, Ali proved more influential in death than in life. Tradition elaborated his life into an epitome of Arab chivalry and Islamic virtue and wisdom. A collection of wise sayings and stories was attributed to him. His memory served as a rallying point for all opposition, and ultimately his martyrdom and that of his two sons provided the foundation for the aberrant Shiite sects of Islam which made an important contribution to the overthrow of the Umayyad Caliphate.

The central doctrine of Shi'a is the belief that the Prophet conferred the mantle of authority on Ali and his sons and descendants by Muhammed's daughter Fatima. As Imams, Ali and his descendants were vested with infallibility in interpreting the Qur'an and, in political theory, exercised both spiritual and temporal authority in contrast to the caliph's limitation to temporal authority. Obviously all the caliphs, except Ali, were usurpers, and opposition to them carried a divine sanction. For this reason, most rebellious movements in Islamic history have appealed to Shiite support for legitimacy.

The tribal obligation to avenge Ali fell first on his eldest son, Hasan, who had strong support in the Mesopotamian garrisons and various parts of Arabia. But Hasan loved life and the harem and agreed to being bought off by the wily Mu'awiyah. About 8 years later he died, possibly poisoned. At Mu'awiyah's death in 680, Ali's second son, Husayn, was persuaded to claim the Caliphate. His death and internment at Kerbela where he had been leading a motley host inspired by belief in his divine protection furnished a second shrine for Shiite pilgrimages. On the anniversary of Husayn's martyrdom Shiite pilgrims lacerate themselves, sometimes to the point of death, as penance for the failure of their ancestors to come forth and defend him. Yet, paradoxically, Shi'a authorizes dissimulation of one's faith for self-protection.

Three major subdivisions of Shi'a exist today. The descendants of the younger son of Husayn subsequently established themselves as Imams of Yemen with religious views not far from the Sunnite positions. The Isma'ili sect or "Seveners" traced the imamate from Ali and his two sons through seven generations and believe that the savior or *mahdi* (divinely guided one) is present but hidden from human view. The present leader of this sect is the fourth Aga Khan and forty-ninth in descent from Fatima. The most influential sect is the Imami or "Twelvers" which passed over one childless eldest son because of his bibulous habits. Most Iranians and nearly half the people of Iraq belong to this sect. Both the Isma'ili and Imami sects believe that their last imam will someday reappear as the mahdi to win the allegiance of all mankind and prepare the world for the final day of judgment. That this messianic doctrine should prevail in Iran, the home of Zoroastrianism, and among nearly half the people of neighboring Iraq, which contains the most sacred Shiite places of pilgrimage, should not be surprising. Meanwhile, for the Imami sect the ulema and ruler of Iran act in the mahdi's behalf, but with limited power. As a result, the Iranian religious leaders exercise a great deal of influence. Descendants of Husayn bear the honored title of Sayyid and descendants of Hasan are Hashemites with the title of Sharif. Hashemites, though mostly Sunnite in religion, provided the ruling families of the modern states of Iraq and Jordan.

As governor of Syria, Mu'awiyah had appreciated the advantages of the Byzantine system of government, as well as Byzantine naval and military organization. Already he had drawn on experienced Syrian Christian administrators to staff his government. Already his victorious fleet had been built in Byzantine arsenals according to Byzantine design and manned largely by Syrian and Egyptian crews. Already Syrian Christians and converts had been recruited for an army organized on the Byzantine model rather than the Arab tribal divisions.

As caliph, Mu'awiyah merely completed the reforms he had already undertaken as governor and sought to extend them to the rest of Islam. But he was no dogmatist and was always ready to adapt for the time being to the circumstances in any area as long as the long-term trend was in the direction of the centralization and consolidation of the authority of the Caliphate. The treasurership, a post second in importance only to command of the army, was entrusted to the Christian grandfather of St. John of Damascus. Since Arab illiteracy and inexperience compelled a reliance on former Byzantine civil servants, Greek remained the language of administration. Of necessity, the court physician, was a Christian. The fact that a Greek treatise on medicine was the first scientific work translated into Arabic indicates the Arab's special concern for health and life. Although preaching preparation for the day of judgment and fear of God, Islam as taught and practiced by the Prophet had been far from otherworldly in emphasis. The court poet, whose poems praising the caliph's achievements are still admired by Muslim students, also was a Christian. Even his favorite wife and mother of his successor was a Christianized Arab.

In short, the transfer of the Caliphate from Medina to Damascus symbolically represented the shift of emphasis initiated by Mu'awiyah from the desert to the settled centers as a source of inspiration and support. Nevertheless, he and his successors reflected their continued attachment and affection for the desert by building pleasure palaces on the desert fringe for rest and relief from the burdens of office. Despite the Prophet's injunction against depictions of life as an infringement on God's monopoly of creation, Syrian artists decorated these resorts with hunting scenes and portrayals of plump dancing girls. Truly this was an era of transition and transformation.

THE SECOND WAVE OF EXPANSION

Following up his victory at sea, Mu'awiyah concentrated his major military efforts against Islam's strongest foe, Byzantium. His reorganized and well-paid army was exercised by annual expeditions north of the Taurus Mountains, mainly in quest of plun-

der. In spite of the losses and hardships suffered by the people of Asia Minor, however, their non-Semitic heritage and their orthodox Christianity caused them to remain loyal to Byzantium. Unlike Syria-Palestine and Egypt, here the forces of Islam were not greeted as liberators. In a sense, the loss of Syria-Palestine and Egypt with their hostile populations had been a blessing in disguise for the Byzantine state, a shedding of liabilities comparable to those of Turkey as a result of World War I. Nevertheless, the city itself was twice threatened. During the winter of 668 to 669 Mu'awiyah's army camped at Chalcedon just across the straits and from 674 to 679 his navy has based in the Sea of Marmora. These and later attacks were thoughtfully timed to coincide with Slavic assaults on Byzantine territory. Only the invention of "Greek fire" which burned on water forced the withdrawal of the Muslim navy.

Although the Umayyads followed no clear-cut policy, they generally did not encourage conversions. After all, conversion meant a double loss for the state: the loss of the poll tax and the obligation to support the converts and their families as brothers. A later Umayyad caliph ineffectually sought to exclude non-Muslims from public office and placed special disabilities on them, but these measures only reflected the progress in "civilizing" Islam and Arabicizing the state. A growing supply of educated Muslims was available and was pressing for government appointments. The prohibition against translating the Qur'an was advancing the use of Arabic, and more and more Arabs were becoming literate in their own language. The need for converts to learn Arabic to understand the Qur'an inspired linguistic studies and standardization. A Persian composed the first standard text of Arabic grammar.

Although Mu'awiyah reserved his greatest military efforts for Byzantium, his desire to consolidate his control resulted in the resumption of the advance of Islam along the paths of lesser resistance to the east and the west, which was prosecuted vigorously by his abler successors beginning with Abul Malik (685–705). In the Maghrib (the Arab "Far West") the forces of Islam operating from the Tunisian base of Kairwan (founded in 670) gradually overcame the resistance of the equally warlike Berber tribesmen. Although the Arabs enjoyed no tactical advantage over these camel-using nomads, the task was eased by the affinity between the Arab and Berber way of life. Once subdued, the Berbers supplied a reservoir of able warriors for the further advance of Islam. A later commander, Musa ibn-Nusayr, who masterminded the conquests in the west, was a former Christian captured as a boy by Khalid while studying the Gospels in a Mesopotamian church. In 711 he sent his Berber lieutenant Tariq with a force of 7000 mostly Berber troops on a probing expedition across the narrow straits into Spain. The name of Gibraltar is derived from Jebal Tariq, meaning "mountain of Tariq." So little resistance was encountered from the weak and divided Visigothic kingdom that Musa soon followed with the main force. In 718 Muslim forces began to cross the Pyrenees and conquer southern France. Finally, on a frigid October day in 732, near Tours, the soldiers of Charles Martel dressed in wolf-skins checked the advance of Islam. During the night the Muslim army withdrew from the field. This skirmish has been magnified in Western annals into a decisive battle, a reputation it scarcely deserves. In exactly a century after the death of the Prophet the banner of Islam had been carried thousands of miles across North Africa, through Spain, to central France. Islam had reached the limits of profitable expansion in the west. The uncomfortably cold climate plus the poor prospects for plunder did not justify a further effort.

In the east, Muslim forces crossed the Oxus River and raided Bukhara in 674, meeting for the first time the Turkish people who were destined to play such an important part in the later history of Islam. Later, the caravan cities of Kashgar and Tashkent (presently in Russia) marked the limits of Arab expansion in central Asia. After 700, Afghanistan was reduced to tributary status, and other forces conquered Sind and the southern Punjab in India.

Unlike some barbarian conquerors, the Arabs were not destructive, but tolerant and, in fact, eager to learn from the superior cultures of their subjects. Undoubtedly the teachings of the Prophet which gave credit to his Christian and Hebrew predecessors contributed significantly to this attitude. In any case, the Arabs had interacted and traded with their civilized neighbors for millennia. The Umayyads wisely followed the Byzantine and Persian models of provincial administration with only minor modifications. Five viceroyalties were established with subordinate provinces under governors being set up as new territories were consolidated. Syria and Palestine formed one viceroyalty. An eastern viceroyalty, including Mesopotamia, Iran, eastern Arabia, central Asia, and the Indian territories, had its capital at Kufa. As the last two areas were consolidated, they received governors. The bulk of Arabia constituted the Hejaz viceroyalty. Egypt was a single viceroyalty. The fifth viceroyalty, ruled from Kairwan, was the Maghrib, although the emir of Spain was all but independent of the viceroy. An imperial system of post roads tied this far-flung empire to the capital. An associated function of the postal service, as in the past, was to supply intelligence to the caliph about activities in the provinces. In consolidated provinces the political, fiscal, and religio-juridical duties were normally separated and entrusted to different individuals by the caliph. Since Muslim law was derived from the Qur'an and the *hadith*, theologians were appointed as judges. They also had the duty of administering religious trusts (*waqf*) and the estates of orphans and the insane. After meeting all local expenses, the tax collector forwarded the remainder to Damascus.

The vast amounts of tribute and booty

delivered to Damascus more than sufficed to meet the needs of the Umayyads and encouraged extravagance and corruption of which the Prophet would scarcely have approved. As befitted such an imperial capital, Damascus was adorned with gorgeous mosques and public buildings, drawing eclectically on the diverse skills and arts of the subject peoples. Conquest yielded vast numbers of slaves, both male and female, to serve every Arab inclination. Female slaves, whose offspring by free men were free, made a great contribution to reducing the barrier between conqueror and conquered. Gradually ethnic distinctions diminished in importance, and an Arab was identified by the profession of Islam and Arabic speech, regardless of racial origin. The introduction of eunuchs also encouraged intermingling by allowing the fuller development of the harem as an institution. For an ordinary official to maintain a hundred or more slaves was not unusual, but how the caliph accommodated his one-fifth share of the 30,000 virgins reportedly taken from the Spanish nobility is beyond imagination. The last three Umayyad caliphs were sons of slaves, and this tradition was continued by their successors.

Slavery, however, should not be mistaken as the foundation of the Arab economy. For the most part, they were personal servants, and many were subsequently freed because the Qur'an described such a charitable act as especially pleasing to God. Furthermore, slavery involved no racial or personal stigma because the Qur'an made clear that such a condition was the result of God's will. In the annals of Islam many of the most brilliant contributions in politics, the sciences, and the arts were made by slaves and freedmen.

Besides women, which the Prophet had permitted, many of the Umayyad caliphs overindulged in wine, which had been forbidden, and in even less defensible vices. Such worldly and sacrilegious behavior was denounced by some brave theologians as leading straight to eternal damnation. Of greater importance, it furnished grounds for the justification of rebellion against the ungodly Caliphate. Many non-Arab converts were discontented with the disabilities they suffered and humiliated by their subordination as clients of Arab tribes. Furthermore, the domination of administration by Syrians was particularly galling to qualified Mesopotamians and Iranians and made the eastern viceroyalty a natural recruiting ground for rebels. Nor were the Arab tribes united behind the Umayyads. From the beginning, Mu'awiyah had gained his strongest support from the south Arabian tribes settled in Syria. The northern tribes had tended to settle in Mesopotamia and Iran creating a division into two opposed camps. Finally, the completion of Arab expansion left inadequate outlets for their martial energy and desire for plunder. All the ingredients for revolution were present. All that was needed was a dynamic leader who could fuse together the dissident Arabs, non-Arab converts, and Shiites into an effective force. A descendant of a paternal uncle of Muhammed, abu al-Abbas, provided this leadership and gave his name to the new dynasty.

The services of the Umayyad Caliphate in its prime, however, should not be forgotten. It established a strong, central government by utilizing the administrative skills and productive talents of its non-Muslim subjects. This effective regime enabled the Islamic state to resume its expansion, restoring political unity to an even larger Middle East than that of the equally tolerant Persian Empire overthrown by Alexander the Great. With unity, trade flourished as never before, and the general level of prosperity for most of the area reached a new peak. But most important, governmental policies facilitated the "civilizing" of Islam and the Arabicization of this vast area so that, in spite of subsequent political fragmentation, it continued to prosper as a single social, economic, and cultural entity bound together by a common language, a common law, and a common faith.

SIGNIFICANT DATES

c.	571–632	Muhammed, the Prophet of Allah
c.	610	The First Revelation
	622	Hijrah—year one of the Islamic Era
	630	Surrender of Mecca
	632–661	Classical Caliphate—the first wave of expansion
	661–750	Umayyad Caliphate at Damascus—the second wave of expansion
	732	Battle of Tours—the peak of Islamic conquest

SELECTED READINGS

*Andrae, Tor, *Mohammed: The Man and His Faith.* New York: Harper & Row, 1960.

*Arberry, A. J., trans., *The Koran Interpreted.* New York: Macmillan, 1964.

———, ed., *Religion in the Middle East.* 2 vols.; Cambridge: Cambridge University Press, 1969.

Arnold, Thomas W., and Guillaume, Alfred, eds., *The Legacy of Islam.* London: Oxford University Press, 1931.

*Brockelman, Carl, *History of the Islamic Peoples.* New York: G. P. Putnam's Sons, 1960.

*Cragg, Kenneth, *The Call of the Minaret.* London: Oxford University Press, 1964.

Fisher, Sidney N., *The Middle East.* New York: Knopf, 1959.

*Gibb, H. A. R., *Mohammedanism.* London: Oxford University Press, 1962.

*Guillaume, Alfred, *Islam.* Baltimore: Penguin Books, 1954.

*Hitti, Philip K., *The Arabs: A Short History.* Chicago: H. Regnery, 1962.

———, *History of the Arabs.* 10th ed.; New York: Macmillan, 1956.

———, *History of Syria.* New York: Macmillan, 1957.

*———, *Islam and the West.* Princeton: Van Nostrand, 1962.

———, *Lebanon in History.* London: Macmillan, 1957.

*———, *The Near East in History.* Princeton: Van Nostrand, 1961.

*Kirk, George E., *A Short History of the Middle East.* 7th rev. ed.; New York: Praeger, 1964.

*Lewis, Bernard, *The Arabs in History.* New York: Harper & Row, 1968.

*Pickthall, Mohammed Marmaduke, trans., *The Meaning of the Glorious Koran.* New York: Mentor Book, 1953.

*Watt, W. Montgomery, *Muhammad: Prophet and Statesman.* London: Oxford University Press, 1961.

Yale, William, *The Near East.* Rev. ed.; Ann Arbor: University of Michigan Press, 1968.

CHAPTER ELEVEN

ISLAMIC CIVILIZATION: 750–1500

The Umayyads had established a secular autocracy ruling over a mixture of cultures in which the Arabs and Islam were merely the dominant elements. Islam, the state, was their primary concern. Only one caliph had made a serious effort to promote Islam, the religion, and this effort had been short-lived. Therefore, abu-al-Abbas, as a revolutionary, was able to rally support by the pledge to advance Islam, the religion, through the establishment of a theocracy for the welfare of all Muslims, not just Arabs. Since Islam had gained more converts in Mesopotamia and Iran, this appeal could be combined with their resentment of political subordination to Syria.

In 747 the rebellion began in Khurasan (northeastern Iran) under the leadership of a Persian convert and Abbasid agent, abu-Muslim al-Khurasani. Soon the capital city, Merv, and most of Iran were in his hands. Backed up by this success, abu-al-Abbas led the rising in Mesopotamia, and in October 749 was proclaimed caliph in the Kufa mosque. The last Umayyad caliph could marshal only 12,000 Syrian troops who were decisively defeated in January 750.

Abbas, appropriately entitled al-Saffah (the bloodshedder), allowed his lieutenants to pursue and ruthlessly liquidate the Umayyad family and officials. The fleeing caliph was discovered and decapitated in Egypt. Eighty members of the caliphal family were invited to a banquet and treacherously attacked while eating. The hosts then covered the bodies and finished their dinner amid the groans of the dying. Even the tombs of the caliphs were desecrated. Only one important Umayyad, Abd-al-Rahman, succeeded in escaping the net of Abbasid agents and, after five years of adventures, reached Spain and established the Umayyad dynasty of Cordoba (756–1031) which, by the introduction

of eastern irrigation techniques, gave Spain greater prosperity than it had enjoyed before or since. At the very outset, the Abbasid Caliphate, though not Islam, thus suffered an important loss in the Far West.

THE ABBASID CALIPHATE IN ITS PRIME

In obedience to his revolutionary pledge to champion Islam, the religion, Abbas as caliph (750–754) called on the theologians and jurists to evolve a system of administrative law and justice known as the *shari'a* to be enforced throughout the state. Muslims, most of whom were not drawn from the Arab aristocracy, were appointed to administrative posts. The ideal, never perfectly achieved, was the establishment of a universal theocracy with a single religion and culture. At best, this goal could be achieved in the cities tied together by trade. The rural population from which this urban civilization drew its sustenance, although superficially accepting Islam, was bound to cling to its locally varying cultures and languages. Even the eclectic Islamic civilization that developed in the cities always demonstrated regional variations. The only universal bond was Arabic as the language of administration, trade, and intellectual endeavor. Therefore, the civilization common to all Islam, regardless of political or religious divisions, was for the most part based on Arabic as a written language and limited to the literate minority.

Caliph Abbas and his brother and successor, al-Mansur (754–775), fully realized that Islamic law and piety alone would be an inadequate support for their dynasty. A feature of the Abbasid regime was the constant attendance on the caliph of the executioner who acted instantly at his command. Al-

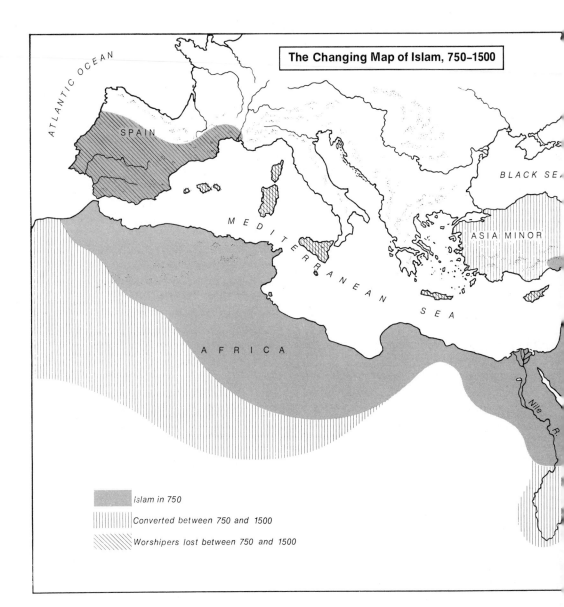

The Changing Map of Islam, 750–1500

ATLANTIC OCEAN

SPAIN

BLACK SEA

MEDITERRANEAN SEA

ASIA MINOR

AFRICA

Nile R.

Islam in 750

Converted between 750 and 1500

Worshipers lost between 750 and 1500

Mansur soon found it necessary to dispose of revolutionary associates who were discontented with their rewards or the failure to gain their religious objectives. On a visit to the court abu-Muslim was executed to gain control of Khurasan. In addition, the two Shiite leaders, both grandsons of Hasan, were eliminated as religious rebels.

Furthermore, although Islamic cultural development under the Abbasids was built on the integration already pioneered under the Umayyads and drew on all the cultural

heritages within the realm, a shift in emphasis from west to east, from Syria to Mesopotamia, from the Byzantine to the Persian model, was apparent from the outset. The founder of the Abbasid Caliphate died in his early thirties after a brief reign, but his brother, al-Mansur, confirmed this tendency that was already indicated by the source of revolutionary strength. On the bank of the Tigris he constructed the permanent capital, Baghdad, not far from the former Sassanid capital which served as a source of building

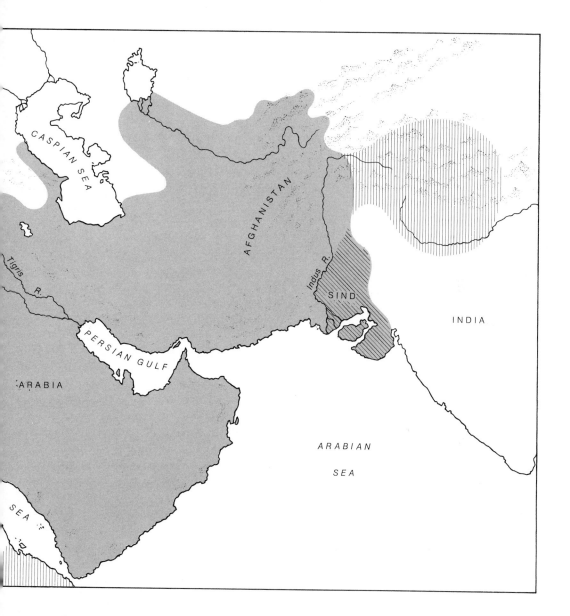

materials. By this step, as much as any other, the predominant commitment to the Iranian heritage was made. This act was reinforced by the utilization of Iranian officials, Iranian titles, Iranian concubines, Iranian dress, and, indeed, every refinement of Iranian life from wine and women to art and architecture. With one major exception, all important military effort was expended in the east. Western Islam could not help feeling neglected, and this sense of neglect fostered movements for political separation. Why should rev-

enues from the Maghrib support the opulent court in distant Baghdad without any compensating service? Governors sent from Baghdad were tempted in time to drop the caliph's name from the Friday prayer in the mosque. This was the equivalent of a declaration of independence.

An important Iranian administrative adoption was the vizir, a single minister responsible for the entire administration and subordinate only to the caliph. Al Mansur appointed the Shiite son of a Buddhist priest,

Khalid ibn-Barmak, as the first vizir, and the vizirate became hereditary in his family. The all-powerful Barmakids amassed unprecedented fortunes and gained renown for their patronage of individuals, religion, the arts, and public works. "Generous as a Barmakid" is a saying still heard today. Such a combination of wealth and popularity posed a threat to the Abbasids. In 803 the famous caliph Harun al-Rashid ordered the execution of the Barmakid vizir whose head was impaled on the main bridge and the two halves of his body on two other bridges in Baghdad. The rest of the family was rounded up and their fortunes confiscated, perhaps to defray some of the costs of the caliph's luxurious court. The Barmakids were destroyed, but the vizirate in other hands continued as the first office in the realm.

Like its Umayyad predecessor, the Abbasid Caliphate reached its zenith in less than a century but, instead of being overthrown, it endured through long centuries of decline when it was reduced to little more than an institutionalized figurehead. The vigorous second caliph not only built the fabled Baghdad, which in less than a century harbored a population of one million as "the emporium of the East," but also destroyed Shiite opposition, extended the eastern frontiers, built roads and mosques to tie the realm together physically and ideologically, and expended large sums, rehabilitating and expanding the irrigation of Mesopotamia to provide material support for the capital.

Byzantium had taken advantage of the internal dissension to assume the offensive against Islam in 745. Indeed, the Byzantine attack contributed to the success of the Abbasid rebellion. The first two caliphs were too occupied in consolidating their victory and retreated along the whole line of the frontier in Asia Minor. Finally, the third caliph gave the command to his son, Harun, who demonstrated his military talents by ravaging Asia Minor and bringing his army before the walls of Byzantium in 782. Byzantium regained its Asian territories only by agreeing to a treaty that stipulated semiannual payments of tribute. During Harun's reign as caliph (786–809) another Byzantine ruler made the mistake of repudiating this arrangement. Again, Byzantine territories were overrun and in 806 the emperor and his household were forced to pay a humiliating tax to obtain peace.

The fabled wealth and magnificence of Baghdad reached its pinnacle under Harun and his son, al-Mamun (813–833), reflecting the importance of the city as the center of imperial power and trade. This eastern-oriented civilization drew on all the cultural streams attracted to its crossroads capital, but especially on Iran which had been throughout its history an important crossroads in its own right. Iran was by its very location subject to, and a source of influence on, its neighbors to the north, the east, and the west. Sumerians had found timber and minerals in its highlands and obtained lapis lazuli by trade with Afghanistan. The founders of the Indus civilization probably had come from the Iranian area. The Indo-Aryans had passed through Iran from the north en route to India, and their Persian cultural cousins had created the largest and most durable Middle Eastern empire before Islam. Persian expansion had stimulated the emerging Indian civilization, and, in turn, India had made important material and cultural contributions to Iran, Islam, and the West. The most important overland trade routes from the Far East and India traversed Iran, exercising significant influence on Iranian cultural development. Western commentators, concentrating on Islamic contributions to the West, have tended to single out and stress the scientific and philosophical accomplishments, especially those of Greco-Byzantine origin. They have generally neglected to explain the selective nature of these borrowings from the Greco-Byzantine heritage and their function as secondary ornaments of the diadem of Islam and Islamic civilization.

Islam was, and is, essentially a religiously oriented civilization, especially concerned with man's welfare on earth in preparation for his life to come. When it emerged out of the desert, Islam carried not only a spiritual message but also a set of regulations for man, society, and the state formulated in terms of a tribal society. Obviously these rules for the regulation of human relationships were inadequate and sometimes inappropriate for the more sophisticated settled societies conquered by Arab forces. The Umayyad Caliphate had sought to put off the problem by minimizing integration and by administering each community according to its traditional system, but the settlement of Arabs in these lands led to gradual integration and raised immediate problems for the Islamic community that had to be dealt with.

Since the teachings of the Prophet had provided no basis or precedent for legislation, Islamic theologians as judges drew on the sayings (*hadith*) ascribed to the Prophet and his companions to supplement Qur'anic prescriptions. In verifying *hadith*, Muslim theologians evolved an interesting historiographical technique. They carefully checked the chain of transmission and evaluated the reliability of the transmitters, but generally ignored the content of the *hadith* itself. In other words, they rigorously tested the source, but not the substance, of *hadith*. By the end of the Umayyad era, however, the technique of supplementing the Qur'an with *hadith* had been exhausted and new solutions were desperately needed.

THE SHARI'A

This situation brought about the formulation of four schools of jurisprudence, none of which notably indicates any borrowing from Roman law. All four schools, of course, accepted the Qur'an as the fundamental source of law and the *hadith* as a secondary source, although they differed in their evaluation of the latter. Where they differed most, however, was in the extent to which they accepted or rejected three additional devices: personal opinion, reasoning by analogy, and consensus of opinion.

Personal opinion, which could not violate the spirit of Qur'anic law, was utilized in cases for which no Qur'anic basis could be found. Although the validity of this device was widely questioned, its supporters cited the fact that the Prophet had allowed its use as a last resort. As such, personal opinion became a source of new law. Reasoning by analogy with the Qur'an or *sunna* became another source of new law. Consensus of opinion of the jurists or of the whole Islamic community, however, proved to be the most liberal device for adaptation to changed circumstances, though theoretically it was also limited by the Qur'an and the *sunna*. This source of new law was based on the saying of the Prophet: "My community shall not agree on an error." It followed that whatever the jurists agreed on or the community at large accepted must be true and, indeed, divinely ordained. Consensus of opinion canonized the texts of the Qur'an and the *hadith* and later confirmed the non-Arab Ottoman rulers as caliphs, among many other uses.

The oldest juridical school was established by the grandson of a Persian slave, abu-Hanifa (d 767). He and his disciples used both personal opinion and reason in developing analogies with the Qur'an and *sunna*, creating new law on the basis of what Western lawyers would call legal fictions. When *hadith* conflicted with each other, he utilized personal opinion to determine which was preferable, but his followers tended to abandon personal opinion for analogy. Today Sunnite Muslims in Turkey, central Asia, and India acknowledge the Hanifite form of the *shari'a*.

The second school, founded in Medina by Malik ibn-Anas (715–795), was naturally more conservative. Both personal opinion and analogical deduction were rejected as valid sources of new law. Since this school sought its answers in the *hadith*, it was confronted with the problem of evaluating this vast body of sayings. To do this, Malik developed the idea of relying on a consensus of jurists' opinions. Whichever *hadith* were acceptable to the majority of jurists were acknowledged as legally valid. The Malikite school still prevails in the Maghrib.

A pupil of Malik, al-Shafii (767–820), sought to find a middle ground between his master's doctrine and that of the Hanifite school. He drew on both and was critical of both. Consensus alone, he argued, could not make a questionable *hadith* legally binding. Unless they could be supported by rational analogy, such *hadith* could be utilized by jurists only as an advisory aid in arriving at a judgment, not as absolute law. As employed by him, both analogy and consensus were restricted in their application. Consensus had to have almost universal acceptance by jurists to be a valid source of law. One result was that his school reduced the number of legally binding *hadith*. On the other hand, it introduced greater flexibility in arriving at judgments by using questionable *hadith* as an advisory aid in arriving at judgments. Furthermore, he acknowledged the validity of the consensus of opinion of the entire community. In practice, the consensus of the community, as in the election of a caliph, meant no more than its passive acceptance. His school is now the dominant one among Sunnites in Palestine, lower Egypt, east Africa, southern Arabia, and Southeast Asia.

Al-Shafii's pupil, Ahmad ibn-Hanbal (d 855), was the founder of the fourth and most conservative school of jurisprudence. Taking his cue from the critical attitude of his master, he was even more critical, drawing up a famous list of only 28,000 acceptable *hadith* on which he commented. He rejected interpretation both by rational analogy and by consensus because they were subject to abuse and insisted on absolute and literal conformity to the law of the Qur'an and his selected list of "unquestionable" *hadith*. The rigor of his position was undoubtedly a reaction to the Mutazilite theological rationalism which was flourishing at the court under the patronage of Caliph al-Mamun. His uncompromising doctrine led to persecution and imprisonment. Today his tomb is a place of pilgrimage, but the Hanbalite school is followed only by the orthodox Wahhabi of Arabia.

These four schools of jurisprudence, which together compose the *shari'a*, had by the tenth century developed sufficiently to meet the needs of the communities they served, and the jurists by consensus agreed that the era of interpretation by personal opinion and reasoning had come to an end. Since then, no basic alteration of the *shari'a* has taken place.

One way in which the greatly changed conditions of modern times might be met would be to reopen the *shari'a* to juridical interpretation. In this way the problems of today and tomorrow might be dealt with without overthrowing Islamic law. Thus far, however, the forces of conservatism have been too strong to permit such a logical development, and the secular governments of Muslim states have been compelled to supplant the *shari'a* in whole or in part. Such traumatic steps naturally militate against a smooth transition and contribute to internal dissension and political instability.

The *shari'a* lays down the laws governing the entire life and conduct of a Muslim. The categories covered can perhaps be best illustrated by listing the chapter headings of an Islamic lawbook. The first chapter concerns the relationship of man to God and prescribes devotional duties, not rights. The second chapter is entitled "family law" and concerns the relationship of the individual and the family, legislating in great detail on the subjects of marriage, divorce, and inheritance. The third chapter covers the relationships between man and man and contains laws concerning property and contracts. The fourth chapter is entitled "penal law" and covers the relationship of the individual and the state. The fifth chapter prescribes the rules for the organization and procedure of the courts, and the sixth chapter deals with foreign relations, especially holy war.

From another point of view the jurists recognized five degrees to inspire ethical conduct in human actions: absolute duties supported by rewards and punishments;

meritorious acts carrying rewards but no punishment if not done; permissible acts which the law neither prescribed nor proscribed; censurable acts involving blame but not punishment; and condemned acts entailing penalties. Thus, Islamic law, rooted in religion, has a far broader conception of its functions than any secular code of law which merely places statutory limits on human actions beyond which positive penalties are imposed. Islamic law is concerned with every aspect of human behavior: good, bad, and indifferent. It, therefore, has an ethical foundation rather than merely a statutory basis, and it is hard to change because it is so thoroughly intertwined with the whole Muslim way of life. Conversely, it is a stiff barrier to bringing about change in other aspects of the Muslim life-style.

THEOLOGICAL DEVELOPMENT

Since both Islamic law and Islamic theology drew on the same sources, the Qur'an and the Prophet's *sunna*, the two were inextricably entwined. Indeed, the judges were theologians who specialized in the law. While the jurists tended to limit their primary attention to the law, the theologians took the whole subject of Islam as their domain. Like the jurists, the theologian received challenging queries in the conquered lands but, unlike the jurists, they proved less willing in the long run to allow adaptations, with the result that greater sectarianism was encouraged. The greatest challenges came not from Judaism and Christianity, which had been already condemned as erring distortions of God's message, but from Greek philosophy.

Abbasid wealth and intellectual curiosity subsidized the translation of Aristotelian, Neoplatonic, and Neopythagorean treatises. This work was performed by Nestorian Christians residing near Baghdad of whom the outstanding figure was Hunayn ibn-Ishaq (809–873), a court physician who was interested in both Greek medicine and Greek philosophy. Caliph al-Mamun, who eagerly sought support for his rationalist Mutazilite views in Greek philosophy, put him in charge of the "House of Knowledge" founded in 830. Hunayn would first make a translation from the Greek into his native Syriac and then have his son do the translation from Syriac into Arabic. In addition to the medical works of Hippocrates and Galen, translations of Plato's *Republic* and Aristotle's *Categories* and *Physics* were completed under his supervision. This era of translations which gained momentum with the accession of the Abbasids in 750 was for the most part completed by the time of Hunayn's death.

The rise, zenith, and decline of the Mutazilite (schismatic) doctrine also fell within these years. Armed with Greek logic, its advocates challenged, in favor of free will, the predestinarian doctrine that followed from the conception of God as the sole creator and destroyer of all things. The Qur'an had explicitly stated that God not only created heaven and earth and everything therein, but also decreed the birth and death and the material condition, whether free or slave, rich or poor, of every individual. This doctrine explains why Muslims preface every statement about future action with the phrase, "God willing." This formula acknowledges the belief that their destiny and life itself are in the hands of God. The Mutazilites also attacked the doctrine that the Qur'an is the eternal and uncreated word of God as logically inconsistent with the unity of God. Caliph-al-Mamun, who was the greatest patron of the translation of Greek works and an ardent supporter of the Mutazilites, would not appoint a judge who believed in the uncreated nature of the Qur'an.

Mutazilite doctrines, if they had prevailed, would have seriously undermined, if not destroyed, Islam because they denied its fundamental tenets. Fortunately, Islam gained an effective and convincing champion in al-Ashari (874–935) who was able to use their own tools of logic against them, learned during a 40-year membership in the Mutazilite community. By numerous citations from the Qur'an he demonstrated that God held individuals responsible for good and evil acts. In other words, while God was the sole creator and distributor of material things, the individual was spiritually and morally responsible for the way in which he utilized these blessings. Man was free to believe or not to believe and free to do good or evil deeds in full awareness of a final judgment. Each individual would be rewarded or punished according to his own deeds (Qur'an 2:128, 135). With reference to the uncreated nature of the Qur'an he argued that the Mutazilites erred by trying to understand God in human terms. God and his attributes are eternal and not anthropomorphically limited by time and space or life and death. Al-Ashari had successfully defended Islamic orthodoxy against Mutazilite criticisms.

Islam's greatest and most sensitive theologian, however, was al-Ghazzali (1058–1111) whose intellectual and spiritual struggles are reminiscent of those of the Christian theologian St. Augustine. His intellectual curiosity was boundless, as he investigated every position he came across from atheism to intense religiosity.

He started his career as a professor of Sunnite theology according to the Asharite doctrine at the recently established Nizamiya college at Baghdad, but his inquiring mind soon became filled with doubts. He turned to Sufism in search of direct knowledge of God. Again, the eternal truth he sought eluded him, and he turned for a time to skepticism. His tortured soul could still find no satisfaction, and broken in body and spirit, he abandoned worldly things and wandered for 12 years over the lands of Islam in quest of peace of mind. Finally, he became convinced of the inadequacy of the human mind to know God because it is entrapped by life and limited to human experience.

God can be approached only through faith and not intellect. Intellect should be used to demonstrate its own weakness and inadequacy. Once intellectual self-conceit has been destroyed, then one can turn with pure faith to God. Al-Ghazzali incorporated these views in a highly intellectual work on

"the revivification of the sciences of religion" which is still revered as the outstanding exposition of Sunnite theology. He argued that the purpose of education is not merely to impart knowledge but more importantly to awaken the moral consciousness of the student so that he can appreciate the limitations of human knowledge and can be led to a higher ethical quest. He employed Greek logic to reduce the role of philosophy to no more than a subordinate support for religion. At the same time, his account of his own experiences and their usefulness to him gave respectability to mysticism in the eyes of orthodox theology.

SUFISM

In every higher religion mere compliance with the devotional requirements has proven unsatisfactory to a substantial number of sensitive souls. By asceticism and mysticism these individuals seek a personal, spiritual communion with God. In Islam the followers of this path are called Sufis, after *suf* (wool) which denotes their emulation of the garb of Christian monks. However, Buddhism as well as Christianity and other local pre-Islamic practices contributed diverse elements to the various forms of Sufi development. For many centuries Sufism was represented only by individual examples of extreme spirituality. Not until the twelfth century did fraternal orders with prescribed techniques and monastic-type centers develop to regularize and perpetuate this practice on an organized basis. Therefore, rather than being a separate sect, Sufism represented a supplement to prescribed ritual, enabling its devotees through emotional mysticism and love to attain a sense of personal relationship with God. Sufis may be found among the adherents of both the Sunnite and Shiite sects.

The Sufi orders each have their unique characteristics, and new ones were formed as late as the nineteenth century. Various mystifying feats are performed by some orders to demonstrate their subordination of the flesh, to induce a transcendent condition, and to raise funds. Everyone has heard of the whirling dervishes. The number and peculiarities of Sufi orders are too numerous to be catalogued, but some of their contributions deserve mention.

First, they furnished a legitimate outlet for pent-up religiosity in a systematic fashion. Many local orders allowed lay participation in rituals which incorporated ancient local practices that bridged the gap between them and Islam. Their founders were venerated as saints who provided intermediaries between man and God. The introduction of saints, as well as some rituals, helped to minimize the distinction between Islam and Christianity for former Christians. The tombs of saints as places of pilgrimage are conveniently dotted throughout Islamic lands. Only the puritanical Wahhabi of Arabia wholly reject the cult of Sufi saints. Sufi mysticism inspired much of Islam's finest poetry both in Arabic and Persian. Finally, Sufism influenced three of Islam's greatest philosophers, al-Farabi, ibn-Sina, and the incomparable al-Ghazzali.

THE SCIENCES

The vast translation work accomplished mainly between 750 and 870 was by no means limited to philosophy or to Greek works. Muslim scholarship selectively drew on those achievements of past cultures which were indicated by Islamic inclinations and deficiencies. Greek literature held no attraction for people with a highly developed poetic and romantic heritage of their own. On the other hand, the inclination to preserve their lives and make the most of them stimulated an intense interest in Greek medicine, especially since the Islamic emphasis on bodily resurrection prohibited anatomical investigation. The leading physicians were initially Christians who based their practice on Greek medicine. Caliph al-Mansur summoned to the court the Nestorian Christian dean of the Sassanid academy of medicine at Jundi-Shapur, ibn-Bakhtishu, and he and his

descendants for six generations were the leading physicians in Baghdad. His grandson, who served Harun, is credited with the psychological cure of a favorite slave who was afflicted with hysterical paralysis by pretending to disrobe her in public.

Although at first largely staffed by Nestorians, hospitals copied the Persian model and set up separate wards for patients afflicted with different diseases. Medical practice emphasized clinical observation, and al-Razi (865–925), a noted physician, distinguished measles from smallpox. Other significant discoveries were made by this empirical technique. Al-Razi is reported to have hung pieces of meat in various parts of Baghdad to determine by the rate of putrefaction the healthiest site for a new hospital. His comprehensive treatise was later translated and used as a medical text in the medieval West. The most comprehensive medical work, however, was the product of ibn-Sina (Avicenna, 980–1037), better known as a philosopher. Besides providing careful clinical descriptions of a number of diseases, it contained a list of 760 drugs with their uses. The emphasis on medical rather than surgical treatment stimulated the study of botany as well as mineralogy, and a later work covered 1400 items, including 200 previously unidentified plants.

The same quest for medical cures encouraged the development of alchemy, and many physicians, such as al-Razi, were also alchemists. Among other things, anxious caliphs subsidized searches for the elixir (*al-iksir*) that could prolong life. Jabir ibn-Hayyan (Geber, fl 776) utilized experimentation to lay the foundations of chemistry. He explained the two basic techniques of chemistry—calcination and reduction—and advanced the procedures of melting and crystallization. He and his successors distinguished a number of different chemicals. Commonly alchemy has been ridiculed for its fruitless pursuit of the means of transmuting base metal into gold, but in this age when nuclear physics has discovered the means of altering basic elements, per-this age when nuclear physics has discovered the means of altering basic elements, perhaps ridicule should be replaced by the recognition of a scientific quest that failed.

A complex of factors, reflecting both the religious and physical needs of the vast realm of Islam and its civilization, stimulated the pursuit of knowledge in astronomy and astrology, mathematics, and geography. All of these related sciences were drawn on to perform the religious requirement of determining the direction of Mecca for the correct orientation of mosques. In addition, the doctrine that God determined the life and death and welfare of each of his creations encouraged the development of the ancient pseudoscience of astrology, with the consequent advancement of the true sciences of astronomy and mathematics on which astrology was based. The demand of astrological theory for precise determinations of time and place promoted calendrical studies and the accurate determination of longitudes and latitudes. Also trade and communications over great distances, both by land and by sea, within and beyond the confines of Islam, provided an additional stimulus for these inquiries. Engineering requirements for urban development and for the full use of water resources by irrigation to gain the maximum agricultural support for this urban civilization supplied further inducements to scientific development. The fruits of trade and empire that poured into the caliphal coffers from all directions supported this quest, as well as the luxuries, vices, and other cultural refinements of the court at Baghdad.

The Muslims as heirs of the ages not only synthesized and transmitted the vital contributions of Greeks, Egyptians, and Mesopotamians but also creatively combined with these contributions a new, fertilizing stream from India whose significance has not yet been fully evaluated. Just when, why, and how Indian astronomical and mathematical development took place remains obscure. Some have argued for indigenous development and others for Hellenistic inspiration via trade, but what is

certain are the positive contributions to Islamic mathematical and astronomical advances in the form of the so-called "Arabic" numerals and invaluable astronomical tables, using the Indian city of Ujjain as a base. Islam's first outstanding mind in these fields, al-Khwarismi (d c 850), synthesized Greek and Indian mathematics and astronomy in a systematic presentation that used the Indian numerals in the solution of quadratic equations. He also established algebra which derives from the first words (al-Jabr) of the title of his book on reduction and cancellation. With other scholars he labored in Caliph al-Mamun's "House of Knowledge" and the observatory associated with it. The caliph, as an informed layman, was more interested in practical applications than in theory and assigned them engineering problems and the determination of the precise length of a terrestrial degree. The latter operation, of course, postulated the sphericity of the earth. Another innovation derived from India, which was successfully opposed by the orthodox, was the replacement of the Arab lunar calendar with a solar calendar.

The interest of Islamic rulers in mathematics and astronomy continued unabated under al-Mamun's successors and produced a number of figures who expanded the achievements in these fields. Especially notable is al-Biruni (973–1048) who measured latitudes and longitudes with greater precision and examined the theoretical problem of the earth's revolution on its axis. Like all the outstanding Islamic scholars, he sought universal knowledge and, among other accomplishments, made significant contributions to physics. The crowning figure in Islamic mathematics and astronomy, however, was Umar Khayyam (1044–1123) who enjoyed the patronage of Nizam al-Mulk, the Iranian vizir of the rude Seljuk Turks. This cultured vizir founded the famous Nizamiya college which for a long time attracted the best minds in Islam. In 1074 he summoned the best astronomers, including Umar Khayyam, to work on a more accurate calendar in a new observa-

which had an error of only one day in 5000 years compared with the error of one day in 3330 years in our Gregorian calendar.

Although Umar Khayyam is famous in the West as a romantic poet, extolling the hedonist pleasures of wine and women in true Iranian style, his reputation in Islam is soundly founded on his mathematical genius, and the poetry attributed to him is rated no better than average. That he should also have shone as a poet is only another example of the wide range of qualifications expected of outstanding men, which included proficiency in theology, logic, medicine, and astronomy, as well as poetry. His principal mathematical contribution was the solution of cubic equations in which he utilized intersecting conic sections. He systematically defined the forms of cubic equations and geometrically demonstrated the solution of each one.

Islamic achievements in the sciences, of which the preceding samples will serve as examples, developed first in the east under Abbasid auspices because here was located the chief source of patronage and the combined heritages, including the Indian, on which they were constructed. Most of this work to which Arabs were culturally less inclined was done by non-Arab Muslims, principally Iranians. Generally speaking, Arabs found theology, literature, and the social sciences a more congenial area for scholarship. As political fragmentation undermined the Abbasid Caliphate, scientists and scholars discovered new patrons at the courts of successors in the east, and in the west at the Fatimid court in Egypt, and especially at the brilliant and tolerant court of Cordoba in Spain. The cultural unity of Islam, in spite of its political divisions, is well illustrated by the freedom with which scholars traveled from court to court throughout the lands of Islam. Indeed, it may be said that the creation of a number of competing courts provided a positive stimulus to scholarship and science through alternative sources of patronage.

HISTORY AND GEOGRAPHY

As a teleological religion with a historical founder who had looked to the past for precedents, Islam, like Christianity, stimulated the study of history. At an early date, historical methods were evolved for the collection and evaluation of the sayings of the Prophet and his companions. Naturally, the life of the Prophet became a major subject of study, and the outstanding events and actions in the course of imperial expansion were celebrated in poetry and prose. Ambitious courtiers penned flattering accounts extolling the accomplishments and virtues of the caliphs. Finally, the records of administrators drawn from the subject peoples provided copious source material for later historians.

With the completion of imperial conquest and the conversion of the bulk of the conquered peoples the need was felt for comprehensive accounts of the achievements of Islam and for comprehensive descriptions of its diverse peoples and features. The first history of this complete type was compiled in 15 volumes by al-Tabari (838–923), who traveled extensively in search of material. His annalistic history was organized chronologically. The first topical study was composed in 30 volumes by an even greater traveler, al-Masudi (d 956), who journeyed as far as Ceylon and Zanzibar in quest of knowledge. His work was more than a history, containing extensive discourses on physical and cultural geography. Among other interesting observations, his keen eye uncovered the fact that what is now dry land had once been covered by the sea and vice versa. The greatest of Muslim geographers, Yaqut (1179–1229), who was born of Greek parents, compiled a geographical dictionary that incorporated historical and scientific as well as geographical knowledge.

Geographical information—and oftentimes fantasy—was brought back from lands far beyond the confines of Islam by adventurous Muslim merchants. The adventures attributed to Sinbad the Sailor were compiled and embellished from these reports. Most of this material on non-Muslim lands, however, was accurate and was incorporated into guides for future travelers and pilgrims by land and by sea.

LITERATURE AND THE ARTS

In literature and the arts, the Abbasids, as might be expected, were predominantly influenced by colorful Iranian precedents. Mosques and public buildings further developed the ovoid or elliptical dome, the spiral tower, and the brilliant glazed wall tiles and metalled roofs favored by the Sassanids. Observing the Qur'anic prohibition of representations of living things, the mosques were adorned with artistic renderings of Arabic script, known as "arabesque." No such restraint, however, limited the Iranian artisan in the decorations of palaces which included nude female figures as well as other scenes drawn from life. Miniatures, for which Iranian art later became famous, started their development in the illumination of secular manuscripts such as the animal fables of Indian origin. By the twelfth century, if not earlier, Chinese influences transmitted by trade and the Turks was apparent in ceramics as well as other art forms, although they always retained distinguishing Iranian characteristics.

The Prophet had frowned on music, wine, and unregulated lust, but the irrepressible Arab inclination toward these pleasures combined with the refined techniques for exploiting them that had been discovered among the conquered peoples—especially the Iranians—proved too strong a temptation, at least for the Arab aristocracy. The well publicized indulgences in this respect of the tolerant and secularly minded Umayyad dynasty was not surprising, but a higher standard of conduct was expected of the self-proclaimed protectors and champions of Islam, the Abbasids. With a few exceptions, however, the Abbasid caliphs not only matched, but far surpassed their pre-

decessors in the cultivation of these arts of living. After all, they had the Iranians as tutors and, perhaps, no other aristocracy has ever demonstrated a greater zest for the full enjoyment of life. The Arab poetic and musical talents were married to Iranian instruments and subsidized by caliphal wealth. Fantastic gratuities and the favor of becoming boon companions of the caliph attracted the very best musical talent to Baghdad. The great names were individual performers, but the demand for background and extravaganzas led to musical notation, musical theory, and musical directors. Many of the most prominent philosophers and physicians, such as al-Kindi, al-Farabi, ibn-Sina, and ibn-Rushd (Averroes), were also noted musical theorists, illustrating the high place gained by music in Islamic civilization. The descriptions in the *Arabian Nights* and the 21-volume *Book of Songs* further testify to the prominence and splendor of dramatic and musical presentations at the caliphal courts. The natural accompaniments of this light and lively music were wine and women, and both were provided in abundant variety.

The caliphs might piously uphold the prohibition of wine and instruct their police to ferret out offenders, but they and their wealthy subjects practiced no such abstention at their frequent banquets and revels. Observing the behavior of their betters, less favored commoners saw little reason for abstinence, and Jewish wine merchants and Christian monasteries provided private facilities for Muslim tipplers.

For the first century and a half of the Abbasid Caliphate women still moved fairly freely in society, and there was an abundance of slave women at court of all shades: black, white, and yellow. Indeed, only three of the Abbasid caliphs were sons of free women. Even as slaves, many were prominent and talented, exercising an important influence in affairs. The seclusion and degradation of women was a later development.

The plentiful and varied supply of the opposite sex, however, proved inadequate to sate the refined erotic tastes of the court.

From the Iranians the Arabs learned the art of dressing beardless youths in female costumes, and much amorous poetry was addressed to such handsome boys. But the jaded senses of the court craved fresh titillation, and some clever courtier devised the reverse, creating a corps of slender female pages dressed like boys. Whatever moral judgment may be made about the life of the court, it cannot be accused of a lack of imagination.

The point needs to be made that for the most part Islamic arts and sciences were for the very few—the aristocracy and the wealthy merchants. The vast bulk of the population was illiterate and impoverished by taxation levied to support the opulent pleasures of their betters. Only the art and architecture of the mosques were designed to be shared by both rich and poor. Only in the mosques did rich and poor meet and pray as spiritual equals. Of course, enlightened caliphs and landlords invested in improvements on their rural estates, but mainly for selfish reasons. Disease and death, poverty and illiteracy pinned the peasant to the earth but, as a Muslim, he knew it was the will of Allah and looked forward confidently to paradise—while the rich appeared to enjoy the promised pleasures in the fabled gardens they constructed on earth. Materially Islam favored the few; spiritually it catered to all.

EDUCATION

Education was inspired by and centered around religion. That the Prophet held literacy in high regard is testified to in the Qur'an and by sayings attributed to him. As a written document, the Qur'an contains the essence of the Islamic faith and way of life, and a knowledge of it is essential to every Muslim. For most Muslims, however, this knowledge was limited to memorization of substantial passages. The memorization of the whole Qur'an is an especially meritorious accomplishment still recognized and honored by public parades. Oral and written instruction was provided by theologians who at-tached themselves to particular mosques, but only at the well-endowed urban mosques did this evolve into systematic schooling. In any case, few of the children of the poor could afford the time necessary for a full course of instruction. Learned theologians who on their travels stopped over at mosques enlivened intellectual life by delivering lectures and telling stories to the audiences that flocked to hear them. Wealthy families employed tutors, sometimes non-Muslims or slaves, to give elementary instruction to their children.

Until the establishment of the Nizamiya in 1065 with accommodations and scholarships for students, higher education was obtained by entering the household and service of a noted scholar as an apprentice. For example, the education of ibn-Sina (Avicenna, 980-1037) began with the memorization of the Qur'an. Next, he studied mathematics in classes given by Mahmud, the geometrician. Then, he entered the household of an astronomer. In his spare time he studied theology and logic under several masters. Finally, he studied medicine and completed his education at the age of sixteen. Few students could be expected to have the ability, the dedication, the time, and the resources to complete such a program of study. The Nizamiya type of theological seminary was far better suited to most students, and the number of similar establishments modeled after it testifies to its popularity. A scholarly traveler from Spain in the late twelfth century listed thirty such colleges (*madrasas*) in Baghdad, twenty in Damascus, and six in Mosul.

In addition to supporting theological colleges, the great mosques, well-endowed with perpetual trusts, were the logical beneficiaries for collections of manuscripts that had been acquired by scholars and wealthy men. Accompanied by trust funds for their care, these collections developed into catalogued libraries with hundreds of thousands of volumes which covered a far wider intellectual spectrum than that normally included in the curriculum of the associated *madrasas*. These libraries enabled intellectually curious students to expand greatly their scholarly attainments by independent study. Ibn-Sina, mentioned above, educated himself in medicine by such self-study in a library.

Booksellers who copied and sold the latest and most up-to-date works were naturally vital to scholarship. That booksellers and their clerks should frequently become significant scholars and authors is not surprising. They had to be literate and the copying of manuscripts was bound to educate them. A most important stimulus to the production of books and the development of libraries was the knowledge of the manufacture of paper. This precious knowledge, ultimately transmitted to the West, was acquired from two Chinese prisoners captured at the battle in 751 that drove Chinese dominion out of central Asia. They first practiced their craft in Samarkand, and by the end of the century a paper mill was operating in Baghdad. Gradually this industry spread through Islam until by the mid-twelfth century it reached Spain.

Whatever the weaknesses and deficiencies of Islamic education, the tremendous significance of its achievements cannot be denied. At a time when the West was sunk in a morass of appalling ignorance, it not only preserved for transmission the accumulated heritages of its conquered peoples, but it also incorporated Indian accomplishments and creatively advanced and enriched the combined heritages that the West was destined to inherit. The debt owned to Islamic scholarship is amply illustrated by many terms of Arabic origin found in current usage in mathematics and astronomy, medicine and chemistry, and commerce and the arts, both fine and industrial.

POLITICAL DISSOLUTION

At the very time when the religion of Islam was gaining the conversion of the bulk of the conquered peoples; when the language of the Qur'an was achieving universal usage in administration, trade, and scholarship; when social distinctions based on nationality were being blurred by blending and were being replaced by a universal hierarchy of status, whether Muslim or non-Muslim, free or slave, rich or poor; when trade was growing in volume and scope and shifting from non-Muslim to Muslim hands; when intellectual creativity was scoring its greatest triumphs in the arts and sciences; during these very same centuries the political unity of Islam was undergoing progressive deterioration and disintegration. Why? How can this apparent paradox be explained?

Modern communist theory asserts that once its ideological objectives are universally achieved political power will no longer be needed and the state will wither away. In practice, the course of Islamic development would appear to provide a historical example of such a theory. Once this dynamic movement had exhausted its imperialistic momentum and a substantial degree of ideological universality had been attained in the religious, cultural, social, and economic realms, the prime purpose of political unity seemed to have been fulfilled and the need for political universality was no longer deemed essential. There was no driving desire for new conquests, and each unit, such as Spain, gradually gained confidence in its ability to manage its own affairs without recourse to the support of a central authority. Despite the Abbasid Caliphate's pretensions to theocratic authority, Islam had no religious hierarchy to support its claims. On the passing of the Prophet all that had been left on earth was a brotherhood of spiritual equals. At best, the institution of the Caliphate had been an earthly device to advance the common cause and secure the common ends of the faithful. With these ends achieved and no dangerous foes left, how could the continuance of a centralized autocracy be justified?

Is a substantial degree of ideological universality necessarily inconsistent with the continuance of political unity? The case of the repeated resurrections of Chinese political unity would appear to refute this postulate. Yet the course of the Chinese dynastic cycle in which political unification was regularly followed by progressive decentralization and the ultimate overthrow of central authority presents periodic examples of this process of political dissolution. Moreover, the static and secular Confucian ideology stands in contrast to the dynamic and mystical Islamic and communist ideologies which feel imbued with a mission to change the world. While Confucianism ostensibly sought guidance in the past, the latter have their eyes on a utopian future either in this world or the next. The latter, as political forces, appear well fitted to Machiavelli's assertion that political entities have only two alternatives—to expand or to decay. Whatever conclusion may be reached, this problem warrants serious consideration.

With the political, cultural, and economic shift of the center of Islam to the more prosperous east it was, perhaps, natural that the first secessions would occur in the west. During these centuries the significantly smaller volume of trade in the Mediterranean helps, in part, to explain the lesser concern of the Abbasids with the west, although Egypt and Syria continued to be important producing and trading centers. Of course, the Umayyad regime established in Spain in 756 refused to acknowledge Abbasid authority. Within a few years the first Shiite regime, which lasted nearly two centuries, gained control of Morocco. The governor sent to North Africa by Caliph Harun in 800 exercised virtual independence, and his successor expanded Islam by the conquest of Sicily in 902 and from there to Malta and Sardinia. These conquests were retained until the Normans arrived in the eleventh century. The governor sent to Egypt in 868 made his post hereditary and paid mere lip service to Baghdad.

After several short-lived dynasties the Shiite Fatimid dynasty, which first emerged in North Africa in 909, conquered Egypt in 969. Claiming descent from Fatima through Husayn and Isma'il, the Fatimid rulers asserted that they were the expected Imams with infallible authority to rectify Islam. Among their achievements was the construction of Cairo as their capital and the foundation of al-Azhar, the oldest and most respected university of Muslim scholarship in Islam today. At its height under al-Aziz (975–996), Fatimid authority was recognized from Syria and the Yemen in the east to the Atlantic in the west. Only the Sunnite court of Cordoba rejected his demand for submission.

The next imam-caliph, al-Hakim (996–1021), may have been insane. His uncontrollable temper brought death to one vizir after another and intense persecution of Christians and Jews. Finally, following extreme Isma'ilite belief, he proclaimed himself the incarnation of God, a step that may explain his persecution. This action left a permanent mark on history. The Druze sect in Lebanon was founded by his missionary Darazi. In 1171 the Fatimid dynasty was ended when the later nemesis of the Crusaders, Saladin, gained power and acknowledged Abbasid suzerainty in the Friday prayer. This measure did not bring his domain of Egypt and Syria under Abbasid control, but it did return Egypt to the Sunnite fold.

Meanwhile, in the east even more complex and significant developments were reducing the Abbasid caliphs to powerless puppets. The story is too involved for detailed treatment here. But, in essence, two dominant themes were emerging. First, the Iranian people, remembering their proud imperial heritage, were reasserting themselves, often drawing on Shiite doctrines for cohesion and inspiration. Second, warlike Turkish-speaking peoples were infiltrating the region from central Asia.

The first break followed the typical pattern already observed. In 820 a trusted general was appointed governor of the key frontier province of Khurasan. Before long he dropped the caliph's name from the Friday prayer and passed his power on to his heirs. Until 872 this dynasty ruled northeastern Islam.

Meanwhile, the next caliph, distressed

at this loss and at his dependence on an Iranian bodyguard of doubtful loyalty, took the fateful step of importing Turkish slaves and mercenaries to displace the Iranians. In due course, the cure proved worse than the disease. First, the increasing reliance on barbaric Turks antagonized the Iranians and united them in hostility to the Caliphate. The Samanid dynasty (c 904–999), which ruled the Iranian homeland from the Indian frontier to the gates of Baghdad, represented a restoration of the Iranian aristocracy. Second, as the Turkish mercenaries came to prevail at court, they used their military control to reduce the caliphs to puppets whom they replaced at will. In view of such impotence at the heart of Islam, the founder of Fatimid Egypt felt safe in declaring himself Imam-Caliph in 909, and the Umayyad emir of Spain followed suit by proclaiming himself caliph in 929. But worse was yet to come.

The next Iranian dynasty, the Buwayhid (945–1055), which was Shiite, gained the submission of the Abbasid Caliphate and the title of "commander of the commanders." Although the first Iranian dynasty reduced the Abbasid domain and the second utterly humiliated the Abbasids, their rulers were cultured Iranians who patronized scholarship and the arts and invested in economic improvements. The Samanids facilitated the education of ibn-Sina by granting the precocious teenager free access to the royal library and encouraged the revival of Iranian literature whose most famous fruit was the nationalistic epic poem by Firdawsi (940–1020), the Shah-Nama (Book of Kings). In 60,000 couplets Firdawsi, though a Muslim, glorified the Zoroastrian heritage and the great deeds of Iranian kings and heroes down to the Islamic conquest.

But the pressure of the Turks from the north was growing. Perhaps they were attracted by the accomplishments of their predecessors at Baghdad. In any case, they had accepted Sunnite Islam and were now eager to play a role in its politics, especially against the Shiites. Already they were seizing frontier regions from the weakening grip of the

Buwayhids. One Turkish leader, Mahmud of Ghazni (997–1030), had inherited from his father, a former slave and mercenary in the service of the Samanids, the control of Khurasan and Afghanistan. From his mountain stronghold in Afghanistan he launched devastating raids on infidel India and annexed the Punjab.

Of more enduring significance, however, were the Seljuk Turks who slowly, but steadily, extended their authority over central Asia and Iran. When their chieftain, Tughril Beg, brought his army before the walls of Baghdad in December 1055, the Abbasid Caliph welcomed him as a liberator and named him Sultan (he with authority). Under two able successors, Alp Arslan (1063–1072) and Malik Shah (1072–1092), Abbasid authority was reestablished over all of eastern Islam. In addition, Alp Arslan decisively defeated Byzantium at the battle of Manzikert (1071) opening Asia Minor to a continuing Turkish inundation that permanently changed its character. With them, these Turkish settlers, only recently rude nomads, carried their adopted Iranian culture which soon submerged Byzantine culture. Under Iranian preceptors the temporarily reunited eastern area of Islam flourished culturally and economically with Iranian influences in the ascendant. This was the era that saw the founding of the Nizamiya, where al-Ghazzali taught, and the achievements of Umar Khayyam. But this unity was not destined to last.

The tribal heritage of the Seljuks led them to distribute their lands as fiefs which contributed to rivalry and the creation of autonomous principalities. Only exceptionally strong rulers could hold together such a state, and none arose after Malik Shah. In Asia Minor the Seljuk Sultans of Rum maintained themselves until superseded in 1302 by the Ottoman Turks. In the thirteenth century another Turkish leader, the Shah of Khwarism, flying the banner of Shi'a, was about to take control of the remaining Seljuk states in the east and put an end to the Abbasid Caliphate when a new, unstoppable force poured forth from eastern Asia. This was more than 60,000 battle-hardened nomad warriors under the command of Chingiz Khan, "the scourge of God." Islam had already been assaulted in the west by the infidel Crusaders, but the Christian attack had been a mere summer shower compared with the storm that now burst on Islam. That Islam survived at all was due more to the strength of its religion than to the strength of its arms, another example of the durability of civilizations in the face of assaults by less sophisticated peoples.

THE MONGOLS

Although the Mongols may be viewed as just another wave of barbarian conquerors from the nomadic steppelands of inner Asia, the vast extent of the ephemeral empire created by Chingiz and his successors added a new dimension to the history of the East. Hitherto a hazardous and intermittent caravan trade had made possible a limited exchange of goods between China and the Middle East, but trade by sea, with all its dangers, was safer. Once the Mongol conquests had united under a single suzerainty the Chinese and Middle Eastern centers of civilization and the lands between, overland trade along well maintained and policed routes flourished as never before—or since. Even Western missionaries and merchants, like the Polos, could travel in complete safety through the domains of the tolerant and cosmopolitan Mongol khans, who did not hesitate to employ talent wherever they found it. Men and ideas were freely exchanged from one end of the Mongol Empire to the other. Islam as a religion gained a permanent foothold in China, and China inspired new artistic advances in the Middle East. The world view of mankind was greatly expanded—at least for a while. Perhaps it was unfortunate that this experiment in cosmopolitanism did not endure. In due course, however, the open-minded, uncivilized Mongol rulers fell captive to the civilizations of the lands that they had occupied and grew culturally apart.

The empire dissolved into its component parts, and localism reerected the old regional barriers.

The immediate impact of the Mongols, however, was not so promising. Like the ancient Assyrians, Chingiz and his generals employed the strategy of terror in the hope of discouraging resistance. Although the accounts are certainly exaggerated, the Middle East had probably never before suffered such destruction and bloodshed. Apparently Chingiz Khan was enraged by the confiscation of a Mongol caravan in violation of a trade agreement and determined to destroy the Shah of Khwarism and all he possessed. In 1219 he unleashed his forces. The caravan cities of Bukhara, Samarkand, Balkh, and Herat were plundered and burned and their inhabitants either slaughtered or enslaved. The Shah's power was completely broken, and he fled and died. His son retreated into India, and Chingiz sent a flying column in pursuit, which plundered the Punjab. Another Mongol horde devastated northern Iran, while a third force, destined to be known as the Golden Horde, went north of the Caspian Sea and defeated Russian and Bulgar armies. For the most part this initial Mongol attack had been a probing and plundering expedition. Before the conquests could be consolidated, a more immediate threat required the long march of Chingiz and his best troops back to Mongolia in 1223 to 1225. There he died in 1227 at the completion of a brilliant campaign. The subsequent campaigns of his heirs, which followed the same proven pattern, may be passed over until his grandson, Hulagu, established the Il-Khanate of Iran (1256–1349).

In the course of consolidating his authority, Hulagu destroyed the hitherto impregnable mountain fortress and headquarters of the Assassins in 1256. The Assassins, so called after the drug, hashish, were an extremist Isma'ilite group founded as a desperate reaction to the Sunnite Seljuk successes. The devotees, with the promise of immediate salvation, were ready to sacrifice their lives in the assassination of influential "heretics" at the master's command. Their fanatical courage may have been reinforced with drugs. In any case, for more than two and one-half centuries they had terrorized the Middle East.

After a month's siege, Baghdad fell on February 1, 1258. The caliph and his court were killed, and the city was turned over to the victorious troops for indiscriminate plunder and slaughter. The stench of rotting corpses was so strong that the city had to be temporarily evacuated. Thus was the Abbasid Caliphate ended after a reign of 500 years.

The only power that proved capable of checking the Mongol advance was the Mamluk dynasty (1250–1517) of slave and mercenary warriors which had only recently taken control of Egypt and Syria from the last of Saladin's successors. Like his predecessors, Saladin had used mercenaries and slaves to provide a professional bodyguard; the last of his successors overdid the practice and became dependent upon them. Military leaders had been granted estates in return for a specified contingent of trained warriors. These lords found it to their advantage to obtain and train slaves to fulfill their military obligation. In this way, fresh blood from all nationalities was continuously imported to rejuvenate the armed forces. The first Mamluk Sultan, for example, had been a slave in the royal bodyguard. In the Mamluk Sultanate the succession passed usually, not to a son, but to a mercenary or slave of proven ability. In 1260 and again in 1277 the Mamluk army repulsed Mongol attacks on Syria, and these actions kept Africa free of Mongol devastation. At the same time the Mamluks gradually eliminated the last Crusader footholds in the Levant.

Probably the Mongols found the hotter lowlands uncongenial. In any case, the Il-Khanate and its successors generally limited their attentions to the highlands of the Middle East, finally ending the vassal Seljuk Sultanate of Rum in Asia Minor in 1302. In Iran and central Asia they patronized the further expansion and development of Islamo-Iranian culture and beautified cities such as Tabriz, Shiraz, Herat, Merv, and Samarkand. To their discredit, they neglected the maintenance of the complex irrigation system of the Tigris-Euphrates valley which had made it the second richest region of the entire Middle East. Today the restoration of this area which is the heart of Iraq has not yet been completed.

Like their Turkish predecessors, the tribal background of the Mongols contributed to the deterioration of the central authority of the Il-Khans, but in the later fourteenth century another military genius, claiming descent from Chingiz Khan, created a temporary empire of vast extent that was ruled from his capital city of Samarkand. Timūr the Limper (Tamerlane, 1336–1405), usurped control of central Asia in 1369, gradually conquered Iran and Mesopotamia, marched to Moscow, and forced the submission of the Golden Horde, invaded northern India with an army of 90,000 and captured Delhi, the capital of the Sultanate, delivered an almost mortal blow to the rising power of the Ottoman Turks, and was ambitiously planning the conquest of China when he died. At Timūr's death most of his conquests, which had not been administratively consolidated by the restless military adventurer, were lost; but his successors were able to control most of Iran until the opening of the sixteenth century when the irrepressible Iranian spirit regained a native dynasty.

Under Mongol and Timurid auspices the rejuvenation of Iranian culture continued. The Mongol trade routes to China contributed further significant Chinese influence in the arts. In religion Iranian national feeling increasingly identified itself with the Shiite version of Islam and incorporated Iranian mystical tendencies in the formation of Sufi orders in the twelfth and thirteenth centuries. Sufism was also a convenient vehicle for accommodating Turkish and Mongol tribal cults following conversion to Islam.

The effect of Sufism as an expression of Iranian national feeling is especially reflected in the works of the great Iranian poets and writers who built on the tradition begun by Firdawsi. Nizami, who died early in the thirteenth century, holds the title of Iran's master of romantic poetry. Al-Rumi (d 1273) was the founder of the noted Sufi order that produced whirling dervishes and, therefore, his poems are filled with Sufi mysticism. Two outstanding figures, Saadi (c 1184–1291) and Hafiz (d 1389), were both born in and inspired by the lovely garden city of Shiraz in southwest Iran considered by Muslims as one of the four earthly paradises. The moralistic Saadi's masterpiece was the *Gulistan* (*Rose Garden*), which stood as a model for later Iranian prose. Although he was a theologian by profession, Hafiz stands out as Iran's greatest lyric poet philosophizing about nature and life in all its abundance and brevity. The single moment of exceptional beauty was captured in his poems as well as the refined Iranian pleasures that were associated with wine, women, and song. His love poems with their realistic, although restrained, sensualism were later interpreted as expressions of Sufi mysticism. Finally, Jami (1414–1492) must be mentioned as one who summed up the achievements of his predecessors, in all of which—poetry and prose, epic and lyric, romance and mysticism—he sought to excel.

In the fine arts this era was prolific in decorative achievements, incorporating Chinese motifs and techniques which eased the former rigidity in style and composition. Especially notable is the continued development of miniature painting technique in manuscript illuminations. With the ardor of the newly converted, the Mongol rulers expended vast efforts and sums on the construction of more magnificent mosques than those of their predecessors—many of which had been destroyed in the course of conquest. The problem of mounting a round dome on a square base had already been solved under the Turks through the use of a pointed arch, an improvement on the squinch. Now no architectural difficulty limited the production of monumental structures.

By the end of the fifteenth century several tendencies had become apparent in the political, religious, and cultural evolution of Islam, that are not altogether outmoded as yet. After nearly nine centuries of Islam the ancient political division of the Middle East with a shifting frontier in Mesopotamia was reemerging in an enduring form with the eastern part dominated by a reborn Iran and the western part ruled by the Ottoman Sultans from the old imperial capital of Byzantium. Perhaps the recurrence of this division is instinct with more than a temporal foundation. This separation of Islam into two parts was supplemented by a religious division: the east predominantly Shi'a and the west Sunni. The cultural difference, however, was one of tones and shades only. Iranian influence had too thoroughly permeated the whole of Islam to allow a sharper distinction.

A more significant sign in the long run was the dynamic development being generated in the Christian West, whose ultimate impact could scarcely have been foreseen by even the most perceptive Muslim in 1500. The Spanish peninsula had been totally regained for Christendom in 1492. Spanish vessels in search of a shortcut to China had discovered a whole new area for expansion, the Americas. But of more immediate importance to the economy of Islam, the Portuguese navigator, Vasco da Gama, had returned from India around the southern tip of Africa with a fantastically profitable cargo of Eastern products. By this step, Islam had been outflanked in its traditional role as a crossroads of commerce until the opening of the Suez Canal—and the full profit of this achievement was not to accrue to Islam until 1956. Again events have temporarily closed this canal which has contributed so much to restoring the crossroads character of the Middle East.

SIGNIFICANT DATES

750–1258	Abbasid Caliphate
750– 850	The peak of Abbasid power
756–1031	Umayyad (Sunnite) dynasty of Cordoba in Spain
786– 809	Harun al-Rashid
813– 833	Al-Mamun and Mutazilite rationalism
c. 750– 900	Evolution of the Shari'a (Islamic jurisprudence)
909–1171	Fatmid (Shiite) dynasty of North Africa and Egypt
1044–1123	Umar Khayyam, the mathematician
1055–1157	Sultanate of the Seljuk Turks
1058–1111	Al-Ghazzali, the theologian
1071	Battle of Manzikert: destruction of Byzantine grip on Asia Minor
1157–1219	Rise and fall of Shah of Khwarism (Shiite) in East
1171–1250	Saladin and Ayyubid (Sunnite) dynasty of Egypt
1219	Beginning of Mongol conquests
1256–1349	Mongol Il-Khanate founded by Hulagu
1258	Mongol Capture of Baghdad: end of Abbasid Caliphate
1250–1517	Manluk ("Slave") dynasty of Egypt-Syria: puppet Abbasids
1326–1512	Rise of the Ottoman Turks
1336–1405	Timūr the Limper (Tamurlane)
1369–1497	Timūrid dynasty ruled Eastern Islam
1501	Foundation of native Safawid (Shiite) dynasty in Iran.

SELECTED READINGS

See Chapter Ten for additional accounts.

*Arberry, A. J., *Sufism: An Account of the Mystic in Islam*. New York: Hillary House, 1956.

Bishai, Wilson B., *Islamic History of the Middle East*. Boston: Allyn & Bacon, 1968.

Glubb, Sir John Bagot, *The Great Arab Conquests*. Englewood Cliffs, N.J.: Prentice-Hall, 1963.

*Grunebaum, Gustave E. von, *Medieval Islam: A Study in Cultural Orientation*. Chicago: University of Chicago Press, 1953.

*————, ed., *Unity and Variety in Muslim Civilization*. Chicago: University of Chicago Press, 1955.

Khadduri, Majid, *War and Peace in the Law of Islam*. Baltimore: Johns Hopkins University Press, 1955.

*Kritzeck, James, ed., *Anthology of Islamic Literature*. New York: Holt, Rinehart and Winston. 1964.

*Nicholson, Reynold A., *A Literary History of the Arabs*. 2nd ed.; Cambridge: Cambridge University Press, 1962.

*Runciman, Steven A., *A History of the Crusades*. 4 vols.; Cambridge: Cambridge University Press, 1951–1958.

Schacht, Joseph, *An Introduction to Islamic Law*. Oxford: Clarendon Press, 1964.

Watt, W. Montgomery, *Islamic Philosophy and Theology*. Edinburgh: Edinburgh University Press, 1962.

————, and Cachia, P., *Islamic Spain*. Edinburgh: Edinburgh University Press, 1965.

CHAPTER TWELVE
MUSLIM AND BRITISH INDIA TO 1858

India's wealth served as a magnet for innumerable invasions, but only three of these invasions have significantly affected the course of Indian civilization—the Aryan, the Muslim, and the British conquests. The rest of the invaders, when they remained, were in due course digested by Indian culture and were given a place in the social hierarchy, so that today their origins cannot be easily ascertained. In spite of the reputed tolerance and flexibility of Indian culture, the other three conquerors presented too sharp a cultural contrast for easy absorption. Of the three, only the Aryans represented a folk movement that completed the destruction of the pre-existing civilization. To what extent the Indo-Aryan civilization that grew up in the Ganges valley reflected a reassertion of the older, submerged civilization is not certain. In contrast, the Muslim and British conquests were carried out by professional elites of limited numbers who were seeking political control primarily for the purpose of material gain. Although they had religious and cultural fanatics in their ranks and although they ultimately had a significant cultural impact, the initial objectives of both were limited to attaching themselves as parasites to draw sustenance from the vast and prosperous Indian host.

The first Muslim invasion was precipitated by piratical attacks on the ships of Arab merchants. In 711 an expeditionary force was sent to the mouth of the Indus, and in only 2 years conquered Sind and the southern Punjab.

Despite the attraction of Indian wealth, this easy conquest was not followed up probably because India presented no military threat. After Islam had effectively demonstrated its readiness to protect its merchants, Indian tolerance prevailed and Arab traders developed a lucrative commerce with complete security. Moreover, Islam's military energy was fully engaged elsewhere. By the time these other tasks were completed, Islamic expansionism had lost its momentum, and the Abbasid caliphs were fully occupied by internal problems.

Not Arabs, then, but Turkish converts and their Mongol kinsmen were, as military adventurers, to carry the banners of Islam throughout India. These were trained professional warriors and not rude nomads seeking a new home. India's wealth attracted their raids, and these raids led to permanent conquest only when the advantages of the systematic exploitation of Indian wealth were realized.

THE ISLAMIC CONQUEST

In the year 986 a former Turkish slave soldier from Khurasan, Sabuktegin, made his first raid into the Punjab. With the prestige and booty obtained he was enabled to build up a state in Afghanistan with its capital at Ghaznī. But he could maintain his dominion only by repeated raids for fresh resources. In 991 he defeated a Rājput confederacy and captured the city of Peshāwar. His son, Mahmūd of Ghaznī, who succeeded him in 997, made almost annual raids during the winter months, retiring with his loot to the mountains as soon as the weather became uncomfortably hot. Again, the Rājput rulers pooled their resources and confronted Mahmūd's troops with a vast host, but again the flexible tactics of the Turks proved their superiority over the large, but unwieldy, Indian force which relied on elephants to break the enemy line. While a line of wagons bore the brunt of the main Indian assault, maneuverable squadrons of expert cavalry rained arrows on the flanks. Finally, the Rājput commander's elephants pan-

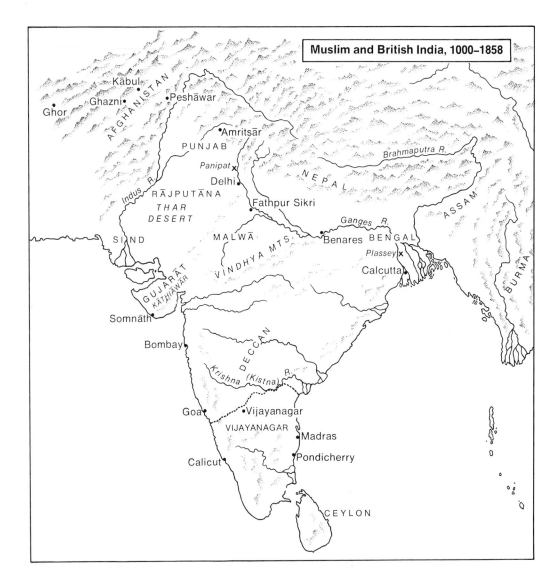

Muslim and British India, 1000–1858

icked, and immediately the rest of the army fled and the slaughter began. In battle after battle this identical pattern repeated itself. Indian generals, including later Muslim ones, never learned how to deal with a mobile force. Indian military conservatism captured its conquerors.

After a number of years the Punjab had been exploited, and Mahmūd had to go farther afield for fresh sources of plunder. He invaded the upper Ganges where even larger cities with greater loot were taken and suc-

ceeded in 1026 in crossing the great Thar Desert and storming the city of Somnath, sacred to Shiva, on the Kāthiāwār coast. As a devoted Muslim, Mahmūd felt an obligation to destroy all idols that fell into his hands. Such iconoclasm undoubtedly also provided psychological justification for the depredations of this not uncultured man.

With his plunder he beautified and made a cultural center of his capital, inviting noted scholars to enjoy his patronage. Best known is al-Bīrūnī who made a thorough study and analysis of all the facets of Indian civilization and its works. This scholarly work, which is not content with a simple relation of facts, is an invaluable source of information for the condition of Indian civilization on the eve of conquest. A fully developed caste system was already firmly established as the basic means of organizing society. He notes the inordinate pride and sense of superiority that led Hindus to hold everything and everyone alien in contempt. He attributes this hatred of *mlechchas* ("barbarians") to the incompatibility of the Islamic and Hindu religions, which had been only too well demonstrated by his patron. Finally, he observes the pacifism and lack of willingness to die for their ideals that characterized Indian intellectuals.

On Mahmūd's death in 1030, India gained a respite of 150 years. His successors were less vigorous and content to live off his accumulated glory and treasure until they lost what was left to the rising Afghan power of Ghor. Meanwhile, new Rājput families had arisen as a result of their continual wargames to replace those destroyed by Mahmūd.

In contrast with Mahmūd, Muhammed of Ghor was a methodical conqueror, not just a raider. From 1175 to 1190 he consolidated his control of the Punjab, eliminating the last of Mahmūd's descendants who had taken refuge there. In 1191 he turned to the east. His first expedition was almost his last. As in Mahmūd's time, the Rājput rulers settled their differences for the time being and combined their forces to meet the invader in the restricted area through which an army must pass to enter the Ganges valley. In the ensuing conflict Muhammed was wounded and his disheartened troops broke and fled. The less mobile Rājput forces, however, were unable to capitalize on their victory by pursuit, and Muhammed returned the next year to the same field of battle with a stolid determination to avenge his defeat. The Rājputs were routed and destroyed, and the whole Ganges basin was opened to the conquest

that was carried out mainly by his generals. By the end of the century all of northern India, except Rājputāna, Mālwā, and part of Gujarāt, had been reduced to subjection. Iconoclasts like their predecessor Mahmūd, Muhammed, and his generals destroyed Hindu idols and temples and all but exterminated the Buddhists in their last centers of strength in the eastern Ganges. The survivors took refuge in Tibet. Assassinated in 1206, Muhammed was succeeded by his chief general and former slave, Kutb-ud-din Aibak, the first ruler of the Slave dynasty of Delhi (1206–1292).

THE DELHI SULTANATE

The political details of intrigue and civil strife among the generals that accompanied every succession need not detain us. More important was the relationship that evolved between the rulers and the ruled. The major problem confronting the conquerors was how to maintain their identity and vitality as a ruling minority in a wholly alien environment. In this task they were aided by the almost total rejection of Islam by the Hindus who retreated into the protective isolation of the caste system, "rendered unto Caesar" the tribute that was demanded, and sought only to coexist in peace. This negative attitude toward government was not new, but was only reinforced by the arrival of Islam. The defeat of the Rājputs may in large part be attributed to the general Hindu indifference to the fate of their rulers. The compartmentalized hierarchy of caste represented a system of social, economic, and political decentralization that permitted the Muslims to confiscate the property of wealthy individuals without fear of stirring up a general insurrection. In addition, the essentially self-governing castes facilitated the task of administration. Only one group needed to be treated with a measure of respect because of its spiritual influence—the brāhman class. Generally they were exempted from the poll-tax that was levied on nonbelievers and, in return, cooperated with the new rulers.

The cultural isolation of the Muslims by the Hindus aided the ruling class in maintaining its identity and encouraged it to turn to Iran for cultural tutelage. In any case, they had to look to external sources for fresh recruits to maintain their military vitality, which tended to be sapped by the debilitating factors of climate and luxury. The influx of Iranian culture and Turkish soldiers was given an added impetus by the Mongol invasions that made India a place of refuge from their ravages. Chingiz Khan sent a flying column in pursuit of the crown prince of Khwarism as far as Peshāwar, but took no further interest in India. The art and architecture of the Delhi Sultanate clearly followed Iranian models, introducing the dome, the arch, and the minaret. The use of Hindu temples as a plentiful quarry of building material and the employment of Hindu artisans produced a blending of styles in which Muslim features were dominant. The Hindu influence is evident in the variation in buildings from place to place according to local traditions, materials, and needs. It is also apparent in the luxuriant decoration that contrasts with the comparatively more austere Iranian practice. Unlike art, the literature that flourished with the influx of refugees was purely Iranian, although gradually a new language called Urdu evolved, based on a western Indian dialect and supplemented by a large infusion of words of Iranian and Arabic origins.

In the religious realm the need to maintain Islam's identity and distinction from the many forms of Hinduism encouraged a watchful conservatism that relied on theologians to keep the doctrine unadulterated. Ultimately, however, a common ground was found in Hindu devotional *bhakti* and Iranian Sufism. Both shared the urge for union with the divine and Iranian Sufis found it difficult not to cross the narrow line to pantheism of the Indian variety. But this movement did not blossom until the Mughal period, and will be

discussed with it. Under the Delhi Sultanate the corruption of the faith was not yet a problem and was carefully guarded against. Among the precautions taken was the distinction, subsequently maintained, between the first-class immigrant Muslims and the second-class Indian converts.

Thus, aided by the Hindu attitude and Iranian refugees, the Muslim conquerors had little difficulty in securing their dominion in northern India and in maintaining their identity and vitality. As long as they recognized the rules of coexistence and did not seek the enforced conversion of all Hindus, their political authority was acceptable. As long as they merely collected the customary taxes and left the caste authorities free to govern their members without interference, they had little to fear from the Indian people.

By the end of the thirteenth century Muslim power had been established and its limits defined. Now Islam was ready for further expansion in India. The Deccan, south of the Vindhya Mountains, was invaded and the remaining Hindu principalities in the north were attacked. When the fall of the great Rājput fortress of Chitor appeared inevitable, the defenders demonstrated their irreconcilability by performing for the first, but not the last, time the Hindu rite of *Jauhār*. All the women burned themselves to death and the men sallied forth to meet death by the sword rather than suffer the fate of surrender. By 1327 virtually all of India had been subjected politically to the Delhi Sultanate. Among the Hindus there was so little sense of unity and common interest that some rulers had collaborated with the Muslims against their traditional Hindu foes.

This first unification of India under the Muslims could not last. The land was so vast and communications so poor that governors had to be granted virtual autonomy. The process by which governors made their posts hereditary and asserted their independence, already observed in the Middle East, was repeated in the Indian subcontinent. No matter how able the sultans were—and this was by no means always the case—or how efficient an administration was developed, decentralization followed its natural course with Shiite doctrines often being adopted for political purposes. A Hindu state, Vijayanagar (1336–1565), gained control of the southern portion of the peninsula and carried on a continuous struggle with the Muslim states of the Deccan.

In northern India the abler sultans sought by administrative reforms along absolutist lines to offset the centrifugal tendencies. Hereditary landholdings were reclaimed by the state. Borrowing from Indian tradition, an extensive and complex system of spies, informers, and agents provocateur was developed. Rigid enforcement of Islamic laws, such as the prohibition of alcohol and gambling, was attempted, but without avail. The centrifugal tendencies repeatedly reasserted themselves. Moreover, the Mongols and their successors were a constant threat.

After the death of the exceptionally able Firuz Shāh in 1388 internal strife attracted the plundering horde of Timūr. In 1398 he invaded India and sacked Delhi after a military victory that had been facilitated by the Indian army's adoption of traditional Indian tactics with their reliance on lumbering war elephants. Like previous raiders, Timūr retired before the onset of hot weather. In his path he permitted greater destruction and slaughter than India had ever seen. Timūr's successors exploited India until 1451 when a short-lived, but able, dynasty filled the gap before another Turko-Mongol adventurer, Bābur, intervened to establish the Mughal (Mongol) dynasty (1526–1857). Once again the old central Asian tactics made it possible for a numerically inferior force to gain a decisive victory at the historic field of Panipat in the narrow passage between the Indus and Ganges basins.

Islam had brought the art of historical writing to India. Some of the accounts are little more than annals and many others are fulsome accounts intended to win the pa-

tronage of the ruler; but others, such as that of the renowned traveler, Ibn Batuta, who visited India in the fourteenth century, are impartial and enlightening analyses. The sensitive and intellectual Bābur, however, added a new and invaluable dimension with his informative *Memoirs*. In this work the adventures, hardships, and character of an exceptionally talented man during his rise to power are intimately revealed.

THE MUGHAL DYNASTY (1526 – 1857)

In 1494 at the age of twelve this descendant of Timūr on the paternal side and Chingiz Khan through his mother succeeded his father as ruler of the central Asian principality of Ferghana whose center was situated in a small, but esthetically stimulating mountain valley. After overcoming the efforts of three uncles to unseat him, he set out at the age of fifteen to win his fortune as the heir of Timūr and in 1497 gained for the first time Timūr's capital, Samarkand. As his *Memoirs* relate, he was overwhelmed by the beauty and perfection of the buildings and gardens of "silken Samarkand." But his fortune was not to be so easily made. When he fell ill and was reported to have died, rebellions broke out and, deserted by most of his men, he wandered as a fugitive undergoing all manner of hardships. This hardening experience is reminiscent of the similar travails of Chingiz Khan in his youth, and for both men it provided invaluable training in character and leadership. Both gained a deep insight in judging men but, while Chingiz learned the need for ruthlessness, Bābur's natural humaneness was reinforced. His refusal to permit his troops to engage in rapine and slaughter was unique among Asian military leaders.

After capturing Kābul in 1504 with a force of less than 300 loyal followers, he consolidated his control of Afghanistan before launching probing attacks in 1519 into India proper. To the Indian people he proclaimed:

"Our eye is on this land and on this people; raid and rapine shall not be." At the critical battle of Panipat in 1526 Bābur commanded less than 12,000 seasoned warriors, but among them were a trained troop of matchlockmen and an artillery battery under a Turkish officer which tore great gaps in the massed charge of the Indian army. The victory, however, was gained by a traditional cavalry charge. Immediately thereafter he occupied the major cities and declared himself sultan, but with his mountaineer background he found both the climate and the customs distasteful and only accepted his role as a command of Allah. The people he described as unhandsome, unfriendly, unkind, impolite, dull-witted, and without any genius or skill in mechanics or architecture. Moreover, India lacked all the good things with which he was familiar, such as good horses, good meat, good bread, ice water, baths, and even candles. During the wet season moisture ruined bows, coats of mail, books, clothes, and furniture. During the dry season the north winds filled the air with choking dust. India's only redeeming features were its vast size and wealth.

His troops were no less disenchanted and pleaded for plunder and a return to Kābul, but Bābur was more successful than Alexander in persuading them to face up to their responsibilities. Now that empire had been achieved after undergoing so many hardships and such great dangers in battle, he argued, it would be shameful to flee from its fruits and retreat to Kābul. He offered anyone who wished the opportunity to return, but that person could never again call him his friend. After this harangue, the discontented had no choice but to abandon, however reluctantly, any thought of mutiny.

Physically exhausted by his strenuous life of adventure and hardship this truly great man died in 1530 at the age of forty-seven, before he had consolidated his conquests, but the *Memoirs* remain as a perpetual memorial to his character and qualities.

The difficulties of his successor Humāyūn, who was forced to flee to Safawid Iran to get aid in regaining his inheritance, though fascinating, cannot be related here. Suffice it to say that Iranian Shiite doctrines were not without influence during the long rule of his unorthodox and inquisitive son, Akbar (1556–1605), who was only thirteen years old at his accession. Akbar's guardian, who secured his succession by a military victory at Panipat, was an Iranian Shiite.

His primary responsibility, recognized by this vigorous and sensitive grandson of Bābur, was the consolidation of Mughal control and the elaboration of an efficient system of administration. Both of these tasks he fulfilled effectively. Yet the personality of this obviously able ruler has rightly baffled his biographers.

As a boy he had little interest in his studies and even refused to learn how to read and write. Perhaps the pedagogy and curriculum repelled him. Certainly he possessed exceptional intellectual curiosity which was aided by a fantastic memory. He also inherited his family's strong sense of beauty, especially of the beauties of nature which he sought to recreate in the construction of his gemlike capital of Fathpur Sikri. He was interested in science and mechanics. His deepest interest, however, was reserved for his quest for the Truth, chiefly by the investigation of all the philosophies and religions that came within his purview, including Roman Catholicism. His inclination was toward mysticism, both of the Sufi and Hindu varieties. Dissatisfied with all the formal religions investigated, he devised his own eclectic religion which supposedly combined the best features of all, but it was mainly limited to the circle of the court and died with him. Whether his religious tolerance came from conviction or the desire to unite the disparate spiritual forces within his realm cannot be clearly determined. At any rate, he eliminated the poll tax on non-Muslims at a substantial loss of revenue and conciliated Hindus by filling a large proportion of administrative posts with Rājputs. Perhaps his own doubts best illustrate his attitude.

> Men fancy that outward profession to the mere letter of Islam, without a heartfelt conviction, can profit them. I have forced many Hindus by fear of my power to adopt the religion of my ancestors, but now that my mind has been enlightened by beams of Truth, I have become convinced that in this distressful place of contrarieties where the dark clouds of conceit and the mists of self-opinion have gathered round you, not a step can be made without the torch of proof. That belief can only be beneficial which we select with clear judgment. To repeat the words of the Creed, to perform circumcision, or to lie prostrate on the ground from dread of kingly power is not seeking God:
>
> (Quoted by Rawlinson, *India*, pp. 311–312)

Naturally his views alarmed the Muslim theologians, who did not fare well in debates with the representatives of other religious doctrines, and a conservative reaction developed in search of a ruler who would uphold the letter of Islamic law. Finally, it should be noted that spiritual sensitivity was no check on his warlike propensities. No Mughal was a more vigorous warrior or glorified more in being in the forefront of battle. There was nothing effete about Akbar. Moreover, he did not shrink from ruthlessness and slaughter whenever he considered it politically expedient. After reducing the last pockets of resistance in northern India, he initiated the conquest of the Muslim states of the Deccan, a policy that was ultimately to prove fatal to the Mughals, but, as his boon companion and biographer has reported, Akbar believed a ruler must "ever be intent on conquest, otherwise his enemies rise in arms against him" (quoted by Rawlinson, *India*, p. 304). As an administrative policy he paid high salaries to his officials and opposed hereditary grants of land as contrary to the maintenance of centralized authority. These realistic domestic and foreign policies would have won the approval of the author of the *Arthashāstra*.

Under his successors, Jahāngīr and Shāh Jahān, the Mughal era reached its zenith. Jahāngīr shared to a degree his father's tolerance and Shāh Jahān's orthodoxy was not oppressive. The latter's rule cannot be passed over without mention of the magnificent tomb constructed in memory of his beloved wife, the Tāj Mahal, which is the supreme expression of Mughal architecture perfectly combining Iranian style and Indian craftsmanship.

The intolerant orthodoxy and tremendously costly campaigns of the last renowned Mughal ruler, Aurangzīb (1659–1707), impoverished the empire and undermined what respect for Muslim authority had been built up by the policies of the earlier Mughals. When Shāh Jahān's health failed in 1657, his sons engaged in a bitter struggle for power. In essence the struggle was reduced to two sons, Dārā Shikōh, who represented the religious liberalism of Akbar, and Aurangzīb behind whom gathered all the forces of Sunnite Muslim reaction. Naturally the Rājputs supported the former, but in battle the victory went to the latter. Dārā Shikōh was subsequently captured and assassinated, and his son died in a dungeon 2 years later. The deposed emperor and father was placed in comfortable imprisonment where he died in 1666.

At last having secured the throne at the cost of the blood of his family, Aurangzīb gradually unfolded his program of reformation. In his personal life he adhered strictly to Qur'anic law and expected all Muslims equally to conform. Drinking and gambling were rigorously suppressed. Artists and musicians sought in vain for wealthy patrons. All apostates were arrested, tried, and executed. No deviations from the commands of the Prophet were tolerated by the ulema who at last had a ruler who would back them to the hilt.

By itself this disciplining of Muslims might have strengthened Islam in India because it represented attention to the old problem of maintaining the identity and vitality of the conquerors, but the same spirit that inspired this reformation of the Muslim community led to a persecution of Hinduism. Although Shāh Jahān's order prohibiting the construction of new Hindu temples had been a serious restraint, Aurangzīb shattered the unwritten rule of coexistence by his order of 1669 which prescribed the demolition of all Hindu schools and temples and the suppression of their religious teaching and practices. The triumphant Muslim religious leaders saw to it that this edict was carried out to the letter. Untold numbers of temples were torn down, frequently being replaced by mosques.

This attack on Hinduism was not only contrary to the rule of coexistence it was also contrary to common sense. The fact that the overwhelming majority of Indians had clung to Hinduism through four and one-half centuries of Muslim domination should have demonstrated the unshakeable strength of their beliefs. The emperor and his advisers would have been wise to remember Akbar's dictum that compulsory conversions are worthless. But they were not content with the destruction of the spiritual edifices of Hinduism. By a series of decrees Hindus were attacked in the economic realm as well. Hindu members of the civil service were dismissed, but this order had to be modified when it was realized that the bureaucracy could not function with such a depletion of its ranks. A 5 percent surtax was assessed on the imports of Hindu merchants. Finally, the poll tax on non-Muslims was revived, a measure that fell on every Hindu. The only result of such an irrational policy was the outbreak of innumerable rebellions which were bloodily suppressed.

But all the rebels could not be captured and killed. Hindu militancy had been reawakened in place of the traditional pacifism. Rebel leaders evolved a guerilla-type of warfare, striking out at unguarded spots and

causing economic disruption that sapped the financial strength of the Mughal Empire. In the Deccan the Marāthā power grew under able leaders. In the Punjab Sikh militarism became the inveterate foe of the Muslims. But the greatest folly was Aurangzīb's attacks on the Rājputs whose valiant and vigorous sons had been a vital source of civil servants and soldiers for the Mughals since the time of Akbar. The emperor's own son who commanded the expedition into Rājputāna protested strongly against the attack on such a race of heroes and finally deserted to their side in the vain hope of overthrowing his father. But even the defection of a favorite son could not shake the fanatical determination of a ruler like Aurangzīb.

In the midst of these difficulties, Aurangzīb decided to revive Akbar's program of conquering the peninsula which had languished under his less militant heirs. Four years were consumed in assembling a vast host and its supplies and moving them to the base of operations in the Deccan. After 6 years of campaigning all the cities of the south had been reduced to submission by the sheer weight of numbers, and Aurangzīb could claim sovereignty over the whole of India from its southern tip to Kābul in Afghanistan. But it was a hollow boast.

The Mughal Empire was on the verge of collapse. The accumulated resources of his predecessors had been exhausted by his monumental campaigns, while the depredations of the growing number of rebels were creating economic anarchy and were sharply reducing the revenues of the government. By itself the conquest of the south was not necessarily ill-advised, although it is doubtful whether the Mughals could have devised an effective enough system of administration to hold together these far-flung possessions for any length of time. Under normal conditions incoming revenues would have offset before long the severe drain on the empire's resources. But combined with the policy of Hindu persecution and the inability to suppress the rebellions that this policy precipitated, the cumulative effect of the conquest was disastrous. As soon as his forces withdrew from any region, fresh rebellions broke out. Approaching his ninetieth year and death, the aged emperor revealed deep doubts about his policies and fear for the welfare of his successor in a letter to a son. Thus, before his death, he realized the probable futility of his life's work, placing his trust in Allah, the faithful, and his sons.

The Mughal dynasty lingered on for another 150 years until officially deposed for alleged conspiracy in the Sepoy Mutiny of 1857. Almost immediately, however, its actual authority began to be compromised by the establishment of virtually independent principalities, and court intrigues reduced the emperors to puppets who were elevated and deposed at will. In the political chaos that ensued it is perhaps not surprising that the new rulers, both Muslim and Hindu, continued to recognize in name at least the suzerainty of the Mughals and to look to them as a source of legitimacy for their titles and honors. In this manner, a shadow empire persisted until finally extinguished by the British Rāj.

MUGHAL ART AND LITERATURE

Although the Mughal rulers spent little on internal improvements, such as irrigation works and roads, they lavished patronage on the arts which reflect increasing sophistication and technical skill and, with the exception of Akbar's reign, the growing artistic domination of Iranian style. With his expressed disdain for India and its arts, Bābur imported artists from the whole Islamic world to make his new home habitable. He and his successors were especially interested in the construction of formal gardens in which they could escape the drab monotony of the north Indian countryside.

The uniqueness of Akbar's eclecticism is witnessed by the very state of preservation of his city of Fathpur Sikri, which was deserted by his successors. The Tāj Mahal of Shāh Jāhān stands out as the most impressive representation of Mughal architecture,

but a number of other examples match its beauty on a smaller scale. Its coordinated gardens and pools typify the Mughal blending of architecture and landscaping. The Tāj Mahal has been described as purely Iranian, but a closer examination reveals extensive Hindu influence in the decorative details.

In painting, greater blending is apparent, perhaps because of the reliance on Indian artists. Painting reached its peak under Akbar's indolent, but esthetically inclined son, Jahāngīr, in a blend of Iranian, Indian, and European influences. Europe contributed perspective, shading, and an almost photographic naturalism in subjects and details which had previously been absent.

Literature of every variety flourished, especially under Akbar's patronage when it enjoyed its greatest freedom. Notable are the translations of the Indian classics which made these works available to open-minded Muslim seekers of Truth and the voluminous *Life of Akbar* by his liberal companion and adviser, Abul Fazil. In addition to Akbar's life this work includes a history of his predecessors and a detailed description of all aspects of contemporary Indian life and administration.

SIKHISM

The major religious developments have already been sketched. One important development, the effort to synthesize Islam and Hinduism, warrants separate attention because it produced Sikhism, which still can count more than 6 million dedicated believers. The initial inspiration for this effort at synthesis came from a low caste weaver of Benares, Kabīr (1440–1518), whose popular devotional verses reflect Sufi influence. Essentially he was an iconoclast denying the need for temples, idols, or prophets. God, he taught, is omnipresent only awaiting recognition and devotion.

His influence on Sikhism is evident from the number of his verses included in the Sikh "bible," but the founder of Sikhism was the Punjabi Hindu, Nānak (1469–1538). After a normal early life Nānak's spiritual discontent led him to take up the wandering life of a Sufi in search of Truth. His travels took him throughout India, to Ceylon, and even to Mecca. He finally returned to devote the last 15 years of his life to teaching his beliefs. His central doctrine was the unalloyed worship of God, the creator and disposer of all things. Islamic influence is also apparent in his cardinal declaration: "There is but one God whose name is true, the Creator." Like Kabīr, he rejected formalistic worship and rites and denied that knowledge of God was the exclusive possession of any religion. Virtuous conduct and humility are the only true guides to God and his mercy. Love, sincerity, justice, modesty, courtesy, truth, and charity in every thought and action are more important than any form of worship.

On this foundation the *gurus* who followed Nānak developed the unique practices and attitudes that came to distinguish Sikhism clearly from both Islam and Hinduism. Nānak himself took the first step by opting for the active life and by rejecting his son's ascetic quietism. Sikhism evolved its own system of writing, its own ritual and scripture, and its own center at Amritsār, which is named after the Sikh temple there. Communal life was encouraged by the establishment of a common meal to which all contributed and of congregational worship. As the order grew in numbers, and secular power, the predominance of Hindu converts led to the incorporation of Hindu customs and an increasing alienation from Islam. The fourth *guru* after Nānak was executed for participation in an unsuccessful rebellion and thus became Sikhism's first martyr.

The next two *gurus* were military as well as spiritual leaders and converted Sikhism into a military organization to combat Aurangzīb's persecution. In 1699 the sworn brotherhood of fighting Sikhs was founded with an initiation and communion ceremony. As in Islam, those Sikhs who died in battle were assured of entrance into paradise. Thus the corporate sense of the Sikhs was given a more clearly institutionalized expression. They were now a living and self-perpetuating community of militant saints who held themselves aloof from both Hindus and Muslims.

The Sikhs were to offer the last and most vigorous resistance to British dominion, but once they were quelled they proved to be loyal subjects and provided some of the best recruits for the Anglo-Indian army. Honorable defeat did not destroy Sikhism or its military qualities. Because of their location in the Punjab the Sikhs suffered heavily in the disorders that followed India's independence and sought recognition for a separate Sikh state. Ironically, then, Sikhism, which was pioneered as an effort to reconcile Islam and Hinduism by drawing on both, became a separate and exclusive community within the Indian body politic.

THE ISLAMIC IMPACT

Although the Islamic conquest failed to break the hold of Hinduism on the spirit of the mass of the Indian people, it was not without a deeply significant impact, as is most clearly shown by the present political division of the subcontinent. In spite of Islam's egalitarian appeal to the downtrodden members of India's caste-ridden social hierarchy, it never secured the conversion of as much as one quarter of the population. This religious defeat stands in contrast to its enduring success throughout the Middle East.

As the present boundaries of Pakistan indicate, Islam as a religion gained its greatest acceptance in the Indus valley and in Bengal. Ever since the shift of the center of gravity to the Ganges valley in ancient times the Indus valley had been a peripheral and semidetached region more deeply influenced by the recurrent invasions from the northwest than by the radiation of Indian civilization from its Ganges center. Moreover, Islam was established in this region for a longer time. Bengal, too, was peripheral and subordinate to the center of Indian civilization in the middle and upper reaches of the Ganges. In Bengal Islamic arms delivered the coup de grace to an already decadent Buddhism. Buddhism like Islam was egalitarian and was opposed to caste, which may have encouraged conversions. In addition, many prominent Bengali brāhman families, such as the Tagores and the Roys, demonstrated a tolerant willingness to get along with the conquerors, although they remained faithful to Hinduism. On the basis of this experience these same families, suspected of dangerous deviation by strict Hindus, showed a similar open-mindedness toward Western culture. For this flexibility they were richly rewarded by both the Muslim and British rulers and were able to make important contributions to India's ultimate reawakening. Finally, as a peripheral area, Bengal was not hit by the first waves of ardent Muslim crusaders and, therefore, when it was incorporated, calmer political considerations prevented the devastation that had hardened the hearts of Hindus in the upper and middle Ganges.

This peripheral thesis may seem to be refuted by the limited success of Islam in the peninsula, but it should be recalled first that Tamil-Land in the lower peninsula was never reduced for any prolonged period of time and second that the peninsula after the eighth century A.D. was the chief source of Hindu revival and development. Shankara, the father of Advaita Vedānta, and many other Hindu leaders were products of the peninsula. Popular *bhakti* Hinduism with its egalitarian and antibrāhman tendencies arose in the south and spread throughout India. In short, in the south Islam was up against what had become the most vigorous and creative strain of Hinduism.

Furthermore, the basic incompatibility of prophetic Islam and mystic Hinduism, despite the synthesizing efforts of a Nānak or an Akbar, encouraged the further development of the established caste system as a protective and self-governing device and reinforced the Hindu sense of spiritual superiority and the common rejection without serious investigation of everything alien. Both of these features represent an introverted attitude that was adopted as a defensive mechanism for cultural self-preservation. So long as the Muslims accepted the role of a ruling caste and stayed within the limits of the unwritten rule of coexistence, they were tolerated. When Aurangzīb overstepped these bounds, rebellions and decentralization were the inevitable result. Acceptance of the same role made possible the British Rāj, although like the Muslims they sought to eradicate Hindu practices equally repulsive to Muslims and Christians, such as *suttee* (the immolation of widows on the husband's funeral pyre), infanticide, and child marriage.

Although Aurangzīb's policies produced the political divisions that tempted the French and the British to intervene in internal affairs and ultimately made possible the piecemeal conquests of British governors, India's political disunity should not be wholly blamed on Mughal ineptness. Had the Muslims never come to India, the same condition in all likelihood would have existed. Long before, India had demonstrated its inability to construct an enduring political unity. Long before, Indian civilization had decided to give first consideration to spiritual affairs, and their hereditary brāhman representatives had relegated worldly affairs, and especially politics, to the bottom of the ladder of values. The caste system had evolved as a substitute for and a buffer against centralized political authority and had effectively performed most of the functions normally associated with the state. Governments were tolerated and taxes were dutifully paid so long as they did not interfere with local caste government, but there was no deep loyalty to these political entities. States and princes might come and go, but the caste-organized society continued and evolved with little or no reference to them. On the other hand, without Aurangzīb the Mughals might have achieved and maintained a sufficient measure of political control to discourage intervention by the agents of French and British trading interests.

Although the Muslims introduced Persian culture, which strongly influenced the arts patronized by the ruling class, they did little to alter the social and economic life of India being content to inherit without significant change the established and accepted system of exploiting the peasantry. Where their Rājput predecessors had plowed back a substantial portion of their revenues into productive public works, the Muslims had little to show in justification of their tax collections other than a multitude of magnificent mosques, palaces, fortifications, and tombs. A few of the wiser Delhi sultans had maintained state granaries to supply food at reasonable prices whenever nature turned against the peasants, but most of the Muslim rulers neglected even this elementary precaution. Famines struck one part of India or another almost annually and carried off untold numbers who, after meeting the demands of the government, had few surpluses to fall back on. But the fertility of India's people proved more reliable than that of its soil, and the human losses were soon recouped. Muslim fatalism, reinforced by the religious barrier, combined to prevent the development of any humanitarian concern for Hindu subjects. What social security the Hindu had was to be found within his family and his caste. This scene of general poverty is only relieved by the growth in the volume of trade that was created by the increasing prosperity of the West. But again, the profit went primarily into the treasure chests of wealthy merchants whose privileges were protected by their caste; the artisan remained as impoverished as the peasant. By sheer numbers and industriousness the artisans and peasants collectively bore the burden of India on their individually weak backs.

THE ARRIVAL OF THE WEST

At the very time when the Mughal conqueror Bābur was reveling in the beauties of his first conquest, Timūr's capital city of Samarkand, three small ships carrying 160 men and commanded by the Portuguese navigator, Vasco da Gama, made their landfall at the port of Calicut on the southwest coast of India. The year was 1498. Neither then nor for several centuries to come was the significance of this arrival of the West generally appreciated by either the rulers or the people of India. Despite da Gama's forthright declaration that his objectives were "Christians and gold," no one was alarmed. After all what was there to fear from these few bold men and their puny ships. India had never suffered an invasion by sea; the very idea was preposterous. They would humor these strange men and benefit as much as possible from their trade. In the long run, however, this seaborne invasion was destined under British direction to be more complete and thorough than any of its predecessors. Of the major Eastern civilizations only the Indian was to be subjected to total conquest by a Western power. This dubious distinction was not to be without significant results.

Following the collapse of the Roman Empire in the West, Europe had continued to deteriorate, showing clear signs of recovery and growth only in the tenth and eleventh centuries. Two overt symptoms of its reviving strength and energy were the Norman liberation of Sicily in the eleventh century and the initiation of the Crusades. The Crusades failed largely because of a complex conflict of interests, which cannot be examined here, but one significant interest was the desire of the Italian merchants to find a more direct and less costly supply of Eastern products. This interest documents the growing prosperity of Europe and its growing demand for luxury goods of Eastern origin. In spite of all obstacles the volume of East-West trade continued to grow, reaching a peak during the thirteenth and fourteenth centuries when the Mongols policed safe caravan routes across the breadth of Asia. The roles of middleman and producer enriched the merchants and rulers of the Middle Eastern crossroads and offset to a large degree the other symptoms of internal decay from which Islam was suffering. Subsequently the supply of Eastern products was periodically interrupted by the internal problems of Islam, and the rise of the Ottoman power and its assault on Europe by land and sea added to the difficulties of the merchant. The growing demand for Eastern products, the uncertainty of supply, the exorbitant charges demanded by the Ottoman Turks and the Mamluk Sultans of Egypt, and the increasing hostility between Christians and Muslims—all of these factors combined to stimulate an interest in finding a new route to the Eastern sources that would outflank Islam. During the fourteenth and fifteenth centuries several speculative treatises on how this aim might be accomplished are evidence of this interest. By way of Islam Western, navigators had gained knowledge of the essential tools: the astrolabe and the compass.

The peoples of the Iberian Peninsula whose long struggle to expel the Muslims had built up a militant spirit and crusading momentum were, perhaps, the most logical choice to strike out in a new direction. The trading cities of northern Italy were too deeply committed to making their traditional trading pattern work, in spite of growing obstacles, and the states of France and England were still preoccupied with solving the internal problems of nation-building. Since the early fifteenth century the Portuguese, who preceded the Spanish in freeing their land of Muslim domination, had taken to the sea, probing southward along the African coast. Prince Henry the Navigator (d 1453) should be mentioned as an important patron and planner of this overseas exploration, which

was so methodical that the Portuguese could not be diverted by the dreams of Columbus. The Spanish rulers did not enter the picture until Columbus gained their patronage, and the discovery of the New World fully absorbed Spanish energies until they occupied the Philippines in the later sixteenth century.

The fantastic profits earned by Vasco da Gama's cargo guaranteed a prompt return in greater strength to Indian waters. Before long, a combination of crusading spirit and economic interest encouraged the Portuguese to sever the maritime link between India and the Middle East. Recognizing this threat, the Ottoman and Mamluk rulers collaborated in putting a naval force in the Indian Ocean that defeated a Portuguese squadron in 1508. In the next year, however, a reinforced Portuguese force decisively defeated the Muslim navy. Albuquerque, who arrived as viceroy, systematically developed a string of fortified bases from Arabia to Malaya to assure Portuguese control of trade. Portuguese success, it should be understood, was not due to any great technical superiority but rather to their determined spirit and unified planning. Indeed, in the Mediterranean the Spanish were unable to break Ottoman naval power even after the apparently decisive battle of Lepanto in 1571.

In India, operating from their island headquarters at Goa, the Portuguese merchants drove an extremely lucrative trade with the great Hindu state of Vijayanagar to which they supplied horses from Arabia to mount the cavalry and other goods in return for gold, precious stones, and tropical products. In other words, the Portuguese enjoyed a "favorable" balance of trade and much of the profit stayed in Goa supporting a luxurious life which, together with the climate, undermined Portuguese vigor. When Vijayanagar was destroyed in 1565 by a coalition of the Deccan sultanates, Portuguese profits dwindled, and by the time the Dutch and the

English appeared at the end of the century the Portuguese colonies in India were already in an advanced state of decay. The principal handicap of little Portugal, with a population of less than one and a half million, was a shortage of surplus manpower to support its overseas enterprises. For example, lack of men forced it to surrender to the Dutch the distribution of Eastern products in northern Europe, and also the crews of ships sailing to the Indies had to be filled out with English and Dutch sailors. These sailors returned home with stories of the weakness of the Portuguese as well as valuable navigational information.

Although one avowed objective was "Christians," profits initially diverted attention from missionary endeavor until the 1540s. Then the inquisition was installed in Goa, and a new breed of dedicated missionaries, the Jesuits, appeared on the scene. The well-educated and flexible Jesuits sought to advance the Christian cause by studying local religious practices and adapting them to Christian usages. In India this adaptation went further than elsewhere. Jesuit missionaries first adopted the robes of the brāhman and utilized Hindu terminology. To reach the people who in southern India have been, and still are, antibrāhman, others took the role of Hindu holy men. Although this technique gained substantial numbers of nominal Christians, missionaries of other orders legitimately complained that this form of Christianity, incorporating many pagan practices, was little more than another Hindu sect. Ultimately the Jesuits were suppressed, but their groundwork, supplemented by successors, resulted in the creation of a significant Roman Catholic community, especially strong in southern India today.

During the seventeenth century, supported by charters that granted monopoly rights, the Dutch and English East India companies, as well as others, established fortified trading stations on the coasts of India in emulation of the Portuguese models.

The last to enter the Indian picture was the French company in the later seventeenth century. Following the Portuguese example, all of them trained small contingents of Indian troops, called sepoys, to reduce military costs and utilized Indians as affiliated merchants to arrange for the production and collection of Indian goods and the sale of European products.

In contrast with the Portuguese, these trading companies felt no burning desire to spread Christianity. Indeed, missionary activity was frowned on as possibly disruptive to trade. Not until 1813 was the English East India Company compelled to admit missionaries as a condition for the renewal of its charter. In any case, English missionary fervor did not become aroused and organized until the 1790s. Even if the companies had entertained more ambitious territorial or religious plans, their realization was unlikely in the seventeenth century, which was the heyday of the Mughal Empire.

The chief posts of the English East India Company became Bombay on the west coast, Madras in the southeast, and Calcutta in the Ganges-Brahmaputra delta. Although those Englishmen who survived the climate returned home with tremendous fortunes, the Europeans as a whole had not yet exercised a significant impact on India. The demand for European goods was inadequate, and the trade had to be balanced by the sale of European specie. This unfavorable condition raised questions about the value of the Indian trade and was a factor in the Dutch withdrawal in order to concentrate their energies on the East Indies. Not until the Industrial Revolution reversed the cotton trade and the development of a Chinese market for Indian-grown opium was this trading picture significantly altered. Meanwhile, amid the political fragmentation accompanying the collapse of the Mughal Empire, an able and enterprising agent of the French Company, François Dupleix, pioneered the technique of effective intervention in Indian politics which was destined under reluctant English auspices to bring the British Rāj to the whole of India.

Dupleix demonstrated conclusively that a small, well-equipped, well-trained, and well-led European force was more than a match for the motley armed hosts of any Indian ruler. With little difficulty he placed his puppets on Indian thrones as allies and added their resources to his own. It soon became evident that if the English company wished to survive, it must emulate his strategy and enter the Indian political arena. By 1751 Dupleix had won control of a major portion of peninsular India, but in that year the British found a match for him in Robert Clive who gained an important victory. Clive, however, was not the sole cause of Dupleix's downfall. Neither the French company nor the French government supported him, and in 1754 he was recalled in disgrace. The Seven Years War (1756–1763) revived French activities in India, but Clive with the aid of the British navy proved equal to the test. In 1757, at the battle of Plassey, Clive, commanding a total force of 3000 men including 950 Englishmen, defeated the French-advised governor of Bengal whose army counted 50,000 infantry and 18,000 cavalry. Clive's casualties totaled 22 killed and 49 wounded! France's Indian ambitions were finally terminated by the capture of their post at Pondicherry in 1761. Perhaps even more important was the virtual destruction of the army of the Marāthā Confederacy in January of the same year at Panipat by an Afghan adventurer. With the defeat of Marāthā arms no significant military force was left in India, other than the British.

ESTABLISHMENT OF THE BRITISH RĀJ

The establishment of British dominion throughout India was a long drawn-out affair, not so much because of the military difficulties encountered as because of the indecision and vacillation of the Company and the British government. Its piecemeal nature involved a profusion of fascinating, but bewildering, actions and names, only a few of which will be mentioned here to illustrate the general problems.

The major problem was the reluctance of both the Company and the government to accept additional administrative responsibility with the accompanying commitment to maintain larger military forces for the defense of new territories. The Company, whose London directors' chief concern was the payment of regular dividends to the shareholders, naturally sought to avoid expensive military operations and commitments. As the government took an increasing interest in Indian government following the loss of the American colonies, it proved almost equally unwilling to extend British dominion except in reaction to potential threats from Napoleon or Russia. In other words, both the Company and the government sought a maximum of profit with a minimum of risk and expense. As a result, all governors had explicit instructions to do no more than defend existing possessions. But in defending Company possessions more than one victorious governor felt the military need to add new territory as a compensating buffer or to reduce the defeated Indian ruler to vassal status by a dependent treaty that added a new military commitment. More than once the government created confusion and chaos by repudiating these arrangements when it learned of them.

This brings up a second major problem—the problem of communications between London and India. Until the inauguration in 1843 of steamship service via the Red and Mediterranean Seas, dispatches delivered by sailing ship around Africa required six months each way. Since the governor could not expect to receive instructions in less than a year, he was forced to act on his own judgment in meeting crises. Even with the information provided by the dispatches, the London directors and the government had inadequate knowledge of the problems confronting the governor. In any case, by the time instructions from London arrived, conditions in India had often undergone a drastic change. In addition, when the governor-general and major officials became government appointees in consequence of Pitt's Act of 1784, the nobles appointed as governor-generals often had no connection with the Company and viewed their responsibilities in purely political and administrative, rather than economic, terms.

A third major problem was the development of an administration adapted to Indian experience. The English with their conception of individual ownership of landed property failed in India, as elsewhere, to appreciate the conception of the joint interest of ruler and peasant in the land without either one having exclusive title to it. They felt compelled to settle the title on someone, if only to establish legal responsibility.

In 1765 Clive extracted from the Mughal Emperor, still titular ruler of India, the right to collect taxes in Bengal and neighboring territories to the west in return for an annual payment of £260,000. This was the Company's first acquisition of extensive territorial responsibility. So elated at the prospects was the revenue-hungry government that in 1767 an act of parliament required the Company to pay £400,000 annually into the British treasury. Relying on traditional methods, collections failed to measure up to expectations. In addition, the Company soon became involved in a bitter struggle against a coalition of peninsular princes. As a result, the Company not only was unable to meet the governmental assessment but also was forced to negotiate a £1,400,000 loan from the government. To meet these financial difficulties, an experienced Company officer, Warren Hastings, was assigned in 1772 to the Presidency of Bengal, while the government of Lord North, equally concerned, drew up legislation that increased the government's role in Indian affairs.

Hastings' task has been likened to the cleansing of the Augean stables. Englishmen had always looked on the underpaid Company service as an opportunity to acquire by their own wits a personal fortune, and the Company, always in need of recruits, had never discouraged this attitude. In an effort to improve collections in Bengal, English district agents had been assigned to supervise the native collectors. Naturally these agents looked on these appointments as a golden opportunity for legalized larceny. Hastings embittered these men by regulating their activities and by setting up judges who were assisted by Indians learned in local customary law to protect the peasants. In 1772 Lord North's Regulating Act represented the first recognition of responsibility by the British government. By its terms Hastings was made governor-general with authority over all Company interests in India, and all political dispatches had to be submitted to the government's scrutiny; but at the same time the governor-general was saddled with a council that could veto his proposals by a majority vote. Three councillors, who were without Indian experience and failed to appreciate the need in administration to deviate from British practice and to conform with Indian custom, hamstrung Hastings until one of them died 2 years later, giving him control of his council. The ringleader, however, on his return to England dedicated himself to a vendetta against Hastings whom he depicted to the Whig leaders, Edmund Burke and Charles James Fox, as an irresponsible despot. In 1784 Hastings was recalled and in 1788 subjected to a 7-year-long impeachment. Ultimately he was acquitted, but he had exhausted his resources in his defense. His trial, at least, illustrated English concern for just and responsible government of subject peoples.

William Pitt's India Act of 1784 represented a further step in the development of government responsibility for India. It established a Board of Control to oversee political, military, and financial affairs and provided for governmental appointment of the governor-general and the major officials. In addition, it laid down the misguided regulation to avoid all entanglement in Indian politics. Most unfortunate, however, was the directive, which the first of a long series of noble governor-generals, Lord Cornwallis of Yorktown fame, was required to implement, settling title to the land in the hereditary tax collectors of Bengal and fixing the amount of taxes owed. The result was to deliver the peasants to the oppression of these extortionate landlords. Elsewhere, fortunately, this example was not followed, and for the most part title was settled in the peasant proprietors in those areas that were brought directly under Company administration.

Instead of preserving peace, the nonintervention directive encouraged depredations by ambitious Indian princes who believed they had nothing to fear from the Company and discouraged peaceful princes who would have welcomed a defensive alliance. These circumstances forced Cornwallis into one punitive war, but the basic policy was not altered until French intervention was again fostered by the visionary schemes of Napoleon.

In 1798 Napoleon ferried an army to Egypt with grandiose plans, and the Marquis of Wellesley accompanied by his younger brother, the future Duke of Wellington, arrived in India as governor-general with orders to counter the machinations of French agents. In a series of brilliant campaigns during his governorship from 1798 to 1805 all significant Indian military power was broken, and Company dominion by dependent alliances was extended over most of India east of the Indus valley and the Punjab. But his aggressive policy, denounced by the directors, led to his recall under threat of impeachment and the reinvocation of the policy of nonintervention. His subsidiary alliances were renounced, and the princes of Rājputāna who had aided him were left to the tender mercies of the resurgent Marāthās. Political anarchy and banditry ravaged India and spilled over into Company territory during the next 8 years of "isolationism." Finally, in 1813, the futility of this policy was realized, and Lord Hastings (no relative of Warren Hastings) was sent out with a free hand to establish law and order. By 1819 the British Rāj had been reestablished and, subsequently, in reaction to Russian expansion, it was expanded to include the Indus valley and the Punjab, while a friendly ruler was maintained in Afghanistan. During these same years Assam and all but the interior of Burma were brought under the Indian administration.

From the preceding account, the reluctance of the Company and the government to extend the territorial commitment in India is evident. Until 1813 only European threats to the Company's economic control could stir the English to action. If it had not been for the vacillation in policy, law and order could easily have been established 50 years earlier, and the Indian people would have been spared the untold hardships and loss of life and property caused by the chaos and devastations of this era of uncertainty and vacillation.

The year, 1813, was indeed a crucial turning point in the evolution of the British attitude toward India. In that year the renewal of the East India Company's charter provided for the end of the Company's monopoly of the Indian trade, a clear sign of its declining influence and the growing role of the government. Although the government was now dominant in fact, this position was not recognized in theory until 1858 after the suppression of the Sepoy Mutiny. In 1813, if not before, India had become the premier gem in the British Imperial diadem, and almost every subsequent imperial action can be related to the paramount interests of protecting India and enhancing its trade. Whether it was checking Russian expansion or securing lines of communication, the bulk of British foreign and imperial policy throughout the nineteenth century can be explained in terms of Britain's obsessive interest in India.

THE BRITISH IMPACT

Even more importantly for India, the charter of 1813 opened the gate to the mounting zeal of the British missionary movement. Before long the missionaries were sending reports to their humanitarian supporters at home castigating the atrocious Hindu practices, such as *suttee*, infanticide, and *thuggee* (the ritual murder of wayfarers as sacrifices to Kali, the goddess of destruction), and urging the advancement of British civilization to rescue the Indians from alleged barbarism. By the late 1820s these complaints began to bear fruit because the humanitarian movement was gaining important influence in the home government.

Hitherto, the Company, with its primary interest in trade, had sought to minimize friction and to interfere as little as possible with the Indian way of life. As many Indians as possible had been utilized in trade and administration. Company employees had been notorious for adopting Indian custom and dress and even taking Indian wives. Scholarly officials had studied the Indian classics and had begun recovering India's pre-Muslim past, thereby stimulating the Indians' interest in their own history and preparing the ground for the development of nationalistic sentiment. Private and public support of education had been devoted to traditional Hindu and Muslim types of schooling.

Now under the impetus of British pride in its position as the premier power and home of the humanitarian movement this sympathetic attitude was rejected in favor of bringing to India the presumed advantages of Christian ethics and British culture. And this movement was not without influential support from a few prominent Indians with English educations, especially the scions of Bengali brāhman families who had previously demonstrated adaptability by serving Muslim overlords. The renowned Rām Mohun Roy (1772–1833), who will be considered later in connection with the evolution of Indian national feeling, accepted Christian ethics while he rejected its theological dogmas, urged the government to suppress practices such as *suttee*, and argued the advantages of an English education.

These ideas, which had previously received scattered support, picked up momentum with the appointment in 1828 of the reform-minded Lord William Bentinck as governor-general. Among other reforms he abolished *suttee* and outlawed the practitioners of *thuggee*. But the most decisive step, taken in 1835, was the resolution giving all governmental support to English education at the higher levels. The primary factor in securing the passage of this resolution was the eloquent, if poorly informed, appeal of the famous historian and prose stylist, Thomas Babington Macaulay. In his own words, "a single shelf of a good European library was worth the whole native literature of India and Arabia." Although the full effect of this decision was not realized for many years, it provided educated Indians, hitherto divided by 14 major languages, with a common means of communication and exposed them to the liberal views of nineteenth-century English writers. As the number of English-educated Indians grew, they expressed complaints against the disparity between English political and social theory and English practice in India and founded English and vernacular newspapers to propagate their views. These views, however, did not gain a significant corporate voice until the later nineteenth century.

The British impact on India during the years between 1813 and 1857 was not only political and cultural but was extended to the economic realm as well. Until 1813 the Company had shipped specie to India to cover its purchases of cotton goods and other products, compensating itself by the resale of Indian importations in the European market. Subsequently the increasingly efficient cotton mills of Lancashire became able to undersell the products of the Indian artisan in his home market, and by the end of this period had partially destroyed this important source of supplemental income for Indian peasants. During the same years other products of England's Industrial Revolution penetrated the Indian market, displacing other handicrafts and reversing the balance of trade. By the later nineteenth century India was reduced to a greater dependence on agriculture for its livelihood than it had ever known, and the growing population fostered by the maintenance of law and order increased the pressure on its agricultural resources. In short, in the eyes of perceptive Indian nationalists India was not only suffering political and social oppression but also was being economically exploited and impoverished. Actually most educated Indian leaders of the nineteenth century, ensconced in the civil service, appreciated the advantages as well as the disadvantages of the British Rāj and agitated for moderate reforms. Not until the last decade did embittered nationalists make their influence felt. But the seed had been planted by the government's sponsorship of English education, and it was only a matter of time before the plant grew and blossomed.

THE SEPOY MUTINY

Lord Dalhousie (1848–1856) was a most vigorous governor-general whose measures contributed significantly to the growing anxiety and tension that exploded in the blind and unplanned Sepoy Mutiny of 1857. He relentlessly pressed the campaign against *suttee* and infanticide and issued laws that permitted widows to remarry and guaranteed the inheritance rights of Christian converts. The latter law, combined with growing missionary work caused the alarmed Indians to believe that there was a concerted plan for their enforced conversion. In an active and well-intentioned program of constructing irrigation works, railroads, and telegraph lines Dalhousie recklessly trod on Indian religious beliefs, giving further alarm to the Indian people. He expanded the government support of English education, planning to extend

it from primary school to the university level, and actively encouraged the education of women, previously restricted to training as housewives. All of these reforms violated in one way or another traditional Indian attitudes, yet Dalhousie bulled ahead with them heedless of the repeated warnings of his experienced advisors. Finally, he brought a number of principalities under direct administration, in part, by a rigorous application of the "doctrine of lapse" whereby a vassal's territory reverted to his immediate overlord on the ruler's death without heirs of his own body. The customary practice of recognizing an adopted son's right of inheritance was renounced. Although some of those thus dispossessed played leading roles in the mutiny, the general loyalty of the princes discounts this action as a major factor.

Undoubtedly Dalhousie's actions contributed to the growing anxiety of the Indian people, but an assortment of immediate factors precipitated the outbreak among some, but by no means all, of the Indian soldiers in government service. One factor was the prediction spread throughout the army that a century after Plassey the British Rāj was destined for destruction. Another factor was the growing fear of conversion or discharge which was unwittingly fostered by the preaching of the Gospel to sepoys by ardent British officers. A much more important and realistic consideration, however, was the sharp reduction of the ratio of British to sepoy troops to less than one to six, occasioned by the need for reinforcements in the Crimean War. After Dalhousie's departure this ratio was further drastically reduced by the withdrawal of six British regiments for service in Persia. Never before had the British garrison been allowed to become so weak. This condition was an open invitation to any dissident sepoys. Under the circumstances the absence of a more general rebellion is the surprising fact. The immediate factor, however, was the story of pig and beef fat used to grease new cartridges whose ends had to be bitten off to be fired. The story was only too true, and the sepoys, whether Muslim or Hindu, had been religiously defiled. The cartridges were ordered withdrawn from use, but the damage had already been done.

The episodes of massacre and heroic valor possess a special fascination. However, what needs emphasis is that the mutiny, largely confined to the sepoys in the Ganges valley and without large-scale popular support, was not a nationalistic uprising but was, instead, a blind outbreak of contagious madness based on accumulated grievances and encouraged by temporary British military weakness. The armies of Bombay and Madras, the recently conquered Sikhs, and the Gurkha troops recruited in Nepal remained loyal and fought against their rebellious countrymen. Dalhousie's telegraph wires helped to organize the British counterattack which within five months regained control. The new governor-general, "Clemency" Canning, gained his nickname for his refusal to yield to the British outcry for vengeance.

Nevertheless, the shock of the short-lived Sepoy Mutiny permanently altered the relationship of ruler and ruled. The distrust and fear imbedded in the hearts of the British community by these events could not be dispelled and resulted in a social barrier between Englishman and Indian. No longer were the old friendly and informal relationships possible. Like the Muslims before them, the British were isolated as a ruling caste to be tolerated for the time being. No liberal pronouncements by Queen Victoria could alter this development. The mutiny had created scars that could only be removed by independence.

Initially the establishment of law and order by the British Rāj had been welcomed by most princes and probably most of the people as the only solution to chaos. But when the "hands-off" policy was replaced by a policy of reforms according to English values, doubts and fears began to permeate the minds of thoughtful and suspicious Indians. Now the mutiny had aroused a compli-

mentary suspicion and fear in the British community. Henceforth mutual distrust could make possible no more than a temporary working accommodation between ruler and ruled in India.

In this chapter the story of India under alien rule has been surveyed and analysed from the initial Muslim conquest at the end of the twelfth century through the Sepoy challenge to the British Rāj in 1857. After the initial shock of conquest, Muslim political authority was passively accepted so long as the new ruling caste, whether united or divided, agreed to the limitation of its function to the political realm and did not interfere significantly with the traditional Hindu way of life. In fact, on this basis of mutual understanding the Muslims for almost 500 years enjoyed the cooperation of the class and caste leaders and the military support of the Rājput warriors. In village and town, life went on as before with little interference and even less assistance from above. Of course, Islam was not without influence. In certain regions, such as the Punjab and Bengal, substantial numbers were attracted by the egalitarian doctrines of Islam. In these areas and in the cities magnificent mosques were erected to serve the faithful, both immigrants and converts. Among the upper Hindu classes the Muslim practice of veiling their women was introduced. But on the whole the separation between a Muslim ruling caste and a vast Hindu subject population was mutually recognized. Only when Aurangzīb challenged this working arrangement in a misguided effort to create throughout India a truly Islamic state was the Indian spirit roused to opposition and active rebellion. Once roused, however, it soon demonstrated the fundamental weakness of the Mughal Empire whose authority rested on a tolerant policy and a recognition of its limited political role.

In the ensuing breakdown of political unity and struggle for power, the French and English companies were tempted to join the Indian carrion feeding on the corpse of the

Mughal body politic. Whether, left to their own devices, Indian leaders could have resolved the problem of political disunity is highly unlikely in view of their previous record. In any case, the instinctive need felt by English merchants for law and order led the company and then the government step by step into the Indian vacuum until they created a greater unity and order than India had yet known.

The British Rāj, established with such apparent ease, was deceptive. The Hindu soul, already awakened from its torpor by Muslim persecution, was unwittingly provided with fresh fuel by the introduction of alien and unsettling Western ideas and values. As yet, the leading Hindu minds, with traditional tolerance, were still wrestling with these new conceptions, while most of

the defeated Muslims rejected them without inspection. The Sepoy Mutiny was merely an unplanned explosion without significant intellectual leadership but, underneath the surface, Hindu intellectuals, dismayed at India's degradation, were searching with typical adaptiveness for some new synthesis that, while retaining the essence of the Hindu heritage, could effectively meet the challenge of the West. By 1858 only a few small symptoms of this intellectual ferment had made an appearance; like an iceberg, most of its future strength was still submerged. After the suppression of the mutiny both the British and the Indians were slow in recognizing the potentialities of this quest whose roots went back to the time of Aurangzib—a quest whose development we shall subsequently examine.

SIGNIFICANT DATES

712	Muslim conquest of Sind
997–1030	Rule and raids of Mahmud of Ghazni
1192	Decisive victory of Muhammed of Ghor
1206–1526	Delhi Sultanate
1327	Peak of Muslim conquest of India
1336–1565	South Indian Hindu state of Vijayanagar
1398	Sack of Delhi by Timūr
1526–1857	Mughal Dynasty founded by Bābur
1469–1538	Nānak, Founder of the Sikhs
1556–1605	Rule of Akbar
1659–1707	Rule of Aurangzīb; Collapse of Mughal Power
1498	Arrival of Vasco da Gama at Calicut
1757	Battle of Plassey
1772–1784	Governorship of Warren Hastings
1784	Pitt's India Act
1786–1793	Governor-Generalship of Lord Cornwallis
1798–1805	Governor-Generalship of Marquis of Wellesley
1813	End of Company's Trade Monopoly
1813–1823	Governor-Generalship of Marquis of Hastings
1818	Final Defeat of Mārathās
1828–1835	Governor-Generalship of Lord Wm. Bentinck
1828	Rām Mohun Roy founds Brāhmo Samāj
1843	Annexation of Sind
1848–1856	Governor-Generalship of Earl of Dalhousie
1849	Final Defeat of Sikhs and Annexation of the Punjab
1857	Sepoy Mutiny
1858	End of East India Company

SELECTED READINGS

See Chapter Three for general accounts.

Ahmad, Aziz, *Studies in Islamic Culture in the Indian Environment*. Oxford: Clarendon Press, 1966.

Bearce, G. D., *British Attitudes Towards India, 1784–1858*. London: Oxford University Press, 1961.

*Edwardes, Michael, *A History of India*. New York: Grosset and Dunlap, 1970.

Embree, Ainslie T., *Charles Grant and British Rule in India*. London: Allen and Unwin, 1962.

Furber, Holden, *John Company at Work*. Cambridge, Mass.: Harvard University Press, 1948.

Graham, G. S., *Great Britain and the Indian Ocean*. Oxford: Clarendon Press, 1967.

Harlow, V. T., *The Founding of the Second British Empire*. 2 vols.; New York: Longmans Green, 1952–1964.

*Lach, Donald F., *India in the Eyes of Europe*. Chicago: University of Chicago Press, 1968.

Majumdar, R. C., *History of the Freedom Movement*. 3 vols.; Calcutta: Firma K. L. Mukhopadhyay, 1962–1963.

————, *The Sepoy Mutiny*. Calcutta: Firma K. L. Mukhopadhyay, 1963.

Moreland, W. H., *India at the Death of Akbar*. Delhi: Atma Ram, 1962.

Pandey, B. N., *The Introduction of English Law into India*. London: Asia Publishing House, 1967.

Russell, Ralph, and Islam, Khurshidul, *Three Mughal Poets*. Cambridge, Mass.: Harvard University Press, 1968.

Sadiq, Muhammad, *History of Urdu Literature*. London: Oxford University Press, 1964.

Sardesai, Govind S., *A New History of the Maratha People*. 3 vols.; Bombay: Phoenix, 1957–1968.

Seal, Anil, *The Emergence of Indian Nationalism*. Vol. 1; London: Cambridge University Press, 1968.

Singh, Khushwant, *A History of the Sikhs*. 2 vols.; Princeton: Princeton University Press, 1963–1966.

*Spear, Percival, *A History of India*, Vol. II. Baltimore: Penguin Books, 1966.

————, *The Twilight of the Mughals*. Cambridge: Cambridge University Press, 1951.

Stokes, Eric, *The English Utilitarians and India*. Oxford: Clarendon Press, 1959.

*Tinker, Hugh, *South Asia*. New York: Praeger, 1966.

*Woodruff, Philip, *Men Who Ruled India*. 2 vols.; New York: Schocken Books, 1964.

CHAPTER THIRTEEN

BARBARIANS IN EAST ASIA: MONGOLS, MANCHUS AND WESTERNERS

We left China under the Southern Sung dynasty (1127–1279) on the verge of conquest by the Mongols led by the able successors of Chingiz Khan. In spite of the loss of the Yellow River homeland of Chinese civilization to tribesmen from the northeast who established the Chin dynasty in northern China, the Southern Sung by diligent development of the resources of southern China had secured a greater income and supported a larger army than any of its predecessors. This economic expansion had been substantially aided by the southward migration of many well-to-do Chinese who brought with them capital, retainers, and the techniques of intensive farming. No Chinese dynasty was richer in scholarship, philosophy, and both the industrial and fine arts. Therefore, the Mongol conquest of this strong and wealthy state was no mean accomplishment.

THE MONGOLS

Although the conquest of China was the Mongol's most impressive achievement, they operated on a far larger stage, affecting directly or indirectly the entire East, and even penetrating and creating alarm in the West. Reference has previously been made to the contest between "the desert and the sown," between the pastoral nomadic and the settled agricultural ways of life. Much of the time the two contrasting economies, where they directly confronted each other, complemented each other, exchanging goods and services with a minimum of friction; but frequently this peaceful relationship was ruptured by climatic changes or by the actions of ambitious or shortsighted individuals on either side.

Although greatly inferior in population and organization, the feuding tribes under a dynamic leader could cooperate in assembling highly mobile armies of experienced warriors which were more than a match for the larger bodies of infantry on which the agricultural states predominantly relied. The nomad's life of herding, hunting, and tribal warfare produced the world's finest cavalry. When the use of the stirrup became general by the fourth century, these expert horsemen, trained by a lifetime in the saddle, could stand in their stirrups and discharge from their powerful compound bows armor-piercing arrows with devastating accuracy at ranges up to 600 feet. The famous "Parthian shot" refers to firing the bow over the shoulder while withdrawing, a maneuver at which the Mongols were also expert. Hunting and raiding had accustomed them to close cooperation in small units of five to a hundred horsemen, charging, scattering, and reforming at a variety of signals given by their commanders. Each warrior had a string of three or more mounts to carry his needs and, in dire straits, to provide sustenance. Normally, however, they lived off the land utilizing their remounts for maximum mobility. On one occasion a Mongol army covered 270 miles in three days, catching the enemy completely unprepared. Is it any wonder that such space-consuming forces could create an empire extending from the Pacific to Europe? To oppose such horsemen with mounted farmers proved impractical and, for the most part, China depended for its cavalry on the employment of contingents from allied nomads on the frontier, units of questionable loyalty.

THE MONGOL CONQUESTS

Many reasons have been put forward to explain the rise and the success of the Mon-

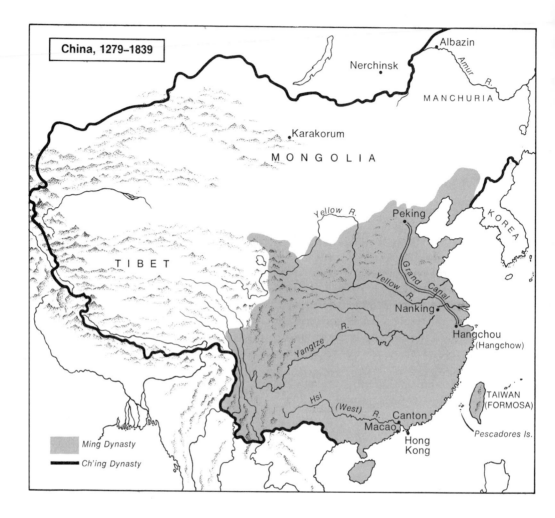

China, 1279–1839

Albazin
Nerchinsk
MANCHURIA
Amur R.

Karakorum
MONGOLIA

Yellow R.
Peking
KOREA

TIBET

Yellow R.
Grand Canal
Nanking

Hangchou
(Hangchow)

Yangtze R.

Hsi (West) R.
Canton
Macao
Hong Kong
TAIWAN (FORMOSA)
Pescadores Is.

Ming Dynasty
Ch'ing Dynasty

gols under the initial leadership of Chingiz Khan (named Temüjin, he received this title from a Mongol assembly in 1206), but few of them seem to stand up under analysis. The first point to be recognized is that there was nothing original in either the strategy and tactics of his forces or the organization and administration of his conquests; in every instance he drew on the proven practices of previous nomadic leaders. His warriors were grouped in the standard units of tens, hundreds, and thousands, and arms and equipment were standardized to simplify the problems of production and supply. In battle, the old nomadic tactics of the feigned rout and the flanking movement by his best

troops, known as the "Standard Sweep," were most commonly used. His campaign strategy called for the customary use of cunning, intrigue, treachery, and mobility to deal with his foes one by one before they had time to combine their forces. In victory over urban areas, he followed the nomadic practice of slaughtering all captives who could not be usefully employed because the marginal steppe economy could not support any surplus population. Of course, news of this practice sometimes had the psychological effect of inducing submission rather than resistance by other cities. His extensive use of spies, rumormongers, and psychological warfare to ease the path of conquest was no novelty in the arsenal of nomadic warfare. His employment of captives as a screen for his troops when storming a fortified city was also nothing new. Like his predecessors, he did not hesitate to take advantage of military talent and techniques wherever he found them, especially in that most difficult and distasteful aspect of warfare for nomads —the siege.

In administration, he also followed precedent by employing educated and experienced civil servants who were picked from the conquered. The construction of post roads to speed communications throughout his far-flung domains had been part of the program of former nomad conquerors, although on a smaller scale. His law code which established uniform regulations and punishments followed precedent. Finally, the division of his realm among his male heirs by his principal wife was in full accord with tribal custom.

In short, any explanation of Mongol success that singles out the genius of Chingiz Khan as the chief factor must be based on less tangible considerations, such as his personality, his ability to pick out able and loyal lieutenants, his uncanny timing in campaigns and battles, the boldness and daring of his vision, and the thoroughness with which he enforced his authority and carried out his decisions—not on any originality in his techniques. Even the story of his youthful hardships and narrow escapes as a hunted fugitive and of his long and arduous rise to power, both of which sharpened his wits and taught him many lessons in leadership, was by no means unique in tribal annals.

His father, a Mongol chieftain, died while he was still a boy, too young and inexperienced to be accepted as a leader. Escaping and eluding those who sought to liquidate him, he demonstrated over the years an ability to survive that attracted followers willing to obey his iron discipline and join their fortunes to his. The mere fact of this ordeal, in combination with his personality, built up a determination to conquer or die

that led him from conquest to conquest. In any case, even if he had been content with regaining his tribal territory, fear of vengeance inspired his old foes and despoilers to combine and intrigue against him. Destiny had marked out his course, although the outcome was still in doubt.

There were plenty of precedents for the creation of a nomadic empire. Ever since the collapse of the Han dynasty, "barbarian" states had been formed, including substantial portions of northern China, but in the illiterate Mongol society little but legends could be known about them. More to the point was the current rule of northern China by Tungusic tribesmen, ancestors of the Manchus. And even more pertinent was the example of the Mongol power to the south whose relative wealth rested on control of the northern trade route to the West, as well as that of other "barbarian" powers who controlled the southern and western parts of the trade routes.

Nominally the future world-conquerer had inherited the position of adopted son and vassal of the Mongol ruler to the south, and his mind readily grasped the addition to military power provided by the control of trade. Indeed, all his subsequent campaigns, after overthrowing his overlord, can be explained in terms of expanding his control of trade, as well as of securing plunder to reward his warriors. Especially is this motivation evident in the direction of his final campaign against the rebellious Tibetan power that controlled the southern route. His successors might become more interested in establishing territorial states supported by land taxes, but Chingiz Khan, following nomadic precedent, was more concerned with building his personal military power supported by levies on the growing East-West trade which he did his best to foster. Without this military might which he transmitted to his heirs their ambitions could never have been realized. He was a typical nomad leader who sought to exploit the trade ties between the civilizations without abandoning the nomad's way of life; his successors ultimately became part of the civilizations they conquered, a guarantee of their eventual overthrow.

Another explanation of Mongol success asserts that it was made possible by the preceding "barbarian" blows suffered by the civilizations, and certainly there is a sound basis for this argument. In the previous centuries Turkish-speaking nomads from the western steppes had infiltrated and gained control of most of the territories of Islam, and in the Far East other barbarian invaders had forced the Sung dynasty to relinquish the Yellow River cradle of Chinese civilization. On the other hand, the military superiority demonstrated by their success should have made these invaders abler defenders of their adopted civilizations, despite the softening effects of their new life. Most were familiar with nomad-type warfare and enjoyed much greater resources and superior technology. Moreover, the Shah of Khwarism, who had just gained supremacy in Iran, was still a nomad power, and he and his troops possessed the fanatical inspiration of recent converts to Islam. Yet, in fact, except for fortified cities, these "civilized" powers presented to Chingiz Khan even less of a challenge than the barbarian powers that he had recently overcome. In the Middle East the Mongol advance was checked only by the professional army of the Egyptian Mamluk regime and in China the stoutest resistance was offered by the Southern Sung regime to campaigns and sieges that lasted more than 25 years (1251–1279). Therefore, any explanation of Mongol success based on the weakened and divided nature of the opposition must be subject to serious reservations.

Greatest credit must be given to the determination, personal magnetism, and self-discipline of Chingiz Khan, as well as to his skill and good luck. With iron discipline he welded together the centrifugally minded Mongol and allied tribesmen into a mobile, streamlined fighting machine that obeyed his commands without question. The maintenance of Mongol momentum under his successors may be ascribed to his establishment of a select group of the ablest young warriors who were even more rigorously trained under his personal supervision and who furnished skilled and loyal officers as needed. The status of a member of this elite corps took precedence over the captain of 1000 horsemen. The effectiveness of this centralized organization of the empire is reflected in its duration for more than a century in spite of the centrifugal tendencies of the tribal way of life.

Although the uncertainties and destruction that accompanied conquest may have temporarily disrupted trade, the Mongols' greatest contribution was the fostering of a greatly increased exchange of goods and ideas via the secure routes that they established across the steppes of central Asia. During the century of Mongol domination, merchant adventurers like Marco Polo and even churchmen could undertake the journey to China with every expectation of returning safely to their homelands. Marco Polo is renowned not for the uniqueness of his trips but for the descriptive report that he wrote. In fact, many Europeans traveled to and from distant China during the era of Mongol supremacy. The subsequent interruptions of the flow of goods and ideas were to contribute to the quest for a sea route. At the time, however, the exchange between China and the Middle East was larger and more significant than it had ever been.

Under the tolerant Mongol rule Islam became permanently established in southwestern and northwestern China, while conversely Chinese influence on the fine and industrial arts of Iran is most impressive. In the eighth century, Islam had gained from China the secret of making paper; now even more dynamic and influential Chinese inventions were transmitted westward, for instance, printing, paper money, and gunpowder. In short, the Mongol regime contributed to the advancement of that basic trend which has been noted as early as prehistoric times, the enlargement of the area and volume of intercourse and exchange of peoples, goods, and ideas. For this service to mankind it deserves to be remembered.

THE YÜAN DYNASTY (1271–1368)

The conquest of the Southern Sung was completed under the leadership of Chingiz Khan's most talented grandson, Khubilai, who became Great Khan in 1260 and the first ruler (1271–1294) of the Yüan Dynasty. Still fired by the Mongol drive for military expansion this vigorous ruler sent forth expedition after expedition, by land and by sea, but without enduring results. As has already been mentioned, two unsuccessful assaults were launched against Japan utilizing the navy inherited from the Sung. Other naval expeditions brought back envoys and exacted tribute from a number of states in Southeast Asia and both coasts of India. By land, repeated expeditions into Vietnam and Burma made the imperial presence felt, but they tended to bog down in the unfamiliar and difficult terrain and climate.

As Great Khan, as well as Emperor of China, Khubilai possessed a far broader outlook than his introverted Sung predecessors. After all, China was only the richest portion of his vast domain. Large numbers of non-Chinese were employed to staff his Chinese civil service, especially the top echelon. The embittered hostility of the Confucian scholar class of southern China encouraged a stratification of the bureaucracy with Mongols in key positions, non-Chinese (predominantly Muslim) at the next level, northern Chinese whose adaptability had been demonstrated by service to the "barbarian" Chin dynasty holding secondary positions, and southern Chinese filling a quota of less than 25 percent at the bottom. As a result of the subordination of the best qualified Confucian scholar-officials in their own land, seditious senti-

ments were widespread and rebellion was an ever-present menace, as Marco Polo reported.

Mongol garrisons were maintained at major cities to discourage outbreaks and were regularly rotated before they were enervated by urban luxury. Recognizing the need of keeping in touch with the steppe source of Mongol strength, Khubilai built a new capital at Peking (also called Khanbaligh, "the Khan's city," and transcribed as Cambaluc by Marco Polo) and erected a summer capital in eastern Mongolia. To transport the grain tax and other needs to the new center two and one-half million laborers dug a connecting canal from the terminus of the Grand Canal at the Yellow River.

Unemployed, but talented, Chinese scholars developed two significant additions to Chinese literature, the drama and the novel, which had begun to take shape as early as the T'ang dynasty. Previously these two literary forms employing, as they did, the vernacular language to appeal to a wider audience had tended to be shunned by the Confucian scholars, who were trained in composition in the classical literary language. The Mongol reliance on non-Chinese officials, untrained in the classical language, encouraged the employment of a more popular style even in government documents. The drama evolved for the entertainment of urban and court audiences, while the novel derived from the tales of storytellers who traveled from market to market regaling the peasants. This contrast is apparent in their themes, style, and language. The drama is a more sophisticated, stylized art form drawing on romantic and military adventures and frequently reflecting the clash between individual desires and Confucian social precepts. The novel, while also dealing with heroic adventures, uses more earthy language and humor and more often concerns peasants and their problems. Both forms have been carefully sifted under Communist auspices to discover suitable presentations of class struggle, with more fruitful results in the case of the novel.

THE MING AND MANCHU DYNASTIES

By the mid-fourteenth century the descendants of Khubilai Khan were so absorbed by intrafamily struggles for power that they neglected the maintenance of their authority in central and southern China. As a result, rebel movements arose and grew in strength, especially in the Yangtze valley. Also the famine and destruction caused by an abnormal sequence of droughts and floods in the north undermined the regime both psychologically and economically, The rebel leaders, many of whom were of humble origins, sought patriotic support by advocating the expulsion of aliens and the establishment of a native dynasty which would restore the ethnocentric outlook of the Sung. Some even claimed descent from the Sung. As usual, secret societies, religious prophesies, and superstitious appeals were drawn on to reinforce and broaden the base of a leader's support.

Out of the struggle for survival among these warlords, Chu Yüan-chang (1328–1398), an orphaned peasant who had learned to read and write as a novice in a Buddhist monastery, ultimately emerged victorious and founded the Ming (Brilliant) dynasty (1368–1644). Most decisive in his rise to power was the capture of Nanking in 1356, which served as a strong, centrally located base of operations. After 12 years spent in consolidating his control over central and southern China, he advanced against the Mongols and captured Peking. Although the Mongols were expelled from China proper, their power was not broken and they remained a major menace. In partial recognition of this fact a succeeding Ming emperor moved his capital from Nanking to Peking in 1421, constructing what remains today one of the most impressive capital cities in the world.

With the Ming emphasis on a conservative restoration, there were no substantial innovations in the government and culture of the Middle Kingdom. In government, the Mongol tendency of concentrating more authority in the hands of the ruler and of exercising a more direct control over the provinces was perpetuated and enhanced by the Ming emperors. But the relatively small size of the bureaucracy belied these autocratic pretensions. As before, the effectiveness of the central government at the local level depended on the voluntary and unpaid cooperation and services of the scholar-landlord class in return for the privileged status it enjoyed.

One unique, though temporary, phenomenon sponsored by the second vigorous Ming ruler should be mentioned. Following the maritime interests of the Southern Sung and Khubilai Khan, seven major naval expeditions were dispatched under the command of the Muslim eunuch, Cheng Ho, between 1405 and 1433 for the political purpose of impressing the states along the maritime trade routes and of securing recognition of Chinese suzerainty.

These were no small-scale explorations, but mighty flotillas of ships up to 400 feet long that transported as many as 28,000 men across the vast distances of the south Asian seas. In comparison, the ill-fated Spanish Armada more than a century and a half later carried fewer men on a much shorter voyage. The impression made on local rulers can be imagined when this fleet hove into sight, dropped anchor, and discharged more than 20,000 troops in full battle array. These voyages reached Hormuz and Aden at the mouths of the Persian Gulf and Red Sea, as well as various points on the African coast, and carried back to the Ming court envoys and tribute from some 50 states, as well as exotic items such as zebras and giraffes.

Although Chinese capability for exploration was clearly demonstrated by these feats of seamanship, this was not their purpose. For the most part, Cheng Ho stuck closely to the established routes of trade. Nor was their purpose particularly to foster trade, to conquer, or to colonize. Under Sung auspices merchants from southern China had greatly expanded their role in maritime trade and established overseas colonies numbering in the thousands in the chief trading centers of Southeast Asia. On the Confucian social scale the despised merchant was near the bottom, and he operated overseas at his own risk. The antitrade attitude of the Ming era is illustrated by its failure to exploit, as the Southern Sung had done, this potential source of tax revenue. Nevertheless, Cheng Ho, it will be recalled, did support Malacca against its enemies in return for concessions to Chinese merchants. Whether this policy derived more from considerations of power than of trade is open to debate. But from the government's point of view overseas trade was of negligible importance because China had little need of imports. This attitude was later to be reflected in China's reaction to Western trade.

The main purpose of these expeditions was to enforce the political conception of the Middle Kingdom by which all known states should acknowledge the suzerainty and supremacy of China and its ruler, the Son of Heaven, as the single source and center of world civilization. It is remarkable that at this time of Ming naval power the Chinese coastal trade was plagued by Japanese and Chinese pirates, forcing the transport of grain revenues to Peking by canal, but in spite of protests to the Japanese government they were recognized as freebooters posing no challenge to the Chinese conception of suzerainty. These spectacular and costly voyages were suddenly and permanently terminated primarily because they had served their purpose but also because all imperial resources were needed to construct the magnificent new capital at Peking and to meet the revived Mongol menace.

In the arts, no civilization that could create such a masterpiece of architectural and landscape design as the imperial palace

at Peking can be considered esthetically moribund. In other media, however, though many individual works of genius can be singled out, Chinese creative talents may be judged as having passed their zenith. The emphasis on seeking models of perfection in the achievements of the past tended to stifle originality. Although the porcelain ware produced at the imperial kilns was technologically superior, the multicolored decoration sometimes used does not possess the esthetic appeal of the austere monochromes of the Sung.

In literature and philosophy, the same backward-looking emphasis on past perfection produced massive compilations and a profusion of scholarly commentaries on previous works but discouraged the striking out on new paths. In volume this age of analysis probably surpassed the total production of the more than 2000 years of Chinese civilization that preceded it. Yet the one influential development in philosophy, the promotion of Confucianist "Idealism" by Wang Yang-ming (1472–1529) against the orthodox "Rationalism" of Chu Hsi, was significantly little more than a restatement of the position of a contemporary opponent of Chu Hsi.

Generally, Wang opposed Chu Hsi's stress on dualism in favor of emphasis on the unity of reality. Even limited truth could not be found by external examination, but only by intuitive introversion. In support of this view he made much of Mencius' statement; "All things are complete within me." His stronger stress on meditation and intuition narrowed the gap between his school of Confucianism and Buddhism, especially the Ch'an sect. Although his impact in China—where Buddhism had long since passed its prime—was limited, his views gained a wide vogue in Japan, where Zen Buddhism in particular was enjoying a vigorous development.

In due course the familiar factors of the dynastic cycle came into play, leading to an increasing decentralization with the consequent deterioration in imperial revenues at a time of growing pressure on the frontiers. Finally, a rebel leader overthrew the Ming dynasty, opening the way for another "barbarian" dynasty which was headed by the Manchus, Tungusic tribesmen whose able leaders had for several generations been building a unified military power that incorporated Mongolian and Chinese contingents. The young commander of the forces defending the Manchu frontier, Wu San-kue, for reasons both personal and political came to terms with a more "civilized" Manchu leader, destroyed the untutored rebels, and served his Manchu masters well in the extended conquest of the rest of China.

Emulating their Mongol predecessors, the Manchus, after 40 years occupied in the consolidation of their authority over the whole of China, established garrisons at key points and placed their most skilled administrators in the top posts of the Chinese civil service. Thanks to their close association with the Chinese in southern Manchuria during their rise to power, they were much more deeply imbued with Chinese culture than the Mongol conquerors had been. Chinese scholar-officials had been employed to educate their leaders and to organize a Chinese-style governmental system to overcome the decentralizing tendencies of tribalism. Indeed, following the conquest, the Manchu emperors recognized the threat of absorption and loss of identity by decreeing the retention of Manchu garb for their people and distinguishing features for their Chinese subjects, such as the plaiting of the hair in a queue. In addition, the Manchurian homeland was set off as a preserve where the vigor of tribal life and hunting might maintain the martial virtues and provide a source of warriors accustomed to life in the saddle.

Another means of maintaining their military ability was a renewal of imperial expansion, especially during the reigns of the two ablest and longest-lived Manchu emperors, K'ang-hsi (1661–1722) and Ch'ien-lung (1736–1795). In any case, their associ-ation with the eastern Mongol tribes attracted them into an involvement with Mongols farther to the west. Moreover, the relationship of the western Mongols with Tibetan Buddhism compelled the Manchus to seek control of Tibet. The end result of Manchu imperialism was to incorporate within the Chinese empire more territory and more people than it had ever previously encompassed, except under the Mongols, and ultimately to bring the Chinese government into contact with the advance echelons of Russian imperialism which were expanding across the Siberian steppes.

These impressive, but costly, exploits, as well as the inevitable softening of the Manchu martial fiber despite the efforts to check it, combined to stir up the internal dissidence that was symptomatic of the declining phase of a dynastic cycle. Even before the abdication of Ch'ien-lung after ruling for a Chinese cycle of 60 years the frequency of rebellions signaled the deterioration of the authority and control of the central government and the increasingly desperate situation of the peasantry, who were squeezed between population growth and the exploitation of the privileged scholar-landlord class. Therefore, before Westerners, armed with the technological advantages of the Industrial Revolution, began to press forcefully for special privileges, the alien Manchu regime was encountering significant internal troubles that would undermine its capability for resistance.

CHINA AND THE WEST (1516 – 1839)

Although during this era China engaged in trade with the West for more than three centuries, the Western impact was negligible until the last half century. In fact, during the eighteenth century the reverse was the case; Chinese government and philosophy, and things Chinese, enjoyed a wide vogue among the upper classes of the West. Philosophers of the Enlightenment saw in the Confucian state an ideal example of rational organization that was staffed with a bureaucracy selected according to merit. Chinese porcelain ware, wallpaper, and other goods were clearly superior in quality to their European equivalents. Formal gardens were enriched by a wide variety of novel Chinese plants and flowers and had to be decorated with pagoda-type structures to be stylish. Not until China's weakness was exposed when confronted in the nineteenth century by the advancing technology of the West, did a reversal of attitude take place. Initially Jesuit and other Roman Catholic missionary scholars transmitted to the West very favorable and even flattering reports of Chinese civilization during the heyday of the Manchu dynasty. Later, during the nineteenth century the decline of the Manchu regime exasperated merchants and other aggressive Westernizers, who wrote exceedingly critical accounts of China's "backwardness"—that is, its reluctance to abandon its time-honored way of life in favor of Western ways.

From the beginning the Chinese government kept the West at arm's length, restricting the traders' residence and place of trade and applying to them the traditional system of group responsibility. Only for a brief period under one of the strongest Manchu emperors were these limitations relaxed. In short, the Middle Kingdom did not welcome Western traders with open arms.

The vast Chinese Empire produced within its boundaries almost all its essential needs, and Chinese overseas merchants were fully capable of supplying the need for tropical products from Southeast Asia. Therefore, first the Portuguese, and then their successors, were viewed as interlopers whose reputation for piracy and the use of force preceded them. Furthermore, their early actions in relations with China did nothing to discredit these reports. Finally, the Chinese government saw no reason to alter its traditional method of treating all alien regimes as tributaries of the single center and source of civilization, the Middle Kingdom ruled by the Son of Heaven. Westerners

found such an unequal approach to international relations not only unfamiliar but intolerable. Not until the nineteenth century, however, when the volume of trade with China grew rapidly thanks to the expanding Chinese demand for opium, was any Western government prepared to use force.

After seizing the transit port of Malacca in the Malay Peninsula from the Muslims in 1511, the Portuguese were not slow in pressing on to China. The friendly relations that they established with the Chinese community in Malacca, in contrast to their unremitting hostility toward the Muslims, undoubtedly encouraged them to send a squadron to reconnoiter the Chinese coast in 1516. The next year another expedition transported an envoy to Canton who finally gained permission to go to Peking in 1520, but the era of good feelings soon came to an end. The Portuguese policy of securing fortified bases of operation had led them to select an island off Canton as a point of rendezvous and rest. Now a vigorous commander secured this position by building a fort and by subjecting the Chinese population to Portuguese rule. The reaction of the Chinese government was amazingly prompt. An expedition razed the fort and expelled the garrison, and the envoy was returned to Canton in chains where he subsequently died in 1523.

For the next 35 years the Portuguese carried on an illicit trade from fortified island bastions off various Chinese ports. One by one, however, these posts were lost to Chinese forces until the Chinese government decided that the Portuguese could be more easily controlled if they were granted a single base for closely regulated trade. Thus, in 1557, the Portuguese gained the right of residence at Macao which was separated from China Proper by a wall manned by Chinese troops. Actually, however, Macao served primarily as a way station until the closure of Japan because the Portuguese had few goods that the Chinese were interested in purchasing.

A century after the arrival of the Portuguese the Dutch and the English put in a forceful appearance on the Chinese scene. In 1604 Dutch ships arrived at Macao in search of trade, but the Portuguese persuaded the Chinese authorities that they were pirates. A Dutch attack on Macao in 1622 confirmed this view of their character. Thereafter, the Dutch carried on an illicit trade first from a fortified base in the Pescadores and then from a base on Formosa that they established in 1630. This outpost was lost in 1662 to the renowned Chinese pirate and Ming champion, Koxinga, but the Dutch gained favor with the Manchu regime by offering their assistance in the suppression of Koxinga's successors. Ultimately, in 1683 Koxinga's grandson surrendered in return for acceptance as a duke of the realm, and Taiwan (Formosa) was for the first time made a part of the Chinese Empire.

Meanwhile, the first English effort to open up trade was even less tactful and auspicious than that of the Dutch. In 1637 Captain John Weddell arrived at Macao with the written consent of the Portuguese viceroy at Goa to conduct trade. The local Portuguese, however, sought to discourage him by every possible delaying tactic. Finally, exasperated at these delays, Captain Weddell sailed up to Canton, fired broadsides, and forced trade. As a result, the English did not gain permission to trade until 1699.

As elsewhere in the East, the Portuguese actively supported Jesuit missionary activity in China. Thanks to the Jesuit policies of adapting the Christian message to local customs and practices and of offering their services to the local rulers, Roman Catholicism gained substantial acceptance in China in a comparatively short time. The able Jesuit, Matteo Ricci, well-versed in European science and technology, laid the foundations for this early success, and his story is an excellent illustration of Jesuit missionary technique.

Arriving in China in 1583, he soon adopted Buddhist garb and dedicated himself to a study of Chinese religion and philos-

ophy for 11 years. By 1594 he had made himself a Chinese scholar and, realizing that Buddhism no longer commanded respect, switched to the dress of a Confucian scholar. In 1601 he obtained permission to reside in Peking where he offered his services to the government and concentrated on converting influential scholar-officials. This task was facilitated not only by the respect he commanded as a Confucian scholar but also by his adoption of Chinese terminology and his toleration of ancestor worship as not essentially inconsistent with Christian doctrine. When he died in 1610, his broad-minded policy left Christianity firmly established at court with the right for missionaries to travel and preach in the provinces as well. His Jesuit successors proved equally well-educated and even secured official positions in the central government. When the Manchu regime took over, the skills and talents of Jesuit missionaries continued to be recognized and utilized.

During the seventeenth century, however, Spanish Franciscan, Dominican, and Augustinian missionaries penetrated China from their base in the Philippines. Appalled at the Jesuit compromises in China, as elsewhere—especially the acceptance of ancestor worship—they laid their complaints before the papacy, initiating the long and damaging Rites Controversy. In the early eighteenth century two papal embassies were sent to China to eradicate these Jesuit "abuses." K'ang-hsi was enraged at this attempted interference in the affairs of the Middle Kingdom by a "barbarian" prince and announced that no alien decrees contrary to his wishes could be enforced in China, especially if they were deemed by him to be subversive of Chinese customs. Christian missionaries were given the choice of conforming to his will or of leaving the country. Since the papal edict condemning the Jesuit accommodations did not become final until 1742, many missionaries found it possible to comply with the imperial position.

While the other Westerners approached

by sea, Russian adventurers reached the northwestern land frontier of the Chinese Empire in the mid-seventeenth century. Their effort to open diplomatic relations foundered on the issue of acknowledging Chinese suzerainty. Yet they pressed ahead, erecting forts in the Amur River valley. K'ang-hsi responded to this encroachment by dispatching an army that captured the Russian post at Albazin in 1685. This clash led to negotiations in which the Jesuits served as intermediaries. In 1689 the Treaty of Nerchinsk, the first between China and a Western state, was concluded defining the boundary generally along the northern watershed of the Amur River and providing for limited overland trade with Peking and the mutual extradition of criminals. As a result, the Russians had to evacuate their posts in the Amur Basin and to accept a frontier that provided the basis for Communist Chinese charges of Russian Imperialism in subsequent acquisitions.

By 1757 a tightly-regulated system, known as the Co-hong, had been established to control the overseas Western trade at the single port of Canton and to keep their representatives at arm's length from the government. This system, with some modifications, remained in force until the "opening" of China as a result of the Opium War (1839–1842).

The Co-hong was composed of those Chinese merchants who were licensed to deal with Western traders. Their number varied, but normally one or more merchants were responsible for all the relations with the traders of a single Western state. Furthermore, in return for their monopoly the Co-hong was responsible as a group for Western behavior. Not only did they handle all trade but they also collected all taxes, took care of all the needs of their customers during the trading season from August to April, and were responsible for settling any issues that might arise. If a Western state failed to comply with the rules, the Chinese merchant was required to stop all trade with its merchants.

No European was allowed to conduct relations directly with any official of the Chinese government. During the trading season only male agents were granted passes to reside in the narrow factory area at Canton, although occasionally they might enjoy escorted outings in Canton's parks and gardens. Their wives and families had to stay in Macao to which they, too, had to retire at the close of the trading season.

During the eighteenth century the volume of Western trade with China grew rapidly as the taste for Chinese tea spread in the West. Tea came to account for more than one half of Western purchases from China. Until the development of a large Chinese market for opium, however, the trade was handicapped by the lack of enough items salable in China to balance it. As a result, Western merchants had to ship large amounts of specie to China to pay for their purchases. Although Western traders became increasingly exasperated at their diplomatic, legal, and commercial disabilities, conflict was finally precipitated by the opium issue. Therefore, a brief sketch of the growth of this problem is necessary.

The smoking of a mixture of tobacco and opium appears to have been initiated about 1650 by the Dutch on Formosa as a specific remedy against malaria. By 1700 this combination was being used for its narcotic effect. In 1729, when the annual importation totaled about 200 chests of 130 to 150 pounds each, the problem was extensive enough to gain recognition in an imperial edict that prohibited the establishment of new opium dens and the retail sale of opium for smoking. Nevertheless, the heavy duty was too lucrative to lead to a ban on importation. Instead, the government sought to prevent the local growth of the opium poppy. By 1800, however, the ill-effects of this habit, which had by then produced an annual importation of less than 5000 chests, could no longer be ignored. An imperial edict forbade both the importation and production of opium for the welfare of the Chinese people. But the traffic in opium had become too valuable to both Westerners and Chinese to be cut off by such an order. The largest importer, the English East India Company, which obtained its supply of opium from India and retained its monopoly of British trade with China until 1834, officially complied with the edict by employing non-Company vessels to smuggle its opium into China with the connivance of Chinese officials. Western shippers, including Americans, discharged their opium into hulks moored below Canton whence Chinese smugglers ferried it to delivery points on shore. So successful was this smuggling operation that by 1830 it had grown to 18,000 chests a year, creating for the first time an adverse balance of trade for China. But this was not the end of the story. When the Chinese government finally felt compelled to take forceful action in 1839, some 40,000 chests were shipped to the China market, but more vigorous enforcement of the prohibition by Chinese officials had already reduced sales in 1838.

On gaining independence, Americans had not been slow to enter the China trade. In 1784 the American ship, *Empress of China*, arrived at Canton, and by 1790 the Americans were second only to the English in the China trade. Although American merchants had thus developed rapidly a major stake in this trade, their government was unwilling to support them or other governments in pressing for a revision of the conditions of trade. From its point of view American merchants who engaged in trade with a country with which the United States did not have diplomatic relations did so at their own risk.

Nevertheless, the dynamic changes taking place in the West under the impact of the Industrial Revolution made other nations, especially Great Britain with its unquestioned supremacy on the high seas, less willing to tolerate the antiquated and humiliating terms imposed by Imperial China. The problems that the Westerners found most galling can be briefly described.

First in importance was the refusal of the Chinese government to agree to diplomatic intercourse on the basis of equality or, indeed, to permit any direct correspondence with Chinese officialdom. The British and other governments repeatedly sent embassies to Peking, most of which foundered on the issue of acknowledging the suzerainty of the Middle Kingdom by the performance of the kowtow. Fundamentally, the traditional attitudes of China and the West toward foreign relations were irreconcilable without a resort to force but, if the Chinese government could have been persuaded to accept the Western point of view, the other major differences could have been settled by negotiation.

A second source of irritation was the conflict between Western and Chinese juridical practices and conceptions. Westerners found wholly unfamiliar the Chinese application of group responsibility for the personal crime of one of their nationals. For example, if an American sailor sneaked ashore in search of excitement, killed a Chinese, and got back to his ship, he had to be identified and surrendered to Chinese justice or else all trade with American nationals might be stopped. Furthermore, Westerners failed to understand or appreciate Chinese judicial procedures and penalties. The Chinese definition of murder included any act that might possibly result in death. If an intoxicated sailor got into a fight that ended in the death of a Chinese, the death penalty was assessed. Thus, many cases defined in Western law as accidental manslaughter were deemed to be murder in Chinese law. Westerners scarcely appreciated the customary leniency toward foreigners of reducing the penalty for murder from decapitation to strangulation. Moreover, Chinese procedure authorized the use of various refined forms of torture to extract confessions, a practice that had generally gone out of favor in the West by the nineteenth century. Finally, Westerners were unhappy about having to submit any property or financial disputes to Chinese jurisdiction.

A third complaint was the legal limitation of trade to the city of Canton and the humiliating restrictions placed on it. Of course, from the Chinese point of view the permission to trade extended to these "barbarians" whose governments refused to pay tribute in acknowledgment of the suzerainty of the Middle Kingdom was an act of generosity and toleration that might be withdrawn at any time. In other words, it was a privilege, not a right, and the restrictions were essential to the control of contact with such "uncivilized" peoples. After all, they supplied nothing necessary to the Chinese economy, and the revenue for the government, while significant, was not essential. On the other hand, their bold disregard of the imperial edict against the importation of opium not only demonstrated their fundamental lawlessness but was producing an embarrassing drain of specie from China.

Although these problems supplemented the opium issue in bringing about the ensuing conflict, the real reasons were the fundamental changes taking place during these years both in the West and in China. While the Western nations were making rapid advances toward greater economic, political, and military strength which increased their sensitivity and belligerence, the outbreak of rebellions in China in the last years of the eighteenth century indicated that the Manchu dynasty had entered the declining phase of the dynastic cycle. A Manchu regime whose mandate was being questioned by increasing instances of internal dissent confronted a vigorous, expansionist West no longer willing to endure the terms of trade under which it had operated for more than a century.

In the final analysis, however, the precipitating factor was the opium issue whose seriousness had been recognized by years of debate at the imperial court over various proposed solutions. One group of officials advocated legalizing opium and placing a heavy duty on its importation to meet, in part, the growing economic difficulties of the imperial government. Another group, appealing to the moral responsibility of the emperor for the welfare of his people, advocated a full enforcement of the prohibition, even if it meant termination of trade with the West, pointing out that their opponents' proposal would not solve the problem of the drain of specie. Late in 1838 the emperor finally decided in favor of those advocating enforcement.

On March 10, 1839 the High Commissioner, Lin Tse-hsu, arrived in Canton empowered to "investigate and act." Just eight days later, on March 18, he acted by placing troops around the factories and ordering the Western merchants to surrender all opium stocks for destruction and to sign bonds against future importations on pain of death. Since the situation was hopeless, more than 20,000 chests of opium, worth 6 million dollars, were surrendered which, much to the amazement of Western merchants accustomed to dealing with corrupt Chinese officials, were totally destroyed by mixing the opium with lime. On the surrender of the opium the forceful commissioner permitted living conditions to return to normal and promised the resumption of trade once the bonds were signed. All except the British complied, although the Americans so qualified their acceptance that its effectiveness was questionable.

The British were compelled to withdraw to the island of Hongkong where their position was precarious until the arrival of two British warships in September. British merchants were galled at the necessity of employing American merchants to dispose of their cargoes and to obtain supplies and return cargoes for a commission. Nevertheless, although no other Western government would actively support the British, almost all Western merchants were sympathetic with the British stand. Finally, on November 3, the two British warships initiated hostilities by sinking four Chinese war junks. The so-called Opium War which was to revolutionize the relationship between China and the West had commenced.

THE REUNIFICATION OF JAPAN

When the Portuguese first reached Japan in 1543, they found the islands engulfed in bitter strife among a number of great lords (daimyō) whom they described as "petty kings." Initial observation might suggest that Japan, like Europe, was being divided into "nations" under rulers who of necessity were concentrating power in their hands to meet the challenge of survival. For more than a century feudal rights and status had been eroded by lords who sought to mobilize and develop all the resources and talents within their domains. Peasant infantrymen had replaced the mounted samurai as the backbone of military strength. Merchants organized in guilds received noble protection and encouragement to enhance the wealth of the daimyō. The feudal-type manor tended to be replaced by a village form of social and political organization which was directly regulated and taxed by the great lord. As a result of these social, economic, and political changes and the lords' quest for talent, social mobility had been greatly accelerated. Already the ruthless struggle for survival had extinguished many noble families and had created many new ones which had risen through their ability to adapt to the demands of this era of dynamic change. An untold number of peasant origin had gained recognition and wealth by superior talent and intelligence. The prestige attached to noble lineage undoubtedly led to the fabrication of pedigrees which, in many cases, concealed more humble origins. Although the Portuguese observers, who found so many familiar features in Japanese life, expected the political divisions to persist as in Europe, the greater cultural uniformity throughout Japan precluded such a result. It was only a question of when and by whom reunification would be accomplished. As it turned out, Japan was on the eve of this development at the hands of three great leaders of differing, but complementary, talents: Oda Nobunaga, Toyotomi

Hideyoshi, and Tokugawa Ieyasu. For an understanding of the result, their respective achievements must be briefly described.

Oda Nobunaga (1534–1582) was the scion of a new family that had recently gained a comparatively small territory including what is today the important city of Nagoya. His renown rests on his skill and ruthlessness as a warrior. His career of conquest began with the decisive defeat in 1560 of the leading daimyō in the area. In Japan, as elsewhere, nothing succeeds like success, and this and subsequent victories brought him a growing flood of new supporters. In 1568 he was strong enough to occupy the imperial capital, Kyōto, and to name a puppet as shōgun. A few years later, when this puppet proved uncooperative, Nobunaga simply removed him and thus, without fanfare, brought an end to the Ashikaga Shogunate. During the rest of his life, he and his generals and allies were kept busy consolidating their control of the central heartland of Honshū.

Among the most ardent opponents who challenged Nobunaga's rise to power were the militant Buddhist monasteries and communities. Therefore, over the objections of some of his advisors, he determined to break their power once and for all by a merciless program of destruction. A significant by-product of his hostility toward the Buddhists was his friendly attitude toward the Christian missionaries which facilitated the rapid rate of conversions. Perhaps this friendliness was also generated by his eagerness to gain knowledge of Western technology, especially regarding firearms.

In 1582, while Hideyoshi was engaged in a campaign in the west, Nobunaga was treacherously assassinated by one of his generals who hoped to consolidate his control before Hideyoshi could return. But he misjudged his major rival. On receipt of the news Hideyoshi promptly negotiated a truce, left posthaste for Kyōto picking up 30,000 reinforcements already en route to join him, and took the assassin by surprise before he could assemble an adequate force. Although

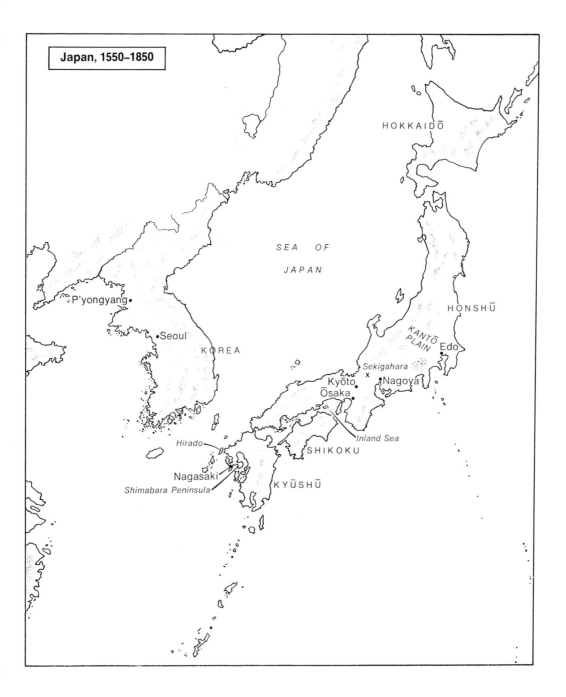

Japan, 1550–1850

Hideyoshi secured the guardianship of Nobunaga's infant grandson and control of Kyōto, more than 2 years were consumed in negotiations and fighting before he gained recognition from all of Nobunaga's vassals.

These years were the real test of the talents of this leader of peasant origin. His father had given up farming for a military career in the Oda service. Hideyoshi (1536–1598) followed in his father's footsteps at the age of twenty-two and demonstrated such exceptional ability that he was rapidly promoted to positions of command. Soon he was Nobunaga's most trusted general and chief advisor. His rise is the outstanding example of the social mobility of these turbulent times.

After gaining the recognition and support of Ieyasu, Nobunaga's major vassal, Hideyoshi proceeded to complete the reunification of Japan in less than 6 years by a combination of shrewd diplomacy and military campaigns. In contrast with his former master, Hideyoshi never committed his fortunes to decision by battle when essentially the same ends might be obtained by negotiation. Furthermore, when victorious, instead of destroying his foes, he added their strength to his by generously granting them new fiefs or lesser portions of their old estates. Foreknowledge of his generosity weakened resistance and facilitated settlements by negotiation.

Once he had completed the task of reunifying Japan, he was confronted with the problem of how to employ the surplus of warriors he commanded and how to consolidate his power by stabilizing Japanese society. Already in 1588 he had decreed the limitation of sword bearing to the samurai class and the surrender of arms held by peasant soldiers. Ironically he had cut off the avenue to advancement that had made possible his own rise to power, but his chief concern was to end the disorders of the past by restoring the traditional stratification of society with each class restricted to its specific function. Subsequent edicts froze samurai, farmers, and merchants in their respective professions by forbidding them to engage in any other.

For the same reason he cast a suspicious eye on the potentially subversive and disruptive growth of Christianity and reversed Nobunaga's policy of generous toleration. In 1587 his emissary roused the Jesuit leader in the middle of the night with a list of queries that indicate some of Hideyoshi's misgivings about Christian practices. On what grounds, he asked, was force authorized to gain converts? Why were Buddhists persecuted and their temples desecrated and destroyed? Why did Christians eat useful animals, such as cattle? Why were Portuguese merchants allowed to enslave Japanese and carry them off for sale? Without awaiting official answers to these questions, Hideyoshi issued two days later a decree ordering all missionaries to leave Japan within 20 days on pain of death. Furthermore, any ship bringing missionaries was to be confiscated.

In fact, however, Christian strength, even among his most important supporters, was too great for the immediate enforcement of this edict. By serving notice on both missionaries and Japanese converts that they must henceforth be more circumspect and restrained in their activities, the threatened prohibition served Hideyoshi's purpose. Not until his authority was secure and some Spanish Franciscans ignored his orders, did he take positive action.

In the 1590s the first Spanish Franciscans arrived from their Philippines base and were granted permission to remain so long as they did not actively propagate their faith. Before long they violated this stipulation. In 1596 typhoon damage forced the Manila galleon, *San Felipe*, to seek refuge in Japan. In reaction to Japanese seizure for salvage the Spanish commander spread out a map illustrating the vast extent of the Spanish Empire and explained that it had been built on the initial achievements of missionaries. Implicit was the threat of military retaliation and conquest.

As soon as Hideyoshi learned of these boasts, the 6 Spanish Franciscans in Japan were arrested and publicly crucified along with 3 Portuguese Jesuits and 17 Japanese converts. In addition, a fresh edict of expulsion was issued, but only 11 of about 100 Jesuits left Japan, the rest finding secret refuge among Japanese converts. Had Hideyoshi lived, their situation might have become untenable.

Meanwhile, Hideyoshi, once entrenched in power, had been able to implement a dream of external conquest that he had entertained at least as early as 1578. This dream, probably based on an inadequate knowledge of the vastness of the undertaking, envisioned the conquest of China, the source of so many significant elements in Japanese civilization. In addition, such a military adventure was probably, in part, inspired by the opportunities for plunder and bloodletting which might ease the social and economic strain created by his liberal policy toward defeated foes. Too many daimyō were in straitened circumstances because of the necessity of supporting their traditional body of retainers on estates that had been drastically reduced in size. Civil warfare was the traditional Japanese solution to such a situation. Hideyoshi may have thought that this prospect could be forestalled by external conquest. In any case, a united and peaceful Japan possessed far more samurai warriors than it needed.

In 1590 Hideyoshi announced his intention to the Korean king and requested an alliance and the right of passage for his troops through Korea. The Korean king replied in no uncertain terms that he would not consider such unfilial conduct toward his "parent" and suzerain, the Chinese emperor. On May 25, 1592, the first of 160,000 troops landed in Korea. Without meeting any significant organized resistance the capital city of Seoul was entered 18 days later, while the court, retreating to P'yongyang, sent desperate appeals for aid to its Chinese overlord. In spite of increasing resistance the Japanese armies pressed the attack and completed the conquest of Korea in six weeks. Belatedly the Ming emperor responded to his vassal's appeal, but the inadequate Chinese army of only 5000 was easily disposed of by the Japanese. Meanwhile, Hideyoshi had remained in Japan with a reserve force of 100,000 warriors ready to be dispatched if needed.

Although the Japanese samurai with their long swords and Western muskets proved invincible in land battles, they had not learned of Korea's radical innovation in naval warfare, the "tortoise" boat. A long, heavily-built hull supported a superstructure that was covered with iron plates and spikes and was equipped with ramming beaks. Oarsmen enabled these first "ironclads" to be propelled backward or forward with relative speed. At about the time the first Japanese troops were entering Seoul, Admiral Yih with a contingent of these unique vessels delivered the first of a series of decisive defeats that gave the Koreans control of the 120 miles of sea separating Japan from Korea. The tactics that he devised were ideally suited to the maximum utilization of his new weapon. A screen of sailing ships would entice the Japanese ships into pursuit by feigning flight. Before they realized the deception, the Japanese ships were being rammed and sunk by the tortoise boats while Japanese fire arrows and guns rattled harmlessly off their armor plate. As a result, Hideyoshi found it extremely difficult to supply and reinforce his forces in Korea.

After his armies ambushed a Chinese army of 43,000 men in 1593, he turned confidently to his proven skill in negotiation. When after three years the Chinese emperor refused to recognize Japanese suzerainty and conceded to him only the title of "King of Japan," Hideyoshi ordered a renewal of the war in 1597 which ended only with his death in the following year. With the possible exception of bloodletting none of his objectives had been achieved. And, unfortunately for his infant heir, most of the blood spilled had come from his most loyal supporters. Some of the more powerful lords, such as Tokugawa Ieyasu, stayed at home consolidating their positions. Plunder scarcely met the costs of the conflict. For the Ming dynasty, as well, the costs of defending its vassal proved disastrous, paving the way for its overthrow by the Manchus. Of course, as the battleground for Chinese and Japanese armies, Korea was pillaged and ravaged by both sides.

Like Nobunaga, Hideyoshi at his death had to entrust his five-year-old son to a board of guardians of whom Tokugawa Ieyasu (1542–1616) was the strongest. Of the three ambitious men who collaborated in the reunification of Japan he was the youngest, the most patient and conservative, and in the long run the most durable. As the head of a minor feudal family he had to operate with caution to survive in this era of feudal turmoil. Although he was a redoubtable warrior renowned for his terrifying war cry in battle, he always recognized that a feudal lord's power ultimately depended on the size of his estate and the resources he could command. While his colorful colleagues engaged in daring and dramatic exploits, he generally conserved his strength and concentrated on enhancing it by deliberate steps.

In 1560, when his overlord was defeated by Nobunaga, he took his first step by switching his allegiance to the victor. For this and subsequent services he was generously rewarded with new estates. After Nobunaga's assassination in 1582 he at first sought to counter Hideyoshi's assertion of supremacy but, recognizing that the risks were too great, he came to terms in 1585. As a reward for his loyal support in the conquest of the Kantō, he was granted in 1590 most of the estates in this largest arable area in Japan. Perhaps Hideyoshi thought he was weakening his vassal by removing him from his home estates, but Ieyasu recognized the much greater potential of the Kantō Plain. While Hideyoshi was chasing Chinese dragons in Korea, he built himself a great castle at Edo (modern Tōkyō) and consolidated his control of the entire plain.

At Hideyoshi's death in 1598 Ieyasu's estate was the largest in Japan, even larger than that which Hideyoshi left to his five-year-old son. In the subsequent intrigue the other great lords attempted to reconcile their differences in order to present a united front against him, but at the decisive battle of Sekigahara (October 21, 1600) Ieyasu's diplomacy had prearranged desertions at the critical moment. Although his supremacy was not officially confirmed by the imperial grant of the title of shōgun until 1603, his victory had gained him de facto control, and he immediately proceeded to consolidate his authority.

The Tokugawa regime delineated by Ieyasu demonstrated little originality. The techniques of feudal organization and control worked out by his predecessors were merely elaborated methodically to guarantee Tokugawa authority for the next two and a half centuries. Although from the point of view of social and economic development feudalism was already an anachronism and although the state-wide peace which the Tokugawa regime provided may seem inconsistent with a military organization, it would be a mistake to expect the tradition bound outlook of the Japanese people ever to consider any radical break with the past. Even today the attitudes inherited from the Tokugawa era are significantly reflected in modern Japanese behavior and practices.

After Sekigahara, and even after gaining the title of shōgun, Ieyasu's authority was by no means unquestioned. Heeding the lesson of his predecessors' failure to pass on their power to their sons, Ieyasu in 1605 set a precedent by officially abdicating as shōgun in favor of his chosen son. In fact, he continued to run the government until his death in 1616, but meanwhile his son gained the experience under his father's tutelage that precluded any challenge at his death.

A greater danger, however, was the continued existence of Hideyoshi's son and heir. In addition to his extensive estates he commanded Japan's leading commercial city, Ōsaka, and the loyalty of its great

Buddhist monastery of the True sect. Cautiously Ieyasu bided his time until by various measures he had reduced the rest of the daimyō to complete submission. Finally, in 1614 he felt the time was ripe to eliminate this threat. His judgment was substantiated by the failure of any important daimyō to support his foe, though 90,000 warriors—mostly dispossessed daimyō and samurai—did come to his defense. A month-long siege failed, but Ieyasu was able to negotiate a peace, turning over to his forces' control of the outer walls and moats. The following summer Ieyasu treacherously renewed the assault and forced the defenders to sally forth where they were more easily destroyed. Thus this greatest single menace to Tokugawa supremacy was entirely eradicated before Ieyasu's death at the age of seventy-three.

THE CLOSING OF JAPAN

Meanwhile, he gradually came to the conclusion that the subversive potentialities of unrestricted foreign trade outweighed any benefits that might accrue to the shogunate. Initially he had hoped to attract Western merchants to Edo, but despite his concessions they clearly preferred to trade at the closer, established stations in Kyūshū. Moreover, many Christians were among the supporters of Hideyoshi's son, and a petty plot was even uncovered among Ieyasu's Christian retainers. Not only were the Christians proving difficult to discipline but also the damaging effects of an adverse balance of trade were beginning to be appreciated.

The chief attraction of the Japanese trade for Western merchants was the opportunity to sell Western and Asian products for cash which could be used to purchase Chinese silks and other Asian products. The Japanese had few products that Western traders were interested in purchasing. Already the drain of specie was significantly apparent. Therefore, economic considerations reinforced the fear of the Christian menace to the stability of the Tokugawa regime in inspiring the steps that culminated in the closing of Japan.

In 1606 Ieyasu issued his first anti-Christian edict, and in 1612 he began to enforce them, executing any of his retainers who refused to renounce Christianity. In 1614 all foreign missionaries who could be discovered were expelled, but none of them were executed while he lived. In 1617 the first executions of missionaries since Hideyoshi's times took place, but not until 1622 did Ieyasu's successor commit the shogunate to a thorough eradication of Christianity, largely out of fear of the Christians' possible collaboration with a Spanish invasion. Suspects were tested by the simple device of being ordered to tread on some sacred symbol, such as a representation of Christ or Mary. All kinds of torture were used to extract recantations. All those who clung to their faith were burned at the stake, a technique ironically borrowed from the inquisition and adapted to Japanese purposes.

During these same years increasing limitations were placed on overseas trade, whether conducted by foreigners or by Japanese. In 1636 an edict terminated all Japanese trading overseas. The construction of oceangoing ships was prohibited, and all Japanese overseas were forbidden to return to Japan on pain of death. All foreign merchants, including Chinese, were restricted to Nagasaki and Hirado, and all trade was placed under strict shogunal control to forestall the strengthening of any of the less reliable daimyō. The door that was being gradually closed was slammed shut as a result of a rebellion in 1637, originally against oppression, that developed into a Christian last stand. About 20,000 warriors with their families held out in an old castle on the Shimabara Peninsula in Kyūshū against an army of 100,000 and the firepower of a Dutch ship until the spring of 1638. The Portuguese, whose sympathy for the Shimabara rebels had not been concealed, were expelled in 1639. When they attempted to reopen relations in 1640, the four envoys and 57 crewmen were put to death. Only 13 were spared to carry the news of Japanese determination back to Macao. In 1641 the Dutch were removed to Nagasaki where they and the Chinese were permitted to carry on a limited and closely controlled trade. Even this restricted trade, however, resulted in a serious drain of specie, and the shogunate was subsequently compelled to place quotas on the export of silver and copper.

Thus within one century Japan shifted from the one extreme of open hospitality to the other extreme of almost complete isolation—an isolation greater than at any time in the past. This policy did provide the stability that made possible more than two centuries of internal peace, but it also removed the alien stimuli and ideas that might have kept Japanese development abreast of the West. When Japan's doors were again opened, an arduous program of modernization was required to catch up with the West. This rejection of the West, however, fitted into the general pattern that shaped the Tokugawa program. The overriding objective that determined every action was the elimination of every potential menace to the absolute authority of the shogunate within the reactionary framework of Japanese feudalism. Obviously, alien influences were potentially subversive.

FEUDAL ABSOLUTISM

As overlord of a unique feudal system of decentralization, almost every specific measure of Ieyasu was aimed at the elimination of social disorder and the prevention of any menacing concentration of power. In essence, then, most of the rules and regulations were negative rather than positive in nature. He accepted and reinforced Hideyoshi's program of rigid social stratification and group responsibility. He followed his predecessor's policy of confiscating part or all of his enemies' fiefs and of redistributing them to reliable supporters with the general purpose of eliminating any potentially hostile concentrations of estates. The daimyō were classified as "inner" or "outer" daimyō according to which side they had been on at Sekigahara, and the fiefs of central Japan and the Kanto were awarded to the "inner" daimyō or his own family. At the same time the more important "outer" daimyō gained as neighbors reliable and watchful "inner" daimyō. In emulation of Hideyoshi, Ieyasu also exhausted the surplus resources of questionable daimyō by assigning to them expensive public works, such as the repair of a temple or the construction of a road.

Not content with these checks, Ieyasu and his successors devised a number of additional safeguards. Each lord had to spend about half his time at court at an expense that placed a heavy drain on his income. This requirement made him an "absentee" landlord increasingly dependent on administrators drawn from the ranks of his samurai. Moreover, during his sojourn on his fief the lord had to leave his family in Edo as hostages for his good behavior. Each fief was isolated by the rule that no outsiders were to reside there. So accustomed did the lords become to the amenities of life in Edo that they came to view the sojourns on their estates as a form of exile. Furthermore, all marriages between daimyō families required the approval of the shogunate. All suspicious or unusual activity in a neighboring fief was to be reported. In other words, each lord was required to inform on his neighbor. But this was not enough; a secret service was established to check on the behavior of all lords.

In a united nation at peace the occupation of a warrior class was a subject of concern. Ieyasu admonished all samurai to lead a frugal life and to keep practiced in arms in the event of a call to duty. But these commands did not solve the problem of a warrior elite without any opportunity to exercise its talents. Hideyoshi had undertaken a foreign adventure, which somewhat eased the problem by reducing the number of samurai, but Ieyasu and his successors were too conservative to contemplate such a solution.

Instead, the samurai were encouraged to devote their spare time to Confucian-style scholarship, especially the study of ethics and of the past. In particular, Ieyasu as a man of action deprecated poetry and esthetics in favor of political history, both Japanese and Chinese, with an emphasis on those topics that concerned the problems of government. In the long run such samurai scholarship became subversive of the Tokugawa regime as it uncovered the fact that the shogunate was essentially a usurpation of imperial authority. In addition, these studies focused attention on the extent of Chinese influence on Japanese civilization. Two broad schools evolved, one emphasizing the Chinese heritage and the other emphasizing the native heritage with special reference to Shintō. Buddhism, whose political power had already been destroyed in the process of reunification, suffered further deterioration from the emphasis on Confucian studies and ethics, while Shintō was released from its subordination to Buddhism.

Most samurai, however, had neither the talent nor the inclination to absorb their energies in scholarship. Moreover, those who accompanied their lords to Edo found it difficult to resist the expensive temptations of the city and obey the order of frugality and simplicity. The "outer" daimyō were squeezed between the costs of residence in Edo, which required about 50 percent of their incomes, and the obligation to maintain their samurai on estates drastically reduced in size. As a result, they attempted to reduce the allotments of the samurai, if not the number they had to support. In the absence of the attrition of war, families expanded, increasing the demands on the fixed income of the samurai.

After several generations many retainers of "outer" daimyō were compelled by a combination of inadequate income, family increase, and the acquisition of expensive tastes to find some solution to their economic needs. The easiest answer was the resort to moneylenders in return for a lien on their allotments. Such a step, however, only encouraged the samurai to live for a time beyond their incomes. In due course many were reduced to pensioners limited to an allowance set by their creditors of the despised merchant class. Occasionally the shogunate sought to resolve this dilemma by a general cancellation of debts. Instead of alleviating their economic difficulties, however, such measures only made the terms of the moneylenders more stringent. Many samurai were forced into marital alliances with the families of their merchant creditors, even though such a prohibited relationship involved loss of status. Some foresighted samurai, appreciating the economic transformation taking place, abandoned their status altogether and fully committed their futures to the hurly-burly world of commerce. In any case, as managers of their lords' estates, "samurai of the robe" had already gained substantial business experience in dealings with merchants for the sale of the surplus production to raise the cash to meet their lords' expenses at Edo. As this commercial operation implies, the lords, too, were gradually compelled by their need of money into dependence on mercantile agents, though their elevated status required them to operate indirectly through their trusted samurai administrators.

A related problem which created disturbances for several generations concerned former samurai, called rōnin, who had lost their lords through death and confiscation of fiefs. Following his victory at Sekigahara, Ieyasu had confiscated 91 of 214 daimyō estates, and his successors condemned additional daimyō for infractions of the rigorous rules of the Tokugawa regime, awarding their fiefs to faithful followers. If the lordless samurai could not find a new lord, these victims of a change beyond their control were forced to shift for themselves as displaced persons. Untrained for any other occupation and unwilling to adapt to a lesser status, many turned to banditry, creating serious disturbances wherever they operated. Most famous is the story of the Forty-Seven Rōnin which in dramatic form epitomizes the ideal of samurai loyalty to their lords.

In 1710 their lord was provoked into drawing his sword and wounding a shogunal official within the palace at Edo. For this violation of the house law he was condemned to commit suicide, and his fief was confiscated. His samurai, now masterless rōnin, deliberated on what course of action to take, and 47 of them agreed to dedicate themselves to avenging their lord. After almost two years of deception and planning they gained their vengeance and subsequently committed suicide in atonement for their crime. No other story better illustrates the ideal of absolute loyalty and duty to the lord and to shogunal regulations which enabled the anachronistic, and even reactionary, feudal system of the Tokugawa regime to function effectively.

SOCIAL AND ECONOMIC CHANGES

Although the paradoxical combination of absolute authority at Edo with a decentralized feudal system entrapped in their own toils the shogunate, the daimyō, and the samurai, it provided the very conditions most conducive to the flourishing of the most lowly regarded class, the merchants. In spite of the intense and dedicated effort to maintain an outmoded social and political order, the ruling classes suffered continuous social deterioration and economic decline throughout the Tokugawa era, while the prospering merchants carried through a social and economic transformation that prepared Japan for its reemergence in the mid-nineteenth century.

Before reunification, the political divisions and disorders had compelled the artisans and merchants to organize guilds and gain the protection of the great lords in return for a share in their profits. After reunification, the establishment of law and order throughout Japan reversed the relationship, making the lords dependent on them for financial support. By the same token it opened up a nationwide market for mercantile development and exploitation. The roads built to accommodate the constant travels of lords and retainers between their fiefs and Edo also facilitated trade, and supplying the needs and other appetites of the ruling class on its travels and, in Edo, provided a wholly new economic opportunity. Finally, the feudal emphasis on the agrarian base of society left the artisans and merchants largely free of the burden of taxation that fell most heavily on the peasantry. When serious efforts were attempted to rectify this imbalance, the commercial classes were too well entrenched and too influential and essential for such reforms to be applied in an effective or enduring way.

During the first half of the Tokugawa period, peace and a doubling of arable land supported a population increase of at least 50 percent. A census in 1721 indicates a growth from 15 to 20 million in 1600 to about 30 million, making Japan more populous at that date than any European state. During the second half of the Tokugawa era the population remained fairly stable despite continued economic development, though at a slower pace. The first half of the Tokugawa era was characterized by the rapid growth of the major urban centers, especially Ōsaka and Edo, which became the commercial entrepots, respectively, of the southwestern and northeastern halves of Japan. Thanks to its strategic location at the head of the Inland Sea, Ōsaka had gained a population of about 350,000 during this period of rapid development and continued to grow more slowly during the second half of the period. With its additional attraction as the political capital, Edo could count almost a million residents.

During the second half of this period the continued development of the major urban centers was restrained by a number of factors. First, the financial difficulties of the shogunate inspired a number of "reform" efforts that could be most effectively enforced in the cities. Second, the major merchants tended to form associations to protect themselves against both the government and new competition. Thus mercantile conservatism replaced the open exuberance of the early era of rapid development. Third, they had already captured and organized the national marketing of the major products, and the opportunities for expansion or new development were limited. For example, the rice merchants of Ōsaka and Edo had gained control of all the national surpluses and were trading in futures by the end of the seventeenth century. Any differences in prices on the two markets were soon adjusted by an exchange of claims. In a similar fashion banking facilities developed out of moneylending, and the money market, which tended toward inflation as a result of debasement, was stabilized by cooperation in banking operations. Finally, the higher standard of living achieved in the cities gradually spread to the towns and villages where the major economic development during the second half of the Tokugawa era took place. Transportation costs, the local availability of raw materials, and low wages encouraged the investment of surplus capital in local enterprises, such as sake brewing, silk weaving, and various food preparations for local distribution. Local opportunity combined with the stabilization of the population to diminish the incentives for migration to the cities.

The economic development and change throughout this era were reflected in significant social and cultural changes. In the cities the wealth building of the merchants and the increasing financial dependence of the ruling classes on them undermined the feudal social order upheld by the shogunate and placed emphasis on income in cash rather than in kind. Although the merchant families emulated the Zen-Confucian ethics of their betters, stressing frugality, duty, loyalty, and self-discipline, they were less wedded to this ideal and used their surplus cash to encourage the production of more colorful art and luxurious entertainment for their moments of relaxation. In fact, their wealth made the lowly merchants the fashioners, if not the arbiters, of taste—and the ruling class, despite the sumptuary laws, found these innovations almost irresistible.

CULTURAL DEVELOPMENT

The higher standard of living and the accumulation of relative wealth stimulated the development of a more colorful, less restrained, bourgeois culture in the cities, catering to the needs and desires of a much larger number of customers with money to spend. Notable creations were the amusement quarters in which were conveniently concentrated theaters, restaurants, teahouses, and bathhouses to provide relaxation and diversion for tired businessmen and other well-to-do male patrons. Professional female entertainers were connected with each of these establishments, and the quality of their accomplishments was determined by the customer's pocketbook. In a society in which marriages were arranged for the mutual benefit of the families, and the training of women emphasized household management and modest subservience rather than cultural attainments, social mingling of married couples was discouraged. Under these circumstances, the development of extramarital facilities for social intercourse between the sexes was natural. It should be stressed that the amusement quarters came into existence primarily to fill the need for cultural exchange and stimulation unavailable in the home. Prostitution was a secondary and subordinate factor in a society devoid of sexual inhibitions. The most intelligent and talented of the girls obtained by contract from poor peasant families were trained to be geishas (accomplished persons). Frequently a wealthy patron became so enamored of a particular geisha that he would purchase her contract and support her for his exclusive use, or sometimes even make her his wife.

Two new dramatic forms, the Kabuki and the puppet theater, evolved to attract the newly rich who found the Nō drama too formal and austere. The first Kabuki troupe appears to have been formed by a Shintō priestess primarily to parade the charms of the male and female members. Alarmed by this blatant display, the shogunate forbade female participation, and henceforth feminine roles were performed by male actors in an exceptionally realistic manner. To enhance the dramatic effect, a runway through the audience, colorful scenery, and the revolving stage were introduced. Many Nō plots were adapted for Kabuki presentation. In addition, historical incidents that lent themselves to the emotional tension favored by Kabuki were utilized as, for example, the story of the Forty-Seven Rōnin. Equally popular, however, were dramatic portrayals of the conflicts between duty and passion in the lives of both the merchant and ruling classes. In both the Kabuki and contemporary life impossible love affairs could only be resolved by joint suicides, the highest form of high drama. The frequency of this theme in all literary forms highlights the tension between the rigorous regulation of behavior and natural inclinations that has left its mark on Japanese character.

Meanwhile, the shogunal restrictions placed on the Kabuki stimulated the development of the puppet theater. Initially the puppets were small, but the demand for realism promoted their growth into figures two thirds human size which required several men to manipulate. Some of the most famous playwrights wrote for the puppet theater. Not only were puppet dramas borrowed by the Kabuki but also the jerky movements of the puppets influenced the Kabuki acting style.

The expansion of literacy promoted by urban growth stimulated literary activity that catered to bourgeois interests with less restraint than the stage. An additional factor encouraging literary production was the development of printing. True to Lady Murasaki's dictum that life as it is should be portrayed with all its vices and vanities, the best

authors bored to the core of Tokugawa life, especially in the cities, deftly exposing and satirizing its fetishes, foibles, and contradictions. Among other themes the tyranny of money as the real standard of urban life and the tendency of sons to fritter away their father's fortunes in the pursuit of happiness in the "fleeting world" of the amusement district were singled out for dissection. The transparent disguises of samurai, for whom the amusement quarters were officially off limits, and their pretensions were held up to ridicule. An interesting phenomenon, paralleled in other cultures, is the fascination of the Japanese urban elite with the works of those writers who most ruthlessly exposed and satirized its weaknesses.

In poetry an even briefer form, the seventeen-syllable *haiku*, gained a popularity it still enjoys. Although it did not depend on a classical education, it did demand the ultimate in wit and skill with words, talents admired in urban life. Urbanites, then as now, craved new fads and fashions. At the end of the seventeenth century the composition of *haiku* became such a fad—a measuring stick of modernity—but, unlike other fashions, it proved durable.

Art, too, tended to reflect the interests of the larger urban market, especially in the evolution of wood-block printing into a fine art. The hereditary schools continued to find a market for their works, but the more colorful and flamboyant art patronized by the newly risen leaders of the sixteenth century continued to be favored, though with greater restraint, by the newly rich merchants. The life and personages of the amusement quarters and scenes along the busy highways furnished a new array of subjects for artistic treatment. The larger market encouraged the development of wood-block printing, as well as of mass production techniques in industrial arts, to make esthetically satisfying works available at costs that would produce even greater sales. As a result, art became "popularized" during the Tokugawa era, reaching a much broader segment of the people. Yet, in keeping with the Japanese heritage, color and mass production seldom violated the ingrained esthetic canons of artistic taste.

SOCIAL AND ECONOMIC CHANGE IN THE COUNTRY

In the countryside a combination of factors also forced significant social changes. The more than two centuries of Tokugawa peace allowed population growth to increase the pressure on the land bringing about more intensive development and competition. For the first half of the period rapid urbanization provided an outlet for surplus population as well as a new market for more diversified agricultural production. The daimyōs' need for surpluses to be converted into cash stimulated a quest for ways to expand production, including land reclamation, improved irrigation technology, a greater use of fertilizers, and seed selection. The shogunal restrictions on imports to stem the drain of specie encouraged home production of former import items, such as silk. In return, the cities gradually infiltrated the towns and then the villages with the taste for a higher standard of living.

One social result of an increasingly competitive rural economy was the gradual breakdown of the traditional extended family into smaller self-supporting family units. The young couples who left home to farm reclaimed or improved lands often fared better than those who stayed behind on exhausted lands. Freed of the requirement to support marginal members, the smaller family units might accumulate surplus cash to invest in improvement of their land, in additional land, or even in some village enterprise, such as sake brewing or silk weaving. Some families prospered, while less fortunate ones fell into the grip of moneylenders and were ultimately reduced to tenancy. Even then the intelligent landlord invested in improvements that would increase his income.

Such growing social stratification among the peasantry generated both the need for and a supply of wage laborers. Increasing competition in the countryside also inspired the formation of cooperatives to regulate and protect the gains made, much as merchant associations had been formed earlier in the cities. At the same time, the economic distress of those who were not faring so well was reflected in localized rural riots seeking debt cancellation and other aid. On the other hand, some aggressive family firms which got their starts in rural enterprise successfully challenged the conservative city merchants and built national businesses.

THE END OF ISOLATION

By the nineteenth century the economic opportunities provided by internal peace had been fully exploited, and the consequent social change had made the centralized feudalism of the Tokugawa regime even more unrealistic and anachronistic. The major economic handicap was the isolation of Japan from the world market which could have furnished a safety valve to meet the problems of overproduction or underproduction and the wider market to stimulate more rapid economic growth and diversification. The first century of internal peace and isolation may have been beneficial, but the second century was damaging in its effects by encouraging conservative and restrictive practices that stifled much of the earlier economic initiative.

On the other hand, the isolation of Japan was by no means absolute, and a small number of scholars kept abreast of Western development via "Dutch learning." In 1720 the shogunate removed the ban on foreign books, other than religious works, and supported study of the Dutch language. As in the case of Confucian studies, criticism subversive of the Tokugawa regime was stimulated by the knowledge about other nations and other ways, and this criticism was sometimes combined with the growing nationalistic feeling among intellectuals. Most important for the future, however, was the existence of a small body of men well informed about both Western government and Western science. When the black ships of the United States compelled Japan to open its doors, the Americans were surprised at the Japanese familiarity with world geography and the principles of science. Thus Japan possessed a small cadre of informed advisors to direct its first steps on the path of modernization.

From the late eighteenth century both the repeated attempts of Western powers to open Japan and internal criticism of the policy of isolation, mostly sponsored by the "outer" daimyō, put increasing pressure on the shogunate. Yet the shogunate, justifiably fearful of any alteration of the Tokugawa system, clung doggedly to its outmoded policies. The acquisition of California immediately increased the interest of the American government in gaining ports of call in the Japanese islands. Indeed, for many years American whalers and traders had been importuning their government for aid in opening Japan. In 1849, the American government informed the European governments of its firm intention to accomplish this objective, and the Dutch transmitted the news to the shogunate. After some delays, Commodore Matthew G. Perry arrived at the foot of the bay south of Edo on July 8, 1853, in command of a squadron of four ships, two of which were powered by steam. For six days he firmly refused to be diverted and threatened to sail to Edo if a principal minister did not come to receive a letter he carried from the President to the Emperor. Finally, the letter requesting "friendship, commerce, a supply of coal and provisions, and protection for our shipwrecked people" was delivered, and Perry sailed, promising to return in a year for a reply.

Unequipped to oppose such a formidable force, the shōgun's court was thrown into a quandary and made the tactical error of consulting the daimyō and the imperial court at Kyōto. Although the daimyō opposed any concessions, the emperor was persuaded to agree to a limited and temporary arrangement until the shogun could prepare to repel the West. However, by even seeking the advice of the great lords and the emperor the already questionable authority of the shogunate had been seriously undermined. By its own admission the shogunate was no longer absolute and independent.

Only seven months later, hastened by information of a proposed Russian attempt to forestall the American one, Perry reappeared with a reinforced squadron of seven ships. After six tedious weeks of negotiation a treaty was concluded which was differently understood by each party. Two ports of call were opened where necessary supplies could be purchased and goods exchanged, "under such regulations as shall be temporarily established by the Japanese government for that purpose." According to the Japanese interpretation this clause did not establish a right to trade. In addition, after 18 months the United States might appoint a resident agent if "either of the two governments" felt such a step was necessary. The shogunate believed that the implementation of this clause required their consent; in other words, that "either" meant "both." Most important of all, the treaty included the standard most favored-nation clauses by which any additional concessions gained by another power automatically accrued to the United States.

The dilemma of the shogunate was not for long limited to the Americans. Within two years the British, Russians, and Dutch demanded and procured similar treaties. The gate forced open by the Americans was soon battered down, and the Japanese were confronted not just with the Americans but with the entire West. Any hope that they may have harbored of extricating themselves from the American relationship was submerged by the combined presence and pressure of the West. Any alteration of the relationship established by the treaties would require a much longer range plan which would involve substantial internal change. Before 1860 some thoughtful Japanese leaders began to appreciate these facts.

On the eve of being forcefully exposed to the industrializing West, both China and Japan were suffering a deterioration in their central governments. China had entered the declining phase of the dynastic cycle, as indicated by the frequency of rebellions, but there was no question in the minds of the indispensable scholar class of the validity and superiority of the Confucian system of government. The Western assault was just another barbarian attack from a new direction which must be resisted and, if possible, repulsed. On the other hand, the weakness of the Tokugawa Shogunate reflected the deepening contradiction between the social and economic realities and the antiquated feudal structure of power. This contradiction had been apparent from the establishment of the reactionary Tokugawa regime and was only enhanced by the social and economic changes unwittingly fostered by shogunal policies. The opening of Japan was a blessing in disguise because it unleashed the too long stifled energies of a vigorous people and allowed them once again to borrow and adapt those features of Western culture and technology best suited to Japan's renewed and dynamic development. In other words, the Japanese people were prepared, and indeed overdue, for another round of dynamic evolution; the stable Chinese society, convinced of the superiority of its civilization, could only be altered significantly by revolution—a revolution that was to be staved off until the twentieth century.

SIGNIFICANT DATES

China

c. 1167–1227	Chingiz Khan, founder of Mongol Empire
1279	Completion of conquest of Southern Sung by Khubilai Khan
1271–1368	Yüan (Mongol) dynasty
1368–1644	Ming dynasty
1405–1433	Naval expeditions of Cheng Ho
1421	Transfer of Ming capital to Peking
1472–1529	Wang Yang-ming, Neo-Confucian "Idealist"
1516	Portuguese arrival in China
1557	Portuguese residence at Macao
1644–1911	Ch'ing (Manchu) dynasty
1683	Chinese annexation of Taiwan (Formosa)
1689	Treaty of Nerchinsk with Russia
1720–1842	Co-hong limitation of trade to Canton
1796	Edict against importation of opium
1839–1842	The Opium War

Japan

1543	Portuguese arrival in Japan
1560–1590	Reunification by Oda Nobunaga and Hideyoshi
1592–1598	Korean expeditions of Hideyoshi
1600	Battle of Sekigahara
1603–1867	Tokugawa Shogunate established by Ieyasu
1637–1638	Shimabara Rebellion
1639	Closure of Japan
1854	Opening of Japan by Commodore Perry.

SELECTED READINGS

See Chapters Four and Eight for general accounts.

*Birch, Cyril, trans., *Stories from a Ming Collection*. New York: Grove Press, 1968.

*Chang, Carson, *Wang Yang-ming: Idealist Philosopher of Sixteenth Century China*. New York: St. John's University Press, 1962.

*Ch'u, T'ung-tsu, *Local Government in China under the Ch'ing*. Stanford: Stanford University Press, 1962.

DeBary, William Theodore, ed., *Self and Society in Ming Thought*. New York: Columbia University Press, 1970.

*Fairbank, John K., ed., *Chinese Thought and Institutions*. Chicago: University of Chicago Press, 1967.

*Franke, Wolfgang, *China and the West*. New York: Harper and Row, 1967.

*Latham, Milton R. E., trans.. *The Travels of Marco Polo*. Baltimore: Penguin Books, 1958.

Michael, Franz. *The Origin of Manchu Rule in China*. Baltimore: Johns Hopkins Press, 1942.

*Prawdin, Michael, *The Mongol Empire*. 2nd ed.; New York: Free Press, 1967.

Spuler, Bertold, *History of the Mongols*. Berkeley: University of California Press, 1970.

*Waley, Arthur, *Yuan Mei: Eighteenth Century Chinese Poet*. Stanford: Stanford University Press, 1970.

*———, trans., *Monkey*. New York: Grove Press, 1958.

Wang, Chi-chen, *Dream of the Red Chamber*. New York: Twayne Pubs., 1971.

See Chapter Nine for general accounts.

*Bellah, Robert, *Tokugawa Religion*. Boston: Beacon Press, 1970.

*Benedict, Ruth, *The Chrysanthemum and the Sword*. Cleveland: World Publishing, 1967.

Boxer, C. R., *The Christian Century in Japan, 1549–1650*. Berkeley: University of California Press, 1951.

*DeBary, William Theodore, trans., *Five Women Who Loved Love*. Rutland, Vt.: Tuttle, 1956.

*Duus, Peter, *Feudalism in Japan*. New York: Random House, 1969.

Hall, John W., *Tanuma Okitsugu, 1719–1788*. Cambridge, Mass.: Harvard University Press, 1955.

*Henderson, Harold G., *An Introduction to Haiku*. New York: Doubleday and Co., 1958.

Hibbett, Howard, *The Floating World in Japanese Fiction*. London: Oxford University Press, 1959.

*Keene, Donald, *The Japanese Discovery of Europe, 1720–1830*. Stanford: Stanford University Press, 1969.

*———, trans., *Four Major Plays of Chikamatsu*. New York: Columbia University Press, 1961.

Michener, James, *The Floating World.* New York: Random House, 1954.

Pritchard, Earl H., *Anglo-Chinese Relations during the 17th and 18th Centuries.* New York: Octagon Books, 1970.

Sansom, George B., *The Western World and Japan.* New York: Knopf, 1950.

*Scott, Adolphe C., *The Kabuki Theatre of Japan.* New York: Macmillan, 1966.

Sheldon, Charles David, *The Rise of the Merchant Class in Tokugawa Japan.* Locust Valley, N.Y.: J. J. Augustin, 1958.

*Smith, Thomas C., *The Agrarian Origins of Modern Japan.* New York: Atheneum, 1966.

*Statler, Oliver, *Japanese Inn.* New York: Pyramid, 1962.

CHAPTER FOURTEEN

ISLAM UNDER TURKS AND PERSIANS

Since the thirteenth century both the Indian and Chinese civilizations had fallen victims to alien conquerors. But while the Indians failed to convert their Muslim conquerors and tolerated them as a segregated ruling caste, the Chinese were partially successful in capturing their conquerors, who did not possess such a strong ideology of their own. The heartland of the more youthful Islamic civilization, too, had not escaped nomadic conquest, but, like the Chinese, the Muslims experienced a substantial measure of success in Islamicizing the invaders. Thus the three major civilizations of the East were each confronted with barbarian conquerors from the Asian interior.

The most important area of initial contact for Islam was the northern steppe frontier of Iran, a region of interpenetration throughout the ages. Indeed, the vitality of the Iranian people with their proud imperial heritage had continuously been revitalized by fresh infusions of warlike nomads from central Asia, and the new wave of Turkish-speaking tribesmen only served to reinvigorate Iranian national feeling which had already been stimulated by the challenge of Islam.

In fact, Persian civilization had already significantly modified Islam, and the forms of Islam that were most successful among the Turks, with their primitive tribal religious practices, incorporated Christian, Zoroastrian, and Indian mystical and magical accretions. These more radical, yet comprehensive, expressions in the form of Sufism were more readily adaptable to tribal shamanism than orthodox Sunnite ritual. A Sufi holy man, like his shaman predecessor, could by his personal magnetism inspire to exceptional valor his band of "warriors of the faith," who would be incapable of comprehending the complexities of Sunnite doctrine

as they had been elaborated under the influence of urban civilization. After al-Ghazzali's reconciliation of Sufi mysticism and Sunnite orthodoxy tribal leaders could proclaim themselves champions of Sunnite Islam, while their followers were really fanatical disciples of Sufi holy men on whom the mantle of Islam rested only lightly.

Ultimately, as the tribesmen settled down, tribal Sufism interacted with the more sophisticated urban Sufi orders catering to merchant and artisan associations. Although most of these Sufi orders expressed allegiance to the Sunnite school, basic contradictions existed in their general assertion of spiritual descent from Ali, the progenitor of the Shi'a, and in the belief that they were not bound by the Qur'anic injunctions and ritual requirements of Sunnite doctrine. Wine, drugs, and music—all denounced or frowned on by the Prophet—were variously employed to induce the ecstatic state of personal communion with the divine. In addition, the belief in the immanent nature of God undermined the orthodox distinctions between good and evil, right and wrong. If God was present in every thing, evil and wrong could only be apparent and not real. Such heterodox subtleties, however, were undoubtedly unappreciated by the mass of the members of Sufi orders.

Turkish warriors, as previously mentioned, were first introduced as slaves and mercenaries into the Abbasid Caliphate, but before long, the centrifugal characteristics of tribal custom brought about the breakdown of political unity. When another Turkish leader of the steppe, the Shah of Khwarism, was on the verge of reuniting eastern Islam, the Mongol armies destroyed him and plundered Iran. Under the Mongol Il-Khanate the Seljuk Turk sultanate of Rum retained control of Anatolia as a tributary state until it, too, was destroyed in 1302. The destruction of this last Seljuk Turk regime opened the way for the rise of the Ottoman Turks who revived the advance of Islam against the "land of war" (*dar al-harb*) by leading unattached Turkish warriors of the faith, driven into Anatolia by the Mongols, in the conquest of the Byzantine Empire in Europe. Meanwhile, Turkish warriors as slaves and mercenaries were a major element in the military forces of the Egyptian Ayyubid dynasty, founded by Saladin and its Mamluk successor. In short, the Asian Middle East and its Egyptian adjunct had fallen almost wholly into the military control of Turkish and Turko-Mongol warriors who had been, at least, superficially converted to Islam and Islamic civilization. Only the Arabs of the desert and the resilient Persians continued to resist. Of course, the Persians enjoyed the advantage that the Islamic civilization adopted by the barbarians was largely a Persian product and the newcomers needed their services. Ultimately a resurgent Persia overthrew its Turko-Mongol overlords and under the banner of Shi'a divided the world of Islam with the Sunnite Ottomans.

THE OTTOMAN CONQUESTS

The origin of the Ottoman Turks is obscure. According to legend they arrived in Anatolia as a small band of horsemen only in the later thirteenth century and, for military services rendered, were granted territory on the Byzantine frontier by the Seljuk sultan. In this location they were expected to guard the interior against any Byzantine assault. However, such a small number, as they appear to have been, could never have undertaken any conquests without the support of the other tribal warriors of the faith whom they attracted to their banners following the collapse in 1302 of the Seljuk regime. Even with this support little could have been accomplished if the Byzantine Empire had not been in such an advanced state of decrepitude, largely dependent on mercenaries

which its shrunken resources could ill afford to maintain. Moreover, warriors of the faith could be attracted by the prospects of plunder in Christian territory, while attacks on fellow Muslims in Anatolia could not ethically yield such fruits. Therefore, the conditions for the Ottoman rise to power, and the direction of their conquests, were largely determined by a complex set of factors that prevailed in both Anatolia and the Byzantine and Balkan area.

First, Ottoman leadership was prescribed by the strategic situation on the Byzantine frontier straddling the main lines of communication with the Muslim world. Second, a supply of warriors eager for plunder was available in anarchic Anatolia and was only awaiting dynamic leadership. Third, the weakened Byzantine Empire not only could offer no effective resistance, even to small forces, but also sought mercenary troops to defend its remaining European territories. Finally, the Orthodox Christian peasantry of the Balkan Peninsula were so oppressed by monastic and absentee landlords and by alien, and especially Latin, rulers that they welcomed the Ottomans as liberators with a better reputation for justice and tolerance.

The base of the Ottoman emirate was initially located about midway between the Byzantine cities of Nicaea and Brusa in Asia Minor. Brusa surrendered in 1326 and Nicaea in 1331, not as a result of direct siege or attack but by being isolated by the unimpeded occupation of the surrounding area on which these cities depended. Constantinople could not assemble the forces necessary to expel the interlopers, and the cities could discover no alternative to submission. Following up these successes, the Ottoman leader effectively occupied the rest of Byzantine Asia Minor, doled the land out in fiefs that were directly held by warriors of the faith, and assumed the title of sultan.

Interestingly enough, the Ottoman's entrance into Europe was by the invitation of a Byzantine usurper to serve as mercenaries

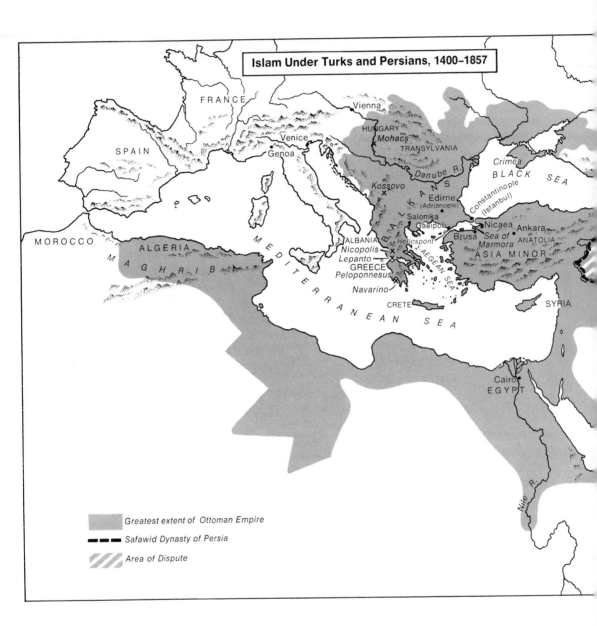

Islam Under Turks and Persians, 1400–1857

Greatest extent of Ottoman Empire
Safawid Dynasty of Persia
Area of Dispute

in advancing his successful bid for power. Six thousand Ottoman warriors campaigned as far as Adrianople and the Black Sea before installing their employer in Constantinople. So effective had they proven to be that 4 years later 20,000 were hired to check a Serbian advance on Salonika. A third time the Ottomans were paid to aid this same Byzantine emperor by silver plate taken from the churches of Constantinople. As a result of this service they learned of both the weakness and the wealth of the dwindling empire. Such a temptation could not long be resisted.

In 1354 the next Ottoman sultan crossed the Hellespont as an invader and established a fortified base for subsequent conquests at Gallipoli. From this position the next sultan, Murad I (1359–1389), rapidly expanded Ottoman territory in Europe. In 1362 historic

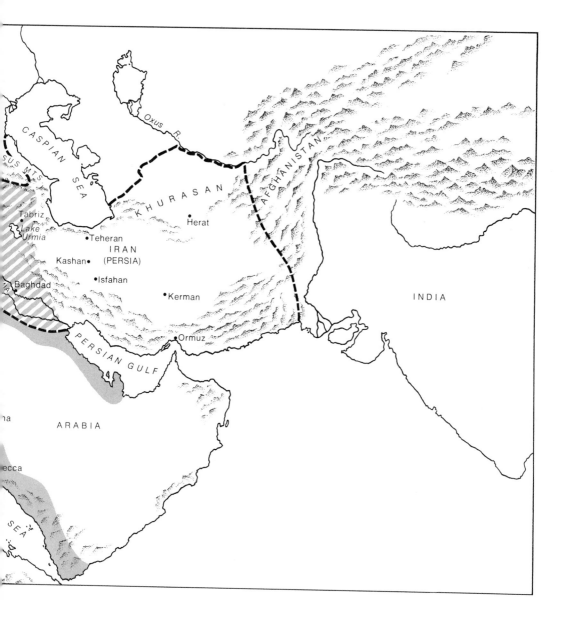

Edirne (Adrianople) was captured and subsequently became the temporary capital of the Ottoman Empire whose territories had by now become more extensive in Europe than in Asia. These European conquests were consolidated by the establishment of Turkish colonies and the transfer of Balkan peoples to vacated lands in Asia Minor. In further campaigns, which occupied the balance of his reign, a Latin crusade to regain

Edirne was disastrously defeated, and Serbians, Bulgarians, and Macedonians were reduced to tributary status and were required to furnish troops for his armies. In the year of his death Ottoman supremacy was confirmed by the decisive defeat of a coalition of these discontented vassals at the great Battle of Kossovo. These victories were greatly facilitated by the divisions within the Christian camp between the Latin and Orthodox churches and between oppressive lords and exploited peasants.

Of greater importance for the future of the Ottoman Empire was Murad I's development of an elite corps of enslaved soldiers, recruited from his Christian captives and known as the Janissaries (New Troops). In the long run, the domination of the government by this body and the breakdown of its rigorous regulations proved to be a major factor in the undoing of Ottoman power. Of course, the employment as soldiers of slaves who had been obtained by warfare or by purchase was nothing new in the Islamic world. What was new was the systematic development of a ruling institution in which slaves fulfilled almost all secular administrative, as well as the major military, functions, while freeborn Muslims were limited to the religious and auxiliary military aspects of government.

The European conquests yielded significant numbers of Christian captives who, according to the shari'a, could be enslaved. As his share, Murad received one fifth of these slaves. Later, however, the supply of captives proved inadequate to meet the needs of the ruling institution, and the legally questionable practice of levying promising youths between ten and twenty years of age from the sultan's Orthodox Christian subjects was instituted.

Most of these youths were entrusted to enfeoffed warriors for several years of religious and military training. They were then transferred to barracks schools for further education and training. The most talented were given further training in administration and then progressed up the administrative ladder to the top posts in the government, while the rest were enrolled in the renowned Janissary corps of infantry or the regular cavalry. As slaves, not only the career, but the very life, of each one was wholly dependent on loyal and satisfactory service to the sultan. Such an institution, which did not reach its full development until the later fifteenth century, was ideally suited to a militant frontier empire, a major portion of whose subjects were infidels—especially after the vigor of its warriors of the faith was sapped by the fruits of conquest. The esprit de corps of the Janissaries was maintained during its heyday by good pay and treatment and by the prohibition of marriage before retirement and of engaging in any business activity. In addition, it was fortified by association with the Bektashi brotherhood of Sufism which broadly recognized the common truth of Christianity and Islam and practiced Christian-type rituals. Such a commanding institution, however, tended to get out of hand when inflationary pressures led to successful demands for bonuses for its support. Discipline eventually broke down, eroding the rigor of the regulations, and abuses made its privileges less tolerable to freeborn Muslims. By the eighteenth century the whole edifice was thoroughly corrupted and infiltrated by freeborn Muslims, but the institution, although completely subverted from its original form and purpose and militarily of little value, was too well entrenched to be abolished before 1826.

To return to the course of conquest, Murad's son and successor, Bayezid the Thunderbolt (1389–1402), set the precedent, supported by the ulema as necessary to the welfare of the realm, of killing his brother. From then on, until the rule of succession was shifted to the senior member of the family, all but one of a sultan's sons could look forward to the probability of following their father to the grave. At least this practice eliminated the problem of pretenders and consequent civil strife.

Bayezid's reign was filled with campaigns and victories—until the final battle of his life. He consolidated his father's conquests and even advanced into Hungary, inspiring another crusade in which Western chivalry was again destroyed at the Battle of Nicopolis on the Danube in 1396. Also he turned his arms from Christian Europe to Muslim Anatolia, relying mainly on the Janissaries and contingents from his Christian vassals because Muslim warriors saw little profit and no religious merit in attacking their co-religionists. Muslims were shocked at this use of formerly Christian troops by a Muslim ruler to conquer fellow Muslims, and their alienation prepared his ultimate defeat by Timur. Meanwhile, Bayezid besieged Constantinople for 8 years after a new ruler failed to acknowledge his tributary status.

The failure of the siege was largely due to Ottoman impotence at sea. Turkish cavalrymen found no attraction in the high seas and depended primarily on Greeks to supply their need for sea transport. Without seapower, however, Constantinople and the islands of the Aegean could not be conquered. In recognition of this fact the Ottomans subsequently developed a navy, but it remained an artificial creation that was designed and manned mostly by non-Turkish subjects.

Although this siege had to be raised, Bayezid's other successes encouraged him to overestimate his strength and assume an insolent attitude toward Timur which could only result in war, once the "World-shaker" felt free to act. In July 1402, their forces collided outside Ankara in Anatolia. The unreliable Muslim Anatolian troops, placed in the forefront, deserted, and this defection of a quarter of his army determined the outcome. Bayezid himself was captured and, in despair, committed suicide less than a year later.

Between the loss of its Anatolian conquests and a struggle for the succession, the prospects of the Ottoman sultanate appeared bleak, but no force emerged to challenge it in its moment of weakness and division. Timur withdrew to prepare for an attempt to conquer China, and the West was torn by its own internal disputes. Within the European domains the enfeoffed warriors of the faith remained strong enough to prevent any rebellions, while the tributary vassals saw no advantage in questioning their relationship to the Ottomans. In 1413 the era of weakness ended with the accession of Bayezid's youngest son, Mehmed I (1413–1421).

Although assaults on Christendom were resumed, most of his efforts were devoted to the rehabilitation of his realm. The reign of his successor, Murad II (1421–1451), was filled with many campaigns both by land and by sea. Most significant was the reassertion of Ottoman authority throughout the empire and especially the effective challenge to Venetian naval superiority. These victories at sea sealed the fate of Constantinople which was successfully taken early in the reign of his successor, Mehmed II the Conqueror (1451–1481).

Mehmed II prepared for the siege by fortifications that cut off any possibility of supplies from the Black Sea, by the casting of great cannon that fired stone balls 30 inches in diameter, by further building up the fleet, and by assembling an army of 150,000 of whom one third were highly trained, crack troops. The once proud imperial capital, stripped of its territories and dependent on the activities of its merchants, could muster only 5,000 able-bodied men out of a shrunken population of 60,000 to defend its extensive walls. This inadequate number was reinforced by only 3,000 Western troops, including a valiant Genoese contingent of 700 men. In spite of the apparently hopeless situation, the troops withstood attack after attack for almost two months, inflicting heavy casualties, until they were finally overwhelmed in a last, all-out attack ordered on May 29, 1453. For three days the city was turned over according to custom to the troops to pillage. Then Mehmed restored order and labored by attractive inducements and outright deportation to repopulate the city and to renew its splendor as the capital of a great empire straddling both the East and the West. Thus the capture of Constantinople proved not the end but, instead, the beginning of a new era of glory for this imperial city.

The Orthodox hostility to Rome reflected in the cry, "Better Islam than the Pope," had already eased the course of Ottoman conquest, and the Ottoman record of tolerance and justice had validated this view. Now Mehmed further verified this trust by appointing an eminent Orthodox churchman as Patriarch and by confirming the privileges of the Orthodox clergy and church throughout his realm. This enlightened act of statesmanship, which assured the support of his Orthodox subjects, stands in contrast with the intolerance that plagued the Latin West in this and succeeding centuries.

Following the fall of Constantinople, the Conqueror utilized his superiority on land and sea to establish direct Ottoman administration over most of the Balkans and Greek peninsulas. In a drawn-out naval contest the Venetians, who were unwilling to challenge Ottoman seapower in a pitched naval battle, were forced to surrender most of their outposts in return for the right to trade. Mehmed had consolidated the Ottoman Empire. His successors used the superior armed forces he had perfected to expand its frontiers in Europe and the Middle East.

These achievements, which brought the empire to its zenith, were carried out not by his son but by his grandson, Selim I (1512–1520), and his great-grandson, Sulayman the Magnificent (1520–1566). At the time of Selim's accession the bulk of Islam was divided and dominated by three major powers: the newly risen Safawid dynasty of Iran as champions of Shi'a, the well-established, but decaying, Sunnite Mamluk regime of Egypt and Syria, and the avowedly Sunnite Ottoman Turks who nevertheless sheltered many Sufi orders. For religious reasons the Safawid state founded by the able and aggressive Shah Isma'il (1501–1524) was the most intolerant and dangerous. Against its cavalry Selim directed his professional army supported by the largest stand of artillery in the world. At a battle above Lake Urmia in 1515 the valiant, but inferior, Persian army was routed, and Selim followed up this victory by occupying part of Armenia, Mesopotamia, and even the Safawid capital of Tabriz.

Rightfully conjecturing that he might be the next victim, the Mamluk sultan attempted mediation so that he and the Shah might subsequently combine their resources for a common defense. Selim was not deceived and promptly declared war. Although the Mamluks had been the first to utilize gunpowder and cannon, the present sultan disdained these unchivalrous weapons and relied on the traditional prowess of his cavalry. In battle the issue was never in doubt. Then Selim marched to Cairo where his artillery put an end to the Mamluk sultanate. Along with Egypt and Syria Selim gained control of the Islamic homeland with the sacred cities of Medina and Mecca, as well as the Abbasid descendant whom the Mamluks had maintained as nominal caliph. Thus Selim's conquests acquired for the Ottomans the prestige of possessing the most sacred centers and symbols of Islam.

In 1518 the Greek corsair, Barbarossa, turned over to the Ottomans his conquest of Algeria. The Ottoman navy, which had previously played only a subordinate and supporting role to the army, gained almost equal stature under the command of this vigorous admiral who secured a seat in the sultan's diwan (council). His fleet, manned mainly by Greeks and Italians, dominated the Mediterranean, ravaging the Spanish coast and acquiring for the Ottomans most of the North African coast, except Morocco.

In Europe the armies of Selim's successor, Sulayman, met no united resistance in the capture of Belgrade and the conquest of most of Hungary because the mighty Hapsburg emperor, Charles V, was internally crippled by the Reformation and externally preoccupied by the challenge of France. French determination to check the growth of Hapsburg power even led to a new departure in European international relations, an alliance with the Ottoman Empire. Only the deep divisions wrought by the Reformation and the increasingly competitive nation-state system could have forced such a radical innovation. The prompt result was the Battle of Mohács in 1526 which destroyed

Hungarian resistance. Next, when the Hapsburgs successfully challenged Sulayman's vassal ruler of Hungary, the sultan did not stop his counterattack until his armies reached the walls of Vienna in the fall of 1529. But he only had light artillery, his heavy artillery having been mired down by heavy rains. The siege had to be raised, but the expedition had succeeded in consolidating his control of Hungary. Henceforth the Holy Roman Emperor had the obligation of defending Christendom against the "terrible Turks." All intermediate powers had been destroyed. Once again, in 1683, an Ottoman army was to besiege Vienna but, compared to the youthful vigor of Sulayman and his armies, that was a last-gasp effort of a decaying military machine.

THE OTTOMAN REGIME

Sulayman's reign represents both the peak of Ottoman development and the beginning of many of the practices that under impotent heirs were destined to corrupt the empire and to account for its designation in the nineteenth century as "the Sick Man of Europe." Therefore, his reign is a logical point at which to pause and examine the strengths and weaknesses of the empire's unique institutional structure.

The key figure of the Ottoman system was the sultan and, according to his character and ability, the empire prospered or deteriorated. But, like all Muslim rulers, his power was severely limited by the religion of Islam and its laws which were interpreted and applied by the ulema. Even the *Kanuns* (obviously derived from the Greek word for "rule" or "law"), which the sultans issued to regulate matters not clearly covered by the *shari'a*, required the approval of the ulema as being consistent with Islamic law. Sulayman was entitled "al Kanuni" for his painstaking codification of these supplementary rules. Thus, in ruling their freeborn Muslim subjects, at least, the sultans had to share authority and to cooperate with the leading representatives of the ulema. Thanks to the conquests in Europe, however, a large proportion of their subjects were non-Muslims, and the unique ruling institution was almost wholly staffed by slaves drawn from the Christian population. Therefore, except for the sultan, the government of this Turkish state was almost exclusively in the hands of former Orthodox Christians of non-Turkish origin. Indeed, most of the sultans were born of slave mothers of non-Turkish blood. Moreover, the ruling institution was essentially a military machine fashioned for, and by, the conquest of non-Muslim territories. This military character explains its success during the era of conquest, and its subsequent deterioration once the limits of empire had been reached.

At first, the main source of military strength had been the Turkish cavalryman who was rewarded by the grant of a fief to support himself and the armed retainers he was required to bring with him when called to the colors. Unlike European feudalism, each fief was held directly from the sultan and its retention depended on able military service. Exceptional ability or valor might be rewarded by the grant of additional nonhereditary estates. This feudal cavalry was still a major element in Sulayman's armies and could muster as many as 150,000 skilled horsemen. Its martial spirit was maintained by frequent and extended campaigns and by the opportunity for plunder furnished by fresh conquests. However, the ruling institution composed of slaves had already supplanted the feudal warriors in importance and prestige, supplying even the officers who supervised them in peacetime and commanded them on campaigns. Although the feudal cavalry continued for a century to play an important military role, its members naturally resented their subordination to the ruling institution, especially as it became more corrupt, and lost their élan as the opportunities for new plunder dwindled and disappeared.

Since the Ottoman regime was essentially a military government designed for war, all members of the ruling institution were regarded as warriors, even when they devoted their talents to administration, and military discipline applied to the whole organization from the grand vizir to the lowliest soldier. The governors and other officials of every province and district operated military governments that were primarily concerned with enforcing Ottoman authority and with providing the men and resources for war. All members were salaried, even when their incomes were derived from the temporary grants of fiefs. The maintenance of such an institution required a large revenue.

Less than half of the lands of the empire were granted out as hereditary fiefs; the rest paid taxes into the imperial treasury, although most of this revenue was probably consumed by local expenses. The guilds and individuals of the towns and cities also were assessed a variety of taxes, and varying amounts were levied on internal trade; but again, most of this was probably expended on the maintenance of garrisons, thus relieving the central government of this direct cost. Nevertheless, each province had a fixed sum that had to be remitted regularly to Constantinople. Of course, during the era of conquests large amounts were gained as booty, and the termination of new conquests appears to have tipped the fiscal scales against the Ottoman regime, encouraging debasement that in the long run only aggravated the fiscal situation through inflation.

The smallest, yet most renowned, element of the ruling institution was the Janissary infantry corps that in Sulayman's day numbered only 12,000 and, subsequently, during its heyday grew to no more than 30,000 fighting men. Because of its exceptional military effectiveness it enjoyed special privileges which it abused and exploited during its extended period of deterioration. It was organized into as many as 196 companies stationed in barracks in the cities of the empire where its members acted as a police force and as a check on the governors.

The imperial capital and neighboring cities contained the largest proportion and the most highly regarded of these companies. All their needs were supplied by artisans and merchants under contract so that the rule against engaging in nonmilitary activities could be maintained.

An elite cavalry corps, divided into six divisions, was another exclusively military branch of the ruling institution that was recruited from slaves. The full members, plus their retainers, totaled 50,000 expert horsemen. Finally, a number of specialized units, such as the artillerymen, rounded out the strictly military arm of the ruling institution.

The administrative, as well as the military, aspects of the ruling institution gained their authority from the sultan who, after Sulayman, became increasingly secluded from his subjects in the imperial palace (*seray*). The palace, following Persian precedent, was divided into three main parts, progessively more secluded: the outer court where the sultan could meet his officers and foreign dignitaries yet keep them at a distance, the inner court where he lived attended by household officers and slave pages in training, and the harem to which only the sultan, his concubines, his sons and female relatives, and the eunuchs who guarded and served them were admitted. In the harem the sultan was treated with great deference. His women were not to look on him unless commanded, and the clatter of his silver-soled slippers on the marble floors was the signal for them to scatter and hide. Normally the sultan only kept four concubines at a time. When replaced, they were freed from slavery. Since these ex-concubines retained the privilege of access to the harem, their hands in marriage were eagerly sought for the influence that they might wield over increasingly secluded sultans, either directly, or through the chief eunuch who became more and more important.

Until Sulayman, the vigorous sultans who built up the empire kept a close personal control over the government making, or at least confirming, all appointments. To conserve his energy, Sulayman delegated broad areas of authority to handpicked officials who were retained in office as long as they functioned efficiently. He also accepted gifts from appointees to help meet the mounting costs of the ruling institution. During his reign the invidious practice of farming the collection of taxes was developed. Under the constant and vigilant surveillance of an active ruler like Sulayman such measures might even contribute to better government, but under less energetic and knowledgeable successors they were subject to great abuses.

The chief minister was the grand vizir who with the sultan's signet ring acted as his deputy, issuing commands and making appointments, subject only to the sultan's veto. Below the grand vizir the secular administration was divided into two broad categories which, for clarity, may be designated as the treasury and the secretariat. Titles and the functions attached to them might change, but this basically triangular organization persisted throughout the life of the empire. The treasury received and disbursed all revenues, turning over any surplus to the private purse of the sultan. When deficits were incurred—and these became frequent after the close of the era of conquests—they were covered by "loans" from the sultan. Indeed, the unsuccessful efforts to solve the fiscal dilemmas largely explain the growth of the corruption that undermined the effectiveness of the central government and turned the empire into the "Sick Man of Europe." The secretariat handled the correspondence and drew up the orders (*fermans*) of the imperial government which were verified by the sultan's monogram. In the provinces and districts small-scale replicas of the imperial administration were established, including the use of identical titles. The size of the palace of a provincial governor (*pasha*) was naturally dependent on the resources of his province.

The sultan and his ruling institution of slaves were balanced and checked by the religious institution staffed by freeborn Muslims learned in Islamic theology and jurisprudence and called as a group the ulema. At the head of this institution was the Shaykh al-Islam who ranked for ceremonial purposes on a par with the grand vizir, and even the sultan. The grand vizir had to keep in constant touch with him on state affairs, and the sultan had to make periodic visits to him. War could not be declared without his approval. He might declare a sultan deposed on the basis of a violation of the *shari'a* of which he was the supreme interpreter. But the fact that each Shaykh was appointed and subject to dismissal by the sultan normally insured the sultan's supremacy. The Shaykh's main function was to make sure that every decision conformed with Islamic law. Therefore, it was logical that Sulayman in establishing this post appointed the Grand Mufti (consultative jurist) of Constantinople rather than the chief Kadi (judge) who was a member of the imperial diwan and thus a part of the ruling institution.

The muftis as spiritual heirs of the founders of the *shari'a* schools of law played a unique role in the Islamic system of jurisprudence. Exceptionally learned from a long career as students and professors in the *madrāsās*, they did not sit in judgment like the kadis but, instead, were available for consultation on any point of law, for a fee. Their answers, called *fetwas*, answered the questions submitted to them. Although "the door of interpretation" had theoretically been closed in the tenth century, they could, in fact, make new interpretations by selection from a host of precedents. As developed, every major city in the empire had one or more muftis, all subordinate to the Shaykh al-Islam, but there was no rigid hierarchy to limit flexibility and independence. Since they were unsalaried and thus theoretically independent, the people have tended to view them and their decisions with great respect.

Status in the ulema derived from education and professorial experience in the *madrāsās*, especially those endowed by the sultans in the capital. Elementary education was wholly unsponsored by the state. The well-to-do employed tutors for their children; the rest, if they could afford the fees, could send their children for group instruction by private teachers in what have been called Qur'an schools attached to every mosque. Generally, instruction in these schools was limited to learning the Arabic alphabet and to memorizing passages of the Qur'an in Arabic, although more able and dedicated teachers might add some mathematics or other useful subjects. In Arabic-speaking lands such instruction might develop literacy, but in non-Arabic-speaking areas it served only the religious purpose of indoctrination and the social purpose of instilling discipline and respect for elders. Plentiful evidence shows that the rod was not spared. All other knowledge and skills had to be gained by apprenticeship.

Higher education, which produced the ulema, was provided in the endowed *madrāsās* attached to major mosques. They represented different levels of instruction, and the student might graduate from one after another before completing his education. Originally non-theological subjects were taught according to the special interests of the professors, but by the seventeenth century the *madrāsas* had degenerated into strictly theological seminaries that were dedicated to the production of new recruits for the ulema. What non-theological studies remained were given in the palace schools that were reserved for trainees of the ruling institution. The advancement of learning was further stifled by the corruption in the awarding of professorships and by the ban on printing or the importation of printed books. In the final analysis, however, in spite of educational deterioration, the ulema effectively performed their fundamental function of maintaining the unity of the Muslim brotherhood encompassed by Sunnite orthodoxy. Indeed, they advanced the cause by

reducing their differences with Sufism through joining and gaining prestige within these orders. Thus, while intellectual deterioration within the ulema may have matched the political and economic deterioration within the empire during the seventeenth and eighteenth centuries, the ideological unity within the Sunnite realm was upheld and even reinforced.

Of course, at its greatest extent the empire included a large proportion of non-Muslim subjects only indirectly affected by the religion of their ruler. From the earliest days of Islamic imperialism the general policy had been to deal with subjects, both Muslim and non-Muslim, as corporate groups. This policy probably reflected both the tribal heritage of Islam and the policies of the rulers that the Islamic conquerors replaced. In any case, it was simpler to deal with the representatives of groups, whether tribal, occupational, or religious, than with each of the individuals involved. This corporate approach to the administration of its predecessors was emulated by the Ottoman regime. Like the Umayyads, the Ottoman sultans ruled a very large non-Muslim population which they saw no great advantage in attempting to convert, especially after the development of a ruling institution that was dependent on a continuing supply of Orthodox Christian recruits. Therefore, after the conquest of Constantinople they established three largely self-governing religious communities (*millets*) under heads appointed by the sultan: the Orthodox Christian, the Jewish, and the Armenian Christian communities.

Following the fall of Constantinople, the Conqueror named a highly regarded Orthodox churchman to be the patriarch of the whole "Roman community" (as the Ottomans termed the body of Orthodox Christians) with the rank of pasha and civil authority over the entire *millet* that resided within the empire. Although the Ottomans fixed the tax assessment, the patriarch was held responsible for apportioning and collecting it. Naturally, the Orthodox church gained freedom of worship, subject to the patriarch's orders, and protection against attacks by the Latin church. Generally, the situation of the church can be considered better under the Ottomans than under the later Byzantine rulers who, in their desperation for Western military aid, were prepared to surrender to the Latin church. A questionable exception to this improved condition was the youth levy for the ruling institution which was assessed only on the Orthodox community as residents of what was, and might still be, considered the "land of war." Those youths taken were lost to the church, but many parents appear to have vied to have their sons chosen for such a privileged career.

Almost immediately, a second *millet* was tacitly established by the appointment of a chief rabbi with similar powers and responsibilities for the Jewish community. In fact, Jews gained favored status with the chief rabbi, ranking ahead of the Orthodox patriarch, and second only to the head of the ulema. So much better was their treatment within the Ottoman Empire that a flood of refugees from European persecution poured in during the later fifteenth century, the largest influx coming from Spain. Thanks to their superior medical knowledge, Jews were regularly appointed court physicians, and many with other skills also secured important posts in the government. The varied skills of these immigrants served not only the government but also contributed significantly to the flourishing conditions of the entire empire during its heyday. The Sephardic Jews from Spain, besides becoming the most numerous, were the best educated and thus were attracted to the cities whose economies they stimulated. They excelled in commerce and, because of their linguistic knowledge, served as interpreters in contacts with Europeans. One group gained renown for its knowledge of the manufacture of arms. The capital acquired the largest Jewish community in the world, and Salonika became virtually a Jewish city.

The establishment of the Armenian Christian *millet* presented a problem because their centers had not yet been taken and their head, the Catholicos, resided outside of the empire. In 1461, however, the Armenian bishop of Brusa was named patriarch with residence in Constantinople and powers similar to the Orthodox patriarch and the chief rabbi.

Although the *millet* system provided an attractive measure of autonomy and religious freedom for Christians and Jews, these religious minorities did suffer disabilities vis-à-vis the Muslims in an Islamic state. Not only were special taxes, such as the poll tax, assessed but in any legal dispute with a Muslim their evidence was not recognized, though most Muslim judges sought to uphold justice. Furthermore, their generous treatment lasted little more than a century. Sulayman's second successor reactivated the sumptuary laws which required non-Muslims to wear distinctive clothing and other badges of inferiority. The same ruler, angered by the growing arrogance of the Janissaries, undermined the system of recruitment from the Orthodox community by enrolling so many others that the size of the corps was doubled. Freeborn Muslims in ever greater numbers sought the privileged status of a Janissary, completely subverting the basic principle of the ruling institution, though nominally these Muslim volunteers were deemed slaves of the sultan. The termination of the youth levy, combined with fear of a Western counterattack, tended not only to lower the regard for all non-Muslims but also to generate a positive hostility toward them as a potential fifth column. These Muslim fears were reinforced by the dominant role that they had achieved in trade with the West. Finally, the liberal treatment accorded the Jews had reawakened messianic dreams, and movements, within their *millet*.

Millet status should not be confused with the special privileges extended to citizens of Western states in concessionary agreements called capitulations (from the

Latin, *Capitula*, meaning "chapters"), which were granted usually for commercial purposes. These agreements can be traced back to the thirteenth century. The Conqueror made such an arrangement to retain the services of Genoese residents in the foreign quarter of the capital. By its terms the Genoese gained security for their persons and property, freedom of trade and travel, and the right to try cases in their own courts according to their own laws in return for the payment of a poll tax. As a result of his French alliance, Sulayman made a similar agreement covering French merchants. Later in the sixteenth century other European states secured the same type of trade concessions which provided extraterritorial privileges.

THE DETERIORATION OF THE OTTOMAN REGIME

This is the sad story of the long-term decay of a once powerful and efficient system of government. Although a vast number of complex factors arose and contributed in many ways to this decline, most of them can be ignored and the essence of the tale can be related briefly because it all stemmed from one factor—the failure to reform and adapt effectively to changed circumstances.

During the two centuries of their rise to power the Ottomans evolved a unique and effective military machine fashioned for, and by, conquest. It fed on fresh conquests and, when the limits of expansion in terms of existing communications were reached, as witnessed by Sulayman's inability to bring his artillery before the walls of Vienna in 1529, the regime was in trouble. Without fresh plunder to feed it, financial problems began to undermine it. Instead of being reformed along peacetime lines, it was allowed to feed on itself with the inevitably fatal result of destroying its one strong point, its military efficiency. Every temporary solution, such as currency debasement, only further weakened it in the long run.

Instead of disciplining or disbanding the expensive and dictatorial Janissaries with their repeated demands for bonuses and salary increases to compensate for inflation, the corps was thrown open to untrained and undisciplined freeborn Muslim recruits who only increased the payrolls and pressures while destroying the corps' effectiveness on the battlefield. The rules against marriage and participation in business and the austerity of barracks life fell into desuetude, and merchants and artisans eagerly sought the privileges and exemption from taxation that membership conferred. In battle the once well-drilled Janissaries were now no more than a rabble.

A change in the law of succession early in the seventeenth century from the son to the eldest prince of the blood brought to the throne many pitiful figures who had spent their whole lives in seclusion. By this gambit the grand vizirs gained full responsibility for the government, but the insecurity of their tenure, subject to the whims of palace intrigue, incapacitated even the ablest from carrying out effectual reforms. Most destructive, however, was the growth of corruption and consequent maladministration that was encouraged by the financial needs of the government. Imperial appointments went to the highest bidder, and to make the sales as frequent as possible the term of appointment was reduced in most instances to one year. Needless to say, appointees had to recoup the cost of their gifts within that year. Likewise, the farming of taxes was placed on the auction block. Such thoroughgoing corruption in the ruling institution could not avoid infecting the religious institution, and professorships, judgeships and, indeed, every appointive position within it were similarly put up for sale. Courtiers usually won the tax-farming contracts which they then subcontracted for all the traffic could bear. Thus the burden on the peasantry, called *raya* meaning "flock to be fleeced," grew in oppression.

While its soul was being consumed by unprecedented corruption, the Ottoman Empire was also confronted by the challenge of the nation-states of Europe. This challenge was both political and economic because the economic changes that had undermined the guilds in the West allowed the rise of a middle class of enterprising merchants and entrepreneurs who sought the protection of their interests both at home and abroad from the central government. Thus the economic changes not only made possible but required the development of strong regimes that could command the resources of their people. In contrast, the Ottoman Empire did not, and by its very diverse nature could not, undergo any such transformation. It remained a loose assemblage of varied and divergent corporate groups based on religion, occupation, or region and was held together only by the military monopoly of the ruling institution—and during the seventeenth and eighteenth centuries this military strength was being rapidly dissipated.

In these circumstances of internal deterioration and external pressure what is amazing is the persistence of the empire, despite substantial territorial losses, through the nineteenth and into the twentieth century. Internally this persistence may be explained by the failure of the diverse corporate groups, until the later nineteenth century, to overcome their differences and to develop common interests and objectives. Each group clung desperately to its rights and privileges and viewed with suspicion every proposal to subordinate it to a larger unity. Indeed, major groups which were too influential to be ignored collaborated to frustrate every effort at reform. In addition, almost every crisis produced a vigorous sultan or grand vizir who, at least, prevented the worst from happening. External political pressure was alleviated during the seventeenth and eighteenth centuries by the preoccupation of the European states with their internal contests for power and, subsequently, by their mutual jealousies and fears regarding each other's acquisitions from the "Sick Man of Europe."

Economic inroads and spoliation, however, were not so easily checked. The Otto-

mans never demonstrated any understanding of economic principles, especially those associated with the Commercial Revolution in the West. As an imperial power, their economic theory was limited to the acquisition of surpluses by plunder and tribute to feed their military machine. For a fee the management of trade was left to the corporate groups that specialized in it. From the beginning the carrying trade was monopolized by Westerners, first the Venetians and then their successors. Although an effective navy was created that even after the disastrous Battle of Lepanto in 1571 continued by a supreme effort to dominate the eastern Mediterranean, the land-loving Turks never appreciated the importance of developing a merchant marine to support their naval arm. In the farther East the stronger Dutch and English successors of the Portuguese effectively reduced the volume of transit trade passing through Ottoman hands to Europe. In any case, the bullion paid by European merchants for these goods immediately passed to the East to pay for more imports, not only for sale to Europe but also for internal consumption. Meanwhile, the capitulations limited import duties on European goods to no more than 3 to 5 percent ad valorem, leaving the more heavily taxed artisans of the Ottoman Empire unprotected against European competition. These trading conditions reduced the empire to a supplier of raw materials and specie, with a few exceptions, in return for European manufactures.

Within the empire the production and exchange of goods began to shrink and deteriorate in quality from the opening of the seventeenth century with consequent economic hardship and a probably large and continuous decline in population. For reasons not yet explained, outbreaks of the bubonic plague, which had disappeared in Europe, regularly ravaged the cities of the empire during the eighteenth and the first half of the nineteenth centuries. Other diseases, largely controlled in the West, also took their toll. Frequent famines, due in part to govenmental irresponsibility and the neglect of irrigation works, carried away many more. Along the fringes of the Desert Bay many formerly prosperous farming communities were abandoned and recaptured by the desert. Official exploitation compelled by corruption and annual appointments probably contributed to a general lowering of the standard of living which, in turn, weakened resistance to the devastations of disease and famine. The extent of depopulation cannot be statistically demonstrated, but it certainly complemented the economic decline in weakening the empire.

INTERACTION WITH THE WEST

In discussing the internal deterioration of the Ottoman Empire, notice has already been taken of Western economic influence. Therefore, this section is limited to a brief analysis of political and cultural factors and the reactions to them.

In spite of mounting internal difficulties, the frontiers established by Sulayman were maintained throughout the sixteenth and seventeenth centuries, mainly as a result of the preoccupation of the European nations with their own relationships. Nevertheless, one ambitious and vigorous vizir, recognizing that Ottoman military strength had been built on conquest and its fruits, sought in 1683 to revitalize the martial spirit of the empire by a fresh round of European conquests. If he had not been blind to the relative conditions of military strength in Europe and the empire, he would have realized that what Sulayman had not been able to accomplish at the peak of Ottoman vigor was certainly impossible a century and a half later. Yet he was desperate and saw no other avenue of reform as he looked around at the reactionary conservatism and corruption of the standing army, the administration, and even the ulema who all collaborated to stifle every lesser effort at reform. Dreaming of vast conquests north of the Danube and east of the Rhine, he led a host of nearly 200,000 ill-trained, ill-equipped, and ill-disciplined troops to the second siege of Vienna, the key to the realization of these dreams. Although from Sulayman's time the superiority of the pike to the scimitar as a complement to the musket had been repeatedly demonstrated, the Ottoman armies still clung to this antiquated combination that had once proved invincible. As before, Vienna was caught unprepared and was almost starved into surrender before an adequate relieving army could be assembled. Even if the Ottomans had gained the city, however, they would have been in equally desperate straits from a shortage of supplies, and the result would have been the same. The brilliantly led relief force almost annihilated the confused and misled Ottoman army. Yet in the subsequent struggle, which was not to end till the Peace of Karlowitz in 1699, fresh levies were raised to meet repeated defeats, interspersed with a few successes. By the terms of peace the Ottoman Empire suffered its first large territorial losses, almost the whole of Hungary and Transylvania to the Hapsburgs and the Greek Peloponnesus to the Venetians.

Throughout the eighteenth century the Ottomans still failed to appreciate the necessity for reform. Indeed, several military successes made possible by the continued preoccupation of the European states with internal conflicts encouraged renewed faith in their outmoded ways. In any case, while the facade of unity was maintained, the extent of real Ottoman authority was sharply reduced by the rise of nearly autonomous provincial rulers both in the European and Asian provinces. Their continued recognition of the sultan's suzerainty was, in most cases, a convenient expedient for legalizing the power that they had seized.

Meanwhile, the expanding Orthodox Christian state of Russia had joined the list of Western powers who were anxious for Turkish territory, and especially access to the Mediterranean. In the second half of the eighteenth century, Catherine the Great and her brilliant general, Marshal Suvorov, overran the Ottoman territories along the north shore of the Black Sea. In 1774 the Treaty of Kuchuk Kainarji confirmed most of these gains, granted Russian commercial vessels the right of free navigation in Turkish waters, and gave Russia the right to make direct complaint regarding the Russian church to be built in Constantinople. This last point was expanded by later interpretations to justify the Russian assertion of a right of protection over all Orthodox Christians and their interests within the Ottoman Empire. Although defeats and losses of territory should have stimulated Ottoman leaders to study and adopt, at least the military techniques responsible for Western superiority, their response was almost wholly negative, rejecting everything of Christian origin and rejecting every reform in favor of retaining their vested interests in the corrupt and tottering administration. Some leaders, however, began to realize at the end of the century the need at least to eradicate the most obvious weaknesses, such as the greedy and militarily useless Janissaries, and they gained an enlightened, if not very forceful, champion in Sultan Selim III (1789–1807). In 1793 he issued the New Regulations to reform the army along Western lines, to revise commercial relations with the West, and to develop an effective system of taxation, but the combined opposition of the ulema, the Janissaries, and other vested interests brought this effort to nought, except for the formation of a Western-style corps of 12,000 men that proved its superiority in the field.

In contrast to the Western assaults on the European frontiers of the Ottoman Empire, Napoleon's expedition to Egypt brought Western arms into the Islamic homeland for the first time since the Crusades and began a century and a half of increasing Western pressure and direct interventions. In addition, it introduced French revolutionary ideas which began the fermentation of new political and intellectual thought that, in time, developed a broader base for reform and revolution. But even the shock of Napoleon's operations in Egypt and Syria could not overcome the reactionary opposition to reform, and Selim was deposed by the Janissaries in 1807 and strangled a year later to forestall his restoration.

After a brief interlude of coups d'état his more daring and ruthless nephew and disciple, Mahmud II (1808–1839), succeeded to the sultanate with a firm determination to take whatever steps were necessary to reassert the authority of the sultan and to revitalize the machinery of the Ottoman Empire. Although he did regain direct control of many areas in Europe and Asia and brought about the long-overdue extinction of the Janissaries by a bloody massacre in 1826, his reign almost witnessed the overthrow of the Ottoman Empire at the hands of his Egyptian governor, the even more vigorous modernizer, Mehemet Ali (1805–1849).

MEHEMET ALI OF EGYPT

This illiterate son of an Albanian fisherman who did not speak Arabic may seem an unlikely prospect to bring unity and modernization to Arabic-speaking Egypt, but he had already demonstrated his qualities of leadership by being appointed second in command of the small Albanian contingent sent to the Egyptian theater in 1799 to oppose Napoleon. In the turmoil and intrigues that followed the withdrawal of foreign forces he emerged victorious in 1805. His seizure of power was recognized the following year by his appointment as governor by the sultan. He suppressed and eradicated the Mamluk chieftains, who had been exploiting the impoverished peasantry, confiscating their fiefs and bringing most of the land under the direct control of the state. During his 44-year rule, he secured a governmental monopoly of all major crops and initiated extensive internal improvements such as the development of irrigation to make possible multiple crops and the introduction of new seeds and crops like cotton and rice. With the greatly increased revenues that these reforms and innovations produced, he financed army modernization, the construction of a navy, and a program of imperial expansion. In addition, he purchased factories, advanced education by establishing schools of engineering and medicine and by financing the advanced study of students in Europe, and established the first Arabic press and newspaper. For the most part he employed French advisors and professors to the growing irritation of the British whose strategic interest in a Middle Eastern route to India was developing.

In 1824 Sultan Mahmud appealed to his powerful governor for military assistance against Greek rebels. His son Ibrahim, who commanded the forces that had already conquered Crete, landed in the Peloponnesus in 1825 and swiftly suppressed the rebels. Britain, France, and Russia, allied by their mutual alarm at the success of the combined Egyptian and Turkish forces against the Greeks, demanded a truce pending negotiations. When the Greeks continued fighting, Ibrahim landed troops and in an accidental naval battle at Navarino (1827) the Egyptian fleet was destroyed.

Although the fleet was destroyed, the army was later evacuated intact and the indomitable pasha demanded his promised reward of Syria. When Sultan Mahmud, miscalculating his determination, refused the request, Ibrahim's forces were unleashed and, after two decisive victories, overran both Syria and Anatolia. On Britain's refusal to intervene in his behalf the Sultan turned in desperation to Russia which was only too willing to oblige. Now thoroughly alarmed at the Russian threat, Britain and France combined to persuade Mehemet Ali to accept Syria in settlement of his claims, and peace was restored for the time being. But the aging sultan was determined not to accept these defeats at the hands of his governor. Feverishly he rebuilt his army and navy and, feeling that he had not long to live, committed them to battle prematurely in 1839. Again, Ibrahim decisively defeated the Ottoman army, but most amazing was the voluntary surrender a week later of the Ottoman navy.

On the same day, July 1, 1839, Sultan Mahmud died after a long and troubled reign to be succeeded by a boy, Abd al-Mejid (1839–1861). But the real power was initially in the hands of the reformer, Reshid Pasha, who persuaded the young sultan to issue a decree calling in general terms for a reform program along Western lines. In the succeeding years this decree led to specific steps that produced a stronger government which was responsive to assemblies and councils that represented, at least, the most powerful elements in the state. It also produced mixed courts for commercial disputes and the establishment of technical schools on Western models. Meanwhile, joint European intervention in which British forces played the leading role were again required to turn back Mehemet Ali. This time he was forced to disgorge all his extra-Egyptian conquests in return for the sultan's recognition of his hereditary right to rule Egypt. In spite of this reverse this remarkable man had laid the foundations of the modern Egyptian state and its economy and had established a dynasty that lasted until 1952.

Relative peace prevailed for more than a decade until a minor dispute over whether certain holy places in Palestine should be controlled by Latin or Orthodox Christians escalated as a result of diplomatic blundering into the Crimean War (1853–1856) in which the major contestants were the French and British versus the Russians. This was a useless war that should have been avoided, but it is significant to note that in its engagements with the Russians the reformed Ottoman army acquitted itself creditably. Moreover, the Russian threat to Constantinople was checked even if the sultan was henceforth dependent on the support of Britain and France. In return, they insisted on reissuance of the earlier reform decree. The military has usually been of necessity the initial area of greatest Western influence in non-Western lands. Foreign training and advisors have usually exposed army officers more fully to Western political, as well as military, ideas. In this respect the Ottoman empire was no exception.

Since the Ottoman Turks inherited the fully developed cultures of the Middle East, there was little that they could add of a creative nature. Their most significant works represented a blend in which the Persian heritage was dominant. The arts were generously patronized, but the results are generally unimpressive except, perhaps, for the architectural perfection of the multitude of buildings which were designed and built by the long-lived Sinan (1589–1679), who began his career as an Orthodox Christian conscript in the Janissaries. The Sulaymaniya mosque in Constantinople, incorporating the best elements from each heritage and designed to surpass the Byzantine Santa Sophia, is probably his major masterpiece.

The even fuller utilization of military and naval technology borrowed from the West largely accounts for the Ottoman rise to power, but thereafter the achievements of the West were rejected and despised until, with Napoleon's arrival in 1798 and subsequent Western intervention, they could no longer be ignored if the empire was to survive. The employment of French military advisors led to the study of the French language by army officers and administrators which reached significant proportions in the reign of Sultan Mahmud II. Knowledge of French threw open the gates to the liberal French writings of the nineteenth century.

Up to the end of the Crimean War, however, these alien ideas reached and infected only a few. Not until the 1860s were the floodgates opened by the introduction of Western subjects and texts and the development of the first Western-type schools, other than the few technical schools. Not until the 1870s did substantial numbers of Tur-

kish students return from France imbued with radical Western ideas. Therefore, 1856 is a logical point at which to end this part of our study of the Ottoman Empire. The progressive sultans, Selim III, Mahmud II, and Abd al-Mejid had prepared the ground for the reception of Western ideas, but the time was not yet ripe for this preparation to bear more than the first few fruits, mainly in the military and commercial realms.

THE SAFAWID DYNASTY (1501 – 1736)

After many centuries of domination by alien rulers of Arab, Turkish, and Mongol origin the resilient Persian people finally gained a native dynasty that maintained its vigor for more than a century and repelled the attacks of Sunnite Turks from both the west and the north on this land of Shiite "heresy." The story of Shiite Persia can be more briefly told than that of the Ottoman Empire, first, because it represents the culmination of the long struggle of the Persian spirit to reassert itself, and second, because its developments in many ways paralleled those of its disciples and prime foes, the Ottomans.

Iran's geographical position has been a major, though often unappreciated, asset. Its northern frontier, east and west of the Caspian Sea, has exposed it to the initial impact of nomadic tribesmen from central Asia in all their pristine vigor. The necessity of absorbing and semicivilizing these barbarian invaders before they pressed onward to the more civilized centers to the east or west repeatedly revitalized the martial spirit and blood of these unwitting defenders of civilization. In addition, its geographical position placed it astride the major overland trade routes between East and West, and the mixed and vigorous Persian peoples benefited both economically and culturally from the mounting volume of trade that was stimulated by the growing prosperity in the

West, until technological improvements in sea transport diverted this trade to sea routes. From another point of view, Iran enjoyed the less remote stimulus of having as immediate neighbors two regions of early and advanced civilizations, Mesopotamia and India. Again, Iran not only protected these civilizations by bearing the initial impact of central Asian invaders but also provided overland routes for the exchange of goods and ideas between them. The influential Persian role in blending Indian and Middle Eastern contributions to bring Islamic civilization to its zenith was no mere accident.

Under the Sassanids the scholars and artisans of Iran had already demonstrated their special talent in incorporating Indian, Mesopotamian, and even some Chinese cultural and scientific ideas and practices; and the Arab conquerors were to be captured by this heritage. The ease with which the Arabs overthrew the Sassanid ruler, captured his capital, and overran Iran reflected no breakdown in Persian vitality but rather the alienation of its local leaders from a regime that had located its center in Mesopotamia and valued Iran principally as a source of warriors for its exhausting and futile contest with the Byzantine Empire. As soon as the Arab conquest was completed, the resilient spirit of the aristocratic leaders, the scholars, and the people who supported them began to reassert itself, first politically, and then culturally and religiously, within the framework of the Islamic empire.

There is no need to relate in detail the Persian revival that culminated in the restoration of Persian independence under the Safawids. It will be enough to recall the major stages leading to this achievement. The rebellion that installed the Abbasid caliphate with its Persian cultural orientation began in the northeastern frontier province of Khurasan under the leadership of a convert to Islam. Persian scholars and scientists soon demonstrated their skills and, thanks to the freedom and safety of communications

throughout the Islamic world, placed a Persian imprint on Islamic civilization, as far away as the distant and independent court of Cordoba in Spain. Not content, however, with political subordination to the Caliphate in Baghdad, a governor of Khurasan less than a century after the establishment of the Abbasids effectively asserted his independence by dropping the caliph's name from the Friday noon prayer. A succeeding dynasty, the Samanid (c 904–999), for a time ruled the whole of Iran and represented the reaction of the Persian aristocracy to their replacement by Turkish mercenaries in the caliph's bodyguard and in military and political commands. The Buwayhid dynasty (945–1055) secured the submission of the Abbasids and the title of "commander of the commanders," but of more permanent significance it raised the banner of Shi'a for both political and religious reasons. Shi'a was not only the traditional vehicle for political opposition, but its mystical doctrines, as well as their individualistic expression in the various forms of Sufism, were more closely related to the pre-Islamic religious experience of the Persians. The reconciliation of Sunnite and Sufi practices by the Persian theologian and philosopher, al-Ghazzali (1058–1111), was truly only another expression of the Persian religious outlook. These Persian dynasts need also to be remembered for their patronage of the Persian literary renaissance whose first great representative was Firdawsi (940–1020), author of the epic Shah-Nama (Book of Kings) glorifying the pre-Islamic accomplishments of Iran. The promising political revival in Persia was cut off and submerged by the Turkish and Mongol inundations which did not spend their force until the later fifteenth century, but paradoxically, these rude conquerors, civilized by Persian preceptors, patronized the full development of the Persian literary revival that was complete before the Safawids restored Persian political independence and unity. Thus the establishment of Safawid Persia was only the final and long delayed act in the political realm that confirmed what Persian genius had already accomplished in the cultural realm.

Shah Isma'il (1501–1524), founder of the Shiite Safawid dynasty, was the descendant of a renowned Sufi who claimed the added aura of descent from Ali, the progenitor of Shi'a. Thus to his appeal as a successful warrior he joined the religious sanction of holiness, a by no means novel combination in Middle Eastern annals. In battle after battle he eliminated the last of the Timurids and attained full control of Iran by 1502. Then he began to build an empire by a series of campaigns northward to the Oxus, eastward into Afghanistan, and westward into Mesopotamia and Anatolia where he was welcomed by colonies of his family's Sufi order. The only remaining power that could challenge his authority was the Sunnite Ottoman Empire under the equally ambitious Selim the Grim. North of Lake Urmia the Ottoman army equipped with muskets and artillery so decisively defeated his cavalry in 1515 that he lost not only his Mesopotamian and Anatolian conquests but also his capital city of Tabriz. Instead of discrediting his leadership, however, this defeat rallied the people to his championship of the Persian cause under the banner of Shi'a. So hostile was the countryside that Selim had to evacuate the city and retreat to the more friendly environment of Anatolia. Isma'il's son, Shah Tahmasp (1524–1576) and Sulayman resumed the struggle. Although Sulayman's superior armies were able to march at will through western Iran, taking city after city, and although the Shah's defense problem was complicated by repeated incursions by the Uzbek tribesmen of central Asia, Sulayman was unable to shake the loyalty of the people and was forced to retire after each invasion without any significant gains.

The peak of the Safawid dynasty was reached under the enlightened, but ruthless, Shah Abbas (1587–1629). At the beginning of his reign the outlook was not good. A large part of Khurasan had been lost to the Uzbeks,

and the western provinces were controlled by the Ottomans. In addition, the Shah was almost totally dependent on the seven Turkish tribes, known as the "Red Heads," whose 70,000 horsemen had originally brought the Safawids to power. Concentrating his energies on the prime task of ejecting the alien interlopers, he made peace with the Ottomans, confirming their gains on the western front, to be free to deal with the Uzbeks. By 1597 he had driven them out of Iran, restoring much of the prestige of his dynasty with the Persian people. He could now give his attention to the Ottomans, but he first recognized the need to reorganize and modernize his armies for this task. Already he had followed the example of the Ottomans by recruiting, mainly from Georgian and Armenian converts, a salaried army of 10,000 cavalrymen and 20,000 infantrymen designated the "Friends of the Shah." This force, which relieved him of dependence on tribal loyalty, was now equipped with firearms. Two English brothers, Robert and Anthony Sherley, who arrived in 1598 with 26 followers, were responsible for manufacturing the Shah's artillery and training his artillerymen.

In 1602, Shah Abbas felt prepared to renew hostilities with the Ottomans. In the next year he won a decisive victory near Lake Urmia, not far from the spot where the first Safawid had suffered such a great defeat. This victory recovered most of the western region, but the Shah, not content with restoring the frontier, took Mesopotamia and other areas from the Ottomans in subsequent campaigns.

His cordial relations with the English led him to favor the East India Company with the lion's share of the increased volume of trade that he fostered. The Portuguese in the fortified base at Hormuz which they had held since 1507 resented this intrusion on their monopoly. In 1622 a Persian army with the support of the English East India Company expelled the Portuguese and, in return for their aid, the English were awarded special privileges that assured their predominance in the Persian market.

Under Safawid patronage this era saw the peak of perfection in the production of Persian rugs and other textiles and the organization of these industrial arts in specialized centers, such as Tabriz, Kashan, Isfahan, Kerman, and Herat, whose products are still renowned. On the less glorious side it must be acknowledged that this perfection was achieved by the exploitation of children many of whom ruined their eyesight as well as their health in the intricate tasks that only little fingers could perform. Shah Abbas unsuccessfully attempted to revitalize ceramic art by importing 300 Chinese potters. The chief fruit was the further introduction of Chinese stylistic motifs which appeared in carpet, textile, and painting designs as well.

In literature and the fine arts the era of greatest creativity had already passed before the rise of the Safawids. In spite of liberal Safawid patronage authors, poets, and painters were unable to surpass or even to equal the achievements of the past. The last, and perhaps the greatest, Persian miniature artist, Bihzad, was still alive at the death of the first shah, but his successors made no new contributions of significance. One notable poet began the movement, reflecting national feeling, to purge the Persian language of Arabic words which influenced Ottoman writers later to pursue the same course. Poetry was generally not of outstanding quality, in part, because the Safawids preferred to patronize Shiite theological development. Persian literary and artistic development continued to depend on aristocratic and royal patronage. It remained art for the few with the exception of the construction of mosques.

Shah Abbas established Isfahan as his capital and lavished attention on its beautification with colorfully decorated mosques, palaces, and gardens. Those that are preserved make Isfahan Iran's premier tourist attraction today. Under Abbas this planned city is said to have accommodated 600,000

residents and to have been furnished with 162 mosques, 273 public baths, and 1802 inns as well as 48 theological seminaries. Every home is asserted to have possessed its own garden court, while across the river were garden palaces without comparison throughout the world. Shah Abbas' beneficence was not limited to his capital. Other cities possess mosques and public buildings built by him. More important, however, as a reflection of his concern for the general welfare, are the canals, inns, and other public works he constructed.

The dedication of the Safawids to the solid establishment of Shi'a as the state religion of Iran led to the theological development of a religious hierarchy similar to that of the Ottomans and enjoying even greater power and prestige. So thorough was their work that no successor could shake it. At the head of the hierarchy stood the Shaykh al-Islam and below him were graded positions according to educational and professorial accomplishment in the state-supported theological colleges. The best minds were thus attracted to theological and related judicial careers. An orthodox legal system was expounded and, as under the Ottomans, a body of legal consultants interpreted the juridical questions submitted to them. In fact, the similarity of the Persian religious institution to that of the Ottomans is striking. Thus both Persian Shi'a and Ottoman Sunni evolved religious hierarchies that were a far cry from the simple religion of the Prophet and became in time major strongholds of conservatism, opposing every effort at modernization as a threat to their vested interests.

For more than a century after the death of Shah Abbas his weak, dissolute, or vicious descendants neglected the welfare of the people, which he had fostered by numerous public works, and surrendered themselves to the life of the harem. Again, the parallel to Ottoman decline is inescapable. In the Safawid case, however, the decay was more rapid and disastrous. First, the external conquests were lost, and then Afghan and Turkish chieftains arose to challenge the obviously weakening grip of the Safawids. In 1722 an Afghan chieftain sacked Isfahan. Out of the anarchy arose a militarily brilliant leader of the Turkish Afshar tribe of Khurasan who, finally in 1736, was elected by the Persian nobles to succeed the last Safawid as Nadir Shah. As a Sunni he accepted the crown only on condition that the Persian school of Shi'a join the Sunnite community as a fifth orthodox school. Such a proposal was preposterous and ultimately failed. Nevertheless, as a general Nadir Shah was outstanding. Not only did he drive out the Afghans and reunite the country, but he also carried Persian arms farther afield than they had been since the days of the ancient Persian Empire. In one notable campaign in 1739 he destroyed a huge Indian army, sacked Delhi, and carried away among the spoils the jewel-encrusted Peacock Throne, built for Shah Jahan and the Koh-i-noor (mountain of light), the fabulous diamond that is now part of the British crown jewels. But these brilliant exploits proved ephemeral. Shortly after his assassination in 1747 his conquests were lost, and Iran was plunged into worse chaos than before, the only vestige of order being maintained by the chiefs of the Zand, a nomadic tribe of southern Iran. Finally, in 1796, a new dynasty was founded by Aga Muhammad, chief of the Turkish Qajar tribe, which had been a major contestant for power with the Zand and was one of the "Red Head" tribes that had originally brought the Safawids to power.

THE QAJAR DYNASTY (1796 – 1925)

Fortunately, the successors of the first shah, who was assassinated by two condemned victims only a year after gaining the throne, were not as depraved as he was. After capturing the last Zand leader in Kerman and torturing him to death, he had punished the city for providing refuge by blinding 20,000 of its inhabitants. Aga Muhammad's

depravity, which caused many such acts of cruelty, has been attributed to the bitterness engendered by his castration at the age of five by political foes.

Although his successors were not so vicious, Iran was little better off under shahs whose continuance in power depended on a collaboration with the aristocracy and the religious hierarchy in the exploitation of the people. The shahs were crippled by their dependence for military strength on the doubtful loyalty of the nobility. As long as these nobles were unimpeded in the exploitation of their own domains and were rewarded frequently by gifts, they supported the government of the shahs, which was little less corrupt than that of the Ottomans. Under such a regime Iran enjoyed internal peace, but no progress. Meanwhile, this once powerful state was reduced to a pawn in the conflicting imperialisms of the Western powers.

Under the next shah, Fath Ali (1797–1834), Iran was first drawn into Napoleon's ambitious scheme to invade British India. By a treaty concluded in May 1807, Napoleon provided a general and 70 officers to reorganize the Persian army, ostensibly to regain Georgia from Russia and then to spearhead a proposed invasion of India. Two months later Napoleon's treaty with the tsar killed this plan, but the French officers arrived at Teheran to the thorough alarm of the British who regained their predominance by providing British officers and a subsidy in return for the dismissal of the French. The British had now come to the conclusion that the neutralization of Persia was essential to the defense of India. Following further Russian acquisitions, Fath Ali accepted a treaty in 1814 that barred all agreements with powers hostile to Britain in return for a £150,000 annual subsidy plus additional aid in case of attack, but the Persian government never gained much benefit from this defensive alliance. Another war with Russia caused the loss of more territory, and the treaty of Turkoman Chai (1828) by which it was concluded also provided for a huge indemnity and capitulations like those with the Ottoman Empire. Justifiably indignant at the lack of British support, the next shah was cool toward them, although he was in no position to repudiate the connection.

The fourth shah, Nasir ad-Din (1848–1896), was by all accounts the most open-minded and ablest of the Qajar dynasty. During his first 4 years he and his incorruptable chief minister, Mirza Taqi Khan, the son of a cook who had risen through innate talent, attempted the fiscal and military reforms essential to the Shah's emancipation from dependence on noble support. The effort failed and the progressive minister had to be dismissed and eventually executed in the face of the reactionary opposition of nobles and officers who had vested interests in the existing system of corruption. One enduring success with long-range significance must be mentioned: the opening of a polytechnic institute in 1851 which served as a military academy where sons of the aristocracy were given a knowledge of the West. Except for Persians who studied abroad, the institute remained for the rest of the century the chief avenue for the transmission of Western ideas which gradually built up a realization of the need for reform, especially among army officers.

Although the shah's concern for the welfare of his people and his state was thus checked, there was no relaxation of foreign pressure. From 1849 to 1854 Russian campaigns east of the Caspian Sea announced the Russian approach to the northeastern frontier of Iran. When the shah was succeeding in a campaign to regain Afghanistan, a British declaration of war compelled him to evacuate and forced him to accept in 1857 a treaty by which Persia recognized the independence of Afghanistan and granted capitulations that threw the door open to extensive British economic penetration. Previously Britain and Russia had been content with vying for Iranian trade. Henceforth Persia was almost impotent in the face of Anglo-Russian competition to reduce it to a puppet

through control of the Iranian economy. After 1857 Persia was thus exposed to far greater Western influence and ideas, and its reaction to them requires separate treatment.

Before concluding our study of premodern Iran, however, one internal development rooted in its religious heritage should be mentioned. Both Persian Shi'a and Sufism had been inspired by the deep-felt need of the individual for intermediaries in the relationship between man and God. One result had been the canonization of a host of holy men and the erection of shrines which became places of pilgrimage for the faithful. The Safawid construction of a Shiite hierarchy and its increasing worldliness and venality were bound to stir feelings of spiritual discontent which only awaited an inspired leader for crystallization. Added factors were the social discontent with exploitation by the privileged classes and the mystical significance attached to the approaching thousandth anniversary of the disappearance of the twelfth imam whose reappearance as the *mahdi* (messiah) was anticipated.

An inspired member of the Shiite clergy, Ali Muhammed, who claimed descent from Ali and Fatima, capitalized on a combination of these factors to create a new religious movement whose popular appeal rapidly gained a large number of dedicated followers. On May 23, 1844, the thousandth anniversary of the disappearance of the twelfth imam, he was greeted by his followers as the expected *mahdi* and was soon given the ancient tribal Sufi title of the *Bab* or "Door" between this world and the next. Henceforth his movement was labeled Babism. He appealed to the downtrodden by condemning class and sex distinctions, while he attacked the religious hierarchy by preaching with Sufi fervor obedience to the spirit rather than to the letter of religion. So intoxicated did he become with his success that he next depicted himself as the "mirror" through which true believers might behold God. From this position it was but a short step to his final heresy, his assertion of being the incarnation of God.

Thoroughly alarmed by the popularity and fervor of this direct challenge to both state and church, the shah authorized the execution of the Bab in 1850 and the subsequent massacre of 40,000 of his followers. As later revised and expanded by a follower, entitled Baha'-ullah (Splendor of God), the religion called Baha'ism gained a worldwide following and preached universal brotherhood and peace. It can count among its monuments an impressive temple in Wilmette, Illinois. For Iran, however, Babism is significant for its revelation of the extent of social, economic, religious, and political discontent. This movement served as a warning to the privileged classes to be on their guard, while it added to the inclination of many educated Iranians to give greater attention to the deep-seated need for reform, if not revolution.

SIGNIFICANT DATES

1302	Mongol overthrow of Seljuk sultanate of Anatolia (Rum)
1326	Capture of Brusa, first capital of Ottoman sultanate
1362	Capture of Edirne (Adrianople), the second capital
1389	Battle of Kosovo confirms Balkan conquests
1389–1402	Reign of Bayezid the Thunderbolt
1402	Ottoman defeat by Timur and loss of Anatolia
1451–1481	Reign of Mehmed II the Conqueror
1453	Capture of Constantinople, the third capital
1512–1520	Selim I: conquest of the Arab Middle East
1520–1566	Sulayman the Magnificent: zenith of Ottoman Empire
1529	First siege of Vienna
1683	Second siege of Vienna
1699	Peace of Karlowitz: first large territorial losses
1774	Treaty of Kuchuk Kainarji: loss of Black Sea territories
1798–1801	Napoleonic episode
1805–1849	Mehemet Ali, founder of Egyptian dynasty
1826	Massacre of Janissaries by Mahmud II
1830	Independence of Greece: loss of Algiers to France
1841	Mehemet Ali reduced to hereditary rule of Egypt by British intervention
1853–1856	Crimean War
1501–1736	Restoration of Persian state under Shiite Safawids
1514	Ottoman victory north of Lake Urmia
1587–1629	Reign of Shah Abbas I: zenith of Safawids
1736–1747	Rule and conquests of Nadir Shah, the Afsharid
1796–1925	Qajar dynasty with capital at Teheran
1814	British defensive treaty providing subsidy for Shah
1828	Treaty of Turkoman Chai granting capitulations to Russia
1850	Execution of Ali Muhammed, founder of Babism
1857	Treaty of Paris granting capitulations to Great Britain

SELECTED READINGS

Anderson, M. S., *The Eastern Question*. New York: Macmillan, 1966.
Arberry, A. J., ed., *The Legacy of Persia*. Oxford: Clarendon Press, 1953.

*Gibb, Hamilton A. R., *Studies on the Civilization of Islam.* Boston: Beacon Press, 1962.

———, and Bowen, Harold, *Islamic Society and the West.* London: Oxford University Press, 1957.

*Gotein, Solomon D., *Jews and Arabs: Their Contacts through the Ages.* New York: Schocken Books, 1955.

*Guerdan, René, *Byzantium: Its Triumphs and Tragedy.* New York: G. P. Putnam's Sons, 1962.

Hourani, Albert H., *Syria and Lebanon.* London: Oxford University Press, 1946.

Hurewitz, J. C., *Diplomacy in the Near and Middle East.* Vol. 1, 1539–1914. Princeton: Van Nostrand, 1956.

Issawi, Charles, ed., *The Economic History of the Middle East, 1800–1914.* Chicago: University of Chicago Press, 1966.

*Levy, Reuben, *The Social Structure of Islam.* Cambridge: Cambridge University Press, 1962.

Rivlin, Helen Anne B., *The Agricultural Policy of Muhammad Ali in Egypt.* Cambridge, Mass.: Harvard University Press, 1961.

Safran, Nadav, *Egypt in Search of Political Community.* Cambridge, Mass.: Harvard University Press, 1961.

Stavrianos, L. S., *The Balkans Since 1453.* New York: Rinehart, 1958.

*Stoianovich, Traian, *A Study in Balkan Civilization.* New York: Knopf, 1967.

Temperley, Harold, *England and the Near East: The Crimea.* London: Longmans Green, 1936.

Wilber, Donald N., *Iran: Past and Present.* Princeton: Princeton University Press, 1958.

Wittek, Paul, *The Rise of the Ottoman Empire.* London: Royal Asiatic Society, 1958.

Yale, William, *The Near East.* Chicago: University of Chicago Press, 1968.

PART FOUR
WESTERN IMPACT AND EASTERN REACTION

Opium War. British ships destroying Chinese war junks in Anson's Bay, January 7, 1841.
(*Radio Times Hulton Picture Library*)

Commodore Perry's landing in Japan, July 14, 1853. (*Culver Pictures*)

Sepoy mutineers storm battery at Lucknow, July 30, 1857. (*Culver Pictures*)

First boat through the Suez Canal, August 15, 1865. (*Culver Pictures*)

Mehemet Ali, ruler and modernizer of Egypt (r. 1805–1847). (*Radio Times Hulton Picture Library*)

Gopal Krishna Gokale, moderate reformer and leader of the Indian National Congress. (*Radio Times Hulton Picture Library*)

Midhat Pasha, Ottoman Modernizer. (*Radio Times Hulton Picture Library*)

Li Hung-chang, Chinese self-strengthener.
(*Charles Phelps Cushing*)

King Mongkut (Rama IV) of Siam
(r. 1851–1868), ardent Westernizer noted
for employing Anna Leonowens to teach his
children. (*Radio Times Hulton Picture Library*)

Prince Itō of Japan, framer of the first constitution. (*Culver Pictures*)

In the first half of this book the rise of the major Eastern civilizations has been described and analyzed with special attention to the distinguishing features of enduring significance. As each of these civilizations developed, its influence spread to its immediate neighbors and was diffused farther afield through the expansion of trade. From the earliest times, even before the rise of civilizations as they have been defined, the growing area of trade and the mounting volume of the exchange of ideas, as well as goods, provided a stimulus to both economic and political growth that supplied the incentives and the conditions for the creation of empires.

Eastern civilizations were all agricultural with the life of their urban centers dependent on the surpluses produced by intensive farming that generally stressed water control. While the attributes of civilization could be easily adopted by settled peoples or by peoples living in regions adaptable to settled agriculture, nomads occupying land suitable only for grazing had but two broad alternatives. They could develop a symbiotic relationship in which they exchanged their surplus livestock and manpower for products of the neighboring civilization, or they could employ their military talents to conquer and exploit part or all of the civilized area. Thus was established the dynamic relationship of "the desert and the sown," normally peaceful, but frequently exploding into violence. Until the development of modern firearms and motorized transport the warlike nomads enjoyed a definite military advantage, whenever they could overcome their tribal feuds and combine their forces.

With the growth of commerce between civilizations whose trade routes passed through nomad territories, the tribesmen gained an additional advantage which they exploited from the tenth to the seventeenth centuries, reducing to submission each of the mainland civilizations. Each "barbarian" conquest brought greater or lesser changes to the conquered civilizations, but in each case the nomads in an alien environment were ultimately taken captive by the civilization. Nothing is more notable in their histories than the innate strength and resilience of the Eastern civilizations.

In the same way that the tribal nomads as "have-nots" were attracted by the wealth of the civilizations step by step from trade to conquest so, too, the Western "nomads of the sea" proceeded from trade to conquest. From the sixteenth to the eighteenth centuries Westerners were primarily interested in trade on the best terms that they could obtain. Over the long sea routes from their homelands it was difficult to mount any significant political pressure except against weak and divided states. Then came the Industrial Revolution which gave the West technological advantages both in commerce and in war, more than compensating for the disadvantage of distance. An even greater advantage was the enterprising and progressive spirit that was responsible for the Industrial Revolution as well as for other social and political changes. Never before had the agricultural civilizations of the East been confronted by such a dynamic force. The Industrial Revolution demanded economic penetration, not just external trade, and Western governments were called on to furnish whatever military pressure was needed to achieve this objective.

By the mid-nineteenth century, among the major centers of civilization only anarchic India had been conquered, but all, to a greater or lesser degree, had suffered political humiliations by Western powers and were destined to suffer further humiliations in the years to come. More important, however, was the realization by a few intellectual and political leaders of the need to adapt to this new and dynamic challenge. The story of the next century centers on their efforts to discover the extent of change and adaptation necessary to meet and repel the challenge of the West without surrendering their treasured heritages. It is also the story of the incorporation of more and more of their people in this struggle, utilizing so far as feasible the borrowed device of Western nationalism. Finally, it should be emphasized that the story has not yet ended. The struggle continues today—and will continue tomorrow. Our task is to understand and appreciate its roots and its meaning for each of these peoples. While the future is unknown, each of the Eastern civilizations has already demonstrated its resilience, even under the disrupting force of the Western impact.

Part Four, which concludes with the Japanese victory over Russia in 1905, which raised new hopes and more optimistic aspirations throughout Asia, is principally concerned with two complementary aspects of this picture: the accelerated internal impact of the West, especially after the opening of the Suez Canal, and the emergence of organized reactions and adaptations to the challenge of the West. These reactions or efforts to find a solution, it will be noted, ran the gamut from one extreme of a total, conservative rejection of the West and things Western, through moderate and radical reform that proposed a lesser or greater adaptation while clinging to Eastern cultural roots, to the other extreme of a revolutionary rejection of the past. By 1905 only Japan had achieved a measure of success, breaking the shackles of unequal treaties and proving itself in battle against a Western power, through a creative and pragmatic mixture of moderate and radical reform. Meanwhile, the pressure and presence of the West in Asia continued to grow throughout this period, increasing the urgency felt in many quarters for some sort of a solution.

CHAPTER FIFTEEN

CHINA UNDER FIRE: 1839 – 1905

The Opium War (1839–1842) was only the opening episode in a century of humiliations that was suffered by the proud Chinese state and civilization at the hands of the West and its able emulator, Japan. By the end of the nineteenth century China even appeared destined for dismemberment into colonies of the various imperial powers. And only in recent years, first under Nationalist and then under Communist auspices, has this most populous state begun to reassert its place in the world. Few Westerners, then or now, realized how deeply wounded the Chinese were by these experiences, and how determined they are to regain their ancient position and prestige. They were and are convinced of the superiority of their civilization which they expect the rest of the world to recognize, respect, and emulate—whether in a Confucian or Communist guise.

According to the Chinese conception of international relations all peoples who were non-Chinese in culture were barbarians, the degree of their barbarousness being determined by the extent to which they recognized Chinese supremacy and conformed to the Confucian code of the ethical relationship between superior and inferior. Obviously such a conception of international relations was wholly at odds with the Western conception of a comity of nations with equal rights. In addition, Chinese ethics (in contrast with those of the West) put commerce and profits at the bottom of the scale of values. As Commissioner Lin Tse-hsu made clear in a letter to Queen Victoria, he believed China had no need of Western trade, while the West was dependent on trade with China, a gracious privilege it was abusing by permitting the smuggling of poisonous opium into China.

Although throughout the era covered by this chapter the overwhelming majority of Confucian scholar-officials clung doggedly to their convictions and proved unwilling to adapt in any significant way to the challenge of the Western barbarians, a few from the very beginning recognized the necessity of some modification in the traditional outlook, even if it only meant military modernization as defense against this new threat from the sea. Commissioner Lin, for example, immediately recognized that British intransigence had created a new frontier to defend. As a first step he resorted to the purchase or lease of Western cannon and ships but, for the long run, he initiated a compilation of all the information he could obtain about the West, inspired by the Confucian precept that knowledge of the enemy is the fundamental weapon in any arsenal. Following the outbreak of full-scale hostilities, he was dismissed and disgraced for failing to maintain peace and suppress the opium traffic. Two years later, in a letter to a friend he argued the necessity of constructing and maintaining a modern navy for the permanent defense of China's long sea frontier. Meanwhile, another scholar, drawing on Lin's preliminary work, compiled a monumental illustrated *Gazeteer of the Maritime Countries* whose central theses were (1) the need to master the techniques discovered by the West in its drive for power and profits and (2) the discovery of Western weaknesses that China might exploit. In contrast with China, the West, he asserted, is characterized by division and disunity. With amazing prescience he foresaw the possibilities of alliances with Russia or the United States to pit one power against another in the same way that China had traditionally defended its northwestern frontier by pitting one nomadic group against another.

The war itself was not very impressive. The British soon discovered that to bring to

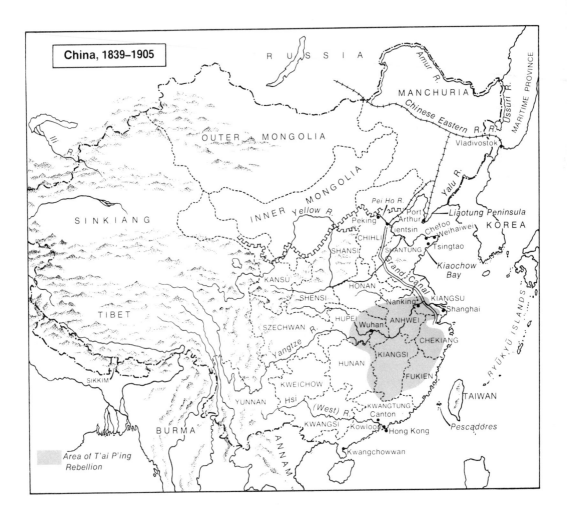

China, 1839–1905

Area of T'ai P'ing
Rebellion

its knees the government of sprawling, decentralized China with its more than 300 million people was no mean task for only 4000
soldiers backed up by 15 warships. They had
no difficulty blockading one port city after
another. Indeed, they were sometimes welcomed for the business they brought. Local
officials did not want to jeopardize their positions by serious warfare. Moreover, the emperor came to believe the British grievances
principally concerned commissioner Lin's
actions and authorized negotiations to ward
off further conflict. The British problem was
to discover a critical position in navigable
waters. At last this was found in 1842 when
reinforced British forces advancing up the

Yangtze severed China's north-south artery,
the Grand Canal. In view of the prospective
loss of all grain revenues from the south, the
Chinese government capitulated and signed
the Treaty of Nanking in August, 1842.

THE FIRST TREATY SETTLEMENT

By the terms of the treaty, five ports
(Canton, Amoy, Foochow, Ningpo, and
Shanghai) were opened for trade and residence and the monopolistic merchant association (Co-Hong) was abolished, allowing
negotiations on equal terms between the
officials of the British and Chinese governments. The island of Hongkong was ceded in

perpetuity to provide a port where the British "may careen and refit their ships." China had to pay $6 million for the destroyed opium, $3 million to cover debts owed by Chinese merchants, and $12 million for the expense of Britain's military effort. Finally, the Chinese government was obligated to publish a fixed set of tariffs. The Treaty of the Bogue in 1843 confirmed a tariff rate averaging 5 percent ad valorem, but more importantly infringed on Chinese sovereignty and freedom of action by a most-favored-nation clause and a somewhat vague assertion of extraterritoriality in criminal cases. In 1844 the American Treaty of Wang-hsia secured all the benefits of the British military effort by means of the most-favored-nation clause and further spelled out the conditions of extraterritoriality in both criminal and civil cases. Extraterritoriality, as defined, provided for the trial in the consular court of the foreign resident of all criminal cases according to the law of his homeland and for full consular assistance in civil cases. In fact, however, this right was regularly abused and the Chinese litigant rarely received justice. Finally, the American treaty provided for revision in 12 years, if either party deemed it necessary.

This first treaty settlement with the maritime countries of the West was concluded when the French obtained imperial edicts granting Roman Catholics the right to build churches, preach, and gain Chinese converts in the treaty ports. Another edict extended this right to Protestants. Furthermore, it was implicitly understood that missionaries might operate outside the treaty ports if they created no civil disturbance.

As it operated in practice, this first treaty settlement, extracted by British force, soon proved unsatisfactory to both parties. Chinese officials were frequently unwilling to implement its provisions, especially in hostile Canton, and the central government, viewing it as only a temporary concession, was unwilling to enforce compliance. Moreover, the infringements on Chinese sover-

eignty were resented and evaded by the Chinese in reaction to their abuse by Westerners. Such negative attitudes, however, were not always the case. Shanghai welcomed the opportunity to gain a share of foreign trade, and its strategic location at the mouth of China's greatest inland waterway, the Yangtze River, made it exceptionally attractive to Western merchants who were granted national and international settlements, governed by Westerners, adjacent to the Chinese city. Because of Canton's intransigence Shanghai soon became the chief base of foreign trading operations.

For the most part, however, the relationship between China and the West became increasingly cold, a condition for which Western abuses and arrogance were as much to blame as Chinese unwillingness to accept the altered relationship dictated by the treaties. In addition to the unjust exploitation of extraterritoriality, the coolie trade, the "convoying" of Chinese coastal trade, the more widespread smuggling of opium, and the open defamation and disregard for Chinese culture and customs by both missionaries and merchants further convinced the Chinese of the essential barbarity and unethical cupidity and rapacity of Westerners. The coolie trade developed to fill the need for cheap and industrious laborers for hard and distasteful tasks in various parts of the world. Theoretically, Chinese coolies voluntarily signed contracts to be shipped out for a specified term of years. In practice, all kinds of deception, including kidnapping, were utilized to meet the ever-growing demand for cheap Chinese labor overseas. Ships were overloaded with human cargo, sanitation was neglected, and as a result many Chinese died in transit, while many more never survived the often inhuman working conditions. To their credit the British and Americans objected to the inhumane aspects of this trade in human flesh which was practiced mainly by Spanish and Portuguese operators, but they could do little to police it. The "convoying" of coastal shipping was an ill-disguised "protection racket," scarcely justified by the prevalence of pirates. Indeed, the Westerners who engaged in this practice were only more powerful pirates with their heavy armament. The smuggling of opium into China was a growing cancer thanks to the expanded opportunities provided by the treaty settlement, which had neglected the issue, except for the indemnity to compensate for the opium destroyed by Commissioner Lin. Finally, no other attitude than defamation of Chinese religious practices could reasonably be expected from the missionaries of such a fundamentally intolerant faith as Christianity. On the credit side of the ledger they initiated significant steps in public health and education. In addition, their concern with reaching the people stimulated study of the Chinese language which made them invaluable as interpreters both for their governments and their merchants. Often these studies counteracted their initial disdain for Chinese civilization.

During these initial years of more open contact between China and the West it is important to recognize that these contacts were primarily limited to the treaty ports. The great mass of the Chinese people had no contact with Westerners and learned little or nothing of their ways. If they heard of them at all, the accounts were adverse, emphasizing their inferiority as barbarians whose selfish greed was supported by reliance on brute force. In the same way, the emperor and the central government remained equally ignorant of the West and convinced of its barbarity because official contact was limited to the treaty ports, and Chinese officials, anxious to justify their inability to deal effectively with Western officials, wrote distorted reports to Peking.

Before many years had passed the Western powers, especially Britain, began to realize the inadequacies of the treaty settlement and the need for revisions. A clause in the American treaty provided the opportunity for renegotiation after 12 years. On the

basis of the most-favored-nation concept the British began to press for revision in 1854.

T'AI P'ING REBELLION (1850 – 1864)

Meanwhile, the Manchu regime, which since the 1790s had been suffering all the typical symptoms of dynastic decline due, in large part, to a vast population increase, was confronted by the largest of a series of rebellions. Ironically, the leader of the T'ai P'ing (Great Peace) Rebellion, Hung Hsiu-ch'üan, was a frustrated civil service examination candidate who received solace from a Baptist missionary and came to believe he had a divine mission to end idolatry in China. Thus Christianity provided the ideological inspiration for the vast devastation and estimated loss of 20 million lives caused by the suppression of this rebellion which came close to overthrowing the Manchu dynasty. Indeed, in the initial stages of the rebellion some missionaries, believing that it offered a great opportunity to advance the cause of Christianity in China, were sympathetic to the insurgents, but in time they were turned off by Hung's arrogant rejection of their religious guidance. Although he emphasized Christian ethics, especially modified versions of the Lord's Prayer and the Ten Commandments, and condemned with puritanical zeal gambling, adultery, opium, and alcohol, he formulated on the basis of his visions a new trinity of God, the father, Christ, the divine elder brother, and Hung, the divine younger brother, which the missionaries found repulsive.

At first the "God Worshippers Society" was formed in Kwangsi Province for self-protection as well as for propagation of its beliefs. Hung preached a primitive economic communism, and in June 1850, he ordered his followers to surrender their wealth to a common treasury from which all would draw essential needs. In 1851 a formal declaration of revolution called for the establishment of a "Heavenly Kingdom of Great Peace" under the "Heavenly King," Hung Hsiu-ch'üan, and the decision was made to march northward. On the way recruits from other rebellious secret societies swelled the ranks despite Hung's insistence that they subscribe to his religious doctrines. In 1853 his forces took Nanking which then served as the T'ai P'ing capital while his armies dominated the Yangtze basin cutting off a major portion of the imperial government's revenue. One column, hoping for popular support that did not materialize, was sent against Peking and overwhelmed near Tientsin. When another rebel force seized Shanghai in 1853, the foreign settlements gained a measure of self-government and agreed to collect the customs duties on behalf of the Chinese government. Thus was begun the foreign management of the maritime customs. The replacement of Chinese by Western officials soon resulted in sharply increased customs revenues for the Manchu government.

T'ai P'ing doctrine called for an egalitarian society to be administered by a military hierarchy, an interesting precedent that the modern communist regime has not neglected to recognize. All land theoretically belonged to the people as a whole, and families were to be allocated the use of plots whose size would be determined by the appraised productivity of the land and by the size of the family. All surplus beyond the needs of the family would be deposited in a public storehouse to meet the needs of the whole community. Precedents for such an idea existed in an ancient Chou classic and the reform effort of Wang Mang. The T'ai P'ing regime never developed sufficient administrative talent and stability, however, to put it into effect on more than a local, experimental basis. Twenty-five families were grouped under a master sergeant who was the civil and religious authority as well as military commander of this basic unit in the administrative hierarchy.

The situation of the Manchu regime was critical when patriotic scholars, such as Tseng Kuo-fan and his lieutenants, Li Hung-chang and Tso Tsung-t'ang, organized effective local opposition to the rebels. They won peasant and gentry support by upholding traditional Confucian values and social stability against the disruptions and ravages of the T'ai P'ing rebels. In time their practical successes in contrast with the impotence of imperial forces gained official recognition in imperial appointments. Appreciating the value of Western arms and leadership, they later collaborated with the "Ever-victorious" army organized by the Westerners at Shanghai, which gained its greatest victories under its British commander, "Chinese" Gordon. This Western support, however, was not secured until a new and more humiliating set of treaties was inflicted on the Chinese Empire by the military collaboration of the recent allies in the Crimean War, Britain and France.

THE ANGLO-FRENCH WAR AND THE SECOND TREATY SETTLEMENT

To enforce their will on the Chinese government at a time when it was crippled by the T'ai P'ing Rebellion as well as other rebellions may seem particularly unchivalrous, but the time of China's greatest internal embarrassment happened to coincide with the time when these Western powers were no longer willing to brook any further delay in securing what they deemed to be essential treaty revisions. In 1856 two incidents, a presumed insult to the British flag and the execution of a French priest, provided convenient pretexts for the already agreed on assault. Under the circumstances the resistance of the Chinese court was surprising and can only be explained by its continued ignorance of the West.

The full attack was delayed until 1858 by the Sepoy Mutiny in India, but then the combined forces captured the fortifications defending the approach to Peking. The emperor had no choice but to capitulate, and the first set of treaties, the Treaties of Tientsin, were negotiated, including new treaties with the United States and Russia, which had refused an invitation to send military forces but had sent observers. The treaties provided for the exchange of ratifications at Peking. When the Western powers returned in 1859, they found that the fortifications had been rebuilt and strengthened in the interim. Only the American envoy agreed to the Chinese insistence that another route to Peking be taken. The Anglo-French forces were repulsed in their effort to retake the forts. Determined to impress on the Chinese government the futility of such resistance to Western demands, the allies returned with larger forces in 1860 and continued the assault until Peking was captured. Actually the mighty walls of the imperial capital could have been effectively defended, but the court had fled and the residents threw open the gates to prevent further bloodshed. In retaliation for capturing and killing some members of a party under a flag of truce the Summer Palace was put to the torch. Now new treaties had to be negotiated with the incensed allies. The Russians, who cunningly posed as mediators, were repaid for services rendered by the cession of all territory north of the Amur River and the maritime provinces east of the Ussuri River, including the port of Vladivostok (Ruler of the East). This was the first, but not the last, time that China was to turn to the Russians in the hope of support in checking Western and Japanese encroachments.

In view of Chinese obstructionism the new treaties added surprisingly little to the Tientsin treaties. Additional indemnities were of course required. Tientsin, the gateway to Peking, was added to the list of ten ports previously scheduled to be opened to Western trade and residence, exposing the whole Chinese coast and permitting penetration of central China through four ports on the navigable Yangtze. An area in the imperial capital was set aside for the establishment of Western embassies to maintain direct contact and pressure on the central government. Foreigners with valid passports gained the right to travel freely throughout the interior of China under the protection of the Chinese government—a protection the weakening authority of the central government proved often unable to provide. This provision, employed mostly by missionaries, became a fruitful source of "incidents" that further undermined the dwindling prestige of the Manchu regime. Missionaries gained toleration outside the treaty ports for themselves and their Chinese converts and, by interpretation, the right to rent property in perpetuity. These advantages were increasingly abused by recourse to the missionaries' embassies whenever they felt that their interests were being restricted by the local magistrates. Since the central government could not resist these demands, the local magistrate, in his own self-interest, found it necessary to obey the commands of the missionary. This exploitation of treaty privileges gained converts but did nothing to enhance the respect for Christianity, its missionaries, or its converts. The British treaty gained the cession of part of the Kowloon Peninsula opposite Hongkong. Finally, the tariffs were revised, and the opium trade was legalized by placing a tariff on it.

The chief results of this second treaty settlement were twofold. Many more Chinese were exposed to Western influence under revised extraterritorial provisions that gave greater opportunities for abuses. Also Western manufactures were furnished with a larger area of exploitation, undermining native handicrafts and distorting the Chinese economy. Second, the weakness of the Manchu regime became more manifest, even to itself. Undoubtedly it would have been overthrown if it had not been for the seizure of power by the Empress-Dowager Tz'u Hsi who employed the best talent wherever she found it, such as Li Hung-chang (1823–1901) and Tso Tsung-t'ang (1812–1885). In any case, the Manchu regime had to rely more and more on loyal Chinese scholar-statesmen who had proven themselves and had built up regional military forces in the suppression of the T'ai-P'ing and other rebellions.

THE BEGINNING OF MODERNIZATION

Chinese eyes had been partially opened to the need for meeting the West on its own terms by what was called "self-strengthening." With the reluctant approval of the Empress-Dowager Western arms and training were supplied to the regional military forces at the request of enlightened officials, while a growing list of shrewd Chinese entrepreneurs established enterprises within the extraterritorial protection of the foreign settlements and joined their foreign friends in exploiting their own people. Many learned the new techniques while serving as agents for the sale of foreign products outside the treaty ports.

Two leading figures in bringing about small steps toward modernization were Sir Robert Hart, the British Inspector-General of the Maritime Customs, who was a trusted advisor because of his sympathy for China's problems, and the exceptionally able scholar-official, Li Hung-chang. A school for interpreters in Peking was developed by Hart into Tung-wen College in 1865 by the addition of a science department financed by the customs revenues. In 1872 Li arranged for 30 young men to study in the United States. By the time the program was terminated in 1881, 120 Chinese students had benefited from this foreign exposure to begin the erosion of China's cultural introversion. The termination of this student program, it should be noted, was the direct result of the humiliating American insistence on legislation suspending Chinese immigration for 10 years with no intention of permitting it to be resumed. Thus the comparative goodwill previously enjoyed by Americans was extinguished.

Li also encouraged the construction of arsenals and shipyards and the purchase of foreign naval vessels and the hiring of foreign officers to begin the development of a modern navy. Clashes of authority soon led to the dismissal of the foreign officers, but naval vessels continued to be added until China had a respectable fleet, at least in terms of tonnage. The same interest led him to be a chief sponsor in the formation of the China Merchants Steam Navigation Company in 1873 which competed with Western operators for the control of modern shipping on coastal and inland waters and also provided valuable training and experience in the operation of modern machinery. Hart persuaded the government to permit a modern survey of coastal waters and the establishment of a modern postal system. In 1878 Li opened a coal mine to fuel his ships which, in turn, led him to press for China's first permanent railroad in 1881 to carry the product to Tientsin. From this modest beginning other railroads were gradually built to facilitate internal transportation. The major deterrent to more rapid development was the Chinese lack of capital combined with a fundamental distrust of foreign investors. Again Li played a decisive role in the construction in 1882 of the first telegraph line between Shanghai and Tientsin. Both railroads and telegraph lines faced stiff opposition from the superstitious peasantry who objected to the disturbance of ancestral burial areas and the consequent release of evil spirits, or other adverse effects. Another open-minded scholar-official, Chang Chih-tung (1837–1909), put in operation in 1890 the Hanyang Iron Works which was the basis for the development of China's largest industrial complex in the Wuhan area of the Yangtze basin.

As can readily be appreciated, these first steps were the work of only a very small number of perceptive and vigorous individuals who were mainly motivated by the desire to build their regional strength and to make immediate profits. After the traditional method of the salt monopoly most large enterprises were sponsored and supervised by officialdom, which alone could supply protection and profitable government contracts, though merchants were called on for capital and management. Consequently competition was limited and efficiency suffered. Both the court and the bureaucracy clung to the old, familiar ways and opposed, sometimes with great vehemence, even these innovations. Although the treaty settlement had banned the use of the term, "barbarian," in all official correspondence, it had not eradicated this attitude toward Westerners and their magical and fiendish devices. Nor had the government genuinely altered its attitude toward international relations. A special board of foreign affairs, the Tsungli Yamen, had been set up in part to preclude direct contact with the court. An audience with the emperor was not granted until 1873 and then it was purposely assigned to the hall where tributary missions were normally received. The only concession on this occasion was the omission of the prescribed kowtow. Not until 1877 was the first Chinese diplomatic mission established abroad.

In 1867, on the advice of Sir Robert Hart, an interesting experiment in the hope of improving relations with the West was attempted. The American minister, Anson Burlingame, whose sympathy for Chinese problems had been evident during his tour of duty, agreed to head a delegation to see what could be done to secure more equal treaties or, at least, to give the Western governments and peoples a less prejudiced picture of China. The mission received a warm welcome in the United States and secured a convention granting reciprocal rights, including immigration. Burlingame's depiction of China as ready and willing to deal with the West on an open and equal basis reflected his ardent hopes rather than the actual situation. He gained substantial sympathy for China in Britain and France—but no concessions. His reception by Bismarck was definitely cool, and this disappointed emissary of goodwill

died of pneumonia in St. Petersburg, bringing a frustrating end to this experiment.

MANCHU MILITARY REVIVAL

Meanwhile, the stamping out of the T'ai P'ing rebellion in 1864 did not bring an end to China's internal difficulties. A number of lesser rebellions, as well as widespread banditry, had been encouraged by the dislocations caused by the T'ai P'ing success and the general weakening of governmental authority. Those officials who had demonstrated their ability against the T'ai P'ing rebels were naturally called on to deal with these problems. A bandit rebellion noted for its cavalry gained cohesion in Shantung and neighboring provinces in 1851 and spread to nine provinces before it was effectively extinguished, mainly by Li Huang-chang and Tso Tsung-t'ang. A Muslim rebellion in remote Yünnan in southwest China was finally crushed in 1873. Most dramatic, however, was the suppression of a number of Muslim uprisings stretching from Shensi Province to the western extremities of the empire in a long series of brilliant campaigns from 1868 to 1878 under the command of Tso Tsung-t'ang. Before long he had regained Shensi, and as he pressed westward, he went beyond the ability of the government to keep him supplied. For whole seasons he had to cut back his operations while his troops planted and harvested crops to feed themselves in subsequent campaigns. Replacements had to be recruited from tribesmen and trained in modern arms. His ability in overcoming such hardships and handicaps is reminiscent of the similar campaigns of the Han and T'ang dynasties. His chief opponent, Yakub Beg, who enjoyed British and Russian sympathy and possibly support, died in 1877, possibly of unnatural causes. With the final dispersal of tribal resistance, Tso's battle-hardened veterans confronted the Russians, who had occupied the Ili basin supposedly to preserve Chinese sovereignty. When they refused to evacuate immediately, Tso Tsung-t'ang was ready and willing to drive them out, but the Chinese government, seriously handicapped by disastrous famines that carried off millions of Chinese and reduced imperial revenues between 1876 and 1878, preferred to negotiate for a Russian withdrawal. The first treaty negotiated ceded three quarters of the area to Russia as well as indemnifying it for occupation costs. The Chinese government refused to ratify it and war seemed imminent, but neither government wanted war. In 1881 a new treaty provided for the restoration of most of the region to China, although the indemnity was increased and Russia gained more liberal trading and residence privileges in Sinkiang. The exploits of Tso Tsung-t'ang had saved the western territories of the Chinese Empire and contributed to an unfortunate sense of self-confidence and even complacency in the empire's ability to cope with any Western challenge.

In other areas, however, further inroads were made and concessions were extracted in this era of temporary Manchu revival. Neither Britain, France, nor Japan recognized or appreciated the loose suzerain-tributary relationship that existed between China and its vassals, Burma, Annam (roughly North Vietnam), and Korea. In addition, other incidents caused by Chinese ignorance of Western motives led to the extraction of other concessions. The mutual lack of understanding created both by imperial isolation and Western arrogance could only contribute to a further deterioration of Manchu prestige at home and increased hatred and fear of the Westerner by the Chinese people. By themselves, the incidents and aggression are not so important as their cumulative effect in building up the degree and extent of Chinese alienation toward the West and its student, Japan. Therefore, they will only be mentioned briefly here.

As has already been suggested, the missionary effort was vastly expanded following the second treaty settlement. Their numbers increased at least fivefold and their converts tenfold. Many of the new missionaries who poured into China were less well trained and held the Chinese government and civilization in lower esteem. Many made important contributions to education and public health, but they also did not hesitate to take advantage of the diplomatic pressure they could exert to advance their cause. The first major incident, however, reflected Chinese ignorance and fear.

A French order of nuns had established an orphanage in Tientsin. Unfortunately for their vocation, the Chinese family system provided few subjects for their loving care. As a result, they paid for children, which may have encouraged kidnapping, and sought critically ill children to give them the benefits of baptism. Since many of their charges died, rumors spread to the effect that the nuns used their eyes and hearts to make an elixir of life. Chinese feeling was whipped into mob action in 1870 and resulted in the massacre of ten nuns, two priests, and the French consul who had sought to protect them, as well as an untold number of Chinese converts. For the Chinese government the results were the execution of the accused leader, reparations, and the dispatch to Paris of a formal mission of apology. This and other incidents in the interior led the Chinese government repeatedly to seek some modification of the treaty guarantees for missionaries, but without avail.

In 1876 the murder of a British consular officer connected with an expedition that was surveying a trade route between Burma and Yünnan forced the Chinese, in the Chefoo Convention, to open more ports and to grant trading concessions besides indemnifying the victim's family. However, the stiffer British demands to improve diplomatic communications were diverted into meaningless verbiage. In spite of severe famine a revivified Chinese regime was no longer ready to give in to the first foreign push, and the British were no longer anxious to deliver ultimatums.

Less important on the surface but more important for its deeper implications about the imperial system was the foreign enchroachment on traditionally tributary states. In Southeast Asia the British from their Indian base had, since 1826, periodically bitten off large chunks of Burma, completing their dinner in 1886 in the face of China's inability to aid its vassal. In this instance the problem was partially solved by Chinese recognition of British sovereignty in return for the continuance of the decennial Burmese tribute missions, in theoretical recognition of Chinese suzerainty, and a British agreement not to force the opening of Tibet. Yet, four years later, China was compelled to recognize a British protectorate over Sikkim, a tiny Chinese tributary on the Tibetan frontier.

Less tactful and peaceful was the French determination to terminate Chinese suzerainty over Annam. In view of stiff Annamese resistance to the French, China honored its obligation as suzerain by sending Chinese troops. In Annam the French found the going difficult and even suffered a major defeat before agreeing to a treaty in 1885 in which China surrendered its suzerainty. Nevertheless, this was China's first treaty without an indemnity, a recognition of the partial revival of Chinese prestige. The impunity with which French forces attacked and blockaded various points on the coast of China exposed the inadequacy of Chinese military and naval development, but the complacency of the Manchu court continued until it was rudely shattered a decade later by the rapidly rising power of Japan.

SINO-JAPANESE RELATIONS AND THE FIRST SINO-JAPANESE WAR (1894–1895)

The 1868 Restoration of titular authority to the Japanese emperor was accomplished by a relatively small group of samurai statesmen who were united by the single goal of ending the humiliating provisions of the unequal treaties forced on Japan by the Western powers. Although they might differ among themselves about the timetable and the extent of accommodation with the West, all these leaders clearly perceived that Western influence rested on the technological superiority of its military strength, which had to be matched and exercised for Japan to gain recognition as an equal. The first opportunity to flex its military muscle abroad occurred when a ship from the Ryūkyū islands, which sent tribute to both China and Japan, was wrecked on the wild southeast coast of Taiwan and some of the crew were consumed by their cannibal captors. When the Chinese government as sovereign refused satisfaction, war fever ran high in Japan and was further fostered by the Korean refusal to consider negotiation of a trade treaty. However, calmer heads prevailed, and the Japanese government limited itself to a punitive expedition against the cannibals. In 1881 China recognized Japanese suzerainty over the Ryūkyūs and paid reparations to the bereaved families of the sailors who had died.

Of greater, though related, significance was the problem of Korea. In the sixties and seventies, not only Japan but also several Western powers had repeatedly attempted to establish treaty relations both for trade and security. In each case they had been staved off by reference to Peking as Korea's suzerain. In 1875 a Japanese surveying ship was fired on, and the Japanese government now felt prepared to demand concrete results. Two missions were dispatched, one to Peking and one to Korea, backed up by armed forces. In the face of Japanese determination China suggested that Korea negotiate a treaty. The most important feature of the treaty of 1876 was the first article which asserted that "Korea, being an independent state, enjoys the same sovereign rights as Japan." This clear refutation of China's suzerainty went unchallenged by the Chinese who apparently did not appreciate its significance and felt confident of Korea's loyalty. Both China and Korea soon realized their error, but it was too late for a repudiation. In the belief that there was some added safety in numbers, Li Hung-chang recommended for Korea a policy of making treaties with all interested powers. All these treaties followed the Japanese model, recognizing the sovereign status of Korea. The stage was set for an Sino-Japanese struggle for control of Korea and its faction-ridden court.

The intrigue and counter-intrigue, plot and counterplot, and the alternation of armed clashes and negotiations are too involved to relate here. Suffice it to say that Li Hung-chang was entrusted with the task of restoring Chinese authority and the actions of his able protege, Yüan Shih-k'ai, led step by step to the escalation of the contest into the first Sino-Japanese War (1894–1895), which proved so disastrous to China. In 1885 the tension of the Sino-Japanese confrontation in Korea was temporarily relieved by the Li-Itō Convention by which each party agreed to withdraw its troops to leave Korea free to reorganize its army with the aid of foreign advisors other than Chinese or Japanese, to give prior notice in writing if either party felt circumstances required the reintroduction of its troops, and to withdraw such troops just as soon as the difficulty had been overcome. This agreement with its equal terms further confirmed the Japanese contention that Korea had no special position as a vassal in its relationship with China. On the other hand, the faction of the Korean court that was in power, the actions of Yüan Shih-k'ai as the Chinese Resident, and Chinese correspondence continued to affirm the Chinese conviction in its suzerain status. Thus the conditions for future misunderstanding and conflict continued to be effective in fact, if not in theory. Meanwhile, the penetration of Russian influence through the provision of military advisors and an attempt to secure an ice-free Korean naval base contributed to the growth of international concern and turbulence over the status of Korea. During these years Japan built up its economic position until it was clearly dominant in Korea's foreign trade.

The immediate factor which precipitated war was the apparent inability of the Korean government to suppress a rebellion by the reactionary, antiforeign Tonghak religious sect. In response to a Korean appeal for military assistance Li dispatched 1500 troops and only notified the Japanese *after* they had shipped out. The Japanese immediately countered with a much larger body of troops. Before either military force landed, the Korean army had put down the rebellion, and the Korean government sought the withdrawal of both forces. Instead of complying, the Chinese and Japanese, each equally suspicious of the other's motives, reinforced those troops that were already there. Neither country wanted to take the first overt act, but finally a Japanese naval force intercepted and sank a Chinese troopship that was carrying further reinforcements to Korea.

Most Western observers thought that little Japan with an army of only 120,000 men was exceedingly brash in challenging the "Sleeping Dragon" with its unlimited human resources. On paper both the Chinese army and navy appeared superior. But this assessment did not take into account the Japanese superiority in quality in both arms and training and the decentralized character of the Chinese government, which made it impossible to command the concentration of its resources. Within the Chinese bureaucracy the conflict was viewed as "Li's war," and the personal jealousy of his prominence made his discomfiture, even at the sacrifice of Chinese prestige, a factor inhibiting cooperation. The ease and rapidity with which the Japanese forces swept from victory to victory amazed Western observers and, it would seem, the Japanese themselves.

The northern portion of the Chinese navy was immediately defeated and forced to take refuge in port. The commanders of the southern elements of the Chinese navy simply withheld their forces from the conflict. Thus Japan enjoyed from the beginning a complete command of the high seas greatly facilitating the support of its land forces. The latter swept through Korea, crossed the Yalu River into Manchuria, and with all organized opposition destroyed soon threatened the imperial capital. The Chinese government had no choice but to sue for peace. Before accepting these overtures, however, Japan diverted forces to secure control of Taiwan and the Pescadores Islands.

Li Hung-chang was charged with the task of negotiating with the Japanese the Treaty of Shimonoseki. The terms were partly moderated as a result of an attempt to assassinate him, but they still were steep. The Manchu regime was compelled to acknowledge Korea's total independence, to cede Taiwan, the Pescadores, and southeastern Manchuria (the Liaotung Peninsula), and to pay a large indemnity. Subsequently Russia in combination with its French ally and a Germany interested in keeping Russia's ambitions directed eastward did compel Japan to give up the Liaotung Peninsula in return for an additional indemnity. Finally, Japan felt no qualms about demanding the full privileges of extraterritoriality from China, although its entire modernization program had been inspired by the determination to rid itself of such unequal provisions.

REACTIONARIES, REFORMERS AND REVOLUTIONARIES

For China the most important result of the war was the total destruction of the partially restored prestige of the Manchu dynasty and the revelation of its inherent weakness, not only to the foreign powers but also to the Chinese people. Henceforth, the foreign powers felt uninhibited in pressing their demands on China. Only a thorough overhaul of the government aimed at centralizing the authority of Peking held any hope of salvaging the situation, but neither the Empress-Dowager, who had temporarily relinquished her authority, nor the scholar-officials, many of whom had already followed Li's lead in creating military forces person-

ally loyal to them, were prepared to accept such drastic changes. To many Westerners and Chinese alike the dynasty had already lost the "Mandate of Heaven"; the only remaining question was when and how it would be overthrown. Nevertheless, a number of scholar-officials tried to prop up the dynasty by proposals of greater or lesser reforms, while other individuals worked for revolution.

In each Eastern civilization's reaction to the Western impact, the entire spectrum was represented from a reactionary rejection of everything Western as essentially corrupt and barbaric, through reformers ready to borrow and adapt various Western techniques and ideas, to revolutionaries the most extreme of whom advocated a total rejection of their heritages in favor of the new Western dispensation. In this regard China was no exception. Because Western historians have been chiefly concerned with positive reactions to the spread of Western civilization, little or no notice has been taken of the reactionaries. Therefore, one should keep in mind that their convictions were held by the overwhelming majority of scholar-officials throughout the interaction of China and the West discussed in this chapter. Even after the disaster of the first Sino-Japanese war, one highly regarded scholar could denounce everything Western, including machinery because it disrupted the ancient handicrafts and created unemployment. On the other hand, as early as the Opium War, Commissioner Lin had drawn on the Confucian dictum to know one's enemy by securing all the information that he could get about the West. In addition, he had recognized the necessity of a Western-style naval force to meet the unprecedented barbarian challenge to China's sea frontier. But, except for a few disciples who had experienced Western naval and military superiority at first hand, his pleas fell on deaf ears until China was again assaulted by the allied forces of Britain and France. Even then, only a handful of enlightened scholar-officials, largely on their own initiative, began the first reluctant steps toward the development of modern military and naval forces and the establishment of the essential industries to support them, prior to the Japanese attack. Although achievements were limited, the number who wrote about the problems sharply increased.

Most of them advocated Westernization only in the material fields of armaments and industrial technology while they proclaimed the superiority of Chinese civilization in the moral and ethical areas, which merely required revitalization in accordance with Confucian precepts. The most prominent proponent of this position, Chang Chih-tung, summed it up in the slogan, "Chinese learning for substance, Western learning for function." Generally, this school of thought supported the Confucian conception of a government of men rather than laws with officials trained in traditional ethics and dedicated to the moral regeneration of society. Western civilization motivated by the quest for profits and power might gain temporary advantages, but lacking the moral virtues of humanity and righteousness it could never establish the larger social harmony and political unity that the propagation of Confucian virtues could provide. To these men the existing political divisions and the egocentric and lawless competition among Western states was proof positive of Chinese moral superiority. Of course, they recognized the contemporary lapse in virtuous conduct and the prevalence of official venality, but this condition was attributed to the ruling dynasty which, in the final analysis, was responsible for screening and appointing all officials. Although the solution recommended rejuvenation of the dynasty's attention to its function to educate and appoint officials of demonstrated virtue, such writing sometimes came close to suggesting revolution.

More radical reform was advocated mostly by southern Chinese scholars of the Canton region which had the longest experience of contact with the West. In the later

nineteenth century they received the added stimulus of translations of seminal Western works as well as opportunities for study abroad. Finally, the additional humiliations shocked them into a realization that the halfway measures of moderate reformers were demonstrably inadequate. Although they avowed their loyalty to Confucianism, their desperate reformulations tended to violate one or another of its sanctified dogmas. In fact, like Confucius, they were attempting to use their interpretation of the past to justify innovations in the established structure of society and state. In this sense, they were unwitting revolutionaries, and later some passed into the revolutionary fold.

Their most notable representative, because he gained the temporary support of the emperor, was K'ang Yu-wei (1858–1927). As the offspring of a scholar-official family, he was given a typical classical education, but reacted against it, first by questioning his teacher's evaluation of various classics, and then by abandoning his studies in favor of a quest for intuitive insight along Ch'an Buddhist lines. The fruit of his meditation was the conviction that he was endowed with a special mission to save his people. Then he resumed his studies on a selective basis, seeking evidence that Confucius had been a reformer who advocated the need for change to meet the altered circumstances of his times and that contemporary Confucian practice was a far cry from the teachings of the sage. At the same time, he absorbed every bit of Western learning he could get his hands on to discover how best to meet the West on its own terms. Following China's defeat by Japan, K'ang's reform program jelled; modernization was its keynote and Japan was its principal model. To justify the drastic changes in Confucian terms, he published in 1897 his first major work, *Confucius As a Reformer*, to demonstrate that if Confucius were alive he would propose similar changes. To make his reforms palatable, he sought to expand the concept of Confucianism to accommodate all the innovations he proposed as being in accord with Confucianism and not just alien Western importations.

In a more radical work that was not published in full during his lifetime K'ang drew on the Confucian virtue of humanity to envision a future utopia encompassing all mankind in a communal and egalitarian recognition of brotherly love that would virtually eliminate the need for government except at the local level. Not only would national boundaries be erased, but the family would be abolished, leaving the care of children and the aged to ultra-hygienic public institutions. The result would be the extension of the benefits of an updated Chinese civilization to the whole world. Such a glorified picture was essentially an expression of Chinese nationalism which did violence to the emphasis of Confucius on the family and social stratification according to the rules of filial piety. Its relevance as a precedent for Chinese communism and the commune is obvious, though K'ang was by no means a Marxist. Indeed, his chief concern was how to fit Western nationalism, which he recognized as the chief spring of Western power, into the traditional Chinese framework.

In June 1898, K'ang secured the emperor's authorization to initiate his "Hundred Days of Reform" on the basis of a memorial to the throne presented in January. In this memorial he made clear that the existing condition of international competition demanded pragmatic changes of traditional institutions, if China were to survive, and to this end he urged the following of Japan as a model because of its similarity in culture and its manifest success.

Despite the pragmatic approach indicated in his memorial, when the inexperienced K'ang came to power, he demonstrated little restraint and less tact in implementing his program in a flood of imperial edicts that thoroughly alarmed and alienated the bureaucracy. His goal was to centralize authority and prepare for the establishment of a constitutional monarchy and a parliamentary system through a public school system, a public press, and elected local assemblies. Civil service examinations were to include Western as well as Chinese learning. The central government was to promote and control agriculture, industry, commerce, communications, and finance through a number of bureaus. The army and navy were to be strengthened and reorganized under national authority. Not only were the ancient institutions of China in jeopardy but, of more importance, the vested interests of the venal bureaucracy in the decentralized system of administration.

Their one hope was the Empress-Dowager, the "Old Buddha" as she was known, who had kept a close watch on the liberated emperor. K'ang and the emperor were soon aware of the mounting opposition to the reforms and ordered Yüan Shih-k'ai to liquidate her chief supporter. Instead, he revealed the plan and assisted Tz'u Hsi in seizing the emperor and reestablishing her regency. K'ang Yu-wei escaped abroad, but many of his followers were put to death. Most of the reform edicts were repealed. Thus ended the "Hundred Days of Reform" which attempted too much in too short a time. Like previous reforming efforts, it failed because it lacked the support of enough of the bureaucracy, the true source of power in Imperial China. A gradual program under strong imperial leadership might have succeeded in transforming the outlook and attitudes of the bureaucracy, but by 1898 it was too late for a gradual reformation, and the belated efforts of the Empress-Dowager were bound to fail.

A growing number of Chinese scholars and leaders foresaw and were preparing for the overthrow of the Manchu dynasty during the latter years of the nineteenth century. Some followed the traditional path by building up their individual military strength and wealth in preparation for a struggle for power, while others set forth revolutionary proposals and sought to implement them. Among those with the "forward look" of the revolutionary, mention must be made of Liang Ch'i-ch'ao (1873–1929), a close associate of K'ang who, in exile, expressed his revolutionary enthusiasm in widely read and respected writings. Even today Chinese communist scholarship honors him in debates about his contribution to progressive thought. In essence he argued for a new, public morality based on the interests of the nation as a whole in this fiercely competitive world of contesting nation-states. He recognized that some aspects of Chinese civilization must be worth preserving since it had endured so long, but he was extremely vague as to what these ancient assets might be. Clearly his eyes were set on the future and no halfway measures would satisfy him, only total revolution and the renovation of Chinese morality in terms of the welfare of the nation. In his journal entitled *A People Made New* he concluded:

> Thus I know why the so-called new methods nowadays are ineffectual. Why? Because without destruction there can be no construction. . . . What, then, is the way to effect our salvation and to achieve progress? The answer is that we must shatter at a blow the despotic and confused governmental system of some thousands of years; we must sweep away the corrupt and sycophantic learning of these thousands of years.
>
> (Translated in deBary, *Sources of Chinese Tradition*, p. 759)

Obviously these are the words of a revolutionary person which a communist can admire. But when it came to action, Liang's sensitivity made him shrink from violence. Although he was revered for his writings, the responsibility for political action was accepted by another Chinese revolutionary from the Canton region, Sun Yat-sen (1866–1925). Although Sun's successes were not achieved during the era under considera-

tion, his revolutionary activity began in 1895 and his basic program was roughly formulated by 1905.

The distinctive characteristic of Sun was the extent of Western influence on his thought, thanks to a Western education beyond the elementary level. Unlike his contemporaries as reformers and revolutionaries, he was no Chinese scholar versed in the classics. Nevertheless, as the child of a peasant family in the Canton area, he was a product of popular Chinese culture. After a secondary education in Hawaii, he returned and completed a medical education in Hongkong. From the beginning he was driven by a burning desire to alleviate the suffering of his people. A voracious reader of Western political, social, and economic tracts, he attempted to adapt the concepts that most impressed him to Chinese conditions, as he understood them. His unquestionable revolutionary ardor and the simplicity of his program, uncluttered with superfluous philosophizing and classical allusions, made a broader appeal than the highly intellectualized writings of many of his contemporaries. No Chinese could doubt his sincerity, and this was the secret of his popularity.

His program was summed up in the "Three People's Principles" clearly enunciated for the first time in 1905 in the publication of the revolutionary society, the T'ung-meng hui (League of Common Alliance), he had just formed among Chinese students in Japan. These principles were (1) nationalism, (2) constitutional democracy, and (3) "equalization of land rights," which meant a land reform program to end excessive landlordism. Nationalism, of course, was nothing new. Many other reformers had seen the necessity of domesticating this alien Western concept. Where Sun differed was in his conviction that such a unification of public sentiment could only be aroused by an emphasis on an anti-Manchu movement, in which even Westerners were invited to participate, for the overthrow of this alien and evil dynasty that had corrupted the "natural democracy" of Chinese civilization. After the overthrow of the Manchus, Sun shifted his emphasis to anti-imperialism to stimulate nationalism. Constitutional democracy, which in later elaboration became less democratic and more Chinese in character, was already conceived as requiring three stages of development before it could be achieved: (1) military government, (2) political tutelage during which local self-government would be permitted, and (3) a constitutional republic. Land reform, which was to become the central feature of what he later termed the "People's Livelihood," reflected the influence of socialistic ideas on his thought. This principle was then, and remained, the vaguest part of his program. In addition to defining the objectives of revolution, Sun made an important contribution to raising the means for it among the overseas Chinese communities in the course of his constant travels.

THE PAPER DRAGON

The transition from rejection of the West through various reformist positions to the advocacy of revolution by a growing number of Chinese intellectuals was accelerated in the last years of the nineteenth century, not only by the increased knowledge of the West available in translations but also by the utter contempt of the West for a China revealed to the whole world as a "paper dragon" by the easy victories of Japan. Concession after concession and humiliation after humiliation were inflicted on a helpless dynasty whose total incapacity to protect its subjects encouraged the spread of an equivalent attitude of disdain among them for Manchu authority. The whole story cannot be told here, but the highlights must be surveyed to give some comprehension of the hopeless depth to which Manchu prestige had sunk.

After the tripartite intervention had restored the Liaotung Peninsula to Chinese sovereignty, the parties to it were not slow in presenting their bills for services rendered. France and Russia demanded the privilege of loaning the sum needed to meet the first installment of the Japanese indemnity, secured by the Chinese maritime customs. Then Great Britain, concerned by the growth of Franco-Russian influence at Peking, joined Germany in forcing further loans which were secured by the salt tax and internal transit charges (*likin*) in the Yangtze region as well as the maritime customs. More important, however, were Russian agreements that secured land and concessionary rights for a trans-Manchurian railroad to Vladivostok, the reservation of Manchuria for future railroad and mining development, and a Russo-Chinese defensive alliance. In essence, Manchuria was being reduced to a Russian sphere of influence, if not a protectorate. The French, also, obtained a rectification in their favor of the Indo-Chinese boundary and a more specific statement of their prior rights to carry out future developments in the neighboring provinces of Kwangtung, Kwangsi, Kweichow, and Yünnan. Thus, in both the north and the south, China was compelled to concede exclusive privileges that established "spheres of influence" and limited its freedom of action. But, unfortunately for the Manchus, this process had only begun. The West in the last years of competing imperialism in the nineteenth century had already raised its national flags over every undefendable piece of land in the world; only the crumbling Manchu empire offered any further opportunities.

The German empire had just committed itself to challenging Britain's command of the high seas and sought in China a suitable base for a Pacific squadron. Kiaochow Bay on the southern coast of the Shantung Peninsula had been selected as most desirable after an extensive survey. Late in 1897 the murder of two German priests furnished the pretext for pressing the German demand on the Chinese government. In March 1898, China was compelled to grant a 99-year lease to the bay and surrounding territory, to acknowledge the province as a German sphere of influence, and to pay a large indemnity. This concession precipitated a general scramble for leases and spheres in which even the British, who opposed the idea of spheres, participated for self-protection. Russia secured a 25-year lease on ice-free Port Arthur at the tip of the Liaotung Peninsula and further rights in its Manchurian sphere—concessions especially galling to the Japanese who had been forced to relinquish this conquest on the ostensible grounds that it posed an intolerable menace to China's independence. The British, fearful of this Russian advance, obtained a lease on the inadequate port of Weihaiwei on the north side of the Shantung Peninsula for as long as the Russians held Port Arthur. They also extracted a 99-year lease on the balance of the Kowloon Peninsula opposite Hongkong and an acknowledgement of the Yangtze basin as its exclusive sphere. Also the French advanced their influence in southern China by a 99-year lease on a port in Kwangtung Province. Not to be outdone, Japan gained recognition of the Chinese province opposite Taiwan as its sphere for development. A halt was finally called to these concessions when China felt strong enough to refuse an Italian request for a naval base. Meanwhile, to avoid clashes, the imperial powers made bilateral agreements defining their respective spheres without even going through the motions of consulting China and gaining its consent.

The initial financial penetration of their respective spheres took the form of railroad construction to tap the resources and markets in the interior. In addition, the United States, which with Britain had always favored an "open door" policy giving no special advantages to any nation in any part of China, renewed its interest and stake in East Asia following its acquisition from Spain of the Philippines. The "open door" policy was nothing new having been enshrined in the most-favored-nation clauses in every Western treaty, but now it was threatened by the special concessions and spheres granted to

the various powers. In 1899 Secretary of State John Hay sent notes to all the involved powers requesting acceptance of the principle of equal economic opportunity and equal treatment for all others within the leased areas and spheres of influence of each power. With favorable responses from each one, though the Russian reply was far from clear, Hay declared the "open door" to be operative. Although the Hay notes explicitly recognized the spheres of influence, they reduced the exclusive incentives for investment. Notice that no guarantees of Chinese administrative and territorial integrity were included; this feature of American diplomacy, though an implied consequence, was reserved for explicit statement in the second round of "open door" notes.

THE BOXER REBELLION

The humiliating defeat by Japan, the subsequent sharply accelerated tempo of Western penetration in missionary as well as political and economic forms, widespread famines against the effects of which the missionary employed every means at his disposal to protect his converts, and the overthrow of K'ang Yu-wei's reform efforts—all combined to inspire militancy among the increasingly desperate peasants in northern China where piracy and banditry grew rapidly. Instead of suppressing bandits, the government attracted them into militia organizations which provided a larger and semilegal vehicle for venting their hostilities. Through the militia the traditional secret societies gained a larger audience among whom to propagate their panaceas. Whether the peasants, the militia, the bandits, and the secret societies were incited more by antiforeign or by anti-Manchu feelings is an open question, but the extent of disillusionment with the dynasty appears to have been underrated in the face of the Manchu success in convincing them that the Westerners and their Chinese "running dogs" were the common foe of peasant and

ruler. Sporadic anti-Christian and antiforeign outbreaks by these groups, dubbed
"Righteous Fists of Harmony" or "Boxers"
by the West, became widespread in 1899.
Officials who demonstrated sympathy by in-
action had to be removed at the request of the
Western governments, but they were treated
as heroes by the court, conveying an impression of imperial approval. Western troops
were sent to protect the legations at Peking
from mob action, and on June 17, 1900 the
Western powers felt that security required
the storming of the shore batteries protecting
the approach to Tientsin and Peking. By the
Chinese this action in addition to previous
clashes with an international force was understood as a declaration of war; the legations were besieged with the aid of imperial troops and a relief column was forced to
retreat to Tientsin. The so-called "Boxer Rebellion" had begun.

An adequate relief expedition was slow
in being assembled because the Japanese,
who had the most troops immediately available, were reluctant to take a major role. A
conglomerate expedition of which almost one
half was Japanese finally reached Peking and
relieved the legations in mid-August. Then,
with the widely admired exception of the
well-disciplined Japanese force, the foreign
troops engaged in an orgy of looting and rapacity of the most disgraceful nature—another example of Western barbarism to reinforce existing Chinese opinion. Meanwhile,
on the excuse of Chinese inability to maintain
order, Russian troops occupied Manchuria,
laying the foundation for the Russo-Japanese
war. In the Boxer madness 231 foreigners
and an untold number of Chinese Christians
were slain.

China might have been carved up on the
spot if the foreign powers had not viewed
their action as the suppression of a rebellion
rather than a war, and if they had not been
mutually suspicious of each others' intentions. Moreover, American insistence on
a moderate settlement was not without influence. After all, the United States and its

merchants had everything to lose and nothing to gain from such a division because it
had no leasehold or sphere of influence.
While the military operations were still in
progress, Hay sent out his second round of
"open door" notes which secured acceptance
of the principle of preserving China's territorial and administrative integrity. Even so, the
terms of the Boxer settlement of 1901, in addition to normal demands, saddled China
with an exorbitant indemnity of 333 million
dollars, a figure out of all proportion to the
costs and damages. Even though Japan had
provided the largest contingent, less than 8
percent of this sum was deemed adequate to
cover expenses. The United States only
asked for 7 percent, which proved more than
enough to cover costs and damages, the rest
being later assigned to a fund to pay the expenses of Chinese students in American institutions. Most greedy was Russia with 29
percent while it continued to occupy Manchuria. To secure the payment of this huge
indemnity, in 39 annual installments, every
source of Chinese revenue was attached and
for the most part placed under Western management.

THE LAST ATTEMPT AT IMPERIAL REFORM

However distasteful to her, the "Old
Buddha" finally accepted the idea of modernization along the lines laid out by K'ang
Yu-wei. Although she denied the relationship, her reforms, carried out with great reluctance over a period of years, bear a striking resemblance to his. First, a model army
of six divisions was organized by Yüan
Shih-k'ai, and four of them were later transferred to a ministry of war to form the nucleus of a proposed national army of 36 divisions. This military buildup was particularly
stimulated by the Russo-Japanese war during which China was a helpless bystander of
a conflict conducted mainly on Chinese soil.
Administrative reorganization sought to
clean out the deadwood in the central gov-

ernment in preparation for the exercise of greater authority over the provinces, but the effort to exert this central control was not implemented until after 1905. In that year an imperial edict abolishing the traditional civil service examinations struck a vital blow at the Confucian hierarchy. In practice, however, the Empress-Dowager for many years had gone outside the scholar class in her quest for able subordinates. Meanwhile, Chang Chih-tung and other progressive officials were encouraged to finance, from provincial revenues and without recourse to foreign loans, railroad construction, mining, and other essential economic improvements.

All these reforms, and those to come, while laudable, were too little and too late to save the dying dynasty. The Boxer rebellion had demonstrated large-scale discontent among the stolid northern Chinese to complement the rebellious record of long standing among the more volatile Chinese of central and southern China. Moreover, the government proved completely impotent in dealing with the foreigners' abuses of their treaty privileges, which increased rather than diminished during these years. The growing numbers of Chinese students returning from periods of study abroad found little in the Manchu regime to commend it, even when the ban on mixed marriages was lifted. For a livelihood they might serve it, but they felt no loyalty to it. It remained an alien regime on which all China's woes were blamed.

In 1905 China stood at the crossroads, if it had not passed them. Japan's victory over Russia demonstrated, not only to China but to all Asia, how successful an integrated modernization program could be and stimulated hope where despair had prevailed, reinforcing the position of reformers and revolutionaries throughout Asia. In contrast to Japan, the reactionary element had dominated the Chinese attitude toward the West during the nineteenth century with only minimal concessions to the pleas of moderate and radical reformers. The conviction of the

Chinese scholar-official class in the ethical superiority of Chinese civilization had only been confirmed by the bald use of power by the West to extract and support concessions. Equally if not more important to them was the threat that more than superficial reforms posed to their vested interests in the opportunities for individual aggrandizement presented by the weakening grip of the Manchu dynasty. Indeed, the program of centralization favored the employment of Manchu over Chinese officials.

In fact, the Manchus might have been overthrown already if the advantageous treaties had not given the foreign powers a vested interest in maintaining them. Certainly the Western administration of the maritime customs service had furnished the dynasty with greater revenue than Chinese administration would have provided. But after 1895 imperial revenues were increasingly hypothecated to meet foreign debt payments, and the remainder available to finance modernization suffered a relative decline, despite a great increase in the volume of trade. To add to imperial problems, China was economically weakened by an increasingly adverse balance of trade. From 1895 a growing number of intellectuals turned to a revolutionary solution of the woes of China and its impoverished peasantry.

China's reaction to the increasing impact of the West took three forms that will be observed in every Eastern civilization: (1) rejection of the West and an emphasis on the revitalization of its ancient heritage of ideals and values, (2) reformism that searched for some compromise incorporating essential Western institutions, and (3) revolution jettisoning more or less of the ancient heritage as outmoded in the modern world. In the other civilizations, representatives of each of these attitudes will be found, but the one that predominates will vary both in time and place. These reactions and the extent to which they have modified the ancient heritages up to the present will be our primary concern.

SIGNIFICANT DATES

1839–1842 Opium War
1842–1844 First treaty settlement
1850–1865 T'ai P'ing Rebellion
1856–1860 Anglo-French War and second treaty settlement
1867 Burlingame Mission
1868–1878 Western campaigns of Tso Tsung-t'ang
1870 Tientsin massacre
1876 Chefoo Convention
1885 French conquest of Indo-China
1885 Li-Itō Convention
1894–1895 First Sino-Japanese war
1897–1898 Imperial scramble for leaseholds and spheres
1898 "Hundred Days of Reform" (K'ang Yu-wei)
1899–1900 "Open Door" notes of John Hay
1900–1901 "Boxer" Rebellion
1904–1905 Russo-Japanese War
1905 Abolition of traditional civil service examinations
1905 Founding of T'ung-meng hui (Sun Yat-sen)

SELECTED READINGS

*Chang, Chung-li, *The Chinese Gentry: Studies on their Role in Nineteenth-Century China.* Seattle: University of Washington Press, 1955.

*Chang, Hsin-pao, *Commissioner Lin and the Opium War.* New York: Norton, 1970.

*Fairbank, John K., *Trade and Diplomacy on the China Coast: The Opening of the Treaty Ports, 1842–1854.* Stanford: Stanford University Press, 1969.

*———, *The United States and China.* Cambridge, Mass.: Harvard University Press, 1958.

*Feuerwerker, Albert, *China's Early Industrialization.* New York: Atheneum Pubs., 1970.

*———, ed., *Modern China.* Englewood Cliffs, N.J.: Prentice-Hall, 1964.

*Hsiao, Kung-chuan, *Rural China: Imperial Control in the Nineteenth Century.* Seattle: University of Washington Press, 1967.

Hsü, Immanuel C. Y., *China's Entrance into the Family of Nations.* Cambridge, Mass.: Harvard University Press, 1960.

———, *The Rise of Modern China.* New York: Oxford University Press, 1970.

Kuhn, Philip A., *Rebellion and its Enemies in Late Imperial China.* Cambridge, Mass.: Harvard University Press, 1970.

*Levenson, Joseph R., *Confucian China and its Modern Fate: A Trilogy.* Berkeley: University of California Press, 1968.

*———, *Liang Ch'i-ch'ao and the Mind of Modern China.* Berkeley: University of California Press, 1967.

Lo, Jung-pang, *K'ang Yu-wei*. Tucson: University of Arizona Press, 1967.

Michael, Franz, *The Taiping Rebellion*. Seattle: University of Washington Press, 1966.

Purcell, Victor, *The Boxer Uprising*. Cambridge: Cambridge University Press, 1963.

*Schiffrin, Harold Z., *Sun Yat-sen and the Origins of the Chinese Revolution*. Berkeley: University of California Press, 1968.

*Schurmann, Franz, and Schell, Orville, eds., *Imperial China*, Vol. I of *The China Reader*. 3 vols.; New York: Random House, 1967.

*Schwartz, Benjamin, *In Search of Wealth and Power: Yen Fu and the West*. Cambridge, Mass.: Harvard University Press, 1964.

*Sharman, Lyon, *Sun Yat-sen*. Stanford: Stanford University Press, 1968.

Shih, Vincent Y. C., *The Taiping Ideology*. Seattle: University of Washington Press, 1967.

Spector, Stanley, *Li Hung-chang and the Huai Army*. Seattle: University of Washington Press, 1964.

*Tan, Chester C., *The Boxer Catastrophe*. New York: Columbia University Press, 1955.

Teng, S. Y., *The Taiping Rebellion and the Western Powers*. New York: Oxford University Press, 1971.

*Waley, Arthur, *The Opium War*. New York: Norton, 1970.

*Wright, Mary C., *The Last Stand of Chinese Conservatism: The T'ung-chih Resoration, 1862–1874*. New York: Atheneum, 1966.

CHAPTER SIXTEEN
THE JAPANESE "MIRACLE" TO 1905

In the swift success of its adaptation to the Western challenge Japan stands in unexampled contrast, not only to China but to every other Asian civilization. In the brief span of 50 years it threw off the humiliating restrictions of unequal treaties and gained recognition as a world power to be reckoned with in international affairs. Many reasons, all valid in part, have been advanced to explain this exceptional achievement. But none of them, individually or in combination, can account for it without the single-minded leadership of the handful of samurai statesmen who engineered the Restoration. Fired by the determination to succeed where the Tokugawas had failed at the task specified by the full title of Shōgun, "Barbarian-subduing Generalissimo," they focused every effort on the one goal of removing the shackles of the unequal treaties and of gaining recognition as a major power. They might quarrel—even to the death—about the timing and the means, and they might make mistakes, but they never differed over the end to which all were committed. Of course, the unique characteristics of Japanese civilization, its history, and its people made possible their achievement; but without their dedicated leadership failure would have been more likely than success.

Only once before had Japan become aware of its backwardness through the loss of its foothold in Korea, and on that occasion it had undertaken a massive "modernization" program, borrowing and adapting during the seventh and eighth centuries the features of Chinese civilization most useful in centralizing power in the state. In the seventeenth century, Japan, recently unified under Tokugawa leadership, had been strong enough to repel the West, as it had earlier expelled the Mongols. In 1854, however, Japan was no match for the advances in Western technology, and the initial treaties that partially opened Japan were soon followed by the demand for the customary concessions which the Tokugawa Shogunate was unprepared to resist.

THE FAILURE OF THE TOKUGAWA SHOGUNATE

According to the American understanding of Perry's treaty, Townsend Harris arrived in 1856 as the United States' first consul-general, much to the annoyance and embarrassment of the shogunate which had taken no steps to fulfill its promise to "expel the barbarian." Within two years, by patience, tact, and references to the possible use of force by other powers Harris secured a new treaty that clarified in America's favor the previous misunderstandings, opened additional ports, established extraterritoriality, fixed a low tariff, and permitted the exchange and export of specie. The last provision led to a damaging drain of Japanese coins until the ratio of gold and silver was adjusted to the international rate. In the long run, however, extraterritoriality and the loss of tariff autonomy were the most damaging to Japanese pride and to their pocketbook. Without the protection and revenue that an adequate tariff could have provided, modernization and its financing were much more difficult. This treaty was soon followed by similar treaties with the other powers which, through inclusion of the standard most-favored-nation clauses, enmeshed Japan in European toils beyond any hope of a simple solution. What is more, the shogunate had been unable as yet to take any significant steps toward the necessary military and naval modernization because of financial difficulties, as well as indecision, and antishogunal feeling and intrigue, already significant before Perry's

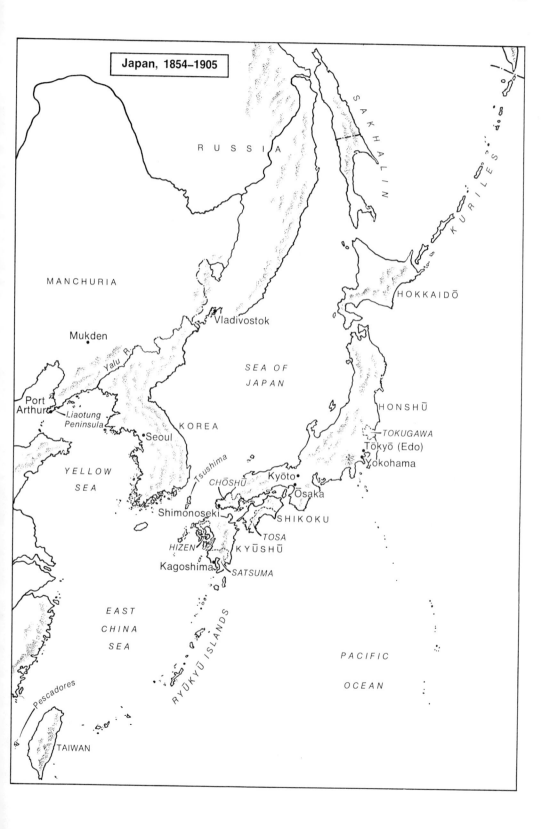

Japan, 1854–1905

arrival, grew with every passing day and every concession.

Even before the opening of Japan much controversy had been aroused over the issues of the shogunate and the seclusion policy. Shortly after his accession in 1846 the Emperor Kōmei took the unprecedented step of instructing the shōgun to adhere to the seclusion policy. Some thoughtful teachers, however, realized that more than words would be needed to hold the aggressive Western powers at bay. Sakuma Shōzan (1811–1864) and his disciple, Yoshida Shōin (1830–1859), were the two most influential figures who altered their attitudes with typical Japanese pragmatism to face the reality of the situation.

Sakuma early recognized the need for military and educational modernization for the purposes of defense, although he favored seclusion until the 1858 treaty definitely opened Japan. After that date, he worked for reconciliation and collaboration between emperor and shōgun to mobilize the human and material resources of the nation. For favoring reconciliation, which was anathema to the ambitious western clansmen, he was assassinated by Chōshū samurai, but his famous slogan, "Eastern ethics and Western science," characterized the moderate outlook of the leaders who engineered Japan's modernization.

His dynamic and daring disciple, Yoshida Shoin of Chōshū, whose brief career ended at the age of thirty on the shōgun's block, had an even more demonstrable relation to Japan's future leaders; among his pupils were such prominent leaders as Kido, Itō, and Yamagata. So eager was he to learn about the West that he attempted unsuccessfully to stow away on one of Perry's ships. In contrast with his more moderate mentor he was an impatient revolutionary who saw nothing but ineptitude and corruption in the political structure of Japan. Drawing on Mencius' justification of rebellion against unworthy rulers, he denounced not only the shogunate but the whole hereditary aristocracy and the feudal system, not be-

cause he was a champion of social justice but because he saw in the ruling class nothing but luxury, indolence, and incompetence. In fact, he looked to the best samurai, true to the code of bushidō, to lead the people of Japan to its imperial destiny. What he sought was a regeneration of the Japanese spirit under dynamic leadership that was unfettered by convention. Knowledge without the will to implement it, he argued, was useless. Brief as his life was, no other individual had a greater influence in inspiring that single-mindedness and "resolute will" among the creators of modern Japan.

With their martial heritage and training the samurai vented their frustration at their country's impotence in more and more frequent acts of violence, and the emperor did nothing to discourage them. Both Westerners and any Japanese who were suspected of being pro-Western were attacked without distinction. In 1860 the chief minister of the shogunate was assassinated. In addition, the daimyō began to disregard the rules requiring residence in Edo and the leaving of their families as hostages when they visited their estates. In further defiance of Tokugawa regulations, the leading daimyō and their retainers consorted and intrigued at the imperial court. The shogunate, fearful of rebellion, felt unable to enforce the rules. Encouraged by these signs of weakness, the emperor in 1862 released the daimyō from the residence rules, ordered the shōgun to consult the daimyō on important affairs of state, and set June 25, 1863, as the date for expelling the barbarians. In the year 1862 an Englishman was cut down for failing to give way to the procession of the Satsuma daimyō. The British demanded an indemnity and execution of the guilty samurai. After extended talks the shogunate agreed to pay the whole indemnity but admitted its inability to bring the murderer to justice. On June 25, 1863, the prescribed date for expelling barbarians, Chōshū batteries opened fire on every Western ship passing through the straits of Shimonoseki.

The inability of the shogunate to discipline or control the two great estates of Satsuma and Chōshū was now manifest. The British, drawing on their long experience in dealing with non-Western peoples, realized that the time had come for the application of force to command respect. In August 1863, a British flotilla entered the port of Kagoshima, the Satsuma capital, sank all ships, and silenced the shore batteries. In the process fires broke out that destroyed most of the city. When individual retaliation by the United States and Holland failed to discourage the Chōshū attacks on shipping, the British, Dutch, French, and Americans sent a joint task force in 1864 to bring this vassal of the shōgun to heel. Not only were the Chōshū ships and shore batteries destroyed, but landing parties decisively defeated the Chōshū samurai, forcing the daimyō to open the straits and the port of Shimonoseki to trade.

Instead of withdrawing in bitterness from further contact, the Satsuma and Chōshū daimyō and their officials pragmatically recognized the inadequacy of their armed forces and took immediate steps to rectify their deficiencies. Satsuma established cordial relations with the British and specialized in mastering naval technology. As a result, Satsuma samurai were most influential in the development of Japan's navy and supplied practically all its flag officers. Chōshū, on the other hand, was most impressed by the defeat of its samurai army and promptly created a peasant army trained and equipped on Western lines. As early as 1866 this new army proved its mettle by fighting to a standstill a far larger Tokugawa force of traditional warriors sent at the emperor's command to discipline the rebellious daimyō for their overt opposition to the imperial ratification of the treaties with the West. This imperial ratification, it should be noted, was insisted on by the West when they came to realize that the emperor was becoming more and more the true source of authority.

This military failure of the Tokugawa Shogunate, acting as an imperial agent, sealed its doom. Since 1846 its traditional monopoly of political authority had been repeatedly challenged and eroded by the actions of the emperor, the daimyō, and itself. It had been unable to meet the demand of the slogan—"Revere the emperor and repel the barbarian"—coined by the Mito branch of the Tokugawa family before the opening of Japan. It had failed to fulfill the subsequent modification of this slogan—"Revere the emperor and expel the barbarian." Finally, it had failed to carry out its function as "Generalissimo" to quell the internal dissidence of its vassals. The shōgun had died in the field in the struggle with Chōshū and was succeeded by a member of the Mito branch of the family that was sympathetic to the restoration of authority to the throne. All that remained to be decided was what form the political reorganization of Japan would take.

THE RESTORATION

In 1867 the accession of a fifteen-year-old emperor greatly eased the path for action by the ambitious advisors of the leading dissident daimyō and samurai of Satsuma and Chōshū, Hizen and Tosa, who dominated the imperial court at Kyōto. For a number of years a proposal for the shōgun to surrender his authority to the emperor, while retaining his hereditary estates, had been discussed and considered. Under such an arrangement he would still be by far the greatest lord because of his vast estates and presumably would exercise a strong voice in the councils of the emperor.

In 1866 Satsuma, Chōshū, Hizen, and Tosa had formed an alliance that was financed mainly by the Mitsui interests and supported by some members of the court nobility and the British. The Tosa daimyō favored this moderate proposal, and in response to his suggestion the shōgun surrendered his authority in November 1867, in the avowed hope that "by unity in thought and effort the country can hold its own with all nations of the world." But the power-hungry leaders of Satsuma and the antifeudal Chōshū disciples of Yoshida Shōin were not willing to settle for the supporting role that such a moderate political change would give them. Their troops had occupied Kyōto, and news of an assassination plot persuaded the ex-shōgun to withdraw to Ōsaka from the imperial capital under the cover of night. This irreconcilable hostility was underlined by other incidents, such as the firing of the Edo palace by incendiaries in Satsuma employ, which convinced the Tokugawa samurai that they had no choice but to fight to preserve their estates. In January 1868, after the Meiji (Enlightened Peace) Emperor (1867–1912) issued the Restoration edict, a three-day battle, decided in typical fashion by Tokugawa defections on the second day, sealed the destruction of Tokugawa material strength. Some further desperate last stands were made and the Tokugawa naval commander did not surrender his force until 1869, but the ex-shōgun lost his court rank and was required to retire to his family estate in Mito. The emperor moved into the castle at Edo, which was renamed Tōkyō (Eastern Capital).

THE OLIGARCHY AND ITS PROGRAM

The more vigorous and uncompromising leaders from the allied western fiefs had won out with a minimum of bloodshed, and their program was set forth on their advice in the Charter Oath of the Emperor in 1868.* Although its five articles were expressed in very general terms, they indicated clearly

the direction and purpose of the reformers. The emperor agreed to being guided by public opinion as expressed in deliberative assemblies. This first article did not imply democracy or representative government; it only limited arbitrary imperial authority by prescribing consultation in arriving at decisions. The second article indirectly attacked feudalism by calling for the abolition of class distinctions to create a united nation. The third article reflected the fear of military domination by requiring civil and military officials to act as one. The fourth article sought to clear the path for modernization by prescribing the destruction of outmoded customs and inequitable practices contrary to the principles of nature. The final article clearly set Japan on the road of modernization by proclaiming the intention of seeking knowledge throughout the world for the promotion of the empire.

As the Charter Oath indicated, the new leaders who had come to power as champions of the cry, "Expel the barbarian," had imbibed a healthy respect for Western power and had realized that their goal had to be interpreted in new terms and had to be accomplished over a long period, which involved more than superficial changes and adaptation. The Restoration would require more than a political reorganization; it would require a revolution that would shake the political, social, and economic structure of Japan to its very roots. The problem was how to accomplish such drastic changes without destroying Japanese civilization in the process.

*Some 100 Sat-Chō-Hi-To samurai and a handful of progressive court nobles provided the leaders in the Restoration and modernization of Japan. Of these the most important were Saigō Takamori (1827–1877), Ōkubo Toshimichi (1830–1878), and Matsukata Masayoshi (1835–1924) of Satsuma; Kido Kōin (1833–1877), Yamagata Aritomo (1838–1922), Itō Hirobumi (1841–1909), and Inouye Kaoru (1836–1915) of Chōshū; Ōkuma Shigenobu (1838–1922) of Hizen; Itagaki Taisuke (1837–1919) of Tosa; and Iwakura Tomomi (1825–1883) and Saionji Kimmochi (1849–1940) of the court nobility. Saigō, who defected and led armed oppo-

sition, Kido, and Ōkubo were lost by the end of the first decade. Itagaki and Ōkuma defected to lead separate movements for representative government and, after the constitution, led the opposition in the lower house of the Diet. In 1898, they joined forces temporarily to form a party government that lasted only four months. With the establishment of constitutional government, Itō and Yamagata became the leading members of the Genrō, extraconstitutional advisors of the throne who actually ran the government. In 1916 Prince Saionji joined the Genrō and exercised a moderating influence on the government until his death in November 1940.

The degree of their success borders on a "miracle" which other underdeveloped nations might still study with profit. This revolution was masterminded from above by a handful of men who were united by the end of transforming Japan into a modern and respected nation.

To achieve this end, their first task, similar to that of their forebears in the seventh century, was to restore political and economic authority to the central government without unduly disturbing the aristocratic character of Japanese society. This task was facilitated by the conviction of the divinity of the emperor which had been fostered since ancient times. Aristocratic families came and went, but the imperial line had continued from prehistoric times. The imperial institution plus the renewed emphasis placed on it during the Tokugawa era provided a single figure to whom every Japanese individual, regardless of status, directed his loyalty, creating a greater sense of national consciousness than most nations enjoyed. Thus, reinforced by the imperial cult of Shintō, an imperial request was a divine command. Therefore, those young men who had managed the Restoration and had destroyed Tokugawa influence possessed the unique advantage of being able to invoke the imperial authority of the young Meiji emperor who accepted their guidance.

THE DESTRUCTION OF FEUDALISM

Their first step was the persuasion of their own lords to surrender their estates to the emperor. This surrender was made palatable by the promise of their continuance as imperially appointed governors and a guaranteed salary of 10 percent of their former revenues, which was in most cases greater than their former average net incomes. Almost all of the other lords voluntarily followed this example based on the accompanying declaration: "There is no soil within the Empire that does not belong to the Emperor . . . and no inhabitant who is not a subject of the Emperor." An imperial edict of 1871 completed the process by abolishing all clans and fiefs and by dividing the land into prefectures, while the ex-daimyō were paid off in government bonds, yielding 8 percent interest and titles of nobility. Many of them participated in the economic development of Japan by investing their funds in commerce and industry.

This assumption of political and economic control of the entire country by the imperial government by no means solved its economic problems. The government also assumed the expense of supporting the samurai and their families, who accounted for almost 5 percent of the population. To solve this problem, their stipends were initially cut by as much as 50 percent. In 1873 they were offered the option of commuting their pensions for a lump sum, and almost one third of them in desperation availed themselves of this opportunity until in 1876 commutation—half in cash and half in bonds—was made compulsory. Insult was added to injury by an accompanying decree which forbade the wearing of the traditional two swords identifying their status, except for army, navy, and police officers. Thus the military facet of feudalism was eliminated under the direction of former samurai.

In fact, however, the hardships inflicted on the samurai should not be exaggerated, even though they resulted in a number of desperate revolts by a minority who found it impossible to adjust to their new circumstances. Indeed, the attempt led by the disenchanted Satsuma leader, Saigō Takamori, to remove the "evil" councillors of the emperor provided the first serious test for Japan's conscript army. Many of the samurai found satisfactory employment in government or as managers and entrepreneurs in Japan's economic development. The bureaucracy that grew with the extension of governmental activities was staffed almost entirely by former samurai. An even larger number of samurai were absorbed as officers in the navy, in the conscript army formed in

1872, and in the police force. Others staffed and developed the universal educational system decreed in 1872, and their disciplined dedication produced in 50 years one of the most literate nations in the world. Because of their relationship to the bureaucracy many more became managers of government-sponsored or assisted enterprises, while others used their lump-sum payments to finance their own businesses. Finally, many poorer samurai, already compelled to farm to eke out a living, used their payments to purchase farmland or set up village enterprises. In these ways, ex-samurai almost monopolized the political and economic life of Meiji Japan and pervaded it with their ideals of duty and loyalty which, by example and education, were extended to the whole population. Therefore, Japan's modernization can be said to be predominantly the product of ex-samurai leadership and enterprise, which was supported by the traditional industriousness and obedience of a well-disciplined peasantry.

MODERNIZATION AND ITS PROBLEMS

Although the leaders succeeded during the first decade of the Meiji era in centralizing political and economic control and in sharply reducing the costs of disinherited feudalism, they were still hard-pressed to find the funds for modernization. Three-fourths of the government's revenue came from agricultural taxes. Although the farmers were pleased to get certificates of ownership for their plots, they were extremely unhappy with the high tax assessments that had to be paid in cash, regardless of whether the harvest was good or bad. When the tax payments fell due, they had to sell their crops for what they could get, while the large landlords and merchants could afford to store crops until prices returned to normal. Soon many small farmers fell hopelessly into debt, and growing numbers were forced into ten-

ancy. By 1900, 40 percent leased part or all of their land.

During the first decade of the Meiji era widespread rural disturbances occurred in which former samurai provided leadership, until rural conditions became more stable. Meanwhile, well aware of the further encroachments that foreign debts might bring, the government with a few minor exceptions financed the initial stages of modernization by the taxation of the peasants.

The fifth article of the Charter Oath proclaimed the objective of seeking knowledge throughout the world, and the Restoration regime did not delay in implementing this aim. Of course, Japan already possessed a nucleus of scholars versed in Western knowledge through "Dutch Learning," and a number of others had traveled and studied in the West before the overthrow of the shogunate. These few men, however, were wholly inadequate to organize and direct the forced-draft modernization program that was planned. A veritable flood of carefully screened students was now sent to selected nations to master specific skills. Japan's modernizers, however, could not wait until their return. Foreign advisors were employed and each one had assigned to him 10 or more student "shadows" to learn his specialty so that he could be dispensed with at the earliest possible date.

Top priority in modernization was naturally given to the army and navy and their supporting enterprises. French military advisors were employed to train the army, until the anti-liberal reaction of the mid-eighties brought a switch to German advisors. Both military and naval academies were established. Since Great Britain was clearly supreme on the high seas, Japan turned to Britain for naval advisors and warships. In significant contrast with China, Japan insisted on new construction equipped with the latest advances in naval technology. Moreover, even before the war with China, Japan had enough confidence in its own naval architects to specify modifications of British designs. Although some warships were built in Japanese shipyards, most of the navy that defeated China and then Russia was British built, and British advisors could take some pride in the skill with which their trainees handled their fleet.

Supporting industries sponsored by the government included armaments, shipyards, a merchant marine, and iron and steel works. The new government inherited from the shogunate the Yokosuka Iron Works which it expanded. Since heavy industries like these required a large investment and a long period of development before becoming profitable, private capital could not be lured into them and they had to be financed by the government. Once they were showing a profit, however, the government sold them, often for a small part of their cost, to favored financial combines, such as Mitsui and Mitsubishi. In addition, an economic crisis forced sales to meet other immediate needs of the government. Such sales had the effect of establishing close ties between these family firms and the government with significant side effects, as will be shown, on Japanese political development. In view of the intimate Japanese relationship with the sea throughout its history, the speed with which a competitive merchant marine was developed should come as no surprise. By the end of the century Japanese ships were carrying the bulk of the country's rapidly expanding foreign trade to the great benefit of its foreign exchange. Attention was also given to internal communications which, thanks to the Tokugawa system, were already more developed than in any other Asian country. In 1872 the first railroad connected Tōkyō with its rapidly growing port of Yokohama. By the end of the century Japan possessed a railroad network of more than 1000 miles of government-owned track and 3000 miles of privately owned track. Another area of development was telegraphic and telephonic communication.

Second priority was given to those industries that would yield the quickest profits

and whose products were most salable in foreign markets. In these respects textile production was a natural industry for early development. Modern plants were purchased by the government as models. Despite some initial setbacks, the substantial profits earned in a short period soon attracted private investment, but the extent of modern industrial production during the Meiji era should not be exaggerated. Cheap labor made production in traditional small-scale operations still profitable. The majority of Japan's silks and cottons continued to be produced in the old fashioned way, relying on nimble fingers in cottage-type industry. Another large earner of foreign exchange that was promoted by the government was tea. By the end of the century Japan was the leading exporter of tea. Although Japan's "Industrial Revolution" was yet to come as a result of the limitless demands of the World War I era, it is significant to observe that by 1897 imports of raw materials had multiplied five times and exports of finished good 20 times, while the population had grown from 34 to 50 million, maintaining an abundant supply of cheap labor. Western humanitarian observers might criticize the indentured labor—mostly girls—recruited from the surplus rural population and the evils of the barracks life that they lived at the factory, but the low production cost they made possible secured the worldwide markets that paid for the import of all types of Western products. Moreover, the accumulated savings of these girls gave them a substantial dowry, enabling the arrangement of better marriages when they returned to their villages.

Generally, the balance of trade favored Japan until the first Sino-Japanese war. Then postwar purchases of machinery and raw materials, which accelerated after 1903 in preparation for war with Russia, created an adverse balance which was compensated for by the floating of bond issues until the limitless demands of World War I reversed the balance sharply in Japan's favor.

The motto, "Expel the barbarian," had

been realistically reinterpreted to mean the elimination of the unequal features of the treaties. Initially, foreign diplomatic experts were hired to train a diplomatic corps versed in Western practices, and embassies were opened in major Western nations rapidly.

Again this positive approach is in contrast to China's negative attitude. The Harris treaty had included a clause that authorized negotiations for revision in 1872. In that year Lord Iwakura, the leading member of the court nobility in the Restoration government, headed a large delegation, including prominent figures like Kido and Itō of Chōshū, that visited the capitals of the treaty nations in a futile quest for favorable revisions. He and his associates returned with a better knowledge of Western legal and political institutions and the conviction that no revision was possible until Japan had altered its institutions along Western lines. Kido, who had played the leading role in ending feudalism, immediately memorialized the throne in favor of representative government. In succeeding years memorials by Itagaki of Tosa and others in favor of an elected assembly took advantage of the divisions within the ruling clique over whether to make war on China or not. The result was a compromise governmental reform that established an assembly of imperially appointed prefectural governors and promised elected prefectural assemblies in the near future. At the same time, the war hawks were partially appeased by a punitive expedition against the Taiwanese cannibals—when the Chinese government refused to accept responsibility for the cannibals' consumption of some shipwrecked fishermen from the Ryūkyū islands—over which both countries claimed suzerainty. Itagaki and Saigō temporarily agreed to rejoin the government, but Kido permanently withdrew.

In 1878 Itagaki, who had previously organized a society for political studies, was disappointed by the limitations placed on the prefectural assemblies to be elected the following year, withdrew from the government,

and joined his society to other liberal study groups to form the Jiyūto or Liberal party. Indeed, his party served as a magnet for a strange assortment of antigovernment sentiments, both liberal and reactionary, including irreconcilable ex-samurai who saw their only salvation in representative government. In 1881 Ōkuma of Hizen, another original member of the ruling clique who shared, to a large extent, Itagaki's views and who had been a prime mover in securing the prefectural assemblies, was dismissed when his proposal for a national assembly by 1883 was overruled by his more conservative associates. Instead of taking the logical step of joining Itagaki, he formed his own party, the Kaishintō or Progressive party, to agitate on strictly liberal principles for constitutional reform. This illogical division into two groups seeking identical ends is an early example of a characteristic of Japanese politics, the tendency for cliques to form around individual personalities rather than to unite on the basis of a proclaimed platform of principles. Both men, it should be added, were also motivated to defect and campaign for representative government because of the practical monopoly of power and patronage exercised by the Sat-Chō group. Representative government was viewed as the only means to break this stranglehold for the presumed good of the nation.

CULTURAL WESTERNIZATION AND REACTION

The decade from 1873 to 1883 was a period of extreme Westernization, at least among the educated urban peoples. Everything Western from clothing and food to ideas and attitudes was adopted without discrimination. Even members of the ruling group, such as Itō of Chōshū, caught this extremist fever. American ideas and practices were especially in vogue, thanks in part to the sympathetic attitude of John A. Bingham, the United States ambassador from 1873 to 1885. For example, the educational program was initially fashioned after the decentralized American system as were the national banks, of which each was authorized to issue inconvertible notes. The lifting of the ban on Christianity in 1873 brought a host of missionaries, especially Americans, who founded a large number of schools which spread Western knowledge. Translations of Western works further propagated Western views, especially liberal and radical ideas. There was even the equivalent of the *Ladies Home Journal*, advocating female emancipation in addition to Western feminist information.

Among Japanese proponents of thorough Westernization the popular writer, Fukuzawa Yukichi (1834–1901), exercised the greatest influence. His extended travels abroad equipped him with a fuller firsthand knowledge of the West than that of any of his contemporaries, and his popular style enabled his writings to reach a much wider audience than any other writer. His books reached sales in the millions and freed him to promote his special interests. One of these was Keio University, which specialized in physics, economics, and medicine. Generally, he rejected Japan's heritage, especially Chinese influence, as stultifying with its subordination of the individual to the group and its emphasis on looking to the past as a guide for present action. He was an ardent advocate of individualism as the basic secret and source of Western dynamism and progress. In his *Autobiography* he denounced the exaggerated reverence for families and institutions, noting that Americans honored George Washington for his individual contributions and cared nothing about his inconsequential descendants. He was also a champion of democracy, equal rights for men and women, and monogamy. Until these Western concepts were put into practice, he believed his country would remain "uncivilized." Thus he set goals for Japan that had not yet in fact been achieved in his beloved West. Moreover, he championed spiritual independence and noted its corruption by the

Confucian bureaucratic tradition. No man, he believed, could enter a public career in Japan and remain morally and intellectually a free agent.

One factor in this Westernizing fad was the belief that it would convince the treaty nations that Japan was a genuine convert, ready for acceptance by them as an equal. At great expense a Western-style pavillion was built, and balls were held with Western music, dances, and bustles. But all these efforts were to no avail. None of the other treaty powers was willing to follow the American example of treaty liberalization which would not go into effect until they had made similar revisions.

Meanwhile, the remaining oligarchs headed by the ultraconservative designer of Japan's army, Yamagata, and the more moderate Itō, both of Chōshū, became sufficiently alarmed to place more and more stringent limitations on the freedom of the press. A law of 1875 placed writers and publishers of radical works in jeopardy, and another law placed public and party meetings under close supervision. In 1881 an imperial edict promised a parliament by 1890 and ordered the cessation of all political agitation. When the parties ignored this decree and continued to create unrest, they were ordered in 1883 to dissolve their organizations.

This reaction in the political realm was reflected in other areas. Itō, who had been sent abroad to study Western constitutions, was so impressed by Bismarck and the efficiency of the German empire that the French military advisors, who had incidentally spread liberal political ideas, were replaced by Germans, and the American-style school system was centralized and directed to introduce moral training that emphasized Japanese culture, obedience, and patriotism. Moreover, the emphasis in education was placed on service and subordination to the interests of the group and the state, not on the intellectual liberation of the individual, and for this reason the curricula were tailored to utilitarian considerations, especially at the advanced levels. These ideals were given official expression in the Imperial Rescript on Education of 1890 which stressed the traditional values of filial piety, moderation, private and public morality, and respect and obedience toward the emperor, the constitution, and the laws. In any case, most Japanese were tiring of the liberal Western "binge" and were ready for a reaffirmation of the virtues of Japanese civilization.

THE CONSTITUTION OF 1889

In anticipation of a constitutional regime 500 titles of nobility on the German model were granted to those who were deemed eligible for selection to the future House of Lords, and a cabinet system was instituted in 1885. In 1888 a privy council was formed to revise Itō's constitution in strict secrecy, and a Peace Preservation Law was promulgated, giving the government almost unlimited powers to deal with any disorders. The government was prepared to proclaim its constitution, which was essentially the work of one man and had been drawn up without any general consultations beyond the privy council. Itō had known what kind of constitution he wanted before he set out on his tour of the West and knew that the German constitution came closest to his ideas—a constitution that gave away as little authority as possible. Therefore, German influence on Itō should not be overstressed. The similarities between the two constitutions stemmed mainly from similar conceptions of government.

In 1889 the constitution was promulgated as an imperial gift of grace. Simultaneously the newspapers were ordered to abstain from critical comment until the constitution had been given the fullest consideration, and radical newspapers were simply closed down. The preamble and the first chapter concerning imperial powers were unique, making clear Itō's conception of the indivisibility of sovereignty which resided in the emperor as the "sacred and inviolable" descendant of a line "unbroken for ages eternal." Not only was the emperor to make all appointments and dismissals, declare war, make peace, conclude treaties, and issue ordinances as needed; but he also exercised "the legislative power with the consent of the Imperial Diet." As Ito emphasized in his commentaries, the purpose of the constitution was to strengthen the spirit of national unity by giving the people a voice in the formulation of imperial decisions. He totally rejected the earlier Western conception of the separation of powers as contrary to reason and the Japanese heritage. The emperor was the head and his subjects the body and limbs of the national polity; the constitution was intended to improve the coordination, and thereby the power, of the body politic under the direction of its single head. The emperor appointed and dismissed officials within the limits of the laws he had approved, and therefore all, including the cabinet, were responsible to him. Normally the emperor made laws with the advice and consent of the Diet, but in crises or war he could act without consulting it.

The second chapter specified the rights and duties of subjects with the saving clause, "according to law," which could always nullify the effectiveness of any of these rights. Of course, in time of national emergency or war the emperor by edict could suspend any or all rights, including the constitution.

The third chapter described the Imperial Diet of two houses. The House of Peers was composed of the imperial family, the nobility, and any others the emperor might wish to name to it. The House of Representatives was elected according to the election law, which initially gave the vote to about 5 percent of the adult male population on the basis of a taxpaying qualification. Either house could initiate legislation, but their normal function was to vote on measures submitted by the government. Under normal circumstances an annual three months-session was prescribed. Parliamentary immunity covered activities within the houses but did not extend to external publicity of a member's views. Government officials were authorized to take seats and speak in either house.

In the fourth chapter the emperor's authority to issue ordinances and rescripts was limited by requiring the countersignature of a minister of state. The fifth chapter provided for imperial law courts to be established according to law and for the imperial appointment and dismissal for cause of judges according to law. Ever since the Iwakura mission had revealed that the elimination of extraterritoriality depended on the development of a judicial system acceptable to the West, French and German legal advisors had aided in this task that was now almost completed. British agreement in 1894, a few days prior to the outbreak of the first Sino-Japanese war, to abandon this humiliating infringement on Japanese sovereignty when the other treaty powers did so led to the ending of extraterritoriality in 1899.

The sixth chapter spelled out the limited powers of the Diet over taxation and the budget. First, its approval was needed only for new taxes treaty modifications of existing taxes, and even this power did not extend to administrative fees. All existing obligations and expenditures were outside its purview; only new liabilities and expenditures required its consent. Moreover, since Ito believed that no proper budget could anticipate unforeseen expenses, each one would include a contingency fund. If events called for expenditures in excess of the budget, such expenditures would require subsequent approval. A Board of Audit, established separately by law, would verify and report income and expenditure to the government for submission to the Diet. If a budget were rejected, the previous year's budget would continue in effect. Finally, in an emergency the government could act as necessary by imperial ordinance. Thus, by all these constitutional reservations, the Diet was prevented from crippling the government

through the exercise of the power of the purse. In short, the constitution invited the support of the people's representatives and the lords in the sovereign's singular responsibility for promoting the welfare of the nation.

Naturally liberals like Itagaki and Ōkuma were appalled at the conservative character of this constitution which delegated so little responsibility to the elected representatives of the people. From the very first session the lower house was tempted to act in an irresponsible and obstructionist manner. The power to obstruct without the power to control only encouraged the parties to act irresponsibly. Nevertheless, as conservative as Itō's constitution was, it needs to be recognized that it was as liberal a document as could receive the reluctant acceptance of the even more conservative elements in the ruling clique. The more liberal elements had been long since forced out of the government, and reaction against things Western characterized the years after 1884. As Itō later pointed out, the emperor presided at the privy council meetings concerning the constitution and only his liberal and progressive attitude overcame the objections of the ultraconservative elements.

Prior to the Chinese War, which united the nation and the Diet in an outburst of chauvinistic loyalty, cabinet after cabinet fell in the face of the lower house's criticisms of the budget, and the Diet was dissolved twice in the hope of gaining a more amenable body. Finally, Itō, who headed the third cabinet, had to resort to an imperial rescript ordering the Diet to cooperate with the government. Meanwhile, these difficulties of early constitutional government led to the forming of an extraconstitutional body, the Genrō (Elder Statesmen), composed of the remaining members of the ruling clique, which could stand outside the constitution and advise the emperor on the operation of constitutional government. From their number they recommended the first heads of government (Yamagata, Matsukata, and Itō), and later they effectively nominated the prime ministers who were appointed by the sovereign until after World War I. In an attenuated form this influence continued to be exercised by a younger recruit, Prince Saionji of the ancient Fujiwara family, until the eve of Japan's entrance into World War II.

During these early years of constitutional government the frequent dissolutions made the candidates for election aware of the costliness of the process with two significant consequences. First, they became less eager to force a dissolution and more willing to make an accommodation with the government in return for favors by which they might recoup their expenses. Second, they became susceptible to offers of financial support from wealthy patrons in return for supporting their bids for government contracts. Meanwhile, local bosses who could deliver the votes came to realize that they possessed a salable commodity. Obviously, Japanese politics was rapidly coming of age.

JAPANESE IMPERIALISM: THE FIRST SINO-JAPANESE WAR (1894 – 1895)

By 1894 the Genrō agreed that the program of modernization in the economic, educational, political, and military areas had become sufficiently developed to permit the major test of the army and navy which had been so long delayed with the consequent defections of impatient members of their group. The major purpose of modernization, it will be recalled, was to make Japan strong enough to throw off the degrading shackles of the foreign treaties by building up the country's armed might.

In the 1870s Saigō Takamori, a commander of the combined Sat-Chō-Hi-To forces which had destroyed Tokugawa power and a great bull of a man, had wanted to chastise Korea for treating Japanese envoys with disrespect and was ready to challenge both China and Russia, if necessary. He particularly feared the Russian advance and

wanted to secure control of Korea before Russia did. Fortunately, the emperor stepped in and ordered the war hawks to make no decision until the Iwakura mission, including the more moderate Ōkubo and Itō, had returned. They voted down such premature action, and Saigō withdrew from the government until it agreed to the harmless Taiwan expedition in 1874. Again, in 1875, Saigō was up in arms when Korean batteries fired on a Japanese surveying vessel and a Russian treaty acknowledged Russian control of Sakhalin Island in return for the acceptance of a Japanese claim to most of the Kurile Island chain. But again he was cheated of his war when a show of force secured a treaty of commerce and friendship with Korea. Again he withdrew from the government and was persuaded to lead Satsuma and other samurai, unhappy with the antisamurai decrees, to remove the "evil councillors" of the emperor. The result of this attempt in 1877 to march on the capital was defeated in a 9-months struggle by the conscript army that had been organized, trained, and commanded by General Yamagata of Chōshū. This was the first and only real test that the new army had before 1894. Therefore, both the army and navy entered the war with China virtually untried in combat.

Even in defeat and decapitation at his request by a fellow samurai, Saigō, one of the three main leaders in the Restoration and champion of the samurai and their code of ethics, left an enduring mark on the ideals of modernized Japan and especially on those of the military. In addition to proving the military ability of the conscript army, this man of limited vision, who felt deeply the affront to his caste and the domination of the government by the samurai leaders of Chōshū became, like the "Forty-seven Rōnin," a hero who symbolized the traditional virtues of the Japanese warrior and inspired the intense patriotism that preferred death to dishonor in the service of the emperor. As in his own case, this devotion to the emperor often resulted in antigovernment organizations that were justified by a conviction regarding the need to remove the evil advisors misleading the crown; but it also transmitted to the army and the navy the high ideals of bushidō, best illustrated by the *Imperial Rescript to Soldiers and Sailors* of 1882 regularly read to them while standing at attention.

As the head of state and commander-in-chief, the emperor told them that he depended on them as his limbs and they shared with him in any glory gained for the empire by arms as well as any grief from a loss or setback. Their first duty was loyalty and they should beware of being misled by "current opinions" or of being drawn into politics. After duty, the next most important virtue was valor. A valorous man would never despise an inferior foe or fear a superior and never engage in undisciplined violence. With reference to the traditional emphasis on personal loyalty, regardless of right or wrong, soldiers and sailors were admonished to be faithful and righteous, keeping uppermost in their minds their public duty rather than faithfulness in private relations. Finally, they should practice simplicity and austerity as a safeguard against becoming selfish, effeminate, and extravagant.

Although these injunctions were not fully adhered to later, they do help to explain the admirable conduct of Japan's armed forces in the first Sino-Japanese War, the Boxer Rebellion, and the Russo-Japanese War, which won the respect of friend and foe alike. Indeed, during these early actions when Japan sought recognition as an equal, the disciplined behavior of its troops stood in sharp contrast to the often less than honorable conduct of the forces of the so-called "civilized" Western powers. The later breakdown of discipline, while stemming largely from internal factors, was to a significant degree an embittered response to the continued unwillingness of the West to accept Japan and its people as equals on racial and economic terms. Such unequal treatment hurt their

pride far more than Westerners ever suspected.

The contest with China for influence in Korea has already been sketched in the previous chapter. Japan became increasingly irritated by China's continued assumption of suzerainty, in contradiction to the clause declaring Korea's independence that was included in every foreign treaty, and by China's continued refusal to cooperate in compelling the Korean government to undertake modernization. In fact, China's willingness to admit Western influence, especially Russian, into Korea alarmed the Japanese. After a Korean progressive leader, whom the Japanese had favored, was murdered in Shanghai and his body returned to Korea where it was dismembered and placed on public exhibition, a new Japanese minister presented almost an ultimatum that demanded a total reform of the Korean regime and suggested that such an accomplishment would require the reduction of Chinese influence over the court. Then came the Korean request for Chinese troops to aid in the suppression of the Tonghak rebels and the dispatch of these troops by Li without the prior notification of Japan, prescribed by the 1885 agreement. The Japanese government responded by sending six times as many troops. Despite the Korean government's entreaties for a mutual withdrawal the Chinese government responded in kind, causing a confrontation that reduced to the vanishing point the prospects for a peaceful settlement. Both China and Japan refused to back away from the crisis, and the sinking of a Chinese troopship precipitated the war. The limited Chinese forces committed to the conflict collapsed ignominiously before the superior efficiency and equipment of the Japanese army and navy. Yet Japan's easy victories, it must be recognized, were achieved at the expense of only those forces that Li could command in northern China; the forces of the officials and commanders in central and southern China were cautiously withheld from the fray. Nevertheless, even if all China's armed might had been committed, the deficiencies in command structure, training, and equipment would probably have resulted in a Japanese victory, though at greater cost.

THE RESULTS OF THE SINO-JAPANESE WAR

The Japanese action during the war seemed to insure its predominance in Korea. The Korean government was forced to sign a treaty of alliance that granted free movement of Japanese troops and supplies and later to issue a series of edicts that reformed its social, economic, and political structure, at least on paper. But the Japanese tried to push Korea too far too fast. Almost all the factions at the Korean court were alienated, and in 1896 the Russians, who with Germany and France had just forced Japan to give up the Liaotung Peninsula, were welcomed as champions of the independence of Korea as proclaimed in the peace treaty with China. From this date Russia supplanted China as Japan's competitor for control of Korea.

The Treaty of Shimonoseki, in addition to confirming the long-asserted independence of Korea and to transferring Taiwan and the Pescadores Islands to Japan, provided an indemnity sufficient to stabilize Japan's currency and to make possible the adoption of the international gold standard. Increased confidence in Japan's economic stability improved the terms of trade and thus stimulated an expansion in the volume of trade. In turn, this expansion accelerated Japan's economic growth and industrial development. A subsequent commercial treaty with China not only secured most-favored-nation treatment, giving Japanese citizens full extraterritorial rights, but also the right to establish factories in the open ports and an equality of taxation with Chinese manufacturers. This last provision completely eliminated what little protection Chinese manufacturers gained from the low import tariff. Naturally, the other powers were not unhappy at these concessions, which they shared under the most-favored-nation clauses.

The outbreak of the war had brought an immediate end to the partisan obstructionism in the lower house to Itō's ministry, and the decision for war may have been influenced by the prospect of unifying the nation in support of the government. If anything, the parties and the people proved more wildly chauvinistic than the government. Certainly, the news of the triple intervention forcing Japan to give up the Liaotung Peninsula caused a nationwide outburst of anti-Western indignation. The emperor sought to calm his subjects by advising them that he and they "must bear the unbearable"—the exact words used by his grandson in 1945. The subsequent Russian acquisition of Port Arthur and control of the Liaotung Peninsula was an act of hypocrisy that thoroughly disillusioned the most ardent Japanese advocates of Western morality. If many Japanese had ever had much faith in Western virtue, these acts disabused them of such beliefs. Thereafter Japan would play the game of power politics with as much cynicism as any Western power. Certainly, the scramble for concessions and spheres of influence at the end of the century set a clear example.

In the intellectual, cultural, and esthetic realms the victory over China created a measure of ambivalence toward the West. The victory stimulated self-confidence, but there was also a realization that this success rested on the mastery of Western technology. Until then, scholarly and literary effort had been concentrated on translation, although, since the anti-Western reaction of the mid-eighties, a few writers had pioneered in creative efforts based, for the most part, on Western models. After victory, creative writings increased sharply and tended to eulogize in a romantic fashion the martial virtues of the Japanese people. Of course, translation work did not cease and, in fact, increased in volume. The acceleration of industrialization, especially in preparation for the Russian war, encouraged an esthetically disappointing effort to blend Western and Japanese motifs in the work of artists and artisans. Fortunately, this proved to be a passing fad, produced mostly for overseas consumption, and was rejected, for the most part, by Japanese consumers. This brief Western fadism, limited to the cities, reflected a backwash from a renewed emphasis on the advantages of Western material techniques which were represented by increased imports of Western machinery. This acceleration in industrialization continued after the Russo-Japanese War and resulted in increased foreign borrowing until 80 percent of the national debt was held by Western investors. Subsequently, however, this indebtedness paid off when Japan became largely independent of the West for machinery and began to export industrial plants of its own manufacture. Generally it may be said that Japanese victories reaffirmed the faith in Western material accomplishments, inspired a determination to industrialize more rapidly, even at the cost of Western indebtedness and, as a by-product, created a temporary spate of renewed cultural borrowing. Japan's victories in both wars created optimistic confidence, but they also underlined the technological gap that still had to be filled.

Another important fruit of the first Sino-Japanese War was the tremendous popularity of the victorious army and navy. Whatever their leaders asked to rebuild the navy and enlarge the army was granted. For an elected representative to cast a negative vote would be political suicide. By going to war Ito may have relieved himself of embarrassing obstruction in the Diet, but military victory brought enhanced political power to his military colleague, Yamagata. Also the increased expenditures on armaments enhanced the economic predominance of the great family combines, known as *zaibatsu*, such as Mitsui, Mitsubishi, Sumitomo, and Yasuda, which secured the lion's share of government contracts. Their rivalry for these contracts led them to become involved in politics in support of one or another of the Genrō. For example, Mitsui became closely connected with Itō and his associates and, when Itō took the command of a party in 1900, was expected to furnish financial support at the polls.

With the exception of the short-lived party government of Ōkuma and Itagaki in 1898, the Genrō rotated as prime ministers until 1901. Although Yamagata and Itō thereafter withdrew from direct participation in the political fray, their protégés, General Katsura and Prince Saionji, continued the struggle for domination of the Diet under their direction and guidance. Thus, the persons changed, but the nature of politics and Genrō direction of imperial policy continued as before.

THE RUSSO-JAPANESE CONFRONTATION

Although Yamagata was a military man, he was also a cautious statesman. He had personally experienced the humiliating retaliation of the West against his native Chōshū in 1864, which gave him a healthy respect for Western arms. If possible, he would have preferred an agreement with Russia by which Russia would limit its activities to Manchuria, recognizing Korea as a Japanese sphere. On one occasion, when he visited St. Petersburg, it is said that he was even willing to accept a division of Korea at the 38th parallel. Itō was equally eager for an accommodation and even an alliance with Russia. While the negotiation of the Anglo-Japanese alliance was in progress, he made a trip to St. Petersburg in a final, futile effort to get the tsarist regime to see reason and come to terms. But the Russian court was under the influence of ardent expansionists and was unwilling to negotiate any kind of firm agreement. As a military realist, Yamagata was anxious for an alliance that would preclude a repetition of external intervention during or after a war with Russia.

The British, also alarmed by the growth

of Russian influence at the Chinese court and by the Russian advance represented in Manchuria by the Chinese Eastern Railway and the Liaotung leasehold to be connected by rail with the Chinese Eastern Road, suggested such an alliance in 1898, but the Boer War temporarily diverted British concern from Asia. British alarm was revived by the Russian occupation of Manchuria in connection with the Boxer Rebellion and the obvious reluctance of the Russians to withdraw. In any case, the Boxer affair further demonstrated both Chinese impotence and Japanese military efficiency, reinforcing the already indicated British inclination to look on Japan as the rising power in East Asia. The only other friendly power, the United States, whose recent acquisition of the Philippines gave it a major stake in Asia, proved unwilling to commit itself to an entangling alliance. Negotiations in 1901 led to the Anglo-Japanese alliance of January 1902. Meanwhile, in 1900, Yamagata as prime minister obtained a decisive voice for the military in the cabinet by an imperial ordinance that prescribed that the army and navy ministers must be generals and admirals on the active list and, therefore, subject to military orders. Thereafter, prime ministers had to accept the demands of the armed forces or face the collapse of their ministries. In addition, no new ministry could be formed without appeasing the army and navy.

The terms of the Anglo-Japanese alliance were clearly directed against Russian expansionist ambitions. If either ally, engaged in an Asian war, were attacked by a second power, the other was obligated to enter the war in support of the beleaguered ally. Furthermore, a clause in the treaty recognized the legitimate and special interest of Japan in Korea in return for Japan's recognition of Britain's sphere of influence in the Yangtze basin. Both allies asserted in the preamble their concern for preserving the administrative and territorial integrity of China, a thinly veiled denunciation of Russia's continued occupation of Manchuria.

Obviously this alliance, limited to Asia, was aimed only at Russia and intended to discourage France from supporting the Asian policies of its Russian ally.

Russia responded promptly by agreeing to evacuate Manchuria in three stages over an 18-month period of time. The evacuation of southern Manchuria was carried out on schedule but, instead of withdrawing the troops from Manchuria, most of them were concentrated in northern Manchuria, ostensibly as guards to protect the Chinese Eastern Railway, while the rest were employed to activate an expired timber concession in northern Korea. Again, Japan sought a negotiated settlement by calling for a mutual recognition of the paramount interest of Russia in Manchuria and of Japan in Korea. On several occasions, these extended negotiations seemed on the verge of a successful conclusion when the Russians backed away for one reason or another. The tsar, under the influence of aggressive advisors, was convinced that Japan would never dare to attack Russia, in spite of repeated reports of Japan's military preparations. This conviction accounts in part for the poor state of Russian preparations. Finally, frustrated at the futility of the negotiations, Japan severed diplomatic relations on February 6, 1904.

THE RUSSO-JAPANESE WAR (1904–1905)

On the same day the Russian forces crossed the Yalu and task forces steamed out of Japanese ports. On February 8 Japanese cruisers destroyed three Russian ships, including two cruisers caught in the harbor of Seoul, and covered the unloading of troop transports. That night Japanese destroyers, which had raced ahead, made a damaging torpedo attack on the Russian fleet which was swinging at anchor in Port Arthur with all lights lit. The next day Japanese battleships forced the Russian fleet to retire under the protection of shore batteries where it remained, except for one sortie, until the land siege forced capitulation on December 31, 1904. The balance of the dispersed Russian Pacific fleet, which in total tonnage matched that of Japan, was initially icebound in the port of Vladivostok. Later Japan lost two battleships to Russian mines, but overall the Japanese struck at the strategic moment and secured command of the seas, making possible the landing of their troops wherever they wished. Japan's army of 800,000 with comparatively short lines of communications by sea faced at first only 100,000 Russian troops, which could be reinforced only over the long, single-track, Trans-Siberian Railroad. Eventually Japan committed one and one-half and Russia one million men to the conflict. Japan received some criticism—especially from Russia—for not declaring war till February 10, but most nations, including Britain and the United States, who viewed Japan as the pygmy challenging the giant, lauded what *The Times* of London described as "an act of daring which is destined to take a place of honour in naval annals." In any case, Japan had previously delayed 6 days in declaring war on China, and Russia had immediately sent troops across the Yalu following the break in diplomatic relations.

Japan's major objective was Port Arthur. Japanese armies cleared Korea and swept across the Yalu River by the first of May. Other armies were landed on the Liaotung Peninsula to support the cutting off of this region by the end of May. By the end of July, Port Arthur was under close siege by the forces commanded by the chivalrous advocate of samurai traditions, General Nōgi, while another army drove numerically superior Russian forces back to Mukden. In the 5-month siege of Port Arthur, Japanese casualties of 60,000, including two sons, did not shake Nōgi's dedication to the code of bushido. No looting was permitted, prisoners were treated as honorable warriors, and the final surrender was carried out with dignity and gallantry, the Russian commander presenting his white horse to Nōgi in appreciation of such generous treatment.

With the fall of Port Arthur the Japanese armies could be concentrated against the defenders of Mukden. This battle involving almost three quarters of a million men with a small numerical superiority for the Japanese was waged from February 23 to March 16, 1905. The Japanese gained Mukden, though at a cost of more than 40,000 casualties, and then continued to push the Russians northward some 70 miles in a preview of the trench-type war of attrition. With their Pacific fleet severely damaged and bottled up, the Russians decided to send their European fleet around the world to regain command of the sea. In an age of coal which required frequent refueling and under diplomatic circumstances which left few ports open for refueling and refitting, this expedition was a major undertaking carried out with exceptional skill and efficiency. But the story of this voyage and its epic ordeals must be subordinated to its dramatic and tragic end, the Battle of Tsushima, the perfect demonstration of battleship tactics and the most total major victory in naval history.

The Japanese were fully informed of the progress of the Russian fleet which received worldwide publicity. The fall of Port Arthur left Vladivostok as its single destination. Although confident that the Russian admiral would select the most direct route through the straits of Tsushima separating Korea and Kyūshū, Admiral Tōgō had the other possible passage mined and got the entire Japanese fleet in tiptop condition to meet the Russians. When picket ships reported the approach of the Russian fleet late in May 1905, Admiral Tōgō led his fleet out to block its passage. The Russian admiral had his ships steaming in columns enabling Tōgō to execute the classic battleship tactic of crossing the "T." By this maneuver his entire line could concentrate both their fore and aft batteries on each Russian battleship as it came into range, while the Russian ships could return the fire only with their forward batteries and only when each came into range. The Russian admiral immediately realized his blunder and ordered a column turn in the hope of running parallel to the Japanese. At this point, however, a combination of the newer construction of the Japanese ships and the encrusted hulls of the Russian ships so long at sea gave the Japanese a speed advantage that enabled them to maintain their position until most of the Russian capital ships were crippled. In this 2-day battle in which the Russian exhibited remarkable valor only two ships out of forty escaped under cover of darkness; the rest were sunk, captured, or interned. The Japanese lost only three torpedo boats and suffered only 600 casualties. Japanese command of the sea was now unchallenged. The British were naturally elated because this victory had been achieved by British-built ships commanded by British-trained officers.

The outbreak of the war had been greeted with wholehearted enthusiasm by the Japanese people, with the exception of a handful of socialists, and the course of the war had been supported by them. In contrast, the Russian people, already stirring with revolutionary discontent at tsarist oppression, could see no point in enduring further hardships for distant territory of questionable value. By the spring of 1905 both combatants were at the end of their economic tethers. After the battle of Mukden the Japanese commander had informed Tōkyō of the need for more men and supplies or for peace. In any event, the Japanese leaders, who entered the war with the limited objective of checking the Russian advance in Asia, had the foresight to send a special envoy to Washington to request American mediation at the appropriate moment according to the progress of the war. Immediately after the Tsushima victory this envoy was instructed to ask President Theodore Roosevelt to proffer his good offices.

Representatives of the combatants met at Portsmouth, New Hampshire. In spite of economic exhaustion and revolutionary rumblings the tsarist government wanted to continue the war in the hope of restoring Russia's shattered prestige, while the Japanese government realized that the only alternative to peace was bankruptcy and the possible loss of all its gains. The Russians put their hope in excessive Japanese demands that would swing world sympathy to them—and the Japanese, inexperienced in public relations, did not disappoint them. The initial Japanese demands were so stiff that Russia could confidently reject many of them. Japanese popularity deteriorated as it continued to cling to most of them. The negotiations dragged on until the Russian representative, at what was expected to be the last meeting, made counterproposals confident that they would be unacceptable, particularly the rejection of an indemnity. Much to his surprise, the Japanese representative accepted the terms and the Treaty of Portsmouth ending the Russo-Japanese war was signed on September 5, 1905, just 19 months after its outbreak.

THE RESULTS OF THE RUSSO-JAPANESE WAR

The treaty recognized Japan's "paramount political, military and economic interests" in Korea, the limited objective for which Japan had gone to war. In addition, the southern section of the South Manchurian Railroad and the Russian leasehold on the Liaotung Peninsula were turned over to Japan with the latter subject, of course, to Chinese confirmation. The southern half of Sakhalin was ceded and fishing rights in Siberian waters were granted. Additional clauses in essence recognized northern Manchuria as Russia's sphere and southern Manchuria as Japan's sphere and ostensibly placed reciprocal limitations on their activities in these regions with little more than a pious recognition of China's sovereignty. Thus, in substance, Japan regained control of the Liaotung Peninsula, which the triple intervention of 1895 had compelled it to disgorge.

Although Japan had made substantial gains, securing unquestioned control of Korea and a firm foothold in Manchuria, news of the Treaty generated a storm of public indignation. The Japanese people, uninformed about the government's financial exhaustion and aware only of the dramatic victories of its armed forces, felt that in comparison with the costs of the Sino-Japanese War the rewards were wholly incommensurate with the sacrifice in men and treasure. Certainly the people felt that a thoroughly defeated Russia should have paid a large indemnity to compensate for these costs. In search of a scapegoat, President Roosevelt and the United States were singled out as the villains who had taken advantage of Japanese inexperience in negotiations. Hitherto the United States had been looked on as a friend; hereafter every incident was exploited to contribute to the deterioration of these friendly relations. Reciprocally, every aggressive Japanese action was viewed with increasing concern by the American government which realized that Japan was a rising and ambitious power and no champion of the "Open Door" in Asia.

One result of Japan's victory over Russia, then, was the realization, not only by the United States, but also by the other powers, that a new power had joined their ranks which would not be content with a secondary role in world affairs. A more important result of this military victory of an Asian nation over what was deemed a Western power was the stimulus this example gave to nationalistic movements and revolutions through-

out Asia. The belief in Western invincibility was severely shaken and a new mood of hope and optimism fired the imaginations of progressive Asian leaders. Revolution rocked Russia and brought constitutional monarchy to Persia. Before long, the Young Turks seized power in the dying Ottoman Empire, while Egyptian leaders more openly vented their discontent with British domination. And in India the moderate leaders of the Indian National Congress took a stronger stand but could not appease the radical leaders who adopted violence to underline their demand for immediate independence. China's impotence in the face of a war fought mostly on its territory led directly to the overthrow of the incapable Manchu dynasty in 1912. In short, Japan's example demonstrated that under able leadership Easterners were in no way inferior to Westerners. Since 1905 Eastern leaders in a variety of ways have worked to prove this thesis. Therefore, the Russo-Japanese War was an event of worldwide significance whose repercussions are still being worked out today.

For Japan, of course, this war effort which almost bankrupted the country filled the people with a deep sense of pride and confidence. The victory vindicated the sacrifices its leaders had commanded to carry out the program of modernization. With renewed energy they dedicated themselves to completing the task of catching up with the West. Also, as a proven power, they were more sensitive than ever to Western actions and attitudes that implied any inequality of status.

SIGNIFICANT DATES

	1854	Opening of Tokugawa Japan
	1856	Arrival of Townsend Harris
1863 and		
	1864	Western Chastisement of Satsuma and Chōshū
	1868	Meiji Restoration and Charter Oath
	1872	Conscript army and universal education decreed
	1874	Taiwan expedition
	1876	Opening of Korea
	1877	Revolt of Saigō Takamori

1878	Jiyūtō (Liberal) party of Itagaki
1881	Kaishintō (Progressive) party of Ōkuma
1885	Li-Itō Convention
1889	Proclamation of constitution
1894–1895	First Sino-Japanese War
1902	Anglo-Japanese alliance
1904–1905	Russo-Japanese War

SELECTED READINGS

See Chapter Nine for general accounts.

Akita, George, *The Foundations of Constitutional Government in Modern Japan, 1868–1900*. Cambridge, Mass.: Harvard University Press, 1967.

*Beasley, W. G., *The Modern History of Japan*. New York: Praeger, 1963.

Borton, Hugh, *Japan's Modern Century*. 2nd ed.; New York: Praeger, 1963.

Craig, Albert M., *Choshu in the Meiji Restoration*. Cambridge, Mass.: Harvard University Press, 1961.

Fairbank, John K., et al., *East Asia: The Modern Transformation*. Boston: Houghton Mifflin, 1965.

Hackett, Roger F., *Yamagata Aritomo in the Rise of Modern Japan*. Cambridge, Mass.: Harvard University Press, 1971.

*Hall, John W., and Jansen, Marius B., eds., *Studies in the Institutional History of Early Modern Japan*. Princeton: Princeton University Press, 1968.

*Hearn, Lafcadio, *Japan: An Interpretation*. Rutland, Vt.: Tuttle, 1955.

Hirschmeier, Johannes, *The Origins of Entrepreneurship in Meiji Japan*. Cambridge, Mass.: Harvard University Press, 1964.

Iwata, Masakazu, *Okubo Toshimichi*. Berkeley: University of California Press, 1964.

*Jansen, Marius B., *Sakamoto Ryoma and the Meiji Restoration*. Stanford: Stanford University Press, 1971.

*Keene, Donald, ed., *Modern Japanese Literature: An Anthology*. New York: Grove Press, 1960.

*Lockwood, William W., *The Economic Development of Japan: Growth and Structural Change, 1868–1938*. Princeton: Princeton University Press, 1954.

*Neumann, William L., *America Encounters Japan: From Perry to MacArthur*. New York: Harper and Row, 1965.

Okamoto, Shumpei, *The Japanese Oligarchy and the Russo-Japanese War*. New York: Columbia University Press, 1971.

*Reischauer, Edwin O., *The United States and Japan*. 3rd ed.; New York: Viking Press, 1962.

Silberman, Bernard, *Ministers of Modernization: Elite Mobility in the Meiji Restoration*. Tucson: University of Arizona Press, 1964.

*Smith, Thomas C., *The Agrarian Origins of Modern Japan*. Stanford: Stanford University Press, 1970.

————, *Political Change and Industrial Development in Japan: Government Enterprise, 1868–1880*. Stanford: Stanford University Press, 1955.

Yukichi, Fukuzawa, *Autobiography*. New York: Columbia University Press, 1966.

CHAPTER SEVENTEEN

THE BRITISH EMPIRE IN INDIA AND THE RISE OF INDIAN NATIONALISM

The unplanned outbreak of violence in 1857, known as the Sepoy Mutiny, was a reactionary attempt to expel the British rulers of India, the only major Eastern civilization to be conquered by a Western power. Like the Marāthā rising against the Mughal emperor Aurangzīb, the outbreak was inspired by British unwillingness to limit their role to the exercise of political authority. Instead, since the governor-generalship of Lord William Bentinck (1828–1835), zealous and well-intentioned officials and missionaries had attempted to reform India and bring to it the presumed benefits of Western culture and Christianity. The suppression of the rebellion effectively ended any dreams of immediately ridding India of its alien rulers and returning to the untrammeled traditions of the past, but the atrocities committed in fear and desperation by both sides permanently altered the relationship and attitudes of rulers and ruled. The British reaction, which set the policies subsequently practiced by the rulers, was well-expressed in Queen Victoria's proclamation of 1858.

BRITISH REACTION TO THE SEPOY MUTINY

In the proclamation of 1858 the ideal of reshaping India in the British image, at least in the immediate future, was forsworn. The princes, most of whom had remained loyal, were looked to as partners in maintaining stability and as the source of leadership in a gradual program of improvement. No longer did they need to fear the high-handed actions of a Dalhousie. Full religious toleration and consideration for Indian customs and practices were promised. Qualified Indians were supposed to receive impartial treatment in appointments to governmental posts. This was one assurance only partially fulfilled in practice, at least in the higher echelons of government service, though universities were established to enable Indians to meet the qualifications. Finally, increased attention to internal improvements for the material welfare of the people was pledged, and this pledge was carried out, though the benefits were largely offset by population growth. In brief, the sobering experience of the mutiny led the British to replace the overly optimistic hopes of Macaulay and his associates (that India could be rapidly Westernized and endowed with the blessings of self-government) with the realization that a period of tutelage of unknown duration would be required before the government could lay down the "white man's burden."

Caution was now the keynote. The ratio of British to Sepoy troops was raised to one-to-one in the north and one-to-two in the peninsula. Moreover, the Sepoys were further professionalized by being recruited from traditional warriors such as the Gurkhas of Nepal, the Sikhs of the Punjab, and the Pathans of the northwest frontier. These troops from the perimeter of India developed a high esprit de corps, but were apolitical professionals who could not provide a core for a nationalistic movement. Generation after generation they served as highly skilled and inexpensive soldiers defending British territories and maintaining law and order.

The 1858 Government of India Act placed full responsibility on a secretary of state for India who sat in the cabinet. He was advised by the Council of India, a remnant of Company rule, composed of men with long years of experience in India, but their influence declined after 1870. In India, the

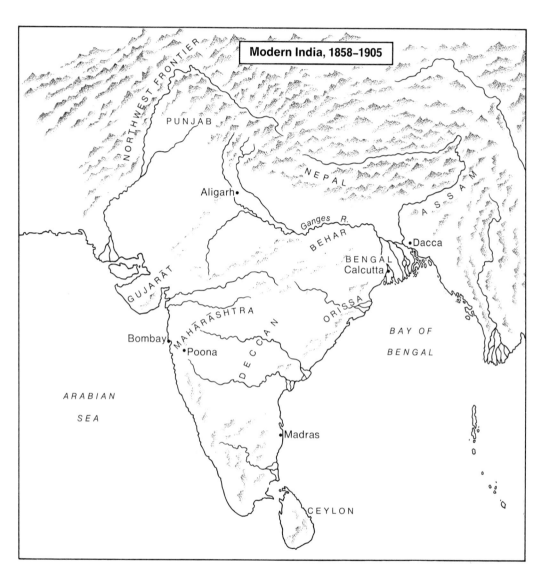

governor-general was called the viceroy when he acted in the name of the Crown. Now that he represented the Crown rather than the Company, the 600 Indian princes felt, as vassals of an individual sovereign, much closer ties of loyalty and proved easier to discipline. The governor-general was assisted by an executive council, which Dalhousie had expanded into a legislative council with added members and a public record of its debates. This practice was formalized in the Indian Councils Act of 1861 providing for six to twelve additional members, of whom at least half must not be officials, and was extended to the provincial governments. In framing this act some had sought a specific provision for Indian members, but the secretary of state defeated the motion on the ground that it would draw an invidious distinction between Her Majesty's subjects. Nevertheless, it was understood that this should be the practice and two Indians were included from the beginning.

The backbone of the British Rāj was the

highly efficient Indian Civil Service selected by competitive examinations since 1853. This elite corps, which numbered about 1000 by 1905, staffed the key posts and included at most less than 30 Indians in its exclusive and well-paid ranks. However, the administrative services by that date employed 4000 Britons and a half million Indians. With the increase in the number of university-educated Indians, the British monopoly of the top positions became a major grievance adding fuel to the nationalistic movement.

Much emphasis—and rightly so—has been placed on the memory of the mutiny as a major factor in developing the social separation of the British as a ruling caste from their Indian subjects. Government officers, businessmen, and planters feared a recurrence of violence and therefore viewed the Indians, and especially Muslims, with distrust. For the same reason the postmutiny government backed away from its former freewheeling reformism and turned conservative, seeking to disturb the status quo as little as possible. The reverse of this was the Indian's tortured memories of the brutal and vengeful retaliation after the mutiny, before "Clemency" Canning could restore order, and the Indian reaction to the increased racial arrogance of the British, stemming from fear and distrust. Thus the social gulf, founded on fear, distrust, and hatred, grew as an aftermath of the mutiny and was reflected in the exclusiveness of British social activities and organizations. The British in India became more concerned with commanding the respect than with gaining the affection of their Indian subjects. However, the British sense of cultural superiority had existed long before the mutiny, as witness the attitude of Macaulay and the reformers. Their condescension in lesser minds had often taken the form of racial arrogance, especially among the planters who poured in after 1850 to establish plantations for tea and other cash crops in hitherto undeveloped Assam.

The British put their hope in the loyal princes to lead the way in further modernization, and a few responded by creating better conditions in their states than in British India. But the overwhelming majority clung to traditional ways, while the British failed to appreciate the importance of the new middle class receiving Western educations in the newly founded colleges and universities. These men with their minds attuned in varying degrees to both worlds were to be the developers of Indian nationalism and the leaders of the future. If the British had recognized this and taken more of them into their fold, the course of Anglo-Indian relations might have been very different. As it was, the British looked to the traditional sources of authority whose failure to provide adequate leadership in 1857 had discredited not only them but also the traditional India associated with them. Nevertheless, the note of caution sounded in the Queen's proclamation set the tone of making haste slowly. Indeed, the British in India proved much less liberal than those at home.

The policy of "enlightened despotism" meant a program of bureaucratic paternalism emphasizing higher education, law reform and enforcement on as just and impartial a basis as possible, and an accelerated program of public works. The universities of Calcutta, Bombay, and Madras, previously planned, were immediately established. Unfortunately, instruction and examination in the English language as well as other handicaps forced a lowering of the standards, compared to those in Britain, and the emphasis on the examinations encouraged "cramming" often with inadequate understanding. Nevertheless, a growing number of college graduates, including some Indian women from mission-sponsored colleges, gained a common language facilitating the exchange of ideas. Moreover, the ideas they imbibed were those derived from the liberal and humanitarian writers of nineteenth century England. As this growing class of English-educated Indians looked around them, they saw obvious discrepancies between these ideas and the condition of India under British rule. Discontent was engendered by the increasing difficulty in finding employment commensurate with their educational attainments. Many entered the lower ranks of the administrative services but were in practice prohibited from admission to its top echelon, especially after the ruling reducing the maximum age for taking the I.C.S. examinations in London from 21 to 19. Others entered the legal and medical professions where their services were certainly needed. Finally, many vented their discontents in the host of English and vernacular journals, even after the strict regulation of the Vernacular Press Act of 1878.

In 1862 the Indian criminal code composed by Macaulay as head of a commission in the 1830s was finally put into effect with variations to meet local conditions. Jurists, both British and Indian, fashioned a complete legal system judiciously blending the best of European and Indian practices. The much more effective enforcement of law throughout British India maintained peace and built up respect for justice, especially as more and more Indian judges were appointed. On the other hand, the increasing rigidity of the legal system tended to eliminate the former flexibility of customary law and contribute to the retention and enforcement of outmoded laws. However, the one really sour note in this story of judicial development along British lines was the virtual rejection of the Ilbert Bill of 1883 introduced by the liberal governor-general, Lord Ripon (1880–1884), which would have authorized Britons to be tried without discrimination before Indian or British judges. The organized agitation of the British community that emasculated this measure had the side effect of illustrating the advantages of organized agitation, which Indian leaders subsequently emulated.

As striking as the attainments in education and justice was the record in public works: notably roads, railroads, and irrigation projects. The telegraph lines had greatly aided the British in organizing their military

response to the mutiny, but in 1857 only 200 miles of railroad track had been laid and all-weather roads were totally inadequate. Irrigation work along the sacred Ganges had been one of Dalhousie's projects that had aroused superstitious opposition. In the area of communications the mutiny stimulated accelerated development to bring all of British India under closer control, and irrigation and flood control projects were undertaken to offset the devastations of flood and famine and to increase the productivity of agriculture.

Within a few years the foundation of a network of national highways designed mostly for strategic purposes had been laid, opening rural India to the penetration of Western products far more extensively than before. Even more dramatic was the government-directed development of a railroad network. The 200 miles of track in 1857 became 4000 miles 12 years later, 25,000 by 1900, and 33,000 by 1905. Since the government planned the railroad network for strategic use and turned over the construction to private enterprise, it more efficiently unified the country than haphazard private development could have done. The roads and railroads enabled educated Indians with English as a common means of communication to travel inexpensively to meetings anywhere in India and thus fostered national feeling. At the same time, poorer Indians took happily to third class rail travel, enduring the pollution of intercaste contact, to attend religious festivals or to seek their fortunes outside the villages of their birth. In short, the development of physical communications gave the Indian people mobility, though it must be observed that inertia, poverty, and fear of the unknown kept the overwhelming majority in their villages from birth to death.

Many Indian writers have denounced the British government for the destruction of native handicraft industries by failing to protect them against the competition of the products of British machines. To the extent that this accusation is valid, it applies, outside Bengal and the immediate environs of Bombay and Madras, mostly to the era after 1858 when the interior was opened by roads and railroads. But such changes as occurred were a two-way proposition. True, the handicraft industries were severely damaged, but only because less expensive manufactured goods were supplied to the Indian consumer. Moreover, the roads and railroads that opened India to British manufactures at the same time furnished a worldwide market for Indian farmers, encouraging the production of cash crops, and also provided a nationwide market for the development of industry in India. In 1880 India had 58 cotton mills and 22 jute mills, and this was only the beginning. By 1905 the former had almost quadrupled and the latter had more than doubled. Of course, much of the capital and ownership of these enterprises came from abroad because of the basic conservativeness of India's commercial class. However, Indian entrepreneurs played a prominent role in cotton manufacturing and the Pārsee Tata family is renowned for pioneering India's iron and steel production. Another index of Indian economic development was the rapid growth in the volume of trade. In 1834 India exported 8 million pounds worth of products against imports of 4½ million pounds; by 1870 these figures had ballooned to 53 million and 33½ million pounds respectively; and by 1905 exports exceeded 100 million and imports 70 million pounds. Although exports regularly exceeded imports, British pensions, profits, and overseas transportation charges balanced the trade.

Certainly the economic opening of India was not without its costs for the Indian way of life. The self-sufficiency of village life became a thing of the past except in remote areas. The extension of irrigation, which covered 14 million acres by 1900 and thus was larger than any other system in the world, could not keep pace with the population growth from 150 million in 1850 to 283 million in 1901. Poverty appears to have been more widespread than ever, and this condition paradoxically can be blamed largely on the railroads and the British program for famine relief. Railroads made it possible to rush food to famine-stricken areas where it was doled out in payment for labor on public works. Thus the natural attrition of excess population during famines was largely eliminated. Without this system the toll during the four year's drought and bubonic plague of 1896 to 1900 would have greatly reduced the 1901 census figure. To attempt to strike a balance between benefits and hardships when so many intangible, as well as tangible, factors are involved is impossible, but it can be said that in the modern world India had to change, and the British made a valuable contribution in guiding and financing this transition.

Furthermore, every British action —whether in the realm of physical communications or the provision of a common language through English education—facilitated the growth of national feeling by breaking down the barriers of geographical, linguistic, racial, and even to some extent caste diversity and divisions. English education in particular provided liberal ideas as ammunition to be used against British rule. The story of India's intellectual revival under the inspiration of an alien ideology presents the already familiar range of reactions from almost total rejection through various forms of compromise to almost complete acceptance of the West. The spiritual heritage and innate tolerance of India, however, as well as the alien occupation of the country, made total rejection or total acceptance infeasible, and some sort of accommodation essential. Thus India's peculiar situation and heritage made for unique and interesting variations on these themes that are still apparent and influential today.

THE INDIAN REACTION

Total acceptance was fostered by a few individuals in the first half of the nineteenth century, but any rejection of the Hindu spiritual heritage was bound to gain few converts. Total rejection under the leadership of orthodox brāhmans, alarmed into active opposition by British reformers and missionaries, received its coup de grace in the suppression of the Sepoy Rebellion. Obviously the future rested with some more moderate position. The first and, in the long run, the most influential figure was the brilliant offspring of a Bengali brāhman family that had previously prospered by accommodating itself to Muslim rule, Rām Mohun Roy (1772–1833), whose major contribution, if only one is to be singled out, was to find in the Hindu heritage a rebuttal to Christianity.

He was a scholar and a linguist, learning Persian, reading Euclid, Aristotle, and the Qur'an in Arabic, and studying the Hindu texts in Sanskrit during his youth. Later he mastered English in the Company's service and picked up a working knowledge of Greek and Hebrew in the course of his biblical studies. In addition to his many accomplishments, such as founding newspapers and preparatory schools for Western studies, he concentrated on finding and promoting the ancient purity of Hinduism, stripped of its popular accretions, as an answer to Christianity, which he believed was the greatest single threat of the West to Indian civilization. His biblical studies led him to accept the humanitarian ethics, which he elaborated in *The Precepts of Jesus*, but to reject Christian doctrines such as the Trinity and the divinity of Jesus. In the Vedānta he discovered these ethics and the concept of a single god manifest in every aspect of nature and founded the Brāhmo Samāj (Society of God) to promote this "pure" form of Hinduism. He denounced as excrescences a whole host of superstitious practices including idol-worship and *suttee*. The Brāhmo Samāj proved an effective counter to the efforts of the missionaries, and his deist-like denunciation of Christian doctrines further enraged them, leading to a running debate in which he fared well.

In the same way that he was ready to accept the ethics of the New Testament as eternal verities, previously preached by Hinduism, he also urged the study of Western science and knowledge but insisted that they, like Christianity, were of Asian origin. He was prepared to acknowledge no debt to the West in the sciences except for "the introduction of useful mechanical arts," and none at all in religion or philosophy. In reply to "A Christian" who warned against being "degraded by Asiatic effeminacy," Roy pointed out that most of the religious figures revered by Christians, including Jesus, were Asians and any reflection on Asians or Asia was a reflection on these prophets and patriarchs.

This reminder of the Asian origin of much of the knowledge, both spiritual and material, deemed Western is something Western students should keep in mind if they wish to understand the refusal of Easterners to acknowledge any type of inferiority. In the subsequent accommodation of Indian reformers to Western influence, Roy's importance cannot be underestimated. Some placed greater emphasis on his wholehearted advocacy of English education, while others followed his stress on spiritual purification; but, whatever their emphasis, the lineage of their thought can be directly traced back to his ideas and represented variations on the themes he set. Attention will be given first to the leading figures in the spiritual reaction, labeled the Hindu Renaissance, and then to the political reaction that produced Indian nationalism.

THE HINDU RENAISSANCE

Debendranāth Tagore (1817–1905), a member of another renowned Bengali family, revitalized the Brāhmo Samāj after assuming leadership in 1843. Like Roy, he worked to check conversions to Christianity and to demonstrate even further the antiquity and truth of Hindu monotheism. To counter the influence of mission schools, he founded a Hindu school, and, as he wrote in his *Autobiography* (p. 39), "Thenceforward the tide of Christian conversions was stemmed, and the designs of the missionaries were knocked on the head." Drawing on intuition and reason, he reconciled to his own satisfaction Western objectivity and Eastern subjectivity to demonstrate the existence and nature of a supreme being.

From the knowledge of what is external, including the body, comes knowledge of the inner self which perceives it; thus each individual is the perceiver, the knower. And what he perceives is not all unregulated chaos but rather demonstrates in many of its aspects a regularity, a design, as in the rising and setting of the sun and moon and in the alternation of the seasons. Such a design, on which our lives depend, cannot be merely an accidental design of matter but rather the design of an infinite mind that brought the universe into existence. By this chain of reasoning Tagore believed that his integration of Western and Indian thought had brought him to a rational explanation of the existence of God that did not rely on faith or idolatry, an explanation that Western deists of the eighteenth century would have understood.

Perhaps to make the Brāhmo Samāj acceptable to as many Hindus as possible, he backed away from Roy's denunciation of idol-worship and returned to the ancient Vedānta doctrine of differing levels of truth. This moderate position taken in 1867 reflected his attitude toward his break with his fiery disciple, Keshub Chunder Sen (1843–1884), under whose leadership, incorporating more and more Christian doctrines, the society was fractured.

While we should never compromise our principles and beliefs, Tagore argued, we should equally demonstrate their strength by tolerating and avoiding alienation of those with other beliefs. There is no need to hurt the feelings of our parents and elders by destroying the images they adore, when all our conscience commands is our abstention from revering them.

Finally, his affirmation of life and its duties is a significant reminder of the realistic approach to this world which is a continuing characteristic of Hinduism. While advocating renunciation as the sole avenue to immortality, he emphasized that such a path did not mean renunciation of this world and its manifold obligations. Instead, as the Gītā had taught, you should be a good husband and father and perform all the duties of a member of the community but remain unattached to the fruits of your actions and free from selfish desire. "When all lusts that dwell in the heart of man are cast out, then the mortal becomes immortal, and even on earth attains God." (deBary, ed., *Sources of Indian Traditions*, p. 614.)

Another dynamic Hindu reformer, Dayānanda Saraswatī (1822–1883), came from a brāhman family of Gujarāt and was outside the circle of English-educated Indians. As a result, he rejected everything Western and furnished a religious foundation for the radical anti-Western branch of the Indian nationalist movement. However, while rejecting Western culture, he was still a religious reformer seeking to get back to the Vedas, as he interpreted them, and to eradicate the burden of corruption acquired in the historical development of Hinduism. In this way, he preached, Mother India would become spiritually rearmed to meet the challenge of the West. With even greater vigor than Roy and his successors, he argued that the Vedas supplied no support for the evils of caste, untouchability, child marriage, female inequality, idol-worship, polytheism, and the horde of other corruptions that had crept into Hinduism. Perhaps his most important contribution was to shift the attitude toward Hinduism from the defensive to the offensive asserting with vigor that the religion of the Vedas, divested of its corruptions, was the one true faith and even extending this claim of Indian preeminence to nonreligious developments. In addition to countering the claims of Christianity he also challenged Islam. To promote commitment to a reformed Hinduism, he founded in 1875 the Ārya Samāj (Society of Aryans), emphasizing the Vedas and their Aryan authors as the sole source of truth. Saraswatī's appeal to the spirit in contrast to Roy's appeal to reason stimulated active proselytizing for members. As a result, it took firmest root in the Punjab where it confronted both Muslims and Sikhs. The anti-Islamic stress of this organization laid the foundation for future communal strife.

On the other hand, Saraswatī did not foresee this consequence because he believed that the religion he taught was based on universal principles acknowledged as true by all mankind and thus should be called the primeval and eternal religion, "above the hostility of all human creeds." He asserted that it incorporated only those views deemed worthy of acceptance "by all men in all ages" and insisted that he had no idea of establishing a new religion. His only aim, he claimed, was to sort out what was true and what was false and to assist others in reaching the same goal. No man worthy of the name could do any less than search for the truth, wherever it might be found, without prejudice and without fear of the unjust, no matter how powerful. At the same time, he should devote all his energy to protecting and advancing the welfare of the righteous, however poor and weak, and to undermining and destroying the wicked rulers of this earth, however strong and influential. The significance of the last assertion for Indian nationalism should not escape notice.

The element of universal truth in every religion implied in the teachings of Saraswatī was discovered in another form through the trances of the gentle, but uneducated, mystic, Shrī Rāmakrishna (1836–1886), to whom God became manifest on different occasions as a Divine Mother, Rāma, Krishna, Muhammed, and Jesus, among others. In each case, he worshiped the deity according to the forms of the religion involved. As a result of these experiences he was convinced, and convinced those who observed him, that the one true God had innumerable manifestations all subsumed in the Indian conception of truth which can free the mind through spiritual communion demonstrating the di-

vine nature in every individual. More even than his disciples this "God-intoxicated" mystic stressed that all paths lead to the one truth. His admirer, Keshub Chunder Sen, was criticized for the narrowness of his outlook.

Freedom or bondage, Rāmakrishna asserted, is no more than a state of mind. If you believe you are free, nothing in this world can bind you. In a Christian book he read he discovered from beginning to end only one theme, that of sin, and in the Brāhmo-Samāj under Sen's tutelage sin was likewise the central concern. "He who repeats day and night: 'I am a sinner, I am a sinner,' becomes a sinner indeed." (deBary, ed., *Sources of Indian Tradition*, p. 642.)

His English-educated disciple, Swāmī Vivekānanda (1863–1902), carried the Indian religious message to the West in an impressive address to the first World Parliament of Religions held in Chicago in 1893 in which he declared himself the spokesman of "the Mother of Religions, a religion which has taught the world both tolerance and universal acceptance." Using as his text the Vedic hymn: "As the different streams having their sources in different places all mingle their water in the sea, so, O Lord, the different paths which men take through different tendencies, various though they appear, crooked or straight, all lead to Thee," he proclaimed the fundamental identity and universality of all religions. For the next three years he became the first Indian to exert a significant impact on the West through lecturing to overflow audiences and founding Rāmakrishna missions dedicated to social service in the United States and Great Britain. His further travels carried him to most parts of the globe. The directness and simplicity of his message that "Man is God" elicited an enthusiastic response, and he did not hesitate to castigate Westerners for their shortsighted materialism.

Upon his return to India Vivekānanda raised a clarion call to young Indians to prosecute the task he had begun. As he saw it, the

Western world was seated on a volcano, about to explode. Its materialistic drive had led it to every corner of the globe, but its soul was empty and torn by nationalistic strife. Now, he asserted, was the time for India's spirituality and philosophy to go forth and conquer the world.

He also recognized the grinding poverty of India's poor and called on the rich to educate and aid the poor. In addition, he appreciated the need to emulate selectively the material accomplishments of the West without sacrificing India's spiritual values. He saw India's future in the regeneration of the Hindu masses and, drawing on the lesson of the Gītā, constantly abjured the people (as did his successor, Gāndhi) to be fearless because fearlessness is the source of strength.

Surprisingly, sympathetic Westerners made an important contribution to the Hindu Renaissance and the consequent growth of Indian nationalism. Initially, a few scholars in the English East India Company's service took a deep interest in recovering India's history and literary heritage. Later, other Western scholars, particularly Germans who felt a special kinship to the Aryans, concentrated on Indian philosophy and other Sanskrit studies in search of cultural links. This Western recognition of the value of ancient Indian civilization was a welcome support to India's ego and aroused Indian scholarship to study with pride its past achievements. Direct Western participation in the Hindu Renaissance began with the founding in New York in 1875 of the Theosophical Society dedicated to the promotion of Hindu ideals and practices, including the concepts of *karma* and transmigration, with an implied criticism of the shallowness of Christianity. In 1882 the society's headquarters was moved to India to draw nourishment from the source of its ideas. Under the leadership of the adventurous and tempestuous Mrs. Annie Besant, who had previously rejected Christianity and accepted socialism, the Theosophical Society played a prominent role in the Indian nationalist movement at the

turn of the century. In 1917 she was even elected to the presidency of the Indian National Congress.

THE MUSLIM RENAISSANCE

The Hindus were accustomed to adjusting to internal challenges and alien conquerors and remained flexible and tolerant so long as their institutions were not too seriously disturbed, but the Muslims as a ruling caste deeply felt the blow of British conquest and withdrew in bitterness rather than accept and cooperate with the conquerors. Their prominence in the mutiny reinforced their separation by convincing the British of their irreconcilable hostility. As a result, the English-educated Hindus monopolized the posts opened to Indians, while the Muslims clung to their traditional religious schools that could not qualify them for British service.

The man who led them out of this seclusion was Sir Seyed Ahmed Khān (1817–1898). He held a subordinate post in the government and, recognizing the futility of the mutiny, remained loyal to the British. Thereafter, he wrote and worked to persuade his fellow Muslims of the necessity of coming to terms with their British rulers and Western learning without jeopardizing their faith in Islam. Like the Hindu reformers, he argued that Islam had become corrupted by many superstitious beliefs and practices and pointed out that in its heyday it had led the world in intellectual and scientific achievement drawing without restraint on the accumulated knowledge of its predecessors. To implement a Muslim revival, he founded in 1877 the Anglo-Oriental College at Alīgarh where Islamic and Western studies were jointly emphasized. In defense of his approach he appealed to reason and the teaching of the Prophet to seek knowledge throughout the world.

In the new college Islamic culture and theology would not be neglected, but pragmatic considerations, if nothing else, required adoption of the English language and the British system of education to qualify graduates for public posts. Such a step, he insisted, did not mean a rejection of Islam but rather its protection in the modern age. Moreover, the Prophet had urged his followers to seek knowledge wherever it was to be found, even if they had to go to China, and in the early centuries of Islam Muslim scholars had heeded this command, drawing on all sources, both Western and Eastern without any ill effects. Now it was time once more for them to go forth fearlessly and take advantage of the scientific progress made in Europe for the benefit of Islam. No Muslim should fear the effect on the faith of such a quest for new knowledge because Islam was a rational religion, not an irrational superstition, and could only be strengthened by the growth of knowledge. Any such fear would only betray a lack of faith in the truth of Islam.

Later he also became concerned by the religious emphasis of the Indian nationalist movement foreseeing the oppression of the Muslim minority if its goal were ever achieved. Therefore, he urged all Muslims to abstain from participation in the Indian National Congress and prophesied the future division of India and consequent bloodshed. As he saw it, any system of representative government that depended on majorities for effective operation required a measure of cohesion and common attitudes in the history, culture, religion, and nationality of its peoples—a condition notably lacking among the peoples of the subcontinent of India. Therefore, the principles and program of the Indian National Congress, he warned, were formulated without regard to the diversity of the Indian peoples both in their historical development and contemporary situation and therefore could not work.

The Muslims, he added, were a united and militant minority accustomed to taking up the sword whenever they were subjected to oppression. Such a disastrous prospect was possible, and even probable, he be-

lieved, if the claim of the predominantly Hindu Congress to represent the ideals and aspirations of the Muslim minority were allowed to prevail.

FOUNDERS OF INDIAN NATIONALISM

Indian leaders, both reactionary and reformist, were stunned into individual resignation by the suppression of the mutiny. Only gradually was the resentment of the Western-educated elite aroused by the failure of the British ruling class to fulfill the Queen's promise to give equal and impartial consideration to qualified Indians in making appointments to government service. In fact, unjust treatment and prejudicial handicaps in the 1870s generated the first signs of an organized nationalist feeling.

As an individual and later as a moderate Congress leader, the Parsee businessman, Dadābhāi Naoroji (1825–1947), honored as "the Grand Old Man of India," first sought to awaken the British people to the inequities of their rule in India. He pointed out the political error of failing to entrust educated Indians with a larger share in government and insisted that for the sake of tranquillity it was in the British interest and according to British colonial experience to give Indians a larger voice in legislation and taxation. He also delineated the argument, used by all succeeding Indian nationalists, that the drain of India's wealth was doing irreparable damage to India and Britain alike. Notable, however, was his fair appraisal and recognition of British contributions—an example not always followed by his less moderate successors. Before an English learned society, he summarized his analysis of the situation in 1871.

He began by expressing his confidence in the British people's traditional sense of fair play and justice, once they were aware of the facts, and then delineated the two major problems, one economic and the other political, in dire need of rectification. The most important problem to Naoroji was "the drain" that must at least be stopped, if not reversed, out of the self-interest of the British rulers in the annual golden egg of £12 million, if not out of the British people's humanitarian concern for the impoverishment of 200 million human beings. Balance must be regained, he argues, just to offset the prospect of more and more devastating famines. Given a respite from "the drain," the Indian people could channel resources into projects for the increased productivity essential to meeting their ordinary needs as well as the extraordinary demands of a costly distant rule. He acknowledged India's debt to Britain for "invaluable moral benefits" and its right to legitimate benefits deriving from its rule, but he insisted that Britain was also obligated to provide the government, and the means, including credit, which would enable the Indian people to pay "the tribute or price" for its rule without dying from famine. The second major problem that he laid before his audience was the need to extend to a people called British subjects the equal rights they deserved as such and to meet in a reasonable way their growing aspirations for "a fair share" in the government of their own country. Such moderate and loyal proposals were received with warm and generous applause by a sympathetic audience, but they proved much less amenable to implementation in the Indian environment.

While Naoroji worked with untiring patience to persuade the British rulers of the errors of their ways, another Indian, embittered by unfair treatment, utilized his oratorical skills to arouse a sense of national unity within India. Surendrenāth Banerjee (1848–1925), nicknamed "Surrender-not" for his unflagging dedication, was one of the first Indians admitted to the I.C.S. Not long after taking up his duties he was dismissed for a minor error which, committed by any of his British colleagues, would have warranted only a reprimand. Not only was the appeal he made in London turned down, but also his application for the bar examinations was refused. He returned to India determined to devote his life to "redressing our wrongs and

protecting our rights, personal and collective." In 1876 he formed the Indian Association of Calcutta with branches in the major cities of the north to put pressure on the government to grant political concessions. However, there was little prospect of success during the viceroyalty of Lord Lytton (1876–1880), the agent of Disraeli's glorification of the empire. In fact, the next year saw the proclamation of Queen Victoria as Empress of India with appropriate fanfare and the reduction from 21 to 19 of the maximum age for the I.C.S. examinations held in London. Banerjee used his new organization to campaign against this additional handicap and sent a futile All-India Memorial against it to the House of Commons. This new regulation, which placed Indian applicants at an additional disadvantage, and the rejection of the appeal against it generated more widespread expressions of nationalistic and anti-British feeling. This feeling was complemented by the anti-Western sentiments of the Hindu Renaissance. Indeed, the growing vigor of attacks on the government by the press inspired the restrictive Vernacular Press Act of 1878. When imprisoned for criticizing a British judge, Banerjee set another precedent for Indian nationalism by welcoming the opportunity to publicize the injustice. The potential divisiveness of the association of religion with nationalism was early recognized in a speech in 1878, that gave credit to Nānak, the founder of Sikhism, as the first champion of an Indian unity transcending social and religious differences. Banerjee now called on all Indians—Hindus, Muslims, Christians, and Pārsees—to bury the hostilities of the past in a common dedication to the welfare of the homeland.

Despite his devotion to the Indian cause and his readiness to suffer incarceration for his beliefs, Banerjee remained in the ranks of the moderates, loyal to Britain and confident that the British sense of justice would eventually rectify India's legitimate grievances without recourse to violence.

For Maharāshtra, the source of militant resistance under the Hindu hero, Shivājī, to the Mughal oppression of Aurangzīb and the last Hindu area to submit to British arms, to be unrepresented in the growth of Indian nationalism is inconceivable. Although Bengal has provided most of the early examples, Mahārāshtra produced two of the most dynamic leaders, the moderate Gopāl Krishna Gokhale (1866–1915) and the uncompromising Bāl Gangādhar Tilak (1856–1920), as well as the ardent advocate of social reform and father of Indian economic studies, Mahādev Govind Rānade (1842–1901). All three were members of the small Chitpavan brāhman caste that had supplied the spiritual leadership and the unifying peshwās (prime ministers) of the earlier Marāthā power. All three settled in the old Marāthā capital city of Poona, and all three supported the Deccan Education Society for the promotion of education and selfless social service and its training institution, Fergusson College. But here the similarity ended. The elder Rānade, barred from political activity by his position as a subordinate judge in the British service, devoted his labors to social reform and economic development and to guiding his political protégés. Gokhale may be considered the exponent of his moderate political views placing confidence in British cooperation to secure social, economic, and political reforms. On the other hand, Tilak, convinced of British perfidy, abandoned hope of gaining such reforms through British cooperation and turned to the promotion of violent anti-British nationalism, first among the Hindu peasantry of Mahārāshtra, and then throughout India.

In the tradition of Rām Mohun Roy, Rānade worked to eradicate the social evils of child-marriage, the non-marriage of widows, female seclusion, and other inequities in the treatment of women, utilizing persuasion and his authority as a judge. Again, by persuasion, he labored to convince orthodox Hindus to recognize the need for ending corrupt practices and purifying the faith. In spite of opposition from men like Tilak, his moderate approach gained results, and in

1887 he founded the Indian National Social Conference, which convened concurrently with the Indian National Congress, to promote social reforms on a nationwide basis.

His other major interest was economic development to alleviate the poverty of the masses. In examining the problem he realistically recognized that Indian conditions precluded a simple emulation of the British system of relying on individual enterprise and concluded that the government must play a prominent role in planning, financing, and managing India's industrial development—an astute preview of what has come to pass since independence. In an essay on "Indian Political Economy" of 1892 he pinpointed the problems and their solution.

Indian social values placed status over contract and combination over competition. Moreover, the economic outlook was generally conservative, unenterprising, and tradition-bound. There was plenty of cheap labor, but it was for the most part unskilled and inefficient. Large-scale cooperation of capital or labor had never occurred, and the traditional institutions and laws, as well as the absence of political stability and security prior to the establishment of British rule, positively discouraged any concentrations of wealth. Finally, Indian religion looked down on the mere pursuit of wealth. Therefore, India was ill-adapted for the promotion of free, competitive enterprise. On the other hand, Rānade noted that even in Europe an expanded role for the state in the regulation and promotion of national enterprise in the national interest was becoming more widely accepted. To limit government to the maintenance of order and defense would be a waste of its potentialities for advancing the welfare of the community as a whole. Specific areas in which he foresaw that state operation could be usefully employed included education, communications, and the pioneering or insurance of risky, but essential enterprises.

Rānade's moderate and pro-British protégé, Gokhale, was India's outstanding political leader until his death in 1915. In 1899 he was elected to the legislative council of the state of Bombay and a few years later was named its representative on the Imperial Legislative Council. In this capacity he did not hesitate to criticize the excessive taxation, especially in depression years, which, he insisted, would be unacceptable in any truly representative system of government. In short, he was denouncing "taxation without representation." Like his mentor, Gokhale was dedicated to social and religious reform, as indicated by his role in the Deccan Education Society whose members took a vow of poverty. He was particularly concerned about the condition of the lower castes, and especially the "Untouchables," a sentiment shared by Rānade and the younger Gāndhi who received advice and support from both in his labors to improve the treatment of Indians in South Africa. In 1905 Gokhale formed the Servants of India Society to recruit nationwide a body of dedicated workers to implement his ideals. His speech defining the society's objectives and the vows required of all members best illustrates the deepest concerns of Gokhale and his supporters.

Great progress, he asserted, had been made in the past 50 years in the development of a sense of Indian unity, transcending religious divisions, to enable a renovated India to move forward and take its place in the community of nations. The Western-educated "brain of the community," in particular, was dedicated to this goal. Although some substantial advances had been achieved in education and local self-government and the people were beginning to be influenced by the Indian press and other informational activities, the time had come for an organization to mobilize devoted workers, willing to sacrifice their personal interests, for a concerted and sustained assault on the ignorance and disabilities of the Indian people, in preparation for attainment of the long-range goal of self-government. Drawing on traditional Indian values, Gokhale appealed for recruits with a love of country as

ardent as the religious spirit. As he put it, "public life must be spiritualized." The tasks of these servants of India would be to develop among the people, by example and precept, a dedication to the country and its political needs that would not shrink from any sacrifice in its cause, to build goodwill and cooperation in the common cause among the various religious and regional communities, and to promote education particularly for raising the status of women and the depressed classes. Every recruit took seven vows similar to those for entrance into a monastic order. First and last he agreed to devote all his energy to the aims of the Society and keep foremost in his thoughts the cause of a united and emancipated India. In addition, he pledged to be pure in his personal life, to avoid personal quarrels and seek no personal advantage, to accept all Indians as brothers, regardless of caste or creed, and to be satisfied with what little support the Society could provide for himself and his family. Such a program of self-denial was well adapted to the spiritual heritage of Indian civilization.

The contrast between Gokhale and Tilak was not as deep as their actions indicated and can be reduced to the difference in their evaluation of the British. Gokhale had an abiding faith in the British sense of justice and commitment to democratic principles, while Tilak was convinced that past performance demonstrated beyond doubt Britain's sole interest in the exploitation of India. Furthermore, Tilak totally rejected the idea that alien rulers could comprehend and alleviate India's ills, and certainly he did not want the Indian people to be in any way indebted to the British for any reforms or favors. Both Gokhale and Tilak saw the need for social and religious reforms, but Tilak's uncompromising nationalism would accept no reforms under British auspices.

In Poona, Tilak set up two newspapers, the Marāthī *Kesari* (The Lion) and the English *Mahratta*, to spread Western knowledge and give Hindu nationalism a popular foundation. In these papers he glorified the Marāthā martial tradition and promoted two annual festivals, one honoring the Māratha hero, Shivājī, and the other the elephant-headed Hindu god, Ganesha, the remover of obstacles. The anti-Muslim, as well as anti-British, nature of these two festivals stirred communal hostility in addition to the anti-cow killing campaign he borrowed from Saraswatī. In his columns he attacked a British reform measure raising the age of consent for marriage, though he personally approved of such a reform, as an example of the arbitrary, anti-Indian rule of the British. If such a reform of a traditional practice were right, it should be done by an independent Indian government. Generally, he denounced those who favored Western culture and used his pen to arouse the people to the glories of Indian civilization. In 1897 two British officials who had used high-handed methods in an attempt to check the spread of plague were murdered shortly after a *Kesari* editorial justified the use of force and assassination against alien oppressors, as Shivājī had done. When his paper went on to condemn the victim's actions as tyrannical, Tilak was sentenced to a year in prison, which only increased his popular appeal. Tilak was the pioneer in transforming Indian nationalism from an association of a handful of Western-educated reformers attempting to persuade the British government to move toward self-government, with little success, into a popular movement supported by a significant number of the Indian people. For this achievement he was given the posthumous title of Lokamānya, "Honored by the People."

THE INDIAN NATIONAL CONGRESS

The vehicle for the organized expression of Indian nationalism has been the Indian National Congress, formed at a meeting of Western-educated leaders in Poona during December, 1885. This body was a direct outgrowth of "Surrender-not" Banerjee's Indian Association of 1876 and the subsequent

difficulties in dealing with Disraeli's viceroy, Lord Lytton, and his popular Gladstonian successor, Lord Ripon (1880–1884). Gladstone, who believed that good government was no substitute for self-government, had asserted: "It is our weakness and our calamity that we have not been able to give to India the blessings of free institutions." Lord Ripon was his agent to initiate steps in this direction. He authorized and encouraged both urban and rural self-government to train the people in the exercise of political responsibility. He aided with public grants the expansion of public and private education at the district level. And he repealed the hated Vernacular Press Act of his predecessor. But his inability to resist the organized agitation of the British community and prevent the emasculation of the Ilbert Bill, providing full equality of Briton and Indian before the law, offset the renovation of the British image his other actions had gained. Although he was given a tumultuous send-off indicating his personal popularity, the British reputation for justice had suffered a damaging blow. Moreover, Indians had been provided not only with a sample of the effectiveness of organized agitation but also with an unquestionable manifestation of the racial arrogance of the British community in India. For the Western-educated elite to jettison the Western ideas and ideals they had learned was impossible; instead, they distinguished between the British bureaucracy and business community in India who failed to live up to these ideals and the British people in whom they placed their faith. At the same time, they realized the need for a national organization.

In 1883, amid the heat of the agitation against the Ilbert Bill, Banerjee formed the Indian National Conference, which met in Calcutta with representatives from all parts of India. At the same time, Allan Octavian Hume, a retired British civil servant concerned about the growing breakdown of communication between the British bureaucracy and the Indian people, sent a letter to all graduates of Calcutta University advocating the formation of an association for the mental, moral, and political regeneration of India. What he had in mind was a formal organization that could provide a channel for a fruitful exchange of views between the government and the people. The Western-organized Theosophical Society, which had recently established its headquarters in India, was also sufficiently disturbed by the growth of misunderstanding and alienation to sponsor a meeting of national leaders at Madras in December, 1884. This meeting led to the issuance of invitations to the meeting the following December at Poona where the organization to be known as the Indian National Congress was officially formed. This meeting, which set forth the platform of the moderate reformers, was attended by 70 delegates, only 2 of whom were Muslims. Although the third annual president was a Muslim and a resolution of the fourth annual meeting gave the Muslims what amounted to a veto, Muslim membership was never numerous, basically because of the opposition of Sir Ahmed Khān and the influence he exercised over educated Muslims.

This first meeting was attended by Hume and other sympathetic Englishmen and received the lukewarm sanction of the new viceroy, Lord Dufferin (1884–1888), who believed such peaceful deliberations were preferable to riots. The tone of the meeting was distinctly moderate, and the delegates went out of their way to affirm their loyalty to the throne. Nevertheless, the first president in his address declared the ultimate goal to be parliamentary self-government, though he too tempered his remark by asking "whether in the most glorious days of Hindu rule you could imagine the possibility of a meeting of this kind" and adding: "It is under the civilized rule of the Queen and the people of England that we meet here together, hindered by none, freely allowed to speak our minds without the least fear or hesitation."

A series of resolutions indicated the problems they believed to be most in need of rectification. One requested a royal commission to investigate the Indian government and another called for a standing committee of the House of Commons to consider complaints. These resolutions illustrate the delegates' dissatisfaction with the government in India and their faith in an informed British government to correct the inequities and prepare India for parliamentary government. Furthermore, their rejection of the autocracy of the past reflects the depth of their indoctrination in British political practices and explains today's determination to make the borrowed system of parliamentary democracy function in practice. Another resolution calling for the abolition of the anachronistic Council of India in London showed the continuing concern about "the drain," composed in large part of "excessive" salaries and pensions. A further resolution asked for the right for the legislative council to review the budget. This privilege later allowed men like Gokhale to criticize the distribution of taxation, which yielded surpluses in years of famine, plague, and depression.

In successive annual meetings attendance grew substantially, but the Congress remained an elite movement, failing to stir up popular support and permitting Lord Dufferin in his final report to describe it as a "microscopic minority" from which little need be feared. Until 1905 its leadership remained moderate, and even conservative, electing three Englishmen as annual presidents. Even after 1900 Lord Curzon, viceroy from 1899 to 1905, could write: "The Congress is tottering to its fall, and one of my great ambitions . . . is to assist it to a peaceful demise." This moderation, however, secured influential support in Britain where in 1888 a Committee for Representative Government was formed to gain public support for its goal. On the other hand, the modest concessions the Congress could extract from a government which, as the preceding statements suggest, did not take it very seriously provided the conditions for the growth of militant, Hindu-oriented nationalism led by fiery dissidents like Tilak who appealed to a growing fund of discontent with British inability to solve the problem of poverty.

Prior to 1905 the one step toward the Congress goal of self-government was the disappointing Indian Councils Act of 1892, which was only passed over substantial opposition in parliament. This act, which implemented most of the modest concessions recommended by Lord Dufferin, was avowedly not intended to represent an advance toward parliamentary government, but simply to give significant interests a voice in the formulation of governmental policy. The membership of the imperial and provincial legislative councils was expanded to accommodate nominees of provincial and municipal councils, chambers of commerce, and other significant groups. Election was involved only in the way these bodies selected their nominees; seating in the legislative councils depended on appointment by the governor or governor-general. In spite of the expansion of these bodies they still retained official majorities, but they were authorized to criticize executive orders and the annual budget. Such criticisms by figures like Gokhale were listened to by the governor-generals and gained important publicity for the Congress through the press reports. The executive council, where administrative decisions were made, remained an exclusive British preserve until 1909.

The year 1892 also saw an economic action that further convinced many Indians that the primary British interest was to exploit India. First, an import duty of 5 percent was assessed on cotton goods to meet a currency crisis. British manufacturers immediately put up a howl at this violation of the principle of free trade with the result that a countervailing excise tax was imposed on Indian cotton goods. Even though both were later reduced to 3½ percent, the cost of cotton cloth to the consumer had been raised and Indian welfare had clearly been sacrificed to that

of British producers. This discrimination against an increasingly impoverished India, the inadequacy of the Indian Councils Act, and the droughts and plague that ravaged India after 1895, all provided fuel for the anti-British campaigns of ardent nationalists like Tilak. The moderates found it increasingly difficult to defend a policy of cooperation with the British Indian government. Faith in British justice was being rapidly eroded. As acts of violence multiplied, the Home government came to realize that it was facing a crisis in India.

To deal with this crisis, the ablest administrator with the widest direct knowledge of Asia and India was selected as the next viceroy. Lord Curzon (1899–1905) had served as undersecretary of state for India, had traveled throughout Asia, and had made four visits to India prior to his appointment. After Lord Dalhousie, he was undoubtedly the most vigorous and imaginative administrator India received as a governor-general. He was sincerely eager to alleviate the ills of India and ready to take whatever steps were necessary—and indeed, a few more. Unfortunately, he was supremely self-confident in his judgment and too aloof to take advice. In addition, he had inherited an explosive situation in which one or two missteps could prove disastrous. While administrative reforms were needed, political reform was the only hope of curing the growing deterioration of Anglo-Indian relations—and such a reform this domineering viceroy was not willing to consider. He was an outstanding representative of the "white man's burden" school of colonial thought.

The drought that confronted him on his arrival called for a massive relief effort. But his success in dealing with it did not satisy him; he was determined to prevent a recurrence and initiated a large-scale expansion of irrigation work and railroad construction. The measure of his achievement was the absence of severe famine, in spite of droughts, until the demands of war caused a breakdown of famine relief in 1943. The distress of the peasants moved him to remit taxes and subsequently to introduce rural cooperative banks to free the peasants from the grip of moneylenders and the fear of eviction. To oversee and guide the peasant base of the Indian economy, he reorganized the department of agriculture and set up a research institute to discover and instruct farmers in more modern techniques. He also provided for governmental support of economic development by forming a department of industry and commerce. Another area that benefited from his personal attention was the army. On several occasions he directly intervened to punish British soldiers, who had escaped penalties for abusing Indians. To reorganize the army he secured Lord Kitchener, hero of the Boer War, as commander-in-chief. Indeed, his insistence on civilian control of the army brought about his resignation in the face of General Kitchener's obstinate refusal to comply. His reorganization of the defense of the Northwest frontier demonstrated exceptional common sense and a touch of military genius. He withdrew the isolated outposts, subject to tribal raids, setting up a no-man's-land and paid tribesmen to police the area, thus diverting their natural inclination for raiding while furnishing them with a rewarding military function to perform. The result was the maintenance of more peaceful conditions at a sharply reduced cost. Another special interest was India's ancient civilization. He set up the Department of Archeology, which twenty years later uncovered the remains of the Indus civilization, and obtained passage of the Ancient Monuments Act to preserve the known works of India's past.

It seems surprising that his sensitivity about Indian culture and the problems of the peasantry was not matched by an appreciation of Indian aspiration for self-government. Perhaps when he looked at the Western-educated leaders of Indian nationalism, he saw in them half-baked converts who would produce only an inefficient imitation of parliamentary government more destructive of Indian welfare than the paternalistic British regime. Certainly, efficiency was the keynote of his administration and the educational reform he put through suggests a measure of contempt for the quality of English education in India. This contempt may very well have extended to the products of this system of education.

In 1901 he called together the principal educational administrators and made clear to them his dissatisfaction with the system. He condemned its imitation of the English system emphasizing literary studies instead of meeting India's need for technically trained personnel and its emphasis on English at the expense of study of Indian languages and literature. In short, in his opinion it was not serving the distinctive needs of the Indian people. Moreover, preparation for the standardized examinations contributed to cramming rather than understanding. Furthermore, he denounced the low academic standards, poor discipline, and incompetent instruction that produced in Bengal alone more graduates than in all England who were unprepared to fill the much fewer opportunities available at the current stage of Indian development. Obviously, he believed that such a system, ungeared to the needs of India, was a fundamental factor in creating economic and political unrest. As he wrote, it was "a huge system of active but often misdirected effort, over which, like some evil phantom, seemed to hover the monstrous and maleficent spirit of Cram." Out of this meeting came a major commitment of public funds to overhaul the educational system from bottom to top for the welfare of India. A universities committee was formed whose recommendations were incorporated in the Universities Act of 1904. This act provided for closer governmental control over what were in fact public institutions by prescribing that the government would appoint the governing boards to assure majorities of educational experts, name their chief administrators, and approve the appointment of all teachers. Their examinations were upgraded, and they were given greater power to improve the instruction of the affiliated schools and colleges through review of accreditation. In addition, the universities were directed to expand their instruction at the graduate level and to provide residential facilities.

These far-reaching reforms were naturally considered a slap in the face by the products of the former system, proclaiming the inadequacy of their education and implying their inferiority. Like any entrenched elite they were enraged by this attack on their prestige and reacted by denouncing every aspect of the act that might win popular support and avoiding any critical imputation of their own competence. The act was seen as an insidious scheme giving the government the power to reduce sharply the number of Western-educated Indians and to insure the perpetuation of British domination in India. The governmental control of higher education was compared unfavorably with its freedom in Britain and declared to be a plot to destroy the Indian movement for self-government by crippling the production of adequately educated personnel. None of the benefits of higher standards and the extension of graduate instruction for future graduates was acknowledged by those deeply hurt by the implication of the act. The measure of goodwill earned by the governor-general's other administrative reforms was entirely dissipated by this act. Even the moderate leaders were incensed and forced to denounce Lord Curzon.

The wrath stirred up by the Universities Act was still in full swing when another administrative reform, the Partition of Bengal in June, 1905, built it into a fury with outbreaks of violence and rumblings of revolution. Admittedly the state of Bengal was an administrative monster with a population of 78 million, including Behār and Orissa. Lord Curzon, interested primarily in adminis-

trative efficiency, was impressed by the facts that the previous neglect of eastern Bengal would be overcome and Assam would gain a seaport in the new capital of Dacca. His administrative mind failed to appreciate the depth of the Bengali feeling of unity that would be violated by partition. Certainly some sort of division was in order for the sake of efficiency, but, instead of separating Behār and Orissā from the state, Bengal proper was divided along communal lines, eastern Bengal with the addition of Assam containing a majority of Bengal-speaking Muslims and western Bengal the bulk of the Bengali-speaking Hindus. What is more, the Bengali-speaking Hindus found themselves outnumbered in their new state by the people of Behār and Orissā. From the Bengali point of view this was a partition of their homeland appealing to religious differences to implement a British policy of "divide and rule." In mass meetings "Surrender-not" Banerjee called upon all Bengalis, both Muslim and Hindu, to unite in the first *swadeshi* movement, a boycott of all foreign goods. The Bengali Hindu press inflamed the people to observe the boycott and a day of mourning for the destruction of the Bengali "nation" with its common traditions, language, literature, and "religion." The 30 million Bengali Muslims were conveniently forgotten as Hindu nationalism became more pronounced, and it must be admitted that the only Muslims distressed by the partition were those 12 million left in the western state.

Tilak recognized the opportunity to convert this localized outburst of Hindu nationalism into a nationwide movement. His fiery pen not only whipped up Hindu and anti-British feeling in his own state of Mahārāshtra but also throughout India. Not only did he support a nationwide boycott of British goods but also demanded British withdrawal and Indian independence. He declared that the British had clearly forfeited their right to rule. Even the moderate champion of cooperation, Gokhale, condemned the government for "its utter contempt of public opinion, its reckless disregard of the most cherished feelings of the people" at the annual meeting of the Indian National Congress.

Indian nationalism was further inflamed by Gandhi's reports of the discriminatory treatment of Indians in South Africa and of Australian and Canadian legislation barring Indian immigrants. Tilak particularly capitalized on these examples of racism to discredit British motives and the British right to rule. But by far the greatest stimulus to Indian nationalism in 1905 was the news of the decisive victories of the Japanese over the Russians. Japanese victory convinced all Asians that they were in no way inferior to the West and wholly capable of ruling themselves. Even Lord Curzon sensed its import when he observed: "The reverberations of that victory have gone like a thunderclap through the whispering galleries of the east." The less dramatic Lord Minto, who arrived in India in November, 1905, to replace Curzon, specifically noted: "The Government of India cannot shut our eyes to present conditions. The political atmosphere is full of change; questions are before us which we cannot afford to ignore, and which we must attempt to answer." Under these much less serene circumstances Congress met, including a large contingent in support of Tilak. As noted in Gokhale's statement, even the moderate majority was deeply disturbed and hard pressed to retain control. Tilak had coined the term, *swaraj*, to describe his demand for independence. Now Congress used *swaraj* in a resolution calling for the first time for dominion-style independence.

By 1905 Indian nationalism was firmly established, though it still was controlled by Western-educated moderates and had only stirred the people in a few states, such as Bengal and Mahārāshtra. Already, however, it had struck an ominous note with its stress on Hinduism and its appeal to Mother India. In the next year, Muslim leaders, alarmed at this trend made manifest by the partition of

Bengal and the tirades of Tilak, set the course of future development by founding the Muslim League.

Nationalism has been defined as a Western import whose religion is secularism. Most of the Western-educated leaders, as we have seen, sought to maintain this definition by appealing for Indian unity, regardless of religion. The Hindu Renaissance, however, combined with the slowness of the Muslim community in coming to terms with the British, created a division between Hindu and Muslim in social, economic, cultural, and political terms that could not easily be overcome. Western historians and archeologists reminded the Hindus that the Muslims, as well as the British, were alien conquerors and revived Hindu pride in the antiquity of Indian civilization. Rām Mohun Roy had founded the Brāhmo Samāj to check the progress of Christianity, but Dayānanda Saraswatī founded the Ārya Samāj to glorify Hinduism and challenge Islam as well as Christianity. Shrī Rāmakrishna and Swāmī Vivekānanda might proclaim the oneness of all religions, but clearly they conceived all other religions as more or less corrupted expressions of Hinduism. Moreover, the latter made a clear call for a Hindu spiritual conquest of the world. Even Gokhale with his broad tolerance saw India's salvation in the spiritual dedication of its leaders.

The spiritual emphasis permeating Indian history and civilization probably precluded any more than lip service to secular nationalism. Nationalism in India had to be associated with religion, which pervaded all Indian thought and life—a fact that the Muslim reformer, Sir Seyed Ahmed Khān, recognized and warned his fellow-Muslims to prepare for. In the Hindu camp Tilak clearly recognized this principle and devoted his life to promoting a Hindu nationalism that was both anti-Muslim and anti-British. After independence, as we shall see, Indian statesmen still proclaimed the secularism of the state, but the fact remains that the man most responsible for this accomplishment was a spiritual leader of the Hindu faith, however tolerant according to Hindu tradition he may have been. Certainly the repeated instances of communal strife belie the words of the constitution and the proclamation of Indian leaders. The subordination of social, economic, cultural, and political practices to the supremacy of religion is the one inescapable characteristic of Indian history and civilization. And the Western concept of nationalism did not have a chance of escaping subordination to religious expression in the Indian environment.

SIGNIFICANT DATES

1857   Sepoy Mutiny
1858   Government of India Act
1861   Indian Councils Act
1875   Founding of Theosophical Society
1877   Founding of Anglo-Oriental College (Muslim)
1878   Vernacular Press Act
1883   Ilbert Bill
1885   Founding of Indian National Congress
1892   Indian Councils Act of 1892
1904   Universities Act
1905   Partition of Bengal
1906   Founding of Muslim League

SELECTED READINGS

*Brown, D. Mackenzie, *The Nationalist Movement: Indian Political Thought from Ranade to Bhave.* Berkeley: University of California Press, 1961.

Gopal, Sarvepalli, *British Policy on India, 1858–1905.* Cambridge: Cambridge University Press, 1966.

Heimsath, Charles H., *Indian Nationalism and Hindu Social Reform.* Princeton: Princeton University Press, 1964.

Kling, Blair B., *The Blue Mutiny.* Philadelphia: University of Pennsylvania Press, 1966.

McCully, Bruce T., *English Education and the Origins of Indian Nationalism.* Gloucester, Mass.: P. Smith, 1966.

*McLane, J., ed., *The Political Awakening in India.* Englewood Cliffs, N.J.: Prentice-Hall, 1970.

Mehrotta, S. R., *India and the Commonwealth 1885–1929.* New York: Praeger, 1965.

Metcalf, Thomas R., *The Aftermath of Revolt: India, 1857–1870.* Princeton: Princeton University Press, 1964.

Natarajan, Swaminath, *A Century of Social Reform in India.* New York: Asia Publishing House, 1962.

Rudolph, Lloyd L., and Rudolph, Susanne, *The Modernity of Tradition.* Chicago: University of Chicago Press, 1967.

Singh, Hira Lal, *Problems and Policies of the British in India, 1885–1898.* Bombay: Asia Publishing House, 1963.

Spear, Percival, *India: A Modern History*. Ann Arbor: University of Michigan Press, 1961.

*Tandon, Prakash, *Punjabi Century, 1857–1947*. Berkeley: University of California Press, 1968.

*Wolpert, Stanley, *India*. Englewood Cliffs, N.J.: Prentice-Hall, 1965.

——, *Tilak and Gokhale*. Berkeley: University of California Press, 1962.

CHAPTER EIGHTEEN

REACTION AND REFORM IN THE MIDDLE EAST: 1856 – 1905

Unlike China, Japan, and India, the Middle East in 1857 was not a unit but rather a disintegrating amalgam in every sense of the term: political, social, economic, and even religious and cultural. Under increasing Western pressure this disintegration was destined to persist to the present day, despite the best efforts of its leaders. The only factors that make it possible to deal with the area as a whole are the Islamic governments, whether Sunnite or Shiite, which prevailed, the common use of Arabic script, even if it was used to write Turkish, Persian, and various dialects, and the common heritage of Islamic civilization, although its condition and interpretation varied widely, even within a particular state. In spite of this division and diversity, however, these common factors command its treatment as a distinctive and distinguishable whole, struggling, perhaps futilely, to maintain and defend its essential unity.

Before attempting to analyze its various problems and the varied efforts to combat them, a survey of the political entities and their internal characteristics may help in setting the stage. At the western extremity of North Africa was the sultanate of Morocco, an Arab-Berber state, more than 60 percent Berber in population, with a history of independence and once the seat of successive empires, which had never been reduced to submission by the Ottoman Empire. Strategically located at the gate to the Mediterranean, it maintained its independence in spite of Spanish acquisitions until its conquest was begun by France in 1901 from the latter's Algerian base. Like the rest of the Maghrib, its coastal regions, and especially the urban centers, were substantially Arabicized,

while the interior was dominated by Berbers, nominally Muslim, but retained many unique customs and practices. To the east of Morocco, Algeria, more than 30 percent Berber and possessing a vast desert hinterland traversed by camel routes to sub-Saharan Africa, had already been detached from the Ottoman Empire and subjugated by France in the years from 1830 to 1848. East of Algeria, Tunisia, the center of the ancient Carthaginian empire, had been the base of Islamic expansion in the West and the most thoroughly Arabicized area, with only 1 percent of the people retaining Berber customs and speech. Nevertheless, this Arab stronghold was occupied with ease in 1881 by the French to secure this flank and to forestall Italian ambitions. Finally, these ambitions were satisfied by the Italian occupation of sparsely populated Libya with its scattered urban centers in 1911. Until then Ottoman suzerainty was recognized by the warrior tribesmen organized under the Sanusi Sufi order, founded in 1837, which controlled and took its toll from the desert trade routes.

Egypt had been all but detached from the Ottoman Empire by the "new pharaoh," Mehemet Ali. Indeed, if the generalship of his son had not been frustrated by foreign intervention, a new and more vigorous empire might have been created, which might have done for Islam what the leaders of the Restoration later did for Japan. Considering however, the irresponsibility of his successors and Anglo-French concern over this route to the East, the likelihood of such an accomplishment seems very meager. By 1879 the financial profligacy of Egypt's rulers brought about Anglo-French management of the foreign debt and three years later British occu-

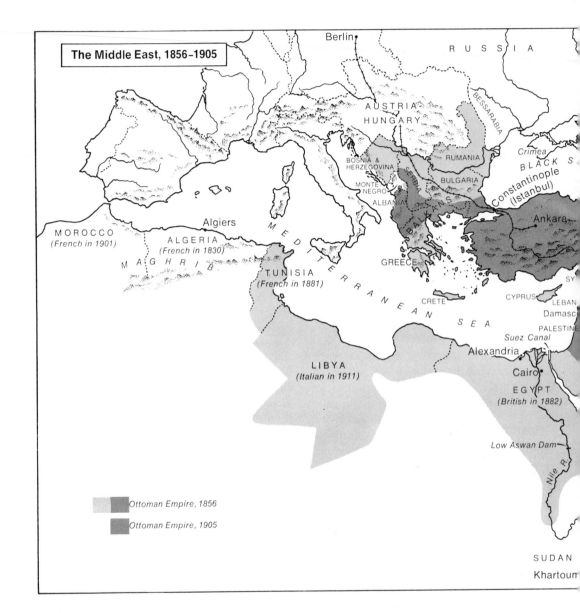

The Middle East, 1856–1905

Berlin

RUSSIA

AUSTRIA
HUNGARY

BESSARABIA

BOSNIA &
HERZEGOVINA

RUMANIA

Crimea

BLACK S.

MONTE
NEGRO

SERBIA

BULGARIA

Constantinople
(Istanbul)

ALBANIA

BALKANS

Ankara

MOROCCO
(French in 1901)

Algiers

ALGERIA
(French in 1830)

MAGHRIB

MEDITERRANEAN

GREECE

SY

TUNISIA
(French in 1881)

CRETE

CYPRUS

LEBAN

Damasc

SEA

PALESTINE

Suez Canal

Alexandria

LIBYA
(Italian in 1911)

Cairo

EGYPT
(British in 1882)

Low Aswan Dam

Nile R.

☐ Ottoman Empire, 1856

☐ Ottoman Empire, 1905

SUDAN

Khartoum

pation. Nevertheless, Egypt's economy had undergone such significant growth that it could support twice the population of 1800. In the period under consideration, Egypt was the most advanced area of the Middle East, economically and intellectually, and this primacy, due first to the works of Mehemet Ali and then the benefits of British stewardship, laid the foundations of its current leadership in the Arab world.

Turning from Africa to Asia, the Ottoman Empire included in addition to the Turkish homeland the Fertile Crescent regions, as well as the Hijaz and the Yemen, with a fluctuating influence over the rest of Arabia depending on the power of the Sa'udi leadership of the puritanical Wahhabi movement. Iraq, divided into three administrative units (*pashaliks*), was a neglected backwater until the advent of Midhat Pasha (1869–1872) who

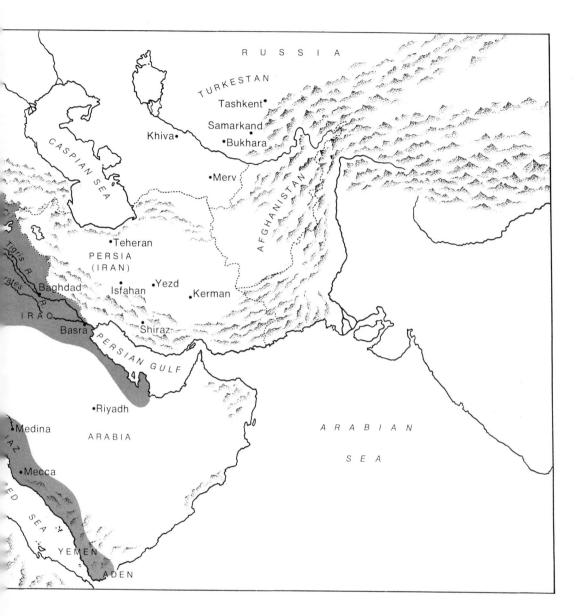

initiated extensive rehabilitation by reopening neglected irrigation facilities and bringing a measure of security by settling some nomadic peoples and policing the rest. After his recall, Iraq, left to the tender mercies of superficially Westernized administrators (*effendis*), soon lapsed into the former corruption, exploitation, and disorder. The dominant foreign power in Iraq and throughout the Persian Gulf was Britain, whose emissaries evinced no territorial interest, except to keep other powers out of the area.

The Levantine region of Syria, Lebanon, and Palestine benefited from Egyptian occupation and the long-term French interest in the Maronite Christians and the Holy Land, which developed discontent with Ottoman rule and a desire for increased trade and modernization. This ferment was especially strong among the Lebanese with a Christian majority and a long record of comparative autonomy. Anti-Christian and anti-Druze outbreaks and massacres led in the 1860s to foreign intervention requiring the Ottoman sultan to appoint Christian governors for a smaller Lebanon. Ottoman concern with the Hijaz centered on the annual pilgrimage to Mecca and the prestige accruing from control of the sacred cities of Medina and Mecca, but authority was vested in the hereditary Hashemite Sharīf descended from the Prophet. Authority over the Imam of the Yemen was even more tenuous, stemming mainly from a mutual desire to curb the aggressive ambitions of the Sa'udi family.

In addition to African and Asian territories, the Ottoman Empire still controlled in varying degrees the bulk of Balkan Peninsula, except Greece. In 1857 these territories included most of present-day Yugoslavia and Rumania, Albania, Bulgaria, and the northern half of Greece. The status of the relationship of the various provinces to Constantinople had already been altered significantly by the penetration of liberal and nationalistic ideals and their support by the often illiberal regimes of the neighboring Russian and Austro-Hungarian empires, whose main interest was to benefit from the dissolution of the European portion of the Ottoman Empire. It was also altered by the rapaciousness of pashas, aided and abetted, rather than deterred, by the local Councils of Notables representing local vested interests. Indeed, the pashas were often hamstrung by these councils and prevented from carrying out reforms in favor of the general welfare. The tendency for nationalistic movements to take root first among the various Christian, as well as linguistic, communities reflects both the former condition of semi-autonomy under the millet system and the quality of religion, in addition to race, as a rallying point for the growth of nationalism. In fact, in many areas, the Muslims, directly dependent on Constantinople, were less favorably situated than their Christian neighbors.

East of the crumbling Ottoman Empire was the shrinking domain of Shiite Persia under the weak Qajar dynasty; it had been reduced to little more than a helpless pawn manipulated by the imperial combatants, Russia and Great Britain. Already Russia had taken large bites of Persian territory west of the Caspian sea and, to the east, was in the process of swallowing the various Turkish tribal groups and their renowned caravan cities that acknowledged Persian suzerainty.

Prior to 1856 the Western powers had been primarily interested in trade on the best possible terms with the Middle East, though Russian, Austro-Hungarian, and French imperial appetites were whetted by nibbling at its weakest extremities. After 1856 economic imperialism sought profitable investment within the area. The ruling classes of the Middle East, shocked at the inability of Islam to ward off the infidels, had already begun to think in terms of selectively borrowing the military and material apparatus of Western technology and therefore proved easy marks for the mighty moneylenders of the West. Since Islam, like early Christianity, condemned usury and its practitioners, the Muslim borrowers disdainfully paid too little attention to the terms of the loans they contracted. The inevitable result was bankruptcy and the insistence of Western creditors upon management of their economies, in addition to further privileges. Greater contact with Westerners and Western education expanded the ranks of those informed not only about Western technological achievements but also about Western political and cultural institutions. Greater knowledge bred a greater discontent with Islam's continued failure to cope with the West and produced a growing realization of the need for much more drastic changes and reforms. Out of this frustration were to come the more radical experiments after 1905. Meanwhile, the seeds planted by the Western impact since 1800 were growing and spreading.

THE TANZIMAT REFORM MOVEMENT IN THE OTTOMAN EMPIRE

As early as the 1790s Ottoman sultans had recognized the need for at least military reform, but had been able to achieve little against the opposition of the vested interests in both church and state. One major accomplishment had been the bloody annihilation in 1826 of the militarily useless and thoroughly corrupt Janissary corps. Further military modernization, however, had met total defeat in 1839 at the hands of the even more modern forces of Mehemet Ali, commanded by his brilliant son, Ibrahim. The new sultan, Abul Mejid (1839–1861), who had succeeded to the throne amid these military disasters, was persuaded by his minister, Reshid Mustafa, to issue in November 1839, the decree that ushered in the reform movement known as the Tanzimāt. In general terms it promised (1) to guarantee to every subject, regardless of race or creed, security of life, honor, and fortune; (2) to establish a uniform and impartial system of assessing and levying taxes; and (3) to set up an equally impartial system for raising troops for military service. As proclaimed, this edict theoretically put an end to the millet system and ended all discrimination between subjects based on religion. Reshid did his best to implement this program by a series of edicts specifying administrative reforms, legal and military equality, and improvements in education, but he met opposition from every group, which minimized the effect of the program. Pashas objected to selection and promotion on the basis of merit and officials generally disliked the idea of fixed salaries and the elimination of corruption. Christians and Jews did not appreciate the privilege of eligibility for military service, and the wealthy members of these communities did not want to be deprived of their virtual monopoly of taxfarming. Some reforms, such as the Councils of Notables attached to each

governor, actually backfired to the disadvantage of the people as a whole. Nevertheless, although most of these reforms failed to secure general acceptance, there was a perceptible improvement in the tone of government. Corruption was at least reduced and arbitrary measures, such as torture, were discontinued because governors could be, and were, brought to book for administrative abuses. Moreover, although Christians and Jews escaped military service, they did receive equal treatment before mixed tribunals in legal disputes with Muslims, though failure to respect this right was a subject of frequent complaints. Improved education, mostly for Muslims, was provided in new schools and colleges. In 1850 a commercial code based on French law was established with mixed tribunals to try cases between Turkish subjects and Europeans. Further reforms were checked by the foreign problems leading to the Crimean War, but after the war, progress was resumed.

In 1856 a new reform decree reasserted the goal of integrating the non-Muslim communities by promising equality in taxation, justice, military service, education, public service, and social respect. The central emphasis on equality indicates the degree to which the previous effort had failed to reach this objective. The balance of the decree called for a thorough program of administrative and legal reforms with the aim of transforming the empire into a modern nation. Although the European powers welcomed this well-intentioned decree and agreed to give the Ottoman government an opportunity to put its own house in order without intervention, the possibility of success depended, as before, on the appointment of able, honest, and dedicated administrators and on the active cooperation of the people.

The supply of Western-educated personnel was larger than before and continued to grow with the expansion and improvement of educational facilities. Not only were many more Western missionary schools established in succeeding years, but also Turkish higher education was expanded by the founding in the late 1860s of a number of schools, notably the Imperial Lycée (1868), the University of Constantinople (1869), and the School of Law (1870). In addition, many Turkish subjects were returning after advanced study in the West, especially France, and many more were going to the West to complete their educations, where they were deeply influenced by Western liberalism, both political and cultural. Yet for most, who secured administrative appointments by bribery, their Westernism was merely a thin veneer reflected principally in Western dress and manners, and they could not resist conformity to the traditional practice of exploiting their often brief tenures of office to recoup their costs and pad their pockets. Moreover, the local notables of both Muslim and non-Muslim communities were not eager to implement reforms that would undermine their positions, while the exploited villagers and townsmen were in most regions so accustomed to the existing system that in their ignorance and apathy they offered no incentive for officials to depart from traditional practices and introduce innovations. Even such an ardent reformer as Midhat Pasha was later discovered, much to the disillusionment of his European supporters, to have engaged in corrupt practices.

Other Western-educated idealists, unwilling to compromise with the existing administrative system and inspired by the concept of nationalism, used their pens to bring about a Turkish intellectual and literary revival. Men like Ibrahim Shinasi and Namik Kemal translated French works into colloquial Turkish and started a Turkish newspaper in which the stilted, Persian-dominated literary style was denounced in favor of popular Turkish language and literature. In addition, they used the paper to promote their ideas of representative government and Turkish nationalism, which provided the intellectual foundation for what came to be known as the Young Turk movement. Their

militant writings led to the suppression of the paper in 1867 and their flight to London and Paris, where they continued their literary assault on the Ottoman regime. Their dedication to revivifying Turkish culture and creating a Turkish nationalism was probably in part a reaction to similar movements among the Greek, Serbian, and Bulgarian subjects of the Ottoman Empire.

The picture, however, of Ottoman administration was not as bleak as the preceding account indicates. In 1858 a new penal code, based on the Napoleonic code, was promulgated and gradually applied throughout the empire, providing the basis of equal justice for all subjects. Christian representatives were appointed to the Grand Council, but since they were drawn from the ruling elite, they were poor champions of the true interests of their people. An attempt was made to implement the pledge of equal military obligation for Christians, but popular opposition, which preferred to pay a tax in lieu of military service, nullified this reform effort to the satisfaction of both Christians and Muslims. More successful was the initiation of tours of inspection in the provinces by major officials of the central government, which provided an outlet for popular complaints, tended to curb administrative abuses, and furnished a wealth of firsthand information for the formulation of reform measures. One result was a more democratic reorganization of the Greek Orthodox, Gregorian Armenian, and Jewish millets, which was intended to check authoritarian oppression by the major prelates and their lieutenants by providing lay participation and to encourage a feeling of common Ottoman citizenship. Ironically, however, the undermining of the vested interests dependent on governmental support had the effect rather of stimulating the development of nationalist and separatist aspirations, at least among the Christian communities.

Another result of the tours of inspection was an administrative reorganization in 1864 enlarging the provinces to conform more closely to regional entities. The governors were given greater latitude in initiating local reforms with the advice of councils including indirectly elected representatives in addition to appointed members. To try out this reform, Midhat Pasha, a Bulgarian Muslim, was named governor of an enlarged province that included most of Bulgaria. Thanks to his ability, honesty, and dedication, this experiment in an unruly frontier province subject to Russian influence was a great success. In four years he united the Bulgarian people in support of the government by dealing out evenhanded justice, by setting up agrarian banks to make loans to the peasants at reasonable rates, by curbing banditry, and by building bridges, roads, schools, and other public works. However, he did not hesitate to crush ruthlessly any revolutionary activities he uncoverd.

Naturally elated by his achievement in Bulgaria, Midhat Pasha returned to Constantinople full of ideas for further reforms too advanced for acceptance by his more conservative colleagues. To get rid of this troublesome associate, they dispatched him in 1869 to work his wonders in Baghdad, the capital of one of the most backward and neglected provinces of the empire. The capital city, itself once the seat of empire, had been allowed to decay into little more than a great refuse heap accumulated through centuries of neglect. In the country nomadic tribesmen grazed their herds in fields that had once supported a large population by irrigated agriculture. Again he went to work with a will. Apathetic townsmen, peasants, and nomads were put to work cleaning up the city and its environs, restoring buildings, constructing roads, and most important of all, opening up the clogged irrigation canals. Some nomads were settled as farmers on the reclaimed lands, while his reformed military force, utilizing conscription, checked the depredations of other nomads and restored a measure of control over them. A savings bank was established extending credit at reasonable rates. Other municipalities were revitalized

and provided with administrative councils. In Baghdad he founded a newspaper, a hospital, an orphanage, and most important for the future, a number of schools. In the city he began a horse-drawn tramway and, before his recall, envisioned a "Euphrates Railway" to supplement the riverine artery of trade. After three years of frenzied effort, marred by some blunders caused by haste, jealous officials secured his recall by Sultan Abul Aziz (1861–1876) who had personally taken the reins of government on the death in 1871 of his progressive grand vizir.

Unfortunately, Midhat Pasha stands almost alone in the ranks of Ottoman officialdom. Other governors of ability were unwilling to risk their careers by bucking the established system of corruption and indolence. Even Midhat Pasha failed to eradicate corruption—and was not entirely unsusceptible to it himself. But compared to most of his colleagues, he was a knight in shining armor. His successors neglected the works he had begun. As governors and officials of the central government they were willing to undertake a variety of constructive projects, often financed by foreign loans, but the funds had a disconcerting habit of being consumed without much in the way of concrete results. This brings up the question of Western financial penetration.

WESTERN ECONOMIC PENETRATION

In 1854 the Ottoman government contracted its first foreign loan to finance some of the added costs of the Crimean War. After the war the Ottoman government recognized the necessity of modernization, not only in the social and political realms, but also in the economic realm. The puzzle that confronted them was how to finance such a program from the meager resources of what was still an overwhelmingly pastoral and agrarian economy and, what was more, a severely impoverished one that barely supplied a subsistence for the vast majority of the people.

The financiers of their former allies, who had already made loans to meet deficits caused by the war effort, had a ready answer: deficit financing covered by foreign loans. In the long run, they argued, the greater revenues made possible by the opening of markets by roads and railroads and by the development of industry would make it easy to pay off the debt. In 1863 the Ottoman Bank was jointly set up by British and French investors with France possessing the controlling interest. It alone could issue banknotes and before long established branches throughout the empire. The dominant French influence in this and other areas reflected the greater long-term French interest in the Ottoman Empire apparent in the political and cultural areas, as well as the economic. French education was already predominant and was confirmed by the use of French instructors and French as the language of instruction in the Imperial Lycée. During the intellectual awakening translators turned first to French works.

In 20 years, from 1854 to 1874, the Ottoman government incurred a foreign debt totaling a face value of 1 billion dollars but yielding, after discounts as high as 50 percent and more, only 600 million. Where did this money go? Most of it went to meet perennial deficits, and only a very small proportion was invested in constructive projects of any type. Thanks to the ancient Capitulations, no tariff protection could be given for the development of industry, and during these years industrialism in the West made such tremendous strides in volume and efficiency that competition without protection was impossible. By 1874 the interest and amortization on the debt amounted to 60 million dollars out of a total imperial income of 80 million. In fact, until 1874 much of the money borrowed had been used to service the debt. Now the Ottoman government was at the end of its economic tether.

In the fall of 1875, just when the Balkan pot had begun to boil over into insurrection in Bosnia and Herzegovina, the government declared its insolvency and decreed a 50 per-

cent cut in interest payments. In the following spring it gave up altogether and suspended payments indefinitely. France, still recuperating from the Franco-Prussian War and the civil strife that followed it, was unprepared to aid French creditors, while Britain, alarmed by the internal difficulties of the Ottoman Empire and the aggressive rumblings of the Russian bear, was unwilling to intervene. Finally in 1881, rather than risk intervention, the autocratic Sultan Abul Hamid II reached an agreement setting up a European consortium representing the creditors to manage a major segment of the economic affairs of his realm. As will be seen, this arrangement forestalled foreign intervention and before long worked out to his advantage.

THE OTTOMAN CONSTITUTION

Since his recall from Baghdad in 1872 Midhat Pasha had been secretly consorting with the liberal Tanzimāt reformers. They were increasingly appalled at the corrupt, irresponsible, and profligate policies of Sultan Abdul Aziz that accelerated the accumulation of debt to accommodate his large harem and its inmates' many importunate relatives and friends. Their appointment to public posts in return for bribes, regardless of qualifications, and the rapid turnover in appointees, though in part a desperate attempt to stave off imminent bankruptcy, was threatening to erase what few improvements in government had been accomplished. In addition, the sultan had appointed a pro-Russian chief minister at a time when the Balkan provinces, Bosnia and Herzegovina and Bulgaria, were seething with unrest. The utter incompetence of the sultan to cope with the mounting crisis in both internal and external affairs inspired direct criticism of the sultan, instead of just his officials, and aroused a deepening concern among conservatives as well as liberals.

The international financial panic of 1873 caused the collapse of several banks with a consequent shortage of money. Drought and famine in 1873 and 1874 in Asia Minor and the Balkans created widespread discontent with the government's inability to supply adequate relief and precipitated outright rebellion in Bosnia and Herzegovina. By the fall of 1875, when their loyal services were most needed, soldiers, sailors, and officials had been paid for more than six months with promissory notes redeemable only at a heavy discount. An attempt to extract additional revenue from the drought-stricken Turkish peasantry to support continued reckless spending met sullen resistance. Finally, on May 2, 1876, the Bulgarian uprising broke out, accompanied by the massacre of all Turks who were not able to escape in time.

The sequence of events made action imperative and secured for Midhat Pasha the support of military officers as well as the Shaykh al-Islam, the head of the religious establishment. With popular discontent at a peak and the support of conservatives who remembered how effectively Midhat had dealt with Bulgarian dissidents, the time was ripe for him and his associates to act. On May 11, 1876, the first step forced the sultan to dismiss his unpopular pro-Russian grand vizir. But Midhat knew he could not succeed by serving a hostile sultan. On the night of May 29 a coup d'état deposed Abul Aziz in favor of Murad V with the approval of a *fetwa* of the Shaykh al-Islam. The new sultan's reign, however, lasted only three months when mental instability made necessary his replacement by his younger brother, Abul Hamid II (1876–1909).

Meanwhile, Turkish troops, mostly irregulars, had crushed the poorly organized Bulgarian rebellion and could not be prevented from retaliating by the massacre of 10 to 20 thousand Bulgarian Christians. News of this action shocked Westerners and led to cries for intervention. Western concern for the Balkan peoples was further inflamed when Serbia and Montenegro declared a religious and racial war in support of the weakening resistance of Slavic Bosnia and Her-

zegovina. The Turkish people were equally aroused, and more volunteers for military service stepped forward than could be used. Serbia and Montenegro were only saved from total defeat by a Russian ultimatum for an armistice, to which the Ottoman government bowed on October 31, 1876, and for a Conference of the European Powers at Constantinople to settle the Balkan problem.

Under the circumstances of this intervention by a hostile West the sultan recognized that drastic measures were necessary to counter this ill feeling and that Midhat Pasha, widely respected by Westerners for his previous record of reform, was the man for the job. Midhat was appointed grand vizir. The European Conferees agreed on a plan that would have increased the territory and autonomy of the defeated Slavs. When it was presented at the first plenary session of the Conference on December 23, Midhat rejected it and countered with the proclamation of a constitution declaring the Ottoman Empire to be "an indivisible whole," a position totally irreconcilable with Western demands, but consistent with the Tanzimāt vision of creating a unified nation out of the diverse peoples of the Ottoman Empire. The constitution included a bill of rights for all subjects, regardless of race or creed, and provided for an elected parliament, an independent judiciary, and substantial provincial decentralization. These liberal features, however, were balanced by the sultan's powers to convoke and prorogue the parliament, to veto any bill, to make all appointments, and to exile anyone he deemed dangerous to the state. This constitution, accepted by a reluctant sultan only to forestall Western demands and break Western unity, reflected the views of a mere handful of reformers and was unsuited to the stage of social, economic, and political modernization reached by the empire.

If anything, the Christian and Muslim communities were more hostile toward each other and less likely to collaborate harmoniously in a parliamentary regime than before. In addition to communal differences, the undeveloped state of internal communications encouraged provincialism, and the impoverished subsistence conditions that prevailed throughout the empire militated against the successful operation of constitutional government. In short, the Ottoman Empire was far from being a nation integrated socially, economically, and politically. The creation of a nation, if at all possible, would require an extended period of enlightened dictatorial direction, such as most Western nations had undergone, to build the essential material foundations and inspire a common loyalty. The need to gain the approval of a divided parliament would only handicap and delay the process of racing to catch up with a revolutionary West gaining added momentum with every new development. Finally, the privileged classes that would dominate a parliamentary regime feared the effect of change on their status; an absolute ruler could more effectively deal with them. Therefore, as soon as feasible, Sultan Abul Hamid II dispensed with parliament, though he continued piously to proclaim the constitution every year.

The constitution may have influenced the British to withdraw their support from the Conference demands, but probably the government of Disraeli was moved more by fear of Russian intentions. The adamant truculence of the Turks, encouraged by the British ambassador and widespread popular support, led Russia to prepare for war by securing Austrian neutrality in return for the promise of Bosnia and Herzegovina. However, Russia made one more try for peace through the London Convention of March 31, 1877, by which the Western powers only asked the Ottoman government to agree to carry out the proposed constitutional reform to the satisfaction of the Western powers. But the Turks rejected even this moderate proposal because it implied a right to oversee and intervene in Ottoman affairs. Thoroughly frustrated by nearly two years of fruitless negotiations, Russia declared war on April 24, 1877.

THE RUSSO-TURKISH WAR OF 1877 – 1878 AND ITS CONSEQUENCES

Initially the war went well for the Russians, who met no serious resistance until they attempted to take the fortress of Plevna, south of the Danube. Repeated attacks on this strategic point along Russia's line of communications were repulsed with heavy losses, and the Russians were forced to settle down for a long siege to starve out the garrison. When Plevna surrendered in December, however, Turkish defenses crumbled and the government was forced to sue for terms. The Treaty of San Stefano, which would have created a monstrous autonomous Bulgarian principality, practically eliminating direct Turkish rule in Europe, was unsatisfactory to both the other Western powers and the other Balkan states. This dissatisfaction immediately produced the Congress of Berlin and its consequent treaty signed on July 13, 1878.

Both before and during the Congress the British prime minister, Disraeli, was the prime mover, and his interpretation of the British interest in keeping any power as far away from the Straits as possible determined the settlement and the separate agreement by which Britain gained Cyprus. Ottoman interests were virtually ignored. The proposed Bulgarian principality was divided into three parts, the most distant part from the Straits gaining full autonomy and the closest remaining under direct Turkish rule. The middle part was granted Christian governors appointed by Constantinople but subject to the approval of the powers. Austrian acceptance of the treaty was purchased by the right to administer, but not annex, Bosnia and Herzegovina. Serbia and Montenegro, outraged at this rejection of their irredentist claim to these regions, were mollified in part by additional territory and independence, but the disregard of ethnic boundaries was to prove a fruitful source of future agitation and wars in the Balkans. Rumania also gained independence. All Russia got was the return of southern Bessarabia and some strategic districts on its Anatolian frontier. Foreseeing the need to make the last concession, the British made a separate agreement with the Ottoman government to resist any further Russian encroachments in return for the right to occupy and administer Cyprus for as long as Russia held these districts.

THE DESPOTISM OF ABUL HAMID (1876 – 1909)

Abul Hamid II and his subjects felt deeply the humiliation of defeat and the loss of territory that was in no way offset by the Bulgarian provisions of the Treaty of Berlin. Any idea of gratitude to the British for salvaging something from the wreckage and giving the Ottoman Empire a reprieve never crossed the sultan's mind; only an intense hatred and fear of the perfidious West haunted his thoughts, along with his other hates and fears. In the mind of the sultan the war and its losses had to be blamed on the liberal policies of Midhat Pasha for which the empire had been unprepared. The parliament was sent packing and Midhat was exiled to the Hijaz where in 1883 he was strangled after previous attempts to poison him had failed.

Obsessed with fear for his life—as well he might be—the sultan retreated into the seclusion of his harem and ruled for the next 30 years in an increasingly despotic fashion. An efficient system of spies and agents provocateur reflected his fears by ferreting out every sign of dissidence and crushing every conspiratorial organization. Assassination was freely used to silence suspects. No one knew whom it was safe to talk to. Christian subjects, because of their Western sympathies and promise of protection, were espe-

cially suspect. Part of the agreement with Britain was a promise to carry out reforms in the governing of the Armenians to preclude any excuse for further Russian encroachment in eastern Anatolia. This pledge, which implied a quasi-British protectorate, made the Armenians a special subject of the sultan's hatred, and their revolutionary machinations gave him an excuse to treat them harshly. Not only were few reforms carried out, but from 1894 to 1896 the sultan felt secure enough to supply arms and encouragement to the Armenians' traditional foes and upland neighbors, the Kurds, who carried out atrocious massacres. Between 10 and 25 percent of the Armenians were killed in these years. In short, this paranoiac despot was obsessed with intense anti-Western, anti-Christian, and anti-liberal fears and hatreds and consumed with the ambition as caliph to eliminate these threats to the Ottoman Empire and to Islam.

Yet, there was an obverse side to this coin. Fear of his spies had a salutary effect on his officials, inspiring less corrupt, even if more ruthless and reactionary, administration. As a result, the reactionary bureaucrats who had wedded their fortunes to Abul Hamid made more regular and larger remittances to the treasury. Fear of spies made liberally minded Turks more circumspect but also stimulated thoughts of revolution in addition to reform. In other words, Abul Hamid's suppression and oppression not only kept reformist feelings alive but tempered reformers into steel-willed revolutionaries awaiting the opportunity to implement their ideas with ruthless vigor and force.

A most important decision of the sultan was the establishment of the European debt commission in 1881 to forestall further intervention. The foreign debt, which by then had reached $1\frac{1}{4}$ billion dollars was reduced to 700 million, or approximately what the Ottoman government had received after discounts. The commission was granted control of the salt monopoly, the tobacco monopoly, the stamp tax, taxes on alcoholic beverages, fisheries, and silk production, and sundry other sources of revenue. To secure a maximum return from these resources, the commission hired foreign experts to modernize and manage production of tobacco, silk, fisheries, and vineyards. These improvements benefited the Turkish producers as well as the European bondholders.

The work of the debt commission reestablished the credit of the Ottoman government enabling the negotiation of further loans for military modernization and public works. In addition, it encouraged foreign capital, especially German, to invest in industries and railroads. Abul Hamid recognized the need for railroads to tie together his Asian territories. As German military advisors were employed because Germany was the one power that had not taken Turkish territory, so German capitalists were invited to construct railroads on a concession basis, first in 1888 from Constantinople to Ankara. In 1889 Kaiser Wilhelm II visited Constantinople, and the following year a Turko-German trade agreement was concluded.

With German military advisors and engineers came German cultural influence, which was more acceptable to the autocratic sultan than French liberalism. British and French capital was permitted to participate, but on a minority basis. Railroad construction agreements for the Anatolian Railway Company included a guaranteed minimum annual revenue per kilometer. As a result, the track tended to meander to tap as many sources of freight, including mineral concessions, as possible. In fact, revenues from the beginning exceeded the minimum guarantee. Moreover, meandering, though it reduced the speed of travel, served the purpose of reaching isolated communities and also often cut costs of construction by avoiding natural obstacles. Railroad planning, however, was significantly handicapped by international strategic interests. A proposal for a Baghdad extension that would have tapped

eastern Anatolia was quashed by Russian objection to bringing a rail line so close to the Russian frontier, and a more westerly route had to be followed. The British, alarmed at the prospect of German penetration of their Iraqi sphere by a railroad terminating at a Persian Gulf port, insisted on prolonged negotiations to secure their commercial and strategic interests and greatly delayed construction. At the outbreak of World War I the renowned "Berlin to Baghdad" railway, conceived as the foundation of Germany's "Drive to the East," had not been completed. Meanwhile, Abul Hamid undertook the construction by the government with German engineers and equipment of the Damascus to the Hijaz route for the ostensible purpose of facilitating pilgrimages to Mecca as part of his Pan-Islamic appeal. Indeed, one third of the cost was met by the voluntary contributions of devout Muslims. In addition, however, this line served the strategic purposes of tying Syria-Lebanon and western Arabia to the empire, of countering French and British influence in this region, and of releasing the empire from dependence on the sea and the Suez Canal routes for the movement of troops.

The sultan's anti-Western, anti-Christian, and antiliberal convictions naturally led him to champion a revitalization of Islam under his leadership as caliph to reverse the tide of Western encroachments on the lands and people of Islam. His Pan-Islamic dream was conceived as a means of not only unifying the Ottoman Empire but also inspiring all Muslims to a general counterattack against the West and its grasping materialism. From the 1870s Ottoman influence was gradually extended into the Arabian interior by supporting the ancestral tribal foes of the Sa'udi champion of Wahhabism. In 1891 this campaign was capped by the capture of the Sa'udi capital, Riyadh. Abul Hamid also refused to authenticate the British occupation of Egypt, mainly from fear of encouraging other interventions, and he secretly supported anti-British activity which, ironically, was generally opposed to the tradition of political autocracy practiced by the sultan and favored a constitutional representative government for an independent Egypt. Other manifestations of his Pan-Islamic attitude were the Armenian massacres, his efforts to cultivate the friendship of the Persian shah, and the war with Greece in 1897 over Crete, which his German-trained and equipped troops would easily have won if it had not been for foreign intervention. His most dramatic step, however, was getting the most dynamic propagator of Pan-Islamism, Jemal al-Din al-Afghani (1838–1896), to take up residence in Constantinople during the last five years of his life.

Jemal al-Din, supposedly born in Afghanistan, had spent his life traveling and preaching throughout Islam and the West a liberal, modernist brand of Pan-Islam emphasizing religious loyalty to the caliph but attacking autocracy as contrary to the spirit of Islam. He wanted to adapt Western science, technology, law, and political liberalism to the needs of a modernized, revitalized, and unified Islamic state capable of defending itself against Western intervention and exploitation. Twice he attempted without success to convert the Persian shah to liberal reforms, but he did gain important disciples here and elsewhere to carry on his work. In Constantinople, though he added luster to Abul Hamid's Pan-Islamism, his continued attacks on the shah led the sultan to place him under close control for the balance of his life.

By ruthless despotism, by public works and railroads, by encouraging foreign enterprise, by modernizing his military forces, and by raising the banner of Pan-Islam and hosting its popular champion, Sultan Abul Hamid II had by 1905 significantly strengthened the Ottoman Empire, but he had also by these same policies unwittingly opened his realm to even greater Western influence and fostered the secret growth of a revolutionary movement whose principal ambition was to remove him and his reactionary officials from

power. After the debacle of the Russian War, which left a permanent imprint on his mind, and the subsequent losses of Tunisia to the French and Thessaly to the Greeks in 1881, he had been strong enough and shrewd enough to prevent further territorial losses. Nevertheless, his autocratic rule had been a holding action creating widespread hostility whose harvest his successors, the Young Turks, were going to reap. Time was running out for Islamic autocracy, and his works sped the process.

EGYPT AND THE POWERS

In Egypt brief periods of anti-Western and especially anti-French reaction, supported by theologians and conservatives, characterized the short reign of Mehemet Ali's immediate successor. He was followed by the pro-French Sa'id (1854–1863), who immediately gave the syndicate headed by his friend, Ferdinand de Lesseps, a 99-year concession to build the Suez Canal, subject to the sultan's confirmation. For this favor he received preferred shares yielding 15 percent of any net profit and agreed to furnish most of the labor. The British, not anxious to see such a link with India in French hands, did everything diplomatically possible to prevent the digging of this artery, but in 1859 the work commenced, to be completed and dedicated a decade later with fantastically expensive fanfare.

At the beginning of his reign Sa'id, like the sultan, fell into the trap of foreign loans to cover the added cost of his contribution to the Crimean War—a trap Mehemet Ali had refused to step into—and his expensive tastes and practices combined with the liberal dismantling of pharaonic controls led him into further loans, creating at his death a foreign obligation of about 60 million dollars. At the same time, Western economic penetration was increased by his encouragement of foreign investments. Compared with his French-educated successor, Isma'il (1863–1879), however, he was a miser.

Isma'il's ambition to modernize Egypt much more rapidly was whetted by the tremendous profits being earned by the greatly expanded demand for, Egyptian cotton during the American Civil War. When the war-caused boom collapsed, he turned to further foreign loans both to continue his programs and to meet payments on the previously accrued debt. Most of the money raised by these loans was dissipated in poorly planned projects and personal luxury. One observer estimated that no more that 10 percent found its way into fruitful projects. A host of foreign adventurers were attracted to Egypt to take advantage of this spendthrift ruler by gaining concessions and then filing suit for breach of contract or some other legal technicality. To meet this problem, mixed tribunals were set up to serve as a model for the introduction in 1883 of a Western-style law code for all cases except those of personal status still judged in religious courts. Another financial blunder was the agreement in 1866 to double the annual tribute paid to the sultan in return for the relatively meaningless title of Khedive. In an effort to meet the rapidly expanding expenses, taxation on the peasantry was increased fivefold. On the credit side, Isma'il increased from 185 to 4817 the number of public schools, built railways and telegraph lines, created a modern postal system, and brought modern amenities to his capital. On the debit side, he employed increasing numbers of Turkish-speaking Turko-Circassians in the government and the army, alienating the Arabic-speaking Egyptians, and took further steps toward free enterprise that permitted alien moneylenders to exploit the peasantry and build landed estates.

The story of the Egyptian march into bankruptcy is tragically similar in time and technique to that of the Ottoman government, but the results were even more disastrous. By 1875 the Khedive needed 20 million dollars just to meet that year's installment on the debt and sold his 44 percent interest in the canal to Disraeli's government to cover the sum. The following year he was totally unable to pay the interest and amortization on the heavily discounted debt of some one half billion and had no choice but to accept an Anglo-French commission for the management of the foreign debt. In 1879, on the grounds of obstruction and covert encouragement of opposition to their measures, the receivers obtained Abul Hamid's reluctant consent to Isma'il's deposition in favor of his son, Tewfik (1879–1892).

EGYPTIAN NATIONALISM

The introduction of Western-style education by Mehemet Ali and his successors created a small intellectual class of Egyptians who increasingly resented their subordination to aliens, whether Turko-Circassian or European. This resentment was particularly strong in the army among the soldiers and junior officers, only a few of whom had recently gained the higher commissions reserved for Turko-Circassians. Some had studied at al-Azhar, the most vital center of Arabic study, where they had listened to the anti-Western and Pan-Islamic teaching of Jemal al-Din. In 1877 Egyptian nationalism gained a vehicle of expression in the first nationalist newspaper. This intellectual elite had the support of a growing discontent among the peasants oppressed by heavy taxation and exploited by aliens. Isma'il's improvement and expansion of communications not only exposed more Egyptians to Western contacts but also facilitated the organization and planning of Egyptian opposition.

To cut costs for the benefit of the foreign creditors, the government at the behest of the Anglo-French commission ordered a drastic reduction in the size of the army. The retirement of 2000 officers without settlement of a year's arrears of pay set off a riot of officers in 1879 forcing the resignation of the ministry, but the consequent replacement of Isma'il with Tewfik only left the Anglo-French commissioners in greater control than before. Nationalist discontent and agitation grew until in 1881 the Khedive, fearful of a rebellion led by the Egyptian officers, agreed to a nationalist-dominated ministry in which Colonel Ahmed Arabi held the important post of Under-Secretary of War.

Colonel Arabi, the son of a small farmer and village shaykh, had studied theology at al-Azhar where he had become acquinted with the liberal movement. Thus, as an anti-Turko-Circassian army officer, as an anti-Western champion of a revitalized Islam, as an advocate of constitutional representative government, and as a man of peasant origin he could rally the support of all discontented elements from the intellectual elite to the peasantry for a strong nationalist movement under the slogan, "Egypt for the Egyptians." The hitherto ineffectual Council of Notables even dared to challenge the Anglo-British commissioners, by voting an independent budget.

Such a threat to the foreign management of Egyptian finances stirred the French government to suggest joint intervention to the British. Although Gladstone's Liberal government was reluctant to take such a step, it agreed when anti-Western activities increased rather than diminished. In February, 1882, Tewfik was forced to accept a full-fledged nationalist ministry. When Colonel Arabi, as War Minister, planned an enlarged army under the command of Egyptian officers, the British and French governments foresaw a complete nullification of their economic reforms and the prospect of anti-Western outbreaks of violence. Naval forces were ordered to Alexandria, the Khedive was asked to dismiss the nationalist regime, and the Ottoman government as suzerain was invited to intervene. Indeed, now that a new French government proved less eager to act, Britain offered to submit the Egyptian problem to a conference of the Western powers at Constantinople. Gladstone, whose liberal principles condemned foreign adventures, was anxious to avoid unilateral action, but the course of events in Egypt forced his hand.

The dismissal of the nationalist regime only stimulated antiforeign feeling in support of Colonel Arabi, manifested in a series of incidents. In the mixed city of Alexandria, headquarters for most of the foreign element, a bloody outbreak in June, following the stabbing of an Egyptian donkey boy by a British Maltese subject, resulted in the deaths of 57 Europeans and 140 Egyptians. Anticipating retaliation, Colonel Arabi rushed the construction of fortifications for the city. When he ignored a British ultimatum to cease these defensive preparations, his fortifications were bombarded on July 11 and a landing party forced him to retire from the city. On the excuse of defense of the Suez Canal, British troops landed at the terminal cities and advanced against Colonel Arabi's "rebel" forces. Near Cairo his army was routed and he was exiled to Ceylon. Thus ended the first Egyptian nationalist effort, though the nationalist movement continued to develop under new leaders during the British occupation.

THE BRITISH OCCUPATION OF EGYPT

Great Britain declared the intention of evacuating Egypt as soon as conditions warranted it, but promptly renounced, much to France's chagrin, the joint management of Egyptian finances and posted Evelyn Baring (later Lord Cromer) of the renowned family of international financiers, as resident consul-general, and de facto ruler of Egypt with the backing of British troops from 1883 to 1907. British management of Egypt has been aptly described as Egyptian hands directed by British civil servants with the overriding objective of creating a viable economy for the repayment of foreign debts. While this economic theme was dominant and interference with Egyptian customs and practices was kept, as in India, to a minimum, the British conscience did lead to some significant social and political reforms.

On the economic side, the foreign debt

and administrative costs were pared down to manageable proportions. Constructive expenditures to increase agricultural production notably included the Delta Barrage (1890) and the low Aswan Dam (1902). As a result of British management, exports and imports tripled during this period. The greatest cost-cutting measure, however, was the evacuation of the Sudan where a fanatical rising against Egyptian oppression had broken out in 1881 under the inspired leadership of the self-proclaimed Mahdi. He had already wiped out an Egyptian army and its British commander before "Chinese" Gordon was dispatched to carry out the evacuation. On the scene, Gordon's humanitarian instincts were so stirred by the atrocities committed on the local inhabitants by the Mahdi's forces that he pleaded for reinforcements to break them and restore a measure of order before carrying out the withdrawal. Gladstone's government, however, was opposed to this plan and delayed sending a relief expedition until it was too late. Just before the relief column arrived, General Gordon and his garrison were overwhelmed at Khartoum in January 1885. More than a decade later this blot on the British escutcheon was removed by the campaigns from 1896 to 1898 commanded by Lord Kitchener, which resulted in the Anglo-Egyptian Condominium (Joint Sovereignty) over the Sudan with Britain as the senior partner.

On the side of social and political reform, with economic overtones, were the abolition of the ancient practice of forced labor, tax reductions in favor of the most hard-pressed peasants, and an assembly with 14 nominated and 16 elected members. This assembly, however, had little power other than to deliberate on and approve governmental measures submitted to it. The British advisors, almost without exception, made all the decisions and oversaw their implementation. In contrast to India, the British did little to foster higher education as a preparation for self-government, except secondary schooling primarily to train civil ser-

vants. Local law and government were left undisturbed in Egyptian hands, British officials intervening only occasionally to prevent gross abuse.

THE REVIVAL OF EGYPTIAN NATIONALISM

The nationalist and reformist movements with their leaders in exile were forced underground, not to reemerge until the accession of the less cooperative Khedive, Abbas II (1892–1914), and the natural liberal inclination of the British brought about a relaxation of controls. Already refugees from the growing repression of Abul Hamid had found a haven in Egypt. Between 1892 and 1900 newspapers published in Egypt increased almost fivefold reflecting the growth of a literate middle class. Three broad schools of thought, not mutually exclusive, can be identified: a Pan-Islamic movement secretly sponsored by Abul Hamid; an Egyptian nationalist movement led by the French-educated Mustafa Kamil and also supported by Abul Hamid and, until the 1904 Anglo-French entente, by the French as well; and finally the reformist movement led by Jemal al-Din's disciple, Muhammed Abduh (1849–1905). The first tended to blend into the second and, under the auspices of Western-educated refugees from Syria and Palestine, to take on a Pan-Arabicist flavor, a preview of the doctrine of today's Egyptian leadership. The publishing activities of Lebanese immigrants, many of whom were Christians, played a major role in Egyptian political and intellectual development. Thus the bond of nationalism was being reduced from the larger and more awkward compass of a common religion to the smaller compass of a common language, Arabic. This shift also made it possible to include non-Muslims, such as the Lebanese Christians.

The more provincial champion, Mustafa Kamil, who had gained recognition for his anti-British crusade while still in Paris, returned to Egypt about 1895, formed the Nationalist Party, and founded a training school for political activists taking up Arabi's slogan of "Egypt for the Egyptians" to describe the initial goal of ridding Egypt of alien oppressors, especially the British occupation. Secondary, but less clearly delineated, Kamil's aims included some form of constitutional government.

Although Lord Cromer was not opposed to orderly evolution toward independence, he was repelled by the emotionalism and radicalism of Kamil's Nationalist party and program, which boded ill for all Europeans, and tended to favor the more moderate Reform Party formed by Muhammed Abuh. Abuh had studied theology at al-Azhar at the time Jemal al-Din was teaching there and became one of his chief disciples, later editing an Arabic newspaper in Paris with him. His dislike of excessive Westernization had swept him into Arabi's revolt for which he suffered exile. Like Jemal al-Din he saw the need to adopt Western science and technology, but unlike his master, whose fundamentalist interpretation of Islam presumed a permanent spiritual opposition to the West, he advocated an intellectual and spiritual rejuvenation by opening the long-closed "gate of interpretation." By this means he sought to bridge the gap between traditional Islam and the realities of the modern world and to minimize the contradictions between the two. As rector of al-Azhar and mufti of Egypt he taught and practiced his more flexible interpretation of Islamic law and doctrine by finding new meanings in the Qur'an and the *hadith* on which the structure of Islam had been built. In short, by reinterpretation he proposed to modernize the social, economic, cultural, and religious structure of Islamic society as the *shari'a* schools had previously done to accommodate Islam to the world it had conquered. By this fresh approach he opened the door for theological adaptation to the modern world—a door that is still only partly opened. His moderation led him to deprecate the use of violence. Indeed, he generally tried to distinguish between religious and political reforms arguing that the one was not essentially linked to the other. Thus he left room for a secular nationalism outside the larger realm of religious loyalty to Islam. In other words, political reform was put in the same class as Western science and technology to be judged separately from the vital issue of Islam.

The Anglo-French Entente of 1904, by recognizing the exclusive British interest in Egypt and the Sudan in return for a free hand in Morocco, terminated French aid to the Nationalist Party. But this loss of support was more than offset the next year by the wave of optimism and increase in indigenous support generated by news of Japan's victory over Russia, one of the chief aggressors against the Middle East. In 1906 the intensity of nationalistic, anti-British sentiment was illustrated by the furious popular reaction to a minor incident. And the following year the British Liberal government saw fit to instruct Lord Cromer's replacement to liberalize the government of Egypt, even at the cost of diminished efficiency.

IRAN

The remoteness of the land of the Shiite shahs did not exempt it from undergoing the economic penetration and territorial imperialism of the West, the growth of a Western-educated elite interested in finding a solution to the country's impotence, and the development of a small literate middle class engaged in business with the Western interests. The degree of influence, however, was less because only two powers, Russia and Britain, were contestants; because, until the discovery of oil, the exploitable resources seemed comparatively meager; and because, though militarily powerless, the rulers of this historically strategic region could maintain their sovereignty by playing Britain's fear of Russian imperialism off against Russia's expansionist policy. Russian seizure of tribal territories in Turkestan could not be prevented, but the British could be depended on to oppose any threat to the territory of Iran proper. During the long reign of Nasir al-Din (1848–1896) foreign control of Iran's economy was greatly expanded, but the pitfall of foreign loans was eluded until 1892 and, along with it, the consequent march to bankruptcy and foreign receivership.

As a representative of the weak Qajar dynasty that ruled in collaboration with the tribal chieftains, the great landlords, and the Shiite hierarchy, Nasir al-Din was comparatively able, recognizing the need of gaining Western knowledge and techniques to strengthen his power and that of the state. At the beginning of his reign, with the aid of an incorruptible minister, he unsuccessfully attempted to assert his authority. The one enduring fruit of this effort was the permanent institute, the Dar al-Funun, where Austrian instructors provided future army officers and government officials, mostly scions of the aristocracy, with the rudiments of Western learning. In connection with this secondary school, basic Western works, especially scientific studies, were translated. But the overall reform program was frustrated by the united opposition of the secular and ecclesiastical elites. Popular discontent with the oppression of the hierarchy in church and state was indicated in popular writings and the wide appeal of the antiecclesiastical Babist movement, but the shah was unable to capitalize on this unrest to gain support for his modernization program. In fact, he was compelled to execute a bloody suppression of the subversive Babists. Power still resided with the hierarchy, not with the people. Throughout this era Persian journalism within Iran was limited to a few, short-lived, government-controlled sheets; only abroad could progressive Persian journals secure publication, such as those edited by Jemal al-Din al-Afghani.

In 1856 a successful campaign to regain control of Afghanistan was frustrated by a British declaration of war commanding withdrawal from what was deemed an important buffer state against threats to British India.

The treaty of the following year, in addition to specifying the independence of Afghanistan, gave Britain full capitulary privileges, opening Iran to British trade and economic penetration. Henceforth Iran was no more than a helpless pawn in the Anglo-Russian rivalry for power. One by one the Iranian dependencies in Turkestan—Tashkent, Samarkand, Khiva, Bukhara, and Merv—were picked off by Russia until the process was virtually completed in 1882. The shah tried to learn about the West and to check its advances by direct negotiations in European visits in 1873, 1887, and 1889. Although he saw and learned a great deal, he could not alter the circumstances and only incurred by his travels expenses that led to the first foreign loan. Direct aggression ceased, but only because Russia had satisfied its territorial ambitions in this direction for the time being and now sought to build up internal influence in emulation of the British. Britain, on the other hand, had no interest in strengthening Iran, which it viewed as a potential threat to India. It was satisfied to keep it a no-man's-land, dominated by British economic interests.

Twice the shah invited Jemal al-Din to advise and assist in the institution of a reform program, but on both occasions his guest's popularity proved too great to endure, especially among the *mujtahids* who headed the religious hierarchy and were incensed at the shah's open-minded support of Christian missions, his concessions to Western economic interests, and his attempts to curb their influence. On the last occasion in 1889 Jemal al-Din was fortunate to escape with his life after being driven out of a shrine to which he had fled for sanctuary. From Basra in Iraq he continued to attack the autocracy of the shah and the grant of a tobacco monopoly to European capitalists to cover his mounting debts. From a *mujtahid* Jemal secured a *fetwa* forbidding the use of tobacco as long as the monopoly was in European hands. This boycott, supported by the Shiite hierarchy, was so effective that the shah had to buy back the tobacco monopoly. When the shah was assassinated in 1896, Jemal, then in Constantinople, was suspected as the prime mover of the plot.

Following the 1857 treaty, British concession hunters converged on Iran, as well as other areas of the East, and the Church Missionary Society stepped up its educational and medical activities in southern Iran, the region under strongest British influence, setting up missions in the fabled cities of Kerman, Yezd, Shiraz, and Isfahan. Roman Catholic and American missionary work in central and northern Iran was also expanded with the blessing and support of the shah. Besides winning acceptance by their medical care, their educational activity greatly broadened the spectrum of Western cultural influence inducing many more students, mostly from prominent families, to go abroad for further study. In this way the small number of graduates of the Dar al-Funun acquainted with Western culture was greatly supplemented, creating broader acceptance of the need for modernization. Most Western-educated aristocrats continued to support the vested interests of their families, but they became increasingly dissatisfied with the impotence of the Qajar dynasty—an impotence that they were unwilling to relate to the continuance of their families' special privileges and interests. The spread of Western cultural influence, however, should not be exaggerated. It was spotty, largely limited to the cities, and not significant in extent until near the end of the century. Nevertheless, it was important in its cumulative effect, even if the peasantry was almost untouched by it.

An early major concession was granted to the British in 1864 for a telegraph line that would ultimately provide a direct connection with London. In the belief that Iran's weakness could be overcome by the swiftest possible introduction of Western technology and financial methods, the shah in 1872 granted a tremendous set of concessions to a persuasive British banker, one of a horde of ambitious concession hunters who inundated Teheran upon learning of the shah's receptiveness. Among the many broad concessions in this agreement were the right to build railroads, the right to develop minerals and oil for 70 years, the right to create a national bank, and the right to manage the customs service for 24 years. If these grants had been put into effect, Iran would have been totally reduced to an economic satellite of Britain. The shah, however, in the course of his first European tour the following year discovered such overt hostility at the Russian court to this package of concessions that he repudiated it upon his return. Subsequently he placated the disappointed British banker by lesser concessions, the most important of which was a charter in 1889 for the establishment of the Imperial Bank of Persia. As was already noted, the grant in 1890 of a tobacco monopoly to a British concern aroused the Shiite clergy to spearhead a nationwide boycott that was so effective that the shah was compelled to buy it back. This repurchase, in addition to other debts incurred, particularly in connection with his tours of Europe, forced the shah to negotiate his first foreign loan in 1892.

Generally, it may be asserted that the successive shahs' efforts to strengthen their regimes and modernize the state, particularly by infringing on the legal jurisdiction of the Shiite hierarchy, created a negative attitude and sullen resentment toward all foreign encroachments. The reaction to the Anglo-Russian struggle for influence in the country may be characterized as a public feeling of "a plague on both your houses" which, on occasion, even after World War II has been expressed in an explosive fashion.

In contrast to the essentially defensive stance of the British, supplemented by peaceful economic penetration, the Russian approach to Iran has been more militant and aggressive in pursuance of its imperialistic ambitions. From 1865 to 1882 Russia was primarily engaged in seizing the Turcoman territories of Iran east of the Caspian Sea. In

1879, however, the shah agreed to the formation in the north of a Persian version of the cossacks, trained and commanded by Russian officers. Before long this unit was the most effective military force in the country. Control of the Caspian Sea was another Russian objective. In 1888 a Russian gained a comprehensive fishing concession, and later a naval base was secured on its southeastern extremity. Russia, alarmed at British financial dominance, presaged by the Imperial Bank, obtained the right to open in 1891 the Discount Bank of Persia.

While Nasir al-Din in his Westernizing policy had attempted to maintain a measure of balance between Russia and Britain, his indolent and spendthrift successor, Muzaffar al-Din (1896–1907), fell under increasing Russian influence, much to the distress of the British and Iranians who feared an emancipation of the shah from the restraints on his power through Russian aid and even a possible sellout of the country. In 1900 a Russian loan of 22 million rubles specified the repayment of all other foreign loans and an agreement not to contract further loans without Russian consent. After paying off outstanding debts and the costs of an expensive European tour, only 6 million rubles were left. Russia promptly extended another loan of 10 million rubles. Meanwhile, Russian domination was further assured by agreements allowing Russia to extend roads into northern Iran, prohibiting railroad concessions to others, and providing a discriminatory tariff in favor of Russian trade.

The fears generated by these actions created the broader base of opposition needed to support the Western-educated liberals' long-held dream of establishing constitutional government. Agitation for a constitution gained the support of some of the religious hierarchy and a few nobles, as well as many merchants whose trade and profits were endangered by the preferential tariff. Naturally, British agents, both public and private, encouraged and aided the agitation as much as they could. The constitu-

tional movement probably would not have been fruitful, however, if it had not been for the catalytic effect of the Russian defeat by Japan in 1905. To the amazement of the Iranians the Russian colossus had been crushed by an Asian people and was internally torn by its own constitutional revolution. The next year, by stopping all economic and public activity in the capital and by retreating to the safety of the British embassy, the reformers and their religious and mercantile allies compelled the shah to proclaim the constitution. The first step toward the creation of a modern nation was thus taken thanks to the temporary alliance of divergent interests and to fortuitous circumstances, but the realization of this dream of an enlightened few was to prove extremely difficult to implement in this ancient land wedded to ancient ways.

By 1856 the Middle East had been fully exposed to the whole spectrum of Western influence, including armed interventions and territorial losses, but only the rulers and a few others yet recognized the need for change and modernization. In 1856 the extent of Western cultural influence was still limited to a very few.

In the next half century the peoples of the Middle East became more and more frustrated at the inability of their rulers to uphold the standard of Islam against the growing pressure of the infidels. More territory was lost. Economic penetration undermined the walls of Islam bringing Westerners into the interior, heavy indebtedness, and even bankruptcy to the Ottoman and Egyptian regimes. The final humiliation was the British occupation of Egypt in behalf of the Western creditors. Cultural penetration grew under the auspices of reformers and reactionaries alike in their desperate efforts to defend Islam against Western assault.

Reaction to the growing Western impact took various forms. First, it is only proper to note that the great mass of the people, struggling to stay alive, knew and cared little or nothing about the West, even though its activities may have affected their livelihood most seriously; only the very few with some knowledge of the West looked beyond their immediate horizons and sought some sort of solution. Reactionaries in church and state continued to reject the West and all it represented as a threat to the traditional order and their particular vested interests in it. Some reactionaries, however, like Sultan Abdul Hamid, were willing to adopt those material attributes accountable for Western wealth and power to build strength for a future counterattack. Abdul Hamid in particular appealed as caliph to all Muslims to accept his authoritarian leadership as the titular head of Islam and to prepare to repel the infidels. Another champion of Pan-Islamic unity and Western technology, Jemal al-Din, attacked autocracy and advocated a liberal constitutional form of government. His disciple, Muhammed Abduh, decried the appeal to religious emotionalism and favored instead the reform of Islam by rational reinterpretation of its positions to conform with the needs of the times. Furthermore, he sought to keep religion and politics separate from each other. Not far removed from this position were the Western-educated reformers who pragmatically supported the introduction of whatever devices and institutions might strengthen the state and its people. The spectrum of their views extended from moderate administrative reform and the adoption of Western technology to radical reform involving the wholesale introduction of Western social, economic, cultural, and political conceptions and practices, especially representative constitutional government and some form of nationalism. Finally, a growing number of would-be reformers, frustrated at their inability to secure from their rulers the desired reforms and at continued encroachment by the West, became revolutionaries conspiring to accomplish their goals by force. Their successes were to come in the years after 1905.

News of the Japanese victory over Russia demonstrated beyond doubt what success a non-Western people could achieve through modernization. A new wave of optimism coursed through the Middle East preparing the way for a broader acceptance of change. The path ahead, as will be seen, was strewn with boulders, but of greater importance, a new hope and enthusiasm had supplanted in many minds the previous mood of frustration and despair.

SIGNIFICANT DATES

1839	Tanzimat reform decree
1854	First Ottoman foreign loan
1854–1856	Crimean War
1856	New Ottoman reform decree
1856	Persian capitulary treaty with Great Britain
1869	Opening of Suez Canal
1875–1876	Balkan rebellions and Ottoman insolvency
1876	Coup d'état of Midhat Pasha: accession of Abul Hamid II: proclamation of constitution
1877–1878	Russo-Turkish War: Congress of Berlin
1881	French seizure of Tunisia: loss of Thessaly to Greece
1882	British occupation of Egypt
1885	Destruction of "Chinese" Gordon at Khartoum
1889	Flight of Jemal al-Din from Persia
1890	Persian concession of tobacco monopoly
1892	First Persian foreign loan

1896–1898   Lord Kitchener regains Sudan: Anglo-Egyptian condominium
1900   Exclusive Russian loan to Persia
1904   Anglo-French entente
1906   Proclamation of Persian constitution

SELECTED READINGS

Ahmed, Jamal Mohammed, *The Intellectual Origins of Egyptian Nationalism*. London: Oxford University Press, 1960.

Baring, Evelyn, Earl of Cromer, *Modern Egypt*. 2 vols.; New York: Macmillan, 1909.

Berkes, Niyazi, *The Development of Secularism in Turkey*. Montreal: McGill University Press, 1964.

Berque, Jacques, *French North Africa*. London: Faber & Faber, 1967.

Blunt, Wilfred S., *Secret History of the English Occupation of Egypt*. New York: Howard Fertig, 1967.

Grunebaum, Gustave E. von, *Modern Islam: The Search for Cultural Identity*. Berkeley: University of California Press, 1962.

*Hourani, Albert, *Arabic Thought in the Liberal Age, 1798–1939*. London: Oxford University Press, 1970.

Kedourie, Elie, *Afghani and 'Abduh*. London: Cass, 1966.

Lerner, Daniel, *The Passing of Traditional Society: Modernizing the Middle East*. Glencoe, Ill.: Free Press, 1958.

Safran, Nadav, *Egypt in Search of Political Community*. Cambridge, Mass.: Harvard University Press, 1961.

*Smith, Wilfrid Cantwell, *Islam in Modern History*. New York: Mentor Book, 1959.

Tignor, Robert L., *Modernization and British Colonial Rule in Egypt, 1882–1914*. Princeton: Princeton University Press, 1966.

*Vucinich, Wayne S., *The Ottoman Empire: Its Record and Legacy*. New York: Van Nostrand Reinhold, 1965.

Zeine, N. Zeine, *Arab-Turkish Relations and the Emergence of Arab Nationalism*. Beirut: Khayat's, 1958.

CHAPTER NINETEEN

COLONIAL SOUTHEAST ASIA TO 1905

The rise of civilizations in this buffer region between the major civilizations of India and China was described in Chapter Seven. From the beginning it was subjected to influences radiating from its great neighbors, but it accommodated them to its own traditions and beliefs creating distinctive cultural amalgams. During the period from the fifteenth to the twentieth century Southeast Asia continued to come under influences from abroad: the spread of Islam and Islamic culture and the more pervasive impact of the West and Western imperialism.

Islam, suitably modified to fit local beliefs and customs, captured the souls of most of the peoples of Malaya and Indonesia, and was making significant gains in the Philippines until it was checked by militant Spanish Catholicism. In the rest of mainland Southeast Asia the established Buddhist doctrines proved relatively immune to the appeals of both Islam and Christianity. Indeed, outside the Philippines Christianity gained few converts, except among primitive peoples.

Western imperialism, however, which reached its greatest intensity after the opening of the Suez Canal in 1869, overran the entire region and subjugated its peoples with the exception of Siam, which was able to play the French off against the British and save most of its territory. Moreover, the economy of each conquered land became increasingly tied to that of the ruling country and its European market. Native reaction, led by the Western-educated elite, was slow in developing and, prior to 1905, achieved organized expression only in the Philippines, the first Southeast Asian country to be subjugated in detail. Another observation was the inability of any of the "twilight" civilizations to radiate an influence of their own outside the confines of Southeast Asia.

MALACCA AND ISLAM

Muslim merchants, both Arab and Persian, had pursued direct trade with Southeast Asia with varying vigor since the seventh century, but had demonstrated little missionary zeal. Prior to the fifteenth century only a couple of city-states in northwestern Sumatra had been converted to the faith. During the fourteenth century the Islamic conquests in India produced conversions to a compatible Sufi-type mysticism among merchants engaged in the Southeast Asian trade of the Gujarāt, Bengal, and Tamil areas. The traders of the first two enjoyed a special advantage because their regions manufactured cotton cloth, a highly desired commodity in Southeast Asia. Each Sufi group under its own inspired shaykh radiated the high morale and infectious zeal of new converts. During the fourteenth century, following the collapse of Shrivijaya and the decline of Mongol prestige, trade via the Malacca strait became extremely hazardous and most merchants preferred the more difficult route via the Sunda strait. In addition, Mongol domination had diverted the bulk of the trade with China to the overland route through central Asia. Revival of the seaborne transit trade depended on the deterioration of Mongol control of the land route and the reassertion of control by some power over the Malacca strait.

The latter end was achieved by the city-state of Malacca, established in 1401 as a significant power at the narrowest point in the passage by a refugee Sumatran noble who had incurred the enmity of both the Thai ruler and the strong Javan successor state of Majapahit. Outside of its strategic location, Malacca was not a promising site. The port was poor and the hinterland could not produce the food to support much of a pop-

Southeast Asia, 1800–1905

ulation. Survival alone depended on finding external support to counter the hostility of the powerful Thai and Javan states. Fortunately, the Malaccan ruler gained the backing of Ming China, which sent naval expeditions to assert Chinese suzerainty along the sea route between 1403 and 1438, by granting preferred treatment to Chinese merchants. The Thai ruler, who had wisely acknowledged Chinese suzerainty, was instructed to give up his claim to suzerainty over southern Malaya. At the same time, Muslim merchants were invited to use the strait, instead of exchanging cargoes at the Muslim city-states of northern Sumatra. Finally, the founder of the Malaccan state accepted conversion to Islam sometime before his death in 1414. By the time Ming naval ambitions waned in the 1430s, Malacca was strong enough to fend off Thai attacks with its contingents of mercenaries paid out of the profits of a prospering trade.

For a century, until the Portuguese conquest in 1511, Muslim Malacca thrived as the entrepot of the Southeast Asian and transit trade. Not only did it provide protection for vessels negotiating the difficult strait, but it also attracted trade by its comparatively low port charges and assessments. In addition to the Chinese ships that brought their cargoes to Malacca for sale, it also collected from Javan intermediaries the highly valued spices of the East Indies for sale to merchants from the west. Each major community in Malacca was regulated by a superintendent according to its particular law and customs, and the population was extremely cosmopolitan in composition, attracted by the diversity of economic opportunities. From this base Islam, with its egalitarian appeal, gradually spread to other ports in Malaya and the Indies in proportion to the volume of trade. Conversion of port rulers was often inspired by the political motive of asserting a measure of independence from Buddhist or Hindu overlords of the interior. The broad advance of Islam, however, occurred after the Portuguese conquest of Malacca and sometimes reflected a reaction to Portuguese ruthlessness and abuses. Like its Hindu and Buddhist predecessors, Islam in the East Indies had to make compromises with the native cultures. In Java, for example, it was unable to supplant the customary law, belief in local spirits, and traditional magical practices.

THE ADVENT OF THE WEST: PORTUGUESE AND SPANISH

Southeast Asia has been described as "the crossroads of religion"; but where Buddhism, Hinduism, or Islam were established, Christianity made little headway. The European impact was greater in the military and economic realms, and with the exception of the comparatively undeveloped Philippines, it did not reach major proportions until the last half of the nineteenth century. Again, with the exception of the Spanish in the Philippines, European interest in Southeast Asia concentrated on the exploitation of trade in tropical products, at first spices and then plantation crops and mineral resources. Until the twentieth century the imperial powers demonstrated little interest in advancing the welfare of their subjects, and even then this concern was expressed in a reluctant and modest fashion largely in re-

action to anti-imperialist manifestations of discontent.

Although some Portuguese officers foresaw the possibility of overextending their resources, Vasco da Gama's voyage to India was rapidly exploited under the dynamic leadership of the second viceroy, Alphonso de Albuquerque (1509–1515). Recognizing the importance of Malacca as the key to the spice trade, he promptly dispatched a naval force that he perhaps hoped would provoke hostility. If this was his aim, he was not disappointed, but retaliation was delayed a year by other pressing problems. In June 1511, he appeared off Malacca with 18 ships and 1400 men, 600 of whom were Indians trained in Western arms. To attack a fortified city the size of Malacca with such a small force might seem foolhardy, but the Portuguese had already learned that their better-built ships and superior gunnery were more than a match for the much larger forces confronting them. Furthermore, they were fired with a fervent ardor to destroy such a stronghold of Islam. Finally, they were aided by some Chinese and Javanese residents unhappy at unfair treatment by the sultan. Even though the attackers were outnumbered 15 to 1, the city fell in August along with its 3000 artillery pieces. Indiscriminate slaughter and looting of Muslims followed, though the Hindu, Buddhist, and Chinese population was spared, as well as the Javanese mercenaries who had defected. Then followed a forced draft refortification before Albuquerque left in February 1512, leaving a garrison of 600 men and 8 ships. As elsewhere, the Portuguese were urged to take native wives to gain converts and produce a future generation of loyal subjects.

Initially the Portuguese sought to emulate the Muslim technique for controlling the trade attracted to Malacca, but opposition and cupidity soon led them to use their superior strength to pursue the trade directly instead of through intermediaries. Portuguese captains bypassed Javanese ports, much to their detriment, to secure spices directly in the Spice Islands, by force when necessary. Efforts to trade directly with China at first backfired, but by 1557 they had been granted their base at Macao. General hatred of the Portuguese was generated by their violent gunboat tactics in the East Indies, while Portuguese soldiers of fortune commanding artillery units gained employment in the armed forces of the mainland states of Southeast Asia. As predicted, Portugal exhausted its human resources in its belligerent trading policy and, by ignoring the welfare of the people, secured no local support to confront other European interlopers when they appeared on the scene.

Spanish interest in the Philippines was stimulated by Magellan's death there while commanding the first circumnavigation of the globe. A dispute over whether these islands and the Spice Islands south of them fell within the Spanish area of exploitation laid down by papal decree led to subsequent expeditions that were frustrated by the Portuguese or natural hazards until 1565. By 1571 Manila was captured from a Muslim ruler and established as the capital of the new territory.

Before the arrival of the Spanish the Philippines were peripheral to Southeast Asia and culturally, politically, and economically undeveloped. Islam had only recently converted the coastal peoples of the southern island of Mindanao and begun to set up scattered outposts in the ports of the islands to the north. A few Chinese merchants had carried on an erratic trade with various parts of the islands, but lack of valuable products to exchange limited its volume. Some Hindu concepts of divine kingship had entered, but the culture was essentially primitive, following animistic and ancestral beliefs in good and evil spirits. Therefore, it offered little resistance to the vigorous propagation of Christianity that was the avowed central goal of the Spanish crown. In Spanish America the spiritual welfare of the Indians had been subordinated to the cupidity of Spanish adventurers. Such was not to be the case in the Philippines, which were designated as a spiritual preserve for the labors of the various monastic orders. At least material considerations were supposed to be subordinated to the counter-Reformation goal of advancing the frontiers of Roman Catholic Christendom.

From the Philippine base missionaries went forth to Indo-China, China, and Japan achieving varying degrees of success. Within the islands, the religious orders, supported by troops, gradually converted the majority of the people, building churches as the most prominent structures in every village. Only the Muslim "Moros" of Mindanao and the more primitive tribesmen in their mountain fastnesses remained outside the orbit of the church. Such extensive occupation of the land and conversion of the people was a unique European accomplishment in the East. For nearly $2\frac{1}{2}$ centuries Spanish Roman Catholic culture permeated the life of the Filipinos making them a people apart, even though native customs and beliefs were never more than superficially suppressed and much blending took place.

In addition to the predominance of churchmen, a major deterrent to the economic development of the Philippines was its location. The only feasible means of communication with the rest of the Spanish world was by ship from Acapulco in Mexico. Since the subsistence economy of the islands produced little of value for trade, Mexican silver had to be diverted from royal coffers to pay for Chinese goods brought to Manila by Chinese merchants. Therefore, economic considerations as well as the dedication of the islands to spiritual endeavor led the Spanish government to limit this trade as much as possible. Licenses for space on the annual Acapulco galleon were further restricted by the rule that the licensee must accompany his cargo. The outward passage to Manila was comparatively easy, but the great circle route back to Acapulco was plagued with storms and many galleons were lost, further limiting interest in the trade to the most adventurous.

Indeed, the hazards of the voyage from Spain limited the number of settlers, few of whom ever returned to their homeland.

Not until the loss of the Spanish colonies in the Americas in the early nineteenth century did the Spanish government relax its monopoly of trade with a consequent increase in its volume and the development of a small middle class, mostly of mixed blood. By the second half of the nineteenth century the discontent of this educated elite with Spanish restrictions on their activities combined with the discontent of Filipino churchmen at their exclusion from the upper echelons of the ecclesiastical hierarchy to produce a rash of religiously oriented rebellions and the growth of national feeling. By fostering political and cultural unification the Spanish rulers were hoisted on their own petard through the generation of a national movement demanding, before the Spanish-American War, a larger role in their own government and even independence. Thus Spanish colonial policy in the Philippines produced the first vigorous expression of nationalism in Southeast Asia. The American successors to Spanish rule were destined to inherit this problem.

THE DUTCH AND THE ENGLISH

In 1580 two events presaged the rise of Dutch and English interest in Southeast Asia: an edict prohibiting the purchase of spices by Dutch rebels at Lisbon, which had just fallen into the hands of the Spanish king, and Sir Francis Drake's return from a marauding voyage around the world with a rich cargo of spices from the East Indies. The actual invasion of this Spanish-Portuguese preserve, however, was delayed for 15 years by several factors. First, the prohibition of Dutch spice purchases was not effectively enforced until 1594, and English energies were absorbed in the conflict with Spain that began with the Spanish Armada in 1588. Second, a detailed sailing manual of Asia with maps by a Dutch traveler was not

published until 1595 and not translated into English until 1598. In the last 5 years of the century a dozen Dutch expeditions were undertaken with minimal success until a 22-ship squadron during 1598–1600 completed a voyage by way of the Cape of Good Hope and the Sunda Strait, earning a fabulous profit. By this route they bypassed the Portuguese strongholds of Goa, Ceylon, and Malacca, sailing directly to the Spice Islands whose inhabitants were eager to do business with any competitor of the brutal Portuguese. In 1602 the Dutch East India Company was formed to finance a systematic development of the spice trade at Portuguese expense. Although the English East India Company had been chartered on the last day of 1600, it was essentially a private operation commanding only a tenth of the assets of the Dutch Company. Therefore, from the beginning it was a small, opportunistic operation, leaving to the Dutch the responsibility for a direct and forceful challenge to the Portuguese position.

In 1602, operating from their base at Bantam in western Java, the Dutch decisively defeated a 30-ship Portuguese fleet and by 1614 had broken Portuguese power, though the stronghold of Malacca did not surrender until 1641 after a long and bloody siege. Meanwhile, the Dutch systematically developed their control of trade from their permanent Javanese headquarters at Batavia.

In contrast with the Portuguese, the experienced and shrewd Dutch merchants gave primary consideration to the development of intra-Asian trade to provide a sound foundation for the few ships that made the annual voyage between Holland and Southeast Asia. Within Southeast Asia trade was fostered between rice-surplus and rice-deficient areas to minimize the amount of bullion needed to pay for the collection of spices. Outside Southeast Asia, spices and other tropical products were exchanged for the products of Persia, India, China, and Japan salable in Southeast Asia and in other

Asian markets. Gujarati and Bengali cottons were obtained for sale throughout the east and Bengali and Chinese silks were exchanged for Japanese silver, gold, and copper. The Dutch trading operations became exceedingly complex, but their character can be indicated by noting that three-fourths of the Dutch Company's trade was limited to Asian markets, the remaining quarter being earmarked for Europe. In spite of the extensive promotion of local trade, however, increasing amounts of bullion had to be brought from Europe to pay for the return cargoes of high-priced spices, silks, porcelains, and tea. To keep the prices of spices high, the Dutch regulated production, even destroying surpluses.

In addition to promoting general trading activities, the Dutch Company introduced new plantation crops, such as sugar and coffee, as it reduced to vassalage the native states of Java and Sumatra during the latter half of the seventeenth and the early eighteenth centuries. Sugar cultivation was entrusted largely to immigrant Chinese on leased land, who were also permitted to gain control of retail trade. The sugar production could not compete in the European market, but it was sold in the Asian arc from Arabia to Japan. Until 1727 Mocha in the Yemen had a monopoly on coffee. As early as 1706 the Dutch experimented with coffee plants requiring three to four years to mature. Local chieftains who could command conscript labor in western Java were offered a guaranteed price for the delivery of dried coffee beans at Batavia. By 1725 coffee was being produced in substantial quantity and contributed to the price break in 1727. But before the break Dutch coffee sales yielded fantastic profits.

While the Dutch Company concentrated on breaking Portuguese power in Southeast Asia, the English Company was performing the same task in western India, eliminating Portuguese and Indian opposition by 1613. Individual English ships with cargoes of cotton cloth and opium conducted daring voyages to all parts of Southeast Asia. Penetration of the Spice Islands over which the Dutch were attempting to assert a monopoly led to Anglo-Dutch hostilities culminating in the "massacre" of two-thirds of the English residents at their factory on Amboina in 1623. In the face of such hostility the English withdrew from direct trade securing their spices elsewhere or through intermediaries. Although the English Company continued to carry on a desultory trade in various parts of Southeast Asia for the next century, it met increasing opposition from the Dutch until events in the last quarter of the eighteenth century reversed the situation.

By then the English East India Company had beaten out its European competitors and was acquiring increasing territory in India. As a commercial enterprise the Company was interested in expanding India's markets, especially eastward, where specie might be earned to counter the imbalance of the trade with Europe. Most pressing, perhaps, was the need to find a commodity salable in China to pay for Company purchases of tea. Like the Dutch, the English had emulated their Portuguese and Arab predecessors by buying opium in Mecca and Aden for sale in Southeast Asia and China. Now the Company capitalized on this opportunity by fostering plantation production of opium in Bengal for sale at annual auctions in Calcutta. So-called "country" vessels, built in India, manned by Indian crews, and commanded by British captains, carried opium, cotton cloth, and other Indian products to markets in Southeast Asia and at Canton in increasing quantities. Heavily armed and constructed of teak, which is much more durable under fire than oak, these Company-licensed ships were ready and able to cope with Dutch or other armed interference with their interloping voyages.

The real turning point, however, leading to British predominance in the markets of Southeast Asia, was the disastrous Dutch involvement in the American Revolutionary War. By the terms of the treaty of Paris the

Dutch were required to give up all monopoly trading claims. The losses of Dutch shipping during the war could not be replaced, and their trade with British-dominated India collapsed. Even their quota of Indian opium was reduced in favor of the "country" traders. Shrewd Dutch investors shifted their capital to the English Company. A lesser blow was the appearance of adventurous American captains who forced trade at gunpoint in Southeast Asian ports. By then, however, internal corruption and irregular practices had already brought the Dutch Company to the verge of bankruptcy; British and American competition only delivered the coup de grace. Bankruptcy was complete by 1791, but the Company was not dissolved and taken over by the Dutch government until 1798.

Meanwhile, the progress toward British predominance in Asian trade was accompanied by the gradual acquisition of outposts in Southeast Asia. In 1786 Penang Island in the Malacca strait was obtained, followed by Malacca itself in 1795 (confirmed in 1824) and a strip of mainland opposite Penang in 1800. Java was occupied from 1811 to 1816 by Company forces under the command of the ambitious expansionist, Sir Stamford Raffles. When Java was returned to the Dutch, much to Raffles disgust, he negotiated the cession of the island of Singapore, which was destined to become the British bastion in Southeast Asia and, with the aid of Chinese immigrants, the commercial center of the region. During the balance of the nineteenth century British control was gradually extended over Burma and the sultanates of Malaya.

While control of Burma may be viewed as an imperialistic extension of Britain's Indian empire, the control of Malaya was part of a policy of securing way stations along the trade routes eastward and westward from India to accommodate its growing supremacy on the high seas and included the acquisition from the Dutch of the Cape of Good Hope and Ceylon, from the French of the island of Mauritius, and from the Chinese of

Hongkong. As its merchant ships became by far the most numerous in Asian trade, Britain's free trade policy, fully implemented after mid-century, inevitably influenced the hitherto closed door policies of the other imperial powers in Southeast Asia. Singapore as a free port attracted an increasing volume of trade. As early as 1797 the Dutch opened Batavia to the trade of other nations, selling the products of its empire there instead of in Amsterdam. Spain also opened the Philippines by mid-century to foreign traders. Only France, which gradually during the second half of the nineteenth century extended its hegemony over what came to be known as French Indo-China, was more interested in prestige than profits and therefore largely uninfluenced by the trend toward free trade.

BRITISH COLONIAL POLICIES

This study's principal concern is the effect of the West on the peoples of Southeast Asia, both the conquered and the Siamese who retained their independence, not the details of conquest and of colonial policies. An understanding of the native reaction and adaptation, however, requires a general appreciation of the major features of imperial activity during the nineteenth and twentieth centuries when the Western impact became pervasive. As was already noted, Spain united and largely converted to the Spanish form of Western civilization the bulk of the backward Philippines, except Muslim Mindanao, providing the conditions for the emergence of Philippine nationalism.

The British record in Burma is a sad exception to their general practice of ruling through local institutions and traditional authorities, chiefly because Burma was treated as an adjunct of India and subjected to an Indian administration, alien to its Buddhist culture and communal social and economic institutions. In the end, Burma represented Britain's greatest failure as an imperial power, with the possible exception of Ire-

land. Even though the British and their Indian collaborators vastly expanded the economy, they and their ways were rejected by
most of the Burmese peoples amid mounting
disorders that the British regime proved
unable to appease or suppress. Finally, on
gaining independence, Burma was to confirm
its hostility by rejecting membership in the
Commonwealth of Nations.

The first Anglo-Burmese War (1824–
1826) was precipitated by Burmese military
expansion across the British-claimed frontier
of India in Assam. In spite of the ravages of
tropical diseases, British naval mobility supported by Indian resources assured victory.
The result was the acquisition of the coastal
regions of Arakan, adjoining India, and Tenasserim with its valuable teak forests to the
east. Neither region was ethnically Burmese,
and the most significant effect of their loss
was the damage to the prestige and authority
of the presumably divinely ordained Burmese rulers. The administration of Arakan
was immediately Indianized, destroying the
authority of the hereditary chiefs, and in due
course Tenasserim suffered a similar fate.
Although the economy and population of Tenasserim expanded substantially under British rule, the results in Arakan were far more
striking. British law and order plus Indian
capital and labor in a few decades increased
Arakan's rice production more than four
times and made it by mid-century the leading exporter of rice in the world.

The second Anglo-Burmese War
(1852–1853) began with a British naval
bombardment of Rangoon after the Burmese
governor had already backed down on the
assessment of fines for alleged port violations by two British merchant ships. This
victory was easier than the first, culminating
in the deposition of the ruler and a further
deterioration of the prestige of the dynasty.
Although the new Burmese ruler refused to
recognize the loss of Lower Burma, the richest part of his domain with much of the coveted teak forests, the British unilaterally
annexed it and proceeded to carry out a com-

prehensive survey and registration of cultivated lands for taxation purposes. At first,
the British operated through selected local
officials, but the close supervision of British
residents tended to limit the local leaders'
traditional authority and undermine their
prestige. The application of Anglo-Indian
law through lowly regarded police under
British direction further restricted their
traditional influence. In addition, the British
sought to build a modernized educational
system on the existing base provided by
Buddhist monks, but lack of cooperation led
them to abandon this effort and to deprecate
traditional Buddhist instruction. Thus the
British alienated the traditional social, political, and religious leaders and disrupted the
ordering of society associated with them.
The one missionary success, conducted
mainly by American Baptists, was among
the still animistic Karens who welcomed
the British as liberators from Burmese persecution. Today the Christian Karens are one
of the most militant anti-Burmese minorities.

On the credit side of the ledger the British stimulated tremendous economic strides
based on their experience in Arakan and Tenasserim. A continuing program of public
works vastly expanded communications and
irrigation. The teak forests were more systematically and less wastefully exploited under
the supervision of a Forestry Department.
Large amounts of virgin land were brought
under cultivation by granting free titles to the
pioneers. In two decades rice production
trebled and population more than doubled,
while trade with independent Burma also
stimulated its economic development. After
1870 the combination of steam navigation
and the opening of the Suez Canal so greatly
enlarged the market for Burman products
that a shortage of both labor and capital developed, filled by the immigration of large
numbers of Indian laborers and money-
lenders. Under boom-time conditions and
the alien Anglo-Indian laws of individual
land tenure, the Burmese social cohesion

based on communal tenure further disintegrated. Although Indian money-lending rates (15 to 36 percent) were lower than Burmese, and Indian lenders preferred not to own land, many developers of virgin lands found themselves reduced by debts to wage labor or forced to sell out and move on to pioneer another area.

The rest of Burma was acquired in a few weeks in the fall of 1885 to forestall the expansion of French influence and proclaimed entirely British on January 1, 1886. The ease of this conquest is explained by the complete collapse of the power and prestige of the Burmese rulers. Kachin (Savage) tribesmen from the northwest were ravaging the land at will, all royal appointments were for sale, and villagers, if they could, had to provide for their own defense against the bandit groups that roamed the land. The whole land was in disorder, and the British heirs found it far more difficult and expensive to restore order than to topple the dynasty. More than 6 years of guerrilla warfare and 40,000 Indian troops, aided by Karen volunteers, were required to enforce British rule and apply Anglo-Indian law and order by the erection of hundreds of fortified outposts protecting the main roads. In 1892 the frontier with French Laos was negotiated as the Mekong River.

Although in Upper Burma peace was established by recognizing the headman of each village under the supervision of a British district deputy commissioner, the alien system of land tenure, law, and court procedure had thoroughly demoralized Lower Burma contributing to an increasing incidence of crime. Individual ownership of land and cash crop farming were beyond Burmese comprehension. Accustomed as they were to communal landholding and subsistence farming, they could not compete effectively with the more sophisticated and acquisitive Indians. The Anglo-Indian legal system bore little relation to their conceptions of justice. Therefore, they saw nothing unethical in wholesale perjury, bribery, and disrespect for judicial procedures outside their experience. More-

over, British disdain for Buddhist education, emulated by Burmese graduates of British-sponsored schools, and British refusal to maintain the Buddhist hierarchy and its discipline contributed to the demoralization of monks who frequently encouraged and sometimes engaged in anti-British and anti-Indian activities. If their religious leaders did not respect British authority, how could ordinary Burmese subjects be expected to do so? Finally, like Buddhism, Burmese culture as a whole deteriorated after the loss of aristocratic and royal patronage and leadership, and this loss was not offset by any widespread Burmese participation in British culture or the economic fruits of Anglo-Indian rule. Between 1870 and 1905 exports multiplied fivefold, but almost all the profits went into the coffers of British and Indian operators. By 1905 the number of government-sponsored secular schools was rapidly catching up with the number of Buddhist schools, but again the principal beneficiaries were the more aggressive Indians.

In 1897 Burma was granted a legislative council, including one Burman and one Shan, with power to initiate legislation, subject to the successive vetoes of the British governor, the governor-general of India, and the secretary of state for India. This was a small beginning toward representative government, but Burma's future progress was to be largely dependent on that of its much larger neighbor, India. By 1905 there was widespread and articulate discontent directed at the British, and especially their Indian associates, but there was no organized national movement. Although Japan's victory was widely acclaimed, it only produced an increase in unorganized disorder and crime with the exception of the moderate and ostensibly nonpolitical Young Men's Buddhist Association founded in 1906. Although a revivified and purified Buddhism was to play a major role in the growth of Burmese nationalism, the YMBA represented only the first modest step. In 1905 there was nothing that can be described as a Burmese nationalist movement, only an unorganized hostility to Anglo-Indian rule expressed in an increasing number of unrelated acts of violence.

Although the Straits Settlements (as the directly ruled areas of Penang Island, mainland Province Wellesley opposite it, Malacca, and Singapore were called after 1826) were subject to the Indian governor-general until 1858, the British policy then and later was far less aggressive and disruptive of Malay institutions than it was in Burma. First of all, British interest, until Chinese tin mining became significant in the 1870s, was limited to providing safe passage and ports of call for the growing trade with Southeast Asia, China, and Japan. In addition, the British saw no profit in jeopardizing their trade with Buddhist Siam by interfering in the affairs of its undeveloped Muslim vassal states in Malaya.

Tin mining on a very small scale and mainly for the Chinese market had for a long time been the single productive export of Malaya, which depended on farming and fishing plus some trading and piracy to provide a mere subsistence. In 1848 the discovery of new rich deposits attracted an increasing number of Chinese mining operators who employed fellow countrymen because the easy-going Malayans were not interested in hard labor. Other Chinese immigrants established themselves in the various sultanates as retailers of British manufactures and money-lenders to the impecunious Malayan farmers and fishermen. Already they had become the major element in the labor and trade of the Straits Settlements. In competition with Indian immigrants, the Chinese proved more industrious and willing to endure hardships. They also proved to be clannish, unassimilable, and prone to form secret societies whose bloody affrays the British authorities generally ignored, permitting them to manage their own affairs in their own way. Most Chinese immigrants arrived as laborers indentured to fellow countrymen who exploited them unmercifully without British interference. Humanitarianism may have been the pre-

vailing creed in Britain, but in Malaya most Englishmen tended to look the other way. The growing shortage of labor encouraged the abuse of the coolie traffic in the 1850s and 1860s when kidnapped Chinese were crammed into the holds of Chinese and European ships with many dying en route from the suffocating, unsanitary conditions. Upon arrival their contracts were sold to the highest bidder, some Chinese buyers paying more than five times the passage cost. There were scarcely any female immigrants, which complicated the social problem, encouraging every variety of vice and crime. One European observer wrote that if Chinese immigration had been unrestricted and had included women, the Malay population of Southeast Asia would have been submerged in a few generations. Until after 1905 the rapidly expanding tin-mining operations were an exclusive Chinese preserve. The more efficient but costly European dredges were only introduced after 1910.

Although British trade in and via Southeast Asia had multiplied many times during the first six decades of the nineteenth century, its growth was nothing compared to the boom after 1870 when the Suez Canal in combination with the long British lead in steam navigation made it profitable to ship bulky cargoes to and from Europe. At last, the British government, pressed by commercial interests, became concerned with improving the chaotic conditions within the tin-producing Malay sultanates. Starting in 1874 subordinate treaties began to be negotiated, backed by Indian troops, giving the British the right to advise the sultans on the regulation of internal affairs and the improvement of their economies. Each of the four treaty states in due course received British residents who oversaw the establishment of orderly government and the development of internal improvements to facilitate the extraction and shipment of tin ore. In 1895 the four states were federated under a resident-general with headquarters at Kuala Lumpur; the resident-general was, in turn, subordinate to the governor of the Straits Settlements acting as High Commissioner for all British interests in Malaya.

The British protectorate did lessen the prestige of the sultans, though the British interfered as little as possible with Malayan customs and practices and favored Malayans in appointments to lower posts in the civil service. A more disturbing factor, however, was the growing proportion of Chinese who by 1905 outnumbered the Malays in the federated states. Generally, the Chinese were nonpolitical, preferring to stay apart and settle their own differences so long as they were unimpeded in pursuing their own enterprises. When clashes with the Malays occurred, the Chinese looked to the British, if they felt unable to secure justice by their own action. In any case, they looked with disdain on the Malayan people and government. By 1905 the immigration of Chinese had created the problem of a plural society of mutually unassimilable cultures, which remains a major handicap to the independent state of Malaysia.

The discovery and exploitation of vast tin deposits were responsible for the growth in wealth and population and the subversion of the simple life of the Malays. This growth was soon to be supplemented by the development of rubber estates, also to serve the demands of a world market. By 1905 the British had encouraged the development in Malaya of the highest per capita income in Southeast Asia, but they had also created a political dilemma of major proportions. The Chinese were more interested in profits than in politics, and the Malays, fearful of the Chinese, looked to the British for protection. There was no nationalist movement, and there could be none until some means of overcoming the mutual mistrust of each community could be found.

DUTCH COLONIAL POLICIES

To the Dutch government, impoverished by its role in the Napoleonic wars, the restoration of its territories in the East Indies meant only one thing: how to make them as profitable as possible. For nearly 15 years, however, the government floundered until it discovered the answer. The general policy of the first governor was liberal and paternal seeking to encourage the peasants by protecting them against excessive exploitation by Europeans, Chinese, and their own chiefs, but it simply could not be effectively enforced because the government lacked the resources to reassert its authority against Anglo-Indian, Chinese, and other interlopers. What coffee and sugar profits were garnered from the short-lived postwar demand were more than consumed by futile efforts to regain monopolistic control of the trade. Adequate public and private capital could not be raised in Holland where by 1820 one-seventh of the urban population had to be supported by public funds. An added burden was the need to repair and develop public works, such as irrigation facilities, but the final blow was a costly guerrilla war from 1825 to 1830 in Java inspired, among other factors, by the reassertion of Dutch authority operating through Chinese tax collectors. Obviously a liberal and paternalistic policy would not produce the necessary revenues and profitable export crops from a peasantry desirous of being left alone to pursue its traditional subsistence farming. A more radical and forceful program was needed and devised by the new governor, Johannes van den Bosch, appointed in 1829.

The Culture Program, a misleading label, proposed a vast expansion in the production of export crops by eliminating the dependence on private enterprise and requiring each community to plant and deliver to the government specified commodities. In theory, about one-fifth of the land or an equivalent in value per capita would be devoted to cash crops to be delivered at government evaluations in lieu of land taxes. In practice, the chiefs became allies of the government by being granted a share of the profits in return for using their traditional authority to secure maximum production. The cooperation of the chiefs was further ensured by bolstering their religiously sanctioned authority in the application of customary law against the attempted inroads of the Muslim ulema. The program was limited for the most part to Java and was most productive in the irrigated interior areas of central and eastern Java, which had hitherto planted little other than rice. Now fabulous amounts of coffee, sugar, tobacco, and indigo, as well as other products, were delivered to the government at fixed values yielding tremendous profits from sales in the European market. In spite of governmental exhortations against peasant exploitation, the temptation was too great for many chiefs to earn more by over-fulfilling their communities' quotas, and in any case crops such as sugar required 50 percent more conscript labor than rice as well as additional labor demands for public works. In some instances, peasants had to devote as much as 200 days of labor a year for the benefit of their chief and the Dutch government. Dutch profits under the Culture Program were so great that in 45 years the Dutch national debt was paid off as well as the cost of the Netherlands railway network.

Such a program of exploitation could not help but have social, economic, and political consequences. The expansion and improvement of the irrigated area, as great as they were, could not keep pace in local needs with a 50 percent increase in population. In spite of the immediate advantages for the chiefs in terms of wealth, their collaboration with the Dutch in the long run undermined their prestige as the religious and social cohesion of the village was eroded by the need to purchase food from outside and by the development of wage labor. As national sentiment developed, the beneficiary of this deterioration of the chiefs' prestige and communal cohesion was Islam with its egalitarian, anti-Dutch, and anti-Western appeal. In the Outer Islands what little development took place generally required immigrant Chinese labor, especially in Sumatra. There was not enough population pressure on the means of subsistence to enforce the Culture system,

and the local rulers for the most part only acknowledged a loose Dutch suzerainty.

Complaints against the Culture Program, inspired ironically by both humanitarian zeal and the eagerness of private enterprise for a share in the profits, were first heard at mid-century, but did not begin to bear fruit until the 1860s when the Liberal Party with a Liberal Program came into power. The so-called Liberal Program gave private enterprise the right to lease land and contract for labor with the chiefs while gradually cancelling Culture programs in various products and limiting others to no more than the originally intended one-fifth of the land of any community. The very profitable sugar and coffee Culture systems were permitted to continue until 1890 and 1917, respectively, but the programs in other products were terminated and turned over to private enterprise in the 1860s and 1870s.

Private enterprise clearly demonstrated its superior efficiency producing by 1885 exports worth ten times as much as in 1860. This dramatic increase was partly the result of free competition and the development of new products in world demand, but it was also in large measure due to the rapid expansion in Asian trade as a whole following the opening of the Suez Canal. Private entrepreneurs pressed into the undeveloped Outer Islands, especially Sumatra, and demanded greater government protection, which led to closer government control of the local rulers. This pressure, reinforced by late nineteenth century imperialism's insistence on the exercise of positive control over claimed territory, produced a debilitating 30-year struggle (1873–1903) to subjugate the fanatical Muslim states of Acheh in northern Sumatra, which absorbed the previous large remittances to Holland and even led to deficits before the Achehnese submitted.

As before, however, the greatest development and the greatest impact on local culture took place in Java where the even more intensive activities of private operators more rapidly broke down the social order than the Culture Program had done. Private operators hired increasing numbers of wage laborers through contracts with community chiefs who also profited as paymasters. More and more Javanese worked outside their communities with which they consequently lost the deep sense of belonging and discipline without finding a satisfactory substitute. After 1890 the growth of the population, which passed 30 million by 1905, exceeded the development of new lands, enabling employers and contractors to exploit the situation. As the writings of disillusioned officials had previously made the Dutch public aware of the evils of the Culture Program, so again peasant complaints were collected by civil servants hostile to private exploitation and used to stimulate agitation in the 1890s, which led to the formulation of a new policy.

The Ethical Policy, formally inaugurated in 1901, was inspired by a laudable concern for the peoples of the East Indies. Legislation included closer regulation of private business, especially the large corporations, educational and other welfare development, larger investments in agricultural improvements and the opening of new lands, and local councils to provide experience in self-government. These reforms, however, made slow progress in the face of native apathy and lack of understanding and the unified resistance of Dutch private operators. The Islamic scholar, Snouck Hurgronje, perceived the decline of the chiefs' and the rise of Islam's prestige and recommended Dutch cultivation of a modernized Indonesian Islamic elite through education and discouragement of most Christian missionary activity among Muslims. Although his teachings converted many young members of the civil service, who tried to implement them, they were too radical for the Dutch people. The Ethical Policy, never effectively implemented, was for the most part abandoned after 20 years.

By 1905 there was no organized national movement in Java, let alone the Dutch East Indies as a whole. Nevertheless, there was a growing number of Indonesians who had secured some knowledge of the West and its ideologies either by education in Holland or association with the Dutch in the lowest levels of the civil service. Those who had studied in Europe, where there was little racial discrimination, found it particularly difficult to adjust to the stratified atmosphere at home, and some found easy answers in socialist and Marxist doctrines. Others, however, found a more naturalized solace in the egalitarian doctrines of Islam, and some had studied the more modern viewpoints taught at al-Azhar in Cairo. The ingredients for the founding of a national movement were present among the educated minority, but it took another six years for them to jell in the initially moderate organization, Sarekat Islam. In a wholly different way, the Dutch had unwittingly undermined the authority of their collaborators, the community chiefs and customary law, and prepared the way for an Islamic revival comparable to the Buddhist revival in Burma. Both movements represented to a considerable degree a rejection of the West and its materialistic culture.

FRENCH COLONIAL POLICIES

French interest in Southeast Asia, commercial, political, and missionary, dated from the seventeenth century, but the most persistent and ultimately decisive factor was the missionary interest sponsored by the Missions Étrangeres. In contrast with the Spanish missionary orders the French society in its constitution emphasized the importance of the ordination and advancement in the hierarchy of native priests. This provision gave them an advantage over their exclusionist Spanish competitors in Vietnam.

During the seventeenth and eighteenth centuries Vietnam was divided between feuding northern and southern dynasties with capitals at Hanoi and Hué and an uncertain boundary not far from the present one. The southern state, however, was then the more vigorous and militant, gaining vitality and new strength from its gradual occupation of the Mekong delta south of Saigon. The northern state, according to contemporary accounts, was more conservative and developed and by far the most civilized region in Southeast Asia, producing silks, porcelains, and finely crafted metal works. Obviously it reflected the long influence of its Chinese neighbor. During the last three decades of the eighteenth century both dynasties were discomfited by a popular rebellion against the oppression of the rulers and the Chinese-style scholar-officials. An indomitable French missionary championed the cause of the last heir to the southern dynasty, in spite of repeated setbacks, from the time they met in 1777 until his death in 1799 after a prolonged bout of dysentery. Finally, in 1802, his protégé succeeded in reuniting all Vietnam and had himself proclaimed emperor. For his faithful French supporter who had secured Western troops and artillery he erected an imposing tomb at which was posted a permanent bodyguard during the ruler's lifetime. Naturally, full toleration was extended to all missionaries, and some of them, as well as French officers, were appointed to top posts in his government. Unfortunately for the French, they were too preoccupied by the Napoleonic wars and their effects to consolidate their position before the emperor's death in 1819. His successor proved less friendly, and after the death of the last important Vietnamese supporter in 1832, Christianity was proscribed and sporadic persecution decimated the missionaries and their native followers.

A wave of executions in the early 1850s, abetted by the pleas of French naval officers for an Asian base, persuaded the prestige-conscious Louis Napoleon to authorize the military operations in 1859 in collaboration with Spain, which led ultimately to the creation of French Indo-China. Vietnamese resistance proved stiffer than anticipated, but reinforcements were poured in, and in 1863 the emperor was forced to accept a treaty giving France control of Saigon and three of the six provinces in the Mekong delta (called Cochin-China), the right of first refusal on future territorial alienations, and a substantial indemnity. The aggressive naval administration was not content with its gains, and by 1867 it had secured control of the rest of the Mekong delta and compelled the weak Cambodian kingdom to shift its vassalage from Siam to France. Further conquest was delayed by the Prussian overthrow of Imperial France in 1870, but the revelation that not the Mekong but the Red river of northern Vietnam, hitherto recognized as a Spanish missionary preserve, was alone suitable for trade with southern China refired imperial ambitions. In 1874 France obtained by treaty the right to use the Red river for trade, but conquest awaited the competitive stimulus of full-fledged European imperialism in the 1880s. The Vietnamese, with the aid of their Chinese suzerain, put up a respectable opposition defeating some French forces in the field, but French attacks on the Chinese coast compelled the Manchu government to concede a French protectorate over Vietnam and the right to trade with Yünnan at a negligible tariff rate. The final act of the naval administration was to round out French Indo-China, except for some further advances in 1907 and 1909, by forcing Siam to surrender Laos in 1893.

The naval administration from 1863 to 1893 proved very costly to France with no compensating economic development of significance. The profits from the export of rice surpluses from Cochin-China, which was directly governed by a host of officers, were more than consumed by the French bureaucracy's salaries and pensions. Northern Vietnam had to be ruled through the emperor and the solidly ensconced, Chinese-style, scholar-official class. Administration was not rationalized and made to pay its way until after 1897 when a civilian governor eliminated a number of superfluous posts, improved tax collections, and took various steps to encourage French investments.

In contrast with the British, the Dutch, and even the Spanish, the French ignored local Asian trade and concentrated on promoting an exclusively colonial economy serving France. As in their other colonies, they were imbued with a deep sense of France's civilizing mission, and what little education they sponsored emphasized French culture. Those Vietnamese who became most Gallicized by study in France were amply rewarded and recognized as citizens and equals. Where the British imperialist sought to instill a sense of awe and respect by adopting a superior attitude, the French rulers were characterized by a sort of cameraderie, which sought to win acceptance rather than respect. Although French scholars made detailed studies of native culture, the government positively discouraged the development of Vietnamese culture that had been showing signs of emancipating itself from Chinese domination just prior to the French conquest.

Cochin-China was so inundated by the French officials who directly ruled it as a colony that the dominant Chinese became too strongly acculturated to create difficulty. In the rest of Vietnam, however, ruled indirectly through the emperor, growing opposition developed by 1905, especially in the north, stemming from a combination of disrespect and hatred for the French in their efforts to supplant the ancient Vietnamese civilization and way of life. But, as elsewhere in Southeast Asia, this opposition still lacked any unity in purpose or organization. Much of it was a traditionalist rejection of the West, but some of the young rebels came from the French-educated minority. A few were already infected with Marxist ideas. Disorganized as this discontent was, it appeared to the French to constitute no threat requiring action.

THE NEW SIAM AND THE WEST (1782 – 1905)

Under the vigorous leadership of the part-Chinese Chakri dynasty a revitalized Siam effectively repelled the Burmese and regained its position as the dominant state in mainland Southeast Asia during the last two decades of the eighteenth century and the first two decades of the nineteenth century. The Chinese strain in the royal line was no accident and remains a prevalent characteristic of the leading families of modern Thailand. The relationship of suzerain and vassal between China and Siam had existed since the founding of the state, and Chinese artisans and merchants had played a significant role in cultural and economic development from the beginning. During and after the disorders caused by the Burmese invasions, Chinese immigration grew rapidly, accounting for some 300,000 of the population by 1850. Of greater importance than their numbers were their monopoly of Siam's economy and utilization of the new capital city of Bangkok as a major base in gaining control of the Southeast Asian seaborne trade after the collapse of the Dutch East India Company. While the employment of the more industrious and highly skilled Chinese laborers often proved more efficient than Siamese conscript labor in public works, other Chinese earned great wealth not only in trade but also as taxfarmers and authorized distributors of illegal opium. Since there were few female immigrants, wealthy Chinese, though clinging to their culture, made matches with influential Thai families to the mutual advantage of both parties. Until the large-scale immigration of Chinese women late in the nineteenth century, such intermarriage provided a measure of assimilation and blurred the ethnic difference, though open hostilities were not unknown.

Siamese culture presented a curious blend of popular animistic beliefs in wandering good and evil spirits, Hīnayāna Buddhism substantially modified to fit Siamese conceptions, and the Cambodian style of divine kingship confirmed by brāhman and Buddhist conducted coronation ceremonies. In addition, Chinese influence can be seen in various practices, especially the strong sense of familial discipline and the consequent obedience of inferior to superior. According to the conception of divine kingship the ruler was the absolute owner and consumer of the land, the people, and its products. Therefore, there was no question of his right to tax and to conscript for labor or military service. Although the people were thus all chattels of the king, about one-third of the population was literally enslaved, though in most instances slavery carried no stigma of inferiority. As in Burma, slaves were allotted for the support of the pagodas. Many other Thai had been enslaved for debt, their owners being required to pay the taxes due from them to the government. Finally, prisoners of war were settled in communities as royal slaves obligated to furnish military service. The divine ruler was absolute in authority, prescribing the law and appointing, promoting, and demoting as he saw fit. Nevertheless, the sacredness of his person created an unbridgeable gulf between the king and his people and precluded direct knowledge and adequate supervision, in spite of the institution of censors, to prevent abuses and exploitation at the provincial and local levels. Furthermore, direct rule was limited to Siam proper; the Muslim sultans of the Malayan peninsula were largely autonomous vassals. The relationship of king and Muslim vassals was mutually beneficial providing for the former the economic advantage of control of major trade routes and for the latter the military protection of their relatively weak sultanates by the leading power in Southeast Asia. This was the general nature of the Siamese state when it was confronted by the challenge of Western imperialism.

On a much lesser scale, the course of Siamese reaction to the Western impact may be compared to that of Japan. Initially, in remembrance of seventeenth century relations, which had almost compromised Siamese independence, and in resentment of British encroachments in Malaya, Siamese policy was extremely cool, if not isolationist, and Chinese merchants, fearful of Western competition, encouraged such a negative policy in every way possible. The only apparent break in this policy was an American commercial treaty of 1833, motivated by the desire for a source of modern arms and a counter to growing British influence in Southeast Asia, but the agreement yielded negligible results in terms of trade, though stepped-up Protestant missionary activity served to introduce Western cultural influence through translations, educational activities, and medical missions. A major beneficiary of this influence was the next ruler who had been passed over in 1824 and had wisely retired quietly to a monastery to study. Through contacts with missionaries he became an enthusiastic student of Western civilization.

Following the accession of this prince as King Mongkut (Rama IV, 1851–1868), a reversal of foreign policy, similar in effect to the opening of Japan, ensued, reinforced by the even stronger interest in Westernization of his younger brother who served as vice-king. Unlike Japan, however, the Westernization program was limited in extent and effectiveness by the absence of broad support beyond the regal brothers and by the traditional restrictions on the direct authority of the crown. Nevertheless, the changes and accomplishments of these years altered the direction of Siamese development.

After a few years' delay a series of treaties, beginning with the British in 1855 and compounding the effects through the customary most-favored-nation clauses, threw Siam open to the West. As usual, the British treaty provided for extraterritoriality, a consulate, a 3 percent tariff, and the rights to lease land, build homes, and travel one day's distance from Bangkok. In addition, it prescribed a modern customs service, a fixed nominal tax on British property, and the free export of gold and rice as well as the termination of the government monopoly of coconut oil. These inroads on Siamese sovereignty were supplemented by various additional provisions in the treaties with other Western powers, such as the customary French insistence on religious toleration and the right of missionaries to travel, reside, and construct churches throughout the country. Moreover, King Mongkut in due course employed some 80 foreign advisors to implement his modernization program. Before long, river steamships and new roads, canals, and bridges appeared. Bangkok was linked to Singapore by telegraph. Western furniture and dress were introduced into the palace of the vice-king who also set up a modern machine shop in pursuance of his special interest in applied science. An American headed the customs service and a British financial advisor advocated a conservative economic policy to the advantage of foreign traders and to the detriment of internal development because, after the salaries of foreign advisors and the costs of government had been met, not much income was left for investment. In the realm of education, Anna Leonowens, the royal tutor whose role has been made famous in the story of *Anna and the King of Siam*, must be mentioned as an illustration of King Mongkut's recognition of the importance of Western learning. In spite of these examples, the pace of modernization was slow and largely limited to the Bangkok area. In most of Siam life went on as before, from the extortionate practices of officials to the customary practices and superstitions of the people. One major change was the shift of emphasis of the Chinese to internal activities as they were gradually squeezed out of their domination of foreign trade.

Mongkut was succeeded after some dissension by the 15-year-old King Chulalongkorn (Rama V, 1868–1910) who demonstrated the influence of Anna's education by pursuing an even more aggressive program of progressive reform. A promising first step was the abolition of the prescribed prostration in approaching his sacred person, but even he could not change the customary attitude toward the ruler and, as the years went by, abandoned the effort. In 1874 a decree freed all children of slaves when they reached the age of 21 though total abolition did not come until 1905. In 1878 a palace school set an example for state-supported

secular education. Moreover, the state financed study in Europe and America of an average of 300 scholars annually. A government printing press turned out text books and the weekly *Royal Gazette*, and genuine freedom of the press encouraged the development of newspapers and periodicals. Many modern buildings were erected in Bangkok by the government. Military and naval modernization was reflected in the construction of an arsenal and drydock. Perhaps most important was the speeding of transportation by the completion in 1900 of a railway extending 200 miles into the interior. Much of this work was financed by the rapid expansion after 1870 of the markets for Asian products. The crown brought more lands under irrigation to meet the increased demand for rice exports, but even by 1905 three-fourths of the potentially irrigable land in the Menam basin had yet to be developed.

The modernization efforts of Chulalongkorn, however, had little effect on the traditional way of life of the rank and file of his subjects. Military modernization did not produce a force capable of dealing with the British and the French who continued to whittle away Siamese territories, but it was strengthened enough to give the government the upper hand in dealing with the large and sometimes rebellious Chinese minority. Attempts at governmental reorganization and reform along European lines did create new organs and titles, but failed to eliminate the traditionally accepted extortionate practices of officialdom in spite of the best efforts of Western advisors. There was, however, enough improvement in administrative efficiency under Western supervision and in the volume of commerce to double treasury receipts between 1896 and 1903. At this time the struggle was begun to get rid of the unequal treaty provisions. The struggle was destined to be a long one, but it did produce a law school in 1897 and the beginning of an overhaul of the legal system with the aid of French advisors to satisfy Western conceptions of justice.

The British were predominant as advisors and in commerce until German shipping surpassed British after 1900. Principal imports were British cotton goods and hardware in exchange for rice and the timber and tin resources developed mostly by British capital. Economic expansion leveled off after 1893 when rice exports reached one half million tons. The main causes were shortages of capital and labor, especially after the termination of slavery and conscript labor. The easygoing Thai peasants were content if they could make a subsistence living and maintain their contributions to Buddhist and other shrines and institutions, while the Chinese had for the most part risen above coolie labor. Even more efficient collection of the traditionally fixed taxes left little surplus, after other commitments, for capital investment. The British refused to consider any increase in the tariffs and agreed in 1905 to only a modest increase in the negligible tax on British properties. The absence of economic expansion anywhere near equivalent to that of Burma reflects a lack of the capital infused into Burma by Indian money-lenders, but their absence from Siam was fortunate for the preservation of the Siamese social order and culture.

By 1905 significant beginnings in modernization had been made, but in view of the continued reverence for the ruler no Western-style nationalist movement could develop. If anything, the conservative elements at the top of Siamese society were alarmed by the liberal designs of the ruler and did their best to short-circuit the effective execution of any reforms that appeared to threaten their positions. In this attitude they were supported by the Buddhist hierarchy who did not like Mongkut's plan to purify Buddhism of its Siamese accretions or his open toleration of Christian missionaries. Chulalongkorn's promotion of free vaccination and other medical modernization alienated the traditional "spirit" doctors who enjoyed great influence among the people. If any form of incipient nationalism existed in Siam,

it was directed against the Chinese, and anti-Chinese feeling, leading to various discriminatory actions, was subsequently to grow in strength, becoming a major factor in developing Thai nationalist feeling.

THE AMERICAN INHERITANCE IN THE PHILIPPINES

When Admiral Dewey's Pacific squadron under orders from the Undersecretary of Navy, Theodore Roosevelt, destroyed the Spanish naval force in Manila Bay on May 1, 1898, the American government became involved with the one active and organized nationalist movement in Southeast Asia. Filipino nationalism, inspired in large part by hostility to ecclesiastical ownership of the best lands and refusal to advance Filipino clerics, had generated a number of priest-led rebellions since the 1840s. To a significant extent this religious unrest had been supplemented by the discontent of a growing Filipino middle class with the failure to gain a fair share of the vast expansion of trade in Asia after 1870. Many Filipino students had gone to Spain where they learned more liberal doctrines of government than were practiced in the friar-dominated government of the Philippines. Most prominent among these students was José Rizal, who was befriended by Marcelo del Pilar, a nationalist leader championing total independence. Rizal gained fame with the publication in 1887 of his novel, *Noli me Tangere (Touch Me Not* or *The Lost Eden)*. In this book he pilloried the stagnant and corrupt ruling society of Manila as completely incapable of initiating the needed reforms. In 1892 he returned and futilely sought to bring about reforms by peaceful petitioning. In spite of his dedication to nonviolence, militant nationalists made him a symbol, and when a large-scale revolution broke out in 1896 on Luzon, he was executed by the Spanish, regardless of the absence of any evidence implicating him in it. The revolution was terminated early in 1898 only by a truce that stipulated the exile of the nationalist commander, Emilio Aguinaldo, in return for a cash indemnity for the rebels and the promise of reforms.

Admiral Dewey welcomed Aguinaldo's assistance in besieging Manila with a Filipino nationalist force under a revolutionary government until the arrival of American troops. Aguinaldo and his followers believed they were fighting for independence; when they learned of the cession of the islands to the United States for 20 million dollars, they were enraged at what they presumed to be American duplicity. Thus the United States fell heir to the problem of Philippine nationalism.

Three and one-half years of guerrilla warfare against the nationalists and an even longer struggle to subdue the Moros proved much more costly in men and material than the brief Spanish-American war. After the termination of military rule in 1901, a civilian commission headed by William Howard Taft recognized the strength of Filipino nationalism by defining the American function as that of trustee to prepare the Philippine Islands for independence. In due course the purchase of the friar-owned lands from Rome was negotiated. This land was then sold in small and large parcels to Filipino farmers and landlords, but many tenants objected to paying for land they believed they rightfully owned. Filipino landlords were put on the Commission in 1901, and the first step toward democracy was the holding of municipal and village elections in 1903. After 1905 more and more positions, both appointive and elective, were opened to Filipinos. The American regime kept its pledge, but the dedication to free enterprise did nothing to deter the development of landlordism in later years.

America's greatest contribution was in education, deemed essential to the establishment of democratic processes. Thousands of teachers and millions of dollars were invested in the development of a universal, state-supported, secular educational system on the American model. Although the use of English in instruction met local opposition, it eventually aided the nationalist movement by overcoming the barrier of local dialects. As in government, Filipino teachers replaced Americans as rapidly as they could be trained. In public health as well, a large investment was made to reduce the high mortality rate. Even Protestant missionaries made some small progress, though Roman Catholicism was too well entrenched to be dislodged from its predominant position. Although the fruit of this program took longer to develop, the character and direction of American rule was clearly delineated by 1905.

Southeast Asia never gained the political unity that its singular title might suggest. The fortunes of the successive states and empires fluctuated according to external interest in trade which generated the surplus income creating prosperity and creative cultural and political development. With the exception of the millennium of Chinese political control of northern Vietnam, its great neighbors exhibited little interest in direct rule and were content with recognition of cultural or political suzerainty, prior to the arrival of European imperialists upon the scene. Ultimately the region was spiritually divided into roughly a Buddhist-dominated mainland and the Muslim-dominated Malayan peninsula and the islands, though this division implied neither political unity nor religious uniformity in either part.

Thus when the Europeans appeared, no major power could contest their gradual assertion of authority, even though their numbers were small. Only a shrunken Siam retained its independence, thanks mainly to the competing ambitions of the British and the French. Only the Spanish in the undeveloped Philippines and the French with less success in more civilized Vietnam made any serious effort to introduce Western civilization before 1905. The British and the Dutch generally limited their interference with native ways to those measures essential to protecting and promoting their own economic interests. Perhaps it is no coincidence that the Spanish who were so deeply dedicated to the goal of converting the pagan Filipinos were the first to reap the harvest of that Western infestation, nationalism.

Outside the Philippines there were by 1905 scattered examples of nationalistic expression, but they were still disparate and unorganized. The growth of nationalism bears a direct relationship to the extent of Western education, and as yet, only a small number of Southeast Asians had been exposed. More time and greater exposure would be necessary for nationalism to mature. Only after the further revelations of World War I did it gain organized and sustained development.

SIGNIFICANT DATES

1401	Founding of Malacca
1403–1438	Voyages of Cheng Ho
1511	Portuguese conquest of Malacca
1571	Spanish conquest of Manila, Philippine Islands
1641	Dutch conquest of Malacca
1786	British get Penang Island as Malayan base
1824–1826	First Anglo-Burmese war
1829	Beginning of Dutch Culture Program
1851–1868	Reign of King Mongkut (Rama IV) in Siam
1852–1853	Second Anglo-Burmese war
1859	Beginning of French conquest of Indo-China
1868–1910	Reign of King Chulalongkorn (Rama V) in Siam
1869	Opening of Suez Canal
1873–1903	Dutch War with Muslim states of Acheh
1885	Chinese recognition of French rule in Vietnam (Annam)
1896–1898	Luzon rebellion of Aguinaido against Spanish rule
1898	American acquisition of the Philippines from Spain

SELECTED READINGS

See Chapter Seven for general accounts.

*Bastin, John, ed., *The Emergence of Modern Southeast Asia, 1511–1957.* Englewood Cliffs, N.J.: Prentice-Hall, 1967.

*Butwell, Richard, *Indonesia.* Boston: Ginn, 1967.

Cady, John F., *A History of Modern Burma.* Ithaca: Cornell University Press, 1958.

————, *The Roots of French Imperialism in Eastern Asia.* Ithaca: Cornell University Press, 1964.

Hahn, Emily, *Raffles of Singapore.* New York: Oxford University Press, 1968.

Harvey, G. E., *British Rule in Burma, 1824–1942.* London: Faber and Faber, 1946.

————, *History of Burma from the Earliest Times to 10 March 1824.* London: Longmans Green, 1925.

Hurgronje, Snouck, *The Achehnese.* 2 vols.; Leyden: Brill, 1906.

*Kartini, Raden Adjeng, *The Letters of a Javanese Princess.* New York: Norton, 1964.

Leur, J. C. van, *Indonesian Trade and Society*. The Hague: W. van Hoeve, 1955.

*Moffat, Abbot L., *Mongkut, The King of Siam*. Ithaca: Cornell University Press, 1961.

Palma, Rafael, *The Pride of the Malay Race: A Biography of José Rizal*. New York: Prentice-Hall, 1950.

*Parkinson, Cyril N., *British Intervention in Malaya, 1867–1877*. London: Oxford University Press, 1960.

Purcell, Victor, *The Chinese in Southeast Asia*. London: Oxford University Press, 1965.

*Ravenholt, Albert, *The Philippines*. Princeton: Van Nostrand, 1962.

*Rizal, José, *The Lost Eden (Noli Me Tangere)*. New York: Norton, 1968.

*———, *The Subversive (El Filibusterismo)*. New York: Norton, 1968.

*Schurz, William Lytle, *The Manila Galleon*. New York: Dutton, 1939.

Skinner, George W., *Chinese Society in Thailand: An Analytic History*. Ithaca: Cornell University Press, 1957.

Swettenham, F., *Footprints in Malaya*. London: Hutchinson, 1942.

Trager, Helen G., *Burma through Alien Eyes, Missionary Views of the Burmese in the Nineteenth Century*. New York: Praeger, 1966.

Tregonning, K. G., *A History of Modern Malaya*. London: University of London Press, 1964.

Vella, Walter Francis, *The Impact of the West on Government in Thailand*. Berkeley: University of California Press, 1955.

———, *Siam under Rama III, 1824–1851*. Locust Valley, N.Y.: J. J. Augustin, 1957.

Wickberg, Edgar, *The Chinese in Philippine Life, 1850–1898*. New Haven: Yale University Press, 1965.

*Yoe, Shway, pseud. for Sir James George Scott, *The Burman: His Life and Notions*. New York: Norton, 1963.

PART FIVE
THE GROWTH OF ASIAN NATIONALISM

Crossing one of many snow-covered mountains during the ordeal of the Long March, 1935–36. (*Eastfoto*)

Rape of Nanking, November 1937. (*Radio Times Hulton Picture Library*)

Sun Yat-sen and Madame Sun (above, left), now a vice-premier of the People's Republic of China, 1924. (*Eastfoto*)

Kemal Ataturk (above, right), founder of the Republic of Turkey.
(*Radio Times Hulton Picture Library*)

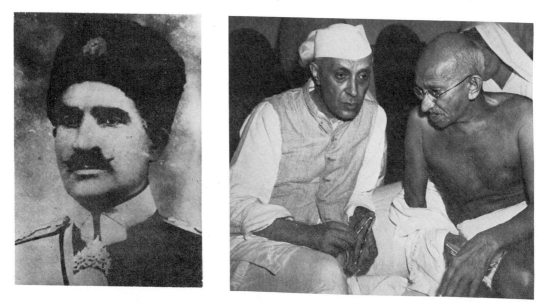

Reza Shah Pahlavi (above, left), founder of modern Iran. (*Keystone Press Agency*)

Mahatma Gāndhi (above, right) with his successor, Nehru. (*United Press International*)

President Yüan Shih-k'ai and his generals (above), March 1912. (*Radio Times Hulton Picture Library*)

King Ibn Saud (left), creator of Sa'udi Arabia. (*United Press International*)

Chiang K'ai-shek and the Soong sisters: (l. to r.) Madame Chiang, Madame H.H. Kung, and Madame Sun Yat-sen. (*Charles Phelps Cushing*)

President Ramon Magsaysay (below) of the Philippines, before his untimely death in a plane crash. (*United Press International*)

General Douglas MacArthur and Emperor Hirohito (above, left). (*International Society for Educational Information, Tokyo*)

Mao Tse-tung and Lin Piao at Yenan. (*Eastfoto*)

The preceding period was characterized by the growing assault of Western imperialism on the East, particularly after the opening of the Suez Canal, fueled materially by the insatiable demands of the Industrial Revolution for markets and raw materials and politically by the competitive stimulus of Western nationalism. In varying degrees Eastern leaders, and particularly the Western-educated elite, reacted against Western penetration by initiating organized efforts to meet the challenge. Only the leadership of Japan, after the Meiji Restoration, dedicated itself and the Japanese people wholeheartedly and exclusively to the task of modernization to "expel the barbarian." Japan's success, culminating in victory over Russia, proved that the task could be done and generated broader support and enthusiasm for nationalist efforts that were aimed at the ultimate goal of freeing their countries from Western domination.

The pace and path of progress toward this goal varied greatly from one country to another, but most Asian countries achieved at least political independence and the termination of unequal treaties within a few years after World War II, and the rest did not lag far behind. Of course, the exhaustion of the Western powers in the two world wars and the consequent ebb of Western imperialism facilitated this achievement. However, the nationalist movements and their search for ways of awakening their peoples contributed to the creation of that sense of nationality so vital to the functioning of states in the modern community of nations. Moreover, they carried out important spadework by exploring the various possible modes of accommodating modernization to the established ideals and values of their respective civilizations. Without their leadership the emancipation of their countries might have been delayed and the pace of modernization would certainly have been slower. Thus the growth of nationalism as a Western transplant with tender roots and an uncertain future was a phenomenon worthy of special attention.

CHAPTER TWENTY

REVOLUTIONARY CHINA: 1905 – 1949

The Japanese victory over Russia was selected as a turning point not only for its catalytic effect on the peoples of the East but also for its worldwide repercussions, which have not yet been exhausted. Of course, any important event can be shown to have had significant results, but this one seems to have been exceptionally productive of momentous consequences. First, victory instilled in the Japanese people the self-confidence in their destiny which eventuated in the Pearl Harbor attack and its consequences. The United States, which hitherto had viewed Japan's modernization with paternal sympathy and benevolence, now looked with concern on Japan's imperial ambitions, which directly challenged the American Open Door policy in Asia. In his own actions President Theodore Roosevelt demonstrated this shift of attitude that put a growing strain on American relations with Japan. Secondly, Japan's victim, Tsarist Russia, was immediately rocked with revolution, presaging the subsequent revolution that brought the Communists to power. Most important, however, was the impetus it gave to the Chinese revolution, which is still in progress under Communist auspices.

In depth and scope the Chinese revolution, so long delayed, has become more far-reaching than any revolution the world has known, challenging every facet of the Chinese heritage and raising a question about the thesis of cultural continuity. Prior to the threat of dismemberment at the end of the nineteenth century, the Chinese (with the exception of a few far-sighted individuals) had rejected the West, even in its material aspects. Between 1900 and 1905 the Empress-Dowager Tz'u Hsi reluctantly authorized the initiation of some reforms, mostly military, but it took the humiliating helplessness of the Manchu regime in the face of the Russo-

Japanese War fought on Chinese soil to drive home the necessity for radical reforms. As it turned out, the forces unleashed by these reforms proved too impatient to accept a gradual transformation, and when the firm hand of the "Old Buddha" was removed by death in 1908, they could no longer be curbed.

THE FINAL MANCHU ATTEMPT AT REFORM

Since Chinese civilization was so thoroughly integrated by the Confucian doctrines of state and society, the most drastic reform measure was the imperial edict of 1905 abolishing the traditional civil service examinations based on stereotyped study of the Confucian classics and substituting knowledge of specified areas of Western learning. This reform did not end overnight the study of the classics, nor did it eliminate the predominance of Confucian scholars in the civil service, but it did remove the incentive for such studies as the major avenue for entrance into the bureaucracy. Now the door to official preferment could theoretically be opened only by Western learning. Where hundreds of students had previously gone abroad for study, now thousands left China each year in quest of the requisite knowledge. Large numbers went to the United States and Europe, but for economical reasons the largest number studied in Japan which, in addition, had clearly demonstrated the successful path to modernization. In Japan many of these students, impatient for change, joined revolutionary organizations, such as Sun Yat-sen's T'ung-meng hui, and gave more attention to revolutionary thought and planning than to their studies. When they returned to China with a superficial knowledge of Western ideas and institutions, only a few actually gained positions in the

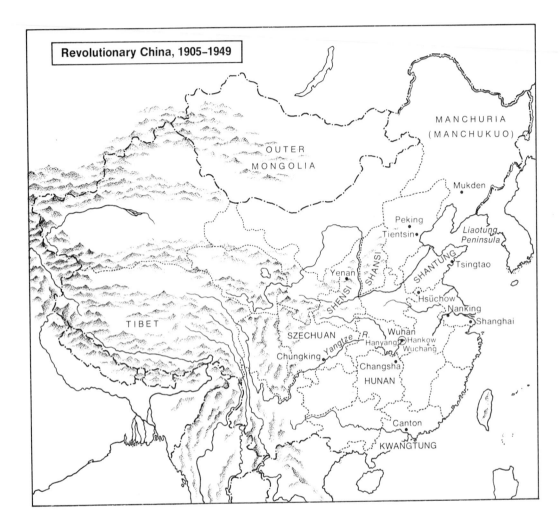

Revolutionary China, 1905–1949

civil service. Such rejection reinforced their revolutionary inclinations and propelled them into anti-Manchu agitation and conspiratorial activities.

Another major reform, intended to strengthen the central government in both internal and external relations, was the creation of a modern national army. This objective, proclaimed as early as 1901 in an imperial edict, was at first entrusted to Yüan Shih-k'ai as governor of Chihli province. By 1906 he had recruited and equipped a model force of six divisions, four of which were then turned over to the central government as the nucleus of a national army planned to number 36 divisions by 1912. Unfortunately this army suffered from its initial mode of development by interested officials; the officers, and to some extent the soldiers, looked first to their commanders, such as Yüan Shih-k'ai, rather than directing their loyalty to the central government. Nevertheless, it was China's first completely modern military force built on Western-style organization, training, and equipment.

Another significant area of attempted reform was the encouragement and support of economic modernization financed as much as possible by Chinese capital. The government realized how seriously China's independence had been compromised by dependence on Western capital, as reflected in the "Rights Recovery" movement after 1905. Politically most important was the development of railroad policy. From 1905 to his death in 1909 Chang Chih-tung was the most influential advocate of provincial financing and control of further railroad construction. Before his death, however, he, as well as the government, had come to appreciate the deficiencies of this program. Adequate sums proved difficult, if not impossible, to raise at the local level, and then these funds under Chinese management tended to be dissipated without accomplishing the planned construction. Efficiency alone demanded centralized administration. Moreover, dependence on local initiative, a traditional tendency in Chinese public works, was recognized as encouraging provincialism at the expense of the pressing necessity to rehabilitate the authority of the central government. Therefore, in 1909 a policy of governmental construction and ownership of railroads was gradually evolved. It went into full effect in 1911 when a loan was negotiated for the completion of the Hankow-Canton and Hankow-Szechuan lines with provisions for the forced purchase of those segments already constructed under provincial auspices. Not only the provincial peoples were alarmed at this assertion of central authority but also the provincial investors were unhappy with the government's decision to issue bonds in payment of only the amount of the actual assets, not the amount originally subscribed. In Szechuan, where the offer totaled less than one third of the original subscription, the combination of popular and investor hostility resulted first in passive resistance, such as a refusal to pay taxes, and then in an attack on the viceroy's headquarters in September 1911. This outbreak, although not truly revolutionary, did reflect the growing discontent with the assertion of central authority and with the assessment of new and increased taxes to meet the costs of the program.

With an appreciation of these factors in mind the aggressiveness of the provincial and national assemblies brought into exis-

tence by the constitutional reform program is not surprising. The pragmatic Chinese could not fail to observe that states with constitutional regimes had been uniformly victorious in recent conflicts. From this observation they concluded that constitutionalism was desirable because it contributed to strengthening the state. In particular they were aware of the successes of Japan against themselves and autocratic Russia. The lesson seemed obvious; a constitutional monarchy fashioned after the Japanese model might well prove the salvation of the Manchu dynasty. Even the authoritarian Empress-Dowager was convinced by the ravaging of the Manchu homeland during the Russo-Japanese War of the need for such an accommodation—so long as she and her successors were assured of retaining executive power. This attitude was made clear in an edict issued following the report of a constitutional commission sent abroad in 1905. "As for ourselves, it is necessary . . . to imitate this government by constitution, in which the supreme control must be in the hands of the Throne, while the interests of the masses shall be given to the elect, advanced to such position by the suffrage of the masses." (*China Year Book*, 1912, p. 353)

On the basis of this declaration the election of provincial assemblies was authorized for 1909 with the promise of a national assembly within nine years. In spite of indirect election by an electoral college in turn elected on a very limited franchise and in spite of a careful delineation of their functions and powers, specifically limited to debate on those issues submitted to them, the provincial assemblies immediately vented their grievances against the central government and its representatives and pressed for the prompt convening of a national assembly. Unfortunately for the Manchu dynasty the death of the "Old Buddha," Tz'u hsi, only one day after the death of the emperor, had removed the one firm hand from the helm of the ship of state and provided another infant emperor under a well-meaning, but ineffective, regent. In addition, the one strong official, Yüan Shih-k'ai, had been forced into retirement in partial compliance with the last wish of the late emperor who had never forgiven his role in ending the Hundred Days of Reform. Under the pressures of a rapidly deteriorating situation, in which regional officials were withholding revenues, the regent conceded the convening of a National Assembly in October 1910.

Although one half of this body was appointed—the rest being elected from the provincial assemblies—it proved far from cooperative. The financial and administrative policies of the government were immediately attacked, and a clear majority demanded a constitution providing for the location of legislative authority in a parliament and executive authority in a cabinet responsible for its actions to the parliament. The regent bowed to these demands by promising a constitution and a parliament by 1913. Finally, before its adjournment in the spring of 1911, the national assembly secured from a reluctant regent agreement in principle to the conception of responsible cabinet government. If the combination of floods, droughts, and consequent famine during 1910 and 1911 had not stimulated widespread support for revolutionary outbreaks, it is conceivable that an orderly transition to constitutional monarchy might have been accomplished; but the prospect seems remote in view of the existence of semi-autonomous regional regimes supported by local armies, the increasing impact of revolutionary agitation, and the growing distrust of the government crippled by a dearth of able and loyal leaders. Chinese distrust of the Manchu regime was further aroused by the growing proportion of Manchus appointed to important positions.

THE FIRST PHASE OF THE CHINESE REVOLUTION

Ever since the last decade of the eighteenth century the Manchu regime had been increasingly confronted by the dilemmas characteristic of the declining phase of a dynastic cycle. Although Western support may have prolonged its life, its demonstrated inability to meet effectively the political, economic, and ideological challenge of the West contributed further to the decline and discrediting of the dynasty. Moreover, the inability of imperial forces to suppress the T'ai P'ing and other rebels and the consequent reliance on able regional leaders with personally recruited armies to carry out this task completed the process of decentralization which made the continuance of the dynasty dependent largely on their loyalty and goodwill.

All the efforts of the Empress-Dowager to pull the fangs of these able officials by moving them around from post to post proved fruitless. The military impotence of the central government and its dependence on these leaders with their personal armies could not be overcome and were only highlighted by defeat in the war with Japan and by the failure of the so-called Boxer Rebellion. The subsequent plan for a national army and the transfer of four divisions from the army of Yüan Shih-k'ai, successor to the personal power of Li Hung-chang, to furnish a nucleus proved similarly futile; officers and men tended to maintain their personal loyalty to their original patron, or whoever directly paid them. When the revolution broke out, the government had no choice but to restore Yüan Shih-k'ai to power. Thus, in effect, a form of warlordism had become established as a predominant factor as early as the T'ai P'ing rebellion, and no governmental program proved capable of checking its course. To support their forces and finance economic developments in their areas, they were permitted to retain imperial revenues. In addition, when normal revenues became inadequate, they were authorized to assess *likin* (transit tolls on trade) to supplement their income. This diversion of imperial revenues forced the court into increasing dependence on foreign loans.

Meanwhile, in spite of a further large

loss of lives in the famines of 1877 and 1878, as well as in local disasters almost annually, the population regained the heavy losses from rebellions and famines and continued to grow. This population growth was not compensated for by any significant increase in the land under cultivation. On the contrary, decentralization and local disorders reduced investment in the maintenance of public works with a consequent decline in productivity and reduction in total acreage. At the same time, supplementary income from handicraft production suffered serious inroads from Western manufactures, while with improvements in communications more and more land was planted with cash crops, further reducing the production of food per capita. In short, by the first decade of the twentieth century the expansion of the population had reached the saturation point and China was becoming dependent on regular importations of food to meet a minimal level of subsistence. Many peasants had been forced off the land to eke out an existence as beggars or bandits. Any widespread crop failure could only result in a heavy loss of life and rebellion. The year 1910, and especially 1911, saw such crop failures, which happened to coincide with a new high point in revolutionary preparations.

Small-scale revolutionary outbreaks, mostly inspired by Sun Yat-sen and largely financed by the contributions of overseas Chinese, had been frequent and futile since his first effort in 1894. After the organization of the T'ung-meng hui and a general statement of revolutionary objectives in 1905, revolutionary preparations became better integrated. Utilizing the traditional techniques of secret societies, local units were formed throughout China, but especially in the central and southern regions. Locally, arms were accumulated and members were recruited with special attention to the military forces. Local rebellions were attempted to test conditions, but no general rebellion seems to have been planned that might jeopardize the overall movement. The outbreak

in the strategic industrial area of Wuhan, which culminated in the overthrow of the Manchu dynasty, appears to have been wholly accidental and unplanned.

A bomb explosion in Hankow on October 9, 1911, not only revealed the local headquarters and arsenal of the revolutionary movement but also led to the seizure of membership lists including the names of officers and soldiers in the garrison force stationed just across the Yangtze in Wuchang. Correctly fearful of arrest and execution (some executions had already been carried out), the troops mutinied on October 10 (the *Double Ten* as it came to be called) and compelled their reluctant commander, Colonel Li Yüan-hung, to lead them in rebellion. Against negligible resistance these troops, reinforced by volunteers, soon secured control of the three cities of the Wuhan complex: Wuchang, Hankow, and Hanyang. News of this success spread rapidly over telegraph wires and inspired a rash of similar rebellions, which were generally successful, except in the north. The problem of establishing a unified revolutionary regime to coordinate these outbreaks appears to support the contention that they were unplanned, or at least premature. Only the self-effacing willingness of Li Yüan-hung to surrender leadership prevented a split into rival regimes. Although a provisional regime in Nanking was permitted to begin negotiations with the imperial government in the name of the revolutionists, no real government was formed until an assembly of delegates elected Sun Yat-sen as president on his return to China late in December.

The revolution and its swift spread caught the Manchu government wholly unprepared. Although the military forces in the north for the most part remained loyal and put down the outbreaks in their areas, their commanders generally refused to march southward against the rebels until their mentor, Yüan Shih-k'ai, was restored to power. In turn, he refused to act until he was invested with the power of a virtual dictator.

Therefore, the government had no recourse but to recall him on his own terms, reconvene the national assembly on October 22, and accept its demands for a constitutional government divesting the monarchy of all real power. These steps were conceded by November 1, and Yüan, who had already been given supreme command of the army and navy, assumed full control on November 8.

On both sides, major military operations, which had already been set in motion, were seriously handicapped by lack of funds. But the failure of Yüan to order his forces to follow up their initial victories, which demonstrated clearly the military superiority of his troops to those of the rebels, must be attributed to more than financial problems; obviously, his continuance in power, in view of his treatment following the death of the Empress-Dowager, depended on keeping alive the rebellion that made his services essential. In addition, he appears to have become convinced that the Manchu dynasty had no future unless it promptly accepted some sort of constitutional regime. Therefore, after the initial successes in the field demonstrated his military strength, he called off his troops and instituted negotiations with the rebels. These extended exchanges finally resulted in an understanding whereby a republic would replace the Manchu dynasty and Sun would step down as president in favor of Yüan. Edicts published on February 12, 1912, provided for the abdication, with generous arrangements for the Manchus, and specifically empowered Yüan to establish a provisional republican government "assuring peace to the people and tranquillity to the Empire." Sun took exceptions to this conferring of power on an individual by the emperor, correctly predicting that it "must surely lead to serious trouble." But he had no other recourse than to accept Yüan's assurances that he would not take advantage of it. Thus, with a minimum of bloodshed, the age of imperial dynasties was ended and a revolutionary quest was begun for the restoration of Chinese prestige—a quest in which China and its peoples are still engaged.

THE ERA OF YÜAN SHIH-K'AI (1912 – 1916)

The proclamation of a republic by no means created a unified state. Regional decentralization had only become more pronounced as a result of the revolution with local leaders acquiring even greater independence, founded on the maintenance of personal armies. Indeed, Yüan's acquisition of the presidency and his continued exercise of power clearly rested on his command of the so-called national army concentrated in the northern provinces. Although his forces were undoubtedly superior in training and equipment to the motley hosts of the other leaders in central and southern China, he lacked the resources to undertake a campaign of unification. The provincial leaders required all the funds they could extract from the peasantry to support their own regimes and, even if they had been so inclined, were not in a position to remit taxes to the central government. Likewise, almost all the revenues Yüan could collect in the provinces under his control had to be devoted to the maintenance and development of his military forces. Therefore, the only practical course open to him was to give official confirmation to those regional leaders he could not entice into coming to Peking to serve his government, as in the case of vice-president Li Yüan-hung, while he negotiated for foreign loans to finance further steps toward unification.

Meanwhile, the organization of a government presented both Yüan and the republicans with difficult problems to resolve. Unfortunately for the republican cause, the masses had not yet gained an appreciation or even a comprehension of republican principles. For them, government was a distinct profession for a specially trained elite and concerned the people as a whole only when it failed to fulfill its designated functions effectively. All they could understand was the concentration of authority in a single figure—be he emperor or warlord or president. Sun had shown an understanding of this problem when he had formed his secret organization, the T'ung-meng hui, and had prescribed a period of political tutelage to prepare the people for the operation of a republican government. Only with great reluctance and misgivings did he agree to amalgamating his society with other republican groups to form an open party, the Kuomintang (Nationalist party), for the promotion of a republican regime to counter the authoritarian inclination of Yüan.

As a military man, Yüan had little sympathy for the ideals of republicanism. As a practical man, he saw little likelihood of their effective implementation at this stage of Chinese development, and his American political advisor, Dr. Frank J. Goodnow, reinforced his conviction that China needed strong leadership along dictatorial lines. A convenient military mutiny in the north gave him an excuse for keeping the government in Peking, the base of his military strength, thus reneging on his agreement to move it to Nanking, the center of republican influence. The Revolutionary Council had no choice but to go to Peking and hope for the best. At the same time, Yüan began to employ to the extent of his resources the traditional practices of bribery and even assassination to eliminate potential opponents. In order not to arouse too much opposition, however, he accepted the Nanking provisional constitution after he was inaugurated as provisional president in March 1912. This constitution sought to check the executive power of the president by requiring every official act to be countersigned by a cabinet responsible to a bicameral legislature. The wily president offset these restrictions, first by securing the appointment of supporters or neutrals to the key cabinet posts, and then, when necessary, by ignoring them altogether.

It was this developing contest for power that led to the formation of the Kuomintang to contest the elections for the legislature. When it was convened in the spring of 1913, Yüan found himself confronted by a much better organized opposition than in the faction-riven Council. On the other hand, the unruly behavior and disruptive demands of both houses played into Yüan's hands by discrediting parliament and parliamentary government in the public eye. An immediate storm of protest arose over confirmation of the foreign reorganization loan, on the basis of the prior approval of the Council, without submitting it to parliament. Although the bulk of the loan was consumed by payments of arrears on foreign debts, enough was left to support an acceleration of Yüan's consolidation of power. A vivid illustration of the extent of his success was the ease with which his forces suppressed a summer revolution in the Yangtze valley in support of the frustrated Kuomintang.

During these months a large committee of both houses was sporadically engaged in drafting a permanent constitution. Again the president outmaneuvered the legislators. On the grounds of the need for foreign recognition, which had been withheld by all the powers except the United States pending the establishment of a permanent government, he persuaded them to rush through the approval of the section dealing with the presidency in time for his formal inauguration on the anniversary of the revolution, October 10, 1913. Once confirmed in authority Yüan was free to act more forcefully. Before parliament was ready to approve the balance of the constitution, he effectively terminated its legislative existence on November 4, 1913 by condemning the Kuomintang for sedition and purging its elected representatives. Thus parliament was left without a quorum. It was officially suspended in January 1914, to meet again only briefly after Yüan's death. The inexperienced republicans, without popular support, had been outwitted by the proven administrator and strongman, ironically backed by the republican powers of the West with vested interests to protect. As always, the Chinese people most desired the restoration of order, and for this they looked to their able and forceful president.

The balance of Yüan Shih-k'ai's career—his march to monarchy and his forced retreat—involved primarily external relations with Japan and the West, complicated by the outbreak of World War I; within China, he had broken all effective opposition. Following his own convictions and the advice of his American advisor, he established a virtual dictatorship supported by a paper constitution that was never fully implemented. His remaining foes with significant military power were bribed into acknowledging his authority, or assassinated. The press was brought under control. Gradually order was restored, even if by force. At the same time, the conservative and reassuring direction of his rule was clearly indicated by renewed emphasis on Confucian morality and resumption of the traditional sacrifices at the altar of Heaven. Obviously, the pace of change was being slowed to an orderly and constructive progress; and for most Chinese, this was a welcome change from the revolutionary disorders of the preceding years.

Although the Western powers, if not Japan, generally favored the restoration of stability because of their economic interests, Russia and Britain remained concerned about the advance of the other in the peripheral regions of China. Taking advantage of the Chinese revolution and Mongolian fears of the growing Chinese encroachment northward, Russian intrigue precipitated a Mongolian declaration of independence. Not long afterward, Tibet expelled the Chinese and to British chagrin made an agreement with the Russian-sponsored Mongol regime. In 1913 President Yüan achieved a modest diplomatic triumph in a convention with Russia agreeing to autonomy, but not independence, and applying only to Outer Mongolia. In 1914 a less favorable convention with Britain defining the status and southern boundary of Tibet was never ratified by the Chinese government. Both of these actions aided in creating popular support for Yüan, but neither one compared with Japanese actions after the beginning of World War I in generating overt expressions of support for his regime.

In seizing the German leasehold at Tsingtao on the southern coast of the Shantung peninsula, Japan deployed more troops and occupied more Chinese territory than could be remotely justified by the size of the German garrison—and continued to occupy much of it long after the Germans capitulated. Then in 1915, when the United States was the only Western power not yet embroiled in the European conflict, Japan delivered the Twenty-One Demands (to be dealt with later) which, if fully implemented, would have reduced China to a Japanese protectorate. These aggressive steps inspired the voluntary formation of defense societies, which raised funds by popular subscription throughout the country and issued statements of patriotic support for Yüan's regime. Even former foes declared their loyalty to the central government in this time of crisis. Yüan naturally interpreted these actions and expressions as an indication of a broadly based, popular acceptance—though they appear to have been generated more by a nationwide sense of a need for unity to repulse the Japanese threat—and, in accordance with the advice of his American advisor, took the steps leading to the proclamation of a new dynasty. Before such a change could be carried out, however, he knew that he needed the approval of the foreign powers, especially Japan, on which he would still be dependent for economic assistance. He was encouraged by the tentative approval of the Japanese government, even though it carried the implied condition that final acceptance would depend on a satisfactory response to the Twenty-One Demands.

In spite of Japan's distrust of Yüan, who had opposed its continental ambitions since the contest for Korea, and in spite of Japan's preference for a weak and disunified China, its government was ready to accept such a change, if it were granted the dominant position in Chinese affairs provided by the Demands. Therefore, as soon as Yüan's unwillingness to comply fully with the Demands became apparent, Japan reversed its policy and worked to undermine his monarchical plans. Whether or not Japan's Western allies, fully occupied by the struggle with Germany and anxious for Japan to play a larger role, might have reacted differently in peacetime to the restoration of monarchy in China remains an open question, but under wartime circumstances they could not risk jeopardizing their Chinese interests by following a policy contrary to the wishes of their Japanese ally. Even though their representatives in China reported no significant opposition to Yüan's plans, they issued joint warnings against them. Even the one power still unengaged in the war, the United States, though it made clear its abhorrence of the Demands, refused to support or oppose Yüan on the ground that the issue was strictly an internal affair to be determined by China and the Chinese people. In contradiction to the reports of the Western representatives and Yüan's own agents Japan warned him of the development of serious opposition that would destroy the law and order he had achieved, and possibly destroy him.

The customary interpretation that both the Western representatives and Yüan were inadequately informed seems highly improbable. What the Japanese were better informed about was their own intrigues to stimulate and support rebellions. When rebellions did break out, the ease with which Yüan's troops defeated and dispersed the largest rebel force confirms the insignificance of the opposition. Undoubtedly Yüan's armies could have suppressed all the revolts, including defections among his own followers, which Japanese subversion had assiduously cultivated, but only at the cost of bankruptcy and a damaging breakdown of the order he had restored. Moreover, there was no assurance that Japan would not decide to play a more direct role in support of the rebels. Finally, there was little prospect of additional foreign loans to finance suppression of the rebels and the restoration of order. Under the circumstances the only prudent course seemed to be to cancel his coronation, accompanied by the face-saving

declaration that he had been misled about the popular will. Unfortunately, such a strategic withdrawal only served to encourage the rebels to demand his total surrender of power and the reinstatement of the constitutional regime with parliament. When, for the welfare of the country, he was about to give in, he suddenly died on June 6, 1916, leaving no clearly designated heir to his military power. The result was more than a decade of disorder during which a host of warlords fought and maneuvered for power at the expense of the Chinese people before at least superficial reunification was achieved.

China could ill afford such a prolonged delay in modernization, while the pace of progress was accelerating elsewhere. When China partially emerged again from its preoccupation with internal turmoil, it found itself even farther behind the economies of Japan and the West, making orderly rather than revolutionary development even more difficult to accomplish.

THE WARLORD ERA AND THE RISE OF KUOMINTANG (1916–1928)

No attempt will be made to describe the complexities of the conflicts and shifting alliances of the northern warlords jockeying for control of Peking, which for diplomatic purposes continued to be viewed as the national capital. Nor will the equally complex maneuverings of the southern warlords be considered. Of more importance was the ruthless exploitation of the peasantry to support the warlords and the military machines that kept them in power. With a few notable exceptions, none of the warlords made any effort to carry out reforms or economic developments for the improvement of the territories under their control. Instead, they collected excessive taxes, often many years in advance, and forced the farmer to divert land from food to profitable cash crops, such as opium, to finance their operations. Obviously such actions enhanced the poverty of the peasantry, already living on the brink of disaster. Many peasant sons welcomed the opportunity to serve in their lord's army where they were at least assured of a full stomach at the expense of their fellow peasants. The irregular requisitions of the poorly disciplined military made every village dread the appearance of a contingent. Only the monopoly of military power and collaboration with the landlord class enabled such a system to function at all. An index of economic deterioration was the growth in food imports. Although almost all of this imported food was consumed in the treaty ports, it reflects the diminishing ability of the countryside to fill the food needs of the cities as well as the growth in their populations as places where there was at least a better opportunity of eking out an existence.

During these years—and especially the war years—Japan continued to take advantage of the needs and weakness of China to expand its economic and political interests. Mention has already been made of the seizure of the German leasehold and properties and the Twenty-One Demands. In 1915 President Yüan Shih-k'ai was compelled to accept most of the Demands, though he refused to accede to the fifth group, which would have established a Japanese hegemony. This agreement confirmed Japan's expanded influence and privileges in Manchuria and Inner Mongolia and its title to the seized German properties and leasehold in Shantung in addition to economic concessions elsewhere. Still Japan was not satisfied, as witnessed by its sabotage of Yüan's bid to revive the monarchy. After his death in 1916—and particularly after China's declaration of war against the Central Powers at American urging— the problems of warlordism and the succession to power gave Japan an ideal opportunity to secure additional concessions. Although China's entrance into World War I secured some financial benefits, such as a five-year suspension on Boxer indemnity payments and an upward revision of the tariff to yield an actual five percent, the

additional revenue by no means met the needs, and greed, of those in control of the government of a fragmented state. The outstretched hands of these Chinese warlords were filled by the so-called Nishihara loans. Ostensibly designed to facilitate Chinese contributions to the allied war efforts, these loans were in fact, gifts, most of which were "secured" by important economic concessions for mines, railroads, and industrial enterprises consolidating Japan's preeminence among foreigners in the Chinese market. To guarantee continuance of the internal turmoil so advantageous to the expansion of Japanese influence, additional funds were also channeled into the war chests of the Manchurian warlord, Chang Tso-lin, and the revolutionary Sun Yat-sen who repeatedly attempted to set up his own regime based in Canton. Sun, it should be recognized, was willing to accept funds from any source to forward his dreams and, in fact, privately admired Japan and its achievements, while he publicly denounced the Peking warlords for selling out the country to Japan. Although Japan pulled in its horns somewhat after the Washington Conference of 1921, it continued less overtly to finance dissension in China.

The Chinese reaction to Japanese encroachment was slow in developing, but when it came, it represented an explosive expression of national feeling whose direction was to prove of tremendous significance for the future of the country. The major factor influencing the Chinese government to enter the war had been the expectation that at the peace table the German properties lost to Japan would be restored, but Japan had protected itself against this eventuality by negotiating secret treaties with its allies to uphold its title to them and the other concessions extracted from China in 1915. At Versailles all the eloquence of the Chinese delegates could not budge the allies. Only the American president backed the Chinese claim, and he, anxious for acceptance of the League of Nations, conceded the point when Japan promised to negotiate separately with

China for the termination of its succession to German political, but not economic, privileges.

News of the rejection of the Chinese claim for the restoration of the German leasehold and properties in Shantung triggered an outbreak of anti-Japanese and anti-imperialistic sentiment and action, known as the May 4th Movement, which became nationwide in scope and is looked back on as the first mass expression of Chinese nationalism. The movement was spearheaded by university students, many of whom had already absorbed leftist doctrines and in any case suspected their government's officials of Japanese collaboration. It soon spread to urban labor, merchants, and chambers of commerce throughout the country and produced the most effective and sustained boycott yet mounted against Japanese goods. The Chinese delegates refused to sign the Treaty of Versailles and returned home to be lionized as national heroes rather than censured, as they expected, for their failure. No matter what personal views government officials may have harbored, they could not afford to act against such a widespread demonstration of national feeling. The boycott was such a blow to the Japanese economy, already reeling under postwar economic disorders, that the government offered to negotiate, as promised, for the surrender of its political rights, but the offer came to naught because the Chinese government had no choice under the circumstances but to insist on an unconditional surrender of all the rights and privileges, economic as well as political.

The importance of the May 4th Movement of 1919 cannot be underestimated. First, it gave new life to Sun Yat-sen's efforts to establish a competing government in Canton, particularly considering the cloud cast over the patriotism of the Peking regime. Second, it provided a stimulus for the subsequent formation of the Chinese Communist Party by those university students and professors who had begun the serious study of Marxist-Leninist writings in 1918. Finally, it supplied the single rallying cry of "Anti-Imperialism" for all dissident factions regardless of their particular ideologies. Around this single theme the conception of China as a nation was formed from the very beginning. The movement magnified the Versailles treaty into the culminating humiliation inflicted upon China by the cynical, imperialist powers, and though Japan was the principal villain, in Chinese eyes all signatories shared the guilt. Even the United States, which had failed to ratify the treaty, was condemned in the eyes of patriotic Chinese because President Wilson, the champion of self-determination and international justice in his Fourteen Points, had surrendered on the Shantung issue. By this general denunciation under the mantle of anti-imperialism there was only one nation left interested in China and untainted by participation in the Versailles settlement to which a nationalist leader could safely turn for aid— Soviet Russia. Therefore, Sun Yat-sen's agreement in January 1923, with the Soviet agent of the Comintern, Adolph Joffe, was no more than a logical consequence of the Chinese reaction to the Versailles treaty.

As early as 1919 the struggling Soviet regime recognized its potential advantage and sought to exploit it by denouncing the imperialist abuses of China and renouncing all Tsarist infringements on Chinese sovereignty, including extraterritoriality. Communist Russia was unable to capitalize on this advantage, however, until after the Washington Conference and the final withdrawal of Japanese troops from the Siberian intervention in 1922. Then Joffe and others were dispatched to regain Russian influence (1) by denouncing the capitalist powers as imperialists, (2) by playing Canton off against Peking and Japan against China, and (3) by cultivating Chinese intellectuals. Although Joffe made little progress in Peking, he was able to reach an agreement with Sun in Shanghai that laid the basis for Russian and Chinese Communist support of the Kuomintang. Sun, correctly suspicious of Communist motives, insisted on a written acceptance of his conviction that the conditions for communism did not exist in China and that the main problem was the achievement of national unification and independence.

Sun's avowed preference for conspiratorial organization and elitist leadership was very well suited to the adoption of communist revolutionary techniques in organizing a centralized and disciplined party structure, and it was in this area that Russian asistance and advice proved most valuable. Sun recognized that his greatest problem was reaching and securing the support of the masses. While communist propaganda techniques proved invaluable in this task, Chinese nationalist scholars also concentrated on this problem and the even broader problem of modifying the Chinese cultural and intellectual outlook to facilitate rapid modernization. Before turning to the political progress of the Kuomintang, attention needs to be given to their endeavors.

Since the turn of the century a rapidly growing number of Chinese students had been exposed to Western education either in missionary and state-supported schools in China or abroad in the schools of Japan and the West. Unfortunately, as is too often the case even today, both texts and instruction were wholly unrelated to the Chinese background and conditions. The results of such an education were most often superficiality, cultural dichotomy, or complete alienation, with the first being the most common consequence. Few students possessed the sensitivity to apply their Western learning to conditions as they existed in China. As was already noted, the abolition of the civil service examinations based on the Confucian classics in 1905 undermined Confucianism as a political institution and threatened it as the basis of the Chinese way of life. But the natural inertia in implementing such a far-ranging change delayed its development until after the revolution and, as a widespread movement, until after the death of Yüan

Shih-k'ai. The Confucian classics continued to dominate instruction even in state-supported schools because not enough teachers versed in Western subjects were available and because the slowness to accept change was reinforced by Yüan's renewed emphasis on Confucian morality. In the frontal assault on Confucianism, which came to be dubbed the New Culture Movement, two figures stood out above the rest: Ch'en Tu-hsiu (1879–1942), future founder of the Chinese Communist party, and the more moderate nationalist, Dr. Hu Shih (1891–1962).

In an article in the December 1916 issue of his magazine, *The New Youth*, Ch'en launched the all-out attack on Confucianism by denouncing the outmoded character of its familial and societal restrictions on the freedom of the individual, both male and female. Although he emphasized individual independence in this article, the influence of Marxist studies is already apparent in his stress on the feudal character of the doctrines of Confucius.

In 1917, Hu Shih, with the backing of Ch'en, initiated a literary revolution, rejecting the classical written language, which even revolutionaries had felt constrained to use in their manifestos, in favor of composition in the contemporary language of the people. Such a step was well justified by the need to reduce illiteracy and to expand communication in a modernized state, but Hu Shih, educated at Cornell and Columbia, was additionally interested in creating a dynamic literary style that could match, if not surpass, the literature of other modern nations. Although the success of his campaign on the second score is open to question, there is no doubt that he broke the grip of the classics and facilitated the development of more widespread literacy. In this work he was aided by others who promoted a mass-education movement with a basic vocabulary of 1300 characters that could be mastered in four and one-half months. With modifications this program has since received even greater emphasis by the Communists.

In 1920 his efforts were recognized when the government directed the progressive introduction, grade by grade, of instruction in the "national language."

The leaders of the New Culture Movement fully realized that Confucianism was a way of life and that a merely destructive attack on it was not enough; a new philosophy of life had to be offered to fill the void. It was in this work that they clearly exposed their commitment to science, social change, and individualism. Hu Shih as a former student of John Dewey was an advocate of pragmatism with its accompanying emphasis on skepticism and materialism. Ch'en was also deeply impressed by Dewey who came to China on a lecture tour during 1919 and 1920. Dewey's philosophy of life may be summed up as follows. While the individual is mortal, society and civilization, which represent the collective lives and cumulative achievements of individuals, persist from generation to generation into infinity. Therefore, individuals should constantly strive to improve society, remembering that any sufferings of the moment will contribute to future happiness. All human institutions are arbitrary constructions designed to preserve society and enhance the individual enjoyment of life. Therefore, they should be freely altered as required by the needs of the times. This skeptical, pragmatic, and materialistic outlook, which looked forward to change, was fully supported in the early writings of Hu Shih who asserted: "Not only do the species change, but truth also changes." A logical corollary of this attack on Confucianism and stress on political, social, and moral relativism was a critical, debunking assault on Chinese history and tradition.

Of course, the subversive character of the New Culture Movement did not go unchallenged. A number of intellectuals were alarmed by this threat to the underlying values of Chinese civilization and came forward in their defense. Others noted the weakness of Western science and materialism as illustrated by the cataclysm of World War I.

While willing to incorporate the material benefits of Western science and progress, they warned against uncritical acceptance of its materialistic values as an example of immoderate extremism bound to founder in its own contradictions. Chinese spiritual and cultural values and identity must not be abandoned in favor of these alien idols with demonstrable feet of clay. On balance, however, the defenders were overwhelmed, and the New Culture Movement won over the bulk of the young intellectuals who generally favored both individual liberation and institutional change. Traditionally the educated class enjoyed great prestige and influence with the Chinese people, but such new and radical views, largely limited to its youthful element, would have been slow in percolating down to the masses under any circumstances. The practice of the new philosophy of life was for the most part restricted to the Western-influenced treaty ports; in most of China the traditional way of life prevailed, including the ritual worship of Confucius. Later, Generalissimo Chiang K'ai-shek (1887–   ) believed he would find the broadest base of support by advocating Confucian morality and purging those with radical views. By these actions he left the Chinese Communist party by default, the sole, substantial, organized entity in support of significant social change. Thus, in the course of events, the New Culture Movement inadvertently cultivated the ground for the ultimate triumph of Chinese communism. Initially, however, nationalism and communism collaborated effectively.

Not long after his agreement with Joffe, Sun sent his military aide, Chiang K'ai-shek, and other Kuomintang supporters to Russia for several months' instruction and training. Chiang, who had received his military training in Japan and had served Sun in several previous attempts to establish a government, returned unconverted and deeply suspicious of Russian motives. He was named director of the Whampoa Military Academy founded to train a nucleus of officers for a new revolutionary army. Immediately he was confronted with the problem of dealing with Russian and Chinese Communist military and civil advisors who sought to install communist indoctrination as an integral part of the cadet's curriculum. Like Sun, Chiang preferred the conspiratorial type of organization based on personal ties of loyalty. By bringing in officers and cadets personally loyal to him and by asserting his authority, he checked communist influence, forcing a division of the academy into a majority group supporting him and a minority communist group. Among the latter were a number of future communist generals, such as Chu Teh (1886–   ) and Lin Piao (1908–   ).

In September 1923, the chief civilian advisor, Michael Borodin, arrived, accompanied by a number of additional organizational experts, both civilian and military. These Russian advisors were supplemented by members of the Chinese Communist party who joined the Kuomintang as individuals, rather than as a group, retaining primary allegiance to the Communist party. Rapidly the Kuomintang was reorganized after the communist revolutionary model with cells at the local level, regional committees and provincial committees with executive power to enforce the party policies and purge any nonconformists, and a party congress to approve the policies and actions dictated by a central executive committee and a supervisory committee. In theory, power came from below through the elected delegates to the party congress, but in practice, policy was determined by the top committees and dictated to the subordinate units. This is what is known in communist parlance as "democratic centralism" and was reinforced by Sun's election as president for life by the first congress in January 1924.

A larger change, however, was wrought in the general outlook, philosophy, and membership of the Kuomintang. Hitherto it had been a comparatively small, secret organization, narrowly based on the support of revolutionary intellectuals and merchants;

now it was transformed into a mass organization with a propaganda appeal to peasants and workers to join in a national revoutionary movement. The admission to membership of both peasants and workers and Chinese Communists, many of whom gained executive positions, gave the party an increasingly leftist orientation which alarmed the conservative elements.

In the hope of peacefully reuniting China for a concerted assault against the imperialistic encroachments on Chinese sovereignty and integrity, Sun traveled to Peking to negotiate a settlement with the northern warlords he had so frequently denounced. His trip was fruitless and he died there in March 1925. Following his death an intricate struggle for power within the party ensued, from which Chiang emerged as the titular head with the grudging acceptance by Borodin and the Communists of his plan for a military campaign to the north.

The strategy for the triumphal march northward to the Yangtze during the fall of 1926 was largely the work of the Russian General Galen, though Chiang was recognized as generalissimo and chairman of the all-important Standing Committee. The troops were divided into two main columns, the one dominated by leftists following an interior route to the Wuhan industrial complex and the other commanded by Chiang and composed largely of his supporters heading for Nanking and Shanghai. The interior column encountered minimal resistance thanks to the agitators who preceded it whipping up popular support by antilandlord, antiwarlord, and anti-imperial propaganda. One of these agitators who was deeply impressed by the potential revolutionary discontent of the peasants was Mao Tse-tung (1893–1977). Once in the Yangtze basin where foreign contacts had been most extensive the anti-imperial appeal proved to be most potent.

The leftist column achieved its objective first, capturing the Wuhan cities after only a semblance of defense and transferring the government promptly to this center. Anti-foreign outbreaks there and in Nanking alarmed the Shanghai businessmen who offered to support Chiang in return for protection against the communist-agitated workers. Fearful of the trend of events and in need of money to pay his troops, Chiang agreed, entered the city in April 1927, and ordered his troops to participate in a bloodbath in which all persons suspected of radical leanings were ferreted out and executed in the streets without even the pretence of a trial. This ruthless action ended all collaboration with the Wuhan regime. When, for obvious reasons, Chiang refused to attend a meeting of the Standing Committee at Wuhan, he was removed from his posts. Relying on his military strength and the material support of the Shanghai business community, he set up his own Nationalist government in Nanking in April 1927. His principal opponent for the succession, the moderately leftist Wang Ching-wei (1883–1944), who had been driven into exile, had returned to head the Wuhan government. Thus the revolutionary movement appeared to be irrevocably split.

At this point, however, the Comintern, encouraged by the apparently favorable course of events, overplayed its hand. A raid by the Peking warlord on the Russian embassy revealed that Borodin was acting under direct orders from Russia, which appeared more interested in the advancement of communism than in the welfare of China. More decisive was the revelation by a Comintern agent to Wang Ching-wei, contrary to the advice of Borodin who knew the limited extent of communist sentiment among the Wuhan leaders, of instructions for prompt progress toward the sovietization of China. Alarmed and shocked by Russia's callous subordination of the Kuomintang goal of national unification to the advancement of communism, in contradiction to the Sun-Joffe agreement, the Wuhan regime, faithful to Sun's program, ordered Borodin and his corps of advisors to leave the country in late July. The Chinese Communists were purged,

either accompanying Borodin on his return to Russia or finding refuge in China beyond the reach of the Kuomintang. Thus Russian impatience and lack of understanding of the Chinese situation, precipitated by the Trotsky-Stalin struggle for power, destroyed in a moment the substantial progress that had been achieved by collaboration with the Kuomintang.

Nevertheless, the expulsion of the Communists did not immediately bring about a reconciliation with Chiang, whom the Wuhan leaders had denounced as a traitor to Sun's principles and just another reactionary warlord. Therefore, to demonstrate his dedication to the cause, Chiang resigned in August as head of the Nanking government and retired with his supporters to Shanghai. Before the end of 1927 the other Kuomintang leaders, who had moved the capital to Nanking, realized that he alone commanded the prestige and military support needed for completion of the initial objective of reunification. He was recalled to power and in 1928 was ready to resume the march northward that had been stalled for a year by intraparty conflicts.

Again, the advance was made by separate columns with that one directly commanded by Chiang following the route closest to the sea. Again, he encountered the greatest resistance, this time from Japanese forces ostensibly dispatched to protect their Shantung properties. In clashes with the Japanese, Chiang's troops were decisively worse. This experience made a permanent impression on Chiang's mind about the inferiority of his forces in equipment and training and in part explains his subsequent reluctance to engage in military resistance to Japanese encroachments. Because of this delay the honor of liberating Peking in June from the control of the "Old Marshall" of Manchuria, Chang Tso-lin, fell to the model warlord of Shansi, Yen Hsi-shan, who had decided to support the Nationalists. In the hope of gaining a successor more amenable to the expansion of their influence in Manchuria the Japanese liquidated the "Old Marshall" by blowing up the railroad car in which he was returning to Mukden, but their plot was thwarted when his son, Chang Hsüeh-liang, known as the "Young Marshall," succeeded to his power and threw in his lot with the Nationalist government on the first day of 1929. In fact, the "Young Marshall" proved to be more vigorous and less cooperative than his father had been, pushing the Japanese into open conquest of Manchuria two and one-half years later.

Meanwhile, the old Kuomintang objective was accomplished of transferring the capital from Peking to Nanking, which incidentally was also the center of Chiang's power. To underline this shift, Peking (Northern Capital) was renamed Peip'ing (Northern Peace), the name by which the Nationalists still refer to it even though it is once more named Peking as the capital of the communist government. In October 1928, a provisional constitution was promulgated according to Sun's program for a period of political tutelage under the direction of the Kuomintang acting through the party congress, the central executive committee, and its standing committee. These party units staffed and supervised the governing organs of which the Central State Council was the most important. In spite of this superstructure of an apparently less authoritarian regime, Chiang in fact monopolized political power by occupying the key posts and manning the rest with his personal supporters.

In theory, the Republic of China had regained the unity lost at the time of Yüan Shih-k'ai's death in 1916. Chiang K'ai-shek headed a party regime dedicated to Sun Yat-sen's plans for a step-by-step implementation of his three principles: nationalism, democracy, and the people's livelihood. He enjoyed the financial backing of the Shanghai business community, notably the Soong banking family, one of whose American-educated daughters he had married in December 1927. (Another daughter, the widow of Sun Yat-sen, had retreated with

Borodin to Russia issuing a denunciation of Chiang as a reactionary warlord). In addition, he enjoyed the goodwill of the Western powers, if not Japan, and controlled two-thirds of the customs revenues from foreign trade. In fact, however, he was merely the strongest and best-financed of the warlords, who acknowledged his regime only so long as their interests were served and their semiautonomous regimes were accepted. His many conflicts in subsequent years with the various warlords fully substantiates this situation. Even the Kuomintang was not united behind his government, the leftist elements, which included most of the intellectuals, even going to the extent of rebellion in alliance with dissident warlords to register their disapproval. By war, bribery, and intrigue, Chiang gradually extended his authority in the ensuing years, but new factors—the peasant-based communist movement of Mao Tse-tung and Japanese militarism concerned at the growth of his power—arose to plague him.

CHIANG K'AI-SHEK, MAO TSE-TUNG AND JAPAN

In view of the weak and divided nature of Chiang's regime in 1929 what was most surprising was not his failures but rather the extent of his success in consolidating his authority by manipulating or eliminating recalcitrant warlords and dissident elements of the Kuomintang. Indeed, the decision of the Japanese military to seize Manchuria in 1931 was motivated by the success of nationalist propaganda in that territory considered by them to be a Japanese preserve, and in 1937 their initiation of the second Sino-Japanese conflict was a further reaction to his elimination of practically all opposition within China, even to the extent of coming to temporary terms with his inveterate foes, the Chinese Communists.

After the debacle of 1927 the Chinese Communist party had been reduced to virtual impotence. Some members sought to follow Marxist doctrine by rebuilding their influence among the urban workers; others retired to the countryside where as agitators in advance of the armies they had achieved an enthusiastic response from oppressed peasants. Among the latter, one who had been deeply inspired by the potentialities of peasant rebellion was the innately rebellious son of a prosperous, but authoritarian, Hunanese farmer, Mao Tse-tung (1893–   ).

As a boy, Mao had been repelled by his father's austerity and severe discipline which, in accordance with traditional Chinese mores, were aimed at improving the family fortunes, even at the expense of abusing his own family and exploiting the misfortunes of his less-disciplined fellow peasants. Mao later depicted himself as the leader of the family opposition against the authority of his father whom he dubbed the "ruling power." In school he rebelled against the authority of his teacher who forced him to read the classics when he preferred the romantic novels telling of peasant resistance to oppression. Indeed, his hatred of authority knew no bounds because he equated every form of it, except his own, with exploitation. In later life it even extended to fellow Communist leaders who were competing with him for authority.

In addition to his dislike for authority and his sympathy for the peasants, Mao demonstrated at an early age organizational and leadership talent. Inspired by works decrying the weakness of China and the humiliations it had suffered at the hands of Japan and the West, he sought out other young men similarly interested in working for the eviction of the powers and the restoration of Chinese prestige. With the revolution he became an ardent supporter of Sun Yat-sen's program but delved even more deeply into socialist literature propagating what he had learned among his growing group of young followers, institutionalized in 1917 as the New-People's Study Society. A number of these disciples subsequently became prominent figures in his development of the Chi-

nese Communist movement, illustrating again the traditional importance of personal ties in Chinese political development.

In 1918 Mao secured a post at the Peking National University Library where he avidly devoured every available piece of socialist and communist writing under the guidance of Li Ta-chao, University Librarian and first champion of the Soviet Revolution. He increasingly engaged in politics attacking the domination of government by militarists supported by members of the landlord class. In addition, he demonstrated his communist indoctrination by organizing during the winter of 1920–1921 the workers of the city of Changsha in his native Hunan. Finally, in May 1921, he was one of the 12 founding fathers of the Chinese Communist party and, after the decision to cooperate with the Kuomintang, became a member of the executive committees of both parties, in addition to other important appointments, including the Communist Politburo. Returning to Hunan in 1925 and 1926 he discovered how easily poor peasants could be inspired to rise against oppressive landlords. In a report to his party's central committee, published in February 1927, before the collapse of Kuomintang-Communist cooperation, he emphasized the fundamental role of the peasants in any successful revolution, insisting that the myriad hosts of poor peasants were in fact the most revolutionary element in Chinese society. Such an assertion was a heretical challenge to the communist proletarian dogma and was therefore rejected, but it demonstrated that Mao had grasped the essence of Chinese revolutionary tradition, which had always depended on the desperation of the peasant masses. Throughout the course of Chinese history dynasty after dynasty had been undermined by peasant rebellions.

After the Kuomintang purge of the Communists Mao took refuge in his native Hunan, planning to implement his dream of a peasant rebellion which, he believed, would spread like a fire throughout the length and breadth of China consuming not only the landlords but also all foreign and domestic exploiters of the Chinese people. His "Autumn Harvest" rebellion in 1927 failed and he lost his position on the Politburo. Still convinced of the correctness of his approach for China in contrast to the doctrinaire reliance of the party leadership in Shanghai on the urban working class, he reformed his depleted ranks and proceeded more gradually to develop his peasant movement. In 1928 he gained an important accretion of military strength when he was joined by Chu Teh, a German-trained officer of the Whampoa Military Academy, with trained lieutenants and a body of troops who had failed to carry out a coup against Chiang. Henceforth Mao and Chu Teh jointly exercised the political and military duties in the expansion of their control over most of Kiangsi and parts of Fukien province.

Under Mao's guidance, guerrilla strategy and tactics were devised to take maximum advantage of a peasant base of support. First, soldiers had to be reeducated to recognize their role as servants and saviors of the people. While the approach of government troops, renowned for their unrestrained rapaciousness, was looked on with terror by the villagers, Red forces came to be viewed as liberators who backed up the poor peasants in dealing with notorious or unrepentant landlords and who aided the villagers in repairing damages or rehabilitating public works. By persuading the peasants to condemn and execute landlords, the Communists made them forever accomplices in crime who could look forward to nothing but the worst from the Kuomintang. Therefore, any village thus "liberated" could be relied on to support the Red forces to the extent of its ability. As an aside, it is interesting to note that the need repeatedly to reeducate both officers and men suggests the difficulty in convincing them, and especially the Kuomintang deserters, of their proper role. After initial terroristic excesses Mao recognized his need for the support of middle and rich

peasants to maintain his troops and developed a more moderate policy inviting their cooperation and even that of well-regarded landlords. This pragmatic policy enabled him to expand the base of support for an enlarged Red army, but it later led to severe criticism of Mao for "rightist deviation."

In 1930, the Politburo, still convinced of the necessity of proletarian seizure of urban bases, ordered the Red armies, of which Mao's was only one, to back the workers by military assaults on key cities. The failure of this policy, in which only Changsha in Hunan was captured and held for a few days by a Red force before being expelled by Nationalist troops, convinced Mao of the correctness of his guerrilla tactics based on encircling the cities from rural bases and avoiding frontal battles, at least until his forces could match those of the Kuomintang in numbers and equipment. He would avoid cities and fixed positions, depending on mobility and peasant support. These tactics, which in the long run have proved so successful in China, were summed up in the now famous aphorism: "When the enemy advances, we retreat; when the enemy halts, we harass him; when the enemy seeks to avoid battle, we attack; when the enemy retreats, we pursue."

In recognition of the growing menace of Mao's movement, Chiang launched one "extermination" campaign after another, whenever he was not diverted by Japanese actions, but from 1930 to 1934 his reliance on traditional tactics was frustrated by Mao's guerrilla tactics, which avoided decisive battles while harassing supply lines and inflicting significant losses on isolated units. Substantial defections also swelled the ranks of Mao's trained troops.

In November 1931, a victorious and confident Mao invited the Politburo to join him in proclaiming a formal Chinese Soviet Republic and in the following year, after the Japanese attack, enhanced the communist appeal to the Chinese intellectuals and people by officially declaring war on Japan, while Chiang pursued a negotiated settlement. During these years, however, the Politburo, which was dominated by recently returned students from Sun Yat-sen University in Moscow, successfully challenged his leadership, criticizing his ideological weakness and reluctance to take the offensive as "rightist deviation." Although Mao retained his post as Chairman of the republic, he temporarily lost control of the Red army.

In 1934, Chiang, following the advice of his German military advisors, altered his tactics. Instead of attempting to find and destroy the forces of his elusive foe in the field, he first sealed off the communist area from essential supplies, such as salt, and then gradually secured a firm control over more and more of it by erecting a network of fortified posts. As the communist area of operations was thus constricted, they were forced to make a decision whether to stand up and fight against superior forces or attempt to break out of the tightening grip of the Kuomintang armies. In pitched battles they had already suffered heavy losses. After weighing the alternatives, they decided to break through in several columns with about 80,000 of their best troops, leaving their peasant supporters to fight a delaying action and then fend for themselves. Thus began the famous Long March of about 6000 miles and more than a year during 1934–1935 through the mountainous terrain of southern and western China until their depleted forces reached the northwest province of Shensi. As they moved forward, skirmishes and battles had to be waged almost daily against their pursuers as well as the troops of the warlords on their line of march with the incidental consequence of breaking their power and extending Chiang's authority over them. In January 1935, at Tsunyi in Kweichow, after the loss of about half of the troops, Mao had gained enough support to demand an enlarged meeting of the Politburo and secured recognition as the head of the Chinese Communist movement. Chou En-lai's switch to Mao's side was an important factor in his success.

Later, when Mao's column met a larger force in western Szechuan its commander was unwilling to recognize Mao's authority and after a long deliberation each went their separate ways, Mao proceeding directly to Shensi province. Although a substantial number of recruits joined his army during the course of the march, the attrition of warfare and weather reduced the original force to only 8000 hardened veterans bonded together much more closely by this common experience of exceptional hardship. Almost all the leading figures of the present regime are veterans of the Long March, and their greatest problem is to instill in the younger generation of recruits to the party the same sense of common comradeship, self-sacrifice, and loyalty it inspired.

Upon the arrival of Mao and his depleted forces in Shensi he was joined by the local communist leader and later by other contingents. Soon he was able to field an army of more than 30,000 with headquarters in the caves of Yenan. Chiang sent Chang Hsüeh-liang, the evicted Young Marshall of Manchuria and deputy commander-in-chief of the Nationalists, and his troops to eliminate the last significant communist army. But Mao's government, which had officially declared war on Japan in 1932, successfully appealed to their strong anti-Japanese feelings for a cessation of hostilities and the formation of a united front against Japanese aggression. The Comintern call for united fronts was well-suited to Mao's needs. All real fighting ceased and the opposing troops openly fraternized with each other.

The growth of anti-Japanese feeling and discontent with Chiang's policy of accommodation was not limited to the followers of the Young Marshall. The seizure of Manchuria had not sated the appetite of the Japanese army. Subsequently they sought to detach five northern Chinese provinces as an autonomous area subject to their influence. Fully aware of his unpreparedness to meet Japanese forces in the field, Chiang negotiated, seeking to yield as little as possible in the hope of buying the time needed to consolidate his authority and build up his military strength. Students and intellectuals, unaware of China's comparative military weakness, became increasingly incensed at what appeared to be a pro-Japanese policy of appeasement, while the growing authoritarianism of Chiang's regime appeared to them to be departing farther and farther from the implementation of Sun Yat-sen's program, as set forth in the provisional constitution of May 1931, adopted prior to the Japanese assault on Manchuria. In particular, the leftist leaders singled out for condemnation his failure to pass or put into effect legislation for the improvement of the people's livelihood. Obviously such reforms could not be enforced in territories under warlord control, but even in those areas directly ruled by Chiang's government little action was taken because of his dependence on the economic support of the business and landlord elements. Furthermore, the vehemence of leftist attacks grew in direct proportion to his increasing reliance on the right wing of the Kuomintang, and reciprocally his shift to the right to staff his government was a direct response to the growing discontent and criticism of the left-wing leaders.

This does not mean that his government was without solid achievements, but for the most part they may be characterized as moderate, gradualist, and conservative in nature. Indeed, the accomplishments of his government were what alarmed the Japanese army leaders and led them to precipitate the second Sino-Japanese War. Mention has already been made of his success in subordinating most of the warlords to his direct control in a multitude of military campaigns. The financing of these operations, however, consumed the bulk of his resources leaving little surplus for reconstruction projects. Nevertheless, thanks to the genius of his brother-in-law, T. V. Soong, as finance minister, the currency was stabilized and payments on the debts inherited from previous regimes were resumed—an amazing feat in

a depression-plagued world, facilitated to a great extent by the attainment of customs autonomy in 1928 as well as a policy of economic austerity. Nevertheless, this achievement was jeopardized by a tendency toward deficit spending. In addition, the late Manchu objective of gaining centralized control of the railroads was accomplished and communications were greatly expanded by the construction of highways initially for the purpose of supporting military operations. Significant progress was also made in army modernization, industrialization, education, public health work including a reduction of opium smoking, and legal reform to gain acceptance by the powers of the termination of extraterritoriality. Unification needs had also spurred the development of radio communications and the establishment of commercial airlines and an air force with Western financial and technical assistance. An indication of the government's concern for the welfare of the peasants was the legalization of cooperatives in 1934, which produced a growth in their numbers in government-controlled territory, and the formation of an agricultural bank to extend credit at reasonable rates. Moreover, planned public works and scientific institutes to develop techniques for agricultural improvement indicated the good intentions of the government once adequate resources became available. On the other hand, the conservative, and even reactionary, inclination of the government was reflected in the formation of the elitist Blue Shirts to ferret out and suppress radicals and the New Life Movement to inculcate outmoded Confucian morality and personal discipline in the young people of China. As might be expected, such political indoctrination was also prescribed for the soldiers and sailors.

Naturally, democratic leaders, who had been frozen out of the government and had set up a semiautonomous regime in Canton supported by the local warlords, rebelled against this trend under the banner of resisting Japan, but in 1936, with surprising ease,

Chiang suppressed them and nominally incorporated the armies of the southern warlords into the Nationalist forces. The two remaining thorns in his side were the Chinese Communists under Mao Tse-tung and the Japanese in the north who were undermining Kuomintang customs revenues by large-scale smuggling operations. Of the two, the Chinese Communist problem appeared capable of solution by military action, but the Young Marshall and his troops, susceptible to the anti-Japanese appeal for a united front, had proved reluctant to fight.

Even if the Communists had been destroyed, however, a victorious Nationalist regime would still not have been free to invest its resources in social and economic reform and reconstruction, presuming it had the inclination to do so; the greater Japanese threat would have compelled Chiang to channel all available income into military preparedness. Indeed, whatever his wishes, the continuous military demands from the time he came to power precluded any significant investment in development that was not directly related to the military task of extending and consolidating his authority. By the same token, these conditions dictated his dependence, whatever his personal views, on those elements able to provide him with the sinews of war. From the beginning he was a military leader who knew of no other way to carry out the Kuomintang goal of national unification than by military means. During the 1930s the Western powers were too preoccupied with their own economic problems to furnish financial and technical assistance on the scale so familiar in our postwar world. As the head of a responsible government, he had to rely on those resources within China that could be tapped to establish a stable regime, and consequently his freedom to experiment was severely limited. In any case, his avowed preference for the Confucian value system and its associated social structure inclined him toward conservatism. On the other hand, his inveterate foe, Mao Tse-tung, as the leader of a rebel movement, remained unfettered by such responsibility and free to experiment within the tradition of peasant rebellion. Even within his own camp Chiang's determination to dispose of the native Communists and his accommodation with the alien Japanese caused serious defections including the resignation of his finance minister and brother-in-law, T. V. Soong. Such were the circumstances that serve as a backdrop for the Sian Incident of December 1936.

THE SIAN INCIDENT AND THE SECOND SINO-JAPANESE WAR

In August 1935, the Comintern, alarmed by the ardent anticommunism and militarism of Germany and Japan, called on all communist parties to work for the formation of popular united fronts in alliance with anti-fascist parties no matter how bourgeois in outlook. Immediately Mao appealed for such an alliance with the Kuomintang against the Japanese asserting "Chinese should not fight Chinese at a time of Japanese aggression." In 1936 he made a formal proposal of "democratic" union to the Kuomintang setting forth its purposes: first, to resist Japan, second, to secure the people's rights, and third, to develop China's economy. In connection with the last point, while emphasizing the needs of the peasants, he stressed the community of interest between peasant and capitalist, both of whom shared the primary need and desire to liquidate imperialism. In this fashion he moderated the communist position on the evils of capitalism in favor of collaboration in defense of the nation. Of course, in the context of Chinese affairs alone, discounting the Comintern directive, a truce was desirable to gain time for rebuilding the Chinese Communist movement and military strength so severely battered by the rigors of the Long March. From Mao's point of view the Comintern's call for united fronts was particularly well-timed, meshing perfectly with his own needs and the general grounds of dissatisfaction with Chiang's

Japanese policy. For the very same reason, Chiang was anxious to knock out the Chinese Communist military force during its period of weakness.

Earlier in 1936, after successfully asserting control over the Canton region, Chiang had flown to the anticommunist headquarters at Sian to organize and give impetus to a final extermination campaign against the last significant stronghold of domestic resistance to his regime, but to no avail. Instead, during the succeeding months, the common hostility to Japanese encroachments on China fostered an accelerated development of fraternization. Determined to reverse this trend, Chiang again flew to Sian in December. When he adamantly refused to listen to the arguments for greater democracy and a united front against Japan, he was arrested ("kidnapped") by his own subordinates throwing the Nanking government into consternation and turmoil. Some, who may have secretly wished for the elimination of the dictatorial Chiang, proposed the bombing of Sian, if he was not immediately released. This proposal was scotched, however, when his wife and brother-in-law flew to Sian placing their lives also in jeopardy. Meanwhile, Chiang stood on his dignity and his inability as commander-in-chief to negotiate with insubordinate officers under his command.

Their ultimate alternative was to kill their unbending prisoner in the hope of establishing a democratic regime, but without clear expressions of support from other Kuomintang leaders such a course was not feasible. Moreover, on the arrival of Madame Chiang and T. V. Soong, Chiang relaxed his position to the extent of listening to the proposals of his subordinates and the Communist representative, Chou En-lai (1898–   ), perhaps out of greater concern for their lives than for his own. Chiang always maintained that he made no concessions or commitments, and no written evidence has emerged to refute his assertion. All that can be said with any certainty is that the suave Chou En-lai convinced the Nationalist officers of the necessity of preserving Chiang's life as the only figure capable of rallying national resistance to Japan. This suggests that Chiang had at least indicated a willingness to enter negotiations for a united front against Japan. Subsequently, the development of secret negotiations, which had reached the point of successful conclusion at the time of the first clash with Japan seven months later, further substantiates such a hypothesis.

On December 25, 1936, Chiang and his relatives flew back to Nanking setting off a widespread popular expression of relief at his salvation. The degree to which he had consolidated his authority was witnessed by the absence of any signs of rebellion during these two weeks of crisis. The Young Marshall voluntarily surrendered himself, was tried and convicted, and then permitted by Chiang to live under comfortable house arrest, though he was never again entrusted with a command. In view of the secret negotiations with the Chinese Communists and the rising tempo of anti-Japanese feeling, Chiang found his room for maneuver with Japan becoming more and more restricted.

When Chinese and Japanese troops clashed, apparently due to a misunderstanding, at a point near Peip'ing on July 7, 1937, neither government wanted war, but both had got into positions from which neither could yield any further concessions to the other. In contrast to the time of the Manchurian episode the Japanese army was under the control of responsible generals, but both military and civil officials felt compelled to insist on the objectives of several years standing: the establishment of truly autonomous government in northern China and joint operations to eradicate the Chinese Communists. As the German-Japanese Anti-Comintern Pact of 1936 demonstrated, Japan's chief concern was to secure its Chinese flank in defense of the extensive Russian and Mongolian frontier of the puppet state of Manchukuo. Normally, Chiang, knowing how unprepared his forces were for war, would have been ready to negotiate on these conditions, but now he was confronted with such a loud anti-Japanese hue and cry that any concessions or collaboration would have been considered treason. Nevertheless, despite the loss of flexibility on both sides, negotiations were undertaken and continued through further clashes in the futile hope that some accommodation could be reached. Meanwhile, to impress on Chiang the seriousness of the Japanese government, troops were moved into the Peip'ing-Tientsin area from Manchukuo, while other military and naval forces massed off Shanghai. Apparently Japan believed that all Chiang needed was "a little convincing" to come to terms. It was this misguided conviction that led a reluctant Japan step-by-step into a deeper and deeper involvement in China. From the beginning, official Japanese policy had no interest in diverting its strength by attempting to conquer China. Even after Chiang retreated into remote Szechuan, the Japanese government still hoped to negotiate a settlement with him. For this reason, as much as the American Neutrality Act of 1937, Japan did not declare war and referred to the limited conflict as the "China Affair." On the other hand, Chiang's need for American arms and material kept him from declaring war. Thus both sides refrained from acknowledging the Second Sino-Japanese War that, with the Japanese attack on Pearl Harbor in December 1941, merged into World War II.

Before major hostilities broke out at Shanghai on August 13, 1937, the Nationalist-Communist negotiations were being rushed to a conclusion. In September, by the terms of agreement, the Communists theoretically acknowledged the Nationalist government, and their army was entitled the Eighth Route Army under the supreme command of Chiang K'ai-shek. The Communists were to cease their political activity, particularly their attack on the landlord class and their redistribution of land. Subsequent negotiations were to work out the details of

Communist participation in the government. In return, the Nationalist regime was expected to do its best to supply arms and other vital needs to the Eighth Route Army. This Kuomintang-Communist alliance was shaky from the very beginning. Chiang was reluctant to supply his sworn enemies, and before long the Communists resumed more moderate land reform along the lines of previous Nationalist legislation that had never been implemented. In addition, their guerrilla tactics led them to set up local elective governments within Japanese-dominated territory contrary to the program and practices of the Nationalist government. The more conventional military practice of the Nationalists precluded any such activity behind enemy lines except in collaboration with those local warlords whose operations had not been extinguished by the Japanese. In spite of heavy casualties, the Nationalist regime was encouraged to cling to conventional tactics by the limited Japanese objectives in China. All they sought was Chinese acceptance of Japanese guidance in the development of a Greater East Asia and an anticommunist alliance. Therefore, each offensive was only intended to bring Chiang to terms, and after each Japanese victory he was permitted to withdraw and reorganize his shattered forces while fresh overtures were made. Moreover, the minimal military commitment of Japan as well as the semimechanized nature of its armies tended to restrict campaigns and occupation to the rail, road, and river arteries, leaving vast hinterlands relatively untouched and capable of resisting foraging parties, if the peasants could be armed and organized along guerrilla lines. Finally, Stalin's Russia, fully aware of the anticommunist obsession of the Japanese, was the major source of foreign aid during the early years of the war until the German assault required all its resources for its own defense. Although almost all the Russian munitions and supplies were delivered to Chiang's government for distribution, he could not afford to jeopardize this aid by taking too strong a stand against the Chinese Communists. Therefore, during the first few years of the struggle the terms of the Kuomintang-Communist agreement were fairly well complied with by both parties, while Chiang's armies bore the brunt of the Japanese assaults.

In Shanghai where full-scale fighting commenced in August 1937, Chiang's best troops surprisingly fought the Japanese to a standstill until in November they were forced to withdraw to Nanking by a flanking movement. The capital city of Nanking, however, fell in less than a month before an all-out attack including the merciless use of aerial bombardment. To impress upon Chiang their determination, the Japanese permitted their troops to engage in an orgy of looting and killing condemned throughout the world as "the rape of Nanking." Instead of breaking the Chinese spirit and forcing Chiang to come to terms, these atrocities boomeranged, uniting the people in support of the Nationalist government and reinforcing the determination to resist Japanese aggression at whatever the sacrifice. After a substantial delay in expectation of a negotiated settlement, the resumption of the offensive along the Yangtze met much stiffer opposition. Only after the almost bloodless capture of Canton in October 1938, cutting the last major overseas supply line, did the vital strategic and industrial center of Wuhan fall. Again, the battered Nationalist armies retreated without significant Japanese pursuit to the remote but rich and populous province of Szechuan establishing the new capital at Chungking.

If the Japanese had wished to commit more military strength to the struggle, they could undoubtedly have advanced into Szechuan, but their principal interests and objectives in China must be kept in mind. Their chief concern remained the threat of Soviet Russia, and this concern was underlined by several clashes with Russian troops along the frontiers of Manchukuo in 1938 and 1939. In support of this interest all they sought in China was an alliance under their leadership, not conquest. When Chiang would not accept satellite status, they proceeded to set up puppet regimes for the exploitation of the Chinese economy. But none of these regimes, dependent on Japanese military backing, secured the hoped for cooperation of the Chinese people. Only after the German attack on Russia eased the communist threat and the Western allies began to restrict the flow of strategic supplies, did Japan begin to readjust its outlook from a defensive to an imperialistic direction—and even then the principal motivation was defensive—to protect its strategic and economic position in a war-torn world.

Meanwhile, the beleaguered regime of Free China, operating on a much less productive base, tended to become more authoritarian and introverted. Although substantial numbers of students and scholars, businessmen and industrialists had retreated to Szechuan with the Nationalists, transferring universities and transporting factories, the loss of urban industrial centers compelled Chiang to rely increasingly for revenue on the land tax collected through the conservative landlord class of Free China. As time passed, their interests came to prevail over the more progressive urban-intellectual elements who were muzzled and suppressed by the secret police, backed by the authoritarian Generalissimo, looking to a revival of the Confucian virtues, especially personal loyalty. He was particularly alarmed by the growing popularity of the Communists among the intellectuals, which was encouraged by their successes in organizing peasant resistance behind the Japanese lines.

The first major clash with the Communists occurred in January 1941, when Nationalist forces destroyed the rearguard of the Communist Fourth Army while reluctantly obeying Chiang's order to evacuate its recently established base of operations in the former Nationalist stronghold south of the lower Yangtze. From this date Chiang became more concerned with containing communist expansion and preserving his military strength for an eventual civil war than with fighting the Japanese. The Communists naturally responded in kind, complaining bitterly of Chiang's refusal to turn over to them a fair share of the meager supplies. Although outright clashes were generally avoided, relations grew cooler with an increasing number of despondent intellectuals defecting to the Communists as the sole hope for a new China. To stem this loss, the secret police was expanded and more stringent controls were enforced. These measures only served to increase the alienation of progressive elements from Chiang's regime. During these years and the early postwar years, the chief effect of increasing authoritarianism was to narrow the base of his support and to generate among the educated the growth of neutralism toward the Nationalist-Communist division; defections to the Communists, at this time only a trickle, became merely a stream until the death-throes of the Nationalist regime were entered in 1948.

A major factor contributing both to disenchantment with Chiang's wartime regime and to the expansion of his authority was the fiscal problem. To compensate for inadequate revenue, the government resorted to printing money at an accelerating pace. In combination with shortages of food and consumer goods, the inevitable result was a sharp inflationary spiral that hit hard government employees, both civil and military, and others living on fixed stipends. Such conditions encouraged individual speculation, corruption, and other selfish practices with a consequent decline in integrity and general morals.

In the spring of 1943, shortly after American and British treaties finally abandoned the rights to extraterritoriality and foreign settlements, Chiang published *China's Destiny* expressing his Confucianist rejection of the West and Western individualism as the source of all China's woes and laying down a statist philosophy for the restoration of China, stressing the ancient Confucian virtues of filial piety, loyalty, and obe-

dience. Businessmen and intellectuals who had aided and abetted the demoralization of China by sponsoring selfish individualism and denigrating the traditional values of the family and the state were singled out for denunciation. In the future all activity would be subordinated to the overriding interests of the nation. Business would be controlled and eventually owned by the state. Education and cultural endeavor would be devoted to inculcating the ancient virtues, and any deviationists would be suppressed. All those with liberal views of any complexion could readily see what the future under Chiang's regime held for them. No work more damaging to the Nationalist cause could have been conceived, especially when it was compared with Mao Tse-tung's *On the New Democracy* published two years earlier.

In this work Mao emphasized the "scientific objectivity" of his brand of communism, which dealt with conditions as they actually existed—not as they should be or might eventually become. According to communist analysis, China was still in the feudal-bureaucratic stage and was far from completion of the capitalist stage of development. Nevertheless, he asserted that under communist leadership both the capitalist and socialist stages could be developed concurrently through the cooperation of the four major revolutionary classes: the proletariat, the peasantry, the intelligentsia, and the national (antiforeign) bourgeois. Although both big business and big industry were scheduled for nationalization and the properties of big landlords for confiscation and redistribution, Mao appealed to businessmen by intimating that there would be a future of undefined duration for private enterprise before the conclusion of the capitalist stage of development. Furthermore, he indicated that their skills and those of the intellectuals and truly democratic party leaders would be needed on a large scale in the government to carry out its tasks of organization and construction. Finally, he made his program even more attractive by asserting his reverence for Sun Yat-sen and insisting that he merely sought to implement Sun's Three People's Principles in accordance with the objective realities of Chinese development. In contrast with Chiang, whose reactionary stance narrowed his base of support, Mao, the pragmatic revolutionary, appealed to as broad a segment of progressive elements as he could possibly include.

POSTWAR NEGOTIATION AND CIVIL WAR (1945–1949)

The facts and factors in the rapid collapse of the Nationalists and the victory of the Communists are too recent and involve too many national interests, including American, for impartial and objective analysis. Instead, a flood of vitriolic literature has for the most part tended to exaggerate one or another set of facts and factors. The student attempting to determine just what happened and why is pulled first this way and then that way by each successive account he examines. Therefore, the account presented here should not be considered more than a tentative interpretation subject to revision.

One point seems unquestionable. The relative strengths of the two contestants had shifted drastically during the course of the war in favor of the Communists. Although the Nationalist regular armies were still much larger (numbering more than three million) and much better equipped for conventional warfare, their morale left much to be desired. A major proportion of the prewar troops had been killed in the heavy fighting of the first years of the war, and their places had been filled by unwilling peasants dragooned into the service by the most brutal methods. The chief benefit of army service for them was the reliability of adequate rations mercilessly requisitioned from their fellow peasants. In contrast, the regular Red armies had grown during the war from 50 to 500 thousand (Mao claimed 910,000), supplemented by untold numbers in local guerrilla and part-time militia units as a source of experienced recruits and supported by a rural base of some 90 million people mainly in rural China north of the Yangtze. These troops had been indoctrinated with the concept of their dependence on the people so well expressed in the slogan: "We are the fish and the people are the water through which we swim." Although the Chinese traditionally feared the approach of soldiers, the approach of Communist troops with their reputation for discipline was far less dreaded than that of Nationalist forces renowned for their ruthless rapaciousness. The disparity in arms, especially artillery, was soon offset in part by the seizure of Japanese equipment surrendered to the Russians in Manchuria.

In addition to superior morale and greater peasant support, Communist armies, accustomed by necessity to guerrilla warfare were prepared to utilize more flexible tactics in contrast to the continued Nationalist reliance on positional tactics. Therefore, in spite of superior numbers, control of the air, and American aid and advice, the Nationalists at the very least no longer enjoyed the overwhelming military superiority they had possessed at the outbreak of the war.

Second, the exigencies of the war had lost for Chiang K'ai-shek the ideological advantage he had once enjoyed. Isolated in the interior, with the consequent loss of maritime revenues, he had been compelled to develop an increasingly austere and authoritarian regime relying on the conservative landlord class to collect the land tax. His wartime writings stilled the hopes of his liberal adherents about their prospects under his regime after the war. Although Chiang expressed concern about the People's Livelihood, the actions of his subordinates toward the peasants belied his words—even if they heard of them. There is no doubt about his personal integrity, patriotism, and dedication, but his subordinates, many of whom were former warlords, had merely used the war to extort even more from the oppressed peasants. Under the circumstances, Communist charges that he was just another warlord, unconcerned with the welfare of the people, found a sympathetic audience.

The relation of these conditions is not intended to suggest that Chiang was licked before he started; only that his position was comparatively weaker in 1945 than in 1937. In fact, he appeared to enjoy many distinct advantages, and even Mao seemed to recognize them by his willingness to negotiate for a settlement. Almost one billion dollars, mostly in unused American credits, plus an untold amount of privately held foreign currency, gave him a strong base for restoring the Chinese economy. Moreover, the cities and industries of central and southern China were surrendered not only essentially undamaged but also with added productive capacity developed during the Japanese occupation. A new asset was the return of Taiwan extensively developed under Japanese rule. In an agreement of August 1945, the Russians promised to turn over industrialized Manchuria to the Nationalists in return for the right to utilize the ice-free ports of the Liaotung Peninsula. Thus even Soviet Russia appeared to recognize the superiority of Nationalist over Communist prospects, though it systematically stripped Manchurian industry of machinery, crippling its immediate potential, before relinquishing control to Nationalist forces. Stalin, despite his avowed disdain for China's "cabbage communists," also permitted surrendered Japanese arms to fall into the hands of the Chinese Communists and impeded in every possible way the Nationalist takeover of Manchuria. Finally, the United States stood ready to support the establishment of a strong Chinese state both by direct aid and by indirect assistance through UNRRA. On the other hand, the American government, in recognition of the greatly enhanced strength of the Communists, favored a negotiated settlement between Chiang and Mao to preclude the revival of a devastating civil war. Therefore, the economic and diplomatic prospects for the establishment of a viable regime looked good, especially if it were more democratic in nature, permitting the participation of parties other than the Nationalists, and particularly the Communists. What the American hopes failed to take into account were the inveterate hostility between Chiang and Mao and the adamant opposition of Chiang to any settlement that would jeopardize Nationalist dominance.

As soon as Japan capitulated, the race was on to take the surrender of Japanese forces and to secure control of as much of China as possible. The Japanese were under orders to surrender only to the Nationalists with the result that they held the cities against Communist assaults until Nationalist forces, transported and supported by American planes, ships, and marines, arrived on the scene. Thus the Nationalists occupied the major cities of northern China, such as Peip'ing and Tientsin, while the Communists gained firm control of the countryside. At the same time, Communists forces under Marshall Lin Piao occupied rural Manchuria and in preparation for the forthcoming struggle carried out a forced draft program of land confiscation and redistribution involving of necessity many brutalities. Against the advice of American military advisors, critical of the strategic division of his forces, Chiang decided that the industrial potential of Manchuria was too great to be ignored and utilized American sea and land transport to move his best divisions to Manchuria. Thanks to Russian removal of all useful machinery as reparations, the prize proved to be an empty one. Communist control of the countryside soon made it a hazardous one, but Chiang adamantly refused to consider evacuation.

In spite of repeated clashes with Nationalist troops the Communists participated in a Political Consultative Conference under the benign mediation of President Truman's emissary, General George Marshall, which in January and February of 1946 arrived at three promising agreements. First came a military truce to be policed by three-man teams, composed of one Nationalist, one Communist, and one American officer. The second agreement sought to provide for an immediate and long-term political settlement. In addition to recognizing existing territorial control, a new state council of 20 Nationalists and 20 from all other parties was given a mandate to draw up a constitution for a government based on the Western concept of a cabinet responsible to a majority in an elected legislature rather than Sun Yat-sen's more conservative proposal for a "democratic" regime. The third agreement stipulated the eventual integration of Communist troops into a Chinese national army of a nonpolitical complexion.

Difficulties immediately broke out, particularly over Manchuria. In other areas disputes also over political control led to armed clashes. Interestingly enough, American truce team officers reported more Nationalist than Communist violations. This apparent anomaly was largely due to the refusal of right-wing Nationalist commanders to accept the truce agreements which seemed to them to represent a betrayal of both Sun's program and Kuomintang objectives. During the balance of 1946 the situation progressively deteriorated with the Communists crying foul and refusing to participate in the Kuomintang-dominated steps toward the establishment of a constitutional facade. Other left-leaning parties, allied as the Democratic League, also refused to participate. By January 1947, when General Marshall returned to the United States in disgust to take up the post of Secretary of State, a full-fledged civil war was under way with no hope of reconciliation.

The demands of the civil war had already undermined the economic stability of the government, and by the beginning of 1947 the exchange rate had reached 7000 yuan to the dollar as compared to 1000 to 1 at the end of the Japanese war. Not long after Chiang's initiation of an all-out offensive in mid-1947 the rate rose to 45,000 to 1 and thereafter accelerated even more rapidly. This inflation was not wholly the result of expenditures on the civil war; it was also stimulated by the corrupt practices of officials handicapped by fixed salaries. Regardless of their integrity—and many had lost their integrity in combatting the hardships of the wartime era and viewed their restoration to positions of power as an opportunity to recoup their fortunes—mere survival forced them to withhold revenues from the central government contributing in this way to the inflationary spiral. In this manner, in spite of about two billion dollars in postwar American aid, the interaction of the financial demands of civil war and the sharp inflationary pressure on military and civil employees resulted in corruption, and even brutality, further undermining the popular respect for the Nationalist government. In addition, governmental stress on industry, especially the large amount of surrendered enterprises retained by the government, and the neglect of rural reconstruction alienated both private businessmen and the peasantry.

To all of these elements, including the politicians of the minor political parties frozen out of governmental appointments, Mao Tse-tung made carefully calculated and effective propaganda appeals. Naturally the peasants were promised land reform, and the Communists could point to a record of action, not just promises, in this field. National (that is, antiforeign) businessmen were attracted by the invitation to cooperate for an untold period in the capitalistic development of the country. Like many professional men and intellectuals, more and more of them saw in the Communist party with its avowed moderate program the only alternative to the increasing inefficiency, corruption, and general deterioration of the Nationalist regime. The middle parties were no more than groups of leaders without followers, offering no realistic alternative.

THE COMMUNIST "LIBERATION" OF CHINA

The ultimate defeat of Chiang K'ai-shek was not immediately apparent, except to the corps of American military, political, and economic advisors frustrated by his refusal to take their advice. On the contrary, the Nationalist offensive of 1947 yielded what seemed to be striking victories, such as the capture of the Communist capital, Yenan. In fact, however, this and other military advances were not so impressive as Chiang sought to make them appear; in true guerrilla fashion, the Communist forces had avoided a direct confrontation with his heavily armed columns and had concentrated instead on harassment of their supply lines. During this same period Chiang proclaimed a new constitution, unacceptable to either the Democratic League or the Communists, and held elections according to its provisions, but under the circumstances of civil war they were scarcely representative of the Chinese people and the Generalissimo continued to exercise dictatorial authority.

By the spring of 1948 even the military position of the Nationalist armies was showing clear signs of deterioration. Isolated in their city strongholds, the dispersed forces throughout north China and Manchuria were losing control of the vital road and rail supply lines, yet Chiang forbade them to attack or even to withdraw until their situations became wholly untenable. By the summer of 1948 the crack Nationalist troops garrisoning the cities of Manchuria had to be supplied by air. During the summer several Manchurian cities were evacuated with a substantial loss of troops and a more vital loss of almost all their heavy American equipment to the Communists. The real blow, however, occurred in November when the too-long delayed orders for the evacuation of Mukden resulted in the surrender of almost all the soldiers and the loss of all their American equipment. Now, adequately supplied with

Japanese and American armaments, the Communist armies were prepared to shift from evasive guerrilla tactics to open battle for the destruction of Chiang's military strength. The contest might have been more even if it had not been for the additional Communist superiority in morale and in the tactical flexibility of their commanders learned from the rigors of guerrilla warfare. Finally, the Communists took maximum advantage of their propaganda assertion of "liberating" the Chinese people from the oppression and exploitation of Chiang K'ai-shek and his ally, the American imperialists, to break down both military and civil resistance. Growing numbers of Nationalist soldiers with their officers defected en masse, while local officials who agreed to cooperate were initially allowed to continue in authority.

The decisive battle of Hsüchou in October–December 1948, won for the Communists, control of China north of the Yangtze and broke the back of Nationalist resistance on the mainland. For this titanic struggle both sides massed more than a million men. Although still superior in equipment and in full command of the air, the Nationalists' morale had reached the breaking point. Most important, however, Chiang and his generals were still wedded to the tactics of fighting in defense of fixed positions. As a result, the mobile, flanking tactics of the Communists precipitated a complete rout.

In recognition of his failure as Generalissimo, Chiang resigned from the presidency in January 1949, to make possible the futile efforts of his subordinates to secure a negotiated settlement. In full command of the military situation, the Communists only utilized negotiations to gain time for the consolidation of control of northern China and the massing of their forces for the "liberation" of China south of the Yangtze. Meanwhile, 500 thousand troops loyal to Chiang were transported to Taiwan along with the remaining financial reserves of $300 million. In December Chiang followed his troops and about one million civilians to their island refuge, and, with the mainland lost, resumed the presidency of the Nationalist government of China in March 1950.

On the mainland, the victorious Communists now took over the responsibility for solving the problems that had frustrated the war-harried Kuomintang regime, problems inherent in the continuing Chinese revolution proclaimed in Sun Yat-sen's Three People's Principles. The extent of Communist success, the methods used, and the degree of continuity with the Chinese heritage will be examined in the final chapter on China.

SIGNIFICANT DATES

1905	Abolition of traditional civil service examinations: founding of T'ung-meng hui
1908	Deaths of Emperor and Empress-Dowager Tz'u Hsi
1909	Election of provincial assemblies
1910	Convening of national assembly
1911	Wuhan incident of October 10 (the Double Ten)
1912–1916	The Chinese Republic under President Yüan Shih-k'ai
1915	Twenty-One Demands
1916	Beginning of New Culture Movement
1916–1928	The Warlord Era and the rise of the Kuomintang
1919	The May 4th Movement
1921	Founding of Chinese Communist party
1923	Sun-Joffe agreement for Russian support
1927	Collapse of Kuomintang-Communist collaboration
1928	Reunification of China by Nationalists
1931	Japanese seizure of Manchuria
1934–1935	The Long March
1936	Sian incident
1937	Second Sino-Japanese War and second united front with Chinese Communists
1941	*On the New Democracy* by Mao Tse-tung
1943	*China's Destiny* by Chiang K'ai-shek
1946	The Marshall mission
1948	Battle of Hsüchou in December
1949	Resignation of Chiang in January and withdrawal to Taiwan in December

SELECTED READINGS

*Barnett, A. Doak, *China on the Eve of Communist Takeover*. New York: Praeger, 1963.

Borg, Dorothy, *The United States and the Far East Crisis of 1932–1938*. Cambridge, Mass.: Harvard University Press, 1964.

*Brandt, Conrad, *Stalin's Failure in China, 1924–1927*. New York: Norton, 1966.

*————, et al., eds., *A Documentary History of Chinese Communism*. New York: Atheneum Pubs., 1966.

*Buck, Pearl, *The Good Earth*. New York: Simon and Schuster, 1939.

*Ch'en, Jerome, *Mao and the Chinese Revolution*. London: Oxford University Press, 1967.

————, *Yuan Shih-k'ai*. Stanford: Stanford University Press, 1961.

Chiang, K'ai-shek, *China's Destiny*. New York: Macmillan, 1947.

*Ch'ien, Tuan-sheng, *The Government and Politics of China, 1912–1949*. Stanford: Stanford University Press, 1970.

*Chow, Tse-tsung, *The May Fourth Movement*. Stanford: Stanford University Press, 1967.

*Clubb, O. Edmund, *Twentieth Century China*. New York: Columbia University, 1964.

*Feis, Herbert, *The China Tangle*. New York: Atheneum Pubs., 1964.

*Fitzgerald, C. P., *The Birth of Communist China*. Baltimore: Penguin Books, 1964.

Gasster, Michael, *Chinese Intellectuals and the Revolution of 1911*. Seattle: University of Washington Press, 1969.

Gillin, Donald G., *Warlord: Yen Hsi-shan in Shansi Province, 1911–1949*. Princeton: Princeton University Press, 1967.

Grieder, Jerome B., *Hu Shih and the Chinese Renaissance*. Cambridge, Mass.: Harvard University Press, 1970.

*Harrison, James P., *The Communists and Chinese Peasant Rebellion*. New York, Atheneum Pubs., 1969.

*Hsu, Kai-yu, *Chou En-lai*. New York: Doubleday, 1969.

*Isaacs, Harold R., *The Tragedy of the Chinese Revolution*. Stanford: Stanford University Press, 1961.

*Jansen, Marius B., *The Japanese and Sun Yat-sen*. Stanford: Stanford University Press, 1970.

*Johnson, Chalmers A., *Peasant Nationalism and Communist Power: The Emergence of Revolutionary China*. Stanford: Stanford University Press, 1966.

*Kates, George N., *The Years that Were Fat: The Last of Old China*. Cambridge, Mass.: M. I. T. Press, 1967.

*Mao Tse-tung, *Selected Works*. 4 vols.; New York: International Pubs., 1954–1960.

*Meisner, Maurice, *Li Ta-chao and the Origins of Chinese Marxism*. Cambridge, Mass.: Harvard University Press, 1967.

*North, Robert C., *Chinese Communism*. New York: McGraw-Hill, 1966.

*Pruitt, Ida, *A Daughter of Han: The Autobiography of a Chinese Working Woman*. Stanford: Stanford University Press, 1967.

Rue, John E., *Mao Tse-tung in Opposition, 1927–1935*. Stanford: Stanford University Press, 1966.

*Schram, Stuart, *Mao Tse-tung*. Baltimore: Penguin Books, 1967.

*————, ed., *The Political Thought of Mao Tse-tung*. New York: Praeger, 1963.

*Schurmann, Franz, and Schell, Orville, *Republican China*, Vol. II of *The China Reader*. 3 vols.; New York: Random House, 1967.

*Schwartz, Benjamin T., *Chinese Communism and the Rise of Mao*. New York: Harper and Row, 1967.

*Sheridan, James E., *Chinese Warlord: The Career of Feng Yu-hsiang*. Stanford: Stanford University Press, 1966.

*Snow, Edgar, *Red Star over China*. New York: Grove Press, 1961.

*Tawney, R. H., *Land and Labor in China*. Boston: Beacon Press, 1966.

*Tsou, Tang, *America's Failure in China, 1941–1950*. 2 vols.; Chicago: University of Chicago Press, 1967.

*U.S. Department of State, *China White Paper: August 1949*. Stanford: Stanford University Press, 1967.

Van Slyke, Lyman P., *Enemies and Friends: The United Front in Chinese Communist History*. Stanford: Stanford University Press, 1967.

*————, ed., *Chinese Communist Movement: A Report of the U.S. War Department, July 1945*. Stanford: Stanford University Press, 1968.

*Wright, Mary C., ed., *China in Revolution*. New Haven: Yale University Press, 1968.

CHAPTER TWENTY-ONE

JAPAN IN VICTORY AND DEFEAT: 1905–1952

Victory over Russia fulfilled the fundamental objectives of the engineers of the Meiji Restoration. The humiliating infringements on Japanese sovereignty of the unequal treaties had been eliminated and the nation had proven in battle its right to rank among the major powers of the world. Thus the modernization program of the aging oligarchs had been vindicated by success.

Nevertheless, the war had revealed significant economic weaknesses involving a distressing dependence on foreign suppliers of strategic goods and finance capital. During their remaining years of direction through World War I the dwindling number of Genrō concentrated attention on overcoming these handicaps with a very substantial measure of success. Another problem that caused them serious concern was the apparent ideological confusion created by the large infusion of Western ideas in the process of rapid modernization. To counter this trend, special attention was given to conservative moral training at the elementary school level, now almost universal, stressing discipline, obedience, and loyalty to the family and the "national polity" symbolized by the emperor. Perhaps it is informative to note that the generation that came of age in the 1930s was the product of this reformed education, though its leaders were exposed to a broader spectrum of ideas at the university level.

During the first three decades after 1905 the Japanese economy moved forward at an accelerated pace toward the goal of full modernization. In spite of some temporary setbacks, Japan achieved by 1936 what may be defined as a mature economy, manufacturing a substantial portion of its machinery needs and even a surplus of light machinery for ex-port. From an exporter of raw and semi-processed materials in payment of imports of manufactured goods Japan was transformed on balance into an exporter of a large amount of inexpensive manufactured goods in payment of imports of essential raw materials and heavy machinery. More important, however, were the political changes, which were not unrelated to economic development.

By 1924 the last of the original oligarchs passed from the scene, leaving only one recently adopted member, Prince Saionji, a protégé of Itō, to exercise what moderating influence he could until his death in 1940. Thus Japan lost the top command which in spite of differences had generally provided a unified leadership. Now the way was open for a contest for authority between the institutionalized groups the oligarchs had fostered to facilitate modernization: the army and navy, the civil bureaucracy, the political parties and politicians, and the zaibatsu industrial combines, which by means of government contracts had come to dominate the modern sector of the economy. The contest for power was not simply between these groups but was much more complex because each one was subdivided into factions that made cross-alliances between the groups. Finally, out of this welter of rivalries the military triumphed, leading the nation first into war with China and then into war with the United States and the Western Allies. The result was devastation and near destruction culminating in the unprecedented experience of an alien occupation.

Yet, by early 1952, when the occupation officially came to an end, a reformed Japan, supported by the resilient spirit of a highly educated, hard-working people, was already

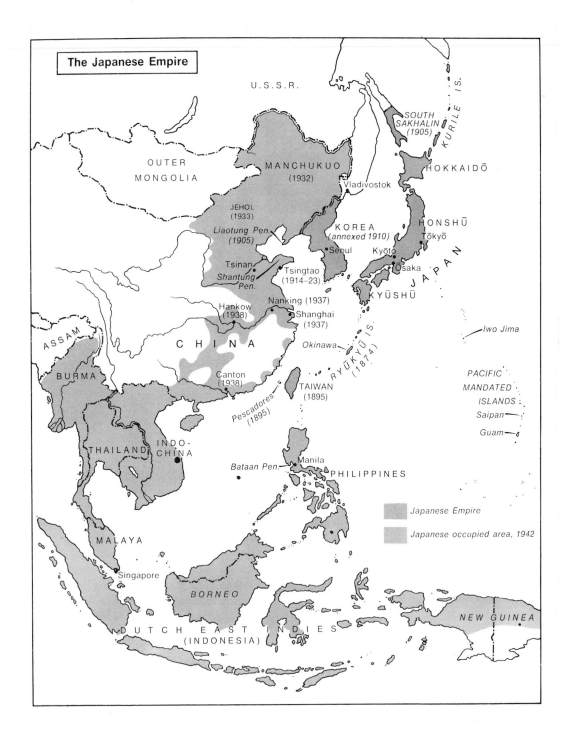

The Japanese Empire

U.S.S.R.

OUTER MONGOLIA

MANCHUKUO (1932)

Vladivostok

SOUTH SAKHALIN (1905)

KURILE IS.

HOKKAIDŌ

JEHOL (1933)

Liaotung Pen. (1905)

KOREA (annexed 1910)

Seoul

HONSHŪ

Tōkyō

Kyōto

Tsinan

Shantung Pen.

Tsingtao (1914–23)

Osaka

JAPAN

KYŪSHŪ

Nanking (1937)

Hankow (1938)

Shanghai (1937)

ASSAM

CHINA

Okinawa

RYŪKYŪ IS. (1874)

Iwo Jima

BURMA

Canton (1938)

TAIWAN (1895)

PACIFIC MANDATED ISLANDS

Saipan

Guam

Pescadores (1895)

THAILAND

INDO-CHINA

Bataan Pen.

Manila

PHILIPPINES

MALAYA

Japanese Empire

Japanese occupied area, 1942

Singapore

BORNEO

NEW GUINEA

DUTCH EAST INDIES (INDONESIA)

clearly on the road to recovery. This rapid rise from the ashes of defeat is eloquent testimony to the fact that the vital "capital" of a modern industrial state is not money or machines but rather the excellence of the education, skills, and dedication of the citizenry. With these thoughts in mind the continued story of the modernization of Japan and its adaptation to Western innovations during these critical years may be surveyed.

THE CHALLENGE OF MAJOR STATUS POWER

Although the fruits of victory were sweet, Japan was financially and physically exhausted and even had been compelled to resort to the London and New York money markets to maintain its war effort. The Treaty of Portsmouth more than met Japan's war aim, securing domination of Southern Manchuria in addition to undisputed control over Korea, but in lieu of a desperately needed cash indemnity to meet the costs of the war Russia had only been willing to surrender the southern half of Sakhalin island. Furthermore, the war had demonstrated an undesirable dependence on Western suppliers for fundamental war materials as well as capital. For example, the navy, whose control of the seas had made possible the victories of the army, had been for the most part built in British shipyards; and steel production, the critical sinew of modern warfare, still fell far short of meeting the growing needs of the nation, even in peacetime. Whatever the cost, the Genrō, who continued to direct the government through World War I, were determined to overcome these deficiencies in Japanese industry. The immediate postwar years witnessed a sharp increase in the rate of economic development. Accelerated purchases of heavy machinery and other essential industrial supplies, financed in part by the floating of bond issues in foreign money markets, generated a spurt in industrial development, but for the first

time created a serious excess of imports over exports and an unfavorable balance of payments that was becoming critical by 1911.

Heavy governmental investment and purchases, exceeding 50 percent of total sales for the modern sector of the economy, furnished the major stimulus to this era of rapid industrial expansion. The capacity of the Yawata Iron and Steel Works, already established in 1901 in reversal of the earlier policy of liquidating government investments, was vastly expanded, and government contracts encouraged the expansion of smaller privately owned operations. After 1906 the government nationalized the trunk lines of the railroad system and stimulated a tripling of the amount of track in subsequent years opening the remotest areas to the national market. Externally, the capital requirements for the development and modernization of South Manchuria and Korea also taxed the financial resources of the nation, while diverting funds from possibly more fruitful internal investments. Military and naval modernization consumed a major portion of the national revenue and was naturally the first area of expenditure in the budget placed under attack in the Diet when the politicians realized in 1911 that the nation was facing a financial crisis.

After 1901 the Genrō no longer served as prime ministers, preferring to pull the strings of government from behind the scenes in true Japanese tradition. Although often differing on policy, the leading Genrō, Itō and Yamagata, compromised their differences for the sake of control and respectively supported their protégés, Prince Saionji and General Katsura rotated peacefully as prime ministers of cabinets above party control until the summer of 1911 when Prince Saionji took office again. His political power, based on leadership of the largest party in the Diet, had been seriously undermined by the assassination of Itō in 1909 by a Korean nationalist after serving as Resident General in Korea. Nevertheless, in view of the financial condition of the country he was determined, backed by Yamagata, to resist the demands of the army and navy for further budget increases. Following months of fruitless negotiations, the army, with Yamagata's consent, destroyed the cabinet by exercising for the first time the power established in 1900 for the army minister to submit his resignation to the emperor while the general staff refused to name a successor. After a number of others refused to form a new government, Katsura was reluctantly recommended to the emperor by the remaining oligarchs. Although he too now favored a policy of economic retrenchment and civil control of the military and was ready to organize a political party to support a more liberal approach to government, the people and the parties distrusted him as a Chōshū military man and a former pawn of Yamagata. He was blamed unjustly for the high-handed way in which Saionji's government had been overthrown, and immediately he confirmed their fears by resorting to imperial rescripts to discipline the navy and to manipulate the Diet.

This political crisis happened to occur at the death of the Meiji emperor in 1912 and was appropriately entitled the "Taishō Crisis" after the regnal name of his successor. At the same time the parties formed a League for the Protection of the Constitution, which promptly called for a "Taishō Restoration." Under this slogan the party leaders argued that the accession of a new ruler should be the occasion for a new round of reforms in a more democratic direction. By means of monster rallies they successfully aroused a united popular and party front against the presumably reactionary Katsura government. Finally, Katsura resigned in 1913 and died within the year.

The significance of the "Taishō Crisis" is difficult to assess because Katsura's three successors as prime minister represent no clear acceptance of party cabinets, and in fact a retrogression from this concept. The first, a rather nondescript Satsuma admiral, had a cabinet composed of almost all party men and did open up many bureaucratic appoint-

ments to party patronage while slashing the budget to relieve the economic pressure on the country's finances. In addition, the limitation on the appointment of army and navy ministers to active duty officers subject to general staff discipline was removed, though no retired officers were ever appointed. The old opposition stalwart and party champion, Ōkuma, who replaced him in 1914, however, proved surprisingly less amenable to direction and control by his party. And his successor in late 1916, another Chōshū general, reverted to the pre-Taishō custom of a nonparty cabinet. Nevertheless, beneath this surface manifestation of retreat the political parties were being strengthened under vigorous leaders in preparation for the first postwar opportunity to reassert themselves with the backing of the zaibatsu, which were growing fat from the tremendous profits of the World War I industrial boom.

The great family combines had been gradually growing both in numbers and in economic strength and influence. As the leaders of modern finance, commerce, and industry, they developed close relationships with prominent leaders of the military and the bureaucracy, frequently cemented by marriage alliances. As the recipients of government contracts they were naturally the principal beneficiaries of the government-sponsored expansion after the Russo-Japanese War and for the same reason were adversely affected by the necessary slowdown in government expenditures after 1911. By 1915, however, they entered their greatest expansion, supplying not only the needs of the Allies but also the consumer requirements of overseas markets that Western manufacturers could no longer meet. As shortages pushed up prices, profits multiplied sixfold creating a large gold reserve. Shipbuilding and shipping, which already carried one-half of Japan's trade, also expanded rapidly as rising freight rates multiplied profits during the war years. The significance of the wartime boom in shipping, commerce, and industry was to turn zaibatsu attention more toward foreign markets, which previously had been incidental to their principal interest in fulfilling the internal needs of a modernizing nation. And their enhanced economic strength made it possible for them to make their influence much more effectively felt in governing circles.

Of course, from the beginning of constitutional government the zaibatsu had been led by self-interest to dabble in politics, financing the election campaigns of individual party politicians and their followers in return for support in securing contracts, and this activity had already furnished the fodder for numerous scandals. In addition, they had not hesitated to bribe bureaucrats in various ways for their benefit. But until after World War I their role was essentially that of clients and supplicants, while Yamagata and his fellow oligarchs still maintained control over the political apparatus. The combination of the passing of the Restoration statesmen, the popularity that the military success of the Allies gave to democracy, the insistent demands of the stronger political parties, and the vastly enhanced economic power of the zaibatsu enabled them to exercise a prominent, if not controlling, influence over the formation of governments and governmental policies. But before turning to the internal developments of the postwar era attention must be given to the imperial and foreign policies between 1905 and 1918.

IMPERIAL AND FOREIGN POLICIES (1905–1918)

During this period foreign policy was principally concerned with securing general recognition of Japan's imperial position, specifically the acceptance of Japan as the successor to all Russian interests and influence in southern Manchuria. Korea presented no immediate problem because no one, other than Koreans, challenged the proclamation of a Japanese protectorate under Itō as Resident-General. Itō took this responsibility to stave off more radical demands for outright

annexation and to promote a modernization program in collaboration with liberal Korean leaders, which he hoped would create a friendly spirit of cooperation and recognition of common interests between the Korean and Japanese peoples. His efforts were frustrated, however, by the maturing nationalistic feeling among Koreans, the tactless and arrogant behavior of Japanese troops, and the obstructionist attitude of the ruler (now called emperor). By 1907 the Korean emperor's hostility became intolerable, and he was forced to abdicate in favor of his feeble-minded son to the accompaniment of a series of rebellions that were ruthlessly crushed. In 1908 Itō had to resign in recognition of the failure of his policy. His subsequent assassination by a Korean patriot while on a tour of inspection in Manchuria provided a convenient pretext for the annexation of Korea in 1910. For the next 35 years Japan attempted the hopeless task of forcefully integrating the Korean people. Although Korea gained many economic benefits as a Japanese province, national feeling proved to be too deeply rooted for such a policy to succeed in spite of heavy expenditures on modernization.

By the terms of the Treaty of Portsmouth Japan succeeded to the Russian leasehold of the Liaotung Peninsula subject to Chinese consent, which was easily obtained, and to ownership of the South Manchurian Railway as well as the less tangible Russian sphere of influence throughout southern Manchuria. On the other hand, Theodore Roosevelt had insisted on an affirmation of the "Open Door" and specific clauses guaranteeing the political independence and territorial integrity of China that might come into conflict with these conceptions. At first, the Japanese government, in desperate need of capital, looked with interest at the proposal of an American railroad magnate, E. H. Harriman, to furnish capital for the joint development of the South Manchurian Railway, but then rejected it, much to Harriman's distress, in favor of raising the necessary capital by a foreign bond issue. Meanwhile, Japanese-American relations were troubled by discriminatory practices in California against Japanese immigrants. President Roosevelt settled this issue with the executive "Gentlemen's Agreement" by which Japan agreed to issue passports only to those returning to previously established homes and to the immediate relatives of those already settled in America and Roosevelt promised to use his good offices to bring an end to discriminatory practices. Related to this settlement was the Root-Takahira Agreement of 1908 by which Japan and the United States mutually recognized each other's existing positions in the Far East. A statement specifying China's "independence and integrity" was included, but the word "territorial" was significantly omitted. Roosevelt realistically recognized that Japan was now a great power that should be treated as an equal, but in accordance with his "Big Stick" policy he directed the American fleet to call at Japanese ports to demonstrate American naval strength. Unfortunately, the Dollar Diplomacy of his successor, Taft, who sought British support for loans to enable China to buy out the Russian and Japanese railroads, ran counter to Roosevelt's advice that it was "peculiarly to our interest not to take any steps as regards Manchuria which will give the Japanese cause to feel, with or without reason, that we are hostile to them."

At the same time that Japanese foreign policy was working for American acceptance of Japan's position in south Manchuria it also sought to mend its fences with its former foe. One secret agreement in 1907 defined the respective spheres of Japan and Russia in Manchuria and another in 1910 even committed them to "common action" against any challenger. British acceptance of Japan's position, if ever in doubt, was confirmed by the renewal of the Anglo-Japanese Alliance in 1911 for ten instead of five years. After American Dollar Diplomacy, ostensibly intended to check Russian and Japanese encroachments on Chinese sovereignty and maintain the "Open Door," had failed in Manchuria, an effort to form a consortium, excluding Russia and Japan, to foster and finance Chinese modernization also proved abortive. Russia and Japan could not be kept out, and Woodrow Wilson, following his election to the presidency, withdrew government support on the ground that such loans secured by Chinese revenues constituted an infringement on Chinese sovereignty and integrity. Finally, the outbreak of World War I presented Japan with the opportunity to become the unchallenged arbiter of East Asia, particularly since the United States was ready to do no more than make disapproving sounds.

After brief hesitation the government of Ōkuma insisted on honoring the Anglo-Japanese Alliance by seizing the German leasehold on the Shantung Peninsula and all German Pacific possessions north of the equator. Then in 1915, following much top-level debate, the Twenty-One Demands were formulated and presented secretly to the Chinese government. All Ōkuma's foreign minister initially sought was a favorable revision of the Sino-Japanese treaties governing Japan's position in Manchuria, particularly an extension from 25 to 99 years of the Liaotung leasehold, and Chinese recognition and clarification in treaty form of Japan's succession to German rights in Shantung; but by the time business, military, and other interests were heard from the demands had been expanded to five groups of which only the first two pertained specifically to Manchuria and Shantung. The fifth group, which the foreign minister refused to label other than "desires," was the most obnoxious, amounting, if they had been accepted, to the virtual reduction of China to a Japanese protectorate. In accordance with long-established practice, the government of Yüan Shih-k'ai allowed these secret demands to leak out in the hope that the Western powers would compel Japan to back down, but although Japan got a bad press, even the

United States, not yet engaged in the war, was unwilling to do more than enunciate a nonrecognition policy. Finally, an ultimatum forced China to consent to a series of treaties incorporating all the demands but putting off the fifth group of "desires" for "future negotiation." Subsequently Japan's foreign ministry employed the leverage of the Allies' need of Japanese support to extract secret treaties from each one accepting Japan's gains and promising to support them at the peace table. Even the United States, anxious to secure its rear upon entry into the war, accepted in the Lansing-Ishii Note of 1917 the idea in the case of Japan's relationship to China that "territorial propinquity creates special interests."

The Genrō, and particularly Yamagata, upset at what they considered the bungling mismanagement of the Twenty-One Demands, brought down Ōkuma's government to be replaced by one headed by a Chōshū general who had gained imperial experience as governor-general of Korea. The new prime minister adopted a policy of attempting to overcome injured Chinese feelings by extending irregular and virtually unsecured loans to finance the warlord successors of Yüan. These "gifts" were named after his able young agent the "Nishihara Loans." The value of these loans to Japan is open to question. While they assured the temporary support of the beneficiaries and secured fresh treaties granting even larger privileges in Shantung and Manchuria, they clearly failed in their avowed objective of winning the goodwill of the Chinese people. On the contrary, they aroused in the minds of students and intellectuals a serious suspicion that their warlord officials were selling China out and thus prepared the way for more widespread anti-Japanese feeling and actions in the postwar era. In turn, Chinese hostility and uncooperativeness in due course raised the hackles of ambitious and belligerent young Japanese army officers stationed in Manchuria and contributed to the opportunistic and forceful actions of the

late twenties and thirties. Of course, to attribute the events of more than a decade later solely to Japanese actions during World War I would be a gross overstatement, but they were contributing factors to the growing alienation between the two countries.

Finally, the aggressiveness of Japanese foreign policy during World War I and the growing influence of the military were reflected in the role played by Japan in the Siberian Intervention of 1918 to 1922. Even more importantly, this intervention reflects another aspect influencing Japan's foreign policy then and later: the deep-seated fear of "dangerous thoughts" emanating from the West, which permeated the thinking of the conservative leadership. Even in the nineteenth century the Restoration oligarchs had on occasion, such as the introduction of the constitution, felt the need to limit the freedom of the press. After the turn of the century the rise of radical and liberal thought had called forth more rigorous repression, especially against Marxist-inspired expressions and activities. Now the spread of the Bolshevik revolution to eastern Siberia brought the challenge to Japan's doorstep and created a sense of alarm that was destined to exercise a deep and continuing influence on Japanese foreign policy. As early as 1917 some leaders entertained the idea of independent or joint Sino-Japanese intervention. All objections were removed, however, when President Wilson, under Allied pressure, agreed to joint intervention, limiting the number of troops to 7000 each and limiting the objectives to securing Allied war supplies piling up in Vladivostok and aiding former Czechoslovak prisoners of war making their way to freedom along the route of the Trans-Siberian Railway. Although the American commander adhered strictly to his instructions in spite of futile Japanese efforts to get him removed, the larger Japanese aim of keeping communism out of East Asia was illustrated by the numerous intrigues of Japanese officers and the expansion of Japanese involvement to 72,000 men, who remained on the mainland until 1922 and did not evacuate northern Sakhalin until 1925. When Japan finally terminated this aggressive intervention, long after the other Allies had withdrawn, it had few gains to show, other than expanded influence in Manchuria, for this very costly military adventure. In fact, the stubborn persistence of the military in continuing this operation helped to discredit the armed forces and their institutionalized influence during the twenties.

THE RISE AND FALL OF ZAIBATSU INFLUENCE AND INTERNATIONALISM (1918 – 1931)

Whatever may be said for or against Japan's activities during World War I, the nation emerged from it tremendously strengthened. As one of the Western Allies, Japan's participation in the war had been minimal and limited to advancing its political interests, permitting large savings and heavy investment in industrial growth under the stimulus of new markets and tremendous profit margins. The boom set in during 1915 and did not collapse until March 1920. During this period industrial employment almost doubled and production more than doubled, multiplying in some industries as much as sevenfold. Inflation pushed up prices faster than wages, and a food shortage precipitated the rice riots of 1918, which toppled the government.

Although large profits encouraged the formation of thousands of new, small-scale enterprises, the great family combines, as the leading operators of the modern sector of the economy, were by far the major beneficiaries of the boom. As controllers of almost all capital and credit, they were enabled to weather the collapse of 1920 and, in addition, to pick up at bargain prices the assets of the less stable, new operators. Subsequently similar financial crises presented them with further opportunities to extend their control of economic activity. Since through their economic strength they played such an important role in the political development of the twenties, an examination of their unique and characteristically Japanese features seems appropriate at this point.

The zaibatsu combines have frequently been mistakenly compared with American monopolies. Only rarely did any such organization monopolize the manufacture of any particular product. Instead, they were primarily vast horizontal trusts financing and coordinating production and trade in a host of products in competition with other combines. Whether a particular organization dated from Tokugawa times (like Mitsui) or not, they were essentially feudal in structure like the former agricultural fiefs, tied together as much by common interests and personal loyalties as by the familiar capitalistic devices of intercorporate stockholding and interlocking directorates of the West. Control of capital and credit through major banks, on the one hand, and marketing facilities, both domestic and foreign, on the other, as well as a supply of technical know-how and managerial talent, were the chief material inducements contributing to the rapid growth of these business giants. But material factors should not be exaggerated; equally important were personal ties and personal loyalty in the Japanese tradition. Switches from employment in one combine to another were tantamount to treason and virtually unheard of, while paternalistic traditions required the employer to retain and maintain an employee regardless of his efficieny or of economic conditions.

Under these circumstances, without considering the excess labor supply maintained by Japan's rapid population growth or the hostile attitude of the government, labor organizers found it very difficult to gain a foothold, and when unions were formed, they were frequently little more than company organs, dependent on the goodwill of the management for whatever benefits they could extend to their members. Furthermore, because labor was cheap and capital expensive, Japanese industry had from the beginning concentrated on textiles which called mainly for a large supply of relatively unskilled labor. Recruiters combed the countryside for tens of thousands of girls to labor under contract in the mills. Such temporary labor, housed in barracks and subjected to company discipline, could scarcely be organized.

Even in the late thirties, production of silk, cotton, woolen, and rayon goods was Japan's largest single industry accounting for more than 30 percent of industrial output, 40 percent of industrial employment, and 60 percent of all exports. Since export was essential and export marketing was in the hands of the zaibatsu, virtually every textile producer submitted to the control of one or another of them, whether or not any direct investment was involved. In return, the producer received technical and managerial assistance, and most important of all, credit to carry him through any economic slump. For the same reasons of self-interest, many other industrial enterprises actively and voluntarily sought out affiliation with one of the financial titans, even though no direct investment was involved. As a result, the economic strength of any particular zaibatsu was actually many times the specific assets appearing on a Western-type balance sheet.

This distinctively Japanese method of financial, commercial, and industrial combination, by which mighty fiefs were created in the modern sector of the economy in competition with each other, was a fitting and logical application of traditional values and practices to the problems of modernization that all Japanese could understand and appreciate, though it might puzzle and bewilder Western observers. Moreover, in capital-short Japan it was also the most rational answer to the need to concentrate savings and invest them for the maximum benefit of the nation. Finally, it was only a logical development that these giants, once they were firmly established, should, like their feudal

predecessors, employ their economic power to influence the operation of government in their own interest; and in the decade of the twenties their influence became a prominent factor in the formation of domestic and foreign policies.

Other institutionalized groups both competing and collaborating among themselves for succession to the mantle of Genrō leadership were the army and navy whose command positions were still dominated by Chōshū and Satsuma men, the national bureaucracy whose influence through appointments and services penetrated every nook and cranny of the country, and the politicians and their parties, which, though more unified, still depended as individuals on the other groups for election support. Above all of them stood the emperor whose "transcendental" authority, symbolizing the unity and continuity of the nation, could, if deemed necessary, be invoked by imperial rescript to uphold and give legitimacy to the position of any group or intergroup faction. But the employment of the emperor's authority for partisan purposes had been abused and was therefore avoided, leaving the groups and factions to work out their differences as best they could.

Once to resist army and navy demands for expansion had been almost unthinkable. After all, their achievements had been chiefly responsible for Japan's recognition as a world power. At great expense the navy had been greatly strengthened since 1905—perhaps too much—by warships built in Japan, and the failure of the opportunistic and expensive activities of the army in Siberia had greatly discredited that branch of the services. In an era of international goodwill, such as seemed to be emerging with the Washington Conference of 1922, both services found it difficult to maintain their strength, let alone increase it. Furthermore, the army in particular suffered from internal discontent on the part of young officers at the attempt to continue Chōshū domination of command and command training.

In retaliation for the uncooperativeness of the other groups with the presumed needs of the services, cliques of young officers, particularly in the army, mounted a general assault on the whole apparatus of constitutional government and the all too evident materialism and self-seeking of bureaucrats, party politicians, and zaibatsu. In the name of the imperial institution and the traditional values and virtues of Japan they called for a purging of the disease of immoral Western individualism and its corrupting attributes and a moral regeneration of the nation under the leadership of the emperor and, of course, officers of superior virtue. Although this appeal failed to gain much support during the twenties, the people, especially in the rural areas that took special pride in their sons in the service, were not unsympathetic to this emphasis on the primacy of family, nation, and morality that was reinforced by moral training in the elementary schools. In addition, many of the young officers came from rural, non-Chōshū backgrounds. Since their entire education tended to stress the traditional Japanese martial virtues and spirit, many became convinced that these values, rather than the complicated modern military equipment deemed essential by most of the top command, were the true source of Japan's victories and military strength. Thus two groups of officers emerged with conflicting views: those who argued the necessity of further mechanized modernization and those who favored a larger army relying more on an emphasis on martial virtues. This division within the army threatened to undermine further the influence of the military in the councils of the nation.

The centralized direction of Japan's modernization led to the creation of a powerful bureaucracy whose elite was drawn primarily from graduates of the Tōkyō Imperial University, and particularly its law school. Through their control of governmental expenditures and appointment of local government officials they wielded great influence over both business and politics. After brief careers characterized by rapid advancement many gained important appointments in zaibatsu organizations or entered politics as representatives of districts for which they had secured benefits. Frequently they made marital alliances with zaibatsu or other prominent families. During the twenties a rapid increase in the percentage of government revenue spent in rural areas reflects not only concern for the sluggishness of the agricultural sector of the economy but also a realistic appreciation of the importance of the rural electorate after the adoption of universal adult male suffrage. With the emergence of party cabinets more and more civil service posts were opened to patronage, which forged another link between the parties and their respective supporters in the bureaucracy, but the independent influence of the bureaucracy was never subordinated to party control—another weakness in the movement toward apparent democracy. A further paradox in this trend was the enactment along with extension of the vote of a Peace Preservation Law to provide more severe safeguards against the growth of "dangerous thoughts." In implementation of this measure the centrally controlled regular and secret police force was substantially enlarged, adding to the prestige and power of the Home ministry, which directed its activities.

Next to their campaign supporters, the zaibatsu, the greatest increase in influence and power after World War I was garnered by the politicians and the parties they put together. Since the institution of constitutional government in 1890, politics in the elected lower house of the Diet had passed through several fairly distinct phases. During the first decade under the loose leadership of the traditional opponents of the conservative oligarchy, Ōkuma and Itagaki, the parties had followed a policy of factious opposition, with the exception of the era of the Sino-Japanese War, in the hope of harassing those in power to accept the principle of party cabinets responsible to a majority in the lower house. The oligarchs had countered with frequent dissolutions, calling for expensive campaigns for reelection, and the thunderbolt of imperial rescripts in an attempt to discipline the lower house. Neither side, however, was able to win a clear-cut victory, and finally Itō had stooped to forming a party in support of his government. Until the "Taishō crisis" of 1912 most politicians had found it more profitable to cooperate with the oligarch-sponsored parties, which in turn supported the rotating, oligarch-sponsored governments of Katsura and Saionji. The years 1913 to 1918, until the rice riots, represented a transitional period during which the Genrō continued to name prime ministers of their choice while admitting party leaders to a greater or lesser role in staffing the cabinets. Finally, following the rice riots, the Genrō were compelled reluctantly to accept the ex-bureaucrat leader of Itō's old party and an elected member of the lower house, Hara Kei, as the first commoner prime minister.

Hara successfully insisted that a majority of the cabinet posts be filled by members of his party. He was hailed by many as the "Great Commoner" and the initiator of a new era in party government. But before accepting these assertions, a closer look at his credentials should be taken. First, he was of higher samurai lineage than any of the Meiji oligarchs, though he was not from one of the estates that had accomplished the Restoration. Thus he was every inch as much of an aristocrat as they were. After a brief career as a journalist he had joined the Foreign Ministry, one branch of the bureaucracy, at 26, rising in a 15-year career to the rank of ambassador to Korea. His bureaucratic connections and proven talent recommended him for appointments as a bank official and president of a company. With both bureaucratic and business backing he entered politics and assisted Itō and Saionji in forming the first major party, of which he became the head when Saionji joined the Genrō. Therefore, although Hara as leader of the strongest party was a champion of party government, he enjoyed cordial relations with the other elite groups and realized the need to arrange a compromise program that would gain the support of important elements in each one for a working coalition. His success in achieving concrete results rested more on his ability in conciliating other groups than on the strict discipline he maintained over his party.

The platform of Prime Minister Hara (September 1918–November 1921) stressed four general themes with an obvious appeal to other groups: "the perfection of national defense, the expansion of education, the encouragement of industry, and the expansion of communications." Certainly the military and the zaibatsu could take no exception to such aims. His ministry saw the continuation of the Siberian Intervention, which he opposed but could not terminate over the objections of the army, the Versailles Peace Conference where Japan's acquisition of German rights in Shantung was upheld but Japan's demand for inclusion of a clause in the League Covenant prescribing racial equality was vetoed by Wilson, the collapse of the war-generated boom in 1920, and finally reluctant agreement to participation in the Washington Conference of 1921–1922. This last action by which he guided Japan's shift from a nationalist to an internationalist foreign policy explains in part his assassination by a right-wing patriot. Domestically his most radical achievement was a reduction of the tax qualification for the vote from ten to three yen, after a universal male suffrage proposal proved unfeasible. By this enlargement of the franchise, which particularly increased the rural vote, he strengthened his own more conservative party while appearing to favor progress toward greater democracy. He also strengthened both his party and his control of its members by securing a large increase in patronage. All told, Hara demonstrated exceptional skill in political manipulation retaining the support in each of the elite groups essential to staying in power, a talent which his deputy and immediate successor as prime minister notably lacked.

Of course, his successor also was blamed for the concessions made at the Washington Conference whereby Japan accepted a lower limit on battleships than the United States and Great Britain (3-5-5 ratio), and also agreed to give up the political privileges in Shantung it had previously secured at great expense and to terminate the Siberian Intervention. In addition, Japan had no choice but to accept the face-saving but meaningless Four-Power Treaty, calling for consultations in any East Asian crisis between Japan, Britain, the United States, and France, in place of the expiring Anglo-Japanese Alliance that the British were unwilling to renew. A final slap at Japanese imperialism in China was the Nine-Power Treaty upholding the time-honored doctrines of the "Open Door" and the maintenance of China's sovereignty, independence, and territorial and administrative integrity.

In spite of the affronts to Japanese sensitivity involved in these agreements, they were generally to Japan's advantage from a strictly rational point of view. The Five-Power Treaty (including France and Italy) limiting battleship construction ended a dangerous naval race with the United States that Japan could ill afford to continue and could not possibly win, while the accompanying agreement prohibiting further British or American naval base development closer to Japan than Singapore and Hawaii assured the Japanese navy of strategic supremacy in the China seas. Japan's political position in Shantung had only stimulated anti-Japanese hostility illustrated in economically damaging boycotts and the creation of more widespread nationalistic feeling in China. Although Japanese withdrawal eliminated neither the anti-Japanese feeling nor nationalistic progress, it did reduce Sino-Japanese tension for the time being and did permit the resumption and continuing growth of trade. The termination of the Anglo-Japanese treaty was a foregone conclusion because of pressure from the United States, Canada, and Australia, fearful of what an embarrassment it might become in the event of a Japanese-American war. In any case, from the British point of view the alliance appeared to

have outlived its usefulness because of the weakness of revolutionary Russia. In fact, the major reason for the convening of the Washington Conference had been to find some graceful way out of this dilemma.

No Japanese statesman was deceived by the face-saving Four-Power Treaty, and some of them welcomed the release from the limitations of an alliance with a Western power. For the latter, the termination of the Anglo-Japanese Alliance was viewed as the final step in the achievement of the Restoration goal of emancipation from the West. At last Japan was a free agent and unfettered master of its own destiny. But others, it should be noted, were concerned at the prospect of diplomatic isolation and wistfully hoped that the trend toward international cooperation, accommodation, and disarmament, which was indicated by the Washington Conference, would be vigorously pursued under the auspices of the League of Nations.

Looked at from this point of view, the Washington Conference symbolized an apparent shift in emphasis from competitive nationalism with its imperialistic accompaniment to internationalism not only for Japan but for all the world powers. But such a shift should not be exaggerated. None of the imperial powers were yet ready to surrender any territory. Only the British showed any willingness to permit progress toward self-government and ultimate independence in certain, selected territories, particularly its recently acquired mandates in the Middle East. Shidehara, Japan's chief negotiator at the Washington Conference and foreign minister, 1924–1927 and 1929–1931, was especially associated in the Japanese mind with this "soft," conciliatory approach to foreign relations, which reflected zaibatsu preference for peaceful, economic competition for overseas markets in place of costly and adventurous militant imperialism. During the war the zaibatsu had gained a taste of how profitable the exploitation of overseas markets could be and were anxious to cultivate this trade, especially after the collapse of the war boom in 1920. The worldwide trend toward internationalism that both victors and vanquished espoused in reaction to the war and for the sake of economic recovery seemed ideally suited to the economic aims of Japan's great business combines. When analyzed in historical perspective, however, the internationalism of the twenties adopted by the powers was a temporary phenomenon dictated by postwar conditions and particular national problems and was not solidly based on genuine acceptance of the new ideals and values that the term implied and that the League of Nations as its instrument symbolized. As soon as internationalism had served its purpose and new problems appeared to call for a revival of nationalistic practices, this promising conception was readily jettisoned after brief hesitation and a few, half-hearted attempts to keep it alive. Nationalism was still king, even in the twenties; realization of the age-old ideal of the brotherhood of man was left for some distant generation to secure. Japan in particular, disillusioned with Western integrity, contained a large and growing number of patriots, organized in sundry societies, who deplored this trend in foreign policy and took advantage of every opportunity to discredit its sponsors.

The short-lived ministry of Hara's successor was followed between 1922 and 1924 by three cabinets reflecting again a retreat from party government and a return to bureaucratic domination. Rather than lose power to the opposition party, Hara's party agreed to support a nonparty admiral as prime minister, but the last of the three cabinets so thoroughly disregarded the parties that they joined in organizing a second "Movement for the Protection of the Constitution" as in the time of the Taishō crisis. In the subsequent general election the united parties thoroughly trounced the government candidates and gained a party government under a coalition cabinet headed by ex-bureaucrat Katō Kōmei (1924–1926) who, like

Hara, had risen in the foreign service and in addition enjoyed zaibatsu support through marriage to a daughter of the head of Mitsubishi.

Thanks to its prolonged absence from power, his party had developed a more liberal image, though its membership was not significantly dissimilar in background and composition. In spite of the coalition character of his government liberalizing measures were enacted, though conservative influence and the need to come to terms with the other groups led to complementary measures to check any movement in a radical direction. The loss of stature of the military service had already been reflected in cutbacks in expenditures even under the nonparty government after Yamagata's death in 1922, but reductions in budget allocations for the services were sharply accelerated by the new regime. Immediately the army lost four divisions. Overall, between 1922 and 1927 the services' share of the budget was pared from 42 percent to 28 percent. Most of the officers, however, were employed as instructors in expanded military training programs in the middle and higher schools, and much of the saving from reduction in the size of the army was expended on mechanization. Moreover, in spite of the cutback, army influence was still extensive; it included more than 200,000 men on active duty, almost 1,500,000 in the various training programs, and more than 3,000,000 in veteran organizations.

Another major liberal measure was the enactment in 1925 of universal suffrage for all males 25 or more years of age, almost quadrupling the electorate as indicated in the first election under its provisions in 1928. At the same time, foreign minister Shidehara was able to persuade the reluctant Peers and Privy Council to accept the negotiation of normal diplomatic relations with Soviet Russia. Opposition to both of these steps was mollified by concurrent passage of a severe Peace Preservation law specifying up to ten years' imprisonment for membership in any organization advocating any change in the "national polity" or the abolition of private property. Thus liberalism was matched with conservatism, reflecting quite accurately the political composition of Japan's leadership.

The Katō government and that of his successor after his death in January 1926, also passed a number of modestly liberal measures for the benefit of the working class and nonrevolutionary unions. Some of the former restrictions on union organization and activity were lifted. A moderate factory law was intended to meet the more serious complaints of foreign competitors. A National Health Insurance law and a Labor Disputes Mediation law at least laid a foundation for meeting some of the common problems of industrialization. But these mass-appeal concessions should not obscure the overriding conservative, business-oriented character of Japanese politics and politicians in the twenties.

A constant flow of corruption scandals raised by the party out of power against the party in power tended to disillusion more and more of the public with the democratic process, particularly in rural areas where tradition was still very strong and economic advance was slower and more erratic. Again, however, this alienation should not be exaggerated. Traditionally the Japanese were accustomed to a hierarchical social structure riddled with economic inequities and irregularities. In practice, villages with shrewd leaders benefited from the democratic process by selling the block of votes under their control, frequently to the highest bidder. Furthermore, during the twenties the government subsidies previously distributed exclusively to strategic industries were increasingly diverted to agriculture for both political and economic reasons. The rise of tenant unions is often cited as a reflection of discontent with the conditions of tenancy which covered 45 percent of all arable land and involved about 55 percent of farm families, but this movement at its peak in 1927 did not include in its membership as much as 10 percent of these families. A symptom of government concern was enactment of a largely ineffective Land Reform law by the Katō regime to enable tenants to purchase from landlords the lands they farmed.

In addition, the village was the principle instrument of relief for industrial unemployment. In times of industrial recession the unemployed workers returned to their rural homes to live with their families. Certainly improvement in the standard of living was much slower in the villages than in the cities, particularly after 1925 when a continuous decline in prices for rice, silk, and other agricultural products set in. Moreover, the army cutback of 1925 adversely affected the country people who looked with high regard on a military career for surplus sons. Rice prices suffered from heavy imports of rice from Korea and other overseas markets carried at very low freight rates as return cargo by Japan's merchant marine, while the decline in silk prices resulted from a fourfold increase in production between 1925 and 1930. Finally, universal education combined with road, rail, radio, and newspaper communications to relieve the isolation of the peasants and develop a greater awareness of their comparative disadvantages.

All these factors contributed to building up rural sympathy and support for the variety of antidemocratic, anti-Western, and promilitary appeals for a return to traditional values under the transcendental leadership of the emperor. On the other hand, it is important to note that even in the general elections of the thirties the rural voters continued to elect the candidates of the much-maligned political parties.

The moderation in foreign policy generally accepted by the elite bureaucrats and ex-bureaucrat politicians who dominated the governments of the twenties was matched by a similiar moderation in their interpretation of constitutional government and specifically the emperor's role in it. The top echelon of the bureaucracy was largely staffed with graduates of the Tōkyō Imperial University and its law school, where the rational constitutional views of Professor Minobe Tatsukichi prevailed. Although he accepted the doctrine of Japan's unique national polity as the "people's greatest glory" and the source of the nation's strength, he adopted the German organic theory of the state as a legal entity in all its parts exercising authority under its constitution and laws. According to this interpretation the emperor was only the highest organ of the state with ultimate executive authority and was definitely limited by the laws enacted under the constitution. Extra-constitutional actions without the consent of the Diet were clearly contrary to the theory of constitutional government.

The moderate, rational, and generally conservative views which predominated in all areas of well-informed thought during the twenties did not go uncontested. Radical views of the right or the left—and sometimes a blend of both—gained a growing following in spite of severe police suppression. Semisecret societies, which had been part of the political landscape since the turn of the century, multiplied rapidly in number and membership after the accession of the Shōwa (Enlightened Peace) emperor in 1926 furnished the occasion to call for a new Restoration. As the Meiji Restoration had destroyed the shogunate and the feudal lords, returning their power and estates to the emperor, so the champions of a Shōwa Restoration demanded the destruction of the power-usurping party politicians and their zaibatsu supporters with a similar restoration of power and property to the imperial institution. In its most radical form the new Restoration would be accomplished by a military coup d'état setting up what amounted to state socialism under the guidance of a committee of patriots, principally drawn from the army. In 1927 one society of army officers, including several on the general staff, carried their planning almost to the point of action.

The broad ideological support for such proposals, beyond the negative factors of political and business behavior, is not far to seek. First, the methods of the Meiji Restoration furnished an ideal precedent and guide for action. Second, the educational reforms of the post Russo-Japanese War years stressing the national polity and absolute obedience to parents and the emperor as the "divine" parent of the nation indoctrinated the mass of the people and weakened the prospects of popular resistance. After 1925 compulsory military training in all middle and higher schools extended and reinforced this indoctrination, though a number of years was needed for this "reform" to develop its full impact. For those highly educated leaders who required a more refined and sophisticated ideological explanation several intellectual formulations sponsored by various societies were already in circulation, of which those of Kita Ikki and Ōkawa Shūmei were most popular.

As early as 1919 Ōkawa had encouraged Kita to write and publish an *Outline for the Reconstruction of Japan*, which was promptly suppressed by the government but continued to circulate in a mimeographed edition. His central thesis argued the subversion of the national welfare under the leadership of self-seeking, Westernized politicians and businessmen. His program of action called for their violent overthrow by patriots led by the army, suspension of the constitution, confiscation of surplus capital and private property over prescribed maximums, and a program of social and economic reforms to realize a genuinely direct relationship between the emperor and his essentially equal people. Proposed reforms included the redistribution of land, old age pensions, and the extension of compulsory education to 16 years of age. Like other radical reformers, he deplored Western influence and proposed the elimination of English language instruction and the game of baseball, but unlike them, he distinguished between Western industry and Western capitalism by advocating industrial expansion under state ownership for the welfare of the nation and the people. While Kita gave primary emphasis to internal reforms to create a unified and harmonious nation in conformance with Japanese tradition, he viewed Japan's reconstruction as preparation for the realization of the nation's destiny, the emancipation from Western domination of fellow Asians, including the peoples of China and India. Indeed, he believed that China and India could never gain independence without the benevolent aid and leadership of a modernized Japan, which he expected them to accept with gratitude.

In contrast to his protégé, Ōkawa Shūmei, a former research director of the South Manchurian Railroad, gave priority to a militant overseas program which, he argued, would then precipitate essential reforms at home. He was less doctrinaire in his opposition to politicians and zaibatsu, only recommending the liquidation of those who refused to become "enlightened." Therefore, he cared little about social reform. Although he was constantly involved in army plots, it is interesting to observe that he survived because his broader attitude left room for cooperative politicians and zaibatsu, while the more radical program of Kita led to his execution in 1936 for participation in an unsuccessful coup. Furthermore, the program of Ōkawa, which comprehended elements from all the elite groups in a traditional harmonious consensus, was followed in the conception of creating a "Greater East Asia Co-Prosperity Sphere." But this diversion anticipates the course of events to which we must return.

Katō's coalition government had shifted under his successor to a strictly partisan party regime that was blamed and forced to resign for the severe financial panic of 1927 caused basically by the joint manipulations of Mitsui and Mitsubishi to destroy another zaibatsu combine. A run on the banks compelled 36 financial institutions, including one major bank, to close their doors before a new government stepped in declaring a 3-week moratorium and employing government funds to salvage the rest. Such a shake-out

was undoubtedly salutary for the inflated economy—the zaibatsu took over the weaker enterprises and the giant Mitsui combine gobbled the chief victim—but, of course, those who were ruined scarcely appreciated the benefits, blaming their misfortune on the parliamentary process and the zaibatsu.

Eager to regain power, Hara's party had accepted as its president in 1925 another Chōshū officer-bureaucrat, General Tanaka, former army minister in Hara's cabinet. His leadership secured for the party important military and bureaucratic backing which sought, among other things, a stronger policy toward China. Lacking a majority in the Diet, his government had to face the first general election under the Universal Suffrage law of 1925, which greatly increased campaign costs. Despite tremendous expenditures, especially by Mitsui, and all the influence the military and the bureaucracy could bring to bear, Tanaka's party lost the election of 1928 and had to hang on as best it could against a hostile lower house. This defeat probably reflected in part the electorate's concern about a government headed by another Chōshū general and backed so strongly by the services, the bureaucracy, and the leading zaibatsu. As never before, the debates of the Diet were filled with irresponsible charges and countercharges against individuals of bribery and worse. Even Tanaka was personally accused of corruption and abuse of power. In the long run these unproven accusations further undermined popular respect for parliamentary government.

But of more immediate concern were the consequences of a stronger policy in China. First, troops sent to protect Japanese citizens and property in Shantung took it on themselves to intercept and check in battle Chiang K'ai-shek's army marching northward to complete the unification of China. The result was an anti-Japanese boycott causing costly dislocations in Japanese trade. Then, early in 1929, the "Old Marshall" of Manchuria, Chang Tso-lin, was killed by a bomb when the train in which he was retreating from

Peking passed under a bridge of the South Manchurian Railroad. The army general staff refused Tanaka's angry demand for a thorough investigation and punishment of those responsible, perhaps from fear of fomenting further indiscipline. When the emperor insisted on a public report, Tanaka, though opposed to military extremism, felt compelled to resign in July 1929.

A new government drawn from the other party brought back the conciliatory internationalist, Shidehara, as foreign minister and in 1930 won a convincing victory at the polls on a platform favoring disarmament, economy, and honesty in government, and a "good neighbor" policy toward China. Obviously a majority of the electorate still favored an internationalist foreign policy. Unfortunately this government did not foresee the impact of the developing worldwide depression. In January 1930, Japan returned to the gold standard which, as expected, stimulated a further increase in export sales; but then in mid-year the world market collapsed. By 1931 exports had dropped 27 percent and Japan's gold reserve was being rapidly depleted. Nevertheless, the government clung doggedly to its hard money policy, alienating the military and the bureaucracy by such steps as cutting salaries 10 percent and paring military expenditures. Japan's acceptance of the London Naval Disarmament treaty of 1930 limiting cruisers to a 7-10-10 ratio, which even Western experts privately admitted was an unfavorable concession, further exacerbated military discontent. They were even more alarmed by rumors that the government was planning to eliminate the general staffs and cut back the scope of military training in the schools. These actual and prospective antimilitary policies served to unite the formerly feuding factions among the officers in joint opposition to the government. The tough-minded prime minister was mortally wounded by an assassin, but the ministry managed to hang on after his death until December 1931, when its other problems were compounded by an in-ability to cope with the independent action of the army in Manchuria initiated in September.

THE TWILIGHT OF PARLIAMENTARY GOVERNMENT AND THE RISE OF MILITARISM

The major achievements of the new party government were immediate repeal of the gold standard and a striking sweep in the ensuing general election. This victory, however, was promptly subverted by divisions into opportunistic factions reflecting the weakness of party unity in the face of rising military influence. In addition, party prestige suffered another blow when departure from the gold standard resulted in tremendous speculative profits for those zaibatsu with inside information, especially the Mitsui giant.

Such publicized irregularities combined with the impact of the depression to permit the revival of military influence and to give credence to the charge of some military extremists that the zaibatsu had purposely planned the depression to enrich themselves. The depression was most severe and enduring in its effect on the rural economy with its dependence on supplemental export crops such as raw silk. In contrast, the industrial sector, dominated by the zaibatsu, began to recover as early as 1932 and was operating at full capacity by 1936, an amazing performance for a country so dependent on foreign trade. But much of the slack in industry was taken up by military procurement and a rapid expansion of economic development in the puppet state of Manchukuo.

The Manchurian "Incident" of September 18, 1931, which led to the creation of Manchukuo (Country of the Manchus), was merely the one successful plot by a military group during that year. The so-called "March Incident" failed to come off only because the moderate General Ugaki refused at the last moment to act as head of a military government whenever a coup had overthrown parliamentary government. Although this unrealized plot was also hushed up for the sake of the prestige of the army, it shook the government and did not discourage the plotters from planning a similar attempt in October, which also failed to materialize.

The new government was soon troubled by peasant assassins from an ultranationalist society who succeeded in killing the governor of the Bank of Japan and the head of the House of Mitsui early in 1932. Then in May 20 naval and army officers went on a rampage murdering the prime minister and attacking banks and party and police headquarters before voluntarily surrendering. The trial turned into a publicity circus for the views of the accused. Expressions of widespread sympathy for their assertions of patriotic motives resulted in absurdly light penalties. Such minimal sentences were an open invitation to future acts of violence and disregard for discipline and authority by young military extremists who looked on themselves as a new breed of dedicated samurai ready to sacrifice their lives for the elimination of corrupt Western influences and the restoration of direct and absolute relations between the emperor and the people without the intervention of such innovations as a constitution, Diet, political parties, and zaibatsu. Warriors and workers, in the service of a divinely ordained and directed emperor, were to constitute the new elite—at least, so the less sophisticated young military extremists believed. This was the outlook of the Kōdō-ha, or Imperial Way Clique, which had a few supporters in command positions, such as Generals Araki and Mazaki; but most of the top officers, distrustful of such an emotional, nonrational approach belonged to the Tōsei-ha, or Control Clique.

While these two factions struggled for supremacy, the government stumbled along from 1932 to 1936 under inadequate cabinets now subject to the influence of one, and then of another, of these groups. As repeated support in general elections showed, however,

the parties were not yet dead, but as time proved, they had been dealt a mortal blow by the events of 1931 and 1932. Not only bureaucrats but also party leaders scrambled for alliances with the military groups, and once this step had been taken, the parliamentary cause was lost.

As before, compromise cabinets were headed by malleable admirals: Admiral Saitō (1932–1934) and Admiral Ōkada (1934–1936). Each appointed some party men from both parties to cabinet posts but were virtually manipulated from behind the scenes by the reviving military. At first the Saitō government appeared to be dominated by the assassins' faction with General Araki as army minister and General Mazaki as inspector-general of military training. Araki took full advantage of his position to publicize the Imperial Way, but his undisciplined associates, discontented with their rate of progress, overplayed their hand. A plot for a general bloodbath liquidating the cabinet and party leaders was discoverd in 1933, but again, to protect the good name of the army, the conspirators were not brought to trial until 1937 and all were virtually acquitted in 1941. Nevertheless, this conspiracy led to the removal in 1934 of General Araki in favor of a Control Clique general, Hayashi. The fortunes of the Imperial Way faction declined rather rapidly while those of the Control faction rose. Hayashi continued as army minister in the even less party-influenced cabinet of Admiral Ōkada. With Araki disposed of, the next target was General Mazaki who was dismissed for alleged complicity in another extremist plot. The remaining influence of the Imperial Way group was broken up by ordering them to posts overseas, or at least ones distant from Tōkyō. But this aggressive policy backfired to the extent that a disgruntled colonel ordered to Taiwan marched into the war ministry and cut down with his sword the Control general responsible for these orders. At his court martial another opportunity was presented to expose the evils of parliamentary government and zaibatsu corruption and to publicize what the Imperial Way group meant by its concept of a Shōwa Restoration. His execution made him a patriotic martyr, providing inspiration for one more major effort.

On February 26, 1936, 1400 troops from the First Division, led by none above the rank of captain, boldly occupied the Prime Minister's residence, the War Office, the Diet, and police headquarters, seeking out for assassination a long list of alleged enemies of the Imperial Way. The prime minister only escaped their swords because his brother was mistaken for him, but many other prominent persons were murdered. Loyal troops were brought into Tōkyō to confront the mutineers who were uncertain what to do next. Then the emperor, in whose name they had acted, ordered them back to their barracks. Their honor compelled them to comply with this imperial command and the mutiny came to an end. The public was shocked at this display of indiscipline, and the Control Clique took full advantage of the public demand for discipline to consolidate its authority over the army. Generals Araki and Mazaki were placed on the inactive list, and 13 young officers, as well as their ideological leader, Kita Ikki, were tried and executed.

Now that the struggle within the army had been concluded in favor of the Control Clique, it could turn to the task of reducing the parties that, although in disarray, were by no means dead, at least in the eyes of the electorate. In 1935 the moderate constitutional theorist and member of the House of Peers, Professor Minobe Tatsukichi, had been attacked in the Diet for his view on the limited constitutional function of the emperor and driven from both political and academic life. This assault on intellectual freedom presaged a broader purge of all nonconformist opinions in the universities. Most party members took their cue from this trend and toned down their public, if not their private, expressions. But in a general election held just before the army mutiny of February 1936, the public rejected the party support-ing a strong foreign policy by returning a large majority for the old internationalist party that campaigned on the issue of parliamentary government versus fascism.

Nevertheless, after the "February Incident," a new cabinet headed by a nonparty bureaucrat capitulated completely to the army's demand for full cooperation. The old ordinance prescribing that only active duty officers subject to the orders of the general staffs serve as army and navy ministers was reissued, placing all cabinets at their mercy. Ironically, this cabinet was to be the first victim of this ordinance. In addition, this cabinet accepted a seven-point program of "national political renovation," committing the government to full support of the army in Manchuria, unrestricted rearmament, increased taxes, and extensive controls over education, trade, industry, and, indeed, every aspect of national life. The ground had already been laid for unlimited naval expansion by giving the specified notice in 1934 that Japan would renounce the Naval Disarmament Treaties. Furthermore, in 1936 Japan became committed to association with the fascist powers by concluding the Anti-Comintern Pact with Germany. But the door was not yet completely closed; if the parties had been willing to close ranks and form a united front, they might still have checked the course toward militarism with the support of the people.

And in the last days of 1936 such a prospect showed signs of realization. Both parties were angered by the secret diplomacy and the subservience of the cabinet to military dictation. Even the party that had favored a strong China policy officially denounced the new controls, the war preparations, and the Anti-Comintern Pact; and one member even dared to make a personal attack on the army minister. After these outbursts in the lower house the army general staff decided that this ministry had outlived its usefulness and brought about its fall by having the army minister resign and refusing to name anyone in his place. A short-lived ministry under a general is notable only because it resorted once more to a general election in the hope of securing a lower house more amenable to direction. Once again the people made clear their preference for parliamentary government by an overwhelming rejection of government-backed candidates. At long last the two parties united against the cabinet and forced its resignation, but time was running out.

Again the sole surviving Genrō since 1924, Prince Saionji, influenced the choice of a new prime minister and this time the mantle fell on his protégé, Prince Konoye, a scion of the venerable Fujiwara family. Konoye had carefully cultivated a wide circle of friends, which made him acceptable to all groups. A prime minister of the highest aristocratic lineage and closely related to the imperial line appeared perfectly suited to realize that traditional ideal of harmonious unity needed in such a time of crisis. Unfortunately, the very qualities that made him so generally acceptable reflected a weakness of character when placed under pressure to make a decision. Less than two months after taking office, Konoye, who sought a peaceful settlement of the Sino-Japanese hostilities that broke out in the Pei-p'ing-Tientsin area in July 1937, was presented with an ultimatum by the army minister: either he should accept the decision to dispatch reinforcements or the army minister would resign. Rather than face up to this challenge, which might bring about the collapse of his ministry, Konoye submitted, virtually assuring an expansion of the hostilities. Once the "China Incident" had clearly developed into the "China Affair," that is, a large-scale, undeclared war, there was no longer any question of a struggle for power; all elite groups cooperated under the overall leadership of the military in an increasingly authoritarian wartime regime.

How can the failure of parliamentary government and the revival of military influence be explained? Many analysts have given major credit to the effects of the depression and the consequent worldwide re-

generation of nationalistic economic policies on a nation so heavily dependent on foreign trade. But while the depression was a severe shock to the Japanese economy, and especially the rural sector, the economy underwent a remarkably rapid recovery when compared with other industrialized nations. By 1936 industry had doubled again and was operating at capacity, and even the rural economy was almost back to normal. At most, the depression can be viewed as a catalyst, accentuating the shortcomings of party government and zaibatsu influence, and providing additional ammunition for the charges already leveled at parliamentary government by civilian and military nationalists. In any case, party politics with cabinets responsible to a majority in the elected lower house of the Diet had gained no more than a tenuous foothold in the twenties and remained in contradiction to the constitutional provision making the prime minister responsible to the emperor. Moreover, prime ministers continued to be named by the emperor on the advice of the Genrō and the Privy Council. In other words, party government, insofar as it was operative, functioned by consent but without constitutional authorization. On the other hand, it is noteworthy that the voters in every general election through 1937 gave their overwhelming support to the parties. If the public will, thus expressed, had been respected, party government would have continued to function. Such an expectation, however, ignores the very real political influence and power of the various elite groups with which each party leader had been compelled to make some sort of accommodation, even in the twenties.

From a more abstract point of view, taking into account cultural and intellectual factors as well as economic and political factors, the disenchantment with party politics and its zaibatsu supporters represents one aspect of a natural reaction to the rapid rate of modernization and the accompanying excessive infiltration of alien Western ideas, values, and institutions that clashed with traditional conceptions and practices. Under such unsettling circumstances the turn to the military as the purest embodiment of traditional virtues was a logical and comprehensible development. Of course, as the preceding account illustrates only too well, the military propagandists of both army cliques took the fullest possible advantage of every opportunity to discredit their foes and publicize their own presumed virtues. This program could not have succeeded, however, if important political leaders, bureaucrats, and zaibatsu had not been persuaded to support them; popular support, even among the more traditionally minded peasantry, was simply inadequate to uphold an assertion of military leadership. In essence, then, the military accomplished a prolonged coup, facilitated by conversions of influential civilians and punctuated by domestic plots and acts of violence of ultranationalist civilian and military extremists and by independent military actions in China that ultimately led to war. Finally, it needs to be noted that the Control Clique of the army, which came to power under the ultimate leadership of General Tōjō, was basically cautious and conservative, anxious to reassert discipline in the ranks, and principally alarmed by the threat of Communist Russia and the possible expansion of its influence in China. The stiffer attitude toward China in 1937 reflected the personal concern of General Tōjō at reports of a rapprochement between Chiang K'ai-shek and Mao Tse-tung following the Sian Incident of December 1936.

THE CHINA AFFAIR AND WORLD WAR II

Military operations cannot be considered except in their broadest general aspects. Japanese objectives in the China campaign were initially limited to compelling the Nationalist government of Chiang K'ai-shek to accept a cooperative, but subordinate, role in a united front against communism, but as Japanese troops advanced the army insisted on stiffer terms. At first, Chiang was not unreceptive to a negotiated settlement, especially after appeals to the League of Nations, Britain, and the United States failed to secure concrete support; but he refused to consider any conditions implying the subordination of the Chinese government to Japanese direction and control. Japan's Anti-Comintern partner, Germany, argued that Japan's attack would only have the reverse effect of pushing China into communist hands in its desperate quest for aid and made every effort to mediate the conflict. Finally, when further negotiation became impossible and Japan turned to the establishment of puppet regimes, Germany had to recall the last of its advisors and cancel valuable contracts with the Nationalist regime, seeking compensation in contracts with the Japanese-sponsored puppet governments.

Once Japanese campaigns had secured the major cities and railroads with the capture of Canton and Hankow in October 1938, the tempo of military effort fell off and Japan concentrated on consolidating its grip and exploiting the resources of the territory it controlled. A "New Order" in East Asia was proclaimed in which Nationalist China could join if it would accept Japanese direction in building in Asia "a new structure of peace based on true justice." The Asia Development Board, also known as the China Affairs Board, sought to unify and rationalize economic activity through two giant holding companies for north and central China. Following the pattern set in Manchukuo, the Japanese government provided one half of the capital while guaranteeing dividends to private investors in the other half.

Generally speaking, the Chinese war and the subsequent occupation of the Chinese heartland did not put an excessive strain on the Japanese economy. On the one hand, defense of the area involved a steady drain on military manpower and material, and substantial capital was diverted to overseas development. On the other hand, men and material gained valuable experience and testing in combat, and the home economy was stimulated by orders for industrial and military equipment as well as by the expanded supply of Chinese resources. Since China, Manchukuo, Korea, and Japan were united in the yen bloc, trade among them did not draw on the foreign exchange reserves. At home, the preparation for war demanded by the military generated a tremendous expansion of heavy industry. But even at the cost of deficit financing this expansion created full employment in a booming economy with which the zaibatsu could have no complaint. On the home front, then, military leadership and its China adventure seemed fully justified by success.

The army, having gained power, now closed ranks, as indicated by General Araki's appointment to the influential cabinet post of Minister of Education. Gradual progress toward the concentration of authority in the cabinet was marked by a 1938 Mobilization law granting the cabinet power to legislate by ordinance and even more by the 1940 dissolution of political parties in favor of the Imperial Rule Assistance Association, a single ideologically unified party under Konoye's leadership to eradicate dissent and guarantee unity in the Diet.

In external relations, however, the course of development was not quite so smooth and ultimately led Japan into an impossible situation. In two probing attacks in 1938 and 1939 to test Russian defenses along the borders of Manchukuo, the Japanese army got bloody noses suggesting that Japan would be well-advised to direct its military ambitions southward. Later, when the Germans launched their attack on Russia, they were deeply disappointed at the Japanese refusal to join in the assault, particularly after German cooperation had enabled Japanese forces to occupy the northern part of French Indo-China. Japanese faith in the good word of Germany, however, had already been shaken by the unexpected Russo-German nonaggression pact of 1939,

and Japanese leaders had determined, in emulation of Germany, to let self-interest alone shape their diplomacy. On September 26, 1940, Japan entered the Tripartite Pact with Germany and Italy, which promised Japan a free hand in Asia and hopefully would discourage America from considering a unilateral attack on Japan. The following day Japan gained permission from the Vichy government of France to "protect" French Indo-China against "Free French" or Allied attack. Japan also gained the friendship of Siam by supporting and then enforcing a settlement of its irredentist claims against the Laotian and Cambodian areas of French Indo-China. During the summer of 1940, when Britain had its back to the wall, Japanese diplomacy was also able to gain the temporary closure of the Burma Road over which a trickle of supplies had recently begun to reach the beleaguered Nationalist regime. These Japanese advances into Southeast Asia without bloodshed had two objectives: first, the cutting of supply routes to Nationalist China, and second, the securing of a guaranteed supply of essential raw materials. Indeed, the latter provided the major motive for Japan's southward expansion, which could prove far more valuable than any adventure in undeveloped eastern Siberia. For this reason, every possible pressure was exerted on the Dutch government, without success, both before and after exile, to guarantee a supply of oil, tin, and rubber from the Dutch East Indies. Consideration of this problem and the overall problem of supplies of strategic raw materials leads directly to the evolution of Japanese-American relations.

Ever since 1905 when the Japanese press had vented its wrath on the "honest broker," President Theodore Roosevelt, for cheating a victorious Japan of its just rewards in the Portsmouth treaty, Japanese-American relations had continuously deteriorated except for a few interludes, such as the generous aid of the American people following the devastating earthquake of 1923. All the incidents contributing to this deterioration cannot be catalogued here, but a few of the major episodes need to be mentioned, such as Taft's Dollar Diplomacy to check the spread of Japanese influence in Manchuria, Wilson's hostility to Japanese claims and his veto of a racial equality clause in the League Covenant at Versailles, the Japanese-American naval race with its potential threat of war, resentment at the naval ratio allocated to Japan at the Washington Conference, the discriminatory character of the American Immigration Act of 1924, Secretary of State Stimson's Non-Recognition Doctrine of Japanese activities in Manchuria, and the continued application of this doctrine to subsequent advances in China. Yet Japan's independence of action as late as 1941 was still severely limited by its dependence on American supplies of strategic materials, particularly scrap iron for its steel mills. American public opinion was horrified by the ruthlessness of Japanese military operations in China, but several incidents involving American property and lives were settled by indemnities. Nevertheless, the American government served notice in July 1939, that the treaty of commerce would not be renewed after it expired in January 1940. This prospect was undoubtedly a factor impelling Japan to develop a more active interest in Southeast Asia. During 1941, however, other developments became interwoven in the complicated web from which the Japanese later in that fateful year could discover no escape.

In the spring of 1941 the pro-German foreign minister of Konoye's second cabinet failed in his effort to persuade Stalin to cut off aid to Chiang K'ai-shek. Indeed, fresh agreements actually stepped up Russian support of Nationalist China. But he did obtain a Russo-Japanese neutrality pact that was followed up with a trade agreement and an adjustment of boundary disputes. Scarcely was the ink dry on this last agreement, however, when Hitler without any notice deceived his Japanese ally again by attacking Russia in June. The Konoye government was deeply embarrassed by this second diplomatic deception and particularly by the foreign minister's support of Germany's brazen request for a Japanese attack on Siberia. Both Konoye and his army minister, General Tōjō, were adamantly opposed to such an action, and the cabinet was dissolved and reconstituted to get rid of the troublesome foreign minister. Immediately the government put into execution the previously agreed plan to extend full control over all French Indo-China.

On July 24, 1941, Japanese troops moved into the south. The Japanese government was taken totally by surprise when the United States, whose previous warnings and threats had all evaporated in nothing more than wordy admonitions, reacted two days later by freezing Japanese assets in concert with Great Britain and the Dominions. The Dutch government in exile also took measures that amounted to a termination of trade with the East Indies in vitally needed products such as oil.

Japan was dependent on supplies of strategic materials from the United States and Southeast Asia. Without them the nation's military capability would gradually wither away with the depletion of its stockpiles, and it would be at the mercy of any foe. For example, oil reserves were sufficient for at most two years and much less in an all-out war with the West. America's unprecedented action had reduced Japan's leaders to three alternatives: (1) a humiliating withdrawal from both French Indo-China and China proper, (2) a possible settlement on less drastic terms with the United States, or (3) war with the West. And a decision one way or another could not be delayed. Therefore, the negotiations with the United States for a settlement of differences, which had been going on in a desultory fashion for more than a year, now took on a new note of desperate urgency. The American government, and particularly Secretary of State Cordell Hull, discounted the possibility of a Japanese attack despite intelligence reports of war preparations and refused to budge from its original demand for total withdrawal from all of China, except Manchukuo. Japan offered to withdraw from French Indo-China, but this concession was not enough. Konoye requested a summit conference with President Roosevelt, but on Hull's advice this request was denied.

At an imperial conference early in September General Tōjō secured reluctant approval of the necessity of war if a settlement with the United States were not reached by mid-October. While Tōjō felt sure of victory, the naval general staff felt less than confident of dealing with the American and British navies and securing the oil of the East Indies before Japan's fuel supply was exhausted. Unwilling to carry out the final decision for war, Konoye resigned on October 16, and the tough-minded Tōjō headed a new government destined to last until 1944. At another imperial conference the decision was made to extend negotiations in the vain hope of reaching a satisfactory agreement by November 25, but that deadline came and went without any moderation in American terms. Finally, an imperial conference on December 1 gave final approval to Tōjō's decision to attack. At dawn on December 7, 1941, Japanese carrier planes caught most of the Pacific fleet in Pearl Harbor and wreaked a more thorough destruction of ships and installations than even the most sanguine admirals anticipated. Fortunately, the American carrier force was at sea and escaped damage. More of the fleet might have been deployed at sea except for a shortage of fuel.

The details of the Japanese conquests and the American counterattack cannot detain us. The well-planned campaigns overran Southeast Asia more rapidly than anticipated, except for the stubborn Filipino-American defense of Bataan and Corregidor. Within a few months Japanese naval forces entered the Indian sea and could easily have extended the scope of conquest, but their goals had already been achieved. Hence-

forth, Japanese strategy sought only to exploit and defend the "Greater East Asia Co-Prosperity Sphere" until the Allies were ready to recognize it in a peace treaty. This strategy was based on the assumption of an Axis victory in Europe. By the time this assumption came into doubt, the opportunity to exploit the period of American weakness had passed, and in fact, the Japanese fleet had already suffered serious losses.

In light of the priority given to the European theater of the war, American reaction in the Pacific was amazingly rapid. In May 1942, a Japanese carrier force covering a troop landing in southern New Guinea clashed with an American carrier force in the Battle of the Coral Sea, the first major engagement between carrier-based planes. Both sides suffered about equally heavy losses in this new type of long-range encounter, but the Americans could claim victory because the Japanese task force withdrew without carrying out its planned landing. In the Battle of Midway of June 1942, the Japanese navy suffered a shattering defeat losing four carriers and two heavy cruisers because American intelligence, by breaking the Japanese code, provided full information on the operation. Thereafter responsibility for mounting a counterattack was divided into three commands: that of Admiral Nimitz with headquarters in Hawaii, which carried out a successful island-hopping advance across the Central Pacific; that of General Douglas MacArthur, which advanced successfully from Australia to the Philippines; and the less successful Indo-Burma command shared by Britain and the United States. The original strategy called on all three to coordinate their advances for the liberation of China, which would then serve as the base for the final attack on Japan, but difficulties in Burma and China forced a modification of strategy in favor of securing island bases from which the Japanese home islands could be brought under attack. Meanwhile, the silent war under the sea was tearing the guts out of the "Co-Prosperity

Sphere." As early as January 1943, American submarines were sinking Japanese shipping ten times faster than it could be replaced and by the end of the year Japanese production was already falling off because of shortages of raw materials from overseas.

By mid-1943 Japanese leaders must have realized individually that there was no prospect of victory, but no one dared to speak of defeat. The Japanese people were kept ignorant of the country's losses, but by the end of the year they could not avoid perceiving the symptoms in everyday life. Meanwhile, Japanese soldiers continued to the very end to fight with epic valor, preferring death to dishonor in the service of their "divine" emperor. Perhaps the supreme expression of self-sacrifice was the thousands of suicide or *Kamikaze* pilots (so called after the "divine wind" or typhoon that had destroyed the Mongol invasion) who crashed their bomb-laden planes into American ships; but their missions were also an admission of Japan's desperate plight by 1944. The war was long since over, but the soldiers of both sides continued to fight and die in ever growing numbers.

With the fall of Saipan after a bloody defense in mid-1944, General Tōjō admitted military failure by resigning under pressure from a group of former ministers who had never wholeheartedly supported the war and now sought some sort of accommodation short of unconditional surrender. Yet the war went on taking a mounting toll both overseas and at home as bombers based on Saipan rained destruction on the industrial cities of Japan. All peace probes failed to yield results, and the German surrender in May 1945 left Japan isolated in its resistance to the combined forces of the Allies. Only the position of the Soviet Union remained in doubt, but the cold reception of all Japanese overtures to mediate left little hope. All that Japanese peace advocates now sought was an assurance that the imperial institution would be preserved, but the Allied declaration at Potsdam did not even grant this con-

cession, demanding total demilitarization, destruction of war industries, trial of war criminals, and democratization during an occupation. The Emperor and the Supreme War Council, with the exception of the military members, were even ready to negotiate on the basis of the Potsdam declaration, but the erroneous impression was conveyed by the press that the government was determined to fight to the bitter end. This impression contributed to President Truman's decision to detonate the first atomic bomb over Hiroshima on August 6. Whether the devastating effect of these bombs or the Russian declaration of war a few hours before the second bomb was dropped on Nagasaki led to the Emperor's decision to insist on surrender over the determination of the military to continue the struggle is a subject of dispute among those who question the contribution of the atomic attacks. Actually, before the bombs were dropped, the Emperor was prepared to accept the terms of the Potsdam declaration, but fearful of the consequences of the intransigence of the military, bowed to their demands. When the United States responded to the request to retain the imperial institution with the vague assurance that "the ultimate form of government of Japan shall . . . be established by the freely expressed will of the Japanese people," the Emperor felt sufficiently reassured to order the military and the people "to bear the unbearable." The military were still not reconciled but the Emperor pointed out that "if we do not terminate the war at this juncture, our unique national structure will be destroyed and our nation will suffer extermination. If we save anything, be it ever so little, we could yet hope to rebuild the nation in the future." Some diehards attempted a coup, and the army minister and some others committed suicide, but the surrender message was dispatched on August 14, 1945. After the formal signing of the surrender document on the battleship *Missouri* on September 2 in Tōkyō Bay, the Japanese people as well as American forces looked forward with anxiety and apprehension to what the occupation might bring.

THE AMERICAN OCCUPATION

In contrast with Europe, plans for the occupation of Japan were slow in being formulated. In the first place, the United States, which had borne the brunt of the war with Japan, insisted on overriding authority, though meeting the objections, chiefly Russian, by agreeing to joint policy and advisory commissions. In practice, the arbitrary exercise of power by General MacArthur, Supreme Commander for the Allied Powers (SCAP), reduced these bodies to virtual impotence.

One vital limiting factor was the wholly inadequate number of personnel trained in the Japanese language and culture. This deficiency forced the decision to govern through Japanese officials and institutions, appropriately modified and controlled, rather than to attempt to govern directly as in Europe. Under SCAP a "braintrust" composed of "experts" on subjects such as agriculture, education, and labor framed and issued directives to Japanese officials for the implementation of the radical reforms prescribed in the *Initial Post Surrender Policy* drawn up by a committee of the American State, War, and Navy departments and supplemented by later edicts.

The provisions of this document reflected both the harshness of those who wished to destroy Japan's potential strength for leadership in Asia in favor of Nationalist China and the liberalism of those idealists who dreamed of transforming Japan into a more advanced democratic paradise than even the United States had yet become. These objectives were to a large degree incompatible and unrealistic. On the one hand, a nation's strength depends much more on the character, skills, and education of its people than on money and machines, which are replaceable. On the other hand, enduring reforms must be carefully adapted to the traditional values and institutions of a people to gain widespread acceptance. Under these circumstances the degree of enduring success that was achieved is truly amazing and owes a great deal to the commanding stature and moderating influence of the Supreme Commander, General MacArthur, who won the respect of the Japanese in the familiar role of "shōgun" and also tempered the ardor of the idealists.

In addition to disarmament and demilitarization, including the return of six and one-half million Japanese soldiers and civilians from overseas, the harsh aspect required the trial of war criminals, the purging from public life of all leaders and officials who had supported or cooperated in the war effort, the dissolution of the zaibatsu organizations, the dismantling of war-connected industries, and reparations in machinery and goods for all Asian countries that had suffered from Japanese aggression. The war crimes trials in Tōkyō dragged on for almost two years before sentencing Tōjō and six others to death and assessing prison terms of various lengths against the rest. Meanwhile, a number of overseas tribunals tried more than 5000 others. Generally these prolonged trials had no significant impact on the Japanese people who remained indifferent and apathetic to the fate of the leaders responsible for the first defeat in Japan's history. Certainly no national sense of war guilt was generated among a people suffering from the economic collapse and consequent hardships of a misguided war policy. The purge of more than 200,000 military and civilian leaders was far more damaging because about 90 percent of the experienced public servants were barred from the civil service and from standing for election to the Diet. A government denuded of trained leadership could scarcely meet the monumental postwar problems effectively. In fact, however, as in the case of purged business leaders, the purged bureaucrats and politicians continued to exercise influence because their appointed or elected successors privately sought their advice. The zaibatsu combines were first attacked through a purge of the top management, but as in government and politics Japanese business relations depended primarily on established personal relationships that largely negated the effect of the purge. Each day the new managers could be seen bicycling to the homes of their former bosses for instructions. After a year's delay the dissolution of the zaibatsu holding companies was ordered as part of a general decentralization policy. Government bonds were issued in payment of the shares which then were offered for sale to the public, but the public had little capital for investment in an uncertain economic future. In any case, Japanese industry had suffered such heavy destruction in the bombing raids of the last year of the war that significant production could not be resumed without large investments of capital.

A year later, at the beginning of 1948, the political deterioration of Nationalist China and the stagnation of the Japanese economy led to a sharp reduction in the number of holding companies marked for dissolution in the hope of restoring confidence in the business community and stimulating a recovery effort. This was the first clear sign of a shift in occupation policy from reform to rehabilitation, and Japanese businessmen, who had been awaiting just such a signal, responded enthusiastically, particularly after mid-year when SCAP extended credit for vital imports. The other policy prescriptions for the destruction of war-related industries and the payment of reparations in machines simply were not implemented to any extent. What heavy industry had escaped severe damage was a necessary base for any economic recovery, and a prostrate economy requiring large shipments of American food to stave off starvation was in no condition to furnish reparations.

The liberal aspect of occupation policy called for sweeping social, economic, and political reforms in the direction of democratization and decentralization. A major step

was an imperial rescript of January 1946, renouncing as false the conception of imperial divinity, a change which, however, did not shake the loyalty and deep respect felt for the emperor. Other measures intended to alter the relationship of the emperor and the people were the abolition of state maintenance of Shintōism to remove the chief support of the imperial cult and the transfer of imperial estates to the state to end the emperor's financial independence of the government. To institutionalize the shift of sovereignty from the emperor to the people a new constitution was needed. When no Japanese committee was willing to make the drastic change of the location of sovereignty to the people, the political "experts" of SCAP drew up the new constitution, which was translated into Japanese, presented by the Emperor, and ratified by the Diet.

In language obviously inspired by the American constitution the preamble made it unquestionably clear that sovereignty resided in "We, the Japanese people, acting through our duly elected representatives. . . ." The emperor was described as no more than a "symbol" of Japanese unity whose very existence was dependent on the will of the people. Abolition of the titled aristocracy, except for imperial princes, was confirmed, and the appointed House of Peers was supplanted by an elected House of Councillors that could delay but not block legislation passed by the House of Representatives. The prime minister, and thus the cabinet, was made subject to the support of a majority in the lower house. An independent Supreme Court was empowered to determine the constitutionality of any law or other official act. Most controversial and embarrassing has been Article 9 renouncing war and the maintenance of armed forces because any amendment of the constitution required the support of two-thirds of both houses and no party has yet been able to muster this many votes in the upper house. Finally, an extensive bill of rights guaranteed to the individual not only those rights familiar to Americans but also many others, such as the right of all adult men and women to vote and the right of labor to organize and bargain collectively.

Long before the promulgation of the new constitution in May 1947, the provisions that it institutionalized had in fact been put into effect. Immediately SCAP had ordered the release of all political prisoners, and labor "experts" advised and assisted labor leaders, including many Communists, in the organization of unions. Socialist and communist organization and activities were given a free rein by the suspension of all limitations on freedom of thought and action. A flood of strikes was a natural consequence, but under the circumstances of economic collapse and vast unemployment collective bargaining could not hope to secure many gains. Therefore, labor naturally turned to political action as the most promising avenue for results. In the first postwar election of 1946 in which all men and women over 20 were eligible to vote the left won one-third of the seats in the lower house including 5 candidates of the Communist party. The Socialists emerged from the first election under the new constitution in 1947 as the largest single party and its leader headed a coalition govenment for 10 months. It fell because divergent views within the coalition, as well as the increasingly conservative attitude of SCAP, prevented the enactment of socialist legislation. During 1947 SCAP became more and more alarmed at the radical and disruptive activities of the left and began to insist on repressive measures. Particularly distressing were Communist domination of labor leadership and calling of a general strike to embarrass the government and SCAP and to set themselves up as champions of national independence.

Other major reforms of the occupation concerned local government, agriculture, education, and even the family. The Home ministry with its control of a national police force was abolished as part of the policy of decentralization that saw the election of pre-fectural governors and other formerly appointed officials and the establishment of police departments under local control after the American model. The agrarian reform program was probably the most successful and enduring project sponsored by the occupation because it dealt effectively with the most exploited sector of the population. Tenancy and high rents were the chief problems in need of solutions. Landlords were required to sell all or most of their land to the government at the prewar rather than the inflated postwar values, and the government then sold it to the tenants on long and easy terms. The amount of leased land was thus reduced from 45 percent to 13 percent of the arable land. The number of farmers who leased all their land dropped from 26 percent to less than 5 percent. Furthermore, legal rent was set at no more than 25 percent of the value of the major crop compared with the previous average of about 50 percent. Naturally landlords were unhappy with these reforms, especially reimbursement at prewar values, which amounted to partial confiscation. Increased land taxes subsequently led to voluntary sales of the remaining leased land to farmers who were able with new mechanized equipment to cultivate enlarged holdings. Although farmers did not care for higher taxes and did their best to evade paying them, they were so fearful of how socialist legislation might affect their gains that they solidly supported candidates of the conservative parties at the polls.

Education was given top priority attention by the occupation "experts" who quite correctly believed that ideological reform was the key to any genuine transformation of Japan into a truly democratic nation. The first step was to purge one-quarter of the teachers too well known for their active support of the war. Then the whole educational system from the elementary through the university level was subjected to a thoroughgoing reorganization in both structure and curricula to reflect American ideas of decentralization, integration of the sexes, and freedom of thought. Both boys and girls received the same education under a coeducational system, and compulsory education was extended to nine years. Plans were initiated for a radical increase in the number of students who could go on to higher education. In an effort to offset the prestige of Tōkyō universities, teachers colleges in the prefectures were converted into universities, and a number of new universities were planned. The former courses in moral training were replaced with social studies using new texts written by American "experts," which stressed the "facts" rather than the myths of Japanese history and treated critically the former emphasis on the martial tradition of Japan. To some, the enforcement of the use of texts arbitrarily rewritten by agents of the occupation seemed inconsistent with the avowed American objective of fostering democratic freedoms. Perhaps most important was the change in teaching philosophy from unquestioning memorization and indoctrination to a positive encouragement in the student of a spirit of curiosity and independent inquiry. Such a reversal of educational doctrine released the teachers from the strait jacket of state-prescribed conformity and encouraged many to express liberal and leftist points of view. Where teachers had previously been impotent in dealing with the central government, the transfer of authority to locally elected boards enabled them to form unions that could exert effective pressure on these less formidable local bodies, and a national teachers union emerged with a pronounced leftist outlook.

The occupation effort to emancipate women and to secure equality of the sexes went beyond granting them the vote and establishing coeducation. A major attempt was made to end the parental arrangement of marriage and to encourage free selection of mates in accordance with American practice. The initial response to this emancipation from parental authority was enthusiastic, especially in the cities, but many Japanese authorities predicted dire consequences from

this revolutionary change in social practice. Actually their predictions did not come true to any serious extent, but gradually the conditions of Japanese life, particularly the need for parental support during the early years of marriage, generated a return to tradition, though the proposed partners gained a greater say in the final decision than in the past.

At the beginning, SCAP policies gave little concern to the problem of economic rehabilitation. In fact, the harsher economic and political directives acted as a positive deterrent to any Japanese efforts at recovery. Cut off from their former overseas sources of raw materials and then purged from their positions, Japanese business leaders could only sit back and observe the continued deterioration of the economy while awaiting a change in occupation policy. Fortunately they did not have very long to wait before the burden of the occupation on the American taxpayer and the revolutionary events in China led the American government to review and modify its policies. No clear date can be set for the shift in policy from reform to recovery, which emerged gradually between mid-1947 and mid-1948. The new emphasis on economic recovery, political stability on the conservative side, and the curbing of leftist activities was not unrelated to the emergence of the cold war and a developing desire to return sovereignty by a peace treaty to a Japan solidly planted in the democratic camp. By the end of 1948 some Japanese steel mills were rolling again with SCAP-arranged, semibarter exchanges of Japanese steel in payment for shipments of American coking coal. Through 1949 and 1950 industrial production and capacity gradually increased with the aid of American credit, stimulating a general improvement in economic activity. Japanese businessmen were depurged and permitted to travel abroad in quest of new foreign trade contacts. The real boost, however, came with the outbreak of the Korean conflict in mid-1950 and the American decision to procure as much of its needs from Japanese suppliers as possible. By the time the occupation was ended in April 1952, Japan was in the midst of a boom which, with the exception of a few shortlived recessions when the economy became overheated, has continued at an accelerating rate. For Japan, then, the best years were yet to come.

As early as 1947, the United States had initiated fruitless negotiations for peace treaties with both Germany and Japan. By 1949 the conclusion was reached that the only feasible course for Japan was a separate peace supported by America's major allies in the cold war. Such a one-sided peace, however, would prove embarrassing to a Japan left defenseless by its constitution because, by relying on American forces for defense, it would have the effect of committing the country to the Western camp. The Japanese were unwilling to jeopardize their neutrality until the North Korean invasion of South Korea raised the specter of invasion by a communist neighbor further motivated by revenge. In August 1950, the conservative government abandoned neutrality and took much more severe steps to suppress the internal activities of the now militant Communist party. At the same time a so-called National Police Reserve of 75,000 men and a Maritime Force of 8000 men were authorized as the nucleus of what later became in fact, if not in name, an army and a navy. Still other obstacles had to be overcome in order to gain enough support for a peace treaty. The Philippines, Australia, and New Zealand, still fearful of a resurgent Japan, were appeased only by bilateral security pacts with the United States. A peace conference was convened in San Francisco, and on September 8, 1951, a peace treaty was signed over Communist objections by 49 nations, followed by a security pact between Japan and the United States authorizing the maintenance of American forces for the defense of Japan.

By the terms of the peace treaty Japan acknowledged the loss of southern Sakhalin, Taiwan, and the Kurile islands and recog-

nized the American trusteeship over the Ryūkyū and other Pacific islands, but the successors to Taiwan and the Kuriles were not specified. The treaty admitted Japan's right as a sovereign nation to provide for its self-defense, and the security pact made it clear that Japan was eventually expected to provide for its own defense. Reasonable reparations settlements were to be separately negotiated. With the securing of the necessary number of ratifications, Japan officially regained its sovereignty on April 28, 1952, though in fact the dismantling of the occupation had begun as soon as the treaty was signed and the Japanese government had been permitted to open direct relations with foreign governments.

In less than a century Japan had advanced from the humiliation of unequal treaties to recognition as a great power, from an agrarian to a fully modernized industrial economy—and then had suffered a devastating defeat and occupation by the world's strongest power before regaining its sovereignty for a fresh start as an equal member of the community of nations. Although the fundamental foundations for modernization were fashioned in the first 50 years, the real process of modernization, particularly in the economic realm, developed in the decades after 1905. Initially the military, vindicated by victory, enjoyed such unchallengeable prestige that no combination of the other elite groups could check their demands as approved by the senior Genrō, General Yamagata, who had even come out of retirement to serve as chief of the army general staff during the Russo-Japanese War. The growing economic strength of the zaibatsu, however, was catapulted upward by the tremendous expansion and profits of World War I. Their financial support of party politicians and bureaucrats, reinforced by the postwar climate in favor of internationalism and democracy, made possible the curbing of military influence and a promising experiment with party government. But the principal source of the parties' strength, the financial backing of the zaibatsu, proved to be their undoing as a continuous barrage of charges of alleged corruption was leveled at whichever party was in power, undermining respect for the parliamentary process. These charges were not made just by disgruntled military leaders and ultranationalist groups who blamed all evils on Western influences, but even opportunistic leaders of the party temporarily out of power were frequently in the forefront in making these irresponsible charges, which generally remained unproven. Thus the politicians themselves were principal participants in their own destruction. On the other hand, the resurgence of the military in the thirties cannot be credited to a popular revulsion against the West and its ideas in the name of Japan's unique national polity; the continued public support of the parties in every election refutes such an argument. The military, inspired by both civilian and military patriots, gradually immobi-

lized the parties and seized power with the support of defectors from the combined opposition of party politicians, bureaucrats, and zaibatsu.

Defeat and foreign occupation discredited the military leaders who had led the nation astray. As the first people to experience the horrors of nuclear war, the popular reaction against war and armament is understandable even in a nation with a strong martial tradition, but it does not mean that the heroic actions and sacrifices of Japan's soldiers and sailors were disavowed or forgotten. Once the worst years of the postwar era had passed, voices were raised again calling for a revitalization of Japan's traditional spirit and values. Japan had once overreached itself, but the energy and ability of its people has brought about an amazing material recovery, even if the ideological future remained uncertain. The problems, achievements, and question marks of the postoccupation years will be examined in a final chapter.

SIGNIFICANT DATES

1905	Treaty of Portsmouth ending Russo-Japanese War
1908	Root-Takahira agreement
1910	Annexation of Korea
1912–1913	Taishō crisis
1915	Twenty-One Demands
1917	Lansing-Ishii note
1918–1922	Siberian intervention
1918–1921	First "party" government under Prime Minister Hara
1921	Washington Conference
1922	Death of last Restoration leader, General Yamagata
1925	Universal adult male franchise
1930	London Naval Disarmament treaty
1931–1932	Manchurian "Incident" and creation of Manchukuo
1936	First Division "mutiny" and anti-Comintern pact
1937	Start of second Sino-Japanese War
1940	Imperial Rule Assistance Associations: Tripartite pact
1941	Pearl Harbor attack of December 7
1942	Battle of the Coral Sea (May) and Battle of Midway (June)
1945	Bombing of Hiroshima (August 9); surrender (August 15)
1945–1952	American occupation
1950–1953	Korean "police action"

SELECTED READINGS

Brown, Delmer, *Nationalism in Japan.* Berkeley: University of California Press, 1955.

*Butow, Robert J. C., *Japan's Decision to Surrender.* Stanford: Stanford University Press, 1967.

*———, *Tojo and the Coming of the War.* Stanford: Stanford University Press, 1969.

Conroy, Francis Hilary, *The Japanese Seizure of Korea.* Philadelphia: University of Pennsylvania Press, 1960.

Dore, Ronald P., *Land Reform in Japan.* London: Oxford University Press, 1959.

*———, ed., *Aspects of Social Change in Modern Japan.* Princeton: Princeton University Press, 1971.

Duus, Peter, *Party Rivalry and Political Change in Taisho Japan.* Cambridge, Mass.: Harvard University Press, 1968.

Feis, Herbert, *Japan Subdued.* Princeton: Princeton University Press, 1961.

*———, *The Road to Pearl Harbor.* New York: Atheneum Pubs., 1962.

Grew, Joseph C., *Ten Years in Japan.* New York: Simon and Schuster, 1944.

*Hersey, John, *Hiroshima.* New York: Bantam Books, 1959.

*Iriye, Akira, *After Imperialism: The Search for a New Order in the Far East, 1921–1931.* New York: Atheneum Pubs., 1969.

Kawai, Kazuo, *Japan's American Interlude.* Chicago: University of Chicago Press, 1960.

*Lockwood, William W., *Economic Development of Japan.* Princeton: Princeton University Press, 1954.

*———, ed., *The State and Economic Enterprise in Japan.* Princeton: Princeton University Press, 1965.

Morley, James W., *The Japanese Thrust into Siberia, 1918.* New York: Columbia University Press, 1957.

Najita, Tetsuo, *Hara Kei in the Politics of Compromise, 1905–1915.* Cambridge, Mass.: Harvard University Press, 1967.

Ogata, Sadako N., *Defiance in Manchuria: The Making of Japanese Foreign Policy, 1931–1932.* Berkeley: University of California Press, 1964.

Scalapino, R. A., *Democracy and the Party Movement in Prewar Japan.* Berkeley: University of California Press, 1953.

*Seidensticker, Edward, *Kafu the Scribbler: The Life and Writings of Nagai Kafu, 1879–1959.* Stanford: Stanford University Press, 1968.

Shigemitsu, Mamoru, *Japan and Her Destiny.* London: Hutchinson, 1958.

Storry, Richard, *The Double Patriots.* Boston: Houghton Mifflin, 1957.

Yoshida, Shigeru, *The Yoshida Memoirs.* Boston: Houghton Mifflin, 1962.

CHAPTER TWENTY-TWO

THE INDIAN STRUGGLE FOR INDEPENDENCE: 1905 – 1947

The events of 1905 both within India and elsewhere transformed the character of the Indian nationalist movement. Hitherto it had been divided into two main streams: the comparatively moderate, Western-educated members of the Indian National Congress seeking British concessions to a long-range evolutionary progress toward dominion-type self-government and those inspired individuals who looked to the Hindu spiritual heritage and sought to revive its pristine vigor and universal appeal by purging it of impurities. Since the first placed its principal faith, with certain reservations, in modernization within the framework of Western, and especially British, achievements, while the second stressed the superiority and even worldwide applicability of the Indian spiritual experience, the two had found few opportunities or possibilities for collaboration prior to 1905.

The most notable exception was Tilak's adamant rejection of all British-sponsored reforms and his publicizing of certain Hindu festivals and practices as well as the exploits of the anti-Muslim, Mahārāshtran hero, Shivāji, to arouse emotional support among the Hindu masses. But Tilak's political influence did not become important until after 1905, and by 1916, when he gained a dominant voice in the Congress, he had substantially moderated his attitude toward the British Rāj.

During 1920, the year of Tilak's death, leadership of the Indian nationalist movement was taken by that charismatic and enigmatic figure, Mohandās Karamchand Gāndhi (1869–1948), who, whether in or out of power, remained the dominant and guiding force in the struggle for independence. Whatever credit may be given to other events, such as the two world wars, in weakening the British position in India, the Mahātma or "Great Soul," as Gāndhi had been dubbed in 1915 by India's poet laureate and first Nobel Prize winner, Rabīndranāth Tagore, gave to Indian nationalism a new dimension by gaining mass participation through combining a uniquely Indian appeal to the spiritual strength of the Hindu people with a rejection of British rule and Western civilization as ethically degenerate and unsuited for the control of India's destiny, or indeed that of any other country. Other nationalist leaders, including his closest associates, might disagree with many of Gāndhi's ideas, but they could not afford to reject the leadership of a man who in thought and action symbolized and inspired the spirit and unity of the Indian people. In life, Gāndhi dominated the Indian independence movement; in death, his ideas and ideals still exercise a pervasive influence.

MODERATES AND EXTREMISTS (1905 – 1916)

The year 1905 proved to be an important turning point in the Indian nationalist movement. Until then, the moderate leadership of the Indian National Congress had placed its faith in British goodwill to deal fairly with Indian demands for constitutional progress. Only Tilak and a few other leaders in Bengal and the Punjab had lost faith in the British and condoned, if not encouraged, anti-British acts of violence. However, the Universities Act of 1904 and then the partition of Bengal in 1905 had shaken the faith of the moderates and stimulated the dominant Congress leader, Gokhale, to demand for the first time *swarāj* (self-government such as other Brit-

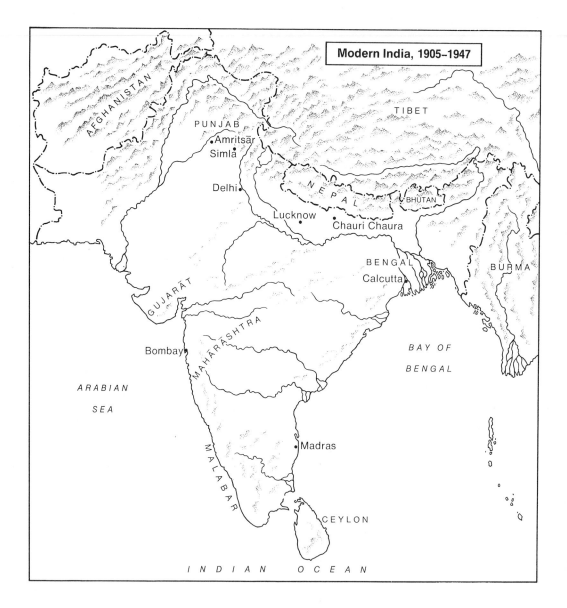

Modern India, 1905–1947

ish colonies enjoyed) in an address at the 1905 meeting of the Congress. Although he continued to favor constitutional progress and to oppose all extremist activism of a violent nature, a sizable and growing number of the membership proved less patient and more willing to listen to the extremist views of Tilak. Agitation against the Bengal partition had generated a *swadeshi* movement (a boycott of British manufactured goods), which was to become an important weapon in the later development of the nationalist movement. Because Bengali Muslims refused to cooperate in the boycott, outbreaks of communal strife were also an important portent for the future. Indeed, fear of Hindu domination at the expense of the Muslim minority caused Muslim leaders to found the All-India Muslim League in 1906. In spite of the signs of new nationalist vigor, which received added impetus from the Japanese victory over Russia, Gokhale saw hope for significant constitutional gains, without violence in the victory of the British Liberal party at the end of 1905 and the appointment of the renowned liberal, Lord Morley, as secretary of state for India.

At the 1906 meeting of the Congress Tilak and the extremists demonstrated their new strength in repeated clashes with Gokhale and the moderates, but a real showdown was put off until the following year. At the 1907 session of the Congress, Tilak's effort to gain the presidency for the deported Punjabi nationalist leader, Lala Lajpat Rai, was frustrated by a parliamentary maneuver. The result was a mad melée within the meeting hall with chairs and sticks being utilized as weapons. This clash produced a secession of the extremists and the framing of a new constitution by the moderate rump specifying the employment of only constitutional procedures for the eventual accomplishment of self-government. This division within the ranks of the Indian National Congress was not healed until 1916, while followers of the extremist leaders, with or without their authorization, engaged in anti-British acts of violence for several years. Their principal weapon was the homemade bomb that initially proved ineffective until more skilled bomb-makers returned after instruction in Paris. By 1910, however, the British authorities had reduced the dimensions of extremist terrorism by capturing and sentencing to death or imprisonment most of the activists as well as the leaders, including Tilak, who were accused of encouraging and condoning the violence of their followers.

Meanwhile, the secretary of state for India, Lord Morley, and the governor-general, Lord Minto, recognized the need to make some concessions to the demands of Indian nationalism. In 1907 Morley named two Indians to the India Council in London, while Minto consulted Indian leaders of all groups to find out what reforms would most effectively meet the varied complaints of the moment. His recommendations, after further modifications, were enacted as the Morley-Minto Reforms of 1909. The fundamental guideline underlying these reforms was the retention of executive authority over all issues in the hands of the British government of India while extending representation to important groups and as large a voice as feasible in decision making to the central and provincial legislative bodies. Another important concession was the appointment of at least one Indian each to the provincial and central executive councils, breaking the British monopoly of this branch of imperial government. Lord Morley specifically denied that these concessions implied any commitment to future progress in the direction of responsible parliamentary self-government, but this statement seems to have been mere politics to gain parliamentary acceptance of the measures. In fact, the admission of Indians to both the legislative and executive branches of what was clearly evolving into a British-style parliamentary system set the path and pattern for future development.

These reforms gave the provincial legislatures an Indian majority elected by such groups as district and municipal administrations, chambers of commerce, landowners, universities, and the Muslim community. Even the central legislature, which was increased to 60 members, gained a nonofficial Indian majority when nonofficial appointees were added to the 27 elected members. Nevertheless, in practice the governor-general's power to appoint a majority placed a positive restraint on this body. The limited and corporate character of the franchise, which was much more restricted for elections to the central legislature, was a far cry from democratic suffrage, but it clearly pointed in this direction for the future.

A major weakness of these reforms stemmed from their underlying principle which, while admitting Indians to a majority role in the legislative process, retained final control in the hands of the British rulers. Although the latter bent over backwards to cooperate with the wishes expressed in the legislatures, on more than one occasion they felt compelled to exercise their power, creating frustration among the Indian legislators and encouraging them to make irresponsible attacks on governmental policies and practices they could not control. In other words, the attempt to blend autocracy with representative institutions was an unnatural and eventually unworkable mixture. At best, it could be justified as a transitional and temporary arrangement.

In the long run, however, a far more serious problem was created by the concession, in deference to the demands of the Muslim League, of separate electorates to assure the Muslim minority of adequate representation in both the provincial and central legislatures. This concession, accepted with great reluctance by Lord Morley, gave official sanction to religion as a basis for political and communal differentiation, contrary to the Western conception of government as a strictly secular operation. But none of the Western nations, with their common Judeo-Christian heritages, suffered from such a deep religious cleavage as India. Moreover, at the time, even the moderate leader, Gokhale, accepted this decision as the only practicable device for securing justice for the Muslim minorities, even though the Muslims were given more seats than their numbers warranted. The seriousness of its divisive effect was not to be generally recognized until further advances toward self-government and communal bloodshed posed a clear threat to Indian unity.

Although Gokhale and the moderates, who now dominated the Congress, had expected more generous concessions from the liberal Lord Morley, they went on record as being deeply satisfied with the reforms—for the time being. Of course, they also expressed the hope that further, liberalizing steps would be taken before long. In 1911 the British government decided on a different approach toward assuaging Indian grievances and generating sentiments of loyalty to the British realm. For the first time the king and queen were brought to India and crowned emperor and empress at a Grand Durbar in Delhi amid all the pomp and pageantry that could be mustered. The Indian people, always attracted by pageantry and a holiday mood poured out by the hundreds of thousands to see and express their loyalty to their titular heads, while the Indian princes particularly welcomed the recognition of their status at a traditional Grand Durbar. Their gratitude was generously expressed a few years later in their contributions to the British during World War I.

This impressive setting was employed to promise the forthcoming rectification of fundamental grievances. Perhaps the most important concession was the repeal of the Bengal partition, which had contributed so heavily to the growth of anti-British feeling and radical Indian nationalism. This action undercut the extremist assertion that no justice could be expected from British rulers. Another change, which appealed more to Muslim than Hindu sentiments, was the removal of the imperial capital from British-dominated Calcutta to Delhi, the former capital of the Mughal dynasty. Other boons included the release of most political prisoners, but not Tilak, and the allocation of additional funds to foster the expansion of education.

These concessions and the Morley-Minto Reforms convinced all but the most radical extremists in the Indian nationalist movement that the British government was just and was ready to make reasonable progress toward the eventual goal of self-government. In any case, Indian nationalism was still limited to the educated elite and could only generate widespread popular support on specific issues with a deep emotional appeal, such as the partition of Bengal. Not until after World War I and the emergence of Gāndhi did it develop massive popular support, and even then this popular commitment proved hard to manage and difficult to maintain for any extended campaign.

The enthusiastic support of Britain's

war effort demonstrated not only the loyalty of most of India's leaders, princes, and people but also the generally salutary effect of the preceding reforms and concessions. Immediately, the British removed all but 15,000 British troops for service in Europe without any repercussions, and the major princes turned over their British-trained forces for service overseas. Later, many of the princes made generous monetary contributions from their own resources, while the Indian legislature took the unprecedented step of agreeing to support Indian troops abroad out of Indian revenues. Moreover, when the prospects of the Western Allies appeared bleakest, the Indian government approved a gift of £ 100,000,000 increasing the country's debt by one-third and, in addition to other exchange problems, creating severe difficulties for the Indian economy at the close of the war. Further important Indian contributions to the war effort were made in the area of essential supplies and munitions stimulating Indian industrialization, particularly the expansion of the recently founded Tata Iron and Steel Works. All told, India provided more than 800,000 soldiers and 400,000 noncombatants during the course of the war and suffered casualties of more than 26,000 killed and 70,000 wounded.

All Indians, however, did not give Britain unquestioning loyalty, and as the war dragged on with heavy Indian casualties, especially at the British defeat in Mesopotamia in 1916, Congress members became restless and demanded prompt progress toward self-government as a reward for loyal support. Even before the war the Ghadr Conspiracy, involving principally Sikhs in the Punjab and overseas in the western United States and Canada, was founded by Har Dayal, one-time lecturer in philosophy at Stanford University. In the newspaper *Ghadr* (Mutiny), which he set up late in 1913 to stir up anti-British sentiments, he placed an advertisement that read: "Wanted: Brave soldiers to stir up *Ghadr* in India; Pay—death; prize—martyrdom; pension

—liberty; field of battle—India." Har Dayal had to flee from the United States and ended up on the Indian section of the German general staff. His lieutenants in America and elsewhere continued the Ghadr agitation and are credited with arranging for passage back to India of as many as 8,000 revolutionaries, mostly Sikhs. A rebellion, planned for February, 1915, was discovered and suppressed by the British. The failure of this effort did not end Ghadr intrigue and plots, but none of them ever bore fruit. Another area of trouble developed in the northwest where Muslim patriots, upset by the state of war between Britain and the Ottoman sultan and caliph, sought to generate a holy war against British India among the tribesmen of the frontier and Afghanistan. Although some military action resulted, it never assumed serious proportions because the emir of Afghanistan remained steadfastly loyal, even in the face of the blandishments of a German-sponsored mission.

Congress restlessness was compounded of various elements that were reinforced by a number of developments during the course of the war. Already mentioned was the initial reluctance of the British to recognize and reward with further steps toward self-government the overwhelming expression of Indian loyalty and the growing dependence of the British war effort on the magnitude of Indian support. Many leaders came to believe that conscienceless British commanders were exploiting Indian troops and labor battalions for the dirty and undesirable tasks of the war. Furthermore, the war itself exposed the internal weakness of European civilization and tended to depreciate the respect previously held by many Indians for its superiority. The mystique that had enveloped the British Rāj was undermined. Two events were destined to alter the leadership and attitude of the Congress. First, in June 1914, Tilak was released after serving six years in prison and then sought respectability and readmission to the Congress by expressing support for the war effort and unequivocally rejecting violence as the avenue to self-government. Second, his principal opponent and unchallenged leader of the moderate-dominated Congress, the veteran Gokhale, died late in 1915 at only 49 years of age, and Tilak, along with a number of his supporters, was taken back into the Congress. Almost immediately he showed some of his old spark by forming a Home Rule League championing self-government at the end of the war. In this effort he was soon joined by the venerable Annie Besant who formed her own Home Rule League in Madras. Both quickly gained enthusiastic middle class support indicating the extent of impatience with the moderates' gradualist program of concessions. At the Lucknow session late in 1916 Tilak not only won the leadership of the Congress but also a Muslim alliance in the Lucknow Pact by granting the Muslim demand for separate electorates. For Tilak, the former Hindu champion and repudiator of faith in British justice, to make such diplomatic concessions, which would formerly have been an anathema to him, was truly surprising. Obviously, imprisonment and age had tempered his youthful militancy, and he was demonstrating the maturity of judgment essential for the all-India leadership he now assumed. But his new moderation was to prove to be his undoing within a few years as a new star arose in the Indian nationalist firmament. Nevertheless, Tilak's achievements during his few years of leadership should not go unappreciated; they broke the grip of the moderates over the Indian National Congress and broke the ground for the broader-based appeal of the inspirational leader, Mahātma Gāndhi. Without this preparation and reorientation Gāndhi's emergence would have been seriously handicapped, if not delayed, and the course of the Indian nationalist movement would have been significantly altered.

At Lucknow Tilak's statesmanship had not only consummated the improbable alliance of the Congress and the Muslim League, based on Muslim fears for the caliphate, but also secured approval of a Congress-League declaration for immediate self-government for all of India. He had broken the domination of the moderates over the Congress and transformed this elitist organization into a suitable vehicle for militant nationalism. It remained for the peculiar genius of Gāndhi to mobilize broad, popular support for the objectives of the Congress. Meanwhile, many of the moderate members, faithful to the evolutionary credo of Gokhale and satisfied with fresh British concessions, defected and in November 1918, formed the Liberal Party in support of British gradualism. The stage was now set for more dynamic development under the leadership of a revolutionized Congress.

THE EMERGENCE OF GĀNDHI AND THE FIRST SATYĀGRAHA MOVEMENT (1917–1924)

The year 1917 witnessed several international and imperial events of great importance to Indian nationalism. Although the Allies had frequently asserted that they were fighting in defense of democracy and the right of self-determination, the suppression of the Irish rebellion of 1916 reinforced doubts about British sincerity. Much more heartening to Tilak and the Congress was the fourteenth point of Woodrow Wilson's 1917 declaration upholding the general principle of self-determination. The Congress seized on this non-British support of its position and gave it widespread publicity in India. In addition, the British government belatedly recognized the need to give some attention to Indian demands. The new secretary of state for India, Edwin Samuel Montagu, a protégé of Lord Morley, announced in August 1917, that Britain's long-term policy called for "the increasing association of Indians in every branch of the administration and the gradual development of self-governing institutions with a view to the progressive realization of responsible government as an integral part of the British Empire." This conservative statement was hedged with further reservations, but Montagu demonstrated his intention of introducing reforms by going to India late in 1917 to confer with the viceroy, Lord Chelmsford. The result was the Montagu-Chelmsford Report of 1918 containing proposals incorporated in the Montagu-Chelmsford Reforms of 1919. Finally, the Russian Revolution of 1917 had an unsettling effect, raising both hopes and fears and suggesting that the world was in ferment and about to witness drastic changes in other areas as well in the near future. All of these developments of 1917 added impetus to the Congress movement under Tilak's leadership, but the results in subsequent years did not measure up to immediate Indian expectations.

The Montagu-Chelmsford Report fell far short of the Home Rulers' demand for immediate responsible self-government and was denounced as inadequate by the December 1918 session of the truncated Congress. In addition, this session called on the British government to release political prisoners and to acknowledge the principle of national self-determination with regard to India. Finally, the recommendations of the Rowlatt Sedition Committee to continue in peacetime the wartime powers of the government to hold political prisoners indefinitely without trial were condemned as an unjust and unwarranted violation of normal British civil liberties. A concurrent meeting of the Muslim League passed similar resolutions and further called on Britain to uphold the Turkish sultan as the Caliph or protector of Islam.

The political demands of Congress and the Muslim League were indirectly reinforced by the growth of broad popular discontent with economic hardships during the last years of the war. The supply of as much grain as possible to the various theaters of the war generated a sharp inflation in the prices of food, as well as other goods and services, and also denuded India of the surpluses needed in case of a crop failure. The

failure of the monsoon in 1918 created a severe famine in many parts of India with which the government was unprepared to cope. Already weakened by famine, the people suffered an inordinately high death toll from an influenza epidemic that swept across India in 1918–1919; inadequate reports indicate that well over five million Indians lost their lives. Despite this reduction in the number of mouths to feed and the return to peace, food prices remained high and in fact the basic cost of living continued to rise. During the war some Indians had made fortunes, but the mass of the people had suffered increasing hardships that showed no immediate abatement after the war. Popular discontent was growing into blind resentment and leaderless unrest. Yet the elite leadership of Congress and the League was separated by too wide a gap from the people for effective collaboration until the unique personality and genius of Gāndhi provided a bridge and united the two, however reluctantly, in the common goal of expelling the British Rāj as incapable of governing in accordance with the traditional values and virtues of Indian civilization. Thus at the critical juncture in the Indian national movement a figure emerged who was able to draw on the wellsprings of the Indian heritage to pull together in a broad-based, general movement the disparate elements of discontent: the modernist, the moderate, the traditionalist, and even for a while, the Muslims.

A more unlikely figure, at least as a young man, to play such a comprehensive and decisive role would be hard to imagine. The youngest son of a Vaishya, rather than a Brāhman, family, which had for several generations provided prime ministers for small principalities in Gujarāt, Gāndhi was a fragile and sensitive child, deeply influenced by the pious Hindu religiosity of his mother. At 18, already a husband and father, he was sent alone to study law in England in preparation for following in his father's and grandfather's footsteps. During the three years in which he completed his program of study he was exposed to other experiences of enduring significance by his own testimony. First, English theosophists introduced him to Sir Edwin Arnold's translation of the Bhagavad Gītā in which the conception of a life of unselfish service particularly impressed him. Second, natural curiosity led him to attend Christian services to hear the sermons of the most renowned preachers of the day and then to study the message of Jesus in the New Testament whose impression upon him is apparent in the many references in his later speeches and writings, especially in support of the doctrine of nonviolence. Finally, after the initial problems of adjustment to a wholly alien environment, he gained such a deep respect for the urbanity and tolerance of Englishmen that only repeated disillusionment later forced him to abandon faith in British justice.

Upon his return, his attempt to develop a law practice in his native Gujarāt was a failure; his mild-mannered way and reedy voice did not carry conviction in courts of law. His career was saved by a Gujarāti Muslim merchant who retained him to handle a complex case in South Africa. Still the English dandy, Gāndhi was deeply shocked at the intolerant treatment he received in South Africa and dedicated himself to organizing the large Indian community of laborers, in addition to building up a lucrative law practice. In 1897 he returned to India in search of backing and developed a close relationship with several nationalist leaders, especially Gokhale, of whom he declared himself to be a disciple. Back in South Africa he devoted himself to fighting discrimination by developing his unique and frustrating technique inadequately labeled "nonviolent noncooperation."

This technique, which erroneously suggests a negative rather than a positive course of action, was inspired by his conviction, based on his interpretation of the New Testament and the Gītā, that the only way to fight evil and injustice was not by physical force but by the "force of truth" (satyā-graha). Such nonviolent "insistence on truth," which drew on traditional Indian values and called for a deeper and more sincere courage than militancy, would, he believed, awaken the British to the error of their ways both in South Africa and India. Initially at least, Gāndhi cannot be described as a radical or an extremist and, looking back to the tolerant treatment he had experienced in England, retained his faith in the British sense of fair play to rectify unjust colonial practices, once massive programs of action had brought them to their attention. Indeed, his loyalty was demonstrated by service in the ambulance corps in both the Boer War and World War I and carrying out a recruiting campaign in India during World War I for which he received an award.

Gāndhi's "nonviolent noncooperation" program, worked out in South Africa, involved progressive steps of mass protest intended as much to educate his people in his doctrine of satyāgraha as to enlighten the ruling class. The first step was a preannounced hartal, or "day of humiliation," on which all Indians were asked to walk out on their jobs and attend mass meetings not only to study their grievances but also to gain indoctrination in the precepts of nonviolent noncooperation. The second step was to take positive action about a specific injustice, such as immobilizing rail transportation with their bodies to protest against discrimination in railroad accommodations. When these efforts failed to secure the desired reforms, the next step was a general boycott of British products. The final step, if all else failed, was outright civil disobedience, such as a refusal to pay taxes. To identify himself with the people, he gradually abandoned English dress and ways in favor of a simple peasant attire and diet, and to gain the popular respect accorded to a spiritual leader, he followed the path of an ascetic, taking a vow of celibacy and devoting at least one day a week to prayer and fasting. By these measures he soon secured a group of dedicated disciples ready to do his bidding in forwarding the cause of Indian emancipation. On the other hand, Gāndhi demonstrated the talents of a politician by his readiness to accept compromise settlements granting substantial elements of his demands. Such was the result of his first major *satyāgraha* campaign in 1913–1914, which greatly alleviated the treatment of Indians in South Africa.

Following this success he went to Britain, but poor health forced his return to India in 1915. His good friend and admirer, Gokhale, urged him to stay out of the political arena for at least a year. Heeding this advice, Gāndhi founded an *āshram*, or retreat, where his disciples and any interested Indian friends could join in studying his teachings and investigating how they could be applied to the problems of India. Attention was particularly directed at the social and economic disabilities of the impoverished masses, and several leaders of upper class backgrounds, such as the younger Nehru, who previously had avoided the unpleasantries of popular contact, were initiated to intimate familiarity with the wretched conditions of the people and persuaded to incorporate a new dimension of social concern for the people's welfare in their campaign for independence. Gokhale's death late in 1915, however, soon led Gāndhi to play a more active role in Indian affairs. Although these were minor, local problems and mostly settled by the mere threat of *satyāgraha*, they did serve to publicize throughout India his unique technique for mobilizing popular resistance to injustice. This publicity proved to be an important preparation for the acceptance of the much larger role of leadership the Mahātma was soon destined to play.

Gāndhi was principally concerned about the amelioration of social and economic injustice, and the technique of *satyāgraha* had been devised to deal with such problems. To the extent that he had yet expressed an interest in politics, he was, like his mentor, a moderate. Indeed, his stress on spiritual strength, in full accord with Indian tradition, implied a subordination of politics that was a source of both strength and weakness in his direction of a national movement for independence. In essence, then, his emergence as a political leader depended on a loss of faith in the British so that he could appear as the leader of a spiritually inspired crusade of nonviolent noncooperation with a British rule genuinely believed to be bereft of all virtue and therefore unworthy of obedience or acceptance. This change of heart was brought about by British actions after World War I. Under other circumstances Gāndhi probably could not have been persuaded to join forces with the nationalist leadership. Thus the British have no one to blame but themselves for the alienation of this remarkable man whose spiritual prestige throughout India gave new life, new meaning, and new direction to the Indian nationalist movement.

The first development that persuaded Gāndhi to take action against the British Rāj was the imminent passage of the Rowlatt Bills in the spring of 1919. These proposals were a reaction to the scheduled expiration six months after the war of the emergency powers that had enabled the Indian government to deal arbitrarily with any individuals suspected of subversive intentions. The government feared that in view of the growing symptoms of widespread discontent, the release of extremists would generate extensive disorders and terrorism with which the normal courts would be unable to cope. Therefore, the Rowlatt Bills authorized the continuance for three years of the wartime powers that the government could implement in case of emergency. Such a proposed abridgment of individual freedom during peacetime by the agents of a nation traditionally committed to safeguarding the rights of the individual came as a profound shock to Gāndhi's faith in British justice. He joined nationalist leaders in a manifesto declaring their determination to sponsor a national movement of nonviolent civil disobedience to any such laws. Thus, on this issue alone, the nationalist movement had captured Gāndhi, and he had converted it to acceptance of his tactics of nonviolent noncooperation. When one of the Rowlatt Bills was enacted, Gāndhi issued a call for a *hartal*, or day of national humiliation, on Sunday, March 30, 1919, during which all work would cease, all businesses would close, and all the people would give themselves over to fasting and prayer for the sake of spiritual purification and in the hope of making the government aware of the injustice of its act.

On that date in the capital city of Delhi violence soon broke out against vendors who failed to observe the *hartal*, and the police, reinforced by troops, fired on the mob, killing eight and wounding a much larger number. Gāndhi, thoroughly dismayed by the violation of the principle of nonviolence, planned to go to Delhi and the Punjab to preach the essential truth of nonviolence, but the government, fearful of his subversive intentions, made the error of arresting him. The inevitable consequence was even more serious and widespread outbreaks with a rising death toll on both sides, which did not cease on his subsequent release from custody and his public denunciation of the use of force. Indeed, the worst and most fateful incident was yet to come.

Amritsār, the sacred city of the Sikhs and center of the Punjab, had already been the scene of bloody riots before General Dyer, in command of 1000 troops, arrived to aid the local forces in restoring order. He immediately issued a proclamation prohibiting public meetings on pain of death. In open defiance of this order, on the next day, April 14, a great crowd of 10,000 persons assembled in a square with only a few narrow exits to listen to speeches. When he learned of the meeting, General Dyer decided that only a bloody lesson could quell unrest. Fifty Gurkha troops were ordered to fire without warning into the unarmed crowd, and they did not cease firing until their ammunition was nearly exhausted. When the fusillade ended, almost 400 Indians had been killed and 1200 wounded. Apparently few bullets had failed to find a mark. The Amritsār Mas-

sacre, following violent outbreaks there and elsewhere, finally persuaded Gāndhi to call off this first national *satyāgraha* movement and to confess publicly to a "Himalayan miscalculation" in initiating such a program before the Indian people were adequately educated in its fundamental precept of nonviolence.

Thus the Mahātma's first campaign in the national arena ended in frustration and disillusionment both for him and for those leaders who had placed their faith in his leadership. For the moment Gāndhi again looked hopefully toward Britain and the implementation of political reforms stemming from the Montagu-Chelmsford Report of 1918. Only another severe shock to his faith in British justice converted him into an irreconcilable foe of the British Rāj.

During the parliamentary debate preceding enactment of the India Act in December 1919, Edwin Samuel Montagu, secretary of state for India, made it clear that the central purpose of the measure was to establish the first stage in a progressive development of self-government for India; Britain was committed to the eventual grant of full responsible self-government whenever circumstances permitted its peaceful realization. On the basis of these assertions Gāndhi, who had by now supplanted Tilak in prestige, persuaded the annual session of the Indian National Congress, held in blood-soaked Amritsār, to accept these reforms as a workable compromise for the time being.

The provisions of the act constituted a sharp advance in practice as well as theory over the Morley-Minto Reforms. The central government was equipped with a bicameral legislature: a council of state and an assembly, with a majority of its members elected by a limited franchise. More striking, however, was the grant of partial responsible self-government at the provincial level where ministers heading "transferred" departments, such as education, public health, and agriculture, were held responsible to majorities in legislatures, where 70 percent of the members were elected. Those heading the more critical "reserved" departments, such as justice and police, were appointed and dismissed at will by the governor. This division of administrative responsibility in the provincial cabinets was dubbed dyarchy and intended to give Indian leaders the needed experience of exercising responsibility in safe areas. Nevertheless, both provincial governors and the governor-general retained the power of overriding the will of their legislatures by "certifying" any measure as either dangerous or essential to public safety, but they carefully refrained from employing this power except in a dire emergency. Even more striking to the average Indian was the vast expansion of the electorate from a meager 33,000 to more than 5 million males who met the low tax-paying qualification; now every Indian knew at least one voter, giving the democratic process greater reality. In spite of the limitation of the electorate, many voters were illiterate and identification symbols had to be devised which tended to reduce resistance on the grounds of literacy to future extensions of the franchise. The communal electorates, inherited from the Morley-Minto Reforms, were reluctantly retained in the face of minority pressure, and indeed, new electorates were devised to represent additional groups, such as Indian Christians and Anglo-Indians.

In looking at the prospects and problems of future Indian self-government the framers of the act recognized that a federal rather than a unitary form of government would be better suited to accommodating in one state the regional and political diversities of India. Therefore, the respective areas of authority of the central and provincial governments were for the first time separated and defined. The central government was empowered to deal with subjects of national concern, such as military and foreign affairs, commerce, and relations with the princely states, while the provincial governments were given control of internal affairs, such as law enforcement, education, and public works.

Naturally it followed that specific revenues had to be allocated to each to support their respective activities. Thus the provincial governments were provided with the means to demonstrate fiscal as well as political responsibility.

Before these reforms became operative, British reaction to the Dyer case destroyed Gāndhi's faith in the British sense of justice and convinced him that British rule was "without virtue" (*asat*) and therefore unworthy of continued loyalty and cooperation. Following an impartial investigation of the Amritsār Massacre, the Indian government, to Gāndhi's satisfaction, had censured Dyer for irrational and unnecessary brutality and dismissed him from the service. After a full floor debate the British House of Commons confirmed this action, though a few voices had been raised in Dyer's defense. But then the healing effect was undone in an emotional outburst of imperial hysteria. Inflammatory articles in the conservative press depicting Dyer as an abused national hero prodded the lords into rejecting the verdict of the lower house in a round of inconsiderate speeches, only too well reported in the Indian press. Moreover, the same British newspapers and periodicals mounted a successful campaign for voluntary contributions to a fund to compensate Dyer for his unjust treatment. Whether or not, as Dyer and the governor of the Punjab claimed, his stern action had prevented more widespread disorders and a greater loss of life is beside the point. This reversal on the part of many representatives of the most influential and respected segments of British society appalled all Indian leaders and intellectuals including the renowned Indian poet, Rabīndranāth Tagore, who denounced it as an "unashamed condonation of brutality ... ugly in its frightfulness." And what is more, their denunciations were echoed by anti-imperialists.

Concurrently, the rise of the Muslim Khilāfat movement presented a unique opportunity for uniting Hindus and Muslims in active opposition to British rule. The Turkish sultan in his role as caliph was accepted as the spiritual head of Sunnite Islam. During the war the British prime minister had publicly upheld the Turkish right to its national homelands in Thrace and Asia Minor, while negotiating secret treaties for the postwar vivisection of the Ottoman realm. After the war, allied occupation of southwest Asia Minor, and the rumored provisions of secret treaties threatened dismemberment of the caliph's temporal base, a prospect which aroused alarm for Islam among Indian Muslims. As a universal spiritual leader, the Mahātma was deeply concerned with countering the progress of Western materialism whose soul-destroying nature, as he saw it, was the principal cause of India's and the world's ills. On the other hand, as a shrewd political leader he fully appreciated the advantages of a Hindu-Muslim alliance in prosecuting a campaign for Indian independence. Which factor, genuine sympathy or political expediency, motivated his support of the Khilāfat movement remains an open question. Probably in his own intuitive and sentient way of thinking he conjoined both in a union without conflict, a feat which Western minds find difficulty in comprehending.

As early as November 1919, when Gandhi still favored cooperation with the Montagu-Chelmsford Reforms, he suggested at a Khilāfat conference the possibility of a united campaign of civil disobedience. In the spring of 1920 the imminent conclusion of a harsh treaty for Turkey led to demands for revision and the proclamation of a one-day fast to be observed by all Indian Muslims. In May, the publication of the abortive treaty of Sèvres, which would have internationalized the Straits and turned over to Greece eastern Thrace and the temporary administration of southeast Asia Minor, confirmed the worst fears of Indian Muslims and galvanized Gandhi into action. In an "Open Letter to All Englishmen in India" he declared that the treacherous dishonoring of the British government's wartime pledge to preserve the

Turkish homelands and the racial arrogance exhibited in British vindication of Dyer's brutality had combined to destroy his faith in British justice and goodwill. Such an immoral government, he asserted, could not be trusted to keep its promise of self-government for India and was unworthy of continued loyalty and cooperation. In August 1920, Gandhi gave a dramatic demonstration of his new conviction by publicly returning all medals and honors he had received from the British government for past services. Convinced of his sincerity, the Khilāfat leaders joined him in proclaiming a Hindu-Muslim campaign of noncooperation. The seal was placed on this alliance when a special session of the Congress in September 1920, accepted his leadership of at least the first steps in a proposed program of "progressive nonviolent noncooperation." Of most immediate significance was nonparticipation by members of Congress and its supporters as either voters or candidates in the November elections, the first to be held under the Montagu-Chelmsford Reforms. In addition, all Indians were urged to boycott government-supported schools, the courts, and all other govenment activities and to emulate Gandhi's moral rejection of the British by returning all British-bestowed honors. If these and subsequent steps were generally observed, Gandhi assured his followers that independence might be achieved in a year.

Actually, as this program was put into operation, the government was deeply alarmed and did seriously consider making generous concessions to the demand for self-government, not out of doubt of its ability to maintain its authority, but out of concern for making its authority dependent on brute force. Ultimately this promising movement failed because it could not command general acceptance and because in its progressive unfolding clear schisms developed in its ranks. Another factor of no small importance was the governor-general's continued adherence to a policy of noninterference over the advice of experienced

provincial governors. Such a policy of ordered restraint undermined the condemnation of British rule on moral grounds and
helped to wean moderate Indian leaders
away from support of Gāndhi's movement.
When violence broke out, the onus for it fell
on Gāndhi's followers. Finally, economic improvement, after the postwar depression, cut
into the broad base of discontent that had
supported the initial enthusiasm for the
campaign.

The first phase of the campaign, a boycott of the elections, was only a qualified success because almost one-third of the electorate turned out to cast their votes. The call
for a surrender of honors and resignation
from governmental posts gained some distinguished supporters but generally failed to
generate among the educated middle class
that spirit of self-sacrifice essential to the
cause of Mother India. Obviously most educated Indians were not yet sufficiently convinced of the validity and rectitude of Gāndhi's position to subordinate personal
interests to the national interest. The withdrawal of students from schools and colleges
secured a much larger, if only temporary,
response, crippling the operation of some
institutions for a brief period. The critical
opposition of such a distinguished supporter
as Rabīndranāth Tagore illustrated a fundamental schism over Gāndhi's repudiation
of Western civilization along with British
government.

Tagore denounced as negative and unrealistic Gāndhi's conviction that India must
purge itself of all Western physical and cultural importations and revive the traditional
Indian way of life in all its pristine simplicity.
Such an introverted program, he argued,
would cripple the country in its future competition with the West. The boycott of the
schools, if it persisted, could only help the
British by reducing the ranks of educated
leaders for the future. Gāndhi's belief that
the industries, "the railways, telegraphs,
hospitals, lawyers, doctors, and such like
have all to go" and that Indians should return

to the spinning wheel and wear only home-
spun cloth, while consistent with his moral
condemnation of the British, seemed to men
of Tagore's outlook wholly contrary to common sense and Indian self-interest. Obviously, Gāndhi had not converted many influential Indian leaders to his view of Britain
and the West as the epitome of evil.

When a full year of noncooperation
failed to produce *swarāj* as promised, popular support began to dwindle. Frustration at
the failure to gain any concrete results led to
outbreaks of violence. Moreover, the Muslim-Hindu entente broke down in the face of
the bloody rampage of fanatical Muslim
Moplahs of Malabar, which was not quelled
before 2000 lives were taken. Realizing that
his movement was faltering and that fresh
pressure would have to be placed on the government, Gāndhi won the approval of the
December 1921 session of the Congress to
initiate the next step in "progressive noncooperation," civil disobedience in the form of
a mass refusal to pay taxes. This new threat
persuaded the government to relax its policy
of restraint and permit the imprisonment of
Congress leaders. Then, on February 4, 1922,
just three days after Gāndhi had issued an
ultimatum, a mob led by members of the
Congress besieged the police station at
Chauri Chaura and incinerated 21 police-
men. Appalled by the news of this atrocity,
the Mahātma called off the whole noncooperation campaign, much to the dismay of
his ardent supporters, such as the younger
Nehru, then languishing in jail, who believed
the movement was just arriving at a decisive
climax. But better than they, Gāndhi sensed
that the time was not ripe for a showdown,
that the ranks of his supporters were split
beyond immediate repair, that more time
would be required to educate all Indians in
the precepts of nonviolent noncooperation.
His movement had failed to achieve the
promised goal, but it did produce enduring
results.

Shortly afterward, his trial and sentencing to six-years' imprisonment for sedition

gratuitously reinforced the popular image of the Mahātma suffering at the hands of a British Pontius Pilate for the welfare of his people. During the campaign he had for the first time generated such a substantial measure of cooperation among all levels of Indian society as to cause serious concern to the government. The Indian people had been led to develop a new sense of national self-esteem and unity under Congress leadership, which forever altered the Anglo-Indian relationship. No longer would Indian nationalists play the role of suppliants seeking concessions from the British; henceforth as representatives of the Indian nation they would negotiate as self-conscious equals with their British counterparts for achievement of the mutually agreed goal of independence. Even though it may not have been immediately apparent, India had come psychologically of age.

THE GĀNDHIAN INTERREGNUM (1922–1928)

While Gāndhi's first *satyāgraha* campaign was in full swing, the government implemented the provisions of the Montagu-Chelmsford Reforms. Despite the Congress boycott, 29 percent of the enlarged electorate turned out to vote. Under Liberal leadership the experiment in dyarchy at the provincial level gained some surprising successes. The Rowlatt Act and other restrictive measures were repealed. Admission to the Indian Civil Service was eased for Indians by holding the annual examinations in Delhi as well as London, and Indo-British parity in its composition became the avowed goal. In addition, the principle of fiscal autonomy for India was conceded, including the right to regulate external trade through a tariff board.

These constructive accomplishments, in conjunction with the fruitlessness of Gāndhi's essentially negative campaign, combined to wean away his moderate, middle class supporters. After his failure and incarceration one element of the Congress formed the *Swarāj* Party to gain election for the declared purpose of crippling the new government. In 1923 a substantial number of Swarājists were elected but not enough to break the ministries and force the governors to resume control of "transferred" departments in more than two provinces. Greater success in the 1926 elections seemed to threaten the whole scheme, but defections among Congressmen anxious to enjoy the fruits of office tempered the results. Indeed, in the central provinces the revolt of this group permitted the restoration of dyarchy. Despite this and other schisms in the ranks of the Congress, it became increasingly apparent that it was and would remain the dominant party with which some further accommodation would have to be made. Moreover, a rash of bloody communal riots in connection with the elections illustrated a growing deterioration of Muslim-Hindu relations. Meanwhile, the Mahātma, released from prison in 1924 after serving only two of his six years' sentence, avoided involvement in politics and concentrated on building popular support and understanding for his ideals by promoting the production and use of native cloth and by championing the elimination of restrictions on association with India's 50 million "Untouchables," the *Harijan* or children of God, as he called them.

In spite of some significant successes in the operation of the reforms and the comparatively peaceful condition of India after the termination of the *satyāgraha* campaign, the need for further change, which might win the cooperation of the Congress, was apparent from the beginning. The operation of even partially responsible governments in the provinces without the participation of the major party was awkward, if not impossible. The reform act had provided for a review after ten years, but the new viceroy, Lord Irwin (1926–1931), recommended an advance in this timetable not long after his arrival. As a result, Sir John Simon headed an all-English commission named in November 1927. News of its all-English composition broke the prevailing calm in India and revived the unity and militancy of the Congress. At its December 1927 session the Congress approved a nationwide boycott of the Simon Commission, reasserted in unequivocal terms the demand for "complete national independence," and subsequently called for an all-parties conference to draft an Indian constitution as a counterattack. In this rekindling of ardent Indian nationalism two young radicals first emerged as prominent leaders, Subāsh Chandra Bose and Jawaharlāl Nehru, the son of the leading figure in the Congress, Motilāl Nehru. Inadvertently the liberal and well-intentioned action of the British government in setting up the Simon Commission provided the stimulus for a new and more dynamic expression of Indian nationalism.

Since the elder Nehru served as chairman and the younger Nehru as secretary of the drafting committee, the product became known as the Nehru Report of 1928, a statesmanlike effort to win as broad support from all elements as possible. Full self-government was demanded, but to appease the Liberals the demand for total independence was moderated to an acceptance of dominion status within the British Commonwealth. On the other hand, the need felt to win the support of all Hindus led the framers of the report to take the calculated risk of alienating Muslims by rejecting separate communal electorates for the representation of minorities. As a result, the future leader of the Muslim campaign for a separate state, Muhammed Ali Jinnāh, walked out of the conference convinced that both religious communities could not coexist within a single independent state. Although the active movement for a Muslim state did not emerge for almost a decade, the alienation from the Congress of a figure like Jinnāh makes the Nehru Report historically a decisive turning point in Hindu-Muslim relations. At the December 1928 meeting of the Congress the young radicals, Nehru and Bose, and their supporters subjected the compromise char-

acter of the report to such a heavy, critical assault that only Gāndhi's intervention staved off a split in the party's ranks. Even then, to gain radical acceptance, Britain was given only one year to grant dominion status or face a mass movement of civil disobedience. Thus the Nehru Report, as a response to the all-English Simon Commission, served as a vehicle for the reemergence in command of a nationalist campaign of the charismatic Mahātma.

ERA OF THE ROUND TABLE CONFERENCES

During 1929 Gāndhi and the Congress sat back and awaited the British response to their ultimatum. One event favorable to the Indian cause was the installation of a Labor government headed by Ramsay MacDonald as a consequence of a general election in May. The Labor party had always advocated a retreat from empire and the new prime minister was noted for his sympathy with the Indian cause. But whatever the predilections of the Labor government it was handicapped in putting them into action by dependence on Liberal votes to maintain a majority. Another encouraging development was Lord Irwin's visit to Britain to inform the new government on the current crisis in India. The viceroy believed that the Congress movement under the Mahātma's spiritual guidance represented a serious issue but that Gāndhi's dedication to nonviolence offered a real opportunity for a negotiated settlement. He returned armed with a declaration, issued on October 31, stating that the goal of Indian constitutional progress was the attainment of dominion status and that Indians had the right to participate in all deliberations affecting their future. By a single stroke both the end and means of Indian constitutional progress had been clarified beyond recall; all that remained to be determined was the timetable, an obstacle that was destined to create many years of political turmoil and even bloodshed. For many years the Congress had demanded round table conferences, and the all-English character of the Simon Commission had been the chief point of criticism. Now the Congress demand had been conceded, though which Indians should serve as delegates would remain a subject of hot dispute with the Congress insisting that it alone was qualified to represent the Indian people.

Apparently Gāndhi and the moderate wing of the Congress were ready to negotiate on the basis of these concessions, but the young radicals were unwilling to compromise. Rather than jeopardize Congress unity, Gāndhi capitulated to their demand that any conference be committed to drawing up a dominion constitution. Young Nehru and Bose, as well as Gāndhi, were well aware that the Labor government, hobbled by dependence on the Liberals, could not possibly accept such a condition. As Gāndhi saw it, however, a greater danger than the collapse of British political sympathy would be a defection of the Congress left wing and its possible resort to unregulated violence. Spurred on by young Nehru, serving his first term as president, the December 1929 meeting of the Congress rejected the gradualist proposal of the British government and approved the initiation of a second *satyāgraha* campaign under Gāndhi's command with the goal of *purna swarāj* or complete independence. January 26, 1930 was proclaimed "Independence Day," a day still celebrated as such.

As was his fashion, the Mahātma retired for several months of meditation on the best course of action, creating a nationwide attitude of expectant suspense. No more electrifying step could have been conceived than his call for defiance of the British-imposed salt tax, which affected every Indian household. To dramatize this first challenge of his campaign, he undertook a 170-mile walk from his retreat to the sea for the symbolic extraction of salt as nature's bounty and necessity, which only an evil government would have the callousness to tax. Accompanied at first only by his disciples he was

daily joined by hundreds and thousands of peasants inspired by association with such a holy man. Although kept fully informed and bombarded by demands for action, the viceroy refused to interfere with the march to the sea. After a brief pause following this symbolic rebellion, tumultous demonstrations in Bombay led to mass arrests, which only served to generate larger and more widespread demonstrations against the government. On May 5, Gāndhi was taken into protective custody and by July, 60,000 of his followers had been jailed to restore relative order in preparation for the first Round Table Conference in the fall. Thus deprived of its leaders, the *satyāgraha* campaign, as predicted, sputtered almost to a halt in spite of inflammatory developments, such as publication of the Simon Report with its limited recommendations for political progress. Furthermore, representatives of all Indian interests, except the all-important Congress, were persuaded to attend the first Round Table Conference. As an infectious element in the Indian body politic, the Congress had been effectively checked and isolated by the viceroy, but deliberation on the future of India without Congress participation seemed somehow unreal.

Nevertheless, this rump conference made significant progress etching out the main features of the 1935 India Act. In the provincial regimes full ministerial responsibility was to replace dyarchy, though the full impact of this concession was tempered by the governors' retention of emergency power to act for the general welfare. In the central government the principle of dyarchy was to be introduced by the governor-general's continued control of vital areas, such as defense and foreign affairs, a condition less than satisfactory to the Congress. Furthermore, the problem of integrating the principalities in an all-India government appeared to be resolved when in a surprise move the princes agreed to participation in a federal form of government placing some restrictions on their independence. Unfortunately, this provision and the reorganization of the central government which depended on it never went into effect because not enough principalities ever acceded to the federation.

Highly satisfied with the outcome of this first conference and the comparative calm in India, the Labor prime minister, Ramsay MacDonald, ordered the release of Gāndhi and other Congress leaders in the hope of inducing them to join in subsequent consultations. Realizing that he had lost the initiative, Gāndhi sought some dramatic means of revitalizing his cause. When non-Congress Indian leaders called on him to make his peace with the viceroy in face-to-face negotiations, Gāndhi saw the opportunity to capitalize on the meetings as confrontations between the Indian people, symbolized by himself, and the British government, symbolized by Lord Irwin. On each of eight occasions during late February and early March 1931, he arrived for his well-publicized meeting a frail figure clad only in the simple *dhoti* of the ascetic and made his way slowly up the Kingsway to the viceroy's palace at Delhi amid the prayers and cheers of thousands of his supporters. Far away at Westminster, even the redoubtable champion of empire, Winston Churchill, appreciated the significance of "a seditious fakir . . . striding half-naked up the steps of the Viceregal Palace . . . to parley on equal terms with the representative of the King-Emperor" and denounced Irwin for his weakness. The upshot of these conversations was the conclusion on March 5, 1931 of the Delhi Pact. In this truce Gāndhi agreed to Congress participation in a second Round Table Conference and called off for the time being his now moribund *satyāgraha* campaign, including the boycott of British goods, which was compounding the already severe effects in India of the worldwide depression. In return, Irwin agreed to release the strictly political prisoners remaining in custody, to cancel the emergency ordinances against civil disobedience, and to make some minor concessions such as modifications of the salt

tax for the benefit of the very poor. This effort to gain Congress cooperation was the final act of statesmanship of this able viceroy who was replaced a month later by a less sensitive and sympathetic successor. Moreover, before the second Round Table Conference convened, the Labor government in Britain fell, a victim of the great depression. Although Ramsay MacDonald continued as prime minister of a national coalition government, his principal support came from the Conservative party, which was less willing to make concessions to the Congress.

At a special session of the Congress, Gāndhi, who had previously surrendered to the radical left rather than risk a split, now appealed to the moderates and won grudging endorsement as the sole delegate of the Congress to the Round Table. Congress radicals might grumble at their loss of command, but after all, their approach had been tried and found wanting. In any case, their former champion, whatever they might think of his "backsliding," still retained undisputed control. The second Round Table Conference, which met in the latter part of 1931, ended in December amid dissension and acrimony and without significant achievement. If blame must be assessed for this failure, it would have to be equally assessed on the uncompromising attitude of Gāndhi, who was convinced that he and the Congress alone spoke for all the people of India, and the similarly strong belief of his opponents, both British and Indian, that he represented no more than a troublesome and disloyal minority, insensitive to the just demands of fellow-Indians. Under the tense and bitter circumstances, both views suffered from exaggeration and distortion. Certainly the Congress did not represent the outlook of all politically conscious Hindus, let alone Muslims, but as the response to the *satyāgraha* campaigns indicated, it did possess a broad appeal to popular discontents in the cities and in the countryside. It is true that in the face of governmental repressions both popular ardor and Congress membership suffered significant attrition, but any organization that could generate such mass enthusiasm and inspire tens of thousands of local leaders with a readiness to risk incarceration could not be passed off as a merely troublesome minority."

Gāndhi's inability to gain any further concessions put the left wing in power again because the only alternatives appeared to be surrender, which was unthinkable. Before he returned from England the *satyāgraha* campaign was renewed, but this time the government struck hard and fast. Within three weeks of his return Gāndhi and many of his lieutenants had been arrested. As in the past, these arrests stimulated more widespread outbreaks, but the government did not falter in its determination to deal firmly with all dissidents. By April more than 34,000 leaders had been jailed and the campaign cooled off, never to regain its old vigor. Although the Mahātma did not officially call it off until 1934, it appeared that the technique of nonviolent noncooperation was no match for a determined government backed by adequate force. On the other hand, it had achieved some results significant for the long-term development of a self-conscious Indian nationality. More Indians than ever before had become actively involved in a common cause under Congress leadership, a fact that was bound to erode traditional parochial outlooks, and many more who feared the consequences of participation became emotionally involved as onlookers. An active role in *satyāgraha* actions inevitably led to the intermingling of castes, particularly if arrested and thrown into jail Hindus could not avoid violation of the rules of pollution. Thus a practical step was taken toward implementing Gāndhi's rejection of caste distinctions and discrimination. Furthermore, women by the thousands emerged from traditional seclusion to play an active part as leaders and followers. Once they had broken away from restriction to the household, no force could contain them. The sharp increase of enrollment in women's schools and colleges reflected this change in the social fabric of Indian life. A new reservoir of potential talent and strength had been tapped.

In 1932 the British awarded separate electorates to the "Untouchables," or "Scheduled Castes" as the British called them, a proposition that Gāndhi had steadfastly opposed at the second Round Table Conference because it implied to his mind a perpetual division of the people. In righteous wrath he undertook a fast to the death that finally forced the untouchable leader to capitulate in return for a guarantee of more seats for his people. Nevertheless, he felt that by this surrender he had betrayed them. On the other hand, Gāndhi, who had always looked on the exclusion of the "Untouchables" as the worst blot on the Hindu escutcheon, considered their inclusion in the Hindu fold essential to the redemption of the Hindus and the unity of the Indian people. By this step he made the eradication of untouchability, as well as caste restrictions, a fundamental plank in the Congress program. His greatest disappointment was his failure to persuade the Muslims to become likewise an integral part of the Indian polity.

Meanwhile, British progress toward the reform of the government of India continued without Congress participation. At the end of 1932 a third Round Table Conference met as a final gesture of consultation with delegates of the various Indian political groups, but the small number of delegates and the absence of the Congress nullified its importance. Subsequently, the real work and struggle took place in the British parliament, while stern repression in India reduced the ranks of the Congress to less than one-half million members. Passage of the Govenment of India Bill was delayed almost two years principally because of the vigorous opposition of Winston Churchill and his supporters to the liberal provisions that committed the government to the ultimate granting of dominion status. Nevertheless, in the final vote in 1935 the measure was approved by substantial majorities in both houses indicating the liberal cast of the British parliament. In the Indian election of 1937 the provisions of the act came into effect for the first time.

In addition to the provisions already mentioned, the act provided for the long overdue separation of Burma from Indian administration. More important for the future of representative government in India was the extension of the provincial franchise by lowering the property qualification to reach some 30 million Indians. By this sweeping step the electorate was increased five times and included roughly one-fifth of the adult population. Separate electorates were retained for Muslims, Sikhs, Europeans, Indian Christians, and other corporate groups, while seats were reserved for the Untouchables and for women.

All the Indian parties voiced disappointment at the extent to which the act fell short of the demand for dominion status, but only the Congress denounced it as unacceptable. Faced with its implementation through elections in 1937, however, the Congress needed to find some more realistic way of coping with an accomplished fact. Under the left-wing leadership of the pragmatic younger Nehru, sponsored by Gāndhi, the battered Congress demonstrated amazing recuperative powers. In 1936, and again in 1937, Nehru was elected to second and third terms as president of the Congress. Whether or not this was Gāndhi's strategy in supporting him, the mantle of responsibility for maintaining Congress solidarity led Nehru to moderate his position. In a manifesto the Congress declared its intention to contest the elections and form ministries but with the avowed purpose of subverting the act and bringing an end to British imperialism. In addition, the manifesto reflected Nehru's concern for social and economic reforms to relieve the poverty of laborers and tenant farmers.

The Congress proved its restored vitality by winning 711 out of 1585 seats and gaining control of the legislatures of 7 of the 11 provinces. At the behest of Nehru and the

Working Committee of the Congress they at first refused to form ministries in the hope of bringing down the whole new edifice, but when Gāndhi persuaded the viceroy to declare that the governors would not use their special powers except under extreme circumstances, they relented and took office. Once in power the Congress ministries demonstrated surprising responsibility, suppressing radical and lawless activities just as sternly as their predecessors and legislating a host of social, economic, and educational reforms. Generally, the Indian Civil Service cooperated in implementing these reforms. On the other hand, the radical left wing, which was beginning to view Gāndhi and Nehru as too conservative, criticized the high command for betrayal of the avowed goal of subverting the government and ending the British regime. The socialist Subāsh Chandra Bose, who was less susceptible to Gāndhi's charms, succeeded Nehru as president in 1938 and successfully campaigned for reelection in 1939 over Gāndhi's candidate on a platform charging a conservative sellout to Britain. Fearful of the revolutionary implications of Bose's leadership, Gāndhi drew on all his prestige in a direct appeal to the Congress and forced an enraged Bose to resign. Subsequently Bose led a Forward Bloc within the Congress until in 1941 he went to Germany in search of fascist support. In 1943 he was employed by the Japanese to command an Indian national army for liberation of his homeland. At war's end he died in a plane crash on Taiwan en route to Japan.

Of far greater importance for the future of India than the quarrels and divisions within the Congress was its irreconcilable attitude toward the Muslim League adopted under Nehru's leadership. Flushed by victory at the polls, the Congress refused to admit Muslims to a share of power in provincial ministries unless they joined the Congress and renounced membership in the League. Since the League under the leadership of Muhammed Ali Jinnāh had campaigned on a platform of cooperation with the Congress, this policy was denounced as a betrayal designed to destroy every other party. Furthermore, the British government was charged with a breach of faith for failure to enforce the Round Table Agreement for the inclusion of minority representatives in provincial cabinets. In view of the apparent weakness of the League as a political organization, perhaps the Congress was justified in taking advantage of this opportunity to consolidate its control of the nationalist movement, but its other actions, bound to give offense to all Muslims, were unforgivably tactless and shortsighted. Legislatures were opened with the singing of the Hindu national anthem, and upon taking office the Congress tricolor flag was hoisted over all public buildings. Patronage was almost monopolized by Congressmen and serious attempts were made to limit school instruction to the Hindi language. No matter how well-intentioned for the unification of the Indian nation, these efforts only served to alarm Muslims, Untouchables, and other minorities as well.

Therefore, when Jinnāh began to assail these abuses of the Congress as indicative of authoritarian and intolerant tendencies, he found a receptive audience. Quite accurately he charged that the provincial ministries were mere puppets of Nehru and the Congress High Command, making any claim of provincial autonomy an illusion. While his accusations of an anti-Muslim plot by the Congress will not stand up to objective examination, the enthusiastic response to his cry of "Islam in danger" was well illustrated by the rapid growth in the membership and influence of the Muslim League. During 1938 Jinnāh's attacks, whetted by success, became even more strident and intransigent, and by the end of the year he was clearly thinking in terms of the creation of some sort of separate Muslim political entity. Reconciliation for cooperation in a unitary state seemed out of the question; at the very least Jinnāh would insist on genuine autonomy for predominantly Muslim regions. Never again

would he place his trust in any pledge of Nehru and the Congress. Thus the future establishment of Pakistan was prefigured. Although the Congress leadership was alarmed at the new strength of the League, it remained blind to the depth of alienation of the large Muslim minority that saw no hope of fair play in a democratic state where the majority ruled.

WORLD WAR II

The events attending the outbreak of World War II illustrated only too well the gulf that had grown between the Congress and the Muslim League during the critical prewar years. For several years, seeing the prospect of a European war on the horizon, the Congress and its leaders made repeated statements indicating opposition to Indian involvement in an Imperialist war, particularly without the declared consent of the Indian people. Ignoring these warnings, the British government went ahead with preparations, dispatching Indian troops to Singapore and Egypt and arming the viceroy with special emergency powers. When Great Britain declared war on September 3, 1939, the viceroy, without consulting Indian political leaders, announced that India as a part of the British empire was automatically at war.

Only the Congress, in accordance with its warnings, took vigorous exception to this unilateral action. Gāndhi and the Congress denounced Nazi aggression but insisted on genuine freedom for India before considering participation as an ally in a struggle in defense of freedom. To this end, the Congress demanded the immediate election of an Indian constituent assembly to draw up a constitution. When the viceroy countered with an offer of "consultations" for the framing of a postwar dominion government, but rejected immediate self-government as impractical, the Congress, after some divisions, rallied behind the Mahātma and the left-wing leadership. Not only was the offer denounced, but on November 8 all eight Congress ministries were ordered to resign. Jubilant at this turn of events, Jinnāh and the League proclaimed December 22 a "Day of Deliverance" from Congress tyranny.

For the balance of the war the Congress boycotted the government and the war effort. By abandoning public office it voluntarily circumscribed its ability to influence the government, except by civil disobedience, a legitimately questionable device during wartime that the British felt fully justified in suppressing without restraint, particularly after Japanese conquests posed a direct threat to India. Only after another unsatisfactory British offer did Gāndhi call in the fall of 1940 for a highly selective, individual application of *satyāgraha* in the hope of avoiding the stigma of subversion, but the government struck hard and fast, arresting more than 14,000 congressmen. Again, in 1942, after the failure of Sir Stafford Cripps' mission to meet the demand for immediate self-government, Gāndhi called on the British to "quit India" or face an all-out program of nonviolent noncooperation. On August 8, the Congress sanctioned what Gāndhi himself called "open rebellion" in the Quit India Resolution, but confronted with the prospect of Japanese invasion from Burma, the government acted even more promptly and firmly. On August 9, Gāndhi, Nehru, and a host of prominent Congress leaders were seized before they could begin to implement a program of civil disobedience. Such unprecedented action precipitated widespread disorders and sabotage that did not remain within the bounds of nonviolence. Telegraph wires were cut, rail and postal stations burned, railroad tracks torn up, and other civil and military facilities destroyed. Before these outbreaks were quelled in September, more than 1000 lives had been lost and 60,000 were imprisoned.

Meanwhile, with the Congress leadership first out of office and then out of circulation altogether, Jinnāh pressed his campaign to organize the Muslim League as the sole voice of what he called the Muslim nation and labored to gain for his followers as strong a position as possible in the provinces and in the central government. His success, largely made possible by the Congress strategy of withdrawal, eliminated almost all remaining prospects of reconciliation. Indeed, by 1942 he was delineating the boundaries for the proposed state of Pakistan, an idea that had received its first important expression as early as 1930 by the noted poet, Sir Muhammed Iqbal, in his presidential address to the League.

In the course of the war India underwent significant social, economic, and military changes that had an important impact on Indian readiness for independence. Despite the disaffection of the Congress, the Indian people made a major contribution to the war effort in both men and materials. The army grew from less than 175,000 to more than 2 million men and the number of Indian commissioned officers from less than 200 to more than 10,000. At the same time, the skills demanded by modern warfare meant that many received important training. Thus at war's end India had gained the prerequisites of a substantial military establishment, adequate for the needs of a new nation. At the same time, military experience and the achievements of Indian arms in North Africa and against the Japanese filled both officers and men with pride and self-confidence.

India also became the principal source of supply for the Middle Eastern and Eastern commands, ultimately meeting 75 percent of the needs. This achievement required a rapid expansion of production facilities, particularly heavy industry, which further strengthened the postwar capability of the Indian economy to meet the responsibilities of independence. The already important steel and cement industries were greatly enlarged and a wholly new aluminium industry was created from scratch. The vast expansion in industrial employment for men and women brought about further erosion of social and caste restrictions as well as providing training in vital skills to both workers and executives. As a result, India gained an adequate reservoir of managers and technicians to operate its economy. An equal, if not more important, consequence was the transformation of India from a debtor to a creditor. Not only was the one and one-half billion dollar public debt wiped out, but also a five billion dollar credit was built up in a blocked account withdrawable after the war in annual instalments. Thus the economic stake of the British in India was all but eliminated, sharply reducing potential opposition to independence and in fact creating a positive interest in getting rid of the burden of governing India.

Although the long-range results of India's wartime role were generally favorable, the immediate economic effects were not always so fortunate. The wartime demands placed on what was essentially a subsistence economy were bound to produce severe strains and dislocations, particularly when Allied purchases were paid for with credit instead of cash. Furthermore, India normally met food deficits by imports of surplus rice, principally from Burma, a source cut off by Japanese conquest in 1942. The sources of consumers goods were also dried up by the war. The consequence was rapid inflation after 1940 in the prices of food and other essential needs as more money chased the shrinking supplies. Since the government was reluctant to impose controls, food prices rose to three times their prewar levels and in 1943 the peasants' temptations to sell their rice at high prices precipitated a famine in Bengal with substantial loss of life before effective action was taken. Contributing to the problem of food distribution were wartime strains on the normal means of transport. The Japanese naval and air threat interrupted the customary sea transport in the Bay of Bengal. As a result, Bombay became the main port and the northern rail lines to the Burma front tended to be monopolized by military traffic. The north-south rail lines, designed only to supplement sea transport, also became over-

burdened. Although the rise in food prices created by these wartime complications actually improved the condition of debt-laden tenant farmers enabling them to pay off debts from the higher prices for their grain, growers of cash crops suffered because of the greater increase in food prices. Laborers also suffered because wages did not increase as rapidly as prices, but worst off were the educated middle class whose salaries fell far behind. On the other hand, their hardships were at least partially offset by the great increase in employment opportunities. An inadequate salary is better than no salary. In a land where unemployment had been endemic, the gainful employment as "white collar" workers of both husband and wife of a middle class family was not uncommon during the war. Indeed, employment opportunities, as well as economic necessity, drew more and more women out of the household, further breaking down their traditional social subordination.

All these developments made the Indians psychologically as well as materially better prepared for independence. Imbued with a sense of corporate accomplishment in the war, they faced the future with self-confidence and even arrogance. Only one blemish—and it was a major one—spoiled this picture of national unity and maturity: the irreconcilable communal distrust of the Congress by the Muslim League. Only the voluntary abdication of public office by the Congress during the war obscured the seriousness of this cancer in the Indian body politic.

THE PATH TO PARTITION AND INDEPENDENCE

The end of the war in Europe in May 1945 found the Indian war effort against Japan at its peak, and no near end in sight. Burma had just been liberated and the attacks on Japanese forces in Malaya and the rest of Southeast Asia were about to begin. No firm date had yet been set for the final, combined Allied invasion of the Japanese homeland.

Under vehement criticism from the Labor party the coalition government of Winston Churchill authorized the viceroy, Lord Wavell, in June 1945, to reoffer the Cripps proposal of 1942 as a basis for negotiation of a postwar government and to affirm that any new constitution would be the work of the Indian people. As a preparatory step, Congress leaders were released from custody and all seats in the executive council were opened to Indians, except that of commander-in-chief, with Congress and League nominees receiving equal representation. At the Simla Conference called to implement this proposal, Jinnāh's unequivocal rejection of it gave a clear preview of the fundamental conflict that was to plague future negotiations. First, he objected to the inclusion of two Muslims on the Congress list of nominees insisting that the League alone must be recognized as the agent of the entire Muslim community. Second, he denounced the principle of League-Congress parity because representatives of other groups on the council might vote with the Congress, placing the League in a minority. Finally, he announced that no proposal would be acceptable that ignored the Pakistan issue. In short, he served notice that the League would not cooperate in any scheme that failed to provide iron-clad guarantees for the equality and autonomy of its Muslim constituents. On this sour note the Simla Conference collapsed in July at the same time that elections in Britain returned the Labor party with a decisive majority. With the Labor party in power, the issue of independence was settled; all that remained to be determined was how it was to be implemented and this determination depended on three Indians: Gāndhi, Nehru, and Jinnāh.

The problem of independence, which the British had deferred until after the war, became immediate upon the Japanese surrender on August 14. The new Labor government announced its intention to carry out its pledge by calling for elections to the central and provincial legislatures, by making another effort to form an all-Indian executive council, and by convening a constitutional assembly at the earliest possible date. Somewhat naively the Laborites apparently expected the Indian parties to sink their differences now that independence was in sight. Anxious to cut expenses, the impoverished British government cancelled orders for goods and began to withdraw its troops from India, thereby reducing Indian fears of military suppression. The consequent economic letdown as much as political discontent precipitated a host of demonstrations, strikes, violent outbreaks, and property destruction during January and February of 1946, including a naval mutiny and the tearing down and burning of the American flag flying over a United States Information Service Office. Contributing factors to this strife were the anti-Western feelings engendered by the trial for treason of Bose's officers whom the Indian public regarded as patriots rather than traitors and the passions aroused by the election campaigns. If nothing else, the elections demonstrated the almost total control of their respective communities by the League and the Congress. Both emerged more confident and uncompromising than ever. In the new legislative assembly, for example, Jinnāh openly threatened civil war unless the League's demand for Pakistan was recognized and accepted.

Alerted and alarmed by these developments, the Labor government dispatched a cabinet mission, dubbed the Cripps mission after its best known member, to speed the negotiations for independence. Moreover, the prime minister declared that Britain would accept whatever form of government the Indian people decided on, even if it meant withdrawal from the British Commonwealth. Such a thoroughgoing commitment and indeed surrender to Indian intransigence cleared the air, at least for the moment, and persuaded the leaders to return once more to the conference table. The result of these deliberations was the publication in mid-May of the cabinet mission's realistic scheme for maintaining Indian unity while meeting the principal objections of the Muslim League. And it came within a hair's breadth of acceptance by both protagonists and their parties.

During the deliberations the Congress had insisted on a freely drafted constitution, unfettered by prior commitments, whose key feature would be a strong, strictly secular, central government. Jinnāh, deeply distrustful of Congress motives and suspicious of a Labor-Congress conspiracy, would not consider any retreat from Pakistan unless prior agreement was reached specifying absolute safeguards for minorities and a weak central government that would leave the constituent states practically autonomous and free to secede from the federation. The recommendations of the cabinet mission essentially sought to assuage the fears and meet the basic demands of the Muslim League within the framework of a unified India. After rejecting the concept of partition as impractical because any division would leave large minorities in each part and disrupt the network of communications, the mission proposed a three-tiered federal scheme with minimal powers assigned to the central government and almost complete autonomy granted to the states. In between, voluntary regional groupings of states would be formed with their own constitutions assigning whatever powers they wished to these governments. The authority of the central government representing the former British provinces and the princely states would be limited to national defense, foreign relations, and communications. As a further safeguard, any legislation affecting communal affairs would require approval by a majority, respectively, of the Muslim and Hindu representatives. Finally, until an elected constituent assembly could give formal expression to these recommendations in a national constitution, an all-Indian executive council with equal representation for Hindus and Muslims would operate an interim government.

The Congress leaders were naturally deeply disappointed with the cabinet mission proposal because their plan for a strong national government was emasculated by concessions to win acceptance from the League. They refused to join the interim government but reluctantly agreed to campaign for seats in the constituent assembly, thereby implicitly accepting the basic recommendations. League adherence raised hopes for success, but then events in July destroyed these expectations.

In an address on July 7, Nehru, serving another term as president of the Congress, declared, "we are not bound by a single thing except that we have decided for the moment to go into the Constituent Assembly." In later statements he made it absolutely clear that the Congress majority in the constituent assembly would be free to draft any kind of constitution it wished without reference to the recommendations of the cabinet mission. Jinnāh, his worst fears confirmed, denounced the Congress' breach of trust, repudiated the League's acceptance of the cabinet mission plan, and called for the creation of an independent Pakistan as the only solution of the Indian dilemma. The League Council not only upheld its leader but also decided that direct action for the achievement of Pakistan could no longer be put off. A Direct Action Day was proclaimed for August 16 when all Muslims were directed to observe a general strike in protest against betrayal by both the Congress and the British government. If any hope remained of reconciling the Hindu and Muslim communities, it was buried in the bloodshed that ensued. In Calcutta alone four days of communal strife took a toll of 4700 dead and 15,000 injured, and in subsequent months further outbreaks throughout India more than doubled these tragic figures. Nevertheless, the British government continued into 1947 desperate but fruitless efforts to salvage the cabinet mission plan in some form or another.

Later in life Nehru admitted that he had committed a serious tactical error and scuttled the one chance for a unified India.

When the weakness of the proposed central government, based on recognition of the Muslim-Hindu schism, is viewed against the need for strong governments to cope with the severe problems presented by independence to India and Pakistan, however, perhaps Nehru's blunder was a blessing in disguise. It seems doubtful that a weak, decentralized regime, plagued by communal distrust and divisions, could possibly have survived.

On February 20, 1947, the British prime minister, thoroughly frustrated by the absence of cooperation from the Indian leaders, announced in the House of Commons his government's firm intention of transferring power no later than June 1948. This declaration was followed by the announcement that Lord Louis Mountbatten would replace Lord Wavell as viceroy. After two months of vain efforts, the new viceroy informed the Indian leaders on June 2 of his genuine regret at being unable to find any solution other than partition. Britain proposed to transfer power to the Dominions of India and Pakistan within the next few months. The Congress reluctantly accepted the inevitability of partition, though Gāndhi vehemently opposed this vivisection of the Indian nation. Although the Muslim League lost much of the territory it originally claimed through the application of local self-determination, it too reluctantly accepted the proposal. All that remained to be done—and it was a monumental task—was the determination of the boundaries and the division of assets and liabilities between the two new states. Nevertheless, this task was accomplished under forced draft in the next two months by a number of Indian committees with the impartial assistance of the viceroy. Meanwhile, the British parliament rushed through the bill authorizing the transfer of power to the two dominions on August 15, 1947, almost a year ahead of the prime minister's deadline. At the same time, the withdrawal of the last elements of the British armed forces was undertaken. At midnight of August 14 the two new regimes were officially proclaimed amid celebrations both at home and abroad.

In their haste to be rid of the burden of India the British had left only two major bits of unfinished business: the fate of the large minorities left behind by partition and the disposition of the princely states. With regard to the latter, the viceroy, now first governor-general of the Dominion of India, had laid down general guidelines based on the previous recommendations of the cabinet mission. British overlordship would lapse with British withdrawal and would not be transferred to either of the new regimes. Thus each prince was theoretically free to accede to either dominion or to attempt to maintain independence. In practice, however, as Mountbatten pointed out to the princes in July, they could not ignore their mighty neighbors, nor could their neighbors be expected to ignore them. They were urged to accept a draft instrument of accession under which they only surrendered authority over defense, foreign affairs, and communications. Upon independence most accepted this course, with only three states creating major problems. The issues involved in these three cases, one of which remains a major bone of contention, will be dealt with later.

Far more tragic was the failure to provide some sort of protection and program of migration for the tens of millions left outside the boundaries of their coreligionists. Most serious was the divided Punjab where warlike Sikh, Muslim, and Hindu communities had historically met, mingled, and hated. Even before independence, the Punjab had a long record as a hotbed of communal strife. With the approach of independence it raged out of control for several months. Villages went up in flames. Men were savagely slaughtered and young women and girls abducted. Unable to find buyers, millions abandoned their meager possessions and sought safety in flight: Hindus and Sikhs streaming eastward toward the Indian frontier and Muslims clogging the roads westward toward Pakistan. Trains carrying refugees were derailed and their passengers massacred, and those on the roads were subjected to almost continuous attack, while

*Gandhi
1/30/48*
↓

native troops either looked on or sometimes took part in the killing.

Both governments were shocked into laying aside their differences for the moment and cooperating in joint efforts to save as many lives as possible. An air shuttle for refugees was established and airdrops of supplies were made to beleaguered columns on foot. Refugee camps were set up for the homeless. By October the worst of the killing was over, but the mass migrations continued. After this nightmare in the Punjab no Muslim could feel safe in the Indian half and no Hindu or Sikh could feel secure in the Pakistani half. By the end of the year more than 11 million were estimated to have crossed the border in both directions. As for the number of dead, the rivers, ditches, and carrion will never reveal their secret. Estimates of the toll range from less than one million to more than two million, a ghoulish score by any count. At first hailed for their swiftness in liquidating their position in India, the British were then severely berated for the haste of their withdrawal. If they had been more deliberate in carrying out the transfer of power, it was argued, they could have policed these anticipated migrations and prevented a bloodbath. What seems to have been forgotten is that these mass movements were precipitated by widespread terrorism, which would only have been deferred until British authority left the scene sooner or later. Bound to their fields, peasants are reluctant to strike out into the unknown, until no alternative remains.

A similar outbreak in divided Bengal was averted largely by the public appeals and fasts of the Mahātma in behalf of nonviolence and brotherly love. By these characteristic actions, and their tragic consequence, this lover of mankind made his final contribution to the people to whom he had dedicated his life. In the process, however, he enraged the extremist Hindu Mahāsabhā and related organizations that were advocating all-out war against Muslims for the recreation of a Hindu empire throughout the Indian subcontinent. On January 30, 1948, while walking to a prayer meeting in New Delhi, the Mahātma was cut down by four shots fired at close range by a Hindu extremist. The assassination of the spiritual leader of Indian nationalism, revered by Muslims as well as Hindus for his great soul and universal message, shocked both communities into a sober realization of the potential consequences of unrestrained passion and hatred. Thus, even his death served the interests of the people he had loved and led, and put the final stamp of greatness on one of the most influential leaders the twentieth century has produced. Indeed, some have suggested that his death, occurring when it did, was fortunate because his mystical appeal, which had done so much to arouse the Indian masses, would have been a distinct embarrassment to the leaders responsible for creating a modern nation.

For better or worse, Western nationalism, transplanted to the Indian environment, has produced the division of the subcontinent into two independent states, and this partition has by no means resolved all the serious ethnic and linguistic, let alone religious, divisions that characterize this vast and second most populous land. In spite of the experience of British rule and institutional development, the two dominions, handicapped by the lowest per capita income in Asia, were confronted with monumental internal problems, in addition to those created by partition. India's and Pakistan's varying approaches to the problems of independence in the modern world will be considered in a final chapter on the subcontinent.

SIGNIFICANT DATES

1905 Gokhale's demand for self-government
1906 Founding of all-India Muslim League
1907 Secession of Tilak and extremists from the Congress

1909   Morley-Minto Reforms
1915   Death of Gokhale and return of Tilak to the Congress
1916   Lucknow Pact of Tilak with Indian Muslims
1919   Montagu-Chelmsford Reforms and Rowlatt Act
1919   Gāndhi's first *satyāgraha* campaign; Amritsār massacre
1920–1922   Second *satyāgraha* campaign
1928   Simon Commission and Nehru Report
1930–1932   Round Table Conferences
1935   Government of India Act
1939   Resignation of Congress ministries
1942   Cripps' Mission and Quit India Resolution
1945   Simla Conference
1947   Labor government's decision to leave India by June 1948
1947   Creation of dominions of India and Pakistan on August 15

SELECTED READINGS

Abbott, Freeland, *Islam and Pakistan*. Ithaca: Cornell University Press, 1968.
*Ashe, Geoffrey, *Gandhi*. New York: Stein and Day, 1968.
Bolitho, Hector, *Jinnah: Creator of Pakistan*. London: J. Murray, 1954.
*Bondurant, Joan V., *Conquest of Violence: The Gandhian Philosophy of Conflict*. Berkeley: University of California Press, 1965.
*Brecher, Michael, *Nehru: A Political Biography*. Boston: Beacon Press, 1962.
*Chaudhuri, Nirad C., *The Autobiography of an Unknown Indian*. Berkeley: University of California Press, 1968.
*Fischer, Louis, *The Essential Gandhi*. New York: Random House, 1962.
*———, *The Life of Mahatma Gandhi*. New York: Macmillan, 1962.
*Gandhi, Mohandas K., *Autobiography: The Story of My Experiments with Truth*. Washington: Public Affairs Press, 1964.
Gokhale, B. G., *The Making of the Indian Nation*. Bombay: Asia Publishing House, 1960.
Nanda, B. R., *The Nehrus: Motilal and Jawaharlal*. London: Allen and Unwin, 1962.
*Nehru, Jawaharlal, *Toward Freedom*. Boston: Beacon Press, 1958.
*Pandey, B. N., *The Break-up of British India*. New York: St. Martin's Press, 1969.
Smith, Wilfred Cantwell, *Modern Islam in India*. London: Probsthain, 1943.
Wasti, S. R., *Lord Minto and the Indian Nationalist Movement*. Oxford: Clarendon Press, 1964.
Wolpert, Stanley A., *Morley and India*. Berkeley: University of California Press, 1967.

CHAPTER TWENTY-THREE

NATIONALISM AND THE STRUGGLE FOR INDEPENDENCE IN THE MIDDLE EAST: 1905–1949

In 1905 those parts of the Middle East that had not yet fallen prey to European imperialism acknowledged the rule of either the Persian shah or the Ottoman sultan, thus roughly reflecting the division between Shiite and Sunnite Islam. Principally because of the impact of the West in all its varied aspects, both regimes recognized the need for modernization, but their efforts in this direction had been frustrated or delayed by a number of factors, including limited resources due to antiquated governmental machinery and the low tariffs of the capitulations, the negative or reactionary attitude of the ruling class, the landlords, the religious hierarchy, and even many townsmen with traditional vested interests to protect, and the apathy and ignorance of tradition-bound villagers and tribesmen who feared and rejected any threat to their customary way of life. Among their Muslim subjects both regimes harbored small, Western-educated elites—mostly army officers—infected with nationalism and eager to implement radical reforms along Western lines, but their very radicalness posed a political threat that neither sultan nor shah could tolerate and that each in his own way felt compelled to suppress. The Ottoman sultan had attempted to overcome the parochialism of the empire by a Pan-Islamic appeal in defense of the faith, but the only consequence of this appeal had been a further stimulation of separatist aspirations among his Christian subjects in the Balkans. Here alone, nationalistic sentiments had percolated down to the masses to any significant extent, aided and abetted by the example and intervention of their fellow Christians in Europe. Modernization efforts were handicapped not only by internal divisions and an archaic institutional structure but also by the lack of communications and educational facilities adequate for the dynamic relationship of immediate stimulus and response between ruler and ruled so essential to the effective functioning of a modern nation-state. Isolated physically, emotionally, and intellectually, the resident of one part of the empire knew little and cared less about what occurred elsewhere, unless it had a direct effect on him. True, news of Japan's victory over Tsarist Russia, which had encroached on the Muslim Middle East as much as any other part of Asia, created widespread interest and excitement, but when the consequent coups in favor of constitutional government took place, few outside the cities became interested or involved.

THE YOUNG TURKS AND THE DISSOLUTION OF THE OTTOMAN EMPIRE

Although the constitutional movement bore its first fruit in Persia, the more radical program and far-reaching consequences of the Young Turk's activities warrant prior consideration. Within a few years they were forced by the reverses they suffered not only to abandon the Ottoman Empire but also under new leadership to abolish the Ottoman Caliphate. In the crucible of war and destruction, however, they forged a new national vitality.

The origins of the Young Turks are somewhat obscure, thanks in large part to Hamidian spies, agents provocateur, and oppression, which brought together in a common cause men with widely differing points of view. Generally, it may be said that they were all ideological heirs of the Tanzimat reformers, had drunk deeply at the wellsprings of Western liberalism, and advocated as a minimal first step the restoration of Midhat Pasha's constitution of 1876. Furthermore, regardless of their personal religious convictions, most of them believed in the French nationalistic idea of an all-powerful secular government in control of the worldly affairs of the state. Once the goal of a constitution was gained, however, they differed on how extensive a role the government could practically undertake in the Ottoman state. Some favored a loose federal union in which the central government would deal only with affairs of a secular and nationwide concern, while the majority wanted a strong centralized regime fully capable of welding into a unified nation the diverse peoples of the Ottoman domain. Assuming Turkish dominance, progressive Muslims and Turkish nationalists tended to support the latter position.

Ever since the tyranny of Abul Hamid had become apparently a permanent program, Ottoman liberals had formed small but short-lived secret associations to keep the idea of constitutional reform alive, only to be uncovered and suppressed by the sultan's ubiquitous spies. As early as 1889 a Committee of Progress and Union secretly recruited students in the Imperial military and civilian academies and colleges and in spite of reprisals attracted new members from other dissident organizations, nicknamed New Ottomans or Young Turks. A planned coup in 1896 was frustrated by arrests, and then in 1897 the wily sultan, by promising amnesty and reform, seized the leadership and emasculated the committee. But his success was only temporary as others both at home and abroad continued the effort to organize all those in favor of reform. A congress was convened in Paris in 1902 and newspapers printed in Europe publicized the need for unity. Nevertheless, the critical developments took place not abroad but in troubled Macedonia, and particularly Salonika, which with its mixed population and economic and strategic importance was coveted by Greece, Serbia, and Bulgaria much to the concern of the powers. Their intrigues and Western intervention aroused anti-Western nationalist feeling among many army and civilian leaders.

In 1906 a small, conspiratorial organization, the Society of Liberty, was formed from these elements in Salonika. At the same time, Mustafa Kemal, who had been arrested for revolutionary activity on the same day he was commissioned in 1905 and then posted to Damascus, founded the secret Fatherland Society among fellow army officers in Syria and soon extended his activities to the army in Macedonia to which he secured a transfer in 1907. Before long a series of mergers amalgamated the various revolutionary groups, and following another congress of Ottoman Liberals in Paris in 1907, both the exile and Macedonian groups agreed to unification in the Society of Union and Progress directed by a central executive committee.

Meanwhile, depressed economic conditions generated widespread popular discontent, which represented potential support. Scattered army mutinies in 1906 seeking back pay alarmed the aging and fearful sultan. Uncertain about the depth of disaffection in the rank and file, he met the demands with concessions instead of the customary suppression. Even those arrested were treated with surprising leniency, only suffering exile or a lesser penalty. Such concessions only encouraged further outbreaks during 1907 in which civilians soon joined in search of redress for local grievances. Obviously, for whatever reasons, the grip of Hamidian tyranny was weakening, a fact that did not long escape the notice of the small revolutionary elite. But the internal weakness of the Ottoman sultanate, which presented them with a golden opportunity, was also destined to invite other attacks on

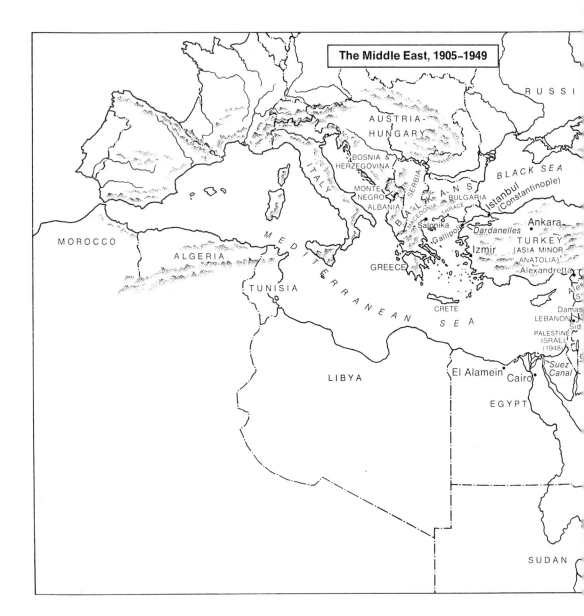

The Middle East, 1905–1949

the empire under a new and uncertain leadership.

In the spring of 1908 mutinies erupted in the Macedonian garrison. Although some military members of the Society of Union and Progress felt compelled to take to the hills, the central committee had done its work well and effectively subverted the command of the Third Army Corps. On July 24 when the sultan received a telegram threatening a march on the capital in support of the demand of the Committee of Union and Progress (C.U.P.) for restoration of the constitution, he immediately capitulated. The next day the announcement of elections for the Chamber of Deputies under the restored constitution, with its guarantees of equality, inspired amazing public displays of fraternal jubilation. Muslims, Christians, and Jews greeted each other with tearful embraces and

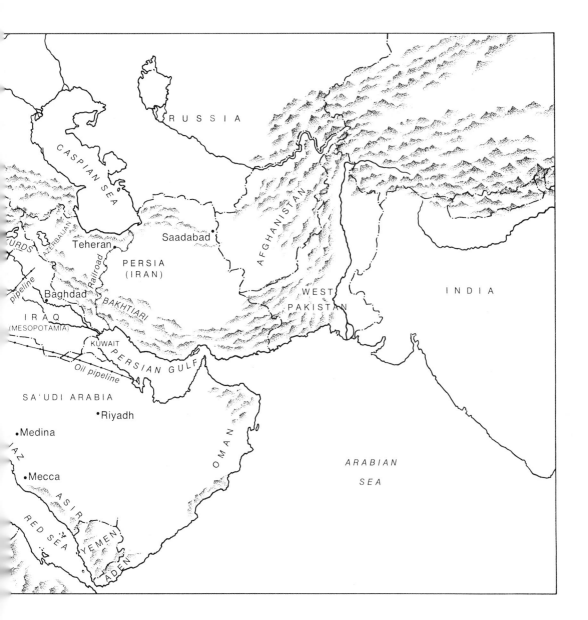

walked arm-in-arm through the streets in celebration of this day of deliverance. The parliament that convened in December included deputies representing all the diverse religious and national components of the empire and reflecting differing political viewpoints. The C.U.P. had enjoyed neither the time nor the strength and experience to organize a victory at the polls. Three major parties soon emerged: the Union and Progress, the Liberal Unionist, and the conservative and Pan-Islamic Muslim Association. Although the Union and Progress party was the largest, it relied on questionable Liberal Unionist support to maintain control. This shaky arrangement was soon jeopardized by Balkan developments that were a serious blow to the prestige of constitutional government and the Young Turks.

On October 5, 1908, the Bulgarian prince unilaterally repudiated the Ottoman connection by taking the title of tsar, and two days later Austria-Hungary also took advantage of the change of government by proclaiming the outright annexation of Bosnia and Herzegovina, which it had administered under Ottoman suzerainty since 1878. Then, on October 12, the people of Crete rebelled and sought union with their countrymen of Greece. To the informed observer none of these events was surprising; the despotism of Abul Hamid had only staved off the inevitable, and these defections were long overdue. Yet the impotence of the new government in dealing with them exposed once and for all the internal decay and weakness of the Ottoman Empire and presaged, indeed invited, the upheavals and assaults yet to come.

These losses, combined with administrative inexperience and the absence of genuine popular appreciation of their goal of equality, discredited the Young Turks and produced a short-lived, conservative countercoup in mid-April of 1909 spearheaded by the First Army Corps stationed at the capital. Amid cries of "down with the constitution," "down with the committee," and "long live the sacred law," their government was turned out, they were forced to seek safety in flight, and Abul Hamid was restored to power. The Third Army, however, remained steadfast in its support of the Young Turks and within two weeks occupied the capital, declared martial law, and restored the parliament. Furthermore, with the backing of a *fetwa* issued by the Shaykh al-Islam parliament deposed the last effective Ottoman sultan and replaced him with a pliant nonentity. Nevertheless, the C.U.P. still remained a small elite without a broad base of support and still had to contend with the Liberal Unionists, whose program of decentralization appealed to the traditional religious and ethnic divisions of the empire, as well as with the reactionary Islamic traditionalists who reflected the outlook of the vast majority of the Muslim population. In addition, fresh blows were about to be struck against Ottoman territories.

In its search for support for its brand of nationalism the C.U.P. after the 1909 coup increasingly appealed to Muslims by advocating a Turkification program, probably because non-Turkish deputies tended to vote as a bloc against all Union and Progress legislation. Such policies, however, were self-defeating, only serving to confirm the suspicions and increase the alienation of non-Turkish peoples. As an omen of things to come, new Arab nationalist groups were organized by disillusioned former members and supporters of the Society of Union and Progress. In Albania the enhanced intervention of the central government precipitated a bloody rebellion that was suppressed in 1911 only after substantial concessions to Albanian autonomy. The failure of the Young Turks to enforce their will in this instance raised the revolutionary temperature of other minorities and the irredentist aspirations of Greece, Serbia, Montenegro, and Bulgaria.

Before their plans could develop, however, empire-hungry Italy struck in the fall of 1911 after Turkish refusal to surrender loosely held Libya. Italian forces easily seized the port cities but found the going tougher in the interior where Turkish leaders, such as Mustafa Kemal, earned military reputations by leading the Sanussi tribesmen in effective guerrilla warfare. Italian naval domination, however, cut off supplies and made prolonged resistance impossible. C.U.P. refusal to admit defeat, rebellion in the Yemen, several minor uprisings elsewhere, and especially the imminence of attack by the Balkan states united all opposition behind the Liberal Unionists in the ouster of the Union and Progress ministry. Although the Liberal Unionist government did secure peace with Italy by abandoning Libya, it failed to forestall the joint Balkan attack one day earlier on October 17, 1912, and it subsequently failed to check the rapid advance of the victorious Balkan allies who overran almost all the remaining European territories in less than a month. When this regime appeared ready to surrender all but the immediate defenses of the capital for the sake of peace, another coup engineered by the Union and Progress party put it in undisputed power through World War I. In a second Balkan war in 1913 among the quarrelsome victors, the C.U.P. regained some of the lost land and some of its lost luster.

The preceding four years of political turmoil disillusioned the Young Turk leadership with constitutional institutions as a vehicle for effective reforms to strengthen the nation. Henceforth the Young Turks enforced their reforms under an increasingly rigorous and ruthless despotism, which dispassionately and ruthlessly punished all dissidents, including any members of the Union and Progress party who wavered in their allegiance. They had discovered the revolutionary axioms that there can be no substitute for power and no toleration for disagreement. Accompanying this shift in internal policy, a parallel shift in foreign policy brought about a return to the Hamidian preference for Germany as the one power with a fairly clean record in its relations with the Ottoman Empire. In any case, the Anglo-Russian entente of 1907, following the earlier Anglo-French entente, effectively neutralized the old policy of playing one aggressor off against the other. Most influential in this shift were the able German military advisors, and in Enver Bey they had an ardent military protégé.

Wisdom should have dictated neutrality during World War I for a country so weakened by repeated blows in recent years, but militant leaders like Enver dreamed of using the war to regain not only recent but also older losses to Great Power imperialism. Furthermore, the Allies refused to bid for the support of a country with so little apparent military potential. The decisive turning point was the "sale" to the Turks of two German cruisers, caught in the Mediterranean at the outbreak of the war, as replacements for two British-built warships that the British refused to deliver. These ships, renamed but still manned by German crews, initiated hostilities late in October 1914, by shelling Russian Black Sea ports.

The details of Turkish participation in the war cannot detain us. Most important was the true birth of the Turkish nation as Turkish troops under German command demonstrated unexpected military capacity and valor. Most notable was the successful defense of the Straits at Gallipoli from February 1915 to January 1916 in which Mustafa Kemal, the future Ataturk, distinguished himself as a military commander. Turkish arms suffered no serious setbacks until the last year of the war, and they tied up more than a million men and mountains of supplies that the Allies could profitably have used in other theaters of the war. Nevertheless, the Turkish war effort inflicted tremendous hardships on its peoples and alienated its Arab and other non-Turkish population, which spelled the death of the Ottoman Empire.

At first, by a Pan-Islamic declaration of a holy war the Turks attempted to win the active support of Muslims both within and without the empire but failed to arouse any significant response. Reluctant Arabs had to be dragooned into the service by ruthless conscription. Overt Arab nationalism received its first expression in 1916 when Sharif Husayn of Mecca raised an army to cooperate with the British in return for their pledge to support the establishment of an Arab nation. Upon the obvious failure of the Pan-Islamic appeal, the increasingly hardpressed Turkish government evolved what was called Pan-Turanism (after Turan, the legendary progenitor of all Turks) by which it sought to bring into one nation the millions of Turkish-speaking peoples ruled by Russia. This sort of Turkish nationalism had long been advocated by the leading intellectual supporters of the Young Turks, such as Ziya Gokalp, Ahmed Emin, and the female novelist Halidé Edib, whose writings promoted the use of the Turkish language and Turkish themes in literature and education. The principal victim of this policy was the suspect Armenian community of about 1,500,000, at least one-third of which was liquidated on the partially justified ground of subversion during wartime. Even the Turks were ashamed of this unnecessarily excessive retribution. The goal of unifying all Turkish-speaking peoples proved unrealistic and unrealizable, though thousands of lives were sacrificed in the effort, but Pan-Turanism did represent a clean break with Ottomanism and thus set the ideological direction leading to the future creation of the Republic of Turkey under the inspired leadership of Mustafa Kemal. The thoroughness of defeat and the harshness of the peace terms the victorious Allies proposed to impose, however, were what gave new life and vigor to Turkish nationalism.

The armistice of October 30, 1918, gave the Allies a free hand by specifying Turkish demobilization and by granting them "the right to occupy any strategic points in the event of any situation arising which threatens the security of the Allies." Both the Turks and their formerly subject minorities held great hopes that a just peace would be based on the twelfth of President Woodrow Wilson's Fourteen Points, guaranteeing a "secure sovereignty" for the Turks and "an absolute unmolested opportunity of development" for the other nationalities of the Ottoman Empire. They hoped that this declaration, to which all the Allies had subscribed, would override the secret treaties for the dismemberment of the Ottoman Empire already revealed by revolutionary Russia. However, it soon became apparent that the old imperialistic inclinations had not yet been subordinated to the Wilsonian ideal.

The Allied occupation of the Ottoman capital was to be expected and indeed welcomed for its monetary infusion into an impoverished economy. Also, continued British occupation of the Arab provinces came as no surprise; in any case, most informed Turks had written them off as casualties of the war

that could not in any event be retained under the Wilsonian doctrine of self-determination. The restoration of the repudiated capitulations and the European-controlled Public Debt Administration, and the revival of concession hunting with the backing of the victors were more disturbing as symptoms of renewed economic imperialism. But much more distressing was the Italian occupation of southern Asia Minor followed in May 1919 by Allied authorization of Greek occupation of western Asia Minor, including the important city of Izmir, as the rumored first step in realizing the Greek dream of restoring its ancient dominion over the Straits and the whole of Asia Minor.

Thoroughly alarmed at the prospect of the vivisection of the Turkish homeland and the impotence of the puppet government to cope with this threat, Mustafa Kemal resigned his commission and convened national congresses at which all Turks were called on to dedicate their lives and fortunes to an Association for the Defense of the Rights of Turkey in Europe and Anatolia. This appeal was perfectly timed as an answer to frustrated Turkish nationalism. The thousands who answered the call made Kemal's forces too strong to crush. Negotiations also proved fruitless; Kemal and his followers refused to compromise. In 1920 the Allies forced the government to accept the Treaty of Sèvres, but patriotic Turks would have nothing to do with terms that all but extinguished Turkish independence. They only demonstrated that no other course was left except rebellion: a rebellion out of which was born the Turkish Republic.

KEMAL ATATURK AND THE REPUBLIC OF TURKEY

Turkish nationalism, nurtured by the writings of Young Turk intellectuals and stripped down to bare essentials by the losses from 1908 to 1919, now became the desperate rallying cry of life or death. At a Grand National Assembly in April 1920,

Mustafa Kemal was elected president with full powers to lead his people to victory or death in the cause of Turkish liberty. On the surface the struggle seemed hopeless, surrounded as the nationalists were by British, French, Greek, and Italian forces. Fortunately, however, the Allies never proved able to cooperate effectively, permitting Kemal to deal with them one by one. Furthermore, the youthful Soviet Russian regime saw a possible advantage in encouraging and aiding the rebels.

First, in the spring of 1920, Kemal's troops forced the French to retire from Turkey proper to Syria. Then, while the Allies debated how to dispose of Turkish territories, they collaborated with Soviet Russian forces in crushing the Armenians in the northeast. British forces in the area, already sharply reduced in size, decided not to intervene. Russo-Turkish collaboration was further confirmed by treaties adjusting the frontier in Turkey's favor and pledging Russian aid to the Kemalists against the imperialist designs of the Western powers. Finally, in March 1921, an agreement was reached with Italy providing for Italian withdrawal in return for limited and specific economic concessions. Thus, at the conclusion of the first year of operations, the Kemalist rebels had eliminated all important hostile forces, except the Greeks, from the Anatolian homeland, and these achievements proved to be a tremendous morale builder against the defeats inflicted by the advancing Greek armies.

Since mid-1920, Greece had accepted the role of agent of the Allies to enforce the provisions of the Treaty of Sèvres. Against Allied advice a general offensive had been undertaken to seize Ankara and break the back of the rebels. In spite of bitter fighting, Kemalist armies were gradually driven back until a combination of overextended supply lines and a bloody stand checked the Greek advance in September 1921. Although it took Kemal almost a year to reorganize his forces, this battle proved to be the critical turning point of the struggle because first France and then Great Britain decided to withhold further support of the Greek war effort and to seek some sort of accommodation with the determined Turkish nationalists whose ultimate victory appeared more and more probable. In October France negotiated a secret treaty of peace and friendship and joined Russia and Italy in supplying munitions to the Kemalists. Belatedly recognizing the writing on the wall, Britain subsequently joined in declaring neutrality, which effectively cut off the British supply of armaments. Nevertheless, Greek generals were reluctant to recognize the necessity of a strategic withdrawal. Finally, on August 26, 1922, the Turks broke through the Greek lines and before long the retreat turned into a rout. Deserted by France and Italy, Britain alone kept forces in position to defend the Straits. Accepting the hopelessness of the British situation, the prime minister agreed to an armistice on October 11, 1922, which provided for a conference to draw up a new peace treaty.

The negotiations between Kemal's regime and the Allies dragged on from November 1922 to July 1923 before the conclusion of the Treaty of Lausanne with the new Turkish Republic, following the deposition of the last Ottoman sultan. The hero of the fight against the Greeks was also the hero of the negotiations, little five-foot four-inch Ismet Inonu, who proved to be more than a match for the most skilled diplomats of Europe. He utilized his slight deafness to advantage by claiming not to hear any proposal of which he did not approve. In any case, he as well as the other delegates knew that the Turks were ready to fight again if they did not get the terms they demanded.

Turkey regained unrestricted sovereignty over all strictly Turkish territory including eastern Thrace and the Straits. The capitulations were finally cancelled and the Ottoman Public Debt Administration was dissolved. An enlightened provision of the treaty called for compulsory exchange of

Turkish and Greek minorities. Although the transfer inflicted personal and economic hardships on its victims, it reduced, if it did not entirely eliminate, the major source of future friction between Greece and Turkey. The Treaty of Lausanne confirmed the creation of the modern state of Turkey. Now Mustafa Kemal and what became known as the Republican People's Party were free to concentrate on the internal struggle to create a modern nation.

Kemal, soon to be known as Ataturk (Father of the Turks), recognized more clearly than most modern leaders of his day that the transformation of the traditional outlook and way of life of the peasant lay at the heart of the struggle. Although conditions forced him to proceed with deliberate haste, he thoroughly exploited his oratorical talent and all the modern communication and educational media Turkey could afford. In addition, as virtual dictator of a single party republic he issued and publicized decrees prescribing simple and, to Western observers, superficial and absurdly naive reforms that he believed to be essential first steps to break the encrusted cake of custom and enforce the Westernization to which the Young Turks were dedicated. At first these reforms affecting every aspect of Turkish life appeared to be haphazard and whimsical, until in 1931 Kemal defined the objectives of Kemalism as republicanism, statism, secularism, populism, nationalism, and reformism.

At the outset, secularism received a partial and tradition-shattering expression in decrees abolishing the caliphate and the ecclesiastical courts administering the *shari'a* or sacred law of Islam. Later another edict, which gave Eastern observers no end of amusement, prohibited the wearing of the fez, traditionally associated with Islam, though it was in fact a Western import, and prescribed that all men's hats must have brims. Nevertheless, traditional institutions and practices could not be eradicated at the stroke of a pen and several years were required before Western-type law codes could

be devised to replace Muslim law. Meanwhile, the otherwise modern republican constitution, adopted in April 1924, declared Islam to be the state religion even though it extended citizenship to all residents without distinction of race or creed; proclaimed all equal before the law; granted freedom of speech, thought, press, and travel; and forbade special privileges for any group or individual. The constitution placed sovereignty in the people, as represented by the Grand National Assembly, whose members were to be elected by universal male suffrage at least every four years. It also established a parliamentary system of government headed by a president and a presidentially appointed prime minister, roles naturally filled by Kemal and his right-hand man, Ismet. As expressions of nationalism, the capital was removed to Ankara from polyglot Constantinople, renamed Istanbul, and Turkish was declared the national language. Not until 1928, after the new law codes were in operation, did Kemal feel that Turkey was ready for a full break with Islam, by amendment of the constitution. Other aspects of secularization included adoption of the Western calendar, Sunday in place of Friday as the day of rest, and in 1935 even the new Western institution of the weekend (*vikend*), which by law lasted from Saturday at 1 P.M. to Sunday at midnight. In addition, women benefited from secularization. Polygamy, which in any event few men had been able to afford, was legally prohibited, and the wearing of the veil, though not banned by law, was officially frowned upon as a symbol of the rejected tradition of the subordination of women. In any case, peasant women had never observed the prescription of the veil to any degree, while the growing number of women who took advantage of expanded educational opportunities was bound to alter the fabric of Turkish society both in urban areas and the countryside. Education underwent secularization as well as vast expansion with the prohibition of religious instruction in both public and private schools. In Kemal's mind, Islam was the chief support of tradition, particularly among the peasants who were his principal concern.

His concern for the peasants, whose blood had created the nation, was most fully expressed in his conception of populism. By this goal he sought to give reality to the constitutional declaration of equality, eradicating all special privileges and providing positive opportunities for peasant participation in a democratic society. While easing the tax burden of the peasants and redistributing land, he also prescribed free, universal education in the primary grades to reduce the burden of illiteracy. Thousands of schools were built at local expense in every village and town, usually after a personal harangue by Kemal or one of his principal deputies. To overcome the shortage of teachers, the development of teacher training schools received special attention. Arabic script had never been well-adapted to the writing of Turkish, and to promote both literacy and nationalism, a modified Roman alphabet was prescribed for all teaching and publications. Such a revolutionary reform created hardship for literate adults who had to learn again to write, but the advantages for both broader-based literacy and for nationalism probably outweighed the disadvantages of this reform.

As the heir of the Young Turks, Kemal's central concern was naturally the development of as strong a feeling of Turkish nationalism as possible. In addition to giving the Turkish language its own alphabet, a purification movement labored to eliminate Arabic words from the vocabulary and even to revive archaic Turkish words. The overall result was a written language much closer to the spoken language. Furthermore, history texts were rewritten slighting the role of the Ottomans and stressing instead the legendary achievements of the Turkish people as a whole. The Sumerians and Hittites, and indeed all who had emerged from the central Asian steppes, were claimed as Turks. Since *adam* is the Turkish word for man, some even

asserted that the first man was a Turk and therefore all mankind was of Turkish origin. Despite the absurdity of such speculations, they did contribute importantly to the popular growth of racial identity and pride. Another dramatic step decreed that every citizen must take a family name from a legally approved list of Turkish words. The assembly bestowed upon Kemal the proud name of Ataturk, "Father of the Turks," and upon Ismet, the name of Inonu, in honor of his military victories there.

The most controversial aspect of Kemal's program was entitled statism, which appears to have evolved out of the economic needs of the new republic, particularly after the onset of the Great Depression. Fully aware of the inroads on Ottoman sovereignty made by Western economic imperialism, Kemal was determined that the Turkish Republic should avoid this fate and pull itself up by its own bootstraps. Foreign exchange was subjected to state control, and more and more foreign trade came under state management through government-to-government trade agreements. Agriculture, the mainstay of his peasant supporters and the principal source of exportable surpluses, naturally was given special attention. A model farm demonstrated the agricultural possibilities utilizing the latest techniques and equipment, but few farmers, even if willing to abandon traditional methods, could afford the necessary capital investment in spite of expanded credit made available through the Bank of Agriculture and the authorization of cooperatives. Indeed, to compensate for the sharp drop in the worldwide market prices for agricultural products a program of government subsidies was initiated in 1932. By careful manipulation of these subsidies the government discovered that it could encourage the production of those crops marketable under its trade agreements and discourage the production of those items for which there was little demand. As a result, the Turkish peasants weathered the depression with small losses and by the late thirties were comparatively prosperous. Nevertheless, it would be a mistake to presume that Turkish farming had undergone any significant degree of modernization; most farmers, even after World War II, continued to work their lands in the same manner their ancestors had followed for untold generations.

More controversial was the application of statism in the industrial sector. Impatient with the reluctance of private capital to invest in industrial enterprise, Kemal gradually expanded the area of governmental ownership and operation. Starting from the inherited base of state monopolies in matches, alcohol, tobacco, and salt, the state acquired and developed railroads, harbors, public utilities, and shipping. The success of these operations in conjunction with the problems of the depression and the growing state role in foreign trade led to the formulation in 1933 of a five-year plan for industrial development in which the government was to take the leading part. The Sumer Bank was founded to build and operate textile, paper, steel, glass, and sugar factories, and in 1936 the Hittite Bank was set up to underwrite the development of the mining and metal industries. Opponents criticized this invasion of the sphere of private enterprise as inspired by either the communist or fascist model, and the criticism rose in intensity as the state, impelled by the need for greater controls, placed the private sector of the economy under increasing regulation. Whether or not Kemal adopted these economic policies out of conviction or the necessities of the times, there can be no dispute about their success in enabling Turkey to weather the onslaught of the Great Depression with a minimum of hardship.

Kemal appears to have been genuinely dedicated to the creation of a functioning democracy, but the difficulties involved in implementing the reforms essential to creating the conditions for democracy prevented him from surrendering dictatorial authority. As early as 1929 he indicated his good intentions y relaxing controls and encouraging the formation of an opposition that took the name of the Liberal party. Unfortunately this experiment coincided with the initial impact of the depression, calling for greater state regulation of the economy. Liberal criticism of these necessary measures stirred up enough response among the commercial classes in the cities to alarm the Republicans. After several political rallies degenerated into riots, Kemal decided that this experiment with democracy was premature and ordered the dissolution of the Liberal party. The course of events prior to his death in November 1938 was not conducive to a fresh effort, and his successor, Ismet Inonu, could plead the dislocations of World War II as an excuse for deferring political liberalization.

In foreign relations Kemal's regime followed an enlightened policy of moderation and friendship to gain breathing space for concentration on the internal problems of nation building. In addition to the already mentioned trade agreements, Turkey entered into pacts of nonaggression and friendship with its neighbors. Only with regard to immediate concerns, such as the Straits and the boundaries with British Iraq and French Syria, did Turkish diplomacy take a more vigorous and demanding stance. By shrewd and skillful diplomacy at Montreux, Turkey secured from the European powers agreement to what amounted for all practical purposes to full, sovereign control over the Straits.

Until the defeat of Hitler's Germany became clear beyond any doubt, the Turkish government, remembering the disastrous consequences of participation in World War I, resisted all overtures and walked the tightrope of neutrality, a role that was especially difficult to maintain after German armies swept through Greece and Bulgaria and up to the Turkish frontiers in 1941. Meanwhile, loans, credits, and export sales at premium prices enabled Turkey to obtain modern arms and equipment for an army that numbered as many as one million men. German setbacks late in 1942 aroused Turkish concern about the possible demands of a victorious Russia and made the government more susceptible to Allied blandishments, particularly American lend-lease. By 1944 all remaining doubts about Allied victory had been erased and Turkey moved step by step into the Allied camp, finally going through the formality of a declaration of war in February 1945. President Inonu must have breathed a sigh of relief after having safely steered the Turkish ship of state through the swirling waters of World War II.

During and after the war American interest and influence in Turkish affairs continued to grow, largely because of the Soviet threat backed up by superior Russian armies along the frontiers. American prodding contributed to Ismet's announcement in 1945 of the government's intention to remove the remaining limitations on the practice of "genuine democracy." Long suppressed opponents of the Republican regime took immediate advantage of this announcement and the relaxation of press controls to publish criticisms, particularly of statist policies, and to form the Democratic party as the organ of all those with grievances against the government. The economic problems of which the Democrats complained stemmed not only from the wartime dislocations but also from the massive military mobilization that Turkey felt compelled to maintain to meet Soviet threats. For a nation of only 24 million people to keep more than one million men indefinitely under arms placed an unreasonable strain on the economy. Obviously, if help was not forthcoming from some quarter, the government would be compelled to come to terms with Russian demands. A partial solution was found when the Truman Doctrine of March 1947 provided $100 million, principally for military modernization. Theoretically Turkey could be defended by a much smaller force if it were equipped with modern arms and strategic roads for the rapid movement of troops from one sector to another. This American aid, which proved to be only the first small installment of a massive assistance program, did serve to keep Turkey in the Western camp and to make it a vital link in the evolving American policy of containment. On the other hand, the growing infusion of American money into the Turkish economy created as many problems as it solved.

Out of the upheavals from 1905 to 1949 the Young Turks and their successors had produced a nation and the most modern state in the Middle East. The loss of non-Turkish territories had been a disguised blessing in facilitating this development. Although the leadership was strongly Westernized and secular in outlook, the bulk of the population had barely begun to break with the traditional way of life. Secularism in particular had not been warmly received by the pious and superstitious peasantry, and the popular reaction against secularism was a factor in the defeat of the Republicans at the polls in 1950. Furthermore, although the Republican elite had carried out the most successful and thoroughgoing revolution in the Middle East, their extended stranglehold on public office had led them to lose touch with the people whose blood and votes had originally put them in power. By 1949 it was time for a change and the Democrats took full advantage of Republican shortcomings.

IRANIAN NATIONALISM

As the one other major independent Islamic state, Shiite Persia underwent a similar experience of foreign encroachment and a native reaction among those most exposed to Western influences, though the extent and intensity, in both instances, were not so severe. Since the path to modernization followed from 1905 to 1949 bore a close resemblance to that of Turkey, the story of Persia (renamed Iran in 1935) may be more briefly told.

In 1905, when Russia's defeat by Japan stirred up as much amazement in Persia as elsewhere in Asia, Russia and Britain were the principal contestants for influence. By means of preclusive loans Russia had recently gained a predominant position in the shah's court, much to the distress of the British and the Persian merchants doing business with them. In December the flogging of several merchants for profiteering, which was nothing unusual, precipitated a demand for the removal of the tyrannical corrupt, and pro-Russian grand vizir by a growing number of merchants, religious leaders, and even high officials, aided and abetted by British agents. When the shah proved obdurate, shops were closed and several thousand sympathetic residents of Teheran took to the streets in support of the demand. When force was threatened, the British embassy offered sanctuary and the shah was ultimately obliged to dismiss his unpopular grand vizir. With their appetites whetted by success, however, the dissidents were encouraged to insist on further governmental reform to restrict the absolute authority of the shah. Again the weak-willed shah was compelled to yield and in October 1906 an elected assembly (*majlis*) met to draw up a constitution. As finally accepted by the shah prior to his death in the following year, the constitution established a cabinet system of government with an appointed premier and a two-house legislature with an appointed upper house and an elected lower house.

As moderate as this constitution was in its restrictions on the authority of the shah, it ran into resistance from the beginning. The Anglo-Russian Entente of 1907, which divided the country into British and Russian spheres with a neutral buffer zone separating them, ended British interest in backing the democrats, while the religious leaders and aristocrats who had supported them soon realized that their vested interests were safer in the hands of the shah. Furthermore, Tsarist Russia, anxious to support the shah against the democrats, supplied Russian officers to organize and command a Cossack-type force that would enable him to enforce 's will and even sent Russian troops to put

down a rebellion in the capital. A flurry of rebellions further alarmed conservative elements and finally persuaded the shah to flee, leaving the throne to a 12-year-old son. Reformist forces gave an American economist, W. Morgan Shuster, extraordinary powers to straighten out Persian finances. Totally ignorant of Persian politics and practices, he proceeded to utilize his authority in a high-handed way that aroused the enmity of Russia as well as influential Persians. As a result, the government, under threat of a Russian invasion, was forced to dismiss him along with all hopes for immediate reform. Conservatives gained control of the regency government and in 1911 dissolved the national assembly (*majlis*). Thus the Persian experiment with constitutional government was aborted.

In the remaining years prior to World War I Russia dominated Persia's northern sphere, which included the capital city of Teheran, while Britain found a good cause for concentrating its interest in the south. And the regime was compelled to subsist on whatever crumbs fell from the tables of the two imperialists. Under these circumstances the Persians welcomed the German "drive to the East" when it reached their land via the Ottoman Empire, but as events demonstrated, not enough time remained for the Germans to establish themselves as an effective counterweight to the entrenched British and Russian positions.

In 1908 the discovery of oil at only 1100 feet north of the Persian Gulf revolutionized the British attitude toward Persia. From a backwater of secondary importance as a buffer between the Indian Empire and Russian expansion it was brought into the mainstream of imperial concern. The mere fact that the Persian Gulf had been left outside the British sphere in the Anglo-Russian division of the previous year shows their former low regard for the area. Now the First Lord of the Admiralty pressed for conversion of the fleet from coal to oil and looked to the development of the easily accessible Persian field as the principal source of supply. In 1909 the Anglo-Persian Oil Company, subsequently renamed the Anglo-Iranian, was formed to develop this resource as rapidly as possible. The British government, in recognition of the strategic importance of what had already been developed into a major oil field, purchased in 1914 a majority interest in the company. Later, discoveries of oil elsewhere in the Middle East proved that the region contained the largest reserves in the world and thereby revolutionized its position in international relations. While oil vastly enhanced the interest of the industrial nations in the Middle East, growing oil royalties provided a fortuitous source of income for the internal development and modernization of those states favored by nature with rich deposits of "liquid gold."

During World War I Persian military impotence invited interested powers to treat its proclamation of neutrality with cavalier contempt. In the northwest, Turkish and Russian armies campaigned back and forth in total disregard of Persian sovereignty. Living off the land, they confiscated crops, leaving the unfortunate people to face famine and starvation. In the south, German agents attempted with some success to stir up tribesmen against the British in the hope of sweeping eastward through Afghanistan to an assault on the Indian empire. The British countered with the organization of the South Persian Rifles, 11,000 tribesmen under English officers. In addition, they felt compelled to divert for the defense of the oil fields troops that might have staved off the 1916 defeat suffered in the Mesopotamian campaign. Foreign depredations and the economic dislocations caused by the war disrupted the Persian economy, generating a devastating inflation that multiplied the prices of food and other essential goods some ten times.

After the war the British thwarted an effort of the moribund regime to gain a hearing for its accumulated grievances at the Paris Peace Conference. They also coerced and bribed the regime into accepting a humiliating treaty that would have reduced the realm to a British protectorate run by British advisors. The *majlis*, however, reflected the rising tide of nationalism by refusing even to consider ratification of this document. As in Turkey and elsewhere, Britain failed to appreciate the effect of the war and wartime propaganda on the growth of nationalistic feeling and backed a discredited regime. Persia was on the verge of revolution against the last representative of the patently corrupt and incompetent Qajar dynasty. All that was needed was a strong leader, and he soon emerged from the ranks of the Cossack brigade, following Soviet withdrawal of support for its Russian officers. The Soviet goal of worldwide revolution against capitalist exploitation led to a repudiation of most Tsarist privileges in Persia, as in other neighboring countries. Extraterritorial rights were renounced, loans cancelled, and concessions surrendered, with the exception of the Caspian Sea fisheries so rich in the production of caviar. It has been suggested that even communism could not eradicate the Russian craving for this luxury.

REZA SHAH PAHLAWI

Reza Khan, a man of little formal education, rose from the ranks of the Cossack brigade on the basis of sheer ability and popularity following the departure of its Russian officers. As a nationalist himself, he could supply the military backing the nationalists needed to seize power. In 1921 his troops swept down on the capital, overwhelmed the police force in a few brief skirmishes, and forced the shah to accept a new cabinet headed by an ardent reformer who was also a fiery journalist. While Reza Khan worked quietly to build up his military power, the impractical prime minister attempted to carry out far-reaching reforms, such as the confiscation of landed estates and the suppression of corruption, far too radical for general acceptance at this initial stage of modernization. After all, many nationalists were also landlords and bureaucrats whose principal goal was the ejection of foreign influence and competition. Discredited by his extremism, the prime minister was forced to flee before the year was out. Thus Reza Khan was left in de facto control, though he did not assume the prime ministership until 1923. Finally, in 1925, the shah, who had fled to Europe, was officially deposed and Reza was enthroned as the first ruler of the Pahlawi dynasty. Like his most successful predecessors, he realized that political power in warlike Persia demanded the elimination of all military forces not directly dependent on his bounty. In successive campaigns his efficient army, equipped with the most modern weapons, brought every dissident element to heel, including the semiautonomous, nomadic tribes such as the Bakhtiari who had frequently intervened effectively in Persian politics. Not for centuries had the realm been so thoroughly pacified and unified.

At the same time, the financial structure of the state underwent a thorough overhaul to provide the resources needed for the support of a modern, centralized government. Again, an American expert, Dr. Arthur C. Millspaugh, was employed under a five-year contract (1922–1927) with almost unlimited authority to put the Persian house in order. Taxes were reformed from top to bottom and they were rigorously collected, much to the dismay of landlords and other privileged individuals who had previously been able to evade payment of their fair share. Corruption, which was part of the way of life, could not be eradicated, but it was substantially reduced. As a result of these financial reforms, the budget was balanced, in spite of the enlarged function of the central government and massive expenditures on modernization of the 40,000 man army. Millspaugh refused to accept a new contract limiting his powers and was dismissed. In any event, his job had been done well.

Reza Shah's approach to modernization was closely similar to that of Kemal whom he admired and, it would seem, emulated. But he was handicapped by his much lesser knowledge of the West and the comparatively more backward and conservative condition of his land and people. Therefore, the overall effect of his efforts at modernization was less thoroughgoing and successful than those of Kemal.

In military affairs, his area of special concern and competence, he did not stint, knowing full well that in Persia political authority traditionally depended on military strength. His typically Persian nationalism showed in his dismissal of foreign military advisors and his refusal to incur foreign debts for any purpose. He was, if anything, more hard-working, energetic, and strait-laced, never giving way to the wild debauchery that characterized Kemal's mode of relaxation. Indeed, he seems to have lacked the ability to attract and delegate responsibility to loyal supporters—perhaps because of the smaller reservoir of trained talent. Instead, he relied more and more on surprise visits to discipline his subordinates, meting out severe punishments to those found loafing on the job. As a result, he took upon himself too much responsibility, which took its toll, leading him to become increasingly introverted and despotic. Over the years the experience of power eroded the affable personality that had once commanded the voluntary loyalty of his troops.

In politics, he was even more dictatorial than Kemal, abandoning the idea of a republic when it became apparent that the people were too deeply wedded to monarchism. When he did not entirely ignore the *Majlis*, it was utilized as only a rubber stamp for his decisions. Rigorous censorship suppressed the expression of any opposition.

The Shiite hierarchy posed the strongest obstacle to reform and the exercise of political authority. Therefore, secularism became a central feature of Reza Shah's reform program. Whether or not he was influenced by Kemal's actions, they at least provided examples. In his case, however, the primary motivation, as in the military sphere, seems to have been the removal of all authority that might compete with his own. The vast estates in perpetual trusts that supported the independence of the religious institution and its schools, hospitals, and other enterprises were seized for the benefit of the state, reducing the religious hierarchy to dependence on governmental stipends. The religious schools through which their doctrines had been propagated were closed, and state-controlled compulsory education was prescribed. Unfortunately, performance could not measure up to promise principally because of the lack of trained teachers to staff the schools. In addition to eradicating the educational influence of Shiite Islam, other popular public activities were banned, including the performances of dervishes and the penitential parades commemorating the deaths of Ali, Hasan, and Husayn. Finally, the legal influence of religious courts was curtailed by the introduction of a secular judicial system on the French model. The effectiveness of these religious reforms varied greatly, being almost negligible in remote regions, but wherever he could apply his authority directly, Reza Shah made it unquestionably clear that he expected absolute obedience and submission. Therefore, the important religious leaders were effectively shackled. On one occasion in 1928 when a preacher dared to criticize the queen for appearing in public without a veil, the shah marched into the mosque without removing his boots and publicly whipped the offender. Obviously the traditional right of sanctuary would no longer be respected. The wearing of the veil was officially proscribed in 1935.

Military preparedness and national independence of foreign influence appear to have been the primary factors in determining the major projects for economic modernization. Although Reza Shah recognized that agriculture was in serious need of reform and development, the ownership of most arable land by absentee landlords, which he proved reluctant to challenge except for his own personal gain, militated against anything more substantial than model farms as examples of what might be done. Instead, road and rail communications received major attention. His pet project was the tremendously difficult and expensive rail line, completed in 1938, traversing the mountains and connecting the Persian Gulf with the Caspian Sea. In less than 900 miles it rose from below sea level to nearly 9000 feet and then descended to sea level passing en route through 224 tunnels and over innumerable bridges. In accordance with his determination to stay free of foreign debt the entire cost of the project was paid for by locally generated funds, principally the earnings of state monopolies of sugar, tea, opium, and oil. This costly engineering feat was strategically justified not only because it provided swift transportation for military forces between the most important regions in the north and the south but also because it gave access to the restless and warlike nomadic tribes. During World War II, it also served as a valuable route for the delivery of American supplies to the beleaguered Soviet Union, though Reza Shah hardly had any such usage in mind. In fact, at the time, both Britain and Russia were opposed to its construction.

In the industrial area, quite a few factories were built for the production of a variety of goods from heavy construction materials to consumers' products. Most of these were state financed and operated enterprises. Although their efficiency was handicapped by a severe shortage of trained technicians and managers, they were able to operate profitably because of the government's control of foreign trade that eliminated foreign competition. Nevertheless, high prices limited the contribution of these facilities to the economy, and the industrialization program must be adjudged unsatisfactory in terms of Iranian needs.

In the light of his heavy emphasis on military development, Reza Shah's conduct of foreign relations was surprisingly moderate. His most vigorous stand was taken on his demand for better terms from the Anglo-Persian Oil Company, but the demands were reasonable and after a belligerent demonstration by the British navy, the company finally signed a revised concessionary agreement in 1933. His one other strong action was the repudiation in 1928 of the capitulations under which foreigners had enjoyed a special, favored status, but this action was no more than an expression of the nationalism that also led in 1935 to the adoption of the broader, generic name of Iran in place of the more parochial Persia. In 1937 Reza Shah hosted at Saadabad the meeting at which a pact was signed with Iran's neighbors, Turkey, Iraq, and Afghanistan, pledging mutual friendship, cooperation, and nonaggression.

During the later thirties, he was increasingly attracted to Nazi Germany, which followed policies he could readily understand and appreciate. Furthermore, the predatory trading policies of the Soviet Union and the general constriction of foreign trade caused by the worldwide depression led him, like Kemal, to look favorably on the generous trade agreements offerd by the Nazi regime. Thousands of Germans of every description inundated the land. Perhaps most flattering were the Nazi scholars who attempted to demonstrate that Iran was the Aryan homeland, still retaining in their purest form elements of ancient Aryan culture. All these factors of mutual attraction contributed to a rapid expansion of trade as well as other exchanges between the two countries until at the outbreak of World War II 45 percent of Iran's foreign trade had been captured by Germany.

The shah's ultranationalism was also reflected in efforts at literary reform and cultural purification. Following up earlier steps in these directions, emphasis on ancient Persian achievements and purging of Arabic loan words from the Persian language were encouraged. As a military man of limited education, however, Reza Shah felt only a small concern for cultural nationalism and not push the program.

Although Reza Shah proclaimed his nation's neutrality, he clearly favored Germany and expected a German victory. When Germany attacked Russia in the summer of 1941, strategic necessity forced Britain and the Soviet Union to violate Iranian neutrality. The shah was compelled to abdicate in favor of his son, Muhammed Reza Shah, who agreed to cooperate with the Allies. For the balance of the war Iran was for all practical purposes an occupied country with Americans playing a major role after their entry into the war. Iran formally declared war on Germany in 1943.

During the war the government and the economy suffered grievous setbacks, almost obliterating Reza Shah's accomplishments. As an almost powerless puppet, the new shah soon lost the respect and control of those elements who had been kept in line by the ruthless dictatorship of Reza Shah. Nomads easily secured arms and ignored the central government, religious leaders once more dared to attack the secular authority of the state, and landowners fell into their old custom of neglecting to pay taxes. Expenditures of more than 30,000 American and Allied troops and the employment of large numbers of Iranians in supply services funneled a tremendous infusion of money into the economy without a compensating supply of consumers' goods. The economic problem was compounded by a crop failure in 1942 and continued food shortages in subsequent years. Consequently, the country suffered another round of severe inflation with prices of essential goods multiplying ten times as they had during World War I. American lend-lease only prevented more drastic hardships. Or course, some wily operators made fortunes, but their publicized successes merely added to the discontents and unrest of the people. Dr. Millspaugh was again invited to stabilize governmental finances, but chaotic conditions and a weak government handicapped his efforts. Other American advisors reorganized the army and the police in the hope of strengthening the government's hand in internal affairs.

While the United States remained pre-occupied with its military functions and British concern was limited to the protection and exploitation of the vital oil resources, the Soviet Union took advantage of its occupation of northern Iran and popular unrest to propagate communism and sponsor the communist-led Tudeh (Mass) party, organized in 1942. Russian subsidies contributed to a surprising proliferation of anti-Western and leftist newspapers and periodicals that fed on the latent discontent. Late in 1944, when the end of the war was in sight, the Russians tightened their grip on the north, barring government tax collectors and foreign journalists, repulsing government troops sent to suppress dissidents, and ignoring all Iranian protests, while Tudeh-sponsored riots racked the capital. Then in the fall of 1945 they backed secessionist movements to establish independent governments by the Turkish-speaking people of Azerbaijan and the Kurds of northwestern Iran. In the spring of 1946 the crisis deepened when British and American troops were withdrawn in conformance with treaty obligations, leaving Iran on its own to deal with the Russian menace. An appeal to the United Nations was thwarted by a Russian veto, which presented the youthful organization with its first crisis. Without external support, except world opinion, the wily Iranian prime minister resorted to diplomatic maneuvers to outwit the communist colossus. He managed to convince the Russian government that he could extract from the *Majlis* the long sought oil concession if Russian troops were withdrawn. To convince the Soviet Union of his sincerity, he included some Tudeh leaders in his cabinet. Then in a swift and complex turn of events the Tudeh members of the cabinet were expelled and the Iranian army overran the two republics, declared martial law, and executed a number of rebel leaders. While the world cheered this victory of David over Goliath, Russia stood immobilized by world opinion and the promise of oil concessions. Keeping his pledge, the prime minister presented the proposed oil agreement to the *Majlis* the following summer where, after appropriate deliberation, it was rejected and the government was directed to find a way of regaining national control over the British oil concession. Russia might fume and foment trouble through its agent, the Tudeh party, but the deed was done. Moreover, as events were to show, the enthusiastic and ardent nationalism stirred up by this controversy presaged trouble for the principal foreign concession, the Anglo-Iranian Oil Company.

Although nationalistic pressure was to be the driving force in the future clash with the British-controlled company, the underlying factor was the postwar economic difficulties and dreams of Iran and the failure to obtain the anticipated Western, and particularly American, aid for a planned, seven-year development program. As early as 1943, following the Teheran Conference, President Roosevelt had indicated that underdeveloped Iran would be an ideal candidate for a demonstration of what an altruistic technical and economic aid program could accomplish. From the Iranian point of view, distant, rich, and productive America, with comparatively clean hands in foreign relations, was the best prospect, if foreign assistance was to be accepted. In 1946, in the midst of its postwar troubles, an Iranian planning board drew up a two billion dollar, seven-year program, inadequately supported by basic research. Thereupon, an American engineering firm was employed to make a thorough feasibility study and present a revised plan. The new plan reduced the projects to ones that could pay for themselves and cut back the expenditures to a total of 650 million dollars of which 250 million was to be financed by a foreign loan. On the basis of this report Iran applied to the International Bank for the loan. While Iran's economic situation worsened, consummation of the loan was delayed by uncertainty about the country's internal stability. The United States authorized a grant of surplus military equipment to bolster Iran's armed forces, but the first shipments did not arrive until 1949.

In any case, the American government was preoccupied by European problems and skeptical about investment in a country so plagued by political instability and corruption.

In 1949 the announcement by President Truman of the Point Four Program for aid to underdeveloped countries raised new hopes and encouraged the shah to visit the United States to make a direct, personal appeal for assistance. The President pledged American support and aid but indicated that the shah should take some concrete steps to improve the investment climate of his country. Upon his return the shah appointed an anticorruption commission as an indication of his intention to institute reforms. He also set an example of land reform for other landlords by beginning a program of dissolving royal estates and selling the parcels of land on easy terms to the peasants who farmed them. The landlords, however, proved less than enthusiastic about following the shah's example. Finally, the Korean conflict, which broke out the following year, absorbed the bulk of American attention and resources and deferred the prospect of substantial American aid for several years.

By 1949, then, Iran had generated a powerful nationalism but had failed to match this spirit with the restoration of an efficient central government and a modernization program comparable to those of Reza Shah. Party politics were explosive, religious leaders used their prestige to add to the political unrest, corruption and inefficiency crippled the bureaucracy, wealthy men with influence ignored the tax collector, and the landless peasant continued to carry the burden of the economy on his weak shoulders. While foreign-owned oil wells pumped Iran's one vital natural resource out of the ground for sale abroad, payments to the government declined because of the British Labor party's restrictive policies on dividends. The target for the concentration of nationalistic frustration with economic stagnation and even delay was obvious.

ARAB NATIONALISM AND THE WEST

Prior to 1905 the signs of nationalism were much less apparent in the Arab provinces of the Ottoman Empire, with the exception of the autonomous provinces of Lebanon and Egypt, which also enjoyed more extensive cultural, commercial, and political relations with the West. In Lebanon, however, the despotic policies of Abul Hamid II had forced most outspoken nationalists and modernists to flee to British-controlled Egypt or European cities. Cairo and Paris became centers of Arab intellectual and nationalist revival. At the time of the Young Turk coup in 1908 some underground groups were operating in Arab cities, and almost without exception they supported the Young Turks until the pro-Turkish policy threatened Arab identity. Suppression of Arab political societies by the increasingly authoritarian Young Turk regime only had the predictable consequence of spawning a host of secret organizations that included many former Arab members of the Society of Union and Progress. In 1913 an Arab congress brought together delegates of various groups and endorsed a joint demand for Arab home rule under a federal structure for the empire. Although the Young Turks ostensibly bowed to this demand, nothing in the way of reform ensued before the war—only more repression. Therefore, at the outbreak of World War I, the Arab provinces were seething with a growing unrest, though activism was limited to a few thousand informed leaders without any substantial popular following. Turko-British hostilities, particularly in the Syria-Palestine theater, justified much more ruthless repression of everyone suspected of subversive intentions, but at the same time British interest in recruiting local support opened a fresh opportunity for Arab nationalism to those peninsular princes who could command a significant body of troops rather than the intellectual dissidents without numerous followers.

Prior to the war, expeditions to the traditional graveyard of Ottoman armies, the Yemen and neighboring Asir, failed to discipline their rulers, and the Young Turks could do no more than acknowledge their exercise of greater autonomy. In 1908 the Young Turks had forced the reluctant sultan to appoint Husayn, the hereditary Sharif of Mecca and head of the Hashemite family descended from the Prophet, as governor of the Hijaz. Without Abdul Hamid's railroad to Medina, which facilitated the support of a strong garrison in the sacred city of Mecca, the Young Turks might have lost control of the spiritual center of Islam. Meanwhile, the champion of the Wahhabi sect, Ibn Sa'ud, continued to build his independent power in central Arabia, pushing back his traditional tribal foes, the Rashids, and expelling Turkish authority from the coast of the Persian Gulf in 1913. His romantic career had begun in 1901 when with a small band of loyal followers he had left sanctuary in Kuwait and seized by stealth his family's former capital of Riyadh. Drawing on the religious appeal of Wahhabism and the personal loyalty of tribal chiefs he expanded his influence. The core of his military strength came from the formation of a brotherhood composed of former bedouins whom he supported in small agricultural settlements.

During the war Ibn Sa'ud accepted a British subsidy but refused to take an active part in the conflict, preferring to husband his resources. On the other hand, the ambitious Husayn, in the famous Husayn-McMahon correspondence, finally agreed in 1916 to lead an armed Arab revolt in return for typically vague British assurances to support the establishment of an Arab state encompassing all Arab lands except those under British control, such as Aden, Oman, Kuwait, and the Syrian coastal strip in which the French were interested. At the same time the British were concluding the secret Sykes-Picot agreement for the division of the whole Fertile Crescent and Desert Bay regions between France and Britain. Husayn did not

learn of this deception until the publication of the secret treaties late in 1917 by the Russian revolutionary regime. Almost simultaneously Arab nationalism received another blow when the Balfour Declaration gave British approval to the creation of a national home for the Jewish people in Palestine so long as "nothing shall be done which may prejudice the civil and religious rights of existing non-Jewish communities ...." Nevertheless, British diplomacy succeeded in retaining the support of Husayn and his forces for the duration of the war by an assurance of British dedication to the doctrine of popular self-determination. Husayn's troops, commanded by his third son, Prince Faysal, effectively protected the desert flank of the British army as it advanced northward through Palestine and Syria. In October 1918, the Arabs liberated Damascus and at the time of the armistice were pressing against the defenses of Aleppo.

Faysal, elated at the prospect of Arab independence, went to the Paris Peace Conference as his father's emissary but soon was disillusioned by the duplicity and broken pledges of the Allies. In mid-1919 an Arab congress met in Arab-held Damascus and demanded an independent state covering Syria, Lebanon, and Palestine under Faysal as constitutional ruler and another state covering British occupied Iraq to be ruled by his elder brother, Prince Abdullah. The delegates also denounced the treacherous Sykes-Picot agreement, the Balfour Declaration, and the mandate concept in terms closely similar to those then being expressed in the Kemalist congress in Turkey. Arab defiance might have paralleled that of the Turks, but their chosen leader, Faysal, was not made of the same stern fiber as Kemal.

Ignoring the Arab nationalist demand for independence, an Anglo-French division of the spoils was reached in September giving Syria and Lebanon to the French, and in December French troops replaced British troops in the occupation of the coastal area. Driven to desperation, the Arab congress proclaimed an independent kingdom of the whole of Syria-Lebanon-Palestine in March 1920. But when the French issued an ultimatum and began a march on Damascus, Faysal capitulated and even ordered the disbanding of his army. In the face of unauthorized resistance the French general ignored Faysal's surrender to the French mandate, fought his way into the city, and soon overran the rest of Syria. For the moment the Arab nationalist movement had been crushed.

Although not officially confirmed by the League of Nations for several years, the French mandate over Syria-Lebanon and the British mandates over Palestine, Transjordan, and Iraq were in fact established, carving the Fertile Crescent and Desert Bay into political units that Arab nationalism has yet to overcome. The French high commissioner then proceeded immediately to subdivide the French area into four units in a policy denounced as one of "divide and rule." Suffice it to say that it did little to foster the larger unity needed to realize the independence a Class A mandate was intended to achieve after a reasonably brief period of tutelage. Each of the units was equipped with a French governor and an administrative staff, more or less French according to the availability of able and trustworthy Arab civil servants. Later, elected councils and even constitutional parliamentary regimes gave the appearance of self-government in response to agitation inspired by Britain's more liberal policies, but the freely exercised authority of the high commissioner, backed up by the French garrison, made the apparent movement toward independence merely a convenient fiction. Just as distressing to many Arab nationalists was the French stress on their "civilizing mission." French was required as a second language in all schools, and the many strictly French schools that were set up received the lion's share of financial support. Textbooks were rewritten to reflect French ideas. Of course, French was established as the official language of the government and the courts. Never-

theless, French rule did contribute important benefits. Communications were expanded, educational facilities multiplied, public health programs eradicated the worst ravages of disease, and the general standard of living improved so substantially that despite population growth emigration declined. To Arab nationalists, however, these material improvements did not compensate for the deprivation of freedom to fashion their own destiny as a nation. Not until after World War II did the states of Syria and Lebanon secure independence from a reluctant France.

In Iraq and Transjordan Britain followed a more liberal course taking seriously its obligation under the Class A mandates to foster progress toward full independence at the earliest possible date. In any case, British strategic interest in these states along the high road to India could most economically be served by stable regimes that looked to Britain for advice and defense. Shackled with the contradictory provisions of the Balfour Declaration, however, the administration of the Palestinian mandate presented Britain with a dilemma that it was never able to resolve.

In 1920, only one month after the announcement of Britain's mandate over Iraq, a costly rebellion broke out testing British resolve and goodwill. In response to this challenge, Sir Percy Cox, who had spent many years in Iraq as a British official and won a measure of popular esteem and affection, was appointed high commissioner and permitted to recruit a staff of old hands in Middle Eastern affairs. Once the rebellion was quelled, Prince Faysal, whom the French had ejected from the kingship of Syria, was named king of what was to become a constitutional monarchy, perhaps as partial atonement for the frustration of his father's dream of an Arab Kingdom and reward for his services during the war. Since several hundred of his officers had settled in Iraq after the dissolution of the Arab army, he enjoyed important local support in addition to military prestige. One of these officers, Nuri es-Said, became the leading figure in Iraqi politics, serving in one important post or another whenever he was not the prime minister. The constitution of 1924 provided for a parliamentary system of government fashioned after the British model. Iraqi politics, however, tended to swirl around a few key figures who rotated portfolios in ever-changing cabinets, while British advisors labored behind the scenes to keep the ship of state on an even keel and to protect British interests against constant Iraqi attacks. Each cabinet would win support by promising to eliminate British influence, a promise it knew it could not fulfill, and then resign to give another combination the opportunity to fail. The appeals to Iraqi nationalism, however, served the useful purpose of submerging the potentially explosive internal divisions between Sunni and Shi'a Muslims, Kurd and Arab, tribesmen and townsmen and of developing gradually a more substantial sense of nationhood. Step by step Britain made concessions. In 1930 a treaty agreement was reached which qualified Iraq for admission as an independent state to the League of Nations in 1932 and termination of the mandate. The central feature of the treaty was a 25-year alliance providing for "consultations" in foreign affairs, the maintenance of British air bases and troops, and a number of other provisions granting Britons a favored position in Iraq. An important factor in the negotiations was the need to defend the rich oil resources discovered when a gusher was struck in 1927 by an international consortium that came to be known as the Iraq Petroleum Company. In 1931 the company negotiated a more comprehensive concession in return for its agreement to build a pipeline to the Mediterranean and to provide assured annual payments against future royalties. Thus the new nation, like Iran before it, gained a valuable, supplemental source of revenue to support its independence.

Transjordan occupied the predominantly desert land stretching between Palestine and Iraq. Again, Britain found it politic to reward the second son of Husayn, Prince Abdullah, with the emirate of this buffer region between the desert and the sown in 1921. As a police force to check Bedouin depredations the British organized and subsidized the famed Arab Legion which in time developed into the best disciplined and most effective military force in the Arab world. Since this impoverished land without any known natural resource to exploit could not support a modern government, it was subsidized and controlled in both internal and external affairs by the British government operating through Emir Abdullah. Genuine independence was not achieved until after World War II and even then as a kingdom it continued to require foreign subsidies.

The perplexing problem of Palestine stemmed directly from the Balfour Declaration of 1917, which had been made under strong Zionist pressure to win the active support of world Jewry for the Allies. Although many orthodox Jews were not sympathetic with the Zionist goal of a national homeland, the Zionists did command the support of much of the wealthiest and most influential elements of the Jewish community in the West and were in a far better position than the Arabs to persuade the British government to see things their way. Furthermore, the British were principally interested in the strategic position of Palestine with regard to Arabia and the Suez Canal and saw an advantage in developing a vigorous, progressive community of Westernized Jews, sympathetic to Western ideas and objectives and dependent on its connection with the West, and particularly Britain.

In 1920, however, the Muslims in Palestine outnumbered the Jews by more than ten to one, and even the Christian community was larger than the Jewish one. Moreover, the 50,000 Jews included some who were culturally Arab and a much larger number of elderly individuals who had only come to pray and die in the Holy Land. At best, the

Zionist base in Palestine was very small. Nevertheless, even before establishment of the mandate the Zionist organization with headquarters in London immediately went to work to raise funds and encourage migration to Palestine on the largest possible scale. Ardent Zionists had no doubt that in time a Jewish national state encompassing the whole area would be created. The vagueness and reservations of the Balfour Declaration were ignored as meaningless verbiage that could not be allowed to frustrate the Zionist goal. From the beginning small clashes occurred and a vital part of Zionist baggage became arms to defend themselves. However, the slowness of the Arab community in recognizing the Zionist threat and in organizing to combat it cannot be stressed strongly enough. The British explained that no more was intended than the provision of a cultural and religious home for the Jews, not a political state, and Arab leaders had no objection to such a proposal. After all, what did they have to fear from a few thousand immigrants, most of whom were unequipped for life outside an urban area? Furthermore, many absentee Arab landlords found it profitable to sell their lands at inflated prices. Only gradually did the Arab community as a whole become alarmed, especially after 1933 when the anti-Semitic policies of the Nazi regime in Germany stimulated a rapid increase in the number of Jewish immigrants. Even then the Arab leadership lacked the resources to finance a campaign such as the Jewish Agency collected annually from world Jewry, particularly in the United States. The main Arab strength was in numbers, which as late as 1939 exceeded the Jews in Palestine by more than two to one.

A pattern soon evolved. An increase in immigration generated objections by the Arab leadership, backed up by riots and violence. The British government restricted immigration until pressure on the home government forced the gates open again. The high commissioners found it impossible to comply with their instructions to cooperate with the Zionists and at the same time pre-serve the rights and position of the Arabs because neither side showed any willingness to compromise. Every British effort to implement some form of self-government in accordance with the provisions of the mandate was thwarted by the refusal of one side or the other to cooperate for fear it would give some advantage to the other. As both Arabs and Jews came to realize that the British government reacted to violence, both increased the resort to this weapon and organized groups equipped and trained to carry out terroristic actions swiftly and effectively. Haganah (Defense), the oldest and largest illegal force, was originally formed under Zionist auspices to defend the scattered and vulnerable Jewish agricultural settlements. Irgun (Zionist Nationalist Army) and the Stern Gang were smaller, more radical groups, unwilling to settle for anything less than a Jewish national state covering the whole of Palestine.

The heavy influx of new settlers after 1933 increased communal tension to the breaking point. Frustrated by the rejection of every proposal for cooperative self-government and by the growing incidence of disorder and violence, a British commission of inquiry in 1936 recommended partition, but all parties—Zionists, non-Zionists, and Arabs—denounced the plan. This impasse set the stage for what was at once a civil war between Arabs and Jews and a rebellion by both against the alleged inadequacies and injustices of British rule, to which the British regime reacted by much more rigorous measures of repression and punishment and a cutback in immigration quotas. Full defiance of the British government by the Zionists was forestalled only by the outbreak of World War II when all parties called off hostilities for the duration.

In 1942, American Zionists, meeting at the Biltmore Hotel in New York, drew up the uncompromising Biltmore Program, demanding unlimited immigration and a Jewish state encompassing all of Palestine. In view of their influence on the American government and the importance of American support during and after the war, the Biltmore Program was tantamount to an ultimatum. Toward the end of the war the pressure built up to accommodate refugees from the Nazi terror by settlement in Palestine. Thousands of displaced persons were illegally smuggled into that troubled land through the efforts of the American-financed Jewish Agency, and positive steps were taken to deter the American government from relaxing the restrictions on immigration into the United States where most Jewish refugees preferred to go. At the end of the war, David Ben-Gurion, the new head of the Jewish Agency in Palestine threatened the British with an all-out struggle if the demands of the Biltmore Program were not met. In preparation for such a struggle the Haganah, as well as the Irgun and the Stern Gang, acquired by one means or another a supply of modern weapons, including even tanks. All three organizations agreed to coordinate their activities and in October 1945 they initiated a round of terrorist attacks intended to intimidate war-weary Britain. Furthermore, President Truman urged the new Labor government to accept the Zionist demand for the immediate admission of 100,000 immigrants. The British were torn between their interest in doing justice to the Arabs, the American-backed Zionist demands, and the need of an impoverished economy for retrenchment. Thus the stage was set for the final act in the drama leading to partition and the creation of the new state of Israel.

As the intellectual center of Arab nationalism, Egypt was as interested as any part of the Arab world, first, in winning freedom from foreign domination, and second, in repelling the progress of Zionism in Palestine. Although officially an autonomous region within the Ottoman Empire, Egypt since the 1880s had been subjected to British control and for all important purposes severed from the sultanate. Therefore, in ensuing years, nationalism tended to concentrate more on the immediate problem of expelling British imperialism rather than on the broader Arab cause. After the death of Mus-

tafa Kamil in 1908, the more volatile Saad Zaghlul took the mantle of leadership over the Egyptian nationalist movement. The British resident, Lord Kitchener, victor over the Mahdi and conqueror of the Sudan, found it impossible to get along with Zaghlul; yet, in 1913, he found himself confronted by this troublesome man as president of the new legislative assembly granted by the British in the hope of staving off nationalist demands. Egypt was on the verge of full-throated resistance when World War I intervened.

Upon Ottoman entrance into the conflict Britain unilaterally proclaimed a protectorate over Egypt and asserted its independence by giving to the puppet ruler the title of sultan. Rigid application of censorship and martial law suppressed Zaghlul's nationalists for the duration, while conscription of men and animals complemented wartime dislocation and inflation in inflicting severe hardship on the people. The wartime disregard for Egyptian sensibilities generated an upsurge in nationalistic feeling among all levels of society, which the British government failed to appreciate.

Immediately after the war, Saad Zaghlul requested permission to lead a delegation (*wafd*) to London for the discussion of nationalist demands which, if conceded, would have amounted to the granting of full independence. However, the British government refused to consider consultations with one who had no official standing in the Egyptian government. Such a high-handed rebuff, however justified, ignited nationalistic enthusiasm for Zaghlul and his party, henceforth known as Wafdists, who rapidly organized mass support among the people. The arrest and deportation of Zaghlul and three other leaders sparked an outbreak of violence and rebellion throughout the land. Although the rebellion was quelled with the aid of reinforcements from abroad, it did awaken the British government to an appreciation of the strength of the nationalist movement.

After further negotiation and agitation Britain proclaimed the termination of its protectorate and the independence of Egypt in

1922 without consultation or agreement with any Egyptian elements. Martial law, under which British authority had been exercised since 1914, was soon ended. However, Britain retained the right to protect and defend its interests until a satisfactory treaty was negotiated with the Egyptian government. Thus, the British continued to exercise the powers of a protectorate in fact, if not in name. In 1923 the king (formerly sultan) issued a constitution of a parliamentary type with a two-house legislature, and elections were held in the fall. Zaghlul and other deported Wafdist leaders returned in time to contest the elections and win an overwhelming majority of the seats in the Chamber of Deputies.

As leader of the anti-British nationalist movement, Zaghlul found it politically impossible to make the concessions necessary to consummate a treaty between England and Egypt. Agitation and violence created crisis after crisis in Anglo-Egyptian relations. Zaghlul died in 1927, but his successor as the head of the Wafdists continued to dominate the unstable political scene whenever free elections gave him an opportunity to demonstrate the popular strength of his party. Finally in 1936 the threat posed by the Italian conquest of Ethiopia and the military tension in Europe overcame anti-British feeling and made Egyptians willing to accept a treaty granting England the right to develop facilities for the defense of Egypt and the Suez Canal. The treaty provided for a 20-year alliance that was more palatable than the actual occupation. Under the Montreux Convention the mixed courts and all extraterritorial privileges were scheduled for gradual abolition over a period of years, and the capitulations were terminated. Sensitive feeling on the Sudan, presumably under a joint condominium since 1899 but actually ruled by the British, was appeased by authorizing Egyptian immigration and the employment of Egyptian troops, if absolutely necessary, to maintain order.

During World War II Egypt again be-

came a major British base occupied by tens of thousands of foreign troops. The British command did not hesitate to use force for the suppression of all real or potential opposition, whether it emanated from the court, the reactionary Muslim Brotherhood, or fascist sympathizers. Even after the Axis threat under the command of General Rommel was decisively thrown back from El Alamein in 1942, the Middle East Command continued to rule Egypt like a conquered land. So little regard was felt for the Egyptian government that no one was concerned with its failure to declare war until early in 1945 simply to qualify for admission as a charter member of the United Nations. The effect of the war on the livelihood of the Egyptian people was mixed. Severe inflation caused suffering to certain sectors of the population, but Allied purchases stimulated production and employment and built up large credits in blocked accounts payable over a period of years after the war. Furthermore, the high-handed practices of the Middle East Command kept at a fever pitch nationalistic resentment at the continued presence of foreign troops on Egyptian soil.

Shortly after the war, these sentiments, capitalized upon by the Wafd opposition and other dissident elements, forced the government to seek treaty revision to move up the date for the final withdrawal of British forces from the whole of Egypt, including the Canal Zone. The negotiations foundered, however, on the issue of the Sudan, where Britain insisted on the Sudanese right of self-determination against the Egyptian claim of sovereignty, and on British reluctance to surrender the defense of the Suez Canal. An appeal to the United Nations failed to win sufficient support, but the actual evacuation of British forces from the rest of Egypt undermined the intensity of anti-British feeling that had broken out in frequent riots. In any case, most Egyptians were equally, if not more, concerned with the corrupt and exploitive character of the inefficient government headed by luxury-loving King Farouk and the critical struggle between Arab and Jew building up to a major crisis in neighboring Palestine.

THE ARAB LEAGUE AND THE PARTITION OF PALESTINE

The hopes raised by the Arab Revolt during World War I for a broader-based Arab unification and independence covering Arabia and the Fertile Crescent had been aborted for the time being by the creation of the British and French mandates. In view of the long record of divisions and personal hostilities that had characterized Arab politics since the early days of Islam, the prospect of maintaining such unity, even if given the chance, seems highly unlikely, particularly when the need to adapt to the modern world is added to the list of difficulties to be overcome. Arab nationalism was fractured into parochial struggles against Western domination with little regard for what was taking place elsewhere, until the growing severity of the struggle in Palestine in 1937 attracted mutual concern for the Arab cause. In 1939 Britain invited the Arab governments to attend a conference on the problem of Palestine, which enhanced their sense of responsibility for the welfare of their hard-pressed brethren.

During the interwar years the one important independent Arab state, the Wahhabi Kingdom of Ibn Sa'ud, expanded its territory and resources. In 1921 his forces, spearheaded by the brotherhood, seized the Rashidi capital, eliminating his traditional family foe. During the same years they also brought to heel all dissident tribes within his imprecisely demarcated realm and extended Sa'udi influence into Asir, which was threatened by the Yemen and the Hijaz of Husayn. In 1924 he took exception to Husayn's presumptuous assertion of succession to the caliphate upon its extinction by the Turkish Republic and easily overran the Hijaz with his disciplined troops. By this conquest he gained control of the sacred city of Mecca and shrewdly cultivated the pilgrimage by

generous treatment to expand his prestige in the Muslim world and supplement his scanty revenues. His consolidated realm, encompassing all of Arabia except Yemen, British Aden, and the British-protected shaykhdoms along the coast, was officially proclaimed in 1932 the Kingdom of Sa'udi Arabia. In 1934 he decisively defeated a Yemeni attack on Asir and granted such generous peace terms that his authority and reputation for chivalry, so important among bedouins, were established beyond challenge. Nevertheless, the expenses of maintaining such a vast state put severe strains on Arabia's small resources, leading him to welcome geological exploration for untapped mineral wealth in the 1930s.

One fruit of this work was the development by a foreign syndicate of a gold mine between Mecca and Medina that yielded several hundred thousand dollars in annual royalties, but far more important for the future was the discovery in 1938 of a major oil deposit inland from the Persian Gulf. Large scale development of this resource, however, had to be delayed by the American concessionaire, the Arabian American Oil Company (Aramco), until after World War II, and even then the full exploitation of this rich oil field had to await the completion of a pipeline to Sidon on the Mediterranean coast after 1949. The infusion of foreign money as well as foreign workers into the primitive economy and desert-type way of life of Arabia, during and after World War II was bound to have a heavy impact on the society and the economy. By 1949, however, the effect appeared to be limited to conspicuous consumption on a vast scale by the extensive royal family and its attendants; the deeper effect on the population at large was as yet scarcely perceptible.

The growing dependence of Britain and Western Europe on the development of major oil deposits in Sa'udi Arabia, Iraq, and the tiny shaykhdom of Kuwait, which almost literally floated on a sea of oil, greatly complicated the British position in Palestine. In addition, the vital importance of the Suez Canal and various pipelines through other Arab states and Palestine for the transportation of oil to the Mediterranean placed a further burden on British diplomacy in the Middle East. Yet postwar Britain was not in a position to antagonize the ardent American support of Zionism. Finally, the demand of its war-weary people for the rapid return of troops from abroad combined with the necessity for the strictest economy to put pressure on the British government for the swiftest possible reduction of the British military presence in the Middle East. Neither the Arab nationalists nor the Zionists, however, would give Britain any respite. Indeed, the accelerating tempo of hit-and-run attacks against British authority made the government realize that the military forces would have to be reinforced if the responsibility for maintaining law and order was to be effectively discharged.

Before the war Britain had invited the Arab states to take an interest in the Palestine dilemma and during the war had encouraged them to initiate positive steps toward cooperation and unity among themselves. Diversity in forms of government and local nationalism presented serious stumbling blocks to the implementation of this goal. In 1942 Nuri es-Said of Iraq suggested the creation of a Greater Syria including Lebanon, Palestine, and Transjordan (a dream Emir Abdullah had long entertained) and the formation of an Arab League as a basis for broader cooperation. Sa'udi Arabia and Egypt, however, were fearful of the challenge that might be presented by a Greater Syria, possibly in alliance with Iraq. Certainly Egypt saw in such an arrangement a potential threat to its predominant position and countered during the following years with suggestions for an Arab League that would not infringe in any way on the sovereignty of its members. Negotiations finally led to the formation of the Arab League by a pact signed March 1945 by Egypt, Sa'udi Arabia, Transjordan, Lebanon, Syria, and Iraq. The

agreement provided for a secretariat with permanent headquarters in Cairo and a council that would hold regular sessions twice a year. Although the principal incentive for the creation of such an organization was the growth of Zionism, it received no mention in the pact whose specific provisions dealt only with economic, social, cultural, and other nonpolitical forms of cooperation. Nowhere in the agreement was there any reference to military cooperation or to Zionism, though these subjects must have occupied an important place in the mind of each signatory. Therefore, from the beginning the Arab League was a weak vehicle for dealing with the leading, immediate concern of every member.

To return to the scene of conflict, British reluctance to alienate the Arabs by any relaxation of immigration restrictions, even in the face of American pressure, led to the sending of an Anglo-American Commission of Inquiry, which carried out an investigation in Palestine early in 1946 amid continued anti-British sabotage and terrorist attacks by the secret military arms of the Zionist organization. In view of the intensity of Arab-Jewish enmity, the commission saw no immediate prospect for the granting of independence, but it did endorse the American recommendation for the prompt admission of 100,000 Jewish immigrants. Britain was caught on the horns of an insoluble dilemma. It was left by the commission's report with the obligation to govern Palestine without the resources to maintain the number of troops adequate for the task. It was confronted by the Arab League's denunciation of large-scale Jewish immigration but was also under the additional pressure of the commission's recommendation to open the floodgates. Furthermore, virtually bankrupt, it was awaiting approval of a vital loan by the American Congress in which Zionist influence was strong.

A subsequent proposal to establish autonomous Arab and Jewish provinces was rejected by both sides principally because it fell short of the demand for immediate independence, but the Zionist organization demonstrated a promising flexibility by retreating from the absolute demand of the Biltmore Program for an independent state encompassing all of Palestine and indicating a willingness to consider partition if the Jewish state included the Negev as an area for future settlement and development. However, the hopes for a negotiated settlement proved to be short-lived. At an international Zionist meeting the radical leaders, headed by Ben-Gurion, showed their strength, and the American Zionist leadership declared its support for the radicals. The consequence was a resumption of terrorism in Palestine.

When a final partition proposal was rejected early in 1947 by both sides, the British government decided to refer the whole, insoluble problem to the United Nations. After investigation, a Special Committee representing eleven nations recommended partition and independence whenever both proposed states agreed to a ten-year economic union under which the more advanced Jewish state would contribute to the development of the poorer Arab state. Since close to 50 percent of the Jewish state would be Arab, there was no chance of Arab approval of this proposal, let alone agreement to the economic union. After explaining the futility of the plan, the British forswore any responsibility for enforcing it and announced their determination to give up the mandate, come what might, by May 15, 1948. In spite of British explanations a two-thirds majority of the General Assembly accepted the partition plan on November 29, 1947. Immediately bloody civil strife between Arab and Jew supplemented anti-British terrorism.

As the tempo of strife grew in ruthlessness and savagery, Arab forces were clandestinely strengthened by a supply of arms and volunteers from the Arab states, while the Zionist organization managed to smuggle an ever-growing amount of arms in support of the Jewish cause. Jewish attacks on Arab communities caused a mounting exodus of terrified Arabs. On the other hand, rigorous disciplinary measures and controls by the Zionists prevented Jews from seeking safety in flight.

A full-fledged civil war was in progress when the Zionists unilaterally proclaimed the creation of the independent state of Israel on May 14, 1948, the eve of the date of partition as proposed by the United Nations. Immediately the United States extended recognition, and the Soviet Union was not far behind. The Arab League had previously declared its total rejection of an independent Jewish state and promptly launched poorly coordinated attacks from all directions. Egyptian armies made a major attack from the south in two columns. The crack troops of the Arab Legion, reinforced by a large, but poorly trained and equipped, Iraqi force, occupied more deliberately the portion of Palestine adjoining Jordan including the old city of Jerusalem. For his own reasons King Abdullah of Jordan preferred to limit his attacks on Israel to steps essential to the protection of that territory he could expect to keep. If Abdullah had unleashed his forces, the fate of Israel would have been in serious doubt. Sporadic and ill-planned attacks from Syria and Lebanon were easily defeated, permitting Israeli commanders to concentrate their smaller forces against the major challenges. Although out-numbered, Israeli troops possessed the advantages of interior lines, a substantial reservoir of World War II veterans skilled in the use of modern weapons, more liberal financing, the do-or-die attitude of desperate men fighting for their very existence, and unity of command compared with the almost complete absence of coordination between the members of the Arab League. Nevertheless, the world was amazed by Israeli ability not only to defend their frontiers but also to win striking victories over the Egyptian forces.

The Security Council of the United Nations immediately dispatched Count Folke Bernadotte of Sweden to mediate the struggle, and he succeeded in arranging sev-

eral short-lived truces before being assassinated by a Stern Gang extremist fearful of
any check on Jewish victories. The abortive
truces actually worked to the advantage of
Israel by undermining what unity of purpose
the Arabs possessed and by giving Israeli
forces time to rearm and regroup before
launching another offensive. Between February and July of 1949 the American successor of Bernadotte, Ralph Bunche, was able to
conclude armistices bringing an end to official hostilities between Israel and the respective Arab states. Under the pressure of
Jewish victories in the field, the Arab states
were forced to agree to significant additions
to the Jewish state as originally proposed in
the partition plan, subject to the negotiation
of a permanent peace. Officially Israel and
the Arab states remain in a state of war. A
major obstacle to peace negotiations has
been the disposition of the approximately
700,000 Arab refugees who fled from Jewish
harassment before and during the war.

By 1949 the Middle East was entering a
new age, an age of concurrent revolution in
the social, economic, and political realms,
though the timetable varied from state to
state. All the Islamic states had gained the
substance of independence with the exception of the Sudan and the French North
African territories, but independence did not
assure modern government and a modern
way of life. These tasks, which may be subsumed under the term, modernization, remained to be accomplished. A major stimulus to modernization was the existence in
their midst of a modern, progressive Jewish
state which had exposed their weaknesses in
the war. In addition, the rapidly expanding
revenues from oil and oil transit were generating much of the necessary capital to finance
development programs in many of these
states. Finally, Western concern for the
maintenance of stability in the oil-rich
Middle East enhanced the prospect of generous development grants and loans from
Western governments and international organizations. Indeed, as we shall see, the extension of cold war competition beyond Turkey was in part a Soviet reaction to increased
American interest and investment in these
strategic borderlands.

SIGNIFICANT DATES

1907	Acceptance of Persian constitution by shah
1908	Coup by Committee of Union and Progress
1908	Discovery of oil in Persia
1911–1912	Italian conquest of Libya
1912–1913	Balkan wars
1916	C.U.P. victories of Gallipoli and Mesopotamia
1916	Husayn, Sharif of Mecca, joins Allies
1917	Balfour Declaration
1920–1923	Turkish independence struggle under Mustafa Kemal
1921	Persian coup of Reza Khan
1922	Grant of Egyptian independence by Britain
1925	Proclamation of Pahlawi Dynasty of Reza Shah
1930	Treaty granting independence to Iraq
1932	Proclamation of kingdom of Sa'udi Arabia
1941	Anglo-Russian deposition of Reza Shah
1942	Biltmore Program
1942	Communist Tudeh (Mass) Party sponsored by Russia
5–1946	Russian effort to detach Azerbaijan
1945	Formation of Arab League
1949	First Arab-Israeli War

SELECTED READINGS

*Antonius, George, *The Arab Awakening*. New York: G. P. Putnam's Sons, 1965.

Banani, Amin, *The Modernization of Iran, 1921–1941*. Stanford: Stanford University Press, 1961.

Binder, Leonard, *The Ideological Revolution in the Middle East*. New York: Wiley, 1964.

Bonne, Alfred, *State and Economics in the Middle East*. London: Routledge & Kegan Paul, 1955.

Browne, Edward G., *The Persian Revolution of 1905–1909*. New York: Barnes and Noble, 1966.

Buber, Martin, *Israel and Palestine: History of an Ideal*. New York: Schocken Books, 1952.

*Cottam, Richard, *Nationalism in Iran*. Pittsburgh: University of Pittsburgh Press, 1968.

Gibb, H. A. R., *Modern Trends in Islam*. Chicago: University of Chicago Press, 1947.

Haim, Sylvia G., ed., *Arab Nationalism: An Anthology*. Berkeley: University of California Press, 1962.

Heyd, Uriel, *The Foundations of Turkish Nationalism: The Life and Teachings of Ziya Gokalp*. London: Luzak, 1950.

Hourani, Albert H., *Minorities in the Arab World*. London: Oxford University Press, 1947.

Hurewitz, J. C., *Diplomacy in the Near and Middle East*. Vol. II; Princeton: Van Nostrand, 1956.

———, *The Struggle for Palestine*. New York: Norton, 1950.

Khadduri, Majid, *Independent Iraq*. London: Oxford University Press, 1960.

Kinross, Lord, *Ataturk*. New York: Morrow, 1965.

Lenczowski, George, *The Middle East in World Affairs*. 3rd ed.; Ithaca: Cornell University Press, 1962.

———, *Oil and State in the Middle East*. Ithaca: Cornell University Press, 1960.

———, *Russia and the West in Iran, 1918–1948*. Ithaca: Cornell University Press, 1949.

*Lewis, Bernard, *The Emergence of Modern Turkey*. London: Oxford University Press, 1961.

*———, *The Middle East and the West*. New York: Harper and Row, 1968.

*———, *Race and Color in Islam*. New York: Harper and Row, 1971.

Longrigg, Stephen H., *Oil in the Middle East: Its Discovery and Development*. London: Oxford University Press, 1961.

Longrigg, Stephen, and Stoakes, Frank, *Iraq*. London: Oxford University Press, 1958.

Millspaugh, Arthur C., *Americans in Persia*. Washington: Brookings Institute, 1946.

Nuseibeh, Hazem Z., *The Ideas of Arab Nationalism*. Ithaca: Cornell University Press, 1956.

Polk, William R., et al., *Backdrop to Tragedy: The Struggle for Palestine.* Boston: Beacon Press, 1957.

Ramsaur, Ernest E., *The Young Turks: Prelude to the Revolution of 1908.* Princeton: Princeton University Press, 1957.

Robinson, Richard D., *The First Turkish Republic.* Cambridge, Mass.: Harvard University Press, 1963.

*Sachar, Abram L., *History of the Jews.* 5th ed.; New York: Knopf, 1967.

Shuster, Morgan W., *The Strangling of Persia.* New York: Century, 1912.

Spector, Ivar, *The Soviet Union and the Muslim World.* Seattle: University of Washington Press, 1959.

*Weizmann, Chaim, *Trial and Error.* New York: Harper, 1949.

*Young, T. Cuyler, ed., *Near Eastern Culture and Society.* Princeton: Princeton University Press, 1951.

CHAPTER TWENTY-FOUR

NATIONALISM AND INDEPENDENCE IN SOUTHEAST ASIA

The diversity and divisions that have characterized this buffer region throughout its history were not significantly reduced by European domination. Indeed, the stress on the economic and even cultural dependence of each area on the homeland of the ruling power may be said to have accentuated these divisions. On the other hand, the more thoroughgoing conquest of their respective territories after 1870 (spurred on by more competitive European nationalism and the profitability of trade in less costly and bulkier cargoes made possible by the Suez Canal and the steamship) undermined or destroyed the authority of traditional rulers, exposed the people and their cultures more fully to the impact of Western ideas and exploitation, and encouraged progress toward thinking in terms of a larger territorial entity. A further challenge to the traditional order was presented by the even larger scale immigration of enterprising Indians and Chinese who came to perform many of the functions of an entreprenurial middle class in a semi-modernized economy. In the case of Malaya, indeed, Chinese immigrants came to constitute so large a proportion of the population that their presence actually deterred the growth of a Malayan nationalist movement. Of course, the differing policies and practices of the respective imperial powers created distinctive conditions in each case for the development of nationalism and progress toward independence. Therefore, the story of each is unique and must be examined separately. Only a few, very broad generalizations can be said to possess any common validity.

By 1905 none of the colonial domains had experienced a long enough period of thoroughgoing Western rule to generate an organized reaction reaching to the grass roots, with the notable exception of the Philippines. Moreover, only a handful of students had yet returned from Europe with educations revealing the discrepancy between European liberalism and imperial practice, and it would take time for them to devise means for expressing their dissatisfaction on more than an individual basis. Although the Japanese victory over Russia did cause a stir and the Japanese example furnished a model for modernization, World War I played a far more important role in awakening Southeast Asians to a realization of the fallibility of their European rulers. Indeed, it is interesting to note that the initial reactions on a significant scale were inspired as much by nativist resentment against the Indian and Chinese coexploiters as by hostility toward Western rule. In Siam, the one remaining independent state, national feeling was aroused far more by the economic dominance of the Chinese community than by the Western infringements on Siamese sovereignty, such as extraterritoriality and tariff restriction. In short, economic and cultural subordination in their own lands furnished the foundations for the political expression of nationalism. Under such circumstances socialist and communist doctrines were enabled to gain a fair foothold.

During the twenties the expansion of the market for Southeast Asian products, particularly in the United States, more or less kept pace with the growing economic needs, though most of the profits went to alien entrepreneurs. The devastating effect of increased dependence on world markets, however, was revealed when the collapse of prices for Southeast Asian products, accompanying the Great Depression, threw much

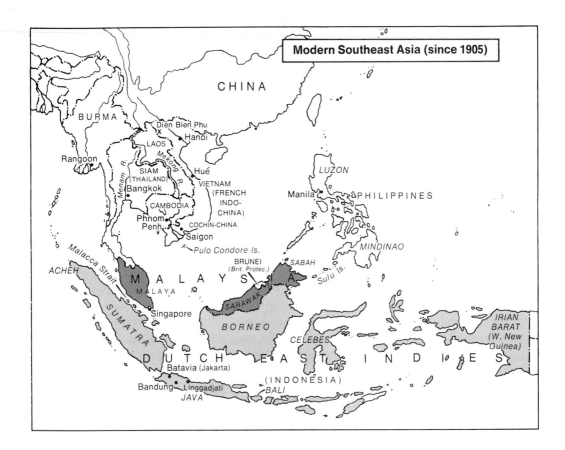

Modern Southeast Asia (since 1905)

of the region back to reliance on a subsistence economy during the thirties. The intensification of economic distress stimulated the growth of nationalistic demands, which each of the imperial powers met in its own way. The final blow to Western imperialism, however, was delivered by the Japanese conquests of 1941–1942 that exposed the weakness of Western garrisons as well as the absence of significant popular support for the colonial regimes.

In their own somewhat clumsy fashion he Japanese conquerors posed as liberators d cultivated the development of carefully trolled anti-Western nationalism under conception of a Greater East Asia Co-erity Sphere. By the end of the war rative self-governing regimes had been in most of the region which, even if little to support the Japanese war ef-

fort, could be expected to resist any reassertion of Western imperialism. After the war, France, Britain, and Holland sought to reestablish their rule over their former domains, and sooner or later each found it expedient to withdraw with greater or lesser grace as the case might be.

In each country, the national enthusiasm generated by the final realization of independence soon turned to disillusionment when the anticipated golden benefits failed to materialize. Political independence, it was soon discovered, did not mean economic independence. For too long the colonial economies had been adapted to dependence on the needs of Western markets. Such economic dependence on Western markets and prices, which were outside their control, constituted a galling limitation on the freedom of action of these new nations. Moreover, any effort to reorder their economies to reduce this dependence would require capital and technical assistance for agricultural and industrial development, and, until Soviet Russia entered the arena, the only source of such aid was the distrusted West. Most of these new nations were further handicapped by an inadequate supply of trained personnel to staff an efficient, modern administration, let alone the infrastructure essential to modernization. Furthermore, those students who went on to advanced education tended to favor law and letters rather than nation-building professions, such as agricultural science and engineering, which were deemed less prestigious. Finally, the open avowal, first by the Chinese Nationalists, and then by the Chinese Communists, of their ambition to reassert China's traditional influence in Southeast Asia reinforced the native hostility toward the alien Chinese minorities and aroused fears of a new Asian imperialism. The more recent efforts to advance the cause of communism in Southeast Asia by violence have done nothing to allay these fears. According to their evulation of the Chinese threat, the leaders of these nations have come forth with a wide spectrum of responses, ranging from cooperation with the Chinese dragon by those who believed that his progress and that of communism were inevitable, through neutralism and compromise based principally on faith in the Chinese pledge to observe the principles of peaceful coexistence, to reliance on the American commitment to come to the aid of those countries prepared to defend their independence.

In the light of the multiplicity of deficiencies and challenges, both internal and external, the progress and successes that these new nations have achieved, however limited, are far more impressive and surprising than their inability to realize in the few years since independence their somewhat extravagant expectations. In the past, nation building has been no easy task and has been frequently punctuated by internal upheavals and external conflict; in today's world of accelerating development and swifter change each new nation must race to keep up, let alone catch up. Under these circumstances instability and radical experiments should not be unexpected as the leadership of each Southeast Asian country seeks to wrench its people out of tradition-bound ways of life into the dynamic interaction and integration between government and people characteristic of a modern nation-state.

THE INDONESIAN STRUGGLE FOR INDEPENDENCE

By 1905 the Dutch had virtually completed the conquest of the Outer Islands, as required by the dynamics of late nineteenth-century imperialism. A bitter 30-year war with the fanatical Achehnese of Sumatra had been concluded putting an end to piracy in the Malacca Straits and also an end to the previous treasury surpluses. Henceforth the taxpayers at home had to contribute regularly to the administration of the Dutch East Indies.

Dutch administration, even in Java, continued to be characterized by indirect rule through rulers and chiefs who accepted a dependent relationship with their Dutch overlords. Under the Liberal policy private operators as well as the government had been permitted to contract with the chiefs for leases of land and the supply of labor. Already the profitable alliance of the chiefs with the Dutch had seriously undermined the popular respect for their traditional authority, while on the island of Java the intensity of private exploitation was breaking down the traditional social structure by reducing the people to increasing dependence on wage labor for their livelihood and by taking many of them away from their villages for extended periods of time. Complaints against abuses by private operators built up in the 1890s into a general attack by concerned, lower-echelon administrators against the neglect of social welfare under the Liberal policy.

Many of these young men were influenced by the Dutch Islamic scholar, Snouck Hurgronje, who recognized the deterioration of the chiefs' traditional authority and urged his countrymen to come to terms with Islam as the one vital and creative force in Indonesian society. He advocated the bringing of the modernized Islamic elite into the colonial administration, support for pilgrims to Mecca and termination of Christian missionary activity, an expanded educational program, and generally a close association with the Muslim leadership in a modernization program under Dutch direction to neutralize the effects on Dutch rule from the Islamic revival he foresaw.

The reformers, however, were just as much influenced by the growing concern for social justice and social welfare that were obviously neglected under the laissez-faire Liberal policy. Private enterprise had thrived at the expense of the natives and had created monster corporations against which the individual was virtually defenseless. Only the government could intervene and discipline the behavior of these financial giants. Only the government was in a position to take positive steps for the social, economic, and educational betterment of the Indonesians. These were the considerations underlying the ethical policy that was implemented with greater or lesser energy from 1901 to 1920 over the bitter objections of the business interests in Indonesia. In essence, the social conscience of the homeland prevailed, at considerable expense to itself, over the predatory instincts of the entrepreneur. In practice, however, many reforms proved difficult to enforce, while in other instances the Indonesians, so deeply bound to their indigenous culture, received the reforms with less appreciation and enthusiasm than anticipated.

Among the measures of the Ethical program, a number sought to regulate the recruitment and employment of labor and the leasing of cultivated land. Others sought to emancipate the peasant from dependence on the Chinese money-lender by providing public credit and encouraging the formation of cooperatives. A major expansion of irrigation facilities was undertaken and a program of agricultural improvement and education was underwritten, while a colonization act was designed to reduce the pressures of overpopulation in Java by subsidizing settlement in the Outer Islands. The effort to decentralize authority by encouraging village "Gatherings" and urban and regional Councils was sabotaged by the insincerity with which it was implemented at all levels and by the inability of the Indonesians to appreciate the liberal theories on which it was based. The government in Holland was certain that it knew what was best for Indonesia and the Indonesians. Batavia was equally certain that reforms were more likely to be implemented under its direction and control. What little authority was left to the "Gatherings" and Councils tended to be usurped by the local Dutch officials who, in effect, recommended to the members the course of action and suggested the wisdom of adhering to their recommendations. Finally, the Indonesian elite who joined their European masters, both official and nonofficial, as members of the Councils found the deliberations and the reform proposals based on Western liberal ideals incomprehensible according to traditional doctrines of aristocratic absolutism and went along with them only because collaboration was the logical avenue to preferment and profit under their Dutch masters. The unwitting results of these restricted efforts at decentralization were to further diminish the authority of the indigenous leadership by subjecting it to group decisions under Dutch direction and to enhance the trend toward centralization when Batavia found it necessary to establish administrative divisions to get the results it sought. In short, real responsibility was never vested in the local Councils nor, for that matter, in the central Council, called the Volksraad, which was authorized in 1916. Their function remained essentially advisory with initiative and decision-making power resting in the Dutch official hierarchy, culminating in The Hague. Neither Dutch officials nor Dutch businessmen ever contemplated the surrender of political or economic control to Indonesians. Indeed, whenever Indonesian aspirations appeared to pose a threat, they were effectively suppressed.

Another major reform effort of the Ethical program aimed at a vast expansion of Westernized education from the village level upward. Thousands of village schools were set up as well as limited facilities for secondary and higher education. However, the program was handicapped from the beginning by inadequate allocations of funds and the generally unenthusiastic and even negative response of villagers who found it difficult to relate the course of study to the customary needs of everyday life. An attempt to stimulate student motivation by propagating Christian values only aroused Muslim hostility. The few who went on to higher education in Holland were appalled on their return at the social subordination they suffered in contrast to the free association with Europeans they had enjoyed, a contrast that was not unique to Dutch colonials. In Europe, Asians were a negligible minority who could without risk be received as social equals, if not actually lionized; in the colonies, the circumstances were reversed. Furthermore, regardless of their educational qualifications, Indonesians found their employment opportunities limited to secondary and minor positions in both government and business where they frequently worked under less qualified Europeans.

While the range of reforms under the Ethical program met only limited success and the Ethical Policy was quietly abandoned after 1920 in favor of administrative efficiency, the productivity of the Islands underwent tremendous expansion, particularly during and after World War I to meet the rapidly accelerating Western demand for products such as tobacco, rubber, tin, sugar, copra, and oil. Most of this development took place

on the Outer Islands where the Ethical Policy was scarcely felt and where large tracts of undeveloped land were available for long-term leases. Javanese productivity and population continued to grow but not at such a rapid and profitable pace because every new step required a proportionately heavier investment to achieve comparable results. Capital from other Western nations supplemented Dutch capital to speed the rate of development, but little of the profits filtered down to the Indonesian peasant and much of the labor for plantation-type development on the Outer Islands was more economically performed by Chinese coolies imported under contract, as was also the case in Malaya. Indonesians proved generally reluctant to abandon their customary rights in rice land in favor of full dependence on wages. Only after 1929 did a provision against goods produced by contract labor in the American tariff force a gradual decline in the utilization of contract labor.

Although the Ethical Policy fell short of liberal expectations and the economic expansion contributed little to the improvement of the peasants' standard of living, Indonesian discontent and national feeling began to receive institutionalized expression after 1905 both in intellectual and more popular, Islamic forms. First to appear was the Budi Ōtomo (beautiful or noble endeavor) group of Western-educated Indonesians, founded in 1908 under the apparent inspiration of Japanese achievement. Generally, they recognized both the unsuitability of Indonesia for any complete transplantation of Western civilization and the inadequacy of traditional Indonesian institutions and culture for meeting the demands of the modern world. Initially they advocated a reexamination of Javanese culture in terms of the needs of modernization without any particular anti-Dutch implications. By World War I, however, the more radical members were urging the adoption of Western techniques to counter Western domination in avowed imitation of the Japanese model. Even the more moderate elements promoted patriotic programs in the new schools, pressed for more vigorous reforms under the Ethical Policy, and made their voices heard in the Volksraad. In time, however, the Budi Ōtomo lost its influence to more radical groups that made it appear conservative.

More important than Budi Ōtomo was the appearance in 1911–1912 of Sarekat Islam, initially an organization of Muslim merchants for the purpose of promoting Islamic loyalty against their Chinese competitors in the batik-cloth trade. Its Islamic appeal aroused an immediate and surprisingly large popular response that embarrassed its essentially nonpolitical and loyal founders. Indeed, the governor-general, concerned about the leadership's ability to control its burgeoning mass membership, denied its first appeal for legal recognition in 1913. On the other hand, the disciples of Hurgronje in the Dutch civil service viewed it favorably as a realization of his predicted Islamic revival and urged Dutch cooperation. Wartime setbacks to the Ethical program, much greater reliance on the United States and Japan to supply Indonesian needs, and the damage to the prestige of Dutch as well as other imperial powers as a result of the war attracted a host of new members, many of whom entertained more radical aspirations and expectations. Modernist Islamic leadership gained control and forced the withdrawal of the more tradition-oriented merchant leaders as well as most peasant members. In addition, Marxist infiltrators alarmed conservative Muslims by their denunciations of capitalism as well as colonialism and their thinly disguised contempt for Islam. Other divisions between the interests of the Outer Islands and Java and between the city and the countryside further complicated the problem of maintaining unity in this first nationalist organization. During the initial postwar years Sarekat Islam did manage to hold together the diversely inspired elements of Indonesian nationalism and to provide a measure of leadership until it was supplanted by the emergence of a number of groups, each of which catered to a particular segment or point of view.

The first defection, which was welcomed, was that of the Communists who established the Indonesian Communist Party (PKI) in 1920 and formally separated from Sarekat Islam in 1922. The Communist leadership adopted an increasingly radical and militant policy that culminated in a disastrous rebellion in November of 1926. Indonesian communism was so thoroughly crushed with the party outlawed that it was not again a factor in politics until the Japanese conquest and liberation from Dutch rule. A further consequence of this rising for Indonesian nationalism as a whole was the weakening of the Dutch reformists and a strengthening of the conservatives who insisted that the government give greater attention to forestalling similar outbreaks in the future. As a result, every new nationalist organization came under close surveillance, and the government did not hesitate to exercise its police power by arresting leaders suspected of subversion.

In 1927, Dr. Sukarno, an engineer, joined other Western-educated activists in founding the Indonesian Nationalist Party (PNI), which sought to follow the example of Gandhi by organizing massive noncooperation with the Dutch regime. His flamboyant oratory and sloganeering attracted the attention of the government and he was arrested and removed from Java in 1930. In 1932 a pro-Marxist Socialist Party was founded by Sutan Sjahrir and Muhammed Hatta, both Sumatrans. Their cooperation with Sukarno, who was released in 1933, only led to the imprisonment of all three. By such prompt repression the government prevented all secular nationalist efforts from developing any significant popular followings prior to the Japanese assault. For the most part, their membership remained limited to students and these had to be circumspect if they hoped for employment after completing their studies.

Meanwhile, the Muslim groups with mass support remained generally loyal and placed their faith in cooperation with the government. If the government had more actively reciprocated this proffer of trust and recruited an Indonesian military force, subsequent events might have followed a different course. At it was, the Muslim community was divided into orthodox and modernist wings, and the Dutch tended to favor the orthodox group because it was more quiescent and less demanding. Orthodox Islam with its mainstrength in the rural areas looked on both pre-Islamic traditions and practices and modernizing efforts that sought to adapt Islam to the modern world as challenges to the true faith. However, not until 1926 did its leaders feel sufficiently pressed by the activities of the reformist Muhammedijah organization, founded as early as 1912, to institutionalize its program by the formation of Nahdatul Ulema. The Muhammedijah leaders, many of whom had studied in Cairo, were advocates of change within the framework of Islam to reach a rational accommodation with the modern world. This meant modern education and social services for Muslims to enable them to play their roles. Therefore, it followed that the Muhammedijah undertook such reforms on its own and continued to give its support for an expansion of the Ethical Policy after the Dutch had largely lost their enthusiasm for such reform programs. By itself, the Muhammedijah was a social service and educational organization—not a political party—but it provided the basis for the founding of the Masjumi Party during World War II.

The suppression of all political expression deemed a threat to Dutch rule was even more vigorously enforced after the onset of the depression thoroughly disorganized the colonial economy, so dependent on world markets for the sale of its raw products. In this respect, the experience of the Dutch East Indies was no different than that of other colonies, except to the extent that its economy was more completely "colonialized." As the market and consequently prices for rubber, oil, tin, and other exports collapsed, plantations and production were sharply cut back by as much as one half, forcing the people to fall back on a subsistence economy. Fortunately, most of them had kept one foot in their paddy fields and thus the retreat was not too hard to accomplish. A traditional subsistence economy has a resilience and flexibility, regardless of governmental competence, which industrialized economies do not enjoy. By 1936, currency devaluation, partial recovery, and preparations for the approaching war revived the demand for colonial products, but one significant casualty of the depression was the open door trade policy because discriminatory regulations were aimed at the sharp rise in cheap Japanese imports.

In spite of this recovery the magical mystique of Western omnicompetence, already shaken in 1905 and during World War I, was more deeply eroded, providing an even broader base of support for nationalistic expressions. Dutch rejection in 1939 of the Volksraad request for a measure of constitutional reform called forth the formation of the Indonesian Political Concentration in which the leadership dared to employ the hitherto forbidden name "Indonesia." Demands presented to the Dutch called for: (1) the name of Indonesia for the islands, (2) an Indonesian as lieutenant-governor, (3) the eligibility of Indonesians for all posts up to assistant directors of administrative departments, (4) the appointment of Indonesians to the Council of the Indies in Holland, and (5) a legislative lower house elected by universal adult suffrage. Finally, under wartime pressure the Dutch government in exile did agree to convene a consultative conference to consider postwar constitutional changes for the entire Dutch empire, but before the meeting could take place the Japanese conquerors arrived and were welcomed by Indonesian nationalists as liberators from Dutch exploitation. By then, the fanatical Achehnese of northwestern Sumatra were already in rebellion.

For a number of years Japan had made careful preparations for its role as a leader of the Greater East Asia Co-Prosperity Sphere.

As early as 1933 selected students undertook the study of Islam and made the pilgrimage to Mecca. In 1938 Indonesian delegates attended, with all expenses paid, an Islamic World Conference sponsored by the Japanese Islamic Association and were told about the divine Japanese Emperor-Caliph. In 1942 Japanese Muslims in the garb of pilgrims from Mecca landed with the army and self-professed Muslim soldiers answered the call to prayer. Europeans were denounced as heretics and publicly humiliated, while every effort was made to cultivate the orthodox Indonesian Muslims as collaborators against both Christians and the more modernist Muslim nationalists. This promising program to win the active support of most Indonesians was compromised, however, by the callous behavior of many Japanese troops and a number of insensitive requirements intended to create loyalty to Japan and the Japanese emperor. Indonesians resented an effort to abolish Arabic script in favor of Japanese. Bowing toward Tōkyō in recognition of the divinity of the emperor suggested Japanese racial and cultural superiority. Forced labor and heavy rice requisitions exceeded the former Dutch exactions and scarcely matched the pretended role of liberators. Late in 1943, when the tide of battle had clearly turned against Japan, the alliance with orthodox Islam was abandoned in favor of association with the new and less fanatical Masjumi Party, an outgrowth of the Muhammedijah, and a secular, puppet organization set up under Sukarno and Hatta. The pro-Marxist Sutan Sjahrir and other radical nationalists maintained an underground movement that could collaborate with Sukarno and Hatta whenever the occasion seemed ripe. At the same time, Sukarno was permitted to recruit an army of about 120,000 officers and men to supplement Japanese defense of the islands. Although the Japanese did not turn over any real political authority to the Indonesians, their destruction of the last remnants of Western prestige and their growing support for secular nationalists under Sukarno's leadership greatly stimulated the spread of nationalistic feeling and prefigured the ultimate failure of Dutch plans to reassert control.

The Indonesian struggle for independence, which was not acknowledged until the end of 1949, is too involved for detailed description. On August 17, 1945, just after Japanese capitulation, Sukarno and his supporters proclaimed the independent Republic of Indonesia and directed their forces to take the surrender of Japanese troops. British forces accompanied by Dutch administrators arrived before Dutch troops and the fighting became extremely confused with even Japanese troops being utilized against the republicans. After a year of struggle the British withdrew and the Dutch conceded in the Linggadjati Agreement of November 1946 de facto Republican authority over the two main islands of Java and Sumatra. The Dutch, however, were not yet ready to admit defeat, and the Indonesians were unwilling to agree to anything less than total sovereignty over all the islands. Therefore, for the next several years continuous guerrilla hostilities and general noncooperation, despite the capture of most of the nationalist leaders, were countered by vigorous Dutch "police actions." Both the United Nations and the United States labored to bring about an end to the hostilities and a peaceful settlement, but the Dutch refused to see the futility of their struggle to reassert control until a round-table conference led to the creation on December 27, 1949 of the United States of Indonesia composed of the Republic plus several Dutch-influenced states. This arrangement did not satisfy President Sukarno and Premier Hatta, and after the dust settled they unilaterally proclaimed a unitary Republic of Indonesia in August 1950.

Thus the Indonesian nationalists finally brought to a successful conclusion their long struggle for independence, succeeding to the entire Dutch East Indies empire with the exception of Western New Guinea (Irian Barat), which was to be a future bone of contention. Now the leadership confronted the problems of giving reality and stability to unified rule over the diverse peoples and interests of the Indonesian archipelago. In other words, the leaders, many of whom had risen on the basis of local support and local interests themselves, faced the task of creating among the people as a whole paramount loyalty and devotion to the new nation. Before long it became apparent that the achievement of political sovereignty by itself was not the panacea many had hoped it would be. Many of the subsequent actions of President Sukarno can be explained in terms of his recognition of the overriding need for a pervasive sense of Indonesian nationalism.

THE PHILIPPINE STRUGGLE FOR INDEPENDENCE

Even though the achievement of Philippine independence took almost as long, the path toward it was greatly smoothed by the publicly proclaimed American policy of preparing and guiding the Filipinos for this eventual goal. In addition, the American government provided exceptionally generous assistance for the promotion of education, public health, and other essential elements of a modern nation-state. Only in its neglect of economic reforms can American stewardship be fairly criticized, and even the shortcomings in this area were not wholly because of American disinterest. Since the ultimate goal was made clear from the beginning, its achievement may be more briefly told.

In the political realm an American Civilian Commission authorized the abolition of military rule and the institution of a civil government under Chief Commissioner William Howard Taft on July 4, 1901. The American Congress enacted an Organic Act for the Philippines in 1902, which permitted the election of a national assembly within two years after the completion of a census. In that fateful year, 1905, the census was completed

and in 1907 the election was held. Six parties were organized to contest the election, but the Nacionalistas, headed by Sergio Osmena and Manuel Quezon, emerged in a dominant position capturing 32 of the 80 seats. In subsequent elections they enlarged their control partly because of their unequivocal championship of independence but more importantly because of their support by the landlord class. Taxpaying and educational qualifications for voting only enhanced their influence. Such an oligarchical control ran counter to the expressed American goal of promoting equality and democracy, yet a reluctant imperial regime felt impelled to cooperate with the more stable elements of Philippine society if it hoped to liquidate its imperial responsibility at the earliest possible date. Its chief hope of overcoming oligarchic domination rested in fostering a massive educational program which in time could alter the social structure. Needless to say, the lack of land reform, for which the American regime has usually been most severely criticized, owed as much, if not more, to Nacionalista opposition. Paradoxically, only a less liberal imperial regime could have ridden roughshod over the landlord class.

In the one area where their interests coincided—church land holding—did the Nacionalistas and their overlords cooperate in a measure of land reform, the Americans because of their belief in the separation of church and state and the Filipinos because of their long-standing hostility to friar landlords and exclusivism. After lengthy negotiations Rome agreed to sell 430,000 acres, nearly 10 percent of the cultivated land and mostly in the rich Manila hinterland, for double the appraised value. When the land was offered for sale on easy terms with priority to the tenants, they objected vigorously to paying for land that they considered rightfully theirs by occupancy. At the same time, purchases were limited to 40 acres for individuals and 2470 acres for corporations, a restriction later extended to all public land for the purpose of frustrating large-scale American investment and development. Since the development of much of the virgin land would require heavy investment, this provision effectively limited the amount of land brought under cultivation, mostly by traditional tenancy arrangements, to a total of only 7.5 million out of 20 million acres of potentially productive land during the era of American rule. American producers of beet sugar, fearful of Filipino competition, were naturally not unhappy with this result, but for Filipinos the extension of tenancy was the unfortunate outcome with consequent agricultural inefficiency. Despite an effort at providing rural credit, most of the former friar lands in time fell back into tenancy. Indeed, thanks to their privileged position, the principal beneficiaries of rural credit were the landlords themselves.

When the anti-imperial Democratic party came to power in 1913, its appointee as governor-general, Francis Burton Harrison, arrived with a determination to accelerate the progress toward independence, regardless of the governmental inefficiency and even corruption it might entail. While Congress wrestled with a new legislative prescription, he signalled his liberalizing intentions by granting Filipinos a majority in the Commission that functioned as an appointed upper house of the Philippine legislature. Furthermore, he alarmed his fellow-Americans resident in the islands by his open and unprejudiced fraternization with what they called his "little brown friends." At the same time, he initiated a program of Filipinizing the civil service which, with the stimulus of generous bonuses voted by the Philippine legislature to those retiring after 10 years, reduced the number of Americans from 2600 in 1913 to 600 in 1921, while the number of Filipino civil servants grew from 6300 to 13,200. Admittedly, administrative efficiency and honesty deteriorated, but Harrison believed that the experience in self-government justified the added costs.

The Jones Act of 1916, though unfortunately not altogether consistent in its pro-

claimed goals and actual provisions, did advance the cause of Filipino self-government, particularly in the way it was implemented by Governor-General Harrison. The preamble, looked to as "the spirit of the law" by Filipino nationalists, committed the United States to granting independence "as soon as a stable government can be established." Just what "stable government" meant, however, was subject to widely varying interpretations. Naturally, the Nacionalistas, who controlled the legislature and filled all key executive positions except the governor-generalship, were convinced that this condition had already been fulfilled, but Harrison's Republican successor, General Leonard Wood, noting what he deemed to be their irresponsible opposition and corrupt practices, was equally certain that they were not yet ready to provide "stable government" up to American standards.

Specifically, the governmental reorganization provided by the Jones Act created a two-house legislature, an elected Senate replacing the Commission and the Assembly being renamed the House of Representatives. The two Nacionalista leaders, Sergio Osmena and Manuel Quezon, became respectively speaker of the House and president of the Senate and controlled legislation through joint caucuses of the party members in both bodies. The franchise was somewhat enlarged by lowering the tax qualification for literate males, but in practice the expansion of tenancy tended to widen the political and social gap between the working class and the elite. At the executive level an appointed cabinet after the American model was established in which all posts except the secretaryship of Education and Health, a direct presidential appointment, were filled by Filipinos. On the other hand, the powers of the governor-general were enhanced by giving him a suspensory veto, subject to presidential confirmation, over all legislation, partially at Harrison's request but more importantly to emulate the American model of a strong executive to counter legislative domination. However, Governor Harrison only exercised this power five times in comparison with the more than 100 vetoes of his successor, Governor Wood. Furthermore, he compromised the powers vested in him by the Jones Act by failing to veto a number of measures, which, in effect, brought the executive branch under legislative supervision and control. In addition to Senate confirmation of appointments, the cabinet members were made answerable to the legislature and given the opportunity to present their cases in person to it. To facilitate coordination between the executive and the legislature a Council of State was accepted by the governor in 1918 composed of the legislative leaders and the cabinet. Until it was suspended in 1925 by Governor Wood, it operated as the dominant policy and decision-making body. Even Governor Wood, anxious to gain the cooperation of Filipino leaders, felt the need of working with this extraconstitutional instrument. When the Council of State was reinstituted in 1928, it was reduced in function to merely an advisory capacity.

Initially, economic development by American private enterprise was handicapped by a stipulation of the Spanish treaty prohibiting discriminatory regulations that might favor American trading or shipping interests. After 1909, however, virtual free trade with the United States encouraged the growth of economic dependence on the American market and American supplies, while the restriction on land sales to aliens led Americans to concentrate on the projected commerce between the United States and the Philippines. This trade was stimulated by the needs of World War I with sugar, mahogany, coconut products, and hemp becoming major exports. During the 1930s mining became another major producer of export sales. As elsewhere in Southeast Asia, enterprising Chinese thrived as the all-important middlemen in this trade. Ultimately three-fourths of all exports went to the United States and almost as high a percentage of imports was supplied by

American producers. American concern about Philippine competition reinforced Filipino demands for independence during the depression.

The ultraliberal trends pioneered by Governor Harrison were checked by Governor Leonard Wood, but not reversed, as charged by his Democratic and Nacionalista opponents. With considerable justification he criticized his Democratic predecessor for moving too fast, raising false hopes, and actually giving modernization a setback by his rapid Filipinization policy. In vain he appealed to responsible Filipino leaders for cooperation. Instead, they sought to frustrate and embarrass him by passing legislation that was either unconstitutional or unworkable. Since both the American and Philippine legislatures refused to provide funds for the expert assistants he needed, he drew on the army for skilled advisors who were promptly denounced as a "khaki cabinet." The Filipino legislators also thwarted his proposal to stimulate economic development by granting long-term leases to American investors who would open up unused land in Mindanao and elsewhere. Wood's death in 1927 brought an end to this impasse, and his successor, Henry L. Stimson, did manage to restore a measure of cooperation, though he was unwilling to go back to the freewheeling liberalism of Harrison.

One further development during the 1920s that needs to be mentioned was the revival of popular rebellions led by religious fanatics claiming magical powers in emulation of their nineteenth century predecessors. While their appeal to popular superstitious beliefs illustrated how little effect American education had yet achieved in the countryside, their denunciations of increased landlordism and its foreign supporters and their call for the violent overthrow of the exploiting class pointed up American neglect in the economic realm and prefigured the peasant discontent that was destined to be the mainstay of the Hukbalahap movement after World War II. Finally, these rebellions represented a traditional nativist reaction to the effects of modernization that in time could find a kindred spirit in the anticapitalist, anti-imperialist tenets of communism. Although they were suppressed and landlordism continued to expand its dominion, their disregarded appeal was pregnant with explosive possibilities for the future.

Although the attainment of self-government and eventual independence owed something to increasingly vigorous Filipino propaganda in the United States, it owed much more to the American agricultural depression that was only intensified by the industrial depression signalled by the 1929 stock market crash. The hostility of American sugar, butter, vegetable oil, and other interests to the favored position of Philippine imports gained general reinforcement from the spreading isolationist sentiment generated by economic nationalism. Even the labor lobby began to complain of unfair competition from Filipino immigrants. The small number of American investors in the Philippines were powerless before this avalanche of opinion that stood behind the Nacionalistas' demand for independence. After several narrowly abortive efforts as early as 1929, the Tydings-McDuffie Act specifying a 10-year transitional period of American sovereignty until total independence was achieved and was accepted in May 1934 by the Philippine legislature. Under its provisions a convention drew up a commonwealth constitution that was approved by all parties, including the Filipino voters, and was proclaimed in force by President Roosevelt in November 1935, with full independence scheduled for July 4, 1945. Meanwhile, a High Commissioner represented American interests in maintaining political and economic stability, regulating trade, managing foreign relations, and protecting the American military presence, though he actually found little opportunity for the exercise of his wide-ranging authority. The constitution followed closely the American model, including the separation of powers and a bill of

rights, but in the hands of the oligarchy, headed by President Manuel Quezon, the government did little to improve the welfare of the people. Indeed, this landlord regime proved so improvident and so incapable of coping with the growing dependence on the American market that High Commissioner Paul V. McNutt suggested a reversal of American withdrawal to stave off the economic and political disaster he foresaw, but no responsible elements in either country were willing to heed his appeal.

In preparation for independence, General Douglas MacArthur, former chief of staff in Washington, was named Field Marshall to organize the armed forces for the defense of the Philippines. Prior to the Japanese attack, insufficient funds and resources were allocated by either the American or Philippine governments to develop an adequate defense, if such could have been mustered in so short a time, against the military might of Imperial Japan. General MacArthur commanded an air force of 60 planes, mostly destroyed in the initial air attacks, an army of some 50,000 ill-equipped Filipino and American troops, which nevertheless held out longer than any other force in Southeast Asia in a valiant and stubborn defense of the Bataan Peninsula (surrendered April 9) and the island fortress of Corregidor (surrendered May 6, 1942), and a small fleet of torpedo boats that enabled the Field Marshall, President Quezon, and Vice-President Osmena to escape capture.

During the three-year Japanese occupation the bulk of the political leaders and the landlords openly, but in most cases reluctantly, collaborated with the conquerors, doing their best to minimize the effects of Japanese dominion. After all, they had vested interests to protect. On the other hand, most of the peasantry, already reduced to tenancy or wage labor and with little to lose but their lives, put up a silent and sullen resistance to Japanese rule and indoctrination, boycotting the schools where Japanese replaced English and producing only enough food for subsistence. At the same time, they gave secret support, refuge, and information on Japanese troop movements to the growing guerrilla resistance forces that were also furnished with American military equipment by MacArthur's command in return for military intelligence. The most notable of these peasant guerrilla organizations was the Hukbalahap or People's Anti-Japanese Liberation Army concentrated in central Luzon around the productive Manila plain and directly drawing its inspiration from the antilandlord Sakdal movement of the 1930s. As its name implies, it, like its namesakes elsewhere in Southeast Asia, was a communist front, though few of the rank and file had much knowledge of communist doctrine. However, the Huk leader, Luis Taruc, had been a communist since 1939.

As elsewhere, the Japanese sought to win the cooperation of the Filipinos by posing as liberators and appealing to their particular interests. Japanese Catholics landed with the troops and denounced the oppression of Protestant America. The collaborationist landlord class was cultivated, and in September 1943, a puppet regime headed by José Laurel was granted "true independence" under a new constitution. But in the Philippines, already a commonwealth and nearing independence, the Japanese liberation proved less convincing than in any other of its conquests. The brutality of Japanese troops soon belied the proclaimed good intentions, and the ideal of a Co-Prosperity Sphere evaporated with the reality of economic decline into a subsistence existence, while all surplus food was requisitioned to feed the army.

In 1944 General MacArthur fulfilled his pledge of "I shall return," and in February 1945, Manila, which had escaped serious damage during the Japanese invasion by being designated an undefended "open city," was virtually leveled by naval gunfire before it was seized by American troops. Quezon had died in 1944 and, therefore, Osmena succeeded him as commonwealth president. Prior to the elections in April 1946, however, General MacArthur gave a clean bill of political health to the reluctant collaborationist, Manuel Roxas, who then led the Liberal party to victory over Osmena and the Nacionalistas. This development was hailed as introducing the American ideal of two-party politics, but since both parties drew their support from the landlord oligarchy it was a difference without great significance for the tenant farmers or the landless poor. Needless to say, the Huks did not welcome the election of a collaborationist and soon turned their terrorist talents against the oligarchic regime. Nevertheless, the United States was determined to honor its pledge and proclaimed the independence of the Republic of the Philippines on July 4, 1946, only one year behind schedule. This act of political liberalism, which marked the world's strongest power as the foremost champion of anticolonialism, was combined with a unique measure of benevolence, the appropriation of more than one billion dollars in aid, and payment of a major part of Philippine war damage claims, both public and private.

In comparison with contemporary colonial regimes American rule may be characterized as exceptionally generous and benevolent. The more thoroughgoing direct rule inherited from the Spanish was extended to include the Muslim Moros of Mindanao and the Sulu islands who had not previously been effectively subdued. In implementation of the pledge to prepare the people for self-government Filipinos were included in the government from the beginning, a direction in which they were moving in any case in the last years of Spanish rule. In addition, a major investment in education not only raised literacy to about 50 percent but also gave the Philippines English as a nationwide language to overcome the divisions created by 8 indigenous languages and more than 40 dialects. Hundreds of American teachers answered the call to institute an American-style system of public education in what has more recently been called the first Peace Corps effort. By 1940 almost all children of first to fourth grade age were in school, though attendance beyond the fourth grade unfortunately fell off sharply in rural areas. Furthermore, public health measures, only reluctantly and suspiciously accepted by Filipinos, had more than doubled the population. As noted, American free trade policy encouraged an excessive dependence on the protected American market, a dilemma recognized at independence by legislation permitting a long delay in gradually applying the full American tariff on Philippine imports. Moreover, this policy of rewarding the production of cash crops as well as the need to win the cooperation of the largely *mestizo* (partly Spanish or Chinese) elite stimulated the further spread of landlordism, while inadequate investment, either public or private, was directed at opening new lands for cultivation. At the same time, tenant farmers, who had to surrender more than half of their crops to landlords, found little inducement to invest in improving productivity.

On balance, however, American performance as an imperial ruler can be compared favorably with those of its more experienced contemporaries. The Philippines faced independence better prepared but substantially alienated from their Southeast Asian neighbors after the unique experience of "three centuries in a Spanish convent and half a century in Hollywood."

THE BURMESE STRUGGLE FOR INDEPENDENCE

British policies toward Buddhist Burma and the mélange of Muslim states in the Malayan peninsula stand in striking contrast to each other, reflecting the differing British approaches toward each of them. In Malaya, Britain was initially concerned only with securing safe passage through the Malacca Straits and then with the development of Singapore as an entrepot for Southeast Asian trade. Not until Chinese-pioneered tin min-

ing grew to major proportions and created internal friction between Chinese entrepreneurs and Malayans did the British feel impelled to intervene, and even then their intervention began on a small scale and expanded only gradually as the need grew for their exercise of police power to maintain a profitable measure of law and order. Regardless of the extent of actual British control, the local ruling houses were left intact as the nominal authorities under British guidance and protection.

The conquest of Burma, however, had grown out of border and trade conflicts with British India and its rule was viewed as a necessary extension and integral adjunct of the British Indian Empire, at least until 1935. In comparison with the political divisions of Malaya, Burma had enjoyed a measure of cultural and political unity under a royal family and aristocracy, no matter how decayed and corrupt, which was spiritually and morally supported and allied with the entrenched Buddhist Sangha or monastic hierarchy. In essence, however, Britain decapitated the Burmese body politic, removing the ruler and the entire administrative hierachy above the village and leaving a writhing, leaderless corpse to adapt as best it could to an alien Anglo-Indian regime. In addition, the Buddhist Sangha, which might have brought moral reinforcement to British rule, was rejected as unprogressive and received no official sanction or support. If left to themselves, the Burmese might have been able to maintain a truncated cultural identity at the village level, but in accordance with laissez-faire doctrine the new realm was thrown open to exploitation and development by profit-motivated Indians and Chinese as well as Englishmen.

First-conquered Lower Burma suffered most from this alien invasion, as Indian capital and labor, aided by government public works, opened up its well-watered lowlands to intensive rice cultivation for export, principally to food-short India. In time, two-thirds of the vast increase in rice production was marketed abroad with almost all the profit going to foreign money-lenders and merchants. Other profitable products for export included teak and oil. The Burmese peasantry, accustomed to an easygoing communal subsistence economy, was thoroughly confused and demoralized by this introduction of a totally incomprehensible economic system, backed up by Anglo-Indian law that rejected communal values and communal use of the land in favor of private proprietorship with full rights of alienation by mortgage and foreclosure or by sale. Many soon lost their traditional fields and were forced to open up new land, which they also frequently lost before establishing legal right by occupancy.

The consequent erosion of communal unity and values without any compensating comprehension and acceptance of the new system proved devastating to the social structure and social order. Since the new legal system was outside their experience, it could not command respect. Perjury and disregard for the law became commonplace. Under the circumstances it is small wonder that a growing number of thoroughly frustrated peasants resorted to violence and banditry aimed principally at Indians and Chinese with the tacit sympathy and even approval of the villagers and Buddhist monks who represented the traditional values of Burmese society. British district deputy commissioners and their staffs, equally frustrated by their inability to maintain order, turned to harsh measures of repression that only further depreciated respect for foreign rule. When the fluctuating rice price, kept artificially low by collusive British buying, collapsed, as it did in 1907–1908 and again in the 1920s and 1930s, peasant distress and disorder were only intensified. Up to 1905 peasant communities in Upper Burma, less amenable to profitable exploitation, had generally managed to maintain their traditional way of life, but in 1908 the insidious process of land alienation began to appear there in significant proportions as well. Thus

one basis of Burmese opposition to Anglo-Indian rule was peasant hostility to the imposition of an alien social and economic order, almost always led by impassioned Buddhist monks, or those who posed as monks, the natural champions of traditional values against the capitalistic, exploitative, and laissez-faire ideals and values of the British. Their desperate actions, however, tended to be directed against their immediate tormentors, the Indians and the Chinese, rather than their British sponsors. Saya San, who led a hopeless rebellion without modern arms in 1930, even revived the traditional kingship in his name with all the sacred symbols and ceremonies pertaining to it.

More properly nationalistic by definition were the organization and activities of those who had received Western educations, no matter how superficial their appreciation of the West. The British never attempted to modernize the Buddhist schools, the carriers of Burmese culture, which reached every Burmese young man. Instead, they preferred to set up a British-type, secular school system capped by the University of Rangoon for the training of future Burmese civil servants on a highly selective basis. Rigorous examinations ruthlessly weeded out the incompetent or unsuitable at each level, but even the small number who completed their educations encountered difficulty in gaining employment, either public or private. Along with unsuccessful candidates they swelled the ranks of semieducated, semi-Westernized discontent.

The first significant organization, which sought to avoid suppression by remaining nonpolitical, was the Young Men's Buddhist Association, founded in 1906 and named in obvious emulation of a notable Western institution. Inspired by Japanese success, its members as a study group hoped to find a workable blend of the best elements in the Buddhist tradition and Western experience. Subsequently, a more encompassing General Council of Buddhist Associations attempted to coordinate this and other expressions of moderate reform and to strengthen their combined influence on the British regime. In spite of a further broadening of its appeal by renaming it the General Council of Burmese Associations in 1921, its advocacy of moderate reform was soon overtaken by the emergence of radical nationalists inspired by the dynamic Gandhian movement in neighboring India.

The first explosive expression of radical anti-British sentiment came in 1920 in a student strike against higher passing standards and closer government regulation prescribed in the charter of the new University of Rangoon. The British government was accused of deceit for proclaiming its eagerness to turn over positions to qualified Burmese, while cutting back on the number who could become so qualified. Most of the secondary schools, where the rate of attrition was as high, were persuaded to join in the boycott modeled on the Gandhian technique. The strike had to be terminated without securing any immediate, significant concessions, but the precedent had been set for political activism on the campus.

The student strike had been part of the general agitation to gain as large a measure of self-government as possible in the postwar governmental reforms being planned for India and Burma. Burmese feelings had been severely injured by the governor's suggestion that because of political apathy Burma was not yet ready for as large a dose of self-government as India. When the long-delayed reforms were finally announced in 1922, Burma received a 130-member Legislative Council with 80 elected members, but 22 of the latter represented special communal and other groups. A modest measure of dyarchy was instituted with two ministers responsible to a majority in the Council, but the government retained control of all vital matters, including finance, and the governor possessed an unlimited veto power. A radical campaign to boycott the first elections met a surprising response; only 7 percent of the eligible voters went to the polls. Since sub-

sequent, unopposed elections did not attract much larger turnouts, perhaps there was something to the governor's charge of Burmese political apathy.

On the other hand, there was little in the political or legislative behavior of those elected to the Council to arouse enthusiasm or instill confidence in either the voters or their British overlords. For the most part, parties tended to fragment into cliques around leaders more noted for their personal magnetism and influence than any evocation of a principled and responsible program. In competition for political support and popularity these leaders frequently proclaimed extreme and irresponsible goals that they knew were impossible to achieve. To maintain any degree of stability, the government found it necessary to limit its proposals to noncontroversial and generally unimportant legislation. In fairness to Burmese politicians, however, it needs to be noted that the number of appointed Councillors plus the representatives of communal and special interests made it practically impossible for any politician to organize a workable majority.

A new round of nationalist activity was touched off by the arrival of the Simon Commission in 1929 to investigate the possibilities of further governmental reform for the entire Indian realm, including Burma. Burmese backing for the boycott of the Commission proclaimed by the Indian Congress was reinforced by a personal visit of Gāndhi. The major issue for Burmese was whether to accept or reject a proposed separation of Burma from India. Many nationalist leaders opposed separation at this time for fear of losing out on whatever reforms were won by India, and a clear majority of the electorate subsequently upheld this position in an ill-advised referendum—ill-advised because the British had already made up their minds in favor of separation.

During these years two important events deserve to be recorded: one of long-range significance to the development of Burmese nationalism and the other illustrating the frustration of the impoverished peasants of Lower Burma. The Saya San Rebellion of 1930–1931 was the direct product of the worldwide agricultural depression of the later 1920s (which collapsed the price of rice and the subsequent industrial depression that compelled immigrant Indian factory workers to compete with Burmese peasants for agricultural employment just for survival). The plight of the peasants was compounded by the reluctant foreclosure of mortgages held by Indian money-lenders on about one-fourth of the developed paddy land. In addition, the government turned a deaf ear to appeals for relief from taxes, particularly the indiscriminate poll tax that hit all, both landed and landless, equally.

At first, rioting and violence were directed against the Indian community. Then the exmonk, Saya San, took command and proclaimed himself the divinely ordained ruler, adopting all the paraphernalia of traditional Burmese kingship. Without modern arms this rebellion was doomed, but his superstitious followers, emboldened by magical charms and favorable astrological forecasts, performed feats of selfless heroism that aroused the sympathy and patriotic feeling of all Burmese. Saya San was captured and tried in 1932. The defense attorney, French-educated Dr. Ba Maw, gained public renown, which accelerated his rise to political prominence.

The second major development was the founding of the Thakin Party among student leaders who found the existing political positions too tame and too self-seeking. The name of the party was derived from the practice of addressing each other as *Thakin* or Master, the Burmese equivalent of *Sahib*, and also from their determination to make the Burmese masters in their own homeland. Since everything British was denounced as the source of Burmese distress, these young, semi-Westernized intellectuals rejected liberalism and looked to socialism and even Marxism for ideological underpinning for their nationalism. In any case, such Utopian

doctrines had more in common with the communal and Buddhist values of Burmese culture than Western liberalism did. Above all, however, they remained ardent nationalists. From their ranks were destined to rise the principal leaders of independent Burma, notably Thakin Nu and Thakin Ne Win.

The young Thakins first gained renown by leading a student strike in 1936 after the University Student Union president, Thakin Nu, was expelled and others disciplined for public criticism of a faculty member. They forced a postponement of the all-important examinations by physically blocking the entrances to the halls. Secondary students soon joined the boycott and all examinations had to be delayed. Again the intimate relationship between higher education and political activism had been demonstrated. The university was the natural training ground for the future leaders of effective nationalism.

The Reform Act of 1935 formally separated Burma from India, under its own administration. Dyarchy was terminated and the entire cabinet was made individually responsible to a majority in the elected House of Representatives of what was now to be a bicameral legislature. This apparently liberal move toward self-government was offset in part by the establishment of a Senate, half-appointed and half-elected by the House, and in part by the extensive veto and control powers retained by the governor. Lack of popular enthusiasm for this new arrangement was illustrated by the poor turnout in the 1936 election. Dr. Ba Maw, who actively wooed the peasants' vote with his Poor Man's Party, won only a disappointing 16 seats. Nevertheless, the continued political fragmentation enabled him to become Burma's first prime minister at the head of a shaky coalition of disparate elements in 1937. Under such circumstances politics remained the name of the game until the Japanese conquest, and the government remained unable to enact much in the way of constructive legislation. As a result, the public continued to hold government in low regard as a plaything of corrupt politicians with little concern for the public welfare.

Dr. Ba Maw finally fell from power in 1939 and before long formed an alliance with the rising Thakins in an ultranationalist program called the Freedom Bloc. Like the Indian Congress, the Freedom Bloc offered cooperation to beleaguered Britain only if genuine progress toward independence was forthcoming. Accused of fomenting treason, Dr. Ba Maw, Thakin Nu, and other leaders were imprisoned in 1940, but 30 Thakins, led by Nu's deputy, Aung San, made good their escape to Japan. They returned in 1942 with Japanese troops and joined in a puppet government headed by Dr. Ba Maw, which secured a proclamation of Burmese independence in 1943. Thakin Aung San commanded the Japanese-sponsored Burma National Army.

As elsewhere, the callous behavior of Japanese troops destroyed whatever faith the Burmans may have had in the high-sounding promises and intentions of Japanese propaganda. Here again, the conception of a Co-Prosperity Sphere foundered on the facts of economic mismanagement and deterioration. More than two million acres of rice land went out of production. Although Dr. Ba Maw had harnessed his star irrevocably to an Axis victory, he did not reveal the secret negotiations of his Thakin associates with the Allies or their organization of the underground Anti-Fascist People's Freedom League. Since the success of the Allied invasion hinged on reaching Rangoon before the beginning of the rainy season in May 1945, the defection of Aung San's army to the Allies in March was a vital turning point, even if it also saved the Thakins from prosecution as traitors.

The impoverished postwar British Labor government was just as committed to getting rid of imperial obligations in Burma as in India. In any case, the British garrison of mainly Indian and African troops could not be relied on in any open challenge to the de facto regime of Aung San, the Burma Na-

tional Army, and the vastly enlarged AFPFL. Although Aung San (aged 32) and a number of his associates were assassinated in July 1947, the Republic of the Union of Burma, led by U Nu, was inaugurated as scheduled on January 4, 1948. In spite of generous terms the deep-seated hostility to Britain caused Burma, unlike India and Pakistan, to reject association in the Commonwealth of Nations, a clear indication of the unique failure of British imperialism in the case of Burma.

MALAYA: AN IMPERIAL FOOTNOTE

As noted, British interest in Malaya expanded only gradually in response to new economic opportunities as each one presented itself. First, they sought bases for the protection of trade in the Malacca Straits. Then Chinese-developed tin mining attracted them into the hinterland where British dredging operations soon exceeded Chinese tin production. Finally, the suitability of soil and climate for the rubber tree led to a vast development of plantations after 1905 and greatly increased the British vested interest in the region, mainly to meet the rapidly growing but erratic demands of the American industrial revolution. Since the Malayan was by nature easygoing, not only capital but also labor had to be imported to power this economic development. By the 1920s Chinese and Indian immigrants outnumbered the native population and by 1941 the Chinese community by itself exceeded the Malayan. As immigrants from more advanced civilizations, both the Chinese and Indians looked down on their Malayan neighbors and maintained their distinctive cultural identities. Thus a complex, plural society arose in which all parties welcomed the impartial mediation of the British government as an umbrella under which each enjoyed the maximum freedom to pursue its interests. Under these conditions nationalism was stifled.

Like the British, the Japanese conquerors were principally interested in exploiting the economic assets of Malaya, although they dealt harshly with the Chinese community here as elsewhere. In reaction, the Chinese mounted a small-scale antifascist guerrilla movement which, though armed by the Allies, fell under communist influence.

After the war the British Labor government was puzzled about how to implement its anti-imperial policy in Malaya and not at all sure that it wished to abandon the strategic Singapore naval base. After numerous reports and one false start, a Federation of Malaya, excluding Singapore, was proclaimed in 1948, and every effort was bent toward preparing Malays for rule in their own homeland. This abandonment of impartiality contributed to a Communist Chinese rebellion that ravaged and terrorized the countryside for the next nine years. Despite the massing of tens of thousands of troops and the ruthless resettlement of 300,000 rural Chinese, the few thousand Communist guerrillas were never totally destroyed. Instead, the so-called Malayan National Liberation Army gave up the direct struggle only when Moscow changed its tactics to peaceful competition. In any case, it proved difficult to supply an armed movement so far removed from communist frontiers. All the rebels did not lay down their arms and occasional headlines verify the continued existence of one to two thousand guerrillas who elude extinction by moving back and forth across the Malaya-Thailand border.

The abatement of guerrilla activity was also related to the agreement of the leading Malay, Chinese, and Indian political parties to bury their differences and join forces in requesting independence in 1955. Under the Malay leadership of the conservative, anti-Communist Tungku Abul Rahman the Federation of Malaya became an independent member of the Commonwealth of Nations in September 1957. But an independent Malayan state without its overwhelmingly Chinese entrepot, Singapore, was an economic and political anomaly. In 1959, the grant of autonomous, self-governing status to Singapore eased the path to negotiation, and in 1963 a larger and looser confederation called Malaysia was conceived, incorporating Chinese Singapore and Malay Sarawak and Sabah on the island of Borneo (the Sultan of Brunei, fearful of exploitation of his oil revenues, abstained) as internally self-governing members. Such a loose organization was bound to generate friction between its members, and Singapore subsequently exercised its right of secession. Nevertheless, under Tungku Abdul Rahman's wise leadership and supported by tin and rubber revenues, the original Malayan Federation has enjoyed striking and irritating prosperity, especially when compared to the economic misfortunes of its much larger neighbor, Indonesia.

THAILAND SINCE 1905

For Siam the year 1905 did not hold the special significance it did for other Asian states because it remained nominally independent and because under progressive kings it had already initiated a modest modernization program, somewhat similar to that of Japan, with the same goal of winning emancipation from the shackles of unequal treaties with the Western powers. Until the 1930s, however, the kings were the principal modernizers; their efforts were partially frustrated by royal princes and aristocrats who feared the loss of their traditional privileges. Moreover, the sacred nature of kingship isolated the rulers from their people and the possibility of popular support against the privileged classes. Thus, in contrast to Japan, the modernization effort lacked the support of the ruling class.

In spite of this handicap some significant advances were made with the aid of Western advisors. Freedom of the press and religious toleration were decreed. The gradual abolition of slavery and conscript labor was completed in 1905. The palace school served as a model for a state-supported educational system, and each year as many as 300 students received royal subsidies for advanced studies abroad. In 1908 French advisors completed a revision of the penal code as a first step in a total revision of the legal system to meet Western objections.

In the realm of economic development, the kings' plans suffered from a shortage of investment capital because of traditional and treaty limitations on royal revenues, corrupt administration, and the expenses of maintaining the royal family and Western advisors. Moreover, with the termination of conscript labor a shortage of cheap labor developed. Nevertheless, progress was made that pales only in comparison with the more rapid pace in neighboring, Western-ruled lands. Modern facilities, including electricity, were introduced to the capital city, Bangkok. Basic railroads were built to tie the remote regions of the state to the capital with the aid of foreign loans and foreign technicians. Irrigation works opened up additional paddy land in the flood plain of the Menam valley, though less than half of the potential paddy land of the area was developed. After all these and other government-sponsored advances are summed up, however, the fact remains that more than 90 percent of foreign and domestic commerce, banking and credit, rice milling, tin mining, and lumbering was in the hands of Chinese and Europeans who took the profits of economic development while contributing an absolute minimum in taxes and customs duties to the revenue of the state.

Such nationalism as did develop in Siam was directed against the Chinese and their domination of the economy. Chinese immigrants had played a leading and generally constructive role for centuries, and until the twentieth century had allowed themselves to be partially assimilated by intermarriage. Every prominent family, including the royal family, possessed more or less Chinese blood. What loyalties long-time immigrants retained were to their families and home provinces, not to the alien Manchu regime. When anti-Manchu revolutionary activities

developed, however, many were stirred into active supporters, visualizing the protection a vigorous new China could extend to them and their interests. With the overthrow of the Manchus, Chinese nationalistic feeling was aroused, and Chinese schools were founded to revitalize Chinese culture and stave off assimilation. Moreover, the increasing immigration of Chinese women, which reached a peak in the 1920s, lessened the incentive for intermarriage. This changed attitude, particularly apparent among more recent immigrants, generated a reciprocal Siamese animosity toward continued immigration and the special privileges of the Chinese community. The new Chinese government policy of "once a Chinese always a Chinese" also created alarm about the future influence of China in the affairs of Siam. Naturally, the growing concern about the special privileges of Chinese spread to those of Europeans and reinforced the long government campaign for revision of the unequal treaties. Siam had employed a succession of foreign experts to work toward this goal, but not until the 1920s, when Woodrow Wilson's son-in-law, Francis B. Sayre, filled this position, were the Western governments, and most importantly Britain, prepared to make concessions. In treaties concluded between 1925 and 1927 the worst features of extraterritoriality and customs restrictions were removed, though total emancipation had to await the years 1937–1939.

Another aspect of modernization and nationalism was the growing frustration with the ineptness and corruption of traditional government felt by those civilian and military figures with Western educations or intimate associations with Western advisors. Their cause was aided by the liberal inclinations of the weak but progressive ruler who had already indicated his readiness to surrender his absolute powers in favor of a constitutional regime. In 1932 the French-educated law professor, Pridi Banomyong, who favored a strong government and a planned economy under the leadership of a

People's Party, and 80 "promoters" engineered a coup. To win the king's approval and to forestall possible foreign intervention, a conservative constitution was adopted. It turned power over to a cabinet responsible to an assembly half elected by indirect suffrage and half appointed by the ruling party. The principal provision of the constitution, which reflected the chief concern of the "promoters," excluded princes from the cabinet. As in the case of Japan, the prior year's budget would continue if the assembly failed to approve the new one. Clearly the Siamese constitution was a partisan instrument designed to legitimize the seizure of power by a small, elite group of civilian and military "promoters" and unfortunately left them free to run affairs as they saw fit as long as they did not fall out among themselves. In essence, a new absolutism had merely been substituted for the old. There was nothing democratic or popular about the coup or the so-called People's Party.

The regime's reliance on military strength was illustrated the next year when Colonel Phibun Songgram and the army elite supplanted Pridi, whose statist economic plans were denounced as communistic. Although he was subsequently rehabilitated and readmitted to the cabinet to retain the support of the intellectual elite, communism was outlawed and suspected Chinese and Vietnamese Communists were expelled from the country. From this date, this conservative regime, primarily motivated by its determination to retain power, tended to be militarist, anticommunist, anti-Chinese, and nationalist in its irredentist objective of regaining lost territories. Income and business taxes, which fell most heavily on the Chinese community, replaced the traditional land tax. A substantial portion of the budget was allocated to military modernization. State-owned and state-supported enterprises reduced the area of alien economic influence and were operated with more or less efficiency for the enrichment of the governing elite. In accordance with the nationalistic emphasis the number of foreign advisors was sharply cut back. Governmental propaganda stimulated popular pride in the superiority of Thai Buddhist culture and sponsored a Pan-Thai irredentist movement. In 1939 Phibun propagated a national code of honor, similar to Japanese bushido, and renamed the realm Thailand (Land of the Free). Thus the course of Siamese development closely paralleled Japan's and predictably Thailand gradually aligned itself with Japan in the coming conflict.

Except for temporary territorial gains, Thailand benefited little from cooperation with the Japanese. Indeed, it suffered only a little bit less than the conquered countries and by 1944 was secretly collaborating with the Allies. Thanks to American sympathy, Thailand escaped major punishment for its alliance with Japan. It repaid its debt to the United States and also maintained its anticommunist stance by joining the Southeast Asia Treaty Organization and later by allowing military bases to be developed on its soil for the struggle against Vietnamese communism. Alignment with the United States, as formerly with Japan, was dictated by continuing fear of its great neighbor to the north and its large Chinese minority. Nevertheless, in spite of some overdue reforms, the elitest regime with its American alliance was susceptible to leftist criticism and subversion, particularly in the neglected northeast region bordering troubled and closely related Laos. Moreover, a small Thai population in southern China has been subject to intensive Chinese communist cultivation. The possibility of expanding to Thailand a form of national liberation warfare is now not so remote as authorities once thought. Today the future of Thailand under a militarily oriented regime is uncertain.

NATIONALISM IN FRENCH INDO-CHINA

The French, famous for the Declaration of the Rights of Man, installed in Indo-China one of the most exploitative and repressive regimes of any of the imperial powers perhaps because in the Vietnamese they confronted the most developed and civilized people in Southeast Asia. A thoroughgoing mercantilism severed trading connections with Asian neighbors as well as other Westerners and subordinated the interests and welfare of Vietnam to those of France. This policy, even more rigorously applied, stifled Vietnamese initiative and pauperized the people in behalf of French investors and their immigrant Chinese vassals in the underdeveloped Mekong delta region. By means of irrigation and flood control works the delta was made to produce an annual surplus of as much as two million tons of rice for export, while within reasonable range of the imperial capital of Saigon more than one million acres were preempted from customary users for French development as rubber and tea plantations. Although northern Vietnam possessed the richest resources in Southeast Asia, both natural and human, for industrial development, industrialization, except for the mining of ores for export, was discouraged to protect the market for French products. At the same time, French pacification and public health measures increased the population pressure on the already crowded means of subsistence forcing impoverished Vietnamese to accept whatever conditions French employers and land developers might prescribe.

French rule was made as direct as feasible and the central administration was staffed with a higher percentage of French civil servants than any other imperial regime in Southeast Asia, while the French military establishment was also proportionately larger. In the south, Cochin-China was under direct rule; in the north, conservative, traditionally educated scholar officials, appointed and dismissed by the French, were permitted to continue their governing roles at the local level. Only gradually were elected local councils authorized, and Indo-Chinese were never granted a majority in the central council, which in any case possessed only advisory powers. All uprisings were ruthlessly suppressed and captured dissidents were transported to Pulo Condore, Indo-China's Devils Island. Even France's dedication to its civilizing mission was reluctantly and minimally implemented. The University of Hanoi, opened in 1907, was closed the following year because of the extent of nationalist agitation until 1918, and in the early 1920s its originally comprehensive curriculum was limited to vocational arts for a negligible student body of less than 1000. Those Vietnamese who returned after completing educations in France were completely frustrated as elsewhere, by the local milieu. Little more than 2000 Indo-Chinese achieved the status of French citizens, the avowed goal of France's civilizing mission.

Under these conditions, combined with traditional political apathy, organized expression of nationalism was at once difficult to develop and inevitable. The longer it was put off the more hostile and radical it could be expected to become. Prior to 1905 traditionalist uprisings in behalf of the Vietnamese imperial family had been put down. After 1905 both reformers and revolutionaries were attracted to Japan to study the Japanese model of modernization. There they met and came under the additional influence of Chinese leaders, such as Liang Ch'i-ch'ao and Sun Yat-sen. Back home, however, their proposals, even those of moderate reform in the direction of modernization, aroused little response from their uninformed countrymen and a positively hostile response from the French government, fearful of making any concessions. During World War I 100,000 Vietnamese soldiers and laborers gained first-hand knowledge of the West through service in France, and many of them returned deeply disenchanted with conditions under French rule. Their numbers swelled the ranks susceptible to nationalist appeals. Several risings generally favoring a Kuomintang-style republic were extinguished and their organizations were destroyed by the French forces. More important in the long run was the development of more radical views by a self-taught young intellectual of exceptional talent, Nguyen Ai-quoc (Nguyen the Patriot), who later became famous as Ho Chi Minh (c 1892–1969).

In 1911 he went to sea as a cabin boy, an experience that vastly broadened his horizon and enabled him to master French and become familiar with several other languages. During a four-year stint as a hotel cook in London (1913–1917) he learned English and became active in anti-imperialist activities among overseas workers. He then moved to Paris where he came under the influence of French leftists and began to demonstrate his intellectual talents by publishing articles in *Le Populaire* and other left-wing journals. At this stage he was a liberal nationalist advocating reform rather than revolution, but within a few years he turned to communism, attending the Fourth Congress of the Comintern in 1922. In 1924 he received some training at the University of Toilers of the East in Moscow before being dispatched to China as Borodin's interpreter. After the collapse of the Kuomintang-Communist alliance he was put in charge of organizing Communist activity throughout Southeast Asia. In 1930 he engineered an abortive rebellion in northern Vietnam and temporarily set up soviet councils in two provinces. His Communist organization survived the brutal French suppression and was again engaged in underground operations by 1933. He had always been a nationalist first and foremost and continued to favor a united front of all anti-French nationalists in carrying out a "bourgeois-democratic" revolution. By maintaining his contacts with non-Communist nationalists he was able to win Kuomintang and American backing and supplies for his leadership of a joint Vietnamese assault on the Japanese in the last days of World War II.

Immediately after the Japanese surrender, the Viet Minh of Ho Chi Minh swept into control of northern Vietnam and on September 2, 1945, proclaimed the Democratic Republic of Vietnam at Hanoi. Elections in November confirmed broad popular support for his nationalist regime of Communists and non-Communists on a platform of "independence and democracy." Meanwhile, French troops backed by British forces regained control of the south and prepared to move northward. Rather than challenge the victorious allies with his new coalition Ho agreed to admit a French garrison in return for recognition of the Democratic Republic of Vietnam as "a free state with its own government, parliament, army, and finances, forming a part of the Indochinese Federation and the French Union." Subsequent negotiations foundered when France detached southern Vietnam as a puppet state under Emperor Bao-Dai, and both sides engaged in bloody hostilities. By the beginning of 1947 a full-fledged civil war was in progress with Ho's guerrilla forces skillfully commanded by Vo Nguyen Giap, a product of Chinese Communist military training. The turning point in this struggle to expel the French came with the Communist conquest of China in 1949, which provided General Giap with a safe sanctuary, a base, and a source of supplies and technical assistance. Still the French, encouraged and supplied by the United States, continued the futile conflict until in 1954 they finally became convinced of the necessity to abandon their Indo-Chinese empire. Negotiations were in progress at Geneva when in May the news of a major French defeat at Dien Bien Phu on the line of communications to Laos removed all remaining doubts.

According to the Geneva Agreement, Laos and Cambodia became independent kingdoms and Vietnam was temporarily divided just north of the imperial capital of Hué in the vicinity of the 17th parallel into Ho's Democratic Republic in the north and Emperor Bao-Dai's Republic in the south, with the Roman Catholic Ngo Dinh Diem as premier. By 1956 the people were to decide at the polls the political future of Vietnam. Meanwhile, an international control commission with members from India, Canada, and Poland would supervise the withdrawal of armed forces and the restoration of peace as well as the provision against external augmentation of military strength. The diverse composition of the commission, however, handicapped its operation and foreclosed the possibility of arriving at a unanimous decision on any critical issue. As an outside but interested party the United States did not sign the Geneva Agreement, though pledging to uphold it. Emperor Bao-Dai's government, refusing to acknowledge even temporary loss of the north, simply declined to sign it.

Under these circumstances the prospects of maintaining peace appeared unlikely from the outset. Ho's forces, which had sponsored a Pathet Lao (Free Laotian) movement late in the conflict, proved reluctant to withdraw from Laos. In like manner, his revolutionary allies as well as other dissidents in South Vietnam distrusted the Bao-Dai regime. This distrust deepened when Ngo Dinh Diem dismissed the emperor, extended his authority by intrigue and armed force with American aid, won popular support at the polls, and then repudiated the possibility of an all-Vietnam referendum as provided in the Geneva Agreement. During 1958 isolated acts of terrorism coalesced into a general pattern of guerrilla insurgency which seemed manageable with increased American assistance. As the dimensions and intensity of the struggle grew, however, Diem's regime felt compelled to abandon a promising reform program and assume more and more dictatorial authority, a prelude to his liquidation by an army coup in 1963. At the same time, as the conflict expanded, so did the American and North Vietnamese commitments to the two sides.

To secure the major supply line to the insurgents in the south, the so-called Ho Chi Minh Trail through Laos, North Vietnamese troops supported a Pathet Lao offensive. The prospect of a total Communist takeover in Laos escalated into another major East-West confrontation in 1962, again settled by a Geneva Agreement providing for restoration of a coalition government headed by the neutralist leader, Prince Souvanna Phouma. By 1964 the Viet Cong controlled most of the countryside in South Vietnam and felt the time was ripe to shift from small-scale guerrilla operations to major military formations for the overthrow of the unstable military regime. For this buildup North Vietnam supplied the heavier weapons, trained officers, and technicians needed. In the spring of 1965 it became clear that the South Vietnamese army would not be able to withstand this assault by itself, and the United States finally decided to commit combat units in addition to the already large contingent of military advisors.

Although escalation and varying tactical experiments have changed the picture from time to time, the overall American military strategy became fairly clear. American forces with their heavier firepower and greater mobility by air assumed the major responsibility for interdicting the vital supply lines from North Vietnam and for breaking up threatening, large-scale military formations in the rugged highlands extending north of Saigon through the narrow waist of Vietnam, while the South Vietnamese army was assigned the principal role in securing and protecting the more heavily populated and productive lowlands along the coast and throughout the Mekong Delta. In response to the growing American troop commitment more and more units of North Vietnam's regular army moved into the south because only they possessed sufficient training and firepower to attempt to cope with the heavily armed American units. Finally, growing antiwar sentiment both within and outside the United States, recognition of the improbability of victory on the battlefield for either side within the scope of current strategy, and a desire to reduce the heavy expenditures in American lives and resources of such an open-ended conflict led to measures intended hopefully to bring it to an end. The bombing of North Vietnam was conditionally terminated, Hanoi was persuaded to meet

American representatives at the negotiating table in Paris, and the administration of President Nixon undertook an intensified program of training and equipping South Vietnamese troops to permit the eventual withdrawal of all American combat forces. How successful such a deescalation of American participation in the Vietnamese struggle will prove to be, only time can tell.

At the date of writing the negotiations in Paris have yet to prove fruitful, but the tempo of the warfare has abated somewhat, at least in terms of American casualties. Meanwhile, the overthrow of Norodom Sihanouk has added the former Communist sanctuary of Cambodia to the area of full-scale warfare. The flow of supplies and reinforcements from the north has not been effectively cut off and appears adequate to sustain this so-called national war of liberation, now involving all of former French Indo-China. Whatever the outcome of this struggle, the future of the Vietnamese and their neighbors in Cambodia, Laos, and Thailand under the shadow of China is uncertain and insecure.

BUNG KARNO'S INDONESIA

Torn by all types of internal divisions as illustrated by the 1955 election, independent Indonesia soon fell under the charismatic leadership of Bung (Brother) Karno and his conception of "Guided Democracy," the only alternative to anarchy. Once united in opposition to any reimposition of Dutch imperialism, the political leaders after 1950 turned into feuding and selfish seekers of power and personal enrichment with little concern for the welfare of the people or of Indonesia as a whole. Imbued with outdated fears of Western imperialism and capitalism, they devoted themselves to emotion-filled propaganda rather than the down-to-earth task of nation building. Indeed, continued hostility toward the Dutch and Dutch interests proved to be the principal cement holding the nation together. The consequences of such hostility and too-frequent resort to the print-

ing press were severe economic deterioration and monetary inflation, only partially offset by American foreign aid. The only major accomplishments were in the fields of education and public health which, each in its own way, contributed to social and economic distress and discontent. When Sukarno took full command in 1957, the nation appeared to Western observers to be on the verge of bankruptcy and general disintegration. What was not yet generally appreciated was the concentration of distress in the burgeoning urban centers and the ability of 85 percent of the population to continue to subsist on their fields in the countryside through any fiscal or political debacle.

Sukarno's seizure of power and proclamation of "guided democracy" were greeted by widespread rebellions of liberal and conservative leaders, both civilian and military, who feared the personal and political consequences of his ultranationalist authoritarianism. However, most of the army under the command of General Nasution remained loyal, and when the rebellions were suppressed, Sukarno was strengthened by the opportunity to exile or imprison thousands of opponents. Another significant result was the fuller recognition by Sukarno of the importance of the army and military power to the maintenance of his authority. Henceforth, the military was allotted the lion's share of the national budget, although it constituted only one of three main elements that he juggled to maintain popular support. The other two were the ultranationalists and the Communist Party (PKI). Whatever his intentions, the necessity of balancing and gaining the continuing cooperation of these three groups seriously limited the possibilities of constructive development.

As Sukarno's program of "guided democracy" was gradually unfolded, it involved a total repudiation of "liberal, Western-style democracy" and free enterprise in favor of his intuitive leadership with the advice of properly attuned, appointed councillors representing functional and regional groupings. The economy was aimed in the direction of a form of socialism tailored to the Indonesian heritage and conditions. A stepped-up anti-Dutch nationalization of major enterprises was tied to an ultranationalist campaign to acquire Western New Guinea (Irian Barat), which won popular support for a military buildup with Soviet aid. In foreign policy Sukarno merely gave a more vigorous and left-leaning expression to anti-imperial "neutralism," while engaging in his own brand of Indonesian imperialism. After his saber-rattling had secured Western New Guinea in 1963 through the good offices of American diplomacy, he poured forth Indonesian indignation and hostility against the creation of Malaysia as a British neo-imperialist plot and went so far as to sponsor rebel attacks on the British garrisons in northern Borneo. Throughout these years he cultivated Indonesian Communists as a counterpoise to army influence.

An assessment of Sukarno's rule must conclude that it differed from its predecessor only in its far greater authoritarianism and more pronounced leftward inclination. Ultranational appeals to emotion and sentiment provided no solution to the pressing problems of nation building. Confiscations of Dutch properties brought no benefits when matched with Indonesian managerial ineptitude. The allocation of as much as 80 percent of the national budget to military preparedness left no resources for social and economic reforms. Increased corruption and fiscal mismanagement only accelerated inflation and sank the new nation deeper into an economic morass. Public welfare continued to be neglected in favor of wasteful expenditures on public buildings intended to enhance the prestige and image of Indonesia and its peerless leader. Asian games were sponsored to supplant the "imperialist-controlled" Olympics, and puritanical prohibitions were directed against Western institutions and practices, such as the Boy Scouts and Western music and dancing, in favor of indigenous Indonesian customs and culture. Meanwhile, Sukarno, named president for life in 1963, lived like a spendthrift playboy on costly junkets around the world and posed as the leader of a third force of nonaligned nations. Yet no group appeared in a position to challenge Bung Karno's popular support by the Indonesian people—or so it seemed in 1965.

At the end of August 1965, however, a confused upheaval began with an alleged Communist, antimilitary coup and ended with a successful military coup and a nationwide anti-Communist pogrom in which more than 100,000 Communists and fellow-travellers were exterminated by aroused Muslims running amok. Thus Muslim fanaticism and the military joined forces in the destruction of the PKI. A military junta attacked Sukarno's associates and gradually took away all his powers and titles. On the shoulders of the military rested the immense burden of bringing fiscal responsibility and administrative reform to a demoralized government and nation. In the wings, the American government discreetly applauded this Communist setback and stood ready to render assistance whenever it might become politically feasible.

THE REPUBLIC OF THE PHILIPPINES

The oligarchy that peacefully succeeded to power in the Philippines in 1946 was immediately confronted with monumental tasks of postwar reconstruction and reform to match its democratic pretensions. Despite the appearance of prosperity created by generous American aid, including war-damage payments, economic recovery was handicapped by popular, and particularly Huk, distrust of collaborationist landlords. Acts of terrorism discouraged landlords from attempting to rehabilitate their estates. In any case, landlords and Huks were far apart in their conceptions of economic justice for the peasantry. Under such conditions private investors were reluctant to rebuild. War-damage payments were largely expended on conspicuous consumption in Manila. Indeed, for a time Manila was the best market for Cadillacs. Against this background of unrest the dependence of the economy on the American market tended to increase rather than to decrease. Further nationalistic resentment was aroused by the retention of American military bases and the requirement of the Bell Trade Act that the government grant equal status to American investors in return for extended, tariff-free access to the American market.

Against the Huks the government unleashed the constabulary without success. Indeed, thanks to popular sympathy, they were enabled to extend their depredations into the city limits of Manila itself. Finally, a capable young politician with popular rather than elitest roots was brought into the government as Defense Minister to cope with the problem. As a first step, Ramon Magsaysay called off the hated constabulary and turned the task of suppression over to the better disciplined army beefed up by American military aid and advisors. A moderate land reform limiting the landlord's percentage of the tenant's crop improved the atmosphere. When a general amnesty plus promises of land and tools was offered, most of the followers of Luis Taruc laid down their arms. On the strength of this achievement Magsaysay was elected to the presidency in 1953, and many observers believed that a new day was dawning for Philippine democracy. The oligarchy, however, still controlled the legislature, and when he died in an airplane crash in 1957, the dreams of drastic change died with him. Nevertheless, Magsaysay's brief regime, as limited as its achievements were, had awakened in the oligarchs a greater sense of responsibility for the public welfare. Although corruption and election irregularities were not eliminated, they were no longer openly condoned and serious attention began to be given to the mounting social and economic problems of the nation.

In foreign relations a growing nationalistic concern with Philippine identification with America rather than Asia was reflected in a "Filipino First" form of economic nationalism aimed at American and Chinese economic domination. New friction arose over American military bases and the special status of American servicemen. At the same time, Philippine initiatives sought to gain acceptance as a Southeast Asian nation. As early as 1954 Manila played host to the eight nations that formed the anti-Communist Southeast Asia Treaty Organization, but this institution was a creation of American diplomacy. In 1961 the Philippines on its own persuaded Malaya and Thailand to join in the Association of Southeast Asia for the mutual cultivation of closer economic and cultural ties. In 1963 President Macapagal, who dreamed of a Pan-Malayan confederation called "Maphilindo," took advantage of common concern over Communist advances to bring together Malaysia and Indonesia in a consultative council in which they agreed to subordinate their differences in favor of "common measures to restrain Chinese expansionism." As yet, none of these Philippine diplomatic initiatives have borne significant or concrete fruit, but they have reinforced the psychological commitment to playing a role as an Asian nation. At the same time, the Philippine government has developed trade relations and common interests with Nationalist China, South Korea, and Japan. Recently it has played a leading part in the formation of the Asian Development Bank in which Japan is a principal investor. Macapagal's successor, President Ferdinand Marcos, who was reelected for an unprecedented second term in 1969, has pursued an even more nationalistic course seeking to break away from the American orbit by withdrawing the Philippine army contingent from Vietnam and proposing trade and diplomatic relations with the Communist world. Whatever the future may hold for Asia, it seems safe to predict that the Philippines will continue to move in the direction of reducing its dependence on the United States and increasing its involvement with its Asian neighbors.

INDEPENDENT BURMA

Unlike the Philippines and Malaya and like Indonesia, the anti-Western feeling of independent Burma was so intense that it turned to socialism and the socialist states as the only alternative for guidance and support in modernization. So strong was anti-British feeling that it alone of all former colonies rejected membership in the Commonwealth. However, the strength of the Buddhist tradition, actively fostered by U Nu, significantly softened the Burmese approach to socialism and to its neighbors. Internal divisions both tribal and political troubled Burma more than Indonesia and made it difficult to maintain the Union of Burma. Christian Karens and primitive Kachins joined small bands of Trotzkyite and non-Trotzkyite Communists in offering continuous guerrilla resistance to the central government.

For the first decade the gentle Thakin, U Nu, and his Socialist Party controlled the government despite little progress in suppressing dissidents or in economic development. His most notable accomplishment was the revitalization of Burmese Buddhism. In 1958 the Thakin army commander, General Ne Win, and an army junta took over temporarily to eradicate corruption, restore administrative efficiency, and stamp out dissidents. In 1960 they believed they had done their job and allowed elections which returned U Nu to power. Frustrated by U Nu's inability to maintain the reforms he had introduced, General Ne Win again seized power on March 2, 1962, but this time he had no intention of giving it back to incompetent civilians.

With the advice of a revolutionary council he scrapped the constitution, dismissed the parliament, and proclaimed what he cal-

led "The Burmese Way to Socialism." With martial abruptness all major trading and industrial activities were nationalized and put under the management of his ablest army officers. Rice marketing was made a government monopoly and the peasants were paid less than one-third of the market value for their crop. The difference was intended to finance economic development. Finally, in 1963, all banks were converted into "People's Banks." Like Sukarno, but without his personal charm, Ne Win demonstrated a puritanical streak by closing dance halls, prohibiting beauty contests and horse racing, and insisting on punctuality and industriousness. Such harshness was not popular with the easygoing Burmese, and economic development showed little improvement. Moreover, the diversion of the ablest army officers to administrative and managerial assignments crippled the antiguerrilla campaign. The incidence of insurgency and crime tended to increase rather than decline.

In foreign policy, Burma, like Indonesia, followed the line of left-leaning nonalignment or neutralism but appeared even more introverted and suspicious of Western intentions. Burma promptly recognized the People's Republic of China and generally treated its great neighbor to the north with respect and circumspection. In contrast with India it agreed to a negotiated settlement of its ill-defined frontier with generally favorable results. Extensive trade and aid agreements were concluded with Russia and China, while American aid, including that of private foundations, was terminated, and even American scholars and journalists were excluded from the country. Nevertheless, as early as 1953 the Communist parties were outlawed, and in the later sixties anti-Peking demonstrations underlined the xenophobic character of Burmese socialism. The lack of significant economic progress, the absence of allies, and the continuance of tribal and political insurgency make Burma an ideal candidate for a Chinese-sponsored war of national liberation whenever the Chinese deem such a move to be strategically desirable.

Since achieving political independence the nations of Southeast Asia, fired by particularistic nationalism, have demonstrated little aptitude for regional cooperation despite the lengthening shadow of China. Only a few of them—the Philippines, Malaysia, and to a lesser extent Thailand—have maintained a degree of internal stability and have achieved reasonable economic progress. Indeed, the very presence of American power in the region may have deterred them from taking more responsibility for their own political welfare. The old lines of economic dependence on Western markets, and particularly the American market, persist with little modification, except for the growing trade with Japan. Outside the expanded urban centers there are few signs of modernization or significant change. Meanwhile, the increasing pressure of population growth has only been partially offset by the increased yields of the "green revolution." Each year the gap tends to widen between them and the industrialized nations.

Nevertheless, the optimist, if he looks hard enough, can discover promising signs of progress and even the beginnings of efforts at regional cooperation. Given enough time and enough external aid, these new nations with vast natural resources may yet find the path to a more prosperous future and escape the role of an enticing vacuum for their great neighbors. From this vantage point, however, the minimal immediate prospect appears to be a growing economic subservience to China or Japan, complemented by a declining dependence on Western markets.

SIGNIFICANT DATES

Indonesia

1908	Founding of Budi Ōtomo
1912	Organization of Sarekat Islam
1916	Authorization of Volksraad
1920	Indonesian Communist Party (PKI)
1926	Nahdatul Ulema, forerunner of Masjumi Party (Orthodox Muslim)
1927	Indonesian Nationalist Party (PNI) of Dr. Sukarno
1932	Socialist Party
1939	Indonesian political concentration
1946	Linggadjati Agreement
1950	Republic of Indonesia
1955	Dr. Sukarno and "guided democracy"
1965	Overthrow of Sukarno and Communist purge by military

Philippines

1907	First national election
1916	Jones Act
1935	Commonwealth Constitution
1946	Independence
1954–1957	Presidency of Ramon Magsaysay
1966–1973	Presidency of Ferdinand Marcos

Burma

1906	Young Men's Buddhist Association
1920	First student strike
1930–1931	Saya San Rebellion
1935	Separation of Burma from India

1936	Student strike led by Thakins
1948–1958	Independent Burma under U Nu
1962	Military regime of General Ne Win

Malaya and Malaysia

1948	Federation of Malaya, excluding Singapore
1957	Federation gains independence
1963	Malaysia including Singapore, Sarawak, and Sabah

Thailand (Siam)

1905	Abolition of slavery and *Corvee* labor completed
1925–1939	Termination of unequal treaties negotiated
1932	"Promoters" coup and "constitution" proclaimed
1939	Siam renamed Thailand

Vietnam, Laos, and Cambodia

1930	First rebellion of Nguyen Ai-quoc (Ho Chi Minh)
1945	Democratic Republic of Vietnam proclaimed
1947–1954	Struggle for independence from French
1954	First Geneve Agreement
1958	Start of struggle for unification of Vietnam
1962	Second Geneve Agreement *re* Laos
1965	Commitment of American troops: bombing of North
1968	Cessation of bombing of North: peace negotiations start

SELECTED READINGS

Bloodworth, Dennis, *An Eye for the Dragon: Southeast Asia Observed, 1954–1970.* New York: Farrar, Straus, and Giroux, 1970.

*Burling, Robbins, *Hill Farms and Paddy Fields.* Englewood Cliffs, N.J.: Prentice-Hall, 1965.

*Buttinger, Joseph, *Vietnam: A Political History.* New York: Praeger, 1968.

*Butwell, Richard, *Indonesia.* Boston: Ginn, 1967.

*———, *Southeast Asia Today and Tomorrow.* Rev. ed.; New York: Praeger, 1969.

———, *U Nu of Burma.* Rev. ed.; Stanford: Stanford University Press, 1970.

Elsbree, Willard H., *Japan's Role in Southeast Asian Nationalist Movements, 1940–1945.* Cambridge, Mass.: Harvard University Press, 1953.

Fall, Bernard B., *The Two Viet-Nams.* Rev. ed.; New York: Praeger, 1967.

Farwell, George, *Mask of Asia: The Philippines Today.* New York: Praeger, 1967.

*Fifield, Russell, *Southeast Asia in United States Policy.* New York: Praeger, 1963.

Fryer, Donald W., *Emerging Southeast Asia.* New York: McGraw-Hill, 1970.

*Geertz, Clifford, *Agricultural Involution: The Process of Ecological Change in Indonesia.* Berkeley: University of California Press, 1963.

*————, *Islam Observed*. Chicago: University of Chicago Press, 1971.

*Gordon, Bernard K., *The Dimensions of Conflict in Southeast Asia*. Englewood Cliffs, N.J.: Prentice-Hall, 1966.

*Grossholtz, Jean, *Politics in the Philippines*. Boston: Little, Brown, 1964.

*Hammer, Ellen J., *The Struggle for Indochina, 1940–1953*. Stanford: Stanford University Press, 1966.

Hanna, Willard A., *Bung Karno's Indonesia*. New York: American Universities Field Staff, 1961.

————, *Eight Nation-Makers: Southeast Asia's Charismatic Statesmen*. New York: St. Martin's Press, 1964.

————, *The Formation of Malaysia*. New York: American Universities Field Staff, 1964.

*Hickey, Gerald C., *Village in Vietnam*. New Haven: Yale University Press, 1967.

Ho, Chi-minh, *On Revolution: Selected Writings, 1920–1966*. New York: Praeger, 1966.

*Kahin, George McTurnan, *Nationalism and Revolution in Indonesia*. Ithaca: Cornell University Press, 1970.

————, ed., *Governments and Politics of Southeast Asia*. 2nd ed.; Ithaca: Cornell University Press, 1964.

*————, and Lewis, John W., *The United States in Vietnam*. New York: Dell, 1967.

*Lacouture, Jean, *Ho Chi-minh*. New York: Random House, 1968.

*Lederer, William J., and Burdick, Eugene, *The Ugly American*. New York: Fawcett, 1960.

*Mehden, F. R. von der, *Religion and Nationalism in Southeast Asia*. Madison: University of Wisconsin Press, 1963.

*Milne, R. S., *Government and Politics in Malaysia*. Boston: Houghton Mifflin, 1967.

Mintz, Jeanne S., *Mohammed, Marx, and Marhaen: Roots of Indonesian Socialism*. New York: Praeger, 1965.

*Newman, Bernard, *Background to Vietnam*. New York: Mentor Book, 1966.

Niel, Robert van, *The Emergence of the Modern Indonesian Elite*. The Hague: W. van Hoeve, 1960.

*Pfeffer, Richard, ed., *No More Vietnams*. New York: Harper and Row, 1968.

*Pomeroy, William J., *The Forest: A Personal Record of the Huk Guerrilla Struggle in the Philippines*. New York: International Pubs., 1963.

*Power, John H., and Sicat, Gerardo P., *The Philippines*. London: Oxford University Press, 1971.

Pye, Lucian W., *Guerrilla Communism in Malaya*. Princeton: Princeton University Press, 1956.

*————, *Politics, Personality and Nation Building: Burma's Search for Identity*. New Haven: Yale University Press, 1962.

*————, *Southeast Asia's Political Systems*. Englewood Cliffs, N.J.: Prentice–Hall, 1967.

*Roy, Jules, *The Battle of Dienbienphu.* New York: Pyramid Pub., 1966.

*Schlesinger, Arthur M. Jr., *Bitter Heritage: Vietnam and American Democracy, 1941–1968.* New-York: Fawcett, 1968.

*Schurmann, Franz, et al., *The Politics of Escalation in Vietnam.* New York: Fawcett, 1966.

Smith, Robert Aura, *Philippine Freedom, 1946–1958.* New York: Columbia University Press, 1958.

Taruc, Luis, *He Who Rides the Tiger.* New York: Praeger, 1967.

*Tilman, Robert O., *Man, State, and Society in Contemporary Southeast Asia.* New York: Praeger, 1969.

Tinker, Hugh, *The Union of Burma.* 4th ed.; London: Oxford University Press, 1967.

Trager, Frank N., ed., *Marxism in Southeast Asia.* Stanford: Stanford University Press, 1959.

*Wilson, David A., *Politics in Thailand.* Ithaca: Cornell University Press, 1966.

*Zagoria, Donald S., *Vietnam Triangle: Moscow, Peking, Hanoi.* New York: Pegasus Pubs., 1967.

PART SIX
INDEPENDENT ASIA

Parade in Tienanmen Square. (*Eastfoto*)

For whatever it may signify, more women have gained posts
of political leadership in the East
than their counterparts in the "more advanced" West.

Madame Indira Gāndhi, Prime
Minister of India. *(Keystone Press
Agency)* Died 10/84 age 66

Golda Meir, Prime Minister of Israel. *(Radio
Times Hulton Picture Library)*

Madame Bandaranaike, Prime Minister of Ceylon.
(Keystone Press Agency)

Chiang Ch'ing, wife of Chairman Mao and the
moving force behind the Great Proletarian Cultural
Revolution. *(Eastfoto)*

President Sukarno, founder of the Indonesian Republic. (*Scheler/Black Star*)

David Ben'Gurion, militant champion, first prime minister, and "Grand Old Man" of Israel. (*Radio Times Hulton Picture Library*)

Ho Chi Minh. (*Novosti from Sovfoto*)

King Hussein of Jordan and
President Nasser of Egypt.
(*Keystone Press Agency*)

Chou En-lai, Mao Tse-tung, and
Lin Piao. (*Eastfoto*)

President Nixon meets Chairman
Mao, February 1972.(*Keystone Press
Agency*)

This final part, which encompasses the sometimes puzzling developments of little more than the past two decades, is too close in time for a clear perspective and must be approached with caution and reservation. Too many questions remain to be answered and too many developments are still in mid-course to justify more than tentative hypotheses or probable conclusions. Whatever seems to be the case today may be overturned tomorrow. However, the story of the civilizations of the East and their interaction with the West would be incomplete without substantial attention to recent developments. Especially does this seem to be the case when the much more rapid and accelerating rate of change since emancipation from Western domination is taken into account. The tentative conclusions set forth in this analysis may very well prove to be wrong in the longer run, but it is hoped that they will provide a basis for thoughtful analysis and evaluation of subsequent developments, whatever course they may happen to take. Indeed, this is the main purpose of this entire study: to provide the Western observer of contemporary developments in the East with a foundation for a deeper and broader understanding and appreciation of the enduring ideals and values that influence the approach and attitude of each of these nations to the problems of today, and tomorrow.

CHAPTER TWENTY-FIVE

REVOLUTIONARY CHINA: A CONTINUED STORY

With the Communist "liberation" of mainland China virtually accomplished by the end of 1949, and the retreat of Chiang K'ai-shek's Nationalist regime to the island bastion of Taiwan, the Chinese revolution, begun in 1911, entered a new and much more dynamic stage of development in both its parts. This development, however, is still in progress and its eventual outcome remains in doubt. All that can be attempted here is a descriptive analysis of these changes, to the extent they can be ascertained, and a concluding examination of the problems and prospects still confronting both regimes. A major concern will be how revolutionary these changes are—that is, to what degree they can be regarded as a complete break with the traditional concepts and practices of Chinese civilization. Naturally, much greater attention will be given to the Communist regime not only because it governs the overwhelming majority of the Chinese people but also because it has attempted by far the more radical program.

To be objective or even accurate about the conditions in the two parts of China is much more difficult than for the preceding period of overt struggle. If anything, the United States government has become more deeply involved and, as a result, has been singled out by the Communists as the number one enemy of China, and indeed of all the oppressed peoples of the world— especially the underdeveloped world. All reports and accounts, regardless of the source, tend to reflect the political orientation of the authors and therefore must be mutually viewed with a healthy skepticism. Moreover, Chinese Communist sources, dictated by the precept of "politics in command," amount to little more than propaganda, whether directed at

the Chinese people or the outside world. Wherever the analyst treads, the ice is very thin and what appears to be the case today may be reversed tomorrow. After these words of warning an effort may be made to assess the massive problems inherited by the Communists and the means employed to resolve them.

RECOVERY AND REHABILITATION (1949 – 1953)

The year of the Communist conquest saw the depth of China's postwar economic dislocation and depression characterized by runaway inflation. Due to the ravages of war the inadequate internal communications by rail and road had suffered severe damage and were in need of heavy investment for rehabilitation, let alone expansion. Industrial production had fallen to almost half its previous peak because of the lack of raw materials, the fiscal chaos, and the flight of capital and management. Although China had never developed a reliable method of measuring agricultural output, food crops were estimated to have fallen off sharply to a total of about 108 million metric tons. Certainly food was in severely short supply in the cities, but such a decline in production seems improbable. Chinese farmers had always tended for taxation purposes to underreport their crops and now, in the midst of political upheaval, may have preferred to hoard their surpluses. Indeed, until the Communist regime began to develop a fairly adequate statistical survey after 1952, "true" output probably exceeded governmental estimates by substantial margins. Thoroughly experienced in deception and difficult to regulate in detail, the Chinese peasant was, and in spite of Communist to-

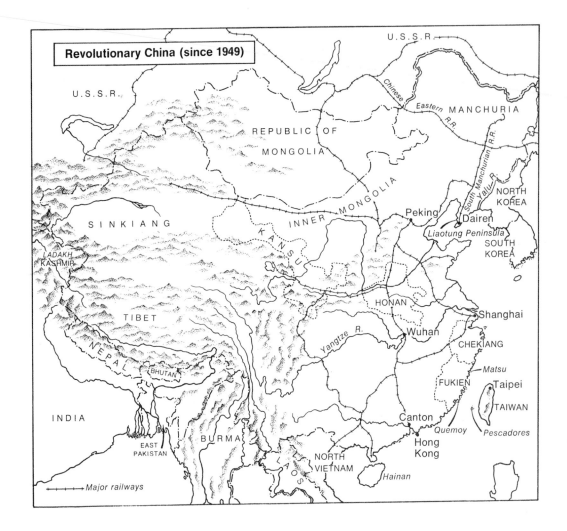

Revolutionary China (since 1949)

talitarian techniques perhaps still is, the best-fed citizen of the state. This is the reward for the hardships of peasant life.

These problems, essentially economic, were offset, however, by a significant number of advantages. The Communist leaders, elated by victory after twenty years of bitter struggle, led four and a half million party members flushed with revolutionary enthusiasm and ready to carry out the orders from above. But Mao Tse-tung, as his writings during the previous decade clearly demonstrate, while unquestionably dedicated to the eventual goal of communism according to the teachings of Marx and Lenin, planned a gradualistic transformation, avoiding Russian errors, yet benefiting from

their experience. Furthermore, his writings make clear that, as a pragmatic Chinese, he fully realized that China's revolution could not slavishly imitate the Russian model but would require necessary modification to fit the Chinese situation. Compared to Lenin and associates, Mao had the advantage of many years of experience in operating a government under the difficult circumstances of civil war. Thus the astute leader who had guided the Communist party to victory after a prolonged struggle was fully prepared to accept the responsibilities of government for which he had schemed and fought so long.

On July 1, 1949, sensing victory, Mao set the stage for the establishment of a new government in a work entitled *On the Peo-*

ple's Democratic Dictatorship advocating the relatively moderate policy of "leaning to one side." By "leaning to one side" Mao meant alliance with the international socialist movement headed by the Soviet Union against "imperialists and their running dogs" within China, that is, those who still chose to support "the bandit regime" of Chiang K'ai-shek. The "people" who would enjoy the freedoms and privileges of the People's Democratic Dictatorship included the working class, the peasantry, the petty bourgeoisie, and the national bourgeoisie. Excluded were "nonpeople" defined as "running dogs of imperialism"—the landlords, bureaucratic bourgeoisie, and Kuomintang counterrevolutionaries. The latter would be tolerated if they behaved themselves, and serious efforts would be made to remold them into "people" through labor. If persuasion failed, however, they would be compelled to work. For any "people" who committed crimes, persuasion in the Chinese tradition of moral superiority was preferred to punishment as a means of convincing them of the antisocial character of their conduct.

Another advantage that had greatly eased the course of Communist conquest was the war-weariness of the Chinese people and their desire for a strong government of any form which held promise of restoring the position of the Middle Kingdom in world affairs. The majority of the people, who had never experienced the benefits of democracy, were ready to accept and obey the directives of an authoritarian regime—if they got results. Mao recognized the overwhelming demand and need for internal peace and national defense by singling out the people's army, the people's police, and the people's courts for priority development as the most vital elements of the future government.

In the economic realm the implementation of socialist objectives was greatly facilitated by the inheritance from the Nationalist government of about two-thirds of China's modern industry, taken over from the Japanese and those accused of collaboration, as well as the entire railroad network. In commerce also the most important operations had been controlled by the Nationalist regime. With his intimate knowledge of the peasants on whom his movement had been built and who constituted 90 percent of the party membership, Mao spoke with authority when he acknowledged the education of the peasants in socialism as the most serious problem confronting the People's Democratic Dictatorship—and so it has proven to be. As he put it:

> The peasant economy is scattered, and the socialization of agriculture, judging by the Soviet Union's experience, will require a long time and painstaking work. . . . The steps to socialize agriculture must be coordinated with the development of a powerful industry having state enterprise as its backbone.

Thus, from the beginning, the greatest challenge to Chinese Communism was recognized and the program for its solution was set forth. The timing of the steps and their coordination with the development of industry, which have seemed to most Western observers erratic, poorly planned, and even disastrous, reflecting a neglect of agriculture and a lack of understanding of its problems, were actually an application of the Chinese Communist strategy of sharp advance and then partial retreat, of struggle and then rectification, yielding a net gain in the progress toward the goal of socialization in this as well as other areas. Most Western analysts, especially American, have stressed and even exaggerated the setbacks while failing to appreciate the substantial advances toward the socialization of agriculture without the attrition suffered by the Soviet Union in similar efforts.

A further advantage was the acceptance of the new regime, however reluctantly, by the vast majority of the educated and progressive elements, including military men, administrators, educators, businessmen, scientists, and technicians. The flight to Taiwan and Hongkong represented only that minority of trained manpower that correctly foresaw little future under the Communists for its individualistic aspirations. Furthermore, pure patriotism—not communism—lured several hundred prominent scholars and scientists into returning from overseas to serve the homeland at great personal sacrifice, especially after the demonstration of military strength in Korea proved that the birth pangs of modern China had at long last spawned an able and effective regime. Thus, as had been the case at the inception of previous dynasties, the Communists had attracted the support of the bulk of the trained manpower so essential to a successful rehabilitation program. On the other hand, few of these intellectuals had been converted to Chinese Communism, and therefore, a host of non-Communist organizations and parties had to be given recognition and a measure of status in what purported to be a united front government. In practice, however, this fiction soon created friction as every activity of the intellectuals came under the scrutiny and direction of comparatively untutored, but ideologically more trustworthy, members of the Communist party. The obvious and only solution was a continuous program of indoctrination by persuasion, which reached periodic peaks of intensity in recurrent rectification drives. Though different in nature and requiring more subtle manipulation, the ideological transformation of the intellectuals has turned out to be almost as difficult a task as the socialization of the peasants. In contrast, the disciplining of the managerial and commercial classes, already accustomed to extensive regulation under the Nationalists, has proven much easier to accomplish.

A final advantage of dubious value was the prompt recognition and promise of support from the acknowledged leader of world communism, the Soviet Union. The Chinese Communist victory had been achieved independently without any significant support during the long years of struggle. Ever since its birth Stalin had viewed Mao's unorthodox movement with suspicion and distrust, but

whatever his personal views and misgivings he had no choice but to welcome the triumph of communism, orthodox or not, in the country with which Russia shared the longest frontier. Nevertheless, it soon became apparent that Stalin was determined to attempt the subjugation of this newest member of the communist club to his direction and control.

After the People's Political Consultative Conference had adopted the Common Program, elaborating on the views already set forth by Mao, and had proclaimed the *People's Republic of China* on October 1, 1949, Mao, who had never left China before, dutifully departed in December on his pilgrimage to Moscow in search of aid. Following nine weeks of secret negotiation, a treaty of alliance and an agreement on economic cooperation emerged which, stripped of the customary glittering generalities and banalities, clearly reflected the clash of two strong wills each unwilling to concede more than an inch or two. The 30-year alliance was defensive against aggression by Japan and any power supporting Japan which, of course, meant the United States. By this treaty China was taken within the protection of the Russian nuclear shield, but nothing more. The economic agreement was equally limited in its provisions and indeed was reminiscent of the ambitions and objectives of Tsarist Russia. While retaining the rights to occupy and use the ice-free port of Dairen on the Liaotung peninsula and to manage the Chinese Eastern railway, Russia promised to furnish the machinery and technical assistance for the rehabilitation of the looted Manchurian mines and industry—at Chinese expense. In addition, joint Sino-Russian enterprises were to be set up for the development of new resources and communications, particularly in the borderlands of Sinkiang, Inner Mongolia, and Manchuria. Finally, a modest credit of 60 million dollars a year for 5 years bearing the low interest of 1 percent was extended for the purchase of Russian equipment and supplies. Not until after Stalin's death in 1953 were these limited economic agreements significantly expanded by his insecure successors, and even then every bit of aid, including military supplies for the Korean conflict, called for repayment in Chinese products on fairly short terms. Thus the Soviet Union's support of its largest partner has been not only limited but also costly. On the other hand, it is only fair to note that this aid and technical assistance laid the vital foundations for modern heavy industry on which the modernization of China depends.

Now that the various advantages of Communist China have been reviewed, its vigorous assault on its problems needs to be examined. Once Nationalist military resistance had been broken, except on Taiwan, the most fundamental problem in need of solution was the fiscal chaos inherited from the Nationalist regime. To the amazement of observers this task was accomplished in less than a year by an assortment of measures characterized by concentration of control of all financial operations. First, the People's Bank of China was founded and empowered to be the sole bank of deposit for governmental funds and the sole bank of issue for legal tender. Through it the government secured the power of life and death over all other banks and financial operations. Second, the new People's Currency was made the sole legal tender for which all existing currency had to be exchanged. This measure helped to reveal the monetary resources of the country. By carefully restricting the amount of currency issued for circulation the government enforced an austerity policy and attempted to check inflation. At the same time, those with savings were induced to invest in National Economic Construction Bonds, while the government reduced expenditures in an effort to balance the budget. For the same reason the taxation structure was simplified by reducing the variety of taxes, and then taxes were more rigorously collected. Finally, the currency was stabilized by giving it a fixed value in relation to grain and other products of common consumption.

While working to restore fiscal stability, the government also directed its attention to the related problem of revitalizing economic activity. The need to rehabilitate the war-torn rail and road system of communications for political as well as economic reasons was recognized and given top priority. The exchange of products between town and country was encouraged in every way with governmental procurement and distribution playing an increasingly important role. Public works to aid agriculture were undertaken, most notable of which was the Huai river flood control and irrigation project. The revival of industrial production was stimulated by governmental contracts and supply of raw materials. Nevertheless, the economy did not begin to hum until the major war effort in Korea late in 1950 furnished both material and patriotic incentives for actively and energetically supporting the new regime. At that time too, the rate of Russian economic assistance was stepped up. By 1953 production in every area had substantially surpassed the pre-1949 peaks.

The patriotic stimulus of wartime tension and demands between 1950 and 1953 enabled the government to accelerate the extension of totalitarian controls and the implementation of its reform program. At the beginning, conditions varied so greatly from area to area that an intermediate tier of six regional administrations was established to exercise most of the functions of the central government. After four years, sufficient control and uniformity had been accomplished to justify elimination of this dangerous policy of decentralization in the 1954 constitution. By the end of 1953 private enterprise and rich peasants still made an important contribution to the economy, but they had all been reduced to a greater or lesser degree of disciplined dependence on the government and the party which presaged their ultimate demise. Active recruitment, especially among the industrial proletariat, had greatly increased the party membership, offsetting to a degree the overwhelming peasant representation, in spite of extensive purges through rectification campaigns of incompetent or ideologically questionable members. Except for two questionable cases in the upper echelon of the party, these purges appear to have been carried out without the violence that had characterized their Russian counterparts, a major credit to the organization and technique of the Chinese Communist party as well as the traditional obedience of the Chinese people to effective authority. Finally, a shrewd policy of harassment by new taxes, employment rules, and other regulations forced foreign entrepreneurs, without any direct threat of confiscation, to abandon operations, plants, and equipment for nominal sums, simply because they could no longer be run profitably.

The united front program, proclaimed at the time of "liberation," envisioned an undefined period of collaboration with all patriotic elements under the leadership of the Communist party to achieve a gradual transformation to socialism and ultimately communism. This transformation is still officially in progress, but the Korean conflict made it possible to speed up the implementation of reforms, though the keynote remained caution. Mao and his experienced associates fully appreciated the immensity of the task confronting them.

The first major reform, bearing no direct relationship to socialism or communism, was the emancipation of women from their traditional inferior status, which had been set forth as a basic objective in the Common Program. The Marriage Law of 1950 was the chief act in implementing this reform. By it, concubinage, child marriage, and arranged marriages were declared illegal. Henceforth marriage was a civil act limited to those who had reached the statutory ages. Unhappy partners of previously arranged marriages were invited to obtain divorces, but the law obliged fathers to support their children until they reached legal age. Initially divorces were granted freely, but since then they have become increasingly difficult to obtain on the ground that plaintiffs by such an action were demonstrating antisocial and selfish characteristics. This attitude is only one reflec-

tion of the puritanical quality of Chinese Communism which places a heavy and traditionally Chinese emphasis on moral regeneration.

More demonstrative of Communist doctrine were the rectification campaigns labeled the "three-anti" and "five-anti" movements. The first was essentially political, aimed at ferreting out and condemning with great fanfare officials (many of whom were holdovers from the Nationalist regime) on the broad charges of corruption, waste, and bureaucratism, which meant treating subordinates and the people as inferiors and not as comrades. At the same time, the people were encouraged to denounce "reactionaries and counterrevolutionaries," even their own parents, who would then be consigned to "reform through labor," practically a death warrant. The "five-anti" movement singled out the bourgeoisie for denunciation on the even vaguer charges of bribery, tax evasion, theft of state property, cheating on labor or materials, and stealing state economic secrets. Again public enthusiasm was whipped up to encourage employees to inform on employers, and public trials were accompanied by public confessions and sentences of varying severity. Many businessmen committed suicide rather than face such an ordeal, others were heavily fined, and the worst offenders were committed to "reform through labor" camps or even executed. The result was a great extension of governmental control, if not outright confiscation, of private enterprise. Many had to borrow from the government banks to pay their fines, which in essence meant their reduction to salaried managers of joint state-private enterprises whose control fell wholly into the government's hands. And, incidentally, the fines helped to replenish the depleted war chest of the regime.

Finally, a land reform decree, more moderate than previous Communist practice for fear of disrupting agricultural production during wartime, attacked the landlord class. Since the Communists had already redistributed land in the north and tenantry was far more prevalent and extensive in the south, central and southern China were primarily affected by this measure. Under its terms rich peasants who farmed part of their land were allowed to hire labor to farm most of the rest, but tenantry in the pure sense of the term was supposed to end. Even absentee landlords living in cities, if they had not been too oppressive in the past, were permitted to retain some of their land to be worked by wage labor. On the other hand, "activist" cadres were sent from village to village to condemn exceptionally evil landlords and usurers. Since these courts were ostensibly unofficial, no records were kept of their sentences, leaving the field open to wide-ranging speculations on the number executed, running from as low as 100,000 to more than 20 million. Of course, the higher figures also include the victims of the "anti" movements who committed suicide, were executed, or subsequently died in labor camps. Every revolution involves a reign of terror whose loss of life rises with its extensiveness.

By 1953, with victory, from the Chinese point of view, over the forces of the United Nations assured in Korea, the stature of the Communist regime guaranteed it against any significant internal opposition. As has previously been noted, nothing succeeds in China like success—and the new government in a few short years had proven itself. After more than a century of humiliation China had found a leadership capable of fighting the combined power of the West to a standstill. Every citizen of the Middle Kingdom could turn with pride and loyalty to such a regime.

Meanwhile, the foundation for more modern, direct control and management had been laid by the census completed in 1953, the most thorough census in the more than 3000 years of Chinese history. Although only estimates, supported by spot checks, were made for the peripheral, low population regions occupied by minority peoples, most of densely populated China proper was directly enumerated by an army of census takers. The result, which exceeded all previous esti-

mates by at least 100 million, probably surprised even the Communist government. A whole series of modern statistical checks were carried out before the final tabulation was released to an amazed world. It was claimed that 583 million were under Communist rule on the mainland. If this figure is accepted, China's greatest asset—and its greatest problem—is its population. Almost one quarter of the human race serves, and is served by, a single authoritarian regime determined to exercise at least a proportionate influence in the world's affairs.

MILITARY AND FOREIGN POLICIES AND RELATIONS (1949–1953)

By the spring of 1950 the new regime had virtually conquered and destroyed all significant resistance throughout all the traditional territories of Chinese rule except the islandlike appendage of Hainan in the extreme southeast whose reduction was in progress, Tibet which had been independent since the revolution, and most important of all, the island of Taiwan plus lesser offshore outposts on which Chiang K'ai-shek and the forces loyal to his Nationalist regime had taken their final refuge and were preparing to make a final stand. In January 1950, President Truman made it absolutely clear that the struggle between the two Chinese governments was strictly an internal affair in which the United States government had no intention of intervening. All military aid and credit for Chiang's refugee regime had been terminated.

Why Mao Tse-tung did not attempt an amphibious assault is a mystery that only future facts will resolve. Perhaps one factor was the hope that Chiang, or his followers, hitherto denounced as "running dogs of American imperialism" and now abandoned by their benefactor, would be amenable to a negotiated settlement appealing to their patriotism. Certainly they were invited to come to terms. A more practical consideration was the costliness of transporting an army in junks across a minimum of 80 miles of open sea, while Chiang had at his command a small navy and the remnants of his air force. Of course, Stalin, if he had wished to do so, could at small cost have offset this Nationalist advantage with a contingent of the Russian air force, but as subsequent events demonstrated he had stronger interests elsewhere and in any case probably preferred to preserve this check on his uncooperative ally. Whatever the circumstances may eventually prove to have been, Chinese Communist troops were being massed in Manchuria before the North Koreans crossed the 38th parallel in June, suggesting that Stalin had persuaded Mao to prepare, if needed, to support that action. Probably little persuasion was necessary because Korea was traditionally an area of Chinese influence and before Japanese expansion had for centuries acknowledged Chinese suzerainty. Meanwhile, scattered contingents continued mopping up operations while another army prepared to invade Tibet, a successful operation launched in October, shortly before Chinese intervention in the Korean conflict.

Until the outbreak of the Korean War and American commitment to the defense of Taiwan as well as South Korea, Chinese foreign policy was moderate, muted, and uncertain, countering charges of being the "running dogs" of Russian imperialism with the weak assertion that it was merely "leaning to one side." Thereafter, denunciations of American imperialism and neocolonialism built up to a crescendo that as yet has seen no more than temporary abatements. Everywhere China turned its eyes, except toward the Russian frontier, the United States stood out as the chief opponent to the reestablishment of traditional Chinese authority and influence. In addition, the United States utilized the full weight of its influence to isolate China by its non-recognition policy and to mobilize opposition to the replacement of Nationalist representation in the United Nations. This American policy has engendered deep-seated bitterness and hatred that may prove difficult to overcome by any change of policy in the foreseeable future.

Late in October 1950, when the counterattacking forces of South Korea and the United Nations under the command of General Douglas MacArthur were nearing the Yalu river boundary of Manchuria in hot pursuit of the routed North Koreans, the People's Republic of China, after several warnings against further advances, committed itself to massive intervention utilizing so-called "volunteers." The overextended United Nations forces were in their turn routed with heavy losses and only with large reinforcements, gradually fought their way back to the 38th parallel, the original line of demarcation between North and South Korea. There both sides dug in during 1951, while long negotiations finally led to a truce in 1953, permitting China to divert more military equipment and supplies to the support of Ho Chi Minh's struggle against the French in Indo-China. At the Geneva Conference of April through July 1954, which provided for the French evacuation of Indo-China, the establishment of the three independent states of Laos, Cambodia, and Vietnam, and the temporary division of Vietnam at the 17th parallel, the People's Republic of China gained recognition as a great power, a stature previously granted to Nationalist China in the formation of the United Nations.

In addition to international prestige China secured a number of other benefits from its successful participation in the Korean conflict. Most obviously its unprecedented victories won the unquestioning support of the Chinese people and consolidated the regime's authority over the mainland. At long last the prolonged Chinese revolution had produced a regime capable of restoring the Middle Kingdom to its rightful position in the world. Moreover, the innate patriotism of millions of overseas Chinese was deeply stirred by this achievement. Many of them, including significantly several hundred highly trained scientists, felt obligated to return voluntarily and offer their services to the fatherland, while millions of others, for one reason or another, felt impelled to make regular and substantial remittances to their ancestral families on the mainland.

A second benefit was the acquisition of modern arms, including an air force, from the Russians. Even though this military equipment was not a gift and eventually had to be paid for, it facilitated the regoranization and modernization of the Chinese army into the major military force in Asia, a potential threat and diplomatic weapon to all its neighbors. No longer were the Soviet Union and the United States the only powers to be reckoned with. Backed up by this military potential, Chinese foreign policy could afford for the next few years to extend its influence by a conciliatory attitude stressing negotiation and peaceful coexistence, while concentrating on internal development to support its military might.

A third benefit, just as important to the Chinese and their leaders as the others, was the replacement of the Soviet Union as the prime protector and benefactor of North Korea. At the same time, Ho Chi-minh's new Communist regime in North Vietnam looked principally to China for economic and political support for its very existence, let alone for its irredentist ambitions. Thus China had won two traditionally dependent states to act as buffers and bases on its northeastern and southeastern frontiers.

The coincidental death of Stalin in 1953 and the consequent struggle for power in the Soviet Union were destined to enhance the influence of China in the communist world, independent of the Korean episode. Stalin had badly miscalculated the results when he proposed to bleed Mao and his men in Korea; the benefits acquired by the wily Mao far exceeded the costs of the war. China emerged from it with so much greater power and prestige, both internally and externally, that the Nationalist charge of being a Russian satellite no longer carried conviction.

COLLECTIVIZATION AND THE FIRST FIVE YEAR PLAN (1953 – 1957)

Freed from the extraordinary costs of a wartime economy and fortified by the vast enhancement of its authority and prestige, both at home and abroad, the Chinese Communist regime proclaimed in September 1953 a shift in emphasis from the "New Democracy" to the "Transition to Socialism." The essential foundations for such an acceleration toward the ultimate goal of communism had been laid during the preceding three years: the identification and disciplining of most hostile elements, the reduction to full governmental control of businessmen and industrialists, and the redistribution of 45 percent of the land to poor peasants and rural laborers totalling close to 70 percent of the rural population.

Such a period, when Communist authority was firmly enough entrenched to permit such a policy change, was also the logical time for replacing the temporary Organic Law and Common Program of 1949 with a "more permanent" constitution. During 1953 a committee headed by Mao drew up a constitution whose final draft was approved in March 1954. Meanwhile, starting in mid-1953, 278 million "people" over 18 years of age elected basic level people's congresses. In turn, these congresses elected delegates to provincial and municipal congresses. Finally, in September 1954, 1226 representatives of the latter, of minority nationalities, of the armed forces, and of overseas Chinese convened as the first National People's Congress and by secret ballot approved the constitution.

The constitution was obviously fashioned after that of the Soviet Union, but it incorporated enough differences to be a unique and distinctive instrument. First, the National People's Congress was unicameral reflecting the Chinese conception of a single, unified, multinational state in contrast with the Russian federation of constituent republics. Although the minority nationalities were guaranteed a measure of autonomy, all legislation was dependent on the approval of the Standing Committee of the National People's Congress and must conform with the national objective of implementing the transition to socialism. Elected to four-year terms, the delegates were to meet for only a few weeks each year, being represented in the interim by a Standing Committee with full power to act in the name of the congress. Another distinctive feature was the greater power vested in the Chairman of the People's Republic of China. Although he was elected by the congress, he was not responsible to it. Moreover, he was concurrently chairman of the National Defense Council, with full authority over the armed forces and nominated the vice-chairman and members of this vital body for approval by the congress. In addition, he nominated the premier who in turn named the members of the State Council, subject to final approval by the congress. On the other hand, neither the congress nor its standing committee could be prorogued, suspended, or dissolved by either the chairman of the Republic or the premier of the State Council. Therefore, the congress only exercised ultimate and not immediate control over the executive as would be the case in a typical parliamentary system of a cabinet responsible to a legislature.

The congress did theoretically control the budget which required its approval and the legal arm of the state by electing the president of the Supreme People's Court and the chief-procurator (that is, state prosecutor) of the Supreme People's Procuratorate. Moreover, the congress had to approve all laws and legislation. But since few laws have been laid down to guide the courts, the administration of justice, in accordance with Chinese tradition, left to judges and juries a wide range of discretion in arriving at judgments limited, of course, by the requirement to conform with the state's ideological dictates of the moment.

The constitution included a long list of civil rights for the "people," such as freedom of speech and assembly and the equality of women, but of greater significance was the emphasis on duties which, in effect, limited the exercise of such rights to activities approved by the government. The right to private property was also circumscribed in fact by the economic aim stated in the constitution that "the policy of the state toward capitalist industry and commerce is to use, restrict, and transform them." A similar transformation was also in progress for agriculture.

Already in December 1951 and again in February 1953 directions had been issued for the formation of mutual aid teams, both temporary and permanent, and lower-level producer's cooperatives in agriculture. Temporary mutual aid teams calling for seasonal sharing of manpower, draft animals, and tools by three to ten families, while introducing the rudiments of collectivization, constituted no significant break with traditional cooperative practices. The permanent mutual aid team, however, demanded more careful accounting with year-round collaboration. The appropriate apportionment and crediting of shared manpower and assets between rich, middle, and poor peasants often became subjects of serious dispute. Many rich peasants, who frequently were more industrious, felt they fared better by hiring labor as needed than by sharing with a team. Lower-level cooperatives, which involved the pooling of land in addition to other communal agricultural assets by 20 to 50 families, were viewed with even less favor by rich peasants because land was always valued by Communists at a lower rate than labor and their relative prosperity was very often the result of better or improved land, not a larger amount of land. Therefore, the comparatively small number of cooperatives existing in 1953 were concentrated mainly in those areas of northern China that were relatively poor and had long been subject to the Communists. Finally, a miniscule proportion of agricultural land, mainly reclaimed land or former Japanese plantation-type operations in Manchuria, was vested in state farms, totally owned and operated by the state with wage labor and imported farm machinery.

The growing reluctance of rich peasants to cooperate and the failure of the 1953 harvest to measure up to expectations, in addition to the ideological desire to advance toward socialism, were all factors in the decision at the end of 1953 to press for the "voluntary" formation of cooperatives and to establish pilot state farms throughout China as examples of the advantages of complete collectivization. Other considerations, political, social, and economic, were of course also important influences. Economically the 1953 census revealed the tremendous and rapidly growing number to be fed, while the plans for industrialization would require increasing withdrawals of acreage for nonfood crops. The only solution seemed to be more intensive cultivation and expanded irrigation to increase productivity per acre because the possibilities of reclaiming new land were limited. It was hoped that by larger scale organization in collectives, China's greatest resource, the underemployed rural population, could be mobilized. Politically there were clear symptoms of backsliding into traditional attitudes and practices on the part of the rich and middle peasants who constituted 30 percent of the rural population. Both politically and socially such antisocial views, which were dangerously infectious, could be eradicated by progressive steps toward collectivization, militantly supported by all the means of persuasion available to a totalitarian state, such as propaganda, mass campaigns, and control of purchase, sales, credit, and taxes. But to carry out such a program, dedicated activists were needed; from 1953 to 1958 party membership, in spite of purges, roughly doubled from 6 to 12 million, and despite intensified efforts to increase the proletarian proportion, the party remained overwhelmingly rural in composition. The difficulty of indoctrinating such a vast and growing body continues to be a major problem of the Communist regime.

The progress toward collectivization during the following years was erratic with periodic relaxations of pressure between campaigns to permit consolidation and a restoration of balance after excesses had stirred up substantial peasant discontent. One such relaxation occurred in 1955 and appears to have reflected a rise in peasant resistance as indicated by only a small increase in the 1954 crop yield. Of course, Communist assertions of adverse weather also were a partially valid explanation. Then, following a sharp increase in the 1955 crop, the program was pressed again until virtually all rural China had adopted lower-level producers' cooperatives by the end of 1956. According to official projections, this progress far exceeded expectations and led the regime to revise its target date.

With the establishment of lower-level producers' cooperatives throughout the land two years ahead of schedule, the decision was made to forge ahead to higher-level producers' cooperatives, distinguished theoretically by eliminating the differentiation in land shares (or virtual expropriation for common use) but factually by being larger organizations (50 to 200 families each) capable of mobilizing a larger work force with more diversified skills to undertake major construction projects. In spite of exceptionally heavy investment during 1956 in the total economy, agricultural productivity showed almost no increase, and again, during 1957, the cautious elements in the hierarchy argued for a relaxation of central pressure to encourage greater peasant cooperation. But this was not to be.

Although a few measures late in 1957 indicated a probable slowdown and decentralization, the victory during 1958 was destined to go to the bold leaders who favored an acceleration, and not a deceleration, of the transition to socialism, regardless of the costs, as the best solution to the political, social, and economic tensions and contradictions created by the progress to date. One rough estimate—and it can be no more than that, subject to widespread regional and local variations—suggests that 40 percent, mainly Communist cadres and the youthful element of the poor peasants, actively favored and supported collectivization, the other 30 percent of poor peasants reluctantly accepted it, and the 30 percent constituting the former rich and middle peasants were dragooned into it by reprisals, or the fear of reprisals. For the latter, collectivization definitely involved social and economic loss, but a general political maxim of Mao Tse-tung applies as well to collectivization; no leader can be always right; any leader whose decisions are 70 percent correct is a successful leader.

Through 1957 at least, the agricultural policies of the Communist regime appear to have been accepted, actively or passively, by the bulk of the rural population. A majority of the peasants probably gained some small improvement in their standard of living at the expense of the more prosperous farmers. On the other hand, discontent with the growing disparity between their standard of living and that of the favored industrial sector was reflected in an excessive migration from the country to the cities. This discontent was reinforced by growing demands for labor on public works, by a program of forced savings, by the shortage of consumer needs, and by the increased governmental control of buying, selling, and credit which, with labor demands, combined to contribute to the shortage of consumer goods by diverting time from and stifling incentive for the production of traditional household crafts.

The blame for these and other shortcomings was placed on incompetent or overzealous cadres who failed to heed the advice of the experienced elders of the community with frequently disastrous results. As the local agents of the regime, they were caught in the middle and subjected to criticism from below and above for any failures. The government constantly preached to them about the evils of arrogance and bureaucratism, reminding them of Mao's aphorism that Communists are like fish in the sea of the peasantry—without their support we will die. Policy directives must be modified to fit local conditions. They must be implemented with the understanding and support of the local sages whose wisdom and leadership must be respected. Yet the policies must be put into effect. The poor cadre—he was damned if he did and damned if he didn't. The only solution was persuasion in long and tedious "struggle" meetings demanding exceptional skill in psychological manipulation, a skill that probably only a few possessed. Indeed, many old hands and new recruits were lacking in basic understanding of Chinese Communist doctrine, let alone appreciation of the reasons for the many bends and shifts in Communist practice.

Although the lack of adequate statistical information delayed until 1955 the announcement of the goals for agriculture and industry of the First Five-Year Plan (1953–1957), Communist ideology required that the overwhelming emphasis be placed on industry, and especially basic heavy industry on which future industrial development depended. For political reasons industrial development was greatly aided by the more liberal and less suspicious successors of Stalin (d. March 1953) who felt a need for the backing of the state representing more than half the population of the Communist world. Irritating encroachments, reminiscent of Tsarist imperial ambitions, were removed when the Soviet Union agreed between 1953 and 1955 to relinquish its share in joint enterprises, its control of the Chinese Eastern Railroad, and its right to maintain an ice-free naval base on the Liaotung Peninsula. China's First Five-Year Plan also happened to coincide with the desire of the new Russian leadership to improve relations both inside and outside the Communist world by an expanding program of trade and aid in competition with the West.

In short order an agreement was reached by which the Soviet Union would provide 141 major modern industrial installations along with the necessary technical advisors. In subsequent agreements through 1957 additional plants were authorized totalling 166 out of 921 major projects scheduled. In addition, East European satellites contracted to supply 68 major industrial installations. Of course, none of these were gifts; all had to be paid for by exports, primarily raw materials, over a relatively short period of time. Most of them served as models that Chinese engineers later showed an exceptional ability not only to duplicate but also to modify and improve. Most were constructed at points strategically located in relation to the sources of raw materials. In any case, the dispersal of industry fitted military considerations and the need to introduce the people of the hinterland to the processes of modernization, in addition to relieving to an extent the burden of distribution on the inadequate and overworked railroad network.

On the other hand, the rapid growth in mining and industrial activity, the inland shift of centers of supply and distribution, and the general reorientation of trade from sealanes to overland routes required a heavy investment in railroad construction. Overburdened old routes needed to be double-tracked to accommodate the heavier traffic and a major accomplishment was the bridging of the Yangtze at the Wuhan rail and industrial center, a project that had been deemed technically unfeasible by Western engineers. This feat, of which the Chinese were inordinately proud, provided an uninterrupted rail route between Peking and Canton. A northward route across Inner Mongolia furnished a shorter connection with the Trans-Siberian Railway through the nominally independent Republic of Outer Mongolia, but perhaps more importantly it enabled the Chinese to reassert influence in this state abandoned on paper, but not in the Chinese heart. Finally, a vital strategic route gradually crept westward along the old caravan route through the Kansu corridor and the vast wastelands of Sinkiang ostensibly to provide another link with Russia but, in fact, to integrate with China proper this potentially mineral rich, non-Chinese frontier region on which Russia had demonstrated designs since the nineteenth century. Far in advance of the railhead large contingents of the army were dispatched to protect the frontier, to police the Muslim peoples, and to begin modern mechanized farming of irrigable land estimated, when fully developed, to be capable of adding 10 percent to China's arable land. At the same time, geological exploration, previously begun by Sino-Soviet teams, revealed vast deposits of uranium, iron, coal, and other valuable ores as well as potentially the largest petroleum reserves outside the Middle East.

Regardless of how Chinese statistical reports are evaluated, industrial and mining production during these five years grew very rapidly in quantity, even if the quality of the products is open to question. Indeed, Russian advisors frequently complained of the neglect of adequate maintenance and quality controls in the drive for production at any costs. The share of the budget allocated to all aspects of economic construction increased from one-third to one-half of the total, and within this category industry's share grew from 46 percent to more than 59 percent with 1956 seeing such heavy investment that it produced a large deficit. Much of private enterprise had already been taken over by the government or forced into joint state-private operation, which in fact meant government control, but in 1953 private enterprise still provided almost 17 percent of the government's revenues. An intensive campaign in 1956 has virtually eliminated, except for the smallest scale, individual activities and handicrafts, yielding only 1 percent of 1957 revenues. A few selected statistics will serve to emphasize the relative growth in key industries between 1953 and 1957. Crude steel production increased from about $1^{1}/_{2}$ to $5^{1}/_{3}$ million tons; coal from 69 to 130 million tons; electric output from 9 to more than 19 billion kilowatt-hours; oil from $^{2}/_{3}$ to $1^{1}/_{2}$ million tons; and cement from less than 4 to almost 7 million tons. However these figures are discounted for exaggeration and inferior quality, they nevertheless reflect a tremendous stride in the march toward modernization, a stride bound to make a deep impression on the visitors who came to China in growing numbers after 1953.

The stepped-up industrialization program presented the government with an even more serious personnel problem than agricultural collectivization. Managerial, technical, and scientific talent had to be identified, trained, and assigned. For the most part, top managerial posts were filled with party stalwarts who, regardless of their ignorance of industrial procedures, could be relied on to maintain ideological doctrines and to press their subordinates to achieve maximum productivity. Many experienced technicians were transferred from light to heavy industry where their skills were upgraded under the guidance of Russian advisors. Institutions of higher learning were directed to produce a larger percentage of technicians, and college graduates were arbitrarily assigned to factories for on-the-job training, those who made good being given rapid promotions. Meanwhile, the number of secondary schools and colleges and the number of students enrolled in technical and scientific curricula were greatly expanded. For qualified research scientists the regime had to depend, for the time being at least, on Western-trained intellectuals, both those inherited from the pre-Communist era and those attracted from abroad by a sense of patriotism.

As an example of the adaptability and persistence of the scholar class, it is interesting to observe that in any list of leading intellectuals in the arts or the sciences, including the new field of nuclear physics, more than 75 percent turn out to be scions of scholar-official families of the imperial era. With the application of universal free education this percentage will in due course drop, but considering the tradition of scholarship in these families and their current predominance in higher education it will probably not drop as rapidly or as much as in other modernizing societies. For some perceptive scholar-official families the "revolution" began in the nineteenth century when they recognized the value of Western achievements and sent their sons abroad to study them, and for more it occurred in 1905 with the abolition of the traditional Confucian civil service examinations. Certainly by 1921, when the Chinese Communist party was founded, most of them had come to recognize the new era and how they needed to train their sons for it. Along this same line of adaptability, it is also interesting to note that 12 percent of the Communist party is drawn from the intellectuals compared to 14 percent

from the proletariat and the balance mostly from the peasantry. The outstanding example of adaptation by an intellectual from a traditional scholar-official family is the suave premier, Chou En-lai.

By 1957, when China was committed to nuclear research and development with Russian cooperation and assistance, it possessed almost as many top quality research physicists as the Soviet Union had in 1947, only a decade earlier. As a point of comparison of research ability, about one-third of the articles in the journal of the Russian nuclear research center at Dubna, where leading Chinese physicists worked with their comrades, were authored by Chinese scientists. Thus it was only a question of when China would, not whether it could, develop a nuclear capability. On the other hand, the political direction has produced a lopsided development of scientific abilities with favored areas forging far ahead while lower priority areas lagged far behind.

As a convinced Marxist, Mao Tse-tung is a firm believer in the dialectical process of change and development and, following a rectification program directed at the intellectuals in 1956, he became concerned at the potentially stifling effect on intellectual interaction of politically dictated thought control and educational manipulation. Whatever other factors both national and international may have motivated him, Mao invited criticism and free intellectual exchange with an aphorism harking back to the philosophical ferment of the preimperial, later Chou dynasty era: "Let a hundred flowers bloom, let a hundred schools of thought contend." The intellectuals, still licking their wounds and fearing reprisals, did not immediately respond until the invitation was reaffirmed more vigorously in the spring of 1957. At first, the criticisms were moderate and restrained, but then, when no penalties were assessed, many gained courage and unleashed their pent-up discontents in a spate of attacks on the entire political apparatus and its agents. Not only were educational policies criticized but also the restrictions on the activities of minority parties and even the precepts of socialism were challenged. Party officials were condemned for incompetence and the government was urged to appoint to positions of authority men of proven talent, regardless of what their politics or party affiliations might be. This was too much. The era of "blooming" was terminated in July with an amended statement emphasizing that "flowers" only should be cultivated—no "weeds" could be permitted to grow in "the garden of socialism." Naturally, several scapegoats among the critics were singled out for throughgoing condemnation; the rest of the adventurous intellectuals were silenced.

Perhaps, as some analysts have suggested, this period of free criticism was purposely created to identify those individuals most hostile to the regime, but I doubt it. The more likely explanation seems to be Mao's concern for intellectual stagnation and his mistaken belief that the intellectuals had been sufficiently converted to be granted this measure of freedom. As his whole career illustrates, Mao was essentially a cautious optimist, always ready to take the calculated risk of a large stride toward his ultimate goal as long as he was sure he could safely retreat if necessary. Indeed, this aggressive, but cautious, optimism has been the major secret of his success as a leader and the success of the movement he led.

Diagnosing the individualistic and anti-socialistic expressions of the intellectuals as the result of ivory-tower isolation and ignorance of the concrete conditions of the masses, Mao and the government decreed a new type of rectification campaign in which teachers, students, and party officials were ordered to the country to do manual labor side by side with the peasants. By this means they would learn the error of their selfish thoughts and return to their posts invigorated to work selflessly and collectively for the welfare of China and all its people. In this way, the paternalistic father of the great Chinese family chastised his bright, but wayward and personally ambitious, sons. The ground was thus prepared for another giant stride.

FOREIGN RELATIONS (1953 – 1957)

Since its establishment the Chinese Communist regime has naturally looked to its elder brother, the Soviet Union, for trade, aid, and diplomatic and military support. The American effort to isolate China did not greatly reduce Chinese trade with the non-Communist world, but the expanding needs of the new regime led to a rapid increase in the volume of trade with the Communist bloc. Under Stalin's more generous successors a peak was reached in 1955 when 80 percent of China's foreign trade was consummated with Communist countries. Since 1953, however, Mao, unwilling to be unduly dependent on the Soviet-dominated bloc and dissatisfied with prices and terms, has bent every effort to develop friendly relations and trade with non-Communist countries to gain leverage in his dealings with Russia and its satellites. Moreover, popular national feeling within China demanded a reduction of Russian influence. To cultivate goodwill two unique programs were undertaken under the direction of Chou En-lai. First, China enunciated five unimpeachable principles that it pledged to observe in its relations with all states that acknowledged them: (1) mutual respect for territorial integrity and sovereignty, (2) nonaggression, (3) noninterference in internal affairs, (4) equality and mutual benefits, and (5) peaceful coexistence. At the same time, every American action calculated to win support directly or indirectly for the containment of communism was dissected and denounced as "neo-colonialism and imperialism." While no better policy could have been designed to appeal to the latent fears and suspicions of the governments of the newly independent, non-Communist countries of Asia and Africa, a second, unorthodox form of diplomacy was fashioned to gain the favor of as many individual officials and nongovernmental groups as possible within both independent states and those colonies striving for independence. China, now ready to display with pride its achievements as a model of how to overcome backwardness in the shortest possible time, reversed itself and issued invitations wholesale to individuals and groups, especially those who were leftist-inclined, for all-expense-paid tours to see at first hand its accomplishments. In spite of the austerity inflicted on its own people, the Chinese government lavished hospitality on its guests, while discreetly keeping to a minimum its propaganda. Upon returning home, these visitors, almost without exception, showed that they were deeply impressed with what they had seen, even if they expressed reservations about the form of government. Thus, the vastly enhanced prestige acquired abroad more than repaid the costs of this program.

The "peaceful coexistence" program won diplomatic recognition, often accompanied by a trade and credit treaty, from a growing number of states and secured for the People's Republic of China a new high in international influence by the deft behavior of Chou En-lai at the 1955 Afro-Asian Conference held at Bandung, Indonesia. The first victory was winning the invitation to attend in place of Nationalist China. At the Conference, Chou had no difficulty in gaining general acceptance for the five principles of peaceful coexistence and a denunciation of imperialism in all its forms. More important was recognition of Taiwan as an integral part of China and the illegality of Chiang K'ai-shek's rebel regime in a joint resolution condemning as equally intolerable the existence of the Western-supported states of Israel and Taiwan. This resolution also served the purpose of providing a common ground of self-interest between the Muslim world stretching from Indonesia to sub-Saharan Africa and China with a minority population of about 10 million Muslims. Chou also paved the way to resolving the problem of the dual citizenship of overseas Chinese that had been maintained since the Chinese revolu-

tion by expressing readiness to conclude an agreement with Indonesia by which, after a reasonable period, Chinese residents must accept one citizenship or the other. The prime condition for such an agreement, which delayed its implementation, was Indonesian nonrecognition and nonintercourse with the Nationalist regime.

By both these programs China made significant gains in its contest with the American colossus, which was slow in devising suitable responses. The effectiveness of the South-East Asian Treaty Organization (SEATO), sponsored in 1954 by the United States to contain mainland China, was successfully undermined, at least among the Southeast Asian nations that soon came to appreciate the need of adapting to the inevitable reassertion of traditional Chinese influence and authority in Asia. Diplomatic recognition by a growing number of new states, as the tide of European imperialism ebbed ever more rapidly, furnished more and more votes supporting the recognition of mainland China's right to membership in the United Nations Organization, in addition to the assured votes of the Communist bloc.

On the other hand, as China's power and prestige arose, symptoms of irritation concerning especially its economic relations with the Soviet Union became more and more frequent. The Chinese complained of the higher prices of essential commodities, such as oil, than those paid by the satellites and even non-Communist Italy. They were particularly irked at the more generous credit and terms extended to non-Communist countries such as India and Egypt for major projects, while China desperately needed additional credit and aid to carry out its industrialization. Later, these projects, which represented Khrushchev's "peace offensive" against the West, provided fodder for the charge of ideological deviation, but for the moment they were used to bargain, with some small success, for an expansion and enlargement of Russian assistance. Meanwhile, the government stepped up its programs to woo non-Communist nations as eventual alternate markets and sources of supply.

As Khrushchev's policies led to difficulties in Russian relations with its satellites, Mao was presented with the opportunity to demonstrate the importance of China's support of Communist solidarity. Khrushchev's deStalinization program of 1956 was disregarded. Theoretical articles in the Chinese press continued to quote Stalin as an authority, though he continued to be subordinate to the trinity of Marx, Lenin, and Mao. Although there had been little love lost between Mao and Stalin, Stalin's statements on the policy of giving primacy to the building of Communism in the Soviet Union were well adapted to the needs of China's current stage of development. When Russia's relaxation of controls generated uprisings and modifications of government and policy in several satellites, Mao, who had always maintained the theory of varying roads to Communism according to the unique conditions of each society, only slowly and ponderously came forth with a declaration supporting the overriding principle of Communist solidarity under the leadership of the Soviet Union at this stage of the world struggle. Undoubtedly, intense negotiations granting new concessions to China preceded this declaration. Perhaps at this time Soviet negotiators agreed to furnish China with the facilities for the creation of a nuclear capability of its own. Certainly during 1957 nuclear reactors were being erected in China under Russian supervision.

The orbiting of Sputnik I on October 4, 1957, which ushered in the Space age, greatly elated Mao. A month later on a visit to Moscow to celebrate the fortieth anniversary of the Bolshevik revolution, he expressed his elation in a speech in which he declared "the East wind prevails over the West wind." Now, he asserted, was the time to pick up the tempo of the world revolution against the exploitation of the people and against the imperialism of the decadent West. The ensuing years showed, much to the alarm of the Russians, that Mao meant every word he said, while the more cautious Soviet leadership, fearful of a nuclear holocaust, was generally more interested in a less belligerent struggle to accomplish the world revolution through peaceful competition with the West.

THE GREAT LEAP FORWARD AND BACKWARD(?) (1958–1961)

During the latter part of 1957 various pronouncements indicating a possible relaxation in the drive for heavy industrialization and more attention to the needs of the consumer, especially the peasant, suggest that a sharp debate about how to meet China's immediate problems was being carried on between the conservative and radical elements in the top echelon of the party. But early in 1958 the victory went to the radicals with the decision for an even more frantic drive to lift China up by its bootstraps to a fully modern state, drawing on the total energies of all the people under the slogan of "politics in command." This was called "the Great Leap Forward."

To understand the reasons for this decision, the basic dilemma confronting the Chinese Communist leadership must be appreciated. By a program of increasing political and economic control the government had collected more than 20 billion dollars to invest in economic development during the First Five-Year Plan. The Russian contribution of more than 2 billion cannot be taken into account because most of it had to be repaid promptly in Chinese raw materials, although the construction of modern plants and the supply of technologists and scientists was of inestimable value to China's modernization. Of the total economic investment, about one-half went into heavy industry, while a mere tithe went into light industry. As a result, industrial production had grown 141 percent, with heavy industry accounting for most of the increase, but agricultural production, in spite of collectivization and a doubling of the irrigated area to more than one-half of the acreage, had grown only 20 percent, barely enough to keep pace with population growth, let alone contribute to the financing of further industrialization. Moreover, agricultural output had failed to increase significantly during 1956 and 1957, and rural discontent had been reflected in a continued migration to the cities in search of more remunerative employment and more of the amenities above mere subsistence. The government's dilemma, then, was how to maintain the momentum of industrial growth, increase agricultural production, and raise morale: and how to accomplish all these ends without adequate capital for investment—a seemingly impossible achievement.

The only answer seemed to be to unleash the potential productivity of China's one great asset—and liability—its vast and underemployed population. This was a crisis appeal fortified by a more belligerent stance in foreign relations to reinforce the people's belief in a beleaguered China caught up in a life or death struggle against the world. Such an effort would require structural changes in society giving greater initiative and responsibility to local leaders, the most notable of which was to be the commune.

One characteristic of the Great Leap Forward with "politics in command" was the repeated upward revision of quotas, accompanied by glowing reports of achievements by local authorities who did not want to be outdone by their counterparts elsewhere. This competitive drive soon got completely out of hand and led to overinflated claims that bore no reasonable relation to real or potential production in many areas. Yet even the top leaders apparently were taken in by these reports, so convinced were they of the untapped potential of China's reservoir of manpower, and reported to the world fantastic results for 1958, such as almost a doubling of grain production to 375 million tons. The following year, after actual deliveries had been appraised, this preliminary estimate was sharply scaled down to 250 million tons, and even this shamefaced admission of a monstrous miscalculation probably exceeded actual grain production by as much or more than 10 percent.

Analysts have advanced various explanations for such a huge discrepancy between estimates and actual harvest. One asserted that estimates were based on seed planted as well as the presumed benefits of improved seed, deep plowing, closer planting, and other new techniques; another claimed that the peasants, without a personal stake in the cooperative's production, were careless or slow in harvesting, thereby wasting or losing a great amount of grain between the field and the granary. While these and other explanations were undoubtedly important contributing factors, probably the greatest villain was the subordination of statistical accuracy to the dynamic doctrine of "politics in command" by which the centrally organized statistical services were directed to support the local authorities in mobilizing and inspiring the people for a maximum productive effort. The fairly well-developed skills and integrity of the statistical service were thus demoralized and sabotaged.

Another aspect of the Great Leap Forward was the local creation with negligible capital of more than three and a half million small-scale, industrial or semi-industrial enterprises both to supplement modern industry and to offset the serious shortage of consumer goods. Most of these so-called factories were no more than organized handicrafts drawing on local skills. The most widely publicized drive aimed at the production of iron in thousands of primitive, "backyard" blast furnaces. This feverish, after-work activity carried out by millions of "volunteers" throughout the country reportedly accounted for about one quarter of 1958's iron and steel production, but in most instances the quality of the product was so inferior that it was scarcely usable for the crudest tools and utensils. Moreover, the experiment proved extremely costly and inefficient in addition to overtaxing the already overburdened transportation system for supply and distribution. As quickly as they had been set up, the backyard furnaces were closed down except for a number with local supplies of coal and iron ore that were enlarged and modernized as permanent producers. This apparent failure, immediately seized on by the Western press as proof positive of the blundering incapacity of Chinese Communist leadership, represented only one part of the general program of increasing production by small-scale, local endeavor and even in itself yielded a number of tangible and intangible benefits.

One tangible benefit was the host of mineral deposits discovered by local exploration which, when tested and verified by trained geologists, furnished a vast increase in the known reserves of natural resources needed to support China's plans for the creation of a modern industrialized economy. Less tangible but perhaps equally significant was the introduction into the mysteries of modern technology of the rural masses who hitherto had considered such skills a supernatural art beyond their abilities or comprehension. Now they gained both an understanding of the process and rudimentary skills in what amounted to a mass educational program. Although the immediate results were disappointing and wasteful, the Chinese people gained an appreciation of the Communist regime's goals of modernization and the problems involved in their achievement. Henceforth, there was no question of China's ability to achieve the regime's objectives; the only question was how long it would take to accomplish production adequate in both quality and quantity. Therefore, to label the Great Leap Forward in industry an unqualified failure appears to have been an exaggeration.

Much more controversial and open to question was the accompanying structural reorganization of agriculture, known as the communes, intended to bring about total mobilization of the productive energies of both the man and womanpower of China. The higher-level cooperatives had combined the labor potential of as many as 200 families but principally for agricultural production and supporting projects, such as minor and

local irrigation and flood control development. Labor for major public works, such as large dams, bridges, roads, and railroads, had been drawn principally from the regular army and those condemned to "reform through labor," while the seasonable character of agriculture left the peasantry still substantially underemployed. Collectivization had significantly undermined the cohesion of the family as the basic social unit, but the mother with young children remained tied down by familial chores. The fullest possible utilization of all potential labor, the subordination of the individual and the last vestiges of the family to the needs and interests of the group and the state, and the eradication of persistent local particularism were all factors contributing to the conception of that much larger entity, the commune, each incorporating an average of 5000 families, though the number of families and territorial size of any one commune varied widely according to local conditions.

As early as April 1958 several experimental communes were "voluntarily" organized in different areas "at the request of the people" according to later propaganda releases, a completely improbable assertion. The most renowned of these was the appropriately named *Sputnik Commune* in Honan province, which was singled out as a model. The commune concept was approved by Mao in August and officially endorsed in September as the next stage in socialist construction. Detailed directions for the "voluntary" formation of communes were published, and all the propaganda stops were pulled in support of their establishment. To the ostensible amazement of the Communist leadership, the recommendations were enthusiastically embraced, and by the end of 1958 almost all of rural China had been "voluntarily" reorganized into more than 26,000 self-governing communes. If nothing else, this achievement suggests the extent to which the Communist party, operating through its millions of cadres, had extended its totalitarian control over the peasantry.

As conceived, the commune pooled all

resources in its area, operated mining, industrial, and commercial enterprises suitable to the area in addition to farming, and took over the functions of local government under a democratic form actually controlled by the local Communist party leadership. Each commune was organizationally subdivided into brigades, roughly corresponding to the former higher-level cooperatives, and these in turn were subdivided into teams equivalent in size to lower-level cooperatives or mutual-aid teams. The commune authorities could dispatch labor, thus mobilized, in large or small groups to work on any planned project anywhere within the commune or even arrange with neighboring communes to exchange labor for an agreed remuneration. To liberate the productive power of women, previously occupied by household chores, mess halls and nurseries were set up. Women were to receive equal credit for equal work and to be directly paid their share at the time of accounting according to a complex system of accumulated work points. The elderly, especially those without families, were taken care of in commune-maintained "happiness homes for the aged." For the time being, each family retained its home and the diminutive plot of land around it supporting a small garden and livestock, though those with larger homes had already been compelled to share them. Ultimate plans called for the construction of apartment buildings with modern facilities both to facilitate communal living and to make the maximum use of all arable land.

Almost immediately complaints were made against overzealous cadres who interpreted the recommendations too generously or applied them too rigorously. Some communes sought to keep children in the nurseries, instead of permitting mothers to pick them up at the end of the workday, on the ground that the trained staffs were better equipped to care for them. The inferior caliber of mass-prepared meals in the mess halls offended the tastes of a people with the world's longest tradition of culinary arts, and they demanded the right to individual prep-

aration of the evening meal at home. Some cadres, believing that true communism had arrived with the communes, applied the doctrine of "to each according to his needs, from each according to his ability" with chaotic results. Members of former cooperatives with better land and production records objected to being penalized for the support of less productive groups within the commune. More serious were the charges of excessive demands for labor and attendance at "educational" meetings to the point of physical collapse and the misdirection of labor to public works at a time when the crops needed care. The worst excesses and errors, however, stemmed mainly from the misunderstanding and inexperience of the cadres and, for the most part, were corrected within a few months, just when the Western press was learning about them and using them to scourge the whole conception of the Chinese commune as a institution for mass enslavement and destruction of the individual and the family. A much more deeply rooted and grosser miscalculation in the organization of the communes did not become apparent for several years.

In a radical effort to overcome local particularism, once and for all, most of the communes, except in the most densely populated regions, were purposely formed to bring together under one regime disparate areas with no historical or natural record of social, economic, or political interdependence and community. In other words, in the hope of breaking down traditional ties, most of the communes were made so large that they encompassed more than one social and trading unit. Moreover, they were often gerrymandered in a manner that split an ancient unit between two communes. Another reason given for the design of such oversize entities was to combine in each commune as varied an assortment of resources as possible to provide the maximum degree of flexibility and self-sufficiency for progessive development. But whatever the reason or reasons for such unnatural combinations, they failed; and in the following years of stress this failure was acknowledged in a reorganization that tripled the number of communes from a low in 1959 of 24,000 to about 74,000. Some of this increase was attributable to the creation of urban communes primarily to release the productive energy of housewives, but most of it reflected the reduction of rural communes to natural size.

In spite of, or because of, the communes agriculture suffered three successive years of serious setbacks from 1959 through 1961 and only gradually recovered in the following years. According to Chinese Communist authorities, the heavy crop losses were almost exclusively caused by abnormally adverse weather accounting for floods or drought over widespread areas, but Western analysts, particularly American, have seen peasant disenchantment with the communes and their inefficient management as the principal explanation for the sharp drop in harvests. Direct evidence is inadequate as yet to form a firm assessment, but what there is suggests that both factors were important. Naturally the government did not publish consolidated data on these harvests, but extrapolation from scattered references makes possible a very rough estimate of the extent of crop losses. During 1959 somewhere between one-quarter and one-third of the crops suffered severe damage or total destruction in spite of monumental mass efforts to save them or replace them by new plantings. Using 220 million tons of grain as the optimum figure for 1958, grain production for 1959 fell somewhere between 150 and 190 million tons, probably about 175 million tons taking into account replanting, but all of this may not have been delivered to granaries due to disrupted or careless harvesting. The devastation of 1960 was described as the worst in almost a century, causing an estimated loss of between one-third and one-half of the crops planted. In areas flooded the previous years the losses were compounded by the lack of time to restore the heavy damage to the poorly engineered reservoirs and irrigation facilities hastily constructed by commune labor. With many more mouths to feed, grain

production may have fallen below the prewar average of 140 million tons. The government boasted that contrary to the custom of pre-Communist famines no one starved to death, thanks to better distribution, but many weak and aged persons, perhaps millions of them, must have died of malnutrition because of the sharply reduced rations, and certainly what reserves there were were exhausted. The crop losses were significantly cut in 1961 yielding a harvest equal to or better than 1959, but the cumulative effect of three successive years of abnormally bad harvests probably made conditions worse than ever. In subsequent years the yields appear to have continually improved, but since the government has not yet seen fit to publish results, it may be assumed that agriculture has not yet matched or surpassed the 1958 claim of 250 million tons of grain.

To add to China's woes, the year 1960 saw the deterioration of Sino-Soviet relations, culminating in an overt split with its Russian supporter signalized by the withdrawal of Soviet advisors and technicians. China was compelled to pursue more vigorously its policy of cultivating trading partners outside the Communist bloc and to draw on its small store of foreign exchange for purchases of grain from Canada, Australia, and other Western sources for delivery in this and succeeding years. The significance of these grain imports, however, should not be exaggerated. As large as they were, they amounted to only 2 to 3 percent of normal production, about the equivalent of normal prewar imports, and could do little more than relieve the shortages in the major cities. Meanwhile, China continued to export substantial amounts of food. Therefore, close examination suggests that these purchases, in view of the deterioration of Sino-Soviet relations, may have been inspired as much by the desire to develop trade relations outside the Communist bloc as by the need for food.

Certainly the poor harvests of 1959 and 1960 combined with the withdrawal of Soviet support, called forth a reorientation of Chinese economic plans along the lines of industrial retrenchment and all-out support of the sagging agricultural sector. Industry was directed to concentrate its efforts on aiding agriculture, while inefficient factories were closed down according to a policy stressing quality rather than quantity. At the same time, the overambitious commune organization had to be relaxed. Administrative responsibility, at least for strictly farming activity, was shifted downward to the brigades (former higher-level cooperatives) and labor could not be diverted to public works without their consent. Furthermore, the production teams were authorized to draw up their production plans for approval by the brigade.

Another step, overpublicized in the West as presaging the abandonment of the communes, was the allotment of private plots to peasant families. For the most part these diminutive plots were drawn from previously unfarmed marginal land; the amount of communal land and the obligation to farm it remained essentially the same. Therefore, the private plots, which could be cultivated in whatever free time was left after all other commune demands had been fulfilled, represented no more than part of a general policy to supplement normal production and provide a new incentive for the improvement of morale. Other parts of this policy included more careful evaluation of labor to reward better workers and an incentive program for the raising of livestock whose numbers had progresively sagged with the advances in collectivization. Finally, rectification and education programs were intensified to deal with backsliders, and almost five million new party members were recruited to fill the expanded need for cadres of the great leap forward and the communes. The aim was to make each one "red and expert," thoroughly indoctrinated in Chinese Communist doctrine and technically proficient for the assigned task.

MINORITY AND FOREIGN RELATIONS (1958–)

Ever since Mao Tse-tung had formed his own movement based on the traditional discontents of the peasantry, he had followed an unorthodox program in practice, if not in theory. From the beginning he justified this deviation with the thesis that there were differing paths to socialism according to the historical and objective conditions existing in each society. In other words, while the end was the same, the means might differ. No matter how convinced a Communist he was, he was first of all a realistic Chinese revolutionary, recognizing, accepting, and capitalizing on the main themes of the Chinese revolution as it had evolved since the turn of the century. The dominant themes were nationalism in reaction to the humiliations inflicted by Western imperialism and a concomitant rejection of Confucianism as a demonstrably bankrupt ideology. In neither instance were Mao and his associates innovators; they only picked up without any real break in continuity the revolutionary trail that Chiang K'ai-shek had lost through his anachronistic emphasis on Confucianism. For this reason, this chapter has been entitled "The Chinese Revolution: A Continued Story." In his writings Mao has drawn liberally from sayings of the past, including some from Confucius, and has stressed the superiority of Chinese civilization reflected in the old conception of the Middle Kingdom.

Upon winning control of the mainland, Mao, though desperate for diplomatic and economic support to build socialism in China, went no further than to say that he was "leaning to one side," a position implying only a tentative commitment and far less than total subservience to Soviet leadership. This strong nationalistic feeling, rooted in the Middle Kingdom concept of China as the center of civilization and dominant force in East Asia, will permit neither Mao nor his successors to settle for anything less than the regaining of China's pre-Western frontiers and sphere of influence, at least until the Chinese people are convinced that their country again holds its rightful place in the world. Although the position of the United States in Asia posed the most immediate threat to China, and the Soviet Union armed with nuclear weapons was the natural ally, no Chinese could forget that Russia had once been a major Western imperialist and still coveted the frontier regions occupied by unintegrated minority peoples. Indeed, Russians held former Chinese territories or, in the case of Outer Mongolia, supported a puppet regime.

Initially the Communist regime had concentrated on creating in Inner Mongolia and the far-flung territories of Sinkiang so-called autonomous regions that were no more than screens for integration. Although minority languages and some other aspects of their cultures were cultivated, the former tribal or "feudal" systems of political and social organization were not tolerated. In the course of suppressing little-known rebellions against the enforcement of the Chinese Communist pattern of organization, tribesmen in the northwest fled across the frontier and were given refuge by the Russians, much to the irritation of the Chinese.

Following the 1950–1951 conquest of Tibet, the next most important minority area, a Preparatory Commission officially headed by the Dalai Lama was set up to bring about the formation of another autonomous region for this vast, but sparsely populated, strategic territory. The feudal hierarchies of the Buddhist lamasaries and a small aristocracy, armed with religious sanctions, were supported in comparative luxury by the traditional heavy exactions on the Tibetan people and were naturally unwilling to surrender these benefits, while the people, long accustomed to this way of life, could comprehend no alternative. Exasperated and impatient at the lack of progress and anxious to integrate this region with its disputed frontier with India, Nepal, and Pakistan, the Chinese government decided in 1959 that persuasion had failed and force must be employed to bring about the essential changes. The Dalai Lama, singled out as the chief obstructionist, escaped the Chinese military net and made good his flight across the frontier into India. For some time thereafter his elusive tribal supporters put up a stiff resistance before finally being ruthlessly suppressed. An International Commission of Jurists weighed the available evidence and condemned Communist policy in Tibet as "cultural genocide," which of course it was. For several years the Panchen Lama, head of the second most important religious sect, was recognized as titular leader, but he too has since been removed and denounced as a reactionary. Information is too scanty and unreliable to judge the Tibetan's reaction to Chinese communist "emancipation," but there seems to be no question that the Chinese are in full control of the entire region.

Such control was verified by the limited Chinese assault on India during the winter of 1962 in an effort to force the Indian government to negotiate a settlement of the frontier dispute on Chinese terms following the recent example of Burma. As heirs of the British the Indian government maintained the unilaterally proclaimed McMahon Line of 1914, which no Chinese regime had ever accepted because it made serious inroads into the former Manchu frontier. Nehru's regime refused to budge and sought military aid successfully from both Russia and the West. Interestingly enough, while the Soviet Union actively gave aid and comfort to India, the Nationalist regime of Chiang K'ai-shek applauded the Chinese Communist stand because the regaining of former frontiers and areas of influence was a national objective transcending the internal political conflict. Since 1962 Nepal and Pakistan have agreed to definitions of their frontiers. The economically hard-pressed but short-lived successor regime of Prime Minister Shastri appeared on the verge of going to the conference table to alleviate the diversion of revenue to military preparedness, but the regime of his successor, Madame Gandhi, has so far put off such a commitment. Ultimately this issue will have to be resolved.

Even before turning to the internal problem of Tibet, Mao took action in the international field to prove that he had meant what he said in his November 1957 speech in Moscow asserting that the time was ripe for pressing the attack against American imperialism and advancing the world revolution. Ho Chi Minh of North Vietnam was equipped and encouraged to expand subversive activities in neighboring Laos and especially American supported South Vietnam; various implied threats and warnings alarmed the government of Thailand, the closest member of SEATO; propaganda calls for Korean reunification and rejection of American puppet status were stepped up; and troops and artillery were massed off the Nationalist-held islands of Quemoy and Matsu, the first of which was subjected to heavy bombardment from August to September of 1958. In provoking this crisis Mao apparently had several objectives: first, he wanted to provide added inspiration to propel the Great Leap Forward; second, he wanted to test the commitment of the Soviet Union under Khrushchev's leadership to the support of China; and third, he wanted to probe the strength of American commitment to the support of Chiang K'ai-shek. The response on the first point was probably satisfactory for the time being, but those on the last two, though anticipated, were certainly disappointing. American policy statements may have been ambiguous, but American action, risking Communist gunfire to protect the delivery of supplies, left no doubt in anyone's mind. The less than enthusiastic backing from Khrushchev, who was leaning strongly toward peaceful coexistence, plus open Russian criticism of China's communes convinced Mao that henceforth China must depend even more than before on its own resources and ability in a growing contest for leadership of the Communist movement. But he believed that China had acquired most of the basic technological know-how to stand on its own feet, and what it still needed in refinements could be purchased on the world market.

During 1956 Mao had developed doubts about Khrushchev's judgment; now these doubts were confirmed. Certainly he was not going to subordinate his interpretation of the correct path for the future to the revisionism of this crude, Johnny-come-lately. What he did not foresee was the forthcoming ordeal of three successive years of crop failures and consequent industrial setbacks. On the other hand, Khrushchev clung to the end to the vain hope that he could discipline this rebellious vassal by economic actions. Neither one would give in, and finally it was Khrushchev who fell from power. Meanwhile, China's nuclear scientists, utilizing the nuclear reactors obtained from Russia, were able to detonate an atomic explosion and become the fifth member of the nuclear club. If nothing else, this event should have made it clear to all that China was determined in the long run to be second to no nation on earth, no matter what the costs to its people.

Since 1960, when Russian technicians were recalled from China, the Sino-Soviet dispute has escalated in bitterness as each side engaged in mutual recriminations and contended for the support of Communists around the world. After several publicized border clashes, there arose even the possibility of war between the two Communist powers. The apparent relaxation in Chinese relations with the United States probably bears a relationship to Sino-Soviet hostility. Meanwhile, the Communist regime gained a diplomatic coup in 1971 when it won recognition as the legitimate representative of China in the United Nations Organization in place of the Nationalist regime.

THE GREAT PROLETARIAN CULTURAL REVOLUTION (1965–)

During the summer of 1966 Western observers became aware of a major new upheaval, entitled the Great Proletarian Cultural Revolution, which represented a reassertion of Mao's leadership. With the benefit of hindsight and Chinese evidence the beginning of this movement was traced back to November 10, 1965, when the Shanghai Party committee, operating under Mao's direction, launched an attack on a 1961 play entitled, *Hai-Jui Dismissed from Office*, as a veiled, reactionary criticism of Mao and Maoism. As the plot gradually unfolded in the following spring, the attack on this play from a provincial headquarters was itself an indirect assault on its sponsors, the Peking Party Committee and government, and in turn the central party and government apparatus headed by Liu Shao-ch'i. Thus what began as an attack against literary revisionism evolved into an all-out struggle for power.

A broader understanding of the Cultural Revolution, however, requires a deeper look into the past to seek out its possible motivations. In December 1958 Mao stepped down as chairman of the People's Republic in favor of Liu Shao-ch'i while retaining the more vital chairmanship of the Chinese Communist Party. Whether this reduction in direct responsibilities was due to ill health, an interest in how Liu would exercise power, or some other reason cannot be determined, but any suggestion that he was forced out seems highly improbable. In any case, in August 1959 he demonstrated his continued strength and his concern for what he had always believed to be the true source of power, the military, when he insisted at the Lushan conference of the Central Committee on the replacement of the Defense Minister who had attacked Maoist policies and favored development of a professional army with his reliable old comrade, Field Marshall Lin Piao. The full significance of this change did not become apparent until the first mass rally of the Red Guards on August 18, 1966, at which Lin Piao appeared as the number two man in the hierarchy and delivered the principal speech, while Liu slipped to eighth place.

Meanwhile, by late 1959 the weaknesses and imminent collapse of the Great Leap Forward, particularly in the agricultural sector, were moving the government toward a reversal of priority from industry to agriculture, as witnessed by a number of articles, though the official decision was not proclaimed until January 1960. At the same time, the emphasis in the "red and expert" dichotomy was shifting from "red" to "expert." During 1960 to 1962, a rectification campaign purged the middle and lower ranks of the Party in favor of "expertness" and in-

cidentally the supporters of Liu Shao-ch'i. In contrast, the army under Lin Piao gave its attention to political indoctrination in the Thoughts of Mao and to the cultivation of "redness" along with a massive utilization of army labor in support of agriculture. Of course, this apparent contradiction between the Party and the army should not be exaggerated; the Socialist Education Campaign, initiated late in 1962 under the sponsorship of the Party at Mao's prodding, ostensibly sought to elevate ideological awareness though it was not pushed as vigorously as previous campaigns. Nevertheless, it may be said that Mao and Lin Piao, on the one hand, and Liu and the Party, on the other, were following divergent courses. Liu's policy was justified by the need for economic recovery, but by 1963 a large measure of recovery had been accomplished and yet Liu's government showed little inclination or ability to reverse the emphasis on "expertness." Furthermore, other veiled attacks generally under the cover of historical analogies against Mao's emphasis on continuous revolutionary struggle, in addition to the play *Hai-Jui Dismissed from Office*, had been appearing since 1961 without any effort at suppression.

Above all, however, Mao was moved by his frequently expressed concern for the maintenance of revolutionary dynamism and by his fear of slipping back into traditional bureaucratic elitism, which he equated with a bourgeois, antirevolutionary elevation of self-interest over the public interest. He was also convinced that the failure of the Great Leap Forward had been due to inadequate stress on ideological preparation of the cadres and the people in favor of economic revolution. The true strength of a people is in its hearts and minds; the body and machines are merely tools to be used or abused. When the heart and mind are set, when they are directed to the common good and not just the individual good, the people can achieve miracles. For these reasons, he called for a proletarian cultural revolution to eradicate old habits, customs, and ways of thought inherited from the old bourgeois culture and singled out the colleges and to a lesser extent the middle schools, which also practiced selective admissions, as the bourgeois strongholds of intellectual self-interest.

Their admissions policies, based on academic achievements, were denounced for giving students of bourgeois and capitalist backgrounds an unfair advantage over bright and dedicated applicants of peasant and working class origins. As a result, admissions were ordered suspended, pending formulation of a revised admissions policy. College administrations and faculties were also castigated for the neglect of doctrinal, and especially Maoist, studies in the curricula. Such conditions, calling for much deeper rectification, were to bring about a closure of the schools for an extended period of time.

To stimulate revolutionary dynamism among the young and to carry out such a far-reaching revolutionary assault on the entrenched authority of the Party, the central government, and the academicians, middle school, and college students were called out as Red Guards to spearhead the Cultural Revolution starting with the first of a succession of mass rallies on August 18, 1966, where they saw Mao and received the silent blessing of "The Great Helmsman." The People's Liberation Army under Lin Piao, as the major organization behind the Cultural Revolution, attempted to remain in the background, organizing, manipulating, and when necessary, policing the youthful ardor of the Red Guards when they got out of hand. Indeed, the role of the army in the Cultural Revolution cannot be underrated. It had undertaken the initial campaign to propagate the Thoughts of Mao among the troops and had published the first edition of the now-famous "little Red Book," *The Thoughts of Mao Tse-tung*. In the early phase of the Cultural Revolution Western analysts noted that editorials, appearing first in the *Liberation Army Daily*, were then reprinted in the *People's Daily*, the central government newspaper. Later, the leading position of Lin Piao and the army was to become even more apparent.

The course of the Cultural Revolution cannot be followed in detail, but its major stages can be mentioned. The attack against "reactionary" intellectuals, sponsored by Mao's wife, Chiang Ch'ing, turned out to be an indirect assault on their sponsors, the Peking and central government hierarchy, headed by Liu Shao-ch'i. After Liu's principal supporters, such as the mayor and deputy-mayor of Peking, the army chief of staff, the principal Party propagandists who controlled the cultural organizations and media, and the editor of the *People's Daily*, had been discredited and dismissed as "anti-Party, anti-socialist monsters," the assault was extended to provincial party leaders and ultimately Liu Shao-ch'i himself, although he was referred to as "China's Khrushchev" rather than by name for a long time. Obviously the aim of this process was to isolate him by destroying the power base he had built up in the Party. However, Liu fought back and the consequence was a factional struggle that went beyond the Party into the government and the army, bringing about sometimes bloody clashes.

When factional strife threatened the stability of the nation, the leaders of the Cultural Revolution moved to a new stage, the formation of revolutionary committees to replace the existing governmental apparatus in the provinces, autonomous regions, and municipalities. Revolutionary committees were supposed to represent in equal proportions the "three-in-one Great Alliance" of (1) the revolutionary mass organizations including as their principal constituent the Red Guards leaders, (2) the revolutionary cadres meaning those local Party and government officials who had supported the Cultural Revolution but in fact incorporating many denounced officials who had been reformed and rehabilitated, and (3) the local army commanders who were needed to restore order and enforce the directives of the revolutionary committees. The Great Alliances were to be formed "in the spirit of compromise," and when their cooperation had produced effective revolutionary committees, the latter would be accredited by the central government. On the surface they were intended to restore harmony, but in fact they were a device to suppress the excessive zeal of the Red Guards whose activities had created even greater factional discord.

More than a year and a half was required before the process of establishing and accrediting revolutionary committees in all 29 provinces, autonomous regions, and municipalities was completed in September 1968. Moreover, in the struggle for chairmanships none was won by a Red Guard and most were taken by military figures since they, in fact, wielded real power. Needless to say, the radical Red Guard leaders were unhappy at what they deemed a reactionary betrayal and they continued to foment local factionalism and disorders. Furthermore, they were alarmed at the formation of more mature peasant and worker teams to investigate and police the schools and colleges. Directives to return to their studies were openly disregarded by large numbers of Red Guards.

With the purge and "reeducation" of party members and the establishment of revolutionary committees completed, the time for formal consolidation of the Party and the government had arrived. In October 1968 the draft of an entirely new party constitution was adopted by the Central Committee and distributed to the whole Party for discussion. The Ninth Party Congress, attended by more than 1500 delegates, adopted it in April 1969. The new constitution is striking for its brevity, totalling only 2700 words, which leaves wide latitude for interpretation and alteration in actual practices. In overall terms it may be characterized as a Maoist constitution proclaiming Mao's thought as the highest theoretical principle guiding the thought and action of the Party. Moreover, it is unique, as constitutions go, for specifically naming Lin Piao as Mao's successor. While the Party has been largely reformed, reeducated, and rehabilitated in the Maoist image, as symbolized by this constitution, the class struggle in the form of a purification campaign of "struggle-criticism-transforma-tion" continues for completion and consolidation of this Great Proletarian Cultural Revolution. Scientists, originally exempted for making important contributions to the state, have more recently been subjected to struggle, and the purification of the peasantry has been intensified. When these and other remaining tasks have been accomplished, some form of National People's Congress will probably be convened to adopt a new constitution for the People's Republic of China.

Meanwhile, border clashes have heated up the Sino-Soviet dispute to a dangerous degree and have accelerated the demands of the Chinese regime on its people for military preparedness and local self-sufficiency in support of a defense in depth. Boundary talks have yet to prove fruitfull despite Chinese willingness to renounce its claims to territories lost to Tsarist imperialism, while a major effort has been undertaken to disperse and remove to interior provinces as many strategic industries as possible, especially nuclear facilities, in anticipation of a Russian preemptive attack. The absence from public view of Lin Piao and the visit of President Nixon reflect in part the depth of the Sino-Soviet dispute and perhaps also presage a further change in the power structure in favor of Chou En-lai.

THE CHINESE REPUBLIC ON TAIWAN

When Taiwan was turned over to the Nationalist government in accordance with the Cairo agreement declaring it to be an integral part of China, the new administration set an example of corruption and exploitation that would have been hard to match anywhere on the mainland. In desperation a popular uprising took place in 1947 which was brutally suppressed. Indeed, the people, though overwhelmingly Chinese, would have welcomed the return of Japanese administration. Some improvement took place under a new governor, but real reform had to await American commitment to the support of Chiang K'ai-shek's refugee regime.

The government of the Republic of China on Taiwan is a fantastic exercise in make-believe, supporting a complete hierarchy of absentee officials for the whole of China and viewing its home island as merely one province. It operates, or rather does not operate, under the 1947 constitution for the very obvious reason that the specified nationwide elections cannot be held. Moreover, the resumption of the presidency by Chiang K'ai-shek after his resignation and his continuation in that office by an assembly that has outlived its elected life are, among other actions, of questionable legality. More important is the stubborn insistence on the unity of China, including the insular province of Taiwan, one point on which Mao and Chiang are in agreement and which made America's Two Chinas policy politically unfeasible.

Meanwhile, the native Chinese who looked with justifiable alarm on the influx of almost two million Nationalist refugees have seen the fostering of genuine economic and political reforms under pressure from Chiang's American benefactor. In the political realm comparatively free provincial and local elections have been held in recent years giving the Taiwanese a real voice in their government. The capital city of Taipei even elected a mayor from an opposition party. In the economic realm, American aid has financed the development of essential industries, such as cement and chemical fertilizers, which not only fill local needs but also provide a surplus for export. In recent years industrialization has moved into high gear, utilizing free ports to attract American and overseas Chinese capital on a large scale. Comparatively much lower wages in Taiwan have even drawn Japanese investment in the production of elements with large labor requirements. Taiwan, with a rapidly growing foreign trade of already almost four billion dollars a year, possesses an economy second in strength in East Asia only to Japan.

A more striking development has been the active and successful implementation of a land reform whose neglect on the mainland had contributed to the overthrow of the Nationalist government. Now 90 percent of the land is owned by those who farm it. In addition, extensive additions to the flood control and irrigation works of the Japanese, again with American aid totalling some one billion dollars before it was phased out in 1965, have increased agricultural productivity to the point where it can more than meet the need for food of the teeming population of 15 million without imports, even though a great deal of arable land is devoted to raising pineapple, sugar cane, and other export crops. All told, despite a tripling of the population under Nationalist rule, Taiwan has gained a higher standard of living and a viable economy which could stand on its own feet if it were not necessary to maintain an abnormally large military establishment. Outside Europe, it is beyond question the most successful example of the American foreign aid program, but this success is primarily due to Chiang's readiness to carry out those reforms that might have saved his government on the mainland. Therefore, the Nationalist government of Taiwan today reflects only a slightly less revolutionary change since 1949 than has taken place on the mainland under Communist auspices, and in many respects it may be considered a greater success, though on a much smaller scale.

Thanks to these changes, when and if Taiwan and the mainland of China are reunited, whether under Nationalist or Communist auspices, the adjustment will not prove too extreme or too difficult, though the Taiwanese would have to give up a substantial degree of economic freedom under a Communist regime. Both regimes are nationalistic, basing their claims on an appeal to China's position in the past. Occasionally popular riots against the American presence and privileges on Taiwan demonstrate that nationalistic sentiments are not limited to the government and its mainland supporters but permeate the entire population. While both claim to be democratic, with somewhat better justification in the case of the Nationalists, both are in fact authoritarian tolerating other parties and dissent only so long as they pose no threat. Although Taiwan has not progressed so far in collectivization, land reform and the encouragement of cooperatives have laid the foundation for possible future development. Finally, both regimes have stressed the importance of industrial modernization and development. When these and other considerations are tallied up, the similarities seem more significant than the differences, especially when the extraordinary traditional ethnocentrism of the Chinese people is taken into account.

Indeed, even before 1949, the Nationalist and Communist positions, if impartially examined, had much more in common than their inveterate hostility toward each other would seem on the surface to suggest. Beyond the issue of whether Chiang or Mao would rule China the major difference lay in their ideologies. Chiang's ideology looked selectively to the past for traditional virtues and values to bolster a new and selfless morality dedicated to the service of the state. This backward-looking idealism, rejecting the West and relying heavily on Confucianist virtues, had already failed China during the nineteenth century and had been denounced by Chinese revolutionaries since the turn of the century. Moreover, it not only contradicted the traditional pragmatic blend of idealism and realism that had characterized China's most successful leaders in the past but also stood in sharp contrast to the actual conduct of Chiang's officers and officials. Therefore, regardless of whatever appeal it may have had, it was unbelievable. An ideology unrelated to the realities and unsuited for the needs of its time can scarcely be expected to gain widespread acceptance.

In contrast, Mao's ideology, borrowed from the most revolutionary thought and action in the West and pragmatically altered to fit China's current condition, realistically stressed the present and the future of China in a modern, industrialized world and looked to the past only for reinforcement and a stylized explanation of the present. Furthermore, Mao was intelligent enough to single out for emphasis those features of Communist doctrine and practice most closely related to the traditional beliefs and practices of Chinese civilization, and, it must be admitted, Communism had much more in common with Chinese experience than the wholly alien, individualistic concepts of Western democracy. For example, the subordination of the individual to the welfare of the group and group collaboration for mutual benefit and protection were nothing new. Even the shift in loyalty from the family to the state, required to meet the challenges of the present, was not altogether unprecedented because Confucianism had placed a high value on loyalty to the prince as the paternalistic authority of that larger entity, the state. Another example was the attention given to the ultimate utopia of Communism when universal harmony and peace would prevail; when all men would be brothers. The concept of universal harmony and peace had always occupied the mainstream of Chinese thought; the only difference was that the world in which it must become operative had undergone vast change and enlargement calling for new and more vigorous measures. Above all, however, Mao's new but recognizable ideology promised to succeed where others had failed in mobilizing the entire energies and talents of the Chinese people to overcome the Western challenge.

At the beginning of this chapter the question was raised of how revolutionary a break with the past the Communist revolution has brought about in China. From the foregoing account it is obvious that, although there has been a great deal of redirection, redefinition, and reorganization, most of the changes were not initiated by the Chinese Communists and their evolution was dictated by the necessity to adapt the traditional values and practices of Chinese civilization to the realities of the modern world. It was no mere coincidence that the Communists completed the massive monument to Sun Yat-sen and named his widow vice-premier of the People's Republic. It was no mere coincidence that the imperial city of Peking was selected as the capital and that its palaces, monuments, and even the imperial tombs were refurbished at considerable expense. Indeed, Communism, as interpreted by Mao, may be described as the most appropriate modern garb for the revitalized Chinese dragon.

It supports an even more authoritarian regime, aided by modern totalitarian techniques and exercising power ostensibly for the general welfare. It supplies a modern, monolithic ideology which, like Confucianism, concerns all aspects of life but enjoys in today's world a far more universal appeal. Where Confucianism passively welcomed converts as civilized persons, Chinese Communism fosters a dynamic missionary spirit useful in advancing Chinese influence and prestige around the world. Like Confucianism it requires the services of a thoroughly indoctrinated elite selected on the basis of ideological merit, not class or caste, and dedicated to permeating society with its views. In time, with the full development of education, this elite will probably acquire the intellectual and cultural stature of the Confucian scholar-officials. The new official, like the old, is judged on his success or failure at his assigned task, guided only by the theoretical writings of Marx and Mao and a constantly changing flood of directives and admonitions from above. Without a fixed and detailed body of rules and laws, China remains a government of men, not laws.

In spite of its very considerable, if not amazing, achievements and its apparent stability the Chinese Communist regime is still confronted with serious problems, both internal and external, which make its future somewhat uncertain. The largest problem underlying all others, is the morale of its people, particularly the peasants, now probably numbering more than 750 million. Can they be persuaded to endure another 20 years of sacrifice and privation, the minimal time needed to modernize the economy? The Chinese people are renowned for their patience and half the population of today has no

memory of any other regime. But the real answer to this problem will depend on the solution of China's second most important problem, the improvement of the character and ability of the average Communist party member. A vast army of better-educated and better-indoctrinated cadres is essential to the totalitarian state that seeks to control and direct the activities of its people in detail. So far, party members freely recruited without much attention to standards of selection, have served as scapegoats at the local level for the miscalculations of the central government. Proper training and selection will take more time. Short of a significant improvement in the standard of living, a major morale booster would be a substantial victory in its militant foreign policy.

Red China's regular army, thoroughly reorganized along modern lines following the Korean conflict, is one of the largest and best-trained in the world numbering about 3,500,000 men; but without the support of an adequate air force and navy it appears limited for the present to land operations, as in Korea and India. Based on present information the Air Force, though sizable, is composed mainly of obsolete Russian-type MIG fighters. Although aircraft plants exist that can reproduce the MIG, it is not certain whether Chinese engineers have developed improvements to produce planes capable of matching up-to-date Russian or American models. In 1966 China successfully tested an intermediate ballistic missile with a nuclear warhead. The only significant element of the Chinese navy is a fleet of about 50 snorkel-type submarines reportedly capable of launching missiles on the surface. Although they could inflict serious damage, in the shallow waters off the China coast where engagements would be most likely to occur, they would be very vulnerable. Finally, Mao and his associates, though talking boldly to maintain tension, have always demonstrated caution in committing their forces to battle until they were reasonably sure of success. Moreover, they can be expected to think twice before inviting destruction of the heavy industrial base built up at such great sacrifice since 1950.

Therefore, the most likely near-term foreign policy triumphs that could be exploited to boost morale appear to be a favorable settlement of the frontier dispute with India and a favorable outcome of the struggle to reunify Vietnam. Another possibility of tremendous impact would be the peaceful return to the fold of Taiwan following the death or disability of the aging Chiang K'ai-shek. The pull of Chinese nationalism should never be underrated. All prominent persons who have returned to the homeland have been treated well, and probably the most important returnee for propaganda purposes was the last acting president of the Nationalist regime on the mainland who lived in self-imposed exile in the United States for 15 years.

In the next generation China seems destined, if it does not stumble, to reassert its influence in all Southeast Asia through cooperative, if not Communist, regimes. Some solution to the unnatural division of Korea may be worked out, though even the possible outlines of such a settlement cannot yet be discerned. Certainly relations with industrial Japan are bound to improve and expand, particularly in the realm of trade. Finally, China's stature and prestige as a world power will spread with the accomplishment of modernization and the present powers will have to adjust their relations with their new partner.

The foregoing favorable forecast is predicated on the satisfactory solution of the succession problem, among others, once Mao and his closest associates have passed from the scene. It must be remembered that the fraternal bonds between them were welded by a long struggle and especially the ordeal of the Long March. A second echelon of leaders about 10 years younger also shared this experience and many more even younger joined the party during World War II and the subsequent civil war before victory was achieved. For the foreseeable future a destructive struggle for power cannot be ruled out, particularly since there are groups among the upper echelon with sharply differing views on strategy. Any strategy based on such an expectation, however, would seem highly unrealistic. Barring some unforeseen mishap, the Chinese Communist Party, as the heir and continuer of the Chinese revolution, is entrenched in power, and under its aggressive leadership China is destined to grow in strength as a principal member of the world community.

SIGNIFICANT DATES

1949	Proclamation of People's Republic of China on October 1
1950	Chiang K'ai-shek resumes Presidency on Taiwan in March
1950	Outbreak of Korean conflict in June
1950	Entrance of Chinese "volunteers" in October
1953	Korean truce
1953–1957	First Five-Year Plan
1954	First Geneva Conference
1955	Bandung Conference
1957	"Hundred Flowers" campaign and its suppression
1958	The Great Leap Forward and the communes
1959	Mao replaced by Liu as head of government
1959	Lin Piao becomes defense minister
1959–1961	Collapse of Great Leap Forward
1964	First nuclear detonation in October
1965	Start of Great Proletarian Cultural Revolution
1969	Adoption of "Maoist" Party Constitution
1969	Sino-Soviet border clashes

SELECTED READINGS

Barnett, A. Doak, *Cadres, Bureaucracy, and Political Power in Communist China*. New York: Columbia University Press, 1967.

*———, *China after Mao*. Princeton: Princeton University Press, 1967.

*———, *Chinese Communist Politics in Action*. Seattle: University of Washington Press, 1969.

*———, *Communist China and Asia: A Challenge to American Policy*. New York: Random House, 1961.

*———, *Communist China: The Early Years, 1949–1955*. New York: Praeger, 1964.

*———, and Reischauer, Edwin O., eds., *The United States and China: The Next Decade*. New York: Praeger, 1970.

*Blum, Robert, completed by A. Doak Barnett, *The United States and China in World Affairs*. New York: McGraw-Hill, 1966.

*Bulletin of Atomic Scientists, *China after the Cultural Revolution*. New York: Random House, 1970.

Chen, Nai-Ruenn, and Galenson, Walter, *The Chinese Economy under Communism*. Chicago: Aldine, 1969.

———, ed., *Chinese Economic Statistics: A Handbook for Mainland China*. Chicago: Aldine, 1967.

*Crozier, Ralph C., ed., *China's Cultural Legacy and Communism*. New York: Praeger, 1970.

*Doolin, Dennis J., *Territorial Claims in the Sino-Soviet Conflict*. Stanford: Stanford University Press, 1965.

*Douglas, Bruce, and Terrill, Ross, eds., *China and Ourselves*. Boston: Beacon Press, 1969.

*Dutt, Vidya Prakash, *China and the World: An Analysis of Communist China's Foreign Policy*. Rev. ed.; New York: Praeger, 1966.

Eckstein, Alexander, et al., eds., *Economic Trends in Communist China*. Chicago: Aldine, 1968.

Fairbank, John K., *China: The People's Middle Kingdom and the U.S.A.* Cambridge, Mass.: Harvard University Press, 1967.

*Fitzgerald, C. P., *The Chinese View of their Place in the World*. London: Oxford University Press, 1964.

Gittings, John, *Survey of the Sino-Soviet Dispute*. London: Oxford University Press, 1968.

*Goldman, Merle, *Literary Dissent in Communist China*. New York: Atheneum Pubs., 1971.

*Griffith, William E., *Sino-Soviet Relations, 1964–1965*. Cambridge, Mass.: M. I. T. Press, 1967.

*———, *The Sino-Soviet Rift*. Cambridge, Mass.: M. I. T. Press, 1964.

Han, Suyin, *China in the Year 2001*. New York: Basic Books, 1967.

Hinton, Harold C., *Communist China in World Politics*. Boston: Houghton Mifflin, 1966.

*Ho, Ping-ti, and Tsou, Tang, eds., *China in Crisis*. 2 vols.; Chicago: University of Chicago Press, 1968.

*Houn, Franklin W., *A Short History of Chinese Communism*. Englewood Cliffs, N.J.: Prentice-Hall, 1967.

Kerr, George H., *Formosa Betrayed.* Boston: Houghton Mifflin, 1965.

Lattimore, Owen, *Nomads and Commissars: Mongolia Revisited.* London: Oxford University Press, 1962.

*Lewis, John Wilson, ed., *Party Leadership and Revolutionary Power in China.* Cambridge: Cambridge University Press, 1970.

*Lifton, Robert J., *Revolutionary Immortality: Mao Tse-tung and the Chinese Cultural Revolution.* New York: Random House, 1968.

*———, *Thought Reform and the Psychology of Totalism.* New York: Norton, 1961.

*Lindbeck, John M., ed., *China: Management of a Revolutionary Society.* Seattle: University of Washington Press, 1971.

*Liu, William T., ed., *Chinese Society Under Communism: A Reader.* New York: Wiley, 1967.

*MacFarquhar, Roderick, ed., *China under Mao: Politics Take Command.* Cambridge, Mass.: M. I. T. Press, 1966.

Mancall, Mark, ed., *Formosa Today.* New York: Praeger, 1964.

*Mao, Tse-tung, *Quotations from Chairman Mao Tse-tung.* New York: Bantam Books, 1967.

*Myrdal, Jan, *China: The Revolution Continued.* New York: Random House, 1971.

*North, Robert C., *Moscow and Chinese Communists.* Rev. ed.; Stanford: Stanford University, 1963.

*Ojha, Ishwer C., *Chinese Foreign Policy in an Age of Transition.* Boston: Beacon Press, 1969.

*Petrov, Victor P., *China: Emerging World Power.* Princeton: Van Nostrand, 1967.

*Pye, Lucian W., *The Spirit of Chinese Politics: A Psychocultural Study of the Crisis in Political Development.* Cambridge, Mass.: M. I. T. Press, 1968.

*Schurmann, Franz, *Ideology and Organization in Communist China.* Rev. ed., Berkeley and Los Angeles: University of California Press, 1969.

———, and Schell, Orville, eds., *Communist China.* Vol. 3 of *The China Reader.*

*Snow, Edgar, *Red China Today: The Other Side of the River.* New York: Random House, 1971.

*Steele, Archibald T., *The American People and China.* New York: Viking, 1967.

*Vogel, Ezra, *Canton Under Communism.* New York: Harper and Row, 1971.

*Wolf, Margery, *The House of Lim.* New York: Appleton-Century-Crofts, 1968.

*Yang, C. K., *Chinese Communist Society: The Family and the Village.* Cambridge. Mass.: M. I. T. Press, 1965.

*Zagoria, Donald S., *The Sino-Soviet Conflict, 1956–1961.* New York: Atheneum Pubs., 1964.

CHAPTER TWENTY-SIX

INDEPENDENT INDIA, PAKISTAN AND CEYLON

In the transfer of sovereignty in India in 1947 one feature stands out above all others. The unhappy necessity of partition not only rent the fabric of unity maintained for a century by the British Rāj but also was sealed in the blood of the countless victims of mutual Muslim and Hindu massacres of those caught on the wrong side of the new frontiers. Despite the Mahātma's pleas for broad-based tolerance, intolerant religious communalism, based on the fears of the Muslim minority, must bear the principal responsibility for the division of the subcontinent and the inveterate hostility between its two parts, only too sadly confirmed by the clashes over Kashmir and more recently former East Pakistan.

Partition also required the rough division of integrated assets and liabilities and the formation of two administrations from the limited human resources of one. In terms of trained talent, India was far better served because the Hindu tradition of cooperation with conquerors had produced many more educated and experienced civil servants than the Muslim community could boast. Furthermore, greater Hindu enterprise brought to the new state of India the overwhelming bulk of business talent as well as 95 percent of the limited amount of modern industry. In the exchange of refugees, Pakistan lost far more skilled persons than it received. After all, India fell heir to all the major urban centers with the exception of Lahore in the Punjab, and Lahore was denuded of its entrepreneurs, both traditional and modern.

Although the Western-educated leaders of both nations owed to British tutelage a genuine dedication to liberal and democratic principles, Pakistan was much more handicapped in implementing these ideals by the personnel shortage and by the militant Islamic condition of its emergence. In fact, the government felt obliged to employ British civil servants and military officers for several years. Having fanned the flame of Islam, Pakistan's leaders also found it difficult to come to terms with the conservative and even reactionary demands of the ulema for a religiously controlled state. The viability of Pakistan was even more seriously threatened by its division into two almost equal parts, separated by more than 1000 miles of impassable Indian territory and by an even greater ethnic, linguistic, and economic gulf between them. Indeed, the sole factor that united the two parts was a common devotion to Islam and a concomitant fear of Hindu domination. Finally, to cap Pakistan's tale of woes, it soon lost the services of its two principal architects, Muhammed Ali Jinnāh, who died exhausted in 1948, and Liāquat Ali Khān, who was assassinated by a disaffected tribesman in 1951, while India enjoyed the unifying and stabilizing leadership of Jawaharlāl Nehru until his death in 1964. Under the circumstances, the mere survival of Pakistan reguires explanation, let alone the measure of progress it has achieved.

THE QUESTION OF KASHMIR

Direct British rule had not extended to the 600 princely states that had retained internal autonomy by acknowledging the paramountcy of the British crown. Since 1857, the rulers of these domains, ranging in size from small estates to realms larger than many European states, had been left alone as loyal supporters of the crown and had not been compelled to join the government as provided in the 1935 India Act. At indepen-

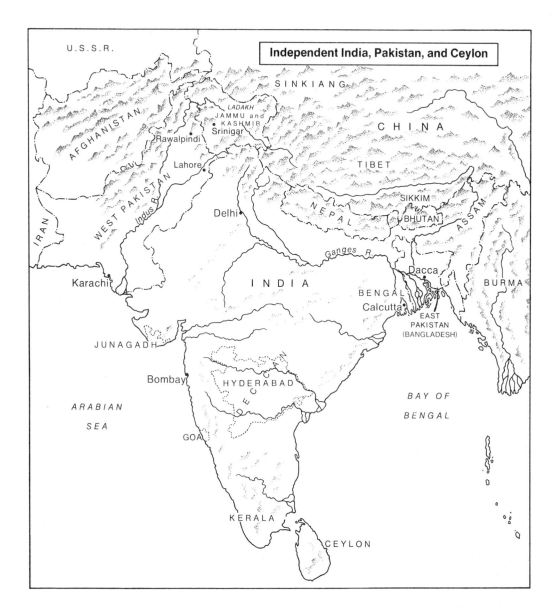

Independent India, Pakistan, and Ceylon

dence they were informed that their relationship with the British crown automatically terminated and were urged to accept the proffered instruments of accession to one or the other of the new states by which they merely transferred control of external affairs and communications from Britain to the new governments. All but a few signed these documents without delay, though within five years they were forced to surrender their lo-

cal authority in return for pensions. Only three states—Junagadh, Hyderabad, and Jammu and Kashmir—created difficulties.

The Muslim ruler of Junagadh, a small state of less than one million population on the coast north of Bombay, exercised his legal right of acceding to Pakistan, even though his realm did not adjoin Pakistan directly and his subjects were overwhelmingly Hindu. When the people demonstrated in protest of his decision, he fled to Pakistan and the Indian army moved in ostensibly to restore order. In response to a protest from Pakistan, based on the legal right of the Nawab of Junagadh to accede to whichever state he wished, the Indian government insisted that no claim of legality by itself could properly supersede the wishes of the people to be expressed in a plebiscite. The plebiscite was duly held under Indian supervision and, as anticipated, upheld accession to India. By itself this action does not seem very striking. Its real significance emerges only in its contrast to the Indian position on Kashmir.

The Muslim ruler of Hyderabad, a state as large as Britain and covering much of the Deccan, wanted to remain independent, even though his realm was surrounded by Indian territory and lacked access to the sea. Under Indian pressure he was ready to delegate control over foreign affairs and communications, but he steadfastly refused to sign a formal document of accession, and made a futile appeal to the United Nations. The Indian government insisted that, regardless of legality, the facts of geography made the existence of an independent state in the heart of India impossible to accept. Finally, after questionable actions on both sides the issue was settled by force when the Indian army invaded Hyderabad in September 1948.

The situation in Jammu and Kashmir (more popularly known simply as Kashmir) represented the opposite side of the coin. The Mahārāja was a Sikh, while his subjects were more than 75 percent Muslim. Furthermore, Kashmir adjoined West Pakistan, its principal roads and trade went to West Pakistan, its rivers irrigated the arid lands to the south, and it represented the "K" in Pakistan. Like the Nizām of Hyderabad, however, the Mahārāja preferred to retain his authority as an independent ruler and refused to accede to either state, although he did make a partial commitment by granting to Pakistan the management of communications and customs duties.

Thereafter the exact course of events is not clear. Apparently a rebellion broke out that the Mahārāja's troops proceeded to suppress. Rebel refugees then won the active support of militant Muslim tribesmen from the Northwest Territory who probably picked up some modern weapons from Pakistani troops while en route to Kashmir. Thus equipped these tribesmen drove back the Mahārāja's forces and were approaching his capital of Srinagar before he signed an instrument of accession to India to gain protection against this wild tribal rampage. Indian troops were flown in on October 27, 1947, just in time to save Srinagar, and they then proceeded to repel the pillaging tribesmen from the lovely Vale of Kashmir. Whatever the role of Pakistan in the tribal invasion of Kashmir, Jinnāh, founder and first governor-general of Pakistan, was stunned by the news of India's action, even when it was accompanied by the promise of a plebiscite after the restoration of order. Only the stern warning of his British commander-in-chief about the consequences of war with India deterred him from ordering Pakistan's smaller army to the support of the tribesmen.

Feeling confident in his case, Nehru charged Pakistan with supporting naked aggression in Kashmir before the Security Council of the United Nations. Pakistan filed a countercharge and pointed out with telling effect Indian inconsistency in now basing its position on the legality of the Mahārāja's accession, an argument which it had rejected in the cases of Junagadh and Hyderabad in favor of the will of the people and the facts of geography. Clearly the latter would fully support the claims of Pakistan. To Nehru's disappointment the Security Council refused to take India's side and instead urged both sides to exercise restraint, while it sought to determine the facts for itself. In 1949 both sides agreed to a cease-fire policed by a U.N. contingent and to a plebiscite under U.N. supervision following a mutual withdrawal of armed forces. As yet, a withdrawal satisfactory to both parties has been impossible to achieve, while India has so transformed its position in Kashmir over the years that a simple plebiscite is no longer feasible or acceptable as a solution. Regardless of justice, possession—and particularly prolonged possession—tends to constitute nine-tenths of international law.

GOVERNMENT AND POLITICS

The constituent assemblies of both new states were immediately confronted with the task of drafting constitutions adapted to their particular conditions and aspirations. Of course, the proclaimed dedication of their leaders to democratic precepts, as learned from their British mentors, precluded any alternative form of government. On the other hand, a full awareness of the under-developed and impoverished circumstances of their people aroused their interest in a strong central government and centralized planning to expedite social change and economic development. In any case, state planning and programs were in vogue throughout the postwar world.

India, under the all-powerful Congress, proceeded with alacrity to fashion the world's lengthiest constitution of 395 articles in 250 pages. In the general form of government it clearly reflected British experience in combination with ideas derived from the Commonwealth and the United States. The Executive was headed by a president, elected to a five-year term by the members of both Houses of Parliament, who, like the British crown, was above party. He could proclaim an emergency for six months under which the constitution gave him extensive powers. Under this provision the Indian president has taken control of states on several occasions for the restoration of law and order. A vice-president, similarly elected, presides over the upper house as in the United States.

The legislature is composed of two houses: a Council of States elected by state legislatures for staggered terms of six years like the American Senate and the Lok Sabhā or House of the People of 500 members elected by universal adult suffrage to represent their constituencies. As in Britain, political power resides in a Prime Minister and Cabinet collectively responsible to the lower house. After the American model a Supreme Court heads up an independent judiciary.

As a federation, the constitution specified the respective jurisdictions of the central and state governments as well as those for which both exercise concurrent responsibility. The president appoints state governors to preside over parliamentary regimes set up according to state constitutions. Under this federal arrangement the central government is not omnipotent and cannot fairly be criticized for the failure of state governments to enact implementing legislation in areas of local responsibility, such as land reform, education, or the specific eradication of social injustice.

The constitution also included a long list of fundamental rights prescribing equality and the protection of minorities in a secular state but reserved its strongest ammunition for carrying out Gāndhi's dream of eradicating Untouchability, the curse of some 50 million Indians at the bottom of the social scale. The abolition of Untouchability was made more than a pious pledge by reserving seats in parliament to be filled only by Untouchables. Subsequent legislation granted them so many special privileges and benefits, such as reserved jobs and scholarships, that many who might otherwise abandon their status are reluctant to do so.

The many advantages and privileges granted to the Untouchables posed a social and political challenge to the middle castes and led them to minimize their differences and cooperate, particularly in the political arena, to secure their common interests against Untouchable domination. Furthermore, the brāhmans in the south, where more positions in college, government, and other traditionally brāhman preserves have been reserved for Untouchables, have tended to migrate to the north where college admissions and government posts remain more open to talent on a competitive basis. Although both caste and Untouchability were denounced, a new division into three caste-like groups appears to be emerging under the impact of this social and political engineering: the specially privileged Untouchables more than 50 million strong, the middle castes with the bulk of the population but still not united, and the educated brāhman and secularist elite seeking a dominant role in government and business.

The constitution also contained an ill-advised provision to replace English with Hindi as the official national language after 15 years of preparation. Hindustani, a mixture of Urdu and Hindi, was a lingua franca widely understood throughout India which Gāndhi had favored as a national language, but purists objected to its Muslim Urdu content and insisted on the adoption of Hindi, an undeveloped, subordinate language, understood by at most one-third of India's people. To make it a suitable vehicle, a language commission was given the task of coining 300,000 new words, a tour de force at best. Southern Indians with their own distinctive languages protested vigorously at what they called Hindi imperialism, and in the 1956 reorganization of states and their boundaries they gained new states roughly conforming to the ranges of their major languages. Fearful of accentuating linguistic divisions that might lead to the dissolution of the Indian nation, Prime Minister Nehru gave way very reluctantly to these demands. Later, in 1965, only bloody riots in which hundreds lost their lives compelled the central government to agree to an indefinite delay in adopting Hindi as the official national language. Meanwhile, English, the language of imperialism but also of Western education and civilization, continues to dominate the field as a national language in competition with revived regional languages. This bitter linguistic competition has unfortunately handicapped students and faculty in both secondary and higher educa-

tion and has even damaged the quality of English instruction.

The Congress Party had almost alone commanded the independence movement, incorporating in its ranks patriots of every political persuasion. Only gradually could opposition parties be formed, largely led by former Congressmen disillusioned with one or another of its policies. By the time of the first elections these parties plus independents denied the Congress a majority of the votes, a condition that persisted in subsequent elections. Nevertheless, the fragmentation of the opposition guaranteed to the Congress a clear majority of seats in the Lok Sabhā. But in the 1967 elections, the first without Nehru's leadership, this majority was whittled down almost to the vanishing point. The divisions of the opposition, however, would appear to assure continued Congress control of the central government for the foreseeable future. More threatening are Congress losses at the state level.

Among the opposition parties no single one has emerged dominant enough to pose a challenge to the Congress. On the extreme right are several Hindu communalist parties, notably the Mahāsabhā and the Jan Sangh, but surprisingly none of these has attracted as much as seven percent of the voters. Also on the right is the newer, modernist, and anticommunal Swatantra or Freedom party, which arose in 1959 to champion individualism and free enterprise against the growing inclination of the Congress toward nationalization, regulation, and socialism. Naturally this party is well financed by concerned businessmen. In the center and left the Socialist Party and its various offshoots have had their thunder stolen by Nehru and the Congress and therefore cannot be considered a significant factor. Finally, the Communist party, despite dependence on foreign direction and the backlash to the Sino-Indian frontier clash, has consistently maintained its role as the major element of the opposition, generally polling close to 10 percent of the vote. Nevertheless, like the Socialist party, the appeal of the Communists is undermined by the strong pro-Untouchable legislation and the socialistic policies of the Congress.

Communist successes in the southwestern state of Kerala perhaps hold some lessons and indications for the future elsewhere in India. Among its features, this state possesses the highest literacy rate (60 percent or about double the national average), the highest population density, the highest rate of educated unemployed, and the largest number of landless poor. As the explosive population growth compounds economic distress and the literacy campaign expands its advance elsewhere, the Communist party may very well become the principal beneficiary in the political realm despite the revitalized religiosity of the people which is more personal than political. After all, Congress policy is also wedded to a strictly secular outlook.

Pakistan, founded on devotion to Islam, encountered much greater difficulty in framing a broadly acceptable constitution. All agreed on an Islamic state, but differed radically on just what this should mean, particularly in terms of the law. The conservative religious leaders insisted that all law conform to the *shari'a*, as interpreted by them. Progressive Western-educated leaders refused to have their actions subjected to such obscurantist dictation. Another major difficulty was the deep-seated differences between the East and West wings of the new state. The more populous, Bengali-speaking East, whose tea and jute provided the bulk of export earnings, feared domination prejudicial to its interests by the predominant leadership of the Urdu-speaking West.

A draft constitution was submitted to the constituent assembly in 1950, but interminable haggling of traditionalists versus modernists and East versus West forestalled approval. In 1956 a second constituent assembly gave its approval to a revised constitution after the West was unified into a single province to put it on a presumably equal footing with the East. The language issue was skirted by declining to designate an official language. The Islamic ultras were appeased for the moment by conceding that state laws must not be in conflict with the *shari'a*. Later, however, irreconcilable differences over interpretation nullified this agreement.

The structure of government under this constitution bore a close resemblance to that of India. The president alone had to be a Muslim, and he enjoyed somewhat more extensive powers than his Indian counterpart. In addition, the two provinces of Pakistan held a bit more comprehensive powers than the Indian states. Nevertheless, in this federation, as in the Indian, the center exercised the balance of power.

The failure of this constitution owed more to politics than to any inherent weaknesses in it. Unlike India, Pakistan soon lost its principal leaders, and with their deaths the Muslim League, a much more elitest organization than the Congress, tended to disintegrate into factions. The comparative shortage of Western-educated leaders and the absence of industry permitted the wealthy and generally conservative landlords to have a greater voice in affairs that they sought to mold according to their personal interests. In other words, political unity and discipline gave way to strident individualism and the unrestrained competition of cliques for personal advantage and profit to the traditional and predictable accompaniment of corruption and maladministration. East Pakistan continued to be distressed at its subordination and the favoritism of the central government toward West Pakistan. Finally, speculative buying, hoarding, and black marketing combined with fiscal mismanagement to create severe inflation, while little attention was given to alleviating the suffering of the refugees and the exploitation of the peasantry. In 1958, a year of upheavals in a number of the new states of Asia, conditions reached such a critical state that the president invited the commander-in-chief of the army, General Ayub Khān, to set up a caretaker regime.

Under martial law the mere threat of summary punishment against merchant speculators brought about almost overnight a drop of 25 percent or more in commodity prices. Convinced as he was of the selfish sinfulness of politicians, Ayub Khān felt he could not stop short of a thorough cleansing of the Augean stables and within three weeks supplanted the president, dissolved the political parties, abolished the constitution, and set up a benevolent dictatorship. At the same time, however, he proclaimed his dedication to democratic principles and pledged to find as soon as possible a democratic solution suited to the conditions of Pakistan. Actually the threat of severe punishment seems to have been sufficient to discipline politicians and civil servants; only a small percentage were convicted and most of these were pardoned.

Another source of opposition to the regime of English-educated Ayub Khān was the wealthy landlords, and the reduction of their influence appears to have been the principal motivation of the land reform for West Pakistan proclaimed early in 1959 (reform of the abuses peculiar to East Pakistan had already been largely accomplished). Under its provisions individual holdings in excess of 500 irrigated or 1000 nonirrigated acres plus 150 acres of orchard land had to be surrendered in return for 4 percent government bonds. However, limited rights of transferring land to immediate members of the family could permit a family to retain as much as 900 acres of the valuable irrigated land. The implementation of this modest reform brought into government hands for redistribution little more than 5 percent of the cultivated land in the West and scarcely compares in its effects with "the land to the tiller" reforms in India. Most peasants remained tenants, though various regulations did improve the conditions of tenancy. Land reform did reduce the direct political influence of the wealthiest landlords over the peasants in their districts but did not significantly lower their income when the interest income from government bonds was taken into account.

On the first anniversary of his regime Ayub Khān announced his idea of basic democracies as his remedy to the problem of government in Pakistan. This conception was inspired by his desire to involve the people at the grass-roots level and thus hopefully avoid the tyranny of politicians and political parties. Under this program the basic units were unions of villages and parts of larger cities of 10 to 15 thousand people each. Each of these units could elect councillors well-known to the voters, and the government could appoint representatives, up to a total of no more than one-half of the elected members, of minorities or special interest groups who could not otherwise get elected. This Union Council would then elect a chairman who received an honorarium and was automatically a member of the council at the next level or circle. This higher council could contain official and nonofficial appointees not to exceed the total of Union Council representatives thus giving the government an even stronger voice. In addition, the circle executive officer was an ex-officio member of this council. The members of the successively higher councils at the district, divisional, and provincial levels were selected in essentially the same manner, though the number and powers of the elected members were further reduced in favor of the appointed officials. In January 1960 the approximately 80,000 Union Councillors, or "Basic Democrats," as they were called, were utilized for the first time as "electors" to indicate by secret ballot their approval of Ayub Khān as president. An almost unanimous vote confirmed him as the first "elected" president of Pakistan.

Subsequently a constitution clearly reflecting Ayub Khān's ideas formally replaced the martial law regime in June 1962. Under this constitution the president was the key figure. In addition to emergency powers, he approved all legislation of the National Assembly. In case of a deadlock he alone could take the issue to the electors. When the National Assembly was not in session or had been dissolved by him, the president could issue ordinances with the full force of law. He was the sole executive authority, and the Council of Ministers or Cabinet, as well as all other officials, was appointed by him and solely responsible to him, not to the National Assembly. The established budget would continue in force; only new expenditures and new taxation required the approval of the National Assembly, thus minimizing the prospects of a paralyzing deadlock.

The 156 members of the National Assembly (half of them including at least three women from each province) were elected by the 80,000 "Basic Democrats" for a five-year term unless the president dissolved this body before then. Each province also elected an assembly of 155 members each (including at least five women from each) in the same manner to assist the presidentially appointed governor in the conduct of provincial government.

An independent judiciary headed by a Supreme Court was provided in the constitution. In addition, an Advisory Council on Islamic Ideology was available to give an opinion on whether or not any law was repugnant to Islam upon referral by the president, governors, or assemblies, but none of these governmental organs were required to submit legislation for its judgment. Finally, both Bengali and Urdu were recognized as official languages.

Clearly this constitution vested predominant power in the hands of President Ayub Khān and his successors, and the effectiveness of any government under it would consequently depend heavily on the character and caliber of whoever occupied the presidential office. Furthermore, despite Ayub Khān's hopes of eliminating political parties, they immediately reemerged and had to be recognized in 1962. It would appear that no functionally democratic system can manage without their organizational services.

In late March 1969, Ayub Khān surrendered the presidency under extreme pressure to General Yahya Khān who forthwith abrogated the constitution, dissolved the National Assembly, and ruled by martial law, promising a new constitution with direct representation according to population, which would favor East Pakistan, once order was restored. In January 1971, a general election based on population was concluded for a National Assembly to draw up a new constitution, while the country remained under martial law. The candidates of the Awami League led by Shaykh Mujibur Rahman swept the polls in more populous East Pakistan and won an absolute majority, campaigning on a platform of autonomy for the East, only a loose association in a limited central government, and nationalization of major enterprises. In the West the party led by Zulfibar Ali Bhutto gained a majority on a platform also calling for nationalization but favoring a strong central government. When Mujibur Rahman insisted that his absolute majority should determine the new constitution, the National Assembly was postponed and the Awami League initiated a program of civil disobedience that turned into a struggle for independence amid reports of atrocities by government forces and Indian aid for the rebels. Finally, direct intervention by the Indian army won independence for the People's Republic of Bangla Desh (Bengal Nation) in December 1971. Yahya Khan resigned in favor of Ali Bhutto as president of West Pakistan.

ECONOMIC PROBLEMS AND PLANNING

Although preindependence India ranked eighth in the world in the size of its industrial plant, industrial production and employment, still accounting for little more than two percent of total employment, made a negligible impact in such a populous land where less than 17 percent lived in cities. Moreover, in the overpopulated countryside miniscule and fragmented plots compelled most peasants to struggle for subsistence alone, resulting in the world's most backward farming methods and lowest productivity. A mere one-third of grain production reached the marketplace, and this supply was very unreliable. Another consequence of subsistence farming was the inadequate development of roads and transport to break down rural isolation. Finally, subsistence agriculture could not produce the tax revenues needed for investment in modernization. Little progress could be anticipated from land reform and heavy investments as long as rural India and Pakistan remained overpopulated in terms of existing modes of agriculture. Therefore, economic planners in both countries, recognizing the well-nigh insuperable obstacles to directly breaking the cycle of agricultural poverty, increasingly preferred to approach the problem obliquely by stressing industrialization, which hopefully would employ the excess rural population and would generate income for subsequent investment in agricultural modernization. Unfortunately, impoverished farmers make poor consumers for industrial products and accelerating rural population growth has more than kept pace with migration to the cities.

Despite these handicaps, however, community development, cooperatives, water control, irrigation, and greater availability of fertilizers and improved seeds have brought notable increases in food production, though both countries still suffer from an annual food deficit made good only by costly imports of millions of tons of grain. In comparison with Pakistan, India boasts a much better record of land reform, with the various states enacting more or less radical measures according to local conditions and needs to implement the slogan of "land to the tiller." This achievement has been largely due to the greater diversity in the educations and occupations of Indian leaders and the absence of

a dominant and entrenched landlord class, such as characterized West Pakistan. Most striking, however, has been the amazing response to the *Bhoodan* (Land Gift) movement of Vinobā Bhāve, a spiritual disciple of Gāndhi. In 1951 terroristic Communist assaults on the landlords of Hyderabad inspired him to take to the road making personal appeals to all landowners to donate land in excess of their personal needs for distribution to the landless poor. His less radical solution gained enthusiastic endorsement from the beleaguered landlords, and Communist influence was promptly dissipated by this preachment so true to the Indian spiritual tradition. After this success Bhāve carried his message of selflessness on foot throughout the land with even greater success, while the more secularly minded leaders of the government looked on in bemused consternation. More than 4 million acres, including 2500 whole villages, were donated for distribution. Such a movement on such a scale is scarcely conceivable in any country other than India.

As in the adoption of a constitution, India preceded Pakistan in the formulation of a plan for economic development. Again, the predominant position of the Congress under Nehru's leadership was largely responsible for this accomplishment. Early in his career Nehru had publicly indicated his belief in the all-important role of the state and his preference for the socialist path to modernization, while preserving and protecting the rights of the individual under a democratic system of government. As he saw it, state planning and direction would be the most economical and speediest device for a country so far behind and so short on capital and human resources.

Nevertheless, the First Five-Year Plan (1951–1956) looked to the private sector for 40 percent of the planned investment of nine billion dollars. Since the private sector was given the principal responsibility for industrial development, the state concentrated on overcoming the aftermaths of war and independence, such as inflation, the rehabilitation of roads and railroads, and the resettlement of 6 million refugees, and on laying the foundations for improved agricultural productivity, mainly by the construction of great dams for water control, irrigation, and the generation of electric power. Of the total state investment, 15 percent was allocated to agriculture, 30 percent to water control and power, only 5 percent to industry and mining, 26 percent to roads and railroads, and 21 percent to social services. In other words, the state wisely devoted its efforts to building up the economic infrastructure outside the scope of private investment. The combined public and private investment was calculated to produce a modest 11 percent increase in national income over the five years of the plan.

Thanks to favorable weather, the high prices for Indian exports (because of the Korean conflict), and the availability of wartime sterling reserves to pay for imports, the Indian economic progress under the First Five-Year Plan exceeded expectations. Agricultural production grew by 22 percent, industrial output expanded by 39 percent, and the increase in national income of 18.5 percent surpassed the goal of 11 percent. Moreover, the investment in the state-owned railroads proved so profitable that surplus earnings became available for investment in other sectors of development. On the ominous side, however, population growth was higher than projected and demonstrated an alarming inclination toward acceleration. Nevertheless, the achievements were substantial enough to justify the enthusiasm with which the Indian government entered upon the much more ambitious Second Five-Year Plan (1956–1961).

This plan projected a doubling of investment in the public sector and a 50 percent increase in the private sector. In 1955 Nehru had made his commitment to socialism more explicit and this commitment was reflected in the planned investment in heavy industry, particularly for a five-fold expansion of steel

production, which accounted for a major portion of the increased industrial investment by the state. In addition, those areas of industry destined for nationalization, those reserved for private enterprise, and those designated for concurrent development were delineated for the guidance of private entrepreneurs, though it was indicated that these guidelines were not inflexible.

Since India was endowed with one of the world's largest deposits of iron ore and coking coal in economical proximity to each other and the world's lowest production cost outside Australia, the government's decision to concentrate on steel was entirely logical. Not only would it reduce the expenditure of foreign exchange on steel imports, but it would also add to export earnings. Furthermore, it would spawn a host of subsidiary enterprises that could expand industrial employment. Less justifiable, however, except on socialist grounds, was state ownership and management in addition to state financing. Three major steel plants with an annual capacity of one million tons each were undertaken, and the honors in providing financial and technical assistance were diplomatically distributed between Russia, Germany, and Britain.

Allocations of the increased expenditures under the Second Five-Year Plan reflect the shift in emphasis. The percentages for transport and communications and for social services increased only slightly to 28.9 and 21.7 percent, respectively, but in view of the doubling of the budget they meant, in fact, an actual increase of more than 100 percent. The biggest increase, of course, was from 5 to 18.6 percent of public expenditure for industry and mining. The reductions to 11.7 percent for agriculture and 19 percent for water control and power still meant actual monetary increases in each of these categories over the first plan. Furthermore, greater attention to bringing water to the fields meant greater immediate benefit for the farmer and agricultural productivity.

Unfortunately, the favorable conditions

during the First Five-Year Plan were reversed during the second. In three years widespread droughts forced the government to divert scarce funds to the purchase of grain from abroad. Nevertheless, agricultural production did manage to register a 20 percent increase by 1961. During the years following the Korean conflict world prices for Indian exports collapsed, reaching a low point in 1958 and sharply cutting export earnings at a time when the prices of essential industrial imports were rising. As a result, heavier drawings than anticipated had to be made on sterling reserves, reducing foreign exchange reserves to a critical level. This combination of circumstances forced a cutback in planned expenditures and the imposition of severe import controls and precipitated a much more ardent appeal for international aid to rescue India from a foreign exchange deficit that by 1961 had grown to about five billion dollars. Fortunately, the challenge of the Russian aid offensive had by this time stimulated a broadening of American interest in foreign aid, and the United States joined other Western Nations in the Aid-India Club to meet a major portion of the Indian deficit. By the close of the Second Five-Year Plan cutbacks reduced the increase in national income from the planned 25 to 20 percent. Moreover, a census revealed an alarming acceleration in population growth as a result of lowered mortality, to an annual rate of 2.8 percent, which effectively lowered the improvement in per capita income. The brightest note was the growth in industrial production by 41 percent which, in view of the shortfall in public investment, was principally due to the larger-than-planned investments in the private sector. Indeed, some critics suggested that greater industrial development might have been made if it had been left to unfettered free enterprise. Certainly the threat of nationalization, strict labor regulations, stringent import controls, and limitations on foreign capital and management did limit and restrain private investment.

Despite the disappointments in the Second Plan and the critical financial problems, the government was sufficiently encouraged to adopt a Third Five-Year Plan (1962–1967) with a proposed two-thirds increase in total investment. Somewhat chastened by its experience, government investment in industry and mining was reduced and the allocations to the various areas were more evenly distributed with a greater, though still small, emphasis on the vital issue of family planning. For almost one-third of public investment, however, the plan looked to foreign aid, particularly from the United States, totalling more than five billion dollars over the five years.

Almost immediately the new plan was in trouble because of problems left over from the previous plan. For example, steel production at the new government plants fell short of planned capacity because of delayed deliveries of equipment, breakdowns, and some errors in planning. This setback meant a reduction in anticipated income. A more vital blow was the Sino-Indian frontier conflict in 1962, which forced the government to more than double military expenditures. Then came the expensive military clash with Pakistan. Finally, severe droughts called for sharply increased importations of grain to stave off starvation and greater expenditures in support of agriculture. In addition, the dwindling of the American grain surplus made a solution of the crisis in Indian agriculture even more pressing.

At a time when India's woes were mounting, the undisputed leadership of the Congress was shaken first by the death of the master pilot, Pundit Jawaharhāl Nehru, and then by the death 18 months later of his less charismatic successor, Lal Bahādur Shāstri. Nehru's daughter, Madame Indira Gāndhi, as prime minister of the second most populous nation in the world has been confronted with the task of maintaining the unity of the Congress and the state during their most severe time of troubles. In the 1967 elections the voters returned only a bare Congress majority to the Lok Sabhā. Nevertheless, the Congress seems too well entrenched and too comprehensive in its appeal to lose control of the center, no matter how many state governments may be lost. Even though its economic planning is sputtering and it is susceptible to a broad spectrum of criticisms, sufficient progress has been made to keep hopes alive.

The circumstances that handicapped the political development and integration of Pakistan also delayed the initiation of its First Five-Year Plan (1955–1960). In fact, the implementation of the plan was further delayed because it did not receive final approval until 1957, less than 18 months before Ayub Khān's takeover. Thus little of the planned development took place prior to the establishment of martial law, and then the initial dislocations and uncertainties of this event tended to limit planned progress. Although some gains were made in land reclamation and even greater gains in industry by the private sector, Pakistan's first plan must be considered a failure. Certainly the poor peasant and townsman were no better off because the small increase in per capita income was exceeded by the rise in the cost of living and because gains in agricultural production were largely offset by accelerated population growth. The principal beneficiaries in Pakistan, as in India, were the emerging middle class and capitalists. Historically, however, this initial result should not be surprising; the same thing happened in the initial stages of the Industrial Revolution in the West. Only gradually did the economic benefits of modernization filter down to the average man.

The Second Five-Year Plan (1960–1965), drawn up and carried out under Ayub Khān's direction, was not only much more effective but also with its public support of private endeavor offered an interesting comparison with the Indian socialistic approach. Like India, Pakistan doubled the proposed investment in its second plan. Moreover, it expanded the plan as it progressed and new opportunities became available. Also like India, it looked to Western aid as a major source of investment capital.

The most striking feature of the plan, and the most successful, was the establishment of a government corporation empowered to finance the expansion and construction of approved private enterprises. In addition, every reasonable incentive was offered to attract foreign capital and industry in contrast to the economic nationalism of India. In brief, Pakistan announced its preference for free enterprise under reasonable restrictions as the swiftest route to modernization. Capitalists, both foreign and domestic, responded with alacrity to this invitation, and after the termination of martial law in 1962 industrial development leaped ahead. Such progress suggests that the arguments of free enterprise critics of Indian planning may have some validity.

On the other hand, the strictly public sector of the plan, which concentrated on improving agricultural production and on carrying on Ayub Khān's proclaimed war against poverty and ignorance, had much less to show for its efforts. In agriculture, the goal of self-sufficiency eluded the planners in Pakistan as in India, and population growth of the same order as India's gobbled up all increases. Popular discontent with the rate of economic progress has been reflected in the 1970–1971 election by the overwhelming success of candidates advocating socialist solutions in both East and West Pakistan. Greater progress was achieved in housing and in finding land for the long-neglected refugees from partition. Schooling was also substantially expanded. However, it is doubtful whether the essential ingredients in the poverty of the growing masses have been significantly alleviated. Of course, the Indo-Pakistani conflict in combination with the cooling of relations with the United States has, as in India, created a sharp increase in the defense portion of the national budget. Consideration of this factor calls for a look at the foreign policies of India and Pakistan.

FOREIGN POLICIES

As the weaker of the two new nations, Pakistan initially tended to lean on Great Britain for support in the international arena and labored to cultivate fraternal relations with its fellow Islamic states, policies that occasionally fell into conflict with each other. Furthermore, in addition to the quarrel with India over Kashmir, a frontier dispute with Afghanistan arose over the lands occupied by the migratory, Pushtu-speaking Pathan tribesmen. Afghanistan challenged the British-established Durand Line, which ran through the Pathan tribal territory, and called for the creation of an independent Pushtunistan, while a plebiscite conducted by Pakistan supported the retention of its position. When Soviet Russia backed up its neighbor, Afghanistan, Pakistan became receptive to American initiatives for a closer relationship, and in 1953 a Mutual Defense Assistance Treaty was concluded over India's objections for the ostensible purpose of bolstering Pakistan's defense against Russian-backed Afghanistan. This agreement led to Pakistan's membership in the American-sponsored CENTO (Central Treaty Organization of Turkey, Iran, Iraq, and Pakistan) and SEATO (Southeast Asia Treaty Organization) designed to check any Russian advance in a weaker imitation of the NATO model. Indeed, Pakistan was the pivotal member linking these two American-sponsored, anti-Communist defense efforts. Although Pakistan obtained a significant amount of American military hardware, it did not receive the diplomatic support it probably expected which armed those Pakistanis who had been critical from the beginning of an alliance with the United States and the West.

When Ayub Khan took over, he was welcomed by the United States as a firm supporter who would restore the political and military prestige of Pakistan. If anything, he was more strongly anti-Communist than his predecessors. In 1960 he even concluded an agreement with India under the auspices of the World Bank for the sharing and development of the waters flowing through Kashmir and proved receptive to the suggestion of joint preparations with India for the defense of the subcontinent against Communist aggression. In addition, he went ahead with plans for a close association with Iran and Turkey. However, it became apparent before long that his principal objective in foreign relations was to gain the necessary security and support to concentrate on internal problems.

In 1962 when the United States began to supply arms to nonaligned India for defense against Communist China, Ayub Khan and his people became alarmed and suggested the possibility of withdrawal from CENTO and SEATO since active alliance with the West did not appear to assure protection against Pakistan's principal foe. At the same time, negotiations with Peking, previously rejected, led to a number of agreements for friendlier relations, including a delineation of the boundary between China and that part of Kashmir controlled by Pakistan. Although these closer ties did not mean any change in attitude toward Communist doctrine, they did contribute to a deterioration in relations with the United States and India, which culminated in the inconclusive 1965 conflict with India.

Thus the number one problem on Pakistan's diplomatic agenda—its relations with India—remains unresolved and has been further aggravated by Indian support of Bangla Desh. This hostility between two nations so intimately intertwined in their territories and their destinies, a tragic consequence of partition and particularly the clash over Kashmir, is a severe economic as well as political handicap for both of them. It has destroyed the economic exchange and cooperation that could have been of so much mutual benefit in their development. It also compels both to divert too much of their limited resources to unproductive and unconstructive military expenditure.

India's foreign policy was largely shaped by Nehru and after his lengthy tenure as prime minister has been continued by his successors without significant modification. Its central feature, a left-leaning neutralism or nonalignment, as Nehru preferred to call it, was dictated by his innate distrust of Western motives, his somewhat uncritical faith in the asserted idealistic objectives of the Soviet Union, and his reluctance to involve India on one side or the other in the developing polarization between East and West. As he saw it, this polarization was an unfortunate exercise in international negativism in a shrinking world crying out for international cooperation and mutual understanding. India's developmental needs required world peace, and hopefully by nonalignment India might be able to contribute diplomatically to the easing of East-West tensions. In any case, an Indian policy of nonalignment, like America's earlier policy of "no entangling alliances," seemed most suitable for advancing the interests of India. For these reasons, Nehru was an ardent supporter of the United Nations and one of the first and warmest advocates of the admission of the People's Republic of China to that body.

The holier-than-thou moral fervor, based on the Indian tradition of toleration and compromise, in which Nehru enwrapped his appeals irritated those Western leaders he took to task, particularly because it did not appear consistent with the selfish and uncompromising positions he took on issues of immediate interest to India, such as Kashmir, Portuguese Indian territories, and even the frontier dispute with China. At worst he seemed to be a fakir and at best guilty of myopic vision.

Naturally he also took up the cudgels on behalf of all those Asian and African peoples struggling for emancipation from Western imperialism and championed the doctrine of self-determination, except in Kashmir. He attacked South Africa's practice of apartheid even more passionately than the leaders of Pakistan and Ceylon, and he led the opposition to South Africa's membership in the Commonwealth. He argued fervently for world disarmament, particularly nuclear disarmament, because as an Asian he felt personally affronted by the singular employment of atomic bombs against Asians. As a panacea for the world's woes, he set forth the *Panch Shila*, or five principles of peaceful coexistence, first incorporated in the Sino-Indian agreement of 1954 over Tibet and further publicized at the Bandung Conference of the following year. These principles called for universal dedication to reciprocal respect for territorial integrity and sovereignty, noninterference in each other's internal affairs, nonaggression, unequivocal recognition of equality between peoples and nations, and peaceful coexistence. And in propagandizing these ideals he belabored the materialism and selfish nationalism of Western governments in contrast to the superior moral and spiritual values of Asia and appealed for a moral regeneration in the West. The outbreak of frontier hostilities with China in 1962 came as a profound shock to Nehru, and he grudgingly had to admit that his dreams of international amity had not been altogether realistic.

Meanwhile, Portugal, unlike France, had proved unwilling to consider the surrender of its enclaves in India. In frustration and perhaps in view of the forthcoming national election, Nehru unleashed the Indian armed forces in 1961 and seized the Portuguese territories including Goa on the west coast south of Bombay. This military action, so apparently inconsistent with his avowed devotion to *Panch Shila* and negotiated settlement of international differences, raised many eyebrows around the world and perhaps encouraged China to employ force the following year in an effort to bring Nehru to the conference table.

Much more important for India, however, was the development of the boundary dispute with Communist China. The cordial relations established between Nehru and Chou En-lai in 1954 and reaffirmed in 1956 had left the precise delimitation of the frontier to future negotiation. In 1957 Chinese engineers found it technically necessary to construct a road linking Sinkiang and Tibet through desolate Ladakh, a lofty Tibetan region loosely tied administratively and economically to Kashmir. So infrequently did Indian authority penetrate this difficult area of great altitude and rarified atmosphere that Chinese construction was not discovered by an Indian patrol until it was nearly completed in 1958. Chinese troops arrested the patrol and a minor exchange of protests followed. In addition, China, which was seeking a precise definition of all its boundaries, subsequently challenged some Indian positions in the northeast as well. Negotiations began in 1960 but foundered on Indian insistence on acceptance of the British boundaries to which it had fallen heir as the basis for negotiations. China berated India for relying on lines established by British imperialism and never ratified by any Chinese government and asserted that since no precise frontier in the modern sense had ever been defined such a national boundary should be the subject of fresh and unfettered negotiation. Furthermore, the Chinese government claimed to be enraged by the refuge and support given by the Indian government to the Dalai Lama and his rebellious supporters when they were defeated and forced to flee from Tibet in 1959. The Chinese tried to persuade Nehru to give ground by pointing to the successful and generally favorable negotiations with Burma and Nepal, but he remained adamant, while the exchange of protests over frontier violations grew in volume. Finally, in October 1962, the Chinese decided on a display of military muscle in the vain hope of bringing Nehru to the conference table on their terms. Whether they had larger objectives in mind is still unproven. What is certain is that open American support and less open Russian aid disappointed their hopes of bringing Nehru

to reasonable terms, despite a surprising unilateral ceasefire, withdrawal, and return of weapons and prisoners of war in November.

Today the dispute remains unsettled and Chinese troops continue to occupy that part of Ladakh vital to the protection of the Sinkiang-Tibet road. The major problem, born with partition, of establishing normal relations between the two new nations of India and Pakistan also remains unresolved. Even the attempts to exercise Indian influence in Nepal have boomeranged, creating fears and suspicions that have made the Nepalese government receptive to Chinese blandishments. Finally, efforts to gain better treatment for Indian emigrants in Ceylon have troubled relations with India's tiny neighbor to the south. Indeed, for whatever lesson may be drawn from it, the record of Indian foreign relations has been much less successful with its immediate neighbors than with more distant peoples. Under Nehru's guidance India may be given major credit as the creator of the Afro-Asian bloc in the United Nations. More significant has been the skillful utilization of the policy of nonalignment to extract from all sides more foreign economic aid than a commitment to one side or the other might have produced, even though the amount of aid has fallen far short of India's needs. In international as in human relations it is sometimes more profitable, although also more risky, to be a courtesan than a bride.

CEYLON: A FOOTNOTE

The predominantly Buddhist island of Ceylon off the southeast tip of India and its eight million people followed in the wake of its great neighbor, gaining independence from Britain in February 1948. A prosperous economy, based on the plantation production of tropical crops for export, such as rubber, tea, cinnamon, cocoa, and coconuts, had created under British tutelage a higher standard of living than India's, which attracted

Tamil-speaking immigrants from the mainland. British rule had also left behind a universal free educational system and a 70 percent literacy rate, the highest in any part of South Asia. Another heritage was the economic and political dominance of a prosperous and generally conservative English-speaking elite. In any case, the economic dependence on export markets to pay for the import of 60 percent of its food needs dictated a cautious foreign policy and membership along with India and Pakistan in the Commonwealth.

By the time of the 1956 election political groupings had reformed around the growing gap between the poor and the rich in a rapidly growing population and around the cultural division between the Buddhist, Singhalese-speaking majority and the Hindu, Tamil-speaking minority. In 1954 the governing United National Party had attempted to meet the economic challenge by a Six-Year Plan of development but as yet could show little progress for its efforts, while the post-Korean war price drop had sharply reduced export earnings. The socialist Freedom Party of Oxford-educated S.W.R. Dudley Bandaranaike came to power on a platform of Singhalese nationalism, radical reforms, left-leaning nonalignment, and the cultivation of trade with the Communist bloc to expand export earnings. Whether intended or not, such a program immediately won American aid in the hope of countering the leftist inclination.

Pro-Singhalese legislation inflamed the Tamils and generated communal riots among these naturally gentle and pacifistic people who were only suppressed by the army after heavy bloodshed. The final act of this drama was the assassination of the prime minister in 1959 and the succession of his widow, Madame Bandaranaike in the following year as the world's first female prime minister. In evaluating the role of Western influence, it is interesting and perhaps ironical to observe the more prominent role in the politics of these new nations won by Western-educated

women than that achieved by their sisters in the West.

Under Madame Bandaranaike the socialist program proceeded to unfold without check. Indeed, in 1963 the nationalization of petroleum refining and distribution in which American companies had a major stake led the American government to attempt to discipline the leftist regime of this small country by cutting off American aid. Mounting economic difficulties and growing discontent with the socialist, pro-Communist orientation of the government gave the more moderate United National Party an opportunity to rebuild its strength, and in elections held in 1965 it was returned to power under the son of its former leader with the support of the influential Buddhist monks who had previously been the main strength of the Freedom Party. Since then, Madame Bandaranaike has regained power but her need to compromise with the opposition has forced her to slow down the progress to socialism, much to the distress of young radicals.

India, Pakistan, and Ceylon—like the new nations of Southeast Asia—have found their efforts to modernize and catch up with the industrial nations frustrated by an accelerating growth in populations that canceled out much of the gains from planned investment. Increasing amounts of foreign aid have not yet enabled them to turn that all-important economic corner. Population increase, it should be stressed, is due not to a higher birth rate but rather to decreased mortality produced by more extensive medical and public health facilities. As a result, the gap between these poor nations and the rich industrial nations has become wider rather than narrower since independence. Yet the faith of both leaders and voters in democratic principles, even in Pakistan, has surprisingly not been fundamentally shaken. Although Western materialism has been severely criticized and various socialist practices have been adopted, none has yet fallen prey to Communist dictatorship, though such an eventuality cannot be precluded if the lag in economic development is not overcome. Some observers place their hopes in new birth control experiments and expenditures, but the effectiveness of such measures will depend on greater and more rapid change in the rural social structure and beliefs than can be anticipated and even then will probably be more than offset by further improvement in the rate of life expectancy. In such over-whelmingly agricultural countries any solution to the economic crisis would seem to require a clear priority on investments in a multifaceted program of social and economic modernization of the agricultural sector. In all of Asia the revolutionizing of the peasantry seems to be the key to the future on which governments may rise or fall, and yet it is in the peasantry that traditional values and practices are most deep-rooted.

SIGNIFICANT DATES

1947	Independence of India and Pakistan on August 14
1948	Deaths of Gāndhi and Muhammed Ali Jinnāh
1951	Bhoodan movement of Vinobā Bhāve
1951–1956	India's First Five-Year Plan
1955–1960	Pakistan's abortive First Five-Year Plan
1956–1961	India's Second Five-Year Plan
1957	Communist election victory in Kerala
1958–1969	Rule of General Ayub Khān
1960–1965	Pakistan's Second Five-Year Plan
1961	Armed seizure of Portuguese enclaves by India
1962	Sino-Indian frontier conflict
1962–1967	India's Third Five-Year Plan
1964	Death of Prime Minister Jawaharlāl Nehru
1965	Frontier war of Pakistan and India
1966	Nehru's daughter, Indira Gāndhi becomes prime minister
1971	East Pakistan becomes the People's Republic of Bangla Desh

SELECTED READINGS

Bhatia, Krishan, *Ordeal of Nationhood: A Social Study of India Since Independence, 1947–1970.* New York: Atheneum Pubs., 1971.

Binder, Leonard, *Religion and Politics in Pakistan.* Berkeley: University of California Press, 1961.

Brown, W. Norman, *India, Pakistan, Ceylon.* Rev. ed.; Philadelphia: University of Pennsylvania Press, 1964.

*Carstairs, Morris G., *The Twice-Born: A Study of a Community of High-Caste Hindus.* Bloomington: Indiana University Press, 1967.

*Korbel, Josef, *Danger in Kashmir.* Rev. ed.; Princeton: Princeton University Press, 1966.

Lamb, Alastair, *The McMahon Line.* 2 vols.; London: Routledge and Kegan Paul, 1966.

*Lamb, Beatrice Pitney, *India: A World in Transition.* Rev. ed.; New York: Praeger, 1968.

*Mandelbaum, David G., *Society in India.* 2 vols.; Berkeley: University of California Press, 1970.

*Minturn, Leigh, and Hitchcock, John T., *The Rajputs of Khalapur, India*. New York: Wiley, 1966.

*Nair, Kusum, *Blossoms in the Dust: The Human Factor in Indian Development*. New York: Praeger, 1962.

*Neale, Walter C., *India: The Search for Unity, Democracy and Progress*. Princeton: Van Nostrand, 1965.

*Palmer, Norman D., *Indian Political System*. Boston: Houghton Mifflin, 1971.

*———, *South Asia and United States Policy*. Boston: Houghton Mifflin, 1966.

*Rosen, George, *Democracy and Economic Change in India*. Berkeley: University of California Press, 1967.

Rowland, John, *A History of Sino-Indian Relations*. Princeton: Van Nostrand, 1967.

*Smith, Donald Eugene, *India as a Secular State*. Princeton: Princeton University Press, 1963.

*Spear, Percival, *India, Pakistan, and the West*. 4th ed.; London: Oxford University Press, 1963.

*Ward, Barbara, *India and the West: Pattern for a Common Policy*. Rev. ed.; New York: Norton, 1964.

Weiner, Myron, *The Politics of Scarcity: Public Pressure and Political Response*. Chicago: University of Chicago Press, 1962.

*Wilcox, Wayne A., *Pakistan: The Consolidation of a Nation*. New York: Columbia University Press, 1966.

CHAPTER TWENTY-SEVEN

REVOLUTIONARY TURMOIL IN THE MIDDLE EAST

The humiliating defeat of the forces of the Arab League by the smaller but determined and highly skilled army of Israel in the Palestine War of 1948 was a traumatic event whose repercussions are far from exhausted today. Indeed, the attitudes and developments, both internal and external, of the Arab-Israeli portion of the Middle East since then may largely be traced to this unresolved confrontation. Under the leadership of European Jews the existence of Israel constitutes from the Arab point of view a Western beachhead in the heart of the Arab world far more discomforting and challenging than the Crusader states of the Middle Ages. Even more intolerable is the Zionist ideology of Hebrew exclusivism. This religious nationalism was physically exhibited by the exodus of over 600,000 Palestinian Arabs who continue to await repatriation in refugee camps and by the second-class citizenship of those Arabs who stayed behind in Israel. Therefore, from the Arab point of view the state of Israel represents not only Western but also Zionist imperialism, aided and abetted by American and European diplomacy and arms. Moreover, the creation of Israel at Arab expense served to expiate the Western sense of guilt for the Nazi extermination of some six million Jews, a crime in which Arabs had no part.

Defeat had also exposed the inadequacy and incompetence of Arab military and political leaders, most of whom had Western educations and a predilection for Western forms of evolutionary development and modernization. Thus the way was opened for younger, more revolutionary leaders to seize power from their elders in a succession of coups. Obviously the liquidation of Israel would require a military solution, and therefore it should come as no surprise that the military were the principal movers and beneficiaries of these upheavals. In any case, the military had traditionally played a leading role in the internal affairs as well as the external relations of Muslim realms. According to traditional Muslim doctrine the main function of government was to enforce the law transmitted by the Prophet and to protect the faithful, and enforcement and protection are essentially military tasks. The Arab peoples were accustomed to military rule. Moreover, these impatient young leaders came mostly from lower class backgrounds and had long chafed and compromised under the domination of a privileged and frequently corrupt elite. Once in power they soon turned to revolutionary social and economic programs to promote what they called social justice. The ideological interpretation of their actions, however, can be overdone. Like their predecessors, what they sought was power: power for themselves and power for their states, though not necessarily in that order. Liberalism and multiparty democracy had proven inadequate and inefficient as vehicles for swift modernization and were further tainted by association with the imperialistic West. Therefore, like their counterparts elsewhere in Asia, these revolutionists turned to authoritarian, single-party regimes as the best means of mobilizing and commanding the undivided energies of all the people under their presumably inspired leadership.

Finally, the conception of a larger, Pan-Arab unity captured their imaginations because the Arab League had failed to provide the coordination and unity essential for the destruction of Israel. As a matter of fact, the Arab League had been originally framed to preserve the independence and integrity of each of its members. Yet, thanks to the traditional personification of leadership, Pan-Arab unification, even among the revolutionary states with parallel goals, has proven as elusive as in the past. The leadership in one state has been unwilling to subordinate itself to the leader of another state, while the concept of collective leadership runs counter to traditional and contemporary Arab practice. Moreover, the age-old contest of Egypt and Mesopotamia for control of the intervening lands of Syria and Palestine has re-emerged in a modern form.

Before looking at the revolutionary upheavals in the Arab world, the slightly less radical developments in Turkey and Iran will be briefly examined.

TURKEY SINCE 1949

By the end of World War II the Turkish Revolution of Kemal Ataturk was already two decades old. Although many of the revolutionary objectives had been only partially fulfilled, the Turkish people were restive and anxious for a change. Under American and domestic pressure Kemal's successor, Ismet Inonu, agreed to a relaxation of political control. In the 1950 election the voters returned the opposition Democratic party on a platform advocating freer enterprise and a relaxation of the restrictions on Islam. The Democrats were particularly successful in wooing the peasants who had been neglected by the bureaucratic Republican politicians.

The United States government welcomed the new government of Prime Minister Adnan Menderes and the establishment of what it called "genuine democracy." This enthusiastic endorsement was demonstrated by opening the floodgates of American foreign aid to a total of two and one-half billion dollars during the 1950s.

The vast infusion of American money and resources into a country of only 24 million people naturally generated an economic boom, but it also created inflation and fiscal dislocations that became increasingly serious after 1954. Numerous new industries were built and existing ones expanded, many of which were scarcely justifiable and viable from a strictly economic point of view. Along with them came many new jobs, which stimulated urbanization. Agricultural production for the market and for export was encouraged by government subsidies, some mechanization, and a road-building program that opened up the rural hinterland. A land reform program, previously enacted by the Republicans, was effectively implemented by the Democratic regime redistributing millions of acres to former tenant farmers. Through 1956 these developments in combination with favorable weather made Turkey a substantial exporter of grain for the first time. Nevertheless, exports could not match imports, and by 1954 the imbalance of trade produced an increasingly critical shortage of foreign exchange.

At the same time, the promised relaxation of restrictions on Islam continued the initial steps in this direction taken by the Republicans. In 1949 a College of Theology at Ankara University and an Institute of Islamic Studies at the University of Istanbul restored respectability and promoted advanced studies for future religious leaders along more modern lines. The ban on religious instruction in public schools was lifted, and the call to prayer and readings from the Qur'an in Arabic could be heard throughout the land on Radio Ankara. The shrines of holy men were reopened, religious orders were once again allowed to operate, and the observance of fast and feast days became more widespread. Although the official separation of church and state was maintained, the retreat from rigorous secularism won general popular support for the Democrats. Indeed, in combination with generous

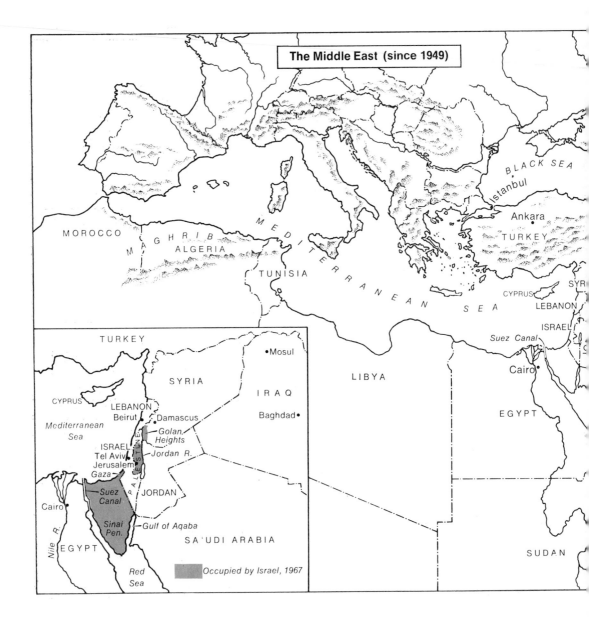

The Middle East (since 1949)

BLACK SEA

Istanbul

Ankara

TURKEY

MOROCCO

MAGHRIB

ALGERIA

TUNISIA

MEDITERRANEAN

SEA

CYPRUS

LEBANON

SYR

ISRAEL

Suez Canal

Cairo

LIBYA

EGYPT

SUDAN

TURKEY

•Mosul

SYRIA

IRAQ

CYPRUS

LEBANON

Beirut •Damascus

Baghdad•

Mediterranean
Sea

Golan
Heights

ISRAEL

Tel Aviv

Jordan R.

Jerusalem

Gaza

Suez
Canal

JORDAN

Cairo

Sinai
Pen.

Gulf of Aqaba

SA'UDI ARABIA

Nile R.

EGYPT

Red
Sea

Occupied by Israel, 1967

support of agriculture it strengthened the Democratic grip on the peasantry.

On the other hand, Menderes' failure to exercise fiscal restraint, probably rooted in part in his faith in the American government coming to his rescue, met with growing criticism from the urban, educated community. In response to charges of fiscal irresponsibility he first argued that economic dislocations were a natural concomitant of accelerated modernization and then instituted more

severe measures of repression than those experienced under the Republicans. Newspaper editors were imprisoned and their organs suspended. Radio stations were forbidden to broadcast any criticisms of the government. Even the military, carefully kept out of politics by Kemal Ataturk, was utilized to harass opposition politicians and to suppress public demonstrations. Defections of liberals from his own party did not deter Menderes. Instead, he merely forbade

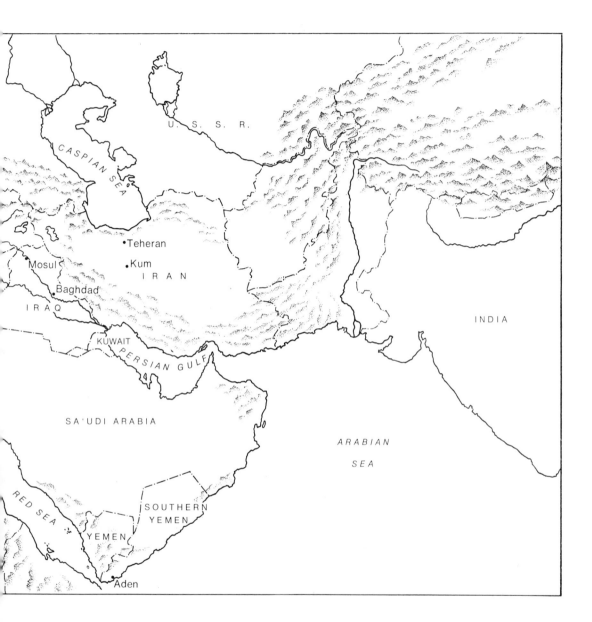

them from joining in a united opposition to his regime. Meanwhile, further reluctant infusions of American money helped him to stave off national bankruptcy. Continued peasant support was reflected in a resounding victory at the polls in 1957, though election irregularities may have contributed to the result.

By 1960, economic disarray, political tyranny, corruption, and harassment of the national hero, Ismet Inonu, reached such

proportions that an internal upheaval threatened to break out. University students and military cadets took to the streets to protest the abuses of the government. Finally, on May 27, 1960, a group of young officers led by General Cemal Gursel seized power and arrested Menderes along with more than 600 of his supporters for crimes against the state. In subsequent trials Menderes and several of his ministers were condemned to death, while almost 500 of his colleagues received prison sentences ranging from one year to life.

Meanwhile, General Gursel headed a 23 man Committee of National Unity pledged to a reform of the government along more democratic lines. In July 1961, a new constitution, characterized by extensive checks and balances, barely won approval from the electorate in preparation for national elections in October. Under its provisions a Senate and a National Assembly replaced the former single-chamber legislature, and an independent Constitutional Court was set up to judge the constitutionality of proposed legislation. A long list spelled out the rights of the individual and the government's obligations to provide for his welfare. The obvious intent of these provisions was to prevent a recurrence of arbitrary rule.

Of the four parties authorized to contest in the elections, the Republican party and the new Justice Party, composed mainly of those former Democrats who had escaped condemnation, garnered the bulk of the votes. Ismet Inonu's Republicans led at the polls with a little more than 40 percent of the vote, drawing their main strength from the cities, while the Justice party demonstrated the continued grip of former Democrats on the peasantry. Since no party had won a majority, Ismet Inonu was called on to form a coalition cabinet that was shaky from the start. Discontent at both extremes posed the threat of renewed civil disturbance, causing the military to continue playing a protective role. After several reshufflings of his government Ismet Inonu was forced to step down, but his successors have been unable to establish any greater political stability, though the economic difficulties inherited from the Menderes regime have been largely resolved. Moreover, American influence has deteriorated, principally as a result of the Turkish belief that the United States favored the Greek position in the strife over the island of Cyprus. Nevertheless, whatever the assessment of the political prospects of Turkey today, it needs to be recognized that from the social and economic point of view Turkey is the most advanced nation in the Middle East in the process of modernization with the unique exception of Israel.

CONTEMPORARY IRAN

Like Turkey, Iran had had its revolution between the wars under the leadership of Reza Shah, founder of the Pahlawi dynasty. Although he admired and emulated Kemal Ataturk, the mere fact of establishing a new dynasty symbolized the lower level of modernization that he was able to accomplish, let alone appreciate. As a comparatively untutored military man his principal concern was power and the consequent breaking down of all important centers of potential opposition, not the conscious institution of an integrated program of social and economic reforms. Large amounts of land were confiscated from recalcitrant landlords, but this change in ownership brought no improvement in the condition of the tenant farmers. Their payments simply went to the royal treasury rather than the former landlord.

As an Allied puppet, his son, Muhammed Reza Shah, was in no position to assert independent authority during the war, and after the war he appeared to prefer to stay above the swirling maelstrom of Iranian politics for fear of losing his crown. At most, he seemed concerned about maintaining his control of the military, the key to power throughout Iranian history. Only when the headstrong policies of Muhammed Musaddiq brought the realm into desperate straits and even threatened his throne, did the young shah decide that the time had come to rule as well as reign. Even then it took some time before he felt strong enough to undertake a radical program of political, social, and economic reforms.

Meanwhile, a succession of postwar prime ministers, dependent on the vested interests represented in the National Assembly (*Majlis*), proved unable to cope with the inflation and economic dislocations inherited from the war and placed their main hope in the prospect of large-scale aid from distant America. Traditional corruption, the refusal of the influential rich to pay their fair share of taxes, and governmental instability made the American government and international bankers skeptical of the value of investing in the ambitious 650 million dollar 7-year development program proposed by the Iranian government. Moreover, during these years American energies and interest were committed to the more critical problems of European recovery and defense. During 1948–1949, as continued deterioration threatened economic collapse, the nation's leaders naturally turned to the possibility of nationalizing or at least extracting more income from Iran's principal resource, the oil that was being exploited under the ownership and operation of the Anglo-Iranian Oil Company. The antiforeign feeling behind this inclination was nothing new and merely represented a restoking of old fires. Of course, by such a move the wealthy vested interests hoped both to forestall radical assaults on their position and to find new wealth-building opportunities for themselves.

Fearful of the consequences for himself, the shah made a sortie into personal diplomacy by traveling to the United States late in 1949 to make a plea for the promised American aid. President Truman was sympathetic but indicated that the Iranian government must take positive steps to improve the investment climate. Upon his return the shah set up an anticorruption commission, pressed for other reforms, and undertook the sale on easy terms of royal estates to their peasant cultivators in the vain hope of persuading other large landowners to follow his example. Before any significant American aid was forthcoming, however, the outbreak of the Korean conflict resulted in an indefinite postponement, while the forementioned economic deterioration continued unabated. Under these circumstances there was nowhere else to turn, and the politically experienced and well-connected champion of

oil nationalization, Muhammed Musaddiq, emerged as the man of the hour.

Iranian public exasperation with the existing distribution of oil profits had first become apparent in mid-1948 when the Anglo-Iranian Oil Company, in which the British Labor government exercised a controlling voice, announced the maintenance of payments at the same level as the previous year despite a doubling of the net profit. Furthermore, Iranians saw little justice in Iran's 20 million dollar share from royalties and taxes when the British government garnered 56 million from dividends and taxes in the same year. Additional complaints were directed at bookkeeping peculiarities and hiring practices detrimental to Iranians. Finally, news of the 50-50 profit split negotiated by Venezuela with American companies and of a similar division under discussion between Aramco and Sa'udi Arabia sharpened the public outcry. The Company did negotiate a new agreement approximating a 50-50 split, but a new oil committee of the *Majlis*, chaired by Musaddiq, rejected it in December 1950. The Company was now ready to make further concessions, but Musaddiq and the *Majlis* were unwilling to settle for anything less than nationalization. Four days after the premier asserted that nationalization was impractical, he was assassinated on March 7, 1951.

Swept up by the emotional impact of this event, the *Majlis* passed the nationalization bill in less than a week. Anti-British strikes and riots in the oil fields and refinery area brought British cruisers into the Persian Gulf. On April 28, 1951, the shah was compelled to accept Musaddiq as prime minister, and the following day he obtained passage of a law calling for the eviction of the Company. Thus was set in motion the crisis that paralyzed Iranian oil production for the next two and one-half years.

As dramatic and colorful as the marches and countermarches of this tension-packed confrontation were, space limitations prohibit a description of them. The main point is that both sides remained obdurate, each believing that its bargaining position was the stronger. Not until the overthrow of Musaddiq in August 1953, could a settlement be reached.

Musaddiq and his supporters were confident that the British Labor government, a champion of domestic nationalization, would understand and appreciate Iran's determination to nationalize the oil industry. The chief issue appeared to be the amount of compensation to the Company and the terms of its payment. Moreover, the Iranian leaders were certain that Britain and Europe depended on the regular delivery of oil from Iran and underestimated the ability of Western oil interests to expand production in places like Kuwait and Sa'udi Arabia as alternate sources of supply. They also failed to appreciate the intimate interrelationships of Western oil companies, regardless of nationality, in the cooperative regulation of production and marketing that made it impossible for Iran to employ the necessary experts and technicians for the independent operation of its oil industry. Indeed, Iran could not even find a market for the oil in storage at the time operations had ceased. In addition, the expectation of American aid to prevent Iran from turning to the Communist camp did not materialize, despite the strong backing given to Musaddiq by the Communist-front Tudeh party. In fact, the American government gave its quiet support to Britain and made it clear that no proposals for aid would be considered until the oil controversy was settled. Finally, to build support for his stand, Musaddiq took such an extreme position and delivered such emotional diatribes against the British that his political survival depended on nothing less than total victory.

On their part, the British made equally serious miscalculations. They were convinced that the desperate plight of Iranian finances would soon force any government to come to terms for the sake of oil revenues. They failed to appreciate the depth of nationalistic feeling aroused by this issue and

how it had united all politically conscious elements from the left to the right in support of Musaddiq. Even the religious establishment, led by the volatile Shiite divine, Mulla Kashani, who was suspected of complicity with the fanatical Fidaiyan-i Islam (Devotees of Islam) in political assassinations, threw its full support and influence to Musaddiq. As for the peasants, oil revenues had never affected their lives, and they continued as before to scratch the same meager subsistence from the soil. Perhaps, as Musaddiq promised, nationalization might at long last bring them some benefits. At the outset, the Company also pointed out the necessity of its services and capital for production and marketing, but Musaddiq was not convinced until he had gone too far to consider retreat.

Fearful of the loss of *Majlis* backing as the financial crisis intensified, Musaddiq demanded and obtained over the objections of many of his supporters virtually dictatorial power to rule by decree in August 1952, and also extracted from the shah the ministry of war in the expectation of gaining control of that decisive instrument in Iranian history, the army. As the number of his critics grew among the elite and even Kashani deserted him, he resorted to press censorship and other arbitrary methods of suppression. In mid-1953 a popular referendum in which he won the support of 99.93 percent of those voting gave him the unconstitutional power to dissolve the *Majlis*, a prerogative of the shah. On August 12, when he announced his intention of carrying out this mandate, the shah attempted to replace him as prime minister with General Zahedi, but Musaddiq brought in troops to defend his position. After committing themselves in this fashion, the shah and General Zahedi had to flee, the former abroad and the latter into the provinces to plan a coup. Such an attack on the shah, however, was going too far. On August 19 mobs led by Zahedi's agents poured into the streets of the capital crying "Long live the Shah." After his tanks won a small-scale battle in the city, General Zahedi appeared and proclaimed the capital secured before nightfall. On August 22 the shah returned in triumph and Musaddiq was arrested, tried, and sentenced to three year's imprisonment for attempted rebellion. Meanwhile, the American government expressed its approval of the coup by making an emergency grant of 45 million dollars on September 5 in the expectation that the oil controversy would soon be settled. As it turned out, this grant was only the first installment of a massive American aid program.

A chastened shah returned to Teheran determined to play a more active political role to secure his throne. The American-trained constabulary was turned loose to ferret out and arrest all Communists and to suppress all opposition. The easygoing political liberty that had previously characterized his reign came suddenly to an end. The management of subsequent elections assured the return of friends of the shah.

After lengthy negotiations the oil dispute was ended on August 5, 1954, when Iran signed an agreement with a consortium of eight major oil companies to produce and market petroleum for the National Iranian Oil Company in return for 50 percent of the profits. Out of its 50 percent profits Iran was obligated to pay 70 million dollars a year for ten years in compensation for nationalization. Thus the original cause of the dispute was settled in Iran's favor, and before long the expansion of the market for oil increased the country's share to more than 300 million dollars annually. In 1956 the last foreign foothold was eliminated when the Russians surrendered their oil concession east of Teheran. In the same year exploration brought in a tremendous gusher near Kum, indicating that Iran's potential reserves had not yet been fully explored. This event also presented the opportunity to bargain for an even larger share of the profits from the new field. In 1957 an Italian company signed a contract returning 75 percent of the profits to Iran.

In the vain hope of countering Iran's movement into the Western camp, the Soviet Union offered to settle all outstanding differences despite the shah's suppression of Iranian Communists. In 1954 a trade protocol was quickly followed by an agreement to return 11 tons of gold and 8 million dollars worth of goods held by Russia since World War II. In addition, the shah and his queen were invited to make a state visit. None of these blandishments, however, succeeded. The shah was convinced at this time that his personal self-interest and the welfare of his realm would be most profitably served by association with the wealthier West. After all, Communists did not hold kings in high regard. When the shah joined the Baghdad pact, an American-sponsored defensive alliance of Iran, Iraq, Pakistan, Turkey, and Britain (later CENTO without Iraq), in the fall of 1955, the Soviet Union cried foul and reasserted its old treaty right to intervene for the protection of Iranian independence, but the shah, fortified by the shipment of American armaments to modernize his army, stood firm. Since then, the Soviet Union has had to settle for the maintenance of the best possible relations it can achieve with Iran.

With the prospect of generous Western grants and loans as well as enlarged oil revenues the shah promptly reactivated the Seven-Year Development Plan. The influx of Western money, material, and personnel soon produced boom conditions in Teheran with the customary opportunities for personal enrichment. Inflationary pressures forced a sharp rise in prices, which encouraged speculation and market manipulation. American governmental concern about getting its money's worth subsequently compelled the shah to take action against the worst speculation and peculation, but with only modest results. Meanwhile, progress was made in modernizing the army, in improving transport and communications, and in constructing major public works, all of which redounded to the credit of the shah and his government.

By 1959 the shah demonstrated growing confidence in his authority by cracking down on recalcitrant army officers, aristocrats, and other critics of his regime. In 1960 a moderate land reform measure that proposed to limit estates to 1000 acres of irrigated land and 2000 acres of unirrigated land was declared contrary to the *shari'a* and the constitution by the head of the Shiite hierarchy, much to the shah's displeasure. The shah also expressed discontent with the *Majlis* and corrupt elections to it by dissolving it and calling for honest elections. Yet the elections held in the early months of 1961 represented no improvement. The shah also showed his distress at the lack of progress in combating illiteracy in the villages by requiring army officer cadets to go and teach in them as members of a Literacy Corps. On November 11, 1961, when the *Majlis* was not in session, he declared his right to initiate legislation and issued a six-point reform program calling for the establishment of village councils, the reform of existing municipal and provincial councils, greater local and provincial initiative, the reform of education and administration, and much more attention to "social justice" in all its aspects, a phrase he may have picked up from the speeches of President Kennedy. Apparently the shah felt strong enough to challenge the vested interests by making direct appeals for popular support. In short, he was preparing to initiate his own revolution. A further indication of the direction of his thinking was his vesting on September 28 of all assets from royal estates in a *waqf* or perpetual trust for educational, charitable, religious, social, and health services under himself and his male successors as chief administrator. It was also evident that a revolution as radical as he envisioned could not be carried out with the existing landlord-dominated *Majlis*. It must either be dispensed with or totally reformed.

The major blow to the landlord aristocrats fell on January 9, 1962, when the Council of Ministers adopted a revised Land Re-form measure. Its chief provision limited the holding of a landlord to a single village, or its equivalent. Orchards, tea gardens, and tree plantations were generally exempted as well as modernized and mechanized farms employing wage labor. A few landlords, either seeing the handwriting on the wall or desirous of exploiting their property more efficiently, had put some of their land into this more profitable type of production. Thus this reform affected principally those estates operated on traditional, sharecropping lines.

The landlords were to be paid in ten annual installments, but the price of their land was based on the taxes they had been paying and thus was far below its true value. The peasants were to pay the government for their land in 15 annual installments. In addition, cooperatives were set up with government support, and only members were eligible to receive land titles. The effect of this land reform proved to be more extensive than anticipated because wherever some land was redistributed local pressure for equal status tended to force landlords unaffected by the reform to also sell out to their tenants. Generally the peasants have demonstrated surprising resourcefulness in coping with the challenges of independent farming and have not needed as much expert advice and assistance as had been expected.

Having won popular support by land reform, even though at first it directly affected little more than 10 percent of the peasants, in January 1963, the shah demonstrated his leadership by gaining overwhelming approval for his reform program in a referendum. Obviously the aristocrats no longer controlled the voting of the people. Another significant advance was the extension of a token vote to women preparatory to their complete enfranchisement. These actions generated riots sponsored by aristocratic and religious leadership against land reform, the enfranchisement of women, the general modernizing tendencies so disruptive to traditional relationships, and most of all the centralization of power in the hands of the shah and the central government. Foreign observers remained skeptical of the shah's ability to carry out his reforms and keep his throne, but as events demonstrated he refused to be deterred from continuing his revolution, though at a more moderate pace.

In 1964 a new *Majlis* was elected by universal franchise. Not only did women vote, but a few stood successfully for election, a radical departure opposed by all conservative elements. The composition of the new *Majlis* with far fewer aristocratic members clearly reflected the victory of the shah's revolution. Although the American government has been confident enough in this reforming monarch to risk its future influence by openly supporting him, the opposition forces remained strong and unconverted. The shah placed his faith in his modernized army, his secret police, and the fickle masses. Maintenance of the army consumes almost one-half of the budget. Yet a group of radical young officers has displayed impatience with the moderate pace of his revolution, posing a threat from the left as well as the right. Only time will tell whether the shah will be able to maintain his control of affairs.

THE ARAB WORLD: THE EMERGENCE OF THE MILITARY

Since the enforced recognition of military defeat at the hands of Israel in 1949, the most common characteristic of the Arab states has been the coming to power of the military by coups and revolutions. After all, the military was the only means of liquidating the wrong suffered by the creation of Israel. But more importantly, it and its radical younger officers represented the only power capable of unseating the moderate middle-class and aristocratic leadership and accomplishing the revolutionary changes believed by them to be essential to rapid modernization. The military revolutionists have not yet seized power in either the more tradi-

tional states, such as Jordan and Sa'udi Arabia, or the more moderate transitional states, such as Lebanon, Tunisia, and Morocco, while the contest for the Yemen remains unresolved. As a result of the dynamic tension between these states and their leaders, the goal of Pan-Arab unity has as yet proved elusive and unattainable. Even the efforts at unifying the revolutionary states have foundered on petty ideological differences and the much more important personal contest for political power. Finally, the position of the military has been vastly strengthened by the Russian decision in 1955 to counter Western influence by vaulting over the northern tier of Turkey and Iran and supplying the revolutionary regimes with armaments, even when they actively suppressed their native Communists. Apparently the Soviet Union was ready to sacrifice local Communist parties for the sake of embarrassing the West. Not only has this policy won a costly measure of success in the Arab world, but it has also raised sufficient anxiety about the dependability of Western backing among the leaders of the northern-tier states of Turkey and Iran to cause them to seek better relations with their mighty neighbor. American domination of the Mediterranean has even been challenged by the goodwill garnered by Russian aid in several of the new nations of the North African Maghrib.

The country to suffer first and most frequently from coups was internally diverse and unstable Syria. The inadequacy of its constitutional regime had been exposed in the mismanagement of its part in the war with Israel, but neither the new regime following the 1949 coup nor its subsequent successors proved capable of overcoming the religious and economic divisions that sapped the energies of the nation. The principal beneficiary of the succession of coups was the military, which alone could hope to discipline the divergent interests and attitudes of the Syrian people. However, Syrian politics did spawn one important contribution to Arab political thought, the Baath (Arab Resurrection) party, which requires more than passing notice.

Baath was the brainchild of Michael Aflaq, a Syrian Christian schoolteacher, who had once flirted with communism. During World War II, when genuine independence was in sight, he and another schoolteacher, who was more interested in the details of organization and administration, founded the movement. The schoolteacher background of the two founders indicates its middle-class intellectual character which limited its popular appeal. As its name suggests, the central feature of Baath philosophy was an Arab renaissance that called for Pan-Arab unity as a basic prerequisite; all other doctrines, such as social justice, were secondary and subordinate goals to this overriding consideration. Thus its appeal was further limited by its implied denigration of Syrian nationalism in favor of the larger philosophical concept of a common Arab nationalism. Not until its merger with the Arab Socialist party in 1953 did the Baath gain a broad political base in Syria.

Meanwhile, in 1947 the Baath had held its first party conference with 200 delegates to consider and approve a constitution. Its key principle called for a unified Arab state stretching from Morocco to Iraq. A politically liberal program was envisioned in which the people would be persuaded and not coerced to accept Baath leadership. The goal of social justice was to be won by various measures such as redistribution of land, nationalization of utilities and major industries, regulation of wages and working conditions, old age insurance, free medical care, and free compulsory education through the secondary level. No incompatibility was seen between socialism and Arab nationalism; both were viewed as complementing and reinforcing each other in the rebirth of the Arab world. At the same time, communism was rejected for its internationalism, which did not square with Arab nationalism, for its doctrine of class struggle, and for its failure to recognize the worth of the individual and the individ-

ual's right to private property consistent with the welfare of all the people. Nevertheless, the Baath welcomed the friendship and cooperation of all other states, whether socialist or not, particularly those that would back the Arabs against their imperialist foes.

Concern about the rising influence of the Soviet Union in Syria as well as agreement with the Pan-Arab aims of Nasser led the Baath to give its support to unification with Egypt in 1958 in the United Arab Republic. Later, when the Baath came to power in both Syria and Iraq in 1963, it also demonstrated its anti-Communist emphasis by vigorous suppression. Its concern for political liberalism also partially explains its support for the liquidation of the union with Egypt in 1961 because of the domineering authoritarianism of Nasser. Subsequently, to counter Nasser's charismatic claim to leadership of the Arab world, the Baath argued for collective leadership. On the other hand, political realities forced it to compromise its liberal principles by association with sympathetic army leaders to gain power and to participate in coups accompanied by purges and bloodbaths in contradiction to the party's avowed preference for persuasion.

The second country to suffer a radical upheaval was Egypt, which had been a major participant in the Palestine war. In addition, Egypt was the most populous Arab nation and served as the intellectual center of the Arab world. Therefore, its participation in revolutionary change and leadership was to be expected. After the war the major organized opposition to the regime of King Faruk was the Muslim Brotherhood, which advocated a revival of dedication to the precepts of Islam in both state and society and championed Pan-Islamic unity. Although its leader disavowed violence or even any desire for political power, he did threaten the use of force if reforms were not instituted and Brothers did play an active role in organizing and carrying out bloody riots. Indeed, it was the growing tendency toward violence by poorly disciplined Brothers that led to a breakdown of association between the Muslim Brotherhood and the Free Officers Society, which engineered the 1952 coup.

After the Palestine War the secret Free Officers Society was formed by several hundred young officers who were disgusted with the demonstrated ineptitude and corruption of the Faruk regime. Beyond these views and the desire for military advancement, the Free Officers Society was unburdened with any ideological convictions or reform program. In fact, it did not even seek political power, but only wanted to throw out the old rascals and restore constitutional life. For the sake of popular acceptance the young officers needed a senior commander as their nominal leader. General Naguib was selected for the job, although Colonel Gamal Abdul Nasser continued to be the leading figure among the young officers. The almost bloodless coup was prematurely precipitated on July 23, 1952, when the king, whose spies had uncovered the details of their organization, was on the verge of suppressing them.

Perhaps surprised at their success and certainly unprepared to rule, the young officers were not sure what to do with the power they had seized. Nevertheless, they were urged on by the applause of liberals, nationalists, socialists, Communists, and the public who greeted the revolution as a "blessed event." Their first decision, arrived at after a long debate, prescribed the exile of King Faruk on July 26. The monarchy was not formally abolished for almost a year. Meanwhile, a Revolutionary Command Council headed by General Naguib was vested with the executive authority of the Free Officers Society and directed to purge the corrupt elements in the political parties, the bureaucracy, and the army. Vacancies in the government were rapidly filled by members of the Free Officers Society to the dismay of the bureaucrats who served under them. In addition, a moderate land reform decree limiting holdings to 250 acres of irrigated fields undermined the political influence of wealthy landlords but benefited less than 6 percent of the impoverished peasants. Like similar reforms elsewhere, land redistribution was tied to compulsory membership in newly formed cooperatives. Other provisions to reduce exorbitant rents and to maintain minimum wages for farm laborers could not be effectively enforced because of the shortage of land and the surplus of labor.

Within a few months the Revolutionary Command Council, frustrated by the obstruction and lack of cooperation of politicians and bureaucrats, abolished, over General Naguib's objections, the political parties, parliament, and the constitution and instituted controls, such as censorship, to throttle all opposition. Naguib's preference for a restoration of constitutional rule produced a clash between him and Nasser, which led to his complete removal from power by the end of 1954. Until his death the fortunes of Egypt were in the hands of Nasser and his close associates.

Shortly after the initial coup Nasser had attempted to explain his ideas and aspirations for Egypt in *The Philosophy of the Revolution*. In this work he rejected the Western conception of parliamentary democracy, which was associated in Arab experience with upper-class domination and corruption, and he called for popular participation in genuine democracy under the inspired leadership of revolutionaries like himself. Under this conception the prime prerequisite of Egyptian unity and discipline required the elimination of all opposition parties in favor of a single National Union. Furthermore, he set up as a revolutionary goal the attainment of social democracy, by which he meant the liquidation of class distinctions based on wealth and privilege. The specific means by which these objectives were to be attained, however, were not yet spelled out and were devised pragmatically in subsequent years. Nevertheless, his basic distrust of the uneducated masses and his consequent conviction in the need for authoritative leadership in a form of "guided democracy" emerged quite clearly from this work that has been compared in significance with Hitler's *Mein Kampf*. Moreover, while his principal concern was Egypt, Nasser also expressed concern for the Arab world as a whole and its need for a hero, a role in which he may privately have envisioned himself. At the very least he believed that Egypt as the intellectual center of the Arab world should lead and provide the leader. Thus, he and the Baath shared many views on revolutionary objectives; where they differed—and differed drastically—was on the procedures for achieving these goals.

On behalf of Egypt Nasser first gained public renown by the successful conclusion in 1954 of a treaty for the final evacuation of British troops. In 1955 when the American government proved reluctant to supply the arms previously promised by President Eisenhower to facilitate the Egyptian negotiations with Britain, Nasser impatiently turned to the Soviet bloc and quickly concluded an agreement for the immediate delivery of arms by Czechoslovakia. Subsequently, when the United States, piqued at Nasser's resort to Communist arms, withdrew its support of Western aid to finance construction of the ambitious High Aswan Dam, the Egyptian leader again succeeded in winning Soviet technical and financial support despite his internal anti-Communist policy. Fortunately for Nasser, his needs coincided with the Russian desire to counteract American influence in the northern-tier states of Turkey and Iran by building up anti-Western feeling in the Arab world.

In 1955 Nasser also displayed his Pan-Arab concern as well as anti-Western sentiments by publicly denouncing the adherence of the Hashemite Kingdom of Iraq to the anti-Communist Baghdad Pact and by discouraging Jordan from following the same course for fear of popular rebellion. In any case, he did not want to see Egypt's traditional competitor for domination of Syria-Palestine strengthened by an infusion of American arms, regardless of the character of its government. Indeed, he did not let his

political convictions stand in the way of concluding a mutual defense pact with the traditionalist regime of Sa'udi Arabia as with Syria. Incidentally, both pacts provided for Egyptian control of joint commands. In addition, Nasser and the Arab League, with its headquarters in Cairo, sponsored fund-raising campaigns in support of revolutionary nationalist movements in Tunisia, Algeria, and Morocco, struggling to throw off the yoke of French imperialism. Finally, Nasser moved onto a larger stage by active participation in the Bandung Conference of Afro-Asian nations in 1955. The conferees expressed their approval for the five principles of peaceful coexistence sponsored by India and China, called for the prompt liquidation of Western imperialism throughout the world, and more specifically declared the continued existence with Western support of Israel and Nationalist China to be equally intolerable. All these actions greatly enhanced the stature of Nasser in Egypt, the Middle East, and the world; but even more dramatic events were yet to come.

Confronted with mounting financial needs, dissatisfied with the Egyptian share of the profits of the Suez Canal Company, and eager to add even further luster to his image as an Egyptian and Arab hero, Nasser decided to risk the consequences of a unilateral declaration nationalizing the Canal in 1956 rather than to wait another 12 years when by treaty it would revert to Egyptian ownership.

The immediate reaction to his seizure of the Canal was probably more drastic than he had anticipated. A joint Anglo-French military assault, ostensibly to protect the Canal, followed an Israeli sweep through the Sinai peninsula to assure access to the East via the Gulf of Aqaba, to counter the rising belligerence of Nasser, and to destroy the new Egyptian military potential built up by Communist arms shipments. Despite Communist armaments, Egyptian defenses rapidly collapsed, and for Nasser, all might have been lost if the United States had not joined the

Soviet Union in backing a Security Council resolution calling for a ceasefire and withdrawal of Anglo-French and Israeli forces. In the subsequent settlement Nasser regained all lost territory and only had to concede free passage in the Gulf of Aqaba for Israeli trade and the installation of a U.N. Peace Force to police this arrangement and the frontier with Israel. Out of the ashes of military defeat Nasser snatched a diplomatic victory that raised his star even higher in the Arab firmament as the Arab champion against Western imperialism in both its Anglo-French and Israeli forms.

Taking advantage of his heightened prestige, Nasser unleashed his propaganda organs to press for Pan-Arab unity and even union under his charismatic leadership. Because of the characteristic political turmoil and expanded Communist influence in Syria this program bore unexpected fruit in February 1958, when the leaders of the Baath party led their country into a union with Egypt in what was called the United Arab Republic, a title that opened up the prospect of further additions. This event proved to be only the first of the striking developments that marked this year of crises and upheavals throughout the Middle East and Asia.

Nasser, it appeared, entered this union somewhat reluctantly, recognizing the divergence and possible incompatability in populations, economies, and political attitudes between its two parts. Although the instrument of union assumed equality, Egypt had five times the population of Syria, a condition scarcely conducive to the practice of genuine equality. Moreover, Egyptians were traditionally accustomed to a government-controlled and directed economy in contrast to the almost uncontrolled Syrian economy. The most dangerous disparity between the two partners, however, was represented by the unitary authoritarianism of Nasser's regime, which tolerated no opposition in comparison with the competitive parties, cliques, and factions that had kept Syria in perpetual political turmoil since independence. From

the beginning, the tendency toward Egyptian domination of the partnership became apparent. The final step that provoked Syrian secession in 1961 was Nasser's decision to apply his doctrine of Arab socialism to Syria. Already alienated by the infiltration of Egyptians into key positions in the government and the army, even the Baath leaders became convinced that union under Nasser was not in the best interests of Syria or their own conception of Arab unity and socialism. Nasser himself did not oppose Syrian secession because this experiment had convinced him that prior social and economic reforms along parallel lines would be a prerequisite to succesful political union. Nevertheless, during 1958 subsequent events offered promise of an early realization of Nasser's dream of Pan-Arab unification.

In neighboring Lebanon the creation of the United Arab Republic spilled over the border stimulating the fervor of those Muslims who had always favored a Greater Syria, including Lebanon, as well as those who responded to Nasser's Pan-Arab propaganda. Even Christian elements in this delicately balanced body politic who had always viewed Lebanon's destiny as part of the Arab world supported the opposition to pro-Western President Camille Chamoun, particularly after his announcement of his intention to seek an unprecedented second term. Arms filtered across the Syrian frontier and by mid-May incidents of violence had built up into what could be defined as a civil war. Since the army refrained from involvement, the fighting on both sides was carried out by largely untrained and undisciplined volunteers. By the time of the Iraq revolution in mid-July the situation of Chamoun's government had so seriously deteriorated— almost the entire frontier was in rebel hands—that the American government responded to his plea by landing 3600 marines. Although the marines basically stayed in camp near the beach, they represented a stabilizing influence that checked Nasser's intervention and permitted an Americanmediated settlement to be concluded by which President Chamoun agreed to step down in favor of the army chief, General Fuad Chehab, who was elected to the presidency by the Chamber of Deputies on July 31. With peace restored, the marines were finally withdrawn on October 24. Since then Lebanon has played a cautiously quiescent role realizing that any other policy would only destroy its delicate political balance and produce destructive internal strife. How long Lebanon can maintain such a truly neutral stance between its Western interests and Arab sympathies, however, is an open question. Meanwhile, during 1958 Iraq was convulsed by revolution and the Jordanian monarchy was seriously threatened. In both instances the military played contrasting, but decisive, roles.

Even before the Suez crisis of 1956 the government of Iraq had drawn upon itself the full wrath of Nasser's propaganda machine for its adherence in 1955 to the pro-Western, anti-Communist alliance of northern-tier states, known as the Baghdad Pact, and the young Hashemite ruler of Jordan, dependent on British financial support, was subjected to dire threats if he dared to join his cousin in such treachery to the Arab cause. During 1957 the more radical and antimonarchical tone of Nasser's utterances persuaded King Sa'ud of Sa'udi Arabia and the Hashemite kings of Iraq and Jordan to set aside their long-standing hostility and make common cause in the so-called "Kings' Alliance." This tentative association, based on common fear of Nasserism, was further strengthened by the creation of the U.A.R., which also precipitated a fortnight later the union of Iraq and Jordan. In emulation of its predecessor, this new union, which by contrast left its members with internal political freedom, declared its readiness to welcome other Arab states as members. Thus, the age-old competition between Mesopotamia and Egypt for the allegiance of the Arab hinterland was once more revived. Although ideological differences provided grist for the propaganda

mills, this division was fundamentally a geopolitical one between these two ancient seats of civilization and could be expected to recur regardless of the ideological positions of the moment.

Nevertheless, a large number of Iraq's intelligentsia were alienated by the comparatively conservative, corrupt, and pro-Western character of the regime under the wily prime minister, Nuri es-Said, a representative of that transitional generation of leaders trained under Western tutelage. These young men, both army officers and politicians, were encouraged by the growth of broader-based revolutionary feeling, particularly in Baghdad, which owed a great deal to Communist and Nasserite propaganda. At dawn on July 14, 1958, elements of Brigadier-General Abul Karim Kassem's 20th Brigade, which were passing through the capital en route to Jordan for the implementation of military union, seized the seats of power, liquidated the royal family and subsequently the feared Nuri Said, allowed the people of the city to run wild, and set up a revolutionary council headed by Kassem with Colonel Abul Salam Muhammed Aref as deputy premier and deputy commander-in-chief. Leaders of the opposition to the former regime, including a Marxist, were taken into the government. The prospect of realizing the dream of Pan-Arab union was heightened when within a few days of the coup Colonel Aref met Nasser in Damascus and signed an agreement pledging close cooperation with the U.A.R. But later developments demonstrated that these steps were designed to win as broad support as possible and to neutralize potential opposition until the new regime was securely established.

The revolutionary character of the new regime was confirmed by the setting up of a People's Court to try supporters of the old regime, by the organization of a citizens' militia called the Popular Resistance Forces to defend the revolution against the remnants of dissent, and by the enactment of a moderate measure of agrarian reform limiting estates to a maximum of 620 irrigated acres and 1240 unirrigated acres. In addition, for the first time Iraq opened diplomatic relations with the Communist world, which led to military and economic aid and an increase in Communist influence within the country along with a reciprocal decline in Western influence. In essence, General Kassem commanded a military dictatorship, comparable to Nasser's, which demonstrated increasingly nationalist proclivities.

The ambition of Colonel Aref for a larger share in power soon provoked a clash between the two men with Kassem gradually adopting a more nationalistic, anti-Nasser position with the support of the Communists, while Aref looked to the Baath for backing. In December Kassem announced the discovery of a conspiracy for his overthrow. With other alleged conspirators Aref underwent a sensational trial for treason in the People's Court and was sentenced to death. The year 1959 also saw a propaganda war that contributed to a sharp deterioration in Iraq-U.A.R. relations and expressions of internal discontent with the growth of Communist influence. During 1960, however, Kassem appeared to regain control by restricting Communist activities and by following a genuine policy of "positive neutralism" between East and West. Thus, like his predecessor, Nuri Said, Kassem moderated his radicalism to secure his position, looked for support to the more numerous elements between the extremes of the political spectrum, and ultimately relied on the loyalty of the army to enforce his will. As a consequence, the promise of radical social and economic reforms on which the revolution had been based failed to materialize, and this failure contributed to the discontents that made possible the successful coup of 1963 led by Aref with Baath backing.

At the same time a Baath coup in Syria held forth the prospect of a union of Iraq and Syria, a potential advancement of Mesopotamian influence, and thus a setback to the progress of Nasserism. In both instances,

however, Baath success was more dependent on the military than its socialist doctrines. In Iraq the supremacy of Aref and the military eclipsed the Baath and doomed the union, while in Syria dependence on the military crippled the reform program. In short, in these and most Arab states the true source of power remained in the hands of the military to which politicians and political parties had to accommodate themselves if they wished to exercise any semblance of power and influence.

Meanwhile, in July 1958, Husayn, the vigorous young Hashemite ruler of Jordan, faced the possibility of the same fate his cousin in Iraq had suffered. Indeed, since coming to the throne, he had come to realize that his survival depended on the crack Arab Legion recruited principally from the traditionalist Bedouin population of his realm, which feared domination by the settled, urban and refugee population situated in the annexed Palestinian territory west of the Jordan. As a result, he had increasingly taken personal control of the government and neglected its parliamentary apparatus. Other than assassination or external intervention, he could depend on the loyal protection of the bulk of the Legion's officers and men, though some officers were subverted by Nasser's agents. It was the fear of external intervention following the bloody coup in Iraq that persuaded the British to fly a contingent of paratroopers to Jordan at the same time that American marines landed in Lebanon. After their withdrawal Husayn came increasingly to rely on American military and economic aid, while continuing to protest his faithfulness to the Arab cause, particularly vis-à-vis Israel, and attempting to minimize and neutralize his differences with Nasser. Fundamentally, however, his government was just as dependent on the military as the radical regimes advocating Arab socialism, a fact of current political life throughout most of the Middle East. The continuing confrontation with Israel further reinforced the role and enhanced the prestige of the military. Even in the more progressive Arab states social and economic modernization was unfortunately handicapped and delayed by the need felt to divert a major portion of each state's revenues into military modernization and preparedness. Paradoxically, the devastating defeats delivered by Israel only served to stimulate a greater reliance and expenditure on the armed forces in preparation for a future conflict to the overall detriment of desperately needed social and economic development. Political liberalism was also a casualty of the apparently irreconcilable Arab-Israeli confrontation, and its effects extended far beyond the immediate neighbors of Israel, suggesting that the conflict itself was only a secondary factor in the prominence of the military in the Arab world.

THE NEWER STATES

Although postwar Britain and France were prepared to surrender their authority in the mandated territories of the Levant as well as in Egypt, the French were less ready to consider cutting loose their closer and more economically integrated colonies in the Maghrib (the Arab Far West): Tunisia, Algeria, and Morocco. The victorious allies also turned over to the United Nations the problem of determining the future of the vast desert realm between Egypt and Tunisia, formerly part of the Italian Empire. Another problem area was the British-controlled Sudan, which Egypt coveted principally because that vital source of life-giving water, the Nile, passed through its territory. Finally, both postwar policy and economic realities have impelled the British government to withdraw from imperial responsibilities as rapidly as possible. The determination to eliminate commitments east of Suez has accelerated the grant of independence to a South Arab Federation composed of the strategic Aden colony and a number of protected principalities along the southern coast of Arabia.

In the Maghrib, more vigorously than in the more remote parts of its colonial empire, France prosecuted its policy of cultural and political assimilation, supported by governmental encouragement of French emigration and settlement through the transfer of fertile Muslim lands to European settlers. Settlement reached larger proportions in Algeria (over 1,000,000), immediately opposite the Mediterranean coast of France, but was also substantial in Tunisia (300,000) and Morocco (200,000). French education was pushed, but colonial administration remained mainly in French hands, leaving these lands at independence with French-speaking and French-educated elites but with a dearth of experienced administrators and technicians. In the postwar period France demonstrated its unwillingness to surrender centralized authority by the rejection of all legislation for Muslim equality and more local self-government and by the brutal suppression of dissidents. As a consequence, organized armed insurrection became the sole recourse for Arab nationalists, breaking out in Morocco and Algeria in 1952 and in Tunisia in 1954.

In Tunisia and Morocco, where French interests were less extensive, the government recognized realities and negotiated its withdrawal by 1956. In Morocco, authority was turned over to the monarchy, which had demonstrated its attraction as the true center of power and loyalty during the resistance, but in Tunisia the socialistic Neo-Destour party headed by Habib Bourguiba gained exclusive control over what amounted to a single-party regime. After surviving Nasser-supported challenges, President Bourguiba consolidated his authority over both the party and the state and took a position in domestic and foreign affairs too moderate to satisfy the more ardent advocates of Arab socialism and Arab nationalism. Although Hassan II of Morocco granted a constitution providing for a parliamentary system of government, his religious authority as a descendant of the Prophet's family and his association with those privileged elements favoring maintenance of the status quo had given him in fact a much more dominant position than the constitution set forth. Through his influence over elections (first held in 1963) the parliament remains so far a servant of the crown, while the King has maintained favor in the Arab world by active support of Arab nationalism. His principal challenge has come from his much more radical neighbor, independent Algeria.

French determination to cling to this last remnant of empire combined with rebel intransigence to produce in Algeria a bloody revolutionary struggle (1954–1962) of unprecedented dimensions in the Arab world. From beginning to end of this total conflict almost one million Algerian lives were lost, directly or indirectly—about one-tenth of the population. One result was the development in the leaders of a more radical revolutionary outlook than the Arab world had yet seen. In France, feeling ran so deep that it took a Frenchman of the heroic stature of General Charles deGaulle to gain acceptance for a negotiated surrender of sovereignty.

In the ensuing struggle for power the mercurial and quixotic Ahmed Ben Bella, who had languished in comfortable French confinement since his dramatic capture in 1956, emerged victorious with the backing of the ablest revolutionary commander, Colonel Houari (Redhead) Boumedienne. By tactics as vicious as any previously employed by the French, Ben Bella disposed of all potential challengers, except Boumedienne, and seized despotic power, while the latter consolidated his control of the military. In domestic policy Ben Bella preached a more radical brand of socialism than Nasser and took steps to nationalize the abandoned landholdings of European settlers and set up cooperative farms. Education was given a number one priority and significant progress was achieved. Nevertheless, few of his economic proposals got far beyond the oratorical stage and total economic collapse was prevented only by foreign aid from the United States, France, and the Communist countries. His foreign policy, if his continuously shifting attitudes can be so defined, was aimed at cultivating as broad support in

both East and West as possible and at building up his image as the outstanding champion of nationalism and national liberation. Even the veteran propagandist, Nasser of Egypt, was put somewhat in the shade by Ben Bella's extravagant and unrealistic promises of finite Algerian aid to revolutionary and antiwhite rule movements throughout Africa.

His irresponsible despotism had brought Algeria to the verge of ruin when in 1965 Colonel Boumedienne at the head of the military carried out a quick and almost bloodless coup on the eve of the second Afro-Asian Conference that Ben Bella was hosting at vast expense to put the final seal on his assertion of power and charismatic leadership. Thus the army that had put him in power took it away, and within Algeria scarcely a hand or voice was raised in his defense. The much less flamboyant, and indeed colorless, Boumedienne proclaimed a moderate policy stressing internal recovery and an Algerian brand of nationalism, but in fact, while avoiding headlines, his regime has proven little less despotic than his predecessor's.

Libya, the vast desert region stretching between Egypt and Tunisia whose few amenities had been devastated by the marches and countermarches of the war, fell temporarily into reluctant British hands as a U.N. trusteeship. The problem was to find an acceptable indigenous authority for this impoverished, illiterate, and almost wholly undeveloped region. In December 1951, the chief of the Muslim Sanussi sect, which exercised the greatest religious and economic influence in the area, was designated king of an independent monarchy. The entire administrative apparatus of the new regime had to be staffed by outsiders, Britons and Arabs from neighboring countries, principally Egypt. In 1959 the discovery of vast reserves of oil revolutionized the future of this poorest of Mediterranean lands. Since then, growing oil revenues have transformed Libya into the second richest Arab country on a per capital basis, second only to Kuwait.

Vast social and economic changes have accompanied this influx of wealth with nomads and farmers abandoning their traditional ways of life for the more glamorous opportunities in the city. The monarchy that seemed so appropriate in 1951 rapidly became an anachronism and was overthrown in 1969 by a military coup, adding another state to the list of military regimes in the Arab world.

The Sudan, once deemed vital to Egypt because of the Nile, was finally permitted by an Anglo-Egyptian agreement of 1953 to determine its own future. On January 1, 1956, independence was proclaimed. As one of the better examples of British tutelage, the Sudan established a parliamentary system with two loosely organized parties, bulwarked by a trained and competent civil service. The northern half of the country also enjoyed a prosperous economy based on irrigated production of long staple cotton. The principal problems were Egyptian relations, resolved in 1959, and of deeper import, the cultural and economic cleavage between the Muslim north and the primitive non-Muslim south. Both problems, as well as corrupt politicians, contributed to a military coup in that year of upheavals, 1958. The military quickly succeeded in negotiating a settlement of the differences with Egypt and in restoring prosperity but was less successful in integrating the south and reconciling the educated elite. In 1964 a popular uprising unseated the military and restored parliamentary government, a unique reversal of the general trend in the Middle East, but in 1969 the military returned to power in another coup.

Lesser areas in the Arabian peninsula that underwent political change in the sixties included Kuwait, the Federation of South Arabia, and the Yemen. The British protectorate over oil-rich Kuwait was relinquished in 1961 and a constitutional monarchy proclaimed in 1962. A threatened absorption of tiny Kuwait by Kassem's Iraq was thwarted by one of the last examples of British saber-rattling, backed up by the United States. Since then, Kuwait has guaranteed its independence by ingratiating itself with the other Arab states through generous loans and grants and by fully supporting the belligerent stance toward Israel. In 1963 the colony of Aden was incorporated into the hodgepodge of protected principalities constituting the Federation of South Arabia. Despite the incongruities and unpreparedness of the Federation, the British government unequivocally committed itself to granting independence and carrying out a total withdrawal. Upon independence on November 30, 1967, it was renamed the People's Republic of Southern Yemen reflecting leftist domination.

Independent Yemen, the most populous state of the peninsula, which harbors irredentist claims against Aden and the Federation, has seen itself racked by civil war during the sixties. In 1962 a successful military coup with the backing of Nasser overthrew the traditionalist religious autocracy of the Imam. With arms aid from Sa'udi Arabia and the loyal support of tribesmen a royalist counterattack was mounted. Only a massive military commitment by Egypt saved the Republicans, but neither side proved capable of extinguishing the other. Sa'udi-Egyptian agreements for the mutual withdrawal of support failed, and the civil war, punctuated by short-lived truces, persisted in a desultory fashion. Final Egyptian withdrawal following the 1967 defeat by Israel only opened the door to Soviet support of the Republicans, a potentially significant strategic advance for Russia.

THE THIRD ARAB-ISRAELI WAR (JUNE, 1967)

Since the creation and defense of the state of Israel in 1948–1949 the Arab world had seen much turmoil and change—independence for the whole Maghrib as well as the Sudan and Kuwait and the rise and spread of both Arab socialism and militarism—but basic objectives, such as the extinction of Zionist Israel and the realization of greater Pan-Arab unity, remained beyond its reach. Arab defeat in 1948–1949 and more decisively in 1956 had not extinguished but rather reinforced Arab determination to persevere. Indeed, the common Arab hostility to Zionism gave substance to the Pan-Arab dream and facilitated the assertion of military authority in government. Unfortunately, it also diverted vital energies and resources from more tangible forms of nation building. Furthermore, no political leader who wished to survive could consider compromise. Popular support required regular declarations of dedication to the ultimate goal of liquidating Zionism.

The long years of truce were frequently troubled by border incidents despite U.N. surveillance. During 1966 and 1967 Arab attacks along the Syrian and Jordanian frontiers, attributed to secret Syrian saboteurs, grew in number and severity along with Syrian diatribes against Israel. Israel sought to discourage these "unofficial" attacks by military assaults of increasing size on border villages. In 1967 Nasser felt impelled to support Syria against an anticipated Israeli invasion by the movement of military forces into the Sinai peninsula as well as by threatening statements. In May the secretary-general of the U.N. acceded to his request for withdrawal of the U.N. force patrolling the Egyptian frontier in the Sinai and the narrow entrance to the Gulf of Aqaba, Israel's outlet to the Indian ocean and the East. The massing of Egyptian forces, 90,000 strong, in the Sinai, the closing of the Gulf of Aqaba, and Nasser's virulent assertions that the end of Israel was at hand thoroughly alarmed the Israelis and created an international crisis, though it is said that Nasser had no intention of fighting. By diplomacy Israel appealed for support to its friends, particularly the United States, which had publicly guaranteed in 1957 the status of the passage into the gulf as an international waterway open to the ships of all nations, but the only responses were vague assurances and admonitions to be patient while negotiations proceeded.

Nevertheless, the government of Israel, fearful of the devastation had a joint Arab assault by a larger, Russian-supplied air force, decided that survival demanded the initial advantage of surprise. Taking advantage of gunfire exchanges along the Gaza front, the Israel air force launched an amazingly successful attack on the morning of June 5, 1967, catching most of the Egyptian air force on the ground and destroying its effective operational capacity for the balance of the brief conflict. Undisputed command of the air greatly facilitated the mobile tactics used to reduce the fixed positions of the Arab forces in the Sinai, West Jordan, and the Syrian heights overlooking Israeli territory. In just six days Egyptian forces were routed from the Sinai, Jordanian troops expelled from West Jordan, and Syrian soldiers compelled to surrender their entrenched positions on the Golan Heights—much to the amazement of the entire world. Only then was a U.N. ceasefire implemented.

Ironically this third humiliation at the hands of the tiny but dynamic state of Israel has only served to further harden Arab hostility and intransigence in its refusal to negotiate a settlement. Russian readiness to rearm the Arab forces has abetted but not determined this hard stance. In an equal sense, Israel is now convinced of the futility of any indirect settlement, such as that in 1957, which falls short of unequivocal Arab acceptance of the existence of Israel, and of its right to exist.

At the time of writing death has removed the charismatic Nasser from the scene, but the parties to this unresolved conflict appear farther apart than ever. As a consequence, both sides must continue to divert vast human and economic resources to military preparedness that could be employed more profitably in internal development. More than two decades after the creation of Israel the Arab world seems very little closer to a solution of its fundamental problems.

SIGNIFICANT DATES

1948	Independence of Israel
1950	Democrats defeat Republicans in Turkish election
1951	Idris named king of independent Libya
1951–1954	Impasse over nationalization of Iranian oil
1952	Military coup of Free Officers Society in Egypt
1954	Nasser takes control of Egypt
1955	Baghdad Pact (CENTO)
1956	Nationalization of Suez Canal: abortive attacks of Israel, Britain, and France
1956	Tunisia and Morocco gain independence from France
1956	Independence of Sudan
1958–1961	Union of Egypt and Syria as United Arab Republic
1958	Overthrow of Iraq monarchy by Kassem
1958	American intervention in Lebanon
1958	British intervention in Jordan
1958–1964	Military rule in Sudan
1959	Discovery of vast oil reserves in Libya
1960	Turkish military coup overthrows Menderes regime
1961	Muhammed Reza Shah takes command of Iran
1961	Independence of Kuwait
1962	Overthrow of Yemen monarchy with Egyptian aid
1962	Algerian independence under Ben Bella
1963	Iraq, coup of Colonel Aref
1965	Algerian coup of Colonel Boumedienne
1967	Third Arab-Israeli War in June
1967	Creation of People's Republic of Southern Yemen
1969	Libyan military coup overthrows King Idris

SELECTED READINGS

Ahmed, M. Samir, *Nasser's Arab Socialism*. Cambridge, Mass.: Harvard University Press, 1966.

*Berger, Morroe, *The Arab World Today*. New York: Doubleday, 1964.

Binder, Leonard, *Iran: Political Development in a Changing Society*. Berkeley: University of California Press, 1962.

————, ed., *Politics in Lebanon*. New York: Wiley, 1966.

*Draper, Theodore, *Israel and World Politics: An Essay on the Roots of the Third Arab-Israeli War*. New York: Viking Press, 1968.

Gallagher, Charles F., *The United States and North Africa*. Cambridge, Mass.: Harvard University Press, 1969.

Gordon, D. C., *North Africa's French Legacy, 1954–1962*. Cambridge, Mass.: Harvard University Press, 1962.

*Halpern, Manfred, *The Politics of Social Change in the Middle East and North Africa*. Princeton: Princeton University Press, 1963.

Hopkins, Harry, *Egypt The Crucible*. Boston: Houghton Mifflin, 1970.

*Hurewitz, J. C., *Middle East Politics: The Military Dimensions*. New York: Praeger, 1969.

*————, ed., *Soviet-American Rivalry in the Middle East.* New York: Praeger, 1969.

Issawi, Charles P., *Egypt in Revolution: An Economic Analysis.* London: Oxford University Press, 1963.

*Karpat, Kemal H., *Political and Social Thought in the Contemporary Middle East.* New York: Praeger, 1968.

————, *Turkey's Politics: The Transition to a Multi-Party System.* Princeton: Princeton University Press, 1959.

Khadduri, Majid, *Modern Libya.* Baltimore: Johns Hopkins Press, 1963.

*Khouri, Fred J., *Arab-Israeli Dilemma.* Syracuse: Syracuse University Press, 1968.

Landau, Jacob M., *The Arabs in Israel.* London: Oxford University Press, 1969.

Laqueur, Walter Z., *Communism and Nationalism in the Middle East.* New York: Praeger, 1957.

————, ed., *The Middle East in Transition.* New York: Praeger, 1958.

*————, *The Road to War.* Baltimore: Penguin Books, 1969.

*————, *Struggle for the Middle East.* Baltimore: Penguin Books, 1971.

Little, Tom, *Modern Egypt.* New York: Praeger, 1967.

*Macdonald, Robert W., *The League of Arab States.* Princeton: Princeton University Press, 1965.

*Mansfield, Peter, *Nasser's Egypt.* Baltimore: Penguin Books, 1965.

Moore, Clement H., *Tunisia Since Independence.* Berkeley: University of California Press, 1965.

*Nasser, Gamal A., *Philosophy of the Revolution.* Buffalo: Smith, Keynes and Marshall, 1959.

Polk, William, *The United States and the Arab World.* Rev. ed.; Cambridge, Mass.: Harvard University Press, 1969.

*Prittie, Terence, *Israel: Miracle in the Desert.* Baltimore: Penguin Books, 1968.

Rivlin, Benjamin, and Szyliowicz, Joseph S., eds., *The Contemporary Middle East.* New York: Random House, 1965.

*Sharabi, Hisham B., *Nationalism and Revolution in the Arab World.* Princeton: Van Nostrand, 1966.

Shwadran, Benjamin, *The Power Struggle in Iraq.* New York: Council for Middle Eastern Affairs Press, 1960.

————, *Jordan: A State of Tension.* New York: Council for Middle Eastern Affairs Press, 1959.

Warriner, Doreen, *Land Reform and Development in the Middle East.* London: Royal Institute of International Affairs, 1957.

CHAPTER TWENTY-EIGHT

THE NEW JAPAN

To speak of a new Japan is somewhat misleading because the industriousness, social discipline, and concern for education, on which its prior modernization was based, have merely reasserted themselves after the blow to Japanese morale of unprecedented defeat and devastation in World War II. No better demonstration can be presented of the concept that the true strength of a nation resides in the character and skills of its people, not in its natural and physical resources. Of course, the comparatively liberal and reformist attitudes of the American Occupation hastened recovery but cannot account for the new heights of economic achievement that have carried Japan to third place, after the United States and the Soviet Union, as an industrial power. Such rapid change and advance in only 20 years have naturally created severe social distortions and tensions as well as a host of political and economic problems, but this fresh example of traditional Japanese adaptability gives one confidence in their ability to resolve these issues in due course.

THE ECONOMIC MIRACLE

Once the harsher attitudes of the Occupation were modified and the Supreme Commander for the Allied Powers (SCAP) began to foster recovery, the Japanese businessman soon demonstrated his talents and resilience. A particular windfall was the Korean conflict of 1950 and the American decision to procure as much of its needs as possible from Japanese suppliers. The substantial profits from these sales were invested in new industrial construction utilizing the most up-to-date technology to supplement the labor-intensive production of small shops with older equipment. By the time independence was regained in 1952, industrial development was forging ahead rapidly, and by 1955, a decade after the war, output had reached the prewar peak, though on a per capita basis population increase left it still short of the former high. Meanwhile, agricultural productivity, benefiting from the Occupation-imposed land reform and the application of chemical fertilizers and insectisides, had reached the highest level per unit in the world, fulfilling the bulk of the food needs of the nation despite increased and more varied dietary standards. Since resource-poor Japan has to import most of its industrial raw materials as well as a great deal of modern machinery, any reduction in food imports is a vital factor in maintaining a reasonable balance of payments.

As early as 1950 many Japanese business leaders expressed concern at excessive dependence on trade with the United States, caused in part by the loss of the China market, and looked forward to the restoration of normal trade with the mainland. Other leaders, recognizing how embarassing trade with Communist China would be for its American ally, urged instead an expansion of trade with the advanced countries of Australasia and Europe to secure a better mix. Almost all agreed at that time that the future of trade with the underdeveloped and unstable countries of Asia and Africa held little promise of significant benefit for Japan.

If the swiftness of Japanese recovery through 1955 amazed Western observers, the almost continuously accelerated growth since then, paced by the world's highest rate of saving and investment, has bordered on the miraculous. So rapid has the advance been that today's statistics are frequently out-of-date tomorrow. Occasionally when the economy has become excessively overheated, with a consequent imbalance in foreign trade, government-imposed restraints have temporarily checked progress to foster consolidation before a fresh advance. Despite these setbacks, however, real economic growth has averaged better than 9 percent annually for the past 15 years, a sustained rate unmatched by any other nation, while the improvement in the real wage of the industrial worker has averaged 5 percent annually doubling per capita income between 1960 and 1967 to more than $1000. Moreover, more modest expectations project a quadrupling of per capita income by 1987 to surpass the present American level. How, one may reasonably ask, can such exceptional past accomplishments and such confident predictions for the future be explained and justified?

While a number of superficial and sometimes transitory advantages must be noted in passing, the real answer resides in the unique combination of the traditional spirit and modern skills of the Japanese people. Indeed, even the superficial advantages often draw heavily on traditional values. The single most important, and perhaps transitory, advantage was a consequence of the war and American postwar strategy: the provision in the new constitution against the maintenance of armed forces. As the situation of the Nationalist Chinese government deteriorated, the United States came to regret this decision, but the popular Japanese reaction against the failure of their military leaders and the development of a new role of moral superiority for Japan toward the arms race between East and West have made it difficult for the conservative government of the Liberal-Democratic party to cooperate with American pressure for rearmament.

The first break came in 1950, when American occupying forces had to be removed to the fighting front in Korea, with the institution of a so-called National Police Force, equipped with tanks and other military-type arms, ostensibly to maintain order within the country. Since then, despite vigorous and sometimes violent opposition, the government has gradually built up a small but ultramodern Self-Defense Force with army, navy, and air arms and the very latest in military technology, except in the dreaded nuclear field. (And the Socialist opposition has even accused the government of secret development in this sensitive area which, of course, it has denied.) As a consequence, Japan's rate of expenditure on military preparedness has been the lowest of any modern nation as a percentage of GNP. Although reliance on an American military umbrella for protection has been the subject of severe controversy, it has contributed to the government's ability to maintain the lowest rate of taxation of any modern nation.

Furthermore, the comparatively small expenditure on social services has also helped in keeping budgetary needs at a low level. However, the need to meet the growing demand for social services comparable with those of the West, as well as the necessity for massive public investment in internal improvements in such a rapidly changing society, promises an early end to this advantage in taxation. Official projections forecast a much larger role for the government in the near future. In any case, the low level of taxation in combination with the traditional frugality of the Japanese people has facilitated the world's highest rate of private saving and investment, averaging one-third of the GNP since 1961. This figure compares with 17 percent in the United States and 25 percent in West Germany, the highest average in the West.

Another initial advantage, which is being rapidly eroded, was the availability of a plentiful supply of cheap yet skilled labor that made it possible for Japanese industry to take advantage of labor-intensive production in such new fields of technology as electronics. Effective birth control, which has limited the population increase to less than 1 percent a year, in combination with the vast expansion in industrial employment is already leading to a shortage of new recruits despite the large scale shift of farm labor to industry. Meanwhile, this shift has been accelerated by the rapid increase in wages and the standard of living reflected in the rise in per capita income. So far the increases in wages have more than been offset by greater procuctivity and by the shifts to new products which Japan was equipped to manufacture most advantageously for the international market, but over the next two decades the anticipated growth in per capita income will all but erase the advantage derived from cheaper labor and will force a reorientation of industry to labor-extensive products, such as petrochemicals and other automated industries, as well as a probable overhaul of employer-employee relations. In addition, the customary practice of retirement at 55 may have to be advanced in view of the prospective labor shortage and the vastly increased life expectancy. Traditionally, however, the Japanese look forward to retirement as the happiest period of their lives, after childhood, when they are relieved of the heavy burden of obligation and revered as elders by their families and the community. This tradition may prove difficult to change. Finally, labor federations, which of necessity have concentrated their efforts in the political arena, may, like American Labor, shift their attention to industrywide bargaining, which employers have to date largely escaped. Indeed, industrial modernization in its manifold aspects poses the greatest challenge to the traditional values of cooperation and reciprocal obligation, which basically explain the rapid pace of recent development.

Another important advantage has been the ready availability of American technological know-how along with substantial infusions of American capital. Of the more than 4000 instances of the acquisition of foreign technology between 1950 and 1967 some 60 percent was purchased or leased on a short-term basis from American sources. By such massive borrowing Japanese industry was vastly aided in reducing the technological gap without being compelled to divert investment funds into costly research and development. In this manner, Japan was en-

abled to undertake at a minimal cost the manufacture of a host of new and sophisticated products for sale at home and abroad. Also, Japanese engineers have often improved on the imported technology and in the last year or two their more advanced technology in several fields has even begun to be sold to Western firms including the electronics titan, IBM. Nevertheless, Japan's comparative neglect of research and development is a subject of growing concern to many leaders in government and industry. They recognize that the maintenance of the country's rapid rate of growth will require a greatly expanded investment in this vital area.

American capital as well as technology has been an important element in fueling Japan's economic development, but Japanese postwar governments, like their predecessors, have been careful to limit foreign ownership to the particular irritation of American industrialists who want to gain a controlling interest and even establish wholly owned subsidiaries. Japanese industrial leaders counter with the argument, possibly specious, that American management techniques would be wholly alien to Japanese values and disruptive of Japan's unique economic order. More important, it would seem, is the unexpressed determination to repel any form of Western economic imperialism and retain the Japanese market for Japanese producers.

In this connection Japan's postwar economic "miracle" is based as much on the cultivation of an expanding domestic consumer market for Japanese products as the essential development of exports to pay for the massive amounts of necessary imports. This development of a domestic consumer market owes its growth and strength to the rising per capita income and standard of living reflected in the now almost universal ownership of TV sets and the progress in transportation. At first the people could only afford bicycles; then in the 1960s the motorcycle became the status symbol; in the last few years automobile sales have leapt forward, illustrating the ability of growing numbers to afford this mode of transportation and incidentally making the inadequacy of Japanese roads a national issue. This attention to the domestic market does not imply any neglect of exports but rather the creation of a better economic balance by the cultivation of broad-based domestic prosperity. Indeed, American ears can attest to the popularity of Japanese motorcycles (as well as their transistor radios), and many are also becoming aware of the recent influx of *Datsun* and *Toyota* automobiles. In fact, the sharply increased sales during 1967 at home and abroad moved the Japanese automotive industry into second place after the United States, while American manufacturers complained bitterly about Japan's refusal to permit them to build and own plants for competition in the expanding Japanese market. The expansion of Japan's exports, which are now more than three times their prewar peak, has been fostered by the government's decision to eradicate the former reputation for shoddy products by specifying quality control and inspection. This policy, carried out in cooperation with the manufacturers, has clearly achieved its goal.

Such a program could probably not have succeeded if it had not been for the continued attention given to the advancement of education and educational opportunity for all its citizens, a policy established early in the Meiji era. Japan has long enjoyed a higher literacy rate than the United States, but more important is the postwar expansion of educational opportunity at the secondary and university levels, originally promoted by the Occupation authorities to foster democratization. Although some American-sponsored reforms were subsequently modified, the consequence has been the graduation at both levels of a larger percentage of the school-age population than any other country except the United States. Furthermore, as comparative testing of secondary level achievement in mathematics indicated, Japanese instruc-

tion produces a larger percentage of high school graduates with a more advanced overall competence than those of any nation tested, including the United States. Since mathematical skills are particularly important to the most sophisticated modern industries, the Japanese educational system can be credited with producing the type of labor needed for the current and future requirements of the most advanced technology conceivable. University instruction in the sciences, however, seems to be in need of reform and development to fill the gap in basic research. Again, the government's responsibility in this area has been recognized and can be confidently expected to be implemented on a growing scale in the future.

After all these and other contributing factors are added up, however, they cannot by themselves explain the amazing economic progress of postindependence Japan. The true source of Japan's material success rests in the vitality and social discipline of its people which draw heavily upon traditional values. Despite the emphasis of the American Occupation on democratization and the incorporation of a long list of rights in the postwar constitution, the Japanese value system continues to place a greater stress on obligations than on rights. Indeed, in the Japanese mind the two are complementary to each other, the exercise of rights depending on the performance of appropriate duties. Such a concept of reciprocity involves more than a material relationship between employer and employee; it also implies a personal and social bond of mutual obligation and concern transcending material considerations. Customarily the worker does not rush away when his workday ends but lingers to inspect the end product in which he takes a personal pride and possibly to exchange views on how to improve production. On the employer's side it is understood that he is obliged to retain employees of proven loyalty, even when technological change makes their continued services no longer rational, and to look after their welfare. On the other hand, workers who accept a better offer from another firm tend to be socially suspect. After a reasonable apprenticeship, employment is looked on as a lifelong commitment. Improvements in productivity are shared by means of semi-annual bonuses amounting sometimes to as much as two months' wages as well as being reflected in annual wage increases. Infirmary and other personal services are normally provided, and social events, such as Shintō festivities and athletic teams, are frequently sponsored by employers. Flower arrangements and other aesthetic adornments along the production line are not uncommon sights, indicating management's appreciation of the total life of their workers. Unions and their leaders generally have a closer affiliation with the particular factory than with the nationwide federations to which most belong. In other words, it is assumed that both employers and employees constitute a group jointly engaged in an enterprise for the mutual benefit of all its individual members. Class distinctions, while recognized and formally maintained in speech and behavior, tend to be subordinated to the common goal. Even competitive striving for promotion tends to be regulated by the rule of seniority. Under the stress of competition some breaks in this pattern of cooperation and mutual loyalty are appearing in areas of short supply, such as research scientists and engineers who are demonstrating more mobility in employment. These initial fissures in the system probably presage a further breakdown of traditional practice in the future.

As one might expect, such responsible cooperation extends beyond employer-employee relations to those between industrial concerns, large and small, and between industry and the government. Relations between large, modern enterprises and their smaller, less modern suppliers and subcontractors are generally close and personal and have normally persisted for generations, sometimes reflecting financial as well as technical support for the small operator.

Wages in the small shops have been customarily lower, but recent competition is tending to reduce this aspect of the so-called "dual economy" and force their owners to invest in modernization as well as expand the size of their operations. Thus, some of the fundamental features of the "dual economy" are being eroded, and further, more rapid erosion can be expected in the future.

Postwar governments, like their predecessors, have actively cooperated in fostering the development of industry by administrative and legislative actions for the welfare of the nation, furnishing some basis for the opposition's charges of corruption and conflict of interest. Indeed, the relationships between business leaders and bureaucrats and politicians of the ruling Liberal-Democratic party have been and are frequently of a personal and intimate nature. Marital links are common, and individuals find no difficulty in moving from one category to another in pursuit of their careers. Indeed, almost all the Liberal-Democrat members of the Diet are former bureaucrats or businessmen. Thus, the tradition of personal relationships and personal loyalty continues to play a prominent role in the otherwise modernized economy of today.

Perhaps the most striking evidence of the spirit of cooperation, however, is the post-Occupation revival of *zaibatsu*-type groupings of commercial and industrial enterprises. Since the public has not been able until recent years to supply adequate amounts of that ingredient essential to modernization, capital, public stockholding has contributed a proportionately much smaller share to capital formation in Japan than in other industrialized states. Instead, this vital function devolved on private financial institutions which constituted the core of prewar *zaibatsu*. The dissolution of the *zaibatsu* decreed by SCAP did little damage to these institutions, and with the revival of the economy, they were enabled to reassert their financial preeminence so that once more they could reform on a somewhat lesser scale the groupings of enterprises. The remerger of the Fuji and Yawata steel companies, dissolved by SCAP, to constitute the second largest steel combine in the world after the United States Steel Corporation is an outstanding example of this process, justified by the alleged necessity of meeting worldwide competition and carried out with the blessing of the government. In addition, however, it needs to be stressed that traditional personal links have greatly facilitated this restoration of *zaibatsu*-type organizations.

Perhaps the best way to picture the economic "miracle" of Japan is a brief enumeration of its achievements. The advance of this nation with only one-half the population of the United States or Russia has been so rapid that few people realize how great it has been. Japanese shipbuilding, utilizing the most advanced technology, leads the world, launching each year as much as fives times the tonnage of its nearest competitor. Connected with this tradition of seafaring, the Japanese fishing industry scours the seas from Africa to the Antartic and regularly places first or second among fishing nations. Japanese industry also leads the world in the production of cameras, plastics, radios, and motorcycles and is surpassed only by the United States in the production of television sets and automobiles. The steel industry, which has been expanding by leaps and bounds, is in third place and pressing the Soviet Union for second place. In other industrial categories the Japanese advance has been equally impressive. While the growing domestic market has provided a sound base for this expansion, the phenomenal growth in export sales from two billion dollars in 1955 to more than eleven billion in 1967 reflects the new prestige of the label, "Made in Japan," which once was synomonous with poor quality. This growth in exports, which is more than double the growth rate of world exports as a whole, also reflects a qualitative shift from light to heavy industrial products. Thus Japan has become, after the United States, the major workshop of the world

with, of course, a special relevance to the Asian world. Whether or not it is ready to accept for Asia the political responsibility normally associated with such economic preeminence will be considered later.

SOCIAL CHANGE

Such vast and rapid economic progress has naturally precipitated significant social change of various kinds whose dimensions cannot yet be clearly discerned and measured with any certainty. Indeed, these changes have been so swift that the Japanese people themselves are bewildered and unsure of where they are and where they are going. Of course, many of these developments, as in education, represent continuations, reassertions, or further development and modification of traditional values and practices in a new setting, but others involve, or appear to involve, breaks with the past. In any case, the Japanese people, who have a record of successful adaptation and integration of alien influences in the past, are engaged in a massive reordering of society on a more comprehensive scale and in a shorter period of time than in any previous confrontation. Again, if their previous experience can be trusted as a guide, they can confidently be expected to work out in their customary pragmatic fashion a successful and satisfying adaptation, blending in a distinctive and creative manner the best elements from the past and the present.

Many of the occupation-imposed reforms in support of democratization and decentralization proved too extreme for full acceptance and have been modified in practice. The transfer of the control of education from the central government to local elected boards ran into trouble when a national Teachers Union, organized in 1947 with American encouragement, became too strong and too radical for control by the local authorities. As a consequence, school boards are now appointed by local officials, such as governors or mayors, who can call upon governmental authority as needed. In addition, curricula and teaching methods were revolutionized to encourage student individualism rather than conformity, texts were rewritten to remove all nationalistic emphases, and courses inculcating ethics and discipline were eliminated. Even fencing and wrestling, which were thought to contribute to martial spirit, were temporarily banned. Since these reforms were seen as major contributors to a sharp rise in juvenile delinquency and other forms of antisocial behavior, they have been significantly modified as part of the ruling party's program of revitalizing national pride. One hour a week in elementary and junior high school is prescribed for "moral education" to instill patriotic pride and civic responsibility. Textbooks now require approval by the Ministry of Education and include a growing number of examples of national heroes and patriotic acts from the past. In fact, the so-called "reverse course" in education and other areas would undoubtedly be much more reactionary if it were not for the vigorous opposition of the Socialist and other left-wing parties. Nevertheless, there is no diminution in the dedication to the advancement of education as a principal national priority. In a nation deficient in natural resources the importance of human resources is fully recognized and fostered.

More than 5 percent of the GNP is invested in education in addition to the fees paid by parents that increase as the students progress up the educational ladder. Education through the high school level is rapidly becoming universal, and 25 percent of college-age youth are enrolled in institutions of higher learning. The American effort to popularize prefectural universities, however, has not reduced the special prestige attached to graduates of the traditional centers in Tōkyō and Kyōto. Each year hundreds of thousands of applicants go through the "examination hell" to gain admission to the colleges of their choice and more than 100,000 enter the ranks of a new kind of *ronin* (masterless *samurai*), cramming for a year or more to make a sec-

ond or third effort. Much more than in the United States, career opportunities depend on graduation from the leading universities. The notable rise in the suicide rate after announcement of the examination results is no coincidence.

A statistical index of Japanese educational achievement and cultural vitality may be obtained by an examination of the publication record. Per capita consumption of newspapers, periodicals, and books surpasses that of Americans and most Europeans as well. Less measurable but clearly apparent is the superior cultural diet provided by the publishers. As in other areas, the unselfconscious association side-by-side of the traditional and the modern, the Eastern and the Western, is a striking feature. The Japanese see no incongruity in this association and freely move from one genre to the other without any conscious uneasiness or concern.

Occupation policy also sought to break down the unity of the family and particularly the vast authority of the head of the family in favor of individual freedom. Constitutional reforms and revisions of the civil law went far toward removing the legal constraints on the individual. Women were given equal status with men in social and economic as well as political affairs. They gained the vote, equal rights to own and inherit property, and equal status in marriage. Moreover, the Occupation discouraged arranged marriages and encouraged the exercise of the new legal rights as in divorce proceedings. Initially, Japanese women responded enthusiastically to their liberation, but in time this enthusiasm was tempered by the cool light of reality. Nevertheless, the past could not be totally recaptured, no matter how much men may have desired it. More important than laws, however, in confirming these changes in a modified form has been the rapid progress of industrialization and urbanization that compelled a loosening of family ties and adaptation to a crowded, competitive urban environment.

After 1950 young people from rural areas were drawn at an accelerating rate into the cities to man the machines of industry. Today about 75 percent of the population lives in urban areas. while less than 20 percent draws its livelihood from the soil. Moreover, only 8 percent of students intend to pursue careers in agriculture. As a consequence, the farms of the future will have to become larger and more mechanized or agricultural output will decline, forcing the diversion of more export earnings to pay for larger food imports. Tōkyō, the world's most populous city, now harbors almost 12 million people within the city limits and more than 15 million in its metropolitan area. Moreover, the east coast of Honshū and northern Kyūshū are developing into an almost continuous urban and industrial strip.

The rate of urban growth over the past decade has been so rapid that public facilities, such as sanitation and roads, have fallen far behind the needs of the cities, both new and old. Skyrocketing land values have encouraged the construction of compact apartment complexes where young couples are enabled to live apart from their families with a consequent erosion of traditional social norms. To pay the rents, more and more wives must seek employment, though the number still falls far short of American practice. Confidential surveys reveal that husbands are increasingly helping their wives in household tasks, but in public the formalities of the traditional relationship are maintained. While the Japanese go to work in Western garb, most—particularly the women—still prefer traditional dress at home. Indeed, an ironic by-product of rising affluence is the need to import silk to meet the demand for expensive silk kimonos. Moreover, no matter how modern their relationship may be in other respects, many wives must still accept the tradition of husbands seeking extramarital entertainment and companionship.

Arranged marriage, which the Occupation tried to eradicate, has revived in a modified form. Parents employ skilled matchmakers to select suitable partners. Such selection not only pleases the parents but also insures that the potential partners come from compatible social and economic backgrounds. In contrast to the finality of this arrangement in the past, however, the prospective couple, after introduction, have dates in public places for a brief period to assure that they are personally compatible. Yet few of these arranged engagements are subsequently broken. Despite the pervasiveness of American influences, which are only too apparent in the cities, the continuing high value placed on the family makes compatibility more important in marriage than Western ideals of romantic love. Divorce rates have dropped, even when compared with the more distant past, but since many divorces are privately arranged by families without recourse to the courts, the precise situation is difficult to determine. Suicides by lovers whose unions are barred by social differences are frequent enough to reflect the persistence of traditional social controls.

Legalized abortion in Japan, though controversial, has proven itself to be the most effective birth control measure adopted by any society in the postwar era, reducing the natural increase to less than 1 percent a year. Recent estimates indicate that one-half of the conceptions each year are aborted. Now that a labor shortage is developing, strong pressure is building up for partial repeal of this legislation. Undoubtedly the "pill" has already become an important factor in birth control.

One of the most striking changes since the war is apparent in the physical appearance of the postwar generation. Vast improvements in diet and public health facilities have not only altered the physique of the young but also added sixteen years to the average life expectancy. High school seniors today are 4 inches taller and 15 pounds heavier than their predecessors in 1950. Even more striking to American observers is the improvement in the bust dimensions of young ladies, which now match American norms. School desks and theater seats have had to be enlarged to accommodate the "new" Japanese. These changes give a physical as well as an emotional dimension to the "generation gap" about which so much is written in the West as well as in Japan.

The urban areas, where modernization is most pronounced, also reflect more radically the overall changes taking place in Japanese life. In their quest to regain international status and prestige the Japanese people have concentrated their energies on economic achievement so exclusively that materialism has become almost a way of life to which all other interests and values have become subordinated. Now that the goals of this national effort have been largely reached, and even surpassed, they find it difficult to readjust their thinking and accept new goals and responsibilities appropriate to their economic leadership. Observers have noted that the nation suffers from a "lack of direction" or at least, a "lack of new direction." Popular enthusiasm can be marshaled only for concrete objectives, such as the 1964 Olympic Games and Expo 1970 in Ōsaka, the first international fair to be held in any Asian country. In 1967 a large clock was erected to give a day-by-day countdown to this event, still three years away. The broad public support for such endeavors indicates the people's concern for Japan's image and a continuing, unjustified feeling of inferiority. Yet there is a deep-seated reluctance to take on international leadership commensurate with Japan's economic stature, which must be attributed to more than consideration of the material costs involved in such endeavors. Once burned—literally—the Japanese are ardent advocates of pacifism and disarmament, and despite their "un-Asian" degree of Westernization, fancy themselves as providing a natural bridge for promoting understanding between East and West.

Although rising incomes have caused a decline in the proportion of the family budget spent for food from 50 percent to less than 35 percent, the tendency to spend surplus disposable income on conspicuous consumption, such as entertainment, household appliances, and automobiles, reflects the dominance of the materialistic ethos as well as the traditional feeling of uncertainty and insecurity about the future in a land frequented by natural disasters like typhoons and earthquakes. Surplus income and a reduced workweek of five or five and one-half days have also generated what is called the "leisure boom," a mad rush to crowded beaches or mountain spas and equally crammed attendance at every type of monstrous amusement facility the fertile minds of entrepreneurs can conceive. A sports mania involving all sorts of incongruous Western importations, such as skiing, surfboarding, and bowling, has gripped the people, and as observers or participants they jam the artificial facilities constructed for them. Yet it is significant to note that traditional *sumo* wrestling attracts as large or larger audiences as professional baseball. Relaxation of the restrictions on foreign exchange in 1964 stimulated overseas tourism, and Japanese tourists have demonstrated a tendency to be bigger spenders than their counterparts visiting Japan. In these as in all other activities the traditional Japanese penchant for operating in groups is a readily recognizable characteristic.

The expansion in higher education and employment opportunities has accelerated the growth of a middle class and begun the erosion of traditional class distinctions, a process given institutional endorsement by the popular and widely publicized marriage of the Crown Prince to a commoner. In the same way, the availability of better-paying jobs, which has virtually eliminated the supply of domestic servants, has elevated the status of the lower levels of the working class. In other words, industrialization and the consequent urbanization in Japan, as in the United States, are increasing social mobility and eroding the former class and regional distinctions. Of course, the process is not so advanced in Japan and attachment to tradition is much more apparent.

GOVERNMENT AND POLITICS

In transitional societies government is usually the final stronghold of the elite and the last area to undergo radical change. Whether or not this axiom is universally valid, it is ideally exemplified in the case of Japan where the process of modernization had been initiated from above and the ablest and most experienced political leadership remains an almost exclusive preserve of the upper class. This dominance is further reinforced by intimate personal and economic links forged between governmental and business leaders. Although challenged by the left wing, the right wing has retained its total grip on the political reigns of the central government throughout the postwar era with the exception of the socialist-conservative coalition government of 1947–1948. Despite the frequently violent disturbances sponsored by the left, the extraordinary political stability of postwar Japan is underlined by the need for only ten prime ministers. As befitted a nation anxious to regain its independence and prestige in the world, the prime ministers until 1954 were exdiplomats. Since then, when economic advance became the primary concern, they have all been exbureaucrats with strong business connections and experience. Their record of achievement speaks for itself and helps to explain their continued acceptance by the electorate. Nevertheless, the vigor of the left wing opposition has effectively moderated the conservative inclination to turn back the political clock, and in fact, the ruling Liberal-Democratic party has adopted progressive national plans looking to a welfare state, thus stealing much of the Socialist thunder.

The Liberals and Democrats, who entered a marriage of convenience in 1955 in opposition to the Socialists, are the heirs of the major prewar parties and harbor conflicting views on national and international policies which emerge in struggles for control of the party. But beyond this the party is riven into a host of factions attached to individual leaders after the prewar pattern of politics. As a consequence, every struggle for power results in a coalition of leaders motivated more by the need for patronage than promotion of the policies they vocally espouse. Such maneuvers, essential to the formation of a government, open their participants to plausible charges of political expediency and corruption by the left-wing opposition.

Charges of corruption are also supported by the hitherto heavy financial dependence of the Liberal-Democrats on the campaign contributions of big business in return for anticipated administrative favors and legislative goodwill. This sentiment is accentuated by the government's and the nation's overriding concern for economic progress. However, the socialist parties also receive contributions from big business as well as being heavily dependent on the support of organized labor. Therefore, the principal beneficiary of the popular reaction against materialism and its pervasive effects on politics has been the neo-Buddhist Sōka-gakkai movement and its political arm which have undergone a meteoric and alarming growth in the past few years.

The left wing is now divided into the moderate Democratic Socialist Party, a fading group of aging men, the Marxist Japan Socialist Party, whose support has been growing in proportion to the pace of urbanization, and a small Communist Party, troubled by the Sino-Soviet rift. The Democratic Socialist Party with its advocacy of evolutionary change might better be described as a centrist party. It draws its principal support from the second largest and growing labor union federation, but the advancing age of its Diet members and the gradual decline in support at the polls suggest a continued deterioration in its influence.

The Japan Socialist Party lost ground percentagewise in the 1967 election in which it won 140 seats, to be second to the 277 Liberal-Democrats, but the comparative youth and vigor of its representatives and the trend toward further urbanization hold out hope for greater strength in the future. The principal liability in an era of unprecedented prosperity is its Marxist orthodoxy that is frightening to farmers and the urban middle class. However, many younger leaders, recognizing this handicap, are beginning to demonstrate more pragmatic flexibility in expressing their views. In addition, following the Liberal-Democratic example, the Socialists are giving more attention to grass-roots organization. Nevertheless, barring some disaster, the dominance of the Liberal-Democrats seems assured for the foreseeable future despite the continued decline in their popular support to less than 50 percent for the first time since the postwar election of 1946.

The Communists, torn internally by the Sino-Soviet split, managed to keep 5 seats with less than 5 percent of the vote, but they have never attracted as much as 10 percent of the electorate and pose no challenge as a political party. On the other hand, they exercise much greater influence through their infiltration of left-wing and anti-American organizations opposing such things as Japanese rearmament and constitutional revision, American military bases and the security pact, and American nuclear weapons and testing in the Pacific, issues that enjoy broad popular support.

The most striking and significant development of the 1967 national election, however, was the impressive showing of the Kōmeito (Clean Government Party), the political arm of Sokagakkai. Hitherto it had demonstrated its political strength in carefully selected local elections and in national elections to the upper house where it had already become the third largest party, but in 1967 it put up candidates for the all-important lower house of the Diet for the first time. With only 32 candidates in the field it elected 25 and garnered 5 percent of the total national vote—an extremely auspicious beginning. In comparison, the Communists with 123 candidates did not attract as many voters. Should the amazingly rapid growth of its tight-knit and fanatical mother organization continue to win dedicated adherents in large numbers, it could soon become a vital factor in Japanese politics.

Most alarming in the Kōmeito's nationalistic denunciation of the competing political parties and the democratic process as necessarily self-seeking, corrupt, and inimical to the public welfare. The Sōkagakkai (Value-Creating Society) derives its spiritual inspiration from the thirteenth-century Buddhist priest, Nichiren, who set forth a fanatical, intolerant, nationalistic brand of Buddhism, arguing that in that era of worldwide decadence the Japanese spiritual heritage, properly understood and cultivated, was the only repository of virtue and truth. His modern interpreters, looking at today's world threatened by nuclear destruction, see Japan again as the salvation of the world and preach pacifism, brotherly love and mutual aid, and the ultimate elimination of national governments when most of the people of the world become converts to Sōkagakkai. Popular appeal, recognizing the traditional undercurrent of unhappiness in the Japanese people, is based on the doctrine that genuine conversion will bring happiness and prosperity in this life. A cynic may note the wisdom of this appeal to contemporary materialistic expectations. Indeed, the largest numbers of conversions have been made among those who feel left behind in the economic boom. But he must also note that the success of the movement suggests a spiritual void, an erosion of traditional values and a loss of direction in the quest for economic success, which the doctrines of none of the parties have been able to fill.

The rapid growth of the movement is also due to its exceptional missionary drive. Each convert must prove himself by making a number of conversions. Although the leadership rejects coercion, desperate converts have been known to utilize harassment and even violence to fill their quotas.

It is tempting and perhaps worthwhile

to compare the popular distrust of politicians and political processes on which this movement feeds and the identical prewar sentiments that contributed to the demise of democracy and domination by the military. But such a comparison, while illustrative of the persistent Japanese desire for unity and leadership, should not be overdrawn. For one thing, Sōkagakkai, while spiritually militant, is an ardent advocate of pacifism, and furthermore, the economic conditions of the twenties and thirties bear no comparison with those of present-day Japan. More disquieting is the intolerant denunciation of party politics and the refusal to identify with any other party of either the right or the left, although its views on many issues are close to those of the left.

Finally, mention must be made of the revival on a very small scale of ultranationalistic "secret" societies whose existence was highlighted by the assassination in 1960 of the leader of the Socialist Party, Asanuma Inejiro, by a member of one of these groups called the "Great Japan Patriotic Party." Although they have no popular support or direct political representation, they are believed to enjoy association and sympathy with a few conservative politicians. Nevertheless, barring some disaster of monumental proportions, there seems to be no prospect of their wielding any significant influence.

The Liberal-Democrats' hammerlock on political power has made the opposition restive and irresponsible. The attempts to limit local autonomy in favor of centralization for the sake of efficient administration are denounced as a "reverse course," intended to sabotage democracy and return to prewar positions. Efforts to pass laws restraining freedom of assembly and street demonstrations are particularly suspect. The program of gradual rearmament despite the constitutional prohibition against maintaining armed forces and talk of amending the constitution are especially alarming to the left, which entertains the dream of a neutral Japan. Conservative arguments that such measures are essential steps in preparation for full independence are rejected as insincere when compared with the pro-American stance of the regime. From the left-wing point of view a disarmed neutralism is not incompatible with genuine independence and national security if equal relations are maintained with both East and West.

FOREIGN RELATIONS

Foreign relations naturally loom large for a defeated and disarmed nation anxious to regain its independence and status in the world community. An end to foreign occupation of the main islands was achieved with ratification of a peace treaty in 1952, but the Soviet Union had refused to come to terms and in a world divided into armed camps a defenseless Japan had to compromise its independence by accepting a Security Pact stipulating American protection with American military bases on Japanese soil. Moreover, the Ryūkyū and Bonin islands, while recognized as Japanese, continued by the terms of the treaty to be American occupied for defense purposes. Sovereignty over Korea, Taiwan, the former German islands and the Kurile chain was renounced, but because Russia was not a party to the treaty Japan insists that the legal status of the Kuriles is still subject to negotiation. Finally, reparations settlements with the victims of Japanese aggression were left for subsequent negotiation. In agreements with the countries of Southeast Asia, Japan has paid out more than 1.5 billion dollars in goods and services. These reparations have not only ameliorated relations with these countries but also cultivated the growth of trade. Today South and Southeast Asia absorbs one-third of Japan's exports. As Japan prospered and regained self-confidence, those limitations that remained unresolved have become sources of increasing irritation and restiveness.

The Japanese have always viewed Russian ambitions in the East with distrust and fear, and their relationships have been at best uneasy. The Soviet stance during and after the war did nothing to allay this concern. Russian incorporation of the Kuriles and even the small islands immediately off the coast of Hokkaidō made the Soviet Union Japan's nearest neighbor. The Russian-sponsored regime in North Korea with its ambition for control of all of this strategic peninsula was also alarming. Finally, the fact that the Sino-Soviet alliance of 1950 was specifically directed against Japan could not be ignored. All political parties recognized the peril and sought amelioration of relations, with the left wing enjoying strong popular support for its neutralist policy. In 1956 this confrontation was partially relieved by a joint declaration terminating the state of war and restoring diplomatic relations. At the same time, the Soviet Union dropped its reparations claims and its veto of Japan's admission to the United Nations. In addition, a separate agreement gave Japanese fishermen limited rights in the rich, Russian-controlled waters to the north of Japan. But Japanese refusal to confirm renunciation of the Kuriles precluded conclusion of a peace treaty. The Russians subsequently offered to return the small islands, which are really an integral part of Hokkaidō, in exchange for a peace treaty, but the Japanese government has insisted on its claims to at least the southernmost islands of the Kurile chain. While maintaining the legality of their claim to all the Kuriles, the Russians quite sensibly point out that the return of any of them cannot be considered as long as the Security Pact poses the threat of American military bases being constructed on them.

Economic rapprochement, as indicated initially by the fisheries agreement, has been cultivated by both countries for their mutual benefit, particularly since the Sino-Soviet rift increased the Russian interest in winning influence in Japan. To counter the domination of American oil companies, independent Japanese refiners have purchased large amounts of Russian oil, while aggressively developing their own oil leases in the Middle East. Moreover, negotiations, so far unsuccessful, have been in progress for the co-operative development of the natural resources of eastern Siberia, a convenient source of raw materials on which resource-poor Japan has long cast covetous eyes. Ultimate agreement in some form, however, seems probable in view of the benefits for both parties.

Relations with China, or rather the two Chinas, which had been a major prewar market for Japanese exports, have proven more difficult and delicate, particularly in view of the inveterate American hostility to the mainland regime. Even the most conservative Japanese find it difficult to comprehend American feeling toward a people with whom they have had such a long and intimate cultural relationship. Of course, for the left-wing parties the entwined problem of alignment with the United States and nonrecognition of mainland China have been central campaign issues.

Under American auspices Japan promptly recognized the Nationalist regime of Chiang K'ai-shek in return for renunciation of reparations. As the economies of the two countries advanced, the volume of trade has grown, cementing the ties between them. Nevertheless, Japanese businessmen cannot help being attracted by the potentially greater volume of trade with the mainland, and despite Nationalist threats to break relations this trade has gradually increased.

The principal deterrent to closer relations with mainland China has been the continued dependence on the United States in military, and to a lesser extent, economic terms. The left wing of course favors breaking this dependence and dreams of a collective security pact between Japan, the United States, mainland China, and the Soviet Union. Most of the conservatives with their strong links to the business community also favor normalization of relations. Therefore, while continuing to support the American position in the United Nations and the international arena, a compromise policy of "separating economics and politics" has facilitated the unofficial cultivation of trade and closer relations with the mainland. Under this policy many newsmen as well as businessmen have been enabled to visit the mainland and gain firsthand knowledge of what is happening. At the same time, a governmental program for gradual rearmament and the diversification of overseas markets and sources of raw materials is aimed at reducing Japan's dependence on the United States over the long term. The American government, recognizing the conservative government's dilemma and anxious to see Japan play a role in Asia commensurate with its economic strength, has accepted these policies with little complaint.

The mainland Chinese, who would like to lure Japan into their economic orbit, have been naturally unhappy with this cautious approach. In each year's trade negotiations they press for larger concessions. In particular they have sought long-term credit for the purchase of entire plants as a device for tying Japan's fortunes closer to the People's Republic of China. One day soon such demands may succeed.

Peking's development of nuclear weapons, followed by the upheavals of the Cultural Revolution, has intensified popular concern about relations with the Red regime. Public interest in the Cultural Revolution and what it might mean for Japan have been reflected in the numerous headlines and increased amounts of newspaper space devoted to describing and analyzing its ups and downs, twists and turns. The major issue in the 1968 elections for the upper house of the Diet was policy toward the People's Republic of China on which the Socialists challenged the Liberal-Democrats. The increased vote for the Liberal-Democrats undoubtedly indicated popular uncertainty about conditions on the mainland and a concomitant need felt for maintenance of the American alliance.

Another area of traditional concern is Korea, "the dagger pointed at the heart of Japan." Establishment of normal relations even with beleaguered South Korea has not been easy. Forceful separation could not erase Korean distrust of their former masters or Japanese contempt for their former subjects. One incident after another frustrated every effort at reconciliation even at the diplomatic level until 1965 when the two governments persuaded their reluctant peoples to accept a diplomatic and commercial pact. The Korean people, however, remain very suspicious of a reassertion of Japanese influence in their country. Hopefully time and greater contact will heal this mutual alienation for the benefit of both countries.

The overriding importance of relations with the United States is apparent from the frequent references already made. Since the termination of the occupation the intimacy of this relationship has, if anything, increased with the growth of trade and personal contact. Japan has risen from seventeenth place to second place after Canada as a market for American products, while the United States remains Japan's leading customer and source of imports. Moreover, as Japan's economic stature has grown, the unequal relationship of victor and vanquished has evolved toward what is approaching true partnership. The importance of Japan to the United States is evidenced by the visits since 1961 of almost half of the cabinet officers to consult directly with their Japanese counterparts on mutual interests and difficulties. The United States has also championed the acceptance of Japan as an equal and respected member of the international community. It sponsored Japan's admission to the United Nations where since 1956 it has played an exceptionally active and constructive role and in 1964 won Japan's acceptance as the first full Asian member of the rich nations' club, the Organization for Economic Cooperation and Development (OECD). In return, Japan has pledged to work toward the goal of devoting 1 percent of its GNP to foreign aid. The United States has also labored with some success to persuade its European allies to drop their discriminatory restrictions on the import of Japanese products.

Continuing difficulties requiring adjudication and modification include the Security Pact and American military bases in Japan, the return to full Japanese control of Okinawa, imbalances in trade between the two countries and the fearful complaints of American producers of unfair competition from Japanese imports and of the traditional Japanese restraints on foreign investment.

In 1960, revision of the Security Pact, which met many of the Japanese objections, triggered a storm of opposition from the left. Zengakuren-led mass marches of university students sought to upset the democratic process and resulted in bloody clashes with the police. Although the government rammed ratification through the Diet, the consequences were the resignation under fire of the prime minister and the cancellation of President Eisenhower's goodwill visit out of concern for his safety. Since then, similar, smaller storms have been generated by the visits of nuclear warships to American bases in Japan. Roughly one-third of the Japanese people openly oppose the American alliance, while less than half of them can be counted as its active supporters. Of course, this proportion can shift somewhat in response to the current conditions in Asia at any particular time.

The return of the Ryūkyū and Bonin islands has become a burning political issue in recent years, endangering the supremacy of the pro-American Liberal-Democratic party. In response to direct appeals, the United States has returned the Bonins to Japanese rule and has agreed to the return of the Ryūkyūs and Okinawa to full Japanese sovereignty in 1972. With these gains in hand, the Japanese government has turned its full energies toward the Soviet Union for the return of the southern Kuriles.

The problems attendant on the greatly enlarged Japanese penetration of the American market and American producers' enhanced interest in the rapidly growing Japanese economy are too complex and controversial for detailed examination. Suffice it to say that the two economies have become so intimately interrelated that any significant alteration for either one could only result in severe repercussions and hardship. American businessmen charge the Japanese with "dumping," or selling below cost, to maintain production in particular lines, and also complain that Japan's lower labor costs create unfair competition. In fact, although Japanese wages are about one-half the average American rate, the competitive edge of Japanese industry, which must import most of its raw material, is due much more to higher productivity and more modern and efficient industrial installations. For example, the American steel industry admits that it can keep its old customers if the import price is no more than $20 or $30 lower per ton, but when the import price is $45 less, as in the case of Japanese steel, old customers can no longer ignore the economic advantage. Japanese steel plants, almost all built in recent years, utilize the most advanced technology, while 70 percent of the American plants are obsolescent. Moreover, Japanese plants are located on the coast where imported raw materials are discharged from ships without further handling directly into the manufacturing process, and the finished product is loaded for low-cost, direct shipment to American or other foreign ports. Such cost-cutting effiency is bound to result in a large competitive advantage until such time as American industry becomes thoroughly modernized. To forestall more vigorous opposition from American industry and labor, which might compel the American government to impose more costly trade barriers, Japanese industries in certain lines, such as textiles, have been persuaded to agree to voluntary quotas on exports to the United States. (Ironically, Japan's rising standard of living has now made its textile industry vulnerable to lower cost imports from less advanced countries in Asia utilizing textile machinery purchased from Japan.)

The extension of this practice of voluntary quotas to other products, such as steel, may become necessary in the future.

Fearful of economic imperialism, the Japanese have traditionally limited foreign investment to a minority interest, maintaining Japanese ownership and control. American businessmen, conscious of the potential profits to be earned in the expanding Japanese consumers market, have in recent years raised increasingly loud complaints against these restrictions on establishing their own subsidiaries to compete in the Japanese market. Under this growing pressure, concessions have been made. As the Japanese continue to gain confidence in their industrial prowess and economic strength, however, the remaining limitations may be expected to fall. More serious may be the charges of infringements on American patents. In most instances, however, the Japanese have been able to claim significant alteration and improvement on the purloined process. Moreover, they can point to similar theft of Japanese-developed processes by American industry.

Undoubtedly the most significant development in Japanese foreign relations in recent years has been the cautious and gradual acceptance of a leadership role in Asian affairs under continual prodding by its American ally. At first, Japan was too preoccupied with its own recovery and concerned about awakening among its former conquests fears of a new Japanese imperialism. Furthermore, many old hands like former prime minister Yoshida saw little potential development of trade with underdeveloped countries as compared with the advanced economies of Western nations. The successful reparations programs have in large part allayed these fears, and the subsequent growth of trade with South and Southeast Asia, while not so rapid as that with the West, has revived interest in these markets and concern for the internal development of these new nations. Membership in

OECD with its commitment to foreign aid and development led Japan to pledge itself to the development of a major foreign aid program. Obviously the concentration of such an aid program on Asian countries would be most beneficial to Japan, economically and politically.

In the formation of the American-sponsored Asian Development Bank Japan gave clear evidence of its commitment by matching the $ 200 million American contribution to its initial capitalization. As a consequence, a leading Japanese banker was elected to the first five-year term as president of the bank. Japanese representatives have also participated in the meetings of various Southeast Asian regional organizations and prime minister Eisaku Satō has traveled to Asian countries to demonstrate the sincerity of Japanese concern for their welfare.

The move toward an expression of interest in political as well as economic leadership has been so far much more cautious and tentative. Since some Asian countries entertain much stronger anti-Communist sentiments than Japan, the exercise of political leadership presents a more delicate and difficult situation. In any case, the established policy of "separating economics and politics" can only be modified gradually.

In 1966, at a meeting in Seoul, Japan joined Australia, New Zealand, Malaysia, the Philippines, Thailand, South Vietnam, Nationalist China, and South Korea in the formation of the Asia and Pacific Council (ASPAC) on the understanding that its functions were strictly nonpolitical, but in the spring of 1967 the foreign minister urged ASPAC to consider all questions, not simply economic ones, within its competence and indicated Japan's readiness to exercise leadership. Moreover, he suggested the desirability of a broader membership including ultimately even the People's Republic of China. The goal of ASPAC, as Satō saw it in a supporting statement, should be the creation of greater "stability and prosperity" throughout Asia. What they envisioned was a cooperative Asian community tolerant of differing political systems and working together for the mutual advantage and uplift of all its member nations, under Japanese guidance and leadership. Some Western observers could not help recalling Japan's prewar dream of a "Greater East Asia Co-prosperity Sphere." Whatever the future may hold for this "dream," it is significantly symptomatic of Japan's maturity and the readiness of the current Liberal-Democratic leadership to play a larger, outward-looking role in the affairs of Asia.

On the other hand, the Yoshida conception that Japan's future depends on its association and trade with the advanced nations is still maintained as strongly as before. In particular, it is recognized that the underdeveloped countries must rely on them for developmental capital. The proposal of a University of Tōkyō professor for a Pacific-Asia Free Trade Area (PAFTA) was released with the approval of the government as a trial balloon in 1967 to test its reception. Full membership would be limited to the so-called advanced countries of the region—Japan, Canada, the United States, New Zealand, and Australia—but the poor countries could be admitted to associate membership. To start the organization, all the rich nations would not have to join. Indeed, the formation in April 1967 by Japan, Australia, and New Zealand of a Pacific Basin Economic Cooperation Committee was hailed as "a step forward toward realization of an Asia-Pacific sphere." As conceived in the proposal, the rich nations, which are all assumed to have a stake in the stability and prosperity of the entire region, would pool their resources for investment in the rational and orderly development of the poor countries. Behind this plan can be perceived the Japanese concern for the already apparent competition among these developed nations and their entrepreneurs for profitable investment and influence in the underdeveloped nations. In several instances, Japan has lost out to the more generous terms offered by others. In fact, the sweet reasonableness of this Japanese proposal appears to fly directly in the face of today's nationalistic self-seeking and suspicion, which is just as virulent among the underdeveloped as among the developed countries. Canadian and American authorities have expressed their interest in the proposal. It can only be hoped that in due course its consideration will reach the stage of concrete negotiation. Even if nothing comes of this particular proposal, however, it also reflects the promising movement of Japanese leadership from a narrow, self-centered concern to a broader, more constructive outlook.

The "new" Japan has emerged from its ordeal by a host economically stronger and more vigorous than ever. In the process it has tested a host of alien ideas and practices, incorporating some in a more or less modified form and rejecting others. Again the Japanese people have demonstrated, and will continue to demonstrate, their exceptional talent for adaptation, their unique ability to cling to the old and welcome the new without feeling any deep sense of incongruity. Although the Japanese are still uncertain as to goals and values, by now it is clear that they are and will remain distinctively Japanese in spirit and character, regardless of the extent of economic and social change.

SIGNIFICANT DATES

1952   Peace treaty ends Occupation: security pact
1956   Admission to United Nations
1960   Revision of security pact
1964   First Asian member of OECD
1965   Diplomatic and commercial agreement with Korea

1966   Founding member of ASPAC
1968   Return of Bonin Islands
1969   Agreement for return of Okinawa in 1972

SELECTED READINGS

*Dore, Ronald P., *City Life in Japan*. Berkeley: University of California Press, 1965.

*Hall, Robert B., Jr., *Japan: Industrial Power of Asia*. Princeton: Van Nostrand, 1963.

*Kahn, Herman. *Emerging Japanese Superstate*. New York: Prentice-Hall, 1971.

*Maruyama, Masao, *Thought and Behavior in Modern Japanese Politics*. London: Oxford University Press, 1969.

Morris, Ivan, *Nationalism and the Right Wing in Japan*. London: Oxford University Press, 1960.

*Norbeck, Edward, *Changing Japan*. New York: Holt, Rinehart and Winston, 1965.

Olson, Lawrence, *Dimensions of Japan*. New York: American University Field Staff, 1963.

*Osgood, Robert E., et al., *Japan and the United States in Asia*. Baltimore: Johns Hopkins Press, 1969.

*Reischauer, Edwin O., *The United States and Japan*. New York: Viking, 1962.

*Scalapino, Robert A., and Masumi, Junnosuke, *Parties and Politics in Contemporary Japan*. Berkeley: University of California Press, 1964.

*Storry, Richard, *Japan*. London: Oxford University Press, 1965.

*Vogel, Ezra F., *Japan's New Middle Class*. Berkeley: University of California Press, 1967.

*Ward, Robert E., *Japan's Political System*. Englewood Cliffs, N.J.: Prentice-Hall, 1967.

White, James W., *The Sokagakkai and Mass Society*. Stanford: Stanford University Press, 1970.

Yamamura, Kozo, *Economic Policy in Postwar Japan: Growth versus Economic Democracy*. Berkeley: University of California Press, 1968.

*Yanaga, Chitoshi, *Big Business in Japanese Politics*. New Haven: Yale University Press, 1968.

*Yoshino, M. Y., *Japan's Managerial System: Tradition and Innovation*. Cambridge, Mass.: M. I. T. Press, 1971.

INDEX